Economics

Economics

JOHN SLOMAN

with the collaboration of

MARK SUTCLIFFE

1998/99 Updated
Third edition

PRENTICE HALL EUROPE

LONDON NEW YORK TORONTO SYDNEY TOKYO SINGAPORE
MADRID MEXICO CITY MUNICH PARIS

First published 1991
Second edition published 1994 and updated 1995
Third edition published 1997
This updated edition published 1999 by
Prentice Hall Europe
Campus 400, Maylands Avenue
Hemel Hempstead
Hertfordshire, HP2 7EZ
A division of
Simon & Schuster International Group

Typeset in 9¾ on 12pt Garamond
by Goodfellow & Egan Phototypesetting Ltd

Printed and bound in Italy by Vincenzo Bona

Library of Congress Cataloging-in-Publication Data

Available from the publisher

British Library Cataloguing in Publication Data

A catalogue record for this book is available from
the British Library

ISBN 0-13-989708-9 (pbk)

3 4 5 03 02 01 00 99

Contents

24 The balance of payments, exchange rates and international economic relationships 724

25 Economic problems of developing countries 774

Preface

To the student

Economics affects all our lives. As consumers we try to make the best of our limited incomes. As workers – or future workers! – we take our place in the job market. As citizens of a country our lives are affected by the decisions of our government: decisions over taxes, decisions over spending on health and education, decisions on interest rates, decisions that affect unemployment, inflation and growth. As dwellers on the planet Earth we are affected by the economic decisions of each other: the air we breathe, the water we drink and the environment we leave to our children are all affected by the economic decisions taken by the human race.

Economics thus deals with some of the most challenging issues we face. It is this that excites me about economics, and still gives me a buzz after more than 20 years of teaching the subject. I hope that some of this excitement rubs off on you.

The first two editions of *Economics* have been widely used in Britain and throughout the world. Like them, this new edition is suitable for all students of economics at first-year degree level, A level or on various professional courses where a broad grounding in both principles and applications is required. It is structured to be easily understood by those of you who are new to the subject, with various sections and boxes that can be left out on first reading or on shorter courses; yet it also has sufficient depth to challenge those of you who have studied the subject before, with starred sections and case studies that will provide much that is new.

It gives a self-contained introduction to the world of economics and is thus ideal for those who will not study the subject beyond introductory level. But by carefully laying a comprehensive foundation and by the inclusion of certain materials in starred sections that bridge the gap between introductory and second-level economics, it provides the necessary coverage for those of you going on to specialise in economics.

The book is designed with one overriding aim: to make this exciting and highly relevant subject as clear to understand as possible. To this end the book has a number of important features:

- Full and consistent use of colour to guide you through the text and make the structure easy to follow.
- A direct and straightforward written style; short paragraphs to aid rapid comprehension.
- Numerous examples given from around the world: some serious, some lighthearted.
- Summaries at the end of each section (rather than each chapter).
- Definitions of all technical terms at the bottom of the page.
- A comprehensive index, including reference to all defined terms.
- Questions throughout the text (typically one or two per page) to test comprehension and stimulate thought while you are learning.
- Questions at the end of each chapter for either individual or class use.
- Many boxes (around 10 per chapter) providing case studies, person profiles, institutional material, news items, contemporary and historical debates and issues, anecdotes and advanced topics.
- The different types of box are distinguished by different coloured backgrounds and appropriate icons.
- Advanced material in starred sections/boxes, which can be omitted without affecting the flow of argument.
- Many issues are examined in their historical as well as contemporary context.

The book looks at the world from the perspective of the late 1990s. Despite huge advances in technology and despite the comfortable lives led by many people in the industrialised world, we still suffer from unemployment, poverty and inequality, and in many countries (the UK included) the gap between rich and poor has grown much wider; our environment is polluted; our economy still goes through periodic recessions or times of rapidly rising prices; conflict and disagreement often dominate over peace and harmony.

What is more, the world order has been changing. With the collapse of the communist regimes in Eastern Europe, and the division of many of these countries into smaller, and in some cases warring, nations; with the move away from the ideological simplicity of a 'free-market' solution to all economic problems; with growing worries about prolonged recessions in many countries; with disagreements over moves towards greater economic union in Europe; with an uncertain role for the USA; and with an ever deepening crisis for many developing countries; so there are many new economic challenges that face us.

But despite our changing environment, there are certain economic fundamentals that do not change. Despite disagreements among economists – and there are plenty – there is a wide measure of agreement on how to analyse these fundamentals.

I hope that this book will give you an enjoyable introduction to the economist's world and that it will equip you with the tools to understand and criticise the economic policies that others pursue.

Good luck and have fun.

To tutors

This new edition retains many of the popular features of the previous editions:

- A style that is direct and to the point, with the aim all the time to provide maximum clarity. There are numerous examples to aid comprehension.
- All technical terms highlighted in the text where they first appear and defined at the foot of that page. Each term is also highlighted in the index, so that the student can simply look up a given definition as required. By defining them on the page where they appear, the student can also see the terms used in context in the text.
- A wealth of applied material in boxes (207 in all), making learning more interesting for students and, by relating economics to the real world, bringing the subject alive. The boxes allow the book to be comprehensive without the text becoming daunting. Many of the boxes can be used as class exercises and virtually all have questions at the end.
- Starred sections and boxes for more advanced material. These can be omitted without interrupting the flow of the argument. This allows the book to be used by students with different abilities and experience, and on courses of different levels of difficulty.
- An open learning approach, with questions incorporated into the text so as to test and reinforce students' understanding as they progress (suggested answers to all the questions are provided in the Tutor's Guide).
- Summaries given at the end of each section, thus providing a point for reflection and checking on comprehension at reasonably frequent intervals.
- An even micro/macro split. The number of chapters and their order have not changed.

Despite retaining these popular features, there have been many changes to this third edition.

A full colour text

This new edition makes use of a modern, full-colour design. The objective is to make it attractive to students and help them gain a clear impression of the book's structure. Too much colour, if used carelessly, can be 'flashy' and end up being confusing. In this third edition, colour has been used carefully to enhance the clarity of the layout and allow students to orientate themselves within the text. The four different pastel shadings for boxes allow their category to be immediately identified (case study, development of ideas, issues and applications, exploring the theory), and the consistent use of colour in graphs and diagrams makes them easier to comprehend and more appealing. The result, we hope, is that colour makes the book agreeable to use and makes studying economics more enjoyable for your students.

Reduced length

The third edition is some 280 pages shorter than the second edition. This has been achieved by rewriting the text line by line so as to achieve maximum clarity. The result is a slimmer, user-friendly volume, but in which none of the essential breadth and depth of coverage has been lost.

Extensive revision

Economics uses a lot of applied material, both to illustrate theory and policy, and to bring the subject alive for students by relating it to contemporary issues. This has meant that, as with the previous edition, much of the book has had to be rewritten to reflect contemporary issues. Specifically this means that:

- Many of the boxes are new.
- There are many new examples given in the text.
- All policy sections reflect the changes that have taken place in the last three years.
- All tables and charts have been updated, as have factual references in the text.

In addition to updating, there have been other changes:

- Many of the macroeconomic theory sections have been reworked to reflect developments of theory and current debate.
- Various sections (e.g. on elasticity and on inequality) have been reordered and rewritten for ease of comprehension.
- There is increased analysis of the European economy and more use of European examples and data. The result is that this remains the most comprehensive European text of all English language introductory economics textbooks available.
- There are increased numbers of international examples and greater use of international data, plus a general recognition of the process of globalisation as economies become more interdependent.
- Much of the UK material has been put into boxes (e.g. taxation, benefits and money supply) thus making the main body of the text less UK specific.
- In addition to the questions embedded in the text, there are now questions at the end of each chapter. Tutors could set these as work for students at home or in class, or students could simply use them to check their comprehension at the end of a topic.

The result of all these changes, I hope, is a text that your students will find exciting and relevant to today's world.

Suggestions for shorter or less advanced courses

The book is designed to be used on a number of different types of course. Because of its comprehensive nature, the inclusion of a lot of optional material and the self-contained nature of many of the chapters and sections, it can be used very flexibly.

It is suitable for one-year principles courses at first-year degree level, two-year economics courses on non-economics degrees, A level, HND and professional courses. It is also highly suitable for single-semester courses, either with a micro or a macro focus, or giving a broad outline of the subject.

The following shows which chapters are appropriate to which types of course.

Alternative 1: Less advanced but comprehensive courses

Omit all starred sections, starred sub-sections and starred boxes.

Alternative 2: Business studies courses

Chapters 1–3, 5–8, 12–14, 18, 19, 22–4.

Alternative 3: Introduction to microeconomics

Chapters 1–12, 23. The level of difficulty can be varied by including or omitting starred sections and boxes from these chapters.

Alternative 4: Introduction to macroeconomics

Chapters 1, 2, 13–24. The level of difficulty can be varied by including or omitting starred sections and boxes from these chapters.

Alternative 5: Outline courses

Chapters 1, 2, 5, 6, 13, 14, 16, 18, 23, 24 (section 24.1). Omit boxes at will.

Alternative 6: Courses with a theory bias

Chapters 1, 2, 4–9, 11, 13–16, 18, 20, 21, 23, 24. The level of difficulty can be varied by including or omitting starred sections and boxes from these chapters.

Alternative 7: Courses with a policy bias (and only basic theory)

Chapters 1–3, 5, 6, 10–14, (16, 17, 19), 20 (sections 20.3 and 20.4), 22–4.

Companion books and materials

Tutor's Guide

A completely revised Tutor's Guide (previously called Instructor's Manual) is available free only to tutors who adopt the main text for course use. It includes:

- Answers to all questions in the text.
- Answers to all multiple choice questions from section A of each chapter of the Student Workbook and Reader.
- Detailed contents listing of the main text, including reference to all sections, sub-sections and boxes.
- Suggestions on how to use the text.
- Learning objectives that can be used for syllabus design and course planning.
- At least one additional case study per chapter that you can reproduce for classroom use.

Copies of the Tutor's Guide are available from Prentice Hall.

Overhead Masters

A pack of Overhead Masters is available free to tutors who adopt the main text. The pack includes:

- Full-page diagrams that can be used for projecting in lectures and classes.
- Lecture plans in large bold type, that again can be used for projection.

Copies of the pack of Overhead Masters are also available from Prentice Hall.

For tutors using Microsoft Powerpoint® the Overhead Masters are available as a presentation from either your local Prentice Hall office or representative.

Student Workbook and Reader, 3rd Edition (by John Sloman and Mark Sutcliffe)

A new edition of the Student Workbook has been designed to accompany this text. Each chapter of the workbook matches a chapter of *Economics* and consists of five sections.

1. Review questions. This section is a mixture of narrative and questions and goes through all the key material in the textbook chapter. Questions are a mixture of multiple choice, true/false, either/or, filling in blank words or phrases, matching a series of answers to a series of questions, short written answers and brief calculations. Each type of question is clearly marked with an appropriate symbol.
2. Problems, exercises and projects. This section includes multiple-part calculations and exercises, and student projects (including data search exercises, games, role playing and questionnaires).
3. Discussion topics and essays. This includes various thought-provoking questions that can be used for class discussion and more traditional essay questions.
4. Readings. This includes newspaper and journal articles, with questions at the end of each reading.
5. Answers and comments. This includes answers to *and* comments on all questions in section 1 of each chapter (except the multiple-choice questions, whose answers are given in the Tutor's Guide).

Internet information

More information is available on this text and supplements through the Internet. Some supplements are directly available from this page. You should also be able to access further information about other Prentice Hall textbooks and products from this site: http://www.bookshop.co.uk/sloman/.

Test bank

The test bank is a Windows-based package made up of 3,000 questions which tutors can access to compose their own tests. Tutors can select questions in terms of their chapter relevance, level of difficulty and question type. This user-friendly software comes with a full set of instructions and is available free to lecturers using the main textbook for teaching.

WinEcon

The Teaching and Learning Technology Programme (TLTP), backed by the Higher Education Funding Councils, has produced and continues to produce a range of technology-based materials for use in teaching. The Economics Consortium of TLTP has produced a comprehensive computer-based learning programme for introductory economics, known as 'WinEcon'. This Windows-compatible software is available for a nominal fee to all UK higher education institutions on a site-licence basis. The author of this text was involved with the Advisory Group of the Economics Consortium.

This software is designed for use alongside an introductory textbook. Within the software, the student is referred to specific pages of this text for more details of the topic on screen. Therefore, the Sloman *Economics* (3rd edition), the Sloman and Sutcliffe *Student Workbook and Reader* (3rd edition) and the WinEcon software make an ideal integrated economics learning package. Further details on the WinEcon software are available principally from Blackwells Publishers or alternatively from the Centre for Computing in the Social Sciences, University of Bristol. There is also a web site for information on the software: http://sosig.ac.uk/winecon.

Country/regional supplements

A series of supplements which tailor the use of this text to specific areas are either already available or forthcoming shortly. These provide case studies and institutional detail relating to the specific country or countries. During 1997, updated 3rd edition supplements will become available for instructors in the Benelux countries and Singapore. In the near future, these will be joined by Scandinavian and South African supplements. An Irish supplement is also available. All of these can be obtained by tutors using the text: for details please contact your local Prentice Hall representative or your local Prentice Hall office.

Acknowledgements

Writing a textbook like this is a bit like painting the Forth Bridge: no sooner have you completed one edition and the various supplements and you have to start working on the next. Still, the task has been made much easier with the massive amount of help and encouragement I've received from family, friends, colleagues and all the team at Prentice Hall.

First and foremost, I must thank Alison for her patience, humour and support and for making the task bearable. As the book has grown older, so my family has grown larger. In addition to Peter (who is now 23), Michael, Andrew, James and Matthew, there is now little Eleanor, who is a constant delight and into everything. At least I am learning not to leave papers lying around! Thanks to all my family and friends. They all seem remarkably understanding.

As always, the team at Prentice Hall has been first class. Tony Johnston, the editor of this edition, like his predecessors, Peter Johns, Mark Allin and Pradeep Jethi, has been a continuous source of encouragement and good ideas. His friendship and support have been really important to me. Thanks Tony. As an author, you deal mainly with the editor, but the book could not be a success without a massive team effort. In particular I should like to thank Alison Stanford, Ann Greenwood and Stuart Macfarlane in production, Claire Brodmann for design, Ruth Pratten for development work, Allison Peacock in marketing, and John Yates, Clare Grist and Joe Marcelle for overseeing the project: it's no mean task turning a manuscript into a finished book. Finally, as before, I should like to thank the entire international sales force. Their efforts are much appreciated.

A special thanks to Chris Bessant who, in addition to painstakingly copy-editing the manuscript, made many detailed and valuable suggestions for pruning the text. A special thanks too to Greg Mahony, a colleague of mine at the University of the West of England, for reviewing the macro half of the book and providing many useful ideas for improvements.

In producing a new edition, it is important to take into account the reactions of those who have used the book. As with the previous edition, tutors and students have provided valuable comments, by letter, by questionnaire and by direct interview. I really appreciate their views and I have attempted to incorporate their suggestions. Thanks, in particular, to the reviewers of the book. Again, their ideas and suggestions have been invaluable.

The third edition has various supplements. Thanks to all those who have been involved in producing them, and especially to Haico Ebbers, Moore McDowell and Jack Cook for producing the Benelux, Irish and Singapore supplements, respectively, and to Gail Mulvey and John Brookes for compiling the test bank of questions. And, as before, a special thanks to John Mark of the Management Centre, King's College London for producing the appendix on statistical sources.

Finally a million and three thanks (it gets more with each edition) to Mark Sutcliffe for all his ideas and support and for providing a lot of the material for this new edition. Working with him makes a potentially tedious task great fun. For those familiar with earlier editions, the consumption of stickies has continued to decline, but we are not totally cured yet.

Credits

Grateful acknowledgement is made to the following sources for permission to reproduce material in this book previously published elsewhere. Every effort has been made to trace the correct copyright holders, but if any have been inadvertently overlooked, the publisher will be pleased to make the necessary arrangement at the first opportunity.

Crown copyright is reproduced with the permission of the Controller of Her Majesty's Stationary Office; Office for Official Publications of the European Communities; Organisation for Economic Co-operation and Development; The Economist, London.

1 Introducing economics

1.1 What do economists study?

You may never have studied economics before, and yet when you open a newspaper what do you read? – a report from 'our economics correspondent'. Turn on the television news and what do you see? – an item on the state of the economy. Talk to friends and often the topic will turn to the price of this or that product, or whether you have got enough money to afford to do this or that.

The fact is that economics affects our daily lives. Continually we are being made aware of local, national and international economic problems, and continually we are faced with economic problems and decisions of our own.

So just what is economics about? What is this subject you are embarking on – with, no doubt, some trepidation?

Many people think that economics is about *money*. Well, to some extent this is true. Economics has a lot to do with money: with how much money people are paid; how much they spend; what it costs to buy various items; how much money firms earn; how much money there is in total in the economy. But despite the large number of areas in which our lives are concerned with money, economics is more than just the study of money.

It is concerned with the following:

- The **production** of goods and services: how much the economy produces in total; what particular combination of goods and services; how much each firm produces; what techniques of production they use; how many people they employ.
- The **consumption** of goods and services: how much the population as a whole spends (and how much it saves); what the pattern of consumption is in the economy; how much people buy of particular items; what particular individuals choose to buy; how people's consumption is affected by prices, advertising, fashion and other factors.

> ?? Could production and consumption take place without money? If you think they could, give some examples.

But we still have not quite got to the bottom of what economics is about. What is the crucial ingredient for a problem to be an *economic* one? The answer is that there is one central problem faced by all individuals and all societies. From this one problem stem all the other economic problems we shall be looking at throughout this book.

This central economic problem is the problem of *scarcity*. This applies not only in countries like Ethiopia and the Sudan, but also in Britain, the USA, Japan, France and all other countries of the world. For an economist, scarcity has a very specific definition ...

> ?? Before reading on, how would you define 'scarcity'? Must goods be at least temporarily unattainable to be scarce?

The problem of scarcity

Ask people if they would like more money, and the vast majority would answer 'Yes'. They want more money so that they can buy more goods and services; and this applies not only to poor people but also to most wealthy people too. The point is that human wants are virtually unlimited.

Yet the means of fulfilling human wants are limited. At any one time the world can only produce a limited amount of goods and services. This is because the world only has a limited amount of resources. These resources,

DEFINITIONS

Production The transformation of inputs into outputs by firms in order to earn profit (or meet some other objective).

Consumption The act of using goods and services to satisfy wants. This will normally involve purchasing the goods and services.

ISSUES AND APPLICATIONS BOX 1.1

WHAT'S THE LATEST ECONOMICS NEWS?

- Budget news: Chancellor cuts 2p off the basic rate of income tax; government hopes that this will provide an incentive for people to work harder.
- Mortgage interest rates reduced: resulting boost to the housing market expected to lead to higher house prices.
- Recent survey reveals that business confidence is low: fall in investment predicted.
- The country continues to bask in a heatwave: record ice-cream sales reported.
- Floods hit Bangladesh: two-thirds of the country's crops ruined; massive food price rises expected.
- Money supply growing too fast: forecasters predict that inflation will soon begin to rise.
- Further cuts in government expenditure announced: Chancellor claims that this is necessary to allow economy to grow and unemployment to fall. Shadow Chancellor disagrees and claims that the cuts will cause unemployment to rise.
- Record balance of trade deficit announced today: further rises in interest rates seem inevitable.
- Rumours of a takeover bid for ABC plc: ABC shares close 25p up on the day.
- Student grants frozen: Student Union president says that in real terms this represents a further cut.

?? What is it that makes each one of the above news items an *economics* item?

or **factors of production** as they are often called, are of three broad types:

- Human resources: **labour**. The labour force is limited both in number and in skills.
- Natural resources: **land and raw materials**. The world's land area is limited, as are its raw materials.
- Manufactured resources: **capital**. Capital consists of all those inputs that themselves have had to be produced in the first place. The world has a limited stock of capital: a limited supply of factories, machines, transportation and other equipment. The productivity of capital is limited by the state of technology.

So here is the reason for scarcity: human wants are virtually unlimited, whereas the resources available to satisfy these wants *are* limited. We can thus define **scarcity** as 'the excess of human wants over what can actually be produced'.

?? If we would all like more money, why does the government not print a lot more? Could it not thereby solve the problem of scarcity 'at a stroke'?

Of course, we do not all face the problem of scarcity to the same degree. A poor person unable to afford enough to eat or a decent place to live will hardly see it as a 'problem' that a rich person cannot afford a second Rolls-Royce. But economists do not claim that we all face an *equal* problem of scarcity. In fact this is one of the major issues economists study: how resources are distributed, whether between different individuals, different regions of a country or different countries of the world.

But given that people, both rich and poor, want more than they can have, this will cause them to behave in certain ways. Economics studies that behaviour. It studies people at work, producing the goods that people want. It studies people as consumers, buying the goods that they themselves want. It studies governments influencing the level and pattern of production and consumption. In short, it studies anything to do with the process of satisfying human wants.

Demand and supply

We said that economics is concerned with consumption and production. Another way of looking at this is in terms

DEFINITIONS

Factors of production (or resources) The inputs into the production of goods and services: labour, land and raw materials, and capital.

Labour All forms of human input, both physical and mental, into current production.

Land (and raw materials) Inputs into production that are provided by nature: e.g. unimproved land and mineral deposits in the ground.

Capital All inputs into production that have themselves been produced: e.g. factories, machines and tools.

Scarcity The excess of human wants over what can actually be produced to fulfil these wants.

of *demand* and *supply*. It is quite likely that you already knew that economics had something to do with demand and supply. In fact, demand and supply and the relationship between them lie at the very centre of economics. But what do we mean by the terms, and what is their relationship with the problem of scarcity?

Demand is related to wants. If goods and services were free, people would simply demand whatever they wanted. Such wants are virtually boundless: perhaps only limited by people's imagination. *Supply*, on the other hand, is limited. It is related to resources. The amount that firms can supply depends on the resources and technology available.

Given the problem of scarcity, given that human wants exceed what can actually be produced, *potential* demands will exceed *potential* supplies. Society therefore has to find some way of dealing with this problem. Somehow it has got to try to match demand and supply. This applies at the level of the economy overall: *aggregate* demand will need to be balanced against *aggregate* supply. In other words, total spending in the economy will need to balance total production. It also applies at the level of individual goods and services. The demand and supply of cabbages will need to balance, as will the demand and supply of video recorders, cars, houses and haircuts.

But if potential demand exceeds potential supply, how are *actual* demand and supply to be made equal? Either demand has to be curtailed, or supply has to be increased, or a combination of the two. Economics studies this process. It studies how demand adjusts to available supplies, and how supply adjusts to consumer demands.

Dividing up the subject

Eonomics is traditionally divided into two main branches – *macroeconomics* and *microeconomics*, where 'macro' means big, and 'micro' means small.

Macroeconomics is concerned with the economy as a whole. It is thus concerned with **aggregate demand** and **aggregate supply**. By 'aggregate demand' we mean the total amount of spending in the economy, whether by consumers, by overseas customers for our exports, by the government, or by firms when they buy capital equipment or stock up on raw materials. By 'aggregate supply' we mean the total national output of goods and services.

Microeconomics is concerned with the individual parts of the economy. It is concerned with the demand and supply of *particular* goods and services and resources: cars, butter, clothes and haircuts; electricians, secretaries, blast furnaces, computers and oil.

?? Which of the following are macroeconomic issues, which are microeconomic ones and which could be either depending on the context?

(a) Inflation.
(b) Low wages in certain service industries.
(c) The rate of exchange between the pound and the D-Mark.
(d) Why the price of cabbages fluctuates more than that of cars.
(e) The rate of economic growth this year compared with last year.
(f) The decline of traditional manufacturing industries.

Macroeconomics

Because things are scarce, societies are concerned that their resources should be used *as fully as possible,* and that over time their national output should *grow*.

The achievement of growth and the full use of resources is not easy, however, as witness the periods of high unemployment and recession that have occurred from time to time throughout the world (for example, in the 1930s, the early 1980s and the early 1990s). Furthermore, attempts by government to stimulate growth and employment have often resulted in inflation and balance of payments crises. Even when societies do achieve growth it is often short lived. Economies have often experienced cycles, where periods of growth alternate with periods of recession, such periods varying from a few months to a few years.

Macroeconomics, then, studies the determination of national output and its growth over time. It also studies the problems of recession, unemployment, inflation, the balance of international payments and cyclical instability, and the policies adopted by governments to deal with these problems.

DEFINITIONS

Macroeconomics The branch of economics that studies economic aggregates (grand totals): e.g. the overall level of prices, output and employment in the economy.

Aggregate demand The total level of spending in the economy.

Aggregate supply The total amount of output in the economy.

Microeconomics The branch of economics that studies individual units: e.g. households, firms and industries. It studies the interrelationships between these units in determining the pattern of production and distribution of goods and services.

Macroeconomic problems are closely related to the balance between aggregate demand and aggregate supply.

If aggregate demand is *too high* relative to aggregate supply, inflation and balance of payments deficits are likely to result.

- **Inflation** refers to general rise in the level of prices throughout the economy. If aggregate demand rises substantially, firms are likely to respond by raising their prices. After all, if demand is high they can probably still sell as much as before (if not more) even at the higher prices, and thus make more profits. If firms in general put up their prices, inflation results.
- **(Current account) balance of payments deficits**[1] are the excess of imports over exports. If aggregate demand rises, people are likely to buy more imports. In other words, part of the extra expenditure will go on Japanese videos, German cars, French wine, etc. Also if inflation is high, home-produced goods will become uncompetitive with foreign goods. We are likely, therefore, to buy more foreign imports and foreigners are likely to buy fewer of our exports.

If aggregate demand is *too low* relative to aggregate supply, unemployment and recession may well result.

- **Recession** is where output in the economy declines: in other words, growth becomes negative. A recession is associated with a low level of consumer spending. If people spend less, shops are likely to find themselves with unsold stocks. As a result they will buy less from the manufacturers, which in turn will cut down on production.
- **Unemployment** is likely to result from cutbacks in production. If firms are producing less, they will need to employ fewer people.

Macroeconomic *policy*, therefore, tends to focus on the balance of aggregate demand and aggregate supply. It can be **demand-side policy**, which seeks to influence the level of spending in the economy. This in turn will affect the level of production, prices and employment. Or it can be **supply-side policy**. This is designed to influence the level of production directly: for example, by trying to create more incentives for workers or business people.

Microeconomics

Microeconomics and choice

Because resources are scarce, choices have to be made. There are three main categories of choice that must be made in any society.

- *What* goods and services are going to be produced and in what quantities, given that there are not enough resources to produce all things people desire? How many cars, how much wheat, how much insurance, how many pop concerts, how many coats, etc. will be produced?
- *How* are things going to be produced, given that there is normally more than one way of producing things? What resources are going to be used and in what quantities? What techniques of production are going to be adopted? Will cars be produced by robots or by assembly line workers? Will electricity be produced from coal, oil, gas, nuclear fission, renewable resources or a mixture of these?
- *For whom* are things going to be produced? In other words, how is the nation's income going to be distributed? After all, the higher your income, the more you can consume of the nation's output. What will be the wages of farm workers, printers, cleaners and accountants? How much will pensioners receive? How much of the nation's income will go to shareholders or landowners?

All societies have to make these choices, whether they be made by individuals, by groups or by the government. These choices can be seen as *micro*economic choices,

[1] The current account excludes investments and financial movements into and out of the country. Such movements are called the 'capital account' (see section 14.1).

DEFINITIONS

Rate of inflation The percentage increase in the level of prices over a twelve-month period.

Current account balance of payments Exports of goods and services minus imports of goods and services. If exports exceed imports, there is a 'current account surplus' (a positive figure). If imports exceed exports, there is a 'current account deficit' (a negative figure).

Recession A period where national output falls for a few months or more.

Unemployment The number of people who are actively looking for work but are currently without a job. (Note that there is much debate as to who should officially be counted as unemployed.)

Demand-side policy Government policy designed to alter the level of aggregate demand, and thereby the level of output, employment and prices.

Supply-side policy Government policy that attempts to alter the level of aggregate supply directly.

CASE STUDIES — BOX 1.2

LOOKING AT MACROECONOMIC DATA

Assessing different countries' macroeconomic performance

Rapid economic growth, low unemployment, low inflation and the avoidance of current account deficits are the major macroeconomic policy objectives of most governments round the world. To help them achieve these objectives they employ economic advisers. But when we look at the performance of various economies, the success of government macroeconomic policies seems decidedly 'mixed'.

The table shows data for the USA, Japan, Germany and the UK from 1978 to 1998.

Macroeconomic performance of four industrialised economies (average annual figures)

	Unemployment (% of workforce)				Inflation (%)				Economic growth (%)				Balance on current account (% of national income)			
	USA	Japan	Germany	UK	USA	Japan	Germany	UK	USA	Japan	Germany	UK	USA	Japan	Germany	UK
1978–80	6.3	2.1	3.2	5.8	9.7	5.1	4.1	13.2	2.5	4.9	2.9	1.4	–0.2	–0.1	–0.3	0.6
1981–3	8.8	2.4	7.7	11.2	6.6	3.2	5.0	8.4	1.0	3.4	0.3	1.3	–0.5	0.9	0.4	1.8
1984–6	7.1	2.6	6.9	11.4	3.3	1.6	1.4	4.8	4.2	4.1	2.5	3.1	–3.2	3.6	2.9	0.3
1987–9	5.6	2.5	6.0	8.3	3.7	1.2	1.4	5.7	3.7	5.2	2.8	3.7	–2.8	2.8	4.4	–3.0
1990–2	6.4	2.1	4.5	8.5	4.2	2.7	3.8	6.4	0.6	3.7	3.5	–0.8	–1.0	2.2	0.3	–2.2
1993–5	6.1	2.8	8.2	9.5	2.8	0.4	3.0	2.5	2.6	0.8	2.0	2.8	–2.0	2.7	–0.9	–0.8
1996–8	4.9	3.6	10.2	7.1	2.4	0.8	1.6	2.9	3.1	0.6	2.1	2.7	–2.1	2.0	–0.3	–0.1

Sources: *National Institute Economic Review* (NIESR), *Economic Trends* (ONS), *OECD Economic Outlook* (OECD).

??

1. Has the UK generally fared better or worse than the other three countries?
2. Was there a common pattern in the macroeconomic performance of each of the four countries over these seventeen years?

If the government does not have much success in managing the economy it could be for the following reasons:

- Economists have incorrectly analysed the problems and hence have given the wrong advice.
- Economists disagree and hence have given conflicting advice.
- Economists have based their advice on inaccurate forecasts.
- Governments have not heeded the advice of economists.
- There is little else that governments could have done: the problems were insoluble.

since they are concerned not with the *total* amount of national output, but with the *individual* goods and services that make it up: what they are, how they are made, and who gets the incomes to buy them.

Choice and opportunity cost

Choice involves sacrifice. The more food you choose to buy, the less money you will have to spend on other goods. The more food a nation produces, the fewer resources will there be for producing other goods. In other words, the production or consumption of one thing involves the sacrifice of alternatives. This sacrifice of alternatives in the production (or consumption) of a good is known as its **opportunity cost**.

If the workers on a farm can produce either 1000 tonnes of wheat or 2000 tonnes of barley, then the opportunity cost of producing 1 tonne of wheat is the 2 tonnes of barley forgone. The opportunity cost of buying a textbook is the new pair of jeans you also wanted that you have had to go without. The opportunity cost of working overtime is the leisure you have sacrificed.

Rational choices

Economists often refer to **rational choices**. By this is simply meant the weighing-up of the *costs* and *benefits* of any activity, whether it be firms choosing what and how much to produce, workers choosing whether to take a particular job or to work extra hours, or consumers choosing what to buy.

DEFINITIONS

Opportunity cost The cost of any activity measured in terms of the best alternative forgone.

Rational choices Choices that involve weighing up the benefit of any activity against its opportunity cost.

Imagine you are doing your shopping in a supermarket and you want to buy a bottle of wine. Do you spend a lot of money and buy a top-quality French wine, or do you buy a cheap Eastern European one instead? To make a rational (i.e. sensible) decision, you will need to weigh up the costs and benefits of each alternative. The top-quality wine may give you a lot of enjoyment, but it has a high opportunity cost: because it is expensive, you will need to sacrifice quite a lot of consumption of other goods if you decide to buy it. If you buy the cheap bottle, however, although you will not enjoy it so much, you will have more money left over to buy other things: it has a lower opportunity cost.

Thus rational decision making, as far as consumers are concerned, involves choosing those items that give you the best value for money – i.e. the *greatest benefit relative to cost.*

The same principles apply to firms when deciding what to produce. For example, should a car firm open up another production line? A rational decision will again involve weighing up the benefits and costs. The benefits are the revenues the firm will earn from selling the extra cars. The costs will include the extra labour costs, raw material costs, costs of component parts, etc. It will only be profitable to open up the new production line if the revenues earned exceed the costs entailed: in other words, if it earns a profit.

In the more complex situation of deciding which model of car to produce, or how many of each model, the firm must weigh up the relative benefits and costs of each – i.e. it will want to produce the most profitable product mix.

> **??** Assume that you are looking for a job and are offered two. One is more unpleasant to do, but pays more. How would you make a rational choice between the two jobs?

Marginal costs and benefits

In economics we argue that rational choices involve weighing up **marginal costs** and **marginal benefits**. These are the costs and benefits of doing a little bit more or a little bit less of a given activity. They can be contrasted with the *total* costs and benefits of the activity.

Take a familiar example. What time will you set the alarm clock to go off tomorrow morning? Let us say that you have to leave home at 8.30. Perhaps you will set the alarm for 7.00. That will give you plenty of time to get up and get ready, but it will mean a relatively short night's sleep. Perhaps you will decide to set it for 7.30 or even 8.00. That will give you a longer night's sleep, but much more of a rush in the morning to get ready.

So how do you make a rational decision about when the alarm should go off? What you have to do is to weigh up the costs and benefits of *additional* sleep. Each extra minute in bed gives you more sleep (the marginal benefit), but gives you more of a rush when you get up (the marginal cost). The decision is therefore based on the costs and benefits of *extra* sleep, not on the *total* costs and benefits of a whole night's sleep.

This same principle applies to rational decisions made by consumers, workers and firms. For example, the car firm we were considering just now will weigh up the marginal costs and benefits of producing cars: in other words, it will compare the costs and revenue of producing *additional* cars. If additional cars add more to the firm's revenue than to its costs, it will be profitable to produce them.

> **??** How would the principle of weighing up marginal costs and benefits apply to a worker deciding how much overtime to work in a given week?

The social implications of choice

Microeconomics does not just study how choices are made. It also looks at their consequences. Under certain conditions the consequences may be an efficient allocation of the nation's resources.

There are, however, a whole series of possible problems that can arise from the choices that people make, whether they are made by individuals, by firms or by the government. These problems include such things as inefficiency, waste, inequality and pollution.

Take the case of pollution. It might be profitable for a firm to tip toxic waste into a river. But what is profitable for the firm will not necessarily be 'profitable' for society. There may be serious environmental consequences of the firm's actions.

DEFINITIONS

Marginal costs The additional cost of doing a little bit more (or *1 unit* more if a unit can be measured) of an activity.

Marginal benefits The additional benefits of doing a little bit more (or *1 unit* more if a unit can be measured) of an activity.

ISSUES AND APPLICATIONS — BOX 1.3

THE OPPORTUNITY COSTS OF STUDYING ECONOMICS

What are you sacrificing?

You may not have realised it, but you probably consider opportunity costs many times a day. The reason is that we are constantly making choices: what to buy, what to eat, what to wear, whether to go out, how much to study and so on. Each time we make a choice to do something, we are in effect rejecting doing some alternative. This alternative forgone is the opportunity cost of our action.

Sometimes the opportunity costs of our actions are the direct monetary costs we incur. Sometimes it is more complicated.

Take the opportunity costs of your choices as a student of economics.

Buying a textbook costing £21.95

This does involve a direct money payment. What you have to consider is the alternatives you could have bought with the £21.95. You then have to weigh up the benefit from the best alternative against the benefit of the textbook.

> ?? What might prevent you from making the best decision?

Coming to classes

You may or may not be paying course fees. Even if you are, there is no extra (marginal) monetary cost in coming to classes once the fees have been paid. You will not get a refund by skipping classes!

So are the opportunity costs zero? No: by coming to classes you are *not* working in the library; you are *not* having an extra hour in bed; you are *not* sitting drinking coffee with friends, and so on. If you are making a rational decision to come to classes, then you will consider such possible alternatives.

> ?? If there are several other things you could have done, is the opportunity cost the sum of all of them?

Revising for an economics exam

Again, the opportunity cost is the best alternative to which you could have put your time. This might be revising for some *other* exam. You will probably want to divide your time sensibly between your subjects. A *sensible* decision is not to revise economics on any given occasion if you will gain a greater benefit from revising for another subject. In such a case the (marginal) opportunity cost of revising economics exceeds the (marginal) benefit.

Choosing to study at university or college

What are the opportunity costs of being a student in higher education?

At first it might seem that the costs would include the following:

- Tuition fees.
- Books, stationery, etc.
- Accommodation expenses.
- Transport.
- Food, entertainment and other living expenses.

But adding these up does *not* give the *opportunity* cost. The opportunity cost is the *sacrifice* entailed by going to university or college *rather* than doing something else. Let us assume that the alternative is to take a job that has been offered. The correct list of opportunity costs of higher education would include:

- Books, stationery, etc.
- *Additional* accommodation and transport expenses over what would have been incurred by taking the job.
- Wages that would have been earned in the job *less* any student grant received.

Note that tuition fees are not included because it is assumed that these are paid by the student's local education authority.

> ??
> 1. Why is the cost of food not included?
> 2. Make a list of the benefits of higher education.
> 3. Is the opportunity cost to the individual of attending higher education different from the opportunity costs to society as a whole?

Illustrating economic issues: the production possibility curve

Economics books and articles often contain diagrams. The reason is that diagrams are very useful for illustrating economic relationships. Ideas and arguments that might take a long time to explain in words can often be expressed clearly and simply in a diagram. Even when arguments are expressed fully in words, an accompanying diagram can help to make the arguments more precise and easier to grasp.

Two of the most common types of diagram used in economics are graphs and flow diagrams. In this and the

ISSUES AND APPLICATIONS — BOX 1.4

SCARCITY AND ABUNDANCE

Is lunch ever free?

The central economic problem is scarcity. But are *all* goods and services scarce? Is anything we desire truly abundant?

First, what do we mean by *abundance*? In the economic sense we mean something where supply exceeds demand at a *zero* price. In other words, even if it is free, there is no shortage. What is more, there must be no opportunity cost in supplying it. For example, if the government supplies health care free to the sick, it is still scarce in the economic sense because there is a cost to the government (and hence the taxpayer).

Two things that might seem to be abundant are air and water.

Air

In one sense air *is* abundant. There is no shortage of air to breathe for most people for most of the time.

But if we define air as clean, unpolluted air, then in some parts of the world it is scarce. In these cases, resources have to be used to make clean air available. If there is pollution in cities or near industrial plants, it will cost money to clean it up. The citizen may not pay directly – the cleaned-up air may be free to the 'consumer' – but the taxpayer or industry (and hence its customers) will have to pay.

Another example is when extractor fans have to be installed to freshen up air in buildings.

Even if you live in a non-polluted part of the country, you may well have spent money moving there to escape the pollution. Again there is an opportunity cost to obtain the clean air.

Water

Whether water is abundant depends again on where you live. It also depends on what the water is used for.

Water for growing crops in a country with plentiful rain *is* abundant. In drier countries, resources have to be spent on irrigation.

Water for drinking is not abundant. Reservoirs have to be built. The water has to be piped, purified and pumped.

??

1. There is a saying in economics, 'There is no such thing as a free lunch' (hence the subtitle for this box). What does this mean?
2. Are any other (desirable) goods or services truly abundant?

next section we will look at one example of each. These examples are chosen to illustrate the distinction between microeconomic and macroeconomic issues.

We start by having a look at a **production possibility curve**. This diagram is a graph. Like many diagrams in economics it shows a simplified picture of reality – a picture stripped of all details that are unnecessary to illustrate the points being made. Of course, there are dangers in this. In the attempt to make a diagram simple enough to understand, we run the risk of oversimplifying. If this is the case, the diagram may be misleading.

A production possibility curve is shown in Figure 1.1. The graph is based on the data shown in Table 1.1.

Assume that some imaginary nation devotes all its resources – land, labour and capital – to producing just two goods, food and clothing. Various possible combinations that could be produced over a given period of time (e.g. a year) are shown in the table. Thus the country, by devoting all its resources to producing food, could produce 8 million units of food but no clothing. Alternatively by producing, say, 7 million units of food it could release enough resources – land, labour and capital – to produce 2.2 million units of clothing. At the other extreme, it could produce 7 million units of clothing with no resources at all being used to produce food.

The information in the table can be transferred to a graph (Figure 1.1). We measure units of food on one axis (in this case the vertical axis) and units of clothing on the other. The curve shows all the combinations of the two goods that can be produced with all the nation's resources fully and efficiently employed. For example, production could take place at point *x*, with 6 million units of food and 4 million units of clothing being produced. Production cannot take place beyond the curve. For example, production is not possible at point *w*: the nation does not have enough resources to do this.

Note that there are two simplifying assumptions in this diagram. First, it is assumed that there are just two types of good that can be produced. It is necessary to

DEFINITION

Production possibility curve A curve showing all the possible combinations of two goods that a country can produce within a specified time period with all its resources fully and efficiently employed.

Table 1.1 Maximum possible combinations of food and clothing that can be produced in a given time period

Units of food (millions)	Units of clothing (millions)
8.0	0.0
7.0	2.2
6.0	4.0
5.0	5.0
4.0	5.6
3.0	6.0
2.0	6.4
1.0	6.7
0.0	7.0

assumption because we only have two axes on our graph. The other assumption is that there is only one type of food and one type of clothing. This is implied by measuring their output in particular units (e.g. tonnes). If food differed in type, there would be the possibility of producing a greater tonnage of food for a given amount of clothing simply by switching production from one foodstuff to another.

These two assumptions are obviously enormous simplifications when we consider the modern complex economies of the real world. But despite this, the diagram still allows important principles to be illustrated, and illustrated simply.

Microeconomics and the production possibility curve

A production possibility curve illustrates the microeconomic issues of *choice* and *opportunity cost.*

If the country chose to produce more clothing, it would have to sacrifice the production of some food. This sacrifice of food is the opportunity cost of the extra clothing.

The fact that to produce more of one good involves producing less of the other is illustrated by the downward-sloping nature of the curve. For example, the country could move from point *x* to point *y* in Figure 1.2. In doing so it would be producing an extra 1 million units of clothing, but 1 million units less of food. Thus the opportunity cost of the 1 million extra units of clothing would be the 1 million units of food forgone.

It also illustrates the phenomenon of **increasing opportunity costs**. By this we mean that as a country produces more of one good it has to sacrifice ever *increasing* amounts of the other. The reason for this is that different factors of production have different properties. People have different skills; land differs in different parts of the country; raw materials differ one from another; and so on. Thus as the nation concentrates more and more on the production of one good, it has to start using resources that are less and less suitable – resources that would have been better suited to producing other goods. In our example, then, the production of more and more clothing will involve a growing *marginal cost*: ever increasing amounts of food have to be sacrificed for each additional unit of clothing produced.

It is because opportunity costs increase that the production possibility curve is bowed outward rather than being a straight line. Thus in Figure 1.2 as production moves from point *x* to *y* to *z*, so the amount of food sacrificed rises for each additional unit of clothing produced. The opportunity cost of the fifth million units of clothing is

DEFINITION

Increasing opportunity costs of production
When additional production of one good involves ever increasing sacrifices of another.

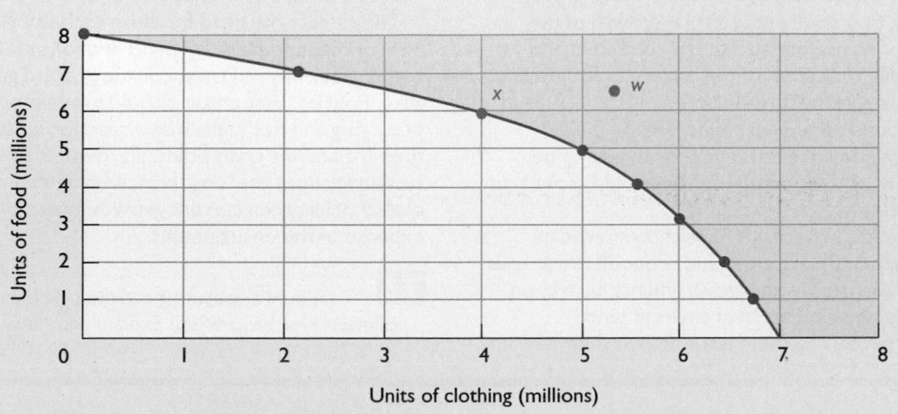

Figure 1.1 A production possibility curve

ISSUES AND APPLICATIONS BOX 1.5

GREEN ECONOMICS
Taking account of environmental costs

People have become concerned by a number of environmental problems in recent years. These include the following:

- *Acid rain.* This is caused by sulphur and nitrogen emissions from power stations, industry and cars. It has been blamed for *Waldsterben* (forest death) in Central Europe and the contamination of many lakes and streams, with the death of fish and plant life.
- *The greenhouse effect.* This is caused by carbon dioxide and other gases emitted again by power stations, various industries and cars. The fear is that these gases will cause a heating of the earth's atmosphere. This will lead to climatic changes which will affect food production. It will also lead to a raising of sea levels and flooding as parts of the polar ice caps melt.
- *Depletion of the ozone layer.* This is caused by the use of CFC gases in aerosols, refrigerators and the manufacture of polystyrene foam. The ozone layer protects us from harmful ultraviolet radiation from the sun. A depletion of this layer could lead to increased skin cancer.
- *Nuclear radiation.* The fear is that accidents or sabotage at nuclear power stations could cause dangerous releases of radiation. The disposal of nuclear waste is another environmental problem.
- *Land and river pollution.* The tipping of toxic waste into the ground or into rivers can cause long-term environmental damage. Soils can be poisoned; rivers and seas can become polluted. It is not just industry that is to blame here. Sewage pollutes rivers and seas. Nitrogen run-off and slurry from farming are also major pollutants.

It was not until the late 1960s and early 1970s that the 'environment' became more firmly part of the political agenda in most European countries. It was largely a response not only to the spectacular growth of the Western economies, but also to the continued and extensive industrialisation of the Eastern bloc countries such as Poland and the former USSR.

'Green groups' sprang up round Europe. These groups realised that, if economic growth was to be sustained, then environmental damage could grow at an alarming rate.

The problems such groups have encountered in attempting to change attitudes and economic strategies have been immense. Certain governments have been reluctant to enter international environmental agreements, perceiving them to be against their national interest. The agreement to cut sulphur dioxide emissions from power stations is one example.

The costs of pollution abatement are high, especially in the short run. As long as these short-run costs are greater than the perceived costs of continuing pollution, then industry and government will continue to incur them. The consequences of this, however, could be devastating and far more costly in the long run, in both a financial and an environmental sense.

What can economists say about the causes of these environmental problems? They have three common features:

- *Ignorance.* It is often not for many years that the nature and causes of environmental damage are realised. Take the case of aerosols. It was not until the 1980s that scientists connected their use to ozone depletion.
- *The polluters do not pay.* The costs of pollution are rarely paid by the polluters. Economists call such costs *external* costs. Because polluters rarely pay to clean up their pollution or compensate those who suffer, they frequently ignore the problem.
- *Present gains for future costs.* The environmental costs of industrialisation often build up slowly and do not become critical for many years. The benefits of industrialisation, however, are more immediate. Thus governments, consumers and industry are frequently prepared to continue with various practices and leave future generations to worry about their environmental consequences. The problem is therefore a reflection of the importance that people attach to the present relative to the future.

Environmentalists recognise these problems and try through the political process and various pressure groups, such as Friends of the Earth and Greenpeace, to reduce people's ignorance and to change their attitudes.

They stress the need for clean technologies, for environmentally sound growth and for greater responsibility by industry, consumers and government alike. Policies, they argue, should prevent problems occurring and not merely be a reaction to them once they are nearing crisis point. If growth is to be sustainable into the long term, with a real increase in the quality of life, then current growth must not be at the expense of the environment.

?? Should all polluting activities be banned? Could pollution ever be justified? Explain your answer.

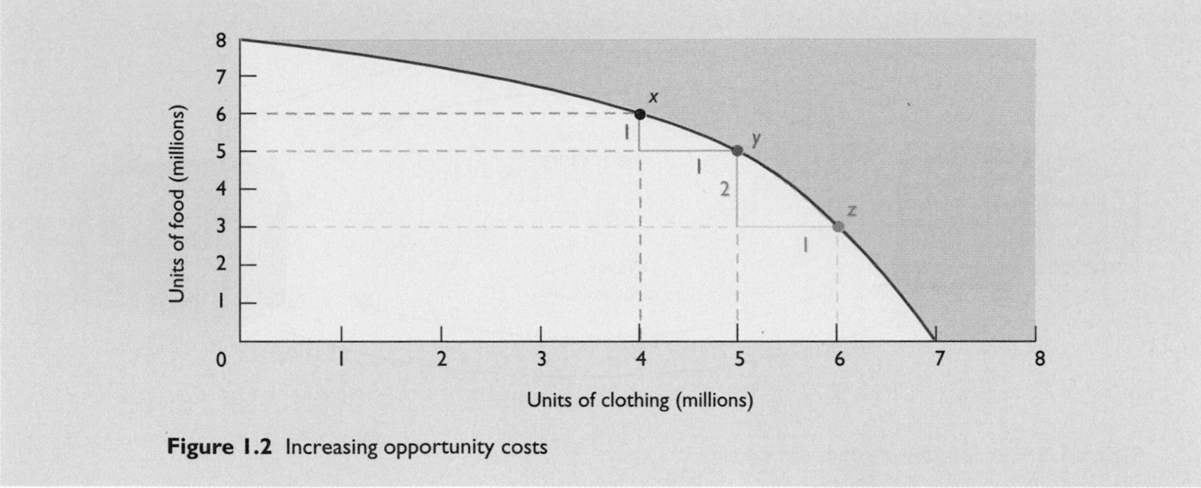

Figure 1.2 Increasing opportunity costs

1 million units of food. The opportunity cost of the sixth million units of clothing is 2 million units of food.

??

1. What is the opportunity cost of the seventh million units of clothing?
2. If the country moves upward along the curve and produces more food, does this also involve increasing opportunity costs?
3. Under what circumstances would the production possibility curve be (a) a straight line; (b) bowed in toward the origin? Are these circumstances ever likely?

Macroeconomics and the production possibility curve

There is no guarantee that resources will be fully employed, or that they will be used in the most efficient way possible. The nation may thus be producing at a point inside the curve: for example, point *v* in Figure 1.3.

What we are saying here is that the economy is producing less of both goods than it could possibly produce, either because some resources are not being used (for example, workers may be unemployed), or because it is not using the most efficient methods of production possible, or a combination of the two. By using its resources to the full, however, the nation could move out on to the curve: to point *x* or *y*, for example. It could thus produce more clothing *and* more food.

Here we are concerned not with the combination of goods produced (a microeconomic issue), but with whether the total amount produced is as much as it could be (a macroeconomic issue).

Over time, the production possibilities of a nation are likely to increase. **Investment** in new plant and machinery will increase the stock of capital; new raw materials may be discovered; technological advances are likely to take place; through education and training, labour is likely to become more productive. This growth in potential output is illustrated by an outward shift in the production possibility curve. This will then allow actual output to increase: for example, from point *x* to point *x′* in Figure 1.4.

DEFINITION

Investment The production of items that are not for immediate consumption.

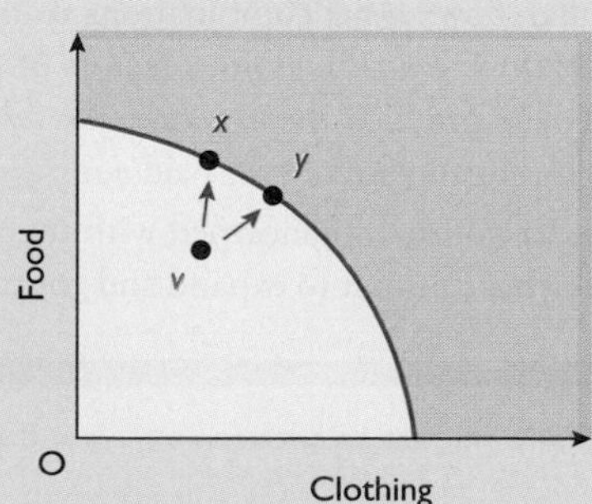

Figure 1.3 Making a fuller use of resources

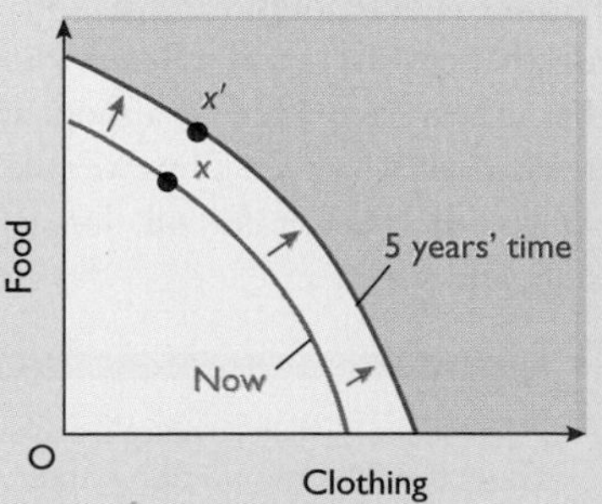

Figure 1.4 Growth in potential output

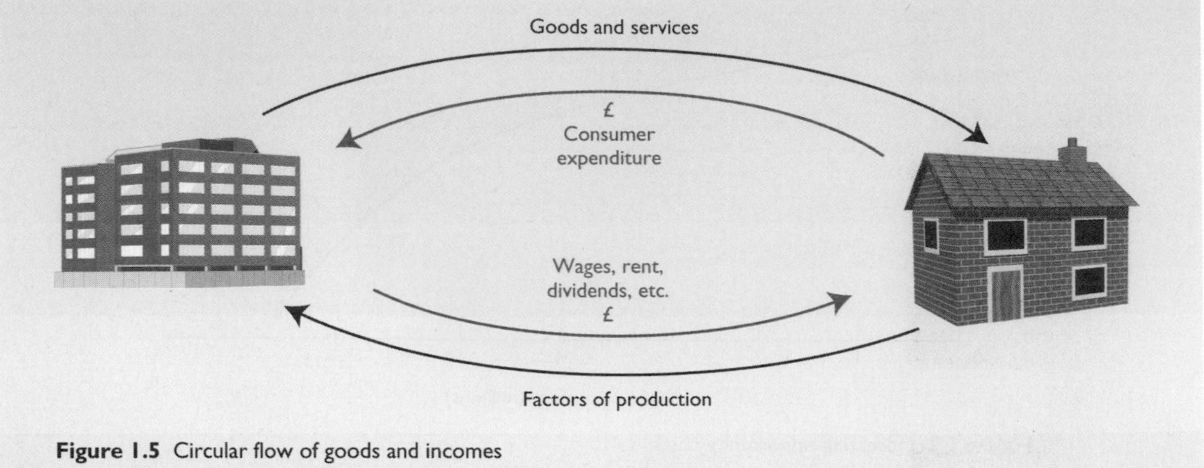

Figure 1.5 Circular flow of goods and incomes

> **??** Will economic growth necessarily involve a *parallel outward* shift of the production possibility curve?

Illustrating economic issues: the circular flow of goods and incomes

The process of satisfying human wants involves producers and consumers. The relationship between them is two-sided and can be represented in a flow diagram (see Figure 1.5).

The consumers of goods and services are labelled 'households'. Some members of households, of course, are also workers, and in some cases are the owners of other factors of production too, such as land. The producers of goods and services are labelled 'firms'.

Firms and households are in a twin 'demand and supply' relationship with each other.

First, in the top part of the diagram, households demand goods and services, and firms supply goods and services. In the process, exchange takes place. In a money economy (as opposed to a **barter economy**), firms exchange goods and services for money. In other words, money flows from households to firms in the form of consumer expenditure, while goods and services flow the other way – from firms to households.

This coming together of buyers and sellers is known as a **market** – whether it be a street market, a shop, an auction, a mail-order system or whatever. Thus we talk about the market for apples, the market for oil, for cars, for houses, for televisions and so on.

Second, firms and households come together in the market for factors of production. This is illustrated in the bottom part of the diagram. This time the demand and supply roles are reversed. Firms demand the use of factors of production owned by households – labour, land and capital. Households supply them. Thus the services of labour and other factors flow from households to firms, and in exchange firms pay households money – namely, wages, rent, dividends and interest. Just as we referred to particular goods markets, so we can also refer to particular factor markets – the market for bricklayers, for secretaries, for hairdressers, for land, etc.

There is thus a circular flow of incomes. Households earn incomes from firms and firms earn incomes from households. The money circulates. There is also a circular flow of goods and services, but in the opposite direction. Households supply factor services to firms who then use them to supply goods and services to households.

This flow diagram, like the production possibility curve, can help to show the distinction between microeconomics and macroeconomics.

Microeconomics is concerned with the composition of the circular flow: *what* combinations of goods make up the goods flow; *how* the various factors of production are combined to produce these goods; *for whom* the wages, dividends, rent and interest are paid out.

Macroeconomics is concerned with the total size of the flow and what causes it to expand and contract.

DEFINITIONS

Barter economy An economy where people exchange goods and services directly with one another without any payment of money. Workers would be paid with bundles of goods.

Market The interaction between buyers and sellers.

SECTION SUMMARY

1. The central economic problem is that of scarcity. Given that there is a limited supply of factors of production (labour, land and capital), it is impossible to provide everybody with everything they want. Potential demands exceed potential supplies.
2. The subject of economics is usually divided into two main branches, macroeconomics and microeconomics.
3. Macroeconomics deals with aggregates such as the overall levels of unemployment, output, growth and prices in the economy.
4. Microeconomics deals with the activities of individual units within the economy: firms, industries, consumers, workers, etc. Because resources are scarce, people have to make choices. Society has to choose by some means or other *what* goods and services to produce, *how* to produce them and *for whom* to produce them. Microeconomics studies these choices.
5. Rational choices involve weighing up the marginal benefits of each activity against its marginal opportunity costs. If the marginal benefit exceeds the marginal cost, it is rational to choose to do more of that activity.
6. The production possibility curve shows the possible combinations of two goods that a country can produce in a given period of time. Assuming that the country is already producing on the curve, the production of more of one good will involve producing less of the other. This opportunity cost is illustrated by the slope of the curve. If the economy is producing within the curve as a result of idle resources or inefficiency, it can produce more of both goods by taking up this slack. In the longer term it can only produce more of both by shifting the curve outwards through investment, technological progress, etc.
7. The circular flow of goods and incomes shows the interrelationships between firms and households in a money economy. Firms and households come together in markets. In goods markets, firms supply goods and households demand goods. In the process, money flows from households to firms in return for the goods and services that the firms supply. In factor markets, firms demand factors of production and households supply them. In the process, money flows from firms to households in return for the services of the factors that households supply.

1.2 Different economic systems

The classification of economic systems

All societies are faced with the problem of scarcity. They differ considerably, however, in the way they tackle the problem. One important difference between societies is in the degree of government control of the economy.

At the one extreme lies the completely **planned or command economy**, where all the economic decisions are taken by the government.

At the other extreme lies the completely **free-market economy**. In this type of economy there is no government intervention at all. All decisions are taken by individuals and firms. Households decide how much labour and other factors to supply, and what goods to consume. Firms decide what goods to produce and what factors to employ. The pattern of production and consumption that results depends on the interactions of all these individual demand and supply decisions.

In practice all economies are a mixture of the two. It is therefore the *degree* of government intervention that distinguishes different economic systems. Thus in the former communist countries of Eastern Europe, the government played a large role, whereas in the United States, the government plays a much smaller role.

It is nevertheless useful to analyse the extremes, in order to put the different **mixed economies** of the real world into perspective. The mixture of government and the market

DEFINITIONS

Centrally planned or command economy An economy where all economic decisions are taken by the central authorities.

Free-market economy An economy where all economic decisions are taken by individual households and firms and with no government intervention.

Mixed economy An economy where economic decisions are made partly by the government and partly through the market.

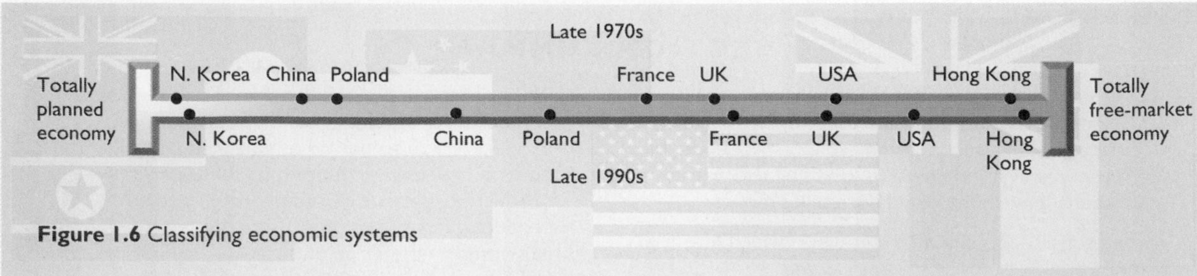

Figure 1.6 Classifying economic systems

can be shown by the use of a *spectrum diagram* such as Figure 1.6. It shows where particular economies of the real world lie along the spectrum between the two extremes.

The diagram is useful in that it provides a simple picture of the mixture of government and the market that exists in various economies. It can also be used to show changes in the mixture over time.

The problem with this type of classification is that it is 'unidimensional', and thus rather simplistic. Countries also differ in the *type* of government intervention as well as the level. For example, governments intervene through planning, through nationalisation, through regulation, through taxes and subsidies, through partnership schemes with private industry, and so on. Thus two countries could be in a similar position along the spectrum but have types of government intervention that were quite different. In one, the intervention could be through the public ownership of industries; in the other, it could be through rules and regulations governing the behaviour of private industries.

Notice that there has been a general movement to the right along the spectrum since the late 1970s. In East European economies this has been a result of the abandonment of central planning and the adoption of a large measure of private enterprise, especially since the late 1980s. In Western economies it has been a result of deregulation of private industry and privatisation (the selling of nationalised industries to the private sector).

?? Do you agree with the positions that the seven countries have been given in the spectrum diagram? Explain why or why not.

The command economy

The command economy is usually associated with a socialist or communist economic system, where land and capital are collectively owned. The state plans the allocation of resources at three important levels:

- It plans the allocation of resources between current consumption and investment for the future. By sacrificing some present consumption and diverting resources into investment, it could increase the economy's growth rate.

  The amount of resources it chooses to devote to investment will depend on its broad macroeconomic strategy: the importance it attaches to growth as opposed to current consumption.
- At a microeconomic level it plans the output of each industry and firm, the techniques that will be used, and the labour and other resources required by each industry and firm.

  In order to ensure that the required inputs are available, the state would probably conduct some form of **input–output analysis**. All industries are seen as users of *inputs* from other industries and as producers of *output* for consumers or other industries. For example, the steel industry uses inputs from the coal and iron-ore industries and produces output for the vehicle and construction industries. Input–output analysis shows, for each industry, the sources of all its inputs and the destination of all its output. By its use the state attempts to match up the inputs and outputs of each industry so that the planned demand for each industry's product is equal to its planned supply.
- It plans the distribution of output between consumers. This will depend on the government's aims. It may distribute goods according to its judgement of people's *needs*; or it may give more to those who produce more, thereby providing an *incentive* for people to work harder; or more likely it will try to find some compromise between the two.

  It may distribute goods and services directly; or it may decide the distribution of money incomes and allow individuals to decide how to spend them. If it does the latter, it may still seek to influence the pattern of expendi-

DEFINITION

Input–output analysis This involves dividing the economy into sectors where each sector is a user of inputs from and a supplier of outputs to other sectors. The technique examines how these inputs and outputs can be matched to the total resources available in the economy.

ture by setting appropriate prices: low prices to encourage consumption, and high prices to discourage consumption.

The free-market economy

Free decision making by individuals

The free-market economy is usually associated with a pure capitalist system, where land and capital are privately owned. All economic decisions are taken by households and firms, which are assumed to act in their own self-interest. These assumptions are made:

- Firms seek to maximise profits.
- Consumers seek to get the best value for money from their purchases.
- Workers seek to maximise their wages relative to the human cost of working in a particular job.

It is assumed that individuals are free to make their own economic choices. Consumers are free to decide what to buy with their incomes. Workers are free to choose where and how much to work. Firms are free to choose what to sell and what production methods to use.

The resulting supply and demand decisions of firms and households are transmitted to each other through their effect on *prices*.

The price mechanism

The price mechanism works as follows. Prices respond to *shortages* and *surpluses*. Shortages cause prices to rise. Surpluses cause prices to fall.

If consumers decide they want more of a good (or if producers decide to cut back supply), demand will exceed supply. The resulting shortage will cause the price of the good to *rise*. This will act as an incentive to producers to supply more, since production will now be more profitable. It will discourage consumers from buying so much. *Price will continue rising until the shortage has thereby been eliminated.*

If, on the other hand, consumers decide they want less of a good (or if producers decide to produce more), supply will exceed demand. The resulting surplus will cause the price of the good to *fall*. This will act as a disincentive to producers, who will supply less, since production will now be less profitable. It will encourage consumers to buy more. *Price will continue falling until the surplus has thereby been eliminated.*

The same analysis can be applied to factor markets. If the demand for a particular type of labour exceeded its supply, the resulting shortage would drive up the wage rate (i.e. the price of labour), thus reducing firms' demand for that type of labour and encouraging more workers to take up that type of job. Wages would continue rising until demand equalled supply: until the shortage was eliminated.

Likewise if there were a surplus of a particular type of labour, the wage would fall until demand equalled supply.

> **??** Can you think of any examples where prices and wages do not adjust very rapidly to a shortage or surplus? For what reasons might they not do so?

The effect of changes in demand and supply

How will the price mechanism respond to changes in consumer demand or producer supply? After all, the pattern of consumer demand changes. For example, people may decide they want more mountain bikes and fewer racers. Likewise the pattern of supply changes. For example, changes in technology may allow the mass production of microchips at lower cost, while the production of hand-built furniture becomes relatively expensive.

In all cases of changes in demand and supply, the resulting changes in *price* act as both *signals* and *incentives*.

A change in demand. A rise in demand is signalled by a rise in price. This then acts as an incentive for supply to rise. What in effect is happening is that the high price of these goods relative to their costs of production is signalling that consumers are willing to see resources diverted from other uses. This is just what firms do. They divert resources from goods with lower prices relative to costs (and hence lower profits) to those goods that are more profitable.

A fall in demand is signalled by a fall in price. This then acts as an incentive for supply to fall. The goods are now less profitable to produce.

A change in supply. A rise in supply is signalled by a fall in price. This then acts as an incentive for demand to rise. A fall in supply is signalled by a rise in price. This then acts as an incentive for demand to fall.

> **??**
> 1. Why do the prices of fresh vegetables fall when they are in season? Could an individual farmer prevent the price falling?
> 2. If you were the owner of a clothes shop, how would you set about deciding what prices to charge for each garment at the end of season sale?
> 3. The number of owners of compact disc players has grown rapidly and hence the demand for compact discs has also grown rapidly. Yet the prices of discs have fallen. Why?

> **DEFINITION**
>
> **The price mechanism** The system in a market economy whereby changes in price in response to changes in demand and supply have the effect of making demand equal to supply.

CASE STUDIES

THE RISE AND FALL OF PLANNING IN THE FORMER SOVIET UNION

Early years

The Bolsheviks under the leadership of Lenin came to power in Russia with the October revolution of 1917. The Bolsheviks, however, were opposed by the White Russians and civil war ensued.

During this period of *War Communism*, the market economy was abolished. Industry and shops were nationalised; workers were told what jobs to do; there were forced requisitions of food from peasants to feed the towns; the money economy collapsed as rampant inflation made money worthless; workers were allocated goods from distribution depots.

With the ending of the civil war in 1921, the economy was in bad shape. Lenin embarked on a *New Economic Policy*. This involved a return to the use of markets. Smaller businesses were returned to private hands, and peasants were able to sell their food rather than having it requisitioned. The economy began to recover.

Lenin died in 1924 and Stalin came to power.

The Stalinist system

The Soviet economy underwent a radical transformation from 1928 onwards. The key features of the Stalinist approach were collectivisation, industrialisation and central planning.

Collectivisation of agriculture

Peasant farms were abolished and replaced by large-scale collective farms where land was collectively owned and worked. Collectivisation initially caused massive disruption and famine, with peasants slaughtering their animals rather than giving them up to the collective. People died in their thousands. Despite an initial fall in output, more food was provided for the towns, and many workers left the land to work in the new industries.

In addition to the collective farms, state farms were established. These were owned by the state and were run by managers appointed by the state. Workers were paid a wage rather than having a share in farm income.

Both collective and state farms were given quotas of output that they were supposed to deliver for which the state would pay a fixed price.

Industry and central planning

A massive drive to industrialisation took place. To achieve this a vast planning apparatus was developed. At the top was *Gosplan*, the central planning agency. This prepared five-year plans and annual plans.

The five-year plans specified the general direction in which the economy was to move. The annual plans gave the details of just what was to be produced and with what resources for some 200 or so key products. Other products were planned at a lower level – by various industrial ministries or regional authorities.

The effect was that all factories were given targets that had to be achieved. It was the task of the planning authorities to ensure that the targets were realistic: that there were sufficient resources to meet the targets. The system operated without the aid of the price mechanism and the profit motive. The main incentive was the *bonus*: bonuses were paid to managers and workers if targets were achieved.

The Stalinist system remained with only minor changes until the 1980s. In the early years, very high growth rates were achieved; but this was at a cost of low efficiency. The poor flow of information from firms to the planners led to many inconsistencies in the plans. The targets were often totally unrealistic, and as a result

The interdependence of markets

The interdependence of goods and factor markets. A rise in demand for a good will raise its price and profitability. Firms will respond by supplying more. But to do this they will need more inputs. Thus the demand for the inputs will rise, which in turn will raise the price of the inputs. The suppliers of inputs will respond to this incentive by supplying more. This can be summarised as follows:

1. Goods market
   - Demand for the good rises.
   - This creates a shortage.
   - This causes the price of the good to rise.
   - This eliminates the shortage by choking off some of the demand and encouraging firms to produce more.
2. Factor market
   - The increased supply of the good causes an increase in the demand for factors of production (i.e. inputs) used in making it.
   - This causes a shortage of those inputs.
   - This causes their prices to rise.
   - This eliminates their shortage by choking off some of the demand and encouraging the suppliers of inputs to supply more.

Goods markets thus affect factor markets.

BOX 1.6

there were frequent shortages and sometimes surpluses. With incentives purely geared to meeting targets, there was little product innovation and goods were frequently of poor quality and finish.

The limits of planning

Although most resources were allocated through planning, there were nevertheless some goods that were sold in markets. Any surpluses above their quota that were produced by collective farms could be sold in collective farm markets (street markets) in the towns. In addition, the workers on collective farms were allowed to own their own small private plots of land, and they too could sell their produce in the collective farm markets.

A large 'underground economy' flourished in which goods were sold on the black market and in which people did second 'unofficial' jobs (e.g. as plumbers, electricians or garment makers).

Gorbachev's reforms

Stalin died in 1953. The planning system, however, remained largely unchanged until the late 1980s.

During the 1970s growth had slowed down and by the time Gorbachev came to power in 1985 many people were pressing for fundamental economic reforms. Gorbachev responded with his policy of *perestroika* (economic reconstruction), which among other things included the following:

- Making managers more involved in preparing their own plans rather than merely being given instructions.
- Insisting that firms cover their costs of production. If they could not, the state might refuse to bale them out and they could be declared bankrupt. The aim of this was to encourage firms to be more efficient.
- Improving the incentive system by making bonuses more related to genuine productivity. Workers had come to expect bonuses no matter how much or how little was produced.
- Organising workers into small teams or 'brigades' (typically of around 10–15 workers). Bonuses were then awarded to the whole brigade according to its productivity. The idea was to encourage people to work more effectively together.
- Stringent checks on quality by state officials and the rejection of substandard goods.
- Allowing one-person businesses and co-operatives (owned by the workers) to be set up.
- A greater willingness by the state to raise prices if there were substantial shortages.

These reforms, however, did not halt the economic decline. What is more there was now an unhappy mix of planning and the market, with people unclear as to what to expect from the state. Many managers resented the extra responsibilities they were now expected to shoulder and many officials saw their jobs threatened. Queues lengthened in the shops and people increasingly became disillusioned with *perestroika*.

Following the failed coup of 1991, in which hard-line communists had attempted to reimpose greater state control, and with the consequent strengthening of the position of Boris Yeltsin, the Russian president and the main advocate of more radical reforms, both the Soviet Union and the system of central planning came to an end.

Russia embarked upon a radical programme of market reforms in which competition and enterprise were intended to replace state central planning (see Box 1.8). The Stalinist system now appears to be but a fading memory.

It is common in economics to summarise an argument like this by using symbols. It is a form of shorthand. Figure 1.7 summarises this particular sequence of events.

Interdependence exists in the other direction too: factor markets affect goods markets. For example, the discovery of raw materials will lower their price. This will lower the costs of production of firms using these raw materials and will increase the supply of the finished goods. The resulting surplus will lower the price of the good, which will encourage consumers to buy more.

?? Summarise this last paragraph using symbols like those in Figure 1.7.

The interdependence of different goods markets. A rise in the price of one good will encourage consumers to buy alternatives. This will drive up the price of alternatives. This in turn will encourage producers to supply more of the alternatives.

?? Are different factor markets similarly interdependent? Give examples.

Conclusion

Even though all individuals are merely looking to their own self-interest in the free-market economy, they are in fact being encouraged to respond to the wishes of others through the incentive of the price mechanism.

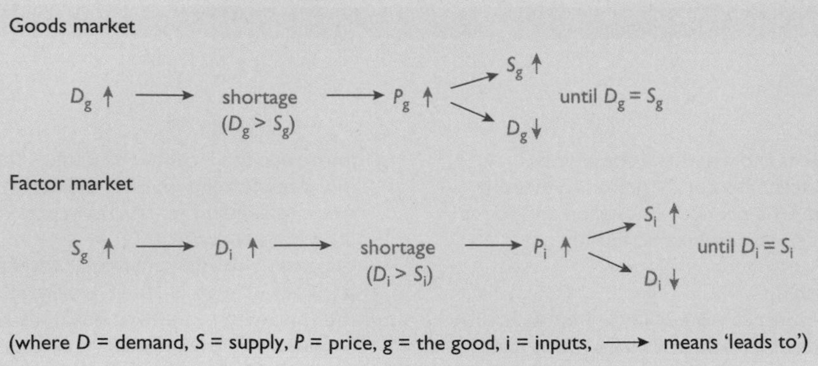

Goods market

$D_g \uparrow$ ⟶ shortage ($D_g > S_g$) ⟶ $P_g \uparrow$ ⟶ $S_g \uparrow$ / $D_g \downarrow$ until $D_g = S_g$

Factor market

$S_g \uparrow$ ⟶ $D_i \uparrow$ ⟶ shortage ($D_i > S_i$) ⟶ $P_i \uparrow$ ⟶ $S_i \uparrow$ / $D_i \downarrow$ until $D_i = S_i$

(where D = demand, S = supply, P = price, g = the good, i = inputs, ⟶ means 'leads to')

Figure 1.7 The price mechanism: the effect of a rise in demand

Assessment of the free-market economy

The fact that a free-market economy functions automatically is one of its major advantages. There is no need for costly and complex bureaucracies to co-ordinate economic decisions. The economy can respond quickly to changing demand and supply conditions.

When markets are highly competitive, no one has great power. Competition between firms keeps prices down and acts as an incentive to firms to become more efficient. The more firms there are competing, the more responsive they will be to consumer wishes.

The more efficiently firms can combine their factors of production, the more profit they will make. The more efficiently workers work, the more secure will be their jobs and the higher their wages. The more carefully consumers decide what to buy, the greater the value for money they will receive.

Thus people pursuing their own self-interest through buying and selling in competitive markets helps to minimise the central economic problem of scarcity, by encouraging the efficient use of the nation's resources in line with consumer wishes. From this type of argument, the following conclusion is often drawn by defenders of the free market: 'The pursuit of private gain results in the social good.' This is obviously a highly significant claim and has profound moral implications.

In practice, however, markets do not achieve maximum efficiency in the allocation of scarce resources, and governments feel it necessary to intervene to rectify this and other problems of the free market. The problems of a free market are as follows:

- Competition between firms is often limited. A few giant firms may dominate an industry. In these cases they may charge high prices and make large profits. Rather than merely responding to consumer wishes, they may attempt to persuade consumers by advertising. Consumers are particularly susceptible to advertisements for products that are new to them and of which they have little knowledge.
- Lack of competition and high profits may remove the incentive for firms to be efficient.
- Power and property may be unequally distributed. Those who have power and/or property (e.g. big business, unions, landlords) will gain at the expense of those without power and property.
- The practices of some firms may be socially undesirable. For example, a chemical works may pollute the environment.
- Some socially desirable goods would simply not be produced by private enterprise. What firm would build and operate a lighthouse?
- A free-market economy may lead to macroeconomic instability. There may be periods of recession with high unemployment and falling output, and other periods of rising prices.
- Finally, there is the ethical objection, that a free-market economy, by rewarding self-interested behaviour, may encourage selfishness, greed, materialism and the acquisition of power.

Assessment of the command economy

Central planning can overcome some of the problems of a free-market economy. Instead of having to rely on the decisions of millions of individuals, decisions that will not always be in the interests of society as a whole, the government could take an overall view of the economy. It could direct the nation's resources in accordance with specific national goals.

High growth rates could be achieved if the government directed large amounts of resources into investment. Unemployment could be largely avoided if the government

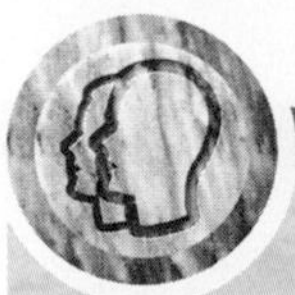

DEVELOPMENT OF IDEAS BOX 1.7

ADAM SMITH (1723–90)
and the 'invisible hand' of the market

Many economists would argue that modern economics dates from 1776. That was the year in which Adam Smith's *An Inquiry into the Nature and Causes of the Wealth of Nations* was published – one of the most important books on economics ever written.

Adam Smith was born in 1723 in Kirkcaldy, a small coastal town north of Edinburgh. His father died when Adam was just a baby, and for most of his life he lived with his mother: he never married. After graduating from Glasgow University at the age of 17, he first became a fellow of Balliol College Oxford, but then returned to Scotland and at the age of 29 became professor of moral philosophy at the University of Glasgow. At the age of 40 he resigned and spent three years touring the continent where he met many influential economists and philosophers. He then returned to Scotland, to his home town of Kirkcaldy, and set to work on *The Wealth of Nations*.

The work, in five books, is very wide ranging, but the central argument is that market economies generally serve the public interest well. Markets guide production and consumption like an *invisible hand*. Even though everyone is looking after their own private self-interest, their interaction in the market will lead to the social good.

In book I, chapter 2, he writes:

> Man has almost constant occasion for the help of his brethren and it is in vain for him to expect it from their benevolence only. He will be more likely to prevail if he can interest their self-love in his favour, and show them that it is for their own advantage to do for him what he requires of them. Whoever offers to another a bargain of any kind, proposes to do this. Give me that what I want, and you shall have this which you want, is the meaning of every such offer; and it is in this manner that we obtain from one another the far greater part of those good offices which we stand in need of. It is not from the benevolence of the butcher, the brewer, or the baker that we expect our dinner, but from their regard to their own interest. We address ourselves, not to their humanity but to their self-love, and never talk to them of our own necessities, but of their advantages.

Later, in book IV, chapter 2, he continues:

> Every individual is continually exerting himself to find out the most advantageous employment of whatever capital he can command. It is his own advantage, indeed, and not that of the society, which he has in view. But the study of his own advantage naturally, or rather necessarily, leads him to prefer that employment which is most advantageous to the society ... he intends only his own gain, and he is in this, as in many other cases, led by an invisible hand to promote an end which was no part of his intention. Nor is it always the worse for the society that it was no part of it. By pursuing his own interest he frequently promotes that of society more effectually than when he really intends to promote it.

He argued, therefore, with one or two exceptions, that the state should not interfere with the functioning of the economy. It should adopt a *laissez-faire* or 'hands-off' policy. It should allow free enterprise for firms and free trade between countries.

This praise of the free market has led many on the political right to regard him as the father of the 'libertarian movement' – the movement that advocates the absolute minimum amount of state intervention in the economy (see Box 11.10). In fact one of the most famous of the libertarian societies is called 'The Adam Smith Institute'.

But Smith was not blind to the drawbacks of unregulated markets. In book I, chapter 7, he looks at the problem of monopoly:

> A monopoly granted either to an individual or to a trading company has the same effect as a secret in trade or manufactures. The monopolists, by keeping the market constantly under-stocked, by never fully supplying the effectual demand, sell their commodities much above the natural price, and raise their emoluments, whether they consist in wages or profit, greatly above their natural rate.

Later on he looks at the dangers of firms getting together to pursue their mutual interest:

> People of the same trade seldom meet together, even for merriment or diversion, but the conversation ends in a conspiracy against the public or in some contrivance to raise prices.

CASE STUDIES BOX 1.8

FREE-MARKET MEDICINE IN RUSSIA

Is the patient recovering?

Reforming the old Soviet Union was never going to be easy. To replace central planning with free markets and enterprise would involve a radical transformation of economic life. But following the rise to power of Boris Yeltsin in Russia in 1991, this is just what was attempted. The following policies were adopted in early 1992:

- Price controls on 90 per cent of items were abolished. But with shortages of most goods, it was hardly surprising that prices rose dramatically.
- Business was given easier access to foreign exchange, and foreign companies were encouraged to invest in Russia.
- The largest privatisation programme in the world was launched. In many of the new private companies, workers were to become the principal shareholders.

These reforms represented a massive shock to the old system. With the virtual abandonment of price controls, prices soared and by the end of 1992 inflation had reached a massive 1354 per cent. These huge price increases led to falling demand, but the disruption to the economy also led to falling supply. In 1992 output fell by nearly 20 per cent and the purchasing power of wages fell by 40 per cent.

The government's budget deficit (the excess of government spending over government tax receipts) rose from 1.5 per cent of national income in the first quarter of 1992 to 15 per cent by the final quarter. Perhaps most significantly, the money supply rose nearly 600 per cent between January and October. Many commentators began to wonder whether the economy could escape the slide into 'hyperinflation' when money would become virtually worthless (see Box 13.7).

Critics argued that the costs of reform were intolerably high. The Russian economy, inherently weak and resistant to change, was unprepared for the radical nature of the policy and as such the reform programme could not be sustained. They highlighted the following weaknesses inherited from the old system:

- Many Russian companies are virtual monopoly producers. If they run into trouble, as many have done, this leads to huge shortages throughout the economy.
- Industry, being used to taking orders from above, has been slow to adapt to economic change and the rigours of the marketplace. Much of it is highly inefficient and wasteful, making a poor use of very scarce resources. Estimates suggest that in 1992 Russia used 15 times as much steel and 6 times as much energy as the USA per unit of national output.
- With the freeing of prices, many firms in a monopoly position simply raised prices and reduced output. That way they could increase profits but with less effort.

Supporters of reform recognised these weaknesses, but maintained that they only strengthened the arguments for changing the old system. In addition, they argued that the reform package of 1991/2 did not go far enough. Price controls on certain goods remained. Price mark-ups in state shops were limited to 25 per cent, and imports were subject to a 20 per cent tariff (customs duty).

Some supporters of reform argued that an economic slump was the medicine required to drive the old sickness out of the system. It would force inefficient producers out of the market, and the competition for survival would lead to greater productivity and ultimately to long-term prosperity.

Six years on, it appeared that the supporters of reform may have been right in their judgements. The Russian economy seemed to have turned the corner. By early 1998, annual inflation had fallen to 10 per cent. This was due in part to the government bringing its expenditure under tighter control, but was accompanied by severe delays in paying pensioners and public-sector workers! The rouble, after a disastrous collapse on the foreign exchange market in 1994, seemed eventually to have stabilised by 1998. Output, having fallen every year since 1992 (and by as much as 13 per cent in 1994), showed its first increase in 1997 (of 0.4 per cent) and was forecast to grow by 1.0 and 3.0 per cent in 1998 and 1999 respectively.

Critics of reform, even in the light of such real gains, still point to the hardship experienced by many Russians. Official unemployment stands at around 9 per cent, with an estimated additional 6 per cent hidden unemployment. In a fifth of all Russian regions, unemployment is over 30 per cent, and in a few over 50 per cent. Those in work have not fared much better. The average real wage fell by some 37 per cent between 1994 and 1996. Many Russians today are faced with severe hardship.

Some, the 'New Russians', have become very wealthy – some legitimately, but some through criminal activities (the rise of the Russian Mafia has been a disturbing development). The rise of the wealthy further serves to highlight the growing divide between rich and poor.

The old certainties have gone. No longer will the state guarantee employment and a moderate standard of living for all. Today's market system in Russia is one where the strong gain and the weak lose.

??

1. In a market economy, would you expect higher prices to lead to lower or higher output?
2. Would increased competition tend to reduce or increase inequality?

carefully planned the allocation of labour in accordance with production requirements and labour skills. National income could be distributed more equally or in accordance with needs. The social repercussions of production and consumption (e.g. the effects on the environment) could be taken into account, provided the government was able to predict these effects.

In practice, a command economy could achieve these goals only at considerable social and economic cost. The reasons are as follows:

- The larger and more complex the economy, the greater the task of collecting and analysing the information essential to planning, and the more complex the plan. Complicated plans are likely to be costly to administer and involve cumbersome bureaucracy.
- If there is no system of prices, or if prices are set arbitrarily by the state, planning is likely to involve the inefficient use of resources. It is difficult to assess the relative efficiency of two alternative techniques that use different inputs, if there is no way in which the value of those inputs can be ascertained. For example, how can a rational decision be made between an oil-fired and a coal-fired furnace if the prices of oil and coal do not reflect their relative scarcity?
- It is difficult to devise appropriate incentives to encourage workers and managers to be more productive without a reduction in quality. For example, if bonuses are given according to the quantity of output produced, a factory might produce shoddy goods, since it can probably produce a larger quantity of goods by cutting quality. To avoid this problem a large number of officials may have to be employed to check quality.
- Complete state control over resource allocation would involve a considerable loss of individual liberty. Workers would have no choice where to work; consumers would have no choice what to buy.
- The government might enforce its plans even if they were unpopular.
- If production is planned, but consumers are free to spend money incomes as they wish, then the government has the problem of avoiding shortages and surpluses, should consumer wishes change.

The mixed economy

Because of the problems of both the purely market and the purely command economies, all real-world economies are a mixture of the two systems. All 'command' economies use the market mechanism to some extent. All 'market' economies involve some degree of government intervention.

The old communist regimes of Eastern Europe were centrally planned economies, and yet planning was not total. Many goods and services were allocated through the market. For example, much of the produce of collective farms was sold on street markets, at prices determined by demand and supply. Even where the production of goods was planned by the state, consumers were free to purchase what they wanted from what was available, and workers had a lot of freedom to choose where to work. These countries could thus be described as **mixed command economies**.

In **mixed market economies**, the government may control the following:

- **Relative prices** of goods and inputs, by taxing or subsidising them or by direct price controls.
- Relative incomes, by the use of income taxes, welfare payments or direct controls over wages, profits, rents, etc.
- The pattern of production and consumption, by the use of legislation (e.g. making it illegal to produce unsafe goods), by direct provision of goods and services (e.g. education and defence), by taxes and subsidies or by nationalisation.
- The macroeconomic problems of unemployment, inflation, lack of growth and balance of payments deficits, by the use of taxes and government expenditure, the control of bank lending and interest rates, the direct control of prices and incomes, and the control of the foreign exchange rate.

Just how the government intervenes, and what the effects of the various forms of intervention are, will be examined in detail in later chapters.

The relative merits of alternative mixtures of government and the market depend on the weight attached to various political and economic goals: goals such as liberty, equality, efficiency in production, the fulfilling of consumer wishes, economic growth and full employment. No one type of mixed economy is likely to be superior in all respects.

DEFINITIONS

Mixed command economy A planned economy that nevertheless makes some use of markets.

Mixed market economy A market economy where there is some government intervention.

Relative price The price of one good compared with another (e.g. good x is twice the price of good y).

SECTION SUMMARY

1. The economic systems of different countries vary according to the extent to which they rely on the market or the government to allocate resources.
2. At the one extreme, in a command economy, the state makes all the economic decisions. It plans how many resources to allocate for present consumption and how many for investment for future output. It plans the output of each industry, the methods of production it will use and the amount of resources it will be allocated. It plans the distribution of output between consumers.
3. At the other extreme is the free-market economy. In this economy, decisions are made by the interaction of demand and supply. Price changes act as the mechanism whereby demand and supply are balanced. If there is a shortage, price will rise until the shortage is eliminated. If there is a surplus, price will fall until that is eliminated.
4. A command economy has the advantage of being able to address directly various national economic goals, such as rapid growth and the avoidance of unemployment and inequality. A command economy, however, is likely to be inefficient: a large bureaucracy will be needed to collect and process information; prices and the choice of production methods are likely to be arbitrary; incentives may be inappropriate; shortages and surpluses may result.
5. A free-market economy functions automatically and if there is plenty of competition between producers this can help to protect consumers' interests. In practice, however, competition may be limited; there may be great inequality; there may be adverse social and environmental consequences; there may be macroeconomic instability.
6. In practice all economies are some mixture of the market and government intervention. It is the degree and form of government intervention that distinguishes one type of economy from another.

1.3 The nature of economic reasoning

Economics is one of the social sciences. So in what sense is it a *science*? Is it like the natural sciences such as physics and astronomy? What is the significance of the word 'social' in social science? What can economists do, and what is their role in helping governments devise economic policy?

Economics as a science

The methodology employed by economists has a lot in common with that employed by natural scientists. Both attempt to construct theories or **models** which are then used to *explain* and *predict*. An astronomer, for example, constructs models of planetary movements to *explain* why planets are in the position they are and to *predict* their position in the future.

Models in economics

In order to explain and predict, the economist constructs models of the economy or parts of the economy. These models show simplified relationships between various economic phenomena. For example, a model of a market shows the relationships between demand, supply and price. Although most models can be described verbally, they can normally be represented more precisely in graphical or mathematical form.

Building models

Models are constructed by making general hypotheses about the causes of economic phenomena: for example, that consumer demand will rise when consumer incomes rise. These hypotheses will often be based on observations. This process of making general statements from particular observations is known as **induction**.

Using models

Explanation. Models explain by showing how things are caused: what are the causes of inflation, why do workers in some industries earn more than others, and so on.

Prediction. Models are sometimes used to make simple forecasts: for example, inflation will be below 5 per cent

DEFINITIONS

Economic model A formal presentation of an economic theory.

Induction Constructing general theories on the basis of specific observations.

ISSUES AND APPLICATIONS — BOX 1.9

CETERIS PARIBUS?

Because of the complexities of the real world, economic models have to make various simplifying assumptions. Sometimes, however, economists are criticised for making unrealistic assumptions, assumptions that make their models irrelevant. The following joke illustrates the point ...

There were three people cast away on a desert island: a chemist, an engineer and an economist. There was no food on the island and their plight seemed desperate.

Then they discovered a crate of canned food that had been washed up on the island. When they realised that they had no means of opening the cans, they decided that each of them should use their expertise to find a solution.

The chemist searched around for various minerals that could be heated up to produce a compound that would burn through the lids of the cans.

The engineer hunted around for rocks and then worked out what height of tree they would have to be dropped from in order to smash open the cans.

Meanwhile the economist sat down and thought, 'Assuming we had a can opener ... '

next year. Usually, however, predictions are of the 'If ... then ... ' variety: for example, if demand for good x rises, its price will rise. This process of drawing conclusions from models is known as **deduction**.

When making such deductions it has to be assumed that nothing else that can influence the outcome has changed in the meantime. For example, if demand for good x rises, its price will rise *assuming* the cost of producing good x has not fallen. This is known as the ***ceteris paribus*** assumption. *Ceteris paribus* is Latin for 'other things being equal'.

Assessing models

Models can be judged according to how *successful* they are in explaining and predicting.

If the predictions are wrong, the first thing to do is to check whether the deductions were correctly made. If they were, the model must be either adapted or abandoned in favour of an alternative model with better predictive ability.

Sometimes an economist will want to retain a model even though it has poor predictive powers if it helps to give some insight into the workings of the economy. For example, a model of some idealised world in which the goals of efficiency, growth and equality were all met might be extremely useful as a yardstick against which to compare the real world and to understand its shortcomings.

Economics as a social science

Despite using similar models to the natural sciences, economics lacks the ability to make precise predictions with accuracy. There are two major reasons for this.

Controlled experiments

It is impossible to conduct controlled experiments in economics.

Physicists can build models and test them using laboratory experiments under tightly controlled conditions. Economists, however, are dealing with a constantly changing environment and complex interactions between individuals, groups, institutions, etc. In order to develop reasonably simple models they have to make simplifying assumptions. But while they may assume that 'other things remain constant', unlike physicists they cannot *actually* hold them constant.

Some natural sciences such as meteorology have this problem too. A vast number of variables affect the course and development of weather systems. Meteorologists thus have to make a large number of simplifying assumptions. Nevertheless weather forecasting has become more accurate in recent years through the use of satellites and computers. So too in economics: with research providing more and more information and with more sophisticated models having been developed, often with the aid of computers, the predictions of economists have become more accurate.

Human behaviour

Although people may behave in broadly similar ways under similar conditions, it is impossible to predict this behaviour with any accuracy. How, for example, will firms react to a rise in the rate of inflation when making their investment decisions? This will depend on unpredictable things such as the state of business confidence.

DEFINITIONS

Deduction Using a theory to draw conclusions about specific circumstances.

Ceteris paribus Latin for 'other things being equal'. This assumption has to be made when making deductions from theories.

For these reasons there is plenty of scope for competing models in economics, each making different assumptions and leading to different policy conclusions. As a result, economics can often be highly controversial. As we shall see later on in the book, different political parties may adhere to different schools of economic thought. Thus the political left may adhere to a model which implies that governments must intervene if unemployment is to be cured; whereas the political right may adhere to a model which implies that unemployment will be reduced if the government intervenes less and relies more on the free market.

It would be wrong to get the impression from this that economists always disagree. There is a popular belief that 'if you laid all the economists of the world end to end they would still not reach a conclusion'. In practice, there is a large measure of agreement between economists about how to analyse the world and what conclusions to draw.

Economics and policy

Economists play a major role in helping governments to devise economic policy. In order to consider this role, it is necessary to distinguish between *positive* and *normative* statements.

A **positive statement** is a statement of fact. It may be right or wrong, but its accuracy can be tested by appealing to the facts. 'Unemployment is rising.' 'Inflation will be over 6 per cent by next year.' 'If the government cuts taxes, imports will rise.' These are all examples of positive statements.

A **normative statement** is a statement of value: a statement about what ought or ought not to be, about whether something is good or bad, desirable or undesirable. 'It is right to tax the rich more than the poor.' 'The government *ought* to reduce inflation.' 'Old-age pensions *ought* to be increased in line with inflation.' These are all examples of normative statements. They cannot be proved or disproved by a simple appeal to the facts.

Economists can only contribute in a positive way to questions of policy. That is, they can analyse the consequences of following certain policies. They can say which of two policies is more likely to achieve a given aim, but they cannot, as economists, say whether the aims of the policy are desirable. For example, economists may argue that a policy of increasing government expenditure will reduce unemployment and raise inflation, but they cannot decide whether such a policy is desirable. Economists, then, as scientists, cannot make normative judgements. They can only do so as individual people, with no more moral right than any other individual.

??

Which of the following are positive statements, which are normative statements and which could be either depending on the context?

(a) Cutting the higher rates of income tax will redistribute incomes from the poor to the rich.
(b) It is wrong that inflation should be reduced if this means that there will be higher unemployment.
(c) It is wrong to state that putting up interest rates will reduce inflation.
(d) The government should raise interest rates in order to prevent the exchange rate falling.
(e) Current government policies should reduce unemployment.

SECTION SUMMARY

1. The methodology used by economists is similar to that used by natural scientists. Economists construct models which they use to explain and predict economic phenomena. These models can be tested by appealing to facts and seeing how successfully they have been predicted or explained by the model. Unsuccessful models can be either abandoned or amended.

2. Being a social science, economics is concerned with human actions. Making accurate predictions in economics is very difficult given that economics is not a laboratory science and has to deal with a constantly changing environment.

3. Economists can help governments to devise policy by examining the consequences of alternative courses of action. In doing this, it is important to separate positive questions about what the effects of the policies are, from normative ones as to what the goals of policy should be. Economists in their role as economists have no superior right to make normative judgements. They do, however, play a major role in assessing whether a policy meets the political objectives of government (or opposition).

DEFINITIONS

Positive statement A value-free statement which can be tested by an appeal to the facts.

Normative statement A value judgement.

Appendix to Chapter 1: Some techniques of economic analysis

When students first come to economics many are worried about the amount of mathematics they will encounter. Will it all be equations and graphs and will there be lots of hard calculations to do and difficult theories to grasp?

As you will see if you glance through the pages of this book, there are many diagrams and tables and several equations. But this does not mean that there are many mathematical techniques that you will have to master. In fact there are relatively few techniques, but they are ones which we use many times in many different contexts. You will find that if you are new to the subject, you will very quickly become familiar with these techniques. If you are not new to the subject, perhaps you could reassure your colleagues who are!

Diagrams as pictures

In many cases, we use diagrams simply to provide a picture of a relationship. Just as a photograph in a newspaper can often provide a much more vivid picture of an event than any description in words, so too a diagram in economics can often picture a relationship with a vividness and clarity that could never be achieved by description alone.

For example, we may observe that as people's incomes rise, they spend a lot more on entertainment and only a little more on food. We can picture this relationship very nicely by the use of a simple graph.

In Figure A1.1, an individual's income is measured along the horizontal axis and expenditure on food and entertainment is measured up the vertical axis. There are just two lines on this diagram: one showing how the expenditure on entertainment rises as income rises, the other how the expenditure on food rises as income rises. Now we could use a diagram like this to plot actual data. But we may simply be using it as a sketch – as a picture. In this case we do not necessarily need to put figures on the two axes. We are simply showing the relative *shapes* of the two curves. These shapes tell us that the person's expenditure on entertainment rises more quickly than that on food, and that above a certain level of income the expenditure on entertainment becomes greater than that on food.

?? What else is the diagram telling us?

If you were to describe in words all the information that this sketch graph depicts, you would need several lines of prose.

Figure 1.5 (the circular flow diagram) and Figure 1.6 (the spectrum diagram) were also examples of sketches designed to give a simple, clear picture of a relationship: a picture stripped of all unnecessary detail.

Representing real-life statistics

In many cases we will want to depict real-world data. We may want to show, for example, how unemployment has changed over the years in a particular country, or how income is distributed between different groups in the population. In the first we will need to look at *time-series* data. In the second we will look at *cross-section* data.

Time-series data

Table A1.1 shows the level of UK unemployment between the first quarter of 1992 and the first quarter of 1996. A table like this is a common way of representing

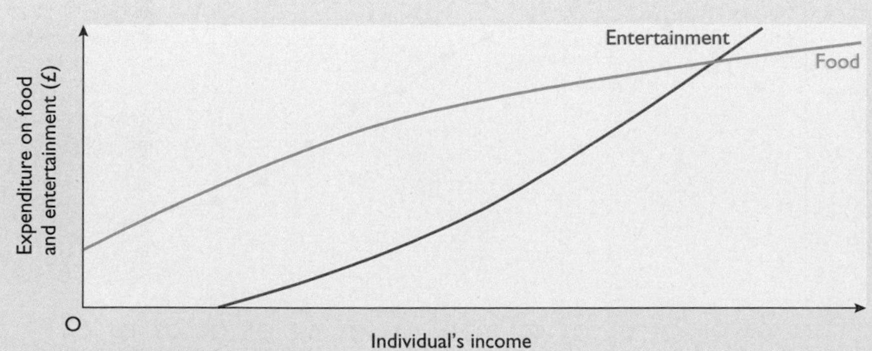

Figure A1.1 Effect of a rise in an individual's income on his or her expenditure on food and entertainment

Table A1.1 UK unemployment, 1992 Q1–1996 Q1: time-series data

	1992				1993				1994				1995				1996
	Q1	Q2	Q3	Q4	Q1	Q2	Q3	Q4	Q1	Q2	Q3	Q4	Q1	Q2	Q3	Q4	Q1
Unemployment (millions)	2.58	2.69	2.76	2.87	2.96	2.95	2.91	2.85	2.78	2.68	2.63	2.51	2.39	2.33	2.31	2.26	2.21

Source: *Economic Trends* (ONS).

time-series data. It has the advantage of giving the precise figures, and is thus a useful reference if we want to test any theory and see if it predicts accurately.

Notice that in this particular table the figures are given quarterly. Depending on the period of time over which we want to see the movement of a variable, it may be more appropriate to use a different interval of time. For example, if we wanted to see how unemployment had changed over the last 50 years, we might use annual figures or even average figures for longer periods of time. If, however, we wanted to see how unemployment had changed over the course of a year, we would probably use monthly or even weekly figures.

?? The table in Box 1.2 shows time-series data for four different variables for four different countries. Would there have been any advantage in giving the figures for each separate year? Would there have been any disadvantage?

Time-series data can also be shown graphically. In fact the data from a table can be plotted directly on to a graph. Figure A1.2 plots the data from Table A1.1. Each dot on the graph corresponds to one figure from the table. The dots are then joined up to form a single line. Thus if you wanted to find the level of unemployment at any time between 1992 Q1 and 1996 Q1, you would simply find the appropriate date on the horizontal axis, read vertically upward to the line you have drawn, then read across to find the level of unemployment.

Although a graph like this cannot give you quite such an accurate measurement of each point as a table does, it gives a much more obvious picture of how the figures have moved over time and whether the changes are getting bigger (the curve getting steeper) or smaller (the curve getting shallower). We can also read off what the likely figure would be for some point *between* two observations.

?? What was the level of unemployment midway between quarter 4 1994 and quarter 1 1995?

It is also possible to combine *two* sets of time-series data on one graph to show their relative movements over time. Table A1.2 shows the figures for UK economic growth for the same time period. Figure A1.3 plots these data along

DEFINITION

Time-series data Information depicting how a variable (e.g. the price of eggs) changes over time.

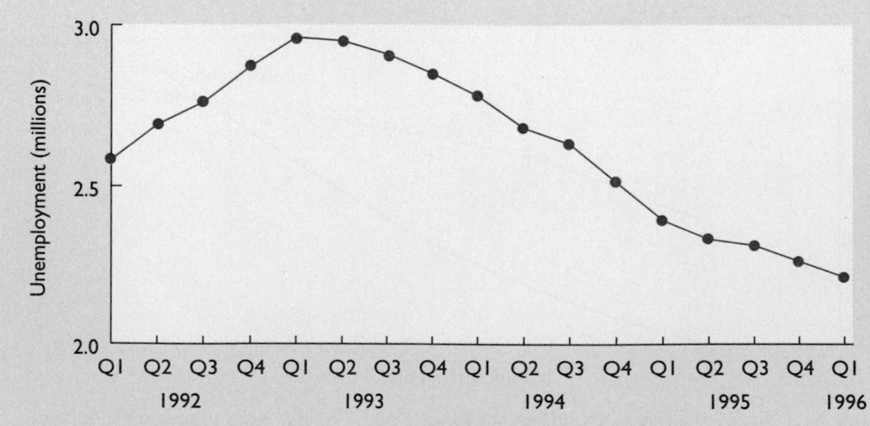

Figure A1.2 UK unemployment, 1992 Q1–1996 Q1: time-series data

Table A1.2 UK economic growth: 1992 Q1–1996 Q1 (% increase over equivalent quarter in previous year)

	1992				1993				1994				1995				1996
	Q1	Q2	Q3	Q4	Q1	Q2	Q3	Q4	Q1	Q2	Q3	Q4	Q1	Q2	Q3	Q4	Q1
Economic growth (%)	−1.5	−0.9	−0.1	0.4	1.6	2.0	2.5	2.9	3.5	4.3	4.1	4.0	3.4	2.5	2.1	2.0	2.0

Source: *Economic Trends* (ONS).

with those from Table A1.1. This enables us to get a clear picture of how unemployment and the rate of economic growth moved in relation to each other over the period in question. Note that we use a different vertical scale for the two variables. This is inevitable given that they are measured in different units.

?? How would it be possible to show three different lines on the same diagram?

All developed countries publish time-series data for the major macroeconomic variables such as national income, prices, employment and unemployment, interest rates, and imports and exports. In the UK the figures are published by the Office for National Statistics and appear in a number of monthly and annual publications such as the *Annual Abstract of Statistics*, *Economic Trends* (monthly), *Economic Trends Annual Supplement*, *Financial Statistics* (monthly) and the *Monthly Digest of Statistics*. International economic statistics are published by, among others, the Organisation for Economic Co-operation and Development (OECD), the International Monetary Fund (IMF), the World Bank and the European Union.

Microeconomic data on the distribution of income, the performance of particular industries, the distribution of household expenditure and so on also appear in the official government statistics. Firms, consumers' associations, charities and other organisations also publish microeconomic statistics.

The appendix at the end of this book looks at the range of readily available microeconomic and macroeconomic statistics. The statistical sources are arranged by subject headings.

Cross-section data

Cross-section data show different observations made at the *same point in time*. For example, they could show the quantities of food and clothing purchased at various levels of household income, or the costs to a firm or industry of producing various quantities of a product.

Table A1.3 gives an example of cross-section data. It shows the distribution of household income in the UK before the deduction of taxes and the addition of benefits. It puts households into five equal-sized groups (or

DEFINITION

Cross-section data Information showing how a variable (e.g. the consumption of eggs) differs between different groups or different individuals at a given time.

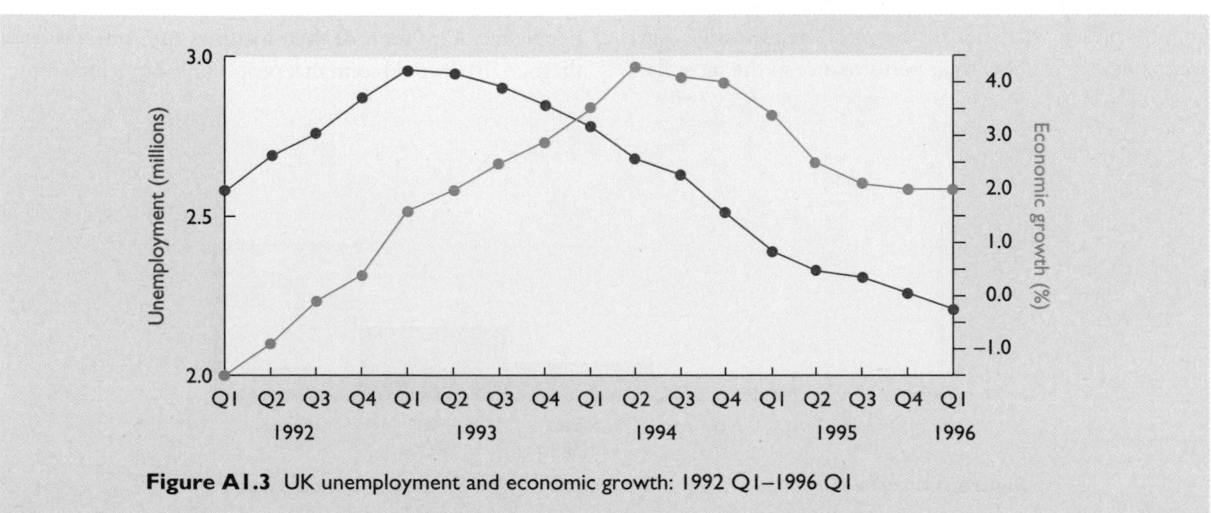

Figure A1.3 UK unemployment and economic growth: 1992 Q1–1996 Q1

Table A1.3 Income before taxes and benefits

	Quintile groups of households					
	Bottom 20%	Next 20%	Middle 20%	Next 20%	Top 20%	Total
1977	3.6	9.9	17.9	25.8	42.8	100.0
1994/5	2.3	6.2	15.1	25.2	51.2	100.0

Source: *Economic Trends* (ONS, December 1995).

'quintiles') according to their income. Thus the poorest 20 per cent of households are in one group, the next poorest 20 per cent are in the next and so on. Looking just at the 1994/5 figures, they show that the poorest 20 per cent earned just 2.3 per cent of total household incomes, whereas the richest 20 per cent earned 51.2 per cent.

Cross-section data like these are often represented in the form of a chart. Figure A1.4 shows the data as a *bar chart*, and Figure A1.5 as a *pie chart*.

It is possible to represent cross-section data at two or more different points in time, thereby presenting the figures as a time series. In Table A1.3, figures are given for just two years. With a more complete time series we could graph the movement of the shares of each of the five groups over time.

?? Could bar charts or pie charts be used for representing time-series data?

Getting a true picture from the statistics

'There are lies, damned lies and statistics.' This well-known saying highlights the abuse of statistics – abuse, unfortunately, that is commonplace. Have you noticed how politicians always seem to be able to produce statistics to 'prove' that they are right and that their opponents are wrong? And it's not just politicians. Newspapers frequently present statistics in the most 'newsworthy' way; companies try to show their performance in the most flattering way; pressure groups fighting for a cause (such as the protection of the environment) again present statistics in the way that best supports their case.

It is not difficult to present data in such a way as to give a grossly distorted picture of reality. Let us have a look at some of the most common examples.

Selective use of data

This is where people choose to look at only those statistics that support their case and ignore those that do not. For example, assume that unemployment has risen but inflation has fallen. The government will highlight the inflation statistics to show how successful its policies have been. The opposition parties will do the opposite: they will concentrate on the unemployment statistics to demonstrate the failure of government policy.

Graphical presentation of data

Two graphs may present exactly the same data and yet convey a quite different impression about them. Figure A1.6 shows how the amount that people buy of a particular foodstuff varies with their income. It is based on the information in Table A1.4.

Diagram (a) shows *exactly the same* information as diagram (b), and yet at a glance it would seem from diagram (a) that people buy a lot more as their incomes rise, whereas from diagram (b) it would seem that people only buy a little more.

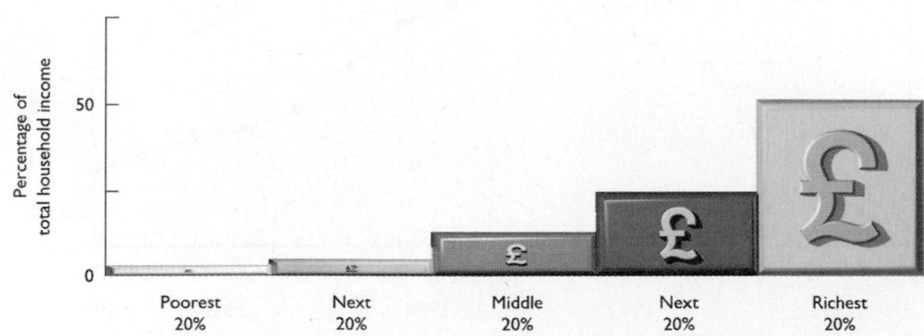

Figure A1.4 The distribution of UK pre-tax income (1994/5): the use of a bar chart

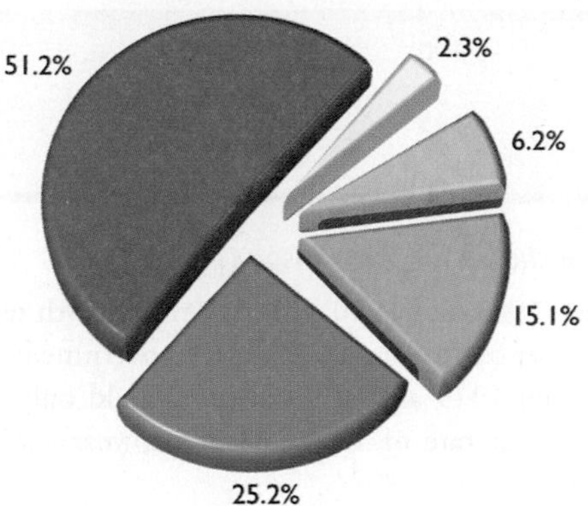

Figure A1.5 The distribution of UK pre-tax income: (1994/5): the use of a pie chart

Clearly the choice of *scales* for the two axes will determine the shape of the graph.

??

1. If the vertical scale for Figure A1.2 ran from 0 to 5 million, how would this alter your impression of the degree to which unemployment had changed?
2. What are the advantages and disadvantages of presenting data graphically with the axes starting from zero?

Use of absolute or proportionate values

'People are paying more taxes now than they did when the government came to office', claims the opposition.

'Since coming into office we have cut taxes substantially', claims the government.

So who is right? Do we pay more or less taxes? Quite possibly they are both right. If incomes have risen, we probably do pay more taxes in total. After all, the more we earn, the greater the sum of money we will be paying in income tax; and the more we spend, the more we will be paying out in VAT. Thus in *absolute* terms we probably are paying more in taxes.

On the other hand, if the government has cut the rates of tax, we may be paying a smaller *proportion* of our income. In other words, a smaller proportion of a larger total can still represent an absolute increase.

Ignoring questions of distribution

'The average person has become better off under this government', claims a minister.

'Poverty has increased steeply under this government', claims the opposition. 'More than half the population are worse off now than when the government came to office.'

Surely, this time one of the claims must be wrong? But again, both could be right. The term 'average' normally refers to the **mean**. The mean income is simply the total national income divided by the number in the population: i.e. income *per head*. If this is what is meant by the average, then the government may well be correct. Income per head may have risen.

If, however, a relatively few people have got a lot richer and the rest have got a little poorer, the **median** income

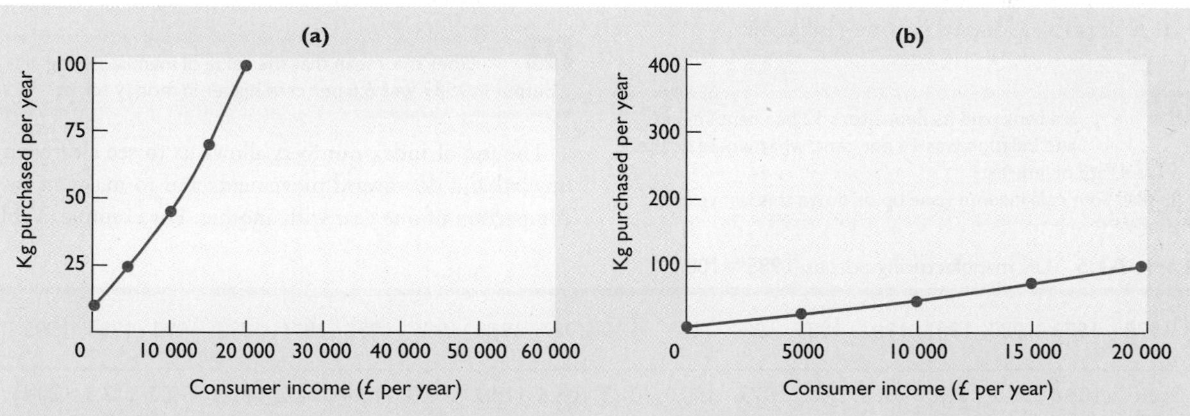

Figure A1.6 The relationship between consumer income and the consumption of a particular foodstuff: using graphs with different scales

DEFINITIONS

Mean (or arithmetic mean) The sum of the values of each of the members of the sample divided by the total number in the sample.

Median The value of the middle member of the sample.

Table A1.4 Annual purchases per person of a particular foodstuff

Consumer income (£ per year)	0	5000	10 000	15 000	20 000
Foodstuff purchased per person (kg per year)	10	25	45	70	100

will have fallen. The median income is the income of the *middle* person. For example, if the population were 50 million, the median income would be the income of the twenty-five millionth richest person. This person's income may have fallen.

Real or nominal values

'Incomes have risen by 5 per cent this last year', claims the government.

'The standard of living has fallen', claims the opposition.

One of the most common abuses of statistics is deliberately switching between real and nominal figures, depending on what message you want to give your audience. **Nominal** figures are the simple monetary values at the prices ruling at the time. For example, if you earned a wage of £100 per week last year and are earning £105 per week this year, then in nominal terms your wage has risen by 5 per cent.

But what if prices have risen by 8 per cent? Your 5 per cent increase in wages will in fact buy you 3 per cent *less* goods. Your **real** wages have gone down by 3 per cent. In other words, to show how much better or worse off a person or nation is, the nominal figure must be corrected for inflation. Thus:

Real growth = Nominal growth – Inflation

??
1. If a bank paid its depositors 12 per cent interest and inflation was 14 per cent, what would be the *real* rate of interest?
2. Has your real income gone up or down this last year?

The time chosen for comparison

'Between 1982 and 1990, Britain's real growth rate averaged 3.5 per cent per year', boasts the government.

'Between 1979 and 1993, Britain could only manage a real growth rate of 1.6 per cent per year', chides the opposition.

Again both are correct, but they have chosen either to include or to ignore the periods from 1979 to 1982 and from 1990 to 1993 when the real growth rate was negative.

Index numbers

Time-series data are often expressed in terms of **index numbers**. Consider the data in Table A1.5. It shows index numbers of manufacturing output in the UK from 1978 to 1995.

One year is selected as the **base year** and this is given the value of 100. In our example this is 1985. The output for other years is then shown by their percentage variation from 100. For 1981 the index number is 91. This means that manufacturing output was 9 per cent lower in 1981 than in 1985. The index number for 1987 is 106.6. This means that manufacturing output was 6.6 per cent higher in 1987 than in 1985.

??
Does this mean that the value of manufacturing output in 1987 was 6.6 per cent higher in money terms?

The use of index numbers allows us to see clearly any upward and downward movements and to make an easy comparison of one year with another. For example, Table

Table A1.5 UK manufacturing output: 1985 = 100

1978	1979	1980	1981	1982	1983	1984	1985	1986	1987	1988	1989	1990	1991	1992	1993	1994	1995
106.1	106.0	96.8	91.0	91.2	93.7	97.6	100.0	101.3	106.6	114.2	119.0	118.4	112.2	111.3	112.7	117.3	120.1

Source: *Economic Trends* (ONS).

DEFINITIONS

Nominal values Money values measured at *current* prices.

Real values Money values corrected for inflation.

Index number The value of a variable expressed as 100 plus or minus its percentage deviation from a base year.

Base year (for index numbers) The year whose index number is set at 100.

Table A1.6 UK manufacturing and service industry output: 1985 = 100

	1978	1979	1980	1981	1982	1983	1984	1985	1986	1987	1988	1989	1990	1991	1992	1993	1994	1995
Output of manufacturing	106.1	106.0	96.8	91.0	91.2	93.7	97.6	100.0	101.3	106.6	114.2	119.0	118.4	112.2	111.3	112.7	117.3	120.1
Output of services	87.1	89.6	89.2	89.5	90.8	93.4	97.0	100.0	104.1	109.6	114.8	117.8	119.1	118.0	117.9	120.6	124.6	128.5

Source: *Economic Trends* (ONS).

A1.5 shows quite clearly that output fell from 1978 to 1981 and did not regain its 1978 level until 1987.

Index numbers are very useful for comparing two or more time series of data. For example, suppose we want to compare the growth of manufacturing output with that of the service industries. To do this we simply express both sets of figures as index numbers with the same base year. This is illustrated in Table A1.6.

The figures show a quite different pattern for the two sectors. The growth of the service industries was much more steady.

Using index numbers to measure percentage changes

To find the annual percentage growth rate in any one year we simply look at the percentage change in the index from the previous year. To work this out we use the following formula:

$$\left(\frac{I_t - I_{t-1}}{I_{t-1}}\right) \times 100$$

where I_t is the index in the year in question and I_{t-1} is the index in the previous year.

Thus to find the growth rate in manufacturing output from 1987 to 1988 we first see how much the index has risen ($I_t - I_{t-1}$). The answer is 114.2 – 106.6 = 7.6. But this does *not* mean that the growth rate is 7.6 per cent. According to our formula, the growth rate is equal to:

$$\frac{114.2 - 106.6}{106.6} \times 100$$

$$= 7.6/106.6 \times 100$$

$$= 7.13\%$$

?? What was the growth rate in manufacturing output from (a) 1982 to 1983; (b) 1990 to 1991?

The price index

Perhaps the best known of all price indices is the **retail price index (RPI)**. It is an index of the prices of goods and services purchased by the average household. Movements in this index, therefore, show how the cost of living has changed. Annual percentage increases in the RPI are the commonest definition of the rate of inflation. Thus if the RPI went up from 100 to 110 over a twelve-month period, we would say that the rate of inflation was 10 per cent.

?? If the RPI went up from 150 to 162 over twelve months, what would be the rate of inflation?

The use of weighted averages

The RPI is a **weighted average** of the prices of many items. The index of manufacturing output that we looked at above was also a weighted average, an average of the output of many individual products.

To illustrate how a weighted average works consider the case of a weighted average of the output of just three industries, A, B and C. Let us assume that in the base year (year 1) the output of A was £7 million, of B £2 million and of C £1 million, giving a total output of the three industries of £10 million. We now attach weights to the output of each industry to reflect its proportion of total output. Industry A is given a weight of 0.7 because it produces seven-tenths of total output. Industry B is given a weight of 0.2 and industry C a weight of 0.1. We then simply multiply each industry's index by its weight and add up all these figures to give the overall industry index.

DEFINITIONS

Retail price index (RPI) An index of the prices of goods bought by a typical household.

Weighted average The average of several items where each item is ascribed a weight according to its importance. The weights must add up to 1.

Table A1.7 Constructing a weighted average index

Industry	Weight	Year 1		Year 2	
		Index	Index times weight	Index	Index times weight
A	0.7	100	70	90	63
B	0.2	100	20	110	22
C	0.1	100	10	130	13
Total	1.0		100		98

The index for each industry in year 1 (the base year) is 100. This means that the weighted average index is also 100. Table A1.7 shows what happens to output in year 2. Industry A's output falls by 10 per cent, giving it an index of 90 in year 2. Industry B's output rises by 10 per cent and industry C's output rises by 30 per cent, giving indices of 110 and 130, respectively. But as you can see from the table, despite the fact that two of the three industries have had a rise in output, the total industry index has *fallen* from 100 to 98. The reason is that industry A is so much larger than the other two that its decline in output outweighs their increase.

The retail price index is a little more complicated. This is because it is calculated in two stages. First, products are grouped into categories such as food, clothing and services. A weighted average index is worked out for each group. Thus the index for food would be the weighted average of the indices for bread, potatoes, cooking oil, etc. Second, a weight is attached to each of the groups in order to work out an overall index.

Functional relationships

Throughout economics we will be examining how one economic variable affects another: how the purchases of cars are affected by their price; how consumer expenditure is affected by taxes, or by incomes; how the cost of producing washing machines is affected by the price of steel; how the rate of unemployment is affected by the level of government expenditure. These relationships are called **functional relationships**. We will need to express these relationships in a precise way. This can be done in the form of a table or a graph or an equation.

Simple linear functions

These are relationships which when plotted on a graph produce a straight line. Let us take an imaginary example of the relationship between total savings in the economy (S) and the level of national income (Y). This functional relationship can be written as:

$$S = f(Y)$$

This is simply shorthand for saying that savings are a function of (i.e. depend on) the level of national income.

If we want to know just *how much* will be saved at any given level of income, we will need to spell out this functional relationship. Let us do this in each of the three ways.

As a table. Table A1.8 gives a selection of values of Y and the corresponding level of S. It is easy to read off from the table the level of savings at one of the levels of national income listed. It is clearly more difficult to work out the level of savings if national income is £23.4 billion or £47.4 billion.

As a graph. Figure A1.7 plots the data from Table A1.8. Each of the dots corresponds to one of the points in the table. By joining the dots up into a single line we can easily read off the value for savings at some level of income other than those listed in the table. A graph also has the advantage of allowing us to see the relationship at a glance.

It is usual to plot the *independent variable* (i.e. the one that does not depend on the other) on the horizontal or x-axis, and the *dependent variable* on the vertical or y-axis. In our example, savings *depend* on national income. Thus savings are the dependent variable and national income is the independent variable.

As an equation. The data in the table can be expressed in the equation:

$$S = 0.2Y$$

This has the major advantage of being precise. We could work out *exactly* how much would be saved at any given level of national income.

DEFINITION

Functional relationships The mathematical relationships showing how one variable is affected by one or more others.

Table A1.8 A savings function

National income (£bn per year)	Total savings (£bn per year)
0	0
10	2
20	4
30	6
40	8
50	10

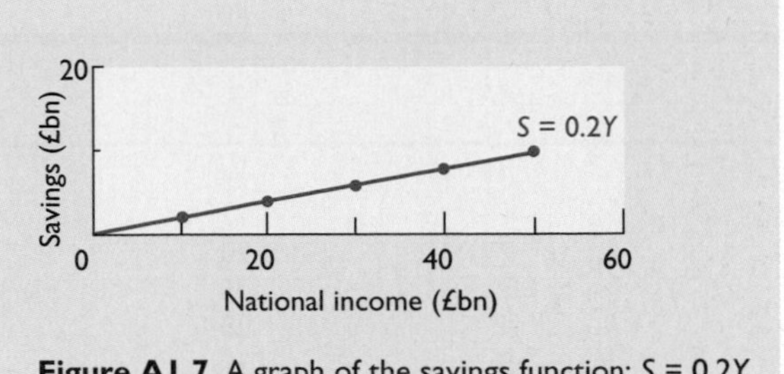

Figure A1.7 A graph of the savings function: $S = 0.2Y$

This particular function starts at the origin of the graph (i.e. the bottom left-hand corner). This means that when the value of the independent variable is zero, so too is the value of the dependent variable. Frequently, however, this is not the case in functional relationships. For example, when people have a zero income, they will still have to live, and thus will draw from their past savings: they will have *negative* savings.

When a graph does not pass through the origin its equation will have the form:

$$y = a + bx$$

where this time y stands for the dependent variable (not 'income') and x for the independent variable, and a and b will have numbers assigned in an actual equation. For example, the equation might be:

$$y = 4 + 2x$$

This would give Table A1.9 and Figure A1.8.

Notice two things about the relationship between the equation and the graph:

- The point where the line crosses the vertical axis (at a value of 4) is given by the constant (a) term. If the a term is negative, the line will cross the vertical axis *below* the horizontal axis.
- The slope of the line is given by the b term. The slope is 2/1: for every 1 unit increase in x there is a 2 unit increase in y.

Table A1.9 $y = 4 + 2x$

x	y
0	4
1	6
2	8
3	10
4	12
5	14
.	.
.	.

?? On a diagram like Figure A1.8 draw the graphs for the following equations: $y = -3 + 4x$; $y = 15 - 3x$.

Note that in the second equation of the question the x term is negative. This means that y and x are *inversely related*. As x increases, y decreases.

Non-linear functions

These are functions where the equation involves a squared term (or other power terms). Such functions will give a curved line when plotted on a graph. As an example, consider the following equation:

$$y = 4 + 10x - x^2$$

Table A1.10 and Figure A1.9 are based on it.

As you can see, y rises at a decelerating rate and eventually begins to fall. This is because the negative x^2 term is becoming more and more influential as x rises and eventually begins to outweigh the $10x$ term.

?? What shaped graph would you get from the equations:

$y = -6 + 3x + 2x^2$; $y = 10 - 4x + x^2$

(If you cannot work out the answer, construct a table like Table A1.10 and then plot the figures on a graph.)

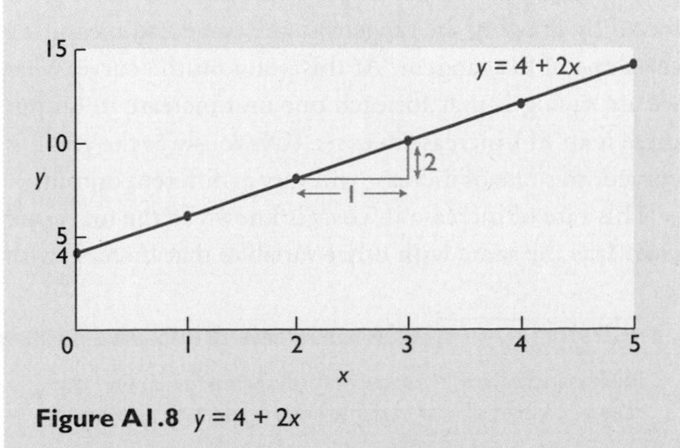

Figure A1.8 $y = 4 + 2x$

Table A1.10 $y = 4 + 10x - x^2$

x	y
0	4
1	13
2	20
3	25
4	28
5	29
6	28
.	.
.	.
.	.

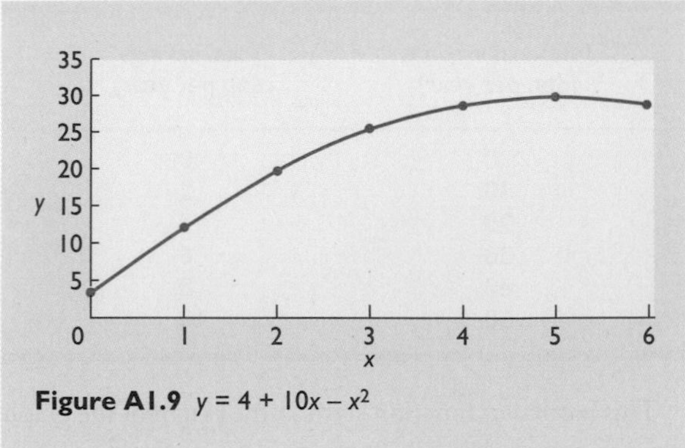

Figure A1.9 $y = 4 + 10x - x^2$

*Elementary differentiation

In several starred boxes we will be using some elementary calculus. The part of calculus we will be using is called **differentiation**. This is a technique to enable us to calculate the rate of change of a variable. The purpose of this section is not to explain why differentiation involves the procedures it does, but simply to state the rules that are necessary for our purposes. You will need to consult a maths book if you want to know how these rules are derived.

First, let us see when we would be interested in looking at the rate of change of a variable. Take the case of a firm thinking of expanding. It will want to know how much its costs will increase as its output increases. It will want to know the rate of change of costs with respect to changes in output.

Let us assume that it faces a cost function of the form:

$$C = 20 + 5Q + Q^2 \quad \textbf{(1)}$$

where C is the total cost of production and Q is the quantity produced. Table A1.11 and Figure A1.10 are derived from this equation.

The rate of increase in its costs with respect to increases in output is given by the *slope* of the cost curve in Figure A1.10. The steeper the slope, the more rapidly costs increase. At point *a* the slope of the curve is 11. This is found by drawing the tangent to the curve and measuring the slope of the tangent. At this point on the curve, what we are saying is that for each one unit increase in output there is an £11 increase in costs. (Obviously as the graph is curved, this rate of increase will vary at different outputs.)

This rate of increase in costs is known as the **marginal cost**. It is the same with other variables that increase with quantity: their rate of increase is known as *marginal*. For example, *marginal revenue* is the rate of increase of sales revenue with respect to ouput.

We can use the technique of differentiation to derive a marginal from a total equation: in other words, to derive the slope of the total curve. Let us assume that we have an equation:

$$y = 10 + 6x - 4x^2 + 2x^3 \quad \textbf{(2)}$$

When we differentiate it we call the new equation *dy/dx*: this stands for the rate of increase in *y* (*dy*) with respect to the increase in *x* (*dx*).

The rules for differentiating a simple equation like equation (2) are very straightforward.

1. You delete the constant term (10). The reason for this is that, being constant, by definition it will not cause an increase in *y* as *x* increases, and it is the *increase* in *y* that we are trying to discover.
2. You delete the *x* from the *x* term which has no power attached, and just leave the number. Thus the term $6x$ becomes simply 6.
3. For any term with a power in it (a square, a cube, etc.), its value should be *multiplied* by the power term and the power term reduced by one. Thus in the term $4x^2$, the 4 would be multiplied by 2 (the power term), and the power term would be reduced from 2 to 1 (but *x* to the power of 1 is simply *x*). After differentiation, therefore, the term becomes $8x$. In the term $2x^3$, the 2 would be multiplied by 3 (the power term), and the power term would be reduced from 3 to 2. After differentiation, therefore, the term becomes $6x^2$.

DEFINITIONS

Differentiation A mathematical technique to find the rate of change of one variable with respect to another.

Marginal cost The rate of increase in costs with respect to output.

Table A1.11 $C = 20 + 5Q + Q^2$

Q	C
0	20
1	26
2	34
3	44
4	56
5	70
6	86
7	104
.	.
.	.
.	.

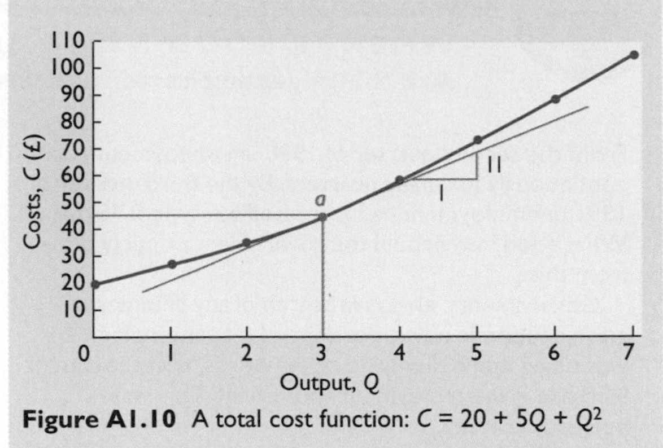

Figure A1.10 A total cost function: $C = 20 + 5Q + Q^2$

Applying these three rules to the equation:

$$y = 10 + 6x - 4x^2 + 2x^3 \quad (2)$$

gives

$$dy/dx = 6 - 8x + 6x^2 \quad (3)$$

To find the rate of change of y with respect to x at any given value of x, therefore, you simply substitute that value of x into equation (3).

Thus when $x = 4$, $dy/dx = 6 - (8 \times 4) + (6 \times 16) = 70$. In other words, when $x = 4$, for every 1 unit increase in x, y will increase by 70.

Returning to our cost function in equation (1), what is the marginal cost equation? Applying the three rules to the equation:

$$C = 20 + 5Q + Q^2 \quad (1)$$

gives:

$$dC/dQ = 5 + 2Q \quad (4)$$

Thus at an output of 3, the marginal cost (dC/dQ) is $5 + (2 \times 3) = 11$, which is the slope of the tangent to point a.

?? What would be the marginal cost equation if the total cost equation were:

$$C = 15 + 20Q - 5Q^2 + Q^3?$$

What would be the marginal cost at an output of 8?

Finding the maximum or minimum point of a curve

The other important use we can make of calculus is to find the maximum or minimum point of a curve. This has a number of important applications. For example, a firm may want to know the minimum point on its average cost curve (a curve which shows how costs per unit of output vary as output increases). Also it is likely to want to know the output at which it will earn maximum profit. Let us examine this particular case.

Assume that the equation for total profit (Π) is:

$$\Pi = -20 + 12Q - Q^2 \quad (5)$$

This gives profit at various outputs as shown in Table A1.12. The corresponding graph is plotted in Figure A1.11.

Table A1.12 $\Pi = -20 + 12Q - Q^2$

Q	Π
0	−20
1	−9
2	0
3	7
4	12
5	15
6	16
7	15
8	12
9	7
10	0

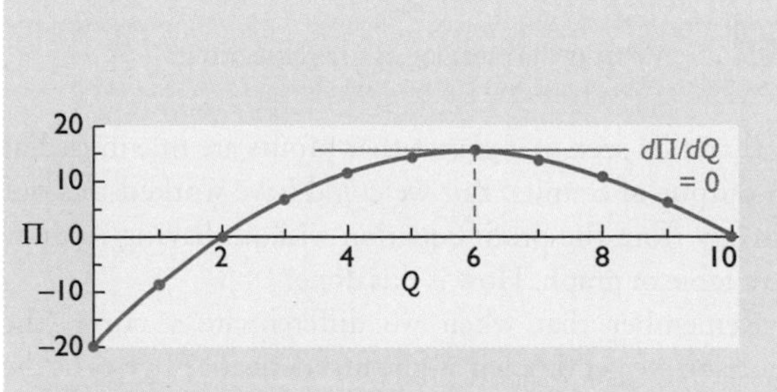

Figure A1.11 A total profit function: $\Pi = -20 + 12Q - Q^2$

ISSUES AND APPLICATIONS *BOX A1.1

WHEN IS GOOD NEWS REALLY GOOD?

Are things getting better or merely getting worse more slowly?

From the second quarter of 1990 unemployment rose continuously for many quarters. By the third quarter of 1991 unemployment had increased by some 0.75 million. What good news could the government possibly draw from this?

Governments, always in search of any glimmer of good economic news, proclaimed that unemployment was rising more slowly (in other words, that the rate of increase in unemployment was falling). This was perfectly correct.

To show this let us assume that N is the number of people out of work. The rate of change of unemployment is therefore given by dN/dt (where t is time). A positive figure for dN/dt represents a rise in unemployment, a negative figure a fall. Its value is given by the slope of the green line in the diagram. From the second quarter of 1990 this figure was positive. Bad news!

But the government sought a rosier interpretation. By using a second-order derivative, d^2N/dt^2, it could show that the rate of increase in unemployment from early 1991 had been falling. The value of this is given by the slope of the red line in the diagram. The government proclaimed that this was evidence that the economy was beginning to recover. Good news!

The use of calculus in this manner is a two-edged sword and such statistical sophistry is open to the political opposition, who could at a later date, if they so wished, claim that a fall in unemployment was bad economic news. Dare they?

?? If the opposition were indeed to claim that a fall in unemployment was bad news, what would have to be the value of d^2N/dt^2: positive or negative?

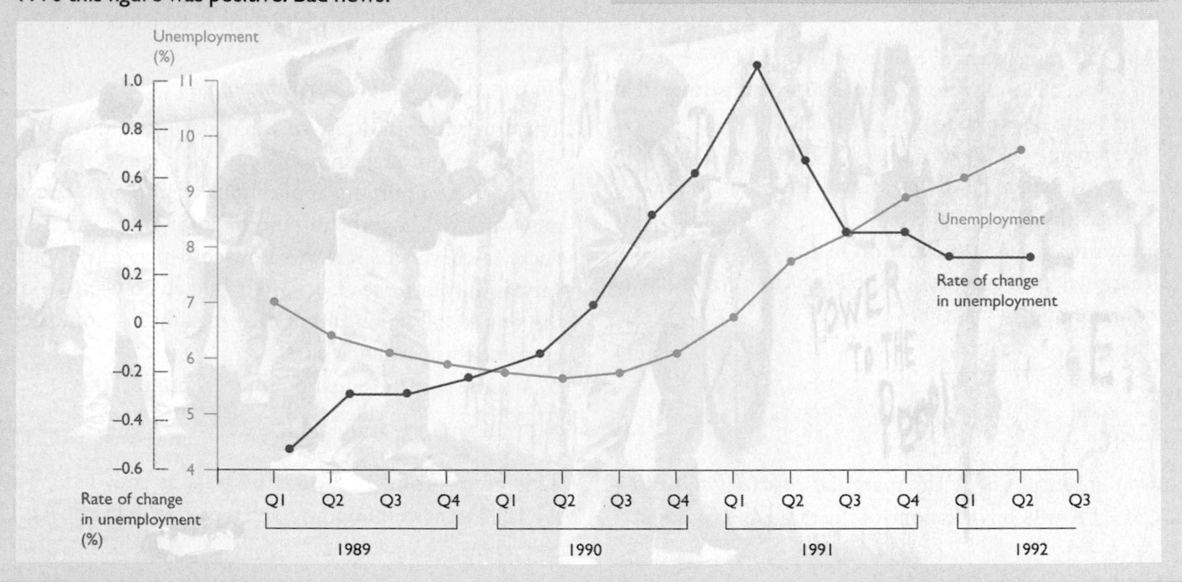

?? What is the meaning of a *negative* profit?

It can be seen at a glance that profits are maximised at an output of 6 units. But we could have worked this out directly from the profit equation without having to draw up a table or graph. How is this done?

Remember that when we differentiate a curve, the equation we get (known as 'the first derivative') gives us the slope of the curve. You can see that at the point of maximum profit (the top of the curve) its slope is zero: the tangent is horizontal. So all we have to do to find the top of the curve is to differentiate its equation and set it equal to zero.

Given that:

$$\Pi = -20 + 12Q - Q^2 \quad (5)$$

then:

$$d\Pi/dQ = 12 - 2Q \quad (6)$$

Setting this equal to zero gives:

$$12 - 2Q = 0$$
$$\therefore 2Q = 12$$
$$\therefore Q = 6$$

Thus profits are maximised at an output of 6 units: the result we obtained from the table and graph.

The second derivative test

There is a problem with this technique, however. How can we tell from equation (6) that we have found the *maximum* rather than the *minimum*? The problem is that *both* the maximum *and* the minimum points of a curve have a zero slope.

The answer is to conduct a **second derivative test.** This involves differentiating the equation a second time. This gives the rate of change of the *slope* of the original curve. If you look at Figure A1.11, as output increases, the tangent moves from being upward sloping, to horizontal, to downward sloping. In other words, the slope is getting less and less. Its rate of change is *negative*. Thus if we differentiate the equation for the slope (i.e. the first derivative), we should get a negative figure.

When we differentiate a second time we get what is called the **second derivative.** It is written d^2y/dx^2.

If we differentiate equation (6):

$$d\Pi/dQ = 12 - 2Q \qquad (6)$$

we get:

$$d^2\Pi/dQ^2 = -2 \qquad (7)$$

(Note that the rules for differentiating a second time are the same as for the first time.) Given that the second derivative in this case is negative, we have demonstrated that we have indeed found the maximum profit point (at $Q = 6$), and not the minimum.

?? Given the following equation for a firm's average cost (AC) – i.e. the cost per unit of output (Q):

$$AC = 60 - 16Q + 2Q^2$$

(a) At what output is AC at a minimum?
(b) Use the second derivative test to prove that this is a minimum and not a maximum.

SECTION SUMMARY

1. Diagrams in economics can be used as pictures: to sketch a relationship so that its essentials can be perceived at a glance.
2. Tables, graphs and charts are also used to portray real-life data. These can be time-series data or cross-section data or both.
3. In order to get a true picture from economic data it is important to be aware of various ways that statistics can be abused: these include a selective use of data, a choice of axes on a graph to make trends seem more or less exaggerated or to make a curve more or less steep, confusing absolute and relative values, ignoring questions of distribution, confusing nominal and real values, and selecting the time period to make the statistics look the most favourable or unfavourable.
4. Presenting time-series data as index numbers gives a clear impression of trends and is a good way of comparing how two or more series (perhaps originally measured in different units) have changed over the same time period. A base year is chosen and the index for that year is set at 100. The percentage change in the value of a variable is given by the percentage change in the index. The formula is:

   $$\left(\frac{I_t - I_{t-1}}{I_{t-1}}\right) \times 100$$

   Several items can be included in one index by using a weighted value for each of the items. The weights must add up to 1, and each weight will reflect the relative importance of that particular item in the index.
5. Functional relationships can be expressed as an equation, a table or a graph. In the linear (straight-line) equation $y = a + bx$, the a term gives the vertical intercept (the point where the graph crosses the vertical axis) and the b term gives the slope. When there is a power term (e.g. $y = a + bx + cx^2$), the graph will be a curve.

*6. Differentiation can be used to obtain the rate of change of one variable with respect to another. The rules of differentiation require that in an equation of the form:

   $$y = a + bx + cx^2 + dx^3$$

   the a term disappears, the bx term simply becomes b, the cx^2 term becomes $2cx$, the dx^3 becomes $3dx^2$ and so on, with each extra term being multiplied by its power term and its power term being reduced by 1.

*7. To find the value of the x term at which the y term is at a maximum or minimum, the equation should be differentiated and set equal to zero. To check which it is – maximum or minimum – the second derivative should be calculated. If it is negative, then setting the first derivative equal to zero has yielded a maximum. If the second derivative is positive, then setting the first derivative to zero has yielded a minimum value.

DEFINITIONS

Second derivative test If on differentiating an equation a second time the answer is negative (positive), the point is a maximum (minimum).

Second derivative The rate of change of the first derivative, found by differentiating the first derivative.

??? END-OF-CHAPTER QUESTIONS ???

1. Imagine that a country can produce just two things: goods and services. Assume that over a given period it could produce any of the following combinations:

Units of goods	0	10	20	30	40	50	60	70	80	90	100
Units of services	80	79	77	74	70	65	58	48	35	19	0

   (a) Draw the country's production possibility curve.

   (b) Assuming that the country is currently producing 40 units of goods and 70 units of services, what is the opportunity cost of producing another 10 units of goods?

   (c) Explain how the figures illustrate the principle of increasing opportunity cost.

   (d) Now assume that technical progress leads to a 10 per cent increase in the output of goods for any given amount of resources. Draw the new production possibility curve. How has the opportunity cost of producing extra units of services altered?

2. Imagine that you won millions of pounds on the National Lottery. Would your 'economic problem' be solved?

3. Assume that in a household one parent currently works full time and the other stays at home to look after the family. How would you set about identifying and calculating the opportunity costs of the second parent now taking a full-time job? How would such calculations be relevant in deciding whether it is worth taking that job?

4. When you made the decision to study economics, was it a 'rational' decision (albeit based on the limited information you had available at the time)? What additional information would you like to have had in order to ensure that your decision was the right one?

5. In what way does specialisation reduce the problem of scarcity?

6. Would redistributing incomes from the rich to the poor reduce the overall problem of scarcity?

7. Assume that oil begins to run out and that extraction becomes more expensive. Trace through the effects of this on the market for oil and the market for other fuels.

8. Give two examples of positive statements about the economy, and two examples of normative ones. Now give two examples that are seemingly positive, but which have normative implications or undertones.

2 Supply and demand

As we saw in Chapter 1, in a free-market economy prices play a key role in transmitting information from buyers to sellers and from sellers to buyers. This chapter examines the price mechanism in more detail.

We ask what determines demand; what determines supply; just what is the relationship between demand, supply and price; how does the price mechanism transmit information; how do prices act as incentives; and how responsive are demand and supply to those incentives.

The markets we will be examining are highly competitive markets, with many firms competing against each other. In economics we call this **perfect competition**. This is where consumers and producers are too numerous to have any control over prices: they are **price takers**.

In the case of consumers, this means that they have to accept the prices as given for the things that they buy. On most occasions this is true. For example, when you get to the supermarket checkout you cannot start haggling with the checkout operator over the price of a can of beans or a tub of margarine.

In the case of firms, perfect competition means that producers are too small and face too much competition from other firms to be able to raise prices. Take the case of farmers selling wheat. They have to sell it at the current market price. If individually they try to sell at a higher price, no one will buy, since purchasers of wheat (e.g. flour millers) can get all the wheat they want at the market price.

Of course, many firms *do* have the power to choose their prices. This does not mean that they can simply charge whatever they like. They will still have to take account of overall consumer demand and their competitors' prices. Ford, when setting the price of its Escort cars, will have to ensure that they remain competitive with Astras, Golfs, Civics, etc. Nevertheless, most firms have some flexibility in setting their prices: they have a degree of 'market power'.

If this is the case, then why do we study *perfect* markets, where firms are price takers? One reason is that they provide a useful approximation to the real world and give us many insights into how a market economy works. Many markets do function very similarly to the markets we shall be describing.

Another is that perfect markets provide an ideal against which to compare the real world. It is often argued that perfect markets benefit the consumer, whereas markets dominated by big business may operate against the consumer's interests. Although these are normative issues, the economist can nevertheless compare the behaviour of prices, output, profit, etc. in different types of market. For example, will the consumer end up paying higher prices in a market dominated by just a few firms than in one operating under perfect competition? Will British Telecom respond to an increase in demand for telephone services in the same way as farmer Giles does to an increase in the demand for cauliflowers?

Markets with powerful firms are examined in Chapters 7 and 8. For now we concentrate on price takers.

DEFINITIONS

Perfect competition (preliminary definition) A situation where the consumers and producers of a product are price takers. (There are other features of a perfectly competitive market; these are examined in Chapter 6.)

Price taker A person or firm with no power to be able to influence the market price.

2.1 Demand

The relationship between demand and price

The headlines announce, 'Major crop failures in Brazil and East Africa: coffee prices soar.' Shortly afterwards you find that coffee prices have doubled in the shops. What do you do? Presumably you will cut back on the amount of coffee you drink. Perhaps you will reduce it from, say, six cups per day to two. Perhaps you will give up drinking coffee altogether.

This is simply an illustration of the general relationship between price and consumption: *when the price of a good rises the quantity demanded will fall*. This relationship is known as the **law of demand**. There are two reasons for this law:

- People will feel poorer. They will not be able to afford to buy so much of the good with their money. The purchasing power of their income (their *real income*) has fallen. This is called the **income effect** of a price rise.
- The good will now be dearer relative to other goods. People will thus switch to alternative or 'substitute' goods. This is called the **substitution effect** of a price rise.

Similarly, when the price of a good falls, the quantity demanded will rise. People can afford to buy more (the income effect), and they will switch away from consuming alternative goods (the substitution effect).

Therefore, returning to our example of the increase in the price of coffee, we will not be able to afford to buy as much as before, and we will probably drink more tea, cocoa, fruit juices or even water instead.

The amount by which the quantity demanded falls will depend on the size of the income and substitution effects.

The size of the income effect depends primarily on the proportion of income spent on the good. Thus the more coffee we buy in the first place, the more likely we will be forced to cut down on the amount we buy if the price goes up. In other words, the bigger the proportion of income spent on the good, the bigger will be the effect of a price rise on people's real income, and the more they will reduce the quantity they demand.

The size of the substitution effect depends primarily on the number and closeness of substitute goods. Thus if you are quite happy to drink tea instead of coffee, a rise in the price of coffee will cause you to cut your consumption of coffee considerably, and correspondingly to increase your consumption of tea.

A word of warning: be careful about the meaning of the words **quantity demanded**. They refer to the amount that consumers are willing and able to purchase at a given price over a given time period (e.g. a week, or a month, or a year). They do *not* refer to what people would simply *like* to consume. You might like to own a Rolls-Royce, but your demand for Rolls-Royces will almost certainly be zero.

The demand curve

Consider the hypothetical data in Table 2.1, which shows how many kilograms of potatoes per month would be purchased at various prices.

Columns (2) and (3) show the **demand schedules** for two individuals, Tracey and Darren. Column (4) by contrast, shows the total **market demand schedule**. This is the total demand by all consumers. To obtain the market demand schedule for potatoes, we simply add up the quantities demanded at each price by *all* consumers: i.e. Tracey, Darren and anyone else who demands potatoes. Notice that we are talking about demand *over a period of time* (not at a *point* in time). Thus we would talk about daily demand or weekly demand or annual demand or whatever.

> **??** Assume that there are 200 consumers in the market. Of these, 100 have schedules like Tracey's and 100 have schedules like Darren's. What would be the total market demand schedule for potatoes now?

DEFINITIONS

The law of demand The quantity of a good demanded per period of time will fall as price rises and will rise as price falls, other things being equal (*ceteris paribus*).

Income effect The effect of a change in price on quantity demanded arising from the consumer becoming better or worse off as a result of the price change.

Substitution effect The effect of a change in price on quantity demanded arising from the consumer switching to or from alternative (substitute) products.

Quantity demanded The amount of a good that a consumer is willing and able to buy at a given price over a given period of time.

Demand schedule for an individual A table showing the different quantities of a good that a person is willing and able to buy at various prices over a given period of time.

Market demand schedule A table showing the different total quantities of a good that consumers are willing and able to buy at various prices over a given period of time.

Table 2.1 The demand for potatoes (monthly)

	Price (pence per kg) (1)	Tracey's demand (kg) (2)	Darren's demand (kg) (3)	Total market demand (tonnes: 000s) (4)
A	4	28	16	700
B	8	15	11	500
C	12	5	9	350
D	16	1	7	200
E	20	0	6	100

The demand schedule can be represented graphically as a **demand curve**. Figure 2.1 shows the market demand curve for potatoes corresponding to the schedule in Table 2.1. This price of potatoes is plotted on the vertical axis. The quantity demanded is plotted on the horizontal axis.

Point *E* shows that at a price of 20p per kilo, 100 000 tonnes of potatoes are demanded each month. When the price falls to 16p we move down the curve to point *D*. This shows that the quantity demanded has now risen to 200 000 tonnes per month. Similarly, if price falls to 12p we move down the curve again to point *C*: 350 000 tonnes are now demanded. The five points on the graph (*A–E*) correspond to the figures in columns (1) and (4) of Table 2.1. The graph also enables us to read off the likely quantities demanded at prices other than those in the table.

??

1. How much would be demanded at a price of 6p per kilogram?
2. Assuming that demand does not change from month to month, plot the *annual* market demand for potatoes.

A demand curve could also be drawn for an individual consumer. Like market demand curves, individuals' demand curves generally slope downward from left to right: they have negative slope.

??

1. Draw Tracey's and Darren's demand curves for potatoes on one diagram. Note that you will use the same vertical scale as in Figure 2.1, but you will need a quite different horizontal scale.
2. At what price is their demand the same?
3. What explanations could there be for the quite different shapes of their two demand curves? (This question is explored in section 2.4 below.)

DEFINITION

Demand curve A graph showing the relationship between the price of a good and the quantity of the good demanded over a given time period. Price is measured on the vertical axis; quantity demanded is measured on the horizontal axis. A demand curve can be for an individual consumer or group of consumers, or more usually for the whole market.

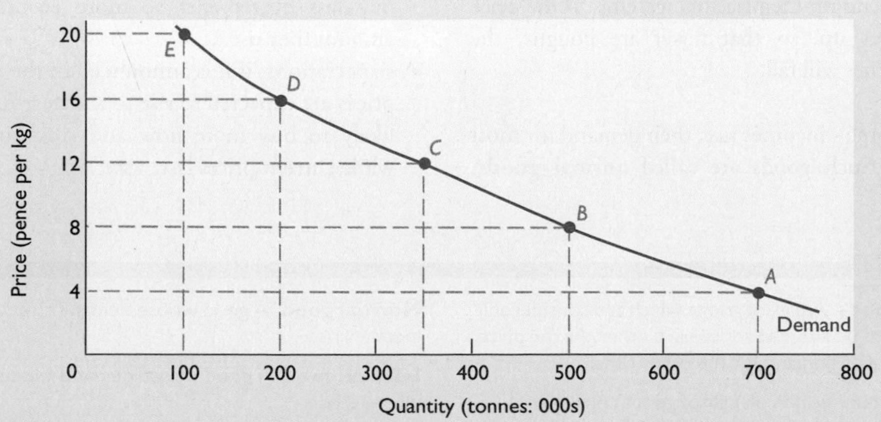

Figure 2.1 Market demand curve for potatoes (monthly)

Two points should be noted at this stage:

- In textbooks demand curves (and other curves too) are only occasionally used to plot specific data. More frequently they are used to illustrate general theoretical arguments. In such cases the axes will simply be price and quantity, with the units unspecified.
- The term 'curve' is used even when the graph is a straight line! In fact when using demand curves to illustrate arguments we frequently draw them as straight lines.

Other determinants of demand

Price is not the only factor that determines how much of a good people will buy. Demand is also affected by the following.

Tastes. The more desirable people find the good, the more they will demand. Tastes are affected by advertising, by fashion, by observing other consumers, by considerations of health and by the experiences from consuming the good on previous occasions.

The number and price of substitute goods (i.e. competitive goods). The higher the price of **substitute goods**, the higher will be the demand for this good as people switch from the substitutes. For example, the demand for coffee will depend on the price of tea. If tea goes up in price, the demand for coffee will rise.

The number and price of complementary goods. **Complementary goods** are those that are consumed together: cars and petrol, shoes and polish, fish and chips. The higher the price of complementary goods, the fewer of them will be bought and hence the less will be the demand for this good. For example, the demand for matches will depend on the price of cigarettes. If the price of cigarettes goes up, so that fewer are bought, the demand for matches will fall.

Income. As people's incomes rise, their demand for most goods will rise. Such goods are called **normal goods**. There are exceptions to this general rule, however. As people get richer, they spend less on **inferior goods**, such as cheap margarine, and switch to better quality goods.

Distribution of income. If national income were redistributed from the poor to the rich, the demand for luxury goods would rise. At the same time, as the poor got poorer they might have to turn to buying inferior goods, whose demand would thus rise too.

Expectations of future price changes. If people think that prices are going to rise in the future, they are likely to buy more now before the price does go up.

> **??** Do all these six determinants of demand affect both an individual's demand and the market demand for a product?

To illustrate these six determinants let us look at the demand for butter:

- Tastes: if it is heavily advertised, demand is likely to rise. If, on the other hand, there is a cholesterol scare, people may demand less for health reasons.
- Substitutes: if the price of margarine goes up, the demand for butter is likely to rise as people switch from one to the other.
- Complements: if the price of bread goes up, people will buy less bread and hence less butter to spread on it.
- Income: if people's income rises, they may well turn to consuming butter rather than margarine or feel that they can afford to spread butter more thickly on their bread.
- Income distribution: if income is redistributed away from the poor, they may have to give up consuming butter and buy cheaper margarine instead, or simply buy less butter and be more economical with the amount they use.
- Expectations: if it is announced in the news that butter prices are expected to rise in the near future, people are likely to buy more now and stock up their freezers while current prices last.

DEFINITIONS

Substitute goods A pair of goods which are considered by consumers to be alternatives to each other. As the price of one goes up, the demand for the other rises.

Complementary goods A pair of goods consumed together. As the price of one goes up, the demand for both goods will fall.

Normal good A good whose demand rises as people's incomes rise.

Inferior good A good whose demand falls as people's incomes rise.

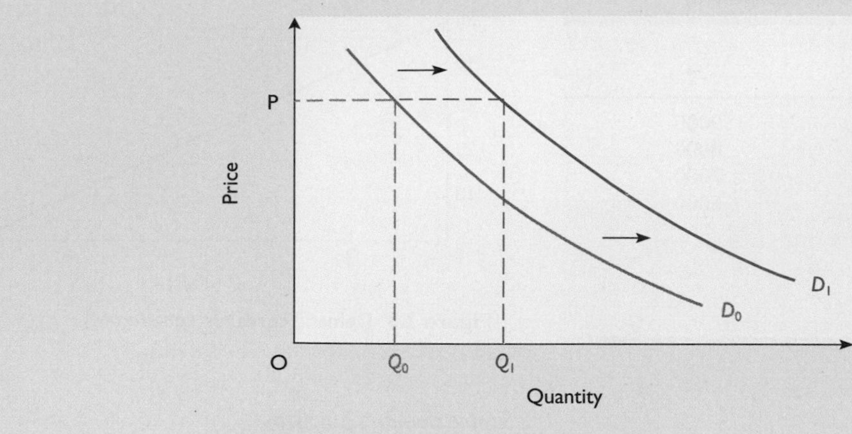

Figure 2.2 An increase in demand

Movements along and shifts in the demand curve

A demand curve is constructed on the assumption that 'other things remain equal' (*ceteris paribus*). In other words, it is assumed that none of the determinants of demand, other than price, changes. The effect of a change in price is then simply illustrated by a movement along the demand curve: for example, from point *B* to point *D* in Figure 2.1 when the price of potatoes rises from 8p to 16p per kilo.

What happens, then, when one of these other determinants does change? The answer is that we have to construct a whole new demand curve: the curve shifts. If a change in one of the other determinants causes demand to rise – say, income rises – the whole curve will shift to the right. This shows that at each price more will be demanded than before. Thus in Figure 2.2 at a price of *P*, a quantity of Q_0 was originally demanded. But now, after the increase in demand, Q_1 is demanded. (Note that D_1 is not necessarily parallel to D_0.)

If a change in a determinant other than price causes demand to fall, the whole curve will shift to the left.

To distinguish between shifts in and movements along demand curves, it is usual to distinguish between a change in *demand* and a change in the *quantity demanded*. A shift in the demand curve is referred to as a **change in demand**, whereas a movement along the demand curve as a result of a change in price is referred to as a **change in the quantity demanded**.

??

1. Assume that in Table 2.1 the total market demand for potatoes increases by 20 per cent at each price – due, say, to substantial increases in the prices of bread and rice. Plot the old and the new demand curves for potatoes. Is the new curve parallel to the old one?
2. The price of pork rises and yet it is observed that the sales of pork increase. Does this mean that the demand curve for pork is upward sloping? Explain.

*Demand equations

We can represent the relationship between the market demand for a good and the determinants of demand in the form of an equation. This is called a **demand function**. It can be expressed either in general terms or with specific values attached to the determinants.

DEFINITIONS

Change in demand The term used for a shift in the demand curve. It occurs when a determinant of demand *other* than price changes.

Change in the quantity demanded The term used for a movement along the demand curve to a new point. It occurs when there is a change in price.

Demand function An equation which shows the mathematical relationship between the quantity demanded of a good and the values of the various determinants of demand.

Table 2.2 Demand schedule for equation (4)

P	Q_d
5	9000
10	8000
15	7000
20	6000
.	.
.	.
.	.
.	.

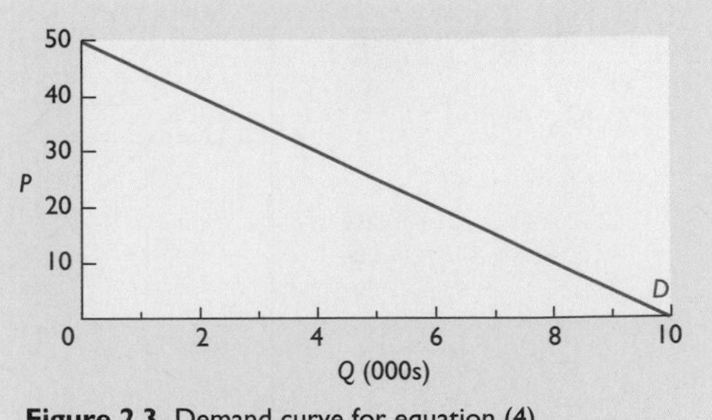

Figure 2.3 Demand curve for equation (4)

General form

$$Q_d = f(P_g, T, P_{s_1}, P_{s_2} \ldots P_{s_n}, P_{c_1}, P_{c_2} \ldots P_{c_m}, Y, B, P^e_{g\,t+1}) \quad (1)$$

This is merely saying in symbols that the quantity demanded (Q_d) 'is a function of' – i.e. depends on – the price of the good itself (P_g), tastes (T), the price of substitute goods ($P_{s_1}, P_{s_2}, \ldots P_{s_n}$), the price of complementary goods ($P_{c_1}, P_{c_2} \ldots P_{c_m}$), total consumer incomes (Y), the distribution of income (B), and the expected price of the good (P^e_g) at some future time ($t + 1$). Equation (1) is thus just a form of shorthand. Expressed in this general form there are no numerical values attached to each of the determinants.

Estimated demand equations

Surveys can be conducted to show how demand depends on each one of a number of determinants, while the rest are held constant. Using statistical techniques called **regression analysis**, a demand equation can be estimated.

For example, assume that it was observed that the demand for butter (measured in 250 g units) depended on its price (P_b), the price of margarine (P_m) and total annual consumer incomes (Y). The estimated weekly demand equation may then be something like:

$$Q_d = 2\,000\,000 - 50\,000P_b + 20\,000P_m + 0.01Y \quad (2)$$

Thus if the price of butter were 50p, the price of margarine were 35p and consumer incomes were £200 million, and if P_b and P_m were measured in pence and Y was measured in pounds, then the demand for butter would be 2 200 000 units. This is calculated as follows:

$$Q_d = 2\,000\,000 - (50\,000 \times 50) + (20\,000 \times 35) + (0.01 \times 200\,000\,000)$$

$$= 2\,000\,000 - 2\,500\,000 + 700\,000 + 2\,000\,000$$

$$= 2\,200\,000$$

Simple demand functions

Demand equations are often used to relate quantity demanded to just one determinant. Thus an equation relating quantity demanded to price could be in the form:

$$Q_d = a - bP \quad (3)$$

For example, the actual equation might be:

$$Q_d = 10\,000 - 200P \quad (4)$$

From this can be calculated a complete demand schedule or demand curve, as Table 2.2 and Figure 2.3 show. As price (P) changes, the equation tells us how much the quantity demanded (Q_d) changes.

??

1. Complete the demand schedule in Table 2.2 up to a price of 50.
2. What is it about equation (4) that makes the demand curve (a) downward sloping; (b) a straight line?

This equation is based on a *ceteris paribus* assumption: it is assumed that all the other determinants of demand remain constant. If one of these other determinants changed, the equation itself would change. There would be a shift in the curve: a change in demand. If the a term alone changed, there would be a parallel shift in the curve. If the b term changed, the slope of the curve would change.

Simple equations can be used to relate demand to other determinants too. For example, an equation relating quantity demanded to income would be in the form:

$$Q_d = a + bY \quad (5)$$

DEFINITION

Regression analysis A statistical technique which allows a functional relationship between two or more variables to be estimated.

ISSUES AND APPLICATIONS *BOX 2.1

THE DEMAND FOR BUTTER[1]

A real-world demand function

The following is an estimate of the UK's market demand curve for butter. It has been estimated (using a computer regression package) from actual data for the years 1969–91.

$$Q_d = 283.8 - 35.4P_b + 89.1P_m - 1.96Y$$

where: Q_d is the quantity of butter sold in grams per person per week.

P_b is the 'real' price of butter: i.e. the price of butter in pence per kg, divided by the retail price index (RPI) (1980 = 100).

P_m is the 'real' price of margarine (calculated in the same way as butter).

Y is the real personal disposable income of households: i.e. household income after tax, expressed as an index (1980 = 100).

From this economists could forecast what would happen to the demand for butter if any of three variables – the price of butter, the price of margarine or income – changed.

?? From this equation, calculate what would happen to the demand for butter if:

(a) The price of butter went up by 1p per kg and the RPI was 100.
(b) The price of margarine went up by 1p per kg and the RPI was 200.
(c) The index of personal disposable incomes went up by 1 point.

There is a serious problem with estimated demand functions like these: they assume that *other* determinants of demand have not changed. In the case of this demand-for-butter function, one of the other determinants *did* change. This was tastes – during the 1970s and 1980s there was a massive shift in demand from butter to margarine, perhaps for health reasons, perhaps because of the advent of 'easy-to-spread' margarines, perhaps because of an improvement in the flavour of margarines. The following table shows this shift.

Consumption of butter, margarine and spreads (grams per person per week)

	Butter	Margarine	Low-fat spreads
1969	174	79	–
1987	61	113	31
1994	39	43	74

Source: *National Food Survey* (MAFF).

Assuming that this shift in taste took place steadily over time, a new demand equation was estimated for the same years:

$$Q_d = 321.4 - 38.5P_b + 16.1P_m - 0.38Y - 5.21TIME$$

where the *TIME* term is as follows: 1969 = 1, 1970 = 2, 1971 = 3, etc.

In the mid-1980s, a new substitute entered the market: low-fat spreads. These have not been on the market long enough to estimate a new demand equation, but clearly they have shifted the demand curve for butter and hence make the estimated equations less reliable for forecasting the demand for butter.

?? 1. How does the introduction of the *TIME* term affect the relationship between the demand for butter and (a) the price of margarine and (b) personal disposable income?
2. Is butter a normal good or an inferior good?

[1] Calculations by W. Thurlow.

?? 1. Referring to equation (5), if the term *a* has a value of –50 000 and the term *b* a value of 0.001, construct a demand schedule with respect to total income (*Y*). Do this for incomes between £100 million and £300 million at £50 million intervals.
2. Now use this schedule to plot a demand curve with respect to income. Comment on its shape.

The branch of economics that applies statistical techniques to economic data is known as **econometrics**. Econometrics is beyond the scope of this book. It is worth noting, however, that econometrics, like other branches of statistics, cannot produce equations and graphs that allow totally reliable predictions to be made. The data on which the equations are based are often incomplete or unreliable, and the underlying relationships on which they are based (often ones of human behaviour) may well change over time.

DEFINITION

Econometrics The science of applying statistical techniques to economic data in order to identify and test economic relationships.

SECTION SUMMARY

1. When the price of a good rises, the quantity demanded per period of time will fall. This is known as the 'law of demand'. It applies both to individuals' demand and to the whole market demand.
2. The law of demand is explained by the income and substitution effects of a price change.
3. The relationship between price and quantity demanded per period of time can be shown in a table (or 'schedule') or as a graph. On the graph, price is plotted on the vertical axis and quantity demanded per period of time on the horizontal axis. The resulting demand curve is downward sloping (negatively sloped).
4. Other determinants of demand include tastes, the number and price of substitute goods, the number and price of complementary goods, income, the distribution of income and expectations of future price changes.
5. If price changes, the effect is shown by a movement along the demand curve. We call this effect 'a change in the quantity demanded'.
6. If any other determinant of demand changes, the whole curve will shift. We call this effect 'a change in demand'. A rightward shift represents an increase in demand; a leftward shift represents a decrease in demand.

*7. The relationship between the quantity demanded and the various determinants of demand (including price) can be expressed as an equation.

2.2 Supply

Supply and price

Imagine you are a farmer deciding what to do with your land. Part of your land is in a fertile valley. Part is on a hillside where the soil is poor. Perhaps, then, you will consider growing vegetables in the valley and keeping sheep on the hillside.

Your decision will depend to a large extent on the price that various vegetables will fetch in the market and likewise the price you can expect to get from sheep and wool. As far as the valley is concerned, you will plant the vegetables that give the best return. If, for example, the price of potatoes is high, you will probably use a lot of the valley for growing potatoes. If the price gets higher, you may well use the whole of the valley, being prepared maybe to run the risk of potato disease. If the price is very high indeed, you may even consider growing potatoes on the hillside, even though the yield per acre is much lower there.

In other words, the higher the price of a particular crop, the more of it you are likely to grow in preference to other crops. This illustrates the general relationship between supply and price: *when the price of a good rises the quantity supplied will also rise.* There are three reasons for this:

- As firms supply more, they are likely to find that beyond a certain level of output, costs rise more and more rapidly.

  In the case of the farm we have just considered, once potatoes have to be grown on the hillside the costs of producing them will increase. Also if the land has to be used more intensively, say by the use of more and more fertilizers, again the costs of producing extra potatoes are likely to rise quite rapidly. It is the same for manufacturers. Beyond a certain level of output, costs are likely to rise rapidly as workers have to be paid overtime and as machines approach capacity working. If higher output involves higher costs of production, producers will need to get a higher price if they are to be persuaded to produce extra output.
- The higher the price of the good, the more profitable it becomes to produce. Firms will thus be encouraged to produce more of it by switching from producing less profitable goods.
- Given time, if the price of a good remains high, new producers will be encouraged to set up in production. Total market supply thus rises.

The first two determinants affect supply in the short run. The third affects supply in the long run. We distinguish between short-run and long-run supply later in the chapter on page 67.

The supply curve

The amount that producers would like to supply at various prices can be shown in a **supply schedule**. Table 2.3

DEFINITION

Supply schedule A table showing the different quantities of a good that producers are willing and able to supply at various prices over a given time period. A supply schedule can be for an individual producer or group of producers, or for all producers (the market supply schedule).

Table 2.3 The supply of potatoes (monthly)

	Price of potatoes (pence per kg)	Farmer X's supply (tonnes)	Total market supply (tonnes: 000s)
a	4	50	100
b	8	70	200
c	12	100	350
d	16	120	530
e	20	130	700

shows a monthly supply schedule for potatoes, both for an individual farmer (farmer X) and for all farmers together (the whole market).

The supply schedule can be represented graphically as a **supply curve**. A supply curve may be an individual firm's supply curve or a market curve (i.e. that of the whole industry).

Figure 2.4 shows the *market* supply curve of potatoes. As with demand curves, price is plotted on the vertical axis and quantity on the horizontal axis. Each of the points *a–e* corresponds to a figure in Table 2.3. Thus, for example, a price rise from 12p per kilogram to 16p per kilogram will cause a movement along the supply curve from point *c* to point *d*: total market supply will rise from 350 000 tonnes per month to 530 000 tonnes per month.

??

1. How much would be supplied at a price of 14p per kilo?
2. Draw a supply curve for farmer X. Are the axes drawn to the same scale as in Figure 2.4?

Not all supply curves will be upward sloping (positively sloped). Sometimes they will be vertical, or horizontal or even downward sloping. This will depend largely on the time period over which firms' response to price changes is considered. This question is examined in the section on the elasticity of supply (see section 2.4 below) and in more detail in Chapters 5 and 6.

Other determinants of supply

Like demand, supply is not simply determined by price. The other determinants of supply are as follows.

The costs of production. The higher the costs of production, the less profit will be made at any price. As costs rise, firms will cut back on production, probably switching to alternative products whose costs have not risen so much.

The main reasons for a change in costs are as follows:

- Change in input prices: costs of production will rise if wages, raw material prices, rents, interest rates or any other input prices rise.

DEFINITION

Supply curve A graph showing the relationship between the price of a good and the quantity of the good supplied over a given period of time.

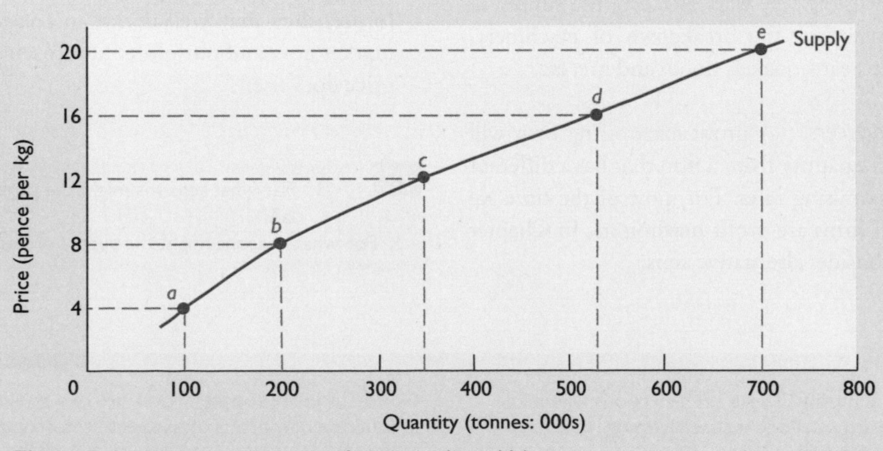

Figure 2.4 Market supply curve of potatoes (monthly)

- Change in technology: technological advances can fundamentally alter the costs of production. Consider, for example, how the microchip revolution has changed production methods and information handling in virtually every industry in the world.
- Organisational changes: various cost savings can be made in many firms by reorganising production.
- Government policy: costs will be lowered by government subsidies and raised by various taxes.

The profitability of alternative products (substitutes in supply). If a product which is a **substitute in supply** becomes more profitable to supply than before, producers are likely to switch from the first good to this alternative. Supply of the first good falls. Other goods are likely to become more profitable if:

- Their prices rise.
- Their costs of production fall.

For example, if the price of carrots goes up, or the cost of producing carrots comes down, farmers may decide to produce more carrots. The supply of potatoes is therefore likely to fall.

The profitability of goods in joint supply. Sometimes when one good is produced, another good is also produced at the same time. These are said to be **goods in joint supply**. An example is the refining of crude oil to produce petrol. Other grade fuels will be produced as well, such as diesel and paraffin. If more petrol is produced, due to a rise in demand and hence its price, then the supply of these other fuels will rise too.

Nature, 'random shocks' and other unpredictable events. In this category we would include the weather and diseases affecting farm output, wars affecting the supply of imported raw materials, the breakdown of machinery, industrial disputes, earthquakes, floods and fire, etc.

The aims of producers. A profit-maximising firm will supply a different quantity from a firm that has a different aim, such as maximising sales. For most of the time we shall assume that firms are profit maximisers. In Chapter 8, however, we consider alternative aims.

Expectations of future price changes. If price is expected to rise, producers may temporarily reduce the amount they sell. Instead they are likely to build up their stocks and only release them on to the market when the price does rise. At the same time they may plan to produce more, by installing new machines, or taking on more labour, so that they can be ready to supply more when the price has risen.

To illustrate some of these determinants let us return to the example of butter. What would cause the supply of butter to rise?

- A reduction in the costs of producing butter. This could be caused, say, by a reduction in the price of nitrogen fertiliser. This would encourage farmers to use more fertiliser, which would increase grass yields, which in turn would increase milk yields per acre. Alternatively, new technology may allow more efficient churning of butter. Or again, the government may decide to give subsidies to farmers to produce more butter.
- A reduction in the profitability of producing cream or cheese. If these products become less profitable, due say to a reduction in their price, due in turn to a reduction in consumer demand, more butter is likely to be produced instead.
- An increase in the profitability of skimmed milk. If consumers buy more skimmed milk, then an increased supply of skimmed milk is likely to lead to an increase in the supply of butter and other cream products, since they are jointly produced with skimmed milk.
- If weather conditions are favourable, grass yields and hence milk yields are likely to be high. This will increase the supply of butter and other milk products.
- If butter producers expect the price to rise in the near future, they may well decide to release less on to the market now and put more into frozen storage until the price does rise.

??

1. For what reasons might the supply of potatoes fall?
2. For what reasons might the supply of leather rise?

DEFINITIONS

Substitutes in supply These are two goods where an increased production of one means diverting resources away from producing the other.

Goods in joint supply These are two goods where the production of more of one leads to the production of more of the other.

Movements along and shifts in the supply curve

The principle here is the same as with demand curves. The effect of a change in price is illustrated by a movement along the supply curve: for example, from point *d* to point *e* in Figure 2.4 when price rises from 16p to 20p. Quantity supplied rises from 530 000 to 700 000 tonnes per month.

If any other determinant of supply changes, the whole supply curve will shift. A rightward shift illustrates an increase in supply. A leftward shift illustrates a decrease in supply. Thus in Figure 2.5, if the original curve is S_0, the curve S_1 represents an increase in supply, whereas the curve S_2 represents a decrease in supply.

A movement along a supply curve is often referred to as a **change in the quantity supplied**, whereas a shift in the supply curve is simply referred to as a **change in supply**.

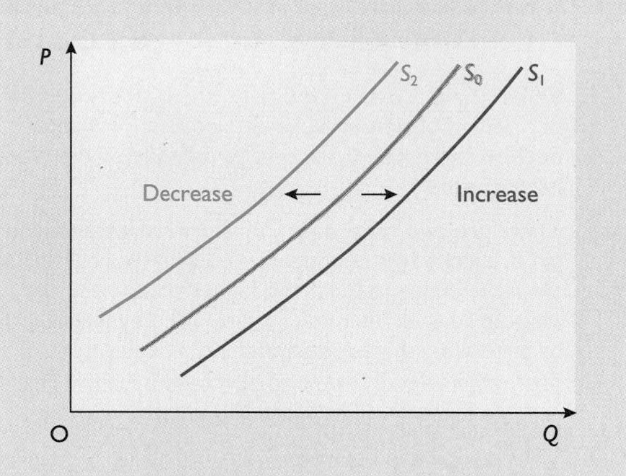

Figure 2.5 Shifts in the supply curve

?? This question is concerned with the supply of oil for central heating. In each case consider whether there is a movement along the supply curve (and in which direction) or a shift in it (and whether left or right).
(a) New oil fields start up in production. (b) The demand for central heating rises. (c) The price of gas falls. (d) Oil companies anticipate an upsurge in demand for central-heating oil. (e) The demand for petrol rises. (f) New technology decreases the costs of oil refining. (g) All oil products become more expensive.

*Supply equations

A general supply function can be written in the form:

$$Q_s = f(P_g, C_g, a_1, a_2 \ldots a_n, j_1, j_2 \ldots j_m, R, A, P^e_{g\,t+1}) \quad (6)$$

In other words, quantity supplied (Q_s) depends on the price of the good (P_g), the costs of production (C_g), the profitability of alternative goods ($a_1, a_2 \ldots a_n$), the profitability of goods jointly supplied ($j_1, j_2 \ldots j_m$), nature and other random shocks (R), the aims of producers (A) and the expected price of the good (P_g^e) at some future time ($t + 1$).

Using survey data and regression analysis, equations can be estimated relating supply to some of these determinants. Note that not all determinants can be easily quantified (e.g. nature and the aims of firms), and thus may be left out of the equation.

The simplest form of supply equation relates supply to just one determinant. Thus a function relating supply to price would be of the form:

$$Q_s = c + dP \quad (7)$$

Using regression analysis, values can be estimated for *c* and *d*. Thus an actual supply equation might be something like:

$$Q_s = 500 + 1000P \quad (8)$$

??
1. If *P* was originally measured in £s, what would happen to the value of the *d* term if *P* were now measured in pence?
2. Draw the schedule (table) and graph for equation (8) for prices from £1 to £10. What is it in the equation that determines the slope of the supply 'curve'?

If any determinant other than price changed, a new equation would result. For example, if costs of production fall, the equation may now be:

$$Q_s = 1000 + 1500P \quad (9)$$

More complex supply equations would relate supply to more than one determinant. For example:

$$Q_s = 200 + 80P - 20a_1 - 15a_2 + 30j \quad (10)$$

where P is the price of the good, a_1 and a_2 are the profitabilities of two alternative goods that could be supplied instead, and j is the profitability of a good in joint supply.

?? Explain why the *P* and *j* terms have a positive sign, whereas the a_1 and a_2 terms have a negative sign.

DEFINITIONS

Change in the quantity supplied The term used for a movement along the supply curve to a new point. It occurs when there is a change in price.

Change in supply The term used for a shift in the supply curve. It occurs when a determinant *other* than price changes.

SECTION SUMMARY

1. When the price of a good rises, the quantity supplied per period of time will usually also rise. This applies both to individual producers' supply and to the whole market supply.
2. There are two reasons in the short run why a higher price encourages producers to supply more: (a) they are now willing to incur the higher costs per unit associated with producing more; (b) they will switch to producing this product and away from now less profitable ones. In the long run there is a third reason: new producers will be attracted into the market.
3. The relationship between price and quantity supplied per period of time can be shown in a table (or schedule) or as a graph. As with a demand curve, price is plotted on the vertical axis and quantity per period of time on the horizontal axis. The resulting supply curve is upward sloping (positively sloped).
4. Other determinants of supply include the costs of production, the profitability of alternative products, the profitability of goods in joint supply, random shocks and expectations of future price changes.
5. If price changes, the effect is shown by a movement along the supply curve. We call this effect 'a change in the quantity supplied'.
6. If any determinant *other* than price changes, the effect is shown by a shift in the whole supply curve. We call this effect 'a change in supply'. A rightward shift represents an increase in supply; a leftward shift represents a decrease in supply.

*7. The relationship between the quantity supplied and the various determinants of supply can be expressed in the form of an equation.

2.3 Price and output determination

Equilibrium price and output

We can now combine our analysis of demand and supply. This will show how the actual price of a product and the actual quantity bought and sold are determined in a free and competitive market.

Let us return to the example of the market demand and market supply of potatoes, and use the data from Tables 2.1 and 2.3. These figures are given again in Table 2.4.

What will be the price and output that actually prevail? If the price started at 4p per kilogram, demand would exceed supply by 600 000 tonnes ($A - a$). Consumers would be unable to obtain all they wanted and would thus be willing to pay a higher price. Producers, unable or unwilling to supply enough to meet the demand, will be only too happy to accept a higher price. The effect of the shortage, then, will be to drive up the price. The same would happen at a price of 8p per kilogram. There would still be a shortage; price would still rise. But as the price rises, the quantity demanded falls and the quantity supplied rises. The shortage is progressively eliminated.

?? Explain the process by which the price of houses would rise if there were a shortage.

What would happen if the price started at a much higher level: say, at 20p per kilogram? In this case supply would exceed demand by 600 000 tonnes ($e - E$). The effect of this surplus would be to drive the price down as farmers competed against each other to sell their excess supplies. The same would happen at a price of 16p per kilogram. There would still be a surplus; price would still fall.

In fact, only one price is sustainable. This is the price where demand equals supply: namely, 12p per kilogram, where both demand and supply are 350 000 tonnes.

Table 2.4 The market demand and supply of potatoes (monthly)

Price of potatoes (pence per kg)	Total market demand (tonnes: 000s)	Total market supply (tonnes: 000s)
4	700 (*A*)	100 (*a*)
8	500 (*B*)	200 (*b*)
12	350 (*C*)	350 (*c*)
16	200 (*D*)	530 (*d*)
20	100 (*E*)	700 (e)

When supply matches demand the market is said to **clear**. There is no shortage and no surplus.

This price, where demand equals supply, is called the **equilibrium price**. By **equilibrium** we mean a point of balance or a point of rest: in other words, a point towards which there is a tendency to move. In Table 2.4, if the price starts at other than 12p per kilogram, there will be a tendency for it to move towards 12p. The equilibrium price is the only price at which producers' and consumers' wishes are mutually reconciled: where the producers' plans to supply exactly match the consumers' plans to buy.

Demand and supply curves

The determination of equilibrium price and output can be shown using demand and supply curves. Equilibrium is where the two curves intersect.

Figure 2.6 shows the demand and supply curves of potatoes corresponding to the data in Table 2.4. Equilibrium price is P_e (12p) and equilibrium quantity is Q_e (350 000 tonnes).

At any price above 12p, there would be a surplus. Thus at 16p there is a surplus of 330 000 tonnes ($d - D$). More is supplied than consumers are willing and able to purchase at that price. Thus a price of 16p fails to clear the market. Price will fall to the equilibrium price of 12p. As it does so, there will be a movement along the demand curve from point *D* to point *C*, and a movement along the supply curve from point *d* to point *c*.

At any price below 12p, there would be a shortage. Thus at 8p there is a shortage of 300 000 tonnes ($B - b$). Price will rise to 12p. This will cause a movement along the supply curve from point *b* to point *c* and along the demand curve from point *B* to point *C*.

Point *Cc* is the equilibrium: where demand equals supply.

Movement to a new equilibrium

The equilibrium price will remain unchanged only so long as the demand and supply curves remain unchanged. If either of the curves shifts, a new equilibrium will be formed.

A change in demand

If one of the determinants of demand changes (other than price), the whole demand curve will shift. This will lead to a movement *along* the *supply* curve to the new intersection point.

For example, in Figure 2.7, if a rise in consumer incomes led to the demand curve shifting to D_2, there would be a shortage of $h - g$ at the original price P_{e_1}. This

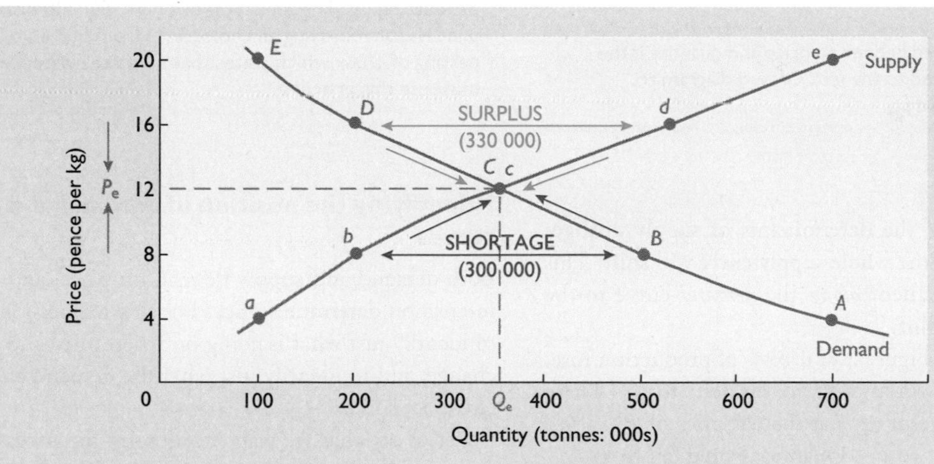

Figure 2.6 The determination of market equilibrium (potatoes: monthly)

DEFINITIONS

Market clearing A market clears when supply matches demand, leaving no shortage or surplus.

Equilibrium price The price where the quantity demanded equals the quantity supplied: the price where there is no shortage or surplus.

Equilibrium A position of balance. A position from which there is no inherent tendency to move away.

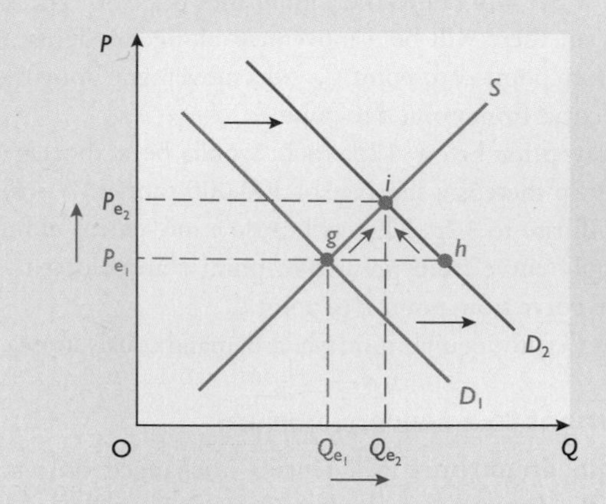

Figure 2.7 Effect of a shift in the demand curve

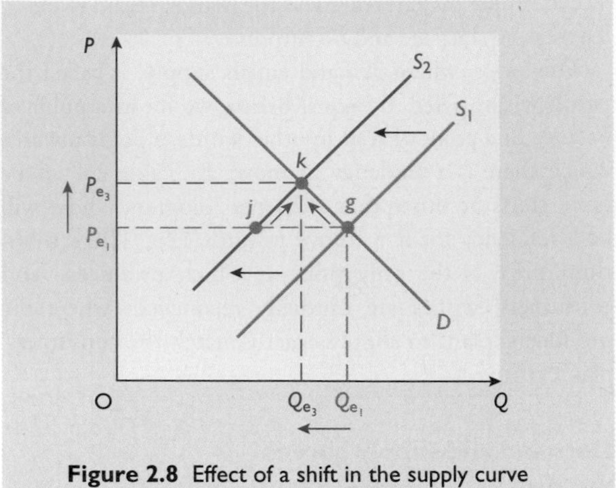

Figure 2.8 Effect of a shift in the supply curve

would cause price to rise to the new equilibrium P_{e2}. As it did so, there would be a movement along the supply curve from point *g* to point *i*, and along the new demand curve (D_2) from point *h* to point *i*. Equilibrium quantity would rise from Q_{e1} to Q_{e2}.

The effect of the shift in demand, therefore, has been a movement *along* the supply curve from the old equilibrium to the new: from point *g* to point *i*.

?? What would happen to price and quantity if the demand curve shifted to the left? Draw a diagram to illustrate your answer.

A change in supply

Likewise, if one of the determinants of supply changes (other than price), the whole supply curve will shift. This will lead to a movement *along* the *demand* curve to the new intersection point.

For example, in Figure 2.8, if costs of production rose, the supply curve would shift to the left: to S_2. There would be a shortage of $g - j$ at the old price of P_{e1}. Price would rise from P_{e1} to P_{e3}. Quantity would fall from Q_{e1} to Q_{e3}. In other words, there would be a movement along the demand curve from point *g* to point *k*, and along the new supply curve (S_2) from point *j* to point *k*.

To summarise: a shift in one curve leads to a movement along the other curve to the new intersection point.

Sometimes a number of determinants might change. This might lead to a shift in *both* curves. When this happens equilibrium simply moves from the point where the old curves intersected to the point where the new ones intersect.

?? What will happen to the equilibrium price and quantity of butter in each of the following cases? You should state whether demand or supply (or both) have shifted and in which direction. (In each case assume *ceteris paribus.*)
(a) A rise in the price of margarine. (b) A rise in the demand for yoghurt. (c) A rise in the price of bread. (d) A rise in the demand for bread. (e) An expected rise in the price of butter in the near future. (f) A tax on butter production. (g) The invention of a new, but expensive, process for removing all cholesterol from butter, plus the passing of a law which states that all butter producers must use this process.

*Identifying the position of demand and supply curves

Both demand and supply depend on price, and yet their interaction determines price. For this reason it is difficult to identify just what is going on when price and quantity change, and to identify just what the demand and supply curves look like.

Let us say that we want to identify the demand curve for good X. We observe that when the price was 20p, 1000 units were purchased. At a later date the price has risen to 30p and 800 units are now purchased. What can we conclude from this about the demand curve? The answer is that without further information we can conclude very little. Consider Figures 2.9 and 2.10. Both are consistent with the facts.

In Figure 2.9 the demand curve has not shifted. The rise in price and the fall in sales are due entirely to a shift in the supply curve. The movement from point *a* to point *b* is thus a movement along the demand curve. If we can

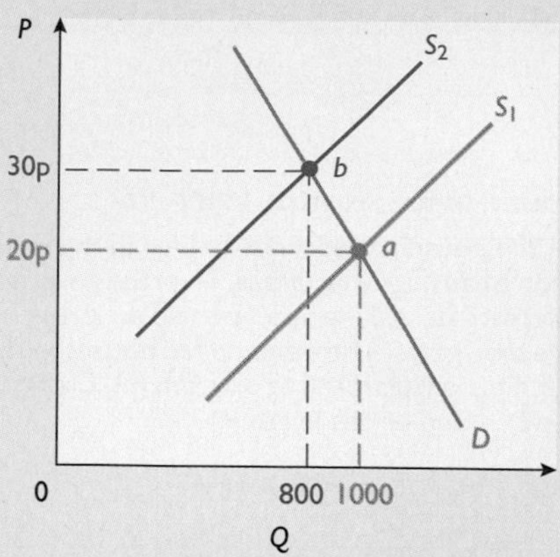

Figure 2.9 Problems in identifying the position and shape of the demand curve: shift in supply curve

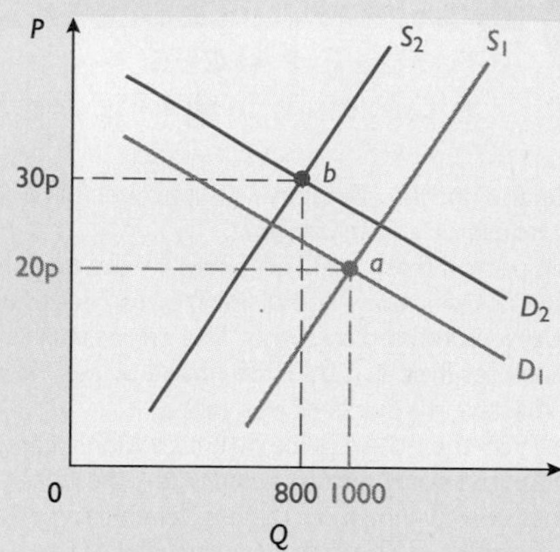

Figure 2.10 Problems in identifying the position and shape of the demand curve: shift in supply *and* demand curves

be certain that the demand curve has not shifted, then the evidence allows us to identify its position (or, at least, two points on it).

In Figure 2.10, however, not only has the supply curve shifted, but so also has the demand curve. Let us assume that people's tastes for the product have increased. In this case a movement from *a* to *b* does *not* trace out the demand curve. We cannot derive the demand curve(s) from the evidence of price and quantity alone.

The problem is that when the supply curve shifts, we often cannot know whether or not the demand curve has shifted, and if so by how much. How would we know, for example, just how much people's tastes have changed?

The problem works the other way round too. It is difficult to identify a supply curve when the demand curve shifts. Is the change in price and quantity entirely due to the shift in the demand curve, or has the supply curve shifted too?

The problem is known as the **identification problem**. It is difficult to identify just what is causing the change in price and quantity.

DEFINITION

Identification problem The problem of identifying the relationship between two variables (e.g. price and quantity demanded) from the evidence when it is not known whether or how the variables have been affected by *other* determinants. For example, it is difficult to identify the shape of a demand curve simply by observing price and quantity when it is not known whether changes in other determinants have *shifted* the demand curve.

SECTION SUMMARY

1. If the demand for a good exceeds the supply, there will be a shortage. This will lead to a rise in the price of the good.
2. If the supply of a good exceeds the demand, there will be a surplus. This will lead to a fall in the price.
3. Price will settle at the equilibrium. The equilibrium price is the one that clears the market: the price where demand equals supply.
4. If the demand or supply curve shifts, this will lead either to a shortage or to a surplus. Price will therefore either rise or fall until a new equilibrium is reached at the position where the supply and demand curves *now* intersect.

*5. It is difficult to identify the position of a real-world supply (or demand) curve simply by looking at the relationship between price and quantity at different points in time. The problem is that the other curve may have shifted (by an unknown amount).

CASE STUDIES BOX 2.2

HOUSE PRICES

A case study in shifting demand curves

Simple demand and supply analysis is a powerful tool for explaining house price movements.

Take the period from 1983 to 1996. At the beginning of the period Britain was recovering from a recession and house prices started to climb. The increase was relatively slow at first, but by 1988 house prices were rising at a massive 40 per cent per year.

Then in 1989 the house price boom suddenly came to an end, and in the south prices actually fell. By 1992 house prices were falling everywhere, leaving over 1.5 million households in homes where the size of the mortgage was larger than the value of the house: they had 'negative equity' in their property.

What was the cause of these movements? The analysis can be divided into two periods: the price boom and the subsequent slump in house prices.

The house price boom: 1983–9

The recovery from recession was faster in the south: people had higher incomes and these were growing faster than in the north. This is illustrated by a large rightward shift in the demand for houses in diagram (a). House prices, which were already higher in the south, thus started to rise rapidly.

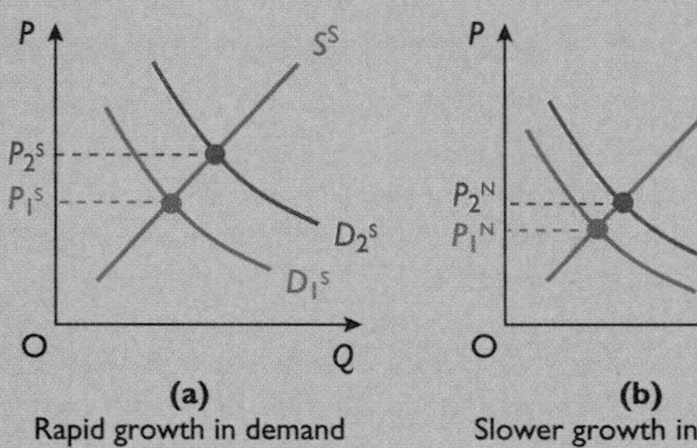

(a) Rapid growth in demand for houses in the south

(b) Slower growth in demand for houses in the north

The recession was deeper and longer lived in the north. Recovery was slow and unemployment remained high. The demand for houses only grew slowly. This is illustrated by a small rightward shift in demand for houses in diagram (b). House prices in the north rose fairly slowly and hence the gap between south and north house prices widened.

After very high mortgage interest rates in 1985, mortgage rates gradually fell. Mortgages were easily obtainable, with banks competing with building societies to lend to house buyers. As house prices rose, so this further increased the demand, as people saw a house as a good investment. People rushed to buy before prices went any higher. Again these effects were bigger in the south, where the price rises were faster.

The house price slump: 1989–96

By mid-1988 house prices were so high in the south that many people had huge mortgages. Then the government raised interest rates. Many people could no longer afford such large mortgages. The demand for houses in the south fell. This is illustrated in diagram (c). Demand shifted to D_3^s, and prices fell to P_3^s.

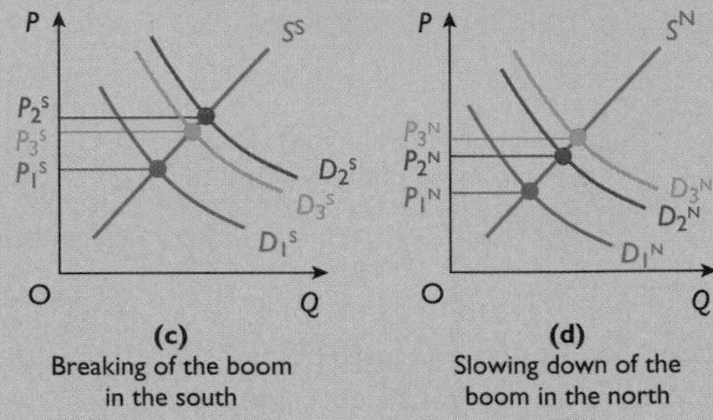

(c) Breaking of the boom in the south

(d) Slowing down of the boom in the north

In the late 1980s, businesses were increasingly being attracted to the north with its plentiful supply of labour, cheaper land and cheaper housing for their employees. Thus by mid-1988 the demand for houses in the north was beginning to rise faster than in the south. This, combined with the fact that people in the north generally had smaller mortgages, meant that the mortgage rate increase had less effect in the north. Thus demand continued to rise in the north (albeit at a slower rate). This is illustrated in diagram (d), with demand rising to D_3^N. As a result, the gap between south and north prices began to narrow.

Between the beginning of 1989 and the beginning of 1992, house prices fell by nearly 25 per cent in the south-east region and by 30 per cent in East Anglia, whereas in Scotland they rose by nearly 30 per cent and in the north of England they rose by 40 per cent.

Then with the deepening recession in all parts of the country in 1992, house prices fell generally. The demand curve in all regions shifted to the left.

After 1992, however, with a fall in interest rates and a gradual recovery in the economy, the housing market should have recovered too. But with many people still in a position of negative equity, and few expecting any significant rise in house prices, demand remained stagnant. Indeed, it was not until 1996 that house prices eventually began to move upwards again.

?? Which way is the *supply* curve for houses likely to shift if (a) builders anticipate a boom in demand; (b) people with houses to sell think that house prices will soon rise rapidly; (c) following a rise in interest rates, people with large mortgages find they are unable to maintain the payments?

2.4

Elasticity

Price elasticity of demand

When the price of a good rises, the quantity demanded will fall. That much is fairly obvious. But in most cases we will want to know more than this. We will want to know by just *how much* the quantity demanded will fall. In other words, we will want to know how *responsive* demand is to a rise in price.

Take the case of two products: oil and cauliflowers. In the case of oil, a rise in price is likely to result in only a slight fall in the quantity demanded. If people want to continue driving, they have to pay the higher prices for fuel. A few may turn to riding bicycles, and some people may try to make fewer journeys, but for most people, a rise in the price of petrol and diesel will make little difference to how much they use their cars.

In the case of cauliflowers, however, a rise in price may lead to a substantial fall in the quantity demanded. The reason is that there are alternative vegetables that people can buy. Many people, when buying vegetables, are very conscious of their prices and will buy whatever is reasonably priced.

We call the responsiveness of demand to a change in price the **price elasticity of demand**, and as we shall see on many occasions throughout this book, it is one of the most important concepts in economics. For example, if we know the price elasticity of demand for a product, we can predict the effect on price and quantity of a shift in the *supply* curve for that product.

Figure 2.11 shows the effect of a shift in supply with two quite different demand curves (D and D'). Curve D' is more elastic than curve D. In other words, for any given change in price, there will be a larger change in quantity demanded along curve D' than along curve D.

Assume that initially the supply curve is S_1, and that it intersects with both demand curves at point a, at a price of P_1 and a quantity of Q_1. Now supply shifts to S_2. What will happen to price and quantity? In the case of the less elastic demand curve D, there is a relatively large rise in price (to P_2) and a relatively small fall in quantity (to Q_2): equilibrium is at point b. In the case of the more elastic demand curve D', however, there is only a relatively small rise in price (to P_3), but a relatively large fall in quantity (to Q_3): equilibrium is at point c.

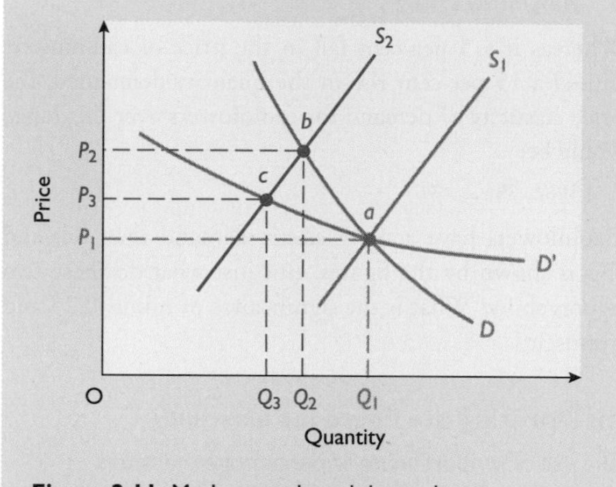

Figure 2.11 Market supply and demand

Measuring the price elasticity of demand

We saw from Figure 2.11 that if we plot two demand curves on the same diagram, the flatter curve will be more elastic than the steeper one. But looking at a curve's slope gives us only a very rough indication of elasticity. It is important to have a much more precise measure.

What we want to compare is the size of the change in quantity demanded with the size of the change in price. But given that price and quantity are measured in different units, the only sensible way we can do this is to use percentage or proportionate changes. This gives us the following **formula for the price elasticity of demand ($P\epsilon_D$)** for a product: percentage (or proportionate) change in quantity demanded divided by the percentage (or proportionate) change in price. Putting this in symbols gives:

$$P\epsilon_D = \frac{\%\Delta Q_D}{\%\Delta P}$$

where ϵ is the Greek epsilon and is the symbol we use for elasticity, and Δ is the capital Greek delta and is the symbol we use for a 'change in'.

DEFINITIONS

Price elasticity of demand The responsiveness of quantity demanded to a change in price.

Formula for price elasticity of demand ($P\epsilon_D$) The percentage (or proportionate) change in quantity demanded divided by the percentage (or proportionate) change in price: $\%\Delta Q_D \div \%\Delta P$.

Thus if a 40 per cent rise in the price of oil caused the quantity demanded to fall by a mere 10 per cent, the price elasticity of oil over this range will be:

$-10\%/40\% = -0.25$

Whereas if a 5 per cent fall in the price of cauliflowers caused a 15 per cent rise in the quantity demanded, the price elasticity of demand for cauliflowers over this range would be:

$15\%/-5\% = -3$

Cauliflowers have a more elastic demand than oil, and this is shown by the figures. But just what do these two figures show? What is the significance of minus 0.25 and minus 3?

Interpreting the figure for elasticity

The use of proportionate or percentage measures

Elasticity is measured in proportionate or percentage terms for the following reasons:

- It allows comparison of changes in two qualitatively different things, which are thus measured in two different types of unit: i.e. it allows comparison of *quantity* changes with *monetary* changes.
- It avoids the problem of what size units to use. For example, an increase from £2 to £4 is 2 price units. An increase from 200 pence to 400 pence is 200 price units. By measuring this change in proportionate or percentage terms the same result is obtained whichever price unit is used, thus avoiding the problems of a merely apparent difference in price change.
- It is the only sensible way of deciding *how big* a change in price or quantity is. Take a simple example. An item goes up in price by £1. Is this a big increase or a small increase? We can only answer this if we know what the original price was. If a can of beans goes up in price by £1, that is a huge price increase. If, however, the price of a house goes up by £1, that is a tiny price increase. In other words, it is the percentage or proportionate increase in price that we look at in deciding how big a price rise it is.

The sign (positive or negative)

Demand curves are generally downward sloping. This means that price and quantity change in opposite directions. A *rise* in price (a positive figure) will cause a *fall* in the quantity demanded (a negative figure). Similarly a *fall* in price will cause a *rise* in the quantity demanded. Thus when working out price elasticity of demand we either divide a negative figure by a positive figure, or a positive figure by a negative. Either way, we end up with a negative figure.

The value (greater or less than 1)

If we now ignore the negative sign and just concentrate on the value of the figure, this tells us whether demand is **elastic** or **inelastic**.

Elastic ($\epsilon > 1$). This where a change in price causes a proportionately larger change in the quantity demanded. In this case the value of elasticity will be greater than 1, since we are dividing a larger figure by a smaller figure.

Inelastic ($\epsilon < 1$). This is where a change in a price causes a proportionately smaller change in the quantity demanded. In this case elasticity will be less than 1, since we are dividing a smaller figure by a larger figure.

Unit elastic ($\epsilon = 1$). **Unit elasticity** is where price and quantity demanded change by the same proportion. This will give an elasticity equal to 1, since we are dividing a figure by itself.

Determinants of price elasticity of demand

The price elasticity of demand varies enormously from one product to another. For example, the demand for a holiday in any given resort typically has a price elasticity greater than 5, whereas the demand for electricity has a price elasticity less than 0.5 (ignoring the negative signs). But why do some products have a highly elastic demand, whereas others have a highly *in*elastic demand? What determines price elasticity of demand?

DEFINITIONS

Elastic demand Where quantity demanded changes by a larger percentage than price. Ignoring the negative sign, it will have a value greater than 1.

Inelastic demand Where quantity demanded changes by a smaller percentage than price. Ignoring the negative sign, it will have a value less than 1.

Unit elastic demand Where quantity demanded changes by the same percentage as price. Ignoring the negative sign, it will have a value equal to 1.

The number and closeness of substitute goods. This is the most important determinant. The more substitutes there are for a good, and the closer they are, the more will people switch to these alternatives when the price of the good rises: the greater, therefore, will be the price elasticity of demand.

Returning to our examples of oil and cauliflowers, there is no close substitute for oil and thus demand is relatively inelastic. There are plenty of alternatives to cauliflowers, however, and thus demand is relatively elastic. Of course, the closeness is very often in the mind of the consumer. Some people may have a particular fondness for cauliflowers. For them demand will be less elastic than for people who are not fussy whether they eat cauliflowers, cabbages, broccoli or any other vegetable.

Similar arguments apply to particular brands of a product. The price elasticity of demand for a given brand of a product will probably be fairly high. If its price goes up, people can simply switch to another brand: there is a large substitution effect. By contrast the demand for a product *in general* will normally be pretty inelastic. If the price of food in general goes up, demand for food will only fall slightly. People will buy a little less since they cannot now afford so much: this is the *income* effect of the price rise. But there is no alternative to food that can satisfy our hunger: there is therefore virtually no *substitution* effect.

The proportion of income spent on the good. The higher the proportion of our income that is spent on a good, the more we will be forced to cut consumption when its price rises: the bigger will the income effect and the more elastic will be the demand.

Thus salt has a very low price elasticity of demand. Part of the reason is that there is no close substitute. But part is that we spend such a tiny fraction of our income on salt that we would find little difficulty in paying a relatively large percentage increase in its price: the income effect of a price rise would be very small. By contrast there will be a much bigger income effect when a major item of expenditure rises in price. For example, if mortgage interest rates rise (the 'price' of loans for house purchase), people may have to cut down substantially on their demand for housing – being forced to buy somewhere much smaller and cheaper, or to live in rented accommodation.

?? Will a general item of expenditure like food or clothing have a price-elastic or inelastic demand? (Consider both the determinants we have considered so far.)

The time period. When price rises people may take a time to adjust their consumption patterns and find alternatives. The longer the time period after a price change, then, the more elastic is the demand likely to be.

To illustrate the effect of time on the price elasticity of demand, let us return to our example of oil. Between December 1973 and June 1974 the price of crude oil quadrupled, which led to similar increases in the prices of petrol and central-heating oil. Over the next few months, there was only a very small reduction in the consumption of oil products. Demand was highly inelastic. Motorists had no alternative fuel to which they could turn. All they could do was to cut the number of journeys (not easy to do for many people) and try to drive their cars more economically. Likewise, those with oil-fired central heating could not suddenly burn gas or coal in their boilers. All they could do was to turn their heating down.

Over time, however, as the higher oil prices persisted, new fuel-efficient cars were developed and many people switched to smaller cars. Similarly, people switched to gas or solid fuel central heating, and spent more money insulating their houses to save on fuel bills. Demand was thus much more elastic in the long run.

?? Demand for oil might be relatively elastic over the longer term, and yet it could still be observed that over time people consume *more* oil (or only very slightly less) despite rising oil prices. How can this apparent contradiction be explained?

Price elasticity of demand and consumer expenditure

One of the most important applications of price elasticity of demand concerns its relationship with the total amount of money consumers spend on a product. **Total consumer expenditure (*TE*)** is simply price times quantity purchased.

$$TE = P \times Q$$

For example, if consumers buy 3 million units (*Q*) at a price of £2 per unit (*P*), they will spend a total of £6 million (*TE*). This is shown graphically in Figure 2.12 as the area of the shaded rectangle. But why? The area of a rectangle is simply its height multiplied by its length. But *TE* is simply price (the height of the blue rectangle) multiplied by quantity (the length of the rectangle).

Total consumer expenditure will be the same as the

DEFINITION

Total consumer expenditure on a product (*TE*) (per period of time) The price of the product multiplied by the quantity purchased: $TE = P \times Q$.

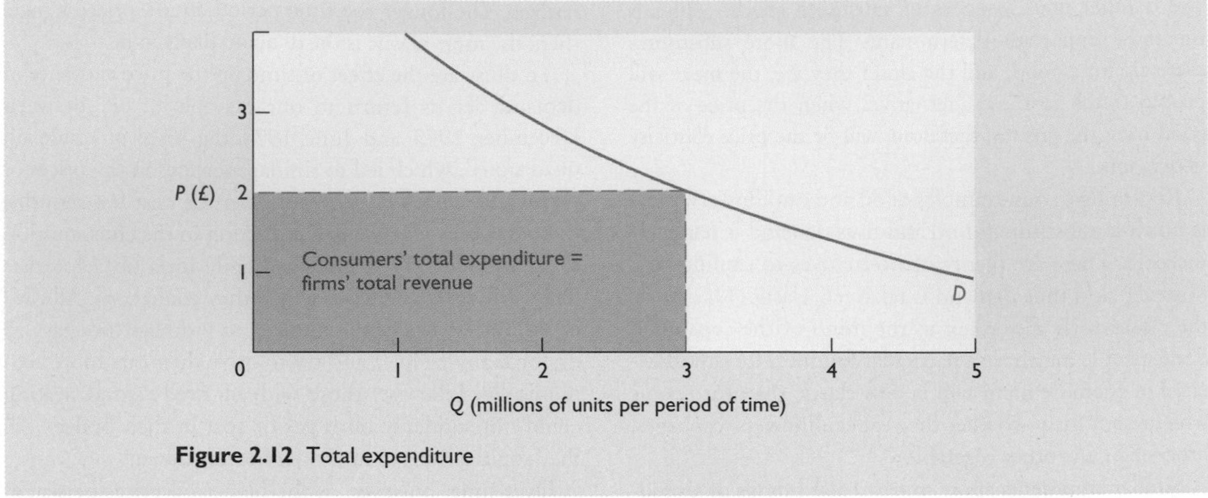

Figure 2.12 Total expenditure

total revenue (*TR*) received by firms from the sale of the product (before any taxes or other deductions).

What will happen to consumer expenditure (and hence firms' revenue) if there is a change in price? The answer depends on the price elasticity of demand.

Elastic demand

As price rises so quantity demanded falls, and vice versa. When demand is elastic, quantity demanded changes proportionately more than price. Thus the change in quantity has a bigger effect on total consumer expenditure than does the change in price. For example, when the price rises, there will be such a large fall in consumer demand that *less* will be spent than before. This can be summarised as follows:

- *P* rises; *Q* falls proportionately more; thus *TE* falls.
- *P* falls; *Q* rises proportionately more; thus *TE* rises.

In other words, total expenditure changes in the same direction as *quantity*.

This is illustrated in Figure 2.13. Demand is elastic between points *a* and *b*. A rise in price from £4 to £5 causes a proportionately larger fall in quantity demanded: from 20 million to 10 million. Total expenditure *falls* from £80 million (the striped area) to £50 million (the pink area)

When demand is elastic, then, a rise in price will cause a fall in total consumer expenditure and thus a fall in the total revenue that firms selling the product receive. A reduction in price, however, will result in consumers spending more, and hence firms earning more.

Inelastic demand

When demand is inelastic it is the other way around. Price changes proportionately more than quantity. Thus the change in price has a bigger effect on total consumer expenditure than does the change in quantity. To summarise the effects:

- *P* rises; *Q* falls proportionately less; *TE* rises.
- *P* falls; *Q* rises proportionately less; *TE* falls.

In other words, total consumer expenditure changes in the same direction as *price*.

This is illustrated in Figure 2.14. Demand is inelastic between points *a* and *c*. A rise in price from £4 to £8 causes a proportionately smaller fall in quantity demanded: from 20 million to 15 million. Total expenditure *rises* from £80 million (the striped area) to £120 million (the pink area).

In this case, firms' revenue will increase if there is a rise in price and fall if there is a fall in price.

?? Assume that demand for a product is inelastic. Will consumer expenditure go on increasing as price rises? Would there be any limit?

Special cases

Figure 2.15 shows three special cases: (a) a totally inelastic demand ($P\epsilon_D = 0$), (b) an infinitely elastic demand ($P\epsilon_D = \infty$) and (c) a unit elastic demand ($P\epsilon_D = -1$).

DEFINITION

Total revenue (*TR*) (per period of time) The total amount received by firms from the sale of a product, before the deduction of taxes or any other costs. The price multiplied by the quantity sold. $TR = P \times Q$.

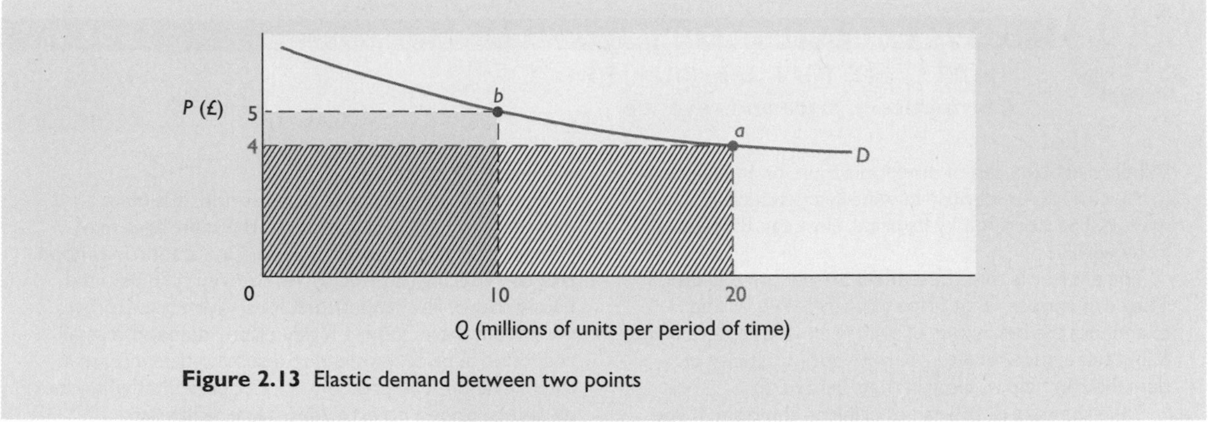

Figure 2.13 Elastic demand between two points

Totally inelastic demand. This is shown by a vertical straight line. No matter what happens to price, quantity demanded remains the same. It is obvious that the more the price rises, the bigger will be the level of consumer expenditure. Thus in Figure 2.15(a), consumer expenditure will be higher at P_2 than at P_1.

> **??** Can you think of any examples of goods which have a totally inelastic demand (a) at *all* prices; (b) over a particular price range?

Infinitely elastic demand. This is shown by a horizontal straight line. At any price above P_1 in Figure 2.15(b), demand is zero. But at P_1 (or any price below) demand is 'infinitely' large.

This seemingly unlikely demand curve is in fact relatively common for an *individual producer*. In a perfect market, as we have seen, firms are small relative to the whole market (like the small-scale grain farmer). They have to accept the price as given by supply and demand in the *whole market*, but at that price they can sell as much as they produce. (Demand is not *literally* infinite, but as far as the firm is concerned it is.) In this case, the more the individual firm produces, the more revenue will be earned. In Figure 2.15(b), more revenue is earned at Q_2 than at Q_1.

Unit elastic demand. This is where price and quantity change in exactly the same proportion. Any rise in price will be exactly offset by a fall in quantity, leaving total revenue unchanged. In Figure 2.15(c), the striped area is exactly equal to the pink area: in both cases total expenditure is £800.

You might have thought that a demand curve with unit elasticity would be a straight line at 45° to the axes. Instead it is a curve called a *rectangular hyperbola*. The reason for its shape is that the proportionate *rise* in quantity must equal the proportionate *fall* in price (and vice versa).

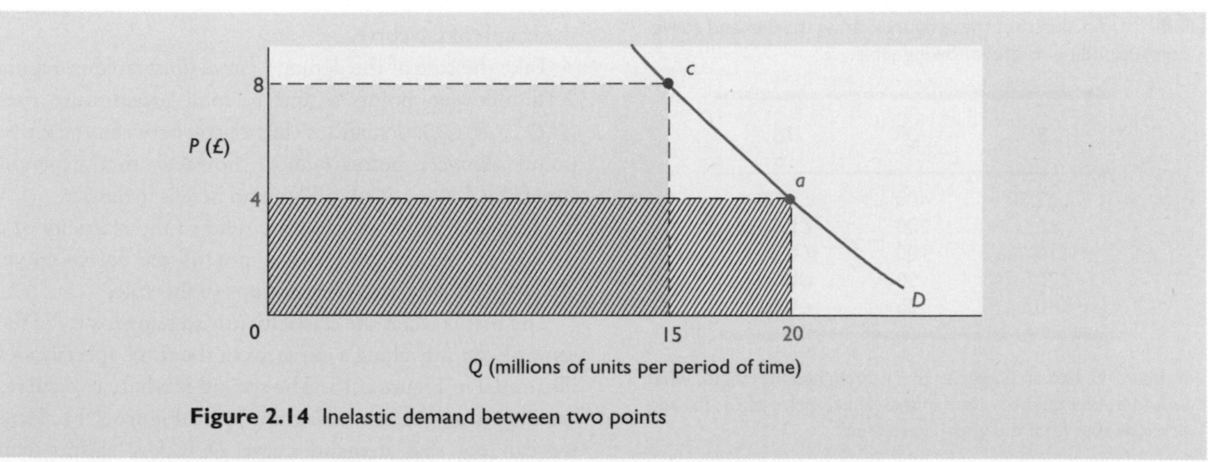

Figure 2.14 Inelastic demand between two points

ISSUES AND APPLICATIONS — BOX 2.3

SHALL WE PUT UP OUR PRICE?

Competition, price and revenue

When you buy a can of drink on a train, or an ice-cream in the cinema, or a bottle of wine in a restaurant, you may well be horrified by its price. How can they get away with it?

The answer is that these firms are *not* price takers. They can choose what price to charge. We will be examining the behaviour of such firms in Chapters 5 and 6, but here it is useful to see how price elasticity of demand can help to explain their behaviour.

Take the case of the can of drink on the train. If you are thirsty, and if you haven't brought a drink with you, then you will have to get one from the train's bar, or go without. There is no substitute. What we are saying here is that the demand for drink on the train is inelastic at the normal shop price. This means that the train operator can put up the price of its drinks, and food too, and earn *more* revenue.

Generally, the less the competition a firm faces, the lower will be the elasticity of demand for its products, since there will be fewer substitutes (competitors) to which consumers can turn. The lower the price elasticity of demand, the higher the price the firm charges is likely to be.

When there is plenty of competition, it is quite a different story. Petrol stations in the same area may compete fiercely in terms of price. One station may hope that by reducing its price by 1p, or even 0.1p per litre below that of its competitors, it can attract customers away from them. With a highly elastic demand, a small reduction in price may lead to a substantial increase in their revenue. The problem is, of course, that when they *all* reduce prices, no firm wins. No one attracts customers away from the others! In this case it is the customer who wins.

??

1. Why may a restaurant charge very high prices for wine and bottled water and yet quite reasonable prices for food?
2. Why are clothes with designer labels so much more expensive than 'own brand' clothes from a chain store, even though they may cost a similar amount to produce?

As we move down the demand curve, in order for the *proportionate* change in both price and quantity to remain constant there must be a bigger and bigger *absolute* rise in quantity and a smaller and smaller absolute fall in price. For example, a rise in quantity from 200 to 400 is the same proportionate change as a rise from 100 to 200, but its absolute size is double. A fall in price from £5 to £2.50 is the same percentage as a fall from £10 to £5, but its absolute size is only half.

??

To illustrate these figures, draw the demand curve corresponding to the following table.

P	*Q*	*TE*
£2.50	400	£1000
£5	200	£1000
£10	100	£1000
£20	50	£1000
£40	25	£1000

If the curve had an elasticity of −1 *throughout* its length, what would be the quantity demanded (a) at a price of £1; (b) at a price of 10p; (c) if the good were free?

The measurement of elasticity: arc elasticity

We have defined price elasticity as the percentage or proportionate change in quantity demanded divided by the percentage or proportionate change in price. But how, in practice, do we measure these changes for a specific demand curve? We shall examine two methods. The first is called the *arc method*. The second (in an optional section) is called the *point method*.

A common mistake that students make is to think that you can talk about the elasticity of a *whole curve*. The mistake here is that in most cases the elasticity will vary along the length of the curve.

Take the case of the demand curve illustrated in Figure 2.16. Between points *a* and *b*, total expenditure rises ($P_2Q_2 > P_1Q_1$): demand is thus elastic between these two points. Between points *b* and *c*, however, total expenditure falls ($P_3Q_3 < P_2Q_2$). Demand here is inelastic.

Normally, then, we can only refer to the elasticity of a *portion* of the demand curve, not of the *whole* curve. There are, however, two exceptions to this rule.

The first is when the elasticity just so happens to be the same all the way along a curve, as in the three special cases illustrated in Figure 2.15. The second is where two curves are drawn on the same diagram, as in Figure 2.11. Here we can say that demand curve *D* is less elastic than

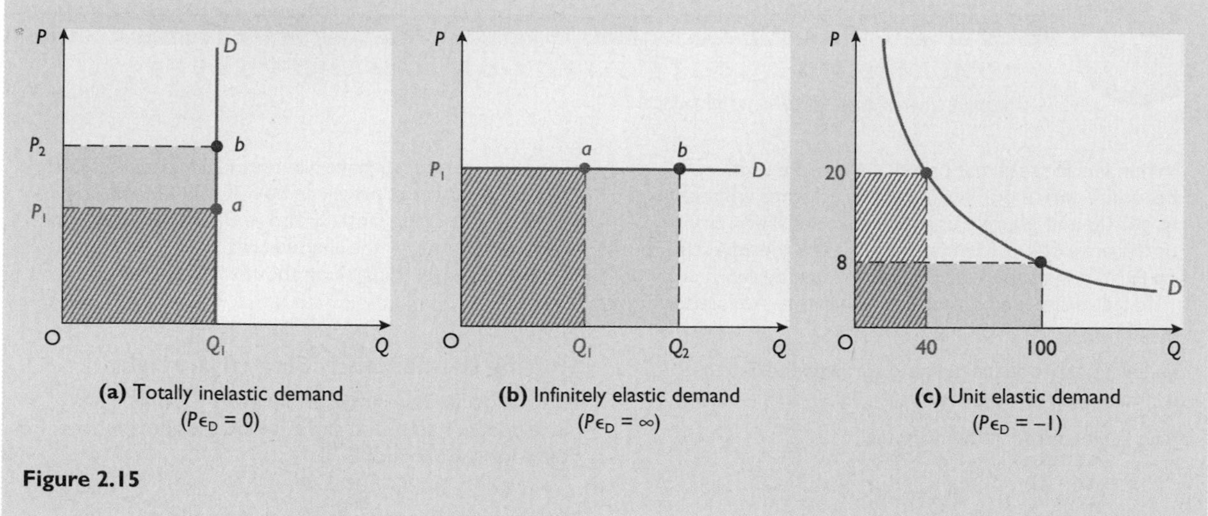

Figure 2.15

demand curve D' at any given price. Note, however, that each of these two curves will still have different elasticities along its length.

Although we cannot normally talk about the elasticity of a whole curve, we can nevertheless talk about the elasticity between any two points on it. This is known as **arc elasticity**. In fact the formula for price elasticity of demand that we have used so far is the formula for arc elasticity. Let us examine it more closely. Remember the formula we used was:

$$\frac{\text{Proportionate } \Delta Q}{\text{Proportionate } \Delta P} \quad \text{(where } \Delta \text{ means 'change in')}$$

The way we measure a proportionate change in quantity is to divide that change by the level of Q: i.e. $\Delta Q/Q$. Similarly, we measure a proportionate change in price by dividing that change by the level of P: i.e. $\Delta P/P$. Price elasticity of demand can thus now be rewritten as:

$$\frac{\Delta Q}{Q} \div \frac{\Delta P}{P}$$

But just what value do we give to P and Q? Consider the demand schedule given in Table 2.5 and graphed in Figure 2.17. What is the elasticity of demand between points m and n? To answer this we need to identify ΔQ and Q, and ΔP and P. Let us start with quantity.

DEFINITION

Arc elasticity The measurement of elasticity between two points on a curve.

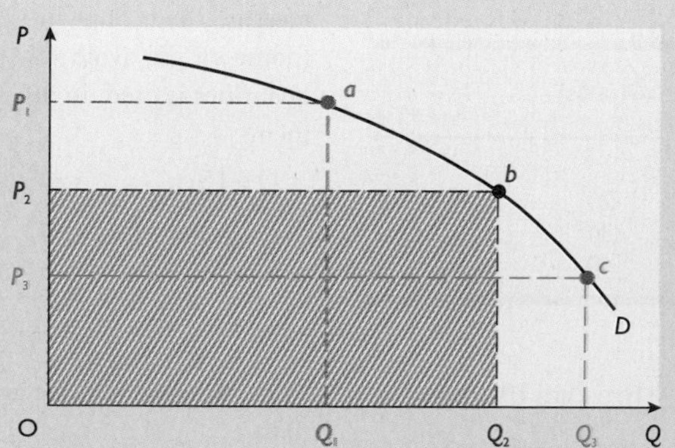

Figure 2.16 Different elasticities along different portions of a demand curve

ISSUES AND APPLICATIONS — BOX 2.4

ADVERTISING AND ITS EFFECT ON DEMAND CURVES

How to increase sales and price

When we are told that brand X will make us more beautiful, enrich our lives, wash our clothes whiter, give us get-up-and-go, give us a new taste sensation or make us the envy of our friends, just what are the advertisers up to? 'Trying to sell the product', you may reply.

In fact there is a bit more to it than this. Advertisers are trying to do two things:

- Shift the product's demand curve to the right.
- Make it less price elastic.

This is illustrated in the diagram.

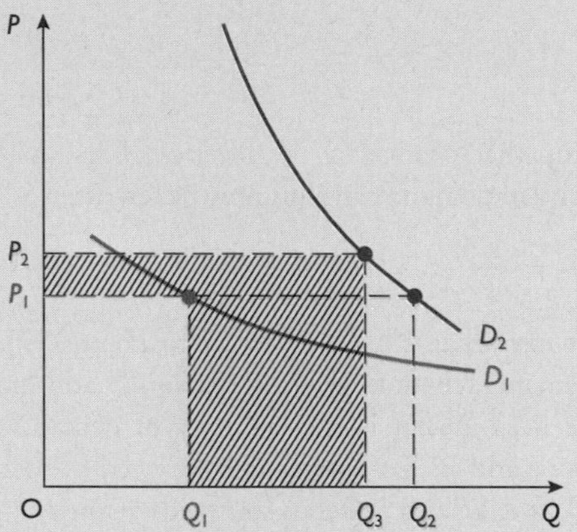

Effect of advertising on the demand curve

D_1 shows the original demand curve with price at P_1 and sales at Q_1. D_2 shows the curve after an advertising campaign. The rightward shift allows an increased quantity (Q_2) to be sold at the original price. If the demand is also made highly inelastic, the firm can also raise its price and still have a substantial increase in sales. Thus in the diagram, price can be raised to P_2 and sales will be Q_3 – still substantially above Q_1. The total gain in revenue is shown by the shaded area.

How can advertising bring about this new demand curve?

Shifting the demand curve to the right

This will occur if the advertising brings the product to more people's attention and if it increases people's desire for the product.

Making the demand curve less elastic

This will occur if the advertising creates greater brand loyalty. People must be led to believe (rightly or wrongly) that competitors' brands are inferior. This will allow the firm to raise its price above that of its rivals with no significant fall in sales. There will only be a small substitution effect because consumers have been led to believe that there are no close substitutes.

??

1. Think of some advertisements which deliberately seek to make demand less elastic.
2. Imagine that 'Sunshine' sunflower margarine, a well-known brand, is advertised with the slogan, 'It helps you live longer'. What do you think would happen to the demand curve for a supermarket's *own* brand of sunflower margarine? Consider both the direction of shift and the effect on elasticity. Will the elasticity differ markedly at different prices? How will this affect the pricing policy and sales of the supermarket's own brand?

Table 2.5

P(£)	Q(000s)
8	10
6	20
4	30
2	40

Quantity

The difference in quantity (ΔQ) between 10 (point *m*) and 20 (point *n*) is 10:

$$\Delta Q = 10$$

But what is the *proportionate* change in Q ($\Delta Q/Q$)? Is it 10/10, taking $Q = 10$ (point *m*) as the base from which to measure the change in Q? Or is it 10/20, taking $Q = 20$ (point *n*)? To avoid this problem the average of the two quantities is used: in other words, the mid-point between them:

$$Q = 15 \qquad \text{i.e.} \left(\frac{10 + 20}{2}\right)$$

$$\therefore \frac{\Delta Q}{Q} = \frac{10}{15}$$

Price

The difference in price between 8 (point *m*) and 6 (point *n*) is 2:

$$\Delta P = -2$$

The *proportionate* change in P is found the same way as the proportionate change in Q.

ISSUES AND APPLICATIONS

BOX 2.5

ANY MORE FARES?

Pricing on the buses

Imagine that a local bus company is faced with increased costs and fears that it will make a loss. What should it do?

The most likely response of the company will be to raise its fares. But this may be the wrong policy, especially if existing services are underutilised. To help it decide what to do, it commissions a survey to estimate passenger demand at three different fares: the current fare of 10p per mile, a higher fare of 12p and a lower fare of 8p. The results of the survey are shown in the first two columns of the table.

Demand turns out to be elastic. This is because of the existence of alternative means of transport. As a result of the elastic demand, total revenue can be increased by reducing the fare from the current 10p to 8p. Revenue rises from £400 000 to £480 000 per annum.

But what will happen to the company's profits? Its profit is the difference between the total revenue from passengers and its total costs of operating the service. If buses are currently underutilised, it is likely that the extra passengers can be carried without the need for extra buses, and hence at no extra cost.

At a fare of 10p, the old profit was £40 000 (£400 000 – £360 000). After the increase in costs, a 10p fare now gives a loss of £40 000 (£400 000 – £440 000).

By raising the fare to 12p, the loss is increased to £80 000. But by lowering the fare to 8p, a profit of £40 000 can again be made.

??

1. Estimate the price elasticity of demand between 8p and 10p and between 10p and 12p.
2. Was the 10p fare the best fare originally?
3. The company considers lowering the fare to 6p, and estimates that demand will be 8½ million passenger miles. It will have to put on extra buses, however. How should it decide?

Fare (pence per mile) (1)	Estimated demand (passenger miles) per year: millions) (2)	Total revenue (£ per year) (3)	Old total cost (£ per year) (4)	New total cost (£ per year) (5)
8	6	480 000	360 000	440 000
10	4	400 000	360 000	440 000
12	3	360 000	360 000	440 000

The base price is taken as the mid-point between the two prices:

$$P = 7 \qquad \text{i.e.} \quad \left(\frac{8+6}{2}\right)$$

$$\therefore \frac{\Delta P}{P} = \frac{-2}{7}$$

Elasticity

Now that we have worked out figures for ΔQ, Q, ΔP and P, we can proceed to work out elasticity. Using the **average (or 'mid-point') formula**, price elasticity of demand is given by:

$$\frac{\Delta Q}{\text{average } Q} \div \frac{\Delta P}{\text{average } P}$$

In our example this would give the following elasticity between m and n:

$$10/15 \div -2/7 = -7/3 = -2.33$$

Since 2.33 is greater than 1, demand is elastic between m and n.

??

Referring to Table 2.5, use the mid-point formula to calculate the price elasticity of demand between (a) $P = 6$ and $P = 4$; (b) $P = 4$ and $P = 2$. What do you conclude about the elasticity of a straight-line demand curve as you move down it?

*The measurement of elasticity: point elasticity

Rather than measuring elasticity between two points on a demand curve, we may want to measure it at a single point: for example, point r in Figure 2.18. In order to

DEFINITION

Average (or 'mid-point') formula for price elasticity of demand ΔQ_D/average Q_D ÷ ΔP/average P.

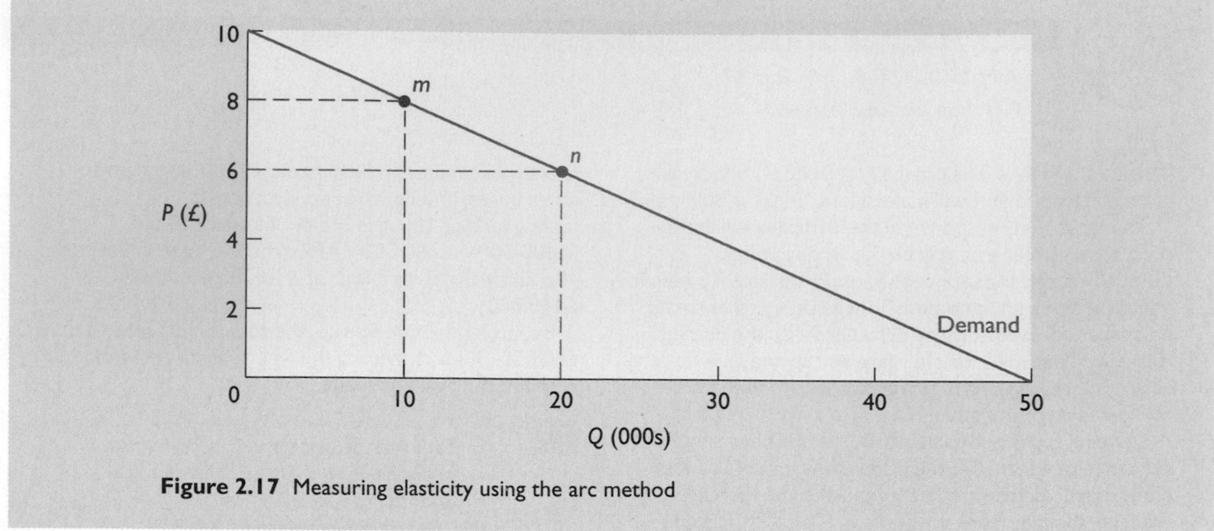

Figure 2.17 Measuring elasticity using the arc method

measure **point elasticity** we must first rearrange the terms in the formula $\Delta Q/Q \div \Delta P/P$. By doing so we can rewrite the formula for price elasticity of demand as:

$$\frac{\Delta Q}{\Delta P} \times \frac{P}{Q}$$

Since we want to measure price elasticity at a *point* on the demand curve, rather than between two points, it is necessary to know how quantity demanded would react to an *infinitesimally small* change in price. In the case of point *r* in Figure 2.18, we want to know how the quantity demanded would react to an infinitesimally small change from a price of 30.

An infinitesimally small change is signified by the letter *d*. The formula for price elasticity of demand thus becomes:

$$\frac{dQ}{dP} \times \frac{P}{Q}$$

dQ/dP is the differential calculus term for the rate of change of quantity with respect to a change in price. And conversely, dP/dQ is the rate of change of price with respect to a change in quantity demanded. At any given point on the demand curve, dP/dQ is given by the *slope* of the curve (its rate of change). The slope is found by draw-

DEFINITION

Point elasticity The measurement of elasticity at a point on a curve. The formula for price elasticity of demand using the point elasticity method is $dQ/dP \times P/Q$, where dQ/dP is the inverse of the slope of the tangent to the demand curve at the point in question.

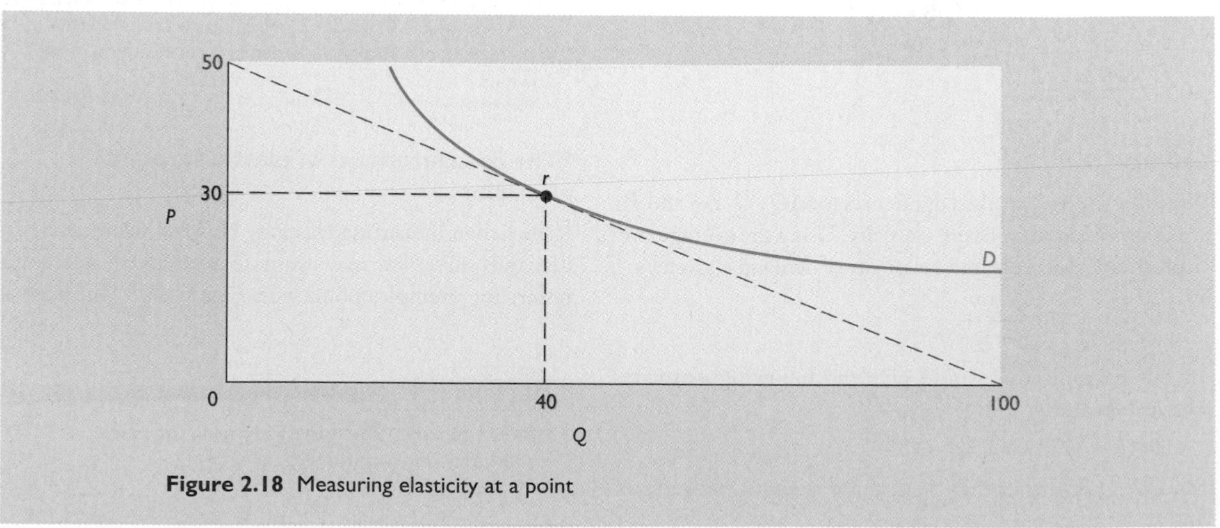

Figure 2.18 Measuring elasticity at a point

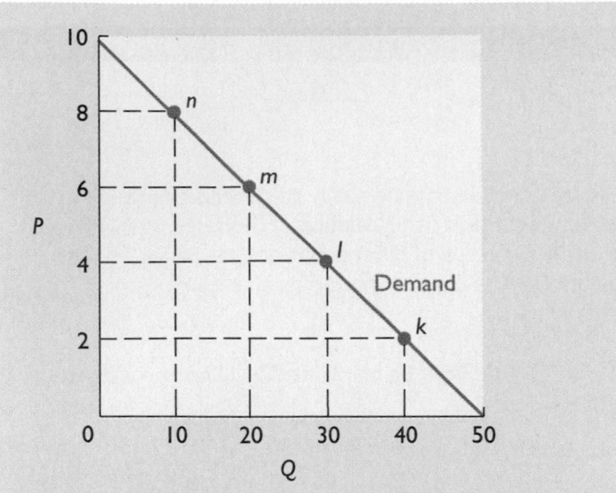

Figure 2.19 Different elasticities along a straight-line demand curve

ing a tangent to the curve at that point and finding the slope of the tangent.

The tangent to the demand curve at point r is shown in Figure 2.18. Its slope is $-50/100$. dP/dQ is thus $-50/100$ and dQ/dP is the inverse of this, $-100/50 = -2$.

Returning to the formula $dQ/dP \times P/Q$, elasticity at point r equals:

$$-2 \times 30/40 = -1.5$$

Rather than having to draw the graph and measure the slope of the tangent, the technique of differentiation can be used to work out point elasticity as long as the equation for the demand curve is known. An example of the use of this technique is given in Box 2.6.

Elasticity of a straight-line demand curve

A straight-line demand curve will have a different elasticity at each point on it. The only exceptions are a vertical demand curve ($P\epsilon_D = 0$), and a horizontal demand curve ($P\epsilon_D = \infty$).

The reason for this differing elasticity is demonstrated in Figure 2.19. Using the point elasticity formula:

$$dQ/dP \times P/Q$$

the slope of the demand curve (dP/dQ) is constant (i.e. $-10/50$). Thus dQ/dP is constant (i.e. $= 50/-10 = -5$).

The value of P/Q, however, differs along the length of the demand curve. At point n, $P/Q = 8/10$. Thus:

$$dQ/dP \times P/Q = -5 \times 8/10 = -4$$

At point m, however, $P/Q = 6/20$. Thus:

$$dQ/dP \times P/Q = -5 \times 6/20 = -1.5$$

?? These questions still refer to Figure 2.19.

1. What is the price elasticity of demand at points *l* and *k* ?
2. What is the price elasticity of demand at the point (a) where the demand curve crosses the vertical axis; (b) where it crosses the horizontal axis?
3. As you move down a straight-line demand curve, what happens to elasticity? Why?
4. Calculate price elasticity of demand between points *n* and *l* using the arc method. Does this give the same answer as the point method? Would it if the demand curve were actually curved?

Price elasticity of supply ($P\epsilon_S$)

When price changes, there will be not only a change in the quantity demanded, but also a change in the quantity supplied. Frequently we will want to know just how responsive quantity supplied is to a change in price. The measure we use is the **price elasticity of supply**.

Figure 2.20 shows two supply curves. Curve S_2 is more elastic between any two prices than curve S_1. Thus, when

DEFINITION

Price elasticity of supply The responsiveness of quantity supplied to a change in price.

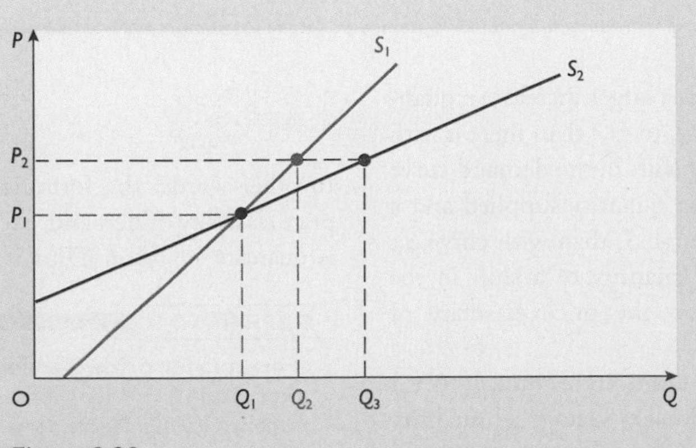

Figure 2.20

EXPLORING THE THEORY *BOX 2.6

USING CALCULUS TO CALCULATE PRICE ELASTICITY OF DEMAND

(A knowledge of the rules of differentiation is necessary to understand this box. No part of the main book uses calculus, but a few boxes will.)

The following is an example of an equation for a demand curve:

$$Q_d = 60 - 15P + P^2$$

(where Q_d is measured in 000s of units). From this the following schedule and graph can be constructed.

P	60	$-15P$	$+P^2$	=	Q_d(000s)
0	60	−0	+0	=	60
1	60	−15	+1	=	46
2	60	−30	+4	=	34
3	60	−45	+9	=	24
4	60	−60	+16	=	16
5	60	−75	+25	=	10
6	60	−90	+36	=	6

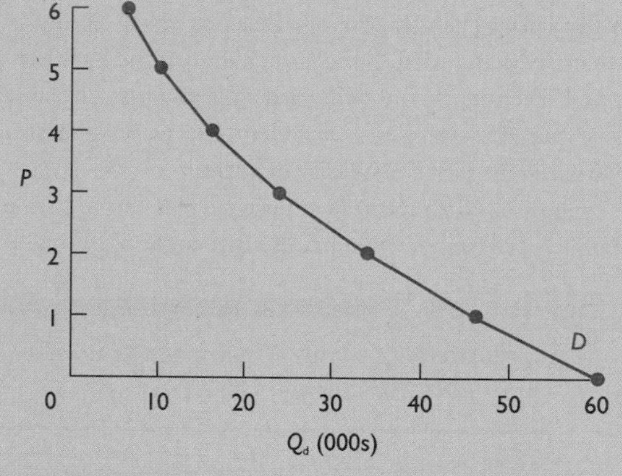

Point elasticity can be easily calculated from such a demand equation using calculus. To do this you will need to know the rules of differentiation (see pages 34–7). Remember the formula for point elasticity:

$$P\epsilon_D = dQ/dP \times P/Q$$

The term dQ/dP can be calculated by differentiating the demand equation:

Given $Q_d = 60 - 15P + P^2$

then $dQ/dP = -15 + 2P$

Thus at a price of 3, for example,

$dQ/dP = -15 + (2 \times 3)$

$= -9$

Thus price elasticity of demand at a price of 3

$= -9 \times P/Q$

$= -9 \times 3/24$

$= -9/8$ (which is elastic)

?? Calculate the price elasticity of demand on this demand curve at a price of (a) 5; (b) 2; (c) 0.

price rises from P_1 to P_2 there is a larger increase in quantity supplied with S_2 (namely, Q_1 to Q_3) than there is with S_1 (namely, Q_1 to Q_2). For any shift in the demand curve there will be a larger change in quantity supplied and a smaller change in price with curve S_2 than with curve S_1. Thus the effect on price and quantity of a shift in the demand curve will depend on the price elasticity of supply.

The **formula for the price elasticity of supply ($P\epsilon_S$)** is: the percentage (or proportionate) change in quantity supplied divided by the percentage (or proportionate) change in price. Putting this in symbols gives:

$$P\epsilon_S = \frac{\%\Delta Q_S}{\%\Delta P}$$

In other words, the formula is identical to that for the price elasticity of demand, except that quantity in this case is quantity *supplied*. Thus if a 10 per cent rise in price

DEFINITION

Formula for price elasticity of supply ($P\epsilon_S$) The percentage (or proportionate) change in quantity supplied divided by the percentage (or proportionate) change in price: $\%\Delta Q_S \div \%\Delta P$.

caused a 25 per cent rise in the quantity supplied, the price elasticity of supply would be:

25%/10% = 2.5

and if a 10 per cent rise in price caused only a 5 per cent rise in the quantity, the price elasticity of supply would be:

5%/10% = 0.5

In the first case, supply is elastic ($P\epsilon_S > 1$); in the second it is inelastic ($P\epsilon_S < 1$). Notice that, unlike the price elasticity of demand, the figure is positive. This is because price and quantity supplied change in the *same* direction.

Determinants of price elasticity of supply

The amount that costs rise as output rises. The less the additional costs of producing additional output, the more firms will be encouraged to produce for a given price rise: the more elastic will supply be.

Supply is thus likely to be elastic if firms have plenty of spare capacity, if they can readily get extra supplies of raw materials, if they can easily switch away from producing alternative products and if they can avoid having to introduce overtime working (at higher rates of pay). If all these conditions hold, costs will be little affected by a rise in output and supply will be relatively elastic. The less these conditions apply, the less elastic will supply be.

Time period (see Figure 2.21)

- Immediate time period. Firms are unlikely to be able to increase supply by much immediately. Supply is virtually fixed, or can only vary according to available stocks. Supply is highly inelastic. In the diagram S_i is drawn with $P\epsilon_S = 0$. If demand increases to D_2, supply will not be able to respond. Price will rise to P_2. Quantity will remain at Q_1. Equilibrium will move to point *b*.
- Short run. If a slightly longer period of time is allowed to elapse, some inputs can be increased (e.g. raw materials) while others will remain fixed (e.g. heavy machinery). Supply can increase somewhat. This is illustrated by S_S. Equilibrium will move to point *c* with price falling again, to P_3, and quantity rising to Q_3.
- Long run. In the long run, there will be sufficient time for all inputs to be increased and for new firms to enter the industry. Supply, therefore, is likely to be highly elastic. This is illustrated by curve S_L. Long-run equilibrium will be at point *d* with price falling back even further, to P_4, and quantity rising all the way to Q_4. In some circumstances the supply curve may even slope downward. (See the section on economies of scale in Chapter 5.)

The measurement of price elasticity of supply

A vertical supply has zero elasticity. It is totally unresponsive to a change in price. A horizontal supply curve has infinite elasticity. There is no limit to the amount supplied at the price where the curve crosses the vertical axis.

When two supply curves cross, the steeper one will have the lower price elasticity of supply (e.g. curve S_1 in Figure 2.20). Any straight-line supply curve starting at the origin, however, will have an elasticity equal to 1 throughout its length, *irrespective of its slope*. This perhaps rather surprising result is illustrated in Figure 2.22. This shows three supply curves, each with a different slope, but each starting from the origin. On each curve two points are marked. In each case there is the *same* proportionate rise in Q as in P. For example, with curve S_1 a doubling in price from £3 to £6 leads to a doubling of output from 1 unit to 2 units.

This demonstrates nicely that it is not the *slope* of a curve that determines its elasticity, but its proportionate change.

Other supply curves' elasticities will vary along their length. In such cases we have to refer to the elasticity

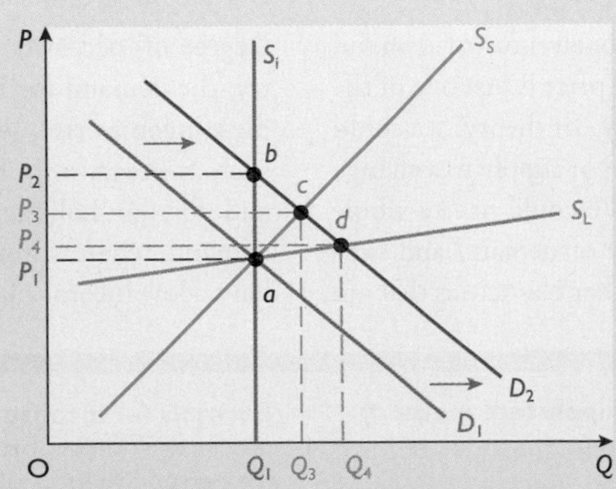

Figure 2.21 Supply in different time periods

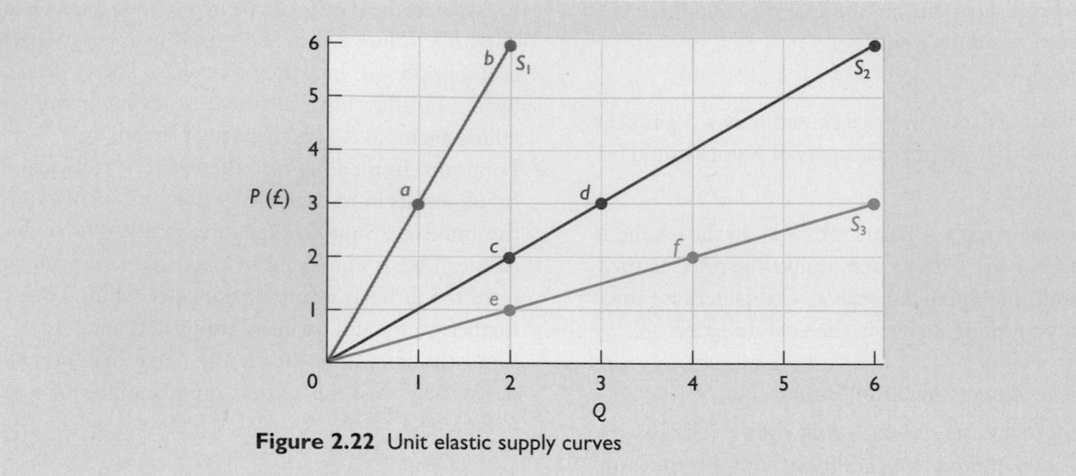

Figure 2.22 Unit elastic supply curves

either between two points on the curve, or at a specific point. Calculating elasticity between two points will involve the arc method. Calculating elasticity at a point will involve the point method. These two methods are just the same for supply curves as for demand curves: the formulae are the same, only the term Q now refers to quantity supplied rather than quantity demanded.

??

Given the following supply schedule:

P:	2	4	6	8	10
Q:	0	10	20	30	40

(a) Draw the supply curve.
(b) Using the arc method calculate price elasticity of supply (i) between $P = 2$ and $P = 4$; (ii) between $P = 8$ and $P = 10$.
*(c) Using the point method, calculate price elasticity of supply at $P = 6$.
(d) Does the elasticity of the supply curve increase or decrease as P and Q increase? Why?
(e) What would be the answer to (d) if the supply curve were a straight line but intersecting the horizontal axis to the right of the origin?

Income elasticity of demand ($Y\epsilon_D$)

So far we have looked at the responsiveness of demand and supply to a change in price. But price is just one of the determinants of demand and supply. In theory, we could look at the responsiveness of demand or supply to a change in *any* one of their determinants. We could have a whole range of different types of elasticity of demand and supply. In practice there are just two other elasticities that are particularly useful to us, and both are demand elasticities.

The first is the **income elasticity of demand ($Y\epsilon_D$)**. This measures the responsiveness of demand to a change in consumer incomes (Y). It enables us to predict how much the demand curve will shift for a given change in income. The **formula for the income elasticity of demand** is: the percentage (or proportionate) change in demand divided by the percentage (or proportionate) change in income. Putting this in symbols gives:

$$Y\epsilon_D = \frac{\%\Delta Q_D}{\%\Delta Y}$$

In other words, the formula is identical to that for the price elasticity of demand, except that we are dividing the change in demand by the change in income that caused it rather than by a change in price. Thus if a 2 per cent rise in income caused an 8 per cent rise in a product's demand, then its income elasticity of demand would be:

$$8\%/2\% = 4$$

Determinants of income elasticity of demand

Degree of 'necessity' of the good. In a developed country, the demand for luxury goods expands rapidly as people's incomes rise, whereas the demand for basic goods, such as bread, only rises a little. Thus items such as cars and foreign holidays have a high income elasticity of demand, whereas items such as potatoes and bus journeys have a low income elasticity of demand.

DEFINITIONS

Formula for price elasticity of supply (arc method) ΔQ_S/average $Q_S \div \Delta P$/average P.

Income elasticity of demand The responsiveness of demand to a change in consumer incomes.

Formula for income elasticity of demand ($Y\epsilon_D$) The percentage (or proportionate) change in demand divided by the percentage (or proportionate) change in income: $\%\Delta Q_D \div \%\Delta Y$.

The demand for some goods actually decreases as income rises. These are inferior goods such as cheap margarine. As people earn more, so they switch to butter or better quality margarine. Unlike **normal goods**, which have a positive income elasticity of demand, **inferior goods** have a negative income elasticity of demand.

> **??** Look ahead to Box 3.4 (page 87). It shows the income elasticity of demand for various foodstuffs. Explain the difference in the figures for fresh potatoes, bread and fruit juices.

The rate at which the desire for a good is satisfied as consumption increases. The more quickly people become satisfied, the less their demand will expand as income increases.

The level of income of consumers. Poor people will respond differently from rich people to a rise in their incomes. For example, for a given rise in income, poor people may buy a lot more butter, whereas rich people may buy only a little more.

Income elasticity of demand is an important concept to firms considering the future size of the market for their product. If the product has a high income elasticity of demand, sales are likely to expand rapidly as national income rises, but may also fall significantly if the economy moves into recession.

Cross-price elasticity of demand ($C\epsilon_{D_{ab}}$)

This is often known by its less cumbersome title of **cross elasticity of demand.** It is a measure of the responsiveness of demand for one product to a change in the price of another (either a substitute or a complement). It enables us to predict how much the demand curve for the first product will shift when the price of the second product changes.

The **formula for the cross-price elasticity of demand** ($C\epsilon_{D_{ab}}$) is: the percentage (or proportionate) change in demand for good a divided by the percentage (or proportionate) change in price of good b. Putting this in symbols gives:

$$C\epsilon_{D_{ab}} = \frac{\%\Delta Q_{D_a}}{\%\Delta P_b}$$

If good b is a *substitute* for good a, a's demand will *rise* as b's price rises. In this case, cross elasticity will be a positive figure. For example, if the demand for butter rose by 2 per cent when the price of margarine (a substitute) rose by 8 per cent, then the cross elasticity of demand for butter with respect to margarine would be:

2%/8% = 0.25

If good b is *complementary* to good a, however, a's demand will *fall* as b's price rises and thus as the quantity of b demanded falls. In this case, cross elasticity of demand will be a negative figure. For example, if a 4 per cent rise in the price of bread led to a 3 per cent fall in demand for butter, the cross elasticity of demand for butter with respect to bread would be:

–3%/4% = –0.75

The major determinant of cross elasticity of demand is the closeness of the substitute or complement. The closer it is, the bigger will be the effect on the first good of a change in the price of the substitute or complement, and hence the greater the cross elasticity – either positive or negative.

Firms will wish to know the cross elasticity of demand for their product when considering the effect on the demand for their product of a change in the price of a rival's product or of a complementary product. These are vital pieces of information for firms when making their production plans.

Another example of the usefulness of the concept of cross elasticity of demand is in the field of international trade and the balance of payments. A government will wish to know how a change in domestic prices will affect the demand for imports. If there is a high cross elasticity of demand for imports (because they are close substitutes for home-produced goods), and if prices at home rise due to inflation, the demand for imports will rise substantially, thus worsening the balance of payments.

> **??** Which are likely to have the highest cross elasticity of demand: two brands of coffee, or coffee and tea?

DEFINITIONS

Normal goods Goods whose demand increases as consumer incomes increase. They have a positive income elasticity of demand. Luxury goods will have a higher income elasticity of demand than more basic goods.

Inferior goods Goods whose demand *decreases* as consumer incomes increase. Such goods have a negative income elasticity of demand.

Cross-price elasticity of demand The responsiveness of demand for one good to a change in the price of another.

Formula for cross-price elasticity of demand ($C\epsilon_{D_{ab}}$) The percentage (or proportionate) change in demand for good a divided by the percentage (or proportionate) change in price of good b: $\%\Delta Q_{D_a} \div \%\Delta P_b$.

ISSUES AND APPLICATIONS BOX 2.7

INCOME ELASTICITY AND THE BALANCE OF PAYMENTS

A problem for certain developing countries

When people are poor they have to spend a large proportion of their income on basic goods such as food. As they get richer, so they can afford to buy an increasing proportion of luxury goods. This means that the income elasticity of demand for basic goods is likely to be low: their demand only rises slowly as incomes rise. The income elasticity of demand for luxury goods, on the other hand, is likely to be high.

This has important implications for international trade. If a country exports basic goods with a low income elasticity of demand, and imports luxury goods with a high income elasticity of demand, it is likely to run into long-term balance of payments problems.

As it grows richer, its demand for imports is likely to grow rapidly. As the rest of the world grows richer, however, so the demand for the country's exports is likely to grow slowly.

This has been one of the problems facing many developing countries. As exporters of commodities such as rice, sugar and tea, they have found that the demand for their exports has grown relatively slowly. As importers of manufactured products, however, their imports have grown relatively rapidly.

This affects their *terms of trade*. The terms of trade are the average price of a country's exports divided by the average price of its imports. If the demand for exports grows only slowly relative to imports, so the price of exports is likely to fall relative to imports: the terms of trade will deteriorate.

In 1991 the terms of trade for developing countries as a whole were only 68 per cent of their 1960 level, whereas the terms of trade for developed market economies were 92 per cent of their 1960 level.[2]

A word of caution: income elasticity of demand is only *one* factor influencing the level of a country's imports and exports, and only *one* factor determining its terms of trade.

?? Would you expect the demand for developing countries' raw material exports to grow rapidly or slowly *over time*? Does their growth over time give a good indication as to their income elasticity of demand?

[2] See *Handbook of International Trade and Development Statistics* (United Nations Conference on Trade and Development, UNCTAD).

SECTION SUMMARY

1. Elasticity is a measure of the responsiveness of demand (or supply) to a change in one of the determinants.
2. It is defined as the proportionate change in quantity demanded (or supplied) divided by the proportionate change in the determinant.
3. If quantity changes proportionately more than the determinant, the figure for elasticity will be greater than 1 (ignoring the sign): it is elastic. If the quantity changes proportionately less than the determinant, the figure for elasticity will be less than 1: it is inelastic. If they change by the same proportion, the elasticity has a value of 1: it is unit elastic.
4. Price elasticity of demand measures the responsiveness of demand to a change in price. Given that demand curves are downward sloping, price elasticity of demand will have a negative value. Demand will be more elastic the greater the number and closeness of substitute goods, the higher the proportion of income spent on the good and the longer the time period that elapses after the change in price.
5. When demand is price elastic, a rise in price will lead to a reduction in total expenditure on the good and hence a reduction in the total revenue of producers.
6. Demand curves normally have different elasticities along their length. We can thus normally refer only to the specific value for elasticity between two points on the curve or at a single point.
7. Elasticity measured between two points is known as *arc elasticity*. When applied to price elasticity of demand the formula is:

$$\frac{\Delta Q_d}{\text{average } Q_d} \div \frac{\Delta P}{\text{average } P}$$

*8. Elasticity measured at a point is known as *point elasticity*. When applied to price elasticity of demand the formula is:

$$\frac{dQ}{dP} \times \frac{P}{Q}$$

where dQ/dP is the inverse of the slope of the tangent to the demand curve at the point in question.

continued

9. Price elasticity of supply measures the responsiveness of supply to a change in price. It has a positive value. Supply will be more elastic the less costs per unit rise as output rises and the longer the time period.
10. Income elasticity of demand measures the responsiveness of demand to a change in income. For normal goods it has a positive value. Demand will be more income elastic the more luxurious the good and the less rapidly demand is satisfied as consumption increases.
11. Cross-price elasticity of demand measures the responsiveness of demand for one good to a change in the price of another. For substitute goods the value will be positive; for complements it will be negative. The cross-price elasticity will be higher the closer the two goods are as substitutes or complements.

2.5 The time dimension

The full adjustment of price, demand and supply to a situation of disequilibrium will not be instantaneous. It is necessary, therefore, to analyse the time path which supply takes in responding to changes in demand, and which demand takes in responding to changes in supply.

Short-run and long-run adjustment

As we saw in the previous section, elasticity varies with the time period under consideration. The reason is that producers and consumers take time to respond to a change in price. The longer the time period, the bigger the response, and thus the greater the elasticity of supply and demand.

This is illustrated in Figures 2.23 and 2.24. In both cases, as equilibrium moves from points *a* to *b* to *c*, there is a large short-run price change (P_1 to P_2) and a small short-run quantity change (Q_1 to Q_2), but a small long-run price change (P_1 to P_3) and a large long-run quantity change (Q_1 to Q_3).

Time lags in production: the cobweb

When goods take a time to produce, there will be a time lag between a change in production decisions and a change in the actual supply coming on to the market. Thus the actual supply at one time will depend on that planned at a previous time. For example, the quantity that farmers harvest now will depend on what they planted earlier.

Since supply decisions depend on price, supply at any time will depend on price at a previous time.

These time lags can lead to price fluctuations. This is illustrated in Figure 2.25: the **cobweb diagram**. Two important assumptions are made:

DEFINITION

Cobweb diagram A diagram showing the path of price and quantity adjustment over time, given a lag between the decision to supply and the goods coming to market. The path has a shape like a cobweb.

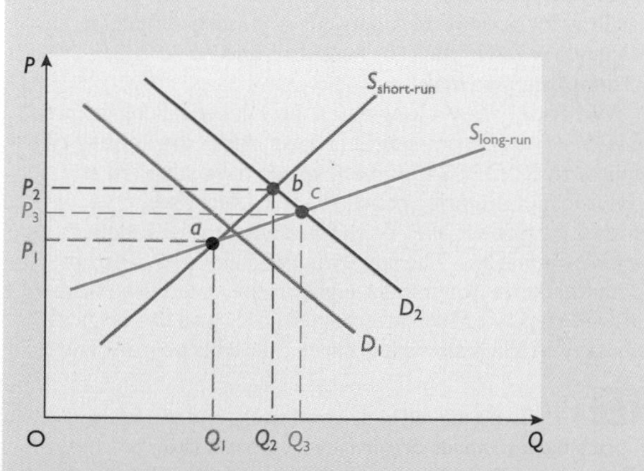

Figure 2.23 Response of supply to an increase in demand

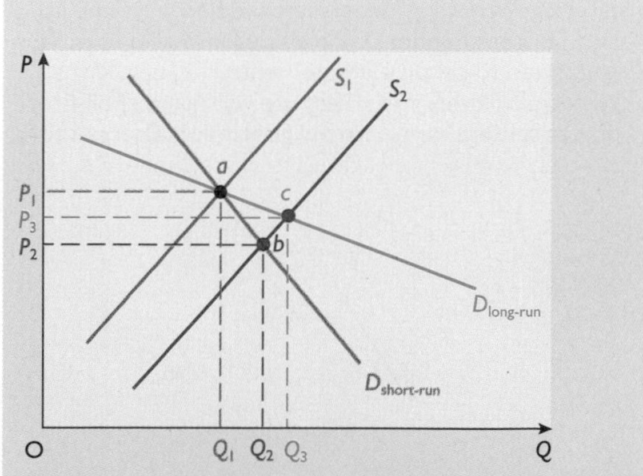

Figure 2.24 Response of demand to an increase in supply

CASE STUDIES BOX 2.8

ADJUSTING TO OIL PRICE SHOCKS
Short-run and long-run demand and supply responses

Between December 1973 and June 1974, the Organisation of Petroleum Exporting Countries (OPEC) put up the price of oil from \$3 to \$12 per barrel. It was further raised to over \$30 in 1979. In the late 1980s the price fluctuated, but the trend was downward. Except for a sharp rise at the time of the Gulf War in 1990, the trend continued in the early 1990s. By 1996 the price was fluctuating around \$16 per barrel: in real terms (i.e. after correcting for inflation), roughly the level prior to 1973.

The price movements can be explained using simple demand and supply analysis.

The initial rise in price

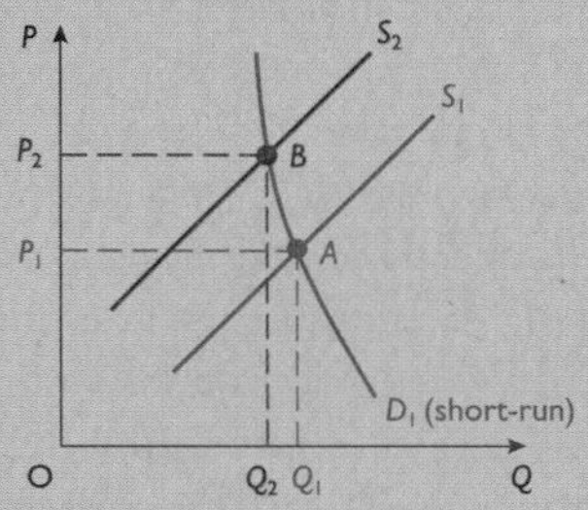

(a) An initial restriction of supply

OPEC raised the price from P_1 to P_2. To prevent surplus at that price, OPEC members restricted their output by agreed amounts. This had the effect of shifting the supply curve to S_2, with Q_2 being produced. This reduction in output needed to be only relatively small because the short-run demand for oil was highly price inelastic: for most uses there are no substitutes in the short run.

Long-run effects on demand

The long-run demand for oil was more elastic. With high oil prices persisting, people tried to find ways of cutting back on consumption. People bought smaller cars. They converted to gas or solid-fuel central heating. Firms switched to other fuels. Less use was made of oil-fired power stations for electricity generation. Energy-saving schemes became widespread both in firms and in the home.

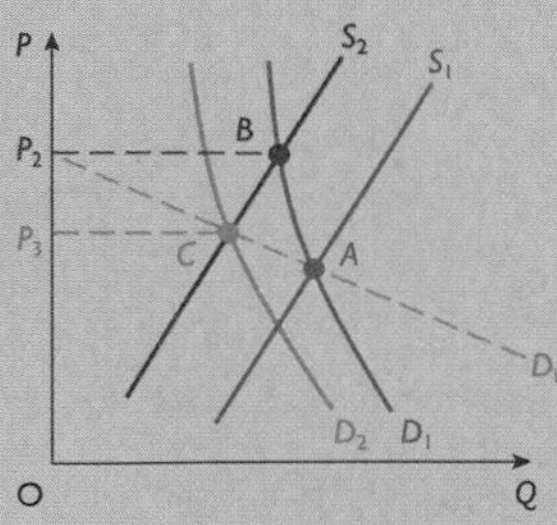

(b) Long-run demand response

This had the effect of shifting the short-run demand curve from D_1 to D_2. Price fell back from P_2 to P_3. This gave a long-run demand curve of D_L: the curve that joins points *A* and *C*.

The fall in demand was made bigger by a world recession in the early 1980s.

Long-run effects on supply

With oil production so much more profitable, there was an incentive for non-OPEC oil producers to produce oil. Prospecting went on all over the world and large oil fields were discovered and opened up in the North Sea, Alaska, Mexico, China and elsewhere.

In addition, OPEC members were tempted to break their 'quotas' (their allotted output) and sell more oil.

The net effect was an increase in world oil supplies. This is shown by a shift in the supply curve to S_3. Equilibrium price thus fell back to P_1 (point *D*).

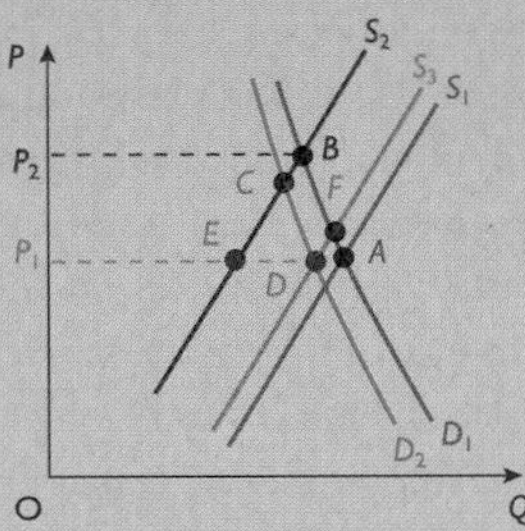

(c) Long-run supply response

Note that the supply curves in these diagrams are all *short-run* supply curves, since each one shows supply for a particular number of oil fields.

Drawing a long-run supply curve is more difficult: it depends when in the story we start and what assumptions we make.

We could draw a long-run supply curve linking points *E* and *F*. The reasoning is as follows. After the limiting of supply to S_2, OPEC members would have supplied at point *E*, had the price remained at P_1. After some years with the price set at P_2 or thereabouts, more suppliers enter the market. The supply curve shifts to S_3. Had the demand curve not shifted, equilibrium would then have moved to point *F*: the intersection of S_3 and the original demand. A long-run supply curve thus links points *E* and *F*.

?? Given the fall in demand to D_2, and the fall in price back towards original levels, what is likely to happen to the position of the (short-run) supply curve?

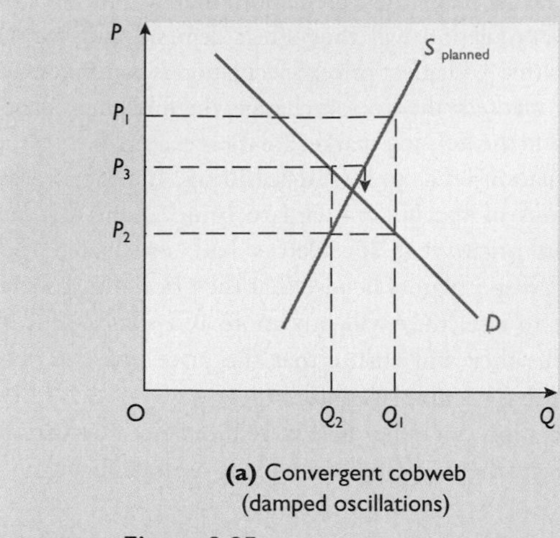

(a) Convergent cobweb (damped oscillations)

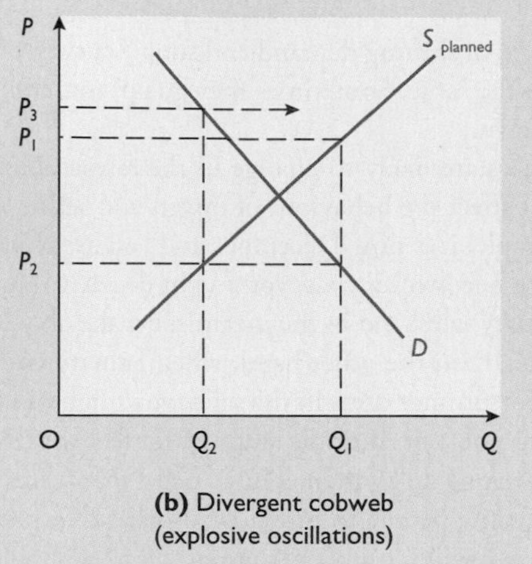

(b) Divergent cobweb (explosive oscillations)

Figure 2.25

- Firms' production plans, once made, are fully carried out: they end up supplying precisely the amount they had planned to.
- There is an initial disequilibrium in the market: either demand or supply has shifted. The result is that price is now above the intersection of the new demand and supply curves.

The diagrams show just the new demand and supply curves. Note that the supply curve is the *planned* supply curve. The *actual* supply coming on to the market will be the amount planned in the previous time period.

Assume that the initial (disequilibrium) price is P_1. At P_1 producers plan to supply Q_1. Thus in the next time period Q_1 is actually supplied. But in order for Q_1 to be sold, price falls to P_2. Producers, seeing that price has fallen to P_2, now only plan to supply Q_2 for the next time period. So in the next time period Q_2 duly comes on to the market. Price now has to rise to P_3 to clear the market.

This process continues with both price and quantity oscillating.

Whether these oscillations get smaller or larger depends on the shape of the demand and supply curves. If the supply curve is steeper than the demand curve (Figure 2.25(a)), the oscillations will be damped: they will get smaller over time. This is called a **convergent cobweb**. If the demand curve is steeper than the supply curve, however, the oscillations will be explosive: they will get larger over time. This is called a **divergent cobweb**.

In practice, cobwebs will not be as clear cut as in the diagram for a number of reasons:

- Producers may anticipate price fluctuations and not simply rely on current prices.
- Demand and supply curves may shift in the meantime.
- There may be a lag in demand adjustment as well as in supply adjustment.
- Plans may not be fulfilled. For example, farmers may experience a better or worse harvest than anticipated.
- Producers may use stocks. They may draw on stocks when prices are high and build stocks when prices are low. Thus supply released on to the market will not fluctuate so much. This in turn will reduce price fluctuations.

?? Go through each of these qualifications and explain how they would affect the cobweb diagram.

Nevertheless cobweb effects have been observed in various markets. Historically, 'hog' cycles and potato cycles have been identified which show clear fluctuations in pig meat and potato prices.

DEFINITIONS

Convergent cobweb A cobweb where the path converges on the equilibrium point. The price oscillations get smaller over time.

Divergent cobweb A cobweb where the path gets further and further away from the 'equilibrium' point. The price oscillations get larger over time.

Speculation

In a world of shifting demand and supply curves, prices do not stay the same. Sometimes they go up; sometimes they come down.

If prices are likely to change in the foreseeable future, this will affect the behaviour of buyers and sellers *now*. If, for example, it is now December and you are thinking of buying a new winter coat, you might decide to wait until the January sales, and in the meantime make do with your old coat. If, on the other hand, when January comes you see a new summer dress in the sales, you might well buy it now and not wait until the summer for fear that the price will have gone up by then. Thus a belief that prices will go up will cause people to buy now; a belief that prices will come down will cause them to wait.

The reverse applies to sellers. If you are thinking of selling your house and prices are falling, you will want to sell it as quickly as possible. If, on the other hand, prices are rising sharply, you will wait as long as possible so as to get the highest price. Thus a belief that prices will come down will cause people to sell now; a belief that prices will go up will cause them to wait.

This behaviour of looking into the future and making buying and selling decisions based on your predictions is called **speculation**. Speculation is often based on current trends in price behaviour. If prices are currently rising, people may then try to decide whether they are about to peak and go back down again, or whether they are likely to go on rising. Having made their prediction, they will then act on it. This speculation will thus affect demand and supply, which in turn will affect price. Speculation is commonplace in many markets: the stock exchange, the foreign exchange market and the housing market are three examples.

Speculation tends to be **self-fulfilling**. In other words, the actions of speculators tend to bring about the very effect on prices that speculators had anticipated. For example, if speculators believe that the price of ICI shares is about to rise, they will buy more ICI shares. But by doing this they will ensure that the price *will* rise. The prophecy has become self-fulfilling.

Speculation can either help to reduce price fluctuations or aggravate them: it can be stabilising or destabilising.

Stabilising speculation

Speculation will tend to have a **stabilising** effect on price fluctuations when suppliers and/or demanders believe that a change in price is only *temporary*.

An initial fall in price. In Figure 2.26 demand has shifted from D_1 to D_2; equilibrium has moved from point *a* to point *b*, and price has fallen to P_2. How do people react to this fall in price?

Given that they believe this fall in price to be only temporary, suppliers *hold back*, expecting prices to rise again: supply shifts from S_1 to S_2. After all, why supply now when, by waiting, they could get a higher price?

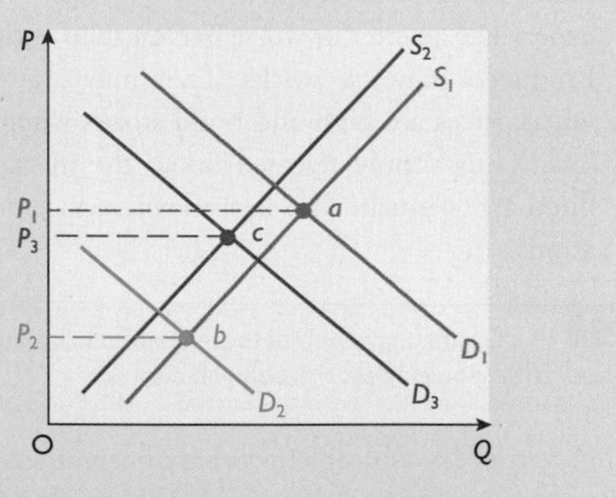

Figure 2.26 Stabilising speculation: initial price fall

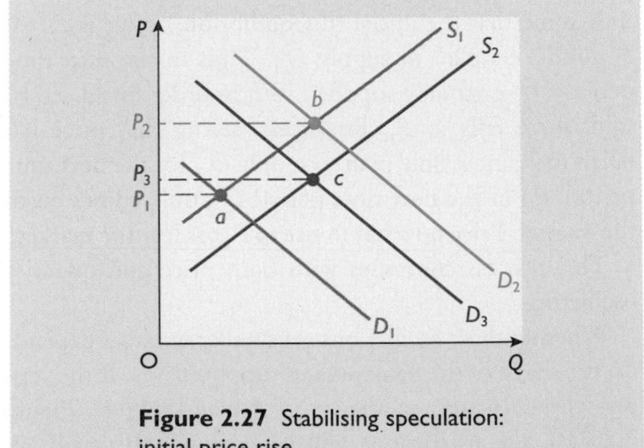

Figure 2.27 Stabilising speculation: initial price rise

DEFINITIONS

Speculation Where people make buying or selling decisions based on their anticipations of future prices.

Self-fulfilling speculation The actions of speculators tend to cause the very effect that they had anticipated.

Stabilising speculation Where the actions of speculators tend to reduce price fluctuations.

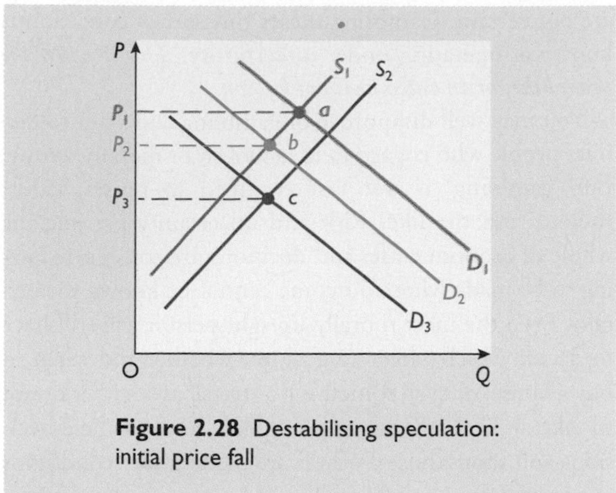

Figure 2.28 Destabilising speculation: initial price fall

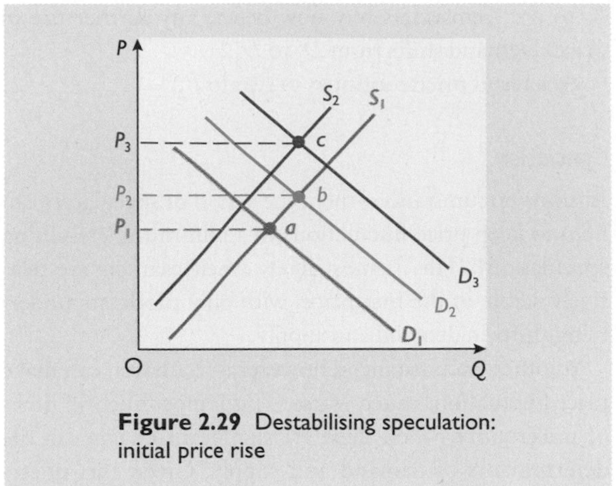

Figure 2.29 Destabilising speculation: initial price rise

Buyers *increase* their purchases, to take advantage of the temporary fall in price. Demand shifts from D_2 to D_3.

The equilibrium moves to point *c*, with price rising back towards P_1.

An initial rise in price. In Figure 2.27 demand has shifted from D_1 to D_2. Price has risen from P_1 to P_2.

Suppliers bring their goods to market now, before price falls again. Supply shifts from S_1 to S_2. Demanders, however, hold back until price falls. Demand shifts from D_2 to D_3. The equilibrium moves to point *c*, with price falling back towards P_1.

A good example of stabilising speculation is that which occurs in agricultural commodity markets. Take the case of wheat. When it is harvested in the autumn there will be a plentiful supply. If all this wheat were to be put on the market, the price would fall to a very low level. Later in the year, when most of the wheat would have been sold, the price would then rise to a very high level. This is all easily predictable.

So what do farmers do? The answer is that they speculate. When the wheat is harvested they know price will tend to fall, and so instead of bringing it all to market they put a lot of it into store. The more price falls, the more they will put into store *anticipating that the price will later rise*. But this holding back of supplies prevents prices from falling. In other words, it stabilises prices.

Later in the year, when the price begins to rise, they will gradually release grain on to the market from the stores. The more the price rises, the more they will release on to the market *anticipating that the price will fall again by the time of the next harvest*. But this releasing of supplies will again stabilise prices by preventing them from rising so much.

Rather than the farmers doing the speculation, it could be done by grain merchants. When there is a glut of wheat in the autumn, and prices are relatively low, they buy wheat on the grain market and put it into store. When there is a shortage in the spring and summer they sell wheat from their stores. In this way they stabilise prices just as the farmers did when they were the ones who operated the stores.

?? Would speculation help to stabilise the price fluctuations associated with the cobweb described in the previous section? How would speculation work here?

Destabilising speculation

Speculation will tend to have a **destabilising** effect on price fluctuations when suppliers and/or buyers believe that a change in price heralds similar changes to come.

An initial fall in price. In Figure 2.28 demand has shifted from D_1 to D_2 and price has fallen from P_1 to P_2. This time, believing that the fall in price heralds further falls in price to come, suppliers sell now before the price does fall. Supply shifts from S_1 to S_2. And demanders wait: they wait until price does fall further. Demand shifts from D_2 to D_3.

Their actions ensure that price does fall further: to P_3.

An initial rise in price. In Figure 2.29 a price rise from P_1 to P_2 is caused by a rise in demand from D_1 to D_2. Suppliers wait until price rises further. Supply shifts from

DEFINITION

Destabilising speculation Where the actions of speculators tend to make price movements larger.

S_1 to S_2. Demanders buy now before any further rise in price. Demand shifts from D_2 to D_3.

As a result price continues to rise: to P_3.

Conclusion

In some circumstances, then, the action of speculators can help to keep price fluctuations to a minimum (stabilising speculation). This is most likely when markets are relatively stable in the first place, with only moderate underlying shifts in demand and supply.

In other circumstances, however, speculation can make price fluctuations much worse. This is most likely in times of uncertainty, when there are significant changes in the determinants of demand and supply. Given this uncertainty, people may see price changes as signifying some trend. They then 'jump on the bandwagon' and do what the rest are doing, and further fuel the rise or fall in price.

> **??** Redraw each of Figures 2.26–2.29, only this time assume that it was an initial shift in supply that caused price to change in the first place.

Dealing with uncertainty and risk

When price changes are likely to occur, buyers and sellers will try to anticipate them. Unfortunately, on many occasions no one can be certain just what these price changes will be. Take the case of stocks and shares. If you anticipate that the price of, say, BP shares is likely to go up substantially in the near future, you may well decide to buy some now and then sell them later after the price has risen. But you cannot be certain that they will go up in price: they may fall instead. If you buy the shares, therefore, you will be taking a gamble.

Now gambles can be of two types. The first is where you know the odds. Let us take the simplest case of a gamble on the toss of a coin. Heads you win; tails you lose. You know that the odds of winning are precisely 50 per cent. If you bet on the toss of a coin, you are said to be operating under conditions of **risk**. *Risk is when the probability of an outcome is known.*

The second form of gamble is the more usual. This is where the odds are not known or are known only roughly. Gambling on the stock exchange is like this. You may have a good idea that a share will go up in price, but is it a 90 per cent chance, an 80 per cent chance or what? You are not certain. Gambling under this sort of condition is known as operating under **uncertainty**. *This is when the probability of an outcome is not known.*

You may well disapprove of gambling and want to dismiss people who engage in it as foolish or morally wrong. But 'gambling' is not just confined to horses, cards, roulette and the like. Risk and uncertainty pervade the whole of economic life, and decisions are constantly having to be made whose outcome cannot be known for certain. Even the most morally upright person will still have to decide which career to go into, whether and when to buy a house, or even something as trivial as whether or not to take an umbrella when going out. Each of these decisions and thousands of others are made under conditions of uncertainty (or occasionally risk).

> **??** Give some examples of decisions you have taken recently that were made under conditions of uncertainty. With hindsight do you think you made the right decisions?

We shall be examining how risk and uncertainty affect economic decisions on several occasions throughout the book. For example, in Chapter 4 we will see how it affects people's attitudes and actions as consumers and how taking out insurance can help to reduce their uncertainty. At this point, however, let us focus on firms' attitudes when supplying goods.

A simple way that suppliers can reduce the problem of uncertainty is by holding stocks. Take the case of the wheat farmers we saw in the previous section. At the time when they are planting the wheat in the spring, they are uncertain as to what the price of wheat will be when they bring it to market. If they keep no stores of wheat, they will just have to accept whatever the market price happens to be at harvest time. If, however, they have storage facilities, they can put the wheat into store if the price is low and then wait until it goes up. Alternatively, if the price of wheat is high at harvest time, they can sell it straight away. In other words, they can wait until the price is right.

Although the keeping of stocks will substantially reduce uncertainty, it can never eliminate it. The farmer when planting the wheat cannot know just how good a harvest it will be. If it is a very good harvest, the market price is likely to remain low for a long time after the harvest, since farmers generally have full barns and are all anxious to sell the moment prices begin to rise. Also there is the problem

DEFINITIONS

Risk When an outcome may or may not occur, but its probability of occurring is known.

Uncertainty When an outcome may or may not occur and its probability of occurring is not known.

EXPLORING THE THEORY — BOX 2.9

SPECULATING AGAINST MARKET MOVEMENTS
Arbitrage in time

Can speculators predict market movements? The following extract from *The Economist*[3] considers the possibilities.

> Soon after the attempted coup in Russia in 1991, a retired hairdresser in Moscow realised that inflation was eating away her pensions and her savings. She had noticed that clothes were always cheaper at one street market than at another one she visited near her daughter's home the other side of Moscow. As a good socialist she had always railed against profiteering middlemen, but she had an idea. She took 2000 roubles from her savings, went to the cheap market and bought a pile of clothes; then she took the metro across the city and sold the clothes for 3000 roubles at the other market. She had discovered *arbitrage*: ... buying something cheaply and immediately selling it more dearly elsewhere.
>
> The hairdresser's opportunity arose because of different prices in different places. There is no accepted name for an arbitrage in time rather than place, but the concept is essentially the same: buying something cheaply now that you know for certain can be sold more dearly later. It is far harder to do because it requires prophetic powers, and yet (in theory) far more opportunities exist for it, because so few people have prophetic powers. It is what most people who trade in financial markets are trying to do, not just those who buy futures contracts. So how do you arbitrage the future?
>
> One way is to get information faster than anybody else. If you know a day in advance that American interest rates will rise, you can buy dollars and make a profit. But not only is that illegal in most markets, it is also governed by the law of diminishing returns. One firm recently spent $35 million on a supercomputer to gain a two-second advantage in arbitraging stock futures in Tokyo. As the speed with which information is assimilated increases, the opportunities for time-arbitraging information decline. A stock price is usually suspended pending a big announcement, allowing the market to react instantaneously.
>
> Classic economic theory suggests there is no other way to beat the market than by getting information faster.
>
> But if that information has already been *predicted* by others, the market will have already adjusted to it. This fact is recognised in 'efficient-market theory'. In its most extreme form the theory states that it is impossible to predict share prices from any information at all ... for if one analyst discovers that the share price always rises on Friday, then he can buy it on Thursday in anticipation. But as his habit spreads, so the price will rise on Thursday instead of Friday and there will be no profit in the tactic.
>
> Current prices, therefore, already reflect all information about the security. Only unpredictable news can cause a change in prices; old news is already discounted. And since unpredictable news is unpredictable, so price changes are unpredictable. It is a 'random walk' in which each price change is unaffected by its predecessor and the system has no memory ...
>
> There are two fashionable ways to criticise the theory. The first is to say it is roughly true, but that no market is perfectly efficient in its handling of information, and there are therefore many loopholes of inefficiency to exploit.
>
> The second approach is to say that there are other ways to beat the market, because time-arbitrage opportunities can also come, not from information advantages, but from ... the heterogeneity of traders – the fact that people reason differently about the information they receive, that they have different time horizons (some are interested in the short term, others in the longer term) and that they have different attitudes to risk.
>
> For example, a fall in French interest rates means lower returns from franc investments for some, but better chances of economic recovery in France for others, depending on their time horizons.
>
> [Put another way], two people can receive the same information at the same instant and still come to opposite conclusions about its likely impact on prices. Neither investor is irrational, although one might be proven wrong. Therefore, a market may well misprice assets, but the mispricing is not because of inefficiency in distributing information but because of different ways of reacting to it.
>
> The same-sized cause can have different-sized effects, depending on the circumstances. A one-point rise in interest rates will have a different effect on financial markets depending on how the markets interpret the authorities' objectives. This makes the mathematics of cause and effect complicated in the extreme.
>
> [An additional problem in predicting financial market behaviour is that conditions change and the causes of such change are not consistent.] Oil prices were a powerful influence on the bond market during the Gulf war but are not now; low interest rates hurt the dollar more a few years ago than they do now; and so on. The world is in a state of perpetual change.
>
> Tomaso Poggio and Jim Hutchinson, who approached the problem from the artificial-intelligence laboratory at the Massachusetts Institute of Technology, think the market can be beaten, but that it will prove difficult because the rules of the game change as fast as you learn them. However rapidly your model updates itself with new information about what moves markets, it is always learning from outdated examples.

?? If information *were* absolutely perfect, could there be any stabilising or destabilising speculation?

[3] 9 October 1993.

that storage costs money. Thus the farmer must weigh up the possible benefits in terms of higher prices of waiting longer before selling against the additional storage costs involved.

SECTION SUMMARY

1. A complete understanding of markets must take into account the time dimension.
2. Given that producers and consumers take a time to respond fully to price changes, we can identify different equilibria after the lapse of different lengths of time. Generally, short-run supply and demand tend to be less price elastic than long-run supply and demand. As a result any shifts in *D* or *S* curves tend to have a relatively bigger effect on price in the short run and a relatively bigger effect on quantity in the long run.
3. If there is a time lag between the decision to supply and the supply coming on to the market, price oscillations are likely to occur. High prices cause producers to plan to supply more. This extra supply when it comes on to the market depresses market price. Producers respond by planning to produce less. When this reduced supply comes to market, market price will rise again. The path that these oscillations trace out on a demand and supply diagram is shaped like a cobweb. These cobwebs can be convergent or divergent depending on the shape of the demand and supply curves.
4. People often anticipate price changes and this will affect the amount they demand or supply. This speculation will tend to stabilise price fluctuations if people believe that the price changes are only temporary. However, speculation will tend to destabilise these fluctuations (i.e. make them more severe) if people believe that prices are likely to continue to move in the same direction as at present (at least for some time).
5. Many economic decisions are taken under conditions of risk or uncertainty. Uncertainty over future prices can be tackled by holding stocks. When prices are low, the stocks can be built up. When they are high, stocks can be sold.

??? END-OF-CHAPTER QUESTIONS ???

1. The weekly demand and supply schedules for T-shirts (in millions) in a free market are as follows:

Price (£)	8	7	6	5	4	3	2	1
Quantity demanded	6	8	10	12	14	16	18	20
Quantity supplied	18	16	14	12	10	8	6	4

   (a) What is the equilibrium price and quantity?

   (b) Assume that changes in fashion cause the demand for T-shirts to rise by 4 million at each price. What will be the new equilibrium price and quantity? Has equilibrium quantity risen as much as the rise in demand? Explain why or why not.

   (c) Now plot the data in the table and mark the equilibrium. Also plot the new data corresponding to (b).

   (d) Referring to the original data, what is the price elasticity of demand between a price of £7 and £5? Is it elastic or inelastic?

   (e) Again referring to the original data and by reference simply to total expenditure, is demand elastic or inelastic with respect to price, between prices of (i) £8 and £7; (ii) £4 and £3? Again with reference simply to total expenditure, what is the price elasticity of demand at a price of £5.50?

2. On separate demand and supply diagrams for bread, sketch the effects of the following: (i) a rise in the price of wheat; (ii) a rise in the price of butter and margarine; (iii) a rise in the price of rice, pasta and potatoes. In each case, state your assumptions.
3. For what reasons might the price of foreign holidays rise? In each case identify whether these are reasons affecting demand, or supply (or both).
4. If both demand and supply change, and if we know which direction they have shifted but not how much, why is it that we will be able to predict the direction in which *either* price *or* quantity will change, but not both? (Clue: consider the four possible combinations and sketch them if necessary: (i) *D* left, *S* left; (ii) *D* right, *S* right; (iii) *D* left, *S* right; (iv) *D* right, *S* left.)
5. Which of the following will have positive signs and which will have negative ones: (i) price elasticity of demand; (ii) income elasticity of demand (normal good); (iii) income elasticity of demand (inferior good); (iv) cross elasticity of demand (with respect to changes in price of a substitute good); (v) cross elasticity of demand (with respect to changes in price of a complementary good); (vi) price elasticity of supply?
6. Is there any truth in the saying that the price of a good is a reflection of its quality?
7. Why are both the price elasticity of demand and the price elasticity of supply likely to be greater in the long run?
8. What are the advantages and disadvantages of speculation from the point of view of (i) the consumer; (ii) firms?

3

Government intervention in the market

The real world is one of *mixed* economies. The government intervenes in many markets, even markets which are highly competitive. This intervention can take a number of forms:

- Fixing prices, either above or below the free-market equilibrium.
- Taxing the production or sale of various goods.
- Subsidising the production or sale of various goods.
- Taking over production. The government could nationalise various industries or run them directly from a government department (e.g. defence and health).
- Regulation. Various laws could be passed to regulate the behaviour of firms. For example, various activities, such as the dumping of toxic waste, could be made illegal; or licences or official permission might have to be obtained to produce certain goods; or a regulatory body could supervise the activities of various firms and prevent any that it felt to be against the public interest (e.g. the production of unsafe children's toys).

Supply and demand analysis is a useful tool for examining the effects of government intervention. Sections 3.1 and 3.2 apply the analysis to two types of intervention: price control and taxation. Finally section 3.3 is a case study which examines the various types of government support for agriculture.

3.1 The control of prices

At the equilibrium price, there will be no shortage or surplus. The equilibrium price, however, may not be the most desirable price. The government, therefore, may prefer to keep prices above or below the equilibrium price.

If the government sets a **minimum price** above the equilibrium (a price floor), there will be a surplus: $Q_s - Q_d$ in Figure 3.1. Price will not be allowed to fall to eliminate this surplus.

If the government sets a **maximum price** below the equilibrium (a price ceiling), there will be a shortage: $Q_d - Q_s$ in Figure 3.2. Price will not be allowed to rise to eliminate this shortage.

Setting a minimum (high) price

The government sets minimum prices to prevent them from falling below a certain level. It may do this for various reasons:

- To protect producers' incomes. If the industry is subject to supply fluctuations (e.g. crops, due to fluctuations in weather) and if industry demand is price inelastic, prices are likely to fluctuate severely. Minimum prices will prevent the fall in producers' incomes that would accompany periods of low prices (see section 3.3).
- To create a surplus (e.g. of grains) – particularly in periods of glut – which can be stored in preparation for possible future shortages.

DEFINITIONS

Minimum price A price floor set by the government or some other agency. The price is not allowed to fall below this level (although it is allowed to rise above it).

Maximum price A price ceiling set by the government or some other agency. The price is not allowed to rise above this level (although it is allowed to fall below it).

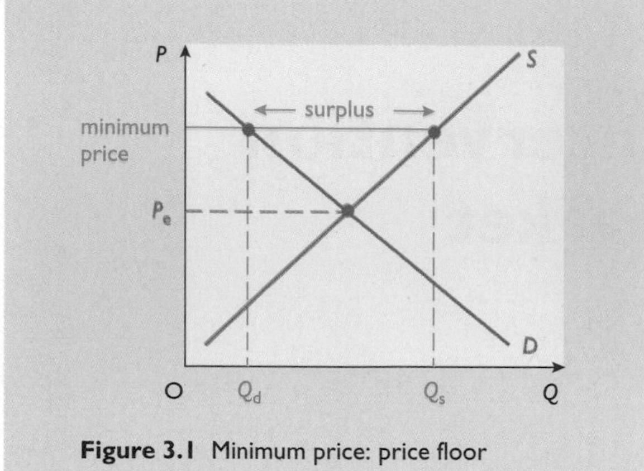

Figure 3.1 Minimum price: price floor

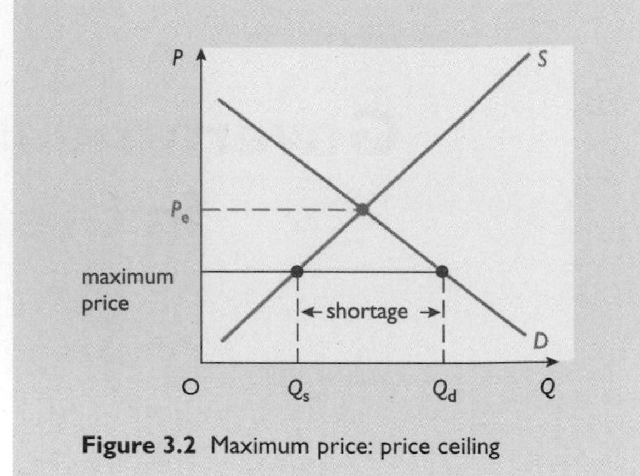

Figure 3.2 Maximum price: price ceiling

- In the case of wages (the price of labour), minimum wages legislation can be used to prevent workers' incomes from falling below a certain level (see Box 10.4).

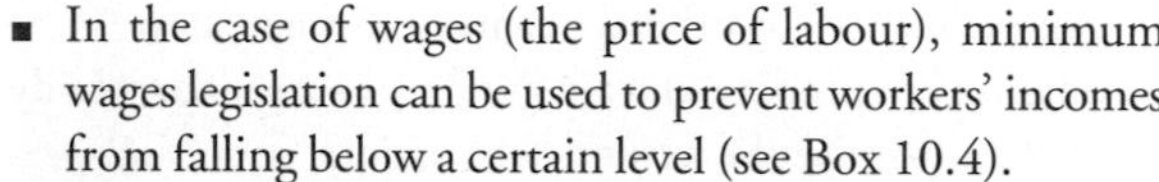

?? Draw a supply and demand diagram with the price of labour (the wage rate) on the vertical axis and the quantity of labour (the number of workers) on the horizontal axis. What will happen to employment if the government raises wages from the equilibrium to some minimum wage above the equilibrium?

The government can use various methods to deal with the surpluses associated with minimum prices.

- The government could buy the surplus and store it, destroy it or sell it abroad in other markets.
- Supply could be artificially lowered by restricting producers to particular quotas. In Figure 3.1, supply could therefore be reduced to Q_d.
- Demand could be raised by advertising, by finding alternative uses for the good, or by cutting down on substitute goods (e.g. by imposing taxes or quotas on substitutes, such as imports).

One of the problems with minimum prices is that firms with surpluses on their hands may try to evade the price control and cut their prices. It is possible that the minimum price was not set by the government, but by an agreement between firms in an attempt to keep their profits up. Here, too, there is the temptation for individual firms to break the agreement and undercut their rivals. This issue is examined in Chapter 7. (Note that in cases where firms can choose what prices to charge, simple supply and demand analysis needs to be replaced by a more sophisticated analysis. This is examined in Chapters 6 and 7.)

Another problem is that high prices may cushion inefficiency. Firms may feel less need to find more efficient methods of production and to cut their costs if their profits are being protected by the high price. Also the high price may discourage firms from producing alternative goods which they could produce more efficiently or which are in higher demand, but which nevertheless have a lower (free-market) price.

Setting a maximum (low) price

The government sets maximum prices to prevent them from rising above a certain level. This will normally be done for reasons of fairness. In wartime, or times of famine, the government may set maximum prices for basic goods so that poor people can afford to buy them.

The resulting shortages, however, create further problems. If the government merely sets prices and does not intervene further, the shortages will lead to the following:

- Allocation on a 'first come, first served' basis. This is likely to lead to queues developing, or firms adopting waiting lists. Queues were a common feature of life in East European countries where governments kept prices below the level necessary to equate demand and supply. In recent years, as part of their economic reforms, they have allowed prices to rise. This has had the obvious benefit of reducing or eliminating queues, but at the same time it has made life very hard for those on low incomes.
- Firms deciding which customers should be allowed to buy: for example, giving preference to regular customers.

Neither of the above may be considered to be fair. Certain needy people may be forced to go without. Therefore, the government may adopt a system of **rationing**. People could be issued with a set number of

DEFINITION

Rationing Where the government restricts the amount of a good that people are allowed to buy.

ISSUES AND APPLICATIONS

BOX 3.1

RENT CONTROL

Cheap housing for all?

The purpose of rent control is to protect the consumer from high rent, as well as to provide cheap housing for the very poor. In practice, however, many economists argue that such rent controls only succeed in making a larger part of the population worse off. How is this so?

Assume that legislation is passed which limits the rent that landlords can charge and this means that rents must be reduced in many cases. The supply of rented property will hardly fall in the short run, as landlords cannot quickly transfer their accommodation to other uses. In the diagram this is shown by the inelastic supply curve S.

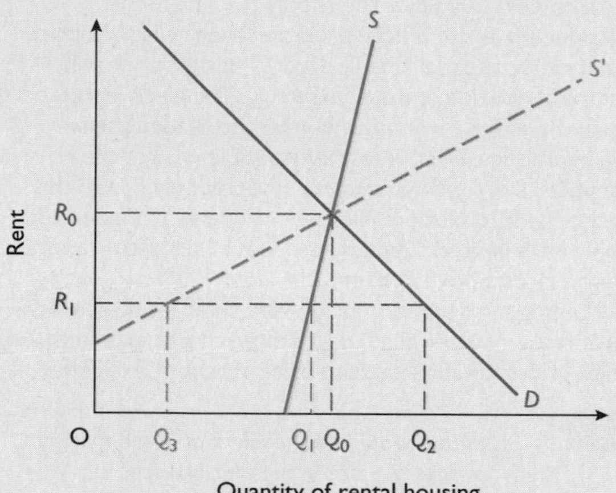

Effect of rent control

With a rent ceiling of R_1 there is a relatively small shortage of rented property with Q_1 supplied and Q_2 demanded. As a result Q_1 households will get accommodation at the lower rent, while others, $Q_2 - Q_1$, will fail to find housing at all.

In the long run, landlords will respond to the lower rent by putting their accommodation to other uses. The supply curve will become flatter and the supply of rented property will fall. The supply curve is now S′.

In the long run, then, at the rent ceiling R_1, the quantity of rental accommodation supplied falls to Q_3. Shortages now increase as less rental housing is available, and more people become homeless – more, perhaps, than in an unregulated market.

Rent controls may have further adverse effects. First, on equity grounds it is somewhat arbitrary as to who gets and who does not get housing at the lower rent. Second, in the long run, those landlords who still keep their property available for rent may cut maintenance costs and let their property fall into disrepair.

Those in favour of rent controls counter these arguments by claiming that the demand and supply curves of rented accommodation are very inelastic.

Take the case of the demand curve. People have got to live somewhere. If rent control is abolished, people will just have to pay the higher rent or become homeless: and given that people will only sacrifice their home as a last resort, demand remains inelastic and rents could rise to a very high level.

??

1. How could housing supplied by the public sector be made to rectify some of the problems we have identified above? (What would it do to the supply curve?)
2. Using supply and demand curves, show the likely effect of rent control on (a) the supply of private flats; (b) the demand for rent collectors.
3. If the government gives poor people rent allowances (i.e. grants), how will this affect the level of rents in an uncontrolled market?
4. The case for and against rent controls depends to a large extent on the long-run elasticity of supply. Do you think it will be relatively elastic or inelastic? Give reasons.

coupons for each item rationed. Alternatively, if many goods were rationed, people could be allocated a certain number of 'points'. This system operated in the UK during the Second World War. Each consumer received a number of points every four weeks to spend as desired. Each rationed product in the points system was given a points value, calculated so as to reflect the expected demand in relation to supply. Thus luxury goods, such as canned salmon, had high points values, whereas cereals had low values.

A major problem with maximum prices is likely to be the emergence of **black markets**, where customers, unable to buy enough in legal markets, may well be prepared to pay very high prices: prices above P_e in Figure 3.2 (see Box 3.2).

DEFINITION

Black markets Where people ignore the government's price and/or quantity controls and sell illegally at whatever price equates illegal demand and supply.

ISSUES AND APPLICATIONS — BOX 3.2

BLACK MARKETS

A consequence of low fixed prices

When the government fixes prices a *black market* is likely to result. A black market is one where sellers ignore the government's price restrictions. But why is it in their interest to do so, given that they probably run the risk of fines or even imprisonment?

Take the case of wartime price controls. The government set maximum prices for many essential items that were in short supply. This is illustrated in the diagram.

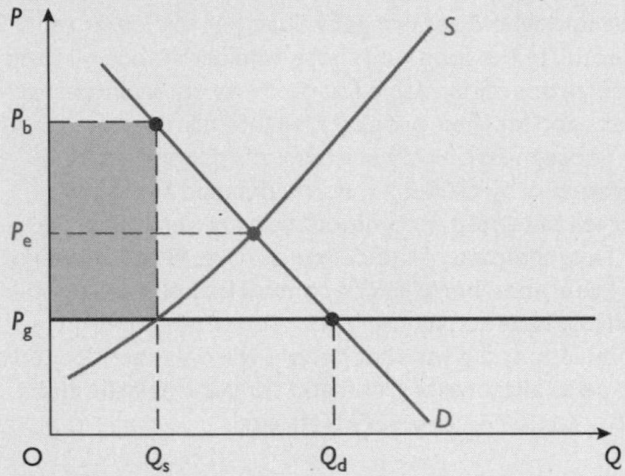

Effect of price control on black-market prices

The unacceptably high equilibrium price is P_e. The price fixed by the government is P_g. But at P_g there is a shortage of $Q_d - Q_s$. To deal with the shortage, either the government will have to accept queues, or shops only selling to 'regular' customers; or alternatively a system of rationing will have to be introduced.

But whichever system is adopted, one thing is clear: many consumers would be prepared to pay a price considerably above P_g in order to get hold of the good. The demand curve shows this: the less the supply, the higher up the demand curve will the equilibrium price be.

This is where black marketeers come in. Provided they can get supplies (maybe by some shady dealing), provided they can have access to consumers, provided consumers are willing to break the law, and provided they can escape detection, black marketeers can charge a price considerably above P_g. But what price can they charge?

Take the extreme case. Assume that the black marketeers buy up *all* the supply (Q_s) from the producers at the official price and then sell it at a price that clears the market. The black-market price will be P_b: at that price demand is equal to Q_s. The black marketeers gain the extra revenue shown by the shaded area.

In practice, of course, many people will get their supplies from official sources, and pay only P_g. On the other hand, if black marketeers are few in number and only have limited supplies, they could sell them at very high prices: above P_b even.

During the Second World War, 'spivs' (as these black marketeers were called) could often charge extortionately high prices for such items as nylon stockings and coffee.

??

1. What would be the effect on black-market prices of a rise in the official price?
2. Will a system of low official prices plus a black market be more equitable or less equitable than a system of free markets?

Another problem is that the maximum prices reduce the quantity produced of an already scarce commodity. For example, artificially low prices in a famine are likely to reduce food supplies: if not immediately, then at the next harvest, because of less being sown. In many developing countries, governments control the price of basic foodstuffs in order to help the urban poor. The effect, however, is to reduce incomes for farmers, who are then encouraged to leave the land and flock into the ever growing towns and cities.

To minimise these types of problem the government may attempt to reduce the shortage by encouraging supply: by drawing on stores, by direct government production, or by giving subsidies or tax relief to firms. Alternatively, it may attempt to reduce demand: by the production of more alternative goods (e.g. homegrown vegetables in times of war) or by controlling people's incomes.

??

Think of some examples where the price of a good or service is kept below the equilibrium (e.g. rent controls). In each case consider the advantages and disadvantages of the policy.

SECTION SUMMARY

1. There are several ways in which the government intervenes in the operation of markets. It can fix prices, tax or subsidise products, regulate production, or produce goods directly itself.
2. The government may fix minimum or maximum prices. If a minimum price is set above the equilibrium, a surplus will result. If a maximum price is set below the equilibrium price, a shortage will result.
3. Minimum prices are set as a means of protecting the incomes of suppliers or creating a surplus for storage in case of future reductions in supply. If the government is not deliberately trying to create a surplus, it must decide what to do with it.
4. Maximum prices are set as a means of keeping prices down for the consumer. The resulting shortage will cause queues, waiting lists or the restriction of sales by firms to favoured customers. Alternatively, the government could introduce a system of rationing. If it does, then black markets are likely to arise. This is where goods are sold illegally above the maximum price.

3.2

Indirect taxes

The effect of imposing taxes on goods

Another example of government intervention in markets is the imposition of taxes on goods. These **indirect taxes**, as they are called, include taxes such as value added tax (VAT) and excise duties on cigarettes, petrol and alcoholic drinks. These taxes can be a fixed amount per unit sold – a **specific tax**. An example is the tax per litre of petrol.

Alternatively, they can be a percentage of the price or value added at each stage of production – an **ad valorem tax**. An example is VAT.

When a tax is imposed on a good, this will have the effect of shifting the supply curve upward by the amount of the tax (see Figure 3.3). In the case of a specific tax, it will be a parallel shift, since the amount of the tax is the same at all prices. In the case of an ad valorem tax, the curve will *swing* upward. At a zero price there would be no tax and hence no shift in the supply curve. As price rises, so the gap between the original and new supply curves will widen, since a given *percentage* tax will be a larger *absolute* amount the higher the price.

But why does the supply curve shift upward by the amount of the tax? This is illustrated in Figure 3.4. To be persuaded to produce the same quantity as before the imposition of the tax (i.e. Q_1), firms must now receive a price which allows them fully to recoup the tax they have to pay (i.e. P_1 + tax).

The effect of the tax is to raise price and reduce quantity. Price will not rise by the full amount of the tax, however, because the demand curve is downward sloping. In Figure 3.4, price only rises to P_2. Thus the burden or **incidence** of such taxes is distributed between consumers and producers. Consumers pay to the extent that price rises.

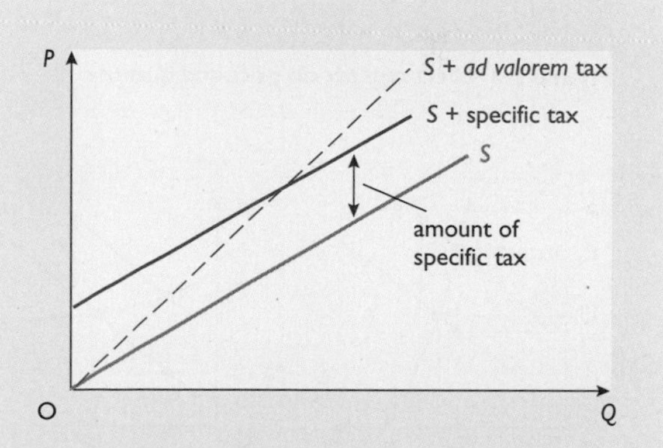

Figure 3.3 Effect of a tax on the supply curve

DEFINITIONS

Indirect tax A tax on the expenditure on goods. Indirect taxes include value added tax (VAT) and duties on tobacco, alcoholic drinks and petrol. These taxes are not paid directly by the consumer, but indirectly via the sellers of the good. Indirect taxes contrast with *direct taxes* (such as income tax) which are paid directly out of people's incomes.

Specific tax An indirect tax of a fixed sum per unit sold.

Ad valorem tax An indirect tax of a certain percentage of the price of the good.

Incidence of tax The distribution of the burden of tax between sellers and buyers.

Producers pay to the extent that this rise in price is not sufficient to cover the tax.

Elasticity and the incidence of taxation

The incidence of indirect taxes depends on the elasticity of demand and supply of the commodity in question. Consider cases (1)–(4) in Figure 3.5.

In each of the diagrams (which are all drawn to the same scale), the size of the tax is the same: the supply curve shifts upward by the same amount. Price rises to P_2 in each case and quantity falls to Q_2; but as you can see, the size of this increase in price and decrease in quantity differs in each case, depending on the price elasticity of demand and supply.

The total tax revenue is given by the amount of tax per unit (the vertical difference between the two supply curves) multiplied by the new amount sold (Q_2). This is shown as the total shaded area in each case in Figure 3.5.

The rise in price from P_1 to P_2 (the red area) is the amount of the tax passed on to consumers and thus represents the **consumers' share** of the tax.

The remainder (the grey area) is the **producers' share**. This is the amount by which the producers' net price ($P_2 - t$) is below the original price (P_1) multiplied by the number of goods sold (Q_2): i.e. $(P_1 - (P_2 - t)) \times Q_2$.

From these diagrams the following conclusions can be drawn:

- Quantity will fall less, and hence tax revenue for the government will be greater, the less elastic are demand and supply (cases (1) and (3)).
- Price will rise more, and hence the consumers' share of the tax will be larger, the less elastic is demand and the more elastic is supply (cases (1) and (4)).
- Price will rise less, and hence the producers' share will be larger, the more elastic is demand and the less elastic is supply (cases (2) and (3)).

Cigarettes, petrol and alcohol have been major targets for indirect taxes. Demand for each of them is high and fairly inelastic. Thus the tax will not curb demand greatly. They are good sources, therefore, of tax revenue to the government (see Box 3.3).

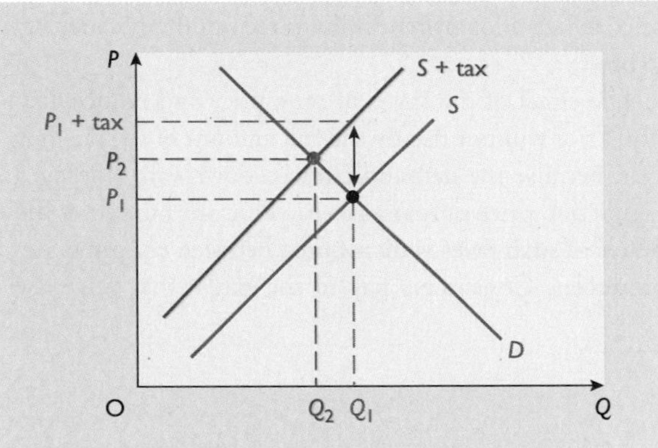

Figure 3.4 Effect of a tax on price and quantity

?? Supply tends to be more elastic in the long run than in the short run. Assume that a tax is imposed on a good that was previously untaxed. How will the incidence of this tax change as time passes? How will the incidence be affected if demand too becomes more elastic over time?

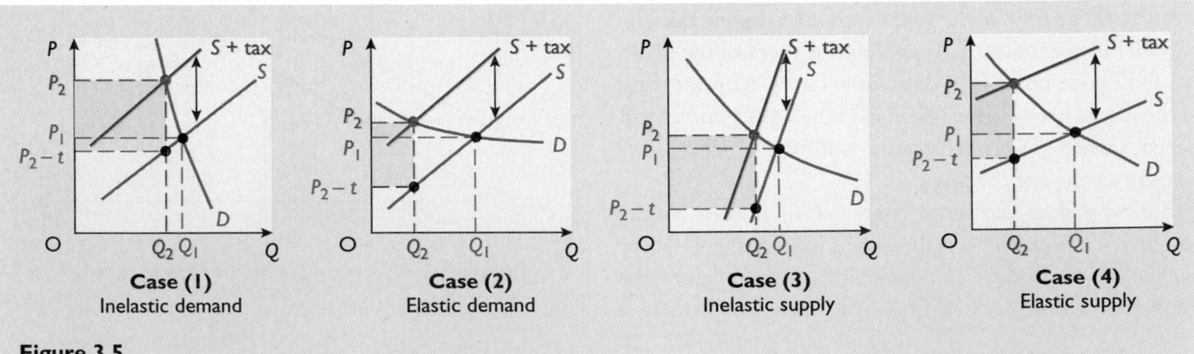

Figure 3.5

DEFINITIONS

Consumers' share of a tax on a good The proportion of the revenue from a tax on a good that arises from an increase in the price of the good.

Producers' share of a tax on a good The proportion of the revenue from a tax on a good that arises from a reduction in the price to the producer (after the payment of the tax).

CASE STUDIES — BOX 3.3

ASHES TO ASHES?
A moral dilemma of tobacco taxes

Consider the following dilemma.

Cigarettes have a fairly price-inelastic demand, and thus placing a tax on them will be an effective means of generating revenue. In the UK in 1996/7, tobacco duties raised £7.7 billion or 2.9 per cent of total tax revenue. This compares with 6.5 per cent for petrol duties, 2.1 per cent for alcohol duties and 0.6 per cent for gambling duties.

Clearly, then, tobacco duties are a major source of revenue for the government. The less people can be put off smoking by the tax, the more revenue will be raised. In fact, if the government were to *encourage* people to smoke, it could thereby raise more revenue. The government thus might want a high and an inelastic demand for tobacco products.

But smoking raises another public issue. Smoking causes ill health. This creates a cost to the country: those who smoke and contract smoking-related diseases demand additional medical resources; also their contribution to society's production is reduced. Smoking also causes a personal cost to the individuals involved.

The anti-smoking lobby argues that the health costs from smoking-related illnesses (which, it should be noted, are notoriously difficult to estimate) far outweigh any revenue benefits. As a result, the non-smoking taxpayer will end up subsidising smokers who have made themselves ill.

In fact the argument presented by the anti-smoking lobby is not as clear-cut as it may seem. The £7.7 billion raised in tax revenue from smoking in 1996/7 covered over a fifth of the total National Health Service expenditure of £33.8 billion. Estimates suggest that less than £1 billion worth of treatment went on those with smoking-related illnesses – in which case the smokers more than paid for themselves!

Indeed, the state and the NHS may acquire further financial benefit from smokers. The benefits stem from the fact that smokers die younger. The NHS gains from avoiding many of the high-cost treatments required by elderly patients. The state gains from having to pay out less in pensions and other benefits.

So here is the dilemma. Should smoking be seen by the government merely as a net source of revenue, in which case the less people are put off smoking by taxes the better, or should the government, in its concern for the health of the nation and its desire to create a smoke-free environment for non-smokers, try to reduce the level of smoking much more substantially, and thereby lose revenue?

??

1. If raising the tax rate on cigarettes both raises more revenue *and* reduces smoking, is there any dilemma?
2. You are a government minister. What arguments might you put forward in favour of maximising the revenue from cigarette taxation?
3. You are a doctor. Why might you suggest that smoking should be severely restricted? What methods would you advocate?

SECTION SUMMARY

1. If the government imposes a tax on a good, this will cause its price to rise to the consumers, but it will also cause the revenue to producers (after the tax has been paid) to fall.
2. The distribution of the burden of the tax between producers and consumers (the 'incidence of tax') will depend on the price elasticity of demand and supply of the good.
3. The consumers' burden will be higher and the producers' burden correspondingly lower, the less elastic the demand and the more elastic the supply of the good. The total tax revenue for the government will be higher the less elastic are both demand and supply.

3.3 Agriculture and agricultural policy

If markets for agricultural products were free from government intervention, they would be about as close as one could get to perfect competition in the real world. There are thousands of farmers, each insignificantly small relative to the total market. As a result farmers are price takers.

Yet despite this high degree of competition, there is more government intervention in agriculture throughout the world than in virtually any other industry. For example, half of the EU budget is spent on agricultural support. This amounted to over £12 000 per farmer in 1996, or

£250 per consumer. Agricultural markets therefore pose something of a paradox. If they are so perfect, why is there so much government intervention?

In this section we will examine this paradox. We will look at why and how governments intervene in agriculture, and in particular at the forms of intervention used in the EU under the Common Agricultural Policy. The section provides a useful case study of the operation of markets and the effects of government intervention.

Why intervene?

What reasons, then, are given for government intervention in agriculture? The following are the most commonly cited problems of the free market.

Agricultural prices are subject to considerable fluctuations. This has a number of effects:

- Fluctuating prices cause fluctuating farm incomes. In some years farm incomes may be very low.
- In other years the consumer will suffer by having to pay very high prices.
- Fluctuating prices make the prediction of future prices very difficult. This in turn makes rational economic decision making very difficult. How is a farmer to choose which of two or more crops to plant if their prices cannot be predicted?
- This uncertainty may discourage farmers from making long-term investment plans. A farmer may be reluctant to invest in, say, a new milking parlour, if in a couple of years it might be more profitable to switch to sheep rearing or arable farming. A lack of investment by farmers will reduce the growth of efficiency in agriculture.

Farm incomes rise less quickly over time than other incomes. Over the years, farming is likely to take a smaller and smaller share of national income. Without intervention, therefore, both the profits of farmers and the wages of farm workers are likely to fall relative to incomes in other parts of the economy, unless there is a substantial movement of the population out of agriculture.

The lack of economic power of farmers. It could be seen to be unfair if farmers are competitive while other sectors are not. A particular complaint of farmers is that they have to buy their inputs (tractors, fertilisers, etc.) from non-competitive suppliers who charge high prices. Then they often have to sell their produce at very low prices to food processors, packers and distributors, who keep the price low to farmers. Farmers thus feel squeezed from both directions.

Traditional rural ways of life may be destroyed. The pressure on farm incomes may cause unemployment and bankruptcies; smaller farms may be taken over by larger ones; and generally, as the rural population declines, village life may be threatened – with the break-up of communities and the closure of schools, shops and other amenities.

Competition from abroad. Farming may well be threatened by cheap food imports from abroad. This may drive farmers out of business. Moreover, if a country becomes too reliant on food imports, there may be severe problems in times of war, or at any other time when supplies may be cut off.

Against all these arguments must be set the argument that intervention involves economic costs. These may be costs to the taxpayer in providing financial support to farmers, or costs to the consumer in higher prices of foodstuffs, or costs to the economy as a whole by keeping resources locked into agriculture that could have been more efficiently used elsewhere.

Causes of short-term price fluctuations

Supply problems

Two aspects of supply help to explain price fluctuations of agricultural products.

Fluctuations in the harvest. A field is not like a machine. It cannot produce a precisely predictable amount of output according to the inputs fed in. The harvest is affected by a number of unpredictable factors such as the weather, pests and diseases. Fluctuating harvests mean that farmers' incomes will fluctuate.

Time lags in supply: the cobweb theory. Crops and animals take time to grow. There is thus a time lag between farmers planning to produce a certain level of output and that output eventually coming to the market. These time lags can cause prices to fluctuate. These fluctuations are explained by the 'cobweb theory', which we examined in section 2.5.

Demand problems

Food, being a basic necessity of life, has no substitute. If the price of food in general goes up, people cannot switch to an alternative: they either have to pay the higher price or consume less food. They might consume a bit less, but not much! The price elasticity for food in general, therefore, is very low.

CASE STUDIES — BOX 3.4

INCOME ELASTICITIES OF DEMAND FOR VARIOUS FOODSTUFFS

The statistics in the table below show the income elasticity of demand for various foodstuffs.

Remember, the income elasticity of demand is:

$$\frac{\%\ \text{change in quantity demanded}}{\%\ \text{change in income}}$$

This means that if the figure is less than 1 (an income-inelastic demand), then a rise in income will give a smaller percentage rise in the demand for that foodstuff. The lower the figure, the greater will be the long-term problems for farmers, since the more slowly will their sales rise.

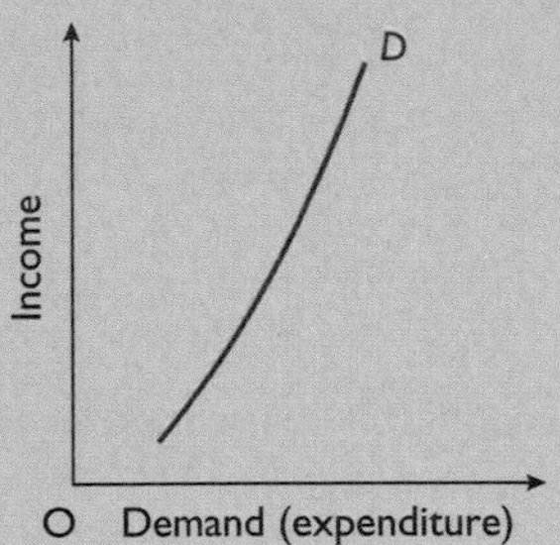

The demand for coffee (with respect to income)

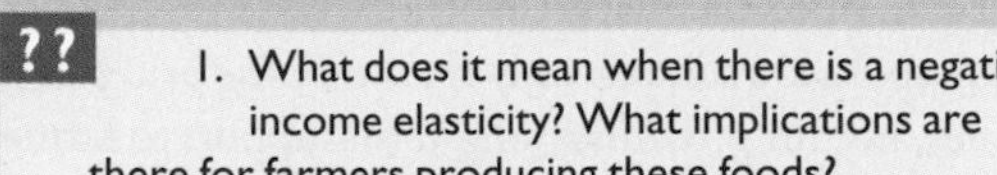

??

1. What does it mean when there is a negative income elasticity? What implications are there for farmers producing these foods?
2. The diagram shows a demand curve for coffee with respect to *income*. The curve is inelastic. (Note that coffee has an income elasticity of 0.23.)
   (a) What would be the effect on this demand curve if there were growing health worries over the consumption of coffee?
   (b) Why might this make the calculation of income elasticity of demand difficult?
3. What would be the shape of the demand curve for tea with respect to income?

Foodstuff	Income elasticity of demand	Foodstuff	Income elasticity of demand
Milk	–0.40	Sugar and preserves	–0.54
Cheese	0.19	Cakes and biscuits	0.02
Eggs	–0.41	Fresh potatoes	–0.48
Carcase meat	–0.01	Fresh green vegetables	0.13
Beef	0.08	Processed vegetables	–0.17
Lamb	–0.21	Fresh fruit	0.48
Pork	–0.05	Fruit juices	0.94
Bread	–0.25	Tea	–0.56
Butter	–0.04	Coffee	0.23
Margarine	–0.44		
		All foods	–0.01

Source: *Household Food Consumption and Expenditure* (ONS).

It is not quite so low for individual foodstuffs, because if the price of one goes up, people can always switch to an alternative. If beef goes up in price, people can buy pork or lamb instead. Nevertheless, certain foodstuffs still have a low price elasticity, especially if:

- They are considered to be basic foods rather than luxuries.
- There are no close substitutes.
- They account for a relatively small portion of consumers' income.

With an inelastic demand curve, any fluctuation in supply will cause a large fluctuation in price. This is illustrated in Figure 3.6.

Causes of declining farm incomes

Demand problems

There is a limit to the amount people wish to eat. As people get richer, they might buy better cuts of meat, or more convenience foods, but they will spend very little extra on basic foodstuffs. Their income elasticity of demand for basic foods is very low.

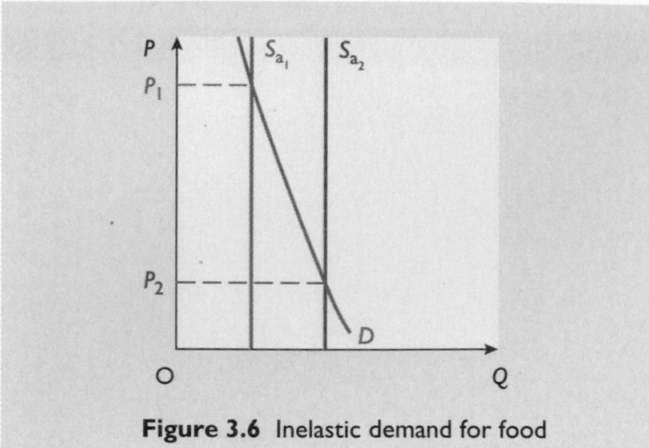

Figure 3.6 Inelastic demand for food

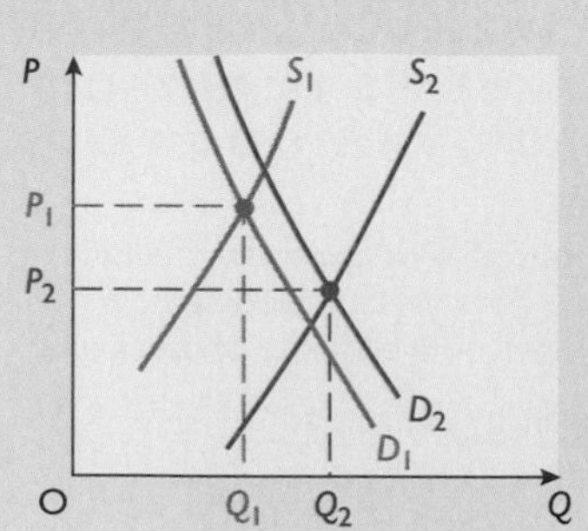

Figure 3.7 Decline in food prices over time

?? Why don't farmers benefit from a high income elasticity of demand for convenience foods?

This very low income elasticity of demand has a crucial effect on farm incomes. It means that a rise in national income of 1 per cent leads to a rise in food consumption of considerably less than 1 per cent. As a result, total farm incomes will grow much more slowly than the incomes of other sectors. Unless people leave the land, farmers' incomes will grow less rapidly than those of the owners of other businesses, and farm workers' wages will grow less rapidly than those of other workers.

Supply problems

Given that demand is sluggish, farmers might seek to increase their profits by reducing costs. That way, they can make more profit without having to sell more. As a result, farmers over the years have strived hard to improve efficiency, and have been keen to invest in new technology and improved farming methods.

However, with a given supply of land, reduced costs mean increased yields and hence increased supply. This, given the price-inelastic demand for food, will lower the price of food, thus largely offsetting any reduction in costs. And given the income-inelastic demand for food, the long-term rise in demand will be less than the long-term rise in supply.

Figure 3.7 shows a basic foodstuff like potatoes or other vegetables. Rising productivity leads to an increase in supply from S_1 to S_2. But given that demand is price inelastic and only shifts slightly to the right over time, from D_1 to D_2, price falls from P_1 to P_2.

Government intervention

There are five main types of government intervention that can be used to ease the problems examined above.

Buffer stocks. The government can buy food and place it in store when harvests are good, and then release the food back on to the market when harvests are bad. These **buffer stocks** are suitable only for *stabilising* prices or farm incomes, not for providing long-term support to farmers.

Subsidies (or tax relief). The government can pay subsidies or grant tax relief to farmers to compensate for low market prices. Subsidies and tax relief can be used to increase farm incomes as well as to stabilise them.

High fixed prices. The government can fix a minimum price for food – normally above the market equilibrium – and buy up any surpluses that result. It will then have either to store the surpluses indefinitely, or find some way of disposing of them: for example, by selling them abroad or giving them away as emergency food aid to famine-stricken countries. Guaranteed prices, like subsidies, can be used to increase farm incomes as well as to stabilise them.

Reducing supply. The government can introduce schemes to reduce the amount of food that farmers are allowed to produce or to sell. The government can also restrict food imports.

Structural policies. The government can provide retraining or financial help for people to leave agriculture. It can provide grants or other incentives for farmers to diversify into forestry, tourism, rural industry or different types of food, such as organically grown crops, or other foods with a high income elasticity of demand.

DEFINITION

Buffer stocks Stocks of a product used to stabilise its price. In years of abundance, the stocks are built up. In years of low supply, stocks are released on to the market.

ISSUES AND APPLICATIONS BOX 3.5

THE FALLACY OF COMPOSITION

Or when good is bad

Ask farmers whether they would like a good crop of potatoes this year, or whether they would rather their fields be ravaged by pests and disease, and the answer is obvious. After all, who would wish disaster upon themselves!

And yet, what applies to an individual farmer does not apply to farmers as a whole. Disaster for all may turn out not to be disaster at all.

Why should this be? The answer has to do with price elasticity. The demand for food is highly price inelastic. A fall in supply, due to a poor harvest, will therefore cause a proportionately larger rise in price. Farmers' incomes will therefore *rise*, not fall.

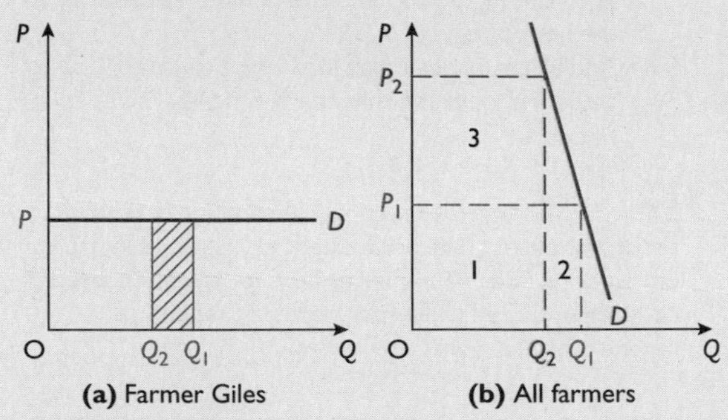

(a) Farmer Giles **(b)** All farmers

Look at diagram (a). Farmer Giles is a price taker. If he alone has a bad harvest, price will not change. He simply sells less (Q_2) and thus earns less. His revenue falls by the amount of the shaded area. But if all farmers have a bad harvest the picture is quite different, as shown in diagram (b). Supply falls from Q_1 to Q_2, and consequently price rises from P_1 to P_2. Revenue thus rises from areas (1 + 2) to areas (1 + 3).

And so what applies to a single farmer in isolation (a fall in revenue) does not apply to farmers in general. This is known as the fallacy of composition: *what applies in one case will not necessarily apply when repeated in all cases.*

What sort of harvest, then, would suit Farmer Giles best? The best possible situation would be for him to have a good harvest and everyone else to have a bad one. That way, price is high and yet he also sells a lot. The worst possible situation would be for him to have a bad harvest and everyone else to have a good one.

But if everyone is to have the same harvest, a generally bad one will be preferable for farmers to a generally good one.

??

1. Can you think of any other (non-farming) examples of the fallacy of composition?
2. Would the above arguments apply in the case of foodstuffs that can be imported as well as being produced at home?

Buffer stocks

Buffer stocks to stabilise prices

If the government merely wants to stabilise prices, it can simply fix a price which balances demand and supply over the long term. Assume that this is P_g in Figure 3.8. At this price demand is Q_d.

If there is a good harvest (S_{a_1}), the government buys up the surplus, $Q_{s_1} - Q_d$, and puts it into store. If there is a bad harvest (S_{a_2}), it releases $Q_d - Q_{s_2}$ from the store on to the market.

Buffer stocks to stabilise farm incomes

If buffer stocks are used to maintain fixed prices (as in Figure 3.8), farmers' *incomes* will still fluctuate, only this time (in contrast to a free market) the bigger the harvest, the *bigger* will farmers' incomes be. Therefore the more the harvest fluctuates, the more their incomes will fluctuate. An alternative, then, is to *vary* the government price in such a way as to keep farmers' incomes stable.

In Figure 3.9 the average annual supply over the years is Q_1. Demand is price inelastic and is shown by the demand curve D. If output were in fact S_{a_1}, in any year, the equilibrium price would be P_1 and the income earned by farmers would be P_1 times Q_1.

Assume now that the government wants to stabilise farm incomes at this level. The curve Y shows all the combinations of P and Q that would achieve this. Note that this is the same as a demand curve with a price elasticity of demand equal to −1 passing through point a. As Chapter 2 explained, a demand curve of unit elasticity gives the same total revenue at any point along it: a given percentage rise in price leads to the same percentage fall in the quantity demanded.

If there is a good harvest (S_{a_2}), output will rise to Q_2. Price must only fall to P_2' (not P_2) if income is to stay constant. But at P_2' only Q_2' is demanded. Thus $Q_2 - Q_2'$ (i.e. $b - c$) must be purchased by the government and put into store.

If there is a bad harvest (S_{a_3}), output will fall to Q_3. Price must only rise to P_3' (not P_3) if income is to stay

DEVELOPMENT OF IDEAS — BOX 3.6

SEVEN YEARS OF PLENTY AND SEVEN YEARS OF FAMINE

Buffer stocks in biblical Egypt

The idea of buffer stocks is not a new one. According to Genesis chapter 41, a buffer stock scheme was employed in the land of Egypt by Joseph.

King Pharaoh had had two dreams. In one, seven fat cows were devoured by seven thin cows. In the other, seven fat ears of corn were devoured by seven thin ears. The only person who could interpret these dreams was Joseph who was in prison. He was thus summoned to Pharaoh and interpreted the dreams as follows:

29. Behold, there come seven years of great plenty throughout all the land of Egypt:

30. And there shall arise after that seven years of famine; and all the plenty shall be forgotten in the land of Egypt; and the famine shall consume the land . . .

35. And let them gather all the food of those good years that come, and lay up corn under the hand of Pharaoh, and let them keep food in the cities.

36. And that food shall be in store to the land against the seven years of famine, which shall be in the land of Egypt; that the land perish not through the famine . . .

46. . . . And Joseph went out from the presence of Pharaoh, and went throughout all the land of Egypt.

47. And in the seven plenteous years the earth brought forth by handfuls.

48. And he gathered up all the food of the seven years, which were in the land of Egypt, and laid up the food in the cities: the food of the field, which was round about every city, laid he up in the same.

53. And the seven years of plenteousness, that was in the land of Egypt, were ended.

54. And the seven years of dearth began to come, according as Joseph had said: and the dearth was in all the lands; but in all the land of Egypt there was bread . . .

56. And the famine was over all the face of the earth: and Joseph opened all the storehouses, and sold unto the Egyptians; and the famine waxed sore in the land of Egypt.

57. And all countries came into Egypt to Joseph for to buy corn; because that the famine was so sore in all lands.

?? Would you expect the demand for corn from the storehouses to be price elastic or inelastic? What implications does your answer have for the price Joseph could have charged if he had wanted to maximise revenue for Pharaoh?

constant. But at P_3', Q_3' is demanded. Thus $Q_3' - Q_3$ (i.e. $d - e$) must be released from the store on to the market.

Conclusions

Buffer stocks can only be used with food that can be stored: i.e. non-perishable foods like grain, wine or milk powder; or food that can be put into frozen storage: e.g. butter and meat.

To prevent stores from mounting over time, the government price will have to be the one that balances demand and supply over the years. Surpluses in good years will have to match shortages in bad years. In this case, then, buffer stocks only stabilise prices or incomes, they do not increase farm incomes over the long term.

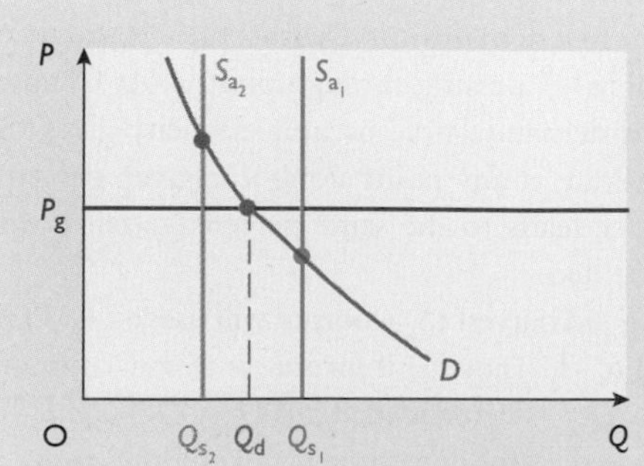

Figure 3.8 Buffer stocks to stabilise prices

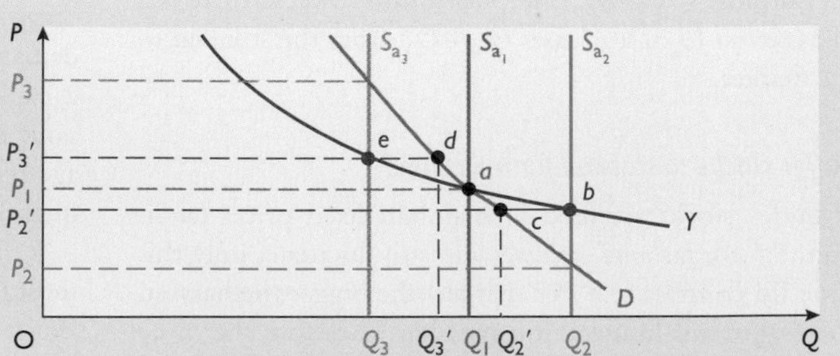

Figure 3.9 Buffer stocks to stabilise incomes

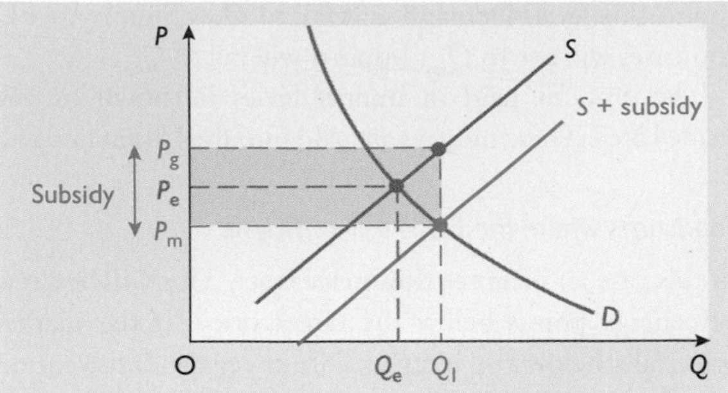

Figure 3.10 Effect of subsidies on foodstuffs in which the country is self-sufficient

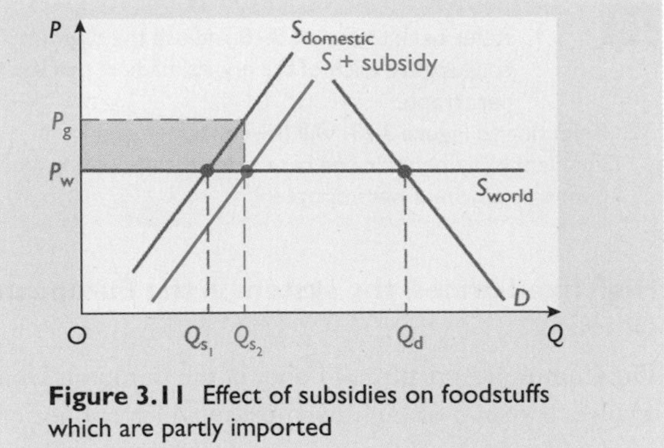

Figure 3.11 Effect of subsidies on foodstuffs which are partly imported

Subsidies

Governments may feel that the market price is too low for farmers. One method of supporting farmers' incomes, therefore, is to pay them a subsidy (per unit produced) which they will receive in addition to the market price. This, of course, will encourage farmers to produce more, which in turn will depress the market price.

Figure 3.10 illustrates the case of a foodstuff where the country is self-sufficient. Without a subsidy the market price would be P_e, where supply equals demand.

Assume now that the government wishes farmers to receive a price of P_g. If farmers do receive this price, they will plan to increase production to Q_1, which will push the market price down to P_m. The size of the subsidy that the government must pay, therefore, will be $P_g - P_m$. The total amount of taxpayers' money spent will be the shaded area. The effect of the subsidy is to shift the effective supply curve downward by the amount of the subsidy, to *S* + subsidy.

When some of the food is imported, the effect is slightly different. Let us assume, for simplicity, that the EU is a price taker in world markets. It will face a horizontal world supply curve of food at the world price. In other words, EU consumers can buy all they want at the world price. In Figure 3.11 the world price is P_w. Without a subsidy, domestic supply is Q_{s_1}. Domestic demand is Q_d. Imports are therefore the difference: $Q_d - Q_{s_1}$.

Assume now that the government wants farmers to receive a price of P_g. At that price domestic supply increases to Q_{s_2}, but the price paid by the consumer does not fall. It remains at P_w. The subsidy paid per unit is $P_g - P_w$. The cost to the taxpayer is again shown by the shaded area.

> **??** The total amount paid in subsidies is greater in Figure 3.10 than in Figure 3.11. Will it always be the case that, for a given after-subsidy price to the farmer (P_g), a greater amount will be paid out in subsidies if the country is self-sufficient in the foodstuff than if it has to import part of the total amount consumed? (Assume that the demand curve is the same in both cases.)

The old UK deficiency payments system

If the aim of subsidies is to guarantee prices to farmers, there is a problem. Actual supply fluctuates and thus diverges from planned supply. If there is a fixed subsidy, therefore, the price the farmer receives will fluctuate along with the market price.

The alternative, then, is to have variable subsidies. This system was used in the UK after the Second World War and continued until entry to the EEC in 1973. The system was one of **deficiency payments**. The government, in consultation with the National Farmers' Union, set guaranteed minimum prices to farmers for a number of products such as wheat, barley, oats, potatoes, eggs, wool and livestock. If the market price for any product fell below the guaranteed price, the difference was paid as a subsidy or 'deficiency payment'. The size of deficiency payment varied, therefore, with the market price, which in turn varied with fluctuations in supply.

An advantage of the system was that the deficiency payment was based on the *average* market price. There was therefore an incentive for farmers to improve quality and get a better than average price without thereby sacrificing any subsidy.

Farmers gained from high stable prices, which both supported their incomes and helped them plan their future investments with more certainty. Consumers gained from low prices. The costs of the deficiency payments were borne by the taxpayer.

> **DEFINITION**
>
> **Deficiency payments** Variable subsidies where the amount paid per unit is that which is necessary to make up the deficiency between the market price and the previously agreed guaranteed price.

??

1. Refer back to Figure 3.10 and use the diagram to illustrate each of the points made in this last paragraph.
2. Referring to Figure 3.11, will the consumer gain from deficiency payments in the case of foodstuffs where the country remains a net importer?

High fixed prices: the system in the European Union

The Common Agricultural Policy of the European Union involves a system of high fixed prices which are not only received by the producer but also paid by the consumer. The EU sets a **target price** for each major foodstuff. This has a different effect depending on whether the EU is self-sufficient in the foodstuff or a net importer.

Foodstuffs where the EU is a net importer

The target price will usually be above the world price. A tax or 'levy' is thus imposed on imports to bring them up to the required price. Given that the world price will fluctuate, this tax has to be variable. The system is thus known as one of **variable import levies.** To work out the size of the necessary levy a **threshold price** is set. This is the port equivalent of the target price. Given that food has to be transported from the port to the market and this costs money, the price at the port (the threshold price) does not have to be quite as high as the target price. The threshold price is thus the target price minus transport costs from the port. Provided, then, that the levy is equal to the difference between the world price and the threshold price, this will bring the EU price of imports up to the target price.

The effects of this system are illustrated in Figure 3.12. To keep the analysis simple, let us assume that transport costs are zero and that therefore the target and threshold prices are the same. If trade took place freely at the world price P_w, Q_{d_1} would be demanded and Q_{s_1} supplied within the EU. The difference $(Q_{d_1} - Q_{s_1})$ would be imported.

If a target price P_t is now set and a levy imposed on imports to raise their price to P_t, domestic prices will also rise to this level. Demand will fall to Q_{d_2}. Supply by EU countries will rise to Q_{s_2}. Imports will fall to $Q_{d_2} - Q_{s_2}$.

The amount paid in import levies is shown by the shaded area. These moneys are paid into the Union budget.

Foodstuffs where the EU is self-sufficient

In this case an **intervention price** is set. This will be a few percentage points below the target price. If the market price falls below the intervention price, the Intervention Boards of the EU will buy up any surpluses at the intervention price. In the case of foodstuffs that can be stored, such as wheat, the surpluses will be put into intervention stores.

The effects of this system are illustrated in Figure 3.13. Assume that the EU demand is D_{EU}. Assume also that the world price is P_w. This will be the equilibrium price, since any surplus at P_w (i.e. $b - a$) will be exported at that price. Thus before intervention, EU demand is Q_{d_1} and EU supply is Q_{s_1}.

Now assume that the EU sets an intervention price of P_i. Given that this is above the equilibrium (world) price, there will be a surplus of $d - e$ (i.e. $Q_{s_2} - Q_{d_2}$). This will be bought by the appropriate Intervention Board. The cost to the EU of buying this surplus is shown by the total shaded area ($edQ_{s_2}Q_{d_2}$). Unless the food is thrown away or otherwise disposed of, there will obviously then be the additional costs of storing this food: costs which could be very high over time, especially if the food has to be frozen.

An alternative to storing the food is for the Boards to sell the surpluses on the world market. In this case the net cost to the Intervention Boards would only be area *edcf*.

??

What will be the amount paid out in Figure 3.13 if instead of the Intervention Boards buying the surpluses, export subsidies were given to farmers so as to guarantee them a price (after subsidy) of P_i?

When surpluses are bought by the EU or export subsidies are given, the money comes from the European Agricultural Guarantee and Guidance Fund (known as

DEFINITIONS

Target price (of a foodstuff in the EU) The price the Union wants producers to receive (and consumers to pay). The Union will intervene through import levies (taxes) or buying up surpluses in order to ensure that price does not fall below the target level.

Variable import levy A tax on imports to bring the price of imported food up to the target price. The size of the tax will vary as the world price varies.

Threshold price The price at which an imported foodstuff enters the EU: the world price plus the variable import levy. The threshold price is set at the target price minus transport costs from the port.

Intervention price The price at which the EU is prepared to buy a foodstuff if the market price is below it.

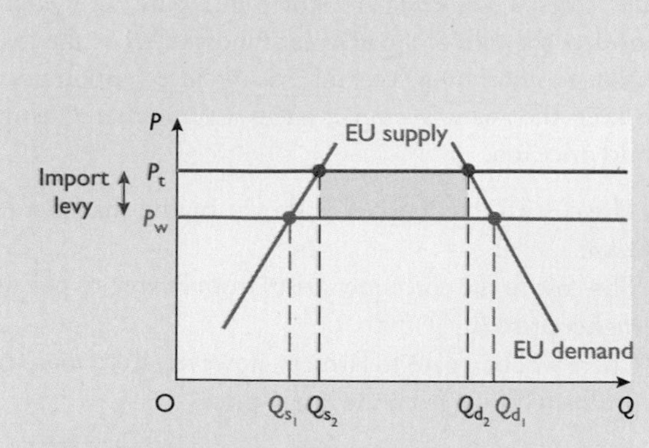

Figure 3.12 The EU system of high prices where some food is imported

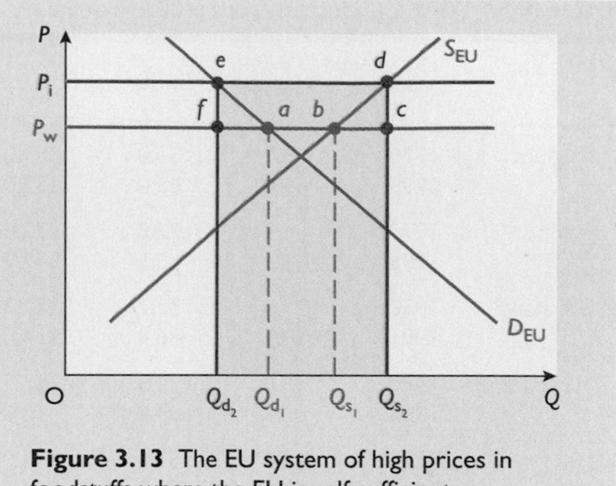

Figure 3.13 The EU system of high prices in foodstuffs where the EU is self-sufficient

FEOGA – the initials of its French name). Originally it was thought that the money earned from port levies would be sufficient to finance these payments. Over the years, however, as the EU has become increasingly self-sufficient in food, and as food surpluses have grown, so member countries have had to make increasingly large additional budget contributions to enable FEOGA to purchase these surpluses.

Justification for the Common Agricultural Policy

The EEC was established in 1957 with the signing of the Treaty of Rome. Article 39 of that treaty set out various objectives of agricultural policy including the following:

- Assured supplies of food.
- A fair standard of living for those working in agriculture.
- A growth in agricultural productivity.
- Stable prices.
- Reasonable prices for consumers.

The CAP has had some success in meeting some of these objectives, but in each case the extent of the 'success' is open to question. Let us examine each in turn.

Assured supplies of food. Memories of a war-ravaged Europe were still fresh in people's minds when the Treaty of Rome was signed. The goal of a guaranteed supply of food was thus seen as very important. The growing self-sufficiency of the EEC in most foodstuffs could therefore be argued to be an important success. It could be a major strategic advantage should the EEC ever be involved in a war, or if world food prices rose substantially.

These arguments are questionable today, however. World food prices have generally been much lower than EU prices, and there is no prospect in the foreseeable future of difficulties in obtaining food imports at reasonable prices.

Fair standard of living for farmers and farm workers. A system of high prices, other things being equal, will give farmers larger incomes. Some farmers have benefited greatly from the CAP, but despite the high prices, average incomes in agriculture have continued to lag behind those of other sections of the economy.

To what extent things would have been even worse for farmers and farm workers without the CAP is difficult to gauge. Prices would have been lower, but whether farm costs would have been higher or lower depends on what would have happened to agricultural productivity and to the prices of farm inputs. Feedstuffs and seeds would have been cheaper, and also probably the price of land. But has the CAP increased or decreased agricultural productivity?

Agricultural productivity. The argument is that higher prices lead to higher profits and therefore more money for farmers to invest in land improvement, agricultural machinery, etc. On the other hand, higher profits may allow farmers to survive without having to become more efficient. The continuance in some EU countries of many small-scale inefficient farms using outdated techniques has been blamed directly on the CAP. Nevertheless, the evidence shows that agricultural yields have improved dramatically over the years, especially in certain crops. Table 3.1 gives some examples of the growth in yields in selected EU countries between 1970 and 1993.

A large proportion of this rise in productivity has been due to technological improvements and a greater use of chemicals. It is difficult, however, to judge the extent to which this greater use has been the direct result of higher food prices rather than the simple availability of new techniques, or competition from other farmers.

Stable prices. By fixing prices which do not fluctuate with demand and supply, stable prices are guaranteed – at

Table 3.1 Yields of selected crops (100 kg/hectare)

	Year	Wheat	Barley	Potatoes
Belgium	1970	39.0	31.0	293.0
	1995	69.8	66.0	352.0
France	1970	34.5	27.8	222.5
	1995	66.2	55.5	342.0
Germany	1970	37.9	32.2	272.3
	1995	68.9	56.4	314.0
Netherlands	1970	45.0	31.9	353.7
	1995	86.6	63.0	410.0
UK	1970	42.0	33.6	275.9
	1995	77.5	57.5	368.0

Source: *Eurostat.*

least for a year. But these stable prices are high prices, so they do not benefit the consumer. They go some way to helping the farmer in making production plans, but only if the prices are not abruptly changed by the EU, and if there are no other shifts in policy that favour one product or another.

But as was demonstrated in Figure 3.8, even if prices are stable, farm incomes will still fluctuate with supply. The better the harvest, the higher will farm incomes be.

Reasonable prices for consumers. In the short run a policy of high prices is inconsistent with reasonable prices for consumers (if 'reasonable' is defined as 'low' or at any rate 'not high'). In the long run, however, it can be argued that, if prices above the market equilibrium encourage investment and productivity increases, then after a number of years they will end up lower than they would have been without the policy.

Criticisms of the CAP

If the arguments in favour of the CAP are questionable, the arguments against are substantial.

Agricultural surpluses (not sold on to world markets)

Apart from the moral question of whether it is right to grow food that is not consumed, especially given the extent of famines and malnourishment in the Third World and the problem of poverty within the EU, there are substantial direct costs of food surpluses. These costs are borne by consumers and taxpayers. They can be divided into static costs (the costs of the CAP with any given demand and supply curves) and dynamic costs (the costs arising from shifts in the curves over time as a result of the CAP).

Static costs. The costs are shown in Figure 3.14, which considers the case of a particular foodstuff. P_e is the free-market equilibrium price, and P_i is the intervention price. To keep the analysis simple, let us assume that P_e is the world price too.

- The cost to the taxpayer is shown by the shaded area, *abcd*.
- The cost to the consumer arises from having to pay the higher price P_i.
- There will be a gain to farmers, however, from the extra profits resulting from the rise in price.

These static costs of the EU system of high prices are likely to be greater than those of *subsidies*. The case of subsidies is illustrated in Figure 3.15. P_f is the price to farmers (which, we will assume, is the same as P_i in Figure 3.14). P_c is the price to consumers. The per-unit subsidy is $P_f - P_c$.

- The cost to the taxpayers is again shown by the shaded area. This time it is $P_f abP_c$. Whether this area is larger or smaller than the shaded area in Figure 3.14 will depend on the price elasticity of demand. The lower the elasticity, the bigger will be the subsidy (and hence the bigger the cost to the taxpayer). In contrast, the lower the elasticity, the lower will be the cost to taxpayers of the EU system, since, with a smaller fall in demand from the rise in price, less will have to be purchased by the Intervention Boards.
- Assuming that the price to farmers is the same in both systems, their gain will be the same.
- Consumers now *gain* from the fall in price from P_e to P_c.

This gain to consumers means that the net cost of subsidies is likely to be much smaller than the net cost of the EU system of intervention prices.

?? Assume that the world price were above point P_e (but still below P_i). Draw a diagram to illustrate the static costs in this case.

Dynamic costs. To the extent that higher prices encourage more investment in farming and therefore greater increases in long-run supply, so surpluses and their attendant costs will increase over time.

- First, there will be the growing cost of purchasing each new year's surplus.
- Second, there will be the growing cost of storing previous years' surpluses.

These costs are costs to the taxpayer, and therefore will be offset to a small extent by an additional net gain to farmers over consumers.

Table 3.2 The cost of price and other market support for agriculture in the EU

Year	Total EU budget (ECU m)	FEOGA Guarantee expenditure		
		Total (ECU m)	% of total EU budget	% of total EU GDP
1977	8924	6830	76.5	0.43
1980	16 301	11 315	69.4	0.50
1984	27 209	18 346	67.4	0.59
1988	41 121	27 687	67.3	0.68
1990	44 379	26 454	59.6	0.55
1992	58 857	32 108	54.6	0.59
1994	59 909	32 970	55.0	0.56
1995	66 758	34 503	51.7	0.58
1996	81 943	40 828	49.8	0.65
1997	82 997	41 805	50.4	0.63

Source: *The Agricultural Situation in the European Union* (Commission of the EU).

The costs of surpluses to EU taxpayers are shown in Table 3.2. The table shows the expenditure of FEOGA on intervention to guarantee high prices, and also on various other forms of market support (e.g. export subsidies). Over half of the expenditure goes on storage and disposal. The figures are given in European Currency Units (ECUs). The ECU is an EU unit of account – a way of valuing EU goods. It is worth approximately 70p, but varies with the exchange rate of the pound.

As the table shows, FEOGA's 'Guarantee expenditure' has accounted for over half of the total EU budget. FEOGA also provides 'Guidance' support for farm modernisation and help for rural communities. This, however, accounts for only some 10 per cent of FEOGA expenditure.

Until recently, agricultural support accounted for a growing proportion of the gross domestic product (GDP) of the EU countries. (GDP is a measure of a country's national output: its measurement is explained in section 14.5.)

Irrational relative prices

Although food prices are kept high generally, some are kept much higher above free-market prices than others. The effect is to cause a misallocation of resources within agriculture. For example, the yellow fields of rape that dominate much of the British landscape have been the direct result of the high levels of support given to oilseed production.

Table 3.3 shows the proportion of total agricultural output (by value) accounted for by various foodstuffs and the proportions of total Guarantee expenditure they receive.

Removes disciplines of markets

Under a system of subsidies, all farm products are sold on the market. Thus the price that farmers are able to receive will depend on the quality of their produce.

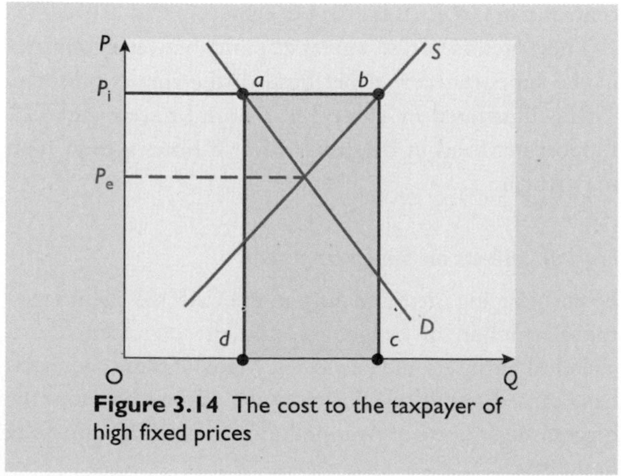

Figure 3.14 The cost to the taxpayer of high fixed prices

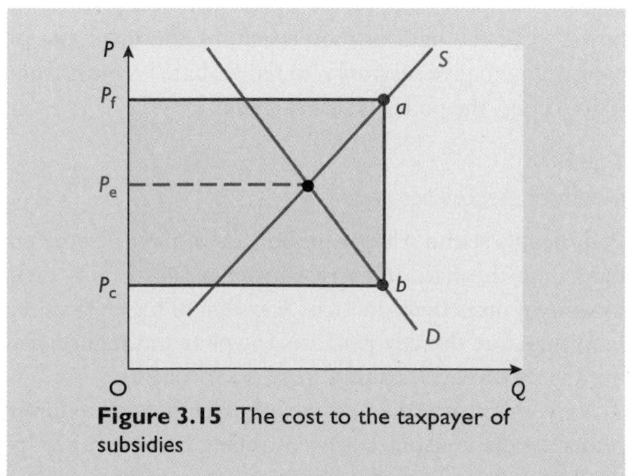

Figure 3.15 The cost to the taxpayer of subsidies

Table 3.3 Unequal support given to different agricultural products in the EU: 1997

	% of total EU agricultural output (by value)	% of FEOGA Guarantee expenditure
Milk products	18.5	8.9
Fruit and vegetables	14.8	3.9
Pigmeat	11.5	0.4
Beef/veal	11.1	14.0
Arable crops	8.8	43.0
Poultrymeat and eggs	6.5	0.4
Wine	5.8	2.2
Potatoes	3.1	0.0
Sugarbeet	2.5	4.5
Sheepmeat	1.7	5.0
Olive oil	1.2	5.0
Tobacco	0.3	2.5

Source: *The Agricultural Situation in the European Union* (Commission of the EU).

Table 3.4 FEOGA support per head of the agricultural workforce in 1995

	FEOGA expenditure per head of the agricultural workforce		
	Guarantee (ECU)	Guidance (ECU)	Total (ECU)
EU (12)	4689	462	5151
Belgium	15 903	392	16 295
Denmark	12 188	146	12 334
France	7756	322	8078
Germany	4495	675	5170
Greece	3127	595	3722
Ireland	10 125	1124	11 249
Italy	2259	305	2564
Luxembourg	2333	1000	3333
Netherlands	7941	54	7995
Portugal	1392	558	1950
Spain	4077	560	4637
UK	5542	139	5681

Source: *The Agricultural Situation in the European Union* (Commission of the EU).

Under the EU system, where prices are guaranteed, food sold into intervention may be of inferior quality. Inspectors thus have to be employed to ensure that a minimum standard of quality of the surplus food is maintained. This further adds to the costs of the surpluses.

Increases inequalities in agriculture

The bigger the farm, the bigger its output, and therefore the bigger the benefit the farmer receives from high prices. Similarly, richer agricultural regions of the EU receive more support than poorer ones. The effect of the CAP, therefore, is to increase inequalities in agriculture. These effects might be seen as beneficial if the aim of the CAP were simply to increase productivity: higher incomes would be the rewards for higher output. But then why give any support at all to the small inefficient farmer? If, however, in the light of food surpluses, the main aim of continuing to give support is to redistribute incomes from rich to poor, the policy is clearly a failure.

Increases inequalities generally

Poor people spend a larger proportion of their income on food than the rich, but pay a lower proportion of their income in taxes than the rich. A system of high prices for food therefore directly penalises the poor and reduces the burden on taxpayers. It thus increases inequality.

A system of subsidies, on the other hand, leads to lower prices for the consumer, the cost being borne entirely by the taxpayer. It therefore leads to greater equality.

Inequitable between member countries of the EU

There are three reasons why the CAP is inequitable between the member countries. The first is that lower levels of support are given to foodstuffs produced in the poorer Mediterranean EU countries.

The second is that the countries which import the most food from outside the EU – countries like the UK – pay the most in import levies into FEOGA. The countries with the greatest food surpluses draw most from FEOGA.

The third is that countries have very different proportions of their workforce engaged in agriculture. In the UK only 2.1 per cent of the civilian working population is employed in agriculture, forestry and fishing. In Belgium the figure is 2.7 per cent; in Germany it is 3.3 per cent; in the Netherlands it is 3.7 per cent; in France it is 4.9 per cent; in Italy it is 7.5 per cent; in Ireland it is 11.1 per cent; and in Greece it is 20.4 per cent.

These factors lead to a great disparity between countries in the support received per head of the rural workforce. This is illustrated in Table 3.4. As can be seen, FEOGA support per head in Belgium is over 8 times greater than in Portugal.

Harmful effects on the environment

By encouraging increased output, the CAP has encouraged the destruction of hedgerows, and the increased use of chemical fertilisers and pesticides. Many of these chemicals have caused pollution. For example, nitrates are now the biggest single cause of river pollution in the UK, especially in the east.

CASE STUDIES BOX 3.7

THE CAP AND THE ENVIRONMENT

A green and unpleasant land?

In many parts of the EU, and in Britain in particular, the rural landscape has changed dramatically over the last twenty years. Hedgerows have been destroyed; woods and copses have been cut down; and what was once a patchwork of small meadows and fields now resembles the Canadian prairies. These have been some of the costs of the drive to increase production of cereals, a drive that has been the response to the high cereal prices set by the EU.

But the costs do not end here. The environment is also under threat from pollutants. Pesticides may kill pests, but they can also kill wild flowers and wild animals and can leave toxic residues in the soil. Fertilisers can leach into rivers. So too can farm waste, such as silage and slurry and dirty water generally from farmyards. The effect can be to pollute drinking water supplies and kill fish and other aquatic life. The practice of stubble burning has increased with the increase in the amount of land used for growing cereals. The resulting smoke can be a public nuisance and the burning can kill wildlife.

Both the EU and individual national governments have recognised these problems and some attempts have been made to tackle them.

- The EU Drinking Water Directive limits the permitted level of nitrates in drinking water supplies to 50 milligrams per litre.
- Pesticides have to be approved by national governments and there are regulations governing their use. In the UK the costs of the necessary testing and monitoring are charged to the pesticide manufacturers. This amounts to more than £5 million per year.
- Governments spend money on research into more environmentally friendly means of controlling pests, with the result that there has been a modest decline in the use of pesticides in most EU countries.
- From 1993 stubble burning has been banned in the UK.
- The EU helps to finance various schemes for environmental protection. In the UK, under the Farm and Conservation Grant Scheme introduced in 1989, grants are available for up to 50 per cent of the cost of equipment to deal with farm effluent. Grants are also available for constructing hedges and stone walls from traditional materials, planting trees as shelter for fields and renovating farm buildings.
- Under the 'set-aside' scheme (see page 98), farmers can be paid to convert arable land to other uses such as woodland or pasture, or simply to let it lie fallow. There are strict limitations on the use of chemicals on such land.
- Grants are also available in the UK under the Farm Woodland Scheme to encourage farmers to plant woods, especially small broad-leaved woods, on land currently used for agriculture.
- Stricter laws against water pollution. The UK 1990 Environmental Protection Act increased the maximum fine from £2000 to £20 000 for each offence.

Despite these various initiatives, the measures have so far had only a very minor impact on the pattern of production. Many environmentalists argue that much more radical steps are needed if the problem is to be taken seriously.

Member countries not 'playing the game'

The CAP is supposed to be a *common* agricultural policy. In practice individual countries have frequently sought to flout its regulations.

In the face of mounting surpluses, countries have sought to protect their own farmers against competition from other member countries. They have used illegal methods (or methods that 'get round' European law) to subsidise their own farmers or to reduce imports from other EU countries.

Effects on the rest of the world

The CAP has had a very damaging effect on agriculture in non-EU countries in two ways.

Import levies. Levies on imported food substantially reduce the amount of food that other countries are able to export to the EU. For example, Australia, a low-cost producer of butter, and once a major exporter to the UK, now finds it impossible to export any butter at all to the EU.

'Dumping' surpluses on world markets. Export subsidies allow EU surpluses to be sold at very low prices on world markets. This has a doubly damaging effect on agriculture in developing countries: (a) exporters of foodstuffs find it very difficult to compete with subsidised EU exports; (b) farmers in the developing countries who are producing for their domestic market find that they cannot compete with cheap imports of food.

Agriculture in the developing world thus declines. Farmers' incomes are too low to invest in the land. Many migrate to the overcrowded cities and become slum dwellers in shanty towns, with little or no paid employment (see

Chapter 25). The neglect of agriculture can then lead to famines if there is poor rainfall in any year. Calls are then made for European (and North American) food surpluses to be used for emergency aid: the same food surpluses that contributed to the problem in the first place!

Reforming the CAP

Proposals for reforming the CAP have been debated within the EU for a number of years. Most have focused on the growing problem of food surpluses and on the resulting demands made on the EU budget. The list of possible reforms is long. The main ones are as follows.

Price reductions. The most obvious solution is a reduction in the levels of intervention prices. In theory this should reduce supply, increase demand and thereby reduce or even eliminate surpluses.

There were some tentative attempts in the 1980s to reduce the rate of increase in intervention prices. Also in 1988 a system of **budget stabilisers** was introduced. These involved automatic price cuts of 3 per cent if *total* EC production exceeded a stated level. To act as a real disincentive to farmers who overproduce, however, price cuts would have to apply to each farm individually. For example, the farmer could be given a lower price for each foodstuff once a certain quota was exceeded. Clearly this would be more expensive to administer.

An alternative is to impose a tax on output, thereby reducing the (after-tax) price to the farmer. Such a scheme was introduced in 1986 when a tax (or **co-responsibility levy** as it is called) of 3 per cent was imposed on cereal production. This was later extended with supplementary levies being imposed on output that exceeded quotas.

The problem with relying solely on substantial price cuts, however, is that many small farmers would be driven out of business: something that the CAP was designed to prevent. Large farms with substantial economies of scale would survive, but the traditional character of the countryside would be further eroded. Politically, it would probably not be possible for large numbers of small farmers to be made bankrupt.

As a result of the difficulties in instituting price reductions, various proposals were put forward to restrict supply.

Production quotas. This system would restrict farmers' permitted output. Quotas have already been introduced for sugar and milk. It is more difficult, however, to have a quota system for grains and vegetables where yields fluctuate with the harvest, and where it would thus be difficult to monitor the system. And if quotas were only applied to a limited range of products, this would merely encourage farmers to switch to other products which may also be in surplus.

Dairy farmers have been bitterly opposed to quotas (introduced in 1984). They naturally see them as a barrier against expansion, efficiency and increased profit. They claim that quotas freeze current production patterns and prevent efficient farmers from entering the market. There is now a trade in quotas, however, as farmers buy and sell their right to produce milk. As a result, milk quotas have become a valuable asset.

Acreage controls. Another way of reducing cereal production has been to reduce the area cultivated. Subsidies are paid to farmers to leave their land fallow. Under this **set-aside** scheme, which was introduced in 1988, farmers withdraw part of their arable land from production, and in return are paid compensation. By the mid-1990s 18 per cent of cereal land in the EU had been taken out of production.

A problem with set-aside is that farmers tend to set aside their least productive land, thereby making little difference to total output. Another problem is that farmers tend to put in extra effort on the remaining land, again hoping to maintain total output. If they are successful, supply will not be reduced and the problem of surpluses will remain. To increase yields they would probably use more chemicals with the attendant problems of pollution.

Diversification. Farmers could be paid subsidies or given tax concessions to encourage them to diversify into food products that are not in surplus, or into forestry, rural industry or tourism. FEOGA Guidance payments can be used for this purpose. Also, set-aside land can be converted to these other uses.

Low-intensity farming. Another option would be to encourage the use of less fertilisers and other chemicals.

DEFINITIONS

Budget stabilisers A system introduced into the EC (EU) in 1988 of limiting total expenditure on agricultural support. Intervention prices were cut when an agreed budget limit was reached.

Co-responsibility levy A tax on food production in the EU so as to reduce the level of agricultural support.

Set-aside A system in the EU of paying farmers not to use a certain proportion of their land.

This would reduce yields per hectare. To some extent this is happening anyway with the shift in consumer preferences towards organic foods. Nevertheless measures could be taken to encourage this trend with the use of subsidies on organically grown food and taxes on various chemicals.

Replacing high prices with subsidies. A more radical possibility, and one that has received little support within the Union, would be to introduce a system like the old UK deficiency payments scheme. This would allow surpluses to be eliminated. It might even be possible to pay a larger per-unit subsidy to smaller farmers. But given the scale of the overproduction, the price inelasticity of demand for food and the extent to which EU prices are above world prices, the necessary size of the subsidies would be very large. This would put a consequently large additional burden on European Union taxpayers. It would be politically difficult given complaints that the current cost of intervention is already excessive.

Income support ('lump-sum' subsidies). Given the size of the surpluses, there is no simple solution. The one most favoured by academic economists, however, is that of a straight grant to farmers, not related to output. Grants protect farmers' incomes, but unlike both high prices and subsidies, grants do not (in theory) encourage them to increase output, since extra output only earns them the market price.

In practice, grants were resisted for many years by politicians, who saw them as 'handouts' for doing nothing at all. Also the worry was that farmers might simply reinvest them in their farms, thereby increasing long-term output.

The MacSharry reforms

Added impetus for reform was given by the negotiations at the so-called 'Uruguay round'[1] of international trade talks (see section 23.2 and Box 23.7). These talks, organised under the auspices of GATT (the General Agreement on Tariffs and Trade), began in 1986. The aim was to reach an international deal on reducing barriers to trade in a wide range of products and services, not least of which was agricultural products. Agriculture, however, proved to be a major stumbling block. The USA claimed that the CAP provided grossly unfair support to European farmers and effectively prevented access to the EC (as it was called then) for a wide range of food imports. The EC, however, was unwilling to scrap the CAP system of price support.

A breakthrough came in May 1992, however, when the EC agriculture ministers agreed a reform of the CAP. After further negotiations between the USA and the EC, an agriculture agreement was reached in November 1992. But it was not until December 1993 that a final GATT agreement was signed, covering a whole range of goods and services.

There were three main features to the 1992 reforms of the CAP (known as the 'MacSharry reforms', after the EU agriculture commissioner):

- A substantial cut in intervention prices, including a 29 per cent cut in cereal prices. The price cuts would be phased in over the period 1993 to 1996. There would be a corresponding cut in export subsidies. (It was assumed that the intervention prices would still be somewhat above world prices.)
- Farmers would then be paid full compensation for their resulting loss of income. Since this income support would be based on average yields in each farming region, it would be independent of any changes in production by individual farmers. The income support would thus provide no direct incentive to increase production.
- In order to receive the income support, all except small farmers would have to agree to set aside 15 per cent of their land.

The effect of these measures has been to reduce farm surpluses. This is illustrated in Figure 3.16. At the old intervention price of P_1, and with demand and supply curves of D and S_1, the surplus was $Q_{s_1} - Q_{d_1}$. Farmers' revenues were *abcd*. The effect of the increased set-aside has been to shift the supply curve of cereals to the left, shown by S_2. This, plus a reduction in the intervention price to P_2, has reduced the surplus to $Q_{s_2} - Q_{d_2}$. Farmers' revenues have been reduced to *a′b′c′d*, but the CAP pays compensation payments for the loss in profits.

In the first three years after these reforms, annual cereal output fell from 180 million tonnes to 160 million tonnes, and intervention stocks all but disappeared. Set-aside land had increased by 30 per cent, and, contrary to the predictions of some analysts, yields had not increased (partly the result of poor weather). In response to this success, land required to be set aside was reduced to 10 per cent in 1995 and to 5 per cent in 1996.

But with crop yields destined to increase in the future, the problem of cereal surpluses has not been completely solved. Also there is the worry among farmers that the level of income support will not keep pace with inflation. Large farmers may be able to compensate for this by increases in efficiency. Small farmers, however, often

[1] It was called the 'Uruguay round' because the negotiations began in Uruguay. They continued at many different locations round the world

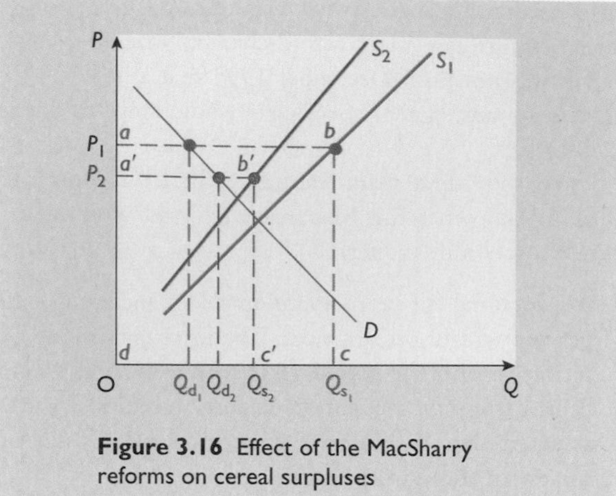

Figure 3.16 Effect of the MacSharry reforms on cereal surpluses

growing crops on more marginal lands and unable to afford the same level of investment per hectare as large farmers, may find that they are unable to survive.

The lower levels of intervention prices help EU consumers, which in turn benefits low-income families relatively more than high-income ones. Taxpayers have to finance the income support, but with less incentive to expand production, this should be less of a burden than that of paying high intervention prices for large food surpluses.

?? Does the requirement to set aside 5 per cent of land reduce output by 5 per cent?

There has also been a shift in emphasis towards viewing agriculture as part of the whole rural environment. This involves increasing the relative size of the Guidance expenditure of FEOGA, and using it for helping to set up alternative rural industries and 'environmentally friendly' farm activities. This expenditure is being co-ordinated with the European Regional Development Fund and the European Social Fund, the aim being to take account of local economic, social and environmental issues when giving support. In other words, there is a shift towards *discretionary* payments and away from automatic (compulsory) market support.

One produce category that did not come under the MacSharry reforms was that of fruit and vegetables. Growers are paid large sums to withdraw produce from the market, much of it totally unfit for consumption. Similarly, tobacco growers in Italy and Greece are paid to produce tobacco, most of which is so high in nicotine that there is virtually no market for it!

Agenda 2000

In July 1997, as part of its proposed plans for expansion of the EU to include various eastern European countries, the European Commission published a document entitled *Agenda 2000*. This contained proposals to extend the MacSharry reforms. These included calls for price cuts to farmers of 20 per cent for grain, 10 per cent for milk and 30 per cent for beef, to take effect from 2000. At the same time there should be an increase in direct income support, targeted mainly at small farmers in outlying regions. There would be ceilings on support given to large farms, forcing grain and cattle agribusinesses to compete at closer to world prices.

The document also called for increased use of less intensive and more environmentally friendly methods, proposing that income support should be paid only to farmers adopting such methods.

Although the 1992 measures had helped to reduce, and in some cases eliminate, food mountains, this had been partly the result of poor harvests. Agenda 2000 warned that unless its recommended price cuts were enforced, large food surpluses would re-emerge. What is more, the ability to export these surpluses at subsidised prices would no longer be an option under the new world trade rules (see Box 23.7).

SECTION SUMMARY

1. Despite the fact that a free market in agricultural produce would be highly competitive, there is large-scale government intervention in agriculture throughout the world. The aims of intervention include preventing or reducing price fluctuations, encouraging greater national self-sufficiency, increasing farm incomes, encouraging farm investment, and protecting traditional rural ways of life and the rural environment generally.
2. Price fluctuations are the result of fluctuating supply combined with a price-inelastic demand. The supply fluctuations are due to fluctuations in the harvest and time lags in supply (the cobweb effect).
3. The demand for food is generally income inelastic and thus grows only slowly over time. Supply, on the other hand, has generally grown rapidly as a result of new technology and improved farm methods. This puts downward pressure on prices – a problem made worse for farmers by the price inelasticity of demand for food.

continued

4. Government intervention can be in the form of buffer stocks, subsidies, price support, quotas and other ways of reducing supply, and structural policies.
5. If buffer stocks are used to stabilise prices, farm incomes will fluctuate *positively* with the harvest. If they are used to stabilise farm incomes, intervention must be such as to allow price to rise (fall) by the same percentage as farm output falls (rises).
6. Subsidies will increase farm incomes but will lower consumer prices to the world price level (or to the point where the market clears). Under the old UK deficiency payments system, subsidies were paid to farmers to make up the deficiency between the expected (post-subsidy) market price and the price the government wished farmers to receive.
7. In the EU prices are kept high to both farmer and consumer. In the case of partly imported foodstuffs, this is achieved by imposing variable import levies. In cases where the EU is self-sufficient, surpluses are purchased at an intervention price.
8. The Common Agricultural Policy of the EU has been justified as providing assured supplies of food, a fair standard of living for farmers, incentives to increase productivity, stable prices, and, in the *long* term, possibly lower prices for consumers.
9. The CAP has been criticised, however, on a number of counts: it leads to food surpluses, the static costs of which are greater than those of subsidies; price support has been unequal as between foodstuffs, with a resulting misallocation of resources; it reduces the incentive to produce high-quality food; it has aggravated inequalities within agriculture; it has been inequitable between member countries; it has encouraged environmental damage; import levies and the surpluses 'dumped' on world markets have had a damaging effect on the agricultural sector of non-EU countries.
10. Reforms have included production quotas, acreage controls (set-aside), taxing output (co-responsibility levies), capping the level of FEOGA expenditure on price support (budget stabilisers), increasing expenditure on rural diversification and restructuring and, since 1992, reducing intervention prices and, in return, paying farmers compensation *unrelated* to current output.

??? END-OF-CHAPTER QUESTIONS ???

1. Assume that the (weekly) market demand and supply of tomatoes are given by the following figures:

Price (£ per kilo)	4.00	3.50	3.00	2.50	2.00	1.50	1.00
Q_d *(000 kilos)*	30	35	40	45	50	55	60
Q_s *(000 kilos)*	80	68	62	55	50	45	38

   (a) What are the equilibrium price and quantity?

   (b) What will be the effect of the government fixing a *minimum* price of (i) £3 per kilo; (ii) £1.50 per kilo?

   (c) Suppose that the government paid tomato producers a subsidy of £1 per kilo. (i) Give the new supply schedule. (ii) What will be the new equilibrium price? (iii) How much will this cost the government?

   (d) Alternatively, suppose that the government guaranteed tomato producers a price of £2.50 per kilo. (i) How many tomatoes would it have to buy in order to ensure that all the tomatoes produced were sold? (ii) How much would this cost the government?

   (e) Alternatively suppose it bought *all* the tomatoes produced at £2.50. (i) At what single price would it have to sell them in order to dispose of the lot? (ii) What would be the net cost of this course of action?

2. Think of two things that are provided free. In each case, identify when and in what form a shortage might occur. In what ways are/could these shortages be dealt with? Are they the best solution to the shortages?
3. If the government increases the tax on wine by 10p, what will determine the amount by which the price of wine will go up as a result of this tax increase?
4. Illustrate on four separate diagrams (as in Figure 3.5) the effect of different elasticities of demand and supply on the incidence of a *subsidy*.
5. Why are agricultural prices subject to greater fluctuations than those of manufactured products?
6. Compare the relative benefits of subsidies and high minimum prices (as under the CAP) to (i) the consumer; (ii) the farmer.
7. The EU is more than self-sufficient in a number of commodities. Does this mean that the objectives of the CAP have been achieved? What has been the cost of achieving this success? What do you think would have happened in the absence of the CAP?
8. In what ways have the MacSharry reforms solved the problems experienced under the CAP?

4 Background to demand

This chapter gives a more detailed explanation of the shape of the demand curve. This explanation involves considering how **rational consumers** behave.

If we had unlimited income (and unlimited time too!), we could consume as much as we wanted. We would not have to be careful with our money. In the real world, however, given limited incomes, given the problem of scarcity, we have to make choices about what to buy. You may have to choose between that new economics textbook you feel you ought to buy and going to a rock concert, between a new pair of jeans and a meal out, between saving up for a car and having more money to spend on everyday items, and so on.

We will be assuming in this chapter that consumers behave 'rationally'. Remember from Chapter 1 how we defined rational choices. It is the weighing-up of the costs and benefits of our actions. As far as consumption is concerned, rational action involves considering the relative costs and benefits to us of the alternatives we could spend our money on. We do this in order to gain the maximum satisfaction possible from our limited incomes.

Sometimes we may act 'irrationally'. We may purchase goods impetuously or out of habit, with little thought to their price or quality. In general, however, it is a reasonably accurate assumption that people behave rationally.

This does not mean that you get a calculator out every time you go shopping! When you go round the supermarket you are hardly likely to look at every item on the shelf and weigh up the satisfaction you think you would get from it against the price on the label. Nevertheless, you have probably learned over time the sort of things you like and the prices they cost. You can probably make out a 'rational' shopping list quite quickly.

With major items of expenditure such as a house, a car, a carpet or a foreign holiday, we are likely to take much more care. Take the case of a foreign holiday: you will probably spend quite a long time browsing through brochures comparing the relative merits of various holidays against their relative costs, looking for a holiday that gives good value for money. This is rational behaviour.

??

1. Do you ever purchase things irrationally? If so, what are they and why is your behaviour irrational?
2. If you buy something in the shop on the corner when you know that the same item could have been bought more cheaply two miles up the road in the supermarket, is your behaviour irrational? Explain.

Two words of warning before we go on. First, don't confuse irrationality and ignorance. We are going to assume that consumers behave rationally, but that does not mean that they have perfect information. How often have you been disappointed after buying something when you find that it is not as good as you had been led to believe by advertisements or by its packaging, or when you find later that you could have bought an alternative more cheaply? Take the case of a foreign holiday. It may not turn out to be nearly as good as the brochure led you to believe. This is a problem of ignorance. You probably nevertheless behaved rationally in the first place, *believing* (albeit wrongly) that you were getting value for money.

Second, the term 'rational' does not imply any moral approval. It is simply referring to behaviour that is consistent with your own particular goals, behaviour directed to getting the most out of your limited income. People may well disapprove of the things that others buy – their clothes, their records, their cigarettes, their cans of lager – but that is making a judgement about their goals: their

DEFINITION

Rational consumer A person who weighs up the costs and benefits to him or her of each additional unit of a good purchased.

tastes or morality. As economists we cannot make judgements about what people's goals *should* be. We can, however, look at the *implications* of people behaving rationally in pursuit of those goals. This is what we are doing when we examine rational consumer behaviour: we are looking at its implications for consumer demand.

There are two major approaches to analysing rational consumer behaviour: the marginal utility approach and the indifference curve approach. These two approaches are described in the two sections of this chapter.

4.1 Marginal utility theory

Total and marginal utility

People buy goods and services because they get satisfaction from them. Economists call this satisfaction 'utility'.

An important distinction must be made between *total utility* and *marginal utility*.

Total utility (*TU*) is the total satisfaction a person gains from all those units of a commodity consumed within a given time period. Thus if Tracey drank 10 cups of tea a day, her daily total utility from tea would be the satisfaction derived from those 10 cups.

Marginal utility (*MU*) is the additional satisfaction gained from consuming one *extra* unit within a given period of time. Thus we might refer to the marginal utility that Tracey gains from her third cup of tea of the day or her eleventh cup.

A difficulty arises immediately with the utility approach to explaining demand, and that is: how do you measure utility? Utility is subjective. There is no way of knowing what another person's experiences are really like. Just how satisfying does Brian find his first cup of tea in the morning? How does his utility compare with Tracey's? We do not have utility meters that can answer these questions!

For the moment, this problem will be ignored, and it will be assumed that a person's utility can be measured in **utils**, where a util is one unit of satisfaction.

Diminishing marginal utility

Up to a point, the more of a commodity you consume, the greater will be your total utility. However, as you become more satisfied, each extra unit that you consume will probably give you less additional utility than previous units. In other words, your marginal utility falls, the more you consume. This is known as the **principle of diminishing marginal utility**. For example, the second cup of tea in the morning gives you less additional satisfaction than the first cup. The third cup gives less satisfaction still.

At some level of consumption, your total utility will be at a maximum. No extra satisfaction can be gained by the consumption of further units within that period of time. Thus marginal utility will be zero. Your desire for tea may be fully satisfied at 12 cups per day. A thirteenth cup will yield no extra utility. It may even give you displeasure (i.e. negative marginal utility).

?? Are there any goods or services where consumers do not experience diminishing marginal utility?

Total and marginal utility curves

If we could measure utility, we could construct a table showing how much total and marginal utility a person would gain at different levels of consumption of a particular commodity. This information could then be transferred to a graph. Table 4.1 and Figure 4.1 do just this. They show the imaginary utility that Darren gets from consuming packets of crisps.

Referring first to the table, if Darren consumes no crisps, he obviously gets no satisfaction from crisps: his total utility is zero. If he now consumes 1 packet a day, he gets 7 utils of satisfaction. (Sorry if this sounds silly, but we will tackle this question of measurement later.) His total utility is 7, and his marginal utility is also 7. They must be equal if only 1 unit is consumed.

If he now consumes a second packet, he gains an extra 4 utils (*MU*), giving him a total utility of 11 utils (i.e. 7 + 4). His marginal utility has fallen because, having already eaten 1 packet, he has less craving for a second. A third

DEFINITIONS

Total utility The total satisfaction a consumer gets from the consumption of all the units of a good consumed within a given time period.

Marginal utility The extra satisfaction gained from consuming one extra unit of a good within a given time period.

Util An imaginary unit of satisfaction from the consumption of a good.

Principle of diminishing marginal utility As more units of a good are consumed, additional units will provide less additional satisfaction than previous units.

Table 4.1 Darren's utility from consuming crisps (daily)

Packets of crisps consumed	*TU* in utils	*MU* in utils
0	0	–
1	7	7
2	11	4
3	13	2
4	14	1
5	14	0
6	13	–1

packet gives him less extra utility still: marginal utility has fallen to 2 utils, giving a total utility of 13 utils (i.e. 11 + 2).

By the time he has eaten 5 packets, he would rather not eat any more. A sixth actually reduces his utility (from 14 utils to 13): its marginal utility is negative.

The information in Table 4.1 is plotted in Figure 4.1. Notice the following points about the two curves:

- The *MU* curve slopes downward. This is simply illustrating the principle of diminishing marginal utility.
- The *TU* curve starts at the origin. Zero consumption yields zero utility.
- It reaches a peak when marginal utility is zero. When marginal utility is zero (at 5 packets of crisps), there is no addition to total utility. Total utility must be at the maximum – the peak of the curve.
- Marginal utility can be derived from the *TU* curve. It is the slope of the line joining two adjacent quantities on the curve. For example, the marginal utility of the third packet of crisps is the slope of the line joining points *a* and *b*. The slope of such a line is given by the formula:

$$\frac{\Delta TU}{\Delta Q} \quad (= MU)$$

In our example $\Delta TU = 2$ (total utility has risen from 11 to 13 utils), and $\Delta Q = 1$ (one more packet of crisps has been consumed). Thus $MU = 2$.

?? If Darren were to consume more and more crisps, would this total utility ever (a) fall to zero; (b) become negative? Explain.

The *ceteris paribus* assumption

The table and graph we have drawn are based on the assumption that other things do not change.

In practice, other things *do* change – and frequently. The utility that Darren gets from crisps depends on what else he eats. If on Saturday he has a lot to eat, and nibbles snacks (not crisps) between meals, he will get little satisfaction from crisps. If on Monday, however, he is too busy to eat proper meals, he would probably welcome one or more packets of crisps.

Each time the consumption of *other* goods changed – whether substitutes or complements – a new utility schedule would have to be drawn up. The curves would shift. Remember, utility is not a property of the goods themselves. Utility is in the mind of the consumer, and consumers change their minds. Their tastes change; their circumstances change; their consumption patterns change.

The optimum level of consumption: the simplest case – one commodity

Just how much of a good should people consume if they are to make the best use of their limited income? To answer this question we must tackle the problem of how to measure utility, given that in practice we cannot measure 'utils'.

One solution to the problem is to measure utility with money. In this case utility becomes the value that people

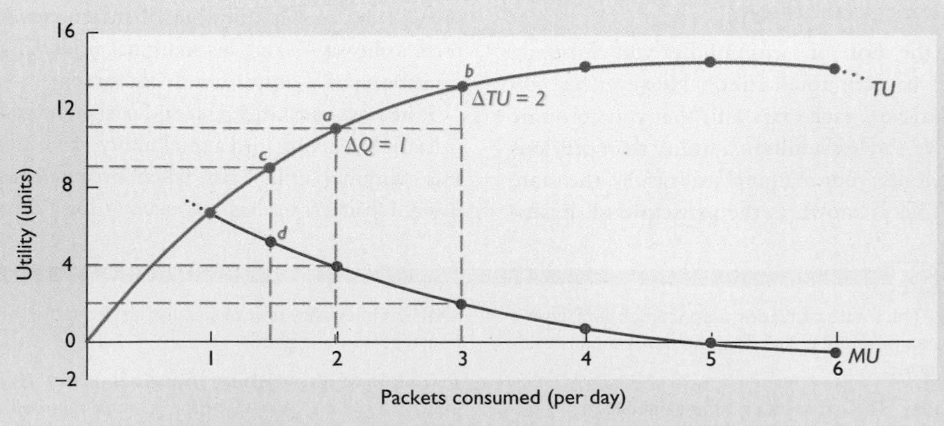

Figure 4.1 Darren's utility from consuming crisps (daily)

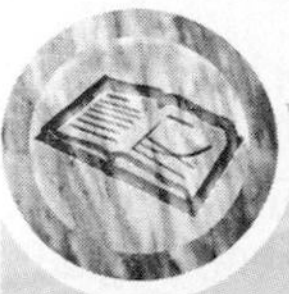

EXPLORING THE THEORY *BOX 4.1

USING CALCULUS TO DERIVE A MARGINAL UTILITY FUNCTION

The relationship between total utility and marginal utility can be shown using calculus. If you are not familiar with the rules of calculus, ignore this box!

A consumer's typical utility function for a good might be of the form:

$$TU = 60Q - 4Q^2$$

where Q is the quantity of the good consumed.

This would give the figures shown in the following table.

Q	$60Q$	$-4Q^2$	=	TU
1	60	− 4	=	56
2	120	− 16	=	104
3	180	− 36	=	144
4	240	− 64	=	176
.	.	.		.

?? Complete this table to the level of consumption at which TU is at a maximum.

Marginal utility is the first derivative of total utility. In other words, it is the rate of *change* of total utility. Differentiating the TU function gives:

$$MU = \frac{dTU}{dQ} = 60 - 8Q$$

This gives the figures shown in the following table.

Q	60	$-8Q$	=	MU
1	60	− 8	=	52
2	60	− 16	=	44
3	60	− 24	=	36
4	60	− 32	=	28
.	.	.		.

Note that the marginal utility diminishes.

The MU function we have derived is a straight-line function. If, however, the TU function had contained a cubed term (Q^3), the MU function would be a curve.

?? Derive the MU function from the following TU function:

$$TU = 200Q - 25Q^2 + Q^3$$

From this MU function, draw up a table (like the one above) up to the level of Q where MU becomes negative. Graph these figures.

place on their consumption. Marginal utility thus becomes the amount of money a person would be prepared to pay to obtain one more unit: in other words, what that extra unit is worth to that person. If Darren is prepared to pay 25p to obtain an extra packet of crisps, then we can say that packet yields him 25p worth of utility: $MU = 25p$.

So how many packets should he consume if he is to act rationally? To answer this we need to introduce the concept of **consumer surplus**.

Marginal consumer surplus

Marginal consumer surplus (MCS) is the difference between what you are willing to pay for one more unit of a good and what you are actually charged. If Darren were willing to pay 25p for another packet of crisps which in fact only cost him 20p, he would be getting a marginal consumer surplus of 5p.

$$MCS = MU - P$$

Total consumer surplus

Total consumer surplus (TCS) is the sum of all the marginal consumer surpluses that you have obtained from all the units of a good you have consumed. It is the difference between the total utility from all the units and your expenditure on them. If Darren consumes four packets of

DEFINITIONS

Consumer surplus The excess of what a person would have been prepared to pay for a good (i.e. the utility) over what that person actually pays.

Marginal consumer surplus The excess of utility from the consumption of one more unit of a good (MU) over the price paid: $MCS = MU - P$.

Total consumer surplus The excess of a person's total utility from the consumption of a good (TU) over the amount that person spends on it (TE): $TCS = TU - TE$.

crisps, and if he would have been prepared to spend £1.20 on them and only had to spend 80p, then his total consumer surplus is 40p.

$$TCS = TU - TE$$

where TE is the total expenditure on a good: i.e. $P \times Q$.

Let us define **rational consumer behaviour** as the attempt to maximise consumer surplus. How do people set about doing this?

People will go on purchasing additional units as long as they gain additional consumer surplus: in other words, as long as the price they are prepared to pay exceeds the price they are charged ($MU > P$). But as more units are purchased, so they will experience diminishing marginal utility. They will be prepared to pay less and less for each additional unit. Their marginal utility will go on falling until $MU = P$: i.e. until no further consumer surplus can be gained. At that point, they will stop purchasing additional units. Their optimum level of consumption has been reached: consumer surplus has been maximised. Were they to continue to purchase beyond this point, MU would be less than P, and thus they would be paying more for the last units than they were worth to them.

The process of maximising consumer surplus can be shown graphically. Let us take the case of Tina's annual purchases of petrol. Tina has her own car, but as an alternative she can use public transport or walk. To keep the analysis simple, let us assume that Tina's parents bought her the car and pay the licence duty, and that Tina does not have the option of selling the car. She does, however, have to buy the petrol. The current price is 70p per litre. Figure 4.2 shows her consumer surplus.

If she were to use just a few litres per year, she would use them for very important journeys for which no convenient alternative exists. For such trips she may be prepared to pay up to £1 per litre. For the first few litres, then, she is getting a marginal utility of around £1 per litre, and hence a marginal consumer surplus of around 30p (i.e. £1 – 70p).

By the time her annual purchase is around 250 litres, she would only be prepared to pay around 90p for additional litres. The additional journeys, although still important, would be less vital. Perhaps these are journeys where she could have taken public transport, albeit at some inconvenience. Her marginal consumer surplus at 250 litres is 20p (i.e. 90p – 70p).

Gradually, additional litres give less and less additional utility as less and less important journeys are undertaken. The 500th litre yields 81p worth of extra utility. Marginal consumer surplus is now 11p (i.e. 81p – 70p).

By the time she gets to the 900th litre, Tina's marginal utility has fallen to 70p. There is no additional consumer surplus to be gained. Her total consumer surplus is at a maximum. She thus buys 900 litres, where $P = MU$.

Her total consumer surplus is the sum of all the marginal consumer surpluses: the sum of all the 900 vertical lines between the price and the MU curve. This is represented by the total *area* between P and MU.

This analysis can be expressed in general terms. In Figure 4.3, if the price of a commodity is P_1, the consumer will consume Q_1. The person's total expenditure (TE) is P_1Q_1, shown by area 1. Total utility (TU) is the area under the marginal utility curve: i.e. areas 1 + 2. Total consumer surplus ($TU - TE$) is shown by area 2.

?? If a good were free, why would total consumer surplus equal total utility? What would be the level of marginal utility?

DEFINITION

Rational consumer behaviour The attempt to maximise total consumer surplus.

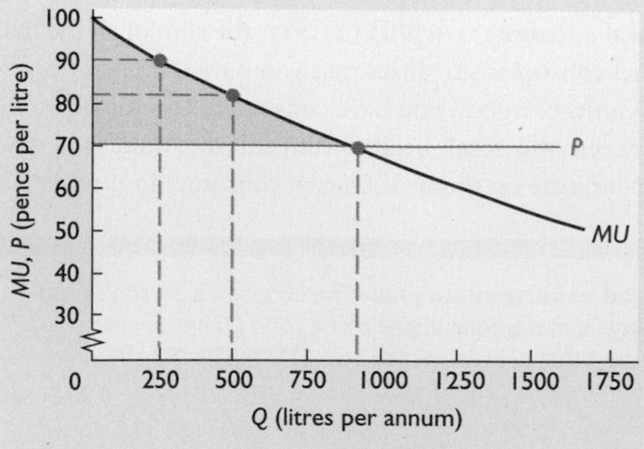

Figure 4.2 Tina's consumer surplus from petrol

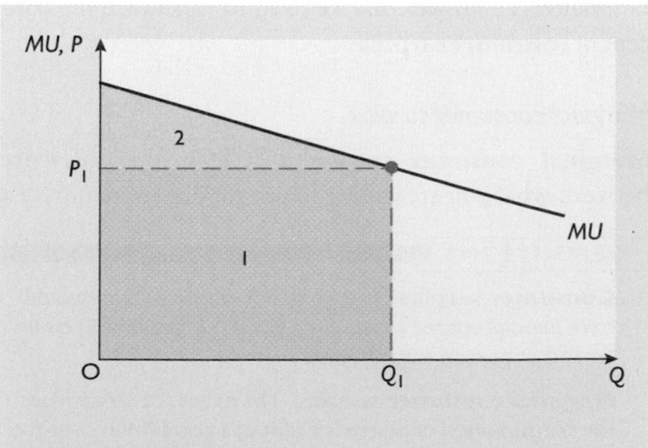

Figure 4.3 Consumer surplus

Marginal utility and the demand curve for a good

An individual's demand curve

Individual people's demand curve for any good will be the same as their marginal utility curve for that good, measured in money.

This is demonstrated in Figure 4.4, which shows the marginal utility curve for a particular person and a particular good. If the price of the good were P_1, the person would consume Q_1: where $MU = P$. Thus point *a* would be one point on that person's demand curve. If the price fell to P_2, consumption would rise to Q_2, since this is where $MU = P_2$. Thus point *b* is a second point on the demand curve. Likewise if price fell to P_3, Q_3 would be consumed. Point *c* is a third point on the demand curve.

Thus as long as individuals seek to maximise consumer surplus and hence consume where $P = MU$, their demand curve will be along the same line as their marginal utility curve.

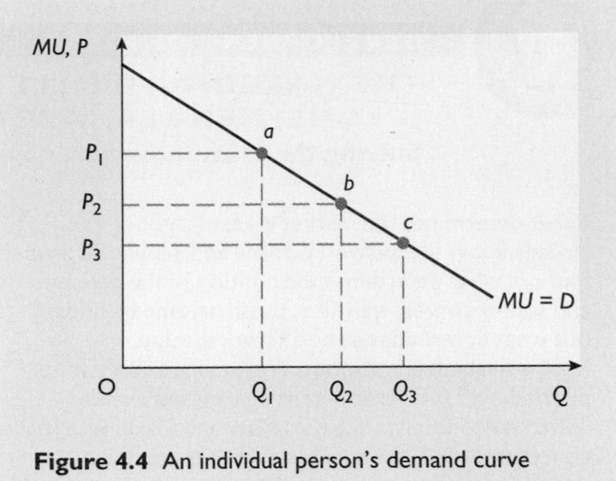

Figure 4.4 An individual person's demand curve

The market demand curve

The market demand curve will simply be the (horizontal) sum of all individuals' demand curves and hence *MU* curves.

The shape of the demand curve. The price elasticity of demand will reflect the rate at which *MU* diminishes. If there are close substitutes for a good, it is likely to have an elastic demand, and its *MU* will diminish slowly as consumption increases. The reason is that increased consumption of this product will be accompanied by *decreased* consumption of the alternative product(s). Since total consumption of this product *plus* the alternatives has increased only slightly (if at all), the marginal utility will fall only slowly.

For example, the demand for a given brand of petrol is likely to have a fairly high price elasticity, since other brands are substitutes. If there is a cut in the price of Texaco petrol (assuming the prices of other brands stay constant), consumption of Texaco will increase a lot. The *MU* of Texaco petrol will fall slowly, since people consume less of other brands. Petrol consumption *in total* may be only slightly greater, and hence the *MU* of petrol only slightly lower.

> **??** Why do we get less consumer surplus from goods where our demand is relatively elastic?

Shifts in the demand curve. How do *shifts* in demand relate to marginal utility? For example, how would the marginal utility of (and hence demand for) margarine be affected by a rise in the price of butter? The higher price of butter would cause less butter to be consumed. This would increase the marginal utility of margarine, since if people are using less butter, their desire for margarine is higher. The *MU* curve (and hence the demand curve) for margarine thus shifts to the right.

> **??** How would marginal utility and market demand be affected by a rise in the price of a complementary good?

Weaknesses of the one-commodity version of marginal utility theory

A change in the consumption of one good will affect the marginal utility of substitute and complementary goods. It will also affect the amount of income left over to be spent on other goods. Thus a more satisfactory explanation of demand would involve an analysis of choices between goods, rather than looking at one good in isolation.

What is more, deriving a demand curve from a marginal utility curve measured in money assumes that money itself has a constant marginal utility. The trouble is that it does not. If people have a rise in income, they will consume more. Other things being equal, the marginal utility of the goods that they consume will diminish. Thus an extra £1 of consumption will bring less satisfaction than previously. In other words, it is likely that the *marginal utility of money diminishes as income rises.*

Unless a good occupies only a tiny fraction of people's expenditure, a fall in its price will mean that their real income has increased: i.e. they can afford to purchase more goods in general. As they do so, the marginal utility of their money will fall. We cannot, therefore, legitimately use money to measure utility in an absolute sense. We can, however, still talk about the relative utility that we get from various goods for a given increase in expenditure.

The following sections thus look at the choice between goods, and how it relates to marginal utility.

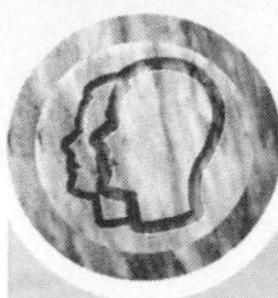

DEVELOPMENT OF IDEAS BOX 4.2

THE MARGINAL UTILITY REVOLUTION: JEVONS, MENGER, WALRAS

Solving the diamonds–water paradox

What determines the market value of a good? We already know the answer: demand and supply. So if we find out what determines the position of the demand and supply curves, we will at the same time be finding out what determines a good's market value.

This might seem obvious. Yet for years economists puzzled over just what determines a good's value.

Some economists like Karl Marx and David Ricardo concentrated on the supply side. For them, value depended on the amount of resources used in producing a good. This could be further reduced to the amount of *labour* time embodied in the good. Thus, according to the *labour theory of value*, the more labour that was directly involved in producing the good, or indirectly in producing the capital equipment used to make the good, the more valuable would the good be.

Other economists looked at the demand side. But here they came across a paradox.

Adam Smith in the 1760s gave the example of water and diamonds. 'How is it', he asked, 'that water which is so essential to human life, and thus has such a high "value-in-use", has such a low market value (or "value-in-exchange")? And how is it that diamonds which are relatively so trivial have such a high market value?' The answer to this paradox had to wait over a hundred years until the marginal utility revolution of the 1870s. William Stanley Jevons (1835–82) in England, Carl Menger (1840–1921) in Austria, and Leon Walras (1834–1910) in Switzerland all independently claimed that the source of the market value of a good was its *marginal* utility, not its *total* utility.

This was the solution to the diamonds–water paradox. Water, being so essential, has a high total utility: a high 'value in use'. But for most of us, given that we consume so much already, it has a very low marginal utility. Do you leave the cold tap running when you clean your teeth? If you do, it shows just how trivial water is to you *at the margin*. Diamonds, on the other hand, although they have a much lower total utility, have a much higher marginal utility. There are so few diamonds in the world, and thus people have so few of them, that they are very valuable at the margin. If, however, a new technique were to be discovered of producing diamonds cheaply from coal, their market value would fall rapidly. As people had more of them, so their marginal utility would rapidly diminish.

Marginal utility still only gives the demand side of the story. The reason why the marginal utility of water is so low is that *supply* is so plentiful. Water is very expensive in Saudi Arabia! In other words, the full explanation of value must take into account both demand *and* supply.

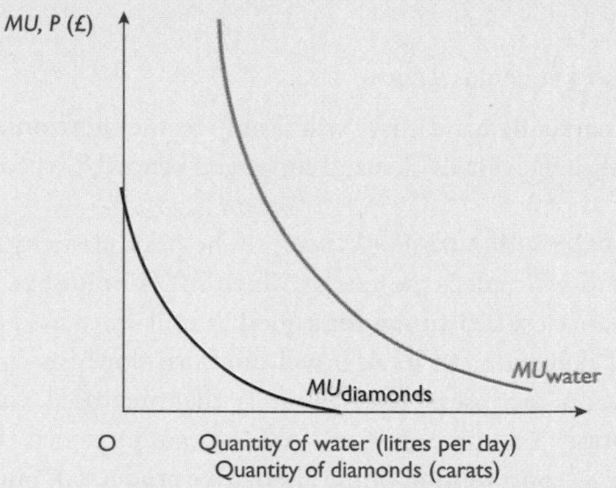

?? The diagram illustrates a person's *MU* curves of water and diamonds. Assume that diamonds are more expensive than water. Show how the *MU* of diamonds will be greater than the *MU* of water. Show also how the *TU* of diamonds will be less than the *TU* of water. (Remember: *TU* is the area under the *MU* curve.)

The optimum combination of goods consumed

We can use marginal utility analysis to show how a rational person decides what combination of goods to buy. Given that we have limited incomes, we have to make choices. It is not just a question of choosing between two obvious substitutes (like carrots and peas or a holiday in Greece and one in Spain), but about allocating our incomes between all the goods and services we might like to consume. If you have, say, an income of £10 000 per year, what is the optimum 'bundle' of goods and services for you to spend it on?

The rule for rational consumer behaviour is known as the **equi-marginal principle**. This states that a consumer will get the highest utility from a given level of income

DEFINITION

Equi-marginal principle Consumers will maximise total utility from their incomes by consuming that combination of goods where:

$$\frac{MU_a}{P_a} = \frac{MU_b}{P_b} = \frac{MU_c}{P_c} \cdots = \frac{MU_n}{P_n}$$

when the utility from the last £1 spent on each good is the same. Algebraically, this is when:

$$\frac{MU_a}{P_a} = \frac{MU_b}{P_b} = \frac{MU_c}{P_c} \ldots = \frac{MU_n}{P_n} \qquad (1)$$

where a, b, c . . . n are the various goods consumed.

All we are describing here is the way in which consumers will achieve the best 'value for money' from their purchases. To explain this consider the following.

What would you do if champagne gave you twice as much satisfaction as sparkling white wine, but cost five times as much? You would buy the sparkling white wine: it would give you better value for money. What would you do if steak cost twice as much as minced beef, but gave you three times as much satisfaction? You would buy the steak. This time the more expensive item gives you better value for money.

What we are doing in each case is comparing the relative marginal utilities of the two items with their relative prices. In the case of steak and mince, when we say that steak gives three times the satisfaction of mince, we are in fact saying:

$$\frac{MU_{steak}}{MU_{mince}} = \frac{3}{1}$$

And when we say that steak costs twice as much as mince we are saying:

$$\frac{P_{steak}}{P_{mince}} = \frac{2}{1}$$

We can generalise from this to any pair of goods a and b that you buy. If:

$$\frac{MU_a}{MU_b} > \frac{P_a}{P_b}$$

you will increase your purchase of good a relative to those of good b. But as you buy more of good a, according to the principle of diminishing marginal utility, the marginal utility of good a (MU_a) will fall. Likewise as you buy less of good b, MU_b will rise. You will stop adjusting the balance of your purchases of goods a and b when the marginal utility ratios are the same as the price ratios: when

$$\frac{MU_a}{MU_b} = \frac{P_a}{P_b}$$

At this point your total utility will be maximised for any given amount of income spent on the two goods.

Another way of looking at the choice between two goods is to compare the ratios of their marginal utility to price (MU/P). If:

$$\frac{MU_a}{P_a} > \frac{MU_b}{P_b}$$

you would consume more a relative to b. This is because you would be getting a greater satisfaction per £1 spent on extra units of good a than you would per £1 spent on good b. In other words, good a would give you better 'value for money' than good b. You would thus buy more a and less b. But as you switched from b to a, the marginal utility of a would fall due to diminishing marginal utility, and conversely the marginal utility of b would rise, until:

$$\frac{MU_a}{P_a} = \frac{MU_b}{P_b}$$

At this point no further gain can be made by switching from one good to the other. This is the optimum combination of goods to consume.

The argument can be extended to any number of goods – a, b, c, d, e, etc. As long as the marginal utility relative to the price of any one good is greater than another, more of it will be consumed. Its marginal utility will fall until:

$$\frac{MU_a}{P_a} = \frac{MU_b}{P_b} = \frac{MU_c}{P_c} \ldots = \frac{MU_n}{P_n}$$

This is the equi-marginal principle given in equation (1) on this page.

The multi-commodity version of marginal utility and the demand curve

How can we derive a demand curve from the above analysis?

For a given income, and given prices of good a and all other goods, the quantity a person will demand of good a will be that which satisfies equation (1). One point on the individual's demand curve for good a is thus determined.

If the price of a good fell, such that:

$$\frac{MU_a}{P_a} > \frac{MU_{b,\,c,\,d,\,etc.}}{P_{b,\,c,\,d,\,etc.}}$$

expenditure would be switched to good a until equation (1) was once more satisfied. A second point has thus been derived.

Further changes in the price of good a would bring further changes in the quantity demanded, in order to satisfy equation (1). Further points on the individual's demand curve would thereby be derived.

If the price of *another* good changed, or if the marginal utility of any good changed (including good a), then again the quantity demanded of good a (and other goods) would change, until again equation (1) were satisfied. These changes in demand will be represented by a shift in the demand for good a.

ISSUES AND APPLICATIONS BOX 4.3

TAKING ACCOUNT OF TIME
Can I spare the time to enjoy myself?

Do you take a taxi or go by bus? How long do you spend soaking in the bath? Do you go to the bother of cooking a meal or will you get a take-away?

We have argued that such decisions, if they are to be rational, should involve weighing up the relative marginal utilities of these activities against their relative marginal costs.

One crucial dimension we have ignored up to now is the *time* dimension. One of the opportunity costs of doing any activity is the sacrifice of time.

A take-away meal may be more expensive than a home-cooked one, but it saves you time. Part of the cost of the home-cooked meal, therefore, is the sacrifice of time involved. The full cost is therefore not just the cost of the ingredients and the fuel used, but also the opportunity cost of the alternative activities you have sacrificed while you were cooking.

Given the high-pressured lives many people lead in affluent countries, a high value is often put on time saved. Fast-food restaurants and supersonic jet travel are symptoms of this lifestyle.

Even pleasurable activities involve a time cost. The longer you spend doing pleasurable activity 'a', the less time you will have for doing pleasurable activity 'b'. The longer you laze in the bath, the less TV will you be able to watch (unless you have a TV in the bathroom!).

Demand under conditions of uncertainty

So far we have assumed that when people buy goods and services they know exactly what price they will pay and how much utility they will gain. In many cases this is a reasonable assumption. When you buy a bar of chocolate you clearly do know how much you are paying for it and have a very good idea how much you will like it. But what about a video recorder, or a car, or a washing machine, or any other **consumer durable**? In each of these cases you are buying something that will last you a long time, and the further into the future you look, the less certain you will be of its costs and benefits to you.

Take the case of a washing machine costing you £400. If you pay cash, your immediate outlay involves no uncertainty: it is £400. But washing machines can break down. In two years' time you could find yourself with a repair bill of £100. This cannot be predicted and yet it is a price you will have to pay, just like the original £400. In other words, when you buy the washing machine you are uncertain as to the full 'price' it will entail over its lifetime.

If the costs of the washing machine are uncertain, so too are the benefits. You might have been attracted to buy it in the first place by the manufacturer's glossy brochure, or by the look of it, or by adverts on TV, in magazines, etc. When you have used it for a while, however, you will probably discover things you had not anticipated. The spin dryer does not get your clothes as dry as you had hoped; it is noisy; it leaks; the door sticks; and so on.

Buying consumer durables thus involves uncertainty. So too does the purchase of assets, whether a physical asset such as a house or financial assets such as shares. In the case of assets the uncertainty is over their future *price*. If you buy shares in a recently privatised industry, what will happen to their price? Will they shoot up in price, thus enabling you to sell them at a large profit, or will they fall? You cannot know for certain.

So how will uncertainty affect people's behaviour? The answer is that it depends on their attitudes towards taking a gamble. To examine these attitudes let us assume that a person does at least know the *odds* of the gamble. In other words, the person is operating under conditions of *risk* rather than *uncertainty*.

?? Define 'risk' and 'uncertainty' (see pages 76–8).

To illustrate different attitudes towards risk, consider the case of gambling that a particular number will come up on the throw of a dice. There is a one in six chance of this happening. Would you gamble? It depends on what odds you were offered and on your attitude to risk.

Odds can be of three types. They can be *favourable* odds. This is where on average you will gain. If, for example, you were offered odds of 10 to 1 on the throw of a dice, then for a £1 bet you would get nothing if you lost, but you would get £10 if your number came up. Since your number should come up on average one time in every six, on average you will gain. The longer you go on playing, the more money you are likely to win. If the odds were 6 to 1, they would be *fair* odds. On average you

DEFINITION

Consumer durable A consumer good that lasts a period of time, during which the consumer can continue gaining utility from it.

would break even. If, however, they were less than 6 to 1, they would be described as *unfavourable*. On average you would lose.

?? Give some examples of gambling (or risk taking in general) where the odds are (a) unfavourable; (b) fair; (c) favourable.

There are three possible categories of attitude toward risk.

Risk neutral. This is where a person will take a gamble if the odds are favourable; not take a gamble if the odds are unfavourable; and be indifferent about taking a gamble if the odds are fair.

Risk loving. This is where a person is prepared to take a gamble even if the odds are unfavourable. The more risk loving a person is, the worse the odds he or she will be prepared to accept.

Risk averse. This is where a person may not be prepared to take a gamble even if the odds are favourable. The more risk averse the person is, the better would have to be the odds before he or she could be enticed to take a gamble. Few people are *totally risk averse* and thus totally unwilling to take a gamble. If I offered people a bet on the toss of a coin such that tails they pay me 10p and heads I pay them £100, few would refuse (unless on moral grounds).

Diminishing marginal utility of income and attitudes towards risk taking

Avid gamblers may be risk lovers. People who spend hours in the betting shop or at the race track may enjoy the risks, knowing that there is always the chance that they might win. On average, however, such people will lose. After all, the bookies have to take their cut and thus the odds are generally unfavourable.

Most people, however, for most of the time are risk averters. We prefer to avoid insecurity. But why? Is there a simple reason for this? Economists use marginal utility analysis to explain why.

They argue that the gain in utility to people from an extra £100 is less than the loss of utility from forgoing £100. Imagine your own position. You have probably adjusted your standard of living to your income (or are trying to!). If you unexpectedly gained £100, that would be very nice: you could buy some new clothes or have a weekend away. But if you lost £100, it could be very hard indeed. You might have very serious difficulties in making ends meet. Thus if you were offered the gamble of a 50:50 chance of winning or losing £100, you would probably decline the gamble.

?? Which gamble would you be more likely to accept, a 60:40 chance of gaining or losing £10 000, or a 40:60 chance of gaining or losing £1? Explain why.

This risk-averting behaviour accords with the principle of *diminishing marginal utility*. Up to now in this chapter we have been focusing on the utility from the consumption of individual goods: Tracey and her cups of tea; Darren and his packets of crisps. In the case of each individual good, the more we consume, the less satisfaction we gain from each additional unit: the marginal utility falls. But the same principle applies if we look at our *total* consumption. The higher our level of total consumption, the less additional satisfaction will be gained from each additional £1 spent. What we are saying here is that there is a **diminishing marginal utility of income**. The more you earn, the lower will be the utility from each *extra* £1. If people on low incomes earn an extra £100, they will feel a lot better off: the marginal utility they will get from that income will be very high. If rich people earn an extra £100, however, their gain in utility will be less.

?? Do you think that this provides a moral argument for redistributing income from the rich to the poor? Does it prove that income should be so redistributed?

Why, then, does a diminishing marginal utility of income make us risk averters? The answer is illustrated in Figure 4.5, which shows the *total* utility you get from your income.

The slope of this curve gives the *marginal* utility of your income. As the marginal utility of income diminishes, so the curve gets flatter. A rise in income from £5000 to £10 000 will cause a movement along the curve from point *a* to point *b*. Total utility rises from U_1 to U_2. A similar rise in income from £10 000 to £15 000, however, will lead to a move from point *b* to point *c*, and hence a *smaller* rise in total utility from U_2 to U_3.

Now assume that your income is £10 000 and you are offered a chance of gambling £5000 of it. You are offered the fair odds of a 50:50 chance of gaining an extra £5000 (i.e. doubling it) or losing it. Effectively, then, you have an

DEFINITION

Diminishing marginal utility of income Where each additional pound earned yields less additional utility.

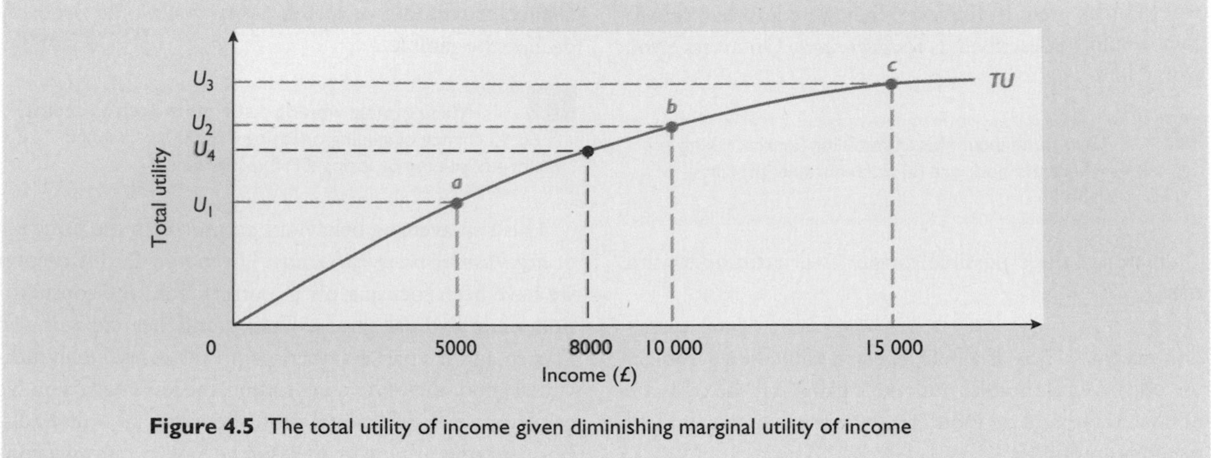

Figure 4.5 The total utility of income given diminishing marginal utility of income

equal chance of your income rising to £15 000 or falling to £5000.

At an income of £10 000, your total utility is U_2. If your gamble pays off and as a result your income rises to £15 000, your total utility will rise to U_3. If it does not pay off, you will be left with only £5000 and a utility of U_1. Given that you have a 50:50 chance of winning, your *average* expected utility will be midway between U_1 and U_3 (i.e. $\frac{(U_1 + U_3)}{2}$) = U_4. But this is the utility that would be gained from an income of £8000. Given that you would prefer U_2 to U_4 you will choose not to take the gamble.

Thus risk aversion is part of rational utility-maximising behaviour.

?? If people are generally risk averse, why do so many around the world take part in national lotteries?

On most occasions we will not know the odds of taking a gamble. In other words, we will be operating under conditions of *uncertainty*. This could make us very cautious indeed. The more pessimistic we are, the more cautious we will be.

Insurance: a way of removing risks

Insurance is the opposite of gambling. It takes the risk away. If, for example, you risk losing your job if you are injured, you can remove the risk of loss of income by taking out an appropriate insurance policy.

Given that people are risk averters, they will be prepared to pay the premiums even though they give them 'unfair odds'. The total premiums paid to insurance companies will be *more* than the amount the insurance companies pay out: that is how the companies make a profit.

But does this mean that the insurance companies are less risk averse than their customers? Why is it that the insurance companies are prepared to shoulder the risks that their customers were not? The answer is that the insurance company is able to **spread its risks**.

The spreading of risks

If there is a one in a hundred chance of your house burning down each year, although it is only a small chance it would be so disastrous that you are simply not prepared to take the risk. You thus take out house insurance and are prepared to pay a premium of *more than* 1 per cent (one in a hundred).

The insurance company, however, is not just insuring you. It is insuring thousands of others at the same time. If your house burns down, there will be approximately 99 others that do not. The premiums the insurance company has collected will be more than enough to cover its payments. The more houses it insures, the smaller will be the variation in the proportion that actually burn down each year.

This is an application of the **law of large numbers**. What is unpredictable for an individual becomes highly pre-

DEFINITIONS

Spreading risks (for an insurance company) The more policies an insurance company issues and the more independent the risks of claims from these policies are, the more predictable will be the number of claims.

Law of large numbers The larger the number of events of a particular type, the more predictable will be their average outcome.

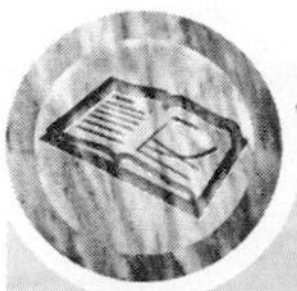

EXPLORING THE THEORY — BOX 4.4

PROBLEMS FOR UNWARY INSURANCE COMPANIES

'Adverse selection' and 'moral hazard'

Adverse selection

This is where the people taking out insurance are those who have the highest risk.

For example, suppose that a company offers medical insurance. It surveys the population and works out that the average person requires £200 of treatment per year. The company thus sets the premium at £250 (the extra £50 to cover its costs and provide a profit). But it is likely that the people most likely to take out the insurance are those most likely to fall sick: those who have been ill before, those whose families have a history of illness, those in jobs that are hazardous to health, etc. These people on average may require £500 of treatment per year. The insurance company would soon make a loss.

But cannot the company then simply raise premiums to £550 or £600? It can, but the problem is that it will thereby be depriving the person of *average* health of reasonably priced insurance.

The answer is for the company to discriminate more carefully between people. You may have to fill out a questionnaire so that the company can assess your own particular risk and set an appropriate premium. There may need to be legal penalties for people caught lying!

?? What details does an insurance company require to know before it will insure a person to drive a car?

Moral hazard

This is where having insurance makes you less careful and thus increases your risk to the company. For example, if your bicycle is insured against theft, you may be less concerned to go through the hassle of chaining it up each time you leave it.

Again, if insurance companies work out risks by looking at the *total* number of bicycle thefts, these figures will understate the risks to the company because they will include thefts from *uninsured* people who are likely to be more careful.

?? How will the following reduce moral hazard?

(a) A no-claims bonus.
(b) The company only being prepared to insure an item for part of its value.
(c) You having to pay the first so many pounds of any claim.
(d) Offering lower premiums to those less likely to claim (e.g. lower house contents premiums for those with burglar alarms).

dictable in the mass. The more people the insurance company insures, the more predictable is the total outcome.

What is more, the insurance company will be in a position to estimate just what the risks are. It can thus work out what premiums it must charge in order to make a profit. With individuals, however, the precise risk is rarely known. Do you know your chances of living to 70? Almost certainly you do not. But a life assurance company will know precisely the chances of a person of your age, sex and occupation living to 70! It will have the statistical data to show this. In other words, an insurance company will be able to convert your *uncertainty* into their *risk*.

The spreading of risks does not just require that there should be a large number of policies. It also requires that the risks should be **independent**. If an insurance company insured 1000 houses *all in the same neighbourhood*, and then there were a major fire in the area, the claims would be enormous. The risks of fire were not independent. The company would, in fact, have been taking a gamble on a single event. If, however, it provides fire insurance for houses scattered all over the country, the risks *are* independent.

??

1. Why are insurance companies unwilling to provide insurance against losses arising from war or 'civil insurrection'?
2. Name some other events where it would be impossible to obtain insurance.

Another way in which insurance companies can spread their risks is by **diversification**. The more types of insurance a company offers (car, house, life, health, etc.), the greater is likely to be the independence of the risks.

DEFINITIONS

Independent risks Where two risky events are unconnected. The occurrence of one will not affect the likelihood of the occurrence of the other.

Diversification Where a firm expands into new types of business.

SECTION SUMMARY

1. The satisfaction people get from consuming a good is called 'utility'. Total utility is the satisfaction gained from the total consumption of a particular good over a given period of time. Marginal utility is the *extra* satisfaction gained from consuming *one more* unit of the good.
2. The marginal utility tends to fall the more that people consume. This is known as the 'principle of diminishing marginal utility'.
3. The utility that people get from consuming a good will depend on the amount of other goods they consume. A change in the amount of other goods consumed, whether substitutes or complements, will shift the total and marginal utility curves.
4. 'Rational' consumers will attempt to maximise their consumer surplus. Consumer surplus is the excess of people's utility (measured in money terms) over their expenditure on the good. This will be maximised by purchasing at the point where the *MU* of a good is equal to its price.
5. In the simple case where the price and consumption of other goods is held constant, a person's *MU* curve will lie along the same line as that person's demand curve.
6. The market demand curve is merely the horizontal sum of the demand curves of all the individual consumers. The elasticity of the market demand curve will depend on the rate at which marginal utility diminishes as more is consumed. This in turn depends on the number and closeness of substitute goods. If there are close substitutes, people will readily switch to this good if its price falls, and thus marginal utility will fall only slowly. The demand will be elastic.
7. Measuring the marginal utility of a good in money avoids the problem of using some imaginary unit such as utils, but it assumes that money has a constant utility. In reality, the marginal utility of money is likely to decrease as income rises.
8. A more satisfactory way of analysing the demand for goods is to look at people's choices *between* goods. A consumer will maximise utility from a given income by consuming according to the 'equi-marginal principle'. This states that goods should be consumed in that combination which equates the *MU/P* ratio for each good.
9. When people buy consumer durables they may be uncertain of their benefits and any additional repair and maintenance costs. When they buy financial assets they may be uncertain of what will happen to their price in the future. Buying under these conditions of imperfect knowledge is therefore a form of gambling. When we take such gambles, if we know the odds we are said to be operating under conditions of *risk*. If we do not know the odds, we are said to be operating under conditions of *uncertainty*.
10. People can be divided into risk lovers, risk averters and those who are risk neutral. Because of the diminishing marginal utility of income, it is rational for people to be risk averters (unless gambling is itself pleasurable).
11. Insurance is a way of eliminating risks for policy holders. Being risk averters, people are prepared to pay premiums in order to obtain insurance. Insurance companies, on the other hand, are prepared to take on these risks because they can spread them over a large number of policies. According to the law of large numbers, what is unpredictable for a single policy holder becomes highly predictable for a large number of them provided that their risks are independent of each other.

*4.2 Indifference analysis

The limitations of the marginal utility approach to demand

Even though the multi-commodity version of marginal utility theory is useful in demonstrating the underlying logic of consumer choice, it still has a major weakness. Utility cannot be measured in any absolute sense. We cannot really say, therefore, by *how much* the marginal utility of one good exceeds another.

An alternative approach is to use *indifference analysis*. This does not involve measuring the *amount* of utility a person gains, but merely *ranking* various combinations of goods in order of preference. In other words, it assumes that consumers can decide whether they prefer one combination of goods to another. For example, if you were asked to choose between two baskets of fruit, one containing 4 oranges and 3 pears and the other containing 2 oranges and 5 pears, you could say which you prefer or whether you are indifferent between them. It does not assume that you can decide just *how much* you prefer one basket to another or just how much you like either.

The aim of indifference analysis, then, is to analyse, *without having to measure utility*, how a rational consumer chooses between two goods. As we shall see, it can be used to show the effect on this choice of (a) a change in the consumer's income and (b) a change in the price of one or both goods. It can also be used to analyse the income and substitution effects of a change in price.

Indifference analysis involves the use of *indifference curves* and *budget lines*.

Indifference curves

A single indifference curve

An **indifference curve** shows all the various combinations of two goods that give an equal amount of satisfaction or utility to a consumer.

To show how one can be constructed, consider the following example. Imagine that a supermarket is conducting a survey about the preferences of its customers for different types of fruit. One of the respondents is Clive, a student who likes a healthy diet and is a regular purchaser of fresh fruit. He is asked his preferences for various combinations of oranges and pears, and asked merely to state which he prefers or whether he is indifferent between them. Starting with the combination of 10 pears and 13 oranges, he is asked to compare this combination with others. Some combinations (such as 12 pears and 15 oranges) he prefers. Others (such as 5 pears and 6 oranges) he likes less than the original combination. Others still (such as 20 pears and 8 oranges) he says he likes the same amount as the original combination. From this is constructed a set of combinations which he likes as much as, but not more than, each other. This is shown in Table 4.2.

Table 4.2 Combinations of pears and oranges that Clive likes the same amount as 10 pears and 13 oranges

Pears	Oranges	Point in Figure 4.6
30	6	*a*
24	7	*b*
20	8	*c*
14	10	*d*
10	13	*e*
8	15	*f*
6	20	*g*

This table is known as an **indifference set**. It shows alternative combinations of two goods that yield the same level of satisfaction. From this we can plot an indifference curve. We measure units of one good on one axis and units of the other good on the other axis. Thus in Figure 4.6, which is based on Table 4.2, pears and oranges are measured on the two axes. The curve shows that Clive is indifferent as to whether he consumes 30 pears and 6 oranges (point *a*) or 24 pears and 7 oranges (point *b*) or any other combination of pears and oranges along the curve.

Notice that we are not saying *how much* Clive likes pears and oranges, merely that he likes all the combinations along the indifference curve the same amount. All the combinations thus yield the same (unspecified) utility.

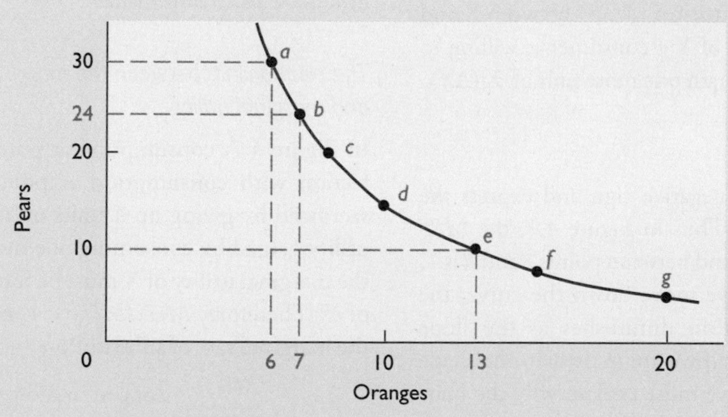

Figure 4.6 An indifference curve

DEFINITIONS

Indifference curve A line showing all those combinations of two goods between which a consumer is indifferent: i.e. those combinations that give the same level of utility.

Indifference set A table showing the same information as an indifference curve.

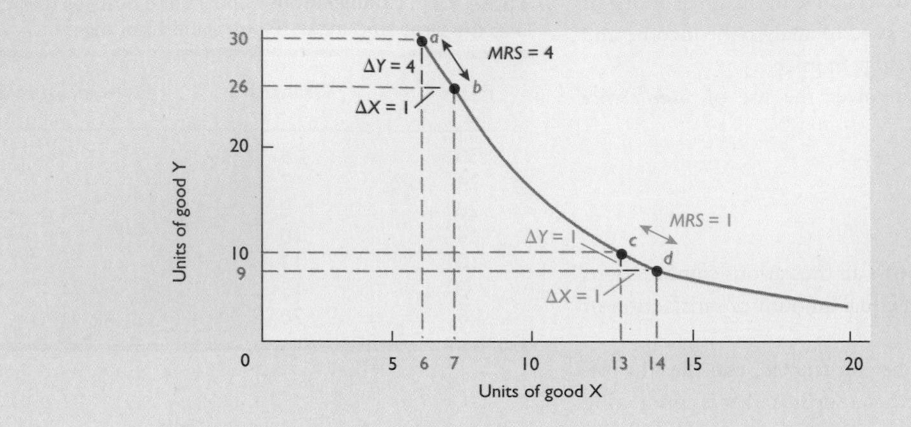

Figure 4.7 Deriving the marginal rate of substitution from an indifference curve

The shape of the indifference curve

As you can see, the indifference curve we have drawn is not a straight line. It is bowed in towards the origin. In other words, its slope gets shallower as we move down the curve. Indifference curves are normally drawn this shape. But why?

To explain the shape of the curve, consider Figure 4.7. It shows an individual's indifference curve for two goods, X and Y.

The slope of the indifference curve is equal to $\Delta Y/\Delta X$. For example, between points *a* and *b*, $\Delta Y = -4$ and $\Delta X = 1$. Thus the slope of the curve between *a* and *b* is $-4/1 = -4$.

Another name for the slope of an indifference curve is the **marginal rate of substitution** (*MRS*) between X and Y. This shows the amount of Y a consumer is willing to give up (ΔY), in order to obtain one more unit of X (ΔX).

$$MRS = \frac{\Delta Y}{\Delta X}$$

(Note that we ignore the negative sign and express the *MRS* as a positive figure.) Thus in Figure 4.7, the *MRS* between points *a* and *b* is 4 and between points *c* and *d* is 1.

It can be seen that, as we move down the curve, the marginal rate of substitution diminishes as the slope of the curve gets less. Thus if we are to explain the shape of the indifference curve, we must explain why the marginal rate of substitution diminishes.

The reason for a **diminishing marginal rate of substitution** is related to the *principle of diminishing marginal utility* that we looked at in section 4.1. This stated that individuals will gain less and less additional satisfaction the more of a good that they consume. This principle, however, is based on the assumption that the consumption of other goods is held *constant*. In the case of an indifference curve this is not true. As we move down the curve, more X is consumed but *less* Y is consumed. Nevertheless the effect on consumer satisfaction is similar. As more X and less Y are consumed, the marginal utility of X will diminish and that of Y will increase. Consumers will thus be prepared to give up less and less Y for each additional unit of X. *MRS* diminishes.

The relationship between the marginal rate of substitution and marginal utility

In Figure 4.7, consumption at point *a* yields equal satisfaction with consumption at point *b*. Thus the utility sacrificed by giving up 4 units of Y must be equal to the utility gained by consuming one more X. In other words, the marginal utility of X must be four times as great as that of Y. Therefore, $MU_X/MU_Y = 4$. But this is the same as the marginal rate of substitution:

$$MRS = \frac{MU_X}{MU_Y} = \text{slope of indifference curve (ignoring negative sign)}$$

DEFINITIONS

Marginal rate of substitution (between two goods in consumption) The amount of one good (Y) that a consumer is prepared to give up in order to obtain one extra unit of another good (X): i.e. $\Delta Y/\Delta X$.

Diminishing marginal rate of substitution The more a person consumes of good X and the less of good Y, the less additional Y will that person be prepared to give up in order to obtain an extra unit of X: i.e. $\Delta Y/\Delta X$ diminishes.

??

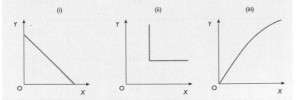

Although indifference curves will normally be bowed in towards the origin, on odd occasions they might not be. Which of the following diagrams correspond to which of the following?

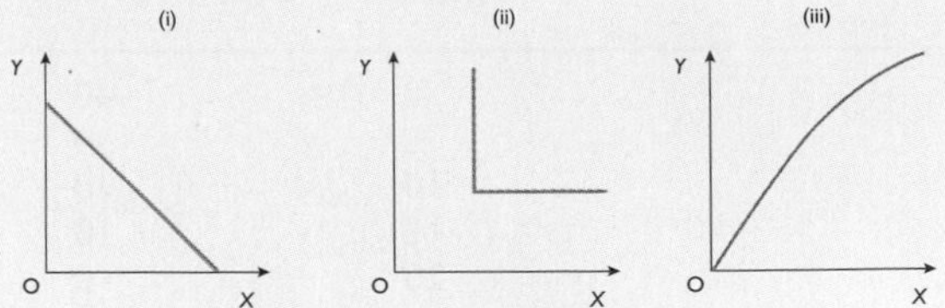

(a) X and Y are left shoes and right shoes.
(b) X and Y are two brands of the same product, and the consumer cannot tell them apart.
(c) X is a good but Y is a 'bad' – like household refuse.

An indifference map

More than one indifference curve can be drawn. For example, referring back to Table 4.2, Clive could give another set of combinations of pears and oranges that all give him a higher (but equal) level of utility than the set shown in the table. This could then be plotted in Figure 4.6 as another indifference curve.

Although the actual amount of utility corresponding to each curve is not specified, indifference curves further out to the right would show combinations of the two goods that yield a higher utility, and curves further in to the left would show combinations yielding a lower utility.

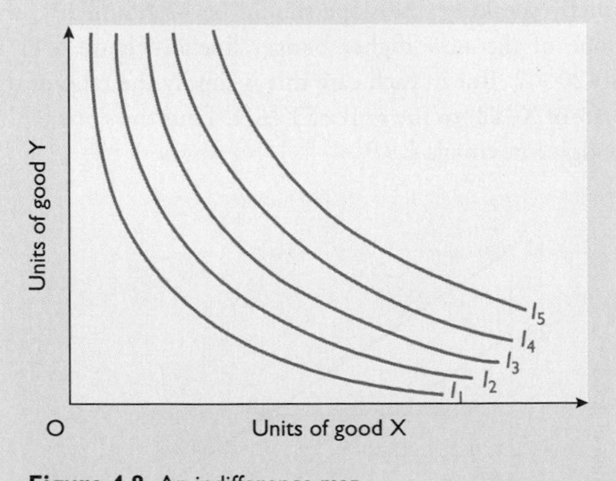

Figure 4.8 An indifference map

In fact, a whole **indifference map** can be drawn, with each successive indifference curve showing a higher level of utility. Combinations of goods along I_2 in Figure 4.8 give a higher utility to the consumer than those along I_1. Those along I_3 give a higher utility than those along I_2, and so on. The term 'map' is appropriate here, because the indifference curves are rather like contours on a real map. Just as a contour joins all those points of a particular height, so an indifference curve shows all those combinations yielding a particular level of utility.

??

1. Draw another two indifference curves on Figure 4.6, one outward from and one inward from the original curve. Read off various combinations of pears and oranges along these two new curves and enter them on a table like Table 4.2.
2. By referring to Figure 4.9 and the three points *a*, *b* and *c* on the two curves illustrated, explain why it would be logically impossible for two indifference curves to cross.

The budget line

We turn now to the **budget line**. This is the other important element in the analysis of consumer behaviour. Whereas indifference maps illustrate people's preferences, the *actual* choices they make will depend on their *incomes*. The budget line shows what combinations of two goods you are *able* to buy, given (a) your income available to spend on them and (b) their prices.

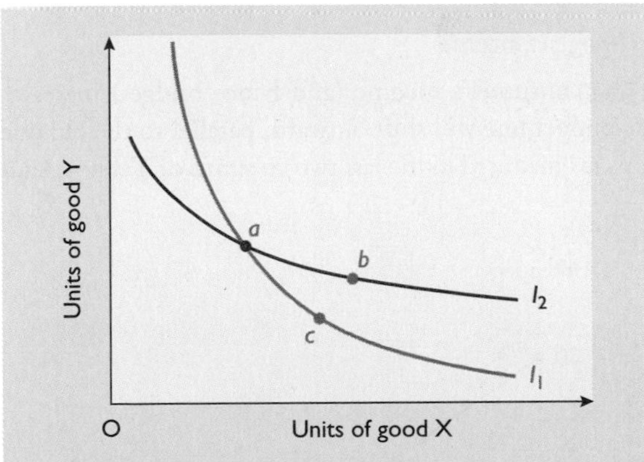

Figure 4.9 The impossibility of two indifference curves crossing

DEFINITIONS

Indifference map A graph showing a whole set of indifference curves. The further away a particular curve is from the origin, the higher the level of satisfaction it represents.

Budget line A graph showing all the possible combinations of two goods that can be purchased at given prices and for a given budget.

Table 4.3 Consumption possibilities for budgets of £30 and £40

Budget of £30			Budget of £40	
Units of good X	Units of good Y	Point on budget line in Figure 4.10	Units of good X	Units of good Y
0	30	*a*	0	40
5	20	*b*	5	30
10	10	*c*	10	20
15	0	*d*	15	10
			20	0

Note: It is assumed that P_X = £2, P_Y = £1.

Just as we did with an indifference curve, we can construct a budget line from a table. The first two columns of Table 4.3 show various combinations of two goods X and Y that can be purchased assuming that (a) the price of X is £2 and the price of Y is £1 and (b) the consumer has a budget of £30 to be divided between the two goods.

In Figure 4.10, then, if you are limited to a budget of £30, you can consume any combination of X and Y along the line (or inside it). You cannot, however, afford to buy combinations that lie outside it: i.e. in the shaded area. The shaded area is known as the *infeasible region* for the given budget.

We have said that the amount people can afford to buy will depend on (a) their budget and (b) the prices of the two goods. We can show how a change in either of these two determinants will affect the budget line.

A change in income

If the consumer's income (and hence budget) increases, the budget line will shift outward, parallel to the old one. This is illustrated in the last two columns of Table 4.3 and in Figure 4.11, which show the effect of a rise in the consumer's budget from £30 to £40. (Note that there is no change in the prices of X and Y, which remain at £2 and £1 respectively.)

More can now be purchased. For example, if the consumer was originally purchasing 7 units of X and 16 units of Y (point *m*), this could be increased with the new budget of £40, to 10 units of X and 20 units of Y (point *n*) or any other combination of X and Y along the new higher budget line.

A change in price

The relative prices of the two goods are given by the *slope* of the budget line. This can be demonstrated with the above example. The slope of the budget line in Figure 4.10 is 30/15 = 2. (We are ignoring the negative sign: strictly speaking, the slope should be –2.) Similarly, the slope of the new higher budget line in Figure 4.11 is 40/20 = 2. But in each case this is simply the ratio of the *price* of X (£2) to the *price* of *Y* (£1). Thus the slope of the budget line equals P_X/P_Y.

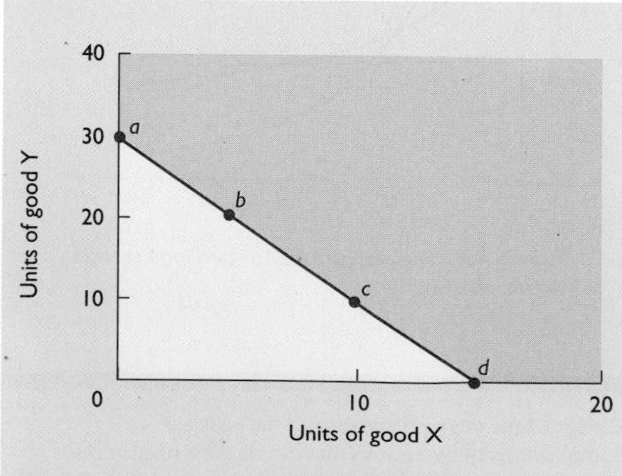

Figure 4.10 A budget line (budget of £30)

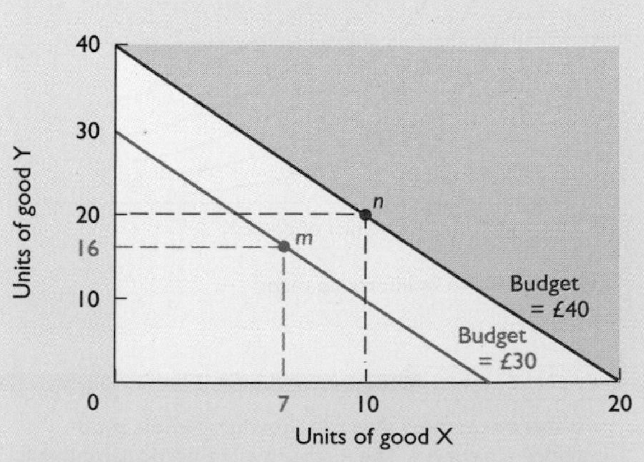

Figure 4.11 Effect of an increase in income on the budget line

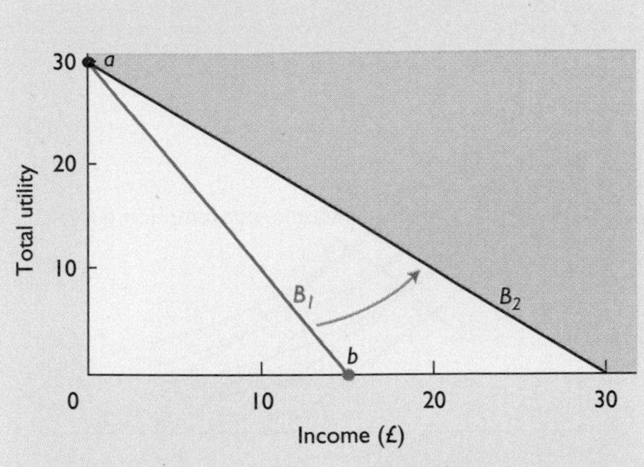

Figure 4.12 Effect on the budget line of a fall in the price of good X

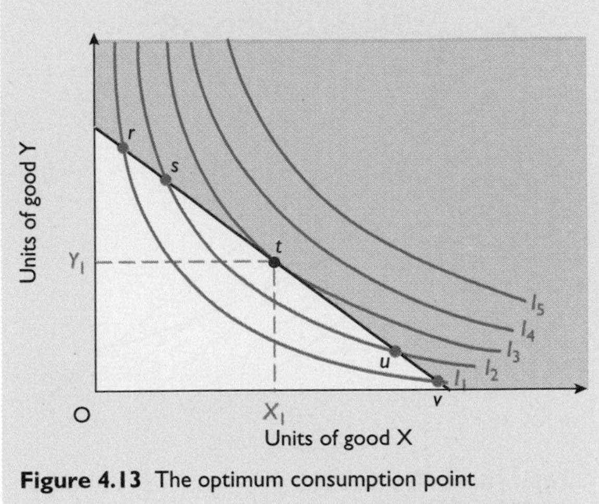

Figure 4.13 The optimum consumption point

If the price of either good changes, the slope of the budget line will change. This is illustrated in Figure 4.12 which, like Figure 4.10, assumes a budget of £30 and an initial price of X of £2 and a price of Y of £1. The initial budget line is B_1.

Now let us assume that the price of X falls to £1 but that the price of Y remains the same (£1). The new budget line will join 30 on the Y axis with 30 on the X axis. In other words, the line pivots outward on point *a*. If the price of Y changed, the line would pivot on point *b*.

??

1. Assume that the budget remains at £30 and the price of X stays at £2, but that Y rises in price to £3. Draw the new budget line.
2. What will happen to the budget line if the consumer's income doubles and the prices of both X and Y double?

Choosing the consumption point

We are now in a position to put the two elements of the analysis together: the indifference map and a budget line. This will enable us to show how much of each of the two goods the 'rational' consumer will buy from a given budget. Let us examine Figure 4.13.

The consumer would prefer to consume anywhere along indifference curve I_5 to anywhere along I_4. Similarly, points along I_4 are preferable to points along I_3. But given the budget line illustrated, it is not possible to consume anywhere along either I_5 or I_4. They are both in the infeasible region.

The consumer can, however, consume at certain points along curves I_1, I_2 and I_3. Consumption could be at point *r* along curve I_1. But to consume this combination of X and Y would not be 'rational'. By moving to point *s* a higher level of satisfaction could be gained, since point *s* is on the higher curve I_2. But point *s* is not the optimum point either. It is possible to gain a higher level of satisfaction still by consuming at point *t* on curve I_3. I_3 is the highest indifference curve that can be reached for this particular budget.

The optimum consumption point for the consumer, then, is where the budget line touches (is 'tangential to') the highest possible indifference curve. At any other point along the budget line the consumer would get a lower level of utility.

If the budget line is tangential to an indifference curve, they will have the same slope. (The slope of a curve is the slope of the tangent to it at the point in question.) But as we have seen:

$$\text{the slope of the budget line} = \frac{P_X}{P_Y}$$

$$\text{and the slope of the indifference curve} = MRS = \frac{MU_X}{MU_Y}$$

Therefore, at the optimum consumption point:

$$\frac{P_X}{P_Y} = \frac{MU_X}{MU_Y}$$

$$\text{i.e. } \frac{MU_X}{P_X} = \frac{MU_Y}{P_Y}$$

But this is the *equi-marginal principle* that we established in the first part of this chapter: only this time, using the indifference curve approach, there has been no need to measure utility. All we have needed to do is to observe, for any two combinations of goods, whether the consumer preferred one to the other or was indifferent between them.

Just as we can use indifference analysis to show the combination of goods that maximises utility for a given budget, so too we can show the *least-cost* combination of goods that yields a *given* level of utility. This is shown in Figure 4.14.

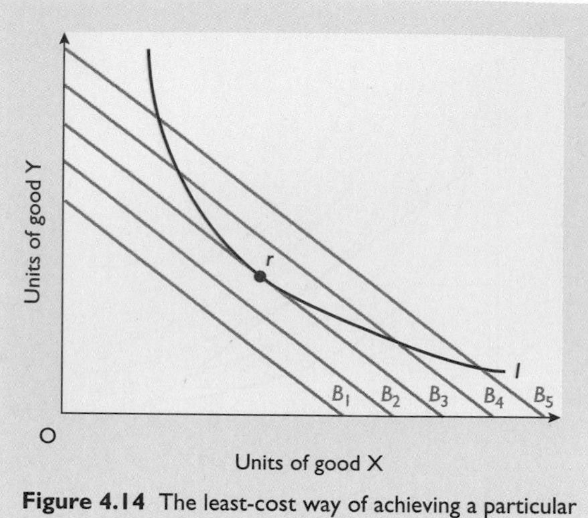

Figure 4.14 The least-cost way of achieving a particular level of satisfaction

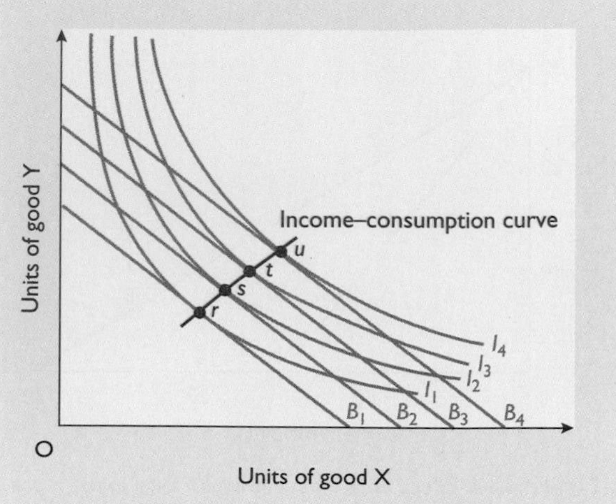

Figure 4.15 Effect on consumption of a change in income

Let us assume that you want to obtain the level of utility indicated by the indifference curve *I*. What combination of the two goods X and Y should you consume? By drawing a series of budget lines on the diagram we can find the least costly way for you to achieve that level of satisfaction. This combination will be at the point where the indifference curve touches the *lowest* possible budget line: i.e. at point *r*. Any other combination of goods along the indifference curve will cost you more: i.e. it will be on a higher budget line.

?? Refer back to Table 4.2 and plot an indifference curve like that shown in Figure 4.6. Assume that pears cost 10p each and that oranges cost 15p. Draw a series of budget lines for different levels of expenditure, making one of them tangential to the indifference curve that you have drawn. Assuming that Clive wants to gain the particular level of satisfaction from eating fruit that is shown by the indifference curve you have drawn, what is the least amount of money he must spend to achieve this? How many pears and how many oranges will he buy?

The following sections show how indifference curves and budget lines can be used to analyse the effect on consumption of changes in income and changes in price.

The effect of changes in income

An increase in income is represented by a parallel shift outward of the budget line (assuming no change in the price of X and Y). This will then lead to a new optimum consumption point on a higher indifference curve. A different consumption point will be found for each different level of income.

In Figure 4.15 a series of budget lines are drawn representing different levels of consumer income. The corresponding optimum consumption points (*r*, *s*, *t*, *u*) are shown. Each point is where the new higher budget line just touches the highest possible indifference curve.[1] The line joining these points is known as the **income–consumption curve**.

If your money income goes up and the price of goods does not change, we say that your **real income** has risen. In other words, you can buy more than you did before. But your real income can also rise even if you do not earn any more money. This will happen if prices fall. For the same amount of money, you can buy more goods than

[1] We can always draw in an indifference curve that will be tangential to a given budget line. Just because we only draw a few indifference curves on a diagram, it does not mean that there are only a few *possible* ones. We could draw as many as we liked. Again it is rather like the contours on a real map. They may be drawn at, say, 10 metre intervals. We could, however, if we liked, draw them at 1 metre or even 1 cm intervals, or at whatever height was suitable to our purpose. For example, if the maximum height of a lake were 32.45 metres above sea level, it might be useful to draw a contour at that height to show what land might be liable to flooding.

DEFINITIONS

Income–consumption curve A line showing how a person's optimum level of consumption of two goods changes as income changes (assuming the prices of the goods remain constant).

Real income Income measured in terms of how much it can buy. If your *money* income rises by 10 per cent, but prices rise by 8 per cent, you can only buy 2 per cent more goods than before. Your *real* income has risen by 2 per cent.

previously. We analyse the effect of a rise in real income caused by a fall in prices in just the same way as we did when money income rose and prices stayed the same. Provided the *relative* prices of the two goods stay the same (i.e. provided they fall by the same percentage), the budget line will shift outward parallel to the old one.

Income elasticity of demand and the income–consumption curve

The income–consumption curve drawn in the upper half of Figure 4.16 shows how Amanda's monthly demand for two goods, bread and compact discs, rises as her income rises.

Directly after leaving school she has a low income and thus has a small monthly budget to spend. As we would expect, she buys few compact discs as they constitute a luxury she can barely afford, whereas she has to eat and bread is a major part of her diet. Initially, then, with a budget of B_1 she consumes at point *a*.

Later, as she moves to better-paid jobs, her budget line shifts to B_2 and then toB_3, and her consumption point rises first to point *b* and then to point *c*. Her purchases of CDs have increased significantly (from Q_{cd_1} to Q_{cd_3}). They have a high income elasticity of demand. Her purchases of bread, however, have hardly increased at all (from Q_{b_1} to Q_{b_3}). Bread, being a basic good, has a low income elasticity of demand.

The lower part of Figure 4.16 shows how Amanda's demand for CDs varies with her income. Each of the points *a*, *b* and *c* corresponds to an equivalent point in the upper part of the diagram. The line joining these points together is known as an **Engel curve**, after the German statistician Ernst Engel (1821–96) who did extensive investigations into the effects of changes in family budgets on family expenditures.

The Engel curve in Figure 4.16 illustrates a good with an income elasticity of demand greater than 1. This means that the proportionate rise in demand from Q_{cd_1} to Q_{cd_2} is greater than the proportionate rise in income from Y_1 to Y_2.

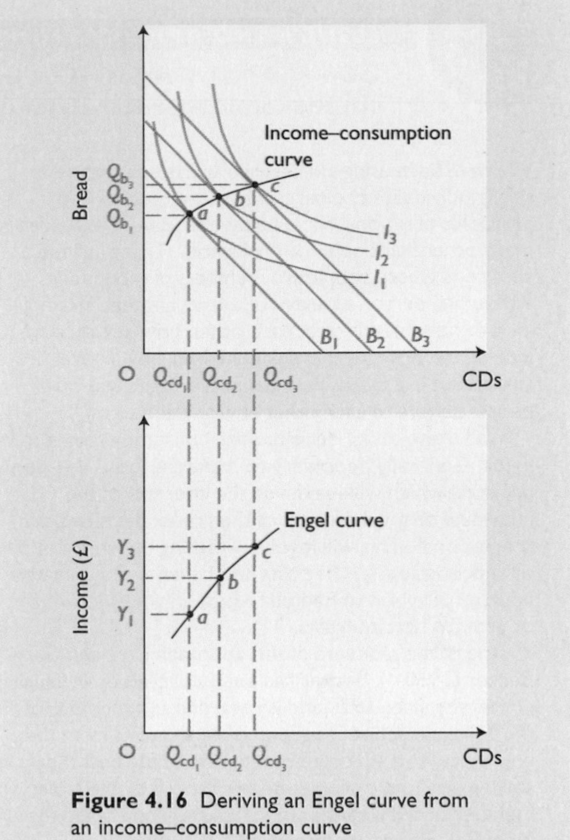

Figure 4.16 Deriving an Engel curve from an income–consumption curve

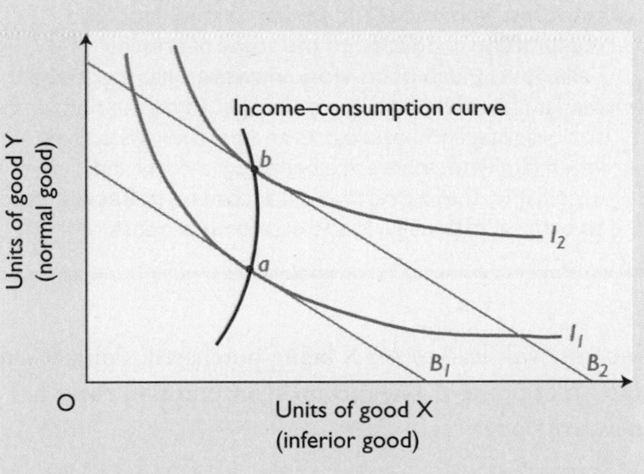

Figure 4.17 Effect of a rise in income on the demand for an inferior good

The effect of a rise in income on the demand for inferior goods

If one of the two goods, X or Y, is an inferior good, such as cheap margarine or inferior cuts of meat, the effect of a rise in income will be to *reduce* the quantity purchased. Remember this is how we *defined* an inferior good in Chapter 2. This is shown in Figure 4.17.

If X is an inferior good and Y is a normal good, an outward movement of the budget line (an increase in

DEFINITION

Engel curve A line showing how much of a good people will demand at different levels of income.

ISSUES AND APPLICATIONS

LOVE AND CARING

An economic approach to family behaviour

We have been using indifference analysis to analyse a single individual's choices between two goods. The principles of rational choice, however, can be extended to many other fields of human behaviour. These include situations where people are members of groups and where one person's behaviour affects another. Examples include how friends treat each other, how sexual partners interrelate, how parents treat children, how chores are shared out in a family, how teams are organised, how people behave to each other at work, and so on.

In all these cases, decisions are constantly having to be made. Generally people try to make the 'best' decisions, decisons which will maximise the interests of the individual or the members of the group, decisions that are 'rational'. This will involve weighing up (consciously or subconsciously) the costs and benefits of alternative courses of action to find out which is in the individual's or group's best interests.

One of the pioneers of this approach has been Gary Becker (1930–). Becker has been a professor at Chicago University since 1970 and is regarded as a member of the 'Chicago School', a group of economists from the university who advocate the market as the best means of solving economic problems (see Box 15.8). He is also a member of the free-market pressure group called the Mont Pelerin Society (see Box 11.10).

Gary Becker has attempted to apply simple economic principles of rational choice to a whole range of human activities: from racial and sexual discrimination, to competition in politics, to the study of criminal behaviour. Much of his work, however, has focused on the family, a field previously thought to be the domain of sociologists, anthropologists and psychologists. Even when family members are behaving lovingly and unselfishly, they nevertheless, according to Becker, tend to behave 'rationally' in the economists' sense of trying to maximise their interests, only in this case their 'interests' include the welfare of the other members of their family.

A simple illustration of this approach is given in the following diagram. It assumes, for simplicity, that there are just two members of the family: Judy and Warren. Warren's consumption is measured on the horizontal axis; Judy's on the vertical. Their total joint income is given by Y_T. The line Y_TY_T represents their consumption possibilities. If Warren were to spend their entire joint income on himself, he would consume at point *g*. If Judy were to spend their entire joint income on herself, she would consume at point *f*.

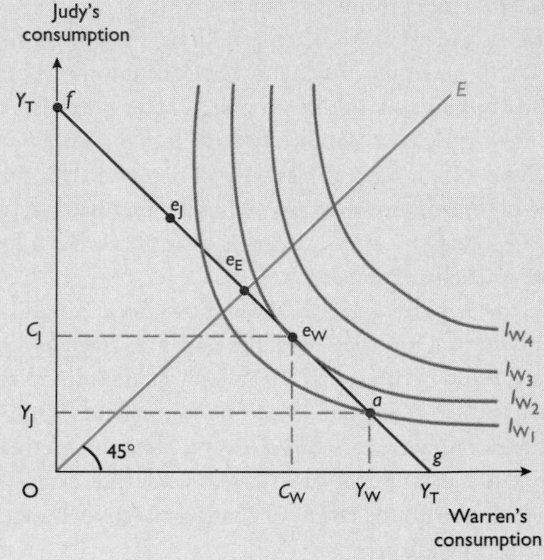

income) will lead to *less* X being purchased. Point *b* is to the *left* of point *a*. The income–consumption curve has a negative slope.

??

1. The income–consumption curve in Figure 4.17 is drawn as *positively* sloped at low levels of income. Why?
2. Show the effect of a rise in income on the demand for X and Y, where this time Y is the inferior good and X is the normal good. Is the income–consumption curve positively or negatively sloped?
3. Sketch an Engel curve corresponding to Figure 4.17. What can we say about the income elasticity of demand for an inferior good?

The effect of changes in price

If either X or Y changes in price, the budget line will 'pivot'. Take the case of a reduction in the price of X (but no change in the price of Y). If this happens, the budget line will swing outwards. This effect is shown in Figure 4.18.

The initial budget line B_1 corresponds to the data in the first two columns of Table 4.3, where the budget was £30, the price of X was £2 and the price of Y was £1. Assume now that the price of X is reduced to £1 while the price of Y remains the same as before (£1). The new budget line B_2 will therefore intersect the X axis at twice the quantity that B_1 does (i.e. 30 units of X), but will continue to intersect

BOX 4.5

Let us assume that Warren works full time and Judy works part time. As a result Warren earns more than Judy. He earns Y_W; she earns Y_J. If each spent their own incomes on themselves alone, they would consume at point *a*.

But now let us assume that Warren loves Judy, and that he would prefer to consume less than Y_W to allow her to consume more than Y_J. His preferences are shown by the indifference curves. Each curve shows all the various combinations of consumption between Warren and Judy that give Warren equal satisfaction. (Note that because he loves Judy, he gets satisfaction from her consumption: her happiness gives him pleasure.)

Warren's optimum distribution of consumption between himself and Judy is at point e_W. This is the highest of his indifference curves that can be reached with a joint income of Y_T. At his point he consumes C_W; she consumes C_J.

If he loved Judy 'as himself' and wanted to share their income out equally, then the indifference curves would be shallower. The tangency point to the highest indifference curve would be on the 45° line *OE*. Consumption would be at point e_E.

Similar indifference curves could be drawn for Judy. Her optimum consumption point might be at point e_J. But if she loved Warren 'as herself', her optimum point would then be at point e_E.

Some interesting conclusions can be drawn from this analysis:

- Income redistribution within the family can be to the benefit of *all* the members. In the case we have been considering, both Warren and Judy gain from a redistribution of income from point *a* to point e_W. The only area of contention is between points e_W and e_J. Here negotiation would have to take place. This might be in return for some favour. 'If you'll let me have the money I need for that new coat, I'll do the washing up for a whole month.'
- In the case of each one loving the other as him- or herself, there is no area of contention. They are both happiest with consumption at point e_E.
- In the case of 'extreme love', where each partner would prefer the other to have more than him- or herself, point e_W would be above point e_E, and point e_J would be below point e_E. In this case each would be trying to persuade the other to have more than he or she wanted. Here a different type of negotiation would be needed. 'I'll only let you buy me that coat if you let me do the washing up for a whole month.'
- Some forms of consumption benefit *both* partners. Household furniture or a new car would be cases in point. Any such purchases would have the effect of shifting the consumption point out beyond line Y_TY_T, and could lead to both partners consuming on a higher indifference curve. This shows the 'economic' advantages of the collective consumption that can be experienced in households or other groups (such as clubs).

??

1. If Judy earned more than Warren, show how much income she would redistribute to him if (a) she cared somewhat for him; (b) she loved him 'as herself'. Draw her indifference curves in each of these two cases.
2. In the case where they both love each other 'as themselves', will their two sets of indifference curves be identical?

the Y axis at the same point. The curve has pivoted on point *a*.

The old optimum consumption point was at *j*. After the reduction in the price of good X, a new optimum consumption point is found at *k*.

??

Illustrate on an indifference diagram the effects of the following:

(a) A rise in the price of good X (assuming no change in the price of Y).
(b) A fall in the price of good Y (assuming no change in the price of X).

A series of budget lines could be drawn, all pivoting round point *a* in Figure 4.18. Each one represents a different price of good X, but with money income and the price of Y held constant. The flatter the curve, the lower the price of X. At each price, there will be an optimum consumption point. The line that connects these points is known as the **price–consumption curve**.

DEFINITION

Price–consumption curve A line showing how a person's optimum level of consumption of two goods changes as the price of one of the two goods changes (assuming that income and the price of the other good remain constant).

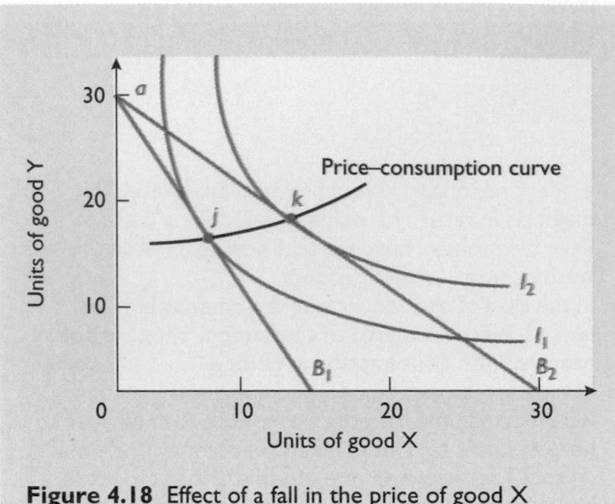

Figure 4.18 Effect of a fall in the price of good X

Deriving the individual's demand curve

We can use the analysis of price changes to show how in theory a person's demand curve for a product can be derived. To do this we need to modify the diagram slightly.

Let us assume that we want to derive a person's demand curve for good X. What we need to show is the effect on the consumption of X of a change in the price of X assuming the prices of all other goods are held constant. To do this we need to redefine good Y. Instead of being a *single* good, Y becomes the total of *all other* goods. But what units are we to put on the vertical axis? Each of these other goods will be in different units: litres of petrol, loaves of bread, kilograms of cheese, numbers of haircuts, etc. We cannot add them all up unless we first convert them to a common unit. The answer is to measure them as the total amount of money spent on them: i.e. what is *not* spent on good X.

With expenditure on all other goods plotted on the vertical axis and with income, tastes and the price of all other goods held constant, we can now derive the demand curve for X. This is demonstrated in Figure 4.19.

We illustrate the changes in the price of X by pivoting the budget line on the point where it intersects the Y axis. It is then possible, by drawing a price–consumption line, to show the amount of X demanded at each price. It is then a simple matter of transferring these price–quantity relationships on to a demand curve. In Figure 4.19, each of the points *a*, *b*, *c* and *d* on the demand curve in the lower part of the diagram corresponds to one of the four points on the price–consumption curve. (Note that P_2 is half of P_1, P_3 is one-third of P_1 and P_4 is one-quarter of P_1.)

?? As quantity demanded increases from Q_1 to Q_2 in Figure 4.19, the expenditure on all other goods *decreases*. (Point *b* is lower than point *a*.) This means, therefore, that the person's total expenditure on X has correspondingly increased. What, then, can we say about the person's price elasticity of demand for X between points *a* and *b*? What can we say about the price elasticity of demand between points *b* and *c*, and between points *c* and *d*?

The income and substitution effects of a price change

In Chapter 2 we argued that when the price of a good rises, consumers will purchase less of it for two reasons:

- They cannot afford to buy so much. This is the **income effect**.
- The good is now more expensive relative to other goods. Therefore consumers substitute alternatives for it. This is the **substitution effect**.

We can extend our arguments of Chapter 2 by demonstrating the income and substitution effects with the use of indifference analysis. Let us start with the case of a normal good and show what happens when its price changes.

A normal good

In Figure 4.20 the price of **normal good** X has *risen* and the budget line has pivoted *inwards* from B_1 to B_2. The consumption point has moved from point *f* to point *h*. Part of this shift in consumption is due to the substitution effect and part is due to the income effect.

The substitution effect. To separate these two effects a new budget line is drawn, parallel to B_2 but tangential to

DEFINITIONS

Income effect of a price change That portion of the change in quantity demanded that results from the change in real income.

Substitution effect of a price change That portion of the change in quantity demanded that results from the change in the relative price of the good.

Normal good A good whose demand increases as income increases.

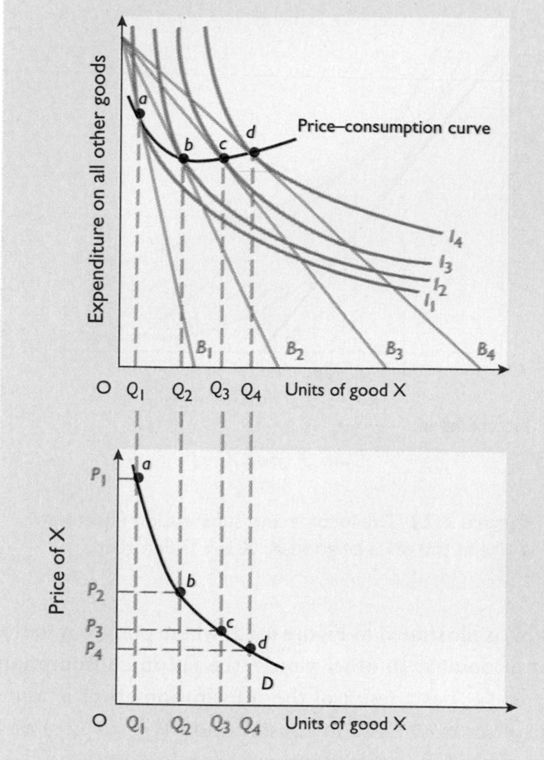

Figure 4.19 Deriving the demand curve for good X from a price–consumption curve

the original indifference curve I_1. This is the line B_{1a}. Being parallel to B_2, it represents the new price ratio (i.e. the higher price of X). Being tangential to I_1, however, it enables the consumer to obtain the *same utility* as before: in other words, there is no loss in *real* income to the consumer. By focusing on B_{1a}, then, which represents no change in real income, we have excluded the income effect. The movement from point *f* to point *g*, therefore, is due *purely* to a change in the relative prices of X and Y. The movement from Q_{x_1} to Q_{x_2}, therefore, is the *substitution* effect.

The income effect. In reality the budget line has shifted to B_2 and the consumer is forced to consume on a lower indifference curve I_2: real income has fallen. Thus the movement from Q_{x_2} to Q_{x_3} is the *income* effect.

In the case of a normal good, therefore, the income and substitution effects of a price change reinforce each other. They are both negative: they *both* involve a *reduction* in the quantity demanded as price *rises* (and vice versa).[2]

The bigger the income and substitution effects, the higher will be the price elasticity of demand for good X.

?? Illustrate on two separate indifference diagrams the income and substitution effects of the following:

(a) A decrease in the price of good X (and no change in the price of good Y).
(b) An increase in the price of good Y (and no change in the price of good X).

An inferior good

As we saw above, when people's incomes rise they will buy less of **inferior goods** such as poor quality margarine and cheap powdered instant coffee, since they will now be able to afford better-quality goods instead. Conversely, when income falls, they will now have to reduce their living standards: their consumption of inferior goods will thus rise.

The substitution effect. If the *price* of an inferior good (good X) rises, the substitution effect will be in the same direction as for a normal good: i.e. it will be negative. People will consume less X relative to Y, since X is now more expensive relative to Y. For example, if the price of inferior-quality margarine (good X) went up, people would tend to use better-quality margarine or butter (good Y) instead. This is illustrated in Figure 4.21. The analysis of substitution and income effects is similar to that of Figure 4.20.

The rise in price of X is signified by an inward pivot of the budget line from B_1 to B_2. As before, the substitution effect is illustrated by a movement along the original indifference curve (I_1) from point *f* to point *g*. The quantity of X demanded falls from Q_{x_1} to Q_{x_2}.

The income effect. The income effect of the price rise, however, will be the opposite of that for a normal good: it will be *positive*. The reduction in real income from the rise in price of X will tend to *increase* the consumption of X, since with a fall in real income *more* inferior goods will now be purchased – including more X. Thus point *h* is to

[2] It is important not to confuse the income effect of a *price* change from the simple effect on demand of an increase in income. In the latter case, a *rise* in income will cause a *rise* in demand for a normal good – a positive effect (and hence there will be positive income elasticity of demand). In the case of a price reduction, although for a normal good the resulting rise in real income will still cause a rise in demand, it is in the *opposite* direction from the change in price – a negative effect *with respect to price* (and hence there will be a negative price elasticity of demand).

DEFINITION

Inferior good A good whose demand decreases as income increases.

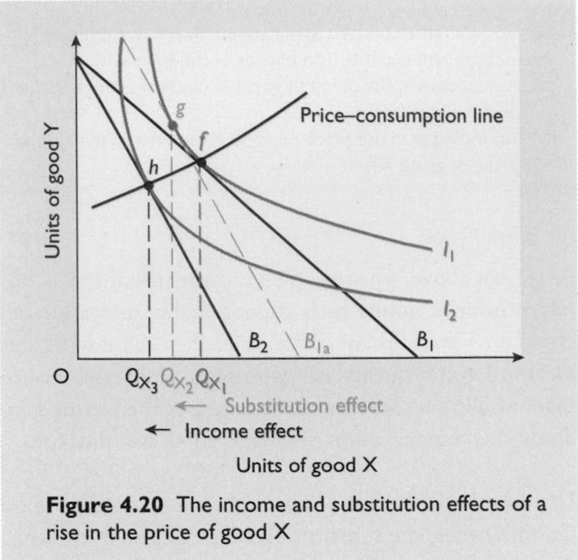

Figure 4.20 The income and substitution effects of a rise in the price of good X

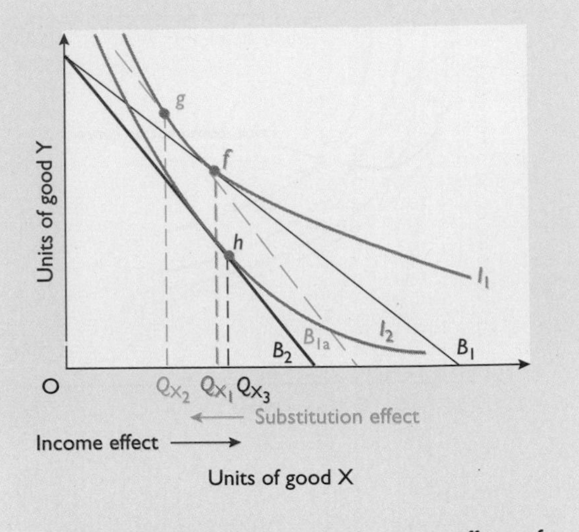

Figure 4.22 The income and substitution effects of a rise in the price of good X: X is a Giffen good

the *right* of point *g*: the income effect increases quantity back from Q_{x_2} to Q_{x_3}.

A Giffen good: a particular type of inferior good

If the inferior good were to account for a very large proportion of a consumer's expenditure, a change in its price would have a significant effect on the consumer's real income, resulting in a large income effect. It is conceivable, therefore, that this large abnormal income effect could outweigh the normal substitution effect. In such a case, a rise in the price of X would lead to *more* X being consumed!

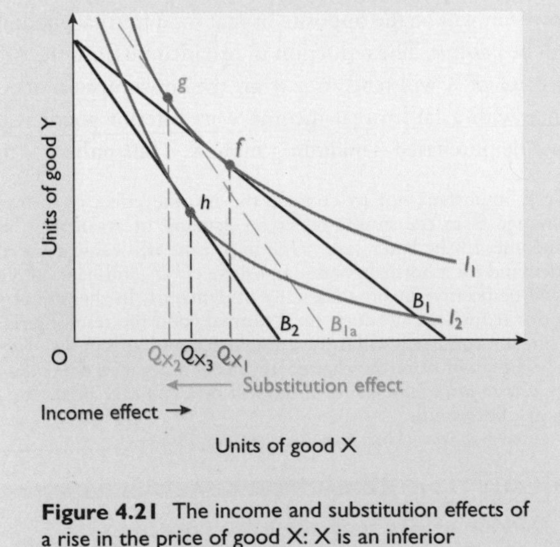

Figure 4.21 The income and substitution effects of a rise in the price of good X: X is an inferior (non-Giffen) good

This is illustrated in Figure 4.22, where point *h* is to the *right* of point *f*. In other words, the fall in consumption (Q_{x_1} to Q_{x_2}) as a result of the substitution effect is more than offset by the rise in consumption (Q_{x_2} to Q_{x_3}) as a result of the large positive income effect.

Such a good is known as a **Giffen good**, after Sir Robert Giffen (1837–1910), who is alleged to have claimed that the consumption of bread by the poor rose when its price rose. Bread formed such a large proportion of poor people's consumption that, if its price went up, the poor could not afford to buy so much meat, vegetables, etc. and had to buy more bread instead. Naturally, such cases must be very rare indeed.

?? Are there any Giffen goods that you consume? If not, could you conceive of any circumstances in which one or more items of your expenditure would become Giffen goods?

The usefulness of indifference analysis

By the use of indifference analysis, it has been possible to demonstrate the logic of 'rational' consumer choice, the derivation of the individual's demand curve, and the income and substitution effects of a price change. All this has been done without having to resort to measuring utility.

DEFINITION

Giffen good An inferior good whose demand increases as its price increases as a result of a positive income effect larger than the normal negative substitution effect.

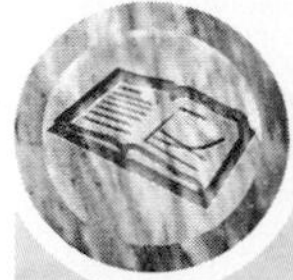

EXPLORING THE THEORY — BOX 4.6

INCOME AND SUBSTITUTION EFFECTS: AN ALTERNATIVE ANALYSIS

Slutsky's approach to defining 'real' income

The analysis of income and substitution effects that we have just been looking at is that developed by Sir John Hicks (we will be giving a 'person profile' of him in Box 20.5). Hicks defined the substitution effect as that which arises *purely* from a change in relative prices. In other words, it is the effect of a price change when *real income is held constant.*

Hicks defined a consumer's real income as constant if the level of *satisfaction* could be maintained constant: in other words, if the consumer can remain on the same indifference curve. With this definition of constant real income, the substitution effect is illustrated by sliding the budget line round the original indifference curve. In Figure 4.20, this resulted in a move from point *f* to point *g* on the original indifference curve I_1.

Hicks' definition, then, of constant real income relies on the *subjective* tastes of the consumer. It will differ from consumer to consumer depending on the shape of each one's indifference curves.

An alternative analysis was the earlier one developed by the Russian economist and mathematician Evgeny Slutsky (1880–1948). Slutsky defined constant real income as that which would allow the consumer to buy exactly the same quantity of goods after a price change as before. This definition does not involve reference to an indifference curve and hence to the subjective tastes of individual consumers.

The Slutsky analysis is shown in the following diagram, which like Figure 4.20 analyses the effect of a rise in the price of good X.

Just as in Figure 4.20, the full effect (i.e. income plus substitution effects) of the price rise is for the quantity of X consumed to fall from Q_{x_1} to Q_{x_3} (a movement from point *f* to point *h*). But this time the income and substitution effects are analysed differently.

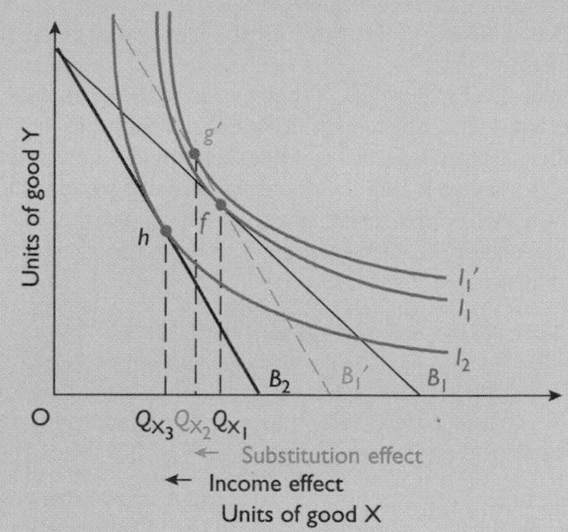

To keep real income constant and thus to isolate the pure substitution effect, the Slutsky approach is to draw a new hypothetical budget line (B_1') through point *f*. By passing through point *f*, it shows that the consumer could (if that was what was wanted) continue to purchase the same amount of the two goods as before. But to illustrate the change in relative prices, B_1' is drawn parallel to the real new budget line B_2. With this hypothetical budget line B_1', the consumer will consume at point *g'* on indifference curve I_1'. The move from *f* to *g'* (i.e. from Q_{x_1} to Q_{x_2}) thus represents the substitution effect.

Slutsky's income effect then becomes the move from *g'* to *h* (i.e. from Q_{x_2} to Q_{x_3}).

?? Show on one diagram both the Hicks and the Slutsky analysis of the income and substitution effects of a *fall* in the price of good X.

Nevertheless there are limitations to the usefulness of indifference analysis:

- In practice it is virtually impossible to derive indifference curves, since it would involve a consumer having to imagine a whole series of different combinations of goods and deciding in each case whether a given combination gave more, equal or less satisfaction than other combinations.
- Consumers may not behave 'rationally', and hence may not give careful consideration to the satisfaction they believe they will gain from consuming goods. They may behave impetuously.
- Indifference curves are based on the satisfaction that consumers *believe* they will gain from a good. This belief may well be influenced by advertising. Consumers may be disappointed or pleasantly surprised, however, when they actually consume the good. In other words, consumers are not perfectly knowledgeable. Thus the 'optimum consumption' point may not in practice give consumers maximum satisfaction for their money.

EXPLORING THE THEORY — BOX 4.7

CONSUMER THEORY: A FURTHER APPROACH

Characteristics theory

Characteristics theory was developed in the mid-1960s by Kelvin Lancaster. He argued that people demand goods not for their own sake, but for the *characteristics* they possess.

Take cars for example. When choosing between the different makes, consumers do not just consider their relative prices, they also consider their attributes: comfort, style, horsepower, durability, reliability, fuel consumption, etc. It is these *characteristics* that give rise to utility.

Characteristics theory, then, is based on four crucial assumptions:

- All goods possess various characteristics.
- Different brands possess them in different proportions.
- The characteristics are measurable: they are 'objective'.
- The characteristics (along with price and income) determine consumer choice.

Let us assume that you are choosing between three different goods or brands of a good (e.g. a foodstuff). Each one has a different combination of two characteristics (e.g. protein and calories). Your choices can be shown graphically.

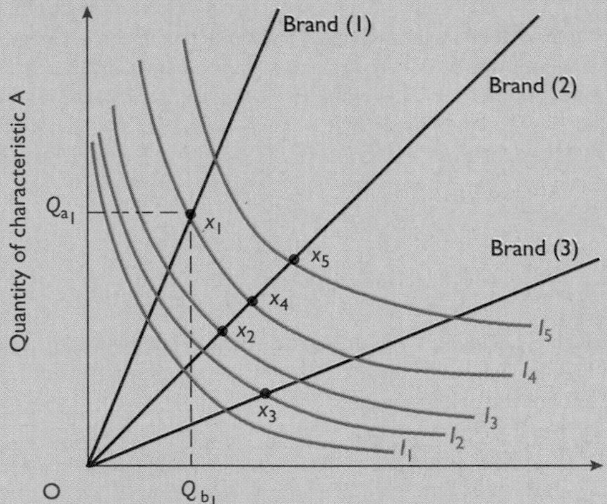

The choice between brands of a product: each brand has different characteristics

The quantities of two characteristics are shown on the two axes. An indifference map can be constructed, showing the different combinations of the two characteristics that yield given levels of utility. Thus any combination of the two characteristics along indifference curve I_4 in the diagram gives a higher level of utility than those along I_3, and so on. The shape of the indifference curves (bowed in) illustrates a diminishing marginal rate of substitution between the two characteristics.

The amounts of the two characteristics given by the three brands are shown by the three rays. The more that is consumed of each brand, the further up the respective ray will the consumer be. Thus at x_1, the consumer is gaining Q_{a_1} of characteristic A and Q_{b_1} of characteristic B.

Assume that, for the same money, the consumer could consume at x_1 with brand (1), x_2 with brand (2) and x_3 with brand (3). The consumer will consume brand (1): x_1 is on a higher indifference curve than x_2 or x_3.

Now assume that the price of brand (2) falls. For a given expenditure, the consumer can now move up the brand (2) ray. But not until the price has fallen enough to allow consumption at point x_4 will the consumer consider switching from brand (1). If price falls enough for consumption to be at point x_5, clearly the consumer will switch.

The characteristics approach has a number of advantages over conventional indifference curve analysis in explaining consumer behaviour.

- It helps to explain brand loyalty. When price changes, people will not necessarily gradually move from one brand to another. Rather they will stick with a brand until a critical price is reached. Then they will switch brands all at once.
- It allows the choice between *several* goods to be shown on the same diagram. Each good or brand has its own ray.
- It helps to explain the nature of substitute goods. The closer substitutes are, the more similar will be their characteristics and hence the closer will be their rays. The closer the rays, the more likely it is that there will be a shift in consumption to one good when the price of the other good changes.
- A change in the quality of a good can be shown by rotating its ray.

There are weaknesses with the approach, however:

- Some characteristics cannot be measured. Such characteristics as beauty, taste and entertainment value are subjective: they are in the mind of the consumer.
- Only two characteristics can be plotted. Most goods have several characteristics.

??

1. Make a list of the characteristics of shoes. Which are 'objective' and which are 'subjective'?
2. If two houses had identical characteristics, except that one was near a noisy airport and the other was in a quiet location, and if the market price of the first house were £80 000 and of the second were £100 000, how would that help us to put a value on the characteristic of peace and quiet?

- Certain goods are only purchased every now and again, and then only one at a time. Examples would include consumer durables such as cars, televisions and washing machines. Indifference curves are based on the assumption that marginal increases in one good can be traded off against marginal decreases in another. This will not be the case with consumer durables.

SECTION SUMMARY

1. The indifference approach to analysing consumer demand avoids having to measure utility.
2. An indifference curve shows all those combinations of two goods that give an equal amount of satisfaction to a consumer. An indifference map can be drawn with indifference curves further to the north-east representing higher (but still unspecified) levels of satisfaction.
3. Indifference curves are usually drawn convex to the origin. This is because of a diminishing marginal rate of substitution between the two goods. As more of one good is purchased, the consumer is willing to give up less and less of the other for each additional unit of the first. The marginal rate of substitution is given by the slope of the indifference curve, which equals MU_X/MU_Y.
4. A budget line can be drawn on an indifference diagram. A budget line shows all those combinations of the two goods that can be purchased for a given amount of money, assuming a constant price of the two goods. The slope of the budget line depends on the relative price of the two goods. The slope is equal to P_X/P_Y.
5. The consumer will achieve the maximum level of satisfaction for a given income (budget) by consuming at the point where the budget line just touches the highest possible indifference curve. At this point of tangency the budget line and the indifference curve have the same slope. Thus $MU_X/MU_Y = P_X/P_Y$ and therefore $MU_X/P_X = MU_Y/P_Y$, which is the 'equi-marginal principle' for maximising utility from a given income that was established in section 4.1.
6. If the consumer's real income (and hence budget) rises, there will be a parallel outward shift of the budget line. The 'rational' consumer will move to the point of tangency of this new budget line with the highest indifference curve. The line that traces out these optimum positions for different levels of income is known as the 'income–consumption curve'.
7. From the income–consumption curve can be derived an Engel curve. This shows how the demand for a single good will vary as income varies. For a normal good, demand will rise as income rises. The Engel curve will be positively sloped. For an inferior good, demand will fall as income rises. The Engel curve will be negatively sloped.
8. If the price of one of the two goods changes, the budget line will pivot on the axis of the other good. An outward pivot represents a fall in price; an inward pivot represents an increase in price. The line that traces the tangency points of these budget lines with the appropriate indifference curves is called a 'price–consumption curve'.
9. By measuring the expenditure on all other goods on the vertical axis and by holding their price constant and money income constant, a demand curve can be derived for the good measured on the horizontal axis. Changes in its price can be represented by pivoting the budget line. The effect on the quantity demanded can be found from the resulting price–consumption curve.
10. The effect of a change in price on quantity demanded can be divided into an income and a substitution effect. The substitution effect is the result of a change in relative prices alone. The income effect is the result of the change in real income alone.
11. For a normal good, the income and substitution effects of a price change will both be negative and will reinforce each other. With an inferior good, the substitution effect will still be negative but the income effect will be positive and thus will to some extent offset the substitution effect. If the (positive) income effect is bigger than the (negative) substitution effect, the good is called a Giffen good. A rise in the price of a Giffen good will thus cause a *rise* in the quantity demanded.
12. Indifference analysis, although avoiding having to measure utility, nevertheless has limitations. Indifference curves are difficult to derive in practice; consumers may not behave rationally; the 'optimum' consumption point may not be optimum if the consumer lacks knowledge of the good; indifference curves will not be smooth for items where single units each account for a large proportion of income.

??? END-OF-CHAPTER QUESTIONS ???

1. Imagine that you had £10 per month to allocate between two goods a and b. Imagine that good a cost £2 per unit and good b cost £1 per unit. Imagine also that the utilities of the two goods are those set out in the table. (Note that the two goods are not substitutes for each other, so that the consumption of one does not affect the utility gained from the other.)

   (a) What would be the marginal utility ratio (MU_a/MU_b) for the following combinations of the two goods: (i) 1a, 8b; (ii) 2a, 6b; (iii) 3a, 4b; (iv) 4a, 2b?

   (b) Show that where the marginal utility ratio (MU_a/MU_b) equals the price ratio (P_a/P_b) total utility is maximised.

   (c) If the two goods were substitutes for each other, why would it not be possible to construct a table like the one given here?

The utility gained by a person from various quantities of two goods: A and B

Good A			Good B		
Units per month	*MU* (utils)	*TU* (utils)	Units per month	*MU* (utils)	*TU* (utils)
0	–	0.0	0	–	0.0
1	11.0	11.0	1	8.0	8.0
2	8.0	19.0	2	7.0	15.0
3	6.0	25.0	3	6.5	21.5
4	4.5	29.5	4	5.0	26.5
5	3.0	32.5	5	4.5	31.0
			6	4.0	35.0
			7	3.5	38.5
			8	3.0	41.5
			9	2.6	44.1
			10	2.3	46.4

Possible combinations of good A and good B (units per month) for a monthly expenditure of £10		Combined *TU* from goods A and B
Good A	Good B	(utils)
5	0	32.5
4	2	44.5
3	4	51.5
2	6	54.0
1	8	52.5
0	10	46.4

2. Is it reasonable to assume that people seek to equate the marginal utility/price ratios of the goods that they purchase, if (a) they have never heard of 'utility', let alone 'marginal utility'; (b) marginal utility cannot be measured in any absolute way?

3. Consider situations where you might consider swapping items with someone. Why are such situations relatively rare?

4. Explain why the price of a good is no reflection of the *total* value that consumers put on it.

5. A country's central bank (e.g. the Bank of England or the Bundesbank) has a key role in ensuring the stability of the banking system. In many countries the central bank is prepared to bail banks out which find themselves in financial difficulties. Although this has the benefit of reducing the chance of banks going bankrupt and depositors losing their money, it can create a moral hazard. Explain why.

*6. Sketch a person's indifference map for two goods X and Y. Mark the optimum consumption point. Now illustrate the following (you might need to draw a separate diagram for each):

   (i) A rise in the price of good X, but no change in the price of good Y.

   (ii) A shift in the person's tastes from good Y to good X.

   (iii) A fall in the person's income and a fall in the price of good Y, with the result that the consumption of Y remains constant (but that of X falls).

*7. Distinguish between a normal good, an inferior good and a Giffen good. Use indifference curves to illustrate your answer.

*8. Assume that commuters regard bus journeys as an inferior good and car journeys as a normal good. Using indifference curves, show how (i) a rise in incomes and (ii) a fall in bus fares will affect the use of these two modes of transport. How could people's tastes be altered so that bus journeys were no longer regarded as an inferior good? If tastes *were* altered in this way, what effect would it have on the indifference curves?

5

Background to supply

The last chapter went behind the demand curve. It attempted to explain just how much of various goods people will buy if they are behaving 'rationally'. As far as consumers were concerned, rational behaviour meant weighing up the *benefits* (utility) of consuming various amounts of goods or combinations of goods against their *costs* (their price).

We now need to go behind the supply curve and find out just how the **rational producer** (or 'firm' as we call all producers) will behave.

In this case we shall be looking at the benefits and costs to the firm of producing various quantities of goods and using various alternative methods of production. We shall be asking:

- How much will be produced?
- What combination of inputs will be used?
- How much profit will be made?

Profit and the aims of a firm

The traditional theory of supply, or **theory of the firm**, assumes that firms aim to *maximise profit*. Although the decision makers in firms may have other aims as well – e.g. pleasant working conditions – under many circumstances it is legitimate to assume that the overriding aim is the maximisation of profits. The advocates of the traditional theory would argue that it enables useful and largely accurate predictions to be made about the behaviour of firms.

The traditional profit-maximising theory of the firm is examined in this and the following two chapters.

First we examine the general principles that govern how much a firm supplies. Then, in Chapters 6 and 7, we look at how supply is affected by the amount of competition a firm faces. Different types of market are examined, right from one extreme where the individual firms are so small that they are totally powerless to influence market conditions, to the other extreme where the firm is a monopoly – the only firm in the market and hence with considerable power.

In some circumstances, however, firms may not seek to maximise profits. Instead they may seek to maximise sales, or the rate of growth of sales. Alternatively, they may have no *single* aim, but rather a series of potentially conflicting aims held by different managers in different departments of the firm. Not surprisingly, a firm's behaviour will depend on just what its aims are. Chapter 8 looks at various **alternative theories** to profit maximisation: each theory depending on the particular aims of the firm.

Profit maximisation

This chapter, then, provides the background to the profit maximising theory of the firm. So just what do we mean by 'profit'?

Profit is made by firms earning more from the sale of goods than the goods cost to produce. A firm's total profit ($T\Pi$) is thus the difference between its total sales revenue (TR) and its total costs of production (TC):

$$T\Pi = TR - TC$$

DEFINITIONS

Rational producer behaviour When a firm weighs up the costs and benefits of alternative courses of action and then seeks to maximise its net benefit.

Traditional theory of the firm The analysis of pricing and output decisions of the firm under various market conditions, assuming that the firm wishes to maximise profit.

Alternative theories of the firm Theories of the firm based on the assumption that firms have aims other than profit maximisation.

(Note that we use the Greek Π (pi) for 'profit' because the letter *P* is normally reserved for 'price' or sometimes, as we shall see later in this chapter, for 'product'.)

In order, then, to discover how a firm can maximise its profit, we must first consider what determines costs and revenue. Sections 5.1–5.4 examine costs. Section 5.5 examines revenue. Finally section 5.6 puts costs and revenue together to examine profit.

5.1 Background to costs: the short-run theory of production

The cost of producing any level of output will depend on the amount of inputs used and the price the firm must pay for them. Let us first focus on the quantity of inputs used.

The production function: using inputs to produce output

As explained in Chapter 1, it is usual in economics to group inputs or *factors of production* into three categories.

Labour. This includes all working people of whatever type: electricians, secretaries, doctors, foremen, unskilled workers, etc.

Land. This includes not only land, but all natural resources.

Capital. This includes all manufactured inputs: plant, tools, machinery, etc. (Note that we are referring here to physical capital, not *financial* capital. In other words, we are not referring to the *money* used to finance investment.)

Some economists include a fourth category: **entrepreneurship**. In a capitalist economy, the owners of firms organise the other three factors, and take the risks of being in business. Entrepreneurship is this organisational activity.

The relationship between output and inputs can be shown in a **production function**. A production function shows the relationship between the amount of factors used and the amount of output generated per period of time (e.g. per day, per month or per year). It can be expressed in algebraic form as follows:

$$TPP = f(F_1, F_2, F_3 \ldots F_n)$$

This merely states that total output – or **total physical product** (*TPP*) – depends on (i.e. is a function of) the quantity of factors (F_1, F_2, etc.) that are used. Numerical examples of production functions are given in the following sections.

Firms are likely to employ many different types of workers, raw materials, tools and machines. In simple economic models, however, it is usually assumed that firms employ only one type of labour, one type of land and one type of capital. In more complex models this assumption can be relaxed.

The simplest model of all assumes just two factors of production: for example, labour and capital or labour and land. In the case of labour and capital the production function would be in the form:

$$TPP = f(K, L)$$

where K and L are the quantities of capital and labour employed.

Although in the case of most firms these two-factor production functions are a considerable abstraction from reality, useful generalisations can nevertheless be made about the relationship between production and costs.

Before we go on, let us review what we have established so far:

- Firms will want to know what output they should produce to maximise profit.
- The level of profit depends on costs and revenue.
- Costs depend on the amount of inputs used.
- The amount of inputs used depends on the amount of output produced.
- The relationship between output and inputs is shown in the production function.

Let us now examine the production function in more detail. To start with we must distinguish between short-run and long-run production functions.

DEFINITIONS

Entrepreneurship The initiating and organising of the production of new goods, or the introduction of new techniques, and the risk taking associated with it.

Production function The mathematical relationship between the output of a good and the inputs used to produce it. It shows how output will be affected by changes in the quantity of one or more of the inputs.

Total physical product The total output of a product per period of time that is obtained from a given amount of inputs.

Short-run and long-run changes in production

If a firm wants to increase production, it will take time to acquire a greater quantity of certain inputs. For example, a manufacturer can use more electricity by turning on switches, but it might take a long time to obtain and install more machines, and longer still to build a second or third factory.

If, then, the firm wants to increase output in a hurry, it will only be able to increase the quantity of certain inputs. It can use more raw materials, more fuel, more tools and possibly more labour (by hiring extra workers or offering overtime to its existing workforce). But it will have to make do with its existing buildings and most of its machinery.

The distinction we are making here is between **fixed factors** and **variable factors**. A *fixed* factor is an input that cannot be increased within a given time period (e.g. buildings). A *variable* factor is one that can.

The distinction between fixed and variable factors allows us to distinguish between the **short run** and the **long run**.

The short run is a time period during which at least one factor of production is fixed. In the short run, then, output can only be increased by using more variable factors. For example, if a shipping line wanted to carry more passengers in response to a rise in demand, it could possibly accommodate more passengers on existing sailings if there was space. It could possibly increase the number of sailings with its existing fleet, by hiring more crew and using more fuel. But in the short run it could not buy more ships: there would not be time for them to be built.

The long run is a time period long enough for all inputs to be varied. Given long enough, a firm can build a second factory and install new machines.

The actual length of the short run will differ from firm to firm. It is not a fixed period of time. Thus if it takes a farmer a year to obtain new land, buildings and equipment, the short run is any time period up to a year and the long run is any time period longer than a year. If it takes a shipping company three years to obtain an extra ship, the short run is any period up to three years and the long run is any period longer than three years.

??

1. How will the length of the short run for the shipping company depend on the state of the shipbuilding industry?
2. Up to roughly how long is the short run in the following cases?
   (a) A mobile disco firm. (b) Electricity power generation. (c) A small grocery retailing business. (d) 'Superstore Hypermarkets Ltd'.
   In each case specify your assumptions.

For the remainder of this section we will concentrate on *short-run* production.

Production in the short run: the law of diminishing returns

Production in the short run is subject to *diminishing returns*. You may well have heard of 'the law of diminishing returns': it is one of the most famous of all 'laws' of economics. To illustrate how this law underlies short-run production let us take the simplest possible case where there are just two factors: one fixed and one variable.

Take the case of a farm. Assume the fixed factor is land and the variable factor is labour. Since the land is fixed in supply, output per period of time can be increased only by increasing the amount of workers employed. But imagine what would happen as more and more workers crowded on to a fixed area of land. The land cannot go on yielding more and more output indefinitely. After a point the additions to output from each extra worker will begin to diminish.

We can now state the law of **diminishing (marginal) returns**. It says that: when increasing amounts of a variable factor are used with a given amount of a fixed factor, there will come a point when each extra unit of the variable factor will produce less extra output than the previous unit.

The short-run production function: total product

Let us now see how the law of diminishing returns affects total output (*TPP*).

In the simple case of the farm with only two factors – namely, a fixed supply of land ($\overline{Ln}$) and a variable supply of farm workers (*Lb*) – the production function would be:

$$TPP = f(\overline{Ln}, Lb)$$

DEFINITIONS

Fixed factor An input that cannot be increased in supply within a given time period.

Variable factor An input that *can* be increased in supply within a given time period.

Short run The period of time over which at least one factor is fixed.

Long run The period of time long enough for *all* factors to be varied.

Law of diminishing (marginal) returns When one or more factors are held fixed, there will come a point beyond which the extra output from additional units of the variable factor will diminish.

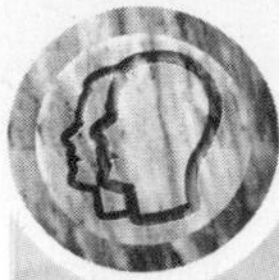

DEVELOPMENT OF IDEAS — BOX 5.1

MALTHUS AND THE DISMAL SCIENCE OF ECONOMICS

Population growth + diminishing returns = starvation

The law of diminishing returns has potentially cataclysmic implications for the future populations of the world.

If the population of the world grows rapidly, then food output may not keep pace with it. There will be diminishing returns to labour as more and more people crowd on to the limited amount of land available.

This is already a problem in some of the poorest countries of the world, especially in sub-Saharan Africa. The land is barely able to support current population levels. Only one or two bad harvests are needed to cause mass starvation. Witness the appalling famines in recent years in Ethiopia and the Sudan.

The relationship between population and food output was analysed as long ago as 1798 by the Reverend Thomas Robert Malthus (1766–1834) in his *Essay on the Principle of Population*. This book was a bestseller and made Robert Malthus perhaps the best known of all social scientists of his day.

Malthus argued as follows:

> I say that the power of population is indefinitely greater than the power in the earth to produce subsistence for man.
>
> Population when unchecked, increases in a geometrical ratio. Subsistence increases only in an arithmetical ratio. A slight acquaintance with numbers will show the immensity of the first power in comparison with the second.[1]

What Malthus was saying is that world population tends to double about every 25 years or so if unchecked. It grows geometrically, like the series: 1, 2, 4, 8, 16, 32, 64, etc. But food output, because of diminishing returns, cannot keep pace with this. It is only likely to grow at an arithmetical rate, like the series: 1, 2, 3, 4, 5, 6, 7, etc. It is clear that population, if unchecked, will soon outstrip food supply.

So what is the check on population growth? According to Malthus it is starvation. As population grows, so food output per head will fall until, with more and more people starving, the death rate will rise. Only then will population growth stabilise at the rate of growth of food output.

Have Malthus' gloomy predictions been borne out by events?

There are two factors that have mitigated the forces Malthus described:

- The rate of population growth tends to slow down as countries become more developed. Although improved health prolongs life, this tends to be more than offset by a decline in the birth rate as people choose to have smaller families.
- Technological improvements in farming have greatly increased food output per hectare. (See Box 5.4 for a relatively recent example.)

The growth in food output has thus exceeded the rate of population growth in advanced countries.

The picture is much more gloomy, however, in developing countries. There *have* been advances in agriculture. The 'green revolution', whereby new high-yielding crop varieties have been developed (especially in the cases of wheat and rice), has led to food output growth outstripping population growth in many developing countries. India, for example, now exports grain.

Nevertheless, the Malthusian spectre is very real for some of the poorest developing countries, which are simply unable to feed their populations satisfactorily. It is these poorest countries of the world which have some of the highest rates of population growth. Kenya, for example, has a population growth of nearly 3½ per cent per annum.

??

1. Why might it be possible for there to be a zero marginal productivity of labour on many family farms in poor countries and yet just enough food for all the members of the family to survive? (Illustrate using *MPP* and *APP* curves.)
2. The figures in the following table are based on the assumption that birth rates will fall faster than death rates. Under what circumstances might these forecasts underestimate the rate of growth of world population?

World population levels and growth: actual and projected

Year	World population (billions)	Average annual rate of increase (%)		
		World	More developed regions	Less developed regions
1950	2.5			
		1.8	1.2	2.1
1960	3.0			
		2.0	1.0	2.4
1970	3.7			
		1.8	0.7	2.2
1980	4.4			
		1.7	0.6	2.1
1990	5.3			
		1.5	0.4	1.8
2000	6.2			
		1.3	0.2	1.6
2010	7.0			
		1.1	0.2	1.3
2020	7.9			
		1.0	0.1	1.2
2030	8.7			

Source: *World Urbanization Prospects* (UN, 1995).

[1] T. R. Malthus, *First Essay on Population* (Macmillan, 1926), pp. 13–14.

Table 5.1 Wheat production per year from a particular farm

	Quantity of variable factor: number of workers employed (*Lb*)	Total physical product: output of wheat in tonnes per year (*TPP*)
a	0	0
	1	3
	2	10
b	3	24
	4	36
	5	40
	6	42
d	7	42
	8	40

The production function can also be expressed in the form of a table or a graph. Table 5.1 and Figure 5.1 show a hypothetical production function for a farm producing wheat. They show how wheat output per year varies as extra workers are employed on a fixed amount of land.

With nobody working on the land, output will be zero (point *a*).

As the first farm workers are taken on, wheat output initially rises more and more rapidly. The assumption behind this is that with only one or two workers efficiency is low, since the workers are spread too thinly. With more workers, however, they can work together – each, perhaps, doing some specialist job – and thus they can use the land more efficiently. In Table 5.1, output rises more and more rapidly up to the employment of the third worker (point *b*). In Figure 5.1 the *TPP* curve gets steeper up to point *b*.

After point *b*, however, diminishing marginal returns set in: output rises less and less rapidly, and the *TPP* curve correspondingly becomes less steeply sloped.

When point *d* is reached, wheat output is at a maximum: the land is yielding as much as it can. Any more workers employed after that are likely to get in each other's way. Thus beyond point *d*, output is likely to fall again: eight workers produce less than seven workers.

The short-run production function: average and marginal product

In addition to total physical product, two other important concepts are illustrated by a production function: namely, **average physical product** (*APP*) and **marginal physical product** (*MPP*).

Average physical product

This is output (*TPP*) per unit of the variable factor (Q_v). In the case of the farm, it is the output of wheat per worker.

$$APP = TPP/Q_v$$

Thus in Table 5.1 the average physical product of labour when four workers are employed is 36/4 = 9 tonnes.

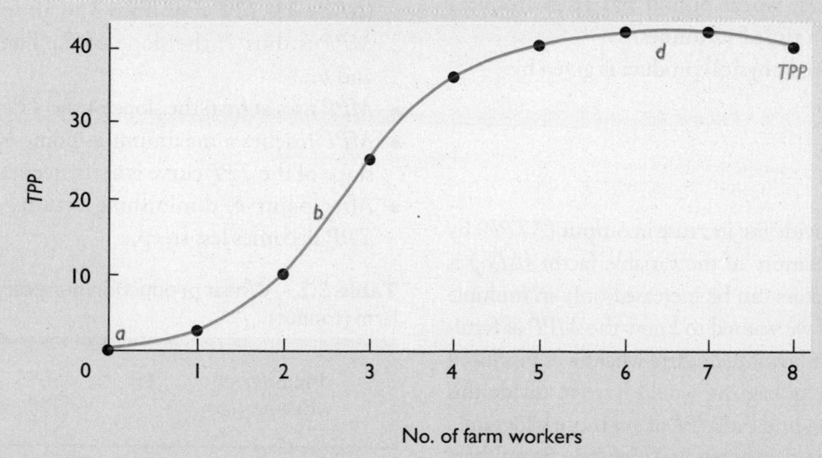

Figure 5.1 Wheat production per year from a particular farm

DEFINITIONS

Average physical product Total output (*TPP*) per unit of the variable factor in question: $APP = TPP/Q_v$.

Marginal physical product The extra output gained by the employment of one more unit of the variable factor: $MPP = \Delta TPP/\Delta Q_v$.

CASE STUDIES BOX 5.2

DIMINISHING RETURNS IN THE BREAD SHOP

Is the baker using his loaf?

Just up the road from where I live is a bread shop. Like many others, I buy my bread there on a Saturday morning. Not surprisingly, Saturday morning is the busiest time of the week for the shop and as a result it takes on extra assistants.

During the week only one assistant serves the customers, but on a Saturday morning there used to be five serving. But could they serve five times as many customers? No, they could not. There were diminishing returns to labour.

The trouble is that certain factors of production in the shop are fixed:

- The shop is a fixed size. It gets very crowded on Saturday morning. Assistants sometimes have to wait while customers squeeze past each other to get to the counter, and with five serving, the assistants themselves used to get in each other's way.
- There is only one cash till. Assistants frequently had to wait while other assistants used it.
- There is only one pile of tissue paper for wrapping the bread. Again the assistants often had to wait.

The fifth and maybe even the fourth assistant ended up serving very few extra customers.

I am still going to the same bread shop and they still have only one till and one pile of tissue paper. But now only three assistants are employed on a Saturday! The shop, however, is just as busy.

?? How would you advise the baker as to whether he should (a) employ *four* assistants on a Saturday; (b) extend his shop, thereby allowing more customers to be served on a Saturday morning?

Marginal physical product

This is the *extra* output (ΔTPP) produced by employing *one more* unit of the variable factor.

Thus in Table 5.1 the marginal physical product of the fourth worker is 12 tonnes. The reason is that by employing the fourth worker, wheat output has risen from 24 tonnes to 36 tonnes: a rise of 12 tonnes.

In symbols, marginal physical product is given by:

$$MPP = \Delta TPP/\Delta Q_v$$

Thus in our example:

$$MPP = 12/1 = 12$$

The reason why we divide the increase in output (ΔTPP) by the increase in the quantity of the variable factor (ΔQ_v) is that some variable factors can be increased only in multiple units. For example, if we wanted to know the *MPP* of fertiliser and we found out how much extra wheat was produced by using an extra 20 kg bag, we would have to divide this output by 20 (ΔQ_v) to find the *MPP* of *one* more kilogram.

Let us return to the data given in Table 5.1. From these figures we can derive figures for *APP* and *MPP*. This is done in Table 5.2.

Note that the figures for *MPP* are entered in the spaces between the other figures. The reason is that *MPP* can be seen as the *difference* in output *between* one level of input and another. Thus in the table the difference in output between five and six workers is 2 tonnes.

These figures can be represented graphically. Figure 5.2 shows *TPP* on one graph and *APP* and *MPP* on another. We can draw a number of conclusions from these diagrams:

- The *MPP* between two points is equal to the slope of the *TPP* curve between those two points. For example, when the number of workers increases from 1 to 2 ($\Delta Lb = 1$), *TPP* rises from 3 to 10 tonnes ($\Delta TPP = 7$). *MPP* is thus 7: the slope of the line between points *g* and *h*.
- *MPP* rises at first: the slope of the *TPP* curve gets steeper.
- *MPP* reaches a maximum at point *b*. At that point the slope of the *TPP* curve is at its steepest.
- After point *b*, diminishing returns set in. *MPP* falls. *TPP* becomes less steep.

Table 5.2 Wheat production per year from a particular farm (tonnes)

	Number of workers (*Lb*)	*TPP*	*APP* (= *TPP*/*Lb*)	*MPP* (= Δ*TPP*/Δ*Lb*)
a	0	0	–	
				3
	1	3	3	
				7
	2	10	5	
b				14
	3	24	8	
				12
c	4	36	9	
				4
	5	40	8	
				2
	6	42	7	
d				0
	7	42	6	
				–2
	8	40	5	

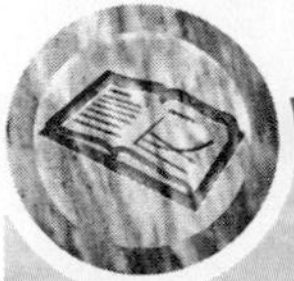

EXPLORING THE THEORY BOX 5.3

THE RELATIONSHIP BETWEEN AVERAGES AND MARGINALS

In this chapter we have just examined the concepts of *average* and *marginal* physical product. We shall be coming across several other average and marginal concepts later on. It is useful at this stage to examine the general relationship between averages and marginals. In all cases there are three simple rules that relate them.

To illustrate these rules, consider the following example.

Imagine a room with ten people in it. Assume that the *average* age of those present is 20.

Now if a 20-year-old enters the room (the *marginal* age), this will not affect the average age. It will remain at 20. If a 56-year-old now comes in, the average age will rise: not to 56, of course, but to 23. This is found by dividing the sum of everyone's ages (276) by the number of people (12). If then a child of 10 were to enter the room, this would pull the average age down.

From this example we can derive the three universal rules about averages and marginals:

- If the marginal equals the average, the average will not change.
- If the marginal is above the average, the average will rise.
- If the marginal is below the average, the average will fall.

??

A cricketer scores the following number of runs in five successive innings:

Innings:	1	2	3	4	5
Runs:	20	20	50	10	0

These can be seen as the marginal number of runs from each innings. Calculate the total and average number of runs after each innings. Show how the average and marginal scores illustrate the three rules above.

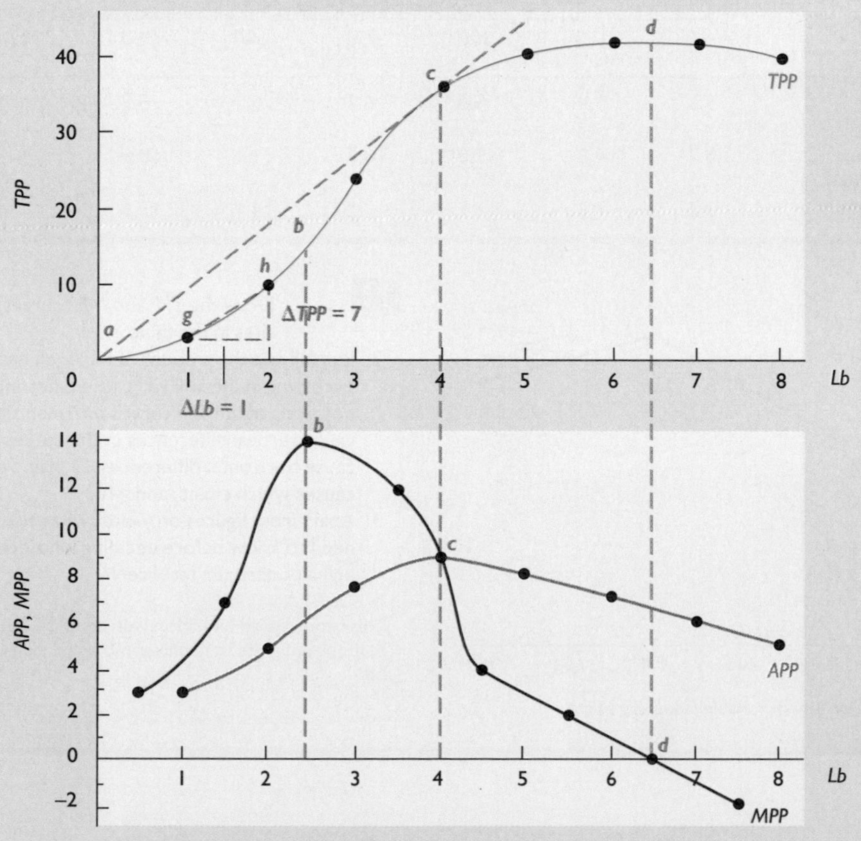

Figure 5.2 Wheat production per year (tonnes)

CASE STUDIES BOX 5.4

DIMINISHING RETURNS TO NITROGEN FERTILISER

Modern trends in agriculture provide a dramatic example of the law of diminishing returns.

Over the last 40 years or so, there have been large increases in yields from grasslands. This has been largely due to huge increases in the use of nitrogen fertiliser. In England and Wales this has risen over the period from around 10 kilograms per hectare to over 100. Some farmers use considerably more.

In 1976 J. Morrison and M. V. Jackson[2] reported on experiments to show the effects on grass yields of different amounts of nitrogen fertiliser.

The experiments were conducted over a four-year period on a number of different sites up and down the country. The findings from three of the sites are shown in the table.

A similar pattern emerges from all the sites. Total output of grass (*TPP*) rises at a roughly constant rate (in other words, *MPP* is roughly constant) with up to about 300 kg/ha of fertiliser. These rises are substantial. Just look at the Gleadthorpe figures! Above 300 kg/ha, however, diminishing returns set in. Additional applications of fertiliser yield less and less extra output: *MPP* falls.

Maximum yield is obtained at around the 600 kg/ha of nitrogen level. Above that, *MPP* is negative.

If the soil has a high *natural* level of nitrogen, the effects of adding nitrogen fertiliser will be more limited. Diminishing returns will set in before the 300 kg/ha level. Consider the graph. It shows the effects of fertiliser on two more sites: Bangor in North Wales and Wenvoe in South Wales.

At Wenvoe there is very little natural nitrogen in the soil. At Bangor, however, the soil supplies about 150 kg/ha of nitrogen. In other respects the sites are similar.

Average (dry matter) grass yields: tonnes per hectare (total physical product: *TPP*)

Site	Nitrogen fertiliser applied: kg/ha/year						Mean rainfall
	0	150	300	450	600	750	May–August (mm)
Cambridge	1.3	3.4	5.6	6.1	6.1	5.9	175
Gleadthorpe, Nottingham	0.7	4.8	9.0	10.7	11.1	10.9	252
South-west Wales (4 sites)	3.2	7.3	11.1	13.2	14.1	13.6	311

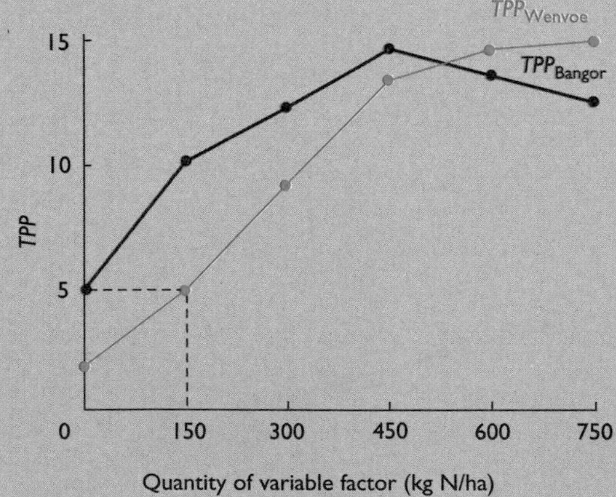

??

1. Draw the *TPP* and *MPP* curves for the three sites in the table.
2. Rainfall and the amount of nitrogen naturally occurring in the soil will cause differences in the positions of the *TPP* curves between sites. One will cause vertical differences in the curves and one will cause horizontal differences. Explain which one causes which effect (and why).
3. Apart from figures on yields, what else will a farmer need to know before deciding whether to use 600 kg/ha of nitrogen fertiliser?

[2] This box is based on J. Morrison and M. V. Jackson, 'The response of grass to fertilizer nitrogen', *Span*, vol. 19 (1976), no. 1.

EXPLORING THE THEORY *BOX 5.5

THE RELATIONSHIP BETWEEN *TPP*, *MPP* AND *APP*
Using calculus again

The total physical product of a variable factor (e.g. fertiliser) can be expressed as an equation. For example:

$$TPP = 100 + 32Q_f + 10Q_f^2 - Q_f^3 \quad (1)$$

where *TPP* is the output of grain in tonnes per hectare, and Q_f is the quantity of fertiliser applied in kilograms per hectare.

From this we can derive the *APP* function. *APP* is simply TPP/Q_f: i.e. output per kilogram of fertiliser. Thus:

$$APP = \frac{100}{Q_f} + 32 + 10Q_f - Q_f^2 \quad (2)$$

We can also derive the *MPP* function. *MPP* is the rate of increase in *TPP* as additional fertiliser is applied. It is thus the first derivative of *TPP*: $dTPP/dQ_f$. Thus:

$$MPP = 32 + 20Q_f - 3Q_f^2 \quad (3)$$

From these three equations we can derive the table shown.

?? Check out some figures by substituting values of Q_f into each of the three equations.

Q_f	*TPP*	*APP*	*MPP*
1	141	141	49
2	196	98	60
3	259	86	65
4	324	81	64
5	385	77	57
6	436	72	44
7	471	67	25
8	484	60	0
9	469	52	–31

Maximum output (484 tonnes) is achieved with 8 kg of fertiliser per hectare. At that level, *MPP* is zero: no additional output can be gained.

This maximum level of *TPP* can be discovered from the equations by using a simple technique. If *MPP* is zero at this level, then simply find the value of Q_f where:

$$MPP = 32 + 20Q_f - 3Q_f^2 = 0 \quad (4)$$

Solving this equation[3] gives $Q_f = 8$.

[3] By applying the second derivative test (see p. 37) you can verify that $Q_f = 8$ gives the *maximum TPP* rather than the *minimum*. (Both the maximum *and* the minimum point of a curve have a slope equal to zero.)

- *APP* rises at first. It continues rising as long as the addition to output from the last worker (*MPP*) is greater than the average output (*APP*): the *MPP* pulls the *APP* up (see Box 5.3). This continues beyond point *b*. Even though *MPP* is now falling, the *APP goes on* rising as long as the *MPP* is still above the *APP*. Thus *APP* goes on rising to point *c*.
- Beyond point *c*, *MPP* is below *APP*. New workers add less to output than the average. This pulls the average down: *APP* falls.
- As long as *MPP* is greater than zero, *TPP* will go on rising: new workers add to total output.
- At point *d*, *TPP* is at a maximum (its slope is zero). An additional worker will add nothing to output: *MPP* is zero.
- Beyond point *d*, *TPP* falls. *MPP* is negative.

??
1. What is the significance of the slope of the line *ac* in the top part of Figure 5.2?
2. Given that there is a fixed supply of land in the world, what implications can you draw from Figure 5.2 about the effects of an increase in world population for food output per head? (See Box 5.1.)

SECTION SUMMARY

1. A production function shows the relationship between the amount of inputs used and the amount of output produced from them (per period of time).
2. In the short run it is assumed that one or more factors (inputs) are fixed in supply. The actual length of the short run will vary from industry to industry.
3. Production in the short run is subject to diminishing returns. As greater quantities of the variable factor(s) are used, so each additional unit of the variable factor will add less to output than previous units: marginal physical product will diminish and total physical product will rise less and less rapidly.
4. As long as marginal physical product is above average physical product, average physical product will rise. Once *MPP* has fallen below *APP*, however, *APP* will fall.

5.2

Background to costs: the long-run theory of production

In the long run *all* factors of production are variable. There is time for the firm to build a new factory (maybe in a different part of the country), to install new machines, to use different techniques of production, and in general to combine its inputs in whatever proportion and in whatever quantities it chooses.

In the long run, then, there are a number of decisions that a firm will have to make: decisions about the scale of its operations, the location of its operations and the techniques of production it will use. These decisions will affect the costs of production. It is important, therefore, to get them right.

The scale of production

If a firm were to double all of its inputs – something it could do in the long run – would it double its output? Or will output more than double or less than double? We can distinguish three possible situations:

Constant returns to scale. This is where a given percentage increase in inputs will lead to the *same* percentage increase in output.

Increasing returns to scale. This is where a given percentage increase in inputs will lead to a *larger* percentage increase in output.

Decreasing returns to scale. This is where a given percentage increase in inputs will lead to a *smaller* percentage increase in output.

Notice the terminology here. The words 'to scale' mean that *all* inputs increase by the same proportion. Decreasing returns *to scale* are therefore quite different from diminishing *marginal* returns (where only the *variable* factor increases). The differences between marginal returns to a variable factor and returns to scale are illustrated in Table 5.3.

In the short run, input 1 is assumed to be fixed in supply (at 3 units). Output can be increased only by using more of the variable factor (input 2). In the long run, however, both input 1 and input 2 are variable.

?? Referring still to Table 5.3, are there diminishing or increasing marginal returns, and are there decreasing or increasing returns to scale?

Economies of scale

The concept of increasing returns to scale is closely linked to that of **economies of scale**. A firm experiences economies of scale if costs per unit of output fall as the scale of production increases. Clearly, if a firm is getting increasing returns to scale from its factors of production, then as it produces more it will be using smaller and smaller amounts of factors per unit of output. Other things being equal this means that it will be producing at a lower unit cost.

There are a number of reasons why firms are likely to experience economies of scale. Some are due to increasing returns to scale; some are not.

Specialisation and division of labour. In large-scale plants workers can do more simple, repetitive jobs. With this **specialisation and division of labour** less training is needed; workers can become highly efficient in their particular job, especially with long production runs; there is less time lost in workers switching from one operation to another; and supervision is easier. Workers and managers can be employed who have specific skills in specific areas.

Indivisibilities. Some inputs are of a minimum size: they are indivisible. The most obvious example is machinery. Take the case of a combine harvester. A small-scale farmer

Table 5.3 Short-run and long-run increases in output

Short run			Long run		
Input 1	Input 2	Output	Input 1	Input 2	Output
3	1	25	1	1	15
3	2	45	2	2	35
3	3	60	3	3	60
3	4	70	4	4	90
3	5	75	5	5	125

DEFINITIONS

Economies of scale When increasing the scale of production leads to a lower cost per unit of output.

Specialisation and division of labour Where production is broken down into a number of simpler, more specialised tasks, thus allowing workers to acquire a high degree of efficiency.

could not make full use of one. They only become economical to use, therefore, on farms above a certain size. The problem of **indivisibilities** is made worse when different machines, each of which is part of the production process, are of a different size. For example, if there are two types of machine, one producing 6 units a day, and the other packaging 4 units a day, a minimum of 12 units would have to be produced, involving two production machines and three packaging machines, if all machines are to be fully utilised.

The 'container principle'. Any capital equipment that contains things (e.g. blast furnaces, oil tankers, pipes, vats, etc.) will tend to cost less per unit of output the larger its size. The reason has to do with the relationship between a container's volume and its surface area. A container's cost will depend largely on the materials used to build it and hence roughly on its *surface area*. Its output will depend largely on its *volume*. Large containers have a bigger volume relative to surface area than do small containers. For example, a container with a bottom, top and four sides, with each side measuring 1 metre, has a volume of 1 cubic metre and a surface area of 6 square metres (six surfaces of 1 square metre each). If each side were now to be doubled in length to 2 metres, the volume would be 8 cubic metres and the surface area 24 square metres (six surfaces of 4 square metres each). Thus an eightfold increase in capacity has been gained at only a fourfold increase in the container's surface area, and hence an approximate fourfold increase in cost.

Greater efficiency of large machines. Large machines may be more efficient in the sense that more output can be gained for a given amount of inputs. For example, only one worker may be required to operate a machine whether it be large or small. Also, a large machine may make more efficient use of raw materials.

By-products. With production on a large scale, there may be sufficient waste products to enable them to make some by-product.

Multi-stage production. A large factory may be able to take a product through several stages in its manufacture. This saves time and cost in moving the semi-finished product from one firm or factory to another. For example, a large cardboard-manufacturing firm may be able to convert trees or waste paper into cardboard and then into cardboard boxes in a continuous sequence.

All the above are examples of **plant economies of scale**. They are due to an individual factory or workplace or machine being large. There are other economies of scale that are associated with the *firm* being large – perhaps with many factories.

Organisational economies. With a large firm, individual plants can specialise in particular functions. There can also be centralised administration of the firms. Often, after a merger between two firms, savings can be made by **rationalising** their activities in this way.

Spreading overheads. There are some expenditures that are only economic when the *firm* is large, for example research and development: only a large firm can afford to set up a research laboratory. This is another example of indivisibilities, only this time at the level of the firm rather than the plant. The greater the firm's output, the more these **overhead** costs are spread.

Financial economies. Large firms may be able to obtain finance at lower interest rates than small firms. They may be able to obtain certain inputs cheaper by buying in bulk.

??

1. Which of the economies of scale we have considered are due to increasing returns to scale and which are due to other factors?
2. What economies of scale is a large department store likely to experience?

Diseconomies of scale

When firms get beyond a certain size, costs per unit of output may start to increase. There are several reasons for such **diseconomies of scale**:

DEFINITIONS

Indivisibilities The impossibility of dividing a factor into smaller units.

Plant economies of scale Economies of scale that arise because of the large size of the factory.

Rationalisation The reorganising of production (often after a merger) so as to cut out waste and duplication and generally to reduce costs.

Overheads Costs arising from the general running of an organisation, and only indirectly related to the level of output.

Diseconomies of scale Where costs per unit of output increase as the scale of production increases.

- Management problems of co-ordination may increase as the firm becomes larger and more complex, and as lines of communication get longer. There may be a lack of personal involvement by management.
- Workers may feel 'alienated' if their jobs are boring and repetitive, and if they feel an insignificantly small part of a large organisation. Poor motivation may lead to shoddy work.
- Industrial relations may deteriorate as a result of these factors and also as a result of the more complex inter-relationships between different categories of worker.
- Production-line processes and the complex interdependencies of mass production can lead to great disruption if there are hold-ups in any one part of the firm.

Whether firms experience economies or diseconomies of scale will depend on the conditions applying in each individual firm.

> ?? Why are firms likely to experience economies of scale up to a certain size and then diseconomies of scale after some point beyond that?

Location

In the long run, a firm can move to a different location. The location will affect the cost of production since locations differ in terms of the availability and cost of raw materials, suitable land and power supply, the qualifications, skills and experience of the labour force, wage rates, transport and communications networks, the cost of local services, and banking and financial facilities. In short, locations differ in terms of the availability, suitability and cost of the factors of production.

Transport costs will be an important influence on a firm's location. Ideally, a firm will wish to be as near as possible to both its raw materials and the market for its finished product. When market and raw materials are in different locations, the firm will minimise its transport costs by locating somewhere between the two. In general, if the raw materials are more expensive to transport than the finished product, the firm should be located as near as possible to the raw materials. This will normally apply to firms whose raw materials are heavier or more bulky than the finished product. Thus heavy industry, which uses large quantities of coal and various ores, tends to be concentrated near the coal fields or near the ports. If, on the other hand, the finished product is more expensive to transport (e.g. bread and beer), the firm will probably be located as near as possible to its market.

When raw materials or markets are in many different locations, transport costs will be minimised at the 'centre of gravity'. This location will be nearer to those raw materials and markets whose transport costs are greater per mile.

> ?? How is the opening-up of trade and investment between eastern and western Europe likely to affect the location of industries within Europe that have (a) substantial economies of scale; (b) little or no economies of scale?

The size of the whole industry

As an *industry* grows in size, this can lead to **external economies of scale** for its member firms. This is where a firm, whatever its own individual size, benefits from the *whole industry* being large. For example, the firm may benefit from having access to specialist raw material or component suppliers, labour with specific skills, firms which specialise in marketing the finished product, and banks and other financial institutions with experience of the industry's requirements. What we are referring to here is the **industry's infrastructure**: the facilities, support services, skills and experience that can be shared by its members.

> ??
> 1. Name some industries where external economies of scale are gained. What are the specific external economies in each case?
> 2. Would you expect external economies to be associated with the concentration of an industry in a particular region?

The member firms of a particular industry might experience **external diseconomies of scale**. For example, as an industry grows larger this may create a growing shortage of specific raw materials or skilled labour. This will push up their prices, and hence the firms' costs.

DEFINITIONS

External economies of scale Where a firm's costs per unit of output decrease as the size of the whole *industry* grows.

Industry's infrastructure The network of supply agents, communications, skills, training facilities, distribution channels, specialised financial services, etc. that supports a particular industry.

External diseconomies of scale Where a firm's costs per unit of output increase as the size of the whole industry increases.

The optimum combination of factors: the marginal product approach

In the long run, all factors can be varied. The firm can thus choose what techniques of production to use: what design of factory to build, what types of machine to buy, how to organise the factory, whether to use highly automated processes or more labour-intensive techniques. It must be very careful in making these decisions. Once it has built its factory and installed the machinery, these then become fixed factors of production, maybe for many years: the subsequent 'short-run' time period may in practice last a very long time!

For any given scale, how should the firm decide what technique to use? How should it decide the optimum 'mix' of factors of production?

The profit-maximising firm will obviously want to use the least costly combination of factors to produce any given output. It will therefore substitute factors, one for another, if by so doing it can reduce the cost of a given output. What then is the optimum combination of factors?

The simple two-factor case

Take first the simplest case where a firm uses just two factors: labour (L) and capital (K). The least-cost combination of the two will be where:

$$\frac{MPP_L}{P_L} = \frac{MPP_K}{P_K}$$

in other words, where the extra product (MPP) from the last pound spent on each factor is equal. But why should this be so? The easiest way to answer this is to consider what would happen if they were not equal.

If they were not equal, it would be possible to reduce cost per unit of output, by using a different combination of labour and capital. For example, if:

$$\frac{MPP_L}{P_L} > \frac{MPP_K}{P_K}$$

more labour should be used relative to capital, since the firm is getting a greater physical return for its money from extra workers than from extra capital. As more labour is used per unit of capital, however, diminishing returns to labour set in. Thus MPP_L will fall. Likewise, as less capital is used per unit of labour, MPP_K will rise. This will continue until:

$$\frac{MPP_L}{P_L} = \frac{MPP_K}{P_K}$$

At this point the firm will stop substituting labour for capital.

Since no further gain can be made by substituting one factor for another, this combination of factors or 'choice of technique' can be said to be the most efficient. It is the least-cost way of combining factors for any given output. Efficiency in this sense of using the optimum factor proportions is known as **technical or productive efficiency**.

The multi-factor case

Where a firm uses many different factors, the least-cost combination of factors will be where:

$$\frac{MPP_a}{P_a} = \frac{MPP_b}{P_b} = \frac{MPP_c}{P_c} \ldots = \frac{MPP_n}{P_n}$$

where a ... n are different factors.

The reasons are the same as in the two-factor case. If any inequality exists between the MPP/P ratios, a firm will be able to reduce its costs by using more of those factors with a high MPP/P ratio and less of those with a low MPP/P ratio until they all become equal.

A major problem for a firm in choosing the least-cost technique is in predicting future factor price changes.

If the price of a factor were to change, the MPP/P ratios would cease to be equal. The firm, to minimise costs, would then like to alter its factor combinations until the MPP/P ratios once more became equal. The trouble is that, once it has committed itself to a particular technique, it may be several years before it can switch to an alternative one. Thus if a firm invests in labour-intensive methods of production and is then faced with an unexpected wage rise, it may regret not having chosen a more capital-intensive technique.

> **??** If factor X costs twice as much as factor Y ($P_X/P_Y = 2$), what can be said about the relationship between the *MPP*s of the two factors if the optimum combination of factors is used?

*The optimum combination of factors: the isoquant/isocost approach

A firm's choice of optimum technique can be shown graphically. This graphical analysis takes the simplest case of just two variable factors – for example, labour and capital. The amount of labour used is measured on one axis and the amount of capital used is measured on the other.

The graph involves the construction of *isoquants* and *isocosts*.

> **DEFINITION**
>
> **Technical or productive efficiency** The least-cost combination of factors for a given output.

Isoquants

Imagine that a firm wants to produce a certain level of output: say, 5000 units. Let us assume that it estimates all the possible combinations of labour and capital that could produce that level of output. Some of these estimates are shown in Table 5.4.

Technique *a* is a capital-intensive technique, using 40 units of capital and only 5 workers. As we move towards technique *e*, labour is substituted for capital. The techniques become more labour intensive.

These alternative techniques for producing a given level of output can be plotted on a graph. The points are joined to form an **isoquant**. Figure 5.3 shows the 5000 unit isoquant corresponding to Table 5.4.

The isoquant shows the whole *range* of alternative ways of producing a given output. Thus Figure 5.3 shows not only points *a* to *e* from the table, but all the intermediate points too.

Like an indifference curve, an isoquant is rather like a contour on a map. And like contours and indifference curves, a whole series of isoquants can be drawn, each one representing a different level of output (*TPP*). The higher the output, the further out to the right will the isoquant be. Thus in Figure 5.4, isoquant I_5 represents a higher level of output than I_4, and I_4 a higher output than I_3, and so on.

??

1. Could isoquants ever cross?
2. Could they ever slope upwards to the right? Explain your answers.

Table 5.4 Various capital and labour combinations to produce 5000 units of output

	a	*b*	*c*	*d*	*e*
Units of capital (*K*)	40	20	10	6	4
Number of workers (*L*)	5	12	20	30	50

The shape of the isoquant. Why is the isoquant 'bowed in' toward the origin? This illustrates a diminishing **marginal rate of factor substitution** (*MRS*). This, as we shall see in a minute, is due to the law of diminishing returns.

The *MRS*[4] is the amount of one factor (e.g. *K*) that can be replaced by a 1 unit increase in the other factor (e.g. *L*), if output is to be held constant. So if 2 units of capital ($\Delta K = 2$) could be replaced by 1 unit of labour ($\Delta L = 1$) the *MRS* would be 2. Thus:

$$MRS = \frac{\Delta K}{\Delta L} = \frac{2}{1} = 2$$

The *MRS* between two points on the isoquant will equal the slope of the line joining those two points. Thus in Figure 5.5, the *MRS* between points *g* and *h* is 2

[4] Note that we use the same letters *MRS* to refer to the marginal rate of *factor* substitution as we did in the last chapter to refer to the marginal rate of substitution *in consumption*. Sometimes we use the same words too – just 'marginal rate of substitution' rather than the longer title. In this case we must rely on the context in order to tell which is being referred to.

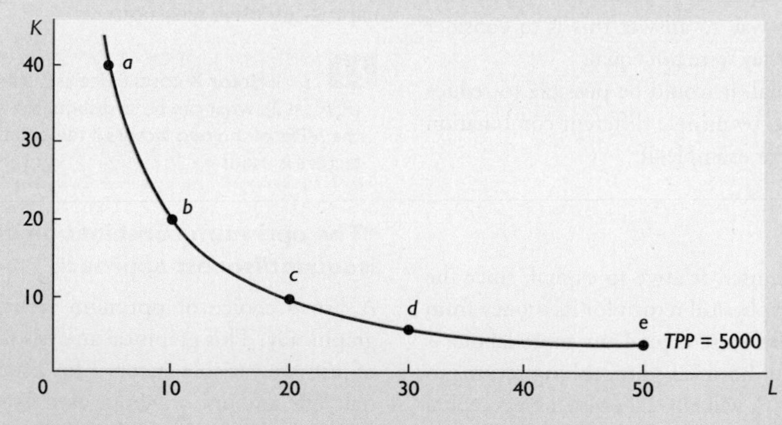

Figure 5.3 An isoquant

DEFINITIONS

Isoquant A line showing all the alternative combinations of two factors that can produce a given level of output.

Marginal rate of factor substitution The rate at which one factor can be substituted by another while holding the level of output constant: $MRS = \Delta F_1/\Delta F_2 = MPP_{F_2}/MPP_{F_1}$

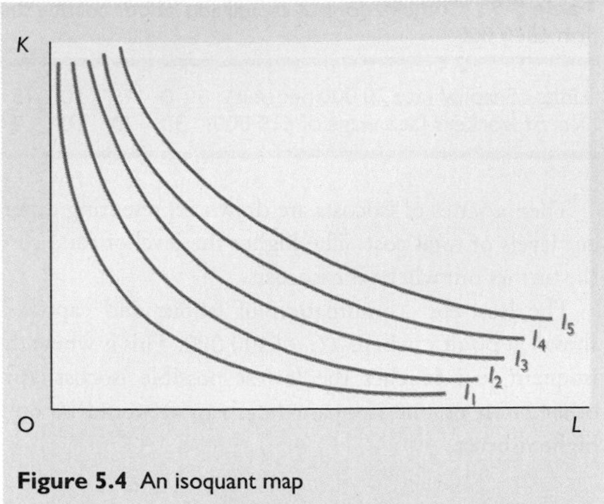

Figure 5.4 An isoquant map

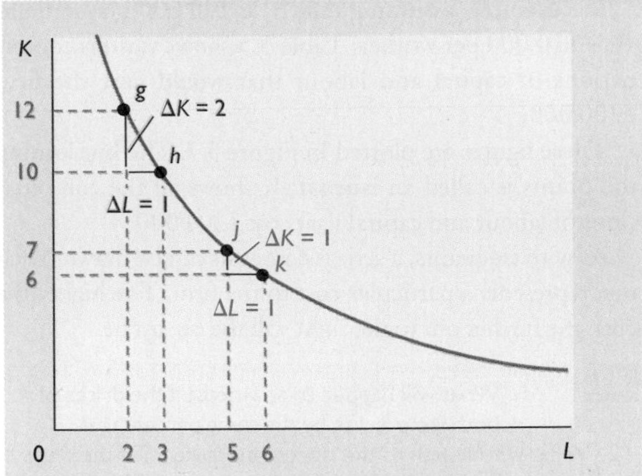

Figure 5.5 Diminishing marginal rate of factor substitution

($\Delta K/\Delta L = 2/1$). But this is merely the slope of the line joining points *g* and *h* (ignoring the negative sign).

When the isoquant is bowed in towards the origin, the slope of the isoquant will diminish as one moves down the curve, and so too, therefore, will the *MRS* diminish. Referring again to Figure 5.5, between points *g* and *h* the *MRS* = 2. Lower down the curve between points *j* and *k*, it has fallen to 1.

?? Calculate the MRS moving up the curve in Figure 5.3 between each of the points: *e–d*, *d–c*, *c–b* and *b–a*. Does the MRS diminish moving in this direction?

The relationship between MRS and MPP. As one moves down the isoquant, total output, by definition, will remain the same. Thus the loss in output due to less capital being used (i.e. $MPP_K \times \Delta K$) must be exactly offset by the gain in output due to more labour being used (i.e. $MPP_L \times \Delta L$). Thus:

$$MPP_L \times \Delta L = MPP_K \times \Delta K$$

This equation can be rearranged as follows:

$$\frac{MPP_L}{MPP_K} = \frac{\Delta K}{\Delta L} \quad (= MRS)$$

Thus the *MRS* is equal to the inverse of the marginal productivity ratios of the two factors.

Diminishing MRS and the law of diminishing returns. The principle of diminishing *MRS* is related to the law of diminishing returns. As one moves down the isoquant, increasing amounts of labour are being used relative to capital. This, given diminishing returns, would lead the *MPP* of labour to fall relative to the *MPP* of capital. But since $MRS = MPP_L/MPP_K$, if MPP_L/MPP_K diminishes, then, by definition, so must *MRS*.

The less substitutable factors are for each other, the faster *MRS* will diminish, and therefore the more bowed in will be the isoquant.

Isoquants and returns to scale. We can use isoquants to illustrate constant, increasing and decreasing returns to scale.

In each of the three diagrams of Figure 5.6 we show the effect of equal percentage increases in the inputs of the two factors (*K, L*). As we increase both by the same proportion, we move up a straight line through the origin (or 'ray'). The ray illustrated in the three diagrams (*R*) is drawn with a slope of 45°, but it could be drawn with any slope.

What happens as we increase capital and labour from 1 unit of each to 2 units to 3 units, and thus move from point *a* to *b* to *c*? In diagram (a) the isoquants are equally spaced. Output increases from 200 to 400 to 600 units. There are *constant returns* to scale. In diagram (b) the isoquants get closer beyond point *b*. As we move from *a* to *b* to *c* this time output increases from 200 to 400 to 700 units. There are *increasing returns* to scale beyond point *b*. Finally in diagram (c) the isoquants get further apart. Output increases from 200 to 400 to 500 units. There are *decreasing returns* to scale beyond point *b*.

?? Draw an isoquant map that illustrates increasing returns to scale up to a certain level of output, and then decreasing returns beyond that.

Isocosts

We have seen how factors combine to produce different levels of output, but how do we choose the level of output? This will involve taking costs into account.

Assume that factor prices are fixed. A table can be constructed showing the various combinations of factors that a firm can use for a particular sum of money.

For example, assuming that P_K is £20 000 per unit and P_L is £10 000 per worker, Table 5.5 shows various combinations of capital and labour that would cost the firm £300 000.

These figures are plotted in Figure 5.7. The line joining the points is called an **isocost**. It shows all the combinations of labour and capital that cost £300 000.

As with isoquants, a series of isocosts can be drawn. Each one represents a particular cost to the firm. The higher the cost, the further out to the right will the isocost be.

??

1. What will happen to an isocost if the prices of both factors rise by the same percentage?
2. What will happen to the isocost in Figure 5.7 if the wage rate rises to £15 000?

The slope of the isocost equals:

$$\frac{P_L}{P_K}$$

This can be shown in the above example. The slope of the isocost in Figure 5.7 is 15/30 = ½. But this is P_L/P_K (i.e. £10 000/£20 000).

Isoquants and isocosts can now be put on the same diagram. The diagram can be used to answer either of two questions: (a) What is the least-cost way of producing a particular level of output? (b) What is the highest output that can be achieved for a given cost of production?

These two questions are examined in turn.

The least-cost combination of factors to produce a given level of output

First the isoquant is drawn for the level of output in question: for example, the 5000 unit isoquant in Figure 5.3. This is reproduced in Figure 5.8.

Table 5.5 Combinations of capital and labour costing the firm £300 000

Units of capital (at £20 000 per unit)	0	5	10	15
No. of workers (at a wage of £10 000)	30	20	10	0

Then a series of isocosts are drawn representing different levels of total cost. The higher the level of total cost, the further out will be the isocosts.

The least-cost combination of labour and capital is shown at point *r*, where TC = £400 000. This is where the isoquant just touches the lowest possible isocost. Any other point on the isoquant (e.g. *s* or *t*) would be on a higher isocost.

Comparison with the marginal productivity approach. We showed earlier that the least-cost combination of labour and capital was where:

$$\frac{MPP_L}{P_L} = \frac{MPP_K}{P_K}$$

In this section it has just been shown that the least-cost combination is where the isoquant is tangential to an isocost (i.e. point *r* in Figure 5.8). Thus their slope is the same. The slope of the isoquant equals *MRS*, which equals MPP_L/MPP_K; and the slope of the isocost equals P_L/P_K.

$$\therefore \quad \frac{MPP_L}{MPP_K} = \frac{P_L}{P_K}$$

DEFINITION

Isocost A line showing all the combinations of two factors that cost the same to employ.

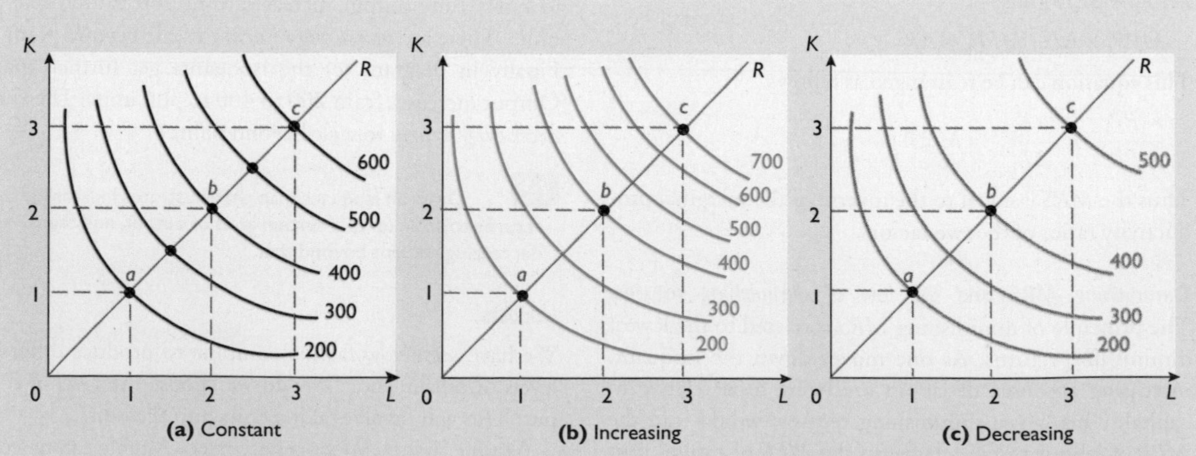

Figure 5.6 Returns to scale

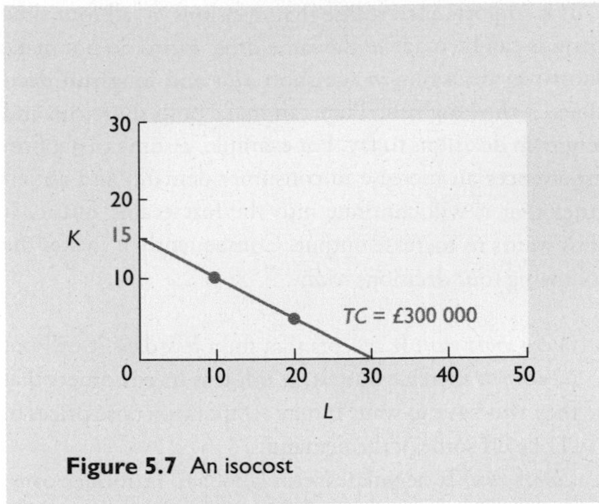

Figure 5.7 An isocost

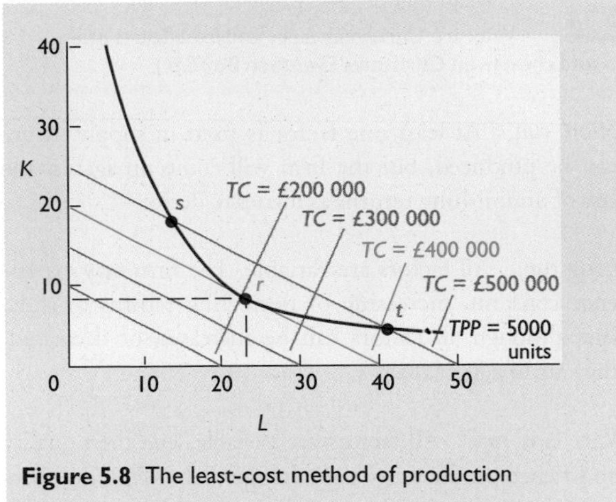

Figure 5.8 The least-cost method of production

$$\therefore \frac{MPP_L}{P_L} = \frac{MPP_K}{P_K}$$

Thus, as one would expect, the two approaches yield the same result.

Highest output for a given cost of production

An isocost can be drawn for the particular level of total cost outlay in question. Then a series of isoquants can be drawn, representing different levels of output (*TPP*). This is shown in Figure 5.9. The higher the level of output, the further out will lie the corresponding isoquant. The point at which the isocost touches the highest isoquant will give the factor combination yielding the highest output for that level of cost. This will be at point *h* in Figure 5.9.

Again this will be where the slopes of the isocost and isoquant are the same: where $P_L/P_K = MRS$.

If the prices of factors change, new isocosts will have to be drawn. Thus in Figure 5.9, if wages go up, less labour can be used for a given sum of money. The isocost will swing inward round point *x*. The isocost will get steeper. Less labour will now be used relative to capital.

Postscript: Decision making in different time periods

We have distinguished between the short run and the long run. Let us introduce two more time periods to complete the picture. The complete list then reads as follows.

Very short run (immediate run). All factors are fixed. Output is fixed. The supply curve is vertical. On a day-to-day basis a firm may not be able to vary output at all. For example, a flower seller, once the day's flowers have been purchased from the wholesaler, cannot alter the amount of flowers available for sale on that day. In the very short run, all that may remain for a producer to do is to sell an already produced good.

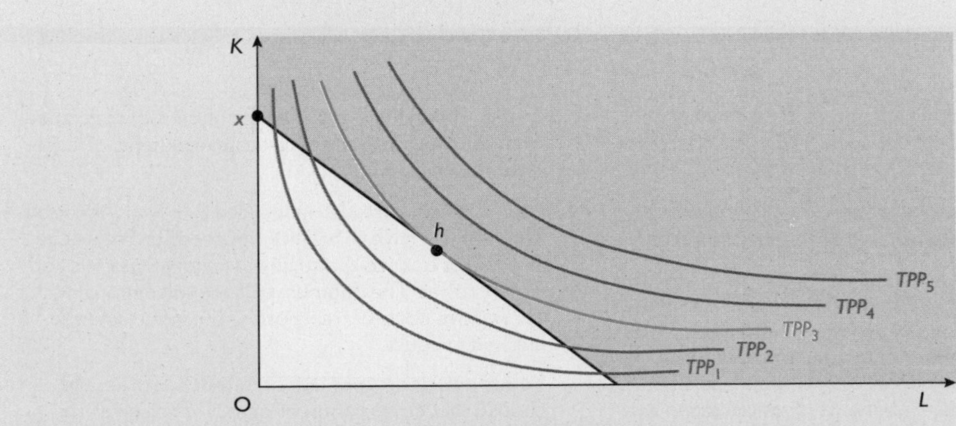

Figure 5.9 Maximising output for a given total cost

??
Why are Christmas trees and fresh foods often sold cheaply on Christmas Eve? (See Box 5.6.)

Short run. At least one factor is fixed in supply. More can be produced, but the firm will come up against the law of diminishing returns as it tries to do so.

Long run. All factors are variable. The firm may experience constant, increasing or decreasing returns to scale. But although all factors can be increased or decreased, they are of a fixed *quality*.

Very long run. All factors are variable, *and* their quality and hence productivity can change. Labour productivity can increase as a result of education, training, experience and social factors. The productivity of capital can increase as a result of new inventions (new discoveries) and innovation (putting inventions into practice).

Improvements in factor quality will increase the output they produce: *TPP*, *APP* and *MPP* will rise. These curves will shift vertically upward.

Just how long the 'very long run' is will vary from firm to firm. It will depend on how long it takes to develop new techniques, new skills or new work practices.

??
1. Could the long run and the very long run ever be the *same* length of time?
2. What will the long-run and very-long-run market supply curves for a product look like? How will the shape of the long-run curve depend on returns to scale?
*3. In the very long run new isoquants will have to be drawn as factor productivity changes. An increase in productivity will shift the isoquants inwards towards the origin: less capital and labour will be required to produce any given level of output. Will this be a *parallel* inward shift of the isoquants? Explain.

It is important to realise that decisions *for* all four time periods can be made *at* the same time. Firms do not make short-run decisions *in* the short run and long-run decisions *in* the long run. They can make both short-run and long-run decisions today. For example, assume that a firm experiences an increase in consumer demand and anticipates that it will continue into the foreseeable future. It thus wants to increase output. Consequently it makes the following four decisions *today*.

- (*Very short run*) It accepts that for a few days it will not be able to increase output. It informs its customers that they will have to wait. It may temporarily raise prices to choke off some of the demand.
- (*Short run*) It negotiates with labour to introduce overtime working as soon as possible, to tide it over the next few weeks. It orders extra raw materials from its suppliers. It launches a recruitment drive for new labour so as to avoid paying overtime longer than is necessary.
- (*Long run*) It starts proceedings to build a new factory. The first step may be to discuss requirements with a firm of consultants.
- (*Very long run*) It institutes a programme of research and development and/or training in an attempt to increase productivity.

Although we distinguish these four time periods, it is the middle two we are primarily concerned with. The reason for this is that there is very little the firm can do in the *very* short run. And in the *very* long run, although the firm will obviously want to increase the productivity of its inputs, it will not be in a position to make precise calculations of how to do it. It will not know precisely what inventions will be made, or just what will be the results of its own research and development.

SECTION SUMMARY

1. In the long run a firm is able to vary the quantity it uses of all factors of production. There are no fixed factors.
2. If it increases all factors by the same proportion, it may experience constant, increasing or decreasing returns to scale.
3. Economies of scale occur when costs per unit of output fall as the scale of production increases. This can be due to a number of factors, some of which result directly from increasing (physical) returns to scale. These include the benefits of specialisation and division of labour, the use of larger and more efficient machines, and the ability to have a more integrated system of production. Other economies of scale arise from the financial and administrative benefits of large-scale organisations.
4. Long-run costs are also influenced by a firm's location. The firm will have to balance the needs to be as near as possible both to the supply of its raw materials and to its market. The optimum balance will depend on the relative costs of transporting the inputs and the finished product.
5. To minimise costs per unit of output a firm should choose that combination of factors which gives an equal marginal product for each factor relative to its

continued

price: i.e. $MPP_a/P_a = MPP_b/P_b = MPP_c/P_c$, etc. (where a, b and c are different factors). If the *MPP/P* ratio for one factor is greater than for another, more of the first should be used relative to the second.

*6. An isoquant shows the various combinations of two factors to produce a given output. A whole map of such isoquants can be drawn with each isoquant representing a different level of output. The slope of the isoquant ($\Delta K/\Delta L$) gives the marginal rate of factor substitution (MPP_L/MPP_K). The bowed-in shape of isoquants illustrates a diminishing marginal rate of factor substitution, which in turn arises because of diminishing marginal returns. If isoquants get progressively closer as you move outwards on the diagram, this illustrates increasing returns to scale. If they get progressively further apart, this represents decreasing returns to scale.

*7. An isocost shows the various combinations of two factors that cost a given amount to employ. It will be a straight line. Its slope is equal to the price ratio of the two factors (P_L/P_K).

*8. The tangency point of an isocost with an isoquant represents the optimum factor combination. It is the point where MPP_L/MPP_K (the slope of the isoquant) = P_L/P_K (the slope of the isocost). By drawing a single isoquant touching the lowest possible isocost we can show the least-cost combination of factors for producing a given output. By drawing a single isocost touching the highest possible isoquant we can show the highest output obtainable for a given cost of production.

9. Four distinct time periods can be distinguished. In addition to the short- and long-run periods, we can also distinguish the very-short- and very-long-run periods. The very short run is when all factors are fixed. The very long run is where not only the quantity of factors but also their quality is variable (as a result of changing technology, etc.).

5.3

Costs in the short run

Having looked at the background to costs in both the short and long run, we now turn to examine the costs themselves. Again we divide our analysis into the short run and the long run. We will be examining how costs change as a firm changes the amount it produces. Obviously, if it is to decide how much to produce, it will need to know just what the level of costs will be at each level of output.

But first we must be clear on just what we mean by the word 'costs'. The term is used differently by economists and accountants.

Measuring costs of production

When measuring costs economists always use the concept of **opportunity cost**. Remember from Chapter 1 how we defined opportunity cost. It is the cost of any activity measured in terms of the *sacrifice* made in doing it: in other words, the cost measured in terms of the opportunities forgone.

How do we apply this principle of opportunity cost to a firm? First we must discover what factors of production it has used. Then we must measure the sacrifice involved in using them. To do this it is necessary to put factors into two categories.

Factors not owned by the firm: explicit costs

The opportunity cost of those factors not already owned by the firm is simply the price the firm has to pay for them. Thus if the firm uses £100 worth of electricity, the opportunity cost is £100. The firm has sacrificed £100 which could have been spent on something else.

These costs are called **explicit costs**, because they involve direct payment of money by firms.

Factors already owned by the firm: implicit costs

When the firm already owns factors (e.g. machinery) it does not as a rule have to pay out money to use them. Their opportunity costs are thus **implicit costs**. They are equal to what the factors could earn for the firm in some alternative use, either within the firm or hired out to some other firm.

DEFINITIONS

Opportunity cost Cost measured in terms of the next best alternative forgone.

Explicit costs The payments to outside suppliers of inputs.

Implicit costs Costs which do not involve a direct payment of money to a third party, but which nevertheless involve a sacrifice of some alternative.

ISSUES AND APPLICATIONS — BOX 5.6

THE FALLACY OF USING HISTORIC COSTS

Or there's no point crying over spilt milk

'What's done is done.'

'Write it off to experience.'

'You might as well make the best of a bad job.'

These familiar sayings are all everyday examples of a simple fact of life: once something has happened, you cannot change the past. You have to take things as they are *now*.

If you fall over and break your leg, there is little point in saying, 'If only I hadn't done that I could have gone on that skiing holiday; I could have taken part in that race; I could have done so many other things (sigh).' Wishing things were different won't change history. You have to manage as well as you can *with* your broken leg.

It is the same for a firm. Once it has purchased some inputs, it is no good then wishing it hadn't. It has to accept that it has now got them, and make the best decisions about what to do with them.

Take a simple example. The local greengrocer in early December decides to buy 100 Christmas trees for £3 each. At the time of purchase this represents an opportunity cost of £3 each, since the £3 could have been spent on something else. The greengrocer estimates that there is enough local demand to sell all 100 trees at £5 each, thereby making a reasonable profit (even after allowing for handling costs).

But the estimate turns out to be wrong. On 23 December there are still 50 trees unsold. What should be done? At this stage the £3 that was paid for the trees is irrelevant. It is a historic cost. It cannot be recouped: the trees cannot be sold back to the wholesaler!

In fact the opportunity cost is now zero. It might even be negative if the greengrocer has to pay to dispose of any unsold trees. It might, therefore, be worth selling the trees at £3, £2 or even £1. Last thing on Christmas Eve it might even be worth giving away any unsold trees.

?? Why is the correct price to charge (for the unsold trees) the one at which the price elasticity of demand equals –1? (Assume no disposal costs.)

Here are some examples of implicit costs:

- A firm owns some buildings. The opportunity cost of using them is the rent it could have received by letting them out to another firm.
- A firm draws £100 000 from the bank out of its savings in order to invest in new plant and equipment. The opportunity cost of this investment is not just the £100 000 (an explicit cost), but also the interest it thereby forgoes (an implicit cost).
- The owner of the firm could have earned £15 000 per annum by working for someone else. This £15 000 then is the opportunity cost of the owner's time.

If there is no alternative use for a factor of production, as in the case of a machine designed to produce a specific product, and if it has no scrap value, the opportunity cost of using it is *zero*. In such a case, if the output from the machine is worth more than the cost of all the *other* inputs involved, the firm might as well use the machine rather than let it stand idle.

What the firm paid for the machine – its **historic cost** – is irrelevant. Not using the machine will not bring that money back. It has been spent. These are sometimes referred to as 'sunk costs'.

Likewise the **replacement cost** is irrelevant. That should be taken into account only when the firm is considering replacing the machine.

Costs and inputs

A firm's costs of production will depend on the factors of production it uses. The more factors it uses, the greater will its costs be. More precisely, this relationship depends on two elements:

- The productivity of the factors. The greater their physical productivity, the smaller will be the quantity of them that is needed to produce a given level of output, and hence the lower will be the cost of that output. In other words, there is a direct link between *TPP*, *APP* and *MPP* and the costs of production.
- The price of the factors. The higher their price, the higher will be the costs of production.

In the short run, some factors are fixed in supply. Their total costs, therefore, are fixed, in the sense that they do

DEFINITIONS

Historic costs The original amount the firm paid for factors it now owns.

Replacement costs What the firm would have to pay to replace factors it currently owns.

not vary with output. Rent on land is a **fixed cost**. It is the same whether the firm produces a lot or a little.

The total cost of using variable factors, however, does vary with output. The cost of raw materials is a **variable cost**. The more that is produced, the more raw materials are used and therefore the higher is their total cost.

?? The following are some costs incurred by a shoe manufacturer. Decide whether each one is a fixed cost or a variable cost or has some element of both.
(a) The cost of leather. (b) The fee paid to an advertising agency. (c) Wear and tear on machinery. (d) Business rates on the factory. (e) Electricity for heating and lighting.
(f) Electricity for running the machines. (g) Basic minimum wages agreed with the union. (h) Overtime pay.
(i) Depreciation of machines as a result purely of their age (irrespective of their condition).

Total cost

The **total cost** (*TC*) of production is the sum of the *total variable costs* (*TVC*) and the *total fixed costs* (*TFC*) of production:

$TC = TVC + TFC$

Consider Table 5.6 and Figure 5.10. They show the total costs for an imaginary firm of producing different levels of output (*Q*). Let us examine each of the three cost curves in turn.

Table 5.6 Total costs for firm X

Output (*Q*)	*TFC* (£)	*TVC* (£)	*TC* (£)
0	12	0	12
1	12	10	22
2	12	16	28
3	12	21	33
4	12	28	40
5	12	40	52
6	12	60	72
7	12	91	103
.	.	.	.
.	.	.	.
.	.	.	.

Total fixed cost (TFC)

In our example, total fixed cost is assumed to be £12. Since this does not vary with output, it is shown by a horizontal straight line.

Total variable cost (TVC)

With a zero output, no variable factors will be used. Thus *TVC* = 0. The *TVC* curve, therefore, starts from the origin.

The shape of the *TVC* curve follows from the law of diminishing returns. Initially, *before* diminishing returns set in, *TVC* rises less and less rapidly as more variable

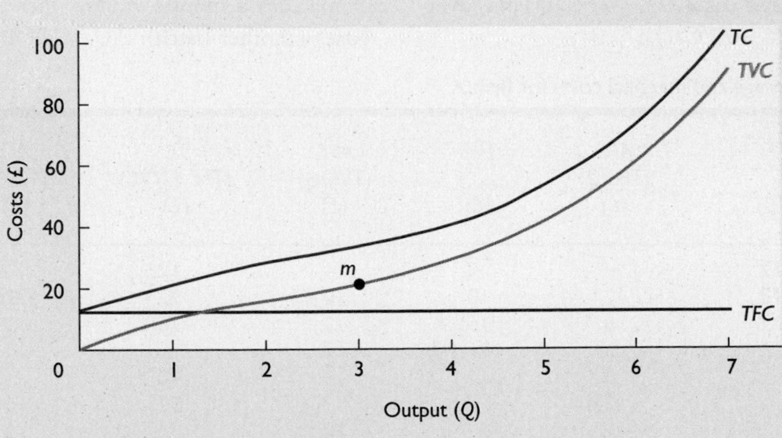

Figure 5.10 Total costs for firm X

DEFINITIONS

Fixed costs Total costs that do not vary with the amount of output produced.

Variable costs Total costs that do vary with the amount of output produced.

Total cost The sum of total fixed costs and total variable costs: $TC = TFC + TVC$.

factors are added. For example, in the case of a factory with a fixed supply of machinery, initially as more workers are taken on the workers can do increasingly specialist tasks and make a fuller use of the capital equipment. This corresponds to the portion of the *TPP* curve that rises more rapidly (up to point *b* in Figure 5.1 on p. 135).

As output is increased beyond point *m* in Figure 5.10, diminishing returns set in. Given that extra workers (the extra variable factors) are producing less and less extra output, the extra units of output they do produce will be costing more and more in terms of wage costs. Thus *TVC* rises more and more rapidly. The *TVC* curve gets steeper. This corresponds to the portion of the *TPP* curve that rises less rapidly (between points *b* and *d* in Figure 5.1).

Total cost (TC)

Since $TC = TVC + TFC$, the *TC* curve is simply the *TVC* curve shifted vertically upwards by £12.

Average and marginal cost

Average cost (*AC*) is cost per unit of production:

$$AC = TC/Q$$

Thus if it cost a firm £2000 to produce 100 units of a product, the average cost would be £20 for each unit (£2000/100).

Like total cost, average cost can be divided into the two components, fixed and variable. In other words, average cost equals **average fixed cost** ($AFC = TFC/Q$) plus **average variable cost** ($AVC = TVC/Q$):

$$AC = AFC + AVC$$

Marginal cost (*MC*) is the *extra* cost of producing *one more unit*: that is, the rise in total cost per one unit rise in output:

$$MC = \frac{\Delta TC}{\Delta Q}$$

To explain this formula, consider the following two examples.

Example 1

A firm is currently producing 100 units of output at a cost of £2000. It now increases its output to 101 units and its total cost rises to £2030. It has thus incurred an extra cost of £30 to produce this 101st unit. Thus the marginal cost of the 101st unit is £30.

Putting these figures into the formula gives:

$$MC = \frac{\Delta TC}{\Delta Q} = \frac{(£2030 - £2000)}{101 - 100} = \frac{£30}{1}$$

But why do we have to divide the rise in cost by 1? In cases like this, where output can be increased one unit at a time, it is obviously not necessary to divide the rise in cost by the rise in output. Marginal cost is simply the rise in costs of producing that extra unit. There are cases, however, where output can only be increased in batches . . .

Example 2

Assume that a firm is currently producing 1 000 000 boxes of matches a month. It now increases output by 1000 boxes (another batch): $\Delta Q = 1000$. As a result its total

Table 5.7 Total, average and marginal costs for firm X

Output (Q) (units)	*TFC* (£)	*AFC* (*TFC/Q*) (£)	*TVC* (£)	*AVC* (*TVC/Q*) (£)	*TC* (*TFC* + *TVC*) (£)	*AC* (*TC/Q*) (£)	*MC* ($\Delta TC/\Delta Q$) (£)
0	12	–	0	–	12	–	
1	12	12	10	10	22	22	10
2	...	6	16	...	28	...	...
3	...	...	21	7	...	...	...
4	...	3	...	...	40	...	7
5	...	2.4	...	...	52	10.4	12
6	...	...	...	10	...	12	...
7	...	1.7	91	13	103	...	31

DEFINITIONS

Average (total) cost Total cost (fixed plus variable) per unit of output: $AC = TC/Q = AFC + AVC$.

Average fixed cost Total fixed cost per unit of output: $AFC = TFC/Q$.

Average variable cost Total variable cost per unit of output: $AVC = TVC/Q$.

Marginal cost The cost of producing one more unit of output: $MC = \Delta TC/\Delta Q$.

EXPLORING THE THEORY BOX 5.7

DERIVING COST CURVES FROM TOTAL PHYSICAL PRODUCT INFORMATION

In section 5.1 we argued that a firm's costs depend on the output of its factors. If we want to know precisely what a firm's cost curves will be, we need to know two pieces of information: (a) how its output varies with the amount of each factor it uses; (b) the price of those factors.

Let us take a simple production function and see how cost curves may be derived from it. Assume that a firm uses just two factors: capital and labour.

Assume that capital is *fixed* in supply at 5 units (column (1)) and costs £60 per unit per week. Thus total fixed costs are £300 (column (4)).

Labour is the variable factor (column (2)). The effects on output (*TPP*) of employing different amounts of labour are shown in column (3).

It is assumed that workers are paid a wage rate of £100 per week. Total (weekly) variable costs, then, are simply the number of workers employed multiplied by this wage rate: column (5) = column (2) × £100.

Total costs are the sum of total fixed and total variable costs: *TC* = column (4) + column (5).

Inputs		Output	Total costs			Average costs			Marginal cost
Capital (units)	Labour (number)	Total physical product (*TPP*) (units)	Fixed (*TFC*) (£) (1) × £60	Variable (*TVC*) (£) (2) × £100	(Total) (*TC*) (£) (4) + (5)	Fixed (*AFC*) (£) (4) ÷ (3)	Variable (*AVC*) (£) (5) ÷ (3)	(Total) (*AC*) (£) (6) ÷ (3)	(*MC*) (£) Δ(6) ÷ Δ(3)
(1)	(2)	(3)	(4)	(5)	(6)	(7)	(8)	(9)	(10)
5	1	100	300	100	400	3.00	1.00	4.00	
									0.67
5	2	250	300	200	500	1.20	0.80	2.00	
									0.67
5	3	400	300	300	600	0.75	0.75	1.50	
									1.00
5	4	500	300	400	700	0.60	0.80	1.40	
									1.67
5	5	560	300	500	800	0.54	0.89	1.43	

To find the three average costs (*AFC*, *AVC* and *AC*) we have to divide the appropriate total cost column by output (column (3)). Thus *AFC* = *TFC*/*TPP* = column (4) ÷ column (3). Similarly, *AVC* = *TVC*/*TPP* = column (5) ÷ column (3). Finally, *AC* = *TC*/*TPP* = column (6) ÷ column (3). Alternatively, *AC* can be found by adding *AFC* and *AVC*: i.e. column (7) + column (8). (Check that this gives the same result.)

Marginal cost can be found by using the formula *MC* = $\Delta TC/\Delta TPP$. In other words, it is the extra cost of producing *one more* unit. Thus when the firm employs a fifth worker, for example, its costs have gone up (ΔTC) by £100 (i.e. the cost of the fifth worker). Its output has increased (ΔTPP) by 60 units (from 500 to 560). Thus if it is costing the firm an extra £100 to produce an extra 60 units, it is costing it £100/60 = £1.67 to produce *one* more unit.

??

1. Draw a graph showing the *AFC*, *AVC*, *AC* and *MC* curves corresponding to the figures in the above table.
2. Calculate a new set of figures for each of the columns (4)–(10) if (a) the price of capital rose from £60 to £100; (b) the wage rate rose from £100 to £150. Why in the case of (a) is the marginal cost not affected?

costs rise by £30: ΔTC = £30. What is the cost of producing one more box of matches? It is:

$$\frac{\Delta TC}{\Delta Q} = \frac{£30}{1000} = 3\text{p}$$

(Note that all marginal costs are variable, since, by definition, there can be no extra fixed costs as output rises.)

Given the *TFC*, *TVC* and *TC* for each output, it is possible to derive the *AFC*, *AVC*, *AC* and *MC* for each output using the above definitions.

For example, using the data of Table 5.6, Table 5.7 can be constructed.

?? Fill in the missing figures in Table 5.7. (Note that the figures for *MC* come in the *spaces* between each level of output.)

What will be the shapes of the *MC*, *AFC*, *AVC* and *AC* curves? These follow from the nature of the *MPP* and *APP* curves that we looked at in section 5.1 above. You may

CASE STUDIES BOX 5.8

PUTTING ON A DUPLICATE

Marginal costs of an extra coach

A few years ago I had to travel to London by coach and decided to book my seat early in case the coach was full. 'There is no need to do that,' I was told, 'because we will always put on an extra coach if there is not enough room on the first.'

Was this an example of 'irrational' behaviour on the part of the coach company? What was the cost of providing me with a seat on that second coach? Would the company have made a loss on my custom?

Let us assume that the cost of putting on a second coach to London holding 50 passengers is £500. *When deciding whether to put on the coach*, what is the marginal cost that the firm must take into account? The answer is that it depends on how many people travel on it. Remember that the formula for marginal cost is $\Delta TC/\Delta Q$. If I have the coach to myself ($\Delta Q = 1$), the marginal cost will be £500. In other words, the coach company is having to pay an extra £500 to let me have a seat. Clearly it will be making a loss by putting on that extra coach.

If, however, 50 people use the second coach, the marginal cost of providing the extra seats is only £10 per seat: $\Delta TC/\Delta Q = £500/50 = £10$. Presumably, with a full coach, the company will make a profit.

Once it has had to put on a second coach and has thus incurred the extra £500 cost, the marginal cost of extra passengers on that coach will be zero. In other words, the marginal cost of the first passenger is £500; thereafter there are no extra costs to be incurred (except maybe for a little extra fuel to cope with the extra weight) until a third coach is put on.

If, then, the question is *whether* to put on a second coach, and if all the company is thinking about is its short-term profits, the marginal cost it will look at is the marginal cost per passenger on it: i.e. $\Delta TC/\Delta Q$. If, however, it has already put on that second coach and it has vacant seats, the marginal cost of taking one more passenger (say, a person arriving at the coach station at the last minute and wanting to buy a ticket on the coach) will be virtually zero.

??

Why may it still make economic sense for the company to put on a coach for just one or two passengers, rather than turning them away?

Recently I again had to travel to London by coach. This time I was advised to book in case the coach was full! Was the coach company being more sensible now?

recall that the typical shapes of the *APP* and *MPP* curves are like those illustrated in Figure 5.11.

Marginal cost (MC)

The shape of the *MC* curve follows directly from the law of diminishing returns. Initially, in Figure 5.12, as more of the variable factor is used, extra units of output cost less than previous units. *MC* falls. This corresponds to the rising portion of the *MPP* curve in Figure 5.11 and the portion of the *TVC* curve in Figure 5.10 to the left of point *m*.

Beyond a certain level of output, diminishing returns set in. This is shown as point *x* in Figure 5.12 and corresponds to point *b* in Figure 5.11 (and point *m* in Figure

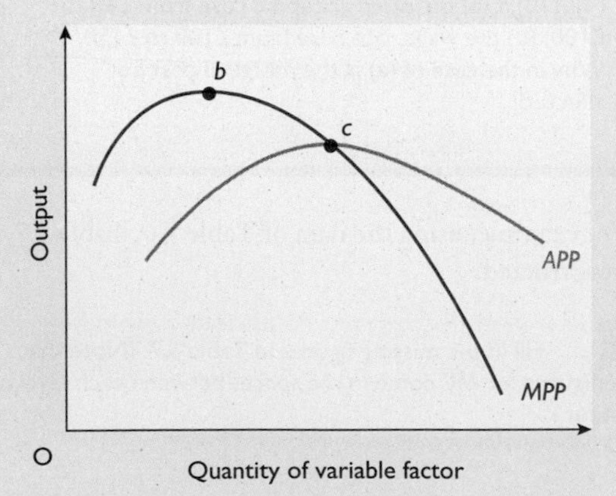

Figure 5.11 Average and marginal physical product

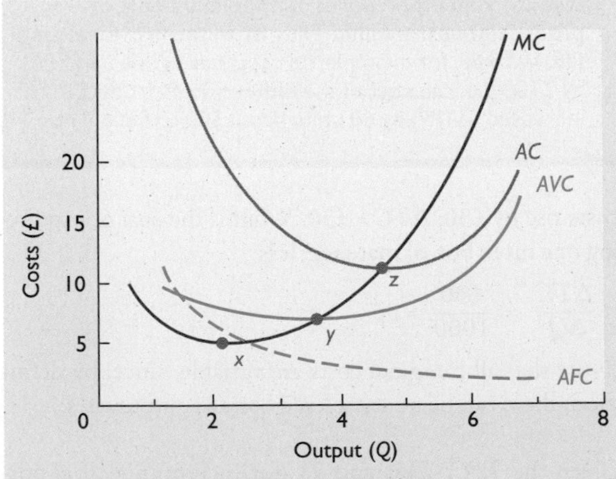

Figure 5.12 Average and marginal costs

5.10). Thereafter *MC* rises as *MPP* falls. Additional units of output cost more and more to produce, since they require ever increasing amounts of the variable factor.

Average fixed cost (AFC)

This falls continuously as output rises, since *total* fixed costs are being spread over a greater and greater output.

Average variable cost (AVC)

The shape of the *AVC* curve depends on the shape of the *APP* curve. As the average produce of workers rises (up to point *c* in Figure 5.11), the average labour cost per unit of output (the *AVC*) falls: as far as point *y* in Figure 5.12. Thereafter, as *APP* falls, *AVC* must rise.

Average (total) cost (AC)

This is simply the vertical sum of the *AFC* and *AVC* curves. Note that as *AFC* gets less, the gap between *AVC* and *AC* narrows.

The relationship between average cost and marginal cost

This is simply another illustration of the relationship that applies between *all* averages and marginals (see Box 5.3).

As long as new units of output cost less than the average, their production must pull the average cost down. That is, if *MC* is less than *AC*, *AC* must be falling. Likewise, if new units cost more than the average, their production must drive the average up. That is, if *MC* is greater than *AC*, *AC* must be rising. Therefore, the *MC* crosses the *AC* at its minimum point (point *z* in Figure 5.12).

Since all marginal costs are variable, the same relationship holds between *MC* and *AVC*.

?? Why is the minimum point of the *AVC* curve at a lower level of output than the minimum point of the *AC* curve?

SECTION SUMMARY

1. When measuring costs of production we should be careful to use the concept of opportunity cost. In the case of factors not owned by the firm, the opportunity cost is simply the explicit cost of purchasing or hiring them. It is the price paid for them. In the case of factors already owned by the firm, it is the implicit cost of what the factor could have earned for the firm in its next best alternative use.
2. In the short run, some factors are fixed in supply. Their total costs are thus fixed with respect to output. In the case of variable factors, their total cost will increase as more output is produced and hence as more of the variable factor is used.
3. Total cost can be divided into total fixed and total variable costs. Total variable cost will tend to increase less rapidly at first as more is produced, but then when diminishing returns set in it will increase more and more rapidly.
4. Marginal cost is the cost of producing one more unit of output. It will probably fall at first (corresponding to the part of the *TVC* curve where the slope is getting shallower), but will start to rise as soon as diminishing returns set in.
5. Average cost, like total cost, can be divided into fixed and variable costs. Average fixed cost will decline as more output is produced. The reason is that the total fixed cost is being spread over a greater and greater number of units of output. Average variable cost will tend to decline at first, but once the marginal cost has risen above it, it must then rise.

5.4 Costs in the long run

When it comes to making long-run production decisions the firm has much more flexibility. It does not have to operate with plant and equipment of a fixed size. It can expand the whole scale of its operations. All its inputs are variable, and thus the law of diminishing returns does not apply. The firm may experience economies of scale or diseconomies of scale, or its average costs may stay constant as it expands its scale of production.

Since there are no fixed factors in the long run, there are no long-run fixed costs. For example, the firm may rent more land in order to expand its operations. Its rent bill therefore goes up as it expands its output.

All costs, then, in the long run are variable costs.

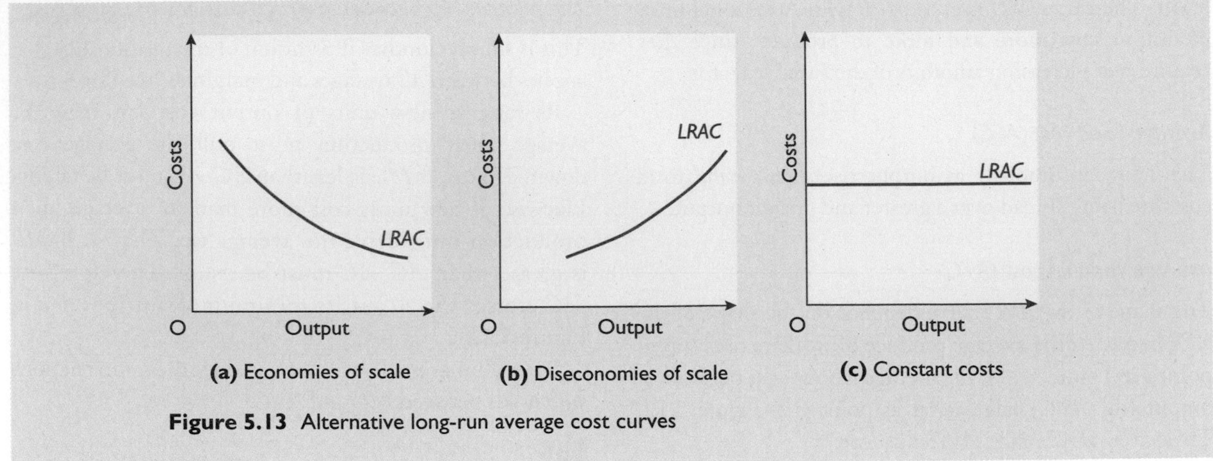

Figure 5.13 Alternative long-run average cost curves

Long-run average costs

Long-run average cost (*LRAC*) curves can take various shapes.

If the firm experiences economies of scale, its *LRAC* curve will fall as the scale of production increases (diagram (a) in Figure 5.13). This, after all, is how we define economies of scale: namely, a reduction in average costs as the scale of production increases. If diseconomies of scale predominate, the *LRAC* curve will rise (diagram (b)). Alternatively, if the firm experiences neither economies nor diseconomies of scale, the *LRAC* curve will be horizontal (diagram (c)).

?? What would the firm's long-run total cost curve look like in each of these three cases?

It is often assumed that as a firm expands, it will initially experience economies of scale and thus face a downward-sloping *LRAC* curve. After a point, however, all such economies will have been achieved and thus the curve will flatten out. Then (possibly after a period of constant *LRAC*) the firm will get so large that it will start experiencing diseconomies of scale and thus a rising *LRAC*. At this stage, production and financial economies will begin to be offset by the managerial problems of running a giant organisation.

The effect of this is to give a ◡ -shaped or saucer-shaped curve, as in Figure 5.14.

DEFINITION

Long-run average cost curve A curve that shows how average cost varies with output on the assumption that *all* factors are variable. (It is assumed that the least-cost method of production will be chosen for each output.)

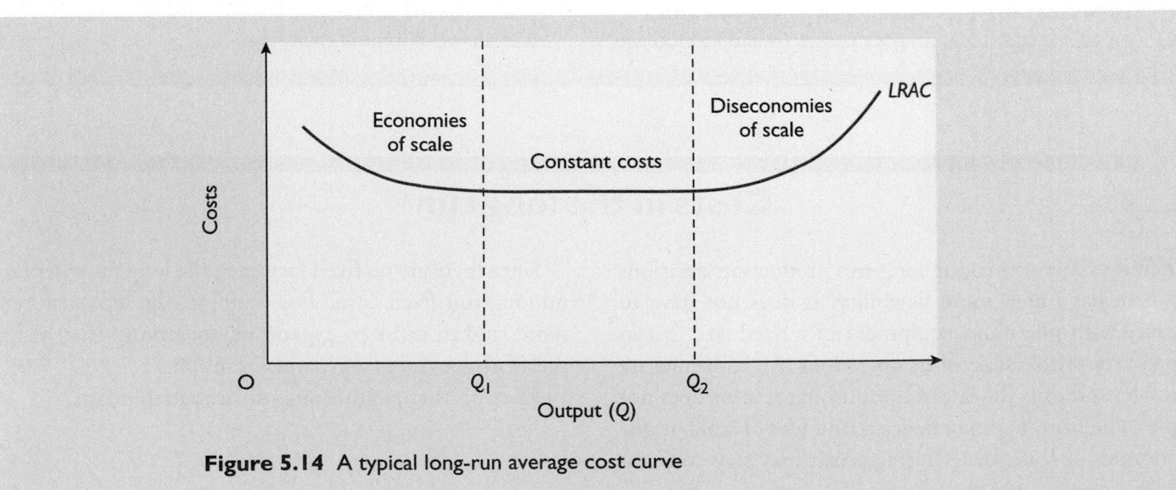

Figure 5.14 A typical long-run average cost curve

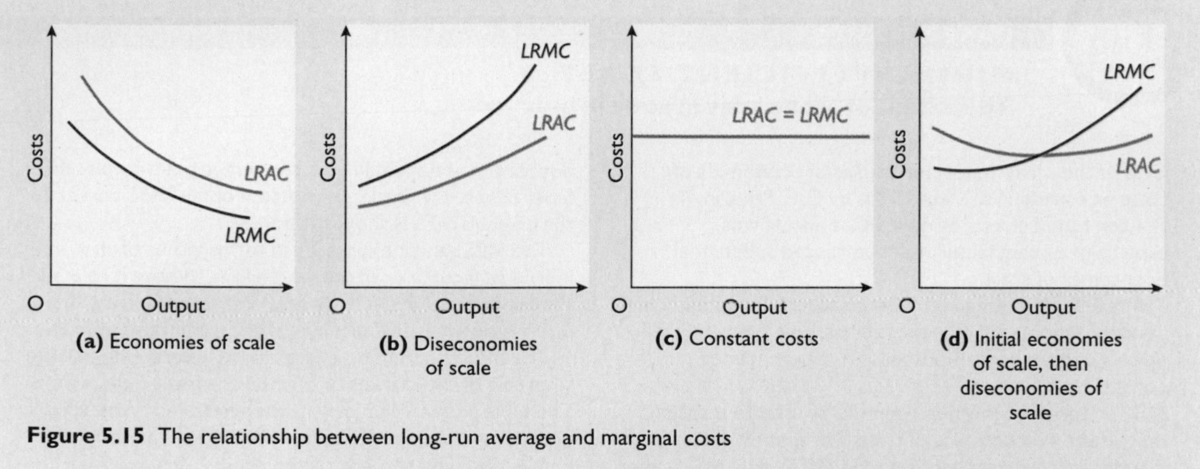

Figure 5.15 The relationship between long-run average and marginal costs

Assumptions behind the long-run average cost curve

There are three key assumptions that we make when constructing long-run average cost curves.

Factor prices are given. At each level of output it is assumed that a firm will be faced with a given set of factor prices. If factor prices *change*, therefore, both short- and long-run cost curves will shift. Thus an increase in nationally negotiated wage rates would shift the curves upwards.

It may be the case, however, that factor prices will be different at *different* levels of output. For example, one of the economies of scale that many firms enjoy is the ability to obtain bulk discount on raw materials and other supplies. In such cases the curve does *not* shift. The different factor prices are merely experienced at different points along the curve, and are reflected in the shape of the curve. Factor prices are still given for any particular level of output.

The state of technology and factor quality are given. These are assumed only to change in the *very* long run. If a firm gains economies of scale, it is because it is being able to exploit *existing* technologies and make better use of the existing availability of factors of production.

Firms choose the least-cost combination of factors for each output. The assumption here is that firms operate efficiently: that they choose the cheapest possible way of producing any level of output. In other words, at every point along the *LRAC* curve the firm will adhere to the cost-minimising formula:

$$\frac{MPP_a}{P_a} = \frac{MPP_b}{P_b} = \frac{MPP_c}{P_c} \ldots = \frac{MPP_n}{P_n}$$

where a . . . *n* are the various factors the firm uses.

If the firm did not choose the optimum factor combination, it would be producing at a point above the *LRAC* curve.

Long-run marginal costs

The relationship between long-run average and **long-run marginal cost** curves is just like that between any other averages and marginals (see Box 5.3). Diagrams (a) to (c) in Figure 5.15 show this relationship in the three cases we looked at in Figure 5.13.

If there are economies of scale (diagram (a)), additional units of output will add less to costs than the average. The *LRMC* curve must be below the *LRAC* curve and thus pulling the average down as output increases. If there are diseconomies of scale (diagram (b)), additional units of output will cost more than the average. The *LRMC* curve must be above the *LRAC* curve, pulling it up. If there are no economies or diseconomies of scale, so that the *LRAC* curve is horizontal, any additional units of output will cost the same as the average and thus leave the average unaffected (diagram (c)).

??

1. Explain the shape of the *LRMC* curve in diagram (d).
2. What would the *LRMC* curve look like if the *LRAC* curve were 'flat bottomed' as in Figure 5.14?

DEFINITION

Long-run marginal cost The extra cost of producing one more unit of output assuming that all factors are variable. (It is assumed that the least-cost method of production will be chosen for this extra output.)

CASE STUDIES

MINIMUM EFFICIENT SCALE

The extent of economies of scale in practice

One of the most important studies of economies of scale was made in the late 1980s by C. F. Pratten.[5] Pratten found strong evidence that many firms, especially in manufacturing, experienced substantial economies of scale.

In a few cases long-run average costs fell continuously as output increased. For most firms, however, they fell up to a certain level of output and then remained constant.

There are two methods commonly used to measure the extent of economies of scale. The first involves identifying a *minimum efficient scale (MES)*. The *MES* is the size beyond which no significant additional economies of scale can be achieved: in other words, the point where the *LRAC* curve flattens off. In Pratten's studies he defined this level as the minimum scale above which any possible doubling in scale would reduce average costs by less than 5 per cent (i.e. virtually the bottom of the *LRAC* curve). In the diagram *MES* is shown at point *a*.

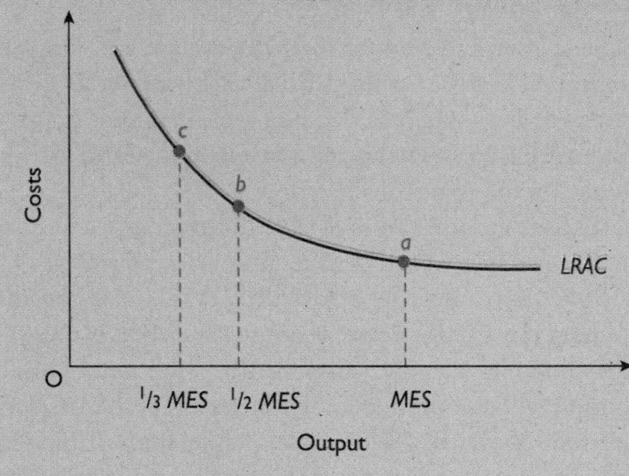

The *MES* can be expressed in terms either of an individual factory or of the whole firm. Where it refers to the minimum efficient scale of an individual factory, the *MES* is known as the *minimum efficient plant size (MEPS)*.

The *MES* can then be expressed as a percentage of the total size of the market or of total domestic production. The table shows *MES* for various plants and firms. The first column shows *MES* as a percentage of total UK production. The second column shows *MES* as a percentage of total EU production.

Expressing *MES* as a percentage of total output gives an indication of how competitive the industry could be. In some industries (such as shoes and tufted carpets), economies of scale were exhausted (i.e. *MES* was reached) with plants or firms that were still small relative to total UK production and even smaller relative to total EU production. In such industries there would be room for many firms and thus scope for considerable competition.

In other industries, however, even if a single plant or firm were large enough to produce the whole output of the industry in the UK, it would still not be large enough to experience the full potential economies of scale: the *MES* is greater than 100 per cent. Examples include factories producing cellulose fibres, and car manufacturers. In such industries there is no possibility of competition. In fact, as long as the *MES* exceeds 50 per cent there will not be room for more than one firm large enough to gain full economies of scale. In this case the industry is said to be a *natural monopoly*. As we shall see in the next few chapters, when competition is

The relationship between long-run and short-run average cost curves

Take the case of a firm which has just one factory and faces a short-run average cost curve illustrated by $SRAC_1$ in Figure 5.16.

In the long run, it can build more factories. If it thereby experiences economies of scale (due, say, to savings on administration), each successive factory will allow it to produce with a new lower *SRAC* curve. Thus with two factories it will face $SRAC_2$; with three factories $SRAC_3$, and so on. Each *SRAC* curve corresponds to a particular amount of the factor that is fixed in the short run: in this case, the factory.

From this succession of short-run average cost curves we can construct a long-run average cost curve. This is shown by the red line in Figures 5.16 and 5.17.

If a firm could only build factories of a particular size, the *LRAC* curve would be 'wavy' as in Figure 5.16. Up to output Q_1, it would be cheaper to use just one factory, but for an output between Q_1 and Q_2 it would be cheaper to use two factories. Likewise between Q_2 and Q_3 it would be cheaper to use three factories.

It is usual, however, to show the *LRAC* curve as a smooth line tangential to the *SRAC* curves (as in Figure 5.17). This is known as the **envelope curve**. The assump-

DEFINITION

Envelope curve A long-run average cost curve drawn as the tangency points of a series of short-run average cost curves.

BOX 5.9

Product	MES as % of production UK	MES as % of production EU	% additional cost at ½ MES
Individual plants			
Cellulose fibres	125	16	3
Rolled aluminium semi-manufactures	114	15	15
Refrigerators	85	11	4
Steel	72	10	6
Electric motors	60	6	15
TV sets	40	9	9
Cigarettes	24	6	1.4
Ball-bearings	20	2	6
Beer	12	3	7
Nylon	4	1	12
Bricks	1	0.2	25
Tufted carpets	0.3	0.04	10
Shoes	0.3	0.03	1
Firms			
Cars	200	20	9
Lorries	104	21	7.5
Mainframe computers	> 100	n.a.	5
Aircraft	100	n.a.	5
Tractors	98	19	6

Sources: C. F. Pratten (1988); M. Emerson, *The Economics of 1992* (Oxford University Press, 1988).

lacking consumers may suffer by firms charging prices considerably above costs.

The second way of measuring the extent of economies of scale is to see how much costs would increase if production were reduced to a certain fraction of *MES*. The normal fractions used are ½ or ⅓ *MES*. This is illustrated in the diagram. Point *b* corresponds to ½ *MES*; point *c* to ⅓ *MES*. The greater the percentage by which *LRAC* at point *b* or *c* is higher than at point *a*, the greater will be the economies of scale to be gained by producing at *MES* rather than at ½ *MES* or ⅓ *MES*. For example, in the table there are greater economies of scale to be gained from moving from ½ *MES* to *MES* in the production of electric motors than in cigarettes.

The main purpose of Pratten's study was to determine whether the creation of a large internal EU market with no trade barriers by the end of 1992 would significantly reduce costs and increase competition. The table suggests that in all cases, other things being equal, the EU market is large enough for firms to gain the full economies of scale *and* for there to be enough firms for the market to be competitive.

??

1. Why might a firm operating with one plant achieve *MEPS* and yet not be large enough to achieve *MES*? (Clue: are all economies of scale achieved at plant level?)
2. Why might a firm producing bricks have an *MES* which is only 0.2 per cent of total EU production and yet face little effective competition from other EU countries?

[5] C. F. Pratten, 'A survey of the economies of scale', in *Research on the 'Costs of Non-Europe'*, vol. 2 (Office for Official Publications of the European Communities, 1988).

tion here is that the short-run fixed factor(s) can be varied by *any* amount in the long run. For example, factories of any size can be built or existing ones can be expanded. The result is that there will be an unlimited number of *SRAC* curves.

??

Will the envelope curve be tangential to the *bottom* of each of the short-run average cost curves? Explain why it should or should not be.

Long-run cost curves in practice

Firms do experience economies of scale. Some experience continuously falling *LRAC* curves, as in Figure 5.13(a). Others experience economies of scale up to a certain output and thereafter constant returns to scale.

Evidence is inconclusive on the question of diseconomies of scale.

There is little evidence to suggest the existence of *technical* diseconomies, but the possibility of diseconomies due to managerial and industrial relations problems cannot be ruled out.

Some evidence on economies of scale in the UK is considered in Box 5.9.

*Derivation of long-run costs from an isoquant map

Cost curves are drawn on the assumption that, for any output, the least-cost combination of factors is used: that is, that production will take place at the tangency point of the isoquant and an isocost: where $MPP_L/MPP_K = P_L/P_K$:

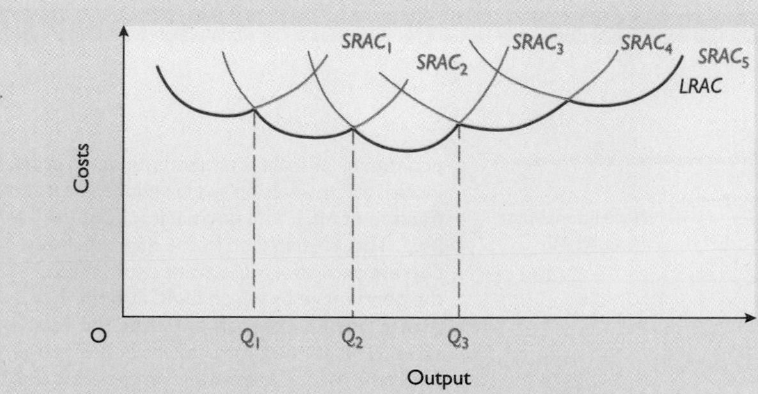

Figure 5.16 Constructing long-run average cost curves from short-run average cost curves: factories of fixed size

i.e. where $MPP_L/P_L = MPP_K/P_K$. By drawing a series of isoquants and isocosts, long-run costs can be derived for each output.

In Figure 5.18, isoquants are drawn for some hypothetical firm at 100 unit intervals. Up to 400 units of output, the isoquants are getting closer together. Thereafter, the gap between the isoquants widens again.

The line from *a* to *g* is known as the **expansion path**. It traces the tangency points of the isoquants and isocosts, and thus shows the minimum-cost combinations of labour and capital to produce each output: the (long-run) total cost being given by the isocost.

Up to point *d*, less and less *extra* capital (*K*) and labour (*L*) are required to produce each extra 100 units of output. Thus long-run marginal cost is falling. Above point *d*, more and more extra *K* and *L* are required and thus *LRMC* rises.

Thus the *isoquant* map of Figure 5.18 gives an *LRMC* curve that is ◡-shaped. The *LRAC* curve will therefore also be ◡-shaped (only shallower) with the *LRMC* coming up through the bottom of the *LRAC*.

?? What would the isoquant map look like if there were (a) continuously increasing returns to scale; (b) continuously decreasing returns to scale?

Using an isoquant map to compare the behaviour of short- and long-run costs

Consider the isoquant map shown in Figure 5.19. It shows a firm currently producing at point *a*. It is produc-

DEFINITION

Expansion path The line on an isoquant map that traces the minimum-cost combinations of two factors as output increases. It is drawn on the assumption that both factors can be varied. It is thus a long-run path.

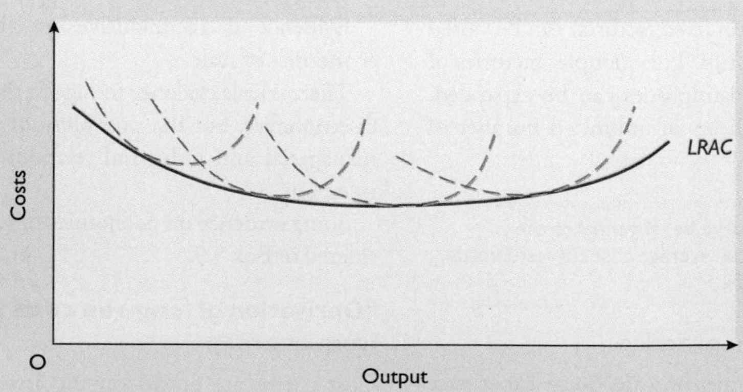

Figure 5.17 Constructing long-run average cost curves from short-run average cost curves: choice of factory size

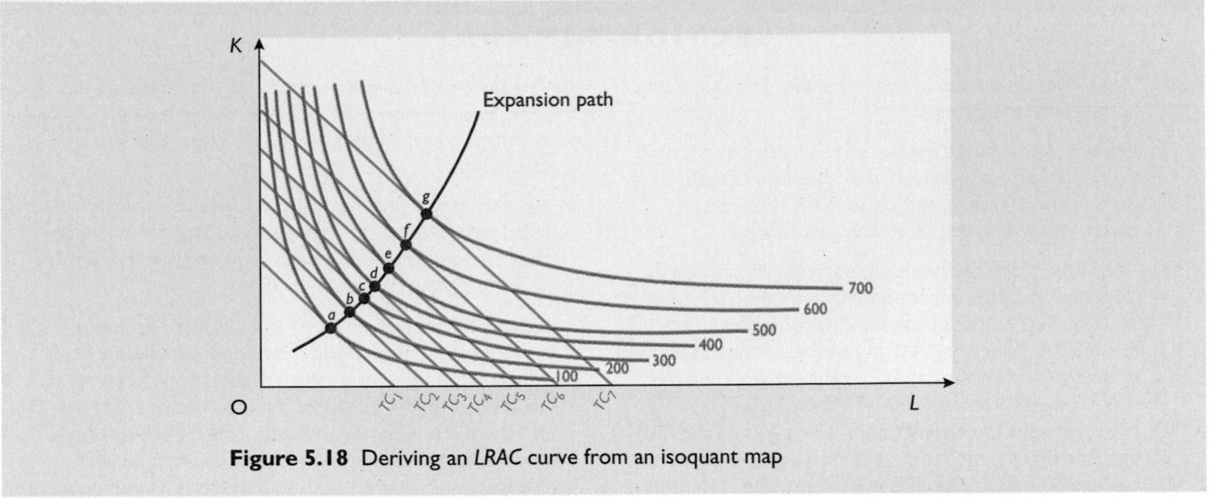

Figure 5.18 Deriving an *LRAC* curve from an isoquant map

ing 200 units of output per time period (shown by the isoquant passing through point *a*) and is using K_1 units of capital and L_1 units of labour. The cost of this much capital and labour is assumed to be £40 000 (shown by the isocost passing through point *a*). Let us assume that the plant which the firm is using is designed to produce 200 units of output at the least possible cost. Therefore point *a* is on the long-run expansion path. Both short-run and long-run average costs are £40 000/200 = £200.

Now let us see what will happen to the firm's costs if it chooses to expand output to 300 units in (a) the short run and (b) the long run.

Short run. In the short run capital is fixed in supply at K_1. If the firm wants to increase output to 300 units, it must therefore take on L_3 labour. It will be producing at point b_S on the 300 unit isoquant. Its total costs will rise to £66 000 (the isocost passing through point b_S). The short-run average cost will rise to £66 000/300 = £220.

Long run. In the long run, if the firm still wants to produce 300 units of output, the firm can increase the amount of capital as well as the amount of labour. It can thus move up the expansion path in Figure 5.19 to point b_L, using K_2 capital and L_2 labour. This time the total cost will only be £60 000. The long-run average cost thus remains at the original £200 (£60 000/300).

?? **Referring again to Figure 5.19 and assuming that the firm is currently producing at point *a* using K_1 capital and L_1 labour, what will be the short-run and long-run average costs of reducing production to 100 units?**

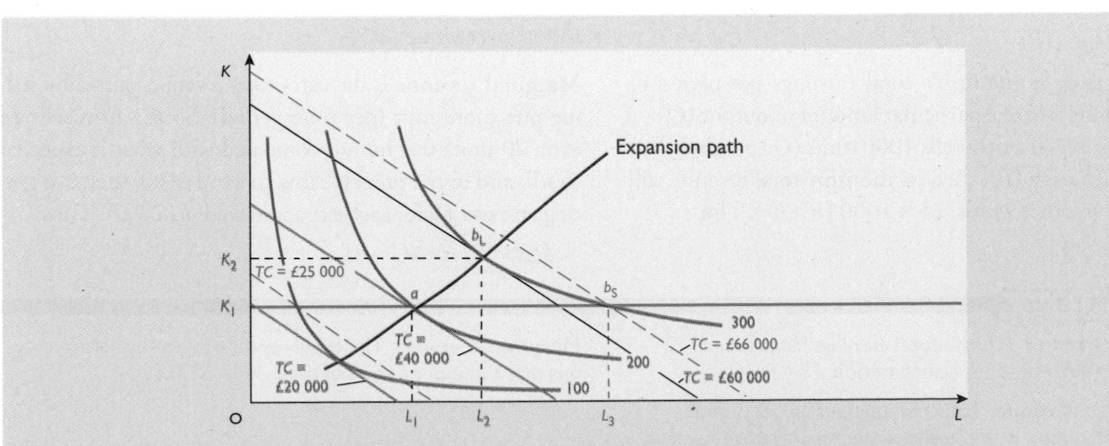

Figure 5.19 Deriving short-run costs from an isoquant map

SECTION SUMMARY

1. In the long run all factors are variable. There are thus no long-run fixed costs.
2. When constructing long-run cost curves it is assumed that factor prices are given, that the state of technology is given and that firms will choose the least-cost combination of factors for each given output.
3. The *LRAC* curve can be downward sloping, upward sloping or horizontal, depending in turn on whether there are economies of scale, diseconomies of scale or neither. Typically, *LRAC* curves are drawn saucer-shaped or -shaped. As output expands, initially there are economies of scale. When these are exhausted the curve will become flat. When the firm becomes very large it may begin to experience diseconomies of scale. If this happens, the *LRAC* curve will begin to slope upward again.
4. The long-run marginal cost curve will be below the *LRAC* curve when *LRAC* is falling, above it when *LRAC* is rising and equal to it when *LRAC* is neither rising nor falling.
5. An envelope curve can be drawn which shows the relationship between short-run and long-run average cost curves. The *LRAC* curve envelops the short-run *AC* curves: it is tangential to them.

*6. Costs can be derived from an isoquant map. Long-run total costs are found from the expansion path, which shows the least-cost combination of factors to produce any given output. It traces out the tangency points of the isocosts and isoquants. Short-run total costs are found by holding one of the two factors constant and reading off the intersections of isocosts and isoquants *at that quantity* of the fixed factor.

5.5

Revenue

Throughout this chapter we are building up a theory of profit maximisation. We are attempting to find the output and price at which a firm will maximise its profits, and how much profit will be made at that level. Remember that we defined a firm's total profit as its total revenue minus its total costs of production:

$$T\Pi = TR - TC$$

We have been looking at costs in some detail. We must now turn to the revenue side of the equation. As with costs, we distinguish between three revenue concepts: total revenue (TR), average revenue (AR) and marginal revenue (MR).

Total, average and marginal revenue

Total revenue (TR)

Total revenue is the firm's total earnings per period of time from the sale of a particular amount of output (Q).

For example, if a firm sells 1000 units (Q) per month at a price of £5 each (P), then its monthly total revenue will be £5000: in other words, £5 × 1000 ($P \times Q$). Thus:

$$TR = P \times Q$$

Average revenue (AR)

Average revenue is the amount the firm earns per unit sold. Thus:

$$AR = TR/Q$$

So if the firm earns £5000 (TR) from selling 1000 units (Q), it will earn £5 per unit. But this is simply the price! Thus:

$$AR = P$$

(The only exception to this is when the firm is selling its products at different prices to different consumers. In this case AR is simply the (weighted) average price.)

Marginal revenue (MR)

Marginal revenue is the extra total revenue gained by selling one more unit (per time period). So if a firm sells an extra 20 units this month compared with what it expected to sell, and in the process earns an extra £100, then it is getting an extra £5 for each extra unit sold: MR = £5. Thus:

$$MR = \Delta TR/\Delta Q$$

DEFINITIONS

Total revenue A firm's total earnings from a specified level of sales within a specified period: $TR = P \times Q$.

Average revenue Total revenue per unit of output. When all output is sold at the same price, average revenue will be the same as price: $AR = TR/Q = P$.

Marginal revenue The extra revenue gained by selling one more unit per period of time: $MR = \Delta TR/\Delta Q$.

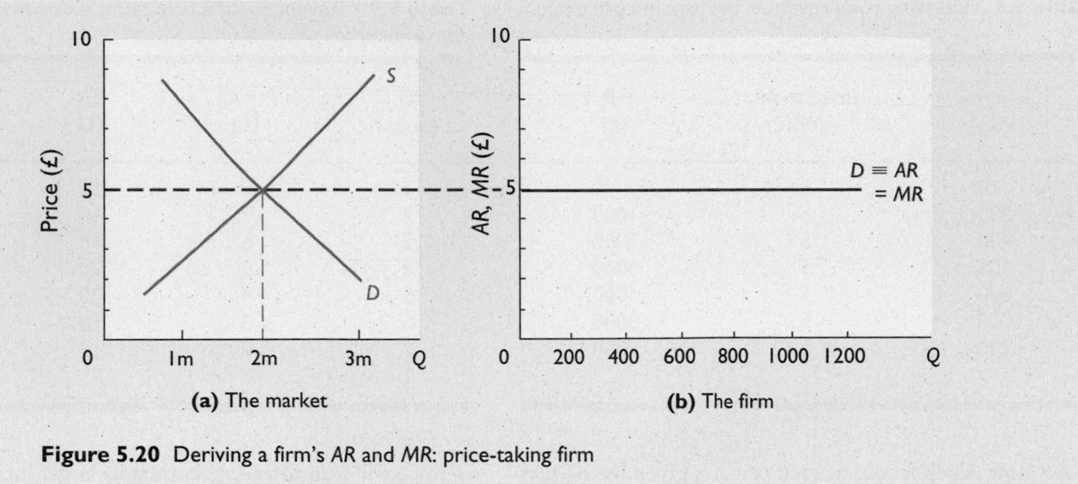

Figure 5.20 Deriving a firm's *AR* and *MR*: price-taking firm

We now need to see how each of these three revenue concepts (*TR*, *AR* and *MR*) varies with output. We can show this graphically in the same way as we did with costs.

The relationships will depend on the market conditions under which a firm operates. A firm which is too small to be able to affect market price will have different-shaped revenue curves from a firm which is able to choose the price it charges. Let us examine each of these two situations in turn.

Revenue curves when price is not affected by the firm's output

Average revenue

If a firm is very small relative to the whole market, it is likely to be a **price taker**. That is, it has to accept the price given by the intersection of demand and supply in the whole market. But, being so small, it can sell as much as it is capable of producing at that price. This is illustrated in Figure 5.20.

The left-hand part of the diagram shows market demand and supply. Equilibrium price is £5. The right-hand part of the diagram looks at the demand for an individual firm which is tiny relative to the whole market. (Look at the differences in the scale of the horizontal axes in the two parts of the diagram.)

Being so small, any change in its output will be too insignificant to affect the market price. It thus faces a horizontal demand 'curve' at the price. It can sell 200 units, 600 units, 1200 units or whatever without affecting this £5 price.

Average revenue is thus constant at £5. The firm's average revenue curve must therefore lie along exactly the same line as its demand curve.

Marginal revenue

In the case of a horizontal demand curve, the marginal revenue curve will be the same as the average revenue curve, since selling one more unit at a constant price (*AR*) merely adds that amount to total revenue. If an extra unit is sold at a constant price of £5, an extra £5 is earned.

Total revenue

Table 5.8 shows the effect on total revenue of different levels of sales with a constant price of £5 per unit. As price is constant, total revenue will rise at a constant rate as more is sold. The *TR* 'curve' will therefore be a straight line through the origin, as in Figure 5.21.

> **??** What would happen to the *TR* curve if the market price rose to £10? Try drawing it.

Revenue curves when price varies with output

The three curves (*TR*, *AR* and *MR*) will look quite different when price does vary with the firm's output.

If a firm has a relatively large share of the market, it will face a downward-sloping demand curve. This means that if it is to sell more, it must lower the price. It could also choose to raise its price. If it does so, however, it will have to accept a fall in sales.

Average revenue

Remember that average revenue equals price. If, therefore, price has to be lowered to sell more output, average revenue will fall as output increases.

Table 5.9 gives an example of a firm facing a downward-sloping demand curve. The demand curve (which

DEFINITION

Price taker A firm that is too small to be able to influence the market price.

Table 5.8 Deriving total revenue: the firm is a price taker

Quantity (units)	Price ≡ *AR* = *MR*(£)	*TR* (£)
0	5	0
200	5	1000
400	5	2000
600	5	3000
800	5	4000
1000	5	5000
1200	5	6000
.	.	.

Table 5.9 Revenues for a firm facing a downward-sloping demand curve

Q (units)	*P* = *AR* (£)	*TR* (£)	*MR* (£)
1	8	8	
			6
2	7	14	
			4
3	6	18	
			2
4	5	20	
			0
5	4	20	
			–2
6	3	18	
			–4
7	2	14	
.	.	.	.

shows how much is sold at each price) is given by the first two columns.

Note that as in the case of a price-taking firm, the demand curve and the *AR* curve lie along exactly the same line. The reason for this is simple: *AR* = *P*, and thus the curve relating price to quantity (the demand curve) must be the same as that relating average revenue to quantity (the *AR* curve).

Marginal revenue

When a firm faces a downward-sloping demand curve, marginal revenue will be less than average revenue, and may even be negative. But why?

If a firm is to sell more per time period, it must lower its price (assuming it does not advertise). This will mean lowering the price not just for the extra units it hopes to sell, but also for those units it would have sold had it not lowered the price.

Thus the marginal revenue is the price at which it sells the last unit, *minus* the loss in revenue it has incurred by reducing the price on those units it could otherwise have sold at the higher price. This can be illustrated with Table 5.9.

Assume that the price is currently £7. Two units are thus sold. The firm now wishes to sell an extra unit. It lowers the price to £6. It thus gains £6 from the sale of the third unit, but loses £2 by having to reduce the price by £1 on the two units it could otherwise have sold at £7. Its net gain is therefore £6 – £2 = £4. This is the marginal revenue: it is the extra revenue gained by the firm from selling one more unit. (Notice that in Table 5.9 the figures for *MR* are entered in the spaces between the figures for the other three columns.)

There is a simple relationship between marginal revenue and *price elasticity of demand*. Remember from Chapter 2 (p. 58) that if demand is price elastic, a *decrease* in price will lead to a proportionately larger increase in the quantity demanded and hence an *increase* in revenue. Marginal revenue will thus be positive. If, however, demand is inelastic, a decrease in price will lead to a proportionately smaller increase in sales. In this case the price reduction will more than offset the increase in sales and as a result revenue will fall. Marginal revenue will be negative.

If, then, at a particular quantity sold marginal revenue is a positive figure (i.e. if sales per time period are 4 units or less in Figure 5.22), the demand curve will be elastic at that quantity, since a rise in quantity sold (as a result of a reduction in price) would lead to a rise in total revenue. If, on the other hand, marginal revenue is negative (i.e. at a level of sales of 5 or more units in Figure 5.22), the demand curve will be inelastic at that quantity, since a rise in quantity sold would lead to a *fall* in total revenue.

Thus the demand (*AR*) curve in Figure 5.22 is elastic to the left of point *r* and inelastic to the right.

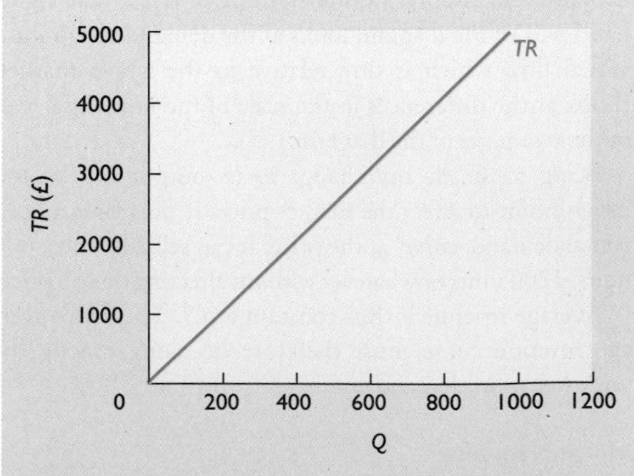

Figure 5.21 Total revenue curve for a price-taking firm

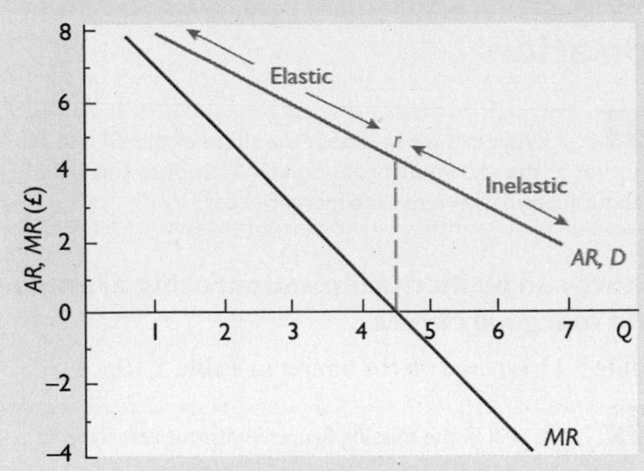

Figure 5.22 *AR* and *MR* curves for a firm facing a downward-sloping demand curve

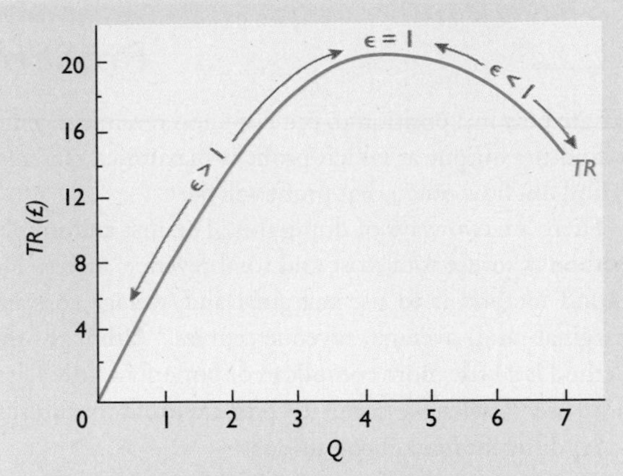

Figure 5.23 Total revenue for a firm facing a downward-sloping demand curve

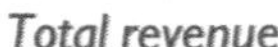

Total revenue

Total revenue equals price times quantity. This is illustrated in Table 5.9. The *TR* column from Table 5.9 is plotted in Figure 5.23.

Unlike the case of a price-taking firm, the *TR* curve is not a straight line. It is a curve that rises at first and then falls. But why? As long as marginal revenue is positive (and hence demand is price elastic), a rise in output will raise total revenue. However, once marginal revenue becomes negative (and hence demand is inelastic), total revenue will fall. The peak of the *TR* curve will be where $MR = 0$. At this point the price elasticity of demand will be equal to -1.

Shifts in revenue curves

We saw in Chapter 2 that a change in *price* will cause a movement along a demand curve. It is similar with revenue curves, except that here the causal connection is in the other direction. Here we ask what happens to revenue when there is a change in the firm's *output*. Again the effect is shown by a movement along the curves.

The effect of a change in any *other* determinant of demand, such as tastes, income or the price of other goods, will shift the demand curve. By affecting the price at which each level of output can be sold, there will be a shift in all three revenue curves. An increase in revenue is shown by a vertical shift upward; a decrease by a shift downward.

?? Copy Figures 5.22 and 5.23 (which are based on Table 5.9). Now assume that incomes have risen and that, as a result, two more units per time period can be sold at each price. Draw a new table and plot the resulting new *AR*, *MR* and *TR* curves on your diagrams. Are the new curves parallel to the old ones? Explain.

SECTION SUMMARY

1. Just as we could identify total, average and marginal cost, so too we can identify total, average and marginal revenue.
2. Total revenue (*TR*) is the total amount a firm earns from its sales in a given time period. It is simply price times quantity: $TR = P \times Q$.
3. Average revenue (*AR*) is total revenue per unit: $AR = TR/Q$. In other words, $AR = P$.
4. Marginal revenue is the extra revenue earned from the sale of one more unit per time period.
5. The *AR* curve will be the same as the demand curve for the firm's product. In the case of a price taker, the demand curve and hence the *AR* curve will be a horizontal straight line and will also be the same as the *MR* curve. The *TR* curve is an upward-sloping straight line from the origin.
6. A firm that faces a downward-sloping demand curve must obviously also face the same downward-sloping *AR* curve. The *MR* curve will also slope downwards, but will be below the *AR* curve and steeper than it. The *TR* curve will be an arch shape starting from the origin.
7. When demand is price elastic, marginal revenue will be positive and the *TR* curve will be upward sloping. When demand is price inelastic, marginal revenue will be negative and the *TR* curve will be downward sloping.
8. A change in output is represented by a movement along the revenue curves. A change in any other determinant of revenue will shift the curves up or down.

5.6

Profit maximisation

We are now in a position to put costs and revenue together to find the output at which profit is maximised, and also to find out how much that profit will be.

There are two ways of doing this. The first and simpler method is to use total cost and total revenue curves. The second method is to use marginal and average cost and marginal and average revenue curves. Although this method is a little more complicated (but only a little!), it is more useful when we come to compare profit maximising under different market conditions.

We will look at each method in turn. In both cases we will concentrate on the short run: namely, that period in which one or more factors are fixed in supply. In both cases we take the instance of a firm facing a downward-sloping demand curve.

Short-run profit maximisation: using total curves

Table 5.10 shows the total revenue figures from Table 5.9. It also shows figures for total cost. These figures have been chosen so as to produce a *TC* curve of a typical shape.

Total profit (*TΠ*) is found by subtracting *TC* from *TR*. Check this out by examining the table. Where *TΠ* is negative, the firm is making a loss. Total profit is maximised at an output of 3 units: namely, where there is the greatest gap between total revenue and total costs. At this output, total profit is £4 (£18 – £14).

The *TR*, *TC* and *TΠ* curves are plotted in Figure 5.24. The size of the maximum profit is shown by the arrows.

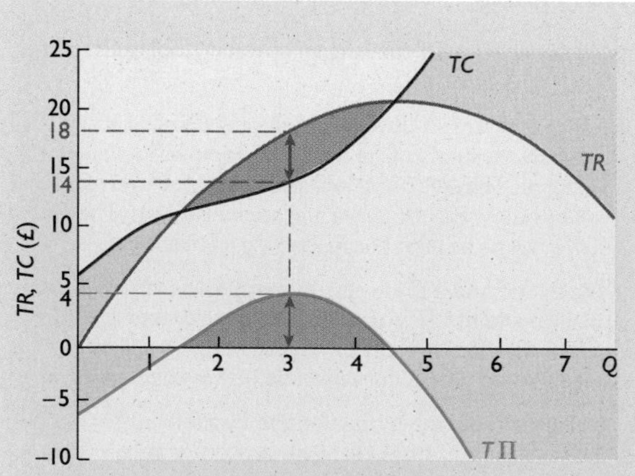

Figure 5.24 Finding maximum profit using totals curves

?? What can we say about the slope of the *TR* and *TC* curves at the maximum profit point? What does this tell us about marginal revenue and marginal cost?

Short-run profit maximisation: using average and marginal curves

Table 5.11 is based on the figures in Table 5.10.

??

1. Fill in the missing figures (without referring to Table 5.9).
2. Why are the figures for *MR* and *MC* entered in the spaces between the lines in Table 5.11?

Finding the maximum profit a firm can make is a two-stage process. The first stage is to find the profit-maximising output. To do this we use the *MC* and *MR* curves. The second stage is to find out just how much profit is at this output. To do this we use the *AR* and *AC* curves.

Stage 1: Using marginal curves to arrive at the profit-maximising output

There is a very simple **profit-maximising rule**: if profits are to be maximised, *MR must equal MC*. From the table it can be seen that *MR* = *MC* at an output of 3. This is shown as point *e* in Figure 5.25.

But why are profits maximised when *MR* = *MC*? The simplest way of answering this is to see what the position would be if *MR* did not equal *MC*.

Referring to Figure 5.25, at a level of output below 3, *MR* exceeds *MC*. This means that by producing more units there will be a bigger addition to revenue (*MR*) than to cost (*MC*). Total profit will *increase. As long as MR exceeds MC, profit can be increased by increasing production.*

At a level of output above 3, *MC* exceeds *MR*. All levels of output above 3 thus add more to cost than to revenue and hence *reduce* profit. *As long as MC exceeds MR, profit can be increased by cutting back on production.*

Profits are thus maximised where *MC* = *MR*: at an output of 3. This can be confirmed by reference to the *TΠ* column in Table 5.11.

Students worry sometimes about the argument that profits are maximised when *MR* = *MC*. Surely, they say, if the last unit is making no profit, how can profit be at a

DEFINITION

Profit-maximising rule Profit is maximised where marginal revenue equals marginal cost.

Table 5.10 Total revenue, total cost and total profit

Q (units)	TR (£)	TC (£)	$T\Pi$ (£)
0	0	6	−6
1	8	10	−2
2	14	12	2
3	18	14	4
4	20	18	2
5	20	25	−5
6	18	36	−18
7	14	56	−42
.	.	.	.

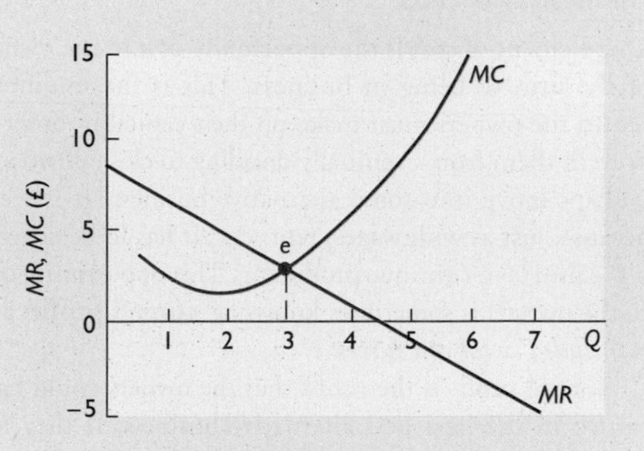

Figure 5.25 Finding the profit-maximising output using marginal curves

maximum? The answer is very simple. If you cannot *add* anything more to a total, the total must be at the maximum. Take the simple analogy of going up a hill. When you cannot go any higher, you must be at the top.

Stage 2: Using average curves to measure the size of the profit

Once the profit-maximising output has been discovered, we now use the average curves to measure the *amount* of profit at the maximum. Both marginal and average curves corresponding to the data in Table 5.11 are plotted in Figure 5.26.

First, average profit ($A\Pi$) is found. This is simply $AR - AC$. At the profit-maximising output of 3, this gives a figure for $A\Pi$ of £6 – £$4^2/_3$ = £$1^1/_3$. Then total profit is obtained by multiplying average profit by output:

$$T\Pi = A\Pi \times Q$$

This is shown as the shaded area. It equals £$1^1/_3 \times 3$ = £4. This can again be confirmed by reference to the $T\Pi$ column in Table 5.11.

?? From the information for a firm given in the table below, construct a table like 5.11.

Q	0	1	2	3	4	5	6	7
P	12	11	10	9	8	7	6	5
TC	2	6	9	12	16	21	28	38

Use your table to draw diagrams like Figures 5.24 and 5.26. Use these two diagrams to show the profit-maximising output and the level of maximum profit. Confirm your findings by reference to the table you have constructed.

Some qualifications

Long-run profit maximisation

Assuming that the AR and MR curves are the same in the long run as in the short run, long-run profits will be maximised at the output where MR equals the *long-run MC*. The reasoning is the same as with the short-run case.

Table 5.11 Revenue, cost and profit

Q (units)	$P = AR$ (£)	TR (£)	MR (£)	TC (£)	AC (£)	MC (£)	$T\Pi$ (£)	$A\Pi$ (£)
0	9	0		6	–		−6	–
			8			4		
1	8	8		10	10		…	−2
			…			2		
2	7	14		12	…		2	1
			4			2		
3	6	18		14	$4\frac{2}{3}$		4	$1\frac{1}{3}$
			2			4		
4	5	20		18	$4\frac{1}{2}$		2	$\frac{1}{2}$
			0			7		
5	4	20		25	5		−5	−1
			−2			…		
6	3	18		36	…		…	…
			…			20		
7	2	14		56	8		−42	−6
.	.	.	.	.	.	.	.	.

The meaning of 'profit'

One element of cost is the opportunity cost to the owners of the firm of being in business. This is the minimum return the owners must make on their capital in order to prevent them from eventually deciding to close down and perhaps move into some alternative business. It is a *cost* because, just as with wages, rent, etc., it has to be covered if the firm is to continue producing. This opportunity cost to the owners is sometimes known as **normal profit**, and is *included in the cost curves*.

Normal profit is the profit that the owners could have earned in the next best alternative business. If they can earn more than normal profit, they will prefer to stay in this business. If they earn less than normal profit, then after a time they will consider leaving and using their capital for some other purpose.

> ?? What determines the size of this 'normal profit'? Will it vary with the general state of the economy?

Given that normal profits are included in costs, any profit that is shown diagrammatically (e.g. the shaded area in Figure 5.26) must therefore be over and above normal profit. It is known by several alternative names: **supernormal profit, pure profit, economic profit, abnormal profit, producer's surplus** or sometimes simply **profit**. They all mean the same thing: the excess of total profit over normal profit.

Loss minimising

It may be that there is no output at which the firm can make a profit. Such a situation is illustrated in Figure 5.27: the *AC* curve is above the *AR* curve at all levels of output.

In this case, the output where $MR = MC$ will be the loss-minimizing output. The amount of loss at the point where $MR = MC$ is shown by the shaded area in Figure 5.27.

When MC = MR at two different outputs

Figure 5.28 illustrates a case where $MR = MC$ at two different points. Which is the one that maximises profit? The answer is Q_2. At Q_1, a move in either direction would *increase* profit (or reduce loss). For example, as output is increased above Q_1, *MR* becomes greater than *MC* and thus output should increase further: *away* from Q_1 and towards Q_2.

The rule for profit maximisation then can be redefined as: the firm should produce where $MR = MC$ *provided that* above that output *MC* exceeds *MR* and below that output *MR* exceeds *MC*.

Whether or not to produce at all

The short run. Fixed costs have to be paid even if the firm is producing nothing at all. Rent has to be paid, business rates have to be paid, etc. Providing, therefore, that the firm is more than covering its *variable* costs, it can go

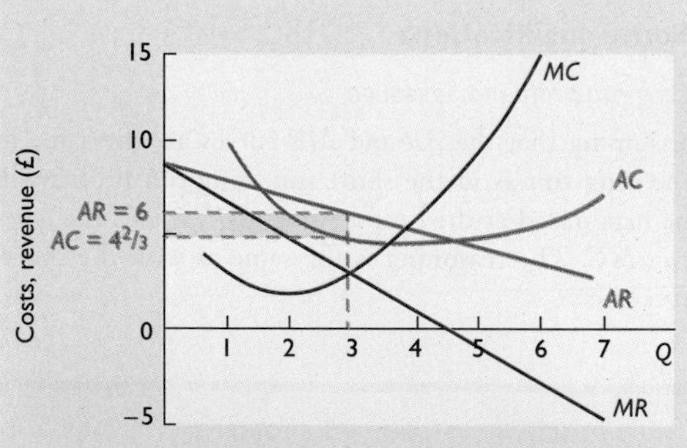

Figure 5.26 Measuring the maximum profit using average curves

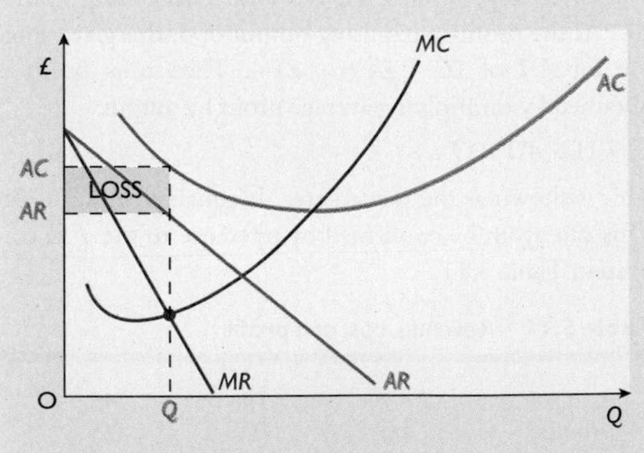

Figure 5.27 Loss-minimising output

DEFINITIONS

Normal profit The opportunity cost of being in business: the profit that could have been earned in the next best alternative business. It is counted as a cost of production.

Supernormal profit (also known as **pure profit, economic profit, abnormal profit, producer's surplus** or simply **profit**) The excess of total profit above normal profit.

EXPLORING THE THEORY *BOX 5.10

USING CALCULUS TO FIND THE MAXIMUM PROFIT OUTPUT

Imagine that a firm's total revenue and total cost functions were:

$TR = 48Q - Q^2$

$TC = 12 + 16Q + 3Q^2$

From these two equations the following table can be derived.

Q	TR	TC	$T\Pi (= TR - TC)$
0	0	12	−12
1	47	31	16
2	92	56	36
3	135	87	48
4	176	124	52
5	215	167	48
6	252	216	36
7	287	271	16
.	.	.	.
.	.	.	.
.	.	.	.

??

1. How much is total fixed cost?
2. Continue the table for $Q = 8$ and $Q = 9$.
3. Plot TR, TC and $T\Pi$ on a diagram like Figure 5.24.

It can clearly be seen from the table that profit is maximised at an output of 4, where $T\Pi = 52$.

This profit-maximising output and the level of profit can be calculated without drawing up a table. The calculation involves calculus. There are two methods that can be used.

Finding where *MR* = *MC*

Marginal revenue can be found by differentiating the total revenue function.

$MR = dTR/dQ$

The reason is that marginal revenue is the rate of change of total revenue. Differentiating a function gives its rate of change.

Similarly, marginal cost can be found by differentiating the total cost function:

$MC = dTC/dQ$

Differentiating TR and TC gives:

$dTR/dQ = 48 - 2Q = MR$

$dTC/dQ = 16 + 6Q = MC$

Profit is maximised where $MR = MC$: in other words, where:

$48 - 2Q = 16 + 6Q$

Solving this for Q gives:

$32 = 8Q$

$\therefore Q = 4$

The equation for total profit ($T\Pi$) is:

$$T\Pi = TR - TC$$
$$= 48Q - Q^2 - (12 + 16Q + 3Q^2)$$
$$= -12 + 32Q - 4Q^2$$

Substituting $Q = 4$ into this equation gives:

$T\Pi = -12 + (32 \times 4) - (4 \times 4^2)$

$\therefore T\Pi = 52$

These figures can be confirmed from the table.

Maximising the total profit equation

To maximise an equation we want to find the point where the slope of the curve derived from it is zero. In other words, we want to find the top of the $T\Pi$ curve.

The slope of a curve gives its rate of change and is found by differentiating the curve's equation. Thus to find maximum $T\Pi$ we differentiate it (to find the slope) and set it equal to zero (to find the top).

$T\Pi = -12 + 32Q - 4Q^2$ (see above)

$\therefore dT\Pi/dQ = 32 - 8Q$

Setting this equal to zero gives:

$32 - 8Q = 0$

$\therefore 8Q = 32$

$\therefore Q = 4$

This is the same result as was found by the first method. Again $Q = 4$ can be substituted into the $T\Pi$ equation to give:

$T\Pi = 52$

??

Given the following equations:

$TR = 72Q - 2Q^2$; $TC = 10 + 12Q + 4Q^2$

calculate the maximum profit output and the amount of profit at that output using both methods.

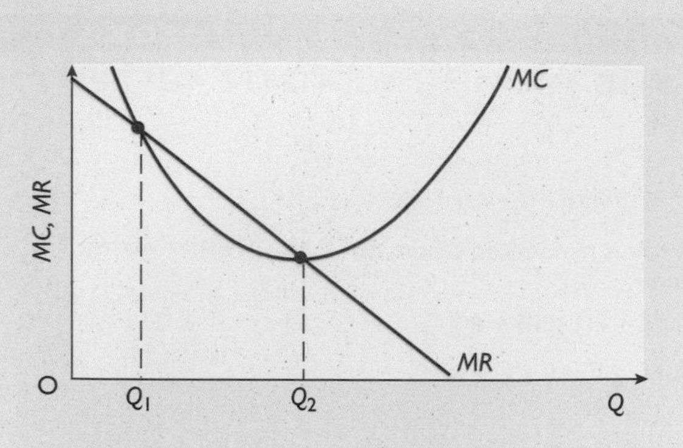

Figure 5.28 Choosing the profit-maximising output when $MC = MR$ at more than one output

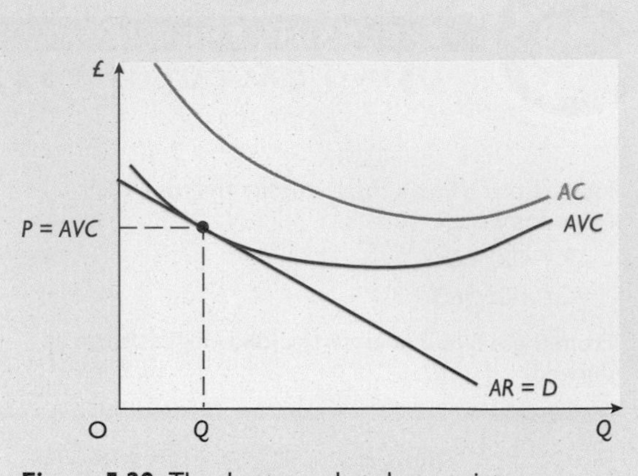

Figure 5.29 The short-run shut-down point

some way to paying off these fixed costs and therefore will continue to produce.

It will shut down if it cannot cover its variable costs: that is, if the *AVC* curve is above, or the *AR* curve below, the position illustrated in Figure 5.29. This situation is known as the **short-run shut-down point**.

The long run. All costs are variable in the long run. If, therefore, the firm cannot cover its long-run average costs (which include normal profit), it will close down. The **long-run shut-down point** will be where the *AR* curve is tangential to the *LRAC* curve.

SECTION SUMMARY

1. Total profit equals total revenue minus total cost. By definition, then, a firm's profits will be maximised at the point where there is the greatest gap between total revenue and total cost.
2. Another way of finding the maximum profit point is to find the output where marginal revenue equals marginal cost. Having found this output, the level of maximum profit can be found by finding the average profit ($AR - AC$) and then multiplying it by the level of output.
3. Normal profit is the minimum profit that must be made to persuade a firm to stay in business in the long run. It is counted as part of the firm's cost. Supernormal profit is any profit over and above normal profit.
4. For a firm that cannot make a profit at any level of output, the point where $MR = MC$ represents the loss-minimising output.
5. In the short run a firm will close down if it cannot cover its variable costs. In the long run it will close down if it cannot make normal profits.

DEFINITIONS

Short-run shut-down point Where the *AR* curve is tangential to the *AVC* curve. The firm can only just cover its variable costs. Any fall in revenue below this level will cause a profit-maximising firm to shut down immediately.

Long-run shut-down point Where the *AR* curve is tangential to the *LRAC* curve. The firm can just make normal profits. Any fall in revenue below this level will cause a profit-maximising firm to shut down once all costs have become variable.

??? END-OF-CHAPTER QUESTIONS ???

1. The following table shows the average cost and average revenue (price) for a firm at each level of output.

Output	1	2	3	4	5	6	7	8	9	10
AC (£)	7.00	5.00	4.00	3.30	3.00	3.10	3.50	4.20	5.00	6.00
AR (£)	10.00	9.50	9.00	8.50	8.00	7.50	7.00	6.50	6.00	5.50

   (a) Construct a table to show *TC*, *MC*, *TR* and *MR* at each level of output (put the figures for *MC* and *MR* mid-way between the output figures).

   (b) Using *MC* and *MR* figures, find the profit-maximising output.

   (c) Using *TC* and *TR* figures, check your answer to (b).

   (d) Plot the *AC*, *MC*, *AR* and *MR* figures on a graph.

   (e) Mark the profit-maximising output and the *AR* and *AC* at this output.

   (f) Shade in an area to represent the level of profits at this output.

*2. Draw the isoquant corresponding to the following table, which shows the alternative combinations of labour and capital required to produce 100 units of output per day of good X.

K	16	20	26 2/3	40	60	80	100
L	200	160	120	80	53 1/3	40	32

   (a) Assuming that capital costs are £20 per day and the wage rate is £10 per day, what is the least-cost method of producing 100 units? What will the daily total cost be? (Draw in a series of isocosts.)

   (b) Now assume that the wage rate rises to £20 per day. Draw a new set of isocosts. What will be the least-cost method of producing 100 units now? How much labour and capital will be used?

3. Choose a particular industry. Identify factors used in that industry that in the short run are (i) fixed; (ii) variable.

4. Taking the same industry, identify as many economies of scale as you can.

5. 'Both short-run and long-run average cost curves may be ◡-shaped, but the explanations for their respective shapes are quite different.' Explain this statement.

6. Why do marginal cost curves intersect both the average variable cost curve and the average cost curve at their lowest point?

7. Draw a diagram like that in Figure 5.26. Now illustrate the effect of a rise in demand for the product. Mark the new profit-maximising price and output. Will the profit-maximising output, price, average cost and profit necessarily be higher than before?

8. Why might it make sense for a firm which cannot sell its output at a profit to continue in production for the time being?

6 Profit maximising under perfect competition and monopoly

6.1 Alternative market structures

As we saw in Chapter 5, a firm's profits are maximised where its marginal cost equals its marginal revenue: $MC = MR$. But we will want to know more than this.

- What determines the *amount* of profit that a firm will make? Will profits be large, or just enough for the firm to survive, or so low that it will be forced out of business?
- Will the firm produce a high level of output or a low level?
- Will it be producing efficiently?
- Will the price charged to the consumer be high or low?
- More generally, will the consumer benefit from the decisions a firm makes? This is, of course, a *normative* question (see section 1.3). Nevertheless, economists can still identify and analyse the effects on consumers of these decisions.

The answers to all these questions depend on the amount of *competition* that a firm faces. A firm in a highly competitive environment will behave quite differently from a firm facing little or no competition.

It is traditional to divide industries into categories according to the degree of competition that exists between the firms within the industry. There are four such categories.

At one extreme is **perfect competition**, where there are very many firms competing. Each firm is so small relative to the whole industry that it has no power to influence price. It is a price taker. At the other extreme is **monopoly**, where there is just one firm in the industry, and hence no competition from within the industry. In the middle come **monopolistic competition**, where there are quite a lot of firms competing and where there is freedom for new firms to enter the industry, and **oligopoly**, where there are only a few firms and where entry of new firms is restricted.

To distinguish more precisely between these four categories, the following must be considered:

- The freedom with which firms can enter the industry. Is entry free or restricted? If it is restricted, just how great are the barriers to the entry of new firms?
- The nature of the product. Do all firms produce an identical product, or do firms produce their own particular brand or model or variety?
- The degree of control that the firm has over price. Is the firm a price taker or does it have the freedom to choose its price, and if it does, how will changing its price affect its profits? What we are talking about here is the nature of the demand curve it faces. How elastic is it? If it puts up its price, will it lose (a) all its sales (a horizontal demand curve), or (b) a large proportion of its sales (a relatively elastic demand curve), or (c) just a small proportion of its sales (a relatively inelastic demand curve)?

Table 6.1 shows the differences between the four categories.

> **??**
> 1. Give one more example in each category.
> 2. Would you expect plumbers and restaurateurs to have the same degree of control over price?

DEFINITIONS

Perfect competition A market structure where there are many firms; where there is freedom of entry into the industry; where all firms produce an identical product; and where all firms are price takers.

Monopoly A market structure where there is only one firm in the industry.

Monopolistic competition A market structure where, like perfect competition, there are many firms and freedom of entry into the industry, but where each firm produces a differentiated product and thus has some control over its price.

Oligopoly A market structure where there are few enough firms to enable barriers to be erected against the entry of new firms.

Table 6.1 Features of the four market structures

Type of market	Number of firms	Freedom of entry	Nature of product	Examples	Implication for demand curve for firm
Perfect competition	Very many	Unrestricted	Homogeneous (undifferentiated)	Cabbages, carrots (these approximate to perfect competition)	Horizontal. The firm is a price taker
Monopolistic competition	Many/several	Unrestricted	Differentiated	Plumbers, restaurants	Downward sloping, but relatively elastic. The firm has some control over price
Oligopoly	Few	Restricted	1. Undifferentiated or 2. Differentiated	1. Cement 2. Cars, electrical appliances	Downward sloping, relatively inelastic but depends on reactions of rivals to a price change
Monopoly	One	Restricted or completely blocked	Unique	British Gas (in many parts of Britain), local water company	Downward sloping, more inelastic than oligopoly. The firm has considerable control over price

The market structure under which a firm operates will determine its behaviour. Firms under perfect competition will behave quite differently from firms which are monopolists, which will behave differently again from firms under oligopoly or monopolistic competition.

This behaviour (or 'conduct') will in turn affect the firm's performance: its prices, profits, efficiency, etc. In many cases it will also affect other firms' performance: *their* prices, profits, efficiency, etc. The collective conduct of all the firms in the industry will affect the whole industry's performance.

Economists thus see a causal chain running from market structure to the performance of that industry.

Structure → Conduct → Performance

First we shall look at the two extreme market structures: perfect competition and monopoly. Then we shall turn to look at the two intermediate cases of monopolistic competition and oligopoly (Chapter 7).

The two intermediate cases are sometimes referred to collectively as **imperfect competition**. The vast majority of firms in the real world operate under imperfect competition. It is still worth studying the two extreme cases, however, because they provide a framework within which to understand the real world. Some industries tend more to the competitive extreme, and thus their performance corresponds to some extent to perfect competition. Other industries tend more to the other extreme: for example, when there is one dominant firm and a few much smaller firms. In such cases their performance corresponds more to monopoly.

Chapters 6 and 7 assume that firms, under whatever market structure, are attempting to maximise profits. Chapter 8 questions this assumption. It looks at alternative theories of the firm: theories based on assumptions *other* than profit maximising.

DEFINITION

Imperfect competition The collective name for monopolistic competition and oligopoly.

6.2 Perfect competition

The model of perfect competition is built on four assumptions:

- Firms are *price takers*. There are so many firms in the industry that each one produces an insignificantly small portion of total industry supply, and therefore has no power whatsoever to affect the price of the product. It faces a horizontal demand 'curve' at the market price: the price determined by the interaction of demand and supply in the whole market.

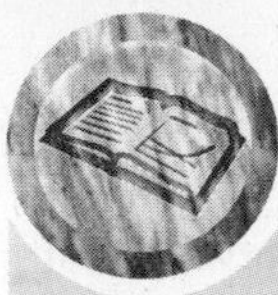

EXPLORING THE THEORY BOX 6.1

CONCENTRATION RATIOS

Measuring the degree of competition

We can get some indication of how competitive a market is by observing the number of firms: the more the firms, the more competitive the market would seem to be. However, this does not tell us anything about how *concentrated* the market might be. There may be *many* firms (suggesting a situation of perfect competition or monopolistic competition), but the largest two firms might produce 95 per cent of total output. This would make these two firms more like oligopolists.

Thus even though a large number of producers may make the market *seem* highly competitive, this could be deceiving. Another approach, therefore, to measuring the degree of competition is to focus on the level of concentration of firms.

The simplest measure of industrial concentration involves adding together the market share of the largest so many firms: e.g. the largest three or the largest five. This would give what is known as the '3-firm' or '5-firm concentration ratio'.

The table shows the 5-firm concentration ratios of selected industries in the UK. As you can see, there is an enormous variation in the degree of concentration from one industry to another.

Industry	5-firm concentration ratio	Industry	5-firm concentration ratio
Tobacco products	99.5	Water supply	49.7
Iron and steel	95.3	Footwear	48.2
Asbestos goods	89.8	Bread, biscuits, etc.	47.0
Motor vehicles and engines	82.9	Carpets	21.8
Cement, lime and plaster	77.7	Clothing	20.7
Grain milling	62.3	Bolts, nuts and springs	11.4
		Processing of plastics	8.8

Source: *Business Monitor PA 1002* (HMSO, 1995).

One of the main reasons for this is differences in the percentage of total industry output at which economies of scale are exhausted. If this occurs at a low level of output, there will be room for several firms in the industry which are all benefiting from the maximum economies of scale. Take the case of tufted carpets. As Box 5.9 showed, economies of scale are exhausted at less than 1 per cent of total industry output. It is not surprising that the largest five firms in the carpet industry account for only 21.8 per cent of output. In the case of steel, however, with a minimum efficient plant size at 72 per cent of industry output, the largest five firms account for 95.3 per cent of output (most of which is produced by one firm, British Steel).

Differences in the extent of economies of scale are not the only cause of differences in concentration. The degree of concentration will also depend on the barriers to entry of other firms into the industry (see page 182) and on various factors such as transport costs and historical accident. It will also depend on how varied the products are within any one industrial category. For example, in categories as large as 'clothing' and 'toys and sports goods' there is room for many firms, each producing a specialised range of products. Within each sub-category, e.g. tennis racquets, there may be relatively few firms producing.

So is the degree of concentration a good guide to the degree of competitiveness of the industry? The answer is that it is *some* guide, but on its own it can be misleading. In particular it ignores the degree of competition from abroad, and from other areas within the country. Thus the five largest UK motor vehicle manufacturers may produce 82.9 per cent of UK vehicle output, but these manufacturers face considerable competition from imported cars and lorries. On the other hand, the five largest water suppliers may account for only 49.7 per cent of UK output, but within their own regions of the country they have a monopoly.

??

1. What are the advantages and disadvantages of using a 5-firm concentration ratio rather than a 10-firm, 3-firm or even a 1-firm ratio?
2. Why are some industries like bread baking and brewing relatively concentrated, in that a few firms produce a large proportion of total output (see Boxes 7.4 and 7.5), and yet there are also many small producers?

- There is complete *freedom of entry* of new firms into the industry. Existing firms are unable to stop new firms setting up in business. Setting up a business takes time, however. Freedom of entry, therefore, applies in the long run. An extension of this assumption is that there is complete factor mobility in the long run. If profits are higher than elsewhere, capital will be freely attracted into that industry. Likewise if wages are higher than for equivalent work elsewhere, workers will freely move into that industry and will meet no barriers.
- All firms produce an *identical product*. (The product is 'homogeneous'.) There is therefore no branding or advertising.
- Producers and consumers have *perfect knowledge* of the market. That is, producers are fully aware of prices, costs and market opportunities. Consumers are fully aware of the price, quality and availability of the product.

These assumptions are very strict. Few, if any, industries in the real world meet these conditions. Certain agricultural markets perhaps are closest to perfect competition. The market for fresh vegetables is an example.

Nevertheless, despite the lack of real-world cases, the model of perfect competition plays a very important role in economic analysis and policy. Its major relevance is as an 'ideal type'. Many on the political right argue that perfect competition brings a number of important advantages. The model can thus be used as a standard against which to judge the shortcomings of real-world industries. It can help governments to formulate policies towards industry.

??

1. It is sometimes claimed that the market for various stocks and shares is perfectly competitive, or nearly so. Take the case of the market for shares in a large company like ICI. Go through each of the four assumptions above and see if they apply in this case. (Don't be misled by the first assumption. The 'firm' in this case is not ICI itself.)
2. Is the market for gold perfectly competitive?

The short run and the long run

Before we can examine what price, output and profits will be, we must first distinguish between the short run and the long run as they apply to perfect competition.

In the **short run** the number of firms is fixed. Depending on its costs and revenue, a firm might be making large profits, small profits, no profits or a loss; and in the short run it may continue to do so.

In the **long run**, however, the level of profits will affect entry and exit from the industry. If profits are high, new firms will be attracted into the industry, whereas if losses are being made, firms will leave.

This leads us to the distinction we made in Chapter 5: that between *normal* and *supernormal* profits. Let us examine them in the context of perfect competition.

Normal profit

This is the level of profit that is just enough to persuade firms to stay in the industry in the long run, but not high enough to attract new firms. If less than normal profits are made, firms will leave the industry in the long run.

Although we shall be talking about the *level* of normal profit (since that makes our analysis of pricing and output decisions simpler to understand), in practice it is usually the *rate* of profit that will determine whether a firm stays in the industry or leaves. The **rate of profit** (r) is the level of profit ($T\Pi$) as *a proportion of the level of capital (K) employed:* $r = T\Pi/K$. As you would expect, larger firms will require to make a larger *total* profit to persuade them to stay in an industry. Total normal profit is thus larger for them than for a small firm. The *rate* of normal profit, however, will probably be similar.

??

1. Why do economists treat normal profit as a cost of production?
2. What determines (a) the level and (b) the rate of normal profit for a particular firm?

Supernormal profit

This is any profit above normal profit. If supernormal profits are made, new firms will be attracted into the industry in the long run.

Thus whether the industry expands or contracts in the long run will depend on the rate of profit. Naturally, since the time taken for a firm to set up in business will vary from industry to industry, the length of time before the long run is reached will also vary from industry to industry.

DEFINITIONS

The short run under perfect competition The period during which there is too little time for new firms to enter the industry.

The long run under perfect competition The period of time which is long enough for new firms to enter the industry.

Rate of profit Total profit ($T\Pi$) as a proportion of the capital employed (K): $r = T\Pi/K$.

ISSUES AND APPLICATIONS BOX 6.2

IS PERFECT BEST?

Be careful of the word 'perfect'.

'Perfect' competition refers to competition that is total. Perhaps 'total' competition would be a better term. There is a total absence of power, a total absence of entry barriers, a total absence of product differentiation between producers, and total information for producers and consumers on the market. It is thus useful for understanding the effects of power, barriers, product differentiation and lack of information.

Perfect does not mean 'best', however.

Just because it is at the extreme end of the competition spectrum, it does not follow that perfect competition is desirable. You could have a perfect bomb – i.e. one that kills everyone in the world. You could have a perfect killer virus – i.e. one that is totally immune to drugs, and against which humans have no natural protection at all. Such things, though perfect, are hardly desirable!

To say that perfect competition is desirable and that it is a goal towards which government policy should be directed are normative statements. Economists, in their role as economists, cannot make such statements.

This does not mean, of course, that economists cannot identify the effects of perfect competition, but whether these effects are *desirable* or not is an ethical question.

The danger is that by using perfect competition as a yardstick, and by using the word 'perfect' rather than 'total', economists may be surreptitiously persuading their audience that perfect competition is a goal we *ought* to be striving to achieve.

??

1. Can economists list advantages and disadvantages of an economic policy?
2. Have economists the right to advise governments?

The short-run equilibrium of the firm

The determination of price, output and profit in the short run under perfect competition can best be shown in a diagram.

Figure 6.1 shows a short-run equilibrium for both industry and a firm under perfect competition. Both parts of the diagram have the same scale for the vertical axis. The horizontal axes have totally different scales, however. For example, if the horizontal axis for the firm were measured in, say, thousands of units, the horizontal axis for the whole industry might be measured in millions or tens of millions of units, depending on the number of firms in the industry.

Let us examine the determination of price, output and profit in turn.

Price

The price is determined in the industry by the intersection of demand and supply. The firm faces a horizontal demand (or average revenue) 'curve' at this price. It can sell all it can produce at the market price (P_e), but nothing at a price above P_e.

Output

The firm will maximise profit where marginal cost equals marginal revenue ($MR = MC$), at an output of Q_e. Note that, since the price is not affected by the firm's output, marginal revenue will equal price. The reason is that the firm is not having to reduce its price in order to sell more. An extra unit produced will therefore earn its full price for

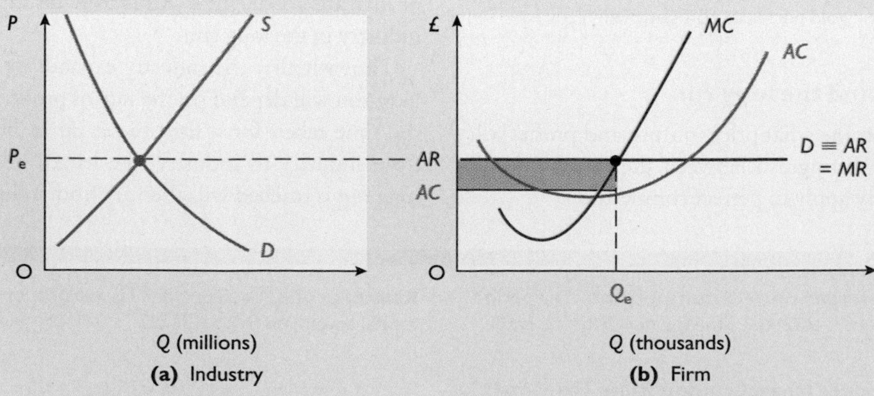

Figure 6.1 Short-run equilibrium of industry and firm under perfect competition

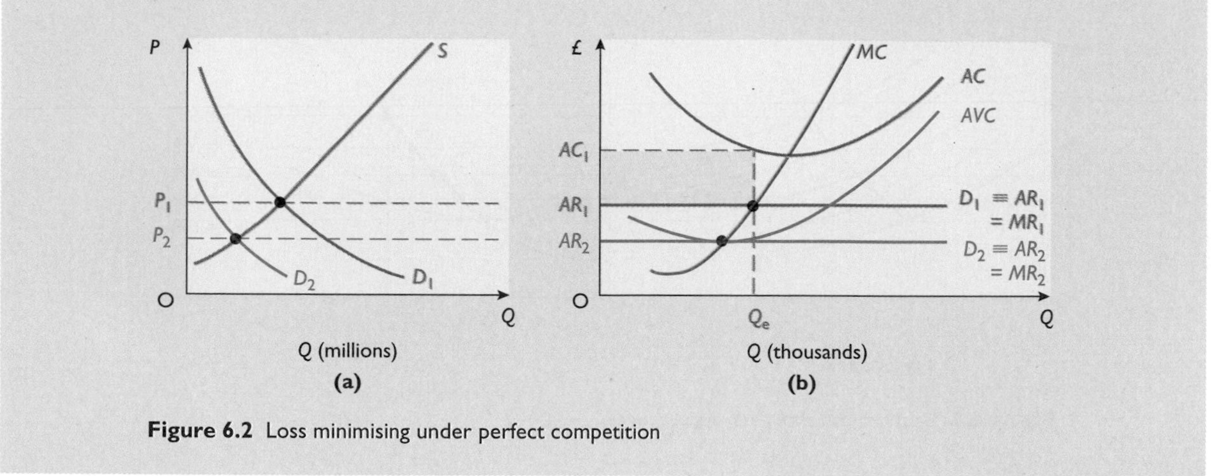

Figure 6.2 Loss minimising under perfect competition

the firm. Thus the firm's *MR* 'curve' and demand 'curve' are the same horizontal straight line.

Profit

If the average cost (*AC*) curve (which includes normal profit) dips below the average revenue (*AR*) 'curve', the firm will earn supernormal profit. Supernormal profit *per unit* at Q_e is the vertical difference between *AR* and *AC* at Q_e. *Total* supernormal profit is the shaded rectangle in Figure 6.1.

What happens if the firm cannot make a profit at *any* level of output? This situation would occur if the *AC* curve were above the *AR* curve at all points. This is illustrated in Figure 6.2, where the market price is P_1. In this case, the point where $MC = MR$ represents the *loss-minimising* point (where loss is defined as anything less than normal profit). The amount of the loss is represented by the shaded rectangle.

As we saw in section 5.6, whether the firm is prepared to continue making a loss in the short run or whether it will close down immediately depends on whether it can cover its *variable* costs.

Provided price is above average variable cost (*AVC*), the firm will still continue producing in the short run: it can pay its variable costs and go some way to paying its fixed costs. It will shut down in the short run only if the market price falls below P_2 in Figure 6.2.

The short-run supply curve

The *firm*'s short-run supply curve will be its (short-run) marginal cost curve.

A supply curve shows how much will be supplied at each price: it relates quantity to price. The marginal cost curve relates quantity to marginal cost. But under perfect competition, given that $P = MR$, and $MR = MC$, *P* must equal *MC*. Thus the supply curve and the *MC* curve will follow the same line.

For example, in Figure 6.3(b), if price were P_1, profits would be maximised at Q_1 where $P_1 = MC$. Thus point *a* is one point on the supply curve. At a price of P_2, Q_2 would be produced. Thus point *b* is another point on the supply curve, and so on.

So, under perfect competition, the firm's supply curve is entirely dependent on costs of production. This demonstrates why the firm's supply curve is upward sloping. Given that marginal costs rise as output rises (due to diminishing marginal returns), a higher price will be necessary to induce the firm to increase its output.

Note that the firm will not produce at a price below *AVC*. Thus the supply curve is only that portion of the *MC* curve above point *e*.

What will be the short-run supply curve of the whole *industry*? This is simply the sum of the short-run supply curves (and hence *MC* curves) of all the firms in the industry. Graphically this will be a *horizontal* sum, since it is *quantities* that are being added.

> **??** Will the *industry* supply be zero below a price of P_5 in Figure 6.3?

The long-run equilibrium of the firm

In the long run, if typical firms are making supernormal profits, new firms will be attracted into the industry. Likewise, if existing firms can make supernormal profits by increasing the scale of their operations, they will do so, since all factors of production are variable in the long run.

The effect of the entry of new firms and/or the expansion of existing firms is to increase industry supply. This is

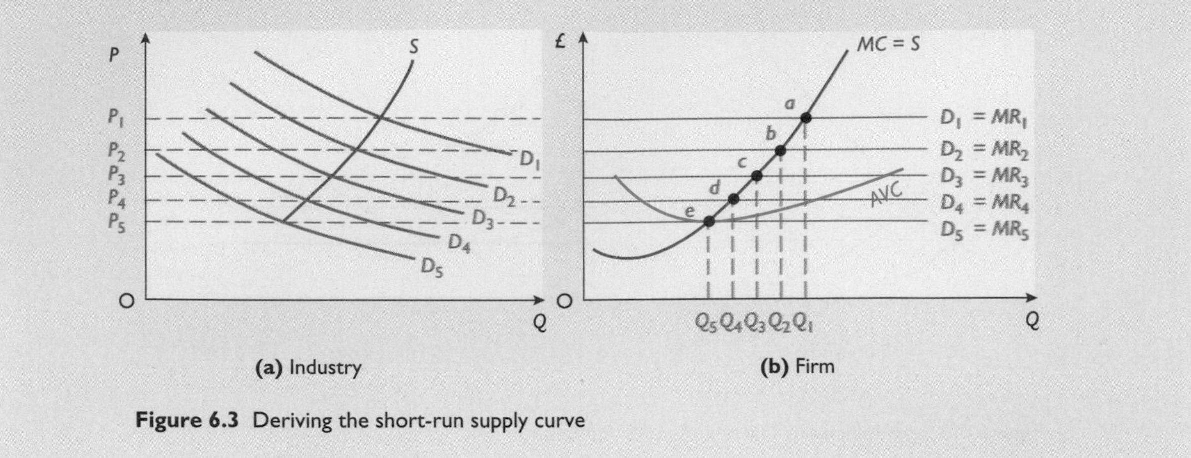

Figure 6.3 Deriving the short-run supply curve

illustrated in Figure 6.4. At a price of P_1 supernormal profits are earned. This causes industry supply to expand (the industry supply curve shifts to the right). This in turn leads to a fall in price. Supply will go on increasing and price falling until firms are making only normal profits. This will be when price has fallen to the point where the demand 'curve' for the firm just touches the bottom of its long-run average cost curve. Q_L is thus the long-run equilibrium output of the firm, with P_L the long-run equilibrium price.

?? Illustrate on a diagram similar to Figure 6.4 what would happen in the long run if price were initially below P_L.

Since the *LRAC* curve is tangential to all possible short-run *AC* curves (see section 5.4), the full long-run equilibrium will be as shown in Figure 6.5 where:

$$LRAC = AC = MC = MR = AR$$

The long-run industry supply curve

If industry demand increased, what would happen to industry price and output in the long run? The long-run supply curve gives the answer.

Each of the diagrams in Figure 6.6 shows an increase in demand. The demand curve shifts from D_1 to D_2. Equilibrium in the short run moves from point *a* to point *b*, where D_2 and S_1 intersect. After the initial rise in price, the resulting supernormal profit attracts new firms into the industry. The short-run supply curve shifts to S_2 and equilibrium moves to point *c*. Thus the long-run effect of the increase in demand has been to move the equilibrium from point *a* to point *c*. This means, therefore, that the *long-run* supply curve will pass through points *a* and *c*. This is illustrated in each of the three diagrams.

If price falls back to its original level (i.e. points *a* and *c* are at the *same* price) the *long-run* supply curve will be horizontal (see diagram (a)). This would occur if there

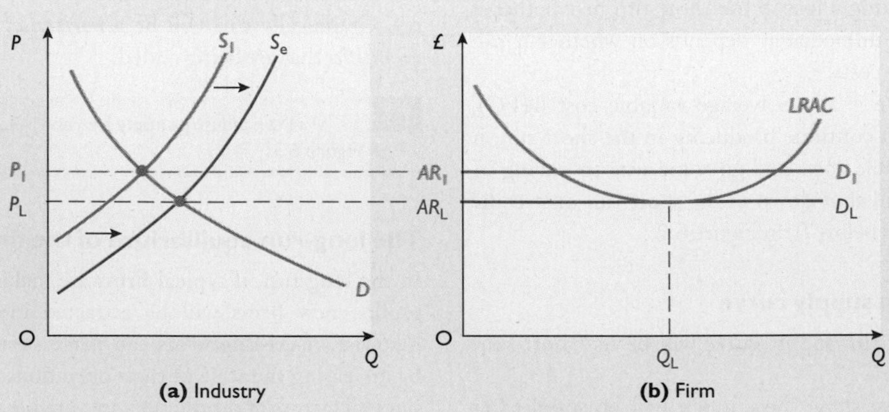

Figure 6.4 Long-run equilibrium under perfect competition

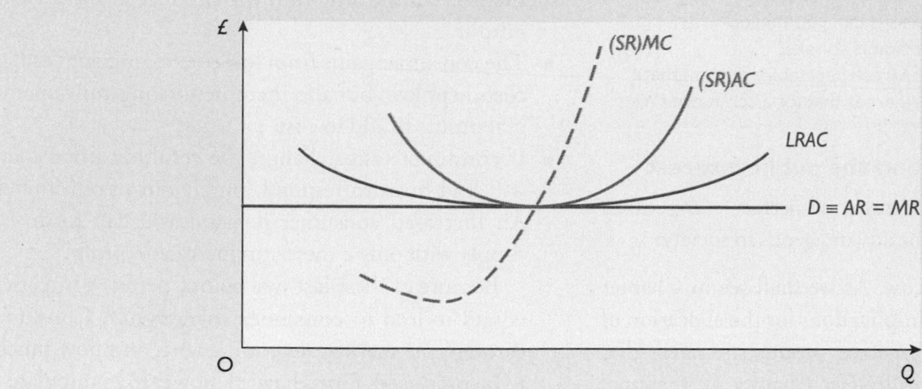

Figure 6.5 Long-run equilibrium of the firm under perfect competition

were no change in firms' average cost curves. Price would simply return to the bottom of firms' *LRAC* curve.

If, however, the entry of new firms creates a shortage of factors of production, this will bid up factor prices. Firms' *LRAC* curve will shift vertically upwards, and so the long-run equilibrium price will be higher. The long-run supply curve of the industry, therefore, will slope upwards, as in diagram (b). This is the case of *increasing industry costs* or *external diseconomies of scale*: i.e. diseconomies external to the firm (see section 5.2).

If the expansion of the industry lowers firms' *LRAC* curve, due, say, to the building-up of an industrial infrastructure (distribution channels, specialist suppliers, banks, communications, etc.), the long-run supply curve will slope downwards, as in diagram (c). This is the case of *decreasing industry costs* or *external economies of scale*.

The incompatibility of perfect competition and substantial economies of scale

Why is perfect competition so rare in the real world – if it even exists at all? One important reason for this has to do with economies of scale.

In many industries, firms may have to be quite large if they are to experience the full potential economies of scale. But perfect competition requires there to be *many* firms. Firms must therefore be small under perfect competition: too small in most cases for economies of scale.

Once a firm expands sufficiently to achieve economies of scale, it will usually gain market power. It will be able to undercut the prices of smaller firms, which will thus be driven out of business. Perfect competition is destroyed.

Perfect competition could only exist in any industry, therefore, if there were no (or virtually no) economies of scale.

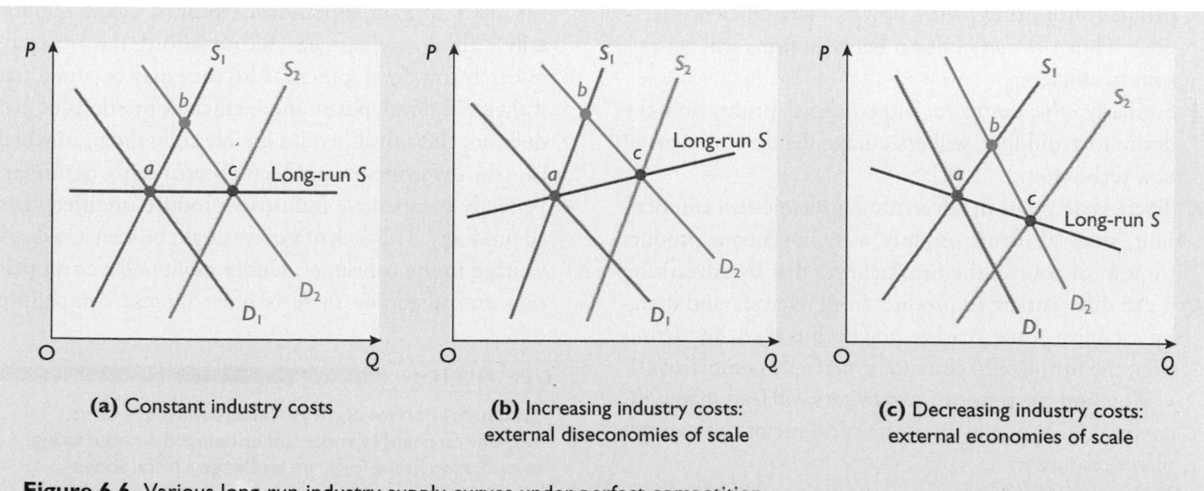

Figure 6.6 Various long-run industry supply curves under perfect competition

??

1. What other reasons can you think of why perfect competition is so rare?
2. Why does the market for fresh vegetables approximate to perfect competition, whereas that for aircraft does not?

Perfect competition and the public interest

There are a number of features of perfect competition which could be argued to be advantageous to society:

- Price equals marginal cost. As we shall see in Chapter 11, this has important implications for the allocation of resources between alternative products. Given that price equals marginal utility (see Chapter 4), marginal utility will equal marginal cost. This is argued to be an *optimal* position.

  To demonstrate why, consider the cases where they are not equal. At levels of output *below* the equilibrium, price is greater than marginal cost. This means that consumers put a higher value on additional consumption than it costs to produce additional output. It could be argued, therefore, that *more* ought to be produced. If, on the other hand, output is *above* equilibrium, price will be below marginal cost. Here it could be argued that *less* should be produced because consumers put a lower value on this additional output than it costs to produce. Clearly, if more should be produced when output is below equilibrium and less should be produced when output is above equilibrium, the equilibrium represents an optimum level of output. As we shall see later, it is only under perfect competition that price will equal marginal cost.
- If a firm becomes less efficient than other firms, it will make less than normal profits and be driven out of business. If it is more efficient, it will earn supernormal profits (until other firms copy its more efficient methods). Thus the competition between firms will act as a spur to efficiency.
- Similarly, the desire for supernormal profit, and the desire to avoid loss, will encourage the development of new technology.
- There is no point in advertising under perfect competition, since all firms produce a homogeneous product (unless, of course, the firm believes that by advertising it can differentiate its product from its rivals' and thereby establish some market power; but then, by definition, the firm would cease to be perfectly competitive).

  This and the previous two factors will lead to low *AC* curves, and hence to an economical use of the nation's scarce resources.
- Long-run equilibrium is at the bottom of the firm's long-run *AC* curve. That is, for any *given* technology, the firm, in the long run, will produce at the least-cost output.
- The consumer gains from low prices, since not only are costs kept low, but also there are no long-run supernormal profits to add to cost.
- If consumer tastes change, the resulting price change will lead firms to respond (purely out of self-interest). An increased consumer demand will call forth extra supply with only a short-run increase in profit.

  Because of these last two points, perfect competition is said to lead to **consumer sovereignty**. Consumers, through the market, determine what and how much is to be produced. Firms have no power to manipulate the market. They cannot control price. The only thing they can do to increase profit is to become more efficient, and that benefits the consumer too.

Even under perfect competition, however, the free market has various limitations. For example, there is no guarantee that the goods produced will be distributed to the members of society in the *fairest* proportions. There may be considerable inequality of income. What is more, a redistribution of income would lead to a different pattern of consumption and hence production. Thus there is no guarantee that perfect competition will lead to the optimum combination of goods being produced.

Another limitation is that the production of certain goods may lead to various undesirable side-effects, such as pollution. Perfect competition cannot safeguard against this either.

What is more, perfect competition may be less desirable than other market structures such as monopoly:

- Even though firms under perfect competition may seem to have an incentive to develop new technology (in order to gain supernormal profits, albeit temporarily), they may not be able to afford the necessary research and development. Also they may be afraid that if they did develop new more efficient methods of production, their rivals would merely copy them, in which case the investment would have been a waste of money.
- Perfectly competitive industries produce undifferentiated products. This lack of variety might be seen as a disadvantage to the consumer. Under monopolistic competition and oligopoly there is often intense competition

DEFINITION

Consumer sovereignty A situation where firms respond to changes in consumer demand without being in a position in the long run to charge a price above average cost.

over the quality and design of the product. This can lead to pressure on firms to improve their products. This pressure will not exist under perfect competition.

The whole question of the efficiency or otherwise of perfect markets and the various failings of real-world markets is examined in more detail in Chapter 11.

At this stage, however, it is important to emphasise that the whole question of advantages and disadvantages is a normative one, and as such it is a question to which the economist cannot give a definitive answer. After all, people have very different views as to what constitutes 'good' or 'bad'.

SECTION SUMMARY

1. The assumptions of perfect competition are: a very large number of firms, complete freedom of entry, a homogeneous product and perfect knowledge of the good and its market by both producers and consumers.
2. In the short run there is not time for new firms to enter the market, and thus supernormal profits can persist. In the long run, however, any supernormal profits will be competed away by the entry of new firms.
3. The short-run equilibrium for the firm will be where the price, as determined by demand and supply in the market, is equal to marginal cost. At this output the firm will be maximising profit. The firm's short-run supply curve is the same as its marginal cost curve (that portion of it above the *AVC* curve).
4. The long-run equilibrium will be where the market price is just equal to firms' long-run average cost. The long-run industry supply curve will thus depend on what happens to firms' *LRAC* curves as industry output expands. If their *LRAC* curves shift upwards (due to external diseconomies of scale), the long-run industry supply curve will slope upwards. If their *LRAC* curves shift downwards (due to external economies of scale), the long-run industry supply curve will slope downwards.
5. There are no substantial (internal) economies of scale to be gained by perfectly competitive firms. If there were, the industry would cease to be perfectly competitive as the large, low-cost firms drove the small, high-cost ones out of business.
6. Under perfect competition, production will be at the point where $P = MC$. This can be argued to be optimal. Perfect competition can act as a spur to efficiency and bring benefits to the consumer in terms of low costs and low prices.
7. On the other hand, perfectly competitive firms may be unwilling to invest in research and development or may have insufficient funds to do so. They may also produce a lack of variety of goods. Finally, perfect competition does not necessarily lead to a fair distribution of income or guarantee an absence of harmful side-effects of production.

6.3 Monopoly

What is a monopoly?

This may seem a strange question because the answer seems obvious. A monopoly exists when there is only one firm in the industry.

But whether an industry can be classed as a monopoly is not always clear. It depends how narrowly the industry is defined. For example, Courtaulds has a monopoly on certain types of fabric, but it does not have a monopoly on fabrics in general. The consumer can buy alternative fabrics to those supplied by Courtaulds. A pharmaceutical company may have a monopoly of a certain drug, but there may be alternative drugs that can be used to treat a particular illness.

To some extent, the boundaries of an industry are arbitrary. What is more important for a firm is the amount of monopoly *power* it has, and that depends on the closeness of substitutes produced by rival industries. The Post Office has a monopoly over the delivery of letters, but it faces competition in communications from telephones, faxes and e-mail.

?? As an illustration of the difficulty in identifying monopolies, try and decide which of the following are monopolies: British Telecom; your local evening newspaper; (see p.185) the village post office; the Royal Mail; Interflora; the London Underground; ice creams in the cinema; Guinness; food on British Rail trains; Tipp-Ex; the board game 'Monopoly'. (As you will quickly realise in each case, it depends how you define the industry.)

The monopolist's demand curve

Since there is, by definition, only one firm in the industry, the firm's demand curve is also the industry demand curve.

Compared with other market structures, demand under monopoly will be relatively inelastic at each price. The monopolist can raise its price and consumers have no alternative firm to turn to within the industry. They either pay the higher price, or go without the good altogether.

The actual elasticity will depend on whether reasonably close substitutes are available in other industries. The demand for a rail service will be much more elastic if there is also a bus service to the same destination.

Barriers to entry

In order for a firm to maintain its monopoly position there must be barriers to the entry of new firms. Barriers also exist under oligopoly, but in the case of monopoly they must be high enough to block the entry of new firms. Barriers can be of various forms.

Economies of scale. If a monopoly experiences substantial economies of scale, the industry may not be able to support more than one producer. In Figure 6.7, D_1 represents the industry demand curve, and hence the demand curve for the firm under monopoly. The monopolist can gain supernormal profit at any output between points *a* and *b*. If there were two firms, however, each charging the same price and supplying half the industry output, they would both face the demand curve D_2. There is no price that would allow them to cover costs.

This case is known as **natural monopoly**. It is particularly likely if the market is small. For example, two bus companies might find it unprofitable to serve the same routes, each running with perhaps only half-full buses, whereas one company with a monopoly of the routes could make a profit.

Even if a market could support more than one firm, a new entrant is unlikely to be able to start up on a very large scale. Thus the monopolist which is already experiencing economies of scale can charge a price below the cost of the new entrant and drive it out of business. If, however, the new entrant is a firm already established in another industry, it may be able to survive this competition.

Product differentiation and brand loyalty. If a firm produces a clearly differentiated product, where the consumer associates the product with the brand, it will be very difficult for a new firm to break into that market. This barrier can occur even though the market is potentially big enough for two firms each gaining all the available economies of scale. In other words, the problem for the new firm is not in being able to produce at low enough costs, but in being able to produce a product sufficiently attractive to consumers who are loyal to the familiar brand.

Lower costs for an established firm. An established monopoly is likely to have developed specialised production and marketing skills. It is more likely to be aware of the most efficient techniques and the most reliable and/or cheapest suppliers. It is likely to have access to cheaper finance. It is thus operating on a lower cost curve. New firms would therefore find it hard to compete and would be likely to lose any price war.

Ownership of, or control over, key factors of production. If a firm governs the supply of vital inputs (say, by owning

DEFINITION

Natural monopoly A situation where long-run average costs would be lower if an industry were under monopoly than if it were shared between two or more competitors.

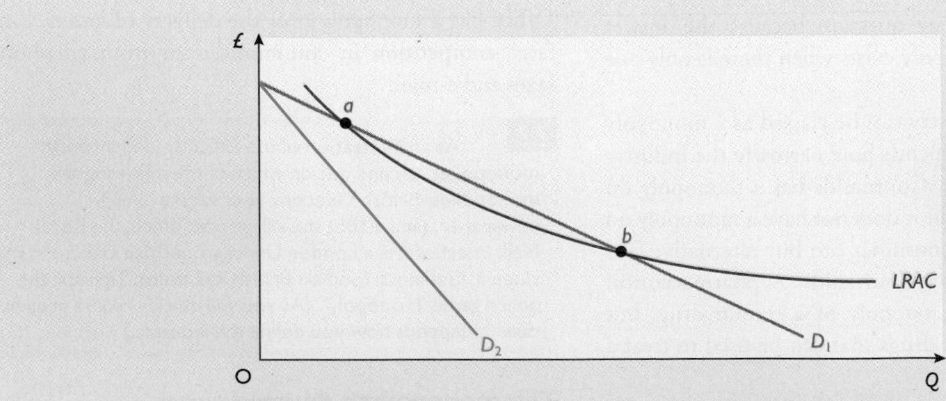

Figure 6.7 Natural monopoly

the sole supplier of some component part), it can deny access to these inputs to potential rivals.

Ownership of, or control over, wholesale or retail outlets. Similarly, if a firm controls the outlets through which the product must be sold, it can prevent potential rivals from gaining access to consumers.

Legal protection. The firm's monopoly position may be protected by patents on essential processes, by copyright, by various forms of licensing (allowing, say, only one firm to operate in a particular area) and by tariffs (i.e. customs duties) and other trade restrictions to keep out foreign competitors.

Mergers and takeovers. The monopolist can put in a takeover bid for any new entrant. The sheer threat of takeovers may discourage new entrants.

Aggressive tactics. An established monopolist can probably sustain losses for longer than a new entrant. Thus it can start a price war, mount massive advertising campaigns, offer an attractive after-sales service, introduce new brands to compete with new entrants, and so on.

Intimidation. The monopolist may resort to various forms of harassment, legal or illegal, to drive a new entrant out of business.

Equilibrium price and output

Unlike the firm under perfect competition, the monopoly firm is a 'price maker'. It can choose what price to charge. Nevertheless, it is still constrained by its demand curve. A rise in price will lower the quantity demanded.

As with firms in other market structures, a monopolist will maximise profit where $MR = MC$. In Figure 6.8 profit is maximised at Q_m. The supernormal profit obtained is shown by the shaded area.

Since there are barriers to the entry of new firms, these supernormal profits will not be competed away in the long run. The only difference, therefore, between short-run and long-run equilibrium is that in the long run the firm will produce where MR = *long-run* MC.

?? Try this brain teaser. A monopoly would be expected to face an inelastic demand. After all, there are no direct substitutes. And yet, if it produces where $MR = MC$, MR must be positive and demand must therefore be *elastic*. Therefore the monopolist must face an elastic demand! Can you solve this conundrum?

Monopoly and the public interest

Disadvantages of monopoly

There are several reasons why monopolies may be against the public interest. As we shall see in sections 12.2 and 12.3, these have given rise to legislation to regulate monopoly power and/or behaviour.

Higher price and lower output than under perfect competition (short run). Figure 6.9 compares the profit-maximising position for an industry under monopoly with that under perfect competition. The monopolist will produce Q_1 at a price of P_1. This is where $MC = MR$.

If the same industry were under perfect competition, however, it would produce at Q_2 and P_2 – a higher output and a lower price. This is where industry supply under perfect competition equals industry demand. (Remember, we showed in section 6.2 that the firm's supply curve

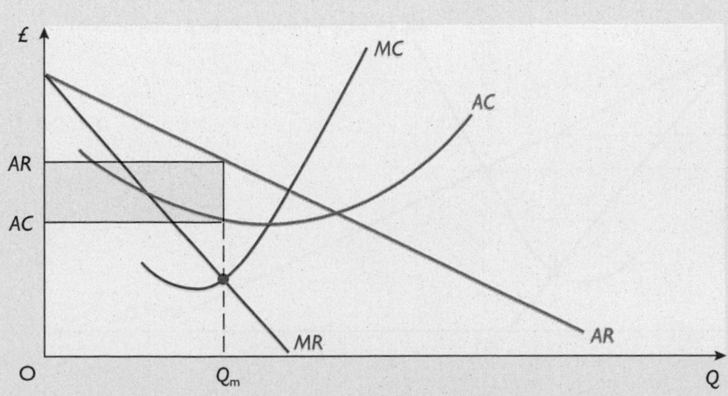

Figure 6.8 Profit maximising under monopoly

under perfect competition is its *MC* curve and thus the industry's supply curve is simply the *industry MC* curve: the *MC* curve shown in Figure 6.9.)

This analysis is based on the assumption that the industry has the *same AC* and *MC* curves whether under perfect competition or run as a monopoly. An example would be the case of potato farmers who initially operate under perfect competition. Then they set up a marketing agency through which they all sell their potatoes. The agency therefore acts as a monopoly supplier to the market. Since it is the same farmers before and after, production costs are unlikely to have changed much. But as we shall see below, even if an industry has *lower AC* and *MC* curves under monopoly than under perfect competition, it is still likely to charge a higher price and produce a lower output.

When we were looking at the advantages of perfect competition, we said that where $P = MC$ could be argued to be the *optimum* level of production. Clearly, if a monopolist is producing below this level (at only Q_1 in Figure 6.9 – where $P > MC$), the monopolist can be argued to be producing at *less* than optimal output. Consumers would be prepared to pay more for additional units than they cost to produce.

Higher price and lower output than under perfect competition (long run). Under perfect competition, freedom of entry eliminates supernormal profit and forces firms to produce at the bottom of their *LRAC* curve. The effect, therefore, is to keep long-run prices down. Under monopoly, however, barriers to entry allow profits to remain supernormal in the long run. The monopolist is not forced to operate at the bottom of the *AC* curve. Thus, other things being equal, long-run prices will tend to be higher, and hence output lower, under monopoly.

Possibility of higher cost curves due to lack of competition. The sheer survival of a firm in the long run under perfect competition requires that it uses the most efficient known technique, and develops new techniques wherever possible. The monopolist, however, sheltered by barriers to entry, can still make large profits even if it is not using the most efficient technique. It has less incentive, therefore, to be efficient (see Box 6.3).

On the other hand, if it can lower its costs by using and developing more efficient techniques, it can gain extra supernormal profits which will not be competed away.

Unequal distribution of income. The high profits of monopolists may be considered as unfair, especially by competitive firms, or anyone on low incomes for that matter. The scale of this problem obviously depends on the size of the monopoly and the degree of its power. The monopoly profits of the village store may seem of little consequence when compared to the profits of a giant national or international company.

?? If the shares in a monopoly (such as a water company) were very widely distributed among the population, would the shareholders necessarily want the firm to use its monopoly power to make larger profits?

In addition to these problems, monopolies may lack the incentive to introduce new product varieties, and large monopolies may be able to exert political pressure and thereby get favourable treatment from governments.

Advantages of monopoly

Despite these arguments, monopolies can have some advantages.

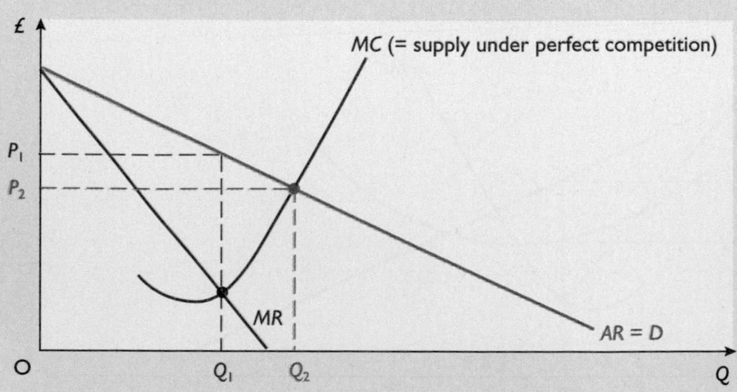

Figure 6.9 Equilibrium of the industry under perfect competition and monopoly: with the same *MC* curve

CASE STUDIES BOX 6.3

COMPETITION IN THE PIPELINE?

Monopoly in the supply of gas

Some of the best examples of monopoly in the UK are the privatised utilities such as telecommunications, water and gas. The government, recognising the dangers of high prices and high profits under monopoly, has attempted to introduce competition in various parts of these industries. But in other parts there is no competition: they remain monopolies.

This mixture of competition and monopoly is well illustrated in the UK market for gas. There are three parts to this market: production; storage and distribution; and supply to customers. In production there is considerable competition, with several companies operating in the North Sea. In storage and distribution, however, there is a monopoly. TransCo International owns the expensive gas pipelines and storage facilities. TransCo was formed in 1996 when British Gas (BG)was split into two parts. The other part, British Gas Energy, is involved in supply to the customer. In supply, the market has been gradually opened up to competition.

First, businesses which used large amounts of gas were allowed to buy from alternative suppliers. Initially competitors to BG could only supply customers consuming more than 25 000 therms per year (the typical household consumes about 600 therms). By 1993 this limit had been reduced to 2000 therms, by which time BG's share of the industrial gas market had fallen to 41 per cent (from virtually 100 per cent in 1990).

Then the market for domestic consumers was opened up to competition. In 1996 competitors to BG Energy were allowed to supply the far south-west of England. This was a trial in preparation for opening up the whole of the British domestic market by 1998.

But how do gas suppliers compete, given that TransCo has a monopoly of the pipelines? The answer is that TransCo is required to allow companies to use its pipelines. It charges them a rent for this service. Producers' supply is metered in; the gas used by companies supplying consumers is metered out. This enables the producing companies to charge the customer-supplying companies, and enables TransCo to work out the amount of rent to charge. Typically this accounts for about 40 per cent of the average household bill.

One reason for splitting BG was the worry that it would charge very high rents to its competitors, thereby giving itself an unfair advantage. In other words, it would use its monopoly in one part of the industry to prevent fair competition in another part.

One solution to this monopoly problem would be for the government to regulate the size of the rent and to insist that BG charged itself the same rent as its competitors. This was the policy in the early 1990s. OFGAS, the regulatory agency set up by the government at the time of privatisation in 1986, attempted to get BG to charge all customers, including itself, the same rent. After the split, TransCo remains regulated to prevent it using its monopoly power to charge excessive rents or to discriminate unfairly between users of its pipelines.

In addition to being responsible for the safety of the gas system, TransCo operates as a 'supplier of last resort'. For example, if there is an upsurge in demand as a result of the weather turning colder, and there is an immediate need to find new supplies in order to avoid households being cut off, TransCo will come into the market and buy gas on behalf of the supplier, thereby ensuring that there is sufficient gas to meet consumer needs. The price it charges to the suppliers is based on the market price for gas: a price that fluctuates daily with demand and supply.

With TransCo's rental charges firmly and fairly regulated, many of the new potential entrants into the gas supply industry are claiming that they will be able to offer domestic consumers savings of anywhere between 10 per cent and 15 per cent on their current bills. We shall see!

??

1. What possible *advantages* to the consumer could there be in (a) TransCo having a monopoly over gas pipelines; (b) BG Energy remaining a monopoly in the supply of gas to domestic households?
2. How would suppliers react if TransCo charged a very high price for providing gas on a last resort basis?

Economies of scale. The monopoly may be able to achieve substantial economies of scale due to larger plant, centralised administration and the avoidance of unnecessary duplication (e.g. a monopoly gas company would eliminate the need for several sets of rival gas pipes under each street). If this results in an *MC* curve substantially below that of the same industry under perfect competition, the monopoly will produce a *higher* output at a *lower* price. In Figure 6.10 the monopoly produces Q_1 at a price of P_1, whereas the perfectly competitive industry produces Q_2 at the higher price P_2.

Note that this result only follows if the monopoly *MC* curve is below point *x* in Figure 6.10. Note also that an industry cannot exist under perfect competition if substantial economies of scale can be gained. It is thus somewhat hypothetical to compare a monopoly with an alternative situation that could not exist. What is more, were the monopolist to follow the $P = MC$ rule observed by

EXPLORING THE THEORY — BOX 6.4

X INEFFICIENCY
The cost of a quiet life

The major criticism of monopoly has traditionally been that of the monopoly's power in selling the good. The firm charges a price above *MC* (see Figure 6.9). This is seen as *allocatively inefficient* because at the margin consumers are willing to pay more than it is costing to produce ($P > MC$); and yet the monopolist is deliberately holding back, so as to keep its profits up. Allocative inefficiency is examined in detail in section 11.1.

Monopolies may also be inefficient for another reason: they may have higher costs. But why?

Higher costs may be the result of *X inefficiency*.[1] Without competitive pressure on profit margins, cost controls may become lax. The result may be overstaffing and spending on prestige buildings and equipment, as well as less effort to keep technologically up to date, scrap old plant, research new products, or develop new domestic and export markets.

Thus the more comfortable the situation, the less may be the effort which is expended to improve it. The effect of this X inefficiency is to make the *AC* and *MC* curves higher than they would otherwise be.

During the early 1980s there were significant reductions in X inefficiency in many countries. With a world-wide recession, and a fall in both sales and profits, many firms embarked on cost-cutting programmes. Much out-of-date plant was closed down, and employment was reduced. Those firms that survived the recession (and many did not) tended to emerge both more competitive and more efficient.

Another example of a likely reduction in X inefficiency is the effect of the Single Market in the EU that was created in 1993. The elimination of customs duties and other barriers to trade between member countries has forced many companies to be more efficient in order to compete with companies in other EU countries.

??

1. How might you measure X inefficiency?
2. Another type of inefficiency is technical or productive inefficiency. What do you think this is? (Clue: it has to do with the proportions in which factors are used.)

[1] This term was coined by Harvey Leibenstein, 'Allocative efficiency or X efficiency', *American Economic Review*, June 1966.

perfectly competitive firms, it would charge an even lower price (P_3) and produce an even higher output (Q_3).

Possibility of lower cost curves due to more research and development and more investment. Although the monopolist's sheer survival does not depend on its finding ever more efficient methods of production, it can use part of its supernormal profits for research and development and investment. It thus has a greater ability to become efficient than has the small firm with limited funds.

Competition for corporate control. Although a monopoly faces no competition in the goods market, it may face an alternative form of competition in financial markets. A monopoly, with potentially low costs, which is currently run inefficiently, is likely to be subject to a takeover bid

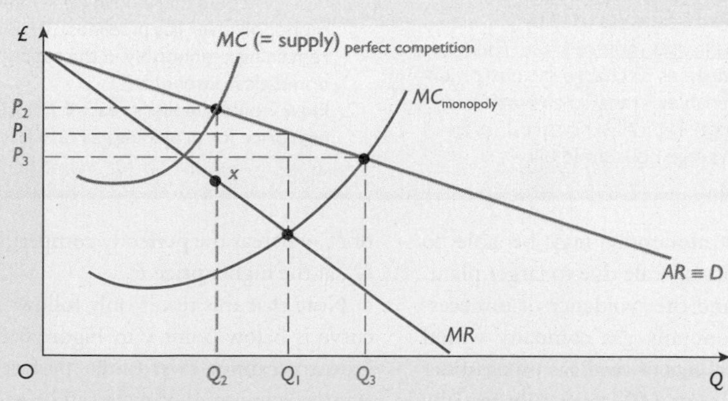

Figure 6.10 Equilibrium of the industry under perfect competition and monopoly: with different *MC* curves

from another company. This **competition for corporate control** may thus force the monopoly to be efficient in order to avoid being taken over.

Innovation and new products. The promise of supernormal profits, protected perhaps by patents, may encourage the development of new (monopoly) industries producing new products.

SECTION SUMMARY

1. A monopoly is where there is only one firm in an industry. In practice it is difficult to determine where a monopoly exists because it depends on how narrowly an industry is defined.
2. Barriers to the entry of new firms will normally be necessary to protect a monopoly from competition. Such barriers include economies of scale (making the firm a natural monopoly or at least giving it a cost advantage over new (small) competitors), control over supplies of inputs or over outlets, patents or copyright, and tactics to eliminate competition (such as takeovers or aggressive advertising).
3. Profits for the monopolist (as for other firms) will be maximised where $MC = MR$. In the case of monopoly, this will probably be at a higher price relative to marginal cost than for other firms, due to the less elastic nature of its demand at any given price.
4. Monopolies may be against the public interest to the extent that they charge a higher price relative to cost than do competitive firms; to the extent that they may cause a less desirable distribution of income; to the extent that a lack of competition removes the incentive to be efficient and innovative; and to the extent that they may exert undesirable political pressures on governments.
5. On the other hand, any economies of scale will in part be passed on to consumers in lower prices, and the monopolist's high profits may be used for research and development and investment, which in turn may lead to better products at possibly lower prices.
6. The relative importance of the advantages and disadvantages of monopoly will vary from industry to industry.

6.4

Potential competition or potential monopoly? The theory of contestable markets

Potential competition

In recent years economists have developed the theory of contestable markets. This theory argues that what is crucial in determining price and output is not whether an industry is *actually* a monopoly or competitive, but whether there is the real *threat* of competition.

If a monopoly is protected by high barriers to entry – say that it owns all the raw materials – then it will be able to make supernormal profits with no fear of competition.

If, however, another firm *could* take over from it with little difficulty, it will behave much more like a competitive firm. The threat of competition has a similar effect to actual competition.

As an example, consider a catering company that is given permission by a factory to run its canteen. The catering company has a monopoly over the supply of food to the workers in that factory. If, however, it starts charging high prices or providing a poor service, the factory could offer the running of the canteen to an alternative catering company. This threat may force the original catering company to charge 'reasonable' prices and offer a good service.

Perfectly contestable markets

A market is **perfectly contestable** when the costs of entry and exit by potential rivals are zero, and when such entry can be made very rapidly. In such cases, the moment the possibility of earning supernormal profits occurs, new firms will enter, thus driving profits down to a normal level. The sheer threat of this happening, so the theory goes, will ensure that the firm already in the market will (a) keep its prices down, so that it just makes normal profits,

DEFINITIONS

Competition for corporate control The competition for the control of companies through takeovers.

Perfectly contestable market A market where there is free and costless entry and exit.

and (b) produce as efficiently as possible, taking advantage of any economies of scale and any new technology. If the existing firm did not do this, entry would take place, and potential competition would become actual competition.

Contestable markets and natural monopolies

So why in such cases are the markets not *actually* perfectly competitive? Why do they remain monopolies?

The most likely reason has to do with economies of scale and the size of the market. To operate on a minimum efficient scale, the firm may have to be so large relative to the market that there is only room for one such firm in the industry. If a new firm does come into the market, then one or other of the two firms will not survive the competition. The market is simply not big enough for both of them.

If, however, there are no entry or exit costs, new firms will be perfectly willing to enter even though there is only room for one firm, provided they believe that they are more efficient than the existing firm. The existing firm, knowing this, will be forced to produce as efficiently as possible and with only normal profit.

The importance of costless exit

Setting up in a new business usually involves large expenditures on plant and machinery. Once this money has been spent, it becomes fixed costs. If these fixed costs are no higher than those of the existing firm, then the new firm could win the battle. But, of course, there is always the risk that it might lose.

But does losing the battle really matter? Cannot the firm simply move to another market?

It does matter if there are substantial costs of exit. This will be the case if the capital equipment cannot be transferred to other uses (e.g. a power station). In this case these fixed costs are known as **sunk costs**. The losing firm is left with capital equipment that it cannot use. The firm may therefore be put off entering in the first place. The market is not perfectly contestable, and the established firm can make supernormal profit.

If, however, the capital equipment can be transferred, the exit costs will be zero (or at least very low), and new firms will be more willing to take the risks of entry. For example, a rival coach company may open up a service on a route previously operated by only one company, and where there is still only room for one operator. If the new firm loses the resulting battle, it can still use the coaches it has purchased. It simply uses them for a different route. The cost of the coaches is not a sunk cost.

Costless exit, therefore, encourages firms to enter an industry, knowing that, if unsuccessful, they can always transfer their capital elsewhere.

The lower the exit costs, the more contestable the market. This implies that firms already established in other similar markets may provide more effective competition against monopolists, since they can simply transfer capital from one market to another. For example, studies of airlines in the USA show that entry to a particular route may be much easier for an established airline, which can simply transfer planes from one route to another (see Box 6.5).

Costless exit can also allow effective potential competition for oligopolies. As we shall see in Chapter 7, if an oligopolistic market is contestable, this will reduce the level of supernormal profits that can be made, just as it does with a monopoly.

> **??** In which of the following industries are exit costs likely to be low: (a) steel production; (b) market gardening; (c) nuclear power generation; (d) specialist financial advisory services; (e) production of a new drug; (f) mobile discos; (g) car ferry operators? Are these exit costs dependent on how narrowly the industry is defined?

Hit-and-run competition

When entry and exit costs are low, and entry can be made speedily, firms may engage in **hit-and-run** tactics. They may enter a market for a short period when high profits can be made and then quickly withdraw again.

For example, a small goods delivery company may set up a rival parcels service to the national postal service at Christmas time over certain major routes if the national service has high (monopoly) postal charges. The fear of such competition may prevent the national service from charging high prices in the first place. Similarly, a local builder serving a small village may suddenly find itself facing competition after a storm from 'cowboy' operators offering to mend roofs cheaply for cash. The fear of this

DEFINITIONS

Sunk costs Costs that cannot be recouped (e.g. by transferring assets to other uses).

Hit-and-run competition When a firm enters an industry to take advantage of temporarily high profits and then leaves again as soon as the high profits have been exhausted.

CASE STUDIES | BOX 6.5

DEREGULATED AIRLINES IN THE USA
A case study of contestable markets?[2]

The airline industry in the United States has been deregulated (i.e. free from government control) for over 16 years, and the impact of this policy on air travel has been dramatic.

Prior to deregulation air routes were allocated by the government with the result that many airlines operated as monopolies or shared the route with just one other airline. Now there exists a policy of 'open skies'. The consequences have been highly significant, with lower fares and, over many routes, a greater choice of airlines. The Brookings Institution calculated that, in the first 10 years of deregulation, the lower fares saved consumers some $100 billion.

Moreover, this has taken place despite a rapid rise in operating costs. But the lower fares and higher costs meant that airlines relied on a growing number of passengers. Not surprisingly, with the recession of the early 1990s many airlines found themselves in trouble. From 1990 to 1992 American carriers made a net loss of about $10 billion. The consequence was that many US airlines went out of business. Gone are famous names such as Eastern and PanAm. In 1992, in the depth of the recession, 32 American carriers went out of business.

Even where routes continue to be operated by just one or two airlines, fares have still fallen if the route is *contestable*: if the entry and exit costs remain low. In 1992, despite the bankruptcies, 23 new carriers were established in North America, and many routes were taken over by existing carriers.

But deregulation has not made all routes more contestable. In some cases the reverse has happened. In a situation of rising costs and falling revenues, there are likely to be takeovers of the vulnerable airlines. Some 7 airlines now account for 90 per cent of American domestic air travel, compared with 15 in 1984. With this move towards greater monopolisation, some airlines have managed to make their routes *less* contestable.

In recent times a system has developed of air routes radiating out from about 30 key or 'hub' airports. With waves of flights scheduled to arrive and depart within a short space of time, passangers can make easy connections at these hub airports.

The problem is that several of these hub airports have become dominated by single airlines which, through economies of scale and the ownership or control of various airport facilities, such as boarding gates or check-in areas, can effectively keep out potential entrants. The problem is worse in airports which are congested and where room for a new entrant could only be made if existing airlines cut back their flights: something they will obviously resist. From 15 of those hub airports, dominated by just one or two airlines, fares are nearly 20 per cent higher than from those airports with more competitors.

So how could routes from these hub airports be made more contestable? Part of the answer may be to deregulate even further. For example, the practice could be ended whereby new take-off or landing slots at certain airports are auctioned among airlines already operating out of that airport.

Part of the answer, however, may be to introduce *new* regulations. During the Reagan and Bush administrations, the airlines were left virtually to their own devices. But President Clinton considered a more interventionist approach. For example, airlines which already have more than a certain percentage of slots could be prevented from obtaining new ones. Also airlines could be prevented from anti-competitive practices, such as big airlines undercutting the prices of small ones so as to drive them out of business. The Department of Justice has begun investigating such cases, and under US law can order airlines to end such practices.

??

1. Make a list of those factors that determine the contestability of a particular air route.
2. Are there any advantages to the traveller of the government allocating routes?

[2] This box is based on material from *The Economist*, 10 March 1990 and 12 June 1993.

may again dissuade the local builder from raising its prices, even if several roofs have been damaged.

?? Give some other examples of hit-and-run competition.

Assessment of the theory

The theory of contestable markets is an improvement on simple monopoly theory, which merely focuses on the existing structure of the industry and makes no allowance for potential competition: no allowance for the size of the barriers to entry and the costs of exit.

Perfectly contestable markets may exist only rarely. But like perfect competition they provide an *ideal type* against which to judge the real world. It is increasingly argued that they provide a more useful ideal type than perfect competition, since the extent of divergence from this ideal provides a better means of predicting firms' price and output behaviour than does the simple portion of the market currently supplied by the existing firm.

One criticism of the theory, however, is that it does not take sufficient account of the possible reactions of the established firm. There may be no cost barriers to entry or exit (i.e. a perfectly contestable market), but the established firm may let it be known that any firm that dares to enter will face all-out war! This may act as a deterrent to entry. In the meantime, the established firm may charge high prices and make supernormal profits.

Contestable markets and the public interest

If a monopoly operates in a perfectly contestable market, it might bring the 'best of both worlds'. Not only will it be able to achieve low costs through economies of scale, but also the potential competition will keep profits and hence prices down.

For this reason the theory has been seized on by politicians on the political right to justify a policy of *laissez-faire* (non-intervention) and deregulation (e.g. coach and air routes). They argue that the theory vindicates the free market. There are two points in reply to this:

- Few markets are *perfectly* contestable. If entry and exit are not costless, a monopoly can still make supernormal profits in the long run.
- There are other possible failings of the market beside monopoly power (e.g. inequality, pollution). These failings are examined in Chapters 10 and 11.

Nevertheless the theory of contestable markets has highlighted the importance of entry barriers in determining monopoly behaviour. The size of the barriers has therefore become the focus of attention of many politicians and academics when considering anti-monopoly policy.

SECTION SUMMARY

1. Potential competition may be as important as actual competition in determining a firm's price and output strategy.
2. The threat of this competition is greater the lower are the entry and exit costs to and from the industry. If the entry and exit costs are zero, the market is said to be *perfectly* contestable. Under such circumstances an existing monopolist will be forced to keep its profits down to the normal level if it is to resist entry of new firms. Exit costs will be lower, the lower are the sunk costs of the firm.
3. Hit-and-run competition can be an important feature of highly contestable markets.
4. The theory of contestable markets provides a more realistic analysis of firms' behaviour than theories based simply on the *existing* number of firms in the industry.

??? END-OF-CHAPTER QUESTIONS ???

1. A perfectly competitive firm faces a price of £14 per unit. It has the following short-run cost schedule:

Output	0	1	2	3	4	5	6	7	8
TC (£)	10	18	24	30	38	50	66	91	120

   (a) Copy the table and put in additional rows for average cost and marginal cost at each level of output. (Enter the figures for marginal cost in the space between each column.)

   (b) Plot *AC*, *MC* and *MR* on a diagram.

   (c) Mark the profit-maximising output.

   (d) How much (supernormal) profit is made at this output?

   (e) What would happen to the price in the long run if this firm were typical of others in the industry? Why would we need to know information about long-run average cost in order to give a precise answer to this question?

2. If the industry under perfect competition faces a downward-sloping demand curve, why does an individual firm face a horizontal demand curve?
3. If supernormal profits are competed away under perfect competition, why will firms have an incentive to become more efficient?
4. Is it a valid criticism of perfect competition to argue that it is incompatible with economies of scale?
5. On a diagram similar to Figure 6.4, show the long-run equilibrium for both firm and industry under perfect competition. Now assume that the demand for the product falls. Show the short-run and long-run effects.
6. Why is the profit-maximising price under monopoly greater than marginal cost? In what way can this be seen as inefficient?
7. On three diagrams like Figure 6.8, illustrate the effect on price, quantity and profit of each of the following: (i) a rise in demand; (ii) a rise in fixed costs; (iii) a rise in variable costs. In each case show only the *AR*, *MR*, *AC*, and *MC* curves.
8. Think of three examples of monopolies (local or national) and consider how contestable their markets are.

7 Profit maximising under imperfect competition

Very few markets in practice can be classified as perfectly competitive or as a pure monopoly. The vast majority of firms do compete with other firms, often quite aggressively, and yet they are not price takers: they do have some degree of market power. Most markets, therefore, lie between the two extremes of monopoly and perfect competition, in the realm of 'imperfect competition'.

There are two types of imperfect competition: namely, monopolistic competition and oligopoly. Under monopolistic competition there will normally be quite a large number of relatively small firms, whereas under oligopoly there will normally only be a few – say, between two and twenty.

> **??** Think of ten different products or services and estimate roughly how many firms there are in the market. (You will need to decide whether 'the market' is a local one, a national one or an international one.) In what ways do the firms compete in each of the cases you have identified?

7.1 Monopolistic competition

We will start by looking at monopolistic competition. This was a theory developed in the 1930s by the American economist Edward Chamberlin. Monopolistic competition is nearer to the competitive end of the spectrum. It can best be understood as a situation where there are a lot of firms competing, but where each firm does nevertheless have some degree of market power (hence the term 'monopolistic' competition): each firm has some discretion as to what price to charge for its products.

Assumptions of monopolistic competition

- There are *quite a large number of firms*. As a result each firm has an insignificantly small share of the market, and therefore its actions are unlikely to affect its rivals to any great extent. What this means is that each firm in making its decisions does not have to worry how its rivals will react. It assumes that what its rivals choose to do will *not* be influenced by what it does.

  This is known as the assumption of **independence**. (As we shall see later, this is not the case under oligopoly. There we assume that firms believe that their decisions *do* affect their rivals, and that their rivals' decisions will affect them. Under oligopoly we assume that firms are *inter*dependent.)
- There is *freedom of entry* of new firms into the industry. If any firm wants to set up in business in this market, it is free to do so.

In these two respects, therefore, monopolistic competition is like perfect competition.

- Unlike perfect competition, however, each firm produces a product or provides a service in some way different from its rivals. As a result it can raise its price without losing all its customers. Thus its demand curve is downward sloping, albeit relatively elastic given the large number of competitors to whom

> **DEFINITION**
>
> **Independence (of firms in a market)** Where the decisions of one firm in a market will not have any significant effect on the demand curves of its rivals.

customers can turn. This is known as the assumption of **product differentiation**.

Petrol stations, restaurants, hairdressers and builders are all examples of monopolistic competition.

> ?? Give some other examples of monopolistic competition. (Try looking through the *Yellow Pages* if you are stuck.)

A typical feature of monopolistic competition is that, although there are many firms in the industry, there is only one firm in a particular location. This applies particularly in retailing. There may be many greengrocers in a town, but only one in a particular street. In a sense, therefore, it has a local monopoly. People may be prepared to pay higher prices there for their vegetables to avoid having to go elsewhere.

Equilibrium of the firm

Short run

As with other market structures, profits are maximised at the output where $MC = MR$. The diagram will be the same as for the monopolist, except that the AR and MR curves will be more elastic. This is illustrated in Figure 7.1(a). As with perfect competition, it is possible for the monopolistically competitive firm to make supernormal profit in the short run. This is shown as the shaded area.

Just how much profit the firm will make in the short run depends on the strength of demand: the position and elasticity of the demand curve. The further to the right the demand curve is relative to the average cost curve, and the less elastic the demand curve is, the greater will be the firm's short-run profit. Thus a firm facing little competition and whose product is considerably differentiated from its rivals may be able to earn considerable short-run profits.

> ??
> 1. Why may a food shop charge higher prices than supermarkets for 'essential items' and yet very similar prices for delicatessen items?
> 2. Which of these two items is a petrol station more likely to sell at a discount: (a) oil; (b) sweets? Why?

Long run

If typical firms are earning supernormal profit, new firms will enter the industry in the long run. As new firms enter, they will take some of the customers away from the existing firms. The demand for the existing firms will therefore fall. Their demand (AR) curve will shift to the left, and will continue doing so as long as supernormal profits remain and thus new firms continue entering.

Long-run equilibrium will be reached when only normal profits remain: when there is no further incentive for new firms to enter. This is illustrated in Figure 7.1(b). The firm's demand curve settles at D_L, where it is tangential to the firm's $LRAC$ curve. Output will be Q_L: where $AR_L = LRAC$. (At any other output, $LRAC$ is greater than AR and thus less than normal profit would be made.)

DEFINITION

Product differentiation Where one firm's product is sufficiently different from its rivals' to allow it to raise the price of the product without customers all switching to the rivals' products. A situation where a firm faces a downward-sloping demand curve.

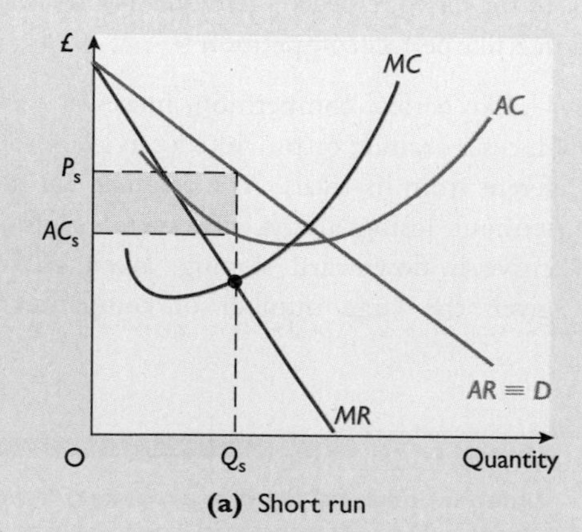

(a) Short run

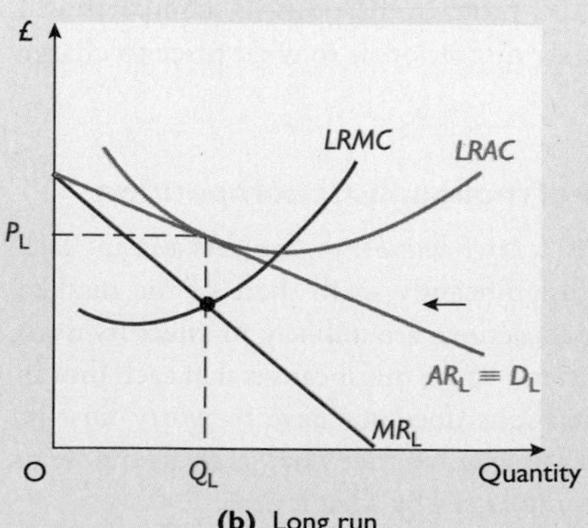

(b) Long run

Figure 7.1 Equilibrium of the firm under monopolistic competition

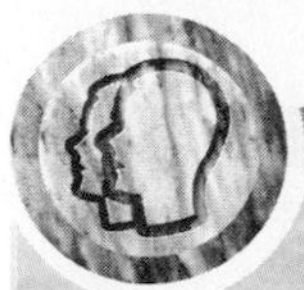

DEVELOPMENT OF IDEAS — BOX 7.1

JOAN ROBINSON (1903–83)
Person profile

At the same time that Edward Chamberlin was developing the theory of monopolistic competition in America, Joan Robinson was developing an alternative theory of imperfect competition in England. There were some differences in their approaches but they both analysed the effects of product differentiation and advertising and thereby extended traditional theory, which had been based almost solely on the two models of perfect competition and monopoly.

Joan Robinson's career, however, was very different from Chamberlin's. He is famous for just one theory; she is famous for the sheer variety and unorthodoxy of her contributions.

She was very much associated with Cambridge. She was a student at Girton College, Cambridge, graduating in 1925. Soon after, she married fellow economist Austin Robinson. After living in India for a time, they returned to Cambridge University where she taught until her retirement in 1971.

During the 1930s she was one of a small group of economists who worked alongside John Maynard Keynes (see Box 15.6), in developing the new macroeconomic theories of employment and money: theories that we shall be looking at in detail from Chapter 15 onwards.

Joan Robinson's contributions to economics were both radical and extensive. She was frequently scathing of traditional economics and of the concerns of economists. For example, she argued that capitalism's failure to eliminate poverty or to aid the development of the Third World were issues which economists should address with urgency.

In 1973, along with John Eatwell, a fellow Cambridge economist, she wrote *An Introduction to Modern Economics*, a book that the authors hoped would revolutionise the teaching of economics. It discarded much of what they considered to be irrelevant in traditional theory (including her early work on imperfect competition!). The book was poorly received, however. Perhaps users of economics textbooks prefer the traditional and familiar!

John Eatwell said of Joan Robinson:

> Her books and articles are often outstanding examples of English prose, and the ideas are novel and exciting, but they do not fit within the framework used by most economists to define their subject.[1]

This non-orthodox approach became very much Joan Robinson's trademark. Such unorthodoxy, however, did not prevent her from being acknowledged as one of the world's most important economic theorists.

[1] J. Eatwell, 'Joan Robinson: Portrait', *Challenge*, vol. 20, no. 1.

??

1. Why does the *LRMC* curve cross the MR_L curve directly below the tangency point of the *LRAC* and AR_L curves?
2. Assuming that supernormal profits can be made in the short run, will there be any difference in the long-run and short-run elasticity of demand? Explain.

Limitations of the model

There are various problems in applying the model of monopolistic competition to the real world:

- Information may be imperfect. Firms will not enter an industry if they are unaware of the supernormal profits currently being made, or if they underestimate the demand for the particular product they are considering selling.
- Given that the firms in the industry produce different products, it is difficult if not impossible to derive a demand curve for the industry as a whole. Thus the analysis has to be confined to the level of the firm.
- Firms are likely to differ from each other not only in the product they produce or the service they offer, but also in their size and in their cost structure. What is more, entry may not be *completely* unrestricted. Two petrol stations could not set up in exactly the same place – on a busy crossroads, say. Thus although the typical or 'representative' firm may earn only normal profit in the long run, other firms may be able to earn long-run supernormal profit. They may have some cost advantage or produce a product that is impossible to duplicate perfectly.
- One of the biggest problems with the simple model outlined in the previous section is that it concentrates on price and output decisions. In practice, the profit-maximising firm under monopolistic competition will also need to decide the exact variety of product to produce and how much to spend on advertising it. This will lead the firm to take part in non-price competition.

CASE STUDIES BOX 7.2

A CASE STUDY IN NON-PRICE COMPETITION
The corner shop and the hypermarket

The general store corner shop run by Mr Brown has recently seen its trade dwindle. This family business, passed from generation to generation, is on the verge of closure. The thorn in Mr Brown's side is a new hypermarket rapidly planned and constructed on a site no more than 2 miles away.

Mr Brown is unable to undercut the hypermarket's prices because he is prevented from making bulk purchases due to his limited storage space. Thus he must consider how he might compete on non-price terms.

Lower prices are not the only advantage the hypermarket has over Mr Brown. It is able to offer a wider range of goods, not only groceries but consumer durables, clothing and hardware. It has superior display and hygiene, easier parking, self-service and longer opening hours as well as credit card facilities. What is Mr Brown to do? What non-price means of competition are open to the small trader?

Mr Brown does surprisingly have a number of options, chief among which is his ability to offer a more personal service, including such things as delivery. Alternatively, he might turn to a local advertising campaign, stressing the shop's convenience and place within the community: i.e. he might try and create a degree of shop loyalty.

Temporary credit and longer hours are further strategies Mr Brown could adopt, fighting the hypermarket on its own terms.

Mr Brown's successes in using these methods will determine his future. One thing is certain: he and others like him will have to be flexible if they are to meet the challenges posed by superstores.

?? Given that many superstores are opening longer hours, providing counter service, home deliveries, etc., do you agree that the only advantage that many small shops have left is their locality?

Non-price competition

Non-price competition involves two major elements: product development and advertising.

The major aims of product development are to produce a product that will sell well (i.e. one in high or potentially high demand) and that is different from rivals' products (i.e. has an inelastic demand due to lack of close substitutes). In the case of shops or other firms providing a service, 'product development' will take the form of attempting to provide a service which is better than, or at least different from, that of rivals: personal service, late opening, certain lines stocked, etc.

The major aim of advertising is to sell the product. This can be achieved not only by informing the consumer of the product's existence and availability, but also by deliberately trying to persuade consumers to purchase the good. Like product development, successful advertising will not only increase demand but also make the firm's demand curve less elastic since it stresses the specific qualities of this firm's product over its rivals' (see Box 2.4).

Product development and advertising not only increase a firm's demand and hence revenue, they also involve increased costs. So how much should a firm advertise, say to maximise profits?

For any given price and product the optimal amount of advertising is where the revenue from *additional* advertising (MR_A) is equal to its cost (MC_A). As long as $MR_A > MC_A$, additional advertising will add to profit. But extra amounts spent on advertising are likely to lead to smaller and smaller increases in sales. Thus MR_A falls, until $MR_A = MC_A$. At that point no further profit can be made. It is at a maximum.

?? Why will additional advertising lead to smaller and smaller increases in sales?

Two problems arise with this analysis:

- The effect of product development and advertising on demand will be difficult for a firm to forecast.
- Product development and advertising are likely to have different effects at different prices. Profit maximisation, therefore, will involve the more complex choice of the optimum combination of price, type of product, and level and variety of advertising.

Monopolistic competition and the public interest

Comparison with perfect competition

It is often argued that monopolistic competition leads to a less efficient allocation of resources than perfect competition.

DEFINITION

Non-price competition Competition in terms of product promotion (advertising, packaging, etc.) or product development.

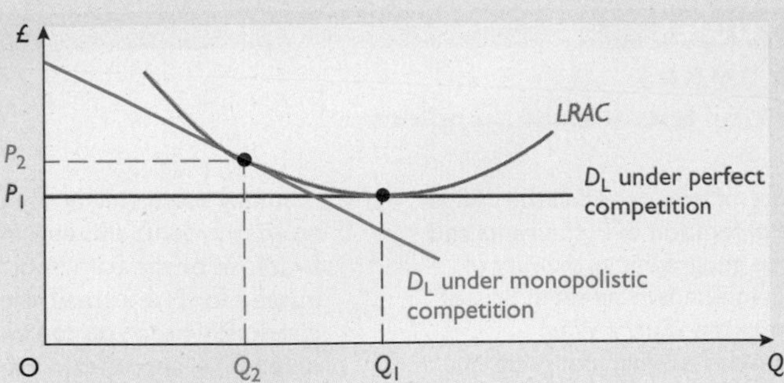

Figure 7.2 Long-run equilibrium of the firm under perfect and monopolistic competition

Figure 7.2 compares the long-run equilibrium positions for two firms. One firm is under perfect competition and thus faces a horizontal demand curve. It will produce an output of Q_1 at a price of P_1. The other is under monopolistic competition and thus faces a downward-sloping demand curve. It will produce the lower output of Q_2 at the higher price of P_2. A crucial assumption here is that a firm would have the *same* long-run average cost (*LRAC*) curve in both cases. Given this assumption, monopolistic competition has the following disadvantages:

- Less will be sold and at a higher price.
- Firms will not be producing at the least-cost point.

By producing more, firms would move to a lower point on their *LRAC* curve. Thus firms under monopolistic competition are said to have **excess capacity**. In Figure 7.2 this excess capacity is shown as $Q_1 - Q_2$. In other words, monopolistic competition is typified by quite a large number of firms (e.g. petrol stations), all operating at less than optimum output, and thus being forced to charge a price above that which they could charge if they had a bigger turnover. How often have you been to a petrol station and had to queue for the pumps?

?? Does this imply that if, say, half of the petrol stations were closed down, the consumer would benefit? (Clue: what would happen to the demand curves of the remaining stations?)

On the other hand, it is often argued that these wastes of monopolistic competition may be insignificant. In the first place, although the firm's demand curve is downward sloping, it is still likely to be highly elastic due to the large number of substitutes. In the second place, although the firm under monopolistic competition will not be operating quite at the bottom of its *LRAC* curve, the nature of the industry may allow some economies of scale to be gained. The *LRAC* curve would thus be lower than in the case of the larger number of smaller firms that would be necessary if the industry were to be perfectly competitive. The size of the economies of scale, if any, will obviously vary from industry to industry.

Furthermore, the consumer may benefit from monopolistic competition by having a greater variety of products to choose from. Each firm may satisfy some particular requirement of particular consumers.

?? Which would you rather have: five restaurants to choose from, each with very different menus and each having spare tables so that you could always guarantee getting one; or just two restaurants to choose from, charging a bit less but with less choice and where you have to book a table quite a long time in advance?

If monopolistic competition brings the disadvantage of excess capacity but the advantage of diversity, is the consumer necessarily worse off under monopolistic competition than under perfect competition? The answer is no. For a start it is rather a bogus question. There is no possibility that industries offering a highly differentiated product could ever be under perfect competition. It is not *logically* possible for a firm *both* to have a horizontal demand curve *and* to provide for some specific demand (like a shop within a few minutes' walk).

DEFINITION

Excess capacity (under monopolistic competition) In the long run firms under monopolistic competition will produce at an output below their minimum-cost point.

CASE STUDIES BOX 7.3

CURRY WARS
Competition hotter than a vindaloo

The growth in the popularity of Indian food in the 1980s and 1990s has led to the proliferation of restaurants and take-away outlets. The close geographic proximity of many such businesses on a well-known street in Bristol led to what became known as the 'Curry War'.

The restaurants had appeared to exist alongside one another quite happily, providing a range of Indian food. In line with the assumptions of monopolistic competition, the restaurants competed in terms of non-price factors such as comfort, advertising and opening hours. Business boomed.

Then with the recession of the early 1990s a price war suddenly erupted. Take-away prices were slashed at first by 20 and 30 per cent, and eventually by 50 per cent at the war's peak. Similar price cuts for dining-in meals were soon to follow. As the war grew more intense, many restaurants saw their profits fall. This was particularly true for those restaurants which tried to resist cutting their prices.

Due to the geographical proximity and cultural links of these businesses, the cut-throat nature of such competition was eventually averted. The local traders' association formed what amounted to a curry cartel. Minimum prices were fixed for curries and prices rose once again.

But as prices in Bristol were rising, prices in other towns were plummeting. On 8 October 1993 *The Independent* reported on a new curry war in Hampstead.

> Mr Khan looked around the Fleet Tandoori, packed, on a Tuesday night, with lager-swilling curry-shovellers, and expressed himself delighted with his night's work.
>
> 'We are doing this for the hard-pressed consumer,' he said. 'We are the consumer's friend. At our prices the consumer can eat at the Fleet for dinner every night for less than the cost of breakfast.'
>
> It may seem unlikely, but if you want a cheap curry to warm you up this autumn, forget Brick Lane, Bradford or the Balti houses of Birmingham. Head instead for Hampstead, the plushest of London districts, where you can indulge in Bombay duck, onion bhaji and vindaloo and still have enough change from a fiver for a packet of extra strong mints ...
>
> ... The opening skirmishes came in September, when the Light of Kashmir restaurant, operating in Hampstead since 1962, started a 'Sunday Madness' promotion, halving, at a stroke, its prices.
>
> ... Within a fortnight, the restaurant had extended its half-price offer to Saturdays and thence to every night of the week ... Two doors down on Fleet Road's parade of shops, on the other side of a Mexican restaurant that offers an 'eat-all-you-like buffet' for just £4.99, is the Fleet Tandoori. A week after the Light started its Seven-Day Madness, a sign appeared outside the Fleet advertising meals at half price.
>
> ... What has upset Mr Khan ... is that all the curry men of Fleet Road are friends and neighbours from way back ... Over the years they have shared staff, poached each other's chefs, cartelled their prices. But the recession put an end to this camaraderie.

??

1. What impact do you think curry wars have on other types of take-away and restaurant meals in the same geographic area? What is the relevance of the concepts of price and cross-price elasticities of demand to these effects?
2. Why are curry wars likely to last only a limited period of time?
3. Collusion between restaurants suggests that they are operating under oligopoly, not monopolistic competition. Do you agree?

Second, even if we identify the cost to consumers from having to pay a price above minimum average cost, this has to be traded off against the gain to consumers from the extra diversity. Only if the cost exceeded the benefit would monopolistic competition be seen as wasteful.

Comparison with monopoly

The arguments here are very similar to those when comparing perfect competition and monopoly.

On the one hand, freedom of entry for new firms and hence the lack of long-run supernormal profits under monopolistic competition are likely to help keep prices down for the consumer and encourage cost saving. On the other hand, monopolies are likely to achieve greater economies of scale and have more funds for investment and research and development.

SECTION SUMMARY

1. Monopolistic competition occurs where there is free entry to the industry and quite a large number of firms operating independently of each other, but where each firm has some market power by producing differentiated products or services.
2. In the short run, firms can make supernormal profits. In the long run, however, freedom of entry will drive profits down to the normal level. The long-run equilibrium of the firm is where the (downward-sloping) demand curve is tangential to the long-run average cost curve.
3. The long-run equilibrium is one of excess capacity. Given that the demand curve is downward sloping, its tangency point with the *LRAC* curve will not be at the bottom of the *LRAC* curve. Increased production would thus be possible at *lower* average cost.
4. In practice, supernormal profits may persist into the long run: firms have imperfect information; entry may not be completely unrestricted; firms may use non-price competition to maintain an advantage over their rivals.
5. Non-price competition may take the form of product development or product promotion (advertising, etc.).
6. Monopolistically competitive firms, because of excess capacity, may have higher costs than perfectly competitive firms, but consumers may gain from a greater diversity of products.
7. Monopolistically competitive firms may have fewer economies of scale than monopolies and conduct less research and development, but the competition may keep prices lower than under monopoly. Whether there will be more or less choice for the consumer is debatable.

7.2 Oligopoly

Oligopoly occurs when just a few firms between them share a large proportion of the industry.

There are, however, significant differences in the structure of industries under oligopoly and similarly significant differences in the behaviour of firms. The firms may produce a virtually identical product (e.g. metals, chemicals, sugar, petrol). Most oligopolists, however, produce differentiated products (e.g. cars, soap powder, soft drinks, electrical appliances). Much of the competition between such oligopolists is in terms of the marketing of their particular brand. Marketing practices may differ considerably from one industry to another.

The two key features of oligopoly

Despite the differences between oligopolies, there are two crucial features that distinguish oligopoly from other market structures.

Barriers to entry

Unlike firms under monopolistic competition, there are various barriers to the entry of new firms. These are similar to those under monopoly (see page 182). The size of the barriers, however, will vary from industry to industry. In some cases entry is relatively easy, whereas in others it is virtually impossible.

Interdependence of the firms

Because there are only a few firms under oligopoly, each firm will have to take account of the others. This means that they are mutually dependent: they are **interdependent**. Each firm is affected by its rivals' actions. If a firm changes the price or specification of its product, for example, or the amount of its advertising, the sales of its rivals will be affected. The rivals may then respond by changing their price, specification or advertising. No firm can therefore afford to ignore the actions and reactions of other firms in the industry.

It is impossible, therefore, to predict the effect on a firm's sales of, say, a change in its price without first making some assumption about the reactions of other firms. Different assumptions will yield different predictions. For this reason there is no single generally accepted theory of oligopoly. Firms may react differently and unpredictably.

DEFINITION

Interdependence (under oligopoly) One of the two key features of oligopoly. Each firm will be affected by its rivals' decisions. Likewise its decisions will affect its rivals. Firms recognise this interdependence. This recognition will affect their decisions.

Competition and collusion

Oligopolists are pulled in two different directions:

- The interdependence of firms may make them wish to *collude* with each other. If they could club together and act as if they were a monopoly, they could jointly maximise industry profits.
- On the other hand, they will be tempted to *compete* with their rivals to gain a bigger share of industry profits for themselves.

These two policies are incompatible. The more fiercely firms compete to gain a bigger share of industry profits, the smaller these industry profits will become! For example, price competition will drive down the average industry price, while competition through advertising will raise industry costs. Either way, industry profits will fall.

Sometimes firms will collude. Sometimes they will not. The following sections examine first **collusive oligopoly** (both open and tacit), and then **non-collusive oligopoly**.

The equilibrium of the industry under collusive oligopoly

When firms under oligopoly engage in collusion, they may agree on prices, market share, advertising expenditure, etc. Such collusion will reduce the uncertainty they face. It will reduce the fear of engaging in competitive price cutting or retaliatory advertising, both of which could reduce total industry profits.

A formal collusive agreement is called a **cartel**. The cartel will maximise profits if it acts like a monopoly: if the members behave as if they were a single firm. This is illustrated in Figure 7.3.

The total market demand curve is shown with the corresponding market *MR* curve. The cartel's *MC* curve is the *horizontal* sum of the *MC* curves of its members (since we are adding the *output* of each of the cartel members at each level of marginal cost). Profits are maximised at Q_1 where $MC = MR$. The cartel must therefore set a price of P_1 (at which Q_1 will be demanded).

Having agreed on the cartel price, the members may then compete against each other using *non-price competition*, to gain as big a share of resulting sales (Q_1) as they can.

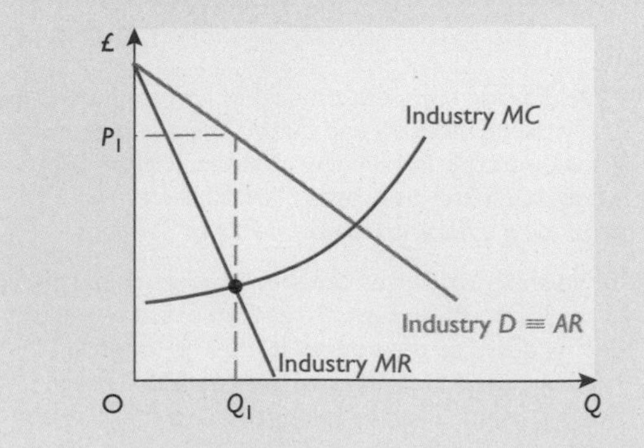

Figure 7.3 Profit-maximising cartel

??
What effect will advertising have on the cartel's *MC* and *AR* curves? How will this affect the profit-maximising output? Is there any problem here for the cartel in fixing the price?

Alternatively, the cartel members may somehow agree to divide the market between them. Each member would be given a **quota**. The sum of all the quotas must add up to Q_1. If the quotas exceeded Q_1, either there would be output unsold if price remained fixed at P_1, or the price would fall.

But if quotas are to be set by the cartel, how will it decide the level of each individual member's quota? One way is to set quotas at the level that will minimise overall industry costs. To do this, each firm should be instructed to produce a level of output such that all firms' marginal costs are *the same*. If they were *not* the same, if firm A's marginal costs were greater than firm B's, total costs would be reduced by switching some of industry production from A to B. In fact, by constructing an industry *MC* curve which is the horizontal sum of the members' *MC* curves, we are assuming that, at any given *industry* marginal cost, each member's marginal cost will be that same level.

The trouble with this cost-minimising solution to carving up the market between the members is that members may have very different costs, in which case the members with lower costs will be given a high quota, whereas the members with high costs may be given a very low quota or

DEFINITIONS

Collusive oligopoly Where oligopolists agree (formally or informally) to limit competition between themselves. They may set output quotas, fix prices, limit product promotion or development, or agree not to 'poach' each other's markets.

Non-collusive oligopoly Where oligopolists have no agreement between themselves, formal, informal or tacit.

Cartel A formal collusive agreement.

Quota (set by a cartel) The output that a given member of a cartel is allowed to produce (production quota) or sell (sales quota).

CASE STUDIES BOX 7.4

OLIGOPOLY OR MONOPOLISTIC COMPETITION?

Big firms and little firms: the case of bakeries

Despite barriers to entry of other *large-scale* firms, many oligopolies face competition at the margin from many small firms. The reason for this is that the small firms often produce a specialist product or serve a local market. These small firms are in a position somewhat like monopolistic competition: they produce a differentiated product and face little if any entry barriers themselves.

A good example of this is bakers. Two giant producers, Allied Bakeries and British Bakeries, produce bread for a nationwide market, with 25 per cent and 22 per cent respectively of the British market in 1995. But then there are thousands of small bakeries, often where the bread is baked in the shop. Their bread is usually more expensive than the mass-produced bread of the two giants, but they often sell a greater variety of loaves, cakes, etc., and many people prefer to buy their bread freshly baked.

In the 1950s and 1960s the giant bakers gradually captured a larger and larger share of the market. This was due to technical developments that allowed economies of scale: developments such as mechanical handling of bread, processes that allowed rapid large-scale proving of dough, and bulk road tankers for flour. Also, with the development of supermarkets where people tended to shop for the week, there was a growth in large-volume retail outlets where there was a demand for wrapped bread with a long sell-by date. These presented real barriers to the small baker.

But then in the 1970s the rise in oil prices and hence the rise in transport costs gave a substantial cost advantage to locally produced bread. What is more, some of the technical developments of the 1960s were adapted to small-scale baking. Finally there was a shift in consumer tastes away from mass-produced bread and towards the more individual styles of bread produced by the small baker.

The effect was a growth in the number of small bakers, who now found that entry barriers were very small.

?? Are the large oligopolistic bakers and the small bakers catering for the same market?

no quota at all. Clearly it would not be in the interests of the high-cost producers to agree to such quotas!

Another method would be for the cartel to divide the market between the members according to their current market share. This is the solution most likely to be accepted as 'fair'.

?? If this 'fair' solution were adopted, what effect would it have on the industry *MC* curve in Figure 7.3?

Collusion and the law

Cartels are effectively prohibited in Britain under Restrictive Trade Practices legislation, unless the firms involved can prove to the Restrictive Practices Court that their agreement is in the public interest. Anti-oligopoly and anti-monopoly legislation is examined in detail in section 12.2.

Where open collusion is illegal, firms may simply break the law, or get round it. There have been various examples of firms breaking the law. For example, construction firms have colluded from time to time when tendering for local authority contracts. They get together beforehand and all agree to put in high-priced estimates for the job. The 'cartel' chooses one firm to get the contract, and that firm therefore puts in a slightly lower (but still high) estimate. On the next occasion the cartel will choose another firm to get the job, and so on, thus dividing the contracts 'fairly' between the 'members'. Such illegal practices are very difficult to prove, provided the firms are careful not to make their agreement too obvious.

Alternatively, firms may stay within the law, but still *tacitly* collude by watching each other's prices and keeping theirs similar. Firms may tacitly 'agree' to avoid price wars or aggressive advertising campaigns.

Tacit collusion: price leadership

One form of **tacit collusion** is where firms set the same price as an established leader. The leader may be the largest firm: the firm which dominates the industry. This is known as **dominant firm price leadership**. Alternatively, the price leader may simply be the one that has

DEFINITIONS

Tacit collusion Where oligopolists take care not to engage in price cutting, excessive advertising or other forms of competition. There may be unwritten 'rules' of collusive behaviour such as price leadership.

Dominant firm price leadership Where firms (the followers) choose the same price as that set by a dominant firm in the industry (the leader).

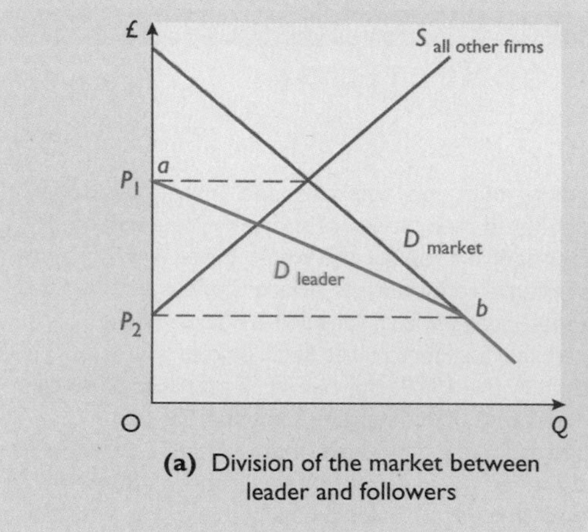

(a) Division of the market between leader and followers

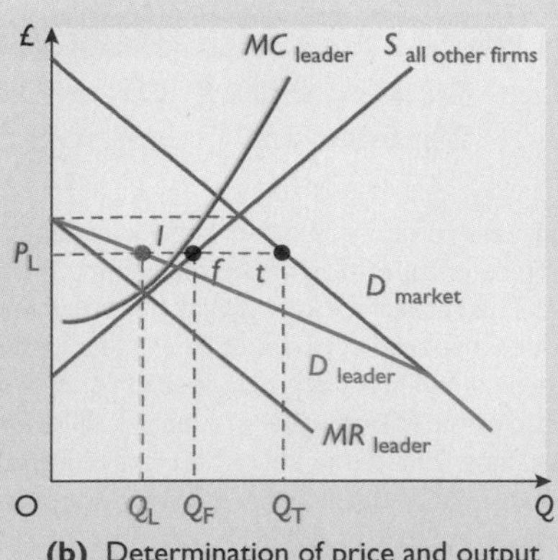

(b) Determination of price and output

Figure 7.4 Dominant firm price leadership

emerged over time as the most reliable one to follow: the one that is the best barometer of market conditions. This is known as **barometric firm price leadership**. Let us examine each of these two types of price leadership in turn.

Dominant firm price leadership

How in theory does the leader set the price? The leader will maximise profits where its marginal revenue is equal to its marginal cost.

In Figure 7.4(a), the total market demand curve is shown. The supply curve of all followers is also shown. These firms, like perfectly competitive firms, accept the price as given, only in this case it is the price set by the leader, and thus their joint supply curve is simply the sum of their *MC* curves – the same as under perfect competition.

The leader's demand curve can be seen as that portion of market demand unfilled by the other firms. In other words, it is market demand minus other firms' supply. At P_1 the whole of market demand is satisfied by the other firms, and so the demand for the leader is zero (point *a*). At P_2 the other firms' supply is zero, and so the leader faces the full market demand (point *b*). The leader's demand curve thus connects points *a* and *b*.

The leader's profit will be maximised where its marginal cost equals its marginal revenue. This is shown in Figure 7.4(b). The diagram is the same as Figure 7.4(a) but with the addition of *MC* and *MR* curves for the leader. The leader's marginal cost equals its marginal revenue at an output of Q_L, (giving a point *l* on its demand curve). The leader thus sets a price of P_L, which the other firms then duly follow. They supply Q_F (i.e. at point *f* on their supply curve). Total market demand at P_L is Q_T (i.e. point *t* on the market demand curve), which must add up to the output of both leader and followers (i.e. $Q_L + Q_F$).

?? Draw a pair of diagrams like those in Figure 7.4. Illustrate what would happen if there were a rise in market demand and no rise in the costs of either the leader or the followers. Would there be an equal percentage increase in the output of both leader and followers?

In practice, however, it is very difficult for the leader to apply this theory. The leader's demand and *MR* curves depend on the followers' supply curve – something the leader will find virtually impossible to estimate with any degree of accuracy. The leader will thus have to make a rough estimate of what its profit-maximising price and output will be, and simply choose that. That is the best it can do!

A simpler model is where the leader assumes that it will maintain a constant *market share* (say, 50 per cent). It makes this assumption because it also assumes that all other firms will follow its price up and down. This is illustrated in Figure 7.5. It knows its current position on its demand curve (say, point *a*). It then estimates how responsive its demand will be to industry-wide price changes and thus constructs its demand and *MR* curves on that basis. It then chooses to produce Q_L at a price of P_L: at point *l* on its demand curve (where *MC* = *MR*). Other firms then follow that price. Total market demand will be Q_T, with followers supplying that portion of the market not supplied by the leader, namely $Q_T - Q_L$.

There is one problem with this model. That is the assumption that the followers will want to maintain a constant market share. It is possible that if the leader raises its

DEFINITION

Barometric firm price leadership Where the price leader is the one whose prices are believed to reflect market conditions in the most satisfactory way.

price, the followers may want to supply more, given that the new price (= *MR* for a price-taking follower) may well be above their marginal cost. On the other hand, the followers may decide merely to maintain their market share for fear of invoking retaliation from the leader, in the form of price cuts or an aggressive advertising campaign.

Barometric firm price leadership

A similar exercise can be conducted by a barometric firm. Although the firm is not dominating the industry, its price will be followed by the others.

It merely tries to estimate its demand and *MR* curves – assuming, again, a constant market share – and then produces where *MR* = *MC* and sets price accordingly.

In practice, which firm is taken as the barometer will frequently change. Whether we are talking about oil companies, car producers or banks, any firm may take the initiative in raising prices. If the other firms are merely waiting for someone to take the lead – say, because costs have risen – they will all quickly follow suit. For example, if one of the bigger building societies raises its mortgage rates by 1 per cent, then this is likely to stimulate the others to follow suit.

Tacit collusion: rules of thumb

An alternative to having an established leader is for there to be an established set of simple 'rules of thumb' that everyone follows. These rules do not involve setting *MC* equal to *MR*, and thus may involve an immediate loss of profit. They do, however, help to prevent an outbreak of competition, and thus help to maintain profits into the longer term.

One example of a rule of thumb is **average cost pricing**. Here, producers simply add a certain percentage for profit on top of average costs. Thus, if average costs rise by 10 per cent, prices will automatically be raised by 10 per cent.

This is a particularly useful rule of thumb in times of inflation, when all firms will be experiencing similar cost increases.

?? If a firm has a typically shaped average cost curve and sets prices 10 per cent above average cost, what will its supply curve look like?

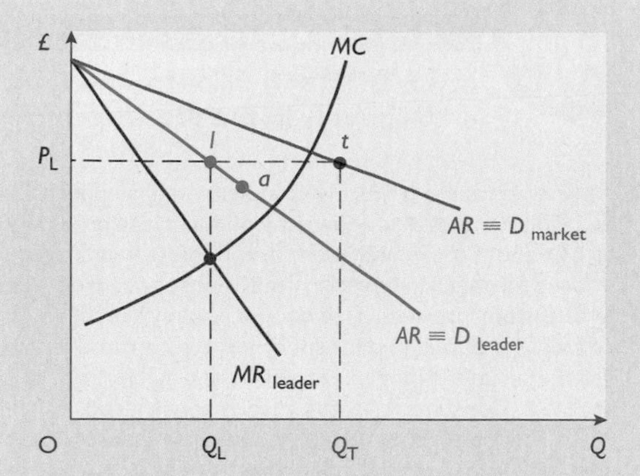

Figure 7.5 A price leader aiming to maximise profits for a given market share

Another rule of thumb is to have certain **price benchmarks**. Thus clothes may sell for £9.95, £14.95 or £19.95 (but not £12.31 or £16.42). If costs rise, then firms simply raise their price to the next benchmark, knowing that other firms will do the same.

Rules of thumb can also be applied to advertising – e.g. you do not criticise other firms' products, only praise your own – or to the design of the product – e.g. lighting manufacturers tacitly agreeing not to bring out an everlasting light bulb.

Factors favouring collusion

Collusion between firms, whether formal or tacit, is more likely when firms can clearly identify with each other or some leader and when they trust each other not to break agreements. It will be easier for firms to collude if the following conditions apply:

- There are only very few firms and hence they are well known to each other.
- They are not secretive with each other about costs and production methods.
- They have similar production methods and average costs, and will thus be likely to want to change prices at the same time and by the same percentage.
- They produce similar products and can thus more easily reach agreements on price.
- There is a dominant firm.

DEFINITIONS

Average cost pricing Where a firm sets its price by adding a certain percentage for (average) profit on top of average cost.

Price benchmark A price which is typically used. Firms, when raising a price, will usually raise it from one benchmark to another.

CASE STUDIES BOX 7.5

IS BEER BECOMING MORE CONCENTRATED?
Oligopoly in the brewing industry

At first glance the UK brewing industry might appear to be highly competitive, with many pubs in close proximity to one another and with many brands of beer and lager offered for sale. However, in reality most pubs are owned by the major brewers. Tied houses, as they are called, account for about 40 per cent of a brewer's turnover, and sell only a limited range of the beers and lagers that are available. Consumer choice is clearly constrained.

The oligopolistic nature of the brewing industry can be seen when we consider the market shares of the leading brewers (see table). In 1985 the three largest brewers held 47 per cent of the market. By 1996 this had grown to 85 per cent. What is also significant is that small independent brewers, which generally operate within a local or regional market, have seen a dramatic fall in their market share. With this huge growth in the market power of the major brewers have come large rises in the price of beer (after taking inflation and tax increases into account).

The Monopolies and Mergers Commission (see section 12.2) investigated the brewing industry and recommended that the brewers should be allowed to own a maximum of 2000 pubs each. This would have involved the brewers selling nearly two-thirds of their pubs (22 000 in all). After complaints from the industry, the government agreed to halve the number sold, but it still hoped that this would increase competition as smaller brewers and other companies and individuals bought these pubs and then stocked a range of beers.

However, the hopes were ill-founded. The pubs that were sold were the least profitable, and many have since closed. There is thus now less competition between pubs. And the brewers, finding a reduction in their scope for achieving economies of scale from *vertical* integration (owning both breweries and pubs), have sought to gain economies of scale from *horizontal* integration (having a larger share of total brewing).

In 1996, for example, Bass (the second largest brewer) announced its takeover of Carlsberg–Tetley (the third largest), giving it a market share of 38 per cent. It now produces such famous brand names as Bass, Carling, Tennent's, Worthington, Tetley, Carlsberg, Castlemaine XXXX, Skol, Burton, Caffrey's and Grolsch.

Small independent brewers are understandably reluctant to expand, faced with the power of such massive competitors in both production and retail, with heavily advertised brands gaining larger and larger shares of the market. The small independents find it impossible to compete in this way.

??

1. What are the barriers to entry in (a) brewing; (b) opening new pubs?
2. Do small independent brewers have any market advantages?

Market shares of the largest brewers

	1985 (%)		1996 (%)
Bass	22	Bass	38
Allied Lyons (Carlsberg)	13	Scottish Courage	32
Grand Met (Watneys)	12	Whitbread	15
Whitbread	11	Guinness Brewing	6
Scottish and Newcastle	10	Others	9
Courage	9		
Others	23		
	100		100
3-firm concentration ratio	47		85
4-firm concentration ratio	58		91

Source: *Mintel*.

- There are significant barriers to entry and thus there is little fear of disruption by new firms.
- The market is stable. If industry demand or production costs fluctuate wildly, it will be difficult to make agreements, partly due to difficulties in predicting and partly because agreements may frequently have to be amended. There is a particular problem in a declining market where firms may be tempted to undercut each other's prices in order to maintain their sales.
- There are no government measures to curb collusion.

?? In which of the following industries is collusion likely to occur: bricks, beer, margarine, cement, crisps, washing powder, blank audio or video cassettes, carpets?

Non-collusive oligopoly: the breakdown of collusion

In some oligopolies, there may only be a few (if any) factors favouring collusion. In such cases the likelihood of price competition is greater.

Even if there is collusion, there will always be the temptation for individual oligopolists to 'cheat', by cutting prices or by selling more than their allotted quota.

Let us take the case of a cartel consisting of five equal-sized firms. The whole cartel is illustrated in Figure 7.6(a). Assume that the cartel sets the industry profit-maximising price of £10. This will give an industry output of 1000 units, which the cartel divides equally between its five members: i.e. each member is assigned a quota of 200 units.

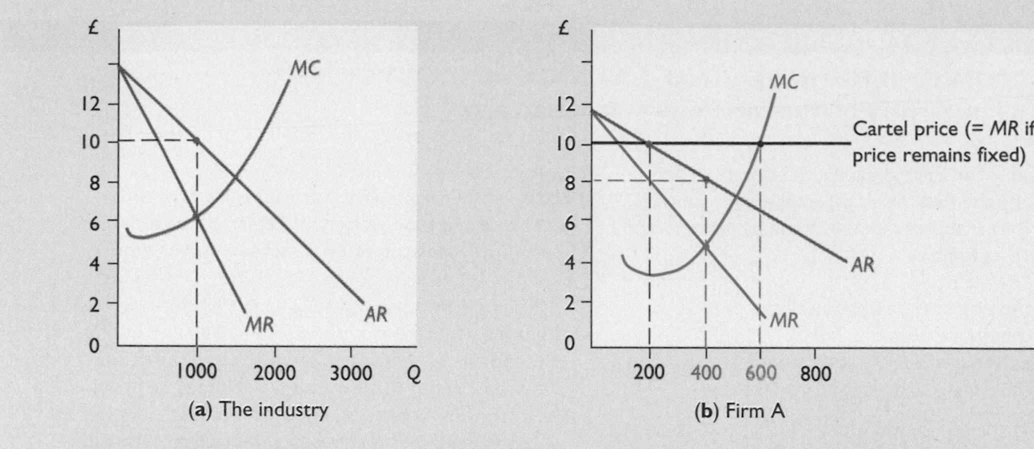

Figure 7.6 The incentive for a firm to produce more than its quota, or to undercut the cartel's price

Now consider Figure 7.6(b). This shows the position for one of the members of the cartel, firm A. Provided the cartel's price remains fixed at £10, then £10 would also be the marginal revenue for the individual firm. This will create an incentive for cartel members to cheat: to sell more than their allotted quota. Firm A would maximise its own profits by selling 600 units, where $MC = P$ (= MR), provided it could do this by taking market share off the other members, and thus leaving total industry output (and hence price) unaffected.

Alternatively, individual members might be tempted to undercut the cartel's price. Again, provided the rest of the cartel maintained its price at £10, firm A would face a relatively elastic demand curve (shown by *AR* in Figure 7.6(b)). A modest cut in its price would attract considerable custom away from the other members of the cartel. Firm A would maximise its profit by cutting price to £8 and thereby increasing its sales to 400 units.

The danger, of course, with either selling above quota or cutting price is that this would invite retaliation from the other members of the cartel, with a resulting price war. Price would then fall and the cartel could well break up in disarray.

When considering whether to break a collusive agreement, even if only a tacit one, a firm will ask: (1) 'How much can we get away with without inviting retaliation?' and (2) 'If a price war does result, will we be the winners? Will we succeed in driving some or all of our rivals out of business and yet survive ourselves, and thereby gain greater market power?'

The position of rival firms, therefore, is rather like that of the generals of opposing armies or the players in a game. It is a question of choosing the appropriate *strategy*: the strategy that will best succeed in outwitting your opponents.

The strategy a firm adopts will, of course, be concerned not just with price but also with advertising and product development.

Non-collusive oligopoly: game theory

The behaviour of a firm under non-collusive oligopoly will depend on how it thinks its rivals will react to its policies.

Economists use **game theory** to examine the best strategy a firm can adopt for each assumption about its rivals' behaviour.

Simple dominant strategy games

The simplest case is where there are just two firms with identical costs, products and demand. They are both considering which of two alternative prices to charge. Table 7.1 shows typical profits they could each make.

Table 7.1 Profits for firms A and B at different prices

		X's price £2	X's price £1.80
Y's price	£2	**A** £10m each	**B** £5m for Y, £12m for X
	£1.80	**C** £12m for Y, £5m for X	**D** £8m each

DEFINITION

Game theory (or the theory of games) The study of alternative strategies that oligopolists may choose to adopt, depending on their assumptions about their rivals' behaviour.

CASE STUDIES

OPEC: THE RISE AND FALL OF A CARTEL

The history of the world's most famous cartel

OPEC is probably the best known of all cartels. It was set up in 1960 by the five major oil-exporting countries: Saudi Arabia, Iran, Iraq, Kuwait and Venezuela. Its stated objectives were as follows:

- The co-ordination and unification of the petroleum policies of member countries.
- The organisation of means to ensure the stabilisation of prices, eliminating harmful and unnecessary fluctuations.

The years leading up to 1960 had seen the oil-producing countries increasingly in conflict with the international oil companies, which extracted oil under 'concessionary agreement'. Under this scheme, oil companies were given the right to extract oil in return for royalties. This meant that the oil-producing countries had little say over output and price levels.

Despite the formation of OPEC in 1960, it was not until 1973 that control of oil production was effectively transferred from the oil companies to the oil countries, with OPEC making the decisions on how much oil to produce and thereby determining its oil revenue. By this time OPEC consisted of thirteen members.

OPEC's pricing policy over the 1970s consisted of setting a market price for Saudi Arabian crude (the market leader), and leaving other OPEC members to set their prices in line with this: a form of dominant 'firm' price leadership.

As long as demand remained buoyant, and was price inelastic, this policy allowed large price increases with consequent large revenue increases. In 1973/4, after the Arab–Israeli war, OPEC raised the price of oil from around $3 per barrel to over $12. The price was kept at roughly this level until 1979. And yet the sales of oil did not fall significantly.

?? Illustrate what was happening here on a demand and supply diagram. Remember that demand was highly inelastic and was increasing over time.

After 1979, however, following a further increase in the price of oil from around $15 to $40 per barrel, demand did fall. This was largely due to the recession of the early 1980s (although, as we shall see later on when we look at macroeconomics, this recession was in turn largely caused by governments' responses to the oil price increases).

Faced by declining demand, OPEC after 1982 agreed to limit output and allocate production quotas in an attempt to keep the price up. A production ceiling of 16 million barrels per day was agreed in 1984.

The cartel was beginning to break down, however, due to the following:

- The world recession and the resulting fall in the demand for oil.
- Growing output from non-OPEC members.
- 'Cheating' by some OPEC members who exceeded their quota limits.

With a glut of oil, OPEC could no longer maintain the price. The 'spot' price of oil (the day-to-day price at which oil was trading on the open market) was falling, as the graph shows.

The trend of lower oil prices was reversed in the late 1980s. With the world economy booming, the demand for oil rose and along with it the price. Then in 1990 Iraq invaded Kuwait and the Gulf War ensued. With the cutting-off of supplies from Kuwait and Iraq, the supply of oil fell and there was a sharp rise in its price.

But with the ending of the war and the recession of the early 1990s, the price rapidly fell again. Today the price of crude oil, in real terms, stands at about $16 per barrel,

Let us assume that at present both firms (X and Y) are charging a price of £2 and that they are each making a profit of £10 million, giving a total industry profit of £20 million. This is shown in the top left-hand box (A).

Now assume they are both (independently) considering reducing their price to £1.80. In making this decision they will need to take into account what their rival might do, and how this will affect them. Let us consider X's position. In our simple example we assume that there are just two things that its rival, firm Y, might do. Either Y could cut its price to £1.80, or it could leave its price at £2. What should X do?

One alternative is to go for the *cautious* approach and think of the worst thing that its rival could do. If X kept its price at £2, the worst thing for X would be if its rival Y cut its price. This is shown by box C: X's profit falls to £5 million. If, however, X cut its price to £1.80, the worst outcome would again be for Y to cut its price, but this time X's profit only falls to £8 million. In this case, then, if X is cautious, it will *cut its price to £1.80*. Note that Y will argue along similar lines, and if it is cautious it too will cut its price to £1.80. This policy of adopting the safer strategy is known as **maximin**. Following a maximin strategy, the firm will opt for the alternative that will *maxi*mise its *mini*mum possible profit.

An alternative strategy is to go for the *optimistic* approach and assume that your rivals react in the way most favourable

BOX 7.6

which in 1973 prices is only about $2.50! However, OPEC still dominates world production, and fresh moves to revive oil prices were made by re-establishing oil quotas.

Oil prices, however, have continued to fall. On the demand side, the development of energy-saving technology plus increases in fuel taxes have led to a relatively slow growth in consumption. On the supply side, the growing proportion of output supplied by non-OPEC members, plus the adoption in 1994 of a relatively high OPEC production ceiling of 24½ million barrels per day, has meant that supply has more than kept pace with demand.

The problem for OPEC is how to constrain output, given the unwillingness of non-OPEC members to adopt quotas and given the chronic tendency of some OPEC members, such as Venezuela and Nigeria, to cheat by producing more than their quota. Typically production by OPEC has been some 1 million barrels per day over the production ceiling.

??

1. What conditions facilitate the formation of a cartel? Which of these conditions were to be found in the oil market in (a) the early 1970s; (b) the mid-1980s?
2. Could OPEC have done anything to prevent the long-term decline in real oil prices since 1981?
3. Many oil analysts are predicting a rapid decline in world oil output from the late 1990s as world reserves are depleted. What effect is this likely to have on OPEC's behaviour?

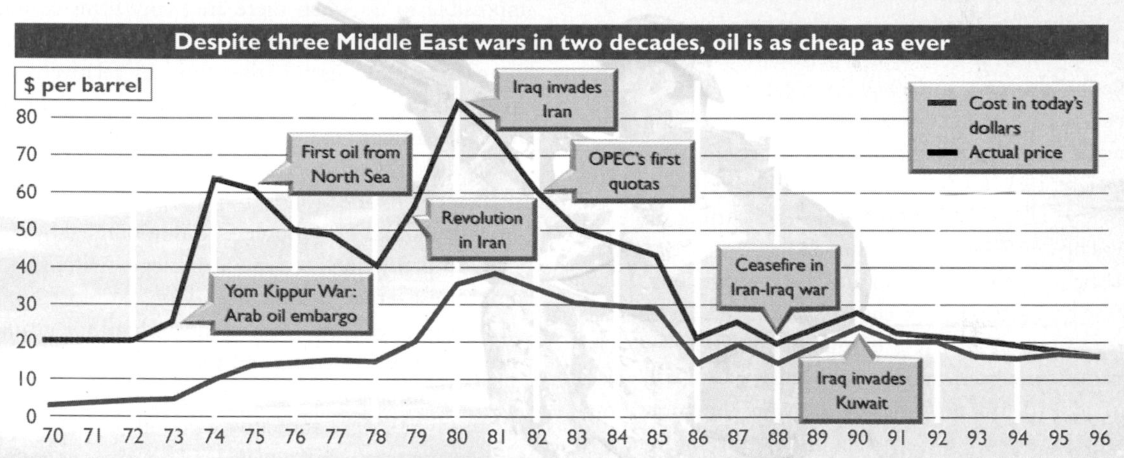

Sources: *The Observer* (12 September 1993); *OECD Economic Outlook* (OECD).

to you. Here the firm will go for the strategy that yields the highest possible profit. In X's case this will again be to cut price, only this time on the optimistic assumption that firm Y will leave its price unchanged. If firm X is correct in its assumption, it will move to box B and achieve the maximum possible profit of £12 million. This strategy of going for the maximum possible profit is known as **maximax**. Note that again the same argument applies to Y. Its maximax strategy will be to cut price and hopefully end up in box C.

Given that in this 'game' *both* approaches, maximin and maximax, lead to the *same* strategy (namely cutting price), this is known as a **dominant strategy game**.

DEFINITIONS

Maximin The strategy of choosing the policy whose worst possible outcome is the least bad.

Maximax The strategy of choosing the policy which has the best possible outcome.

Dominant strategy game Where the *same* policy is suggested by different strategies.

Table 7.2 Profit possibilities for firm X (£m)

		Other firms' responses						
		a	b	c	d	e	f	
Strategies for firm X	1	100	60	−20	10	30	80	(Maximax – a)
	2	40	50	20	30	25	60	(Maximin – c)
	3	90	15	30	25	20	50	(Best compromise)

But, given that both X and Y will be tempted to lower prices, they will both end up earning a lower profit (£8 million profit each in box D) than if they had charged the higher price (£10 million profit each in box A). Thus collusion, rather than a price war, would have benefited both, and yet both would be tempted to cheat and cut prices. This is known as the **prisoners' dilemma**. An example is given in Box 7.7.

More complex games with no dominant strategy

More complex 'games' can be devised with more than two firms, many alternative prices, differentiated products and various forms of non-price competition (e.g. advertising). Table 7.2 illustrates a more complex game.

It shows the profits that will result from three alternative strategies that firm X can pursue (e.g. price cut, advertising campaign, new model) and six possible responses from rivals (e.g. all rivals cutting price, some cutting price, all increasing advertising). It is assumed that firm X can calculate the effects on its profits of these various reactions.

Which strategy will X choose? It may go for the safe strategy – *maximin*. Here it will choose strategy 2. The worst outcome from strategy 2 (response c) will still give a profit of £20 million, whereas the worst outcome from strategy 3 (response b) is a profit of only £15 million, and the worst outcome from strategy 1 (response c) is a loss of £20 million.

Alternatively, firm X may go for a high-risk strategy: the one with highest maximum profit – *maximax*. Here it would choose strategy 1. This has a potential maximum profit of £100 million (response a), whereas the best outcome from strategy 3 is only £90 million (response a), and for strategy 2 only £60 million (response f).

Alternatively, it may go for a **compromise strategy**. Here it could choose strategy 3. The best outcome from strategy 3 (response a) is only slightly lower than strategy 1 (response a) – £90 million compared with £100 million. The worst outcome (response b) is only slightly lower than strategy 2 (response c) – £15 million compared with £20 million.

Alternatively, it may go for a strategy which gives the *best most likely outcome*, or the *best average outcome.*

The advantage of the game-theory approach is that the firm does not need to know which response its rivals will make. It does, however, need to be able to measure the effect of each possible response. This will be virtually impossible to do when there are many firms competing and many different responses that could be made. The approach is only useful, therefore, in relatively simple cases, and even here the estimates of profit from each outcome may amount to no more than a rough guess.

It is thus difficult for an economist to predict with any accuracy what price, output and level of advertising the firm will choose. This problem is compounded by the difficulty in predicting the type of strategy – safe, high risk, compromise – that the firm will adopt.

In some cases, firms may compete hard for a time (in price or non-price terms) and then realise that maybe no one is winning. Firms may then jointly raise prices and reduce advertising. Later, after a period of tacit collusion, competition may break out again. This may be sparked off by the entry of a new firm, by the development of a new product design, by a change in market demand, or simply by one or more firms no longer being able to resist the temptation to 'cheat'. In short, the behaviour of particular oligopolists may change quite radically over time.

Non-collusive oligopoly: the kinked demand curve

In 1939 a theory of non-collusive oligopoly was developed simultaneously on both sides of the Atlantic: in America

DEFINITIONS

Prisoners' dilemma Where two or more firms (or people), by attempting independently to choose the best strategy for whatever the other(s) are likely to do, end up in a worse position than if they had co-operated in the first place.

Compromise strategy A strategy whose worst outcome is better than under the maximax strategy and whose best outcome is better than under the maximin strategy.

ISSUES AND APPLICATIONS — BOX 7.7

THE PRISONERS' DILEMMA

Game theory is not just relevant to economics. A famous non-economic example is the prisoners' dilemma.

Nigel and Amanda have been arrested for a joint crime of serious fraud. Each is interviewed separately and given the following alternatives:

- First, if they say nothing, the court has enough evidence to sentence both to a year's imprisonment.
- Second, if either Nigel or Amanda *alone* confesses, he or she is likely to get only a three-month sentence but the partner could get up to ten years.
- Third, if both confess, they are likely to get three years each.

What should Nigel and Amanda do?

		Amanda's alternatives: Not confess	Amanda's alternatives: Confess
Nigel's alternatives	Not confess	**A** Each gets 1 year	**C** Nigel gets 10 years; Amanda gets 3 months
	Confess	**B** Nigel gets 3 months; Amanda gets 10 years	**D** Each gets 3 years

Let us consider Nigel's dilemma. Should he confess in order to get the short sentence (the maximax strategy)? This is better than the year he would get for not confessing. There is, however, an even better reason for confessing. Suppose Nigel doesn't confess but, unknown to him, Amanda does confess. Then Nigel ends up with the long sentence. Better than this is to confess and to get no more than three years: this is the safest (maximin) strategy.

Amanda is in the same dilemma. The result is simple. When both prisoners act selfishly by confessing, they both end up in position D with relatively long prison terms. Only when they collude will they end up in position A with relatively short prison terms, the best combined solution.

Of course the police know this and will do their best to prevent any collusion. They will keep Nigel and Amanda in separate cells and try to persuade each of them that the other is bound to confess.

Thus the choice of strategy depends on:

- Nigel's and Amanda's risk attitudes: i.e. are they 'risk lovers' or 'risk averse'?
- Nigel's and Amanda's estimates of how likely the other is to own up.

??

1. How would Nigel's choice of strategy be affected if he had instead been involved in a joint crime with Jeremy, Pauline, Diana and Dave, and they had all been caught?
2. Can you think of any other non-economic examples of the prisoners' dilemma?

by Paul Sweezy and in Britain by R. L. Hall and C. J. Hitch. This **kinked demand theory** has since become perhaps the most famous of all theories of oligopoly. The model seeks to explain how it is that, even when there is no collusion at all between oligopolists, prices can nevertheless remain stable.

The theory is based on two asymmetrical assumptions:

- If an oligopolist cuts its price, its rivals will feel forced to follow suit and cut theirs, to prevent losing customers to the first firm.
- If an oligopolist raises its price, however, its rivals will *not* follow suit since, by keeping their prices the same, they will thereby gain customers from the first firm.

On these assumptions, each oligopolist will face a demand curve that is *kinked* at the current price and output (see Figure 7.7). A rise in price will lead to a large fall in sales as customers switch to the now relatively lower-priced rivals. The firm will thus be reluctant to raise its price. Demand is relatively elastic above the kink. On the other hand, a fall in price will bring only a modest increase in sales, since rivals lower their prices too and therefore customers do not switch. The firm will thus also be reluctant to lower its price. Demand is relatively inelastic below the kink. Thus oligopolists will be reluctant to change prices at all.

This price stability can be shown formally by drawing in the firm's marginal revenue curve, as in Figure 7.8.

DEFINITION

Kinked demand theory The theory that oligopolists face a demand curve that is kinked at the current price: demand being significantly more elastic above the current price than below. The effect of this is to create a situation of price stability.

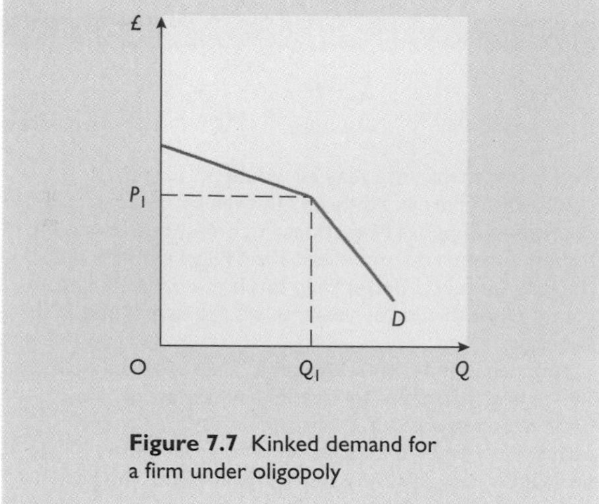

Figure 7.7 Kinked demand for a firm under oligopoly

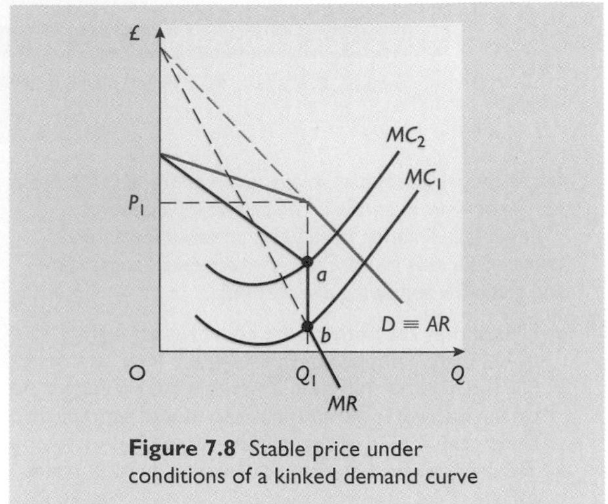

Figure 7.8 Stable price under conditions of a kinked demand curve

To see how this is done, imagine dividing the diagram into two parts either side of Q_1. At quantities less than Q_1 (the left-hand part of the diagram), the *MR* curve will correspond to the shallow part of the *AR* curve. At quantities greater than Q_1 (the right-hand part), the *MR* curve will correspond to the steep part of the *AR* curve. To see how this part of the *MR* curve is constructed, imagine extending the steep part of the *AR* curve back to the vertical axis. This and the corresponding *MR* curve are shown by the dotted lines in Figure 7.8.

As you can see, there will be a gap between points *a* and *b*. In other words, there is a vertical section of the *MR* curve between these two points.

Profits are maximised where $MC = MR$. Thus, if the *MC* curve lies anywhere between MC_1 and MC_2 (i.e. between points *a* and *b*), the profit-maximising price and output will be P_1 and Q_1. Thus prices will remain stable *even with a considerable change in costs*.

Despite its simple demonstration of the real-world phenomenon of price stability, the model does have two major limitations:

- Price stability may be due to *other* factors. Firms may not want to change prices too frequently as it will involve modifying price lists, working out new revenue predictions and revaluing stocks of finished goods, and it may upset customers. Price stability, therefore, is not proof of the accuracy of the model.
- Although the model can help to explain price stability, it does not explain how prices are set in the first place. To do this, some other model would be required. This is a serious limitation in times of inflation, when oligopolists, like other firms, will raise prices in response to higher costs and higher demand. What the model does predict, however, is that the price will be raised only after marginal cost has risen above MC_2 in Figure 7.8, and that once it has been raised, a new kink will form at that price. Price will then remain fixed at that level until higher costs once more force a further price rise.

Oligopoly and the public interest

If oligopolists act collusively and jointly maximise industry profits, they will in effect be acting together as a monopoly. In such cases the disadvantages to society experienced under monopoly will also be experienced under oligopoly (see section 6.3).

Furthermore, in two respects, oligopoly may be more disadvantageous than monopoly:

- Depending on the size of the individual oligopolists, there may be less scope for economies of scale to mitigate the effects of market power.
- Oligopolists are likely to engage in much more extensive advertising than a monopolist (see below).

These problems will be less, however, if oligopolists do not collude, if there is some degree of price competition and if barriers to entry are weak.

Also the power of oligopolists in certain markets may to some extent be offset if they sell their product to other powerful firms. Thus oligopolistic producers of baked beans sell a large proportion of their output to giant supermarket chains which can use their market power to keep down the price at which they purchase the beans. This phenomenon is known as **countervailing power**.

DEFINITION

Countervailing power Where the power of a monopolistic/oligopolistic seller is offset by powerful buyers who can prevent the price from being pushed up.

??

Which of the following are examples of effective countervailing power?
(a) Power stations buying coal from British Coal.
(b) A large office hiring a photocopier from Rank Xerox.
(c) Marks and Spencer buying clothes from a garment manufacturer.
(d) A small village store (but the only one for miles around) buying food from a wholesaler.

In some respects, oligopoly may have *advantages* to society over other market structures:

- Oligopolists, like monopolists, can use part of their supernormal profit for research and development. Unlike monopolists, however, oligopolists will have a considerable *incentive* to do so. If the product design is improved, this may allow the firm to capture a larger share of the market, and it may be some time before rivals can respond with a similarly improved product. If, in addition, costs are lowered by technological improvement, the resulting higher profits will enable the firm to withstand better a price war should one break out.
- Non-price competition through product differentiation may result in greater choice for the consumer. Take the case of stereo equipment. Non-price competition has led to a huge range of different products of many different specifications, each meeting the specific requirements of different consumers.

It is difficult, however, to draw any general conclusions, since oligopolies differ so much in their performance.

Advertising and the public interest

There is no point in advertising under perfect competition, since there is no product differentiation. There is no point in farmer Jones advertising his or her potatoes if they are no different from farmer Brown's. Under monopoly too there is little point in advertising, since, by definition, there are no rivals to compete with (except, perhaps, in other industries).

However, under imperfect competition (both monopolistic competition and especially oligopoly), advertising is often a major means of competing.

Supporters of advertising claim that it is an important freedom for firms. Moreover, they claim that it brings specific benefits for consumers:

- Advertising provides information to consumers on what products are available.
- Advertising may be necessary in order to introduce new products. Without it, firms would find it difficult to break into markets in which there were established brands. In other words, it is a means of breaking down barriers to entry.
- It can aid product development by helping the firm emphasise the special features of its product.
- It may encourage price competition, if prices feature significantly in the advertisement.
- By increasing sales, it may allow the firm to gain economies of scale, which in turn will help to keep prices down.

Critics of advertising, however, claim that advertising imposes serious costs on the consumer and on society in general:

- Advertising is designed to persuade people to buy the product. Consumers do not have perfect information and may thus be misled into purchasing goods which may be inferior in quality to those goods which are not advertised.
- Scarcity is defined as the excess of human wants over the means of fulfilling them. Advertising is used to *create* wants. It could thus be argued to increase scarcity.
- It increases materialism.
- Advertising costs money: it uses resources. These resources could be put to alternative uses in producing more goods.
- If there are no economies of scale, the costs of advertising will tend to raise the price paid by the consumer. Even if the firm has potential economies of scale, it may be prevented from expanding its sales by retaliatory advertising from its rivals.
- Advertising can create a barrier to the entry of new firms by promoting brand loyalty to existing firms' products. New firms may not be able to afford the large amount of advertising necessary to create a new brand image, whereas existing firms can spread the cost of their advertising over their already large number of sales. In other words, there are economies of scale in advertising which act as a barrier to entry.
- People are constantly subjected to advertisements, on television, in magazines, on billboards, etc., and often find them annoying, tasteless or unsightly. Thus advertising imposes costs on society in general. These costs are external to the firm: that is, they do not cost the firm money, and hence are normally ignored by the firm.

??

1. Could annoyance to the public ever rebound as a direct cost to the firm?
2. Choose two products which are extensively advertised. Make out a case for and a case against these particular advertisements.

The effect of advertising on competition, costs and prices is an empirical issue. The evidence, however, is inconclusive. Most of the other questions raised in the above discussion are normative and thus cannot be settled by a simple appeal to facts.

Oligopoly and contestable markets

The new theory of contestable markets has been applied to oligopoly as well as to monopoly, and similar conclusions are drawn.

The lower the entry and exit costs for new firms, the more difficult it will be for oligopolists to collude and make supernormal profits. If oligopolists do form a cartel (whether legal or illegal), this will be difficult to maintain if it very soon faces competition from new entrants. What a cartel has to do in such a situation is to erect entry barriers, thereby making the 'contest' more difficult. For example, the cartel could form a common research laboratory, denied to outsiders. It might attempt to control the distribution of the finished product by buying up wholesale or retail outlets. Or it might simply let it be known to potential entrants that they will face all-out price, advertising and product competition from all the members if they should dare to set up in competition.

The conclusions of the theory, as far as the public interest is concerned, are straightforward. The industry is likely to behave competitively if entry and exit costs are low, with all the benefits and costs of such competition – even if the new firms do not actually enter. If entry and/or exit costs are high, however, the degree of competition will simply depend on the relations between existing members of the industry.

> **??** Which of the following markets do you think are contestable:
> (a) credit cards; (b) brewing; (c) petrol retailing;
> (d) insurance services; (e) compact discs?

SECTION SUMMARY

1. An oligopoly is where there are just a few firms in the industry with barriers to the entry of new firms. Firms recognise their mutual dependence.
2. Oligopolists will want to maximise their joint profits. This will tend to make them collude to keep prices high. On the other hand, they will want the biggest share of industry profits for themselves. This will tend to make them compete.
3. They are more likely to collude if there are few of them; if they are open with each other; if they have similar products and cost structures; if there is a dominant firm; if there are significant entry barriers; if the market is stable; and if there is no government legislation to prevent collusion.
4. Collusion can be open or tacit.
5. A formal collusive agreement is called a 'cartel'. A cartel aims to act as a monopoly. It can set price and leave the members to compete for market share, or it can assign quotas. There is always a temptation for cartel members to 'cheat' by undercutting the cartel price if they think they can get away with it and not trigger a price war.
6. Tacit collusion can take the form of price leadership. This is where firms follow the price set by either a dominant firm in the industry or a firm seen as a reliable 'barometer' of market conditions. Alternatively, tacit collusion can simply involve following various rules of thumb such as average cost pricing and benchmark pricing.
7. Non-collusive oligopolists will have to work out a price strategy. This will depend on their attitudes towards risk and on the assumptions they make about the behaviour of their rivals. Game theory examines various strategies that firms can adopt when the outcome of each is not certain. They can adopt a low-risk 'maximin' strategy of choosing the policy that has the least-bad worst outcome, or a high-risk 'maximax' strategy of choosing the policy with the best possible outcome, or some compromise.
8. Because firms are likely to face a kinked demand curve, they are likely to keep their prices stable unless there is a large shift in costs or demand.
9. Whether oligopoly behaviour is in the public interest depends on the particular oligopoly and how competitive it is; whether there is any countervailing power; whether the firms engage in extensive advertising and of what type; whether product differentiation results in a wide range of choice for the consumer; how much of the profits are ploughed back into research and development; and how contestable the market is. Since these conditions vary substantially from oligopoly to oligopoly, it is impossible to state just how well or how badly oligopoly in general serves the public interest.

7.3 Price discrimination

Up to now we have assumed that a firm will sell its output at a single price. Sometimes, however, firms may practise **price discrimination**. This is where a firm sells the same product to different consumers at different prices. There are three major varieties of price discrimination:

- **First-degree price discrimination** is where the firm charges each consumer the maximum price he or she is prepared to pay for each unit. For example, stallholders in a bazaar will attempt to do this when bartering with their customers.
- **Second-degree price discrimination** is where the firm charges customers different prices according to how much they purchase. It may charge a high price for the first so many units, a lower price for the next so many units, a lower price again for the next, and so on. For example, electricity companies in some countries charge a high price for the first so many kilowatts. This is the amount of electricity that would typically be used for lighting and running appliances: in other words, the uses for which there is no substitute fuel. Additional kilowatts are charged at a much lower rate. This is electricity that is typically used for heating and cooking, where there are alternative fuels.
- **Third-degree price discrimination** is where consumers are grouped into two or more independent markets and a separate price is charged in each market. Examples include different-priced seats on buses for adults and children, and different prices charged by a firm for the same product in different countries. Third-degree price discrimination is much more common than first- or second-degree discrimination.

Conditions necessary for price discrimination to operate

As we shall see, a firm will be able to increase its profits if it can engage in price discrimination. But under what circumstances will it be able to charge discriminatory prices? There are three conditions that must be met:

- The firm must be able to set its price. Thus price discrimination will be impossible under perfect competition, where firms are price takers.
- The markets must be separate. Consumers in the low-priced market must not be able to resell the product in the high-priced market. For example, children must not be able to resell a half-priced child's cinema ticket for use by an adult.
- Demand elasticity must differ in each market. The firm will charge the higher price in the market where demand is less elastic, and thus less sensitive to a price rise.

Advantages to the firm

Price discrimination will allow the firm to earn a higher revenue from any given level of sales. Let us examine the case of third-degree price discrimination.

Figure 7.9 represents a firm's demand curve. If it is to sell 200 units without price discrimination it must charge a price of P_1. The total revenue it earns is shown by the grey area. If, however, it can practise third-degree price discrimination by selling 150 of those 200 units at the higher price of P_2, it will gain the pink area in addition to the grey area in Figure 7.9.

> **??** Explain why, if the firm can practise *first*-degree price discrimination by selling every unit at the maximum price each consumer is prepared to pay, its revenue from selling 200 units will be the grey area plus the pink area in Figure 7.10.

Another advantage to the firm of price discrimination is that it may be able to use it to drive competitors out of business. If a firm has a monopoly in one market (e.g. the home market), it may be able to charge a high price due to relatively inelastic demand, and thus make high profits. If it is under oligopoly in another market (e.g. the export market), it may use the high profits in the first market to

DEFINITIONS

Price discrimination Where a firm sells the same product at different prices.

First-degree price discrimination Where a firm charges each consumer for each unit the maximum price which that consumer is willing to pay for that unit.

Second-degree price discrimination Where a firm charges a consumer so much for the first so many units purchased, a different price for the next so many units purchased, and so on.

Third-degree price discrimination Where a firm divides consumers into different groups and charges a different price to consumers in different groups, but the same price to all the consumers within a group.

CASE STUDIES BOX 7.8

WHAT'S THE TRAIN FARE TO LONDON?
Price discrimination on the trains

Ask the question, 'What's the fare to London?' at ticket enquiries, and you may receive any of the following replies:

- Do you want 1st or standard class?
- Do you want single or return?
- How old are you?
- Do you have a railcard (family, young person's, student, senior citizen's)?
- Do you want a day return, a 'saver' or a period return?
- Will you be travelling back on a Friday?
- Will you be travelling out before 10 a.m.?
- Will you be leaving London between 4 p.m. and 6 p.m.?
- Do you want an 'APEX' ticket (one booked in advance)?
- Do you want to take advantage of our special low-priced winter Saturday fare?

??

1. Look at each of the above questions. In each case decide whether price discrimination is being practised. If it is, is it sensible for train operators to do so? Is it discriminating between people with different price elasticities of demand?
2. Are these various forms of price discrimination in the traveller's interest?

subsidise a very low price in the oligopolistic market, thus forcing its competitors out of business.

Profit-maximising prices and output

Assuming that the firm wishes to maximise profits, what discriminatory prices should it charge and how much should it produce? Let us first consider the case of first-degree price discrimination.

First-degree price discrimination

Since an increase in sales does not involve lowering the price for any unit save the *extra* one sold, the extra revenue gained from the last unit (*MR*) will be its price. Thus profit is maximised at Q_1 in Figure 7.11, where $MC = MR$ (= P of the *last* unit).

Third-degree price discrimination

Assume that a firm sells an identical product in two separate markets X and Y with demand and *MR* curves as shown in Figure 7.12.

Diagram (c) shows the *MC* and *MR* curves for the firm as a whole. This *MR* curve is found by adding the amounts sold in the two markets at each level of *MR* (in other words, the horizontal addition of the two *MR* curves). Thus, for example, with output of 1000 units in market X and 2000 in market Y, making 3000 in total, revenue would increase by £5 if one extra unit were sold, whether in market X or Y.

Total profit is maximised where $MC = MR$: i.e. at an output of 3000 units in total. This output must then be divided between the two markets so that *MC* is equal to *MR* in each market: i.e. $MC = MR = £5$ in each market.

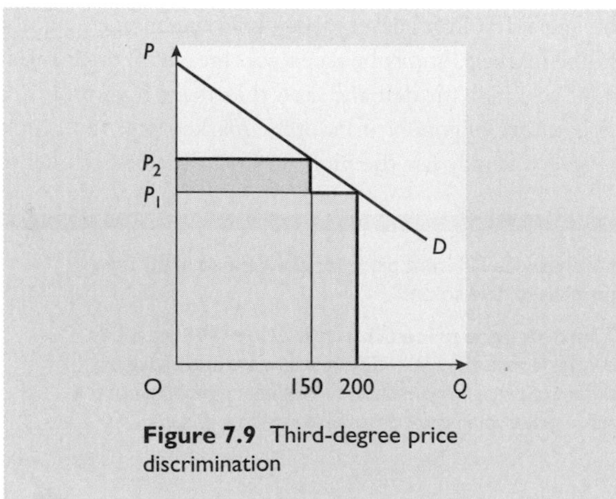

Figure 7.9 Third-degree price discrimination

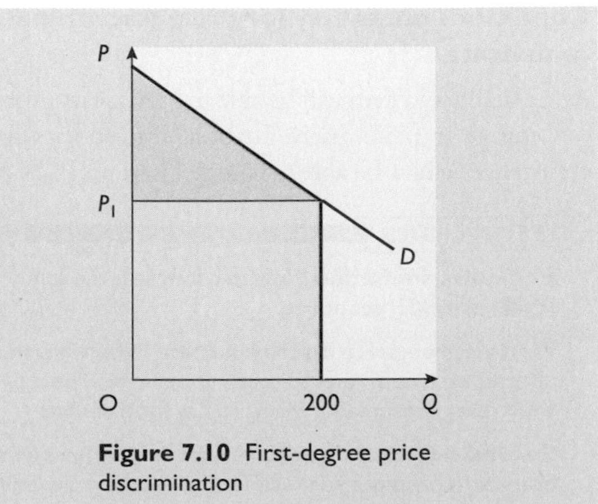

Figure 7.10 First-degree price discrimination

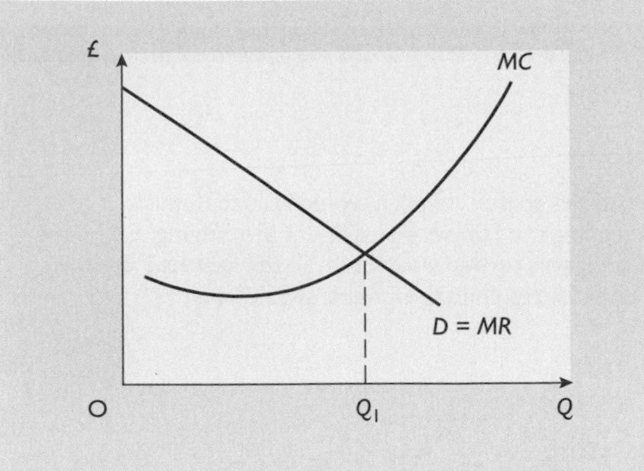

Figure 7.11 Profit-maximising output under first-degree price discrimination

MR must be the same in both markets, otherwise revenue could be increased by switching output to the market with the higher *MR*.

The profit-maximising price in each market will be given by the relevant demand curve. Thus, in market X, 1000 units will be sold at £9 each, and in market Y, 2000 units will be sold at £7 each. Note that the higher price is charged in the market with the less elastic demand curve.

?? How would profit-maximising output and price be determined under third-degree price discrimination if there were three separate markets? Draw a diagram to illustrate your answer.

Price discrimination and the public interest

No clear-cut decision can be made over the social desirability of price discrimination. Some people will benefit from it; others will lose. This can be illustrated by considering the effects of price discrimination on the following aspects of the market.

Distribution

Those paying the higher price will probably feel that price discrimination is unfair to them. On the other hand, those charged the lower price may thereby be able to obtain a good or service they could not otherwise afford: for example, concessionary bus fares for old-age pensioners. Price discrimination is likely to increase output and make the good or service available to more people.

Competition

As explained above, a firm may use price discrimination to drive competitors out of business. This is known as **predatory pricing**. For example, in many towns large bus companies have used profits they make in *other* towns where they have a monopoly to subsidise their bus fares and thereby drive competitors out of business, only then to raise prices above those that the competitors had been charging. On the other hand, a firm might use the profits from its high-priced market to break into another market and withstand a possible price war. Competition is thereby increased.

DEFINITION

Predatory pricing Where a firm sets its prices below average cost in order to drive competitors out of business.

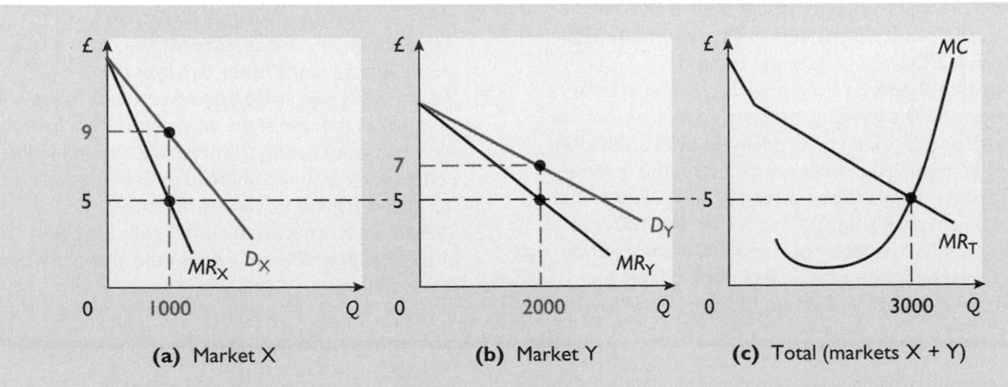

Figure 7.12 Profit-maximising output under third-degree price discrimination

ISSUES AND APPLICATIONS — BOX 7.9

JUST THE TICKET?

Price discrimination in the cinema

One of the commonest forms of price discrimination is where children are charged a lower price than adults, whether on public transport or for public entertainment. Take the case of cinema tickets. In most cinemas children pay less than adults during the day. In the evening, however, many cinemas charge both adults and children the same price.

But why do cinemas charge children less during the day? After all, the child is seeing the same film as the adult and occupying a whole seat. In other words, there is no difference in the 'product' that they are 'consuming'. And why are children charged the higher price in the evenings, given that the seat and the film are the same as during the day?

The answer has to do with revenue maximisation and the price elasticity of demand. Once a cinema has decided to show a film, the marginal costs of an additional customer are zero. There are no additional staffing, film-hire, electricity or other costs. With marginal costs equal to zero, profits will be maximised where marginal revenue is also equal to zero: in other words, where total revenue is maximised.

Take the case of a cinema with 500 seats. This is illustrated in the diagram, which shows the demand and marginal revenue curves of both adults and children. It is assumed that the elasticity of demand for children's tickets is greater than that for adults' tickets. Diagram (a) shows demand during the late afternoon (i.e. after school). Here the demand by children is relatively high compared with adults, but the overall demand is low. Diagram (b) shows demand during the evening. Here there is a higher overall level of demand, especially by adults, many of whom work during the day.

For the afternoon screening (diagram (a)), revenue is maximised from children by charging them a price of £2.00, i.e. at the point on the demand curve where *MR* = 0. At this price 200 child tickets will be sold.

Assuming that the same adult price is charged in both the afternoon and the evening, we need to look at the *total* demand for full-priced tickets (i.e. for both afternoon and evening screenings) in order to ascertain the revenue-maximising price. This will be a price of £3.50, where total adult *MR* = 0 (see diagram (b)). This will lead to 100 adult tickets being sold in the afternoon and 500 in the evening.

But why are reduced-price tickets not available for children in the evening? In diagram (b), the sale of low-priced tickets for children would lead to demand exceeding the 500 seat capacity of the cinema. Each time an adult was turned away because the seat had already been sold to a child the cinema would lose.

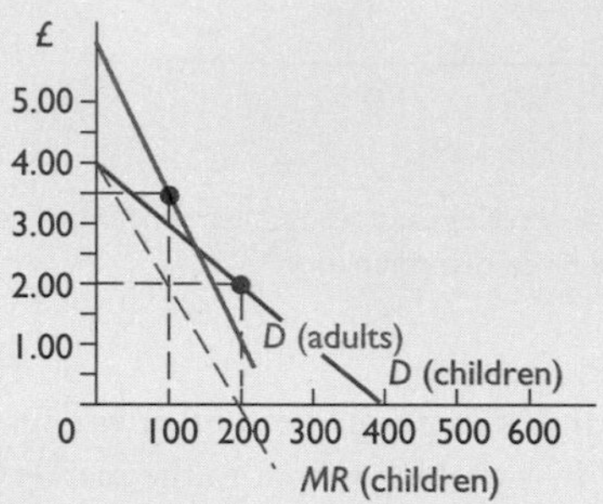

Number of tickets (afternoon)
(a)

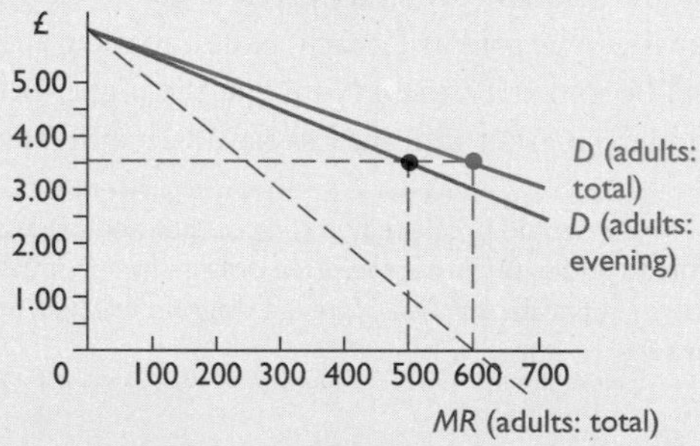

Number of tickets (evening and total)
(b)

??

1. Which type of price discrimination is the cinema pursuing: first, second or third degree? Would it be possible for the cinema to pursue either of the other two types?
2. If all cinema seats could be sold to adults in the evenings at the end of the week, but only a few on Mondays and Tuesdays, what price discrimination policy would you recommend to the cinema in order for it to maximise its weekly revenue?
3. Would the cinema make more profit if it could charge *adults* a different price in the afternoon and the evenings?

Profits

Price discrimination raises a firm's profits. This could be seen as an undesirable redistribution of income in society, especially if the average price of the product is raised. On the other hand, the higher profits may be reinvested and lead to lower costs in the future.

SECTION SUMMARY

1. Price discrimination is where a firm sells the same product at different prices. It can be first-degree, second-degree or third-degree price discrimination.
2. Price discrimination allows the firm to earn a higher revenue from a given level of sales.
3. Under first-degree price discrimination, the profit-maximising output is where $MC = P$. Under third-degree price discrimination, profit-maximising output is where the firm's MC is equal to the overall MR (found by adding horizontally the MR curves in each of the separate markets). This is then divided between the markets by selling that amount in each market where $MC = MR$, at a price given by the demand curve in each market.
4. Some people will gain from price discrimination; others will lose.

??? END-OF-CHAPTER QUESTIONS ???

1. Assume that firm X is considering four possible strategies: 1, 2, 3 and 4. Assume that firm X estimates that there are five possible responses (a, b, c, d and e) that its rivals might make to its actions. It estimates the effects on its profits in the case of each of these five responses to each of its four strategies. Its estimates are given in the following table.

   Profit possibilities for firm X (£m)

		Rivals' responses				
		a	b	c	d	e
Alternative strategies for firm X	1	30	20	80	−10	100
	2	−5	105	40	100	30
	3	90	0	50	45	60
	4	30	15	10	20	25

   (a) Which of the strategies (1, 2, 3 or 4) should it adopt if it is hoping to make the maximum possible profit (maximax)?

   (b) Which of the strategies should it adopt if it is very cautious and decides to assume that the worst will happen (maximin)?

   (c) Which of the strategies might be the best compromise between these two extreme positions? Explain.

2. Assume that a monopolistically competitive industry is in long-run equilibrium. On a diagram like Figure 7.1(b), show the effect of a fall in demand on a firm's price and profit in (i) the short-run and (ii) the long run.
3. In what ways is a monopolistically competitive firm likely to be less efficient than one under perfect competition?
4. Are there any shops in your area that stay open later than others? If so, are their prices similar? Why, do you think, are their prices similar/different?
5. Give three examples of oligopolistic industries. In what ways do the firms in each of these industries compete? Why do they choose to compete in the way that they do?
6. Why, under oligopoly, might a particular industry be collusive at one time and yet highly price competitive at another?
7. What is meant by the *prisoners' dilemma game* when applied to the behaviour of oligopolists? What will determine the outcome of the game?
8. Think of two examples of price discrimination. In what ways do the consumers gain or lose? What information would you need to be certain in your answer?

8

Alternative theories of the firm

8.1 Problems with traditional theory

The traditional profit-maximising theories of the firm have been criticised for being unrealistic. The criticisms are mainly of two sorts: (a) that firms wish to maximise profits but for some reason or other are unable to do so; or (b) that firms have aims other than profit maximisation. Let us examine each in turn.

Difficulties in maximising profit

One criticism of traditional theory sometimes put forward is that firms do not use *MR* and *MC* concepts. This may be true, but firms could still arrive at maximum profit by trial and error adjustments of price, or by finding the output where *TR* and *TC* are furthest apart. Provided they end up maximising profits, they will be equating *MC* and *MR*, even if they do not know it! In this case, traditional models will still be useful in predicting price and output.

The main difficulty in trying to maximise profits is a lack of information.

Firms may well use accountants' cost concepts not based on opportunity cost. If it were thereby impossible to measure true profit, a firm would not be able to maximise profit except by chance.

?? What cost concepts are there other than those based on opportunity cost? Would the use of these concepts be likely to lead to an output greater or less than the profit-maximising one?

More importantly, firms are unlikely to know precisely (or even approximately) their demand curves and hence their *MR* curves. Even though (presumably) they will know how much they are selling at the moment, this only gives them one point on their demand curve and no point at all on their *MR* curve. In order to make even an informed guess of marginal revenue they must have some idea of how responsive demand will be to a change in price. But how are they to estimate this price elasticity? Market research may help. But even this is frequently very unreliable. Such information takes time to acquire and act on, by which time market conditions may have changed, thus making the information out of date. The firm will therefore have to decide whether the possibly small benefit from market research is worth its cost.

The biggest problem in estimating the firm's demand curve is in estimating the actions and reactions of *other* firms and their effects. Collusion between oligopolists or price leadership would help, but there will still be a considerable area of uncertainty, especially if the firm faces competition from abroad. Even other *industries'* products may be substitutes or complements to some degree, and thus will affect the price elasticity of demand for this firm's product.

Game theory may help a firm decide its price and output strategy: it may choose to sacrifice the chance of getting the absolute maximum profit (the high-risk, maximax option), and instead go for the safe strategy of getting probably at least reasonable profits (maximin). But even this assumes that it knows the consequences for its profits of each of the possible reactions of its rivals. In reality, it will not even have this information to any degree of certainty, because it simply will not be able to predict just how consumers will respond to each of its rivals' alternative reactions.

Finally there is the problem of deciding the *time period* over which the firm should be seeking to maximise profits. Firms operate in a changing environment. Demand curves shift; supply curves shift. Some of these shifts occur as a result of factors outside the firm's control, such as changes in competitors' prices and products, or changes in technology. Some, however, change as a direct result of a firm's policies, such as an advertising campaign, the development of a new improved product, or the installation of new equipment. The firm is not, therefore, faced with static cost and revenue curves from which it can read off its profit-maximising price and output. Instead it is faced with a changing (and often highly unpredictable) set of curves. If it chooses a price and output that maximises profits *this* year, it may as a result jeopardise profits in the future.

Let us take a simple example. The firm may be trying to decide whether to invest in new expensive equipment. If it does, its costs will rise in the short run and thus short-run profits will fall. On the other hand, if the quality of the product thereby increases, demand is likely to increase over the longer run. Also variable costs are likely to decrease if the new equipment is more efficient in its use of fuel or raw materials, or requires less labour per unit of output to operate it. In other words, long-run profit is likely to increase, but probably by a highly uncertain amount.

Given these extreme problems in deciding profit-maximising price and output, firms may fall back on simple rules of thumb for pricing.

Alternative aims

An even more fundamental attack on the traditional theory of the firm is that firms do not even *aim* to maximise profits (even if they could).

The traditional theory of the firm assumes that it is the *owners* of the firm who make price and output decisions. It is reasonable to assume that owners *will* want to maximise profits: this much most of the critics of the traditional theory accept. The question is, however, whether the owners do in fact make the decisions.

In **public limited companies** the shareholders are the owners and presumably will want the firm to maximise profits so as to increase their dividends and the value of their shares. Shareholders elect directors. Directors in turn employ professional managers who are often given considerable discretion in making decisions. There is therefore a *separation between the ownership and control* of a firm.

But what are the objectives of managers? Will *they* want to maximise profits, or will they have some other aim?

Managers may be assumed to want to *maximise their own utility*. This may well involve pursuits that conflict with profit maximisation. They may, for example, pursue higher salaries, greater power or prestige, better working conditions, greater sales, etc. Different managers in the same firm may well pursue different aims.

Managers will still have to ensure that *sufficient* profits are made to keep shareholders happy, but that may be very different from *maximising* profits.

Alternative theories of the firm to those of profit maximisation, therefore, tend to assume that large firms are **profit satisficers**. That is, managers strive hard for a minimum target level of profit, but are less interested in profits above this level.

Such theories fall into two categories: first, those theories that assume that firms attempt to maximise some other aim, provided that sufficient profits are achieved (these are examined in section 8.2); and second, those theories that assume that firms pursue a number of potentially conflicting aims, of which sufficient profit is merely one (these are examined in section 8.3).

?? Make a list of six possible aims that a manager of a high street department store might have. Identify some conflicts that might arise between these aims.

The principal–agent problem

The issue of the divorce between the ownership and control of a company is an example of what is known in economics as the **principal–agent problem**. One of the features of a complex modern economy is that people (principals) have to employ others (agents) to carry out their wishes. If you want to go on holiday, it is easier to go to a travel agent to sort out the arrangements than to do it all yourself. Likewise, if you want to buy a house, it is more convenient to go to an estate agent. The point is that these agents have specialist knowledge and can save you, the principal, a great deal of time and effort. It is merely an example of the benefits of the specialisation and division of labour.

It is the same with firms. They employ people with specialist knowledge and skills to carry out specific tasks. Companies frequently employ consultants to give them advice or engage the services of specialist firms such as an advertising agency. It is the same with the employees of the company. They can be seen as 'agents' of their employer. In the case of workers, they can be seen as the agents of management. Junior managers are the agents of senior management. Senior managers are the agents of the

DEFINITIONS

Public limited company A company owned by its shareholders. The shares may be bought and sold publicly – on the Stock Exchange.

Profit satisficing Where decision makers in a firm aim for a target level of profit rather than the absolute maximum level.

Principal–agent problem Where people (principals), as a result of lack of knowledge, cannot ensure that their best interests are served by their agents.

DEVELOPMENT OF IDEAS BOX 8.1

MANAGERIAL UTILITY MAXIMISATION

Williamson's alternative alternative

> The belief that managerial discretion has an important influence on the resource allocation process within the business firm has a long and recurrent history among economists.
>
> O. E. Williamson[1]

Williamson makes reference to a galaxy of famous names in support of his proposition. These include Adam Smith, Alfred Marshall and John Maynard Keynes, all of whom, according to Williamson, questioned the dominant theory of the firm – namely, profit maximisation.

The theory of profit maximisation came under increasing attack during the 1950s and 1960s, when a whole range of new and alternative theories were developed. The common element of these theories was the replacement of profit maximising by a profit 'constraint'.

Provided that *satisfactory* levels of profit were achieved, managers were seen to be free to pursue a whole range of discretionary policies: that is, they were free to maximise their own utility.

Williamson identified a number of factors that would determine a manager's utility. These included the following:

- Salary.
- Job security.
- Dominance – including status, power and prestige.
- Professional excellence.

Of these only salary is *directly* measurable. The rest have to be measured indirectly. One way of doing this is to examine managers' expenditure on various items, and in particular on *staff*, on *perks* (such as a company car and a plush office) and on *discretionary investment*. The greater is the level of managerial expenditure on these items, the greater is likely to be their status, power, prestige, professional excellence and job security.

Increased *spending on staff* often comes from promotion. Power, status and prestige are all enhanced as the staff under the manager's control grow in number. The number of staff is a symbol of the manager's professional importance.

Emoluments (*perks*) in the form of expense accounts, company cars, etc., reflect the manager's position within the firm. The higher the level of perks, the more secure and dominant the manager is likely to be.

Discretionary investment by managers is possible when earnings above the minimum profit constraint are achieved. This allows managers to expand staff and perks and undertake any other projects that the manager wishes to pursue. How the money is invested is at the manager's discretion.

Having identified these factors that influence a manager's utility, Williamson developed several models in which managers maximise their utility function. He used these models to predict managerial behaviour under various conditions and argued that they performed better than traditional profit-maximising theory. To support these claims he conducted a number of case studies. These showed, for example, that staff and perks were cut during recessions and expanded during booms, and that new managers were frequently able to cut staff without influencing the productivity of firms.

Although Williamson's work has produced and stimulated a whole range of investigations into the behaviour of managers, the evidence gathered remains inconclusive. Many economists suggest that the nature of the market in which the firm operates will determine which of the theories is the most relevant: profit maximisation, managerial utility or some other.

?? On what other factors might a manager's utility depend?

[1] *The Economics of Discretionary Behaviour* (Prentice Hall, 1964), p. 3.

directors, who are themselves agents of the shareholders. Thus in large firms there is often a complex chain of principal–agent relationships.

But these relationships have an inherent danger for the principal: there is **asymmetric information** between the two sides. The agent knows more about the situation than the principal – in fact this is part of the reason why the principal employs the agent in the first place. The danger is that the agent may well not act in the principal's best interests, and may be able to get away with it because of the principal's imperfect knowledge. The estate agent trying to sell you a house may not tell you about the noisy neighbours or that the vendor is prepared to accept a much lower price. A second-hand car dealer may 'neglect' to tell you about the rust on the underside of the car or that it had a history of unreliability.

DEFINITION

Asymmetric information Where one party in an economic relationship (e.g. an agent) has more information than another (e.g. the principal).

ISSUES AND APPLICATIONS — BOX 8.2

WHAT DO YOU MAXIMISE?
Or managers are only human too

You are a student studying economics. So what do you maximise?

Do you attempt to maximise the examination marks you will get? If so, you will probably have to spend most of each week studying. Obviously you will have to have breaks for food and sleep, and you will need some recreation, but you will probably still spend a lot more time studying than you do now!

What is more likely is that you will, in some rather vaguely defined way, try to maximise your happiness. Getting a good mark in your exams is just one element contributing to your happiness, and you will have to weigh it against the opportunity cost of studying – namely, time not spent out with friends, watching television, pursuing your hobby, etc.

To argue that managers seek to maximise profits to the exclusion of everything else is rather like arguing that you seek to maximise your exam marks. Managers' happiness (or utility) will depend on their salaries, the pleasantness of their job, their power, their respect, the friendship of their colleagues, etc.

Achieving profits may be an important aim (after all it does contribute to a manager's utility), but the effort required to make extra profits involves an opportunity cost to the manager. For example, the manager may have to work longer hours! Managers are only human too.

??

1. When are increased profits in the manager's personal interest?
2. Do you carefully allocate your time between study and leisure? If not, why not?

In firms too, agents frequently do not act in the best interests of their principals. For example, workers may be able to get away with not working very hard, preferring instead a quiet life. Similarly, given the divorce between the ownership and control of a company, managers (agents) may pursue goals different from those of shareholders (principals). Thus *X inefficiency* is likely to occur.

So how can principals tackle the problem? There are two elements in the solution:

- The principals must have some way of *monitoring* the performance of their agents. Thus a company might employ efficiency experts to examine the operation of its management.
- There must be *incentives* for agents to behave in the principals' interests. Thus managers' salaries could be more closely linked to the firm's profitability.

Alternative theories of the firm therefore place considerable emphasis on incentive mechanisms in explaining the behaviour of managers and the resulting performance of their companies.

In a competitive market, managers' and shareholders' interests are more likely to coincide. Managers have to ensure that the company remains efficient or it may not survive the competition and they might lose their jobs. In monopolies and oligopolies, however, where supernormal profits can often be relatively easily earned, the interests of shareholders and managers are likely to diverge. Here it will be in shareholders' interests to institute incentive mechanisms that ensure that their agents, the managers, are motivated to strive for profitability.

Survival: the ultimate aim?

Aiming for profits, sales, salaries, power, etc. will be useless if the firm does not survive! Trying to *maximise* any of the various objectives may be risky. For example, if a firm tries to maximise its market share by aggressive advertising or price cutting, it might invoke a strong response from its rivals. The resulting war may drive it out of business. Some of the managers may easily move to other jobs and may actually gain from the experience, but the majority are likely to lose. Concern with survival, therefore, may make firms cautious.

Not all firms, however, make survival the top priority. Some are adventurous and are prepared to take risks. Adventurous firms are most likely to be those dominated by a powerful and ambitious individual – an individual prepared to take gambles.

The more dispersed the decision-making power is in the firm, however, and the more worried managers are about their own survival, the more cautious are their policies likely to be: preferring collusion to competition, preferring to stick with products that have proved to be popular, and preferring to expand slowly and steadily.

If a firm is too cautious, however, it may not after all survive. It may find that it loses markets to more aggressive competitors. Ultimately, therefore, if a firm is concerned to survive, it must be careful to balance caution against keeping up with competitors, ensuring that the customer is sufficiently satisfied and that costs are kept sufficiently low by efficient management and the introduction of new technology.

SECTION SUMMARY

1. There are two major types of criticism of the traditional profit-maximising theory: (a) firms may not have the information to maximise profits; (b) they may not even want to maximise profits.
2. Lack of information on demand and costs and on the actions and reactions of rivals, and a lack of use of opportunity cost concepts, may mean that firms adopt simple 'rules of thumb' for pricing.
3. In large companies there is likely to be a divorce between ownership and control. The shareholders (the owners) may want maximum profits, but it is the managers who make the decisions and managers are likely to aim to maximise their own utility rather than that of the shareholders. This leads to profit 'satisficing'. This is where managers aim to achieve sufficient profits to keep shareholders happy, but this is a secondary aim to one or more alternative aims.
4. The problem of managers not pursuing the same goals as the owners is an example of the *principal–agent problem*. Agents (in this case the managers) may not always carry out the wishes of their principals (in this case the owners). Because of asymmetric information, managers are able to pursue their own aims, just so long as they produce results that will satisfy the owners. The solution for owners is for there to be better means of monitoring the performance of managers, and incentives for the managers to behave in the owners' interests.
5. Some alternative theories assume that there is a single alternative aim that firms seek to maximise. Others assume that managers have a series of (possibly conflicting) aims.

8.2 Alternative maximising theories

Long-run profit maximisation

The traditional theory of the firm is based on the assumption of *short-run* profit maximisation. Many actions of firms may be seen to conflict with this aim and yet could be consistent with the aim of **long-run profit maximisation**. For example, policies to increase the size of the firm or the firm's share of the market may involve heavy advertising or low prices to the detriment of short-run profits. But if this results in the firm becoming larger, with a larger share of the market, the resulting economic power may enable the firm to make larger profits in the long run.

At first sight, a theory of long-run profit maximisation would seem to be a realistic alternative to the traditional short-run profit-maximisation theory. In practice, however, the theory is not a very useful predictor of firms' behaviour and is very difficult to test.

One question is whether long-run profit maximisation is merely the result of managers pursuing other aims, or whether it is the prime aim itself.

What is more, 'long-run maximisation' could be an excuse for virtually any policy. When challenged as to why the firms had, say, undertaken expensive research or high-cost investment, or had engaged in a damaging price war, the managers could reply, 'Ah, yes, but in the long run it will pay off.' This is very difficult to refute (until it is too late!).

If long-run profit maximisation *is* the prime aim, the means of achieving it are extremely complex. The firm will need a plan of action for prices, output, investment, etc., stretching from now into the future. But today's pricing and marketing decisions affect tomorrow's demand. Therefore, future demand curves cannot be taken as given. Today's investment decisions will affect tomorrow's costs. Therefore, future cost curves cannot be taken as given either. These shifts in demand and cost curves will be very difficult to estimate with any precision. Quite apart from this, the actions of competitors, suppliers, unions and so on are difficult to predict. Thus the picture of firms making precise calculations of long-run profit-maximising prices and outputs is a false one.

A precise theory of long-run profit maximisation is therefore not useful in explaining how firms actually behave. Either the theory would be too simplistic to be realistic, because there could be no simple formula for predicting price and output and the level of investment, or it would have to be so complex that it would be quite unworkable.

It may be useful, however, simply to observe that firms, when making current price, output and investment

DEFINITION

Long-run profit maximisation An alternative theory which assumes that managers aim to shift cost and revenue curves so as to maximise profits over some longer time period.

ISSUES AND APPLICATIONS — BOX 8.3

WHEN IS A THEORY NOT A THEORY?

Have you heard the joke about the man sitting in a railway carriage who was throwing pieces of paper out of the window? A fellow traveller was curious and asked him why he kept doing this.

'It keeps the elephants down,' was the reply.

'But,' said the other man, 'there are no elephants around here.'

'I know,' said the first man. 'Effective, isn't it?'

Let's reformulate this joke.

Once upon a time there was this boss of a company who kept doing strange things. First he would spend a massive amount of money on advertising, and then stop. Then he would pay a huge wage increase 'to keep his workforce happy'. Then he would close the factory for two months to give everyone a break. Then he would move the business, lock, stock and barrel, to a new location.

One day he was talking to an accountant friend, who asked, 'Why do you keep doing these strange things?'

'I have to do them to make the business profitable,' was the reply.

'But your business *is* profitable,' said the accountant.

'I know. It just goes to show how effective my policies are.'

??

1. Why might it be difficult to refute a theory of long-run profit maximisation?
2. If a theory cannot *in principle* be refuted, is it a useful theory?

decisions, try to judge the approximate effect on new entrants, consumer demand, future costs, etc., and try to avoid decisions that would appear to conflict with long-run profits. Often this will simply involve avoiding making decisions (e.g. cutting price) that may stimulate an unfavourable result from rivals (e.g. rivals cutting their price).

Sales revenue maximisation (short run)

Perhaps the most famous of all alternative theories of the firm is that developed by William Baumol in the late 1950s. This is the theory of **sales revenue maximisation**. Unlike the theory of long-run profit maximisation, it is easy to identify the price and output that meet this aim – at least in the short run.

So why should managers want to maximise their firm's sales revenue? The answer is that the success of managers, and in particular sales managers, may be judged according to the level of the firm's sales. Sales figures are an obvious barometer of the firm's health. Managers' salaries, power and prestige may depend directly on sales revenue. The firm's sales representatives may be paid commission on their sales. Thus sales revenue maximisation may be a more dominant aim in the firm than profit maximisation, particularly if it has a dominant sales department.

Sales revenue will be maximised at the top of the *TR* curve at output Q_1 in Figure 8.1. Profits, by contrast, would be maximised at Q_2. Thus, for given total revenue and total cost curves, sales revenue maximisation will tend to lead to a higher output and a lower price than profit maximisation.

??

Draw a diagram with *MC* and *MR* curves. Mark the output (a) at which profits are maximised; (b) at which sales revenue is maximised.

The firm will still have to make sufficient profits, however, to keep the shareholders happy. Thus firms can be seen to be operating with a profit constraint. They are *profit satisficers*.

The effect of this profit constraint is illustrated in Figure 8.2. The diagram shows a total profit ($T\Pi$) curve. (This is found by simply taking the difference between *TR* and *TC* at each output.) Assume that the minimum acceptable profit is Π (whatever the output). Any output greater than Q_3 will give a profit less than Π. Thus the sales revenue maximiser who is also a profit satisficer will produce Q_3 not Q_1. Note, however, that this output is still greater than the profit-maximising output Q_2.

If the firm could maximise sales revenue and still make more than the minimum acceptable profit, it would probably spend this surplus profit on advertising to increase revenue further. This would have the effect of shifting the *TR* curve upward and also the *TC* curve (since advertising costs money).

Sales revenue maximisation will tend to involve more advertising than profit maximisation. Ideally the profit-maximising firm will advertise up to the point where the

DEFINITION

Sales revenue maximisation An alternative theory which assumes that managers aim to maximise the firm's short-run total revenue.

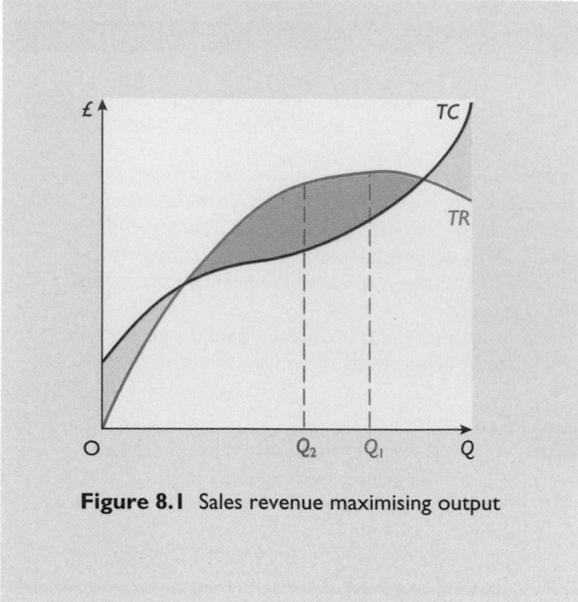

Figure 8.1 Sales revenue maximising output

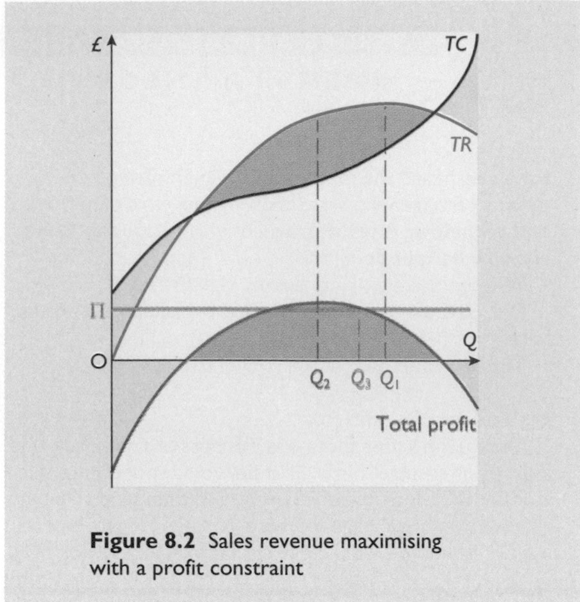

Figure 8.2 Sales revenue maximising with a profit constraint

marginal revenue of advertising equals the marginal cost of advertising (assuming diminishing returns to advertising). The firm aiming to maximise sales revenue will go beyond this, since further advertising, although costing more than it earns the firm, will still add to total revenue. The firm will continue advertising until surplus profits above the minimum have been used up.

> **??** Since advertising increases a firm's costs, will prices necessarily be lower with sales revenue maximisation than with profit maximisation?

Growth maximisation

Rather than aiming to maximise *short-run* revenue, managers may take a longer-term perspective and aim for **growth maximisation** in the size of the firm. They may directly gain utility from being part of a rapidly growing 'dynamic' organisation; promotion prospects are greater in an expanding organisation since new posts tend to be created; larger firms may pay higher salaries; managers may obtain greater power in a larger firm.

Growth is probably best measured in terms of a growth in sales revenue, since sales revenue (or 'turnover') is the simplest way of measuring the size of a business. An alternative would be to measure the capital value of a firm, but this will depend on the ups and downs of the stock market and is thus a rather unreliable method.

If a firm is to maximise growth, it needs to be clear about the time period over which it is setting itself this objective. For example, maximum growth over the next two or three years might be obtained by running factories to absolute maximum capacity, cramming in as many machines and workers as possible, and backing this up with massive advertising campaigns and price cuts. Such policies, however, may not be sustainable in the longer run. The firm may simply not be able to finance them. A longer-term perspective (say 5–10 years) may require the firm to 'pace' itself, and perhaps to direct resources away from current production and sales into the development of new products that have a potentially high and growing long-term demand.

Growth may be achieved either by internal expansion or by merger.

Growth by internal expansion

Internal growth requires an increase in sales, which in turn requires an increase in the firm's productive capacity. In order to increase its *sales*, the firm is likely to engage in extensive product promotion and to try to launch new products. In order to increase *productive capacity* the firm will require new investment. Both product promotion and investment will require finance.

In the short run, the firm can finance growth by borrowing or by retaining profits or by a new issue of shares. Table 8.1 shows that the largest source of finance for investment in the UK is internal funds (i.e. ploughed-back profit). Nevertheless, until the recession of the early

> **DEFINITION**
>
> **Growth maximisation** An alternative theory which assumes that managers seek to maximise the growth in sales revenue (or the capital value of the firm) over time.

Table 8.1 Sources of capital funds of UK industrial and commercial companies

Year	Total from all sources (£ million)	Internal funds[1] (%)	Borrowing from banks, etc. (%)	Shares and debentures (%)	Overseas sources (%)
1970	6336	60.7	22.4	3.2	13.7
1980	28 913	66.1	22.3	4.9	6.7
1986	48 715	58.5	21.6	12.5	7.4
1987	79 475	49.6	21.1	25.3	4.0
1988	99 874	40.8	39.6	11.5	8.1
1989	108 025	32.7	41.7	14.9	10.7
1990	88 058	37.5	33.2	16.2	13.1
1992	53 452	68.3	–5.3	26.8	10.2
1994	82 469	72.9	–2.3	26.9	2.5
1996	114 501	53.0	20.0	19.0	8.0
1997	136 443	41.8	8.6	30.4	19.2

[1] Includes grants and tax relief.

Source: *Financial Statistics* (ONS).

1990s, a growing proportion of company investment was financed by bank borrowing. A growing proportion of investment has also been financed by the issue of new shares and debentures (fixed-interest loan stock).

What limits the amount of finance a firm can acquire, and hence the rate at which it can grow? If the firm *borrows* too much, the interest payments it incurs will make it difficult to maintain the level of dividends to shareholders. Similarly, if the firm *retains* too much *profit*, there will be less available to pay out in dividends. Also if it attempts to raise capital by a *new issue of shares*, the distributed profits will have to be divided between a larger number of shares. Whichever way it finances investment, therefore, the more it invests, the more the dividends on shares in the short run will probably fall.

This could lead shareholders to sell their shares, unless they are confident that *long-run* profits and hence dividends will rise again, thus causing the share price to remain high in the long run. If shareholders do sell their shares, this will cause share prices to fall. If they fall too far, the firm runs the risk of being taken over and of certain managers losing their jobs. The **takeover constraint** therefore requires that the growth-maximising firm distribute sufficient profits to avoid being taken over.

In the long run, a rapidly growing firm may find its profits increasing, especially if it can achieve economies of scale and a bigger share of the market. These profits can then be used to finance further growth.

Growth by merger

A merger may be the result of the mutual agreement of two firms to come together. Alternatively, one firm may put in a takeover bid for another. This involves the first firm offering to buy the shares of the second for cash, to swap them for shares in the acquiring company, or to issue fixed-interest securities (debentures). The shareholders of the second firm then vote on whether to accept the offer. (Technically this is an 'acquisition' or 'takeover' rather than a merger, but the term 'merger' is generally used to include both mutual agreements and acquisitions.)

There are three types of merger:

- A **horizontal merger** is where firms in the same industry and at the same stage of production merge: e.g. two car manufacturers.
- A **vertical merger** is where firms in the same industry but at different stages in the production of a good merge: e.g. a car manufacturer with a car component parts producer.
- A **conglomerate merger** is where firms in different industries merge: e.g. when British Aerospace acquired Austin Rover.

DEFINITIONS

Takeover constraint The effect that the fear of being taken over has on a firm's willingness to undertake projects that reduce distributed profits.

Horizontal merger Where two firms in the same industry at the same stage in the production process merge.

Vertical merger Where two firms in the same industry at different stages in the production process merge.

Conglomerate merger Where two firms in different industries merge.

CASE STUDIES BOX 8.4

THE BODY SHOP
Selling the environment

The Body Shop shot to fame in the 1980s. It stood for environmental awareness and an ethical approach to business. But its success was as much to do with what it sold as what it stood for. It sold natural cosmetics, Raspberry Ripple Bathing Bubbles and Camomile Shampoo, products that were immensely popular with consumers. Its Stock Exchange listing in 1984 was one of the most successful retail flotations in history.

Unlike many other niche market retail operations started in the 1980s, such as The Sock Shop, The Body Shop has avoided financial difficulties. Its profits have increased from a little over £1 million in 1985 to £33.5 million in 1995. Sales, meanwhile, have grown even more dramatically, from £4.9 million to £219.7 million over the same period.

What makes this success so remarkable is that The Body Shop does virtually no advertising. Its promotion has largely stemmed from the activities and environmental campaigning of its founder, Anita Roddick, and the company's uncompromising claims to having a green image and conducting its business operations with high ethical standards. It actively supports green causes such as saving whales and protecting rainforests, and it refuses to allow its products to be tested on animals. Perhaps most surprising in the world of big business has been its high-profile initiative 'trade not aid', whereby it claimed to pay 'fair' prices for its ingredients, especially those supplied by people in developing countries who were open to exploitation by large companies.

The growth strategy of The Body Shop, since its founding in 1975, has focused upon developing a distinctive and highly innovative product range, and at the same time identifying such products with major social issues of the day such as the environment and animal rights.

??

1. What assumptions has The Body Shop made about the 'rational consumer'?
2. How would you describe the aims of The Body Shop?

Merger activity

Merger activity tends to go in waves: several years of low merger activity are followed by periods of feverish activity, where both the number and value of mergers can increase several hundred per cent. These periods tend to correspond to periods when the stock market is buoyant with rapidly rising share prices, and when, therefore, the finance of mergers is easier. These periods in turn tend to correspond to periods of rapid growth in the economy, when business confidence is high. Figure 8.3 illustrates the major booms in UK merger activity that have occurred since the Second World War.

The first of these booms began in the mid-1960s and reached a peak in 1972. Then during the mid-1970s and early 1980s there were relatively few mergers. But in 1983, the value and number of mergers began to increase dramatically. By the late 1980s mergers were occurring at four times the rate of a decade earlier. Then after 1989 merger activity began to slow down along with the slowdown in growth of the economy only to recover again with the economic recovery of the mid-1990s.

The merger boom of the late 1980s was different in a number of ways from the boom of the late 1960s and early 1970s:

- There were some exceptionally large mergers. For example, in the third quarter of 1989, the peak of the merger boom (see Figure 8.4(b)), of 212 mergers, the value of the largest three accounted for 58 per cent of the total.
- There was a marked shift in the method of financing acquisitions after the Stock Exchange crash of October 1987 (see Table 8.2). The percentage of expenditure on acquisitions financed from share issue, which up to then had been increasing, fell from 66 per cent in the first half of 1987 to 9 per cent in the fourth quarter of 1989. With the slow recovery of the stock market, however, in the early 1990s, this figure gradually rose again, averaging 27 per cent from 1992 to 1995.
- There was an increase in the proportion of conglomerate mergers. In the 1960s less than 10 per cent of expenditure on mergers was on conglomerate ones. By the 1980s this had risen to around 30 per cent.

Motives for merger

But why do firms want to take over others? Economists have identified a number of possible motives.

Merger for growth. Mergers provide a much quicker means to growth than does internal expansion. Not only does the firm acquire new capacity, it also acquires additional consumer demand. There is a danger for growth-

Table 8.2 The finance of mergers in the UK (% of expenditure)

	1973	1975	1977	1979	1981	1983	1985	1987	1988	1989	1990	1991	1992	1993	1994	1995	1996	1997
Cash	53	59	62	56	68	44	40	35	70	82	77	70	63	81	64	79	64	37
Issues of shares	36	32	37	31	30	54	52	60	22	13	18	29	36	16	34	20	35	62
Issues of debentures	11	9	1	13	3	2	7	5	8	5	5	1	1	3	2	1	1	1

Source: *Financial Statistics* (ONS).

maximising firms, however, from being taken over themselves. If they are growing rapidly and yet have a relatively low profit and a low stock market value, they will be attractive to predators.

Merger for economies of scale. Once the merger has taken place, the constituent parts can be reorganised through a process of 'rationalisation'. The result can be a reduction in costs. For example, only one head office will now be needed.

Evidence for such motivation is sparse, however. The problem is in separating the desire to reduce costs from the desire to achieve other objectives. Reduced costs are a way of increasing profits and thereby of increasing the rate of growth. It is probably unlikely that managers will want to reduce costs for their own sake.

In fact the evidence suggests that most mergers result in little if any cost savings: either potential economies of scale are not exploited due to a lack of rationalisation, or diseconomies result from the disruptions of reorganisation or a lack of control over the acquired part of the organisation by the parent company. In many cases, managers seem to know little about the businesses their companies have bought. New managers installed by the parent company are often seen as unsympathetic, and morale may go down.

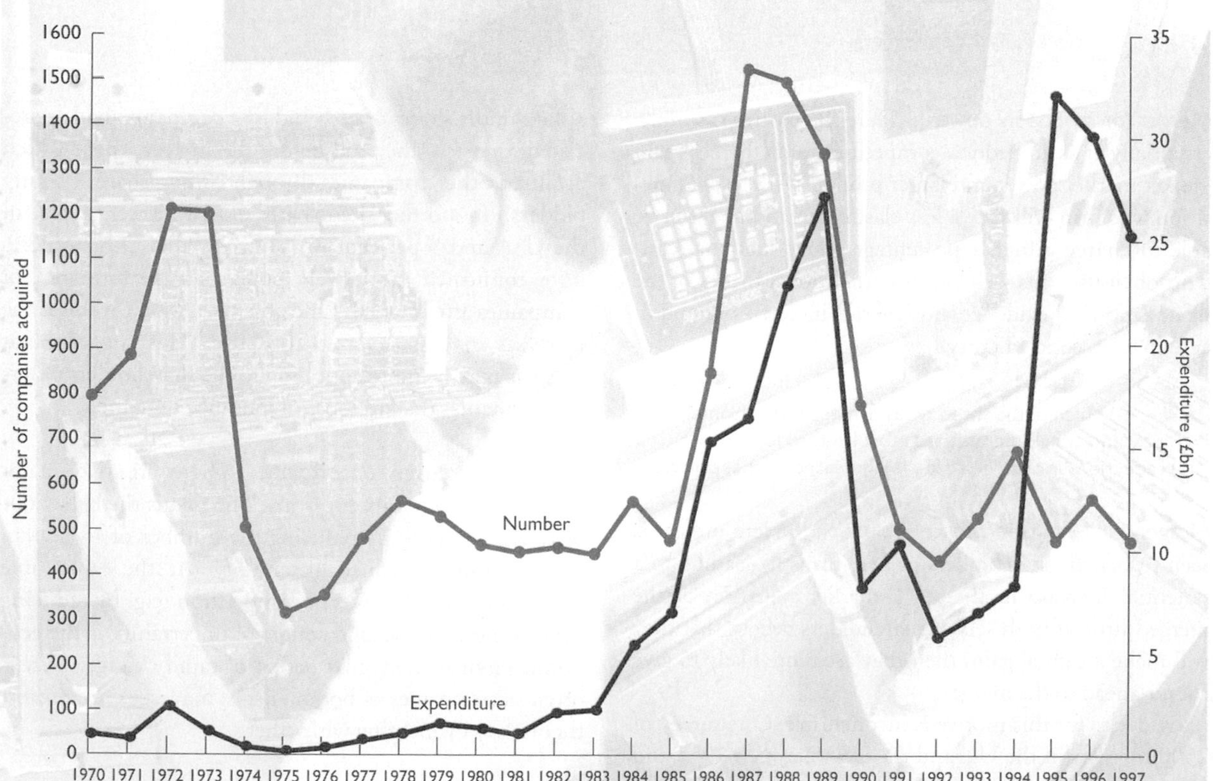

Figure 8.3 Acquisitions and mergers by UK industrial and commercial companies
Source: *Financial Statistics* (ONS).

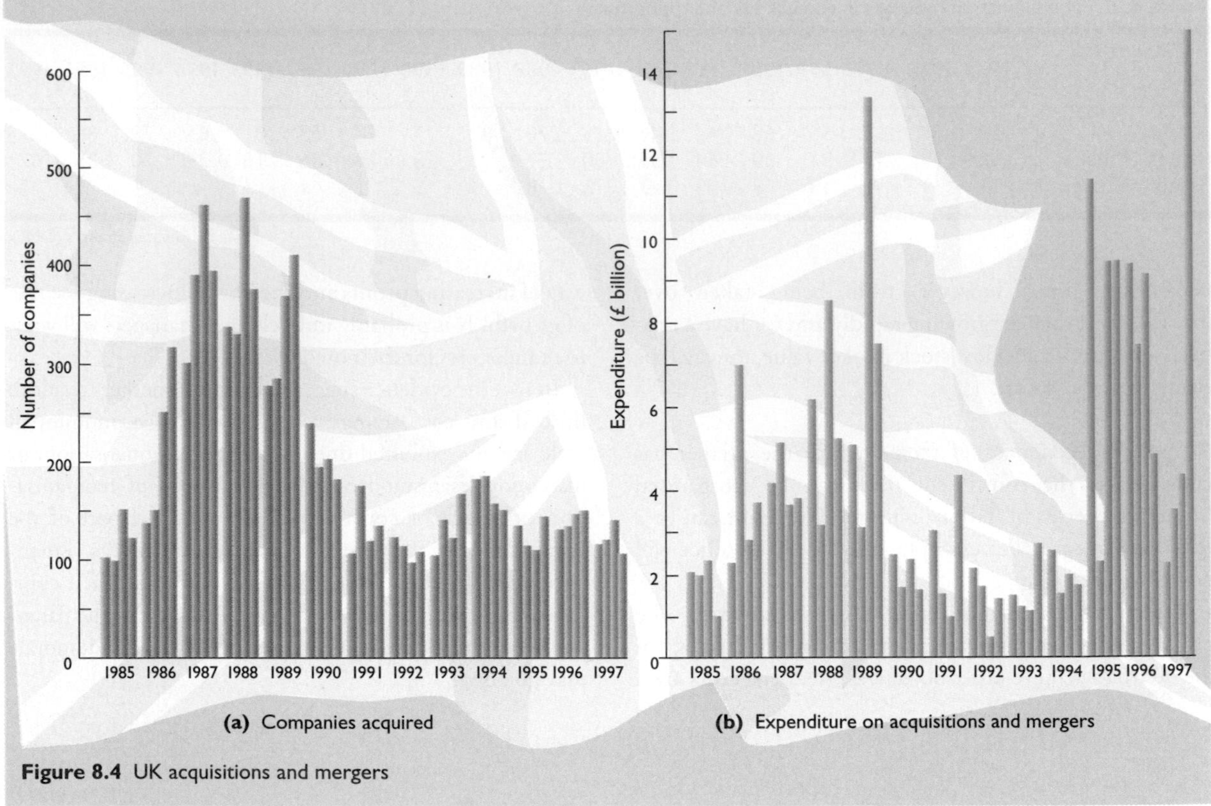

Figure 8.4 UK acquisitions and mergers

Merger for monopoly power. Here the motive is simple: essentially it is to reduce competition and thereby gain greater market power and larger profits. With less competition, the firm will face a less elastic demand and will be able to charge a higher percentage above marginal cost. This obviously fits well with the traditional theory of the firm. Empirical evidence, however, is inconclusive and in certain cases contradictory.

> **??** Which of the three types of merger (horizontal, vertical and conglomerate) are most likely to lead to (a) reductions in average costs; (b) increased market power?

Merger for increased market valuation. Here merger is seen to benefit shareholders of *both* firms by leading to a potential increase in the stock market valuation of the merged firm. If both sets of shareholders believe that they will make a capital gain, then they are more likely to give the go-ahead to the merger.

Evidence for this motive is inconclusive. One survey of 2500 mergers in the UK and the USA between 1955 and 1985[2] showed that, although shares in the companies that were the target of a takeover bid were pushed up by the bid, the shareholders of the bidding companies initially gained (or lost) very little. After two years, however, although the shares of cash-bidding companies had appreciated as fast as they did before the merger, those which acquired other companies through issuing shares ('equity bidders') found that their shares did 18 per cent worse in the USA and 9 per cent worse in the UK. Other studies have confirmed a relatively poor share performance of companies after merger. One possible reason for this is the increases in costs referred to above. This suggests that mergers may be more appealing to the shareholders of target companies than to those of bidding companies.

Merger to reduce uncertainty. There are two major sources of uncertainty for firms. The first is the behaviour of rivals. Mergers, by reducing the number of rivals, can correspondingly reduce uncertainty. At the same time they can reduce the costs of competition (e.g. by reducing advertising). The second source of uncertainty is the economic environment. In a period of rapid change, such as often accompanies a boom, firms may seek to protect themselves by merging with others.

[2] J. Franks, R. Harris and C. Mayer in A. Auerbach (ed.), *Corporate Takeovers: Causes and consequences* (University of Chicago Press, 1989).

CASE STUDIES BOX 8.5

A WARM WELLCOME TO GLAXO!

In January 1995 the drugs manufacturer Glaxo announced its purchase of fellow drugs producer Wellcome. This was the largest acquisition in European history, with Glaxo paying a massive £9.4 billion for its rival. As a result of its purchase Glaxo became the largest pharmaceutical company in the world, with a capital value of £15.5 billion and a yearly turnover of £8 billion.

What is interesting about the global drugs market is its highly competitive structure. Glaxo-Wellcome, the world's number one drugs manufacturing company, commands only 6 per cent of the world market. The vast majority of other firms in this sector tend to operate with a share no larger than 2 per cent.

Prior to the merger with Wellcome, Glaxo was a single-sector company, even within drug manufacturing, producing prescription-only drugs: it had progressively shed its 'over the counter' (OTC) drug production activities during the 1970s. At the same time its growth strategy was very much based upon internal expansion (its last business acquisition being in 1977). Glaxo's rise to prominence as the world's premier drugs company came with the launch of Zantac in 1981, which was to become the world's biggest selling drug. Even sixteen years on, Zantac still accounts for 40 per cent of Glaxo's sales revenue.

Given its dominant market position and largely successful internal growth strategy, why change direction and embark upon a growth strategy in which it had little experience? What benefits could Wellcome offer Glaxo?

What Wellcome did not offer Glaxo was significant diversity. Like Glaxo, Wellcome was a single-sector producer (nineteenth in the world rankings) with most of its business interests in prescription-only drugs. Also like Glaxo, Wellcome was highly dependent upon one drug (Zovirox) for its sales revenue (40 per cent).

The following can be advanced to explain the motives behind Glaxo's expensive acquisition:

- The 1990s saw many drug manufacturers consolidating their market positions. Roche of Switzerland successfully launched a £3.5 billion bid to acquire Syntex, the UK-based drug manufacturer. SmithKline Beecham acquired DPS, a US drug distributor, and Sterling Health, a US drug manufacturer, for £3.3 billion. Glaxo may have felt forced into adopting a fast-growth strategy in order to meet the competition from these newly merged businesses.
- It has been estimated that the acquisition of Wellcome by Glaxo will yield savings in the region of £600 million. The major area in which economies will be gained is research and development. At the time of merger, the two businesses' current R & D costs were £1.2 billion a year.
- Although Wellcome was mainly a prescription-only drug company, it did offer Glaxo some opportunities for developing the OTC side of the market. In 1994 Wellcome entered into a joint venture with Warner-Lambert, a major US OTC producer, to develop and market OTC products, under the name Warner Wellcome. By the end of 1994 this activity had added £300 million to Wellcome's turnover.

But why should Glaxo want to diversify into OTC products? Three reasons have been suggested:

- Governments world-wide are cutting back on their pharmaceutical expenditure as they attempt to control general government spending on health care.
- Zantac and Zovirox, the big earners for Glaxo and Wellcome respectively, were reaching the end of their lives. Patents for both drugs were due to expire in the USA in 1997.
- Changing social trends suggest that individuals are assuming more responsibility for their own health and buying OTC products when possible. Hence this segment of the market has huge growth potential.

Market analysts suggest that by the year 2000, the drugs manufacturing sector will be dominated by a few giant multinational corporations. Glaxo is certainly looking for ways to ensure that it is one of those producers.

??

1. Glaxo has a relatively small share of the total drugs market, and yet could reasonably be described as a monopoly. Explain.
2. If governments are major purchasers of drugs, does this provide effective countervailing power to the drugs companies?

Merger due to opportunity. Sometimes mergers may occur in response to opportunities that may suddenly and unexpectedly arise. Many firms are on the lookout for new markets, new products, new expertise and new ideas. At the same time, managers may be unwilling to plan a strategy of takeovers in advance, in case this encourages other bidders or pushes up the share prices of the target firms. This suggests that the actual mergers that take place will be very difficult to predict.

Other motives. Other motives for mergers include:

- Getting bigger so as to become less likely to be taken over oneself.

CASE STUDIES

MERGER ACTIVITY
A European perspective

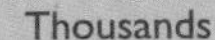

Mergers[3] within Europe have been predominantly horizontal rather than vertical or conglomerate. This has led to a steady increase in concentration within a wide range of manufacturing and service-sector industries in a number of European countries, especially in the UK, France, Germany, Holland and Sweden. Research suggests that such merger activity has led to few gains in efficiency and only minimal improvements in competitiveness.

Main motives for mergers and joint ventures in the EC: 1988/9–1991/2

Strengthening of market position	648
Expansion	419
Restructuring (including rationalisation and synergy)	158
Complementarity	72
Diversification	55
Co-operation	13
Research and development	3
Other	73
Total cases specifying reasons	1441

Source: *Reports on Competition Policy* (Commission of the European Communities, various years).

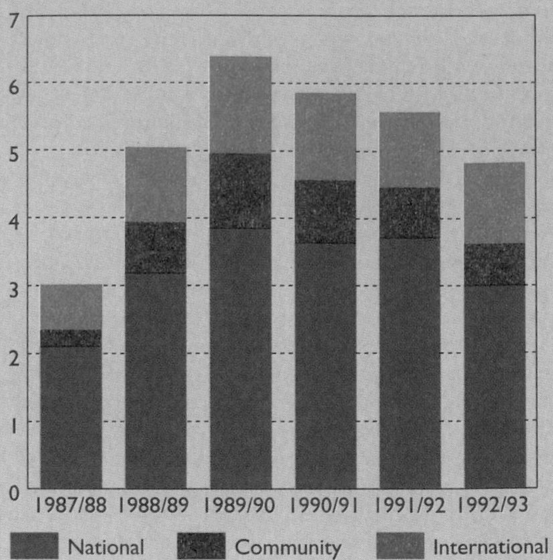

(a) Number of majority acquisitions and mergers involving EC firms

Source: *23rd Report on Competition Policy* (Commission of the European Communities).

Pre Single Market (1993)

The table shows the main motives given for industrial mergers and acquisitions in the EC between 1988/9 and 1991/2. Clearly the desire to gain greater market power and market share was the driving force behind mergers in the EC.

During the 1980s the number of mergers involving EC companies steadily grew. In part this can be explained by the recovery from the recession of the early 1980s and the brighter prospects for business in Europe. It is not surprising, therefore, that the trend reversed in the recession of the early 1990s (see Figure (a)).

For most of the 1980s, the majority of mergers occurring in Europe were within national boundaries. But as inter-EC trade grew and as Europe was increasingly seen by business as a 'single market', so an increasing proportion of mergers were 'cross-border'. The proportion of total EC mergers that were between companies in different member states grew from 8.3 per cent in 1987/8 to 20.5 per cent in 1992/3. This is illustrated in Figure (a).

An important factor explaining the increase in inter-EC mergers was the process of dismantling barriers to trade to create a true 'common market' by 1993 (see section 23.4). Firms took the opportunity to establish a European network and restructure their operations as well as to expand productive capacity.

A notable feature of European merger activity is the size of the firms involved. In 1986–7, 57 per cent of merger activity involved firms with sales over ECU1 billion and 23 per cent over ECU5 billion. By 1990/91 this had risen to 87 per cent and 45 per cent respectively. The larger the firms involved, the more likely they are to be involved in cross-border mergers rather than purely domestic ones. The implication of these trends is that markets are becoming increasingly concentrated. Up to 1993, the sectors most affected by mergers were chemicals, electrical engineering, metals, food and drink, and banking.

Merger activity varied between different European countries.

- In the four largest EC economies – Germany, France, Italy and the UK – although inter-EC country mergers increased, mergers between companies from the same country were still the largest category. In the smaller EC countries, however, mergers with companies in other member states greatly exceeded domestic mergers.
- As far as companies being acquired are concerned,

BOX 8.6

merger activity has been particularly great in France and Germany. As far as acquiring companies is concerned, French, German and UK firms were the major acquirers.

- In the early 1990s there was a large increase in acquisitions of EC companies by Scandinavian countries. The main reason was uncertainty about the likelihood of these countries gaining entry to the EC and therefore the desire of companies to be *inside* the large single market.

Since 1993

When the single market came into being in January 1993, many commentators predicted that there would be a new wave of merger activity as companies, faced with new competition, would be forced to rationalise, or would take the opportunity to expand their operations in other EU countries.

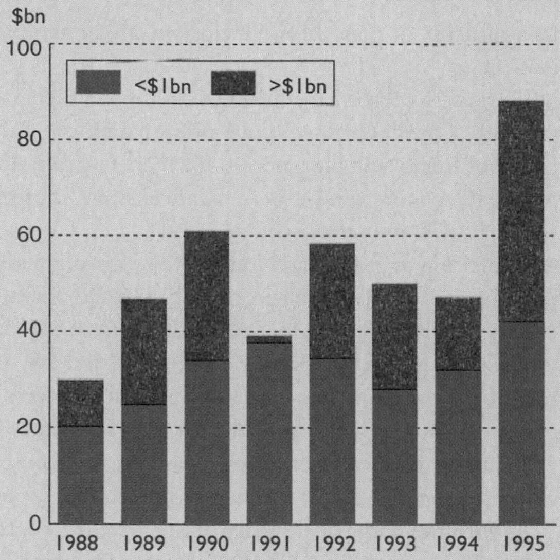

(b) Crossborder mergers and acquisitions in Europe: total value ($bn)

Source: *European Trends* (Economist Intelligence Unit).

As it turned out, the recession gripping Europe caused merger activity initially to decline (see Figure (b)). The main determinant of merger activity in the short run remains the overall state of the economy. When an economy moves into recession, so merger activity also declines. This is also illustrated by US and Japanese investment in Europe in the mid-1990s. Whilst the US economy was recovering from recession after 1992, the Japanese economy was still slowing down. In 1993 and 1994, whilst US-based multinationals were actively acquiring EU companies, Japanese multinationals acquired virtually none.

The upturn in the European economy after 1994 saw a significant rise in merger activity. The USA remained the biggest acquirer of European companies, with the major target being UK firms, followed by French, German and Swedish. The largest merger, however, in 1995 was the domestic UK acquisition of Wellcome by Glaxo – at nearly $15 billion, more than twice the value of the next largest merger (see Box 8.5). This was one of several large mergers in the pharmaceutical industry.

Another sector where restructuring was rife was banking. Bank mergers led to substantial cost savings, as branches were closed and infrastructure shared. In the UK, the Lloyds and TSB banks, the Lloyds bank and Cheltenham and Gloucester building society, and the Halifax and Leeds building societies were all major mergers. Similarly large banking mergers took place in other EU countries.

The other sector where merger activity has shown a marked increase is utilities, such as telecommunications, water and electricity. In the UK, in particular, most of the privatised water and electricity companies have been taken over, with buyers attracted by the sector's monopoly profits. French and US buyers have been prominent.

Despite the growing number of horizontal mergers, there has also been a tendency for companies to become more focused, by selling off parts of their business which are not seen as 'core activities'. For example, not long after its takeover of Wellcome, Glaxo decided to concentrate on the production of *prescription* drugs, and as a consequence to sell its share of Warner Wellcome, which produced non-prescription drugs. Another example was Volvo. After unsuccessfully attempting to merge with Renault in 1993, it subsequently divested itself of several companies that it owned in a variety of industries, ranging from banking and finance to food, matches and pharmaceuticals.

This trend of horizontal mergers and conglomerate and vertical de-mergers has allowed companies to increase their market power in those specific sectors where they have expertise. Consumers may gain from lower costs, but the motives of the companies are largely to gain increased market power – something of dubious benefit to consumers.

?? Are the motives for merger likely to be different in a recession from in a period of rapid economic growth?

[3] When we refer to 'mergers' this also includes acquisitions (i.e. takeovers).

- Defending another firm from an unwanted predator (the 'White Knight' strategy).
- Asset stripping. This is where a firm buys another and then breaks it up, selling off the profitable bits and probably closing down the remainder.
- Empire building. This is where owners or managers like the power or prestige of owning or controlling several (preferably well-known) companies.
- Broadening the geographical base of the company by merging with a firm in a different part of the country or the world.

Most of these theories are in need of greater empirical investigation and support.

??

1. Which of the above theories overlap and in what way?
2. Why, do you think, is it difficult to find adequate empirical support for any of them?

Mergers and the relationship between growth and profit

In order for a firm to be successful in a takeover bid, it must be sufficiently profitable to finance the takeover. Thus the faster it tries to grow and the more takeovers it attempts, the higher must be its profitability.

In addition to being an obvious means to the growth of the firm, mergers may be a means of increasing profits, since mergers can lead to both lower average costs through economies of scale and higher average revenue through increased market power over prices. These profits in turn may be seen as a means of financing further growth.

It can therefore be seen that, whichever way it is financed, growth is closely linked to profits. High profits can help a firm grow. Rapid growth can lead to a rapid growth in profits.

These are not inevitable links, however. For example, long-run profits may not increase if a firm, as part of its growth policy, invests in risky projects or projects with a low rate of return. Expansion alone is no guarantee of profits. Also, high profits will not necessarily lead to growth if a large proportion is distributed to shareholders and only a small proportion is reinvested. High profits may help growth, but they do not guarantee it.

Equilibrium for a growth-maximising firm

What will a growth-maximising firm's price and output be? Unfortunately there is no simple formula for predicting this.

In the short run, the firm may choose the profit-maximising price and output – so as to provide the greatest funds for investment. On the other hand, it may be prepared to sacrifice some short-term profits in order to mount an advertising campaign. It all depends on the strategy it considers most suitable to achieve growth.

In the long run, prediction is more difficult still. The policies that a firm adopts will depend crucially on the assessments of market opportunities made by managers. But this involves judgement, not fine calculation. Different managers will judge a situation differently.

One prediction can be made. Growth-maximising firms are likely to diversify into different products, especially as they approach the limits to expansion in existing markets.

Alternative maximising theories and the public interest

It is difficult to draw firm conclusions about the public interest.

In the case of sales revenue maximisation, a higher output will be produced than under profit maximisation, but the consumers will not necessarily benefit from lower prices, since more will be spent on advertising – costs that will be passed on to the consumer.

In the case of growth and long-run profit maximisation, there are many possible policies that a firm could pursue. To the extent that a concern for the long run encourages firms to look to improved products, new products and new techniques, the consumer may benefit from such a concern. To the extent, however, that growth encourages a greater level of industrial concentration through merger, the consumer may lose from the resulting greater level of monopoly power.

As with the traditional theory of the firm, the degree of competition a firm faces is a crucial factor in determining just how responsive it will be to the wishes of the consumer.

??

How will competition between growth-maximising firms benefit the consumer?

SECTION SUMMARY

1. Rather than seeking to maximise short-run profits, a firm may take a longer-term perspective. It is very difficult, however, to predict the behaviour of a long-run profit-maximising firm, since (a) different managers are likely to make different judgements about how to achieve maximum profits and (b) demand and cost curves may shift unpredictably both in response to the firm's own policies and as a result of external factors.
2. Managers may gain utility from maximising sales revenue. They will still have to ensure that a satisfactory level of profit is achieved, however. The output of a firm which seeks to maximise sales revenue will be higher than that for a profit-maximising firm. Its level of advertising will also tend to be higher. Whether price will be higher or lower depends on the relative effects on demand and cost of the additional advertising.
3. Many managers aim for maximum growth of their organisation, believing that this will help their salaries, power, prestige, etc.
4. Growth may be by internal expansion. This can be financed by ploughing back profits, by share issue or by borrowing. Whichever method a firm uses, it will require sufficient profits, if it is to avoid becoming vulnerable to a takeover.
5. Growth may be by merger. Mergers can be horizontal, vertical or conglomerate. Merger activity tends to occur in waves. For example, there was a major increase in merger activity in the late 1980s. Various motives have been suggested for mergers, including growth, economies of scale, market power, increased share values, reduction in uncertainty, and simply taking advantage of opportunities as they occur.
6. As with long-run profit-maximising theories, it is difficult to predict the price and output strategies of a growth-maximising firm. Much depends on the judgements of particular managers about growth opportunities.
7. Alternative aims will benefit the consumer to the extent that they encourage firms to develop new products and to find more efficient methods of production. They may be against the consumer's interest to the extent that they lead firms to engage in extensive advertising or to merge with a resulting increased concentration of market power.

8.3 Multiple aims

Satisficing and the setting of targets

Firms may have more than one aim. For example, they may try to achieve increased sales revenue *and* increased profit. The problem with this is that if two aims conflict, it will not be possible to maximise both of them. For example, sales revenue will probably be maximised at a different price and output from that at which profits are maximised. Where firms have two or more aims, a compromise may be for targets to be set for individual aims which are low enough to achieve simultaneously and yet which are sufficient to satisfy the interested parties.

Such target setting is also likely when the maximum value of a particular aim is unknown. If, for example, the maximum achievable profit is unknown, the firm may well set a target for profit which it feels is both satisfactory and achievable.

Behavioural theories of the firm: the setting of targets

A major advance in alternative theories of the firm has been the development of **behavioural theories.**[4] Rather than setting up a model to show how various objectives could in theory be achieved, behavioural theories of the firm are based on observations of how firms *actually* behave.

Large firms are often complex institutions with several departments (sales, production, design, purchasing, personnel, finance, etc.). Each department is likely to have its own specific set of aims and objectives which may possibly come into conflict with those of other departments. These aims in turn will be constrained by the interests of shareholders, workers, customers and creditors (collectively known as 'stakeholders'), who will need to be kept sufficiently happy.

[4] See in particular R. M. Cyert and J. G. March, *A Behavioural Theory of the Firm* (Prentice Hall, 1963).

DEFINITION

Behavioural theories of the firm Theories that attempt to predict the actions of firms by studying the behaviour of various groups of people within the firm and their interactions under conditions of potentially conflicting interests.

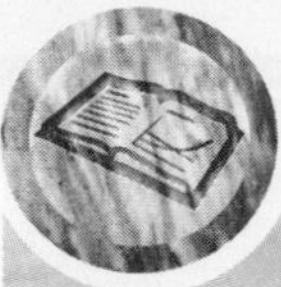

EXPLORING THE THEORY BOX 8.7

TYPES OF THEORY: DESCRIPTIVE AND PRESCRIPTIVE

The behavioural theory does not state how a firm *ought* to behave in order to achieve certain objectives. Rather, it examines just how firms *do* behave. It *describes* their behaviour and looks at the consequences for, say, profit. It is thus a descriptive theory.

The traditional theory of the firm *may* be used in this way. Advocates of the theory may claim that firms do maximise short-run profits, and do equate *MR* and *MC*. Others, however, would claim that the traditional theory is 'prescriptive'. It says what firms must do if they are to maximise profits. 'If you wish to maximise profits then you must equate *MR* and *MC*', or 'If you are a risk-averse oligopolist, and prefer to go for a safe strategy, then you should adopt the maximin alternative.'

??

1. Are the theories of sales revenue maximisation prescriptive or descriptive?
2. If prescriptive theories tell firms what they ought to do, are they normative? Is there a problem here?

Behavioural theories do not lay down rules of how to *achieve* these aims, but rather examine what these aims are, the motivations underlying them, the conflicts that can arise between aims, and how these conflicts are resolved.

It is assumed that targets will be set for production, sales, profit, stock holding, etc. If, in practice, target levels are not achieved, a 'search' procedure will be started to find what went wrong and how to rectify it. If the problem cannot be rectified, managers will probably adjust the target downwards. If, on the other hand, targets are easily achieved, managers may adjust them upwards. Thus the targets to which managers aspire depend to a large extent on the success in achieving *previous* targets. Targets are also influenced by expectations of demand and costs, by the achievements of competitors and by expectations of competitors' future behaviour. For example, if it is expected that the economy is likely to move into recession, sales and profit targets may be adjusted downwards.

If targets conflict, the conflict will be settled by a bargaining process between managers. The outcome of the bargaining, however, will depend on the power and ability of the individual managers concerned. Thus a similar set of conflicting targets may be resolved differently in different firms.

Behavioural theories of the firm: organisational slack

Since changing targets often involves search procedures and bargaining processes and is therefore time consuming, and since many managers prefer to avoid conflict, targets tend to be changed fairly infrequently. Business conditions, however, often change rapidly. To avoid the need to change targets, therefore, managers will tend to be fairly conservative in their aspirations. This leads to the phenomenon known as **organisational slack**.

When the firm does better than planned, it will allow slack to develop. This slack can then be taken up if the firm does worse than planned. For example, if the firm produces more than it planned, it will build stocks of finished goods and draw on them if subsequently production falls. It would not, in the meantime, increase its sales target or reduce its production target. If it did, and production then fell below target, the production department might not be able to supply the sales department with its full requirement.

Thus keeping targets fairly low and allowing slack to develop allows all targets to be met with minimum conflict.

Multiple goals: some predictions of behaviour

Conservatism

Some firms may be wary of unnecessary change. Change is risky. They may prefer to stick with tried and tested practices. 'If it works, stick with it.' This could apply to pricing policies, marketing techniques, product design and range, internal organisation of the firm, etc.

If something does not work, managers will probably change it, but again they may be conservative and only try a cautious change: perhaps imitating successful competitors.

This safe, satisficing approach makes prediction of any given firm's behaviour relatively easy. You simply examine its past behaviour. Making generalisations

DEFINITION

Organisational slack Where managers allow spare capacity to exist, thereby enabling them to respond more easily to changed circumstances.

DEVELOPMENT OF IDEAS

BOX 8.8

J. K. GALBRAITH (1908–)
A lofty view of economics

No review of alternative theories of the firm can be complete without an examination of the contribution of John Kenneth Galbraith, who for decades has attacked the traditional theory of the firm for its unrealistic assumptions. But that is not all he has been famous for.

Tall in stature (6′8″) and deed, Galbraith has been a prolific writer, producing academic works not only in economics, but also in sociology and politics. Not many economists can lay claim to writing best-sellers, yet Galbraith has written five.[5] He has also been a frequent contributor to newspapers, radio and television. With his dead-pan voice and razor-sharp wit he has delighted audiences with acid attacks on big business and free-market capitalism, with its 'private affluence and public squalor'. As a lifelong liberal and an active supporter of Democrat causes, he has been vehemently opposed to the philosophy of the New Right and to leaders such as Ronald Reagan, George Bush and Margaret Thatcher.

As a highly original thinker and maverick he has frequently challenged mainstream economics. This unorthodox approach was apparent in the early years of his career. On appointment as deputy head of the Office of Price Administration during the Second World War, he was a strong advocate of wartime price controls and rationing, and also argued that widespread price fixing should be seriously considered in peacetime too. After all, he maintained, it was no more than large firms already practised as normal business behaviour! His forced resignation in 1943 stemmed largely from the unpopularity of his views.

The great part of Galbraith's career has centred on Harvard, where from 1949 to his retirement in 1975 he was Professor of Economics, although for a period under the Kennedy administration he was US ambassador to India. His active participation in politics as speech writer and adviser to a long line of Democrat politicians, including John F. Kennedy, has ensured that his views have been heard in the highest political circles. In many cases Galbraith has used his political experiences to enhance and develop his theories and to explain the place of power in economic theory – power of the state, power of big business and power of pressure groups.

In *The New Industrial State* (1967) and *Economics and the Public Purpose* (1973), he argued that power structures in big business make the traditional assumptions of profit maximisation irrelevant. And yet, economists continue to assume that firms are profit maximisers:

> The corporate reality is ignored. Discussion begins with the observation: 'Profit maximization, of course, assumed'.[6]

The basis of power in big business is what Galbraith calls the 'technostructure'. This is the experts – the scientists, engineers and economists(!) – and the professional managers:

> As the firm grows larger, the technostructure becomes the effective governing power for reasons that are not mysterious. Unless you have the knowledge that allows you to participate in making decisions and do participate, you can't be influential.[7]

According to Galbraith, the technostructure has its own goals, such as job satisfaction, growth and status, and it will try to shape decisions to achieve these objectives. What has happened is that the capitalists (the owners) have lost power as a result of the increasing complexity of the modern business world. They are no longer in a position to insist on policies of profit maximisation. As Galbraith remarks:

> [The modern large corporation] loses its legitimacy as an entrepreneurial and capitalist institution. It becomes instead an instrument of its own organization ...
>
> Having independent power and being the creation of its own organization, the modern corporation, not surprisingly, serves the purposes of its own management. These purposes are frequently different from those of the public, or substantial parts of it, and the latter are less than pleased. Specifically, the corporate bureaucracy, like all organizations, seeks its own expansion.[8]

Like many of Galbraith's theories, his analysis of the structure of big business challenges the very foundations of traditional economics. But one person's heresy can be another's orthodoxy. Galbraith's theories have much in common with the other alternative theories of the firm we have considered in this chapter. It is just that Galbraith has a way of reaching out to a mass audience with his views: something that no other economist has managed to do, with the possible exceptions of his arch academic 'enemies', Milton Friedman (see Box 15.8) and Friedrich von Hayek (see Box 11.10).

[5] *American Capitalism: The concept of countervailing power* (Houghton Mifflin, 1952); *The Affluent Society* (Houghton Mifflin, 1958: Penguin, 1962); *The New Industrial State* (Houghton Mifflin, 1967; Penguin, 1969); *Economics and the Public Purpose* (Houghton Mifflin, 1973; Penguin, 1975); *The Culture of Contentment* (Sinclair Stevenson, 1992).

[6] *Economics and the Public Purpose* (Penguin, 1975), p. 106.

[7] *Almost Everyone's Guide to Economics* (André Deutsch, 1979), p. 55.

[8] *Annals of an Abiding Liberal* (André Deutsch, 1980), pp. 75, 77.

about all such cautious firms, however, is more difficult. Different firms are likely to have established different rules of behaviour depending on their own particular experiences of their market.

Comparison with other firms

Managers may judge their success by comparing their firm's performance with that of rival firms. For example, growing market share may be seen as a more important indicator of 'success' than simple growth in sales. Similarly, they may compare their profits, their product design, their technology or their industrial relations with those of rivals. To many managers it is *relative* performance that matters, rather than absolute performance.

What predictions can be made if this is how managers behave? The answer is that it depends on the nature of competition in the industry. The more profitable, innovative and efficient are the competitors, the more profitable, innovative and efficient will managers try to make their particular firm.

The further ahead of their rivals that firms try to stay, the more likely it is that there will be a 'snowballing' effect: each firm trying to outdo the other.

?? Will this type of behaviour tend to lead to profit maximisation?

Satisficing and the public interest

Firms with multiple goals will be satisficers. The greater the number of goals of the different managers, the greater is the chance of conflict, and the more likely it is that organisational slack will develop. Satisficing firms are therefore likely to be less responsive to changes in consumer demand and changes in costs than profit-maximising firms. They may thus be less efficient.

On the other hand, such firms may be less eager to exploit their economic power by charging high prices, or to use aggressive advertising, or to pay low wages.

The extent to which satisficing firms do act in the public interest will, as in the case of other types of firm, depend to a large extent on the amount and type of competition they face, and their attitudes towards this competition. Firms that compare their performance with that of their rivals are more likely to be responsive to consumer wishes than firms that prefer to stick to well-established practices. On the other hand, they may be more concerned to 'manipulate' consumer tastes than the more traditional firm.

?? Are satisficing firms more likely to suffer from X inefficiency (see Box 6.4) than firms which seek to maximise profit or sales revenue?

SECTION SUMMARY

1. In large firms, decisions are taken by or influenced by a number of different people, including various managers, shareholders, workers, customers, suppliers and creditors. If these different people have different aims, a conflict between them is likely to arise. A firm cannot maximise more than one of these conflicting aims. The alternative is to seek to achieve a satisfactory target level of a number of aims.
2. Behavioural theories of the firm examine how managers and other interest groups actually behave, rather than merely identifying various equilibrium positions for output, price, investment, etc.
3. If targets were easily achieved last year, they are likely to be made more ambitious next year. If they were not achieved, a search procedure will be conducted to identify how to rectify the problem. This may mean adjusting targets downwards, in which case there will be some form of bargaining process between managers.
4. Life is made easier for managers if conflict can be avoided. This will be possible if slack is allowed to develop in various parts of the firm. If targets are not being met, the slack can then be taken up without requiring adjustments in other targets.
5. Satisficing firms may be less innovative, less aggressive and less willing to initiate change. If they do change, it is more likely to be in response to changes made by their competitors. Managers may judge their performance by comparing it with that of rivals.
6. Satisficing firms may be less aggressive in exploiting a position of market power. On the other hand, they may suffer from greater X inefficiency.

??? END-OF-CHAPTER QUESTIONS ???

1. Assume that a firm faces a downward-sloping demand curve. Draw a diagram showing the firm's *AR*, *MR*, *AC* and *MC* curves. (Draw them in such a way that the firm can make supernormal profits.) Mark the following on the diagram:
   (a) The firm's profit-maximising output and price.
   (b) Its sales-revenue-maximising output and price.
   (c) Its sales-maximising output and price (subject to earning at least normal profit).

   Could the answer to (a) and (b) ever be the same? Could the answer to (b) and (c) ever be the same?
2. Would it be possible for firms to calculate their maximum-profit output if they did not use marginal cost and marginal revenue concepts?
3. What is meant by the principal–agent problem? Give two examples of this problem that you have come across in your own experience.
4. 'A firm will always prefer to make more profit rather than less.' Do you agree with this statement? Is it compatible with alternatives to the profit-maximising theory of the firm?
5. A firm under monopoly or oligopoly that aims to maximise sales revenue will tend to produce more than one that aims to maximise profits. Does this conclusion also apply under (a) perfect competition and (b) monopolistic competition, given that there is freedom of entry?
6. What are the potential costs and benefits of mergers to (i) shareholders; (ii) managers; (iii) customers?
7. Why is it difficult to test the assumption that firms seek to maximise *long-run* profits?
8. Do behavioural theories of the firm allow us to make any predictions about firms' prices and output?

9 The theory of distribution of income

9.1 The market for factors of production

Why do pop stars, footballers and stockbrokers earn such large incomes? Why, on the other hand, do cleaners, hospital porters and workers in clothing factories earn very low incomes? These are the types of question that the theory of distribution seeks to answer. It attempts to explain why some people are rich and others poor.

It does this by examining the incomes earned by the various *factors of production*. In the case of labour, this income takes the form of wages and salaries. In the case of land it is the rent earned by landlords. In the case of capital it is the profits or interest earned by the owners of capital. Notice that we are not talking about the price at which a factor is sold (i.e. the price of land or the price of capital equipment). Rather we are talking about the incomes earned from the use of these factors.

In a free-market economy the distribution of income may be highly unequal. This raises the normative question of whether this inequality is desirable. Although economists cannot answer this question directly, they can examine the causes of the inequality. They can also examine government policies to redistribute incomes, and the consequences of these policies for economic efficiency and growth.

This chapter examines the theory of income distribution. In doing so it concentrates on what determines the rewards to particular factors of production. Chapter 10, on the other hand, looks at income distribution in practice. It looks at inequality and poverty and at government policies to tackle the problem.

Distribution of income in perfect markets

It is useful to make a similar distinction to that made in the theory of the firm: the distinction between perfect and imperfect markets. Although in practice few factor markets are totally perfect, many do at least approximate to it. Also, when we come to study imperfect markets it is useful to have a yardstick against which to judge the effects of such imperfections. Perfect markets provide that yardstick. (A word of caution: as Box 6.2 pointed out, 'perfect' does not necessarily mean 'desirable'.)

Assumptions

The assumptions of perfect factor markets are similar to those of perfect goods markets:

- *Everyone is a price taker.* No one has any economic power to affect factor prices. In the labour market, both employers and workers have to accept the market wage. Similarly, landlords and tenants have to accept the rent of land as given by the market. Likewise those who supply and those who demand capital have to accept the market rate of return on that capital.
- There is *freedom of entry.* There are no restrictions on the movement of labour or capital, or on changes in the use of land. For example, workers are free to move to jobs and areas of the country where wages are higher. There are no barriers erected by, say, unions, professional associations or the government. Of course, it takes time for workers to change jobs and perhaps to retrain. Similarly, the use of land cannot be changed overnight. This assumption therefore applies only in the long run.
- There is *perfect knowledge.* Workers are fully aware of what jobs are available at what wages and with what conditions of employment. Likewise employers know what labour is available and how productive that labour is. Similarly, those who supply and demand other factors are fully aware of their price and quality.
- *Factors are homogeneous.* It is usually assumed that in perfect markets factors of a particular type are identical. For example, it would be assumed that all bricklayers are equally skilled and motivated.

?? Which of the above four assumptions do you think would be correct in each of the following cases?

(a) Shorthand typists.
(b) Shepherds.
(c) Unskilled workers.
(d) Economics teachers.
(e) A hectare of prime agricultural land.
(f) A herd of Friesian cows.
(g) A warehouse.
(h) Oxyacetylene welding equipment.

The workings of the market

In a perfect market, factor earnings are determined by demand and supply. In this way factor markets are very similar to goods markets, but the roles of supplier and demander are reversed. In goods markets, firms supply goods and households demand goods. In factor markets, firms demand factors while households supply them. These demand and supply relationships can be illustrated in the circular flow of income shown in Figure 9.1.

Starting at the bottom of the diagram and moving anti-clockwise, households demand goods and services. The price of each good and service is determined by the interaction of this demand and firms' supply. In the process, money flows from households to firms.

To produce these goods firms need to employ factors of production. The demand for goods thus creates a demand for factors. The demand for factors is thus said to be a **derived demand**. For example, the demand for bricklayers is derived from the demand for new houses. The demand for factors then interacts with their supply by households. This determines the price paid to the factor owners for the use of those factors.

Generally it would be expected that the supply and demand curves for factors of production slope the same way as for goods and services. Take the case of labour. The higher the wages paid for a certain type of job, the more workers will want to do that job. This gives an upward-sloping supply curve of labour. On the other hand, the higher the wages that employers have to pay, the less labour they will want to employ. Either they will simply produce less output, or they will substitute other factors,

DEFINITION

Derived demand The demand for a factor of production depends on the demand for the good which uses it.

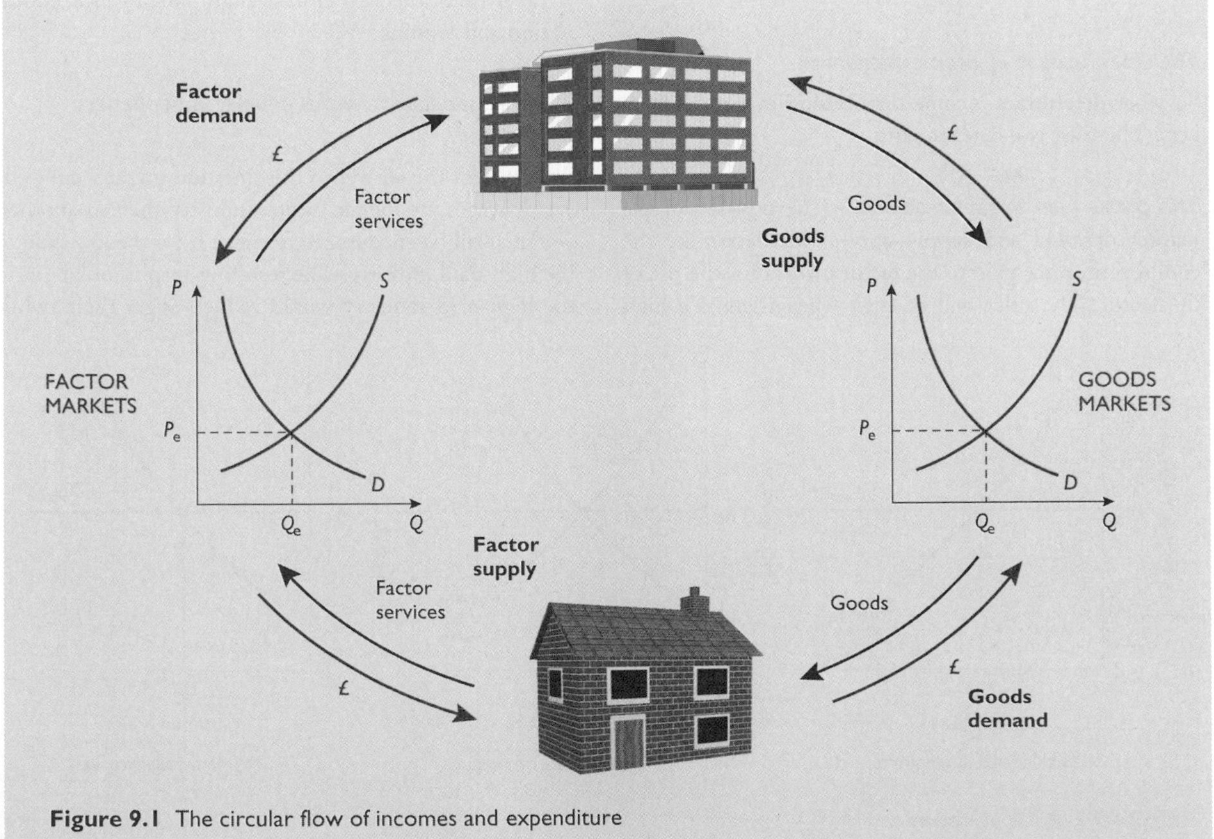

Figure 9.1 The circular flow of incomes and expenditure

like machinery, for labour. Thus the demand curve for labour slopes downwards.

These upward-sloping supply curves and downward-sloping demand curves are for the *whole market*. They determine the market price of each factor. Individual firms and households under perfect competition then have to accept these prices as given (the first assumption we made above). As individuals they have no power to influence them: they are *price takers*. Figure 9.2 illustrates the case of labour.

Diagram (b) shows how the equilibrium hourly wage is determined by the intersection of the demand and supply of labour hours.

Diagram (a) shows how an individual employer has to accept this wage. The supply of labour to that employer is infinitely elastic. In other words, at the market wage W_m, there is no limit to the number of workers available to that employer (but no workers at all will be available below it: they will all be working elsewhere). At the market wage W_m, the employer will employ Q_1 hours of labour.

Diagram (c) shows how an individual worker also has to accept this wage. The demand curve for that worker is also infinitely elastic. In other words, there are as many hours' work as the worker cares to do at this wage (but none at all above it).

The determination of income distribution

So what determines income distribution in perfect markets? There are two determinants.

The prices paid to factor owners. The position of the market demand and supply curves will determine the equilibrium price paid to the factor owners for the use of the factor. The price will be high when there is a high demand for the factor relative to supply. So if, for example, the demand for computer programmers grows faster than their supply, their wages will rise.

To explain the causes of inequality in factor earnings, then, it is necessary to examine what determines the position of the demand and supply curves. This is done in subsequent sections of this chapter.

The ownership of factors of production. There are two aspects to this:

- The *quantity* of factors that people own. Some people own lots of land and capital. Some people own only a little. Others own none: all they have to sell is their own labour. The more factors people own, the more they will earn. Thus however 'perfect' the market, and however equal wages are, inequality will persist if there is an unequal distribution of property.
- The *quality* of factors that people own. Different factors of production have different productivities. The higher the productivity of a factor, the more it will earn for its owner. Thus fertile land or city centre property will earn high rents. Efficient modern capital equipment will earn more than old inefficient equipment. Likewise workers differ in strength, intelligence, education and training.

Is there a tendency towards equality under perfect competition?

At first sight the answer to this question might seem to be yes. If wages are higher in one industry than in another, workers will be encouraged to move from the low-paid to the high-paid industry. The resulting surplus of labour in the high-paid industry would reduce wages there, while

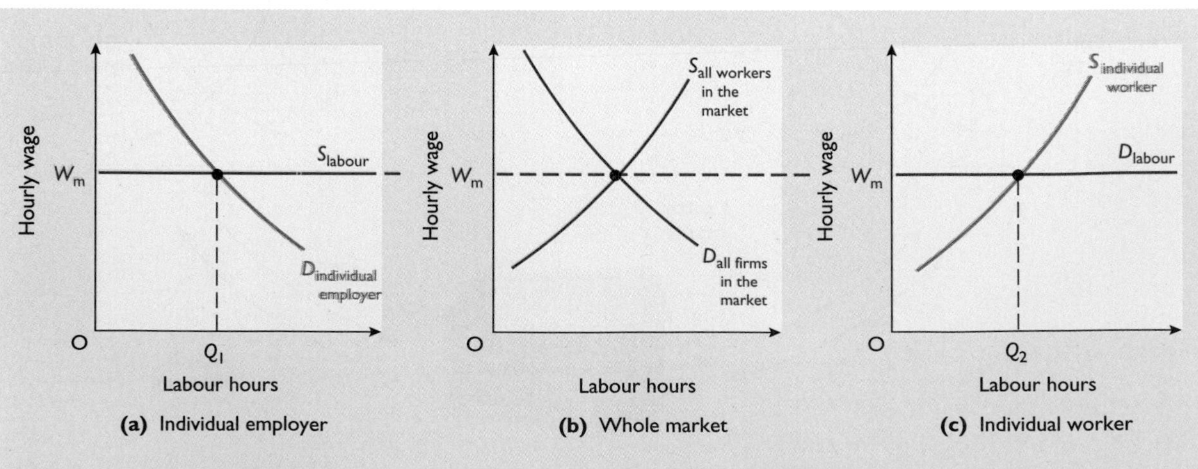

Figure 9.2 A labour market

ISSUES AND APPLICATIONS BOX 9.1

LABOUR AS A FACTOR OF PRODUCTION

Is this any way to treat a worker?

The theory that wages depend on demand and supply is often referred to as the 'neo-classical' theory of wages. Treated as pure theory it is value free and does not involve moral judgements. It does not say, for example, whether the resulting distribution of income is fair or just.

In practice, however, the neo-classical theory is often used in such a way as to imply moral judgements. It is a theory that tends to be associated with the political right and centre: those who are generally in favour of markets and the capitalist system. Many on the political left are critical of its implied morality. They make the following points:

- By treating labour as a 'factor of production', it demeans labour. Labour is *not* the same as a piece of land or a machine.
- It somehow legitimises the capitalist system, where some people own land and capital whereas others only have their own labour. It seems to imply that people have a right to the incomes from their property even if that property is highly unequally distributed among the population.
- It implies that labour has no rights to the goods that it produces. These goods are entirely the property of the employer, even though it is the workers who made them.

Karl Marx (1818–83) was highly critical of these values and the way that the capitalist system led to extremes of wealth and poverty. He argued that labour was the only true source of value. After all it is labour that makes machines, labour that tills the land and makes it yield, labour that mines coal and other natural resources. Property, he argued, is therefore a form of theft. When capitalists extract profits from their enterprises, he continued, they are stealing part of the value produced by labour.

Neo-classical economists defend their position against the Marxist 'labour theory of value' by arguing the following:

- They are merely describing the world. If people want to draw pro-capitalist conclusions from their theory, then that is up to them.
- If the labour theory of value is used in any practical way to evaluate costs and output, it will lead to a misallocation of resources. Labour is not the only scarce resource. Land, for example, is also scarce and needs to be included in calculations of costs, otherwise it will be used wastefully.

?? Assume that it is agreed by everyone that it is morally wrong to treat labour as a mere 'factor of production', with no rights over the goods produced. Does this make the neo-classical theory wrong?

the shortage of labour in the low-paid industry would raise its wages. The differential would be reduced. Similarly, if capital is attracted to industries with a high return, this will depress the return because the increased output will depress industry prices. Likewise if farmers transfer the use of their land to produce more profitable crops, the extra output will reduce the crop's price and hence the return on the land.

But even under perfect competition inequality will persist. One reason is that the costs of supplying factors may differ. In the case of labour, it is far nicer to do a clean and pleasant job than a dirty, unpleasant or dangerous job. Other things being equal, nasty jobs would have to pay more than nice jobs in order to attract labour. Similarly, owners of capital would expect a higher return on risky projects than on totally safe projects.

?? Why, do you think, are some of the lowest-paid jobs the most unpleasant? (The next paragraph might provide part of the answer. When you have read it, consider whether it contains the whole answer.)

The other reason is the unequal ownership of factors, in terms of both quantity and quality. In the long run, all nurses may be paid the same and all brain surgeons may be paid the same, but nurses will not be paid the same as brain surgeons. Two landowners may earn the same rent per acre for the same sort of land, but one farmer may own 10 hectares, whereas the other may own 1000 hectares, and of course many people own no land at all.

Distribution of income in imperfect markets

In real-world factor markets it is usual for one or more of the assumptions of perfect competition to break down.

Various groups have economic power. Large employers, trade unions, large landlords and large owners of capital all may have significant economic power. In general, the greater a group's power and the more it is exercised, the greater will be that group's share of national income.

Markets may be imperfect in other respects:

- There may be *restrictions on the movement of factors* into various firms or industries. For example, trade unions may try to restrict the employment of non-union labour. The government may impose ceilings on rents. Oligopolists may collude to try to prevent new capital entering their industry.

- Firms and households may have *imperfect knowledge.* Workers will not apply for better paid jobs if they do not know such jobs exist. Capitalists will not always make the best investments: they can only really guess at how successful an investment will be.
- People *do not always try to maximise their own economic interest.* Firms may not be profit maximisers. They may not be ruthless employers whose only concern for their workforce is as an 'input' into production. Likewise workers may be motivated by questions of loyalty or commitment rather than by pure selfishness. At the other extreme, employers may treat their workforce badly, even if productivity suffers as a result. They may discriminate between workers on other than economic grounds (e.g. by sex or race). Likewise workers may behave in a belligerent and uncooperative way, even if it means that they lose bonuses or sacrifice their chance of promotion.

To the extent that these imperfections affect the rewards that people earn, so they will affect the distribution of income.

?? If a firm is a profit 'satisficer' rather than a profit maximiser, how will this affect the wages that it pays?

SECTION SUMMARY

1. In perfect markets, factor rewards will be determined by the interaction of the market demand and supply of the factor. Income distribution will depend on the prices of the factors and how their ownership is distributed.
2. Although in perfect markets there will be a tendency for the price of a given type of factor to be equalised by market forces, inequality will persist because of differences in the costs of supplying factors, differences in the quality of factors and inequality in the ownership of factors.
3. In imperfect markets, factor prices (and hence the distribution of income) will be affected by economic power, restrictions on factor movements, imperfect knowledge of market opportunities and non-maximising behaviour.

9.2 Wage determination under perfect competition

Wages under perfect competition will be determined by the interaction of the demand and supply of labour. To explain the distribution of wage incomes, it is thus necessary to examine the determinants of the supply of and demand for labour.

The supply of labour

We can look at the supply of labour at three levels: the supply of hours by an individual worker, the supply of workers to an individual employer and the total market supply of a given category of labour. Let us examine each in turn.

The supply of hours by an individual worker

Work involves two major costs (or 'disutilities') to the worker:

- When people work they sacrifice leisure.
- The work itself may be unpleasant.

Each extra hour worked will involve additional disutility. This **marginal disutility of work** (*MDU*) will tend to *increase* as people work more hours. There are two reasons for this. First, the less the leisure they have left, the greater is the disutility they experience in sacrificing a further hour of leisure. Second, the unpleasantness they experience in doing the job will tend to increase due to boredom or tiredness.

This increasing marginal disutility (see Figure 9.3(a)) will tend to give an upward-sloping supply curve of hours by an individual worker (see Figure 9.3(b)). The reason is that, in order to persuade people to work more hours, a higher hourly wage must be paid to compensate for the higher marginal disutility incurred. This helps to explain why overtime rates are higher than standard rates.

Under certain circumstances, however, the supply of hours curve might bend backwards (see Figure 9.4). The

DEFINITION

Marginal disutility of work The extra sacrifice/hardship to a worker of working an extra unit of time in any given time period (e.g. an extra hour per day).

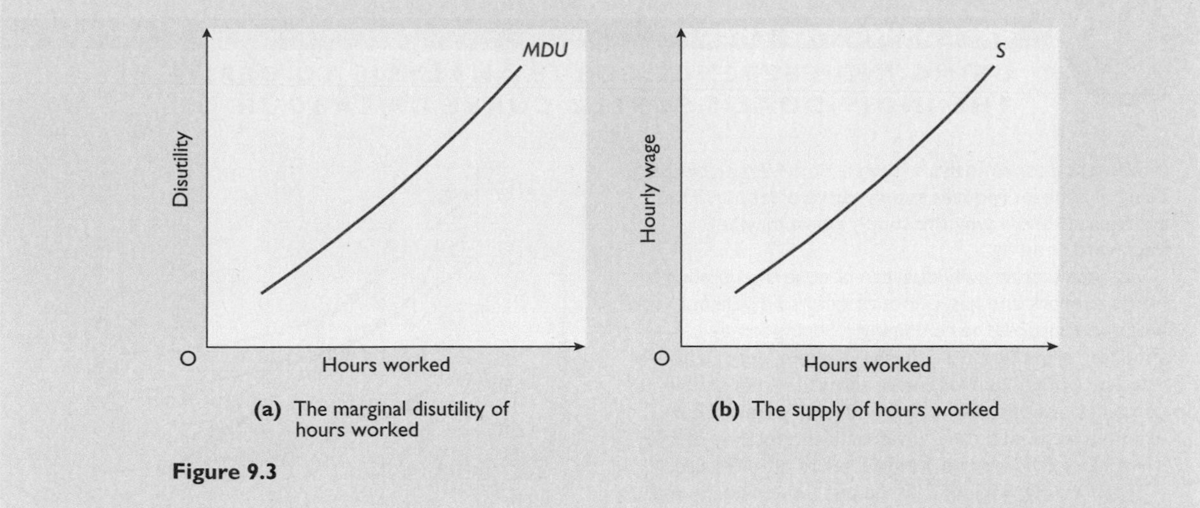

(a) The marginal disutility of hours worked

(b) The supply of hours worked

Figure 9.3

reason is that when wage rates go up there will be two opposing forces operating on the individual's labour supply.

On the one hand, with higher wages people will tend to work more hours, since time taken in leisure would now involve a greater sacrifice of income and hence consumption. They substitute income (i.e. work) for leisure. This is called the **substitution effect** of the increase in wage rates.

On the other hand, people may feel that with higher wage rates they can afford to work less and have more leisure. This is called the **income effect**.

The relative magnitude of these two effects determines the slope of the individual's supply curve. It is normally assumed that the substitution effect outweighs the income effect, especially at lower wages. A rise in wages acts as an incentive: it encourages a person to work more hours. It is possible, however, that the income effect might outweigh the substitution effect. Particularly at very high wage rates people say, 'There's not so much point now in doing overtime. I can afford to spend more time at home.'

If the wage rate becomes high enough for the income effect to dominate, the supply curve will begin to slope backwards. This occurs above a wage rate of W_1 in Figure 9.4.

These considerations are particularly important for a government considering tax cuts. The Conservative government of the 1980s argued that cuts in income taxes are like giving people a pay rise, and thus provide an incentive for people to work harder. This analysis is only correct, however, if the substitution effect dominates. If the income effect dominates, people will work *less* after the tax cut. These questions are examined in Chapter 10.

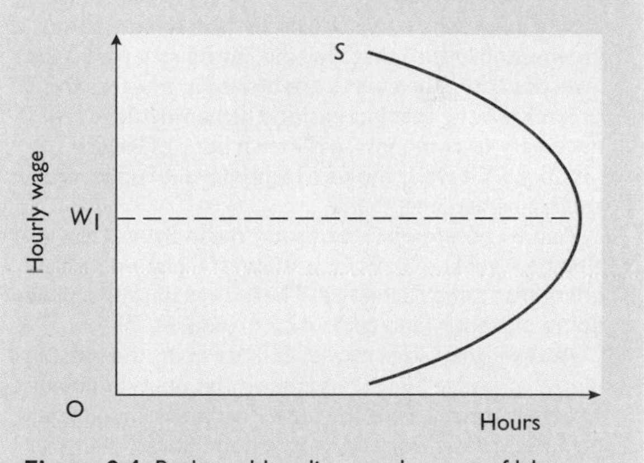

Figure 9.4 Backward-bending supply curve of labour

The supply of labour to an individual employer

Under perfect competition the supply of labour to a particular firm will be perfectly elastic, as in Figure 9.2(a). The firm is a 'wage taker' and thus has no power to influence wages. Take the case of a small firm that wishes to employ a temporary typist and thus goes to a secretarial agency. It has to pay the 'going rate', and presumably

DEFINITIONS

Substitution effect of a rise in wages Workers will tend to substitute income for leisure as leisure now has a higher opportunity cost. This effect leads to *more* hours being worked as wages rise.

Income effect of a rise in wages Workers get a higher income for a given number of hours worked and may thus feel they need to work fewer hours as wages rise.

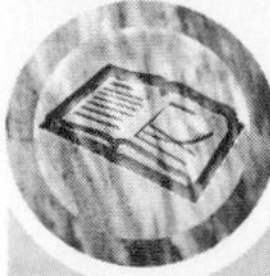

EXPLORING THE THEORY *BOX 9.2

USING INDIFFERENCE CURVE ANALYSIS TO DERIVE THE INDIVIDUAL'S SUPPLY CURVE OF LABOUR

Indifference curve analysis (see section 4.2) can be used to derive the individual's supply curve of labour. The analysis can show why the supply curve may be backward bending.

Assume that an individual can choose the number of hours to work and has 12 hours a day to divide between work and leisure (the remaining 12 being for sleep, shopping, travelling, etc.). In the diagram, with an hourly wage rate of £5, budget line B_1 shows all the possible combinations of daily income and leisure hours. For example, at point *x* the individual has an income of £40 by working 8 hours and taking 4 hours off as leisure.

At an hourly wage of £10 the budget line becomes B_2, and of £12.50, B_3.

The diagram also shows three indifference curves. Each indifference curve shows all those combinations of income and leisure that give the individual a particular level of utility. The curves are bowed in towards the origin, showing that increasingly higher incomes are necessary to compensate for each hour of leisure sacrificed. Curve I_3 shows a higher level of utility than I_2, and I_2 a higher level than I_1.

At a wage rate of £5 per hour, the individual can move along budget line B_1. Point *x* shows the highest level of utility that can be achieved. The individual thus supplies 8 hours of labour (and takes 4 off in leisure).

At the higher wage rate of £10 per hour, the individual is now on budget line B_2 and maximises utility at point *y* by working 9 hours. Thus the higher wage has encouraged the individual to work one more hour. So far, then, the individual's supply curve would be upward sloping: a higher wage rate leading to more labour hours supplied.

At the higher wage rate still of £12.50 per hour, the individual is on budget line B_3, and now maximises utility

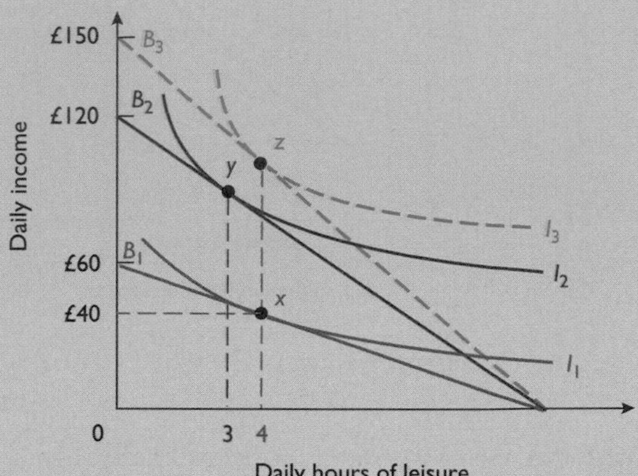

The choice of hours worked at different wage rates

at point z. But this means that only 8 hours are now worked. The supply curve has begun to bend backwards. In other words, the individual is now in a position to be able to afford to take more time off in leisure. The income effect has begun to offset the substitution effect.

??

1. Using the analysis developed in Chapter 4, try to show the size of the income and substitution effects when moving from point *x* to point *y* and from point *y* to point z.
2. Illustrate on an indifference diagram the effect on the hours a person works of (a) a cut in the rate of income tax; (b) an increase in child benefit (assuming the person has children).

will be able to employ as many typists as it likes (within reason) at that wage rate.

The market supply of a given type of labour

This will typically be upward sloping. The higher the wage rate offered in a particular type of job, the more people will want to do that job.

The *position* of the market supply curve of labour will depend on the number of people willing and able to do the job at each given wage rate. This depends on three things:

- The number of qualified people.
- The non-wage benefits or costs of the job, such as the pleasantness or otherwise of the working environment, job satisfaction or dissatisfaction, status, power, the degree of job security, holidays, perks and other fringe benefits.
- The wages and non-wage benefits in alternative jobs.

A change in the wage rate will cause a movement along the supply curve. A change in any of these other three determinants will shift the whole curve.

?? Which way will the supply curve shift if the wage rates in alternative jobs rise?

Elasticity of supply

We concentrate here on the *market* supply curve of labour for a particular type of job.

The determinants of elasticity of supply

How responsive will the supply of labour be to a change in wages? If market wages go up, will a lot more labour become available or only a little? This responsiveness (elasticity) depends on (a) the difficulties and costs of changing jobs and (b) the time period.

Another way of looking at the elasticity of supply of labour is in terms of the 'mobility of labour': the willingness and ability of labour to move to another job. The greater the difficulties and costs of changing jobs, and the shorter the time period involved, the more immobile will labour be, and hence the less elastic will be the supply curve of labour.

Immobility is of two types: geographical and occupational.

Geographical immobility. Sometimes people have difficulty in moving to another part of the country, or are unwilling to do so. The possible reasons for this **geographical immobility** include the following:

- The financial costs of moving home.
- The inconvenience of moving.
- Social and family ties.
- Poor availability of housing or other facilities (e.g. schooling) in the new area.
- The higher cost of living in the new area, including perhaps higher commuting costs.
- Ignorance of available jobs elsewhere in the country.
- Fear of the unknown.

Occupational immobility. Even if there are alternative jobs vacant in the same town, people may be unable or unwilling to change jobs. This **occupational immobility** can be due to the following:

- Lack of qualifications or ability to do alternative jobs.
- Less desirable working conditions or fringe benefits in the alternative jobs.
- Ignorance of available jobs.
- Fear of the unknown.

The mobility of labour is thus higher when there are alternative jobs in the same location, when alternative jobs require similar skills and when people have good information about these jobs. It is also much higher in the long run, when people have the time to acquire new skills and when the education system has time to adapt to the changing demands of industry.

??

1. Assume that there is a growing demand for computer programmers. As a result more people train to become programmers. Does this represent a rightward shift in the supply curve of programmers, or merely the supply curve becoming more elastic in the long run, or both? Explain.
2. Which is likely to be more elastic, the supply of coal miners or the supply of shop assistants? Explain.

Economic rent and transfer earnings

The earnings of a factor of production can be split into two elements. The relative size of these two elements depends on the elasticity of supply of that factor.

Transfer earnings are what a factor must earn to prevent it from moving to an alternative use. In the case of labour it is what people must be paid to persuade them to stay in their present job.

Economic rent is anything over and above transfer earnings.

For example, take the case of Mary Jones. She is the manager of a high street store and earns £20 000 per year. She could earn £15 000 in another job and would indeed transfer to that other job if her salary were cut below £15 000. Thus her transfer earnings are £15 000. The remaining £5000 is her economic rent. Economic rent equals total earnings minus transfer earnings.

Now take the case of a market supply curve – say, the market for nurses. This is illustrated in Figure 9.5. Starting at point a and moving towards point b, as the wage rate is raised so more nurses are attracted to the profession. At each higher wage the *new* nurses attracted are getting just enough to persuade them to transfer into the profession: the wage for them is entirely transfer earnings. But nurses *already* in the profession will get economic rent; after all, they are now getting more than the minimum necessary to keep them in the profession.

Workers' economic rent is thus the difference between the actual wage rate and the point on the supply curve at which they entered the market.

DEFINITIONS

Geographical immobility The lack of ability or willingness of people to move to jobs in other parts of the country.

Occupational immobility The lack of ability or willingness of people to move to other jobs irrespective of location.

Transfer earnings What a factor must earn to prevent it from moving to another use/occupation. Total transfer earnings are the area under the supply curve to the left of current factor employment.

Economic rent The excess that a factor is paid over its transfer earnings. Total economic rent is the area between the supply curve and the factor price.

CASE STUDIES — BOX 9.3

'TELECOMMUTERS'
The electronic cottage

One of the causes of inequality of wages has been the geographical immobility of labour. Within countries this manifests itself in different rates of pay between different regions: often, those regions furthest from the capital city pay the lowest rates.

It also applies between countries. Poorer countries pay lower wages because there is not the mobility of labour between countries to counteract it. Thus in the EU, countries such as Greece, Ireland and Portugal have much lower wages than Germany, France or the Benelux countries. Although there is officially 'free movement of labour' under the terms of the 1993 single market, in practice there are all sorts of social, financial and language barriers that prevent workers in poorer countries moving to higher-paid jobs in the richer EU countries.

Nevertheless within countries people are often prepared to commute long distances in order to earn the higher pay that large cities have to offer. Witness the army of people who travel into London each day from many miles away, getting up early, arriving back late and paying huge sums of money for travelling.

One important development in recent years, however, is helping to reverse this trend. The increasing sophistication of information technology, with computer linking through telephone lines (modems) and fax machines, has meant that many people can work at home. The number of these 'telecommuters' has grown steadily since the information technology revolution of the early 1970s. In 1990 it was estimated that there were some 15 million telecommuters in the USA. The true figure is in fact very difficult to calculate and subject to a whole range of definitional problems concerning 'home working'.

Most telecommuters are in white-collar occupations, ranging from those in direct contact with the office (e.g. computer programmers) to those who process information into a computer system. The impact that such new working practices may have on the work environment is immense.

It has been found that where 'telecommuting networks' have been established, gains in productivity levels have been significant, when compared with comparable office workers. Most studies indicate rises in productivity of over 35 per cent. With fewer interruptions and less chatting with fellow workers, less working time is lost. Add to this the stress-free environment, free from the strain of commuting, and the individual worker's performance is enhanced.

With further savings in time, in the renting and maintenance of offices (often in high-cost inner city locations) and in heating and lighting costs, the economic arguments in favour of telecommuting seem very persuasive.

As well as the immediate economic advantages, such changes in working practices may have significant social effects. On the positive side, telecommuting opens up the labour market to a wider group of workers who might find it difficult to leave the home, groups such as single parents and the disabled. Also, concerns that managers lose control over their employees, and that the quality of work falls, appear unfounded. In fact the reverse seems to have occurred: the quality of work in many cases has improved.

Whether employees feel isolated, as many commentators have predicted, is also unclear. On the one hand, it is true that for some people work is not just a means of earning a living. It is an important part of their social environment, providing them with an opportunity to meet others and to work as a team. For those who are unable to leave the home, however, telecommuting may be the *only* means of earning a living: the choice of travelling to work may simply not be open to them.

Ironically, it appears that whereas the industrial revolution destroyed cottage industries and people's ability to work from home, information technology is doing the reverse, and may in the end contribute to the destruction of the office – at least of large central offices. Small local offices, however, may flourish as the developments in technology mean that people do not have to travel long distances for meetings.

These technological developments have been the equivalent of an increase in labour mobility. Work can be taken to the workers rather than the workers coming to the work. The effect will be to reduce the premium that needs to be paid to workers in commercial centres, such as the City of London.

??

1. *The Economist* on 12 June 1993 reported that 'Saturn, a new car-making subsidiary of General Motors … reckons it has saved $500 000 a year in air fares by installing a video-conferencing link between its factory in Spring Hill, Tennessee, and its Detroit Office.' What effects are such developments likely to have on executive salaries?
2. How are the developments referred to in this box likely to affect relative house prices between capital cities and the regions?

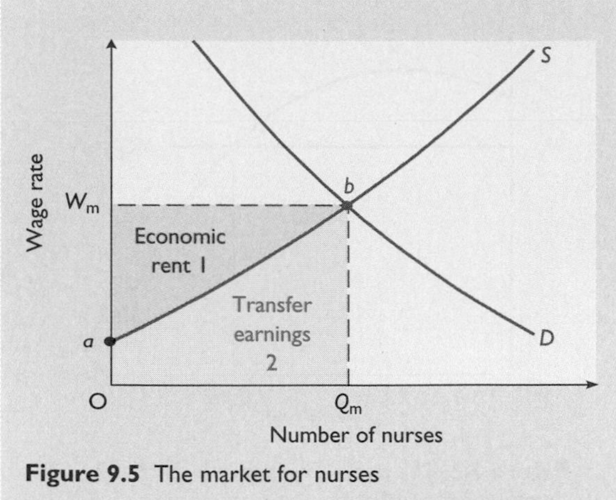

Figure 9.5 The market for nurses

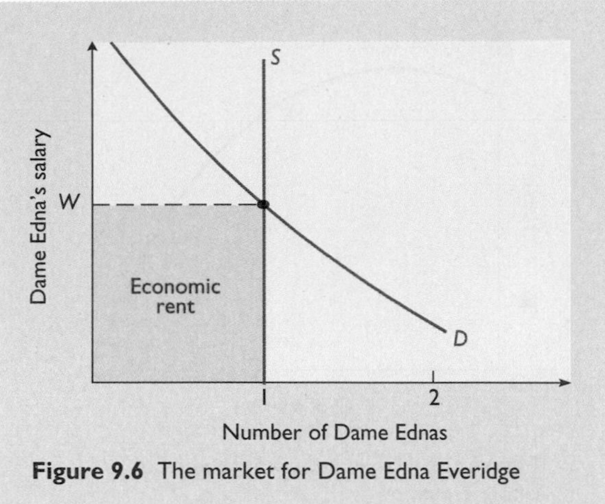

Figure 9.6 The market for Dame Edna Everidge

Thus at the market wage W_m in Figure 9.5, the total economic rent of all those employed is shown by area 1 – the area above the supply curve. Area 2 shows transfer earnings.

The less elastic the supply curve, the greater will be the proportion that is economic rent. Why? The bigger the wage increase necessary to attract extra workers, the more economic rent existing workers will gain.

?? Draw a perfectly elastic supply curve. Will workers receive any economic rent? Explain the reason for your answer.

Now take the extreme position of a totally inelastic supply curve. The simplest example is that of a person with a unique talent, like a famous show business megastar, such as Dame Edna Everidge (see Figure 9.6). The quantity of Dame Ednas is fixed. There is only one: she is unique. As a result her income is determined entirely by demand, and is entirely economic rent. The more popular she is, the higher the demand for her performances and the higher the income she can command. Thus megastars can earn very high incomes.

Conversely, once a star's popularity wanes, his or her income can plummet, as many show business failures can confirm.

Identifying transfer earnings and economic rent. The precise division of a worker's income between transfer earnings and economic rent will depend on the context.

Only a small cut in wages will be necessary before workers are encouraged to move to the same job in another firm in the same town (assuming there are such jobs). In this context the elasticity of labour supply is high. Thus economic rents are low and transfer earnings are high.

The same workers, however, would need a much larger cut in wages to persuade them to move to another town and into a totally new job. Transfer earnings thus tend to be much lower between different occupations. Supply is less elastic and consequently economic rents are correspondingly higher.

Quasi-rent. In the long run, people's economic rent may be competed away as newly trained workers enter the market. In other words, labour supply curves may be inelastic in the short run, but much more elastic in the long run.

Economic rent that applies only in the short run as a result of skill shortages is known as **quasi-rent**.

The demand for labour: the marginal productivity theory

The traditional 'neo-classical' theory of the firm assumes that firms aim to maximise profits. The same assumption is made in the neo-classical theory of labour demand. This theory is generally known as the **marginal productivity theory**.

The profit-maximising approach

How many workers will a profit-maximising firm want to employ? The firm will answer this question by weighing up the costs of employing extra labour against the

DEFINITIONS

Quasi-rent Temporary economic rent arising from short-run supply inelasticity.

Marginal productivity theory The theory that the demand for a factor depends on its marginal revenue product.

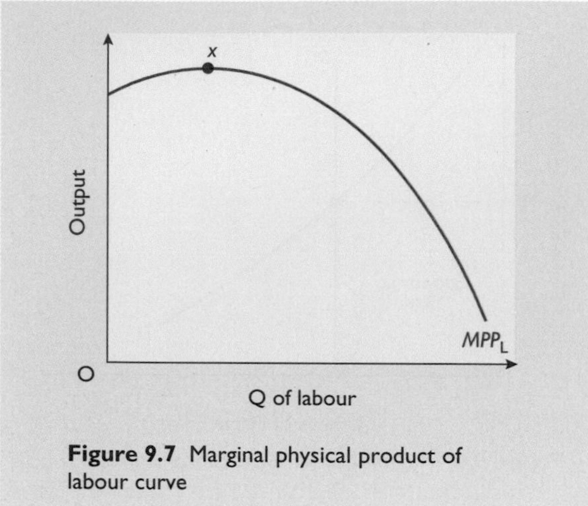

Figure 9.7 Marginal physical product of labour curve

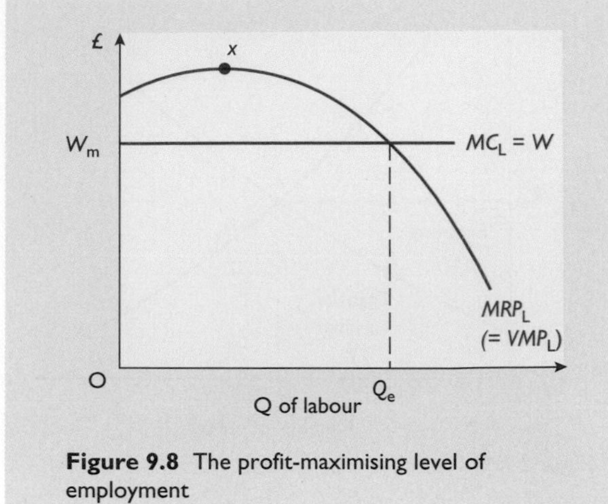

Figure 9.8 The profit-maximising level of employment

benefits. It will use exactly the same principles as in deciding how much output to produce.

In the goods market, the firm will maximise profits where the marginal cost of an extra unit of *goods* produced equals the marginal revenue from selling it: $MC = MR$.

In the labour market, the firm will maximise profits where the marginal cost of employing an extra *worker* equals the marginal revenue that the worker's output earns for the firm: MC of labour = MR of labour. The reasoning is simple. If an extra worker adds more to a firm's revenue than to its costs, the firm's profits will increase. It will be worth employing that worker. But as more workers are employed, diminishing returns to labour will set in. Each extra worker will produce less than the previous one, and thus earn less revenue for the firm. Eventually the marginal revenue from extra workers will fall to the level of their marginal cost. At that point the firm will stop employing extra workers. There are no additional profits to be gained. Profits are at a maximum.

Measuring the marginal cost and revenue of labour

Marginal cost of labour (MC_L). This is the extra cost of employing one more worker. Under perfect competition the firm is too small to affect the market wage. It faces a horizontal supply curve (see Figure 9.2(a)). Thus the additional cost of employing one more person will simply be the wage: $MC_L = W$.

Marginal revenue of labour (MRP_L). The marginal revenue the firm gains from employing one more worker is called the **marginal revenue product** of labour. The MRP_L is found by multiplying two elements – the *marginal physical product* of labour (MPP_L) and the marginal revenue gained by selling one more unit of output (MR):

$$MRP_L = MPP_L \times MR$$

The MPP_L is the extra output produced by the last worker. Thus if the last worker produces 100 tonnes of output per week (MPP_L), and if the firm earns an extra £2 for each additional tonne sold (MR), then the worker's MRP is £200. This extra worker is adding £200 to the firm's revenue.

A related concept is the **value of the marginal product** of labour (VMP_L). This is the MPP_L multiplied by the *price* of the good (rather than its MR):

$$VMP_L = MPP_L \times P$$

As we saw in Chapter 6, under perfect competition $P = MR$, since the firm is a price taker in the goods market. Thus $MRP_L = VMP_L$ under perfect competition. The distinction between MRP_L and VMP_L becomes significant however, when we consider firms operating in imperfect markets (see section 9.3).

The profit-maximising level of employment for a firm

The MPP_L curve is illustrated in Figure 9.7. As more workers are employed there will come a point when diminishing

DEFINITIONS

Marginal revenue product (of a factor) The extra revenue a firm earns from employing one more unit of a variable factor: $MRP_{factor} = MPP_{factor} \times MR_{good}$.

Value of the marginal product (of a factor) The market value of the output produced from employing one more unit of a variable factor: $VMP_{factor} = MPP_{factor} \times P_{good}$.

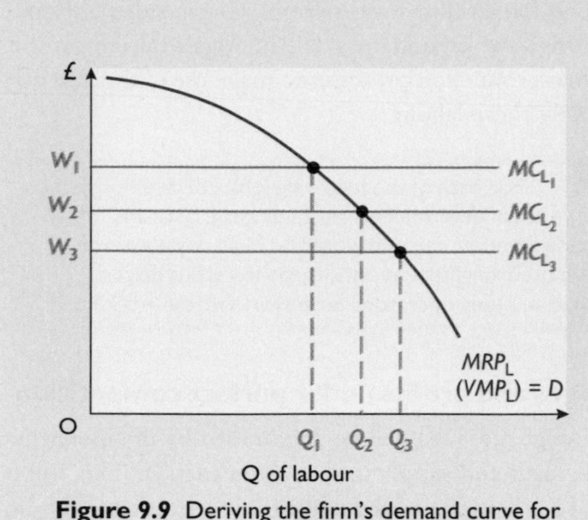

Figure 9.9 Deriving the firm's demand curve for labour

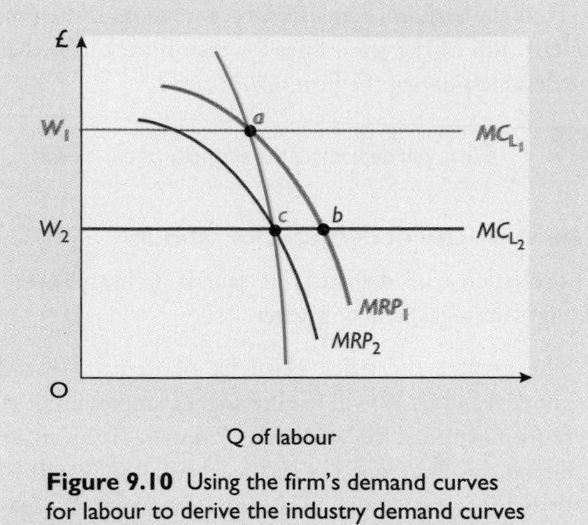

Figure 9.10 Using the firm's demand curves for labour to derive the industry demand curves for labour

returns set in (point *x*). The MPP_L curve thus slopes down after this point. The MRP_L curve will be a similar shape to the MPP_L curve, since it is merely being multiplied by a constant figure, *MR*. (Under perfect competition $MR = P$ and does not vary with output.) The MRP_L curve is illustrated in Figure 9.8, along with the MC_L 'curve'.

?? Why is the MC_L curve horizontal?

Profits will be maximised at an employment level of Q_e, where MC_L (i.e. *W*) = MRP_L. Why? At levels of employment below Q_e, MRP_L exceeds MC_L. The firm will increase profits by employing more labour. At levels of employment above Q_e, MC_L exceeds MRP_L. In this case the firm will increase profits by reducing employment.

Derivation of the firm's demand curve for labour

No matter what the wage rate, the quantity of labour demanded will be found from the intersection of *W* and MRP_L (see Figure 9.9). At a wage rate of W_1, Q_1 labour is demanded; at W_2, Q_2 is demanded; at W_3, Q_3 is demanded.

Thus the MRP_L curve will show the quantity of labour employed at each wage rate. But this is just what the demand curve for labour shows. Thus the MRP_L curve is the demand curve for labour.

There are three determinants of the demand for labour:

- The wage rate. This determines the position *on* the demand curve. (Strictly speaking, we should refer here to the wage rate determining the 'quantity demanded' rather than the 'demand'.)
- The productivity of labour (MPP_L). This determines the position *of* the demand curve.
- The demand for the good. The higher the market demand for the good, the higher will be its market price, and hence the higher will be the *MR*, and thus the MRP_L. This too determines the position of the demand curve. It illustrates just how the demand for labour (and other factors) is *derived* from the demand for the good.

A change in the wage rate will be represented by a movement *along* the demand curve for labour. A change in the productivity of labour or the demand for the good will *shift* the curve.

Derivation of the industry demand curve for labour

This will not simply be the sum of the demand curves of the individual firms. The firm's demand curve is based on a constant *P* and *MR*, no matter how many workers the firm employs (this is one of the assumptions of perfect competition). In Figure 9.10, when the wage rate falls from W_1 to W_2 the firm will employ more labour by moving from *a* to *b* along its demand curve MRP_1.

The trouble with this analysis is that when the wage rate falls it will affect *all* employers. They will all want to employ more labour. But when they do, the total industry output will increase, and hence *P* (and *MR*) will be pushed down. This will shift the firm's *MRP* curve to the left and lead to a lower level of employment at point *c*. Therefore, when we allow for the effect of lower wages on the market price of the good, the firm's demand curve for labour will be the *green* line passing through points *a* and *c*.

Thus the *industry* demand curve for labour is the (horizontal) sum of the *green* lines for each firm, and is therefore less elastic than the firm's *MRP* curve.

?? What will determine the elasticity of this curve?

The elasticity of demand for labour

The elasticity of demand for labour (with respect to changes in wages) will be greater:

- The greater the price elasticity of demand for the good. A fall in *W* will lead to higher employment and more output. This will drive *P* down. If the market demand for the good is elastic, this fall in *P* will lead to a lot more being sold and hence to a lot more people being employed.
- The easier it is to substitute labour for other factors and vice versa. If labour can be readily substituted for other factors, then a reduction in *W* will lead to a large increase in labour used to replace these other factors.
- The greater the elasticity of supply of complementary factors. If wages fall, a lot more labour will be demanded if plenty of complementary factors can be obtained at little increase in their price.
- The greater the elasticity of supply of substitute factors. If wages fall and more labour is used, fewer substitute factors will be demanded and their price will fall. If their supply is elastic, a lot fewer will be supplied and therefore a lot more labour will be used instead.
- The greater the wage cost as a proportion of total costs. If wages are a large proportion of total costs and wages fall, total costs will fall significantly; therefore production will increase significantly, and so too will the demand for labour.
- The longer the time period. Given sufficient time, firms can respond to a fall in wages by reorganising their production processes to make use of the now relatively cheap labour.

?? For each of the following jobs, check through the above list of determinants (excluding the last), and try to decide whether demand would be relatively elastic or inelastic: firefighters; typists; carpenters; bus drivers; Punch and Judy operators; farm workers; car workers.

Wages and profits under perfect competition

The wage rate (*W*) will be determined by the interaction of demand and supply in the labour market. This will be equal to the value of the output that the last person produces (VMP_L or MRP_L).

Profits to the individual firm will arise from the fact that the MRP_L (VMP_L) curve slopes downward (diminishing returns). Thus the last worker adds less to the revenue of firms than previous workers already employed.

If *all* workers in the firm receive a wage equal to the *MRP* of the *last* worker, everyone but the last worker will receive a wage less than their *MRP*. This excess of MRP_L over *W* of previous workers provides a surplus to the firm (see Figure 9.11). In a simple two-factor model (labour and capital), this surplus will be the same as profits less fixed capital costs.

Perfect competition between firms will ensure that profits are kept down to *normal* profits. If the surplus over wages is such that *supernormal* profits are made, new firms will enter the industry. The price of the good (and hence VMP_L and MRP_L) will fall, and the wage will be bid up, until only normal profits remain.

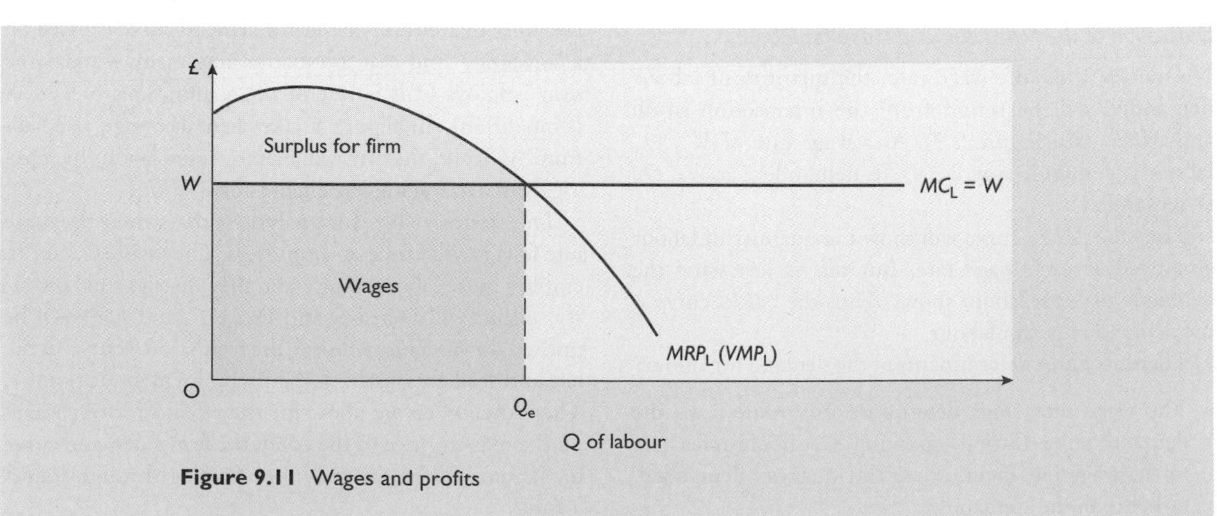

Figure 9.11 Wages and profits

Equality and inequality under perfect competition

The mythical world of perfect wage equality

Under certain very strict assumptions a perfectly competitive market will lead to perfect equality of wages. All workers will earn exactly the same. These strict assumptions are as follows:

- All workers have identical abilities.
- There is perfect mobility of labour.
- All jobs are equally attractive.
- All workers and employers have perfect knowledge.
- Wages are determined entirely by demand and supply.

Given these assumptions, if consumer demand rose in any industry, the demand for labour would rise. As a result, wages would begin to rise. Immediately workers would flood into this industry, attracted by the higher wages. Very quickly, then, the wage would be competed back down to the level in the rest of the economy. Likewise if wages began to fall in any industry, workers would leave, thereby eliminating any labour surplus and preventing the fall in wages.

Under these conditions, therefore, not only would the labour supply curve to a *firm* be infinitely elastic, but so too would the labour supply curve to each *industry* at the universal wage.

Of course, in the real world these conditions do not hold. Huge inequalities of wages exist. A stockbroker in the City can earn fifty times as much as a shop assistant. But even if markets *were* perfect, inequality would be expected to persist.

Causes of inequality under perfect competition

In the short run, inequality will exist under perfect competition because of the time it takes for changes in demand and supply conditions to bring new long-run equilibria. Thus expanding industries will tend to pay higher wages than contracting industries.

But even after enough time has elapsed for all adjustments to be made to changes in demand and supply, long-run wage differentials will still exist for the following reasons:

- Workers do not have identical abilities. Some people are strong while others are weak. Some people are intelligent, while others are not. Some people are dextrous while others are clumsy. Education and training can only go a certain way to eliminating these differences in ability.
- Workers are not perfectly mobile, even in the long run. People have different preferences about where they want to live and the jobs they like to do.
- Jobs differ enormously in terms of the skills they require and in terms of their pleasantness or unpleasantness.

What is more, since demand and supply conditions are constantly changing, long-run general equilibrium throughout the economy will never be reached.

Conclusions: Who are the poor? Who are the rich?

The poor will be those whose labour is in low demand or high supply. Low demand will be due to low demand for the good or low labour productivity. High supply will be due to low mobility out of contracting industries or to a surplus of people with the same skills or qualifications. Thus workers will be poor, for example, who possess few skills, are unfit, are working in contracting industries, do not want to move from the area and will not or cannot retrain.

The rich will be those whose labour is in high demand or low supply. Thus workers who possess skills or talents which are in short supply, especially those skills which take a long time for others to acquire, and those who are working in expanding industries will tend to earn high wages.

Although the movement of labour from low-paid to high-paid jobs will tend to reduce wage differentials, considerable inequality will persist even under perfect competition. It is a fallacy, therefore, to believe that simply by 'freeing up' markets and encouraging workers to 'stand on their own feet' or 'get on their bikes' poverty and inequality will be eliminated.

What is more, in the real world there exist many market imperfections. These tend to make inequality greater. These imperfections are examined in the next section.

Finally, income inequality under capitalism will also be due to unequal distribution of the ownership of land and capital. Even under perfect competition, considerable inequality will therefore exist if wealth is concentrated in the hands of the few.

SECTION SUMMARY

1. Wages in a perfect market will be determined by supply and demand.
2. The supply curve of hours by an individual worker will reflect the increasing marginal disutility of work. Its shape will depend on the relative sizes of the substitution and income effects of a wage change. The substitution effect will be positive. A higher wage will encourage people to work more by substituting wages for leisure. The income effect, however, will be negative. A higher wage will make people feel that they can afford to work less. If the income effect is bigger than the substitution effect, the supply of hours curve will bend backwards.
3. The supply of labour to a particular employer under perfect competition will be infinitely elastic.
4. The market supply will typically be upward sloping. Its elasticity will depend on labour mobility. Immobility is of two types: geographical and occupational.
5. The elasticity of supply will determine what proportion of wages consists of transfer earnings and what proportion consists of economic rent. Transfer earnings are the wages that must be paid to prevent a worker transferring to another job. Economic rent is any wages above transfer earnings.
6. The demand for labour will depend on a worker's marginal revenue product. This is the extra revenue that a firm will gain from the output of an extra worker. The profit-maximising firm will continue taking on extra workers until MRP_L is equal to MC_L (= W under perfect competition).
7. The elasticity of demand for labour will depend on the elasticity of demand for the good, the ease of substituting labour for other factors and vice versa, the elasticity of supply of substitute and complementary factors, wages as a proportion of total costs, and the time period involved.
8. Although market forces will tend to lead to the elimination of differentials as workers move from low-paid to high-paid jobs, nevertheless inequality can persist even under perfect competition. People have different abilities and skills; people are not perfectly mobile; and jobs differ in their labour requirements.
9. Inequality is also caused by market imperfections and by unequal ownership of land and capital.

9.3 Wage determination in imperfect markets

In the real world, firms and/or workers are likely to have the power to influence wages. This is one of the major types of market imperfection.

Firms may have market power in selling goods: in other words, they may be operating under conditions of monopoly, oligopoly or monopolistic competition.

Firms may also have market power in employing labour. When a firm is the only employer of a certain type of labour, this situation is called a **monopsony**. Until recently, British Rail was a monopsony employer of train drivers. A monopsony is more likely to occur in a local market. Thus a factory may be the only employer of certain types of labour in that district. When there are just a few employers, this is called **oligopsony**.

Workers may have market power as members of unions. When a single union bargains on behalf of a certain type of labour, it is acting as a monopolist. When there is more than one union, they are oligopolists.

When a monopsonist employer faces a monopolist union, the situation is called **bilateral monopoly**.

Firms with market power in selling goods (monopoly, etc.)

This section assumes that there is still perfect competition in the labour market, but that there is power in the goods market. This type of situation is not uncommon. Often large firms have considerable market power in selling their output and yet compete for certain categories of labour (e.g. electricians, secretaries) with many other firms.

According to the theory we developed above, an employer will maximise profits by employing labour up to the point where $W = MRP_L$. Where firms operate under *perfect*

DEFINITIONS

Monopsony A market with a single buyer or employer.

Oligopsony A market with just a few buyers or employers.

Bilateral monopoly Where a monopsony buyer faces a monopoly seller.

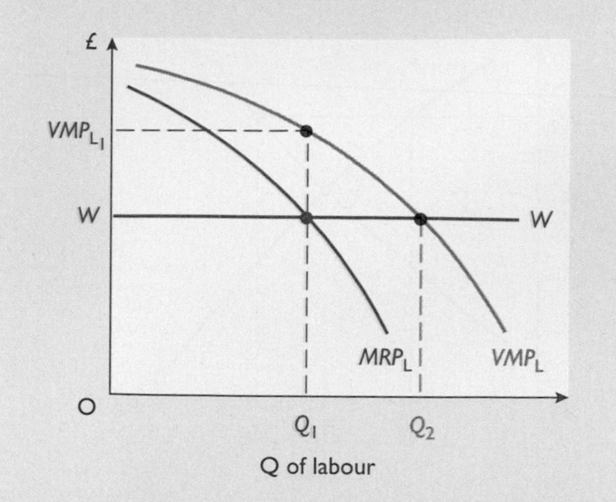

Figure 9.12 Firms with power in the goods market but perfect competition in the labour market

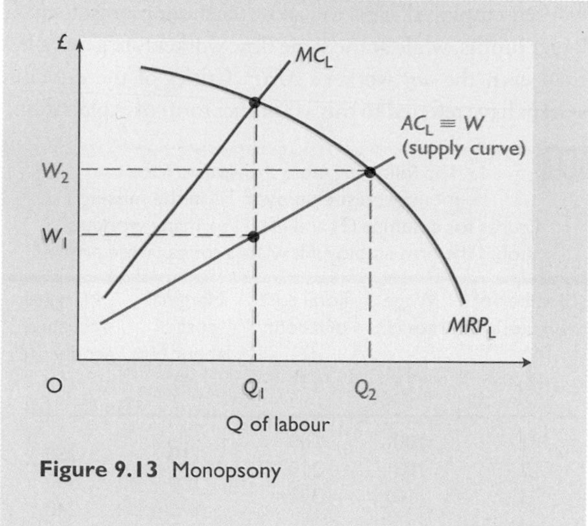

Figure 9.13 Monopsony

competition in the goods market, MR will equal P: they are price takers and thus one more unit sold earns the full market price. Thus, as we saw, MRP_L (i.e. $MPP_L \times MR$) = VMP_L (i.e. $MPP_L \times P$). Therefore if $W = MRP_L$, W also equals VMP_L. In other words, workers will be paid a wage equal to the value of the last worker's output (VMP_L).

Where firms have market *power* in the goods market, however, MR will be *less* than P (see Figure 6.8 on page 183). Thus MRP_L will be less than VMP_L. But this will mean that workers will now be paid a wage less than the value of the last worker's output: ($W < VMP_L$). This has been referred to as one form of 'monopoly exploitation' of labour.

In Figure 9.12 instead of employing Q_2 labour (where $W = VMP_L$) the monopolist will employ Q_1 labour (where $W = MRP_L$). Note that at Q_1, $W < VMP_L$.

Other things being equal, a monopolist will produce less than a competitive industry. There will thus be a lower demand for labour. If a lot of firms employing a particular type of labour have market power in their respective goods markets, the general level of demand for this type of labour will be lower and thus wages will tend to be lower. The ratio of profits to wages in such industries is likely to be higher than under perfect competition, since there is not the competition from new entrants to drive profits down and wages up. This has also been referred to as a form of exploitation of labour.

Nevertheless, economies of scale in such industries may lead to greater output and possibly greater employment (unless the economies of scale involve using less of this type of labour) and hence higher wages. Also the higher profits may lead to higher investment, faster growth and hence higher wages in the long run.

Firms with market power in employing labour (monopsony, etc.)

When only one or a few firms employ a particular type of labour, they have power to influence wages. Thus monopsonists or oligopsonists are 'wage makers' not 'wage takers'. A large employer in a small town, for example, may have considerable power to resist wage increases or even to force wages down.

Such firms face an upward-sloping supply curve of labour. This is illustrated in Figure 9.13. If the firm wants to take on more labour, it will have to pay higher wages to attract workers away from other industries. But conversely, by employing less labour it can get away with paying lower wages.

The supply curve shows the wage that must be paid to attract a given quantity of labour. The wage it pays is the *average cost* to the firm of employing labour (AC_L). The supply curve is also therefore the AC_L curve.

The *marginal cost* of employing one more worker (MC_L) will be above the wage (AC_L). The reason is that the wage rate has to be raised to attract extra workers. The MC_L will thus be the new higher wage paid to the new employee *plus* the small rise in the total wages bill for existing employees: after all, they will be paid the higher wage too.

The profit-maximising employment of labour would be at Q_1, where $MC_L = MRP_L$. The wage paid would thus be W_1.

If this had been a perfectly competitive labour market, employment would have been at the higher level Q_2, and the wage rate at the higher level W_2, where $W = MRP_L$. What in effect the monopsonist is doing, therefore, is forcing the wage rate down by restricting the number of workers employed. This will allow the monopsonist to make larger profits, while at the same time workers are getting less than even the *last* worker's *MRP*. Critics of the capitalist system have referred to this as another form of exploitation.

??

1. The following table shows data for a monopsonist employer. Fill in the missing figures for columns (3) and (4). How many workers should the firm employ if it wishes to maximise profits?

Number of workers (1)	Wage rate (£) (2)	Total cost of labour (£) (3)	Marginal cost of labour (£) (4)	Marginal revenue product (£) (5)
1	100	100		
			110	230
2	105	210		
			120	240
3	110	330		
				240
4	115			
				230
5	120			
				210
6	125			
				190
7	130			
				170
8	135			
				150
9	140			
				130
10	145			

2. Will a monopsony typically be a monopoly? Try to think of some examples of monopsonists that are not monopolists, and monopolists that are not monopsonists.

Labour with market power (union monopoly or oligopoly)

The extent to which unions will succeed in pushing up wage rates depends on their power and militancy. It also depends on the power of firms to resist and on their ability to pay higher wages. In particular, the scope for unions to gain a better deal for their members depends on the sort of market in which the employers are producing.

If the employers are producing under perfect or monopolistic competition, unions can raise wages only at the expense of employment. Firms are earning only normal profit. Thus if unions force up wages, the marginal firms will go bankrupt and leave the industry. Fewer workers will be employed. The fall in output will lead to higher prices. This will enable the remaining firms to pay a higher wage rate.

Figure 9.14 illustrates these effects. If unions force the wage rate up from W_1 to W_2, employment will fall from Q_1 to Q_2. There will be a surplus of people ($Q_3 - Q_2$) wishing to work in this industry for whom no jobs are available.

The union is in a doubly weak position. Not only will jobs be lost as a result of forcing up the wage rate, but there is also a danger that these unemployed people could undercut the union wage, unless the union can prevent firms employing non-unionised labour.

Wages can be increased without a reduction in the level

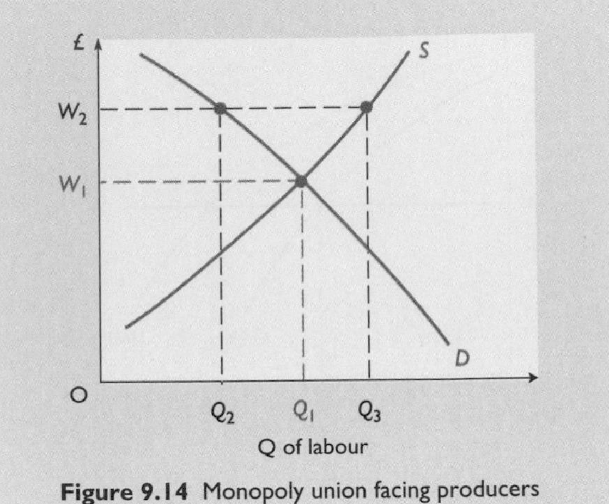

Figure 9.14 Monopoly union facing producers under perfect competition

of employment only if, as part of the bargain, the productivity of labour is increased. This is called a **productivity deal**. The *MRP* curve, and hence the *D* curve in Figure 9.14, shifts to the right.

??

Which of the following unions find themselves in a weak bargaining position for the above reasons?

(a) The seafarers' part of the rail and maritime union RMT.
(b) The shopworkers' union (USDAW).
(c) The National Union of Mineworkers.
(d) The farmworkers' union (part of the Transport and General Workers' Union).

In a competitive market, then, the union is faced with the choice between wages and jobs. Its actions will thus depend on its objectives.

If it wants to *maximise employment*, it will have to content itself with a wage of W_1 in Figure 9.14, unless productivity deals can be negotiated. At W_1, Q_1 workers will be employed. Above W_1 fewer than Q_1 workers will be *demanded*. Below W_1 fewer than Q_1 workers will be *supplied*.

If, on the other hand, it wants to *maximise the total amount of wages* paid by employers, it will continue pushing up the wage rate as long as the demand for labour is inelastic. As long as it is inelastic the increase in wage rates will be proportionately larger than the fall in employment, thereby causing total wage payments to rise. As wages are raised, however, firms will increasingly be forced to cut

DEFINITION

Productivity deal Where, in return for a wage increase, a union agrees to changes in working practices that will increase output per worker.

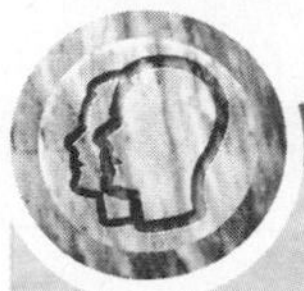

DEVELOPMENT OF IDEAS — BOX 9.4

LIFE AT THE MILL
Monopsony in Victorian times

A dramatic illustration of the effects of extreme monopsony power is that of the textile mill in nineteenth-century England. When a mill was the only employer in a small town, or when factory owners colluded as oligopsonists, and when there was no union to counterbalance the power of the employer, things could be very bad for the worker. Very low pay would be combined with often appalling working conditions.

Friedrich Engels described the life of the textile factory worker as follows:

> The factory worker is condemned to allow his physical and mental powers to become atrophied. From the age of eight he enters an occupation which bores him all day long. And there is no respite from this boredom. The machine works ceaselessly. Its wheels, belts and spindles hum and rattle ceaselessly in his ears, and if he thinks of taking even a moment's rest, the overlooker is always there to punish him with a fine. It is nothing less than torture of the severest kind to which the workers are subjected by being condemned to a life-sentence in the factory, in the service of a machine which never stops. It is not only the body of the worker which is stunted, but also his mind. It would indeed be difficult to find a better way of making a man slow-witted than to turn him into a factory worker.[1]

What were these fines that the overlooker could impose on the worker? Engels quotes an example of some typical factory rules:

> 1st. The door of the lodge will be closed ten minutes after the engine starts every morning, and no weaver will afterwards be admitted till breakfast-time. Any weaver who may be absent during that time shall forfeit threepence per loom.
>
> 2nd. Weavers absent at any other time when the engine is working, will be charged threepence per hour each loom for such absence; and weavers leaving the room when the engine is working without the consent of the overlooker, shall forfeit threepence.
>
> 3rd. Weavers not being provided with nippers or shears, shall forfeit one penny for every day they are so unprovided.
>
> 9th. All shuttles, temples, brushes, oil-cans, wheels, windows, etc., if broken, shall be paid for by the weaver.
>
> 10th. ...The master may discharge any hand without notice, for bad work or mis-conduct.
>
> 11th. If any hand in the mill be seen talking to another, whistling, or singing [he or she] will be fined sixpence.[2]

It will be argued that such rules are necessary to ensure the smooth co-ordination of the various processes carried on in a big, well-run factory. It will be said that stern discipline of this kind is just as necessary in the factory as in the army. That may be true enough, but how can one defend the state of society which can only survive by the exercise of such shameful tyranny?[3]

??

1. Why did competition between employers not force up wages and improve working conditions?
2. Were the workers making a 'rational economic decision' when they chose to work in such factories?

[1] F. Engels, *The Condition of the Working Class in England*, translated by W. O. Henderson and W. H. Chaloner (Basil Blackwell, 1971), pp. 199–200.
[2] These rules appeared in J. Leach, *Stubborn Facts from the Factories*, p. 13, quoted in Engels, op cit., pp. 200–1.
[3] Engels, op cit., pp. 201–2.

back on labour. The elasticity of demand is likely to increase as wages rise. When the elasticity has risen to unity, total incomes of workers will be at a maximum.

Unions may press for a higher wage rate still, even though it will mean that the firm pays out less in total wages. This is likely if unions are merely concerned to *maximise the incomes of remaining members* after **natural wastage**. Natural wastage is when people leave their job not because they have been made redundant, but because they have retired or moved to another job.

Firms and labour with market power (bilateral monopoly)

What happens when a union monopoly faces a monopsony employer? What will the wage rate be? What will the level of employment be? Unfortunately economic theory cannot give a precise answer to these questions. There is no 'equilibrium' level as such. Ultimately the wage rate and the level of employment will depend on the relative bargaining strengths and skills of unions and management.

Nevertheless, economic theory can make some contribution to predicting the outcome of negotiations. It can identify the limits within which the wage rate will be set. The lower limit will be that which a monopsonist would

DEFINITION

Natural wastage Where a firm wishing to reduce its workforce does so by not replacing those who leave or retire.

CASE STUDIES

THE RISE AND DECLINE OF THE LABOUR MOVEMENT?

Perhaps rather surprisingly, the origins of the labour movement do *not* lie within a socialist political movement or among unskilled workers, despite the fact that such workers would probably have had the most to gain from the market power that unions provided.

Instead, the early unions, or 'artisan societies' as they were known, were conservative in their views and had a membership based on skilled handicraft workers – the 'aristocracy of labour'. Their principal interest, like many professional associations today, was to protect their members' incomes by regulating the flow of labour: for example, by insisting that new workers undertook a lengthy apprenticeship.

Unionism among *unskilled* workers developed during the 1880s. Industrialisation had caused the nature of many jobs to change. Technical innovation had brought about a high degree of deskilling, and there was a massive shift of labour from agriculture to industry, expanding the potential union base. Coupled with this there was the capitalist system itself, which in its early years was openly exploitative, with low wages, long hours and poor working conditions. The new unions were thus quite different in character. Their memberships were larger; they were often politically left wing; and they were prepared to use strikes to gain their demands.

Hostility towards these unions from the legal system (strikes were regarded as 'criminal conspiracy') and also from employers meant that membership grew slowly at first. Only 11 per cent (1.6 million) of adult males in manual occupations were in an effective union in 1892. After the First World War, however, membership soared. By 1920, 45 per cent of the total labour force (8.3 million workers) were in trade unions.

But it was after the Second World War that the trade union movement in the UK really became established as a substantial economic and political force. This can be explained by three crucial trends:

- The growth in the public sector meant that government was itself becoming increasingly responsible for determining wages and conditions of service for many workers.
- In their attempt to control inflation in the 1960s and 1970s, governments sought to constrain wage increases ('incomes policy'). To be successful, this required acceptance by the trade union movement.
- The philosophy of many post-war governments was to govern by consent. Social contracts and pacts, and tripartite discussions between government, employers and unions, gave the union movement considerable influence over economic decision making.

Attempts to curb union power during the 1960s and 1970s, including the two Acts, 'In Place of Strife' (1969) and the Industrial Relations Act (1971), attracted fierce and widespread opposition, and as a result legislation was in many cases abandoned or modified. The trade union movement had by the late 1970s become very powerful with over 13 million members (see the diagram).

pay in the absence of a union. The upper limit will be where a firm would be driven into bankruptcy. Also economic theory can examine the consequences of various wage rates for employment.

Strange as it may seem, unions may well be in a stronger position to make substantial gains for their members when they are facing a powerful employer. There is often considerable scope for them to increase wages *without* this leading to a reduction in employment, or even for them to increase both the wage rate *and* employment. Figure 9.15 shows how this can be so.

Assume first that there is no union. The monopsonist will maximise profits by employing Q_1 workers at a wage of W_1. (Q_1 is where $MRP_L = MC_L$.)

What happens when a union is introduced into this situation? Wages will now be set by negotiation between unions and management. Once the wage rate has been agreed, the employer can no longer drive the wage rate down by employing fewer workers. If it tried to pay less than the agreed wage, it could well be faced by a strike, and thus have a zero supply of labour!

Similarly, if the employer decided to take on *more* workers, it would not have to *increase* the wage rate, as

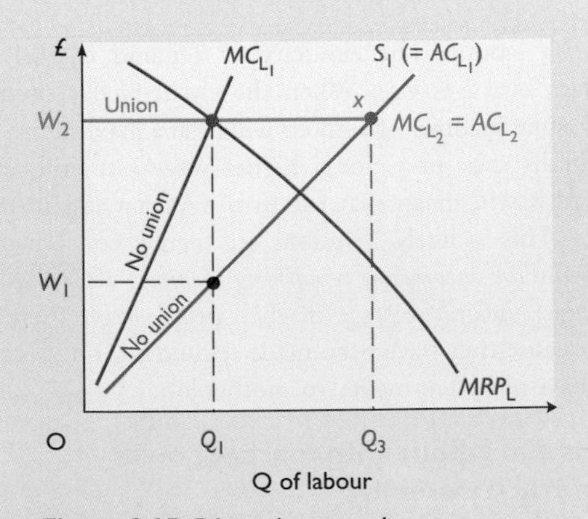

Figure 9.15 Bilateral monopoly

BOX 9.5

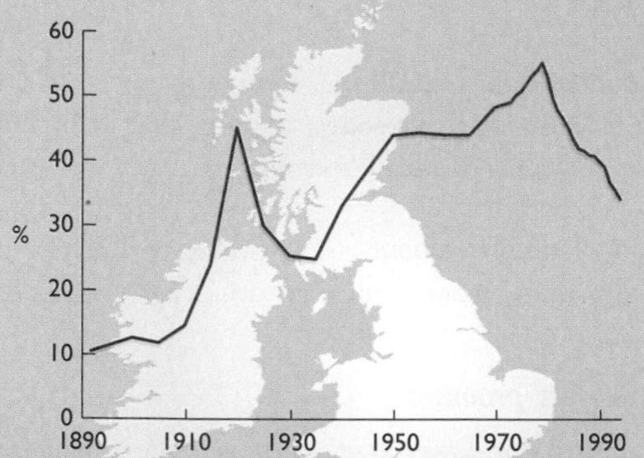

UK trade union membership as % of total employed plus unemployed

Sources: A. Marsh and B. Cox, *The Trade Union Movement in the UK 1992* (Malthouse Press); Department of Employment.

The election of the Conservative government in 1979 ushered in a new wave of trade union reform, eroding and removing many rights and privileges acquired by unions over the years. Trade union membership began to fall. Since 1979 it has fallen by some 5 million. This can be explained in part by the shift from a manufacturing to a service-based economy, a sector which is far less unionised than manufacturing. The main explanation, however, lies in the attitudes of new firms to union recognition, where in many cases a more aggressive management style and a highly competitive environment have made it virtually impossible for unions to gain bargaining rights.

With continued privatisation and the introduction of private-sector management practices, local pay bargaining and contracted-out services into many of the remaining parts of the public sector, trade unionism is still further under threat.

The future of the union movement is unclear. The creation of mega-unions is one possibility, as groups of unions merge in an attempt to retain some form of power and influence. For example, in 1993 a new union, UNISON, was created by an amalgamation of various public-sector unions. It has some 1.5 million members. Many unions have adopted a 'new realism', accepting single-union agreements and supporting flexible working practices and individualised pay packets based on performance. Some commentators have suggested that unions may become little more than advisers to individual employees on questions of law and rights, their influence over pay bargaining simply withering away. Unions are being forced to reconsider their role, however uncertain it may appear to be.

??

1. What professional associations can you identify that have adopted strategies similar to those of the early skilled-worker unions?
2. What factors, other than the ones identified above, could account for the decline in union membership in recent years?

long as the negotiated wage were above the free-market wage: as long as the wage rate were above that given by the supply curve S_1.

The effect of this is to give a new supply curve that is horizontal up to the point where it meets the original supply curve. For example, let us assume that the union succeeds in negotiating a wage rate of W_2 in Figure 9.15. The supply curve will be horizontal at this level to the left of point x. To the right of this point it will follow the original supply curve S_1, since to acquire more than Q_3 workers the employer would have to raise the wage rate above W_2.

If the supply curve is horizontal to the left of a point x at a level of W_2, so too will be the MC_L curve. The reason is simply that the extra cost to the employer of taking on an extra worker (up to Q_3) is merely the wage rate: no rise has to be given to existing employees. If MC_L is equal to the wage, the profit-maximising level of employment ($MC_L = MRP_L$) will now be where $W = MRP_L$. At a negotiated wage rate of W_2, the firm will therefore choose to employ Q_1 workers.

What this means is that the union can push the wage right up from W_1 to W_2 and the firm will still *want* to employ Q_1. In other words, a wage rise can be obtained *without* a reduction in employment.

?? If the negotiated wage rate were somewhere between W_1 and W_2, what would happen to employment?

The union could go further still. By threatening industrial action, it may be able to push the wage rate above W_2 and still insist that Q_1 workers are employed (i.e. no redundancies). The firm may be prepared to see profits drop right down to normal level rather than face a strike and risk losses. The absolute upper limit to wages will be that at which the firm is forced to close down.

Collective bargaining

In collective bargaining there are various threats or promises that unions and management can make. For these to be effective, the other side must believe that they will be carried out.

Union threats

Strikes. This is the union's ultimate weapon. Their effectiveness will depend on the number of workers involved; how crucial they are to the production process; the length of time the strike continues; and the ability of the firm to bypass the strike by drawing on stocks, using non-unionised labour or finding other techniques of production.

Picketing. **Picketing** is where union members gather at the entrance to a firm and attempt to dissuade workers from entering. Workers are often unwilling to cross picket lines, even if they are not directly involved in the dispute. In the case of **secondary picketing** the union pickets a firm not directly involved in the dispute. This was made illegal in the UK by the 1980 Employment Act.

Working to rule. This is where union members are instructed to stick to the letter of their job description and to refuse to take on any extra duties. The effect is to slow down production. Since union members continue to be paid, a union can continue with this type of action for much longer.

Non-cooperation. The union may refuse to co-operate in the introduction of new machines, new work practices and so on. The firm may be able to impose these changes on the workforce, but it would probably get better results with the goodwill of the union.

Union promises

In return for higher wages and for better working conditions, the union may offer a formal no-strike agreement, or an informal promise not to take industrial action; increased productivity; reductions in the workforce; or long-term deals over pay.

Employers' threats

Plant closure. This is the ultimate threat of an employer. It might be taken seriously by the unions if the firm can simply move its business to another plant which does not employ union members, as happened when the major newspapers in England progressively moved out of Fleet Street in the 1980s.

Lock-outs. This is where union members are temporarily laid off until they are prepared to agree to the firm's conditions.

Redundancies. Employers frequently use this threat to try to resist wage increases, arguing that at higher wage rates they cannot afford to employ so many workers.

Using non-union labour. The firm may threaten to bring in non-union labour unless the union agrees to its terms.

Employers' promises

In return for lower wage increases the firm may offer 'perks' such as productivity bonuses, profit-sharing schemes, better working conditions, more overtime, better holidays, security of employment, or a **closed shop**.

Industrial action imposes costs on both unions and firms. It is usually in both sides' interests, therefore, to settle by negotiation. Nevertheless to gain the maximum advantage, each side must persuade the other that it will carry out its threats if pushed.

The approach described so far has essentially been one of confrontation. The alternative is for both sides to concentrate on increasing the total net income of the firm by co-operating on ways to increase efficiency or the quality of the product. This approach is more likely when unions and management have built up an atmosphere of trust over time.

?? Recall the various strategies that rival oligopolists can adopt. What parallels are there in union and management strategies?

The outcome of negotiations

The outcome of negotiations will depend on a number of factors.

DEFINITIONS

Picketing Where people on strike gather at the entrance to the firm and attempt to dissuade workers or delivery vehicles from entering.

Secondary picketing Where workers picket a firm not directly involved in the dispute.

Closed shop Where a firm agrees to employ only union members.

Power

The greater the power of either side to pursue its objectives, the more likely it is to succeed. A *union's* power depends on the following:

- The financial reserves of the union.
- Its size and influence (both with other firms and over public opinion).
- The percentage of the labour force in the union.
- Support from other unions.
- National/local/industrial employment levels. The easier it is for union members to get jobs elsewhere, the less worried they will be by threats of redundancy.

A *firm's* power depends on the following:

- Its financial reserves.
- The willingness of banks or suppliers to extend credit.
- The size of the whole company relative to the part in dispute. A large multinational corporation, for example, may be able to use profits in one part of the organisation to subsidise the part that is making a loss because of the union action.
- Solidarity with other firms involved in the dispute.
- Its ability to substitute machines or non-union labour for the workers in dispute.

Attitudes

The determination of either side to win is crucial. The more solid the support from members and their families, the more likely the union is to succeed. Similarly, the tougher the management and the more determined it is not to give in, the more likely it is to succeed. Of course, if both sides are determined, the dispute can last a very long time, as did the miners' dispute over pit closures in 1985–6.

The union's membership

The wage settlement may be higher if the union represents only some of the workers. If it can secure a higher wage rate for its members, who may be **core workers**, non-members may well lose their jobs, or be replaced by part-time or temporary workers. The core workers can be seen as **insiders**. Their union(s) can prevent the unemployed – the **outsiders** – from competing wages down.

Scope for movement by the employer

When firms are operating in a competitive goods market, and where the wage demand is confined to that one firm only, its scope for giving wage increases is limited. If, however, the firm's rivals are *also* facing similar wage demands, there is more scope for granting them. This scope will depend on the industry-wide demand curve for labour (see Figure 9.14). The less elastic it is (i.e. the fewer the substitutes for the industry's product), the less will a wage rise be at the expense of employment: the more will the wage rise be simply passed on to the consumer in higher prices.

When the firm has market power in the goods market, its demand curve for the good and hence for labour will be relatively inelastic. It therefore has much more scope to grant wage increases.

Efficiency wages

When a firm is considering whether to concede to a union's pay demand, it cannot take marginal productivity as simply given. The wage rate paid may well affect how hard workers work. If the firm pays higher wages, workers may be better motivated; labour turnover may fall; and it may be easier to recruit well-qualified labour. The firm will thus offer a wage increase that balances increased wage costs against gains in productivity. The firm's **efficiency wage rate** will be above the market-clearing wage rate. Outsiders are unable to compete it down.

Bargaining skills

The more skilful the negotiators are on one side, the more likely they are to gain at the expense of the other.

Information

A lot of bargaining involves bluff and counter-bluff. The bargaining position of each side would be strengthened if it had accurate information about the power and motivation of the other.

The role of government

The government can influence the outcome of collective bargaining in a number of ways.

DEFINITIONS

Core workers Workers, normally with specific skills, who are employed on a permanent or long-term basis.

Insiders Those in employment who can use their privileged position (either as members of unions or because of specific skills) to secure pay rises despite an excess supply of labour (unemployment).

Outsiders Those out of work or employed on a casual, part-time or short-term basis, who have little or no power to influence wages or employment.

Efficiency wage rate The profit-maximising wage rate for the firm after taking into account the effects of wage rates on worker motivation, turnover and recruitment.

As provider of social security. The provision or withdrawal of social security benefits affects the ability of strikers to sustain a dispute.

As macroeconomic policy maker. Whatever policies the government adopts to control inflation, if negotiators believe that they will be successful in keeping general wage and price increases down, they will probably reduce the level of wage settlements in individual cases.

As employer. The government may take a tough line in resisting wage demands by government employees, hoping thereby to set an example to employers in the private sector.

As purchaser of supplies from private companies. The government could refuse to purchase supplies from firms which give in to 'excessive' wage demands.

As arbitrator. Past governments have attempted to mediate in disputes which they felt were damaging to the economy. More formally, the government can set up arbitration or conciliation machinery. For example, the Advisory Conciliation and Arbitration Service (ACAS) conciliates in over 1000 disputes each year. It also provides, on request by both sides, an arbitration service, where its findings will be binding.

As legislator. The government can pass laws that restrict the behaviour of employers or unions. It could pass laws that set minimum wages, or prevent discrimination against workers on various grounds. Similarly it could pass laws that curtail the power of unions. Since 1979 the Conservative government in the UK has passed the following Acts:

- 1980 Employment Act. This Act required unions to put closed-shop agreements to a secret ballot. New closed-shop agreements would have to be supported by at least 80 per cent of the workforce. It also severely limited unions' ability to take secondary action against a firm not directly involved in a dispute.
- 1982 Employment Act. This made political strikes, sympathy action and action against other non-unionised companies illegal. Lawful action was confined to that against workers' own direct employers, even to their own particular place of work.
- 1984 Trade Union Act. This made (secret) ballots of the membership mandatory for the operation of a political fund, the election of senior union officials, and strikes and other official industrial action.
- 1988 Employment Act. This made it unlawful for a firm to dismiss any employee for refusing to join a trade union. It also made it unlawful for a union to take industrial action in support of a closed shop, or to take disciplinary action against any member who refuses to join a strike.
- 1990 Employment Act. This made *all* secondary action unlawful. It also made it illegal for firms to deny employment on the grounds that an applicant does not belong to a union.
- 1992 Trade Union and Labour Relations (Consolidation) Act. This specified details for the conduct of union ballots and the regulation of unions' financial affairs. It also made it unlawful for employers to penalise workers for choosing to join or refusing to join a trade union.
- 1993 Trade Union Reform and Employment Rights Act. This effectively ended closed shops by giving employees the right to join any union. It required employers to gain workers' written permission before union dues can be deducted from pay packets. It also required union ballots to be postal.

These Acts have placed union restraint within civil rather than criminal law. This means that if a union is in breach of any of the laws, it will be subject to fines or sequestration of assets, rather than its officials or members being sent to prison. The government was anxious to avoid the creation of martyrs and a hardening of union attitudes.

Other labour market imperfections

The possession of power by unions and/or firms is not the only way in which real-world labour markets diverge from the perfectly competitive model:

- Workers or employers may have imperfect information.
- Wages may respond very slowly to changes in demand and supply, causing disequilibrium in labour markets to persist.
- Firms may not be profit maximisers. Likewise workers may not seek to maximise their 'worker surplus' – the excess of benefits from working (i.e. wages) over the disutility of working (displeasure in doing the job and lost leisure).

Some of the forms and effects of these imperfections are examined in the next three sections.

Imperfect information

In the real world, workers are unaware of many jobs that are available. They may well be willing to move jobs, but end up staying where they are due to ignorance. The effect of this ignorance is to decrease the elasticity of supply of labour. For firms wishing to take on extra labour, the less

CASE STUDIES BOX 9.6

THE 'JAPANISATION' OF EUROPEAN INDUSTRY

New working practices for old

The outstanding economic performance of the Japanese economy since the 1960s has been much envied and in more recent times its methods of production much copied. Japanese investment in Europe, North America and other parts of the world has introduced new working practices which many domestic manufacturers see as the model for the future. The 'Japanese model' of production contains a number of crucial elements:

- A commitment to a constantly improving quality. 'Total quality management' (TQM) involves all employees working towards continuously improving all aspects of quality, both of the finished product and of methods of production. This is achieved where possible through the active involvement of employees within team groups.
- A commitment to eliminate waste. According to the 'just-in-time' (JIT) principle, business should take delivery of just sufficient quantity of parts, at the right time and place. Buffer stocks are not carried, hence the whole system of production runs with little, if any, slack. The adoption of JIT, so far, has not been as extensive as TQM.
- The flexibility of labour. This can refer to flexibility over the tasks that a worker is capable of doing and can be required to do (functional flexibility). It can also refer to flexibility over the pattern of work – hours, shift patterns, days per week, etc. – that the employee must accept (numerical flexibility). Both forms of flexibility are seen as important to productivity.
- A belief in the superiority of team work. Collective effort is a vital element in Japanese working practices. A team could be responsible for the level and quality of its output, and its efficiency of production, or it could simply be a group of workers in which there is job rotation.

How far these practices have filtered through to UK and other European firms from their Japanese rivals is unclear. Recent evidence tends to conclude that, although many indigenous companies have gone some way towards adopting Japanese work practices, few have adopted the Japanese model completely. However, there has been some convergence between UK and Japanese methods, not least because of extensive reform of the trade union movement and the weakening of trade union power in recent years.

?? What are the advantages and disadvantages of Japanese work practices from the point of view of the worker?

the elasticity of supply, the higher the wages they will have to pay to attract a given number of extra workers.

Firms too suffer from imperfect information. They may be ignorant of what quality and quantity of labour is available. In other words, they may not know the position and shape of the labour supply curve. This makes it difficult for them to decide what wage rate to offer when recruiting labour.

Economists have developed **search theory** to explain how workers and firms will deal with this problem of ignorance. Workers will spend time searching for better jobs. This could be after quitting their previous job, or while currently in a job (e.g. by searching through the job advertisements in the local/national newspapers). Likewise employers will spend time searching for suitable labour. Maybe they will advertise and then spend time interviewing a number of applicants.

In both cases search is costly, both in time and effort and in money. If workers give up a job to look for a better one, they lose pay. Even if they do not give up their job, they still have to sacrifice leisure time in searching and perhaps spend money travelling to interviews. Thus rational workers/employers will weigh up the benefits of search (namely, a better job/quality of labour) against the costs of search.

They might decide at the outset that the costs outweigh the benefits. Workers in a good job might say, 'What's the point?' Firms might say, 'We'll make do with the labour we've got.'

If they do decide to search, how long should they carry on? If they perceive that the benefits of continuing searching exceed the costs, then they will carry on. If the costs are perceived to exceed the benefits, however, they will settle for what they can get.

The problem here is that the benefits of searching cannot be calculated in advance. It was because people were ignorant that they were searching in the first place. All they can do, then, is to use their 'judgement' about when to stop – a judgement based on the evidence they have accumulated so far and coloured by either optimism or pessimism.

DEFINITION

Search theory This examines people's behaviour under conditions of ignorance where it takes time to search for information.

What will be the effect of searching on the wage level? This is illustrated in Figure 9.16. This diagram has two curves. The first is the 'wage offered' curve. This shows that, as the period of search increases, the average worker will get better wage offers. This curve will gradually flatten out as the worker's search becomes complete. The top of the curve represents the maximum wage that this type of worker can receive. The second curve shows the wage rate that the worker would accept. As time progresses, and the costs of search increase, so the typical worker would settle at a lower and lower wage. This curve bottoms out as it approaches the minimum that the worker would accept under any circumstances.

As long as the wage offered is below the level acceptable, the worker will continue searching. The worker will stop searching at t_1, and settle for a wage of W_1.

This wage will be higher:

- The more optimistic workers are about finding a high-paid job. This will shift the W_a line up. It will thus also increase the average search time.
- The less the costs of search to workers. More readily available information on jobs, and better social security payments for those who have quit their job to search, are examples of things which reduce the costs of searching. This too will shift the W_a line up.

In both these cases, workers will be prepared to search longer and thus firms will be forced to pay a higher wage to get the required labour.

- The more pessimistic firms are about the difficulties in finding suitable labour. This will shift the W_o line up.
- The higher the costs of search to firms. This too will shift the W_o line up.

??

1. When you finish studying and start looking for a job (assuming you have not already got one), what factors will you take into account when deciding whether to accept a job offer or to continue looking? How will the level of unemployment affect your decision?
2. In what ways could the government reduce the problem of imperfect information?

Persistent disequilibrium

Apart from unions pushing wages above the equilibrium, there are other reasons why an imbalance of demand and supply may persist in a given labour market.

Wages set for a period of time. Typically when wage rates are set through a process of collective bargaining the agreement will last for a period of time – usually a year. But during the year the demand and supply curves of labour could shift, causing a disequilibrium that cannot be corrected until the next wage round.

Custom and practice. A firm may have agreed to a formula for setting various wage rates in its organisation. A higher grade of job may always get, say, 20 per cent more than a lower grade, even though changes in demand and supply may have made this differential no longer appropriate.

A given wage rate covering several types of labour. An employer may pay all its workers the same rate, even though there is a shortage of one type of labour and a surplus of another. For example, many schools cannot recruit maths teachers because they can only pay them the same rate as other teachers, despite the fact that maths teachers are in short supply.

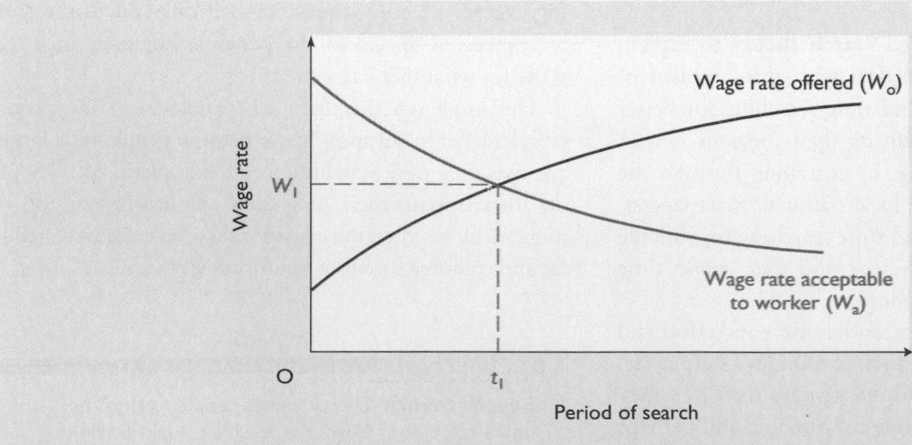

Figure 9.16 Job search by a particular type of labour (average)

National or industry-based wage agreements. When wages are set nationally or centrally within a large organisation they will not reflect the local supply and demand conditions. In some regions there may be a surplus of a given type of labour, whereas in other regions there may be a shortage.

Longer-term considerations. Firms are concerned to gain the goodwill and loyalty of their workforce. Without it long-term profits will fall. Wages that are frequently raised or lowered according to demand and supply, with some workers gaining and others losing, will hardly be seen as 'fair' wages by the workers and could be demotivating. Firms may find it in their long-term interests, therefore, to let disequilibrium wages persist for quite a long time.

Another example is where pay is related to age or length of service. Often younger workers, once they have gained some experience, are more efficient than older workers. Yet it is in the firm's interests to pay more to older workers in order to encourage workers to stay with the company. It gives them more of a 'career structure'.

As we have seen, wage rates that are based on considerations of worker motivation are known as *efficiency wage rates*. Firms are often willing to pay above the market-clearing level in order to attract, retain and motivate workers.

All these considerations mean that the labour market is not like the market for cattle or antiques. It is not like an auction, with wages fluctuating according to demand and supply. Wages tend to be relatively 'sticky'.

Non-maximising behaviour

Not all employers are ruthless profit maximisers. The owners of some small businesses may treat their employees more as family members than as 'factors of production'. They may pay them better wages and give them better conditions of work than they would if they were purely concerned to make money. Large companies too may not squeeze the maximum profit from their workers. Where there is a separation between the ownership and control of a company, profits may take a second place to other goals that interest managers (see Chapter 8). Managers may prefer an 'easy life'. Paying good wages and keeping a contented workforce may give them that easy life. Of course, it could be argued that in some cases keeping a contented workforce is a way of improving productivity, and thus is really only a way of increasing long-run profits.

Not all workers are 'rational economic maximisers' either, carefully weighing up the costs and benefits of each job. Workers may give little thought to such issues, and may simply stay put in a job through 'sheer inertia'. This has the effect of reducing the elasticity of supply of labour, and can therefore increase inequality. If workers are not prepared to leave low-paid jobs, the pay will remain low, and in relative terms will become lower.

Discrimination

This can be another major factor in determining wages. Discrimination can take many forms: it can be by race, sex, age, class, dress, etc.; it can occur in many different aspects of society. This section is concerned with **economic discrimination**. This is defined as a situation where otherwise identical workers receive different pay for doing the same job, or are given different chances of employment or promotion.

Take the case of racial discrimination by employers. Figure 9.17 illustrates the wages and employment of both black and white workers by a firm with monopsony power which practises racial discrimination against black workers. Let us assume that there is no difference in the productivity of black and white workers. Let us also assume for simplicity that there is an equal number of black workers and white workers available at any given wage rate. Finally let us assume that there are no laws to prevent the firm discriminating in terms of either wages or employment.

Figure 9.17(a) shows the *MC* and *MRP* curves for black workers. If there were no discrimination, employment of black workers would be at Q_{B_1}, where $MRP_B = MC_B$. The wage rate paid to black workers would be W_{B_1}.

Figure 9.17(b) shows the position for white workers. Again, if there were no discrimination, Q_{W_1} white workers would be employed at a wage of W_{W_1}: the same wage as that of black workers. (Note that in each case the *MRP* curve is drawn on the assumption that the number of workers employed from the other racial group is constant.)

If the firm now discriminates against black workers, it will employ workers along a lower curve, $MRP_B - x$ (where x can be seen as the discriminatory factor). Employment of black workers will thus be at the lower level of Q_{B_2} and the wage they receive will be at the lower level of W_{B_2}.

How will discrimination against black workers affect wages and employment of white workers? Let us consider two cases.

In the first case assume that the employer practises economic discrimination purely in the negative sense: i.e. it discriminates against black workers but employs white workers on profit-maximising principles. Thus white

DEFINITION

Economic discrimination Where workers of identical *ability* are paid different wages or are otherwise discriminated against because of race, age, sex, etc.

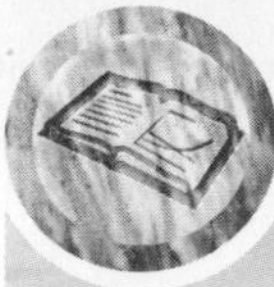

EXPLORING THE THEORY — BOX 9.7

HOW USEFUL IS MARGINAL PRODUCTIVITY THEORY?

Reality or the fantasy world of economists?

The marginal productivity theory of income distribution has come in for a lot of criticisms. Are they justified?

To start with, you cannot criticise something unless you know precisely what it is you are criticising. Marginal productivity theory has been criticised for assuming perfect competition. It doesn't!

Marginal productivity theory merely states that to maximise profits an employer will employ workers up to the point where the worker's marginal cost equals the extra revenue added by that worker: $MC_L = MRP_L$. This applies equally under perfect competition, monopoly and monopsony.

What it does say is that, if there is perfect competition, then the worker's *wage* will equal MRP_L. It certainly does not say that there will always be perfect competition, or that $W = MRP_L$ in other market structures.

A second criticism is that employers simply do not behave in this 'marginal way', weighing up each additional worker's costs and revenues for the firm. There are three possible reasons for this.

Ignorance of the theory of profit maximisation

The employer may use some rule of thumb, but nevertheless is attempting to maximise profits.

This is only a criticism of the theory if the theory is supposed to describe how employers actually behave. It does not. It merely states that, if firms are attempting to maximise profits, they will in fact be equating MC_L and MRP_L, whether they realise it or not!

A worker's marginal productivity cannot be calculated

When workers are part of a team, it is not usually possible to separate out the contribution to output of each individual. What is the marginal productivity of a cleaner, a porter, a secretary, a security guard, or even a member of a production line? Similarly, it may not be possible to separate the contribution of workers from that of their tools. A lathe operator is useless without a lathe, as is a lathe without a lathe operator.

This is a more fundamental criticism. Nevertheless it is possible to amend the theory to take this into account. First, an employer can look at the composition of the team, or the partnership of worker and tools, and decide whether any reorganisations or alternative production methods will increase the firm's profitability (i.e. increase revenue more than costs). Second, the employer can decide whether to expand or contract the overall size of the team, or the number of workers plus machines. Here the whole team or the worker plus machine is the 'factor of production' whose marginal productivity must be weighed against its costs.

Firms are not always profit maximisers

This is only a criticism if the theory states that firms are. As long as the theory is merely used to describe what would happen *if* firms maximised profits, there is no problem.

This criticism, then, is really one of how the theory is used. And even if it is used to predict what will actually happen in the real world, it is still relatively accurate in the large number of cases where firms' behaviour only slightly diverges from profit maximising. It is clearly wrong in other cases.

A final criticism is the moral one. If economists focus their attention exclusively on how to maximise profits, it might be concluded that they are putting their seal of approval on this sort of behaviour. Of course, economists will respond by saying that they are doing no such thing: they are confining themselves to positive economics. Nevertheless the criticism has some force. What an economist chooses to study is in part a normative decision.

?? Do any of the following contradict marginal productivity theory: (a) wage scales related to length of service (incremental scales); (b) *nationally* negotiated wage rates; (c) discrimination; (d) firms taking the lead from other firms in determining this year's pay increase?

workers would be employed up to that point where their *MC* equals their *MRP*. But the fact that fewer black workers are now being employed will mean that for any given quantity of white workers there will be fewer workers employed in total, and therefore, the *MRP* of white workers will have increased. In Figure 9.17(b) the white workers' *MRP* curve has shifted to MRP_{W_2}. This has the effect of raising employment of white workers to Q_{W_2} and the wage rate to W_{W_2}.

Firms may, however, also practise economic discrimination *in favour* of certain groups. Figure 9.17(b) also illustrates this second case, where the employer practises economic discrimination in favour of white workers. Here the firm will employ workers along a higher curve, $MRP_{W_2} + y$, where y is the discriminatory factor. The effect is further to increase the wage rate and level of employment of white workers, to W_{W_3} and Q_{W_3} respectively.

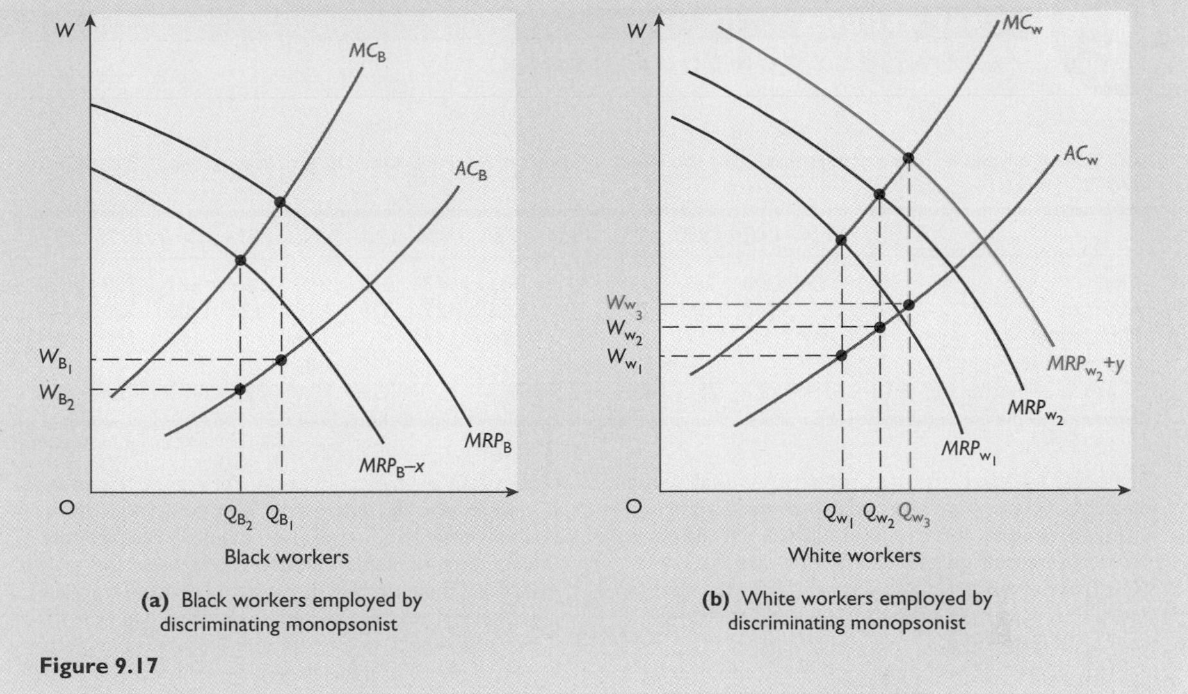

(a) Black workers employed by discriminating monopsonist

(b) White workers employed by discriminating monopsonist

Figure 9.17

> **??** What effect will the discrimination by the firm have on the wages and employment of black workers in other firms in the area if (a) these other firms discriminate against black workers; (b) they do not discriminate?

If the government now insists on equal pay for equal work, then employers which discriminate will respond by further cutting back on black workers. The answer to *this* problem would seem to be for the government to pass laws that insist not only that black workers be paid the same as white for doing the same job, but also that they be treated equally when applying for jobs. The problem here is that an employer which wants to continue discrimination can always claim that the black applicants were less well qualified than the white applicant who got the job. Such laws are, therefore, difficult to enforce.

The type of discrimination considered so far can be seen as 'irrational' if the firm wants to maximise profits. After all, to produce a given amount of output it would be paying out more in wages to employ white workers than black workers. In a competitive market environment such firms may be forced to end discrimination simply to survive the competition from non-discriminating rivals. If, however, the firm has market power, it will probably be making sufficient profits to allow it to continue discriminating. The main pressure here to end discrimination is likely to come from shareholders, unions, customers or race relations organisations.

Not all cases of discrimination result in lower profits, however. A firm may agree not to employ black workers because of pressure from racist white workers. If it ignores this pressure, it might face industrial relations problems and a resulting loss of profits. Discrimination in this case could be part of a profit-maximising behaviour (behaviour, albeit, which condones other people's prejudices).

Other examples of non-economic discrimination stem from unequal educational opportunities. If the educational system discriminates against black children, they are likely to end up with poorer qualifications. They have less **human capital** invested in them. Under these circumstances employers, preferring to employ the best-qualified applicants, are likely to choose white people. This is particularly so in the more highly paid jobs that require a higher level of educational attainment. Tackling this problem at source means tackling weaknesses in the education system or problems of inner-city deprivation. Nevertheless there may still be a benefit to be gained from passing laws that tackle more than just pure economic discrimination. For example, firms could be required to employ a minimum quota of black people. This at least would help to guard against any prejudices of employers against the ability of black workers.

DEFINITION

Human capital The qualifications, skills and expertise that contribute to a worker's productivity.

CASE STUDIES

EQUAL PAY FOR EQUAL WORK!

(a) Average gross hourly earnings, excluding the effects of overtime, for full-time UK employees, aged 18 and over, 1970–97 (pence per hour)

	1970	1974	1978	1980	1982	1984	1986	1988	1990	1992	1994	1995	1996	1997
Men	67	105	200	281	355	417	482	573	689	810	865	887	939	982
Women	42	71	148	206	262	306	358	429	528	638	688	708	750	788
Differential	25	34	52	74	93	111	124	144	161	172	177	179	189	194
Women's earnings as a % of men's	63.1	67.4	73.9	73.5	73.9	73.5	74.3	75.0	76.6	78.8	79.5	79.8	79.9	80.2

Source: *New Earnings Survey* (ONS).

One of the key characteristics shown in table (a) is that female gross hourly earnings relative to male gross hourly earnings increased substantially during the early 1970s. Having peaked at around 74 per cent in the late 1970s, they remained at about that level for the next ten years. They then rose again towards the 80 per cent mark by the late 1990s.

The inequality between male and female earnings can in part be explained by the fact that men and women are occupationally segregated. Seeing that women predominate in poorly paid occupations, the difference in earnings is somewhat to be expected. But if you consider table (b), you can see that quite substantial earnings differentials persist *within* particular occupations.

??

1. If we were to look at weekly rather than hourly pay and included the effects of overtime, what do you think would happen to the pay differentials in table (a)?
2. In table (b), which of the occupations have a largely female workforce?

So why has this inequality persisted? There are a number of possible reasons:

- The marginal productivity of labour in typically female occupations may be lower than in typically male occupations. This may in part be due to simple questions of physical strength. Very often, however, it is due to the fact that women tend to work in more labour-intensive occupations. If there is less capital equipment per female worker than there is per male worker, then it would be expected that the marginal product of a woman would be less than that of a man.
- Women may on average undertake less training than men. If, therefore, the resulting level of skills obtained by women is less than that obtained by men, women will have a lower marginal productivity.

There are various reasons for differences in training and qualifications. The educational system may favour boys rather than girls. Even if this is not deliberate policy, the attitudes of parents, teachers and pupils may be such as to give more encouragement to boys to think of qualifications for a future career. Employers are also more willing to invest money in training men, fearing that women may leave after a short time to have children.

- Women tend to be less geographically mobile than men. If social norms are such that the man's job is seen as somehow more 'important' than the woman's, then a couple will often move if necessary for the man to get promotion. The woman, however, will have to settle for whatever job she can get in the same locality as her partner.
- A smaller proportion of women workers are members of unions than men. Even when they are

Conclusions: Who are the poor? Who are the rich?

To the list we made at the end of section 9.2 we can now add the following factors which will tend to make people poor:

- Lack of economic power, not belonging to a union or belonging to a union with only weak bargaining power.
- Working for firms which operate in a highly competitive goods market.
- Ignorance of better job opportunities.
- Lack of will to search for a better job.
- Discrimination against them by employers or fellow workers.

Thus many people of Asian origin, especially women, working in the garment industry in back-street 'sweatshops' in London and other cities earn pitifully low wages.

Conversely, belonging to a powerful union, working for a profitable employer which nevertheless is not a ruthless profit maximiser, being aware of new job opportunities and having the 'get up and go' to apply for better jobs, and being white, male and middle class are all factors that help to contribute to people earning high wages.

BOX 9.8

members of unions, these are often in jobs where unions are weak (e.g. clothing industry workers, shop assistants and secretaries).

- Part-time workers (mainly women) have less bargaining power, less influence and less chance of obtaining promotion.
- Custom and practice. Despite equal pay legislation many jobs done wholly or mainly by women continue to be low paid, irrespective of questions of productivity.
- Prejudice. Some employers may prefer to give senior posts to men on grounds purely of sexual prejudice.

This is very difficult to legislate against when the employer can simply claim that the 'better' person was given the job.

??

1. If employers were forced to give genuinely equal pay for equal work, how would this affect the employment of women and men? What would determine the magnitude of these effects?
2. What measures could a government introduce to increase the number of women getting higher-paid jobs?

(b) Average gross hourly earnings, excluding the effects of overtime, for selected occupations, full-time UK employees on adult rates, 1997.

Occupation	Men (£ per hour)	Women (£ per hour)	Women's earnings as a % of men's
Nurses	9.82	9.42	95.9
Social workers	10.32	9.71	94.1
Police officers (below sergeant)	12.29	11.25	91.5
Secondary school teachers	15.73	14.17	90.1
Bar staff	4.36	3.87	88.8
Chefs/cooks	5.80	5.00	86.2
Laboratory technicians	9.33	7.95	85.2
Sales assistants	5.39	4.58	85.0
Medical practitioners	21.80	17.85	81.9
Solicitors	21.50	15.22	70.8
Assemblers and lineworkers	7.22	5.10	70.6
Computer operators	8.53	6.35	74.4
Personnel managers	18.00	13.40	74.4
All occupations	9.82	7.88	80.2
Average *gross weekly* pay (incl. overtime)	403.70	297.20	72.7
Average weekly hours worked (incl. overtime)	41.8	37.6	
Average weekly overtime	3.2	0.9	

Source: *New Earnings Survey* (ONS).

SECTION SUMMARY

1. If firms have market power in the goods market, they will tend to produce a lower ouput and hence employ fewer workers. They will maximise profits at the level of employment where the marginal revenue product of labour ($MRP_L = MPP_L \times MR$) is equal to the wage rate.
2. If a firm is a monopsony employer, it will employ workers to the point where $MRP_L = MC_L$. Since the wage is below MC_L, the monopsonist, other things being equal, will employ fewer workers at a lower wage than would be employed in a perfectly competitive labour market.
3. If a union has monopoly power, its power to raise wages will be limited if the employer operates under perfect or monopolistic competition in the goods market. A rise in wages will force the employer to cut back on employment.

continued

CASE STUDIES

FLEXIBLE LABOUR MARKETS AND THE FLEXIBLE FIRM

The last two decades have seen sweeping changes in the ways that firms organise their workforce. Two world recessions combined with rapid changes in technology have led many firms to question the wisdom of appointing workers on a permanent basis to specific jobs. Instead, they want to have the greatest flexibility possible to respond to new situations. If demand falls, they want to be able to 'shed' labour without facing large redundancy costs. If demand rises, they want rapid access to additional labour supplies. If technology changes (say, with the introduction of new computerised processes), they want to have the flexibility to move workers around, or to take on new workers in some areas and lose workers in others.

What many firms seek, therefore, is flexibility in employing and allocating labour. What countries are experiencing is an increasingly flexible labour market, as workers and employment agencies respond to the new 'flexible firm'.

There are three main types of flexibility in the use of labour:

- **Functional flexibility**. This is where an employer is able to transfer labour between different tasks within the production process. It contrasts with traditional forms of organisation where people were employed to do a specific job, and then stuck to it. A functionally flexible labour force will tend to be multiskilled and relatively highly trained.
- **Numerical flexibility**. This is where the firm is able to adjust the size and composition of its workforce according to changing market conditions.

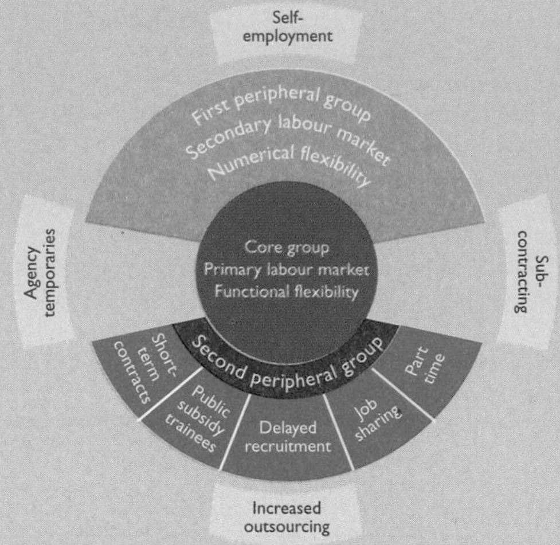

The flexible firm
Source: Institute of Manpower Studies (1984).

To achieve this, the firm is likely to employ a large proportion of its labour on a part-time or casual basis, or even sub-contract out specialist requirements, rather than employing such labour skills itself.

- **Financial flexibility**. This is where the firm has flexibility in its wage costs. In large part it is a result of functional and numerical flexibility. Financial flexibility

4. In a situation of bilateral monopoly (where a monopoly union faces a monopsony employer) the union may have considerable scope to raise wages above the monopsony level, without the employer wishing to reduce the level of employment. There is no unique equilibrium wage. The wage will depend on the outcome of a process of collective bargaining between union and management.
5. Each side can make various threats or promises. A union can threaten strikes or other forms of industrial action such as working to rule. On the other hand, it can offer such things as no strikes, increased productivity, or reductions in the workforce. Management can threaten redundancies, lock-outs, plant closures, or taking on non-union labour. Alternatively, it can offer better working conditions, shorter hours, longer holidays, profit-sharing schemes, job security, etc.
6. The outcome of the bargaining will depend on the relative power of both sides, their attitudes, the scope for movement on the part of the employer, the information each side has about the other, and their bargaining skills. The outcome also depends on the legal framework within which the negotiations take place.
7. Power is not the only factor that makes actual wage determination different from the perfectly competitive model. Firms and workers may have imperfect knowledge of the labour market. Each side will probably have to go through a search procedure. The equilibrium wage will depend on how long and how hard each side is prepared to search.
8. Labour markets do not adjust instantly to changes in demand or supply: disequilibrium can persist. The reasons are that wages are changed only at intervals (typically annually); wages may be set by

continued

BOX 9.9

can be achieved by rewarding individual effort and productivity rather than paying a given rate for a particular job. Such rates of pay are increasingly negotiated at the local level rather than being nationally set. The result is not only a widening of pay differentials between skilled and unskilled workers, but also growing differentials in pay between workers within the same industry but in different parts of the country.

The diagram shows how these three forms of flexibility are reflected in the organisation of a **flexible firm**, an organisation quite different from that of the traditional firm. The most significant difference is that the labour force is segmented. The core group, drawn from the **primary labour market**, will be composed of *functionally* flexible workers, who have relatively secure employment and are generally on full-time permanent contracts. Such workers will be relatively well paid and receive wages reflecting their scarce skills.

The periphery, drawn from the **secondary labour market**, is more fragmented than the core, and can be sub-divided into a first and a second peripheral group. The first peripheral group is composed of workers with a lower level of skill than those in the core, skills that tend to be general rather than firm specific. Thus workers in the first peripheral group can usually be drawn from the external labour market. Such workers may be employed on full-time contracts, but they will generally face less secure employment than those workers in the core.

The business gains a greater level of numerical flexibility by drawing labour from the second peripheral group. Here workers are employed on a variety of short-term, part-time contracts. Workers in the second peripheral group have little job security.

As well as being able to supplement the level of labour in the first peripheral group, the second periphery can also provide high-level specialist skills that supplement the core. In this instance the business can sub-contract or hire self-employed labour, minimising its commitment to such workers. The business thereby gains both functional and numerical flexibility simultaneously.

How far is the flexible firm model being adopted by business in the UK?

Various government measures to reduce 'labour market rigidities' have certainly encouraged firms to move in this direction. These measures include reductions in the power of trade unions and the removal of certain worker rights, such as those relating to unfair dismissal. In response, businesses have attempted to enhance numerical flexibility by reducing job demarcations, introducing non-standard job forms, particularly relating to part-time work, and adopting more flexible payment systems. However, it is unclear as to how far such moves represent a co-ordinated attempt to adopt the flexible firm model.

??

1. Is a flexible firm more likely or less likely to employ workers up to the point where their $MRP = MC_L$?
2. How is the advent of flexible firms likely to alter the gender balance of employment and unemployment?

custom and practice; a given wage rate may cover several types of labour; agreements may be national or industry-wide.

9. Firms may not be profit maximisers and as such may be prepared to continue employing workers beyond the profit-maximising level and paying above the profit-maximising wage.
10. Firms may exercise discrimination (by race, sex, age, etc.) in their employment policy. By discriminating against a particular group, an employer with market power can drive down the wages of the members of that group. Unless firms are forced not to discriminate, equal pay legislation may well lead to a reduction in the employment of members of groups that are discriminated against.

DEFINITIONS

Functional flexibility Where employers can switch workers from job to job as requirements change.

Numerical flexibility Where employers can change the size of their workforce as their labour requirements change.

Financial flexibility Where employers can vary their wage costs by changing the composition of their workforce or the terms on which workers are employed.

Flexible firm A firm that has the flexibility to respond to changing market conditions by changing the composition of its workforce.

Primary labour market The market for permanent full-time core workers.

Secondary labour market The market for peripheral workers, usually employed on a temporary or part-time basis, or a less secure 'permanent' basis.

9.4

Land and capital

The non-human factors of production

In this final section of the chapter we consider the market for *other* factors of production. These can be divided into two broad groups:

- *Land.* This includes all those productive resources supplied by nature: in other words, not only land itself, but also all natural resources.
- *Capital.* This includes all manufactured products that are used to produce goods and services. Thus capital includes such diverse items as a blast furnace, a bus, a cinema projector, a computer, a factory building and a screwdriver. However, it does not include *paper* assets, such as money or shares. These are merely claims on physical assets.

One problem with this classification is that some non-human factors are partly land and partly capital. For example, raw materials when they are delivered to factories have been extracted, processed and transported. They cannot be classified as pure land. Even land itself contains elements of capital if it has been improved from its natural state – say, by levelling or drainage. Nevertheless, the distinction is still useful. It helps to focus on the different properties that different factors can have.

Factor prices versus the price of factor services

A feature of most non-human factors is that they last a period of time. A machine may last 10 years; a coal mine may last 50 years before it is exhausted; farmland will last for ever if properly looked after. We must therefore distinguish between the income the owner will get from *selling* the factor and that which the owner will get from *using* it or *hiring* it out:

- The income from selling the factor is the factor's *price.* It is a once-and-for-all payment. Thus a machine might sell for £10 000, or a hectare of land for £20 000.
- The income gained from using a factor is its *return*, and the income gained from hiring a factor out is its *rental.* This income represents the value or price of the factor's *services*, expressed per period of time. Thus a machine might earn the firm £1000 per year. A hectare of land might earn £2000 rent per year for a landlord.

Obviously the price of a factor will be linked to the value of its services. The price that a hectare of land will fetch if sold will depend on the return or rent that can be earned on that land. If it is highly productive farmland, it will sell for a higher price than a piece of scrubby moorland.

?? When we were looking at wages, were we talking about the price of labour or the price of labour services? Is this distinction between the price of a factor and the price of factor services a useful one in the case of labour? Was it in Roman times?

The profit-maximising employment of land and capital

On the demand side, the same rules apply for land and capital as for labour, if a firm wishes to maximise profits. Namely, it should demand factors up to the point where the marginal cost of the factor equals its marginal revenue product: $MC_f = MRP_f$. This same rule applies whether the firm is buying the factor outright, or merely renting it.

Figure 9.18 illustrates the two cases of perfect competition and monopsony. In both diagrams the *MRP* curve slopes downwards. This is another illustration of the law of diminishing returns, but this time applied to land or capital. For example, if a farmer increases the amount of land farmed while *holding other factors constant*, diminishing returns to land will occur. If the same number of farm workers and the same amount of agricultural machinery and fertilisers are used but on a larger area, then returns per hectare will fall.

In diagram (a) the firm is a price taker. The factor price is given at P_{f_1}. Profits are maximised at Q_{f_1} where $MRP_f = P_f$ (since $P_f = MC_f$).

In diagram (b) the firm has monopsony power. The factor price will vary, therefore, with the amount that the firm uses. The firm will again use factors to the point where $MRP_f = MC_f$. In this case it will mean using Q_{f_2} at a price of P_{f_2}.

What is the difference between buying a factor and renting it? Although the $MRP_f = MC_f$ rule remains the same, there are differences. As far as buying the factors is concerned, the MC_f is the extra outlay for the firm in *purchasing* one more unit of the factor; and the MRP_f is all the revenue produced by that factor over its *whole life* (but measured in terms of what this is worth when purchased: see page 272). In the case of renting, MC_f is the extra outlay for the firm in rent *per period*, while MRP_f is the extra revenue earned from it *per period.*

The demand for capital services

What we are talking about in this section is the hiring of capital equipment for a period of time (as opposed to buying it outright). The analysis is virtually identical to that

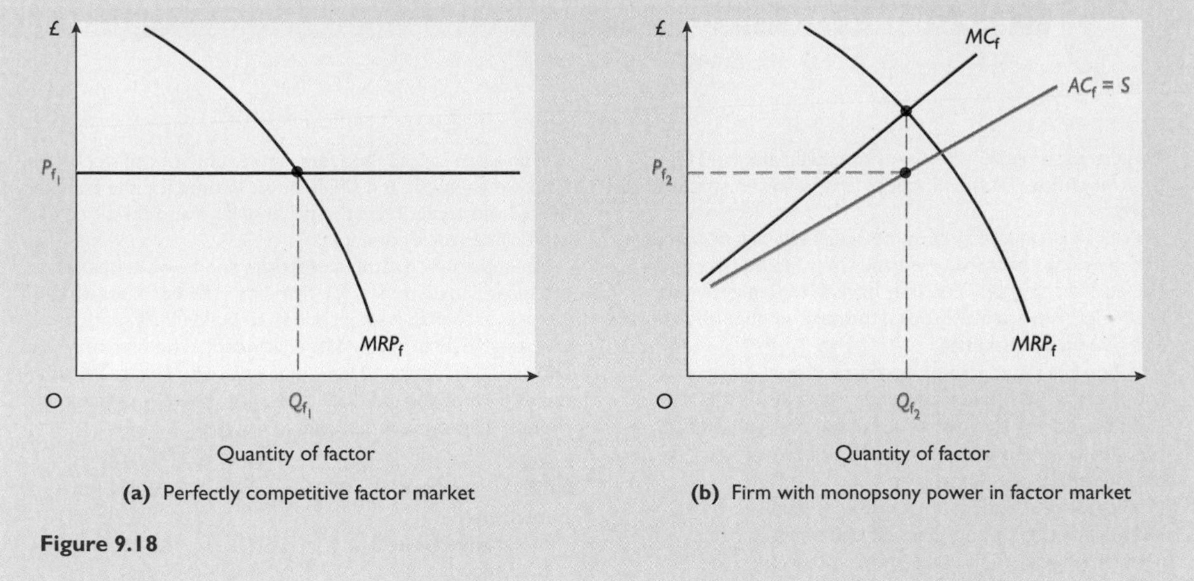

(a) Perfectly competitive factor market

(b) Firm with monopsony power in factor market

Figure 9.18

of the demand for labour. As with labour we can distinguish between an individual firm's demand and the whole market demand.

Individual firm's demand

Take the case of a small painting and decorating firm thinking of hiring some scaffolding in order to complete a job. It could possibly use ladders, but the job would take longer to complete. If it hires the scaffolding for one day, it can perhaps shorten the job by, say, two or three days. If it hires it for a second day, it can perhaps save another one or two days. Hiring it additional days may save extra still. But diminishing returns are occurring: the longer the scaffolding is up, the less intensively it will be used, and the less additional time it will save. Perhaps for some of the time it will be used when ladders could have been used equally easily.

The time saved allows the firm to take on extra work. Thus each extra day the scaffolding is hired gives the firm extra revenue. This is the scaffolding's marginal revenue product of capital (MRP_K). Diminishing returns mean that it has the normal downward-sloping shape (see Figure 9.19). The firm is assumed to be under perfect competition and thus has no power to influence the daily rental charge (R_K). It will maximise profits by hiring the scaffolding for 10 days.

If the firm has monopsony power, the diagram will look like Figure 9.18(b). Most firms that hire capital rather than buying it outright will, however, be small firms, and thus closer to perfect competition.

Market demand

The market demand for capital services is derived in exactly the same way as the market demand for labour (see Figure 9.10 on page 247). It is the horizontal sum of the MRP_K curves of the individual firms, corrected for the fact that increased use of capital will increase output, drive down the price of the good and hence reduce *MRP*. This means that the market demand curve for capital is steeper than the horizontal sum of the demand curves (MRP_K) of all the firms in the market.

?? Under what circumstances would the market demand for renting a type of capital equipment be (a) elastic; (b) inelastic? (Clue: turn back to page 248 and see what determines the elasticity of demand for labour.)

The supply of capital services

It is necessary to distinguish (a) the supply *to* a single firm, (b) the supply *by* a single firm and (c) the market supply.

Supply to a single firm

The small firm renting capital equipment is probably a price taker. If so, it faces a horizontal supply curve at the going rental rate, R_K in Figure 9.19. If, however, it has monopsony power, it will face an upward-sloping supply curve as in Figure 9.18(b).

Supply by a single firm

Again, the firm is likely to be a price taker. It has to accept the going rental rate established in the market. The theory

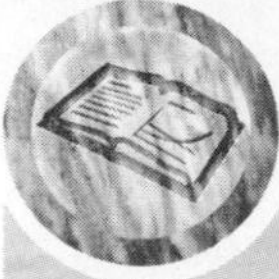

EXPLORING THE THEORY — BOX 9.10

STOCKS AND FLOWS

The discussion of the rewards to capital and land leads to a very important distinction: that between stocks and flows.

A *stock* is a quantity of something held. A landowner may own 200 hectares. A farmer may have a barn with 500 tonnes of grain. You may have £1000 in a savings account. These are all stocks: they are all quantities held at a given point in time.

A *flow* is an increase or decrease in quantity over a specified period. The landowner may buy another 10 hectares during the year. The farmer may use 10 tonnes of grain from the barn each week as animal feed. You may save £10 per month.

Wages, rent and interest are all rewards to *flows*. Wages are the amount paid for the services of a person's labour for a week or month. Rent is the amount paid per period of time to use the services of land. Likewise interest is the reward paid to people per year for the use of their money.

If an asset is sold, its value is the value of the *stock*. It is a simple payment at a single point in time for the transfer of a whole asset. Thus the price of land and the price of capital are stock concepts.

An important example of stocks and flows arises with capital and investment. If a firm has 100 machines, that is a stock of capital. It may choose to build up its stock by investing. Investment is a flow concept. The firm may choose to invest in 10 new machines each year. This may not add 10 to the stock of machines, however, as some may be wearing out (a negative flow).

?? Which of the following are stocks and which are flows?
(a) Unemployment.
(b) Redundancies.
(c) Profits.
(d) A firm's stock market valuation.
(e) The value of property after a period of inflation.

here has a lot in common with perfect competition in the goods market: the supply curve is the firm's *MC* curve, only here the *MC* is the extra cost of supplying one more unit of capital equipment for rent over a given time period.

The problem with working out the marginal cost of renting out capital equipment is that the piece of equipment probably cost a lot to buy in the first place, but lasts a long time. How then are these large costs to be apportioned to each new rental? The answer is that it depends on the time period under consideration.

The short run. In the short run the hire company is not buying any new equipment: it is simply hiring out its existing stock of equipment. In the case of our scaffolding hire firm, the marginal costs of doing this will be as follows:

- Depreciation. Scaffolding has second-hand value. Each time the scaffolding is hired out it deteriorates, and thus its second-hand value falls. This loss in value is called 'depreciation'.
- Maintenance and handling. When equipment is hired out it can get damaged and thus incur repair costs. The equipment might need servicing. Also hiring out equipment involves labour time (e.g. in the office) and possibly transport costs.

These marginal costs are likely to be relatively constant. In other words, for each extra day a piece of equipment is hired out, the company will incur the same additional costs. This gives the supply curve shown in Figure 9.20.

Q_{max} shows the total supply of equipment available for renting over a given time period. R_1 is the marginal cost per period of hiring it out. Thus up to Q_{max} the supply curve is infinitely elastic, whereas at Q_{max} it becomes totally inelastic, since there is no more equipment to hire out. Provided the firm can get a rental above R_1, it will be worth hiring out all its equipment. If, however, the market rental is below R_1, it will be worth the firm selling off its equipment second hand.

?? Assume now that the firm has monopoly power in hiring out equipment, and thus faces a downward-sloping demand curve. Draw in two such demand curves on a diagram like Figure 9.20, one crossing the *MC* curve in the horizontal section, and one in the vertical section. How much will the firm supply in each case and at what price? (You will need to draw in *MR* curves too.) Is the *MC* curve still the supply curve?

The long run. In the long run the hire company will consider purchasing additional equipment. What is the marginal cost of this? There are three elements:

- The opportunity cost of purchasing the equipment. This is the interest that the firm sacrifices by not saving the money in a bank or investing it elsewhere.

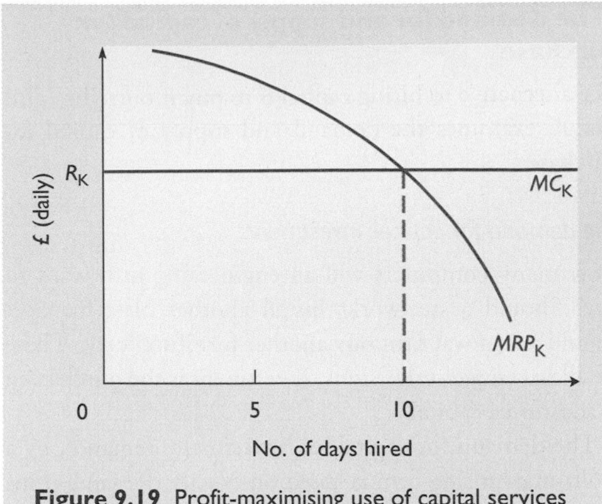

Figure 9.19 Profit-maximising use of capital services by perfectly competitive firm

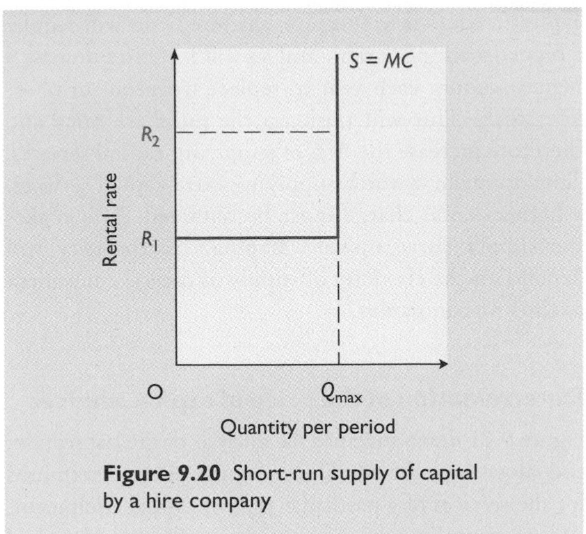

Figure 9.20 Short-run supply of capital by a hire company

- Depreciation. This is the loss in value of the equipment over its life: the difference between its purchase price and its scrap value.
- Maintenance and handling costs. These are the total ongoing costs over the life of the equipment.

These three elements then have to be expressed as a rate *per period*, so that *MC* can be compared with the rent charged to the customer (*MR*). An illustration will make this clearer. Let us assume the following:

- A piece of capital equipment costs £10 000 to purchase. The current rate of interest that the firm could earn by investing elsewhere is 10 per cent per year (i.e. £1000). The opportunity cost of purchasing the equipment is thus £1000 per year.
- The equipment lasts 20 years and has no scrap value at the end. It depreciates at a steady rate of £500 per year.
- Maintenance and handling costs are also £500 each year.

In this example the marginal cost of the equipment per year is £1000 + £500 + £500 = £2000. If, therefore, the equipment earns a rental of more than £2000 per year, it will be profitable to buy the equipment.

It is normal to express this *MC* as a percentage of the purchase price. In this case the *MC* is 20 per cent per year. If the equipment earns a rental of more than 20 per cent of the purchase price, then it is profitable to purchase.

What will the firm's long-run supply curve look like? If the firm is a price taker in purchasing capital equipment, the supply curve will be horizontal, at least up to a fairly high level of output. But it will be vertically higher than the short-run curve (say, going through R_2 in Figure 9.20) because the *MC* now includes the opportunity cost of purchasing new equipment. There will also be no vertical section, since the firm can increase the supply of capital for hire by simply purchasing more. Beyond a certain level of output the curve may begin to slope upward, due to diseconomies of scale and hence rising handling costs.

Market supply

The market supply curve of capital services is the sum of the quantities supplied by all the individual firms. Either it can be the total supply of a particular type of capital (e.g. scaffolding), or more narrowly it can be the supply of a particular type of capital to a certain industry (e.g. the catering industry, or the coal industry).

In the case of the total supply of a particular type of capital, the *short-run* supply curve will be virtually totally inelastic. The reason is that capital is *heterogeneous*: i.e. one piece of capital equipment is not the same as another. If there is a shortage of scaffolding, you cannot use a cement mixer instead: people would fall off!

?? If supply is totally inelastic, what determines the rental value of capital equipment in the short run?

In the case of supply to a particular industry, supply will not be totally inelastic because capital equipment to a limited extent can be transferred from one industry to another. But supply is still pretty inelastic.

In the *long run*, the supply curve of capital services will be more elastic because extra capital equipment can be produced. It will not be horizontal, however, but upward sloping. The reason is that, if the supply of capital services is to increase, the hire firms will require a bigger stock of capital, and so will have to purchase a bigger amount each year to replace worn-out or obsolete stock. This will push up the purchase price and therefore increase the *MC* of supplying capital services. Thus to make it worth supplying extra capital services, a higher rental charge must be obtained. This makes the supply curve upward sloping. Its elasticity will depend on the elasticity of supply of capital equipment to the hire companies.

Determination of the price of capital services

Figure 9.21 draws together the analysis of the last section, and shows how the equilibrium rental rate is determined for the services of a particular type of capital equipment. We are assuming perfect competition. The interaction of demand and supply in diagram (b) gives an equilibrium rate of R_e. This is the rate given to the user of capital services in diagram (a), who demands Q_1. It is also the rate given to the supplier of capital services in diagram (c), who supplies Q_2.

Note that the analysis here parallels that of the determination of the equilibrium wage in a given labour market (see Figure 9.2 on page 238).

?? What will happen to the demand for capital services and the equilibrium rental if the price of some other factor, say labour, changes? Assume that wage rates fall. Trace through the effects on a three-section diagram like Figure 9.21. (Clue: a fall in wages will reduce costs and hence the price of the product, so that more will be sold; and it will make labour cheaper relative to capital.)

*The demand for and supply of capital for purchase

The alternative to hiring capital is to buy it outright. This section examines the demand and supply of capital for purchase.

The demand for capital: investment

How many computers will an engineering firm want to buy? Should a steelworks install another blast furnace? Should a removal firm buy another furniture lorry? These are all **investment** decisions. Investment is the purchasing of additional capital.

The demand for capital, or 'investment demand', by a profit-maximising firm is based on exactly the same principles as the demand for labour or the demand for capital services. The firm must weigh up the marginal revenue product of that investment (i.e. the money it will earn for the firm) against its marginal cost.

The problem is that capital is durable. It goes on producing goods, and hence yielding revenue for the firm, for a considerable period of time. Calculating these benefits therefore involves taking account of their timing.

There are two ways of approaching the problem: the *present value* approach and the *rate of return* approach. In both cases the firm is comparing the marginal benefits with the marginal costs of the investment.

Present value approach. To work out the benefit of an investment (its *MRP*), the firm will need to estimate all

DEFINITION

Investment The purchase by the firm of equipment or materials that will add to its stock of capital.

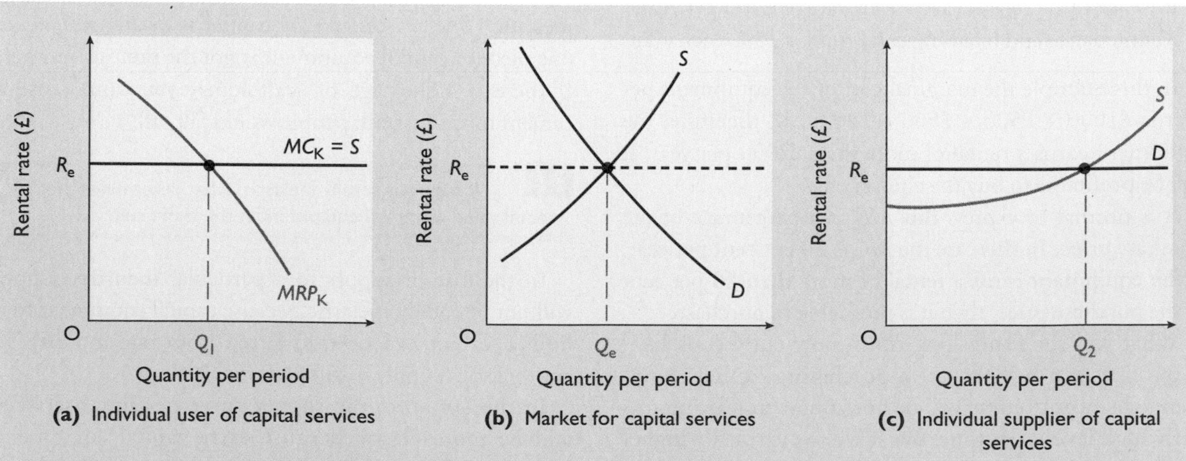

Figure 9.21 Long-run equilibrium rental rate for the services of a particular type of capital

the future earnings it will bring and then convert them to a **present value**. It can then compare this with the cost of the investment. Let us take a simple example.

Assume that a firm is considering buying a machine. It will produce £1000 per year (net of operating costs) for four years and then wear out and sell for £1000 as scrap. What is the benefit of this machine to the firm? At first sight the answer would seem to be £5000. This, after all, is the total income earned from the machine. Unfortunately it is not as simple as this. The reason is that money earned in the future is less beneficial to the firm than having the same amount of money today: if the firm has the money today, it can earn interest on it by putting it in the bank or reinvesting it in some other project.

To illustrate this assume that you have £100 today and can earn 10 per cent interest by putting it in a bank. In one year's time that £100 will have grown to £110, in two years' time to £121, in three years' time to £133.10 and so on. This process is known as **compounding**.

It follows that if someone offered to give you £121 in two years' time that would be no better than giving you £100 today, since, with interest, £100 would grow to £121 in two years. What we say, then, is that, with a 10 per cent interest rate, £121 in two years' time has a *present value* of £100.

The procedure of reducing future value back to a present value is known as **discounting**. When we do discounting, the rate we use is called the **rate of discount**: in this case 10 per cent. The formula for discounting is as follows:

$$PV = \Sigma \frac{X_t}{(1+r)^t}$$

where PV is the present value
X_t is the earnings from the investment in year t
r is the rate of discount (expressed as a decimal: i.e. 10% = 0.1)
Σ is the sum of each of the years' discounted earnings.

So what is the present value of the investment in the machine that produced £1000 for four years and then is sold as scrap for £1000 at the end of the four years? According to the formula it is:

	Year 1		Year 2		Year 3		Year 4
=	$\frac{£1000}{1.1}$	+	$\frac{£1000}{(1.1)^2}$	+	$\frac{£1000}{(1.1)^3}$	+	$\frac{£2000}{(1.1)^4}$
=	£909	+	£826	+	£751	+	£1366
=	£3852						

Thus the present value of the investment (i.e. its *MRP*) is £3852, *not* £5000 as might seem at first sight. In other words, if the firm had £3852 today and deposited it in a bank at a 10 per cent interest rate, the firm would earn exactly the same as it would by investing in the machine.

So is the investment worthwhile? It is now simply a question of comparing the £3852 benefit with the cost of buying the machine. If the machine costs less than £3852, it will be worth buying. If it costs more, the firm would be better off by keeping its money in the bank and earning the 10 per cent rate of interest.

The difference between the present value of the benefits (PV_b) of the investment and its cost (C) is known as the **net present value** (NPV):

$$NPV = PV_b - C$$

If the NPV is positive, the investment is worthwhile.

> **??** What is the present value of a machine that lasts three years, earns £100 in year 1, £200 in year 2 and £200 in year 3, and then has a scrap value of £100? Assume that the rate of discount is 5 per cent. If the machine costs £500, is the investment worthwhile? Would it be worthwhile if the rate of discount were 10 per cent?

Rate of return approach. The alternative approach when estimating whether an investment is worthwhile is to calculate the investment's *rate of return*. This rate of return is known as the firm's **marginal efficiency of capital** (MEC) or **internal rate of return** (IRR).

We use the same formula as for calculating present value:

$$PV = \Sigma \frac{X_t}{(1+r)^t}$$

DEFINITIONS

Present value approach to appraising investment This involves estimating the value *now* of a flow of future benefits (or costs).

Compounding The process of adding interest each year to an initial capital sum.

Discounting The process of reducing the value of future flows to give them a present valuation.

Rate of discount The rate that is used to reduce future values to present values.

Net present value of an investment The discounted benefits of an investment minus the cost of the investment.

Marginal efficiency of capital or **internal rate of return** The rate of return of an investment: the discount rate that makes the net present value of an investment equal to zero.

and then calculate what value of r would make the PV equal to the cost of investment: in other words, the rate of discount that would make the investment just break even. Say this worked out at 20 per cent. What we would be saying is that the investment would just cover its costs if the current rate of interest (rate of discount) were 20 per cent. In other words, this investment is equivalent to receiving 20 per cent interest: it has a 20 per cent rate of return (MEC).

So should the investment go ahead? Yes, if the actual rate of interest (i) is less than 20 per cent. The firm is better off investing its money in this project than keeping it in the bank: i.e. if $MEC > i$ the investment should proceed.

This is just one more application of the general rule that if $MRP_f > MC_f$ then more of the factor should be used: only in this case MRP is expressed as a rate of return (MEC), and MC is expressed as a rate of interest (i).

The profit-maximising position is illustrated in Figure 9.22. As the firm invests more, and thus builds up its stock of capital, so MEC will fall due to diminishing returns. As long as MEC is greater than i, the firm should invest more. It should stop when the stock of capital has reached Q_1. Thereafter it should cut investment to a level just sufficient to replace worn-out machines, and thus keep the capital stock at Q_1.

The risks of investment. One of the problems with investment is that the future is uncertain. The return on an investment will depend on the value of the goods it produces, which will depend on the goods market. But future markets cannot be predicted with accuracy: they depend on consumer tastes, the actions of rivals and the whole state of the economy. Investment is thus risky.

How is this risk accounted for when calculating the benefits of an investment? The answer is to use a higher rate of discount. The higher the risk, the bigger the premium that must be added to the rate.

The supply of capital

It is necessary to distinguish the supply of *physical* capital from the supply of *finance* to be used by firms for the purchase of capital.

Supply of physical capital. The principles here are just the same as those in the goods market. It does not matter whether a firm is supplying lorries (capital) or cars (a consumer good): it will still produce up to the point where $MC = MR$ if it wishes to maximise profits.

Supply of finance. When firms borrow to invest, this creates a demand for finance (or 'loanable funds'). The supply of loanable funds comes from the deposits that individuals and firms make in financial institutions. These deposits are savings, and represent the resources released when people refrain from consumption. In other words, the less people consume, the more loanable funds there will be available to finance investment.

Among other things, savings depend on the rate of interest that depositors receive. The higher the rate of interest, the more people will be encouraged to save. This would be illustrated by an upward-sloping supply curve of loanable funds, as shown in Figure 9.23.

Savings also depend on the level of people's incomes, their expectations of future price changes, and their general level of 'thriftiness' (their willingness to forgo present consumption in order to be able to have more in the future). A change in any of these other determinants will shift the supply curve.

*Determination of the rate of interest

What determines the rate of interest this time? Again the answer lies in demand and supply: the demand and supply of loanable funds.

The long-run position is illustrated in Figure 9.23. The supply curve is the total supply of savings, which in the long run can be used to build up the capital stock. The demand curve includes the demand by households for credit and the demand by firms to finance their investment.

The demand curve slopes downward for two reasons. First, households will borrow more at lower rates of interest. It effectively makes goods cheaper for them to buy. Second, it reflects the falling rate of return on investment as investment increases. This is simply due to diminishing returns to investment. As rates of interest fall, it will become profitable for firms to invest in projects that have a lower rate of return: the quantity of loanable funds demanded thus rises.

Equilibrium will be achieved where demand equals supply at an interest rate of i_e and a quantity of loanable funds $£_e$.

How will this market adjust to a change in demand or supply? Assume that there is a rise in demand for capital equipment, due, say, to an improvement in technology which increases the productivity of capital. There is thus an increase in demand for loanable funds. The demand curve shifts to the right in Figure 9.23. The equilibrium rate of interest will rise and this will encourage more savings. The end result is that more money will be spent on capital equipment.

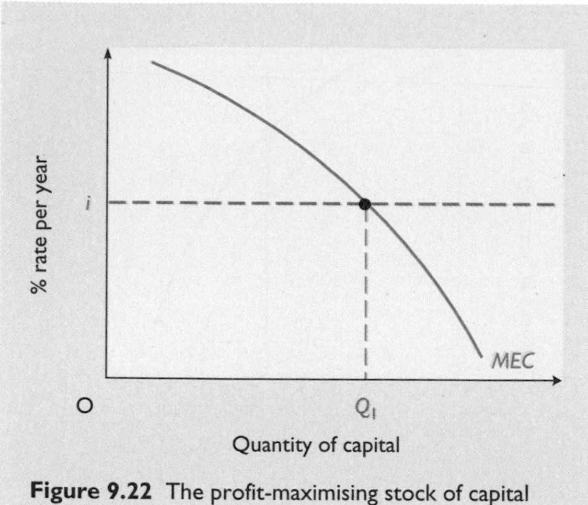

Figure 9.22 The profit-maximising stock of capital

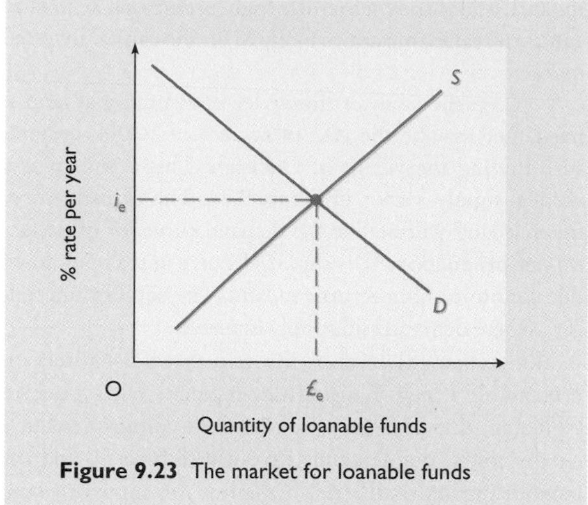

Figure 9.23 The market for loanable funds

Capital and profit

What does the analysis so far tell us about the amount of profit firms will earn? After all, profit is the reward that the owners of firms get from having and using capital.

Remember from Chapter 6 the distinction between normal and supernormal profit. In a perfectly competitive world all supernormal profits will be competed away in the long run.

Another way of putting this is that a perfectly competitive firm in the long run will only earn a **normal rate of return** on capital. This means that the return on capital (after taking risk into account) will be just the same as if the owners of capital had simply deposited their money in a bank instead. If a firm's capital yields a higher rate of return than this normal level (i.e. supernormal returns), other firms will be attracted to invest in similar capital. The resulting increased level of capital will increase the supply of goods. This in turn will lower the price of the goods and hence lower the rate of return on capital until it has fallen back to the normal level.

?? Can a perfectly competitive firm earn a supernormal rate of return on capital if it *continuously* innovates?

If, however, capital owners have monopoly/oligopoly power and can thus restrict the entry of new firms or the copying of innovations – for example, by having a patent on a particular process – they can continue to get a supernormal return on their capital.

If an investment entails *risks*, it will have to bring the possibility of returns higher than the market rate of interest, otherwise no one will be willing to take the risk. If the investor is lucky and the investment pays off, a rate of profit considerably higher than the rate of interest can be earned. This will not be competed away by other firms if they too face similar risks because *on average* such investments only yield an approximately normal rate of return.

An example of a risky investment is prospecting for oil. An oil company may be lucky and have a major strike, but it may simply drill dry well after dry well. If it does get a major strike and hence earn a large return on its investment, these profits will not be competed away by competitors prospecting in other fields, because they too still run the risk of drilling dry holes.

Rent: the reward to landowners

We turn now to land. The income it earns for landowners is the *rent* charged to the users of the land. This rent, like the rewards to other factors, is determined by demand and supply.

What makes land different from other factors of production is that it has an inelastic supply. In one sense this is obvious. The total supply of land in any area is fixed. It is in the very nature of land that it cannot be moved from one place to another!

In another sense supply is not *totally* inelastic. Land can be improved. It can be cleared, levelled, drained, fertilised, etc. Thus the supply of a certain type of land can be increased by expending human effort on improving it. The question is whether *land* has thereby increased, or whether the improvements constitute *capital* invested

DEFINITION

Normal rate of return The rate of return (after taking risks into account) that could be earned elsewhere.

in land, and if so whether the higher rents that such land can earn really amount to a return on the capital invested in it.

To keep the analysis simple let us assume that land *is* fixed. Let us take the case of an area of 10 000 hectares surrounding the village of Oakleigh. This is shown as a vertical supply 'curve' in Figure 9.24. The demand curve for that land will be like the demand curve for other factors of production. It is the *MRP* curve and slopes down due to diminishing returns to land. The equilibrium rent is r_e, where demand and supply intersect.

Notice that the level of this rent depends entirely on *demand*. If a new housing development takes place in Oakleigh, due perhaps to a growth in employment in a nearby town, the demand curve will shift to D_1 and the equilibrium rent will rise to r_{e_1}. But the supply of land remains fixed at 10 000 hectares. Landowners will earn more rent, but they themselves have done nothing: the higher rent is a pure windfall gain.

So why are rents in the centre of London many times higher per hectare than they are in the north of Scotland? The answer is that demand is very much higher in London.

Demand for land depends on its marginal revenue product. Thus it is differences in the *MRP* of land that explain the differences in rent from one area to another. There are two reasons for differences in *MRP*. Remember that *MRP* = *MPP* (marginal physical product of the factor) × *MR* (marginal revenue of the good produced by that factor).

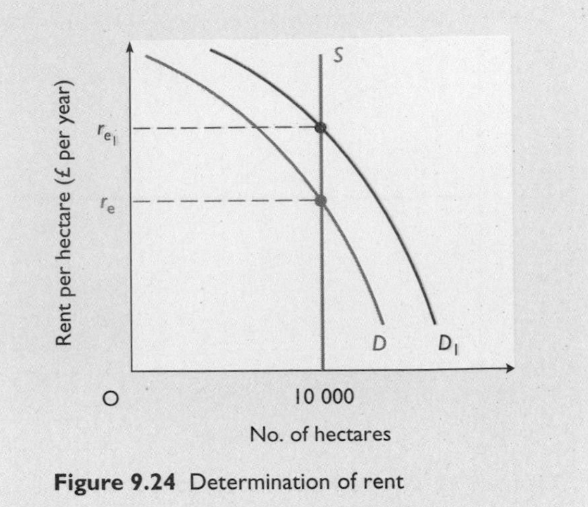

Figure 9.24 Determination of rent

?? 1. We defined the factor of production 'land' to include raw materials. Does the analysis of rent that we have just been looking at apply to raw materials?
2. The supply of land in a particular area may be totally inelastic, but the supply of land in that area *for a specific purpose* (e.g. growing wheat) will be upward sloping: the higher the price of wheat and thus the higher the rent that wheat producers are prepared to pay, the more will be made available for wheat production. Using the concept of transfer earnings, what will determine the elasticity of supply of land for any particular purpose?

Differences in MPP

Land differs in productivity. Fertile land will produce a higher output than deserts or moorland. Similarly, land near centres of population will be of much more use to industry than land in the middle of nowhere.

?? What other factors will determine the *MPP* of land for industry?

Differences in MR

The higher the demand for a particular good, the higher its price and marginal revenue, and hence the higher the demand and rent for the land on which that good is produced. Thus if the demand for housing rises relative to the demand for food, the rent on land suitable for house building will rise relative to the rent on agricultural land.

To summarise: rents will be high on land which is physically productive (high *MPP*) and produces goods in high demand (high *MR*).

The price of land

Not all land is rented: much of it is bought and sold outright. Its price will depend on what the purchaser is prepared to pay, and this will depend on the land's rental value.

Let us say that a piece of land can earn £1000 per year. What would a person be prepared to pay for it? There is a simple formula for working this out:

$$P = \frac{R}{i} \tag{1}$$

where *P* is the price of the land, *R* is the rent per year and *i* is the market rate of interest.

Let us assume that the market rate of interest is 10 per cent (i.e. 0.1). Then according to the formula, a purchaser would be prepared to pay:

$$\frac{£1000}{0.1} = £10\,000$$

Why should this be so? If a person deposits £10 000 in the bank, with an interest rate of 10 per cent this will earn that person £1000 per year. Assuming our piece of land is guaranteed to earn a rent of £1000 per year, then provided

EXPLORING THE THEORY — BOX 9.11

THE ECONOMICS OF NON-RENEWABLE RESOURCES

What happens as stocks diminish?

As world population inexorably rises, so the demands on our planet's resources continue to grow. Some of these resources are *renewable*. Water resources are replenished by rain. The soil, if properly managed, can continue to grow crops. Felled forests can be replanted. Of course, if we use these resources more rapidly than they are replenished, stocks will run down. We are all aware of the problems of seas that are over fished, or rain forests that are cleared, or reservoirs that are inadequate to meet our growing demand for water.

But whereas these resources can be replenished, others cannot. These are known as *non-renewable resources*. What determines the price of such resources and their rate of depletion? Will we eventually run out of resources such as oil, coal, gas and various minerals? To answer these questions, we need to distinguish between the available *stock* of such resources, and their use (a *flow*). The greater their use, the faster the stocks will run down.

Price increases over time

As stocks run down, so the price of the resources will tend to increase. Thus we can all expect to pay more for fossil fuels as remaining reserves are depleted. Owners of the reserves (e.g. mineowners and owners of oil wells) will thus find the value of their assets increasing. But how quickly will prices rise? In a perfect market, they will rise at the market rate of return on *other* assets (of equivalent risk).This is known as the *Hotelling rule*, named after Harold Hotelling who developed the argument in the early 1930s.

To understand why this is so, consider what would happen if the price of oil rose more slowly than the rate of return on other assets. People who owned oil wells would find that the value of their oil reserves was increasing less rapidly than the value of other assets. They might as well sell more oil now and invest the money in other assets, thereby getting a higher return. The extra oil coming to the market would depress the *current* oil price, but also reduce reserves, thereby creating a bigger shortage for the future and hence a higher *future* price. This would cause oil prices to rise more quickly over time (from the new lower base). Once the rate of price increase has risen to equal the rate of return on other assets, equilibrium has occurred. There will no longer be an incentive for the oil to be extracted faster.

The current price

But what determines the current price *level* (as opposed to its rate of increase)? This will be determined by supply and demand for the extracted resource (its flow).

In the case of a resource used by households, demand will depend on consumer tastes, the price of other goods, income, etc. Thus the greater the desire for using private cars, the greater the demand for petrol. In the case of minerals used by firms, demand will depend on the marginal revenue product of the resources. In either case, a rise in demand will cause a rise in the resource's price.

Supply will depend on three things:

- The rate of interest on other assets. As we have seen, the higher the rate of interest, the faster will the resource be extracted, in order that the mineowners (or well owners) can reinvest their profits at these higher rates of interest.
- The stock of known reserves. As new reserves are discovered, this will push down the price.
- The costs of extraction. The lower the costs, the greater will be the amount extracted, and hence the lower will be the market price of the resource.

Are we extracting non-renewable resources at the optimum rate?

If there are limited reserves of fossil fuels and other minerals, do we run the danger that they will soon run out? Should we be more concerned with conservation?

In fact, the market provides an incentive to conserve such resources. As reserves run down, so the price of non-renewable resources will rise. This will create an incentive to discover alternatives. For example, as fossil fuels become more expensive, so renewable sources of energy such as solar power, wind and wave power, will become more economical. There will also be a greater incentive to discover new techniques of power generation and to conserve energy.

Markets, however, are imperfect. As we shall see in Chapter 11, when we consume natural resources we do not take into account the full costs. For example, the burning of fossil fuels creates harmful environmental effects in the form of acid rain and the greenhouse effect, but these 'external' costs are not included in the price we pay.

Then there is the question of the distribution of income between present and future generations. If non-renewable resources are going to be expensive in the future, should we not be conserving these resources *today* in order to help our descendants? The problem is that consumers may well act totally selfishly, saying, 'Why should we conserve resources? By the time they run out we will be dead.'

??

1. Will the market provide incentives for firms to research into energy-conserving techniques, if energy prices at present are not high enough to make the use of such techniques profitable?
2. How will the existence of monopoly power in the supply of resources influence their rate of depletion?

it costs less than £10 000 to buy, it is a better investment than putting money in the bank. The competition between people to buy this land will drive its price up until it reaches £10 000.

This is just another example of equilibrium being where marginal cost equals marginal benefit. This can be demonstrated by rearranging equation (1) to give:

$$Pi = R$$

Remember that the equilibrium price of the land (P) is £10 000 and that the rate of interest (i) is 0.1. If you borrow the £10 000 to buy the land, it will cost you £1000 per year in interest payments (i.e. Pi). This is your annual marginal cost. The annual marginal benefit will be the rent (R) you will earn from the land.

> **??**
> 1. What price would the same piece of land sell for if it still earned £1000 rent per year, but if the rate of interest were now 5 per cent?
> 2. What does this tell us about the relationship between the price of an asset (like land) and the rate of interest?

Conclusions: Who are the poor? Who are the rich?

We have been building up an answer to these questions as this chapter has progressed. The final part of the answer concerns the ownership of land and capital. Many people own no land or capital at all. These people will therefore earn no profit, rent or interest.

For those who are fortunate enough to own productive assets, their income from them will depend on (a) the quantity they own and (b) their rental value.

The quantity of assets owned

This will depend on the following:

- Inheritance. Some people have rich parents who leave them substantial amounts of land and capital.
- Past income and savings. If people have high incomes and save a large proportion of them, this helps them to build up a stock of assets.
- Skill in investment (entrepreneurial skill). The more skilful people are in investing and in organising production, the more rapidly will their stock of assets grow.
- Luck. When people open up a business there are usually substantial risks. The business might flourish or fail.

The rental value

This is the income earned per unit of land and capital. It will depend on the following:

- The level of demand for the factor. This depends on the factor's *MRP*, which in turn depends on its physical productivity (*MPP*) and the demand for the good it produces and hence the good's *MR*.
- The elasticity of demand for the good. The greater the monopoly power that capital owners have in the goods market, the less elastic will be the demand for the product and the greater will be the supernormal returns they can earn on their capital.
- The elasticity of supply of the factor. The less elastic its supply, the more factor owners can gain from a high demand. The high demand will simply push up the level of economic rent that the factor will earn.
- The total factor supply by other factor owners. The further to the left the total factor supply curve, the higher the level of economic rent that each unit of the factor can earn for any given level of demand.

Thus if you are lucky enough to have rich parents who leave you a lot of money when you are relatively young; if you are a skilful investor and save and reinvest a large proportion of your earnings; if you have luck in owning assets that few other people own, and which produce goods in high demand: then you may end up very rich.

If you have no assets, you will have no property income at all. If at the same time you are on a low wage or are unemployed, then you may be very poor indeed.

SECTION SUMMARY

1. It is necessary to distinguish between buying the *services* of land (by renting) or capital (by hiring) from buying them outright.
2. The profit-maximising employment of land and capital services will be where the factor's *MRP* is equal to its price (under perfect competition) or its *MC* (where firms have monopsony power).
3. The demand for capital services will be equal to MRP_K. Due to diminishing returns, this will decline as more capital is used.
4. The supply of capital services to a firm will be horizontal or upward sloping depending on whether the firm is perfectly competitive or has monopsony power. The supply of capital services by a firm in the short run is likely to be infinitely elastic up to its maximum use, and then totally inelastic. In the long run, the supplying firm can purchase additional capital equipment for hiring out. Its decision to do so will depend on its marginal cost. This will normally be expressed as a rate per year, which will take into

continued

account the opportunity cost of borrowing money to make the purchase, the annual depreciation of the equipment, and maintenance and handling costs.

5. The market supply of capital services is likely to be highly inelastic in the short run, given that capital equipment tends to have very specific uses and cannot normally be transferred from one use to another. In the long run it will be more elastic.

6. The price of capital services will be determined by the interaction of demand and supply.

*7. The demand for capital for purchase will depend on the return it earns for the firm. To calculate this return, all future earnings from the investment have to be reduced to a present value by discounting at a market rate of interest (discount). If the present value exceeds the cost of the investment, the investment is worthwhile. Alternatively, a rate of return from the investment can be calculated and then this can be compared with the return that the firm could have earned by investing elsewhere.

*8. The supply of finance for investment depends on the supply of loanable funds, which in turn depends on the rate of interest, on the general level of thriftiness and on expectations about future price levels and incomes.

*9. The rate of interest will be determined by the demand and supply of loanable funds. When deciding whether to make an investment a firm will use this rate for discounting purposes. If, however, an investment involves risks, the firm will require a higher rate of return on the investment than current market interest rates.

10. Rent on land, like the price of other factor services, will be determined by the interaction of demand and supply. Its supply is totally inelastic (or nearly so). Its demand curve will be downward sloping and will equal the *MRP* of land.

11. The price of land will depend on its potential rental value (its marginal benefit) and the repayment costs of borrowing to pay for the land (its marginal cost). Equilibrium will be where the two are equal.

??? END-OF-CHAPTER QUESTIONS ???

1. The wage rate a firm has to pay and the output it can produce varies with the number of workers as follows (all figures are hourly):

Number of workers	1	2	3	4	5	6	7	8
Wage rate (AC_L) (£)	3	4	5	6	7	8	9	10
Total output (TPP_L)	10	22	32	40	46	50	52	52

Assume that output sells at £2 per unit.

(a) Copy the table and add additional rows for TC_L, MC_L, TRP_L and MRP_L. Put the figures for MC_L and MRP_L in the spaces between the columns.

(b) How many workers will the firm employ in order to maximise profits?

(c) What will be its hourly wage bill at this level of employment?

(d) How much hourly revenue will it earn at this level of employment?

(e) Assuming that the firm faces other (fixed) costs of £30 per hour, how much hourly profit will it make?

(f) Assume that the workers now formed a union and that the firm agreed to pay the negotiated wage rate to all employees. What is the maximum to which the hourly wage rate could rise without causing the firm to try to reduce employment below that in (b) above? (See Figure 9.15.)

(g) What would be the firm's hourly profit now?

2. If a firm faces a shortage of workers with very specific skills, it may decide to undertake the necessary training itself. If on the other hand it faces a shortage of unskilled workers it may well offer a small wage increase in order to obtain the extra labour. In the first case it is responding to an increase in demand for labour by attempting to shift the supply curve. In the second case it is merely allowing a movement along the supply curve. Use a demand and supply diagram to illustrate each case. Given that elasticity of supply is different in each case, do you think that these are the best policies for the firm to follow? What would happen to wages and economic rent if it used the second policy in the first case?

3. Why does the marginal revenue product differ between workers in different jobs?

4. For what reasons is the average gross weekly pay of women only 72 per cent of that of men in the UK?

5. Given the analysis of bilateral monopoly, if the passing of minimum-wage legislation forces employers to pay higher wage rates to low-paid employees, will this necessarily cause a reduction in employment?

6. Using a diagram like Figure 9.21, demonstrate what will happen under perfect competition when there is an increase in the productivity of a particular type of capital. Consider the effects on the demand, price (rental rate) and quantity supplied of the services of this type of capital.

7. What factors could cause a rise in the market rate of interest?

8. How is the market price of land related to its productivity?

10

Inequality, poverty and policies to redistribute incomes

10.1 Inequality and poverty

Inequality is one of the most contentious issues in the world of economics and politics.

The political right argues that a certain amount of inequality and poverty is the inevitable price paid for an efficient, growing economy. People need the incentives of high incomes to encourage them to work, train, invest and take risks. This may mean that some people are poor, and most on the right argue in favour of government measures to alleviate poverty. Nevertheless they worry that any significant redistribution from rich to poor may seriously reduce growth and efficiency by undermining incentives. People on the right also argue from a moral standpoint that the freedom to own property and to pass it on to children, and the freedom to keep the bulk of the income from that property, are fundamental rights.

The left, not surprisingly, disagrees. A fundamental tenet of socialism is that the distribution of income should be based on need, rather than on private property ownership and the workings of the market. A truly socialist society would be a much more equal society. Most socialists nevertheless do accept that there will have to be incentives for an economy to function, and that therefore there will have to be some minimum level of inequality.

Whether the current distribution of income is desirable or not is a normative question. Economists therefore cannot settle the debate between left and right over how much the government should redistribute incomes from rich to poor. Nevertheless economists do have a major role to play in the analysis of inequality. They can do the following:

- Identify the extent of inequality and analyse how it has changed over time.
- Explain why a particular level of income distribution occurs and what causes inequality to grow or to lessen.
- Examine the relationship between equality and other economic objectives such as efficiency.
- Identify various government policies to deal with problems of inequality and poverty.
- Examine the effects of these policies, both on inequality itself and on other questions such as efficiency, inflation and unemployment.

Section 10.1 looks at the nature and causes of inequality. Section 10.2 looks at policies to redistribute income, and in particular at the use of taxes and benefits. It also examines the relationship between income redistribution and economic efficiency: for example, will high taxes on the rich discourage them from working and investing?

Types of inequality

There are a number of different ways of looking at the distribution of income and wealth. Each way highlights a different aspect of inequality.

The distribution of income

There are three broad ways of examining the distribution of income. First we can look at how evenly incomes are distributed among the population. This is known as the **size distribution of income**. It can be expressed between *households*, or between *individual earners*, or between *all individuals*. It can be expressed either *before* or *after* the deduction of taxes and the receipt of benefits. For example, we might want to know the proportion of pre-tax national income going to the richest 10 per cent of households.

DEFINITION

Size distribution of income Measurement of the distribution of income according to the levels of income received by individuals (irrespective of source).

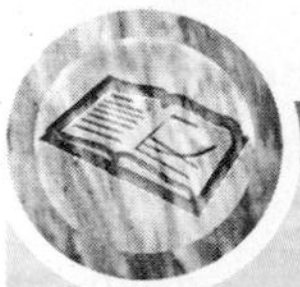

EXPLORING THE THEORY BOX 10.1

HOW CAN WE DEFINE POVERTY?

In attempting to solve a social problem such as poverty, it is normal for the policy-making body to adopt the following four-stage approach:

- The problem is defined.
- The problem is measured.
- The problem's causes are identified.
- Alternative policies are considered to cure the problem.

The importance of defining the problem of poverty correctly is that it determines the subsequent stages: the number of poor, possible causes of poverty and ways of tackling the problem.

There are two ways of looking at poverty.

Absolute poverty (or subsistence poverty)

As its name suggests, this definition involves identifying a poverty line measured in terms of those basic items considered essential to life: items such as adequate clothing, food and shelter.

By defining poverty in absolute terms, it is assumed that all individuals have similar minimum requirements, and that those whose means fall below the required minimum are poor.

Attempts have been made to include minimum social/cultural needs in such definitions: for example, adequate leisure and recreation, education and security.

?? Compile your own list of basic necessities. Are these the same for all people?

Relative poverty

Relative poverty, by contrast, is a far more flexible concept.

The definition is based on judgements, made by each particular society, as to what is considered a reasonable and acceptable standard of living, according to the conventions of the day. Hence an individual who is unable to attain this reasonable and acceptable standard is considered poor. For example, if fridges, TVs and videos are considered part of 'civilised existence', then without them you are considered poor! The standard of living considered to be acceptable by society will differ over time, and from one society to another.

??

1. If poverty is defined in absolute terms, will the list of necessities still vary from society to society?
2. If we use a relative definition of poverty, what difficulties will we encounter in comparing poverty over time?

Then there is the question of distribution between different *factors of production*. This is known at the **functional distribution of income**. At the *broader* level, we could look at the distribution between the general factor categories: labour, land and capital. For example, there is the question of the relative shares of wages and profits in national income. At a *narrower* level, we could look at distribution within the factor categories. Why are some jobs well paid while others are badly paid? Why are rents higher in some areas than in others? This is the type of distribution we looked at in Chapter 9.

Finally there is the question of the **distribution of income by class of recipient**. This can be by *class of person*: women, men, single people, married people, people within a particular age group or ethnic group, and so on. Alternatively it can be by *geographical area*. Typically this is expressed in terms of differences in incomes between officially defined regions within a country.

The distribution of wealth

Income is a *flow*. It measures the receipt of money per period of time (e.g. £10 000 per year). Wealth, by contrast, is a stock (see Box 9.10). It measures the value of a person's assets at a particular point in time. The distribution of wealth can be measured as a size distribution (how evenly it is distributed among the population); as a functional distribution (the proportion of wealth held in various forms, such as dwellings, land, company shares, building society deposits, etc.); or according to the holders of wealth, classified by age, sex, geographical area, etc.

DEFINITIONS

Functional distribution of income Measurement of the distribution of income according to the source of income (e.g. from employment, from profit, from rent, etc.).

Distribution of income by class of recipient Measurement of the distribution of income between the classes of person who receive it (e.g. homeowners and non-homeowners or those in the north and those in the south).

Analysis of incomes below a certain level: the analysis of poverty

A major problem here is in defining just what is meant by poverty. The dividing line between who is poor and who is not is necessarily arbitrary. Someone who is classed as poor in the UK may seem comparatively rich to an Ethiopian. Where the line is drawn is important, however, to the extent that it determines who receives state benefits and who does not.

The extent and nature of poverty can be analysed in a number of ways:

- The number of people or the proportion of the population falling into the category.
- The size distribution of income between poor people.
- The occupational distribution of poverty.
- The geographical distribution of poverty.
- The distribution of poverty according to age, sex, ethnic origin, marital status, educational attainment, etc.

It is not possible in this chapter to look at all aspects of inequality in the UK. Nevertheless some of the more important facts are considered, along with questions of their measurement and interpretation.

The size distribution of income in the UK

Figure 10.1 shows the size distribution of income in the UK. It covers income from all sources. In each chart, households are grouped into five equal-sized groups or **quintiles**, from the poorest 20 per cent of households up to the richest 20 per cent. The following points can be drawn from these statistics:

- In 1996/7 the richest 20 per cent of households earned 51 per cent of national income, and even after the deduction of taxes this was still 44 per cent.
- The poorest 20 per cent, by contrast, earned a mere 2.3 per cent of national income, and even after the receipt of benefits this had only risen to 6.8 per cent.

Inequality has grown dramatically in recent years. Between 1977 and 1996/7 the post-tax-and-benefits share of national income of the bottom 40 per cent of households fell from 23.3 per cent to 18.0 per cent; while the share of the top 20 per cent grew from 36.9 per cent to 44.0 per cent.

Figure 10.2 shows the distribution of income in 1996/7 before and after tax. This time there are ten equal-sized groups or **deciles**. Cash benefits are included in both the before-tax and the after-tax data. The chart dramatically

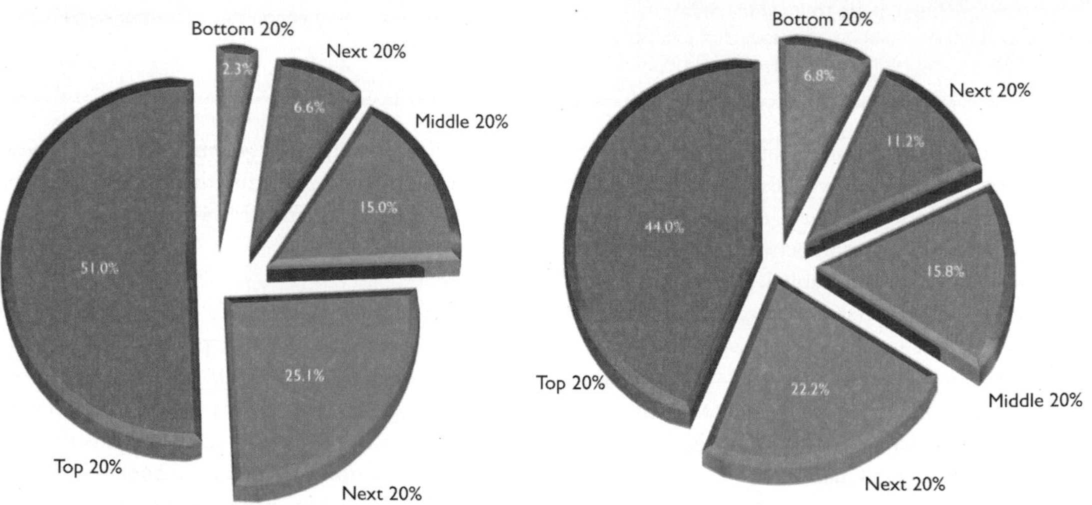

Figure 10.1 Size distribution of UK income by quintile group of households: 1996/7

Source: *Economic Trends* (ONS, April 1998).

DEFINITIONS

Quantiles Divisions of the population into equal-sized groups.

Quintiles Divisions of the population into five equal-sized groups (an example of a quantile).

Deciles Divisions of the population into ten equal-sized groups (another example of a quantile).

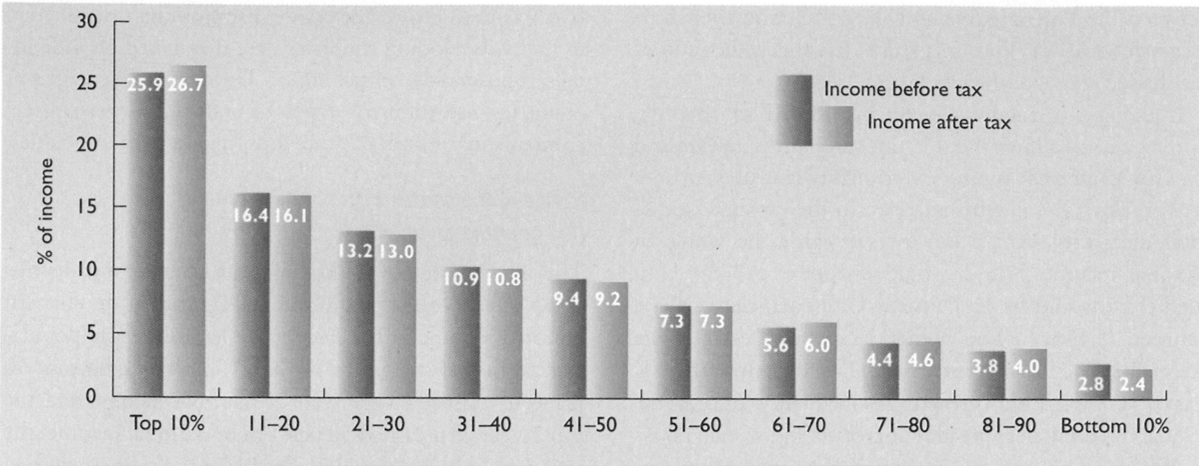

Figure 10.2 Percentage shares of income, before and after tax by decile group of households: 1996/7

Source: *Economic Trends* (ONS, April 1998).

depicts the level of inequality at the top end of the range. The top 10 per cent of households in 1996/7 earned 25.9 per cent of pre-tax income, over nine times as much as the bottom 10 per cent, who earned a mere 2.8 per cent.

As we shall see in section 10.2, by taxing the rich proportionately more than the poor, taxes can be used as a means of reducing inequality. In the UK in recent years, however, taxes have not had this effect. In fact, as Figure 10.2 shows, the effect of taxation is slightly to *increase* inequality, raising the share of the richest 10 per cent from 25.9 per cent to 26.7 per cent and reducing the share of the poorest 10 per cent from 2.8 per cent to 2.4 per cent.

Measuring the size distribution of income

Apart from tables and charts, two of the most widely used methods for measuring inequality are the *Lorenz curve* and the *Gini coefficient.*

Lorenz curve

Figure 10.3 shows the **Lorenz curve** for the UK based on 1996/7 pre-tax incomes.

The horizontal axis measures percentages of the population from the poorest to the richest. Thus the 40 per cent point represents the poorest 40 per cent of the population. The vertical axis measures the percentage of national income they receive.

The curve starts at the origin: zero people earn zero incomes. If income were distributed totally equally, the Lorenz curve would be a straight 45° line. The 'poorest' 20 per cent of the population would earn 20 per cent of national income; the 'poorest' 60 per cent would earn 60 per cent, and so on. The curve ends up at the top right-hand corner, with 100 per cent of the population earning 100 per cent of national income.

In practice the Lorenz curve will 'hang below' the 45° line. Point *x*, for example, shows that the poorest 50 per cent of UK households earned only 24.2 per cent of national income. The further the curve drops below the 45° line, the greater will be the level of inequality.

The Lorenz curve is quite useful for showing the change in income distribution over time. From 1949 to 1979 the curve moved inwards towards the 45° line, suggesting a lessening of inequality. Since then it has moved downwards away from the 45° line, suggesting a deepening of inequality.

The problem with simply comparing Lorenz curves by eye is that it is imprecise. This problem is overcome by using Gini coefficients.

Gini coefficient

The **Gini coefficient** is a precise way of measuring the position of the Lorenz curve. It is the ratio of the area

DEFINITIONS

Lorenz curve A curve showing the proportion of national income earned by any given percentage of the population (measured from the poorest upwards).

Gini coefficient The area between the Lorenz curve and the 45° line divided by the total area under the 45° line.

between the Lorenz curve and the 45° line to the whole area below the 45° line. In Figure 10.3 this is the ratio of the shaded area *A* to the whole area (*A* + *B*).

If income is totally equally distributed so that the Lorenz curve follows the 45° line, area *A* disappears and the Gini coefficient is zero. As inequality increases, so does area *A*. The Gini coefficient rises. In the extreme case of total inequality, where one person earns the whole of national income, area *B* would disappear and the Gini coefficient would be 1. Thus the Gini coefficient will be between 0 and 1. The higher it is, the greater is the inequality. In 1979 the pre-tax Gini coefficient in the UK was 0.30. With the growth in inequality during the 1980s, the coefficient steadily increased and stood at 0.37 in 1996/7. The post-tax coefficient rose even more dramatically – from 0.29 in 1979 to 0.38 in 1996/7.

Gini coefficients have the advantage of being relatively simple to understand and use. They provide a clear way of comparing income distribution either in the same country at different times, or between different countries. They suffer two main drawbacks, however.

First, a single measure cannot take into account all the features of inequality. Take the case of the two countries illustrated in Figure 10.4. If area *X* is equal to area *Y*, they will have the same Gini coefficient, and yet the pattern of their income distribution is quite different.

?? In which country in Figure 10.4 would you expect to find the highest number of poor people? Describe how income is distributed in the two cases.

Second, there is the problem of what statistics are used in the calculation. Are they pre-tax or post-tax; do they include benefits; do they include non-monetary incomes (such as food grown for own consumption: a major item in many developing countries); are they based on individuals, households or tax units? Unfortunately, different countries use different types of statistics. International comparisons of inequality are thus fraught with difficulties.

Ratios of the shares in national income of two quantile groups

This is a very simple method of measuring income distribution. A ratio quite commonly used is that of the share of national income of the *bottom 40 per cent* of the population to that of the *top 20 per cent*. Thus if the bottom 40 per cent earned 15 per cent of national income and the top 20 per cent earned 50 per cent of national income, the ratio would be 15/50 = 0.3. The lower the ratio, therefore, the greater the inequality. Figure 10.5 gives some examples of this ratio from different countries.

??

1. Why, do you think, are the ratios for developing countries lower than those for developed countries?
2. Make a list of reasons why the figures in this table may not give an accurate account of relative levels of inequality between countries.
3. What would the ratio be if national income were absolutely equally distributed?

The functional distribution of income in the UK

Distribution of income by source

Figure 10.6 shows the sources of household incomes in 1965, 1975, 1985 and 1996/7. Wages and salaries constitute by far the largest element. However, their share fell from 76.0 per cent to 64.6 per cent of national income between 1965 and 1996/7. Conversely, the share coming

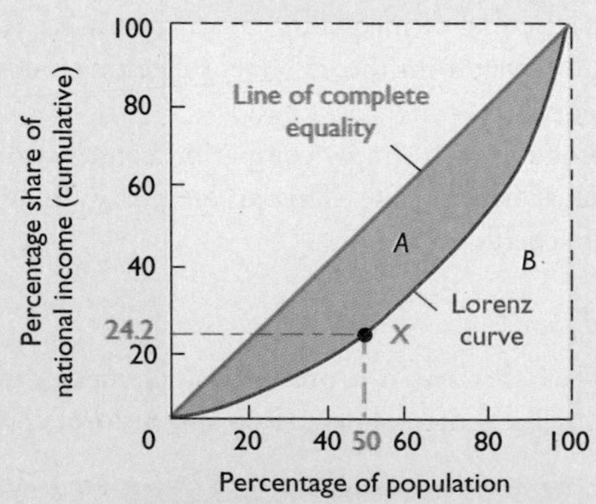

Figure 10.3 Lorenz curve: UK households' pre-tax incomes

Source: *Economic Trends* (ONS, April 1998).

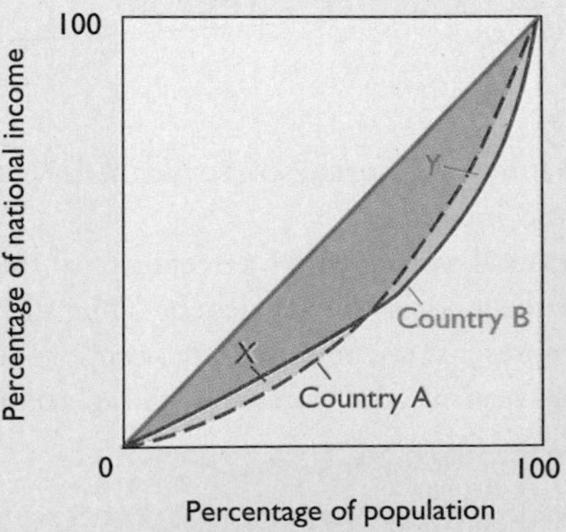

Figure 10.4 Lorenz curves for two countries with the same Gini coefficients

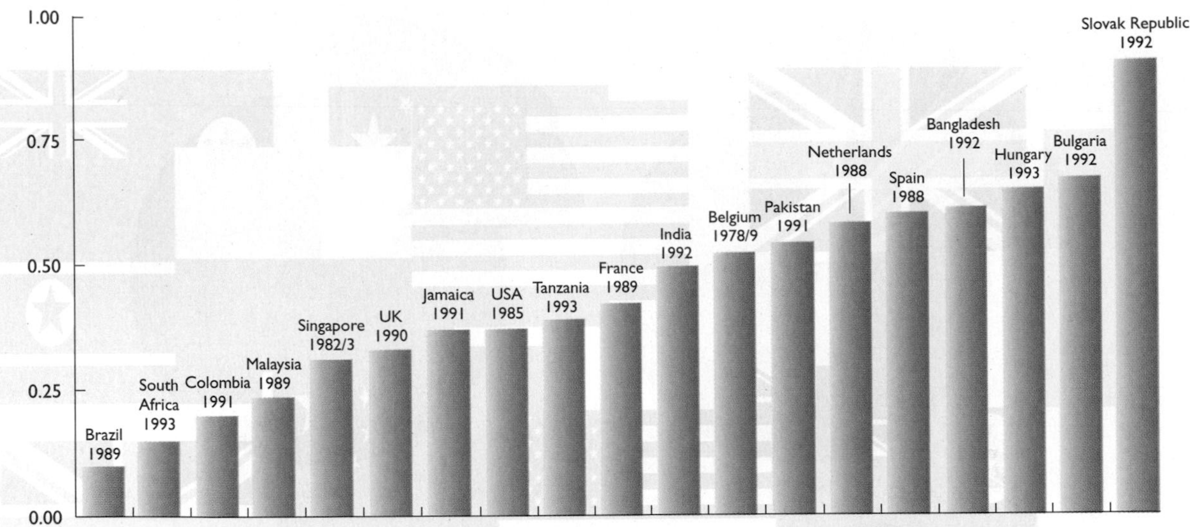

Figure 10.5 Ratio of income shares of bottom 40% to top 20% of households (after taxes and benefits)

Source: *World Development Report* (World Bank, 1997).

from social security benefits and pensions rose from 10.6 per cent to 20.1 per cent, reflecting the higher levels of unemployment in the early 1990s and the growing proportion of the population past retirement age.

In contrast to wages and salaries, investment income (dividends, interest and rent) accounts for a relatively small percentage of household income – a mere 4.5 per cent in 1996/7.

With the growth of small businesses and the increased numbers of people being 'employed' on a freelance basis, so the proportion of incomes coming from self-employment has grown. It rose from 5.7 per cent in 1975 to 9.4 per cent in 1996/7.

The overall shares illustrated in Figure 10.6 hide the fact that the sources of income differ quite markedly between different income groups. These differences are shown in Table 10.1.

Column (1) shows that higher-income groups get a larger proportion of their income from wages and salaries than do lower-income groups. This can be largely explained by examining column (5). As would be expected, the poor tend to get a larger proportion of their incomes in social security benefits than do people further up the income scale.

It is interesting to note that the second poorest 20 per cent of households have a larger proportion of their income from pensions and annuities than any other group. Pensioners are clustered in this group because they tend to be fairly poor (pensions being less than wages), but not as poor as the unemployed or families on low incomes with a large number of dependants.

Table 10.1 Sources of UK household income as a percentage of total household income by quintile groups: 1996/7

Gross household weekly incomes (quintiles)	Wages and salaries (1)	Income from self-employment (2)	Income from investments (3)	Pensions and annuities (4)	Social security benefits (5)	Other (6)	Total (7)
Lowest 20%	3.6	1.3	3.4	5.5	83.7	2.5	100.0
Next 20%	23.9	5.4	4.7	11.9	51.8	2.2	100.0
Middle 20%	56.5	8.6	4.4	11.3	17.5	1.7	100.0
Next 20%	74.5	8.1	3.6	6.3	6.3	1.1	100.0
Highest 20%	75.6	12.0	5.0	4.1	2.3	1.0	100.0
All households	64.6	9.4	4.5	6.5	13.6	1.3	100.0

Source: *Family Spending* (ONS, 1997).

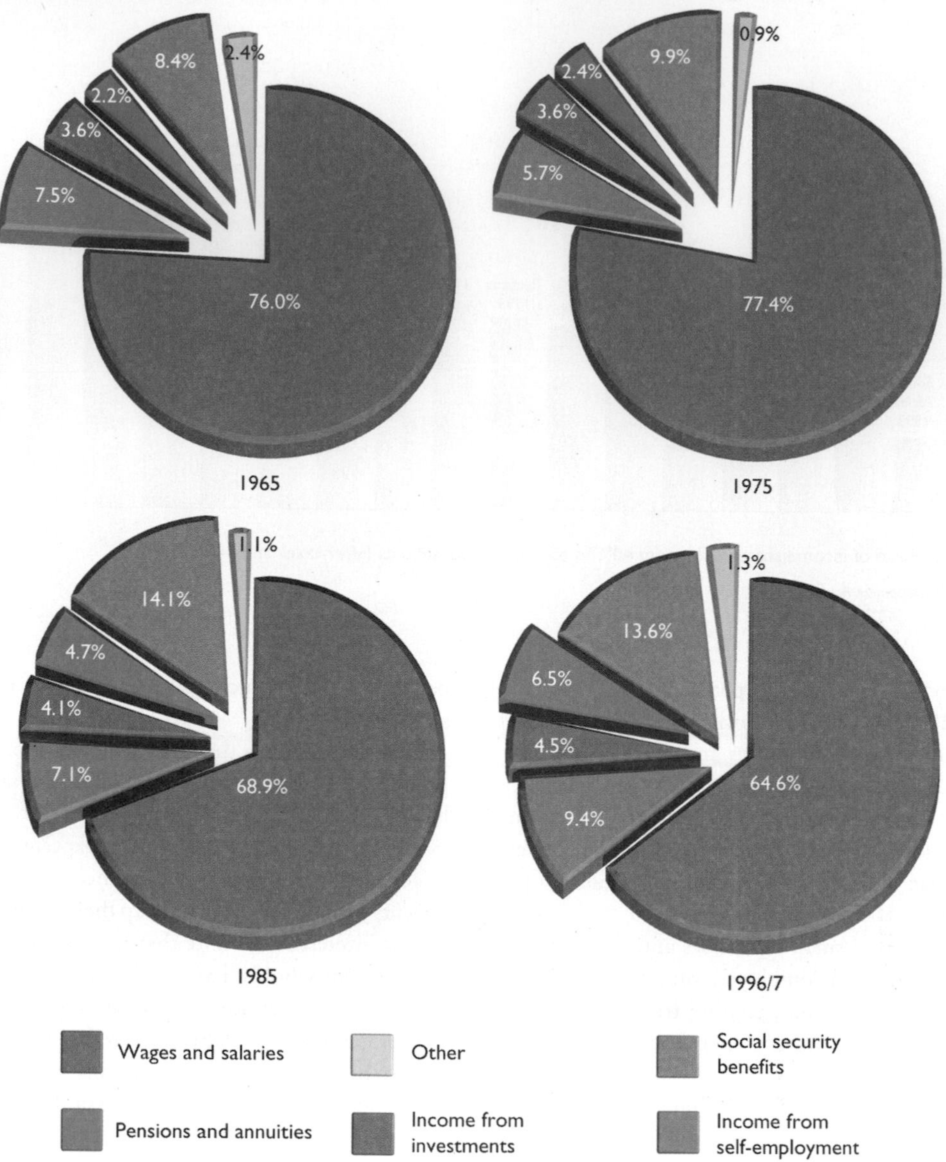

Figure 10.6 Sources of UK household income as a percentage of gross household income
Source: *Family Spending* (ONS, 1997).

One perhaps surprising feature to note is that the proportion of income coming from profits, rent and interest (column (3)) varies little between the income groups. In fact only for those people in the top 1 or 2 per cent is it significantly higher. The conclusion from this, plus the fact that investment incomes account for only 4.5 per cent of household incomes in total, is that incomes from capital and land are of only relatively minor significance in explaining income inequality.

?? Why does the second poorest 20 per cent of households have a larger proportion of income from investments than any other group of households?

The major cause of differences in incomes between individuals in employment is the differences in wages and salaries between different occupations.

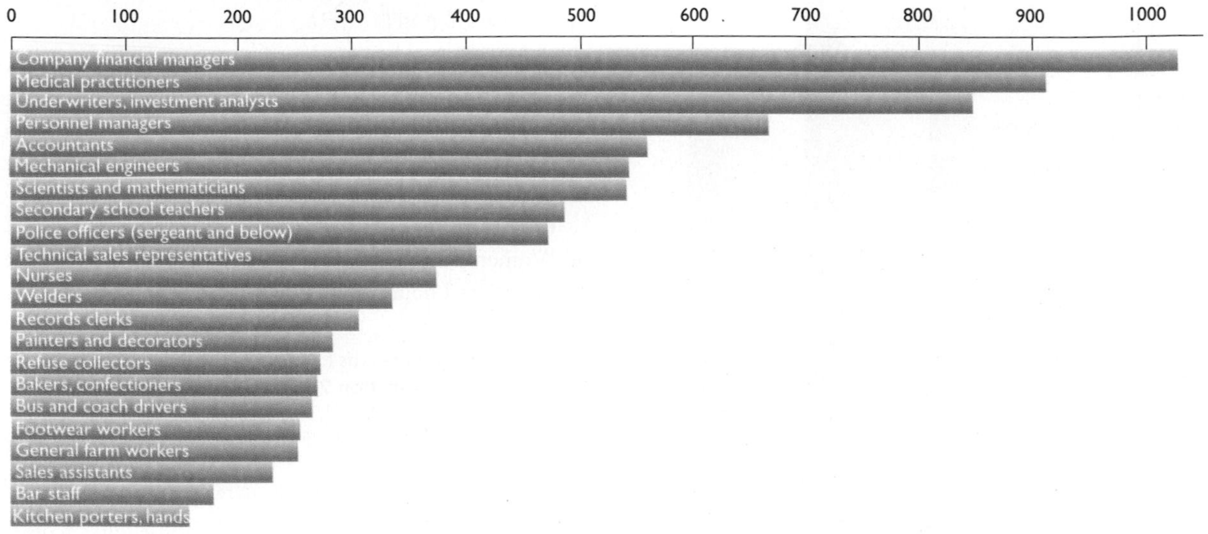

Figure 10.7 Average gross weekly earnings of UK full-time adult male employees (£): selected occupations: 1997

Source: *New Earnings Survey* (ONS, 1997).

Distribution of wages and salaries by occupation

Differences in full-time wages and salaries are illustrated in Figure 10.7. This shows the average gross weekly earnings of full-time adult male workers in selected occupations in 1997. As can be seen there are considerable differences in earnings between different occupations. The causes of differences in wages from one occupation to another were examined in Chapter 9.

> **??** If fringe benefits (such as long holidays, company cars, free clothing/uniforms, travel allowances and health insurance) were included, do you think the level of inequality would increase or decrease? Explain why.

About 10 per cent of the earnings in Figure 10.7 come from overtime (on average about 3.3 hours per week). The amount of overtime worked differs markedly, however, between occupations. Thus it is not just the basic hourly wage rate (or annual salary) that explains differences in earnings from one occupation to another, but also the number of hours worked and the overtime rate.

Since the late 1970s wage differentials have widened. Part of the explanation lies in a shift in the demand for labour. Many firms have adopted new techniques which require a more highly educated workforce. Wage rates in some of these skilled occupations have increased substantially.

At the same time there has been a decline in the number of unskilled jobs in industry and, along with it, a decline in the power of unions to represent such people. Where low-skilled jobs remain, there will be intense pressure on employers to reduce wage costs if they are competing with companies based in developing countries where wage rates are much lower.

As prospects for the unskilled decline in industry, so people with few qualifications increasingly compete for low-paid, service-sector jobs (e.g. in supermarkets and fast-food outlets). The growth in people seeking part-time work has also kept wage rates down in this sector.

Other determinants of income inequality

Differences in household composition

Other things being equal, the more dependants there are in a household, the lower the income will be *per member* of that household. Figure 10.8 gives an extreme example of this. It shows the average household income in the UK in 1996/7 of four different categories of household.

Households with two adults and four or more children had a lower average income than households with only one man and one woman. This means that they had a very much lower income *per member* of the household.

There is a twin problem for many large households. Not only may there be relatively more children and old-age dependants, but also the total household income will be reduced if one of the adults stays at home to look after the family, or only works part time.

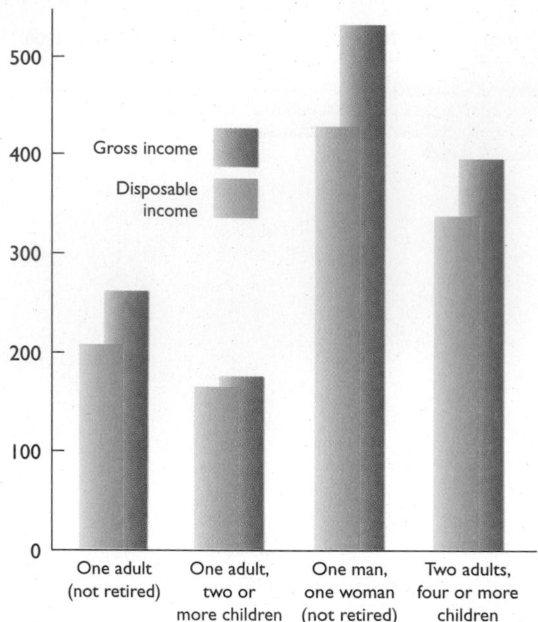

Figure 10.8 Weekly income for different types of UK household (£): 1996/7

Source: *Family Spending* (ONS, 1997).

Differences by sex

Box 9.8 looked at some of the aspects of income inequality between the sexes. Figure 10.9 gives examples of average gross weekly earnings of full-time adult female workers in 1997. The average for all occupations was £297. This compares with £409 for men. There are three important factors to note:

- Women are paid less than men in the same occupations. You will see this if you compare some of the occupations in Figure 10.9 with the same ones in Figure 10.7.
- Women tend to be employed in lower-paid occupations than men.
- Women do much less overtime than men (on average just under 1 hour per week, compared with 3.2 for men).

> **??** List the reasons for each of the three factors above. (Re-read section 9.3 and Box 9.8 if you need help.)

Differences in the geographical distribution of income

Figure 10.10 shows the gross weekly household incomes in different regions of the UK in 1996/7. These incomes reflect the following factors:

- Differences in the types of occupation between areas. This in turn reflects differences in the types of industry in different areas.
- Differences in the relative demand and supply of workers with particular qualifications. Areas with higher unemployment will tend to pay lower average wages. Areas with skill shortages will tend to pay higher average wages.
- Differences in the costs of living between areas. The higher the cost of living, the higher the wage that must

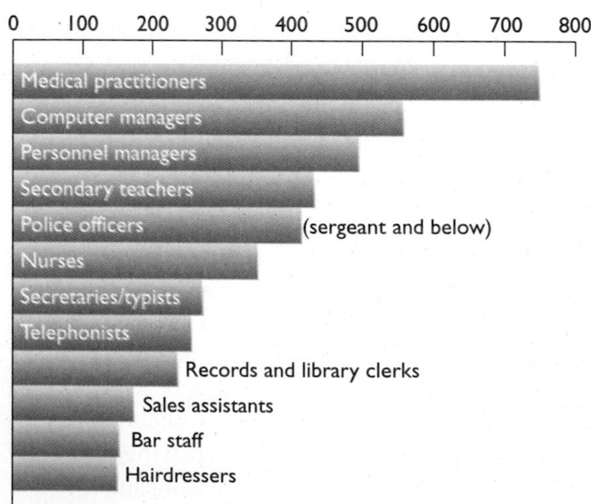

Figure 10.9 Average gross weekly earnings of full-time adult female employees (£): selected occupations: 1997

Source: *New Earnings Survey* (ONS, 1997).

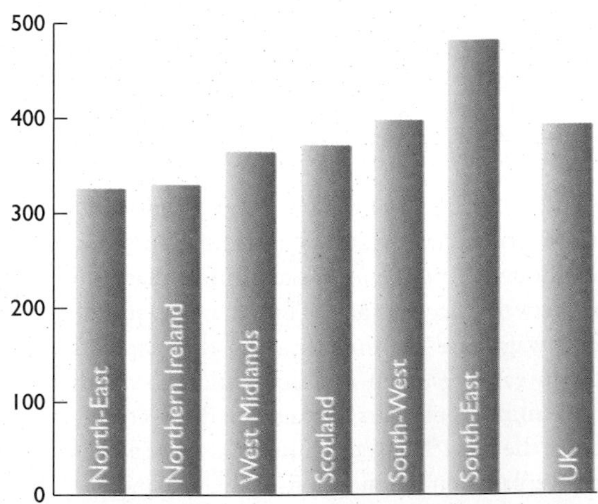

Figure 10.10 Gross weekly household income: selected UK regions (£): 1996/7

Source: *Family Spending* (ONS, 1997).

be paid to attract sufficient labour and the higher the wages that will be demanded by trade unions.

- Differences in household composition between areas. Areas where there are relatively large numbers of owner-occupied houses and two-or-more-earner households will have higher average household incomes.

As can be seen from Figure 10.10, average incomes are significantly lower in the north-east than in the south-east of England. Regional inequality is explored in section 22.3.

The distribution of wealth

Wealth is difficult to measure. Being a *stock* of assets (such as a house, land, furniture, personal possessions and investments), it has an easily measurable value only when it is sold. What is more, individuals are not required to keep any record of their assets. Only when people die and their assets are assessed for inheritance tax does a record become available. Official statistics are thus based on Inland Revenue data of the assets of those who have died that year. These statistics are suspect for two reasons. First, the people who have died are unlikely to be a representative sample of the population. Second, many items may not be included, especially household and personal items, and items passed automatically to the surviving spouse.

Table 10.2 Size distribution of UK wealth

	Proportion of marketable wealth (%)		
	1971	1981	1994
Wealthiest 1%	31	18	19
Wealthiest 5%	52	36	38
Wealthiest 10%	65	50	51
Wealthiest 25%	86	73	73
Wealthiest 50%	97	92	93
Gini coefficient	0.80	0.67	0.69

Source: *Social Trends* (ONS, 1998).

Figure 10.11 and Table 10.2 give official statistics on the UK composition and distribution of wealth. As can be seen from Table 10.2, inequality of wealth is far greater than inequality of income. The wealthiest 1 per cent of the adult population owned 19 per cent of the marketable wealth in 1994, and the wealthiest 10 per cent owned 51 per cent. These figures do not include pension rights, which are much more equally distributed. Even when they are included, how-

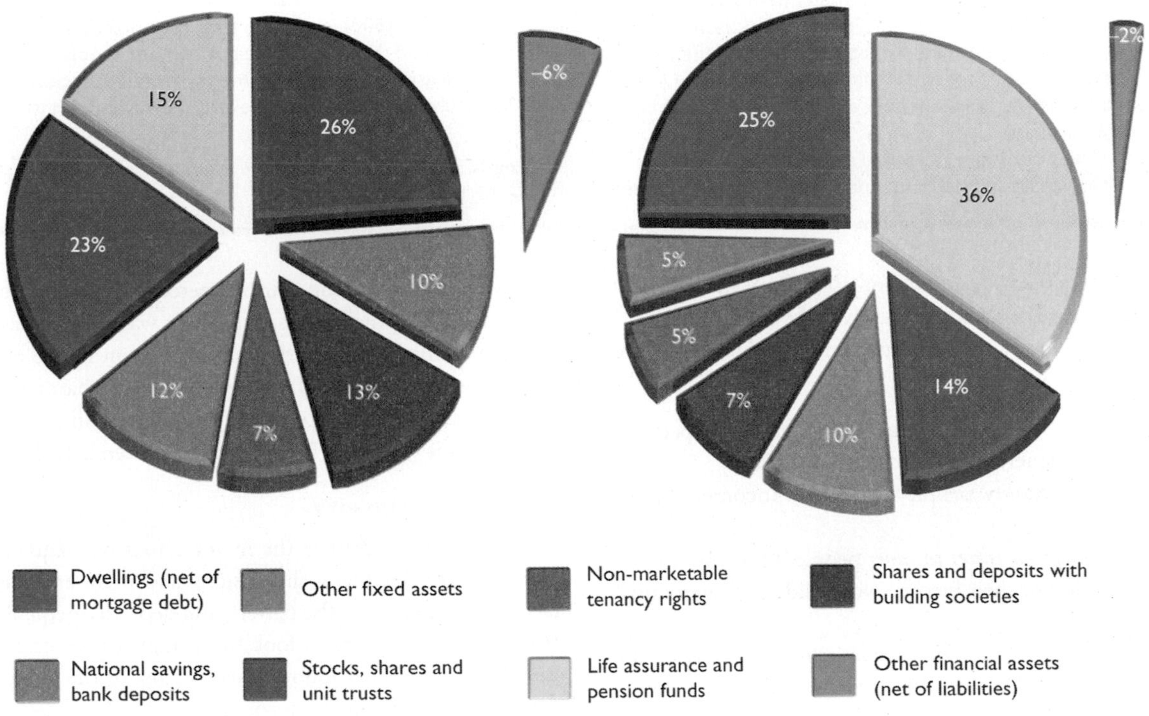

Figure 10.11 Composition of UK wealth: 1971 and 1996

Source: *Social Trends* (ONS, 1998).

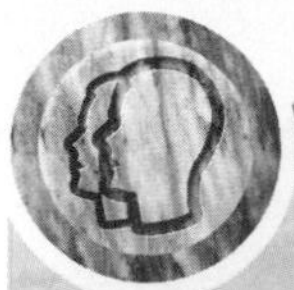

DEVELOPMENT OF IDEAS — BOX 10.2

POVERTY IN THE PAST

Consider from the following passage whether it is reasonable or even possible to compare poverty today with poverty in the 1800s.

> Every great city has one or more slums, where the working class is crowded together. True, poverty often dwells in hidden alleys close to the palaces of the rich; but, in general, a separate territory has been assigned to it, where, removed from the sight of the happier classes, it may struggle along as it can. These slums are pretty equally arranged in all the great towns of England, the worst houses in the worst quarters of the towns; usually one- or two-storied cottages in long rows, perhaps with cellars used as dwellings, almost always irregularly built. These houses of three or four rooms and a kitchen form, throughout England, some parts of London excepted, the general dwellings of the working class. The streets were generally unpaved, rough, dirty, filled with vegetable and animal refuse, without sewers or gutters, but supplied with foul, stagnant pools instead. Moreover, ventilation is impeded by the bad, confused method of building of the whole quarter, and since many human beings live crowded into a small space, the atmosphere that prevails in these working-men's quarters may be readily imagined. Further, the streets serve as drying grounds in fine weather; lines are stretched across from house to house, and hung with wet clothing.
>
> The houses are occupied from cellar to garret, filthy within and without, and their appearance is such that no human being could possibly wish to live in them. But all this is nothing in comparison with the dwellings in the narrow courts and alleys between the streets, entered by covered passages between the houses, in which the filth and tottering ruin surpass all description. Scarcely a whole window-pane can be found, the walls are crumbling, doorposts and window-frames loose and broken, doors of old boards nailed together, or altogether wanting in this thieves' quarter, where no doors are needed, there being nothing to steal. Heaps of garbage and ashes lie in all directions, and the foul liquids emptied before the doors gather in stinking pools. Here the poorest of the poor, the worst-paid workers with thieves and the victims of prostitution indiscriminately huddled together, the majority Irish, or of Irish extraction, and those who have yet sunk in the whirlpool of moral ruin which surrounds them, sinking daily deeper, losing daily more and more of their power to resist the demoralising influence of want, filth, and evil surroundings.[1]

??

1. If we were to measure poverty today and in the 1800s in *absolute terms* (see Box 10.1), in which would there be the greater number of poor?
2. If we measure poverty in *relative terms*, must a society inevitably have a problem of poverty, however rich it is?

[1] F. Engels, *The Condition of the English Working Class* (Progress Publishers, 1973), pp. 166–7.

ever, the wealthiest 1 per cent and 10 per cent still owned 10 per cent and 34 per cent respectively of the nation's wealth.

The four major causes of inequality in the distribution of wealth are as follows:

- *Inheritance:* this allows inequality to be perpetuated from one generation to another.
- *Income inequality:* people with higher incomes can save more.
- *Different propensities to save:* people who save a larger proportion of their income will build up a bigger stock of wealth.
- *Entrepreneurial and investment talent/luck:* some people are successful in investing their wealth and making it grow rapidly.

Even though wealth was still highly concentrated in 1994, there had been a significant reduction in inequality of wealth over time. From 1971 to 1981 the Gini coefficient of wealth fell a full thirteen percentage points from 0.80 to 0.67. A major reason for this was the increased taxation of inherited wealth. Another reason in the early 1970s was a substantial fall in the real value of shares when share prices failed to keep pace with inflation. Since 1981, however, this reduction in inequality has been halted.

Causes of inequality

We turn now to identify the major causes of inequality. The problem has many dimensions and there are many factors that determine the pattern and depth of inequality. It is thus wrong to try to look for a single cause, or even the major one. What follows then is a list of the possible determinants of inequality:

- Inequality of wealth. People with wealth are able to obtain an income other than from their own labour. The greater the inequality of wealth, the greater is the inequality of income likely to be.

CASE STUDIES — BOX 10.3

HOW TO REVERSE BRITAIN'S INCREASED INEQUALITY

Recommendations of the Rowntree inquiry

In February 1995 the Rowntree Foundation published the results of a comprehensive inquiry into Britain's growing inequality since 1979.[2] The findings make grim reading. Inequalities in income had widened further and faster than in any other period in history. The rich had got substantially richer, while the poor had become not only relatively poorer, but *absolutely* poorer.

This growing divide, the report argued, was threatening the whole fabric of society. There was a growing underclass of people with little hope of clawing their way out of their desperate poverty, frequently seeing crime as their only escape route. The poor include the long-term unemployed, pensioners, families dependent on state benefits and young people without the educational attainment to compete in the increasingly competitive labour market. And it is not just the poor who are affected by poverty. Do we want a society, asks the report, where the rich have to build fortresses to protect themselves?

But was this growth in inequality not necessary to provide incentives for people to better themselves and to encourage faster economic growth? The report found no evidence of this. The UK has had a lower rate of economic growth than other countries which had a more equal distribution of income in 1979 and a much more equal distribution in 1995. It is true that more countries had experienced a growth in inequality than a decline (see the diagram), but the UK was second only to New Zealand in the speed at which inequality had increased. In some cases (e.g. Italy), rates of economic growth faster than in the UK have been combined with a reduction in inequality.

The report did not just look at the nature of the problem. It attempted to identify solutions. The following are the major ones:

- Increased expenditure on education and training designed to help the employment prospects of the long-term unemployed and the young who had left school with few if any qualifications.
- Allowing those on benefits to earn a little more or to undertake paid training, without losing all their benefit.
- Providing subsidies for employers taking on the long-term unemployed.
- Providing lump-sum payments to people returning to work.

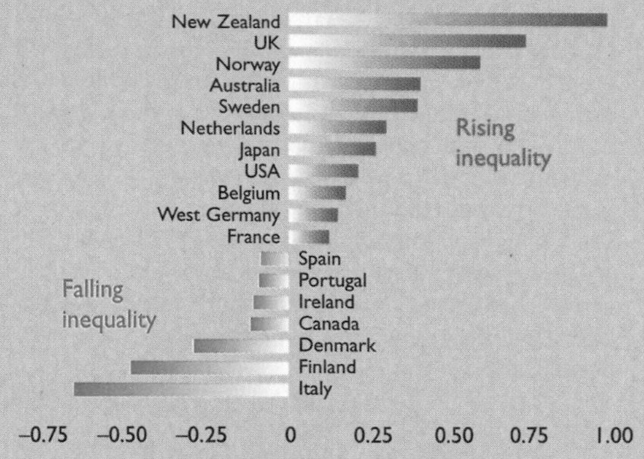

Changes in income inequality: 1979–92

- Making it easier to return to benefits for those losing or quitting their job.
- Targeting tax cuts at the poor and not the rich.
- Improving child-care provision.
- Top-up benefits for those on low incomes.
- Restoration of free school meals for those on Family Credit.
- Support for inner-city areas and estates where levels of poverty and crime are high.
- Government subsidies to local authorities and housing associations for house building, in order to make rents more affordable and to reduce the disincentive of losing housing benefits for those finding work.

The thrust of these recommendations was to encourage employment and improve the lot of low-paid workers. This was seen as a much better alternative than simply increasing benefits, which could well make people more reluctant to get a job. After all, not only would they have to pay taxes, but they would probably sacrifice their benefit – the so-called 'poverty trap' (see pages 312–14).

?? What would be the dangers of paying subsidies to *employers* for taking on the long-term unemployed?

[2] *Income and Wealth* (The Joseph Rowntree Foundation, 1995).

- Differences in ability. People differ in strength, intelligence, dexterity, etc. Some of these differences are innate and some are acquired through the process of 'socialisation' – education, home environment, peer group, etc.
- Differences in attitude. Some people are adventurous, willing to take risks, willing to move for better jobs, keen to push themselves forward. Others are much more cautious.
- Differences in qualifications. These are reflections of a number of things: ability, attitudes toward study, access to educational establishments, the quality of tuition, attitudes and income of parents, etc.

ISSUES AND APPLICATIONS

MINIMUM WAGE LEGISLATION

A way of helping the poor?

> It is a serious national evil that any class of His Majesty's subjects should receive less than a living wage in return for their utmost exertions. It was formerly supposed that the workings of the laws of supply and demand would naturally regulate or eliminate that evil, but whereas in what we call 'sweated trades' you have no parity of bargaining between employers and employed, when the good employer is continually undercut by the bad, and the bad again by the worse, there you have not a condition of progress, but of progressive degeneration.
>
> Winston Churchill (1909)

One way of helping to relieve poverty is for the government to institute a legal minimum hourly wage. A form of minimum wage legislation was introduced in Britain as long ago as 1909 by Winston Churchill, who was at the time President of the Board of Trade in the Liberal government. This involved the setting-up of wages councils. These were independent bodies representing workers in low-pay industries which were poorly unionised. The councils set legally enforceable minimum hourly rates of pay for their respective industries.

In 1993, however, the government announced the abolition of wages councils, and today the UK is one of the few industrialised countries that does not have a legal minimum wage. The Council of Europe defines low pay as anything below two-thirds of the mean wage level. It refers to this as the 'decency threshold'. If a minimum hourly wage were to be based on this, then in the UK it would be set at just under £6, and would raise wages for over 9 million workers. Other studies have identified the low-pay threshold at two-thirds of *median* earnings of *male* workers. A minimum hourly wage set at this level would be about £3.75, and would raise wage rates for only 4 million workers, 70 per cent of whom would be women.

The call for a minimum wage from the political left has grown stronger as the number of low-paid workers has increased. Today there are many people working as cleaners, kitchen hands, garment workers, security guards and shop assistants, who are receiving pittance rates of pay, sometimes less than £2.00 per hour. There are several factors explaining the growth in the size of the low-pay sector.

- *Unemployment.* Very high rates of unemployment since the early 1980s has shifted the balance of power from workers to employers. Employers were able to force many wage rates downwards, especially of unskilled and semi-skilled workers.
- *Growth in part-time employment.* Changes in the structure of the UK economy, in particular the growth in the service sector and the growing proportion of women seeking work, have led to an increase in part-time employment. Many part-time workers do not receive the same rights, privileges and hourly pay as their full-time equivalents.
- *Changes in labour laws.* The abolition of the wages councils and the introduction of various new laws to reduce the power of labour (see page 258) have taken away what little protection there was for low-paid workers.

Assessing the arguments

The arguments against a national minimum wage were put forcibly by Michael Howard in 1992 when he was the Employment Secretary: 'There can be no conceivable justification for a policy which would, on its own, wreck our economy and devastate job prospects.'

So will the imposition of a minimum wage cause unemployment? At first sight the answer would seem to be yes. If it raises wage rates for the poor (and to be effective it must do), then surely the demand for labour will fall and the supply will rise?

Just what will happen to employment depends on two things: the competitiveness of individual labour markets and the elasticity of demand and supply of labour.

In a *competitive* labour market, the level of unemployment created will depend on how much the

- Differences in hours worked. Some people do a full-time job plus overtime, or a second job; others work only part time.
- Differences in job utility/disutility. Other things being equal, unpleasant, arduous or dangerous jobs will need to pay higher wages.
- Differences in power. Monopoly power in the supply of factors or goods, and monopsony power in the demand for factors, is unequally distributed in the economy.
- Differences in the demand for goods. Factors employed in expanding industries will tend to have a higher marginal revenue product because their output has a higher market value.
- Differences in household composition. The greater the number of dependants relative to income earners, the poorer the average household member will be (other things being equal).
- Discrimination, whether by race, sex, age, social background, etc.

BOX 10.4

wage rate rises and on the elasticity of labour demand and supply. The more elastic the demand and supply of labour, the bigger the unemployment effect will be.

Evidence suggests that the demand for low-skilled workers by *individual* employers is likely to be relatively wage sensitive. Often such firms are operating in highly competitive goods/services markets. Any rise in wages, and hence prices, would lead to a large fall in sales and hence employment. But given that *all* firms would face the minimum wage, individual employers would be more able to pass on higher wages in higher prices, knowing that their competitors were doing the same.

When employers have a degree of *monopsony* power, however, it is not even certain that they would want to reduce employment. Remember what we argued in Figure 9.15 (on page 254) when we were examining the effects of unions driving up wages. The argument is the same with a minimum wage. The minimum wage can be as high as W_2 and the firm will still want to employ as many workers as at W_2. The point is that the firm can no longer drive down the wage rate by employing fewer workers, so the incentive to cut its workforce has been removed! Indeed, if the minimum wage rate were above W_1 but below W_2, the firm would now want to employ *more* workers (where the minimum wage rate ($= MC_L$) is equal to the MRP_L). What is effectively happening is that the minimum wage is redistributing the firm's income from profits to wages.

In the long run, the effect on unemployment will depend on the extent to which the higher wages are compensated by higher labour productivity. In several EU countries, where minimum wages have been in force for many years, unemployment has generally been no higher than in the UK, but investment and labour productivity are generally higher.

Recent findings in the USA have suggested that increases in the minimum wage have had a neutral effect upon employment. It has been found that there exists a 'range of indeterminacy' over which wages can fluctuate with little impact upon levels of employment. Even beyond this range, whereas some employers might reduce the quantity of labour they employ, others might respond to their higher wage bill, and hence higher costs, by improving productive efficiency.

Evidence on the employment effects of a national minimum wage appears far from conclusive, certainly where the minimum wage results in fairly modest rises in wage rates. The issue, then, seems to be how *high* the minimum wage rate can be set before unemployment begins to rise.

Beyond the economic arguments, the potentially most powerful claim in favour of a legal minimum wage rate is the moral one: that people working hard in a job should be able to take home a fair wage. Being a moral justification, it is one on which economists can have little say, other than to consider whether in practice a minimum wage rate will indeed help to relieve poverty.

The biggest weakness of a minimum wage as a means of relieving poverty is that it only affects the employed. The main cause of poverty is unemployment. Clearly the unemployed would not benefit from a minimum wage.

Another cause of poverty is a large number of dependants in a family. If there is only one income earner, he or she may be paid above the minimum wage rate and yet the family could be very poor. By contrast, many of those who would be helped by a minimum wage are second income earners in a family.

These are not arguments against minimum wages legislation. They merely suggest that a minimum wage rate cannot be the sole answer to poverty.

??

1. Why is the median wage likely to be lower than the mean wage (and thus a minimum wage based on the median wage be lower than one based on the mean wage)?
2. If minimum wages encourage employers to substitute machines for workers, will this necessarily lead to lower long-term unemployment in (a) that industry and (b) the economy in general?

- Degree of government support. The greater the support for the poor, the less will be the level of inequality in the economy.
- Unemployment. As explained in the previous section, this has become one of the major causes of poverty and hence inequality in recent years.

??

Which of the above causes are reflected in differences in the marginal revenue product of factors?

Government attitudes towards inequality

The political right sees little problem with inequality as such. In fact, inequality has an important economic function. Factor price differences are an essential part of a dynamic market economy. They are the price signals that encourage resources to move to sectors of the economy where demand is growing, and away from sectors where demand is declining. If the government interferes with this process by taxing high incomes and subsidising low incomes, working people will not have the same incentive to gain better qualifications, to seek promotion, to do overtime, or to move for better jobs. Similarly, owners of capital will not have the same incentive to invest.

If inequality is to be reduced, claims the political right, it is better done by encouraging greater factor mobility. If factor supply curves are more elastic (greater mobility), then any shifts in demand will cause smaller changes in factor prices and thus less inequality. But how is greater mobility to be encouraged? The answer, they say, is to create a culture of self-help: where people are not too reliant on state support; where they will 'get on their bikes' and look for higher incomes. At the same time they argue that the monopoly power of unions to interfere in labour markets should be curtailed. The net effect of these two policies, they claim, would be to create a more competitive labour market which would help to reduce inequality as well as promoting economic growth and efficiency.

State support, say those on the right, should be confined to the relief of 'genuine' poverty. Benefits should be simply a minimum safety net for those who cannot work (e.g. the sick or disabled), or on a temporary basis for those who, through no fault of their own, have lost their jobs. Even at this basic level, however, the right argues that state support can be a serious disincentive to effort.

Although many on the political left accept that there is some possibility of a trade-off between equality and efficiency, they see it as a far less serious problem. Questions of efficiency and growth, claims the left, are best dealt with by encouraging investment. This, they argue, is best achieved by creating an environment of industrial democracy where workers participate in investment decisions. This common purpose is in turn best achieved in a more equal and less individualistically competitive society. The left also sees a major role for government in providing support for investment: for example, through government-sponsored research, by investment grants, by encouraging firms to get together and plan a co-ordinated strategy, or by maintaining low interest rates which make borrowing cheaper for investment.

These policies to achieve growth and efficiency, claims the left, will leave the government freer to pursue a much more active policy on redistribution.

SECTION SUMMARY

1. Inequality can be examined by looking at the size distribution of income, the functional distribution of income (whether by broad factor categories, narrow factor categories, occupation or other individual factor reward), the distribution of income by recipient (whether by class of person or geographical area), the distribution of wealth, or the extent and nature of poverty.
2. An analysis of the size distribution of income in the UK shows that inequality has grown.
3. The size distribution of income can be illustrated by means of a Lorenz curve. The greater the inequality, the more bowed the curve will be towards the bottom right-hand corner.
4. Size distribution can also be measured by a Gini coefficient. This will give a figure between 0 (total equality) and 1 (total inequality). It can also be measured as the ratio of the share of national income of a given lower income quantile to that of a higher income quantile.
5. Wages and salaries constitute by far the largest source of income, and thus inequality can be explained mainly in terms of differences in wages and salaries. Nevertheless state benefits are an important moderating influence on inequality and constitute the largest source of income for the poorest 20 per cent of households. Investment earnings are only a minor determinant of income except for the richest 1 or 2 per cent.
6. Apart from differences in wages and salaries between occupations, other determinants of income inequality include differences in household composition, sex and where people live.
7. The distribution of wealth is less equal than the distribution of income. The trend towards greater equality of wealth stopped in the early 1980s.
8. Attitudes towards government redistribution of income vary among political parties. The political right stresses the danger that redistributive policies may destroy incentives. The best approach to inequality, according to the right, is to 'free up' markets so as to encourage greater mobility. The left, by contrast, sees fewer dangers in reducing incentives and stresses the moral and social importance of redistribution from rich to poor. The left argues that growth and employment are best encouraged by direct state support for investment.

10.2 Taxes, benefits and the redistribution of income

In this section we will look at policies to redistribute incomes more equally, and in particular we will focus on the use of government expenditure and taxation. Redistribution is just one of three major roles for government expenditure and taxation. The second is to compensate for the failure of the market to provide an efficient allocation of resources. We examine this role in the next two chapters. The third is to influence the overall level of activity in the economy. Adjusting government expenditure and/or taxation for this purpose is known as *fiscal policy* and is examined in Chapter 17.

The use of taxation and government expenditure to redistribute income

Taxation. By taxing the rich proportionately more than the poor, the post-tax distribution of income will be more equal than the pre-tax distribution.

Subsidies. These are of two broad types. First, *cash benefits* can be seen as subsidies to people's incomes. They include such things as family credit, child benefit and old-age pensions. Second, *benefits in kind* provide subsidised goods and services, which may be provided free (e.g. education and health care) or at a reduced price (e.g. concessionary bus fares for the elderly). Subsidies will lessen inequality if they account for a larger proportion of a poor person's income than a rich person's.

Although we shall focus mainly on use of taxes and benefits, there are two other types of redistributive policy.

Legislation. Examples include minimum wage legislation (see Box 10.4) and anti-discrimination legislation.

Structural. This encompasses a wide range of policies where the government tries to alter those institutions and attitudes of society which increase or at least perpetuate inequalities. Examples of such policies include attacking privileges, instituting universal comprehensive education, encouraging worker share ownership, encouraging industries to move to areas of high unemployment and encouraging the provision of crèche facilities at work.

Before we turn to look at the use of taxation and government expenditure to redistribute incomes, we must first look at what taxes are available to a government and what are the requirements of a good tax system.

The requirements of a good tax system

Whatever the purpose of taxation, when it comes to devising and administering particular taxes there are various principles that many people argue should be observed.

Horizontal equity. According to **horizontal equity**, people in the *same circumstances* should be taxed equally. In other words, taxes should be levied impartially. For example, people earning the same level of income and with the same personal circumstances (e.g. number and type of dependants, size of mortgage, etc.) should pay the same level of income tax.

?? Is it horizontally equitable for smokers and drinkers to pay more tax than non-smokers and non-drinkers?

Vertical equity. According to **vertical equity**, taxes should be 'fairly' apportioned between rich and poor. What constitutes fairness here is highly controversial. No one likes paying taxes and thus a rich person's concept of a fair tax is unlikely to be the same as a poor person's. This whole question of using taxes as a means of redistributing incomes will be examined in detail below.

Equity between recipients of benefits. Under the **benefit principle** it is argued that those who receive the most benefits from government expenditure ought to pay the most in taxes. For example, it can be argued that roads should be paid for from fuel tax. That way those who use the roads the most will pay the most towards their construction and maintenance.

DEFINITIONS

Horizontal equity The equal treatment of people in the same situation.

Vertical equity The redistribution from the better off to the worse off. In the case of taxes this means the rich paying proportionately more taxes than the poor.

Benefit principle of taxation The principle that people ought to pay taxes in proportion to the amount that they use government services.

??

1. Does the benefit principle conflict with either vertical or horizontal equity?
2. Would this be a good principle to apply in the case of health care?

In most cases the benefits principle would be difficult to put into practice. There are two reasons why. First, a specific tax would have to be devised for each particular good and service provided by the state. Second, in the case of many goods and services provided by the state it would be difficult to identify the amount of benefit received by each individual. Just how much benefit (in money terms) do you derive from street lighting, from the police, from the navy, from clean air, etc.?

Cheap to collect. Taxes cost money to collect. These costs should be kept to a minimum relative to the revenue they yield.

Difficult to evade. If it is desirable to have a given tax, people should not be able to escape paying. A distinction here is made between **tax evasion** and **tax avoidance**:

- Tax evasion is illegal. This is where, for example, people do not declare income to the tax authorities.
- Tax avoidance is legal, albeit from the government's point of view undesirable. This is where people try to find ways of managing their affairs so as to reduce their tax liability. They may employ an accountant to help them.

Non-distortionary. Taxes alter market signals: taxes on goods and services alter market prices; taxes on income alter wages. They should not do this in an undesirable direction.

If prices are not distorted in the first place, it is best to use taxes that have the same percentage effect on prices of all goods and services. That way *relative* prices remain the same. For example, VAT in the UK is levied on virtually all goods and services at a single rate of 17½ per cent. If goods were taxed at different rates, this would create distortions, switching consumption and production from goods with high taxes to goods with low taxes.

If, however, the government feels that market prices *are* distorted in the first place, taxes can be used to alter price signals in the desired direction.

??

How can the market distortions argument be used to justify putting excise duties on specific goods such as petrol, alcohol and tobacco? Is this the only reason why excise duties are put on these particular products?

Convenient to the taxpayer. Taxes should be *certain* and *clearly understood* by taxpayers so that they can calculate their tax liabilities. The method of payment should be *straightforward.*

Convenient to the government. Governments use tax changes as an instrument for managing the economy. Tax rates should thus be *simple to adjust*. Also the government will need to be able to *calculate* as accurately as possible the effects of tax changes, both on the total tax yield and on the distribution of the burden between taxpayers.

Minimal disincentive effects. Taxes may discourage people from working longer or harder, from saving, from investing or from taking initiative. For example, a high rate of income tax may discourage people from seeking promotion or from doing overtime. 'What is the point,' they may say, 'if a large proportion of my extra income is taken away in taxes?' It is desirable that these disincentives should be kept to a minimum.

Of course, not all these requirements can be met at the same time. There is no perfect tax. The government thus has to seek a compromise when there is a conflict between any of the requirements. One of the most serious conflicts is between vertical equity and the need to keep disincentives to a minimum. The more steeply the rich are taxed, it is argued, the more serious are the disincentive effects on them likely to be. This particular conflict is examined below.

Types of tax

Taxes can be divided into two broad categories. **Direct taxes** are paid directly by the taxpayer to the tax authorities. Such taxes include personal income tax, tax on companies' income and tax on capital and wealth. **Indirect taxes**, on the other hand, are paid via a middle person. For example, value added tax (VAT) is designed to be a tax on consumption. But you the consumer do not pay it to the

DEFINITIONS

Tax evasion The illegal non-payment of taxes (e.g. by not declaring income earned).

Tax avoidance The rearrangement of one's affairs so as to reduce one's tax liability.

Direct taxes Taxes on income and wealth. Paid directly to the tax authorities on that income or wealth.

Indirect taxes Taxes on expenditure. Paid to the tax authorities not by the consumer, but indirectly by the suppliers of the goods or services.

authorities: it is paid by firms, which then pass it on to consumers in higher prices. You are thus taxed indirectly when you buy goods and services.

Direct taxes

Personal income tax. All types of income are included – wages, salaries, interest, dividends and rent. In most countries, people can earn a certain amount of income free of tax: this is known as their **personal tax allowance**. The size of the allowance will usually vary according to the person's circumstances (e.g. whether they are married or single and whether they have various dependants). In many countries, employees' income tax is paid directly on their behalf by their employers. In the UK this is known as the pay-as-you-earn scheme (PAYE).

The marginal rate of income tax is the rate that people pay on additional income. In most countries, the marginal rate increases in bands as people earn more. Thus in the UK a person earning £4000 per year will only pay 20 per cent on an extra pound earned, whereas a person earning £40 000 will pay 40 per cent on an extra pound earned. In many countries, there is a main marginal rate of tax that most people pay. This is known as the **basic or standard rate of tax.**

The *average* rate is a person's total income tax as a fraction of total income. This will always be less than the marginal rate, since part of a person's income will be tax-free; and for higher tax rate payers, part will be taxed at lower rates.

Individuals' social security contributions. In the UK these are known as national insurance contributions (NICs). These are like income taxes in that they are generally charged as a percentage of a person's income, the marginal rate varying with income. Unlike other taxes, which are paid into a common fund to finance government expenditure, they are used to finance *specific* expenditure: namely, pensions and social security. Although they do not officially count as 'taxes', to all intents and purposes they are so.

Employers' social security contributions. Employers also have to pay social security contributions on behalf of their employees. These are paid per employee. In some countries, small firms pay reduced rates.

Tax on corporate income. In the UK this is known as corporation tax. It is a tax on the profits of limited companies. In most countries, there are lower rates for small companies. Profits can usually be offset against capital expenditure and interest payments when working out the tax liability. This effectively means that profits that are reinvested are not taxed.

Taxes on capital gains. This is a tax payable when a person sells assets, such as property or shares. It is payable on the gain in value of these assets since a set date in the past, or since they were purchased if this was after the set date.

Taxes on wealth. These are taxes on assets held or acquired by individuals. One form of wealth tax in most countries is that on inherited assets or assets transferred before a person's death. Another is taxes based on the value of a person's property. This is a particularly common form of local taxation (the others being local income tax, local business tax and local sales tax).

Poll taxes. These are fixed-sum charges per head of the population, irrespective of the person's income. Very few countries use such taxes as they are regarded as grossly unfair. A poll tax (or 'community charge') was introduced in Scotland in 1989 and in England and Wales in 1990 as the new form of local tax. But it was massively unpopular with the electorate and was replaced by the 'council tax' (based on property values) in 1993.

Indirect taxes

There are three main types of indirect tax, all of which are taxes on *expenditure*.

General expenditure taxes. An example of this is **value added tax** (VAT). This is the main indirect tax throughout the EU. VAT is paid on the value that firms add to goods and services at each stage of their production and distribution. For example, if a firm purchases supplies costing

DEFINITIONS

Tax allowance An amount of income that can be earned tax free. Tax allowances vary according to a person's circumstances.

Basic rate of tax The main marginal rate of tax, applying to most people's incomes.

Value added tax (VAT) A tax on goods and services, charged at each stage of production as a percentage of the value added at that stage.

Table 10.3 Calculating VAT: an example

	Value added (1)		VAT (2)		Value added plus VAT (3)	Price sold to next stage (4)
Firm A sells raw materials to firm B for £11 000	£10 000		£1000		£11 000	£11 000
Firm B processes them and sells them to a manufacturer, firm C, for £19 800	£8000		£800		£8800	£19 800
Firm C sells the manufactured goods to a wholesaler, firm D, for £27 500	£7000		£700		£7700	£27 500
Firm D sells them to a retailer, firm E, for £33 000	£5000		£500		£5500	£33 000
Firm E sells them to consumers for £44 000	£10 000		£1000		£11 000	£44 000
	£40 000	+	**£4000**	=	**£44 000**	

£10 000 and with them produces goods which it sells for £15 000 (before VAT), it is liable to pay VAT on the £15 000 minus £10 000: in other words, on the £5000 value it has added. Suppliers must provide invoices to show that the VAT has already been paid on all the inputs.

The example in Table 10.3 can be used to show how the tax eventually gets passed on to the consumer. For simplicity's sake, assume that the rate of VAT is 10 per cent and that each firm uses only one supplier.

The value added at each stage plus VAT adds up to the total amount paid by the consumer: £44 000 in this case. The total VAT paid, therefore, amounts to a tax on the consumer. In the example, the £4000 VAT is 10 per cent of the (pre-tax) consumer price of £40 000.

The rates of VAT in the various EU countries are shown in the table in Box 23.11 on pages 718–19. Each country has a standard rate and up to two lower rates for basic goods and services.

Many other countries levy general expenditure taxes at a *single* stage (either wholesale or retail). These taxes are called *purchase taxes* and will normally be a percentage of the value of the price of the good at that stage.

Excise duties. These are taxes on particular goods and services, for example petrol and diesel, alcoholic drinks, tobacco products and gambling. They are a single-stage tax levied on the manufacturer. They are paid in addition to VAT.

VAT is an **ad valorem tax**. This means that the tax is levied at a *percentage* of the value of the good. The higher the value of the good, the higher the tax paid. Excise duties, by contrast, are a **specific tax**. This means that they are levied at a *fixed amount*, irrespective of the value of the good. Thus the duty on a litre of unleaded petrol is the same for a cut-price filling station as for a full-price one.

Customs duties. Economists normally refer to these as **tariffs**. They are duties on goods imported from outside the country.

?? To what extent do (a) income tax, (b) VAT and (c) a poll tax meet the various requirements for a good tax system on pages 295–6 above? (Some of the answers to this question are given below.)

The balance of taxation

Table 10.4 shows the balance of the different types of tax in selected countries. Some striking differences can be seen between the countries. In France, income taxes account for only 16 per cent of tax revenue, whereas in the USA they account for 35 per cent. In the UK, social security contributions (national insurance) are a much lower percentage of total taxes than in other countries, whereas indirect taxes are a much higher percentage. In the USA, taxes on corporate income are nearly $2^1/_2$ times greater as a proportion of total taxes than in Germany. In all countries, taxes on capital and wealth are a very small proportion of total taxation.

The table also shows total taxes as a percentage of gross national product or GNP. (GNP is a measure of the

DEFINITIONS

Ad valorem tax A tax on a good levied as a percentage of its value. It can be a single-stage tax or a multi-stage tax (such as VAT).

Specific tax A tax on a good levied at a fixed amount per unit of the good, irrespective of the price of that unit.

Tariff A tax on imported goods.

Table 10.4 Balance of taxation in different countries

Types of tax as % of total tax	France 1983	France 1994	Germany 1983	Germany 1994	Japan 1983	Japan 1994	Netherlands 1983	Netherlands 1994	Sweden 1983	Sweden 1994	UK 1983	UK 1994	USA 1983	USA 1994
Income	15.5	16.4	24.7	23.5	25.3	24.0	22.6	22.6	39.5	37.6	28.7	29.6	37.3	35.0
Social security	43.6	43.7	39.4	40.3	29.8	33.3	45.8	41.7	26.6	27.4	18.0	18.9	24.0	26.1
Corporate income	5.2	5.1	4.6	3.2	17.1	12.9	6.0	7.4	3.5	5.0	10.7	8.3	8.2	9.4
Capital and wealth	0.6	0.9	0.2	0.3	1.0	2.0	0.4	0.6	0.2	0.1	0.6	0.6	0.9	0.9
Expenditure	35.1	33.9	31.3	32.7	26.8	27.8	25.2	27.7	30.2	29.9	42.0	42.4	29.6	28.6
Total taxes as % of GNP	43.4	44.4	40.8	42.3	27.3	28.3	46.9	46.7	51.6	52.2	37.8	33.4	30.7	31.7

nation's income: we will be examining how it is measured in section 14.5.) In Sweden over 50 per cent of the nation's income is paid in tax, whereas in Japan the figure is under 30 per cent. For all countries except the UK and the Netherlands, a higher proportion of national income was paid in taxes in 1994 than in 1983.

Taxes as a means of redistributing income

If taxes are to be used as a means of achieving greater equality, the rich must be taxed proportionately more than the poor. The degree of redistribution will depend on the degree of 'progressiveness' of the tax. In this context, taxes may be classified as follows:

- **Progressive tax.** As people's income (Y) rises, the percentage of their income paid in the tax (T) rises. In other words, the *average* rate of tax (T/Y) rises.
- **Regressive tax.** As people's income rises, the percentage of their income paid in the tax falls: T/Y falls.
- **Proportional tax.** As people's income rises, the percentage of their income paid in the tax stays the same: T/Y is constant.

In other words, progressiveness is defined in terms of what happens to the average rate of tax as incomes rise. (Note that it is not defined in terms of the *marginal* rate of tax.)

??

1. If a person earning £5000 per year pays £500 in a given tax and a person earning £10 000 per year pays £800, is the tax progressive or regressive?
2. A proportional tax will leave the distribution of income unaffected. Why should this be so, given that a rich person will pay a larger absolute amount than a poor person?

An extreme form of regressive tax is a lump-sum tax. This is levied at a fixed *amount* (not rate) irrespective of income.

Figure 10.12 illustrates these different categories of tax. Diagram (a) shows the total amount of tax a person pays. With a progressive tax the curve gets progressively steeper, showing that the average rate of tax (T/Y) rises. The marginal rate of tax ($\Delta T/\Delta Y$) is given by the slope. Thus between points x and y the marginal tax rate is 40 per cent.

Diagram (b) shows the average rates. With a proportional tax a person pays the same amount of tax on each pound earned. With a progressive tax a larger proportion is paid by a rich person than by a poor person, and vice versa with a regressive tax.

The more steeply upward sloping the average tax curve, the more progressive is the tax, and the more equal will be the post-tax incomes of the population.

Problems with using taxes to redistribute incomes

How successfully can taxes redistribute income, and at what economic cost?

Problems in achieving redistribution

How to help the very poor. Taxation takes away income. It can thus reduce the incomes of the rich. But no taxes, however progressive, can *increase* the incomes of the poor. This will require subsidies.

But what about tax cuts? Cannot bigger tax cuts be given to the poor? This is possible only if the poor are already paying taxes in the first place. Take the two cases of income tax and taxes on goods and services.

DEFINITIONS

Progressive tax A tax whose average rate with respect to income rises as income rises.

Regressive tax A tax whose average rate with respect to income falls as income rises.

Proportional tax A tax whose average rate with respect to income stays the same as income rises.

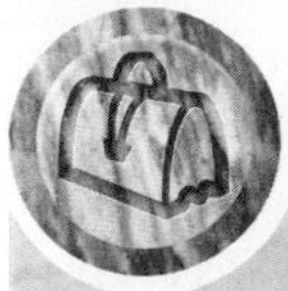

CASE STUDIES

TAXATION IN THE UK

How progressive is it?

Income tax

Everyone can earn a certain amount tax free. This is their *personal allowance*. In 1998/9 this was £4195. An additional tax-free allowance is granted to married couples. Single parents, old people and people with special needs also get additional tax-free allowances.

Above this tax-free level of income, people pay an initial rate of 20 per cent on each extra pound earned. In 1998/9 this was on the next £4300 of income. Beyond this, people then start paying the *basic rate* of income tax. In 1998/9 the basic rate was 23 per cent.

There is an upper limit to income on which the basic rate is paid. Above this, each extra pound earned is charged at the *higher rate* of 40 per cent. In 1998/9 this was paid on any taxable income (i.e. income above the tax-free allowance level) above £27 100.

Income tax in the UK is progressive. In other words, the average rate of tax rises with income. There are two reasons for this:

- Tax allowances account for a larger proportion of a poor person's income than a rich person's.
- Above certain levels of income higher marginal rates of tax are paid.

The diagram and table (a) show the marginal and average rates of income tax in 1998/9. Although income tax is still mildly progressive, it is much less so now than it used to be. This is due to various changes in income tax rates that were made by the Conservative government during the 1980s. One change was a series of reductions in the basic rate: from 33 per cent in 1979 to 25 per cent in 1988 and then to 23 per cent in 1996. This resulted in income taxes accounting for a smaller fraction of total taxation, and since income taxes are more progressive than most other taxes, this in turn led to a reduction in the redistribution of income.

The most dramatic change was introduced in the 1988 Budget. Before that time there were several higher rates of taxation above the 40 per cent rate, up to 60 per cent. In 1988 all rates above 40 per cent were abolished.

Table (a) UK marginal and average income tax rates, and average income tax plus NIC rates: 1998/9

Single persons/married women[1] (annual figures)			
Income (£)	Marginal income tax rate (%)	Average income tax rate (%)	Average income tax + NIC rate (%)
3000	0	0.0	0.0
4000	0	0.0	3.3
6000	20	6.0	11.6
8000	20	9.5	16.2
10 000	23	12.1	19.4
15 000	23	15.7	23.9
20 000	23	17.5	26.2
25 000	23	18.6	27.5
30 000	23	19.4	26.9
40 000	40	24.0	29.6
50 000	40	27.2	31.7
100 000	40	33.6	35.9

[1] Or married men if the wife receives the married couple's allowance.

Source: Author's calculations.

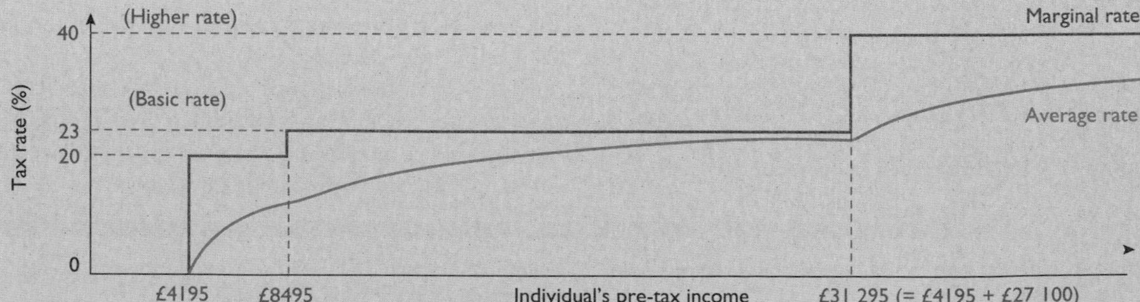

Note: This assumes that the only allowance the person is entitled to is the single person's allowance.

Average and marginal rates of income tax for a single person: 1998/9

BOX 10.5

National insurance contributions (NICs)

These are payments made by individuals and their employers to the Department of Social Security. They are used to finance pensions and social security. Although they do not officially count as taxes, to all intents and purposes they are so. Individuals' contributions are a percentage of their income up to a certain level. Above that no more NICs are paid: i.e. the marginal rate becomes zero (see table (b)).

Table (b) Marginal national insurance rates for individuals: 1998/9

Income per annum (£)	Marginal national insurance rate
0– 3 327	0%
3 328–25 220	10% (plus 2% of £3 327)
25 221–	0%

The combined effect of income tax and employees' NICs is to give a tax that is partly progressive and partly regressive. In 1998/9 the combined marginal rate rose from zero to 33 per cent (i.e. 23 per cent plus 10 per cent) up to the upper limit of NIC. Above this the rate fell to 23 per cent (the marginal NIC rate was zero), rising again to 40 per cent when people reached the higher rate of income tax!

Corporation tax

This is a tax on the profits of limited companies. In 1999/2000 the rate is 20 per cent for companies with profits below £300 000 rising to 30 per cent for those with profits over £1.5 million. Profits can be offset against capital expenditure and interest payments when working out liability to corporation tax. This effectively means that profits that are reinvested are not taxed.

Capital gains tax

This is a tax payable when a person sells assets, such as property or shares. It is payable on the gain in value of these assets (after allowing for inflation) since a set date in the past, or since they were purchased if this was after the set date. It is payable only if a person's capital gains exceed a certain amount in any year. In 1998/9 this amount was £6800. The rate of tax was the same as income tax (20, 23 or 40 per cent, depending on a person's total taxable income). The sale of owner-occupied houses is excluded from the tax. Capital gains tax, being charged at three rates, is mildly progressive.

Inheritance tax

This is a wealth tax paid when assets are transferred from one person to another, either on death or during the donor's lifetime if the donor dies within seven years of the gift. In 1998/9, transfers below £223 000 were exempt. Amounts above this were taxed at a rate of 40 per cent on the excess.

The high threshold means that this tax only has a redistributive effect away from people in receipt of very large inheritances.

Local authority taxes

Local authorities raise part of their revenue from the *council tax*. This is a property tax levied on a household (as opposed to individuals). If there is only one adult living in the property, however, the tax is reduced by one-quarter. Each property is put into one of eight bands (A–H), depending on the property's value. The higher the band, the greater is the tax. The size of the tax varies from one local authority to another depending on their expenditure.

A larger proportion of rich people are home owners. Richer people tend to live in bigger houses. For these two reasons rich people tend to pay more council tax than poor people. Whether the tax is actually progressive or not, however, depends on how much more they pay: do they pay a larger proportion of their income? This varies with (a) the particular local authority in question and (b) the number of occupants in any given house.

Local authorities are also financed partly from general taxation and partly from the *uniform business rate*. This tax on firms is levied at a single rate throughout the country, but varies with the size and value of the business. Businesses are given a 'rateable value' by the Inland Revenue and then all businesses are charged at the same percentage of their rateable value. The moneys from the business rates go to a central pool and then all local authorities draw from this pool according to the size of their population. The money they draw does *not* depend on the amount of business rates paid in their area.

Indirect taxes

These consist of VAT (levied at 17½ per cent on most goods and services), excise duties (on petrol and diesel, alcoholic drinks, tobacco products and gambling), customs duties on goods imported from outside the EU, and levies imposed on agricultural imports (see section 3.3).

Indirect taxes tend to be regressive. The reason is that the rich tend to spend a smaller proportion of their income than the poor: the poor cannot afford to save; the rich can.

continued

CASE STUDIES — BOX 10.5 *continued*

TAXATION IN THE UK
How progressive is it?

The regressive nature of indirect taxes is lessened by two features:

- Some basic goods and services, which are consumed proportionately much more by the poor, are zero rated for VAT. These include food and children's clothes.
- Excise duties (levied on top of VAT) apply only to certain items. Some of these, such as petrol, are consumed proportionately more by the rich. Others, however, such as cigarettes, are consumed proportionately more by the poor.

Indirect taxes used to be less regressive than they are today for the following reasons:

- Before 1973, when VAT was introduced, there was purchase tax on various goods. This was levied at higher rates on luxury goods.
- There used to be more than one rate of VAT (other than zero). There was a basic rate and a luxury rate.
- VAT was raised from 8 per cent to 15 per cent in 1979 and to 17½ per cent in 1991 as part of a general shift from direct to indirect taxes.
- VAT was imposed on domestic fuel in 1994: previously it had been zero rated. The poor spend a larger proportion of their income on domestic fuel than do the rich. In 1998/9, the VAT rate on domestic fuel was 8 per cent.

The relative progressiveness of income tax, NIC and the council tax on the one hand, and indirect taxes on the other, is shown in table (c) for the years 1978 and 1996/7.

??

1. Had taxes become more or less progressive between 1978 and 1996/7?
2. How do you think the 1988 Budget changes affected these figures?

Table (c) Distribution of the tax burden in the UK

Quintile groups of households (ranked by original income)	1978			1996/7		
	Income tax, NICs and rates as % of gross income[1] (1)	Indirect taxes as % of gross income[1] (2)	Total tax as % of gross income[1] (1)+(2)	Income tax, NICs and council tax as % of gross income[1] (1)	Indirect taxes as % of gross income[1] (2)	Total tax as % of gross income[1] (1)+(2)
Poorest 20%	0.6	20.6	21.6	10.2	27.2	37.4
Next 20%	11.1	20.7	31.8	12.9	21.9	34.8
Middle 20%	17.9	18.7	36.6	17.6	18.9	36.5
Next 20%	20.1	17.2	37.3	20.6	16.4	37.0
Richest 20%	23.2	14.8	38.0	23.4	11.8	35.2
All households	18.5	17.1	35.6	19.8	16.1	35.9

[1] Gross income = original income plus cash benefits.

Sources: *Social Trends* (CSO, 1980); *Economic Trends* (ONS, April 1998).

If the government were to cut income tax, then anyone currently paying it would benefit. A cut in tax *rates* will give proportionately more to the rich, since they have a larger proportion of taxable income relative to total income. An increase in personal *allowances*, on the other hand, will give the same *absolute* amounts to everyone above the new tax threshold. This will therefore represent a smaller proportionate gain to the rich. In either case, however, there will be no gain at all to those people below the tax threshold. They paid no income tax in the first place. These poorest of all people therefore gain nothing at all from income tax cuts.

Since taxes on goods and services are generally regressive, any cut in their rate will benefit the poor proportionately more than the rich. A more dramatic effect would be obtained by cutting the rate most on those goods consumed relatively more by the poor.

The government may not wish to cut the overall level of taxation, given its expenditure commitments. In this case it

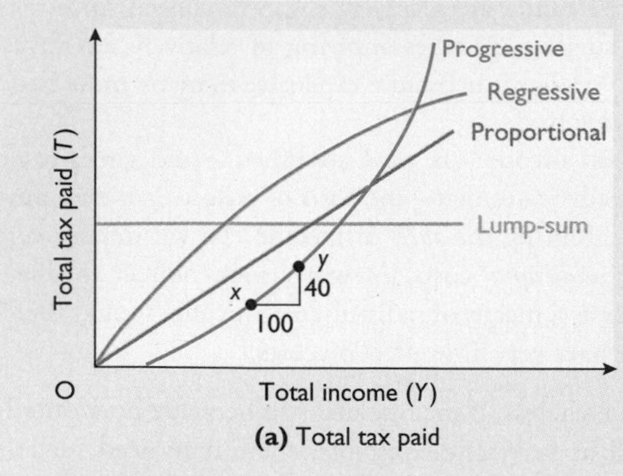

(a) Total tax paid

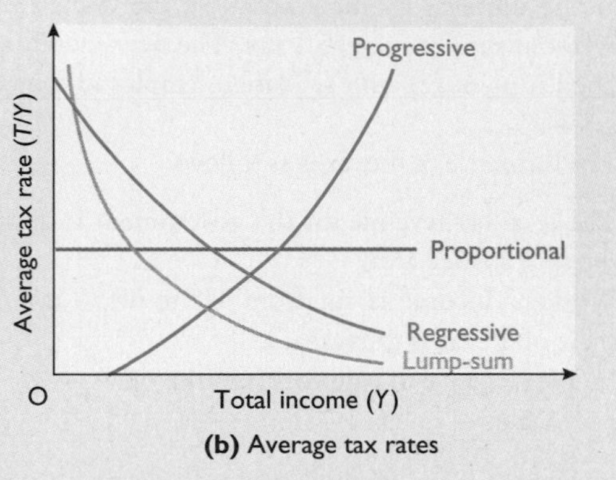

(b) Average tax rates

Figure 10.12

can switch the burden from regressive to progressive taxes. That way at least some benefit is gained by the very poor.

Tax evasion and tax avoidance. The higher the rates of tax, the more likely are people to try to escape paying some of their taxes.

People who are subject to higher rates of income tax will be more tempted not to declare all their income. This tax *evasion* will be much easier for people not paying all their taxes through a pay-as-you-earn (PAYE) scheme. This will include the self-employed, or people doing casual work on top of their normal job ('moonlighting'). Furthermore, richer people can often reduce their tax liability – tax *avoidance* – by a careful use of various allowances (such as mortgage tax relief) and tax loopholes such as being allowed to offset 'business expenses' against income.

Part of the government's justification for abolishing income tax rates above 40 per cent in 1988 was that many people escaped paying these higher taxes.

?? Why may a steeply progressive income tax which is designed to achieve greater *vertical* equity lead to a reduction in *horizontal* equity?

Undesired incidence of tax. High rates of income tax on high wage earners may simply encourage employers to pay them higher wages. At the other end of the scale, tax cuts for low-paid workers may simply allow employers to cut wages. In other words, part of the incidence of income taxes will be borne by the employer and only part by the employee. Thus attempting to make taxes more 'progressive' will fail if employers simply adjust wages to compensate.

The incidence of income tax is determined by the elasticity of supply and demand for labour. In Figures 10.13 and 10.14, the initial supply and demand curves for labour (before the imposition of the tax) intersect at point (1), giving Q_1 labour employed at a wage of W_1. Now an income tax is imposed. This shifts the labour supply curve

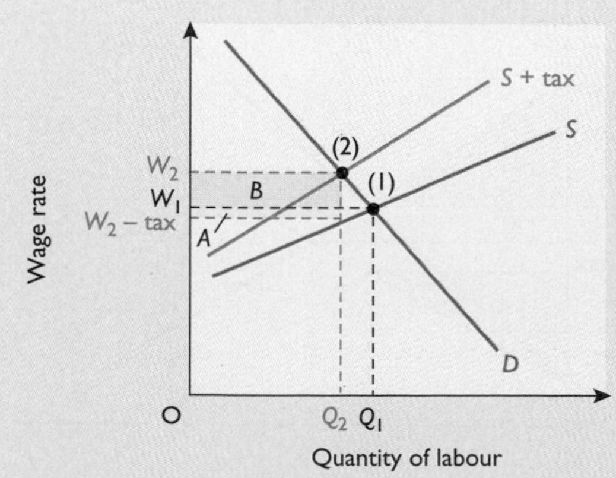

Figure 10.13 The incidence of an income tax: elastic supply of labour

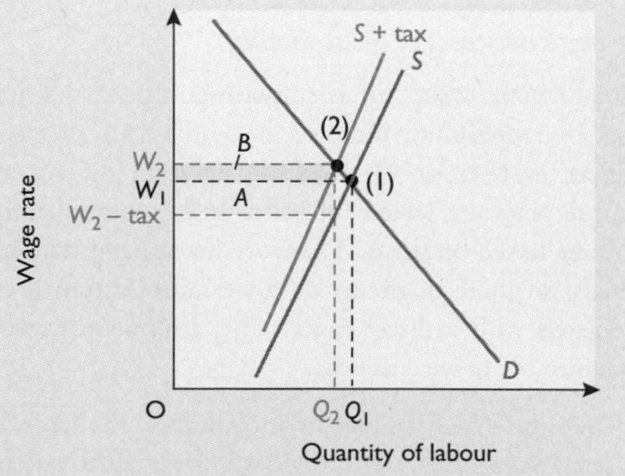

Figure 10.14 The incidence of an income tax: inelastic supply of labour

vertically upwards by the amount of the tax, giving the new labour supply curve, S + tax. The new equilibrium is reached at point (2) with Q_2 labour employed at a (gross) wage of W_2.

The incidence of the tax is as follows:

- The total tax revenue for the government is shown by the total shaded area.
- Workers' income is cut from W_1 to W_2 – tax. Their share of the tax is thus area *A*.
- Employers have to pay workers a rise of $W_2 - W_1$. They pay area *B*.

In Figure 10.13 supply is relatively elastic. In this case the main burden of the tax falls on employers. In Figure 10.14, by contrast, supply is relatively inelastic. Here it is workers who pay the bulk of the tax.

??

1. Do poor people gain more from a cut in income tax with an elastic or an inelastic supply of labour? Is the supply of unskilled workers likely to be elastic or inelastic?
2. Draw two diagrams like Figures 10.13 and 10.14, but this time keep the two sets of supply curves the same in each and vary the slope of the demand curve. How does the elasticity of demand affect the incidence of the income tax?

Of course, income taxes are not just imposed on workers in one industry alone. People, therefore, cannot move to another industry to avoid paying taxes. This fact will cause a relatively inelastic supply response to any rise in income tax, since the only alternative to paying the income tax is to work less. The less elastic this response, the more will the burden of the tax fall on the taxpayer and the more effectively can income taxes be used to redistribute incomes.

The economic costs of redistribution

Administrative costs. It is sometimes argued that using taxes to redistribute incomes is costly because income taxes are more expensive to administer than indirect taxes. Income taxes are levied on individuals whereas indirect taxes are levied on firms. There are fewer firms than individuals, so there ought to be lower administrative costs associated with indirect taxes. This argument, however, has a number of weaknesses:

- With the PAYE system of income tax, the tax is collected from firms, not individuals. Individuals still have to fill in income tax returns and these have to be checked by the Inland Revenue, but with computerisation the PAYE system has been made much more streamlined.
- Excise duties are relatively cheap to collect, since they are single-stage taxes applying to relatively few firms. But VAT is much more expensive as many more firms are involved.
- Unless income tax were abolished – and virtually no one advocates that – the costs of collecting it exist anyway. Raising the *rates* of income tax will impose very few *additional* costs. A swing from indirect to direct taxes as a means of redistributing income should therefore have very little effect on costs.

Nevertheless, if income tax is to be made horizontally as well as vertically equitable, there may need to be a complex system of personal allowances. This *will* raise administrative costs.

Costs of resource reallocation. If redistribution is to be achieved through *indirect* taxes, this can lead to market distortions.

Take first the case of an indirect tax applied to one good only. Assume for simplicity that there is universal perfect competition. Raising the price of this good relative to other goods will introduce a market distortion. Consumption will shift away from this good towards other goods which people preferred less at the original prices. What is more, the loss to consumers and producers (other things being equal) will be greater than the gain to the community from the tax revenue. This is illustrated in Figure 10.15.

With no tax, price will be at P_1 and output at Q_1, where demand equals supply. By imposing a tax on the good, the supply curve shifts upward to S + tax. Price rises to P_2 and output falls to Q_2. Producers are left with P_2 – tax. What are the various losses and gains?

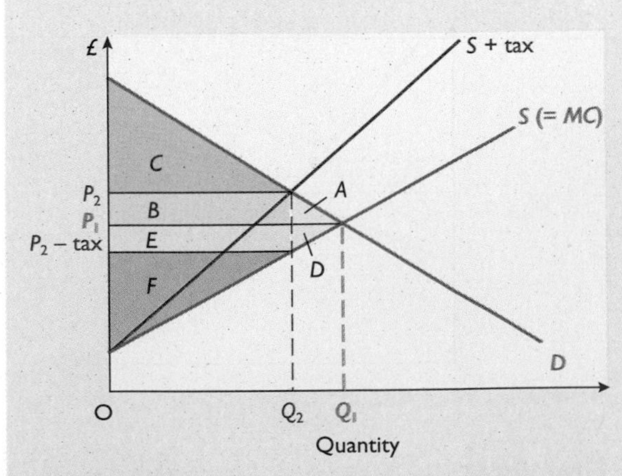

Figure 10.15 Indirect tax applied to good X

Consumers, by having to pay a higher price, lose consumer surplus (see section 4.1). Originally their consumer surplus was areas $A + B + C$. With the price now at P_2, the consumer surplus falls to area C alone. The loss to consumers is areas $A + B$.

Producers, by receiving a lower price after tax and selling fewer units, lose profits. In the simple case where there are no fixed costs of production, total profits are simply the sum of all the marginal profits (P (= MR) – MC) on each of the units sold. Thus before the tax is imposed, firms receive total profits of areas $D + E + F$. After the tax is imposed they receive a profit of area F alone. The loss in profits to producers is therefore areas $D + E$.

The total loss to consumers and producers is areas $A + B + D + E$. The gain to the government in tax revenue is areas $B + E$: the tax rate times the number of units sold (Q_2). There is thus a net loss to the community of areas $A + D$.

However, if the money raised from the tax is redistributed to the poor, their gain in welfare is likely to exceed the loss in welfare from the higher tax. The reason is that a pound sacrificed by the average consumer is probably of less value to him or her than a pound gained by a poor person.

What is more, if the tax is applied at a uniform rate to *all* goods, there is no distortion resulting from reallocation between goods. This is one of the major justifications for having a single rate of VAT.

Of course, in the real world, markets are highly imperfect and there is no reason why taxes will necessarily make these imperfections worse. In fact it might be desirable on efficiency grounds to tax certain goods and services, such as cigarettes, alcohol, petrol and gambling, at higher rates than other goods and services. We will examine these arguments in the next chapter.

Disincentives. A problem with *income* taxes is that, if they lead to less employment, then, other things being equal, less will be produced. Redistribution will be achieved at the expense of total output and consumption. But do high tax rates discourage people from working? It depends on the elasticity of supply of labour.

Critics of high marginal rates of income tax claim that labour supply is relatively elastic. They argue that putting up income tax rates will act as a disincentive and significantly reduce national income.

Those in favour of high income taxes argue that the supply curve of labour is highly inelastic and may even be downward sloping. A rise in taxes will cut people's income. They will not be able to afford to reduce the amount they work and may even have to work harder or longer.

Who is correct? The arguments are examined in the next section.

Taxation and incentives

The whole question of incentives is highly charged politically. According to the political right there is a trade-off between output and equity. High and progressive income taxes can lead to a more equal distribution of income, but a smaller national output. Alternatively, by cutting taxes there will be a bigger national output, but less equally divided. If many socialists are correct, however, we can have both a more equal society *and* a bigger national output: there is no trade-off.

To analyse these arguments we need to return to the distinction between the income and substitution effects of changes in income on the supply of labour.

Income and substitution effects of higher income taxes

Raising taxes does two things.

It reduces incomes. People therefore work *more* in an attempt to maintain their consumption of goods and services. This is the **income effect**.

It reduces the opportunity cost of leisure. An extra hour taken in leisure now involves a smaller sacrifice in consumption. Thus people may substitute leisure for consumption, and work *less*. This is the **substitution effect**.

The relative size of the income and substitution effects is likely to differ for different types of people and different types of tax change.

Different types of people

The *income* effect is likely to dominate for people with long-term commitments: those with families and with mortgages and other debts. A rise in tax rates for such people is likely to encourage them to work more.

DEFINITIONS

Income effect of a tax rise Tax increases reduce people's incomes and thus encourage people to work more.

Substitution effect of a tax rise Tax increases reduce the opportunity cost of leisure and thus encourage people to work less.

DEVELOPMENT OF IDEAS BOX 10.6

THE LAFFER CURVE
Having your cake and eating it

Professor Art Laffer was one of President Reagan's advisers during his first administration (1981–4). He was a strong advocate of tax cuts, arguing that substantial increases in output would result.

He went further than this. He argued that tax cuts would actually *increase* the amount of tax revenue the government earned.

Tax revenue = Average tax rate × Income

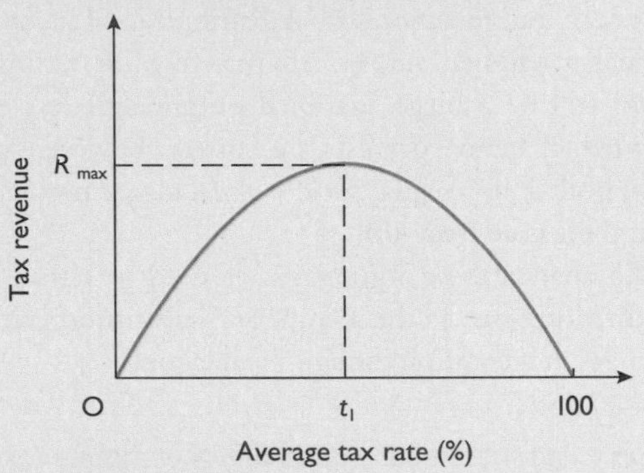

If tax cuts cause income to rise (due to incentives) proportionately more than the tax rate has fallen, then tax revenues will increase. These effects are illustrated by the now famous 'Laffer' curve.

If the average tax rate were zero, no revenue would be raised. As the tax rate is raised above zero, tax revenues will increase. The curve will be upward sloping. Eventually, however, the curve will peak (at tax rate t_1). Thereafter tax rates become so high that the resulting fall in output more than offsets the rise in tax rate. When the tax rate reaches 100 per cent, the revenue will once more fall to zero, since no one will bother to work.

The curve may not be symmetrical. It may peak at a 40 per cent, 50 per cent, 60 per cent or even 90 per cent rate. Nevertheless, Laffer and others on the political right have argued that current tax rates are above t_1. In fact most evidence suggests that current tax rates are well below t_1.

??

1. What is the elasticity of supply of output with respect to changes in tax rates at a tax rate of t_1? What is it below t_1? What is it above t_1?
2. If the substitution effect of a tax cut outweighs the income effect, does this necessarily mean that the economy is to the right of point t_1?

The income effect of a rise in tax rates is also likely to be relatively large for people on higher incomes, for whom an increase in tax rates represents a substantial cut in income. Table 10.5 shows the effect on the incomes of two people of a rise in the tax rate from 25 per cent to 30 per cent. In both cases it assumes that the personal allowances are £4000. For the person on £5000 close to the tax threshold, net income falls by only £50. For the person on £50 000 net income falls by £2300. Such a person may well work harder as a result of the rise in tax.

The *substitution* effect is likely to dominate for those with few commitments: those whose families have left home, the single, and second income earners in families where that second income is not relied on for 'essential' consumption. A rise in tax rates for these people is likely to encourage them to work less.

Table 10.5 Effects of increasing the rate of income tax on the amount of tax people pay

Tax rate	Person on £5000 (taxable income £1000)	Person on £50 000 (taxable income £46 000)
25%	£250	£11 500
30%	£300	£13 800

??

1. Who is likely to work harder as a result of a *cut* in income tax rates, a rich person or a poor person? Why? Would your answer be different if personal allowances were zero?
2. How will tax cuts affect the willingness of women to return to employment after having brought up a family?

Although high income earners may work more when there is a tax *rise*, they may still be discouraged by a steeply progressive tax *structure*. If they have to pay very high marginal rates of tax, it may simply not be worth their while seeking promotion or working harder (see Box 10.6).

Different types of tax

If the government wishes to raise income taxes in order to redistribute incomes, there are three main ways it can do it: raising the higher rates of tax; raising the basic rate; and reducing tax allowances.

Raising the higher rates of tax. This may seem the most effective way of redistributing incomes: after all, it is only the rich who will suffer. There are, however, serious problems:

- The income effect will be relatively small, since it is only that part of incomes subject to the higher rates that will be affected. The substitution effect, however, could be relatively high. There may be little disincentive in raising the higher rate from 40 per cent to 45 per cent, but the problem could be very serious if the rate were raised to very high levels.
- It may discourage risk taking by business people.
- The rich may be more mobile internationally, so there may be a 'brain drain'.

Raising the basic rate of tax. As we have seen, the income effect is likely to be relatively large for those with higher incomes, especially if they have substantial commitments like a large mortgage. For such people, a rise in tax rates is likely to act as an incentive.

For those just above the tax threshold, there will be very little extra to pay on *existing* income, since most of it is tax free. However, each *extra* pound earned will be taxed at the new higher rate. The substitution effect, therefore, is likely to outweigh the income effect. For these people, a rise in tax rates will act as a disincentive.

For those below the tax threshold, the marginal rate remains at zero. A rise in the basic rate might nevertheless deter them from undertaking training in order to get a better wage.

For those people who are not employed, a rise in tax rates may make them feel that it is no longer worth looking for a job. Alternatively they might take a job *more* readily, since there is less point in searching for a well-paid job if a higher proportion of wages is going to be taken in taxes.

Reducing tax allowances. For all those above the old tax threshold there is no *substitution* effect at all. The rate of tax has not changed. However, there is an *income* effect. The effect is like a lump-sum tax. Everyone's take-home pay is cut by a fixed sum, and people will need to work harder to make up some of the shortfall. This type of tax change, however, is highly regressive. If everyone pays the same *amount* of extra tax, this represents a bigger percentage for poorer people than richer people.

For those now brought into tax for the first time, there *will* be a substitution effect. These people may thus be discouraged from working so hard. Those below even the new tax threshold will feel no direct effect, but may be discouraged from seeking better qualifications.

The conclusion from the theoretical arguments is that tax changes will have very different effects depending on (a) whom they affect and (b) the nature of the change.

??

1. Go through each of the above types of tax change and consider the effects of a tax *cut*.
2. What tax changes (whether up or down) will have a positive incentive effect and also redistribute incomes more equally?

One final point should be stressed. For many people there is no choice in the amount they work. The job they do dictates the number of hours worked, irrespective of changes in taxation.

Evidence

All the available evidence suggests that the effects of tax changes on output are relatively small. Labour supply curves seem highly inelastic to tax changes.

Benefits

Benefits can be either cash benefits or benefits in kind.

Cash benefits

Means-tested benefits. **Means-tested benefits** are available only to those whose income (and savings in some instances) fall below a certain level. In order to obtain such benefits, therefore, people must apply for them and declare their personal circumstances to the authorities.

The benefits could be given as grants or merely as loans. They could be provided as general income support or for the meeting of specific needs, such as rents, fuel bills, household items, etc.

Universal benefits. **Universal benefits** are those that everyone is entitled to, irrespective of their income, if they fall into a certain category. Examples include state pensions, and unemployment, sickness and invalidity benefits.

People who are working pay social security contributions (NICs in the UK), based on their earnings. When they retire, become unemployed or fall sick they are

DEFINITIONS

Means-tested benefits Benefits whose amount depends on the recipient's income or assets.

Universal benefits Benefits paid to everyone in a certain category irrespective of their income or assets.

ISSUES AND APPLICATIONS

TAX CUTS AND INCENTIVES

An application of indifference curve analysis[2]

Will tax cuts provide an incentive for people to work harder? This question can be analysed using indifference curves (see section 4.2). The analysis is similar to that developed in Box 9.2. It is assumed that individuals can choose how many hours a day to work.

The position with no income tax

Diagram (a) shows the situation without income tax.

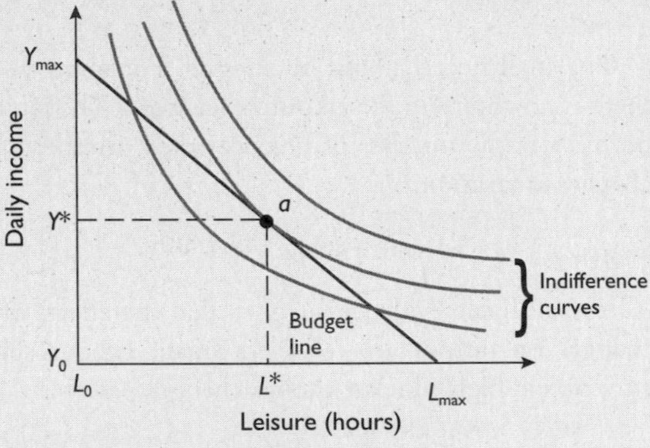

(a) Without income tax

The budget line shows the various combinations of leisure and income open to an individual at a given wage rate.

> **??** Why is the budget line straight? What would it look like if overtime were paid at higher rates per hour?

The indifference curves show all the combinations of income and leisure that give the person equal satisfaction. The optimum combination of income and leisure is at Y^* and L^* where the individual is on the highest possible indifference curve: point *a*.

The position with income tax

Now let us introduce a system of income taxes. This is illustrated in diagram (b).

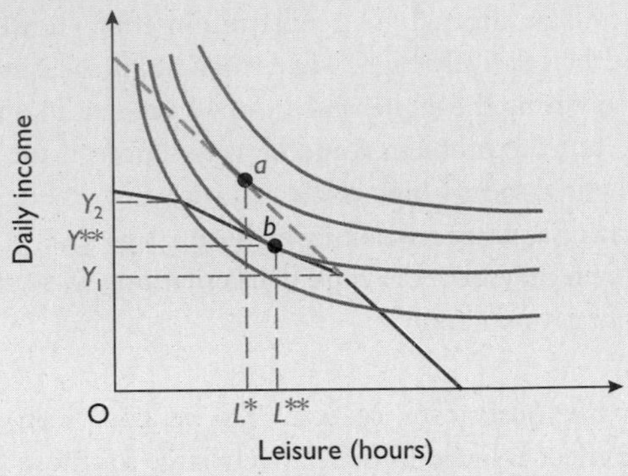

(b) With income tax

Assume that the tax has the following features:

- Up to an income of Y_1 no tax is paid: Y_1 is the individual's personal allowance.
- From Y_1 to Y_2 the basic rate of tax is paid. The budget line is flatter, since less extra income is earned for each extra hour of leisure sacrificed.
- Above Y_2 the higher rate of tax is paid. The budget line becomes flatter still.

The individual illustrated in the diagram will now choose to earn a take-home pay of Y^{**} and have L^{**} hours of leisure: point *b*. Note that this is more leisure than in the no-tax situation (point *a*). In this diagram, then, the tax has acted as a disincentive. The substitution effect has outweighed the income effect.

> **??** Redraw diagram (b), but in such a way that the income effect outweighs the substitution effect.

A cut in the basic tax rate

We can now analyse the effects of tax cuts. A cut in the basic rate is shown in diagram (c).

The tax cut makes the budget line steeper above point *q* (the tax threshold).

entitled to benefits. In many countries, there is a time limit on unemployment benefits. After that, people have to accept whatever work is available or rely on a lower level of social security payments.

Benefits in kind

Individuals receive other forms of benefit from the state, not as direct monetary payments, but in the form of the provision of free or subsidised goods or services. These are known as **benefits in kind**. The two largest items in most

> **DEFINITION**
>
> **Benefits in kind** Goods or services which the state provides directly to the recipient at no charge or at a subsidised price. Alternatively, the state can subsidise the private sector to provide them.

*BOX 10.7

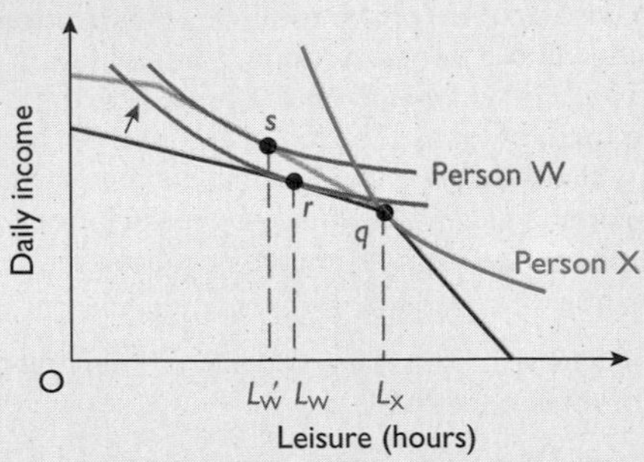

(c) Cut in the basic rate of tax

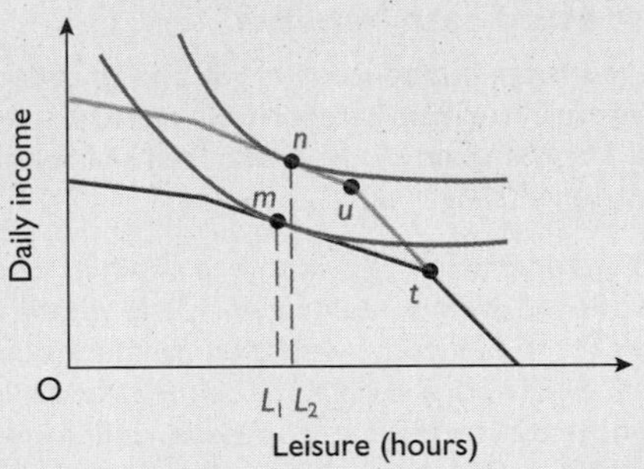

(d) Increase in the tax threshold

For people on the tax threshold – like person X – the cut in the basic rate makes no difference. Person X was originally taking L_x hours of leisure (point *q*) and will continue to do so.

For people above the tax threshold – like person W – the tax cut will enable them to move to a higher indifference curve. Person W will move from point *r* to point *s*. The way this diagram is drawn, point *s* is to the left of point *r*. This means that person W will work harder: the substitution effect is greater than the income effect.

?? Try drawing two or three diagrams like diagram (c), with the tangency point at different points along the budget line to the left of *q*. You will find that the further to the left you move, the *less* likely is the substitution effect to outweigh the income effect: i.e. the more likely are people to work *less* when given a tax cut.

A rise in the tax threshold

Diagram (d) shows a rise in personal allowances while the tax rate stays the same.

The point at which people start paying taxes rises from point *t* to point *u*. The *slope* of the budget line remains the same, however, since the tax *rate* has not changed.

For people paying taxes, the increase in allowances represents a lump-sum increase in income: there will thus be an income effect. But since tax *rates* have not changed, there is no substitution effect. People therefore work less. The person in the diagram moves from point *m* to point *n*, taking L_2 rather than L_1 hours in leisure.

?? Will people actually on the old tax threshold (i.e. those whose indifference curve/budget line tangency point is at *t*) work more or less? Try drawing it.

A cut in the higher rate of tax

It is likely that the income effect of this will be quite small except for those on very high incomes. The substitution effect is therefore likely to outweigh the income effect, causing people to work more.

?? All the above analysis assumes that taxes will not affect people's *gross* wage rates. If part of the incidence of taxes is borne by the employer, so that gross wages fall, after-tax wages will fall less. There will therefore be a smaller shift in the budget line. How will this affect the argument for tax cuts?

[2] This box is based on D. Ulph, 'Tax cuts: will they work?', *Economic Review*, March 1987.

countries are health care and education. They are very differently distributed, however. This difference can largely be explained on age grounds. Old people use a large proportion of health services, but virtually no education services.

Benefits in kind tend to be consumed roughly equally by the different income groups. Nevertheless they do have some equalising effect, since they represent a much larger proportion of poor people's income than rich people's. They still have a far smaller redistributive effect, however, than cash benefits.

Figure 10.16 shows the expenditure on social protection benefits in selected European countries. These include unemployment, sickness, invalidity, maternity, family, survivors' and housing benefits and state pensions. They are mainly cash benefits, but do include some benefits in kind. They exclude health and education. As you can see, the

CASE STUDIES

THE SYSTEM OF BENEFITS IN THE UK

Means-tested cash benefits

Under the system introduced in 1988 and amended in 1996 there are five main categories of means-tested benefits. They are paid by the Department of Social Security (Benefits Agency).

- Income support. This is available to all adults who do not work and are not seeking work, and whose income (or joint income with their partner) is below a certain level, whose savings are below a certain level and who are in certain categories: e.g. unfit for work, looking after a sick or disabled person, or bringing up children on their own. The amount of income support received depends on people's circumstances (e.g. number of children and other dependants, and whether they receive any other income). If a person does receive any other income, then for each £1 earned, income support is reduced by £1. Thus the marginal lost-benefit rate is 100 per cent.
- Income-based jobseeker's allowance. This is for unemployed people and those working less than 16 hours per week. Recipients must be capable of, available for, and actively seeking, work, and have income and savings below certain levels. The amount of benefit depends on the person's circumstances. To be entitled to such benefit, claimants must complete a Jobseeker's Agreement, which sets out the types of work they are willing to do, and their plan to find work. A recipient can earn a small amount each week without losing benefit. Above that, each £1 earned reduces benefit by £1.
- Family credit. This is a tax-free benefit to anyone on low income who is supporting a child, but who works too many hours to be entitled to jobseeker's allowance. If the family's income is below a certain level, they are entitled to the full benefit, whose amount depends on the number of children. As the family's income rises above this level, so the family credit is correspondingly reduced.
- Social fund. This provides money for specific needs. It is primarily for people on income support or jobseeker's allowance. Some people are entitled to grants from the fund. These are people who would otherwise probably have to be in an institution: a hospital, an old people's home, a hostel, etc. The majority of payments from the fund, however, are in the form of loans. The loans are interest free, but they will not be given unless they can be repaid. Repayments are made weekly by making deductions from people's income support or jobseeker's allowance.
- Housing benefit. This is a grant paid to help meet the cost of rents or rates.

Means-tested benefits are thus of two types: *general support* (income support, jobseeker's allowance and family credit) and *payments for specific purposes* (grants and loans from the social fund and housing benefit).

Universal cash benefits (by category of person)

These are benefits that everyone is entitled to, irrespective of their income, if they fall into a certain category. Most of these benefits are 'social insurance' benefits. People who are working pay national insurance contributions, based on their earnings. When they retire, become unemployed or fall sick they are entitled to benefits. Unemployment benefit (known as national insurance based jobseeker's allowance) and sickness benefit are paid only for a certain number of weeks. After that, the unemployed have to rely on income support, and the sick on invalidity benefit.

Child benefit is not regarded as social insurance. It is a flat payment to parents (usually the mother) for each child. Single parents receive an additional payment.

Benefits in kind

The two main types of benefit in kind are education and health. The table shows how the benefits are distributed between different income groups. Benefits in kind are consumed slightly more by poorer households. Poorer households often have more children and suffer from poverty-related diseases. They are also more likely to receive housing benefit and free school meals. Nevertheless, as the table shows, benefits in kind have a much smaller redistributive effect than cash benefits.

benefits vary significantly from one country to another. For example, Sweden provides 50 per cent more social protection than the UK. One note of caution: the expenditure on unemployment-related benefits depends on the level of unemployment, which depends on the state of the economy. Thus the expenditure on social protection in the UK rose from 21.7 per cent in 1989 (a time when the economy was booming) to 27.2 per cent in 1992 (a time of recession).

Benefits and the redistribution of income

It might seem that means-tested benefits are a much more efficient system for redistributing income from the rich to

BOX 10.8

Effects of the 1988 and 1996 measures

In these measures, the government has moved away from payments for specific needs and tried to simplify the system by treating people in broad categories (such as marital status, number of children, etc). This inevitably means that some people with particular needs receive inadequate benefit.

The government has attempted to give more support to some of the poorest of the population, especially through family credit. But it has been unwilling to contemplate a substantial increase in the *overall* level of benefits. The effect, therefore, is that some very poor families have been helped, not at the expense of the rich, but at the expense of the moderately poor and the 'able-bodied' single poor.

There are serious problems too with the system of loans. The obvious point here is that loans only tide people over. They do not redistribute incomes. Then there is the problem of repayment. If income support is designed to cover only the bare essential weekly expenditures, how can people afford to pay back loans out of their income support?

??

1. What categories of poor people would not be entitled to either income support or family credit?
2. What explanation can you give for the different distribution of bus and rail subsidies shown in the table?

Distribution of benefits in the UK: 1996/7 (average per quintile group of households (£ per year))

Benefit	Bottom 20%	Next 20%	Middle 20%	Next 20%	Top 20%	All households
Cash benefits						
Retirement pension	1556	1808	1381	817	537	1220
Job Seeker's allowance	120	53	51	29	25	55
Incapacity benefits	263	414	347	202	78	261
Other contributory	50	71	65	82	78	69
Income support	1182	697	298	130	33	468
Family credit	130	118	35	3	0	57
Child benefit	413	310	297	250	180	290
Housing benefits	729	770	298	83	11	378
Student maintenance awards	80	74	48	40	37	55
Other non-contributory	247	492	546	328	110	344
Total cash benefits	4767	4803	3365	1962	1087	3197
Benefits in kind						
Education	1696	1213	1177	1008	618	1142
National health service	1966	1885	1726	1448	1261	1657
Housing subsidy	87	82	37	17	4	45
Rail travel subsidy	17	23	45	56	133	55
Bus travel subsidy	30	36	25	20	13	25
Free milk and school meals	83	24	9	4	2	24
Total benefits in kind	3879	3263	3019	2553	2030	2949
Total benefits	8646	8066	6384	4515	3117	6146

Source: *Economic Trends* (ONS, April 1998).

the poor: the money is directed to those most in need. With universal benefits, by contrast, many people may receive them who have little need for them. Do families with very high incomes need child benefit? Would it not be better for the government to redirect the money to those who are genuinely in need?

There are, however, serious problems in attempting to redistribute incomes by the use of means-tested benefits:

- Not everyone entitled to means-tested benefits actually receives them. This may be due to a number of factors:
  - Ignorance of the benefits available. This in turn may be due to the complexities of the system.

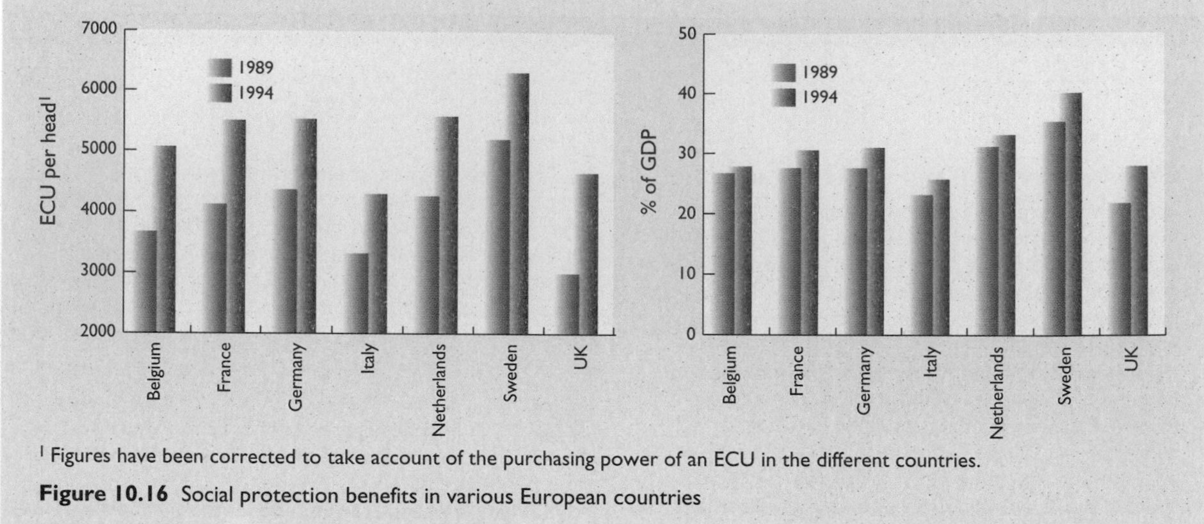

[1] Figures have been corrected to take account of the purchasing power of an ECU in the different countries.

Figure 10.16 Social protection benefits in various European countries

Source: *Basic Statistics of the European Union* (Eurostat, 1997).

– Difficulties in applying for the benefits. People may give up rather than having to face difficult forms or long queues or harassed benefit office staff.
– Reluctance to reveal personal circumstances.
– The perception that the benefits are 'charity' and therefore demeaning.

Thus some of the poorest families may receive no support.

- Even when people do apply for benefits, the need first to discover their personal circumstances may make the application procedure lengthy and unpleasant.
- The level of income above which people become ineligible for benefits may be set too low. Of course, this is partly an argument for raising the level. Even so, there will always be some people just above the level who will still find difficulties. By receiving various universal benefits, however, such as child benefit, or benefits in kind such as health and education, these people's difficulties could be alleviated.
- Means tests based purely on *income* (or even universal benefits based on broad categories) ignore the very special needs of many poor people. A person earning £80 a week and living in a small, well-appointed flat with a low rent will have less need of assistance than another person who also earns £80 per week but lives in a cold, draughty and damp house with large bills to meet. If means tests are to be fair, *all* of a person's circumstances need to be taken into account.

The tax/benefit system and the problem of disincentives: the poverty trap

When means-tested benefits are combined with a progressive income tax system there can be a serious problem of disincentives. As poor people earn more money, so not only will they start paying income taxes and national insurance, but also they will begin losing means-tested benefits. Theoretically, it is possible to have a marginal tax-plus-lost-benefit rate in excess of 100 per cent. In other words, for every extra £1 earned, taxes and lost benefits add up to more than £1. High marginal tax-plus-lost-benefit rates obviously act as a serious disincentive. What is the point of getting a job or trying to earn more money, if you end up earning little more or actually losing money?

This situation is known as the **poverty trap**. People are trapped on low incomes with no realistic means of bettering their position.

In the UK, for some people the marginal rate is 100 per cent. For example, for every extra £1 that a part-time, low-income worker earns, he or she loses £1 in jobseeker's allowance. The disincentive effect is overcome, however, by such people having to be willing to accept more work, and hence more pay, to avoid forfeiting their benefit (see Box 10.8).

The problem of the poverty trap would be overcome by switching to a system of universal benefits unrelated to income. For example, *everyone* could receive a flat payment from the state fixed at a sufficiently high level to cover their basic needs. There would still be *some* disincentive, but this would be confined to an income effect:

DEFINITION

Poverty trap Where poor people are discouraged from working or getting a better job because any extra income they earn will be largely taken away in taxes and lost benefits.

ISSUES AND APPLICATIONS — BOX 10.9

NEGATIVE INCOME TAX AND REDISTRIBUTION

A unified system of tax and social security

The complexities of welfare provision have led many economists to look for a more simplified and effective means to cure poverty and redistribute income, while avoiding the poverty trap. One such solution is the negative income tax system, which works as follows.

First, a minimum income level must be set. This will generally be on or about the poverty line. Let us assume for the sake of argument that this level is £2000. Under the negative income tax system, everyone is entitled to this fixed level of benefit. If you earn nothing, then you just get this £2000.

Second, income tax is paid right from the first pound a person earns. Assume that the tax rate is 25 per cent.

These taxes are then offset against the fixed benefit. If taxes exceed the benefit, a person pays the difference to the tax authorities. If taxes are less than the benefit, the person receives the difference from the tax authorities – a negative tax. The table shows how it works. With earnings up to £8000, people receive a net benefit (a negative income tax). Over £8000, people pay a positive net tax.

A negative income tax system

Earnings (£) (1)	Tax on earnings at 25% (£) (2)	Benefit (£) (3)	Tax minus benefit (£): (2) – (3) (4)	Net income (£): (1) – (4) (5)
0	0	2000	–2000[1]	2000
4000	1000	2000	–1000[1]	5000
8000	2000	2000	0	8000
12 000	3000	2000	1000	11 000
16 000	4000	2000	2000	14 000

[1] Negative income tax.

The level of fixed benefit can be made to vary with people's circumstances. Thus if a single person's benefit were £2000, a married couple's with four children could be, say, £5000.

The advantages claimed for the system are as follows:

- It eliminates the poverty trap. There are no levels of earnings where benefits suddenly disappear.
- It is simple to administer. A single agency – such as the Inland Revenue – is involved.
- It would have a high take-up rate.

There are, however, various problems associated with the system:

- If the tax authorities are responsible for paying a negative income tax, it will be paid in arrears. This could be a major problem for the poor. An alternative is for everyone to receive the full fixed benefit – say, through the Post Office – and then simply to pay taxes on *every* pound earned. The effect is just the same.
- There may still need to be special payments for specific needs: for example, for the sick and for those with housing problems.
- The main problem is the cost. If the marginal tax rate is to be kept low (say, at a standard rate of 25 per cent), and if the basic benefit for the poor is to be sufficiently high (say, £5000), then anyone earning less than *£20 000* will receive a negative income tax payment! This would put a tremendous cost burden on indirect taxes: a burden paid disproportionately by the poor!
- Alternatively, the marginal tax rate could be increased. But then the problem of disincentives is likely to arise.

Thus the conflict between equity and efficiency is not resolved.

?? Draw up a similar table to the one above, only this time assume that the basic benefit is £6000. Assume that the marginal tax rate is 20 per cent up to £10 000 and 40 per cent from £10 000 to £20 000. To what extent would this particular system help to tackle the problems of (a) equity; (b) cost of provision; (c) incentives?

people would not have the same need to work if the state provided a basic income. But there would no longer be the disincentive to work caused by a resulting *loss* of benefits (a substitution effect).

The big drawback with universal benefits, however, is their cost. If they were given to everyone and were large enough to help the poor, their cost would be enormous. Thus although the benefits themselves would not create much disincentive effect, the necessary taxation to fund them probably would.

There is no ideal solution to this conundrum. On the one hand, the more narrowly benefits are targeted on the poor, the greater is the problem of the poverty trap. On the other hand, the more widely they are spread, the greater is the cost of providing any given level of support to individuals. A compromise proposal is that of a **negative income tax**. This is examined in Box 10.9.

Conclusions

Redistribution is not costless. Whether it takes place through taxes or benefits or both, it is possible that there will be a problem of disincentives. Nevertheless the size of the disincentive problem varies enormously from one tax to another and from one benefit to another, and in some cases there may even be an *in*centive effect: for example, when the income effect of a tax outweighs the substitution effect. It is therefore important to estimate the particular effects of each type of proposal not only on income distribution itself, but also on economic efficiency.

Ultimately the questions of how much income should be redistributed and whether the costs are worth bearing are normative questions, and ones therefore that an economist cannot answer. They are moral and political questions. It would be nice if the 'utility' gained by the poor and lost by the rich could be quantified so that any net gain from redistribution could be weighed up against lost output. But such 'interpersonal comparisons of utility' are not possible. For example, the benefit that a person receives from a cooker or an electric fire cannot be measured in 'utils' or any other 'psychic unit'. What people are prepared to pay for the items is no guide either, since a poor person obviously cannot afford to pay nearly as much as a rich person, and yet will probably get the same if not more personal benefit from them.

Yet decisions have to be made!

DEFINITION

Negative income tax A combined system of tax and benefits. As people earn more, they gradually lose their benefits until beyond a certain level they begin paying taxes.

SECTION SUMMARY

1. Government intervention in the economy through taxation and government expenditure has a number of purposes including redistribution, the correction of market distortions and macroeconomic stabilisation.
2. There are various requirements of a good tax system, including horizontal and vertical equity, payment according to the amount of benefit received, being cheap to collect, difficult to evade, non-distortionary and convenient to the taxpayer and the government, and having the minimum disincentive effects.
3. Taxes can be divided into those paid directly to the authorities (direct taxes) and those paid via a middle person (indirect taxes). Direct taxes are of two main types: (a) Taxes on income: these include personal income tax, tax on company profit and on capital gains. Social security contributions (NIC in the UK) are also assessed on a person's income. (b) Taxes on wealth: these include inheritance tax, tax on property and business rates. Indirect taxes include VAT, excise duties and customs duties.
4. Taxes can be categorised as progressive, regressive or proportional. Progressive taxes have the effect of reducing inequality. The more steeply progressive they are, the bigger is the reduction in inequality.
5. There are various limitations to using taxes to redistribute incomes. First, they cannot on their own increase the incomes of the poor. (Cutting taxes, however, can help the poor if the cuts are carefully targeted.) Second, high taxes on the rich may encourage evasion or avoidance. Third, higher income taxes on the rich will probably lead to their employers paying higher (gross) wages.
6. Using taxes to redistribute incomes involves costs: these include administrative costs, costs of resource reallocation and disincentive effects.
7. Raising taxes has two effects on the amount people wish to work. On the one hand, people will be encouraged to work more in order to maintain their incomes. This is the income effect. On the other hand, they will be encouraged to substitute leisure for income (i.e. to work less), since an hour's leisure now costs less in forgone income. This is the substitution effect. The relative size of the income and substitution effects will depend on the nature of the tax change. The substitution effect is more likely to outweigh the income effect for those with few commitments, for people just above the tax threshold of the newly raised tax and in cases where the highest rates of tax are increased.

continued

8. Benefits can be cash benefits or benefits in kind. Means-tested cash benefits include support for poor families and the low paid. Universal benefits include state pensions, unemployment benefits, and sickness and invalidity benefits. Benefits in kind include health care, education and free school meals.
9. Means-tested benefits can be specifically targeted to those in need and are thus more 'cost-effective'. However, there can be serious problems with such benefits, including: limited take-up, time-consuming procedures for claimants, some relatively needy people falling just outside the qualifying limit and inadequate account taken of *all* relevant circumstances affecting a person's needs.
10. The poverty trap occurs when the combination of increased taxes and reduced benefits removes the incentive for poor people to earn more. The more steeply progressive this combined system is at low incomes, the bigger is the disincentive effect.

??? END-OF-CHAPTER QUESTIONS ???

1. Using the data shown on the pie charts in Figure 10.1, construct two Lorenz curves (on the same diagram), corresponding to the before- and after-tax income figures. Interpret and comment on the diagram you have drawn.
2. Can taxes be used to relieve poverty?
3. In what ways might the views of different politicians on what constitutes a 'good' tax system conflict?
4. Distinguish between proportional, progressive and regressive taxation. Could a progressive tax have a constant marginal rate?
5. Consider the cases for and against a poll tax.
6. Under what circumstances would a rise in income tax act as (i) a disincentive and (ii) an incentive to effort?
7. What is meant by the *poverty trap*? Would a system of *universal* benefits be the best solution to the problem of the poverty trap?
8. How would you go about deciding whether person A or person B gets more personal benefit from each of the following: (a) an electric fire; (b) a clothing allowance of £*x*; (c) draught-proofing materials; (d) child benefit? Do your answers help you in deciding how best to allocate benefits?

11 Markets, efficiency and the public interest

In Chapter 10 we examined the problem of inequality and the various redistributive policies that a government could pursue. In this chapter we turn to examine another major area of concern. This is the question of the *efficiency* of markets in allocating resources. The arguments we shall be looking at provide the basis for many of the microeconomic policies adopted by government.

In section 11.1 we show how a *perfect* market economy could under certain conditions lead to 'social efficiency'. In section 11.2 we examine the *real* world and show how markets in practice fail to meet social goals. This second section presents the major arguments in favour of government intervention in a market economy. In section 11.3 we turn to discuss the alternative ways in which a government can intervene to correct these various market failings. If the government is to replace the market and provide goods and services directly, it will need some way of establishing their costs and benefits. Section 11.4 looks at 'cost–benefit analysis'. This is a means of establishing the desirability of a public project such as a new motorway or a new hospital. Finally in section 11.5 we look at the case for *restricting* government intervention. We examine the advantages of real-world markets and the drawbacks of government intervention.

The optimum amount of government intervention depends on two things: first, the *positive* question of the relative successes of government and the market in achieving various social goals; and second, the *normative* question of the relative desirability of various, possibly conflicting, social goals – goals such as efficiency and equity.

11.1 Efficiency under perfect competition

Perfect competition has been used by many economists and policy makers as an ideal against which to compare the benefits and shortcomings of real-world markets.

As was shown in Chapter 6, perfect competition has various advantages for society. Under perfect competition, firms' supernormal profits are competed away in the long run by the entry of new competitors. As a result firms are forced to produce at the bottom of their average cost curves. What is more, the fear of being driven out of business by the entry of new firms forces existing firms to try to find lower-cost methods of production, thus shifting their *AC* curves downward.

Perhaps the most wide-reaching claim for perfect competition is that under certain conditions it will lead to a *socially efficient* use of a nation's resources.

Social efficiency: 'Pareto optimality'

If it were possible to make changes in the economy – changes in the combination of goods produced or consumed, or changes in the combination of inputs used – and if such changes benefited some people without anyone else being made worse off, this would be said by economists to be an **improvement in social efficiency**, or a **Pareto improvement**, after Vilfredo Pareto, the Italian social scientist (see Box 11.1).

DEFINITIONS

An improvement in social efficiency A Pareto improvement.

Pareto improvement Where changes in production or consumption can make at least one person better off without making anyone worse off.

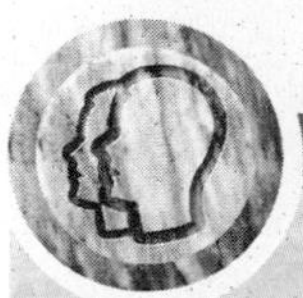

DEVELOPMENT OF IDEAS BOX 11.1

VILFREDO PARETO (1848–1923)

Person profile

Pareto came to economics late in his life: his first writing on the subject did not appear until 1896 when he was 48 years old. He had, however, replaced Leon Walras (see Box 4.2) in the Chair of Economics at the University of Lausanne in 1892 and his economic career had started somewhat earlier. Like many notable economists of the past, Pareto had been trained in a discipline away from economics. He was a successful engineer and mathematician, and later became an iron works manager.

Pareto was Italian by nationality, although he was born in Paris. He was, much to his disappointment, to spend a large part of his life away from Italy. He did, however, involve himself deeply in Italian political, economic and social life, and this was to have a profound influence on his work in a number of ways. His contact with Italian socialism, and late in his life fascism, was to lead to a general disillusionment with political regimes irrespective of their aims.

Pareto's economic and political philosophy was subtly to change his life. In his early writings he expounded a strong belief in economic liberalism, being an advocate of free trade and competition. Such beliefs, however, diminished in later years.

His two outstanding works – the *Cours d'Economie Politique* (1896) and *Manuale d'Economia Politica* (1907) – represent a mixture of economics and sociology (another discipline in which Pareto was to make valuable contributions).

One feature that stands out in these texts is Pareto's belief that, in order for economics to be scientific (i.e. concerned with model building, explanation and prediction), it must be ethically neutral. Values and biases must be kept to a minimum. In this respect Pareto was one of the first advocates of *positive* economics. What is rather surprising given this standpoint is that Pareto is most well known for his work on welfare economics – one of the potentially most value-laden areas of study.

Pareto is often seen as the founder of modern welfare economics. The Pareto criterion, which states that 'in order for a maximum welfare position to be reached then the "ophelimity"[1] of some should not increase to the detriment of others', was intended to represent a neutral standard of welfare, but nevertheless a standard against which the effects of economic changes can be judged to be an improvement or not. This at Pareto's time of writing was a path-breaking piece of work. Although the original Pareto criterion has since been refined and modified,[2] it still represents a crucial historical step in the development of modern welfare economics.

Pareto's contribution to economics has been a lasting one. It is interesting to speculate, however, just how much greater his contribution would have been had he not turned solely to the study of sociology from about 1912.

[1] Pareto uses this term as an alternative to utility.
[2] See, for example, the Hicks–Kaldor criterion in section 11.4 (page 349).

??
Do you agree that, if some people gain and if no one loses, then this will be an 'improvement' in the well-being of society? Would it be possible for there to be an improvement in the well-being of society without there being a Pareto improvement?

When all Pareto improvements have been made – in other words, when any additional changes in the economy would benefit some people only by making others worse off – the economy is said to be **socially efficient**, or **Pareto optimal**. What we shall show is that under certain conditions a perfect market will lead to Pareto optimality.

But a word of caution. Just because social *efficiency* is achieved in a particular market environment, it does not necessarily make that environment *ideal.* It may be a *necessary* condition for an ideal allocation of resources that all Pareto improvements are made: that all waste is eliminated. It is not *sufficient*, however. If, for example, the government redistributed income from the rich to the poor, there would be no Pareto improvement, since the rich would lose. Thus both an equal and a highly unequal distribution of income could be Pareto opti-

DEFINITIONS

Social efficiency A situation of Pareto optimality.

Pareto optimality Where all possible Pareto improvements have been made: where, therefore, it is impossible to make anyone better off without making someone else worse off.

mal, and yet it could be argued that a more equal distribution is socially more desirable. For the moment, however, we will ignore questions of fairness and just focus on social efficiency.

So why may a perfect market lead to social efficiency? The following sections explain.

The simple analysis of social efficiency: marginal benefit and marginal cost

Remember how we defined 'rational' choices. A rational person will choose to do an activity if the gain from so doing exceeds any sacrifice involved. In other words, whether as a producer, a consumer or a worker, a person will gain by expanding any activity whose marginal benefit (*MB*) exceeds its marginal cost (*MC*) and by contracting any activity whose marginal cost exceeds its marginal benefit. Remember that when economists use the term 'cost' they are referring to 'opportunity cost': in other words, the *sacrifice* of alternatives. Thus when we say that the marginal benefit of an activity is greater than its marginal cost, we mean that the additional benefit gained exceeds any sacrifice in terms of alternatives forgone.

Thus the economist's rule for **rational economic behaviour** is that a person should expand or contract the level of any activity until its marginal benefit is equal to its marginal cost. At that point the person will be acting efficiently in his or her own private interest. Only when $MB = MC$ can no further gain be made. This is known as a situation of **private efficiency**.

By analogy, *social* efficiency will be maximised where, for any activity, the marginal benefit to *society* (*MSB*) is equal to the marginal (opportunity) cost to *society* (*MSC*). At this point, Pareto optimality is achieved. But why? If *MSB* is greater than *MSC*, there will be a Pareto improvement if there is an increase in the activity. For example, if the benefits to consumers from additional production of a good exceed the cost to producers, the consumers could fully meet the cost of production in the price they pay, and so no producer loses, and yet there would still be a net gain to consumers. Thus society has gained. Likewise if *MSC* is greater than *MSB*, society will gain from a decrease in production.

It is argued by economists that under certain circumstances the achievement of *private* efficiency will result in *social* efficiency also. Two major conditions have to be fulfilled, however:

- There must be *perfect competition* throughout the economy. This is examined in the following sections.
- There must be *no* **externalities**. Externalities are additional costs or benefits to society, *over and above* those experienced by the individual producer or consumer. Pollution is an example. It is a cost that society experiences from production, but it is not a cost that the individual producer has to pay. In the *absence* of externalities, the only costs or benefits to society are the ones that the individual producer or consumer experiences: i.e. marginal social benefit (*MSB*) is the same as marginal private benefit (*MB*), and marginal social cost (*MSC*) is the same as marginal private cost (*MC*).

To understand just how social efficiency is achieved we must look at how people maximise their interests through the market. We will look first at the demand side and then at the supply side, and then finally put the two sides together.

Achieving social efficiency through the market

Consumption: $MU = P$

The marginal benefit to a consumer from the consumption of any good is its marginal utility. The marginal cost is the price the consumer has to pay.

As demonstrated in Chapter 4, the 'rational' consumer will maximise consumer surplus where $MU = P$: in other words, where the marginal benefit from consumption is equal to the marginal cost of consumption. Do you remember the case of Tina and her purchases of petrol? (See page 106.) She goes on making additional journeys and hence buying extra petrol as long as she feels that the journeys are worth the money she has to spend: in other words, as long as the marginal benefit she gets from buying extra petrol (its marginal utility to her)

DEFINITIONS

Rational economic behaviour Doing more of those activities whose marginal benefit exceeds their marginal cost and doing less of those activities whose marginal cost exceeds their marginal benefit.

Private efficiency Where a person's marginal benefit from a given activity equals the marginal cost.

Externalities Costs or benefits of production or consumption experienced by society but not by the producers or consumers themselves. Sometimes referred to as 'spillover' or 'third-party' costs or benefits.

exceeds its marginal cost (its price). She will stop buying extra petrol when its marginal utility has fallen (the law of diminishing marginal utility) to equal its price. At that point her consumer surplus is maximised: she has an 'efficient' level of consumption.

> **??** Assume that the price of the good falls. How will an 'efficient' level of consumption be restored?

Production: P = MC

The marginal benefit to a producer from the production of any good is its marginal revenue (which under perfect competition will be the same as the price of the good). As demonstrated in Chapter 6, the 'rational' firm will maximise its profit where its marginal revenue (i.e. the price under conditions of perfect competition) is equal to its marginal cost of production. This is the same thing as saying that it will produce where the marginal benefit from production is equal to the marginal cost from production.

Social efficiency in the market: MSB = MSC

Provided the two conditions of (a) perfect competition and (b) the absence of externalities are fulfilled, Pareto optimality will be achieved. Let us take each condition in turn.

Perfect competition. Since $MU = P$ (for each consumer) and $P = MC$ (for each producer), then, since the market price (P) for any good is the same for *all* producers and consumers:

$MU = MC$ (for all producers and all consumers)

No externalities. In the absence of externalities, $MSB = MU$ (i.e. the benefits of consumption within society are confined to the direct consumers) and $MSC = MC$ (i.e. the costs of production to society are simply the costs paid by the producers). Thus:

$$MSB = MU = P = MC = MSC$$

i.e. $MSB = MSC$

Inefficiency would arise if (a) competition were not perfect and hence if marginal revenue were *not* equal to price and as a result marginal cost were not equal to price; or (b) there were externalities and hence either marginal social benefit were different from marginal utility (i.e. marginal *private* benefit) or marginal social cost were different from marginal (private) cost. We examine such 'market failures' in section 11.2.

> **??**
> 1. If monopoly power existed in an industry, would production be above or below the socially efficient level (assuming no externalities)? Which would be greater, *MSB* or *P*?
> 2. Assuming perfect competition and no externalities, social efficiency will also be achieved in factor markets. Demonstrate that this will be where:
>
> $MSB_f = MRP_f = P_f = MDU_f = MSC_f$
>
>   (where *MRP* is the marginal revenue product of a factor, *MDU* is the marginal disutility of supplying it, and *f* is any factor – see section 9.2).
> 3. Why will marginal social benefit *not* equal marginal social costs in the labour market if there exists (a) union monopoly power and/or (b) firms with monopsony power?

Interdependence, efficiency and the 'invisible hand': the simple analysis of general equilibrium

If there is perfect competition and an absence of externalities throughout the economy, then the whole economy, when in equilibrium, will be socially efficient. A state of general Pareto optimality will exist.

No economy, however, is static. Conditions of demand and supply are constantly changing. Fashions change, technology changes and so on. Thus old patterns of consumption and production will cease to be Pareto optimal. Nevertheless, provided there is perfect competition and no externalities, forces will come into play to restore Pareto optimality.

In this perfect market economy, Pareto optimality is restored not by government action, but rather by the individual actions of producers, consumers and factor owners all seeking their own self-interest. It is as if an 'invisible hand' were working to guide the economy towards social efficiency (see Box 1.7).

The economic system will respond to any change in demand or supply by a whole series of subsequent changes in various interdependent markets. Social efficiency will thereby be restored. The whole process can be illustrated with a circular flow of income diagram (see Figure 11.1).

Assume, for example, that tastes change such that the marginal utility of a particular good rises. This is illustrated on the right-hand side of the diagram by a shift in the *MU* curve (i.e. the demand curve) from MU_1 to MU_2 (i.e. D_1 to D_2). This will lead to the following sequence of events, which you can follow round the diagram in an anti-clockwise direction.

Consumer demand

The rise in marginal utility (i.e. the rise in marginal social benefit of the good, MSB_g) leads to increased consumption. The resulting shortage will drive up the market price.

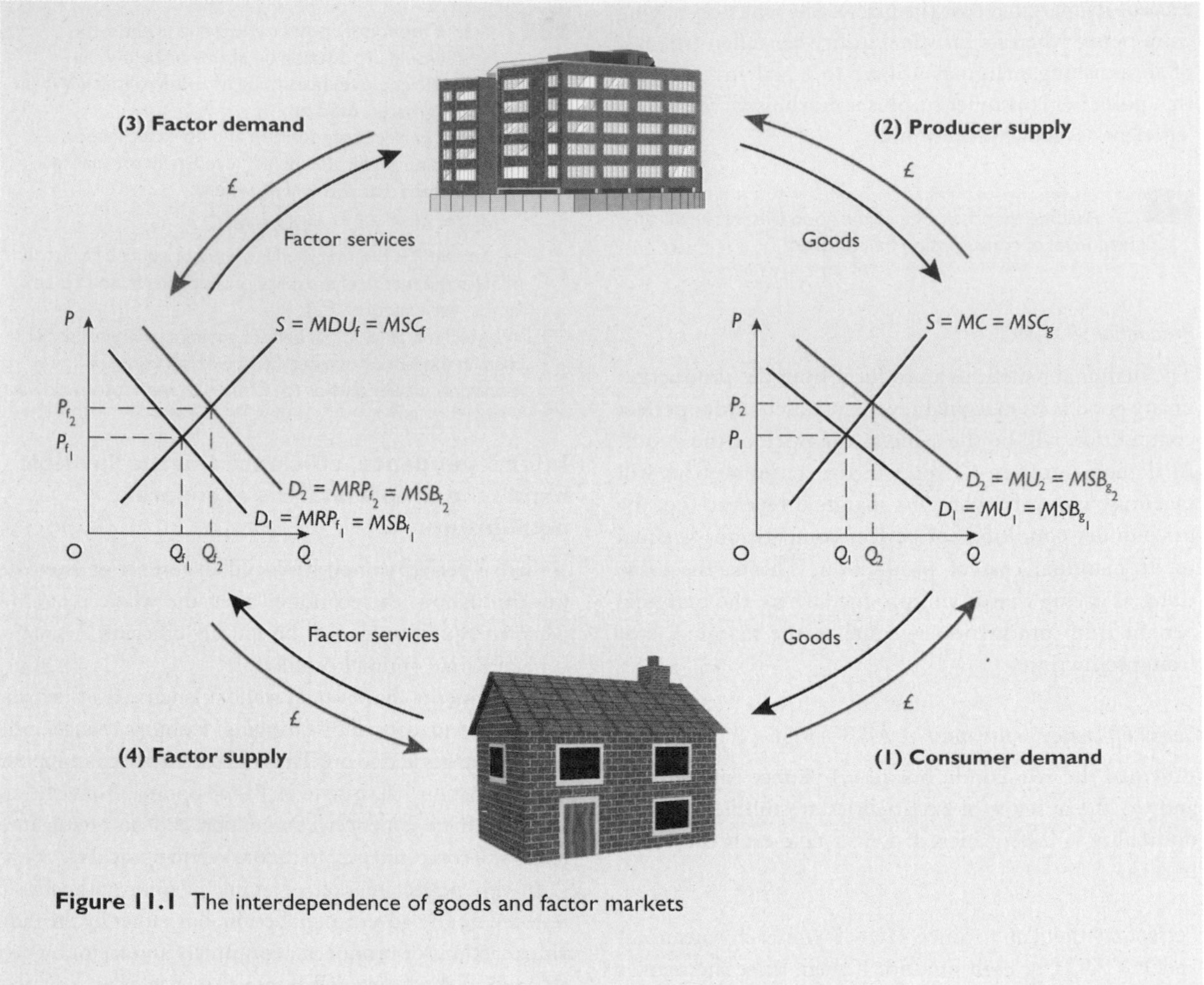

Figure 11.1 The interdependence of goods and factor markets

Producer supply

The rise in the market price will mean that price is now above the marginal (social) cost of production. It will thus be profitable for firms to increase their production. This in turn will lead to an increase in marginal cost (a movement up along the marginal cost curve) due to diminishing returns. There is a movement up along the supply curve. Price will continue to rise until equilibrium is reached at $P_2 Q_2$, where $MSB_{g_2} = MSC_g$.

Factor demand

The rise in the price of the good will lead to an increase in the marginal revenue product of factors that are employed in producing the good. The reason for this is that the marginal *revenue* product of a factor is its marginal *physical* product multiplied by the *price* of the good (see section 9.2). But since the price of the good has now gone up, the output of factors will be worth correspondingly more. The following takes just one factor (f) as an example.

A rise in the value of the factor's output (due to the higher price of the good) will make its marginal revenue product higher than its marginal cost to the firm. This will increase the demand for the factor. Factor demand shifts to D_2 (= MRP_{f_2} = MSB_{f_2}). This in turn will drive up the price of the factor.

Factor supply

The rise in the price of the factor will raise the marginal benefit of supplying it (and hence the marginal social benefit). This will mean that the marginal benefit now exceeds the marginal cost (the marginal disutility, MDU_f) of supplying the factor. There is thus a movement up along the factor supply curve as more units of the factor are supplied. The price of the factor will continue to rise until equilibrium is reached at $P_{f_2} Q_{f_2}$, where $MSB_{f_2} = MSC_f$.

(1) Consumer demand
$MU\uparrow$ (i.e. $MSB\uparrow$) $\rightarrow D\uparrow$ (i.e. D_1 to D_2) $\rightarrow MU > P \rightarrow$ consumption $\uparrow \rightarrow D > S \rightarrow P\uparrow$

(2) Producer supply
$P\uparrow \rightarrow P > MC$ (i.e. $P > MSB$) $\rightarrow$ production $\uparrow \rightarrow MC\uparrow$ (i.e. $MSC\uparrow$)
(movement up along MC and hence MSC curve)

(3) Factor demand
$MRP_f\uparrow$ (i.e. $MSB_f\uparrow$) $\rightarrow MRP_f > P_f \rightarrow$ employment of factor $\uparrow \rightarrow P_f\uparrow$

(4) Factor supply
$P_f\uparrow \rightarrow P_f > MDU$ (i.e. $P_f > MSC_f$) $\rightarrow$ supply of factor $\uparrow \rightarrow MDU\uparrow$
(movement up along MDU and hence MSC_1 curve)

Figure 11.2 The effects of an initial increase in consumers' marginal utility for a good

These effects in the four quadrants of Figure 11.1 are summarised in Figure 11.2.

The process of adjustment does not end here. If supernormal profits are made, new firms will enter. Similarly, if factor rewards are supernormal, new factors will be attracted from other industries. This in turn will affect prices and hence quantities in *other* industries in both goods and factor markets.

In other words, a single change in tastes will create a ripple effect throughout the economy, through a whole series of interdependent markets. Eventually, long-run equilibrium will be restored with $MSB = MSC$ in all markets. The economy has returned to a position of Pareto optimality. And all this has taken place with no government intervention. It is the 'invisible hand' of the market that has achieved this state of social efficiency.

These arguments form a central part of the neo-classical case for *laissez-faire*: the philosophy of non-intervention by the government. Under ideal conditions, it is argued, the free pursuit of individual self-interest will lead to the social good.

?? Trace through the effects in both factor and goods markets of the following:
(a) An increase in the productivity of a particular type of labour.
(b) An increase in the supply of a particular factor.
Show in each case how social efficiency will initially be destroyed and then how market adjustments will restore social efficiency.

The following pages examine social efficiency in more detail. You may omit these and skip straight to section 11.2 (page 324) if you want to.

*The intermediate analysis of social efficiency: marginal benefit and marginal cost ratios

In practice, consumers do not consider just one good in isolation. They make choices between goods. Likewise firms make choices as to which goods to produce and which factors to employ. A more satisfactory analysis of social efficiency, therefore, considers the choices that firms and households make.

Whether as a producer, consumer or worker, a person will gain by expanding activity X relative to activity Y if:

$$\frac{MB_X}{MB_Y} > \frac{MC_X}{MC_Y}$$

The reason is straightforward. Activity X is giving a greater benefit relative to its cost than is activity Y. Only when:

$$\frac{MB_X}{MB_Y} = \frac{MC_X}{MC_Y}$$

can no further gain be made by switching from the one activity to the other. At this point, people will be acting efficiently in their own private interest.

By analogy, *social* efficiency will be maximised when:

$$\frac{MSB_X}{MSB_Y} = \frac{MSC_X}{MSC_Y}$$

This is the requirement for Pareto optimality. If, however:

$$\frac{MSB_X}{MSB_Y} > \frac{MSC_X}{MSC_Y}$$

there would be a Pareto improvement if there were an increase in activity X relative to activity Y. For example, if the marginal benefit to consumers from good X relative to good Y were greater than the marginal cost to producers from good X relative to good Y, then if more X was produced relative to Y, the additional gain to consumers would be greater than the additional cost to producers. Thus consumers could fully compensate the producers (in the price they pay for X) and still have a net gain.

As with the simple analysis of social efficiency, it can be shown that, provided there is perfect competition and no externalities, the achievement of private efficiency will result in social efficiency also. This will be demonstrated in the following sections.

*Efficiency in the goods market (intermediate analysis)

Private efficiency under perfect competition

Consumption. The optimum combination of two goods X and Y consumed for any consumer is where:

$$\frac{MU_X}{MU_Y} \text{ (i.e. } MRS) = \frac{P_X}{P_Y}$$

The *marginal rate of substitution in consumption (MRS)* is the amount of good Y a consumer would be willing to sacrifice for an increase in consumption of good X (i.e. $\Delta Y/\Delta X$). $MRS = MU_X/MU_Y$ since, if X gave twice the marginal utility of Y, the consumer would be prepared to give up two of Y to obtain one of X (i.e. $MRS = 2/1$).

> **??** If MU_X/MU_Y were greater than P_X/P_Y, how would consumers behave? What would bring consumption back to equilibrium where $MU_X/MU_Y = P_X/P_Y$?

Production. The optimum combination of two goods X and Y produced for any producer is where:

$$\frac{MC_X}{MC_Y} \text{ (i.e. } MRT) = \frac{P_X}{P_Y}$$

The *marginal rate of transformation in production (MRT)* is the amount of good Y that the producer will have to give up producing for an increase in production of good X (i.e. $\Delta Y/\Delta X$) if total costs of production are to remain unchanged. $MRT = MC_X/MC_Y$ since, if the marginal cost of good X were twice that of Y, the firm's costs would remain constant if it gave up producing two of Y in order to produce an extra X (i.e. $MRT = 2/1$).)

> **??** If MC_X/MC_Y were greater than P_X/P_Y how would firms behave? What would bring production back into equilibrium where $MC_X/MC_Y = P_X/P_Y$?

Social efficiency under perfect competition

In each of the following three cases, it will be assumed that there are no externalities.

Social efficiency between consumers. If MU_X/MU_Y for person a is greater than MU_X/MU_Y for person b, *both* people would gain if person a gave person b some of good Y in exchange for some of good X. There would be a Pareto improvement. The Pareto optimal distribution of consumption will therefore be where:

$$\frac{MU_X}{MU_Y}_{\text{person a}} = \frac{MU_X}{MU_Y}_{\text{person b}} \ldots = \frac{MU_X}{MU_Y}_{\text{person } n}$$

i.e. $MRS_a = MRS_b \ldots = MRS_n$

But this will be achieved *automatically* under perfect competition, since each consumer will consume that combination of goods where $MU_X/MU_Y = P_X/P_Y$ and all consumers face the *same* (market) prices and hence the *same* P_X/P_Y.

Social efficiency between producers. If MC_X/MC_Y for producer g is greater than MC_X/MC_Y for producer h, then if producer g produced relatively more Y and producer h produced relatively more X, the same output could be produced at a lower total cost (i.e. with less resources). There would be a Pareto improvement. The Pareto optimal distribution of production between firms is therefore where:

$$\frac{MC_X}{MC_Y}_{\text{producer g}} = \frac{MC_X}{MC_Y}_{\text{producer h}} \ldots = \frac{MC_X}{MC_Y}_{\text{producer } n}$$

i.e. $MRT_g = MRT_h \ldots = MRT_n$

This too will be achieved *automatically* under perfect competition, since each producer will maximise profits where $MC_X/MC_Y = P_X/P_Y$ and all producers face the *same* (market) prices and hence the *same* P_X/P_Y.

Social efficiency in exchange. If MU_X/MU_Y (i.e. MRS) for all consumers is greater than MC_X/MC_Y (i.e. MRT) for all producers, then there would be a Pareto improvement if resources were reallocated to produce relatively more X and less Y.

Assume the MRS (i.e. $\Delta Y/\Delta X$) = 3/1 and the MRT (i.e. $\Delta Y/\Delta X$) = 2/1. Consumers will be prepared to give up 3 units of Y to obtain 1 unit of X, and yet producers only have to sacrifice producing 2 units of Y to produce 1 unit of X. Thus consumers can pay producers in full for extra units of X they produce and there will still be a net gain to consumers. There has been a Pareto improvement.

The Pareto optimal allocation of resources is where:

Social MRS ($SMRS$) = Social MRT ($SMRT$)

Assuming no externalities, this will be achieved automatically under perfect competition, since (a) with no externalities, social and private marginal rates of substitution will be the same, and similarly social and private marginal rates of transformation will be the same, and (b) P_X/P_Y is the same for all producers and consumers. In other words:

$$SMRS = MRS_{\text{all consumers}} = \frac{MU_X}{MU_Y}_{\text{all consumers}} = \frac{P_X}{P_Y}$$

and $$SMRT = MRT_{\text{all producers}} = \frac{MC_X}{MC_Y}_{\text{all producers}} = \frac{P_X}{P_Y}$$

i.e. $SMRS = SMRT$

Thus the pursuit of *private* gain, it is argued, has led to the achieving of *social* efficiency. This is a momentous conclusion. It is clearly very attractive to people to think that, simply by looking after their own interests, *social* efficiency will thereby be achieved!

This is illustrated graphically in Figure 11.3. A production possibility curve shows the various combinations of two goods X and Y that can be produced (see page 10). Its slope is given by $\Delta Y/\Delta X$ and shows how much Y must be given up to produce 1 more of X. Its slope, therefore, is the marginal rate of transformation (MRT).

Social indifference curves can be drawn showing the various combinations of X and Y that give particular levels of satisfaction to consumers as a whole. Their slope is given by $\Delta Y/\Delta X$ and shows how much Y consumers are prepared to give up to obtain 1 more unit of X. Their slope, therefore, is the marginal rate of substitution in consumption (MRS).

The Pareto optimal combination of goods is at point S, where the production possibility curve is tangential to the highest possible indifference curve. At any other point on the production possibility curve, a lower level of consumer satisfaction is achieved. The slope of the tangent at S is equal to both MRT and MRS, and hence also to P_X/P_Y.

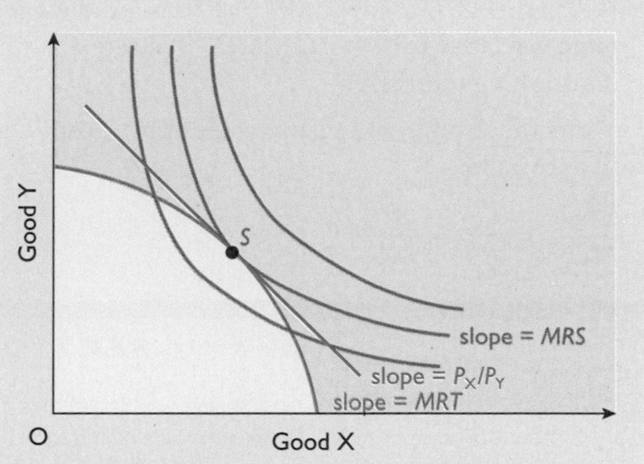

Figure 11.3 The achievement of social efficiency under perfect competition

> **??** If production were at a point on the production possibility curve below point S, describe the process whereby market forces would return the economy to point S.

*Efficiency in the factor market (intermediate analysis)

A similar analysis can be applied to factor markets, showing that perfect competition and the absence of externalities will lead to efficiency in the use of factors between firms.

If MPP_L/MPP_K for firm g is greater than MPP_L/MPP_K for firm h, then if firm g were to use relatively more labour and firm h relatively more capital, more could be produced for the same total input. There would be a Pareto improvement.

The Pareto optimum distribution of factors between firms will therefore be where:

$$\frac{MPP_L}{MPP_K}_{\text{firm g}} = \frac{MPP_L}{MPP_K}_{\text{firm h}} \ldots = \frac{MPP_L}{MPP_K}_{\text{firm } n}$$

But this will be achieved automatically under perfect competition since, as we saw in section 5.2, each producer will be producing where $MPP_L/MPP_K = P_L/P_K$ and each producer will face the same factor prices and hence P_L/P_K.

Provided there are no externalities, and assuming $P_L/P_K = MSC_L/MSC_K$, then:

$$\frac{MSB_L}{MSB_K} = \frac{MSC_L}{MSC_K}$$

*The intermediate analysis of general equilibrium

General equilibrium is where equilibrium exists in all markets. Under perfect competition and in the absence of externalities, general equilibrium will give Pareto optimality.

If any change in the conditions of demand or supply occurs, this disequilibrium will automatically create a whole series of interdependent reactions in various markets.

Assume, for example, that tastes change such that MU_X rises and MU_Y falls. This will lead to the following sequence of events in the goods market:

> $MU_X/MU_Y > P_X/P_Y \rightarrow$ consumers buy more X relative to Y $\rightarrow MU_X/MU_Y\downarrow$ (due to diminishing marginal utility) and $P_X/P_Y\uparrow$ (due to a relative shortage of X and a surplus of Y).

DEFINITION

General equilibrium Where all the millions of markets throughout the economy are in a simultaneous state of equilibrium.

$P_X/P_Y \uparrow \rightarrow P_X/P_Y > MC_X/MC_Y \rightarrow$ firms produce more X relative to Y $\rightarrow MC_X/MC_Y \uparrow$ (due to diminishing returns).

The process of price and quantity adjustment continues until once more:

$$\frac{MU_X}{MU_Y} = \frac{P_X}{P_Y} = \frac{MC_X}{MC_Y}$$

Similar adjustments will take place in the factor market. The price of those factors used in producing good X will be bid up and those used in producing Y will be bid down. This will encourage factors to move from industry Y and into industry X. The whole process of adjustment continues until equilibrium and Pareto optimality are restored in all goods and factor markets.

SECTION SUMMARY

1. Social efficiency (Pareto optimality) will be achieved when it is not possible to make anyone better off without making someone else worse off. This will be achieved if people behave 'rationally' under perfect competition providing there are no externalities.
2. Rational behaviour involves doing more of any activity whose marginal benefit (*MB*) exceeds its marginal cost (*MC*) and less of any activity whose marginal cost exceeds its marginal benefit. The optimum level of consumption or production for the individual consumer or firm will be where $MB = MC$. This is called a situation of 'private efficiency'.
3. In a perfectly competitive goods market, the consumer will achieve private efficiency where $MU = P$; and the producer where $P = MC$. Thus $MU = MC$. In the absence of externalities, private benefits and costs will equal social benefits and costs. Thus $MU = MSB$ and $MC = MSC$. Thus $MSB = MSC$: a situation of social efficiency (Pareto optimality).
4. In perfectly competitive factor markets, the employer will achieve private efficiency where $MRP_f = P_f$, and the factor supplier where $P_f = MDU_f$. Thus $MRP_f = MDU_f$. In the absence of externalities, $MRP_f = MSB_f$ and $MDU_f = MSC_f$. Thus $MSB_f = MSC_f$: a situation of social efficiency in the factor market.
5. Given perfect competition and an absence of externalities, if the equality of marginal benefit and marginal cost is destroyed in any market (by shifts in demand or supply), price adjustments will take place until general equilibrium is restored where $MSB = MSC$ in all markets: a situation of general Pareto optimality.

*6. The rational producer or consumer will choose the combination of any two pairs of goods where their marginal benefit ratio is equal to their marginal cost ratio. Consumers will achieve private efficiency where:

$$\frac{MU_X}{MU_Y}(MRS) = \frac{P_X}{P_Y}$$

Producers will achieve private efficiency where:

$$\frac{P_X}{P_Y} = \frac{MC_X}{MC_Y}(MRT)$$

Thus:

$$\frac{MU_X}{MU_Y} = \frac{MC_X}{MC_Y}$$

In the absence of externalities this will give a situation of social efficiency where:

$$\frac{MSB_X}{MSB_Y} = \frac{MSC_X}{MSC_Y}$$

*7. Similarly, in factor markets, social efficiency will be achieved if there is perfect competition and an absence of externalities. This will be where the *MSB* ratio for any two factors is equal to their *MSC* ratio.

*8. Again assuming perfect competition and an absence of externalities, general equilibrium will be achieved where there is a socially efficient level of production, consumption and exchange in all markets: where the *MSB* ratio for any pair of goods or factors is equal to the *MSC* ratio.

11.2 The case for government intervention

In the real world, markets will fail to achieve social efficiency. Part of the problem is the lack of perfect competition, part is the existence of externalities, and part is the fact that markets may take a long time to adjust to any disequilibrium given the often considerable short-run immobility of factors. What is more, social efficiency (i.e. Pareto optimality) is not the *only* economic goal of society. Markets may also fail to the extent that they fail to achieve objectives such as greater equality, faster growth, full employment, stable prices and the provision of public goods and services such as roads, the police and sewerage systems.

The various possible failures of the market are examined below. They provide the major part of the case for government intervention in the economy.

Externalities

The market will not lead to social efficiency if the actions of producers or consumers affect people other than themselves: in other words, when there are *externalities* (side-effects). Whenever other people are affected beneficially, there are said to be **external benefits**. Whenever other people are affected adversely, there are said to be **external costs**.

Thus the full costs to society (the **social costs**) of the production of any good are the private costs faced by firms plus any side-effects of production. Likewise the full benefits to society (the **social benefits**) from the consumption of any good are the private benefits enjoyed by consumers plus any side-effects.

There are four major types of externality. (In each case we will assume that the market is in other respects perfect.)

External costs of production (MSC > MC)

When a chemical firm dumps waste in a river or pollutes the air, the community bears costs additional to those borne by the firm. The marginal *social* cost (*MSC*) of chemical production exceeds the marginal private cost (*MC*). Diagrammatically, the *MSC* curve is above the *MC* curve.

In Figure 11.4 the socially optimal output for the firm would be Q_2, where $P = MSC$. The firm, however, produces Q_1 which is more than the optimum. Thus external costs lead to overproduction from society's point of view.

The problem of external costs arises in a capitalist society because no one has legal ownership of the air or rivers and can prevent or charge for their use as a dump for waste. Control must, therefore, be left to the government or local authorities.

Other examples include extensive farming that destroys hedgerows and wildlife, acid rain caused by smoke from coal-fired power stations, and nuclear waste from nuclear power stations.

External benefits of production (MSC < MC)

Imagine a bus company that spends money training its bus drivers. Each year some drivers leave to work for coach and haulage companies. These companies' costs are reduced as they do not have to train such drivers. Society has benefited from their training even though the bus company has not. The marginal *social* cost of the bus service, therefore, is less than the marginal *private* cost.

In a diagram like Figure 11.4, the *MSC* curve would be *below* the *MC* curve. The level of output (i.e. number of passenger miles) provided by the bus company would be where $P = MC$, a *lower* level than the social optimum, where $P = MSC$.

Another example of external benefits in production is that of research and development. If other firms have access to the results of the research, then clearly the benefits extend beyond the firm which finances it. Given that the firm receives only the private benefits, it will conduct a less than optimal amount of research.

External costs of consumption (MSB < MB)

When people use their cars, other people suffer from their exhaust, the added congestion, the noise, etc. These 'negative externalities' make the marginal social benefit of using cars less than the marginal private benefit (i.e. marginal utility).

Figure 11.5 shows the marginal utility and price to a consumer of using a car. The distance travelled by this motorist will be Q_1 miles: i.e. where $MU = P$ (where price is the cost of petrol, oil, wear and tear, etc. per mile). The *social* optimum, however, would be less than this, namely Q_2, where $MSB = P$.

Other examples are noisy radios in public places, cigarettes and their smoke, and litter.

> **??** Is it likely that the *MSB* curve will be parallel to the *MU* curve? Explain your reasoning.

External benefits of consumption (MSB > MB)

When people travel by train rather than by car, other people benefit by there being less congestion and exhaust and fewer accidents on the roads. Thus the marginal social benefit of rail travel is *greater* than the marginal private benefit (i.e. marginal utility). There are external benefits from rail travel.

Other examples are deodorants, vaccinations and attractive clothing.

DEFINITIONS

External benefits Benefits from production (or consumption) experienced by people *other* than the producer (or consumer).

External costs Costs of production (or consumption) borne by people *other* than the producer (or consumer).

Social cost Private cost plus externalities in production.

Social benefit Private benefit plus externalities in consumption.

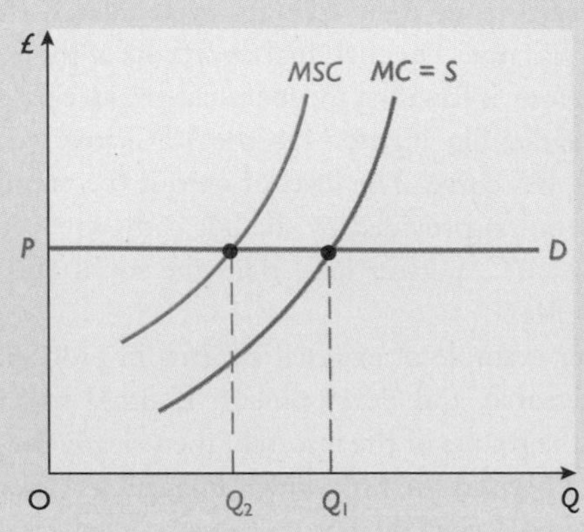

Figure 11.4 External costs in production

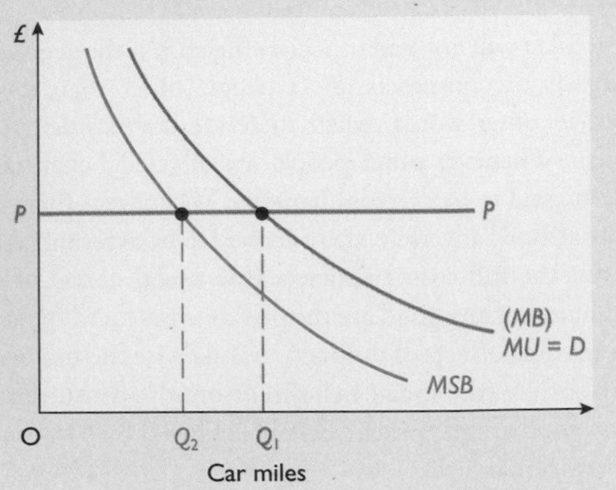

Figure 11.5 External costs in consumption

> ?? On a diagram like Figure 11.5 demonstrate that there will be a less than optimal level of consumption when there are external benefits in consumption.

In general, whenever there are external benefits, there will be too little produced or consumed. Whenever there are external costs, there will be too much produced or consumed. The market will not equate *MSB* and *MSC*.

> ??
> 1. Give other examples of each of the four types of externality.
> 2. Redraw Figures 11.4 and 11.5, only this time assume that the producer (in the first diagram) or the consumer (in the second) has economic power and is thus *not* a price taker. How does the existence of power affect the relationship between the private and the social optimum positions?

Market power

Lack of Pareto optimality

Whenever markets are imperfect, whether as pure monopoly or monopsony or as some form of imperfect competition, the market will fail to equate *MSB* and *MSC*. Pareto optimality will not be achieved.

This is illustrated in Figure 11.6, which shows revenue and cost curves for a monopolist. It assumes no externalities. The socially efficient (Pareto optimal) output is Q_2, where *MSB* = *MSC*. The monopolist, however, produces the lower output Q_1, where *MR* = *MC*.

> ?? Referring back to Figure 9.13 on page 251, and assuming that the MRP_L curve represents the marginal social benefit from the employment of a factor, and that the price of the factor represents its marginal social cost (i.e. assuming no externalities), show that a monopsony will employ less than the Pareto optimal amount of factors.

Deadweight loss under monopoly

Another way of analysing the welfare loss that occurs under monopoly is to use the concepts of *consumer* and *producer surplus*. We examined consumer surplus in Chapter 4 (page 105): it is the excess of consumers' total utility from consuming a good over their total expenditure on it. Producer surplus is just another name for profit, but we measure it by a different method from the one we used in Chapters 5–7. The two concepts are illustrated in Figure 11.7, which is similar to Figure 11.6. The diagram shows an industry which is initially under perfect competition and then becomes a monopoly (but faces the same revenue and cost curves).

Under *perfect competition* the industry will produce an output of Q_{pc} at a price of P_{pc}, where $MC (= S) = P (= AR)$: i.e. at point *a*. Consumers' total utility is given by the area under the demand (*MU*) curve (the sum of all the areas 1 to 7). Consumers' total expenditure is $P_{pc} \times Q_{pc}$ (areas 4 + 5 + 6 + 7). Consumer surplus is the difference between total utility and total expenditure: in other words, the area between the price and the demand curve (areas 1 + 2 + 3).

Producer surplus (profit) is the difference between total revenue and total cost. Total revenue is $P_{pc} \times Q_{pc}$ (areas 4 + 5 + 6 + 7). Total cost is the area under the *MC* curve (areas 6 + 7). Producer surplus is thus the area between the price and the *MC* curve (areas 4 + 5).[3] Total consumer plus producer surplus is therefore the area between the demand and *MC* curves. This is shown by the total shaded area (areas 1 + 2 + 3 + 4 + 5).

[3] Strictly speaking, the area under the *MC* curve is total *variable* cost. Any fixed costs would thus have to be deducted from areas 4 + 5 to get producer surplus. But, since fixed costs do not vary with output, they do not affect the argument about the relative producer surplus under perfect competition and monopoly.

ISSUES AND APPLICATIONS BOX 11.2

CAN THE MARKET PROVIDE ADEQUATE PROTECTION FOR THE ENVIRONMENT?

In recent years people have become acutely aware of the damage being done to the environment by pollution. But if the tipping of chemicals and sewage into the rivers and seas and the spewing of toxic gases into the atmosphere cause so much damage, why does it continue? If we all suffer from these activities, both consumers and producers alike, then why will a pure market system not deal with the problem? After all, a market should respond to people's interests.

The reason is that the costs of pollution are largely *external* costs. They are borne by society at large and only very slightly (if at all) by the polluter. If, for example, 10 000 people suffer from the smoke from a factory (including the factory owner) then that owner will only bear approximately 1/10 000 of the suffering. That personal cost may be quite insignificant when the owner is deciding whether the factory is profitable. And if the owner lives far away, the personal cost of the pollution will be zero.

Thus the *social* costs of polluting activities exceed the *private* costs. If people behave selfishly and only take into account the effect their actions have on themselves, there will be an *overproduction* of polluting activities.

Thus it is argued that governments must intervene to prevent or regulate pollution, or alternatively to tax the polluting activities or subsidise measures to reduce the pollution.

But if people are purely selfish, why do they buy 'green' products? Why do they buy, for example, 'ozone-friendly' aerosols? After all, the amount of damage done to the ozone layer from their own personal use of 'non-friendly' aerosols would be absolutely minute. The answer is that many people have a social conscience. They *do* sometimes take into account the effect their actions have on other people. They are not totally selfish. They like to do their own little bit, however small, towards protecting the environment.

Nevertheless to rely on people's consciences may be a very unsatisfactory method of controlling pollution. In a market environment where people are all the time being encouraged to consume more and more goods and where materialism is the religion of the age, there would have to be a massive shift towards 'green thinking' if the market were to be a sufficient answer to the problem of pollution.

Certain types of environmental problem may get high priority in the media, like acid rain, the greenhouse effect, damage to the ozone layer and brain damage to children from leaded petrol. However, the sheer range of polluting activities makes reliance on people's awareness of the problems and their social consciences far too arbitrary.

?? The following table gives the costs and benefits of an imaginary firm operating under perfect competition whose activities create a certain amount of pollution. (It is assumed that the costs of this pollution to society can be accurately measured.)

(a) What is the profit-maximising level of output for this firm?
(b) What is the socially efficient level of output?
(c) Why might the marginal pollution costs increase in the way illustrated in this example?

Output (units)	Price per unit (*MSB*) (£)	Marginal (private) costs to the firm (*MC*) (£)	Marginal external (pollution) costs (*MEC*) (£)	Marginal social costs (*MSC* = *MC* + *MEC*) (£)
1	100	30	20	50
2	100	30	22	52
3	100	35	25	60
4	100	45	30	75
5	100	60	40	100
6	100	78	55	133
7	100	100	77	177
8	100	130	110	240

CASE STUDIES — BOX 11.3

THE POLICE AS A PUBLIC SERVICE

Could policing be provided privately?

A good example of a public good or service is that of the police. Take the case of police officers on the beat. They are providing a general service to the community by deterring and detecting crime.

If individuals had to employ privately their own police officers, this would create considerable external benefits relative to private benefits. One police officer can provide protection to *many* individuals. But for most people it would be out of the question to employ their own police officer: the private cost would hugely exceed the private benefit. Also, once such privately employed police were on duty catching and deterring criminals, it would not be possible to exclude those people from benefiting who were not employing their own police officers. There would be a 'free-rider' problem.

It obviously makes sense, therefore, that policing should be provided as a public service.

But do all aspects of policing come into this category? The answer is no. When there is a *specific* task of guarding specific property, policing could be provided by the market. This is in fact done by security firms. Security guards are employed by banks, shops, factories, etc. to prevent theft or criminal damage to specific property. In these cases the private benefits are perceived to exceed the private costs.

Should such security services be provided privately or are they better provided by the police? Since the *private* benefits in such cases are large, there is a strong argument for charging the recipient. But why should the service be provided by private security firms? Could not the police charge firms for specific guard duties? The problem here is that, if private security firms were not allowed to operate, the police would have a monopoly and could charge very high prices unless the prices were regulated by the government. Also the quality of the service might be poorer than that provided by private security companies which were competing against each other for business.

On the other hand, the police are likely to have greater expertise to bring to the job. Also there are economies of scale to be gained: for example, the police may have knowledge of criminal activities in other parts of the area which may pose a threat to the particular property in question. Finally, there is the problem that private security guards may not show the same level of courtesy as the police in dealing with the public (or criminals for that matter).

??

1. The police charge football clubs for policing inside football grounds. Do you think this is a good idea?
2. Some roads could be regarded as a public good, but some could be provided by the market. Which types of road could be provided by the market? Why? Would it be a good idea?

What happens when the industry is under *monopoly*? The firm will produce where $MC = MR$, at an output of Q_m and a price of P_m (at point *b* on the demand curve). Total revenue is $P_m \times Q_m$ (areas 2 + 4 + 6). Total cost is the area under the *MC* curve (area 6). Thus the producer surplus is areas 2 + 4. This is clearly a *larger* surplus than under perfect competition (since area 2 is larger than area 5). The consumer surplus, however, will fall dramatically. With consumption at Q_m, total utility is given by areas 1 + 2 + 4 + 6, whereas consumer expenditure is given by areas 2 + 4 + 6. Consumer surplus, then, is simply area 1. (Note that area 2 has been transformed from consumer surplus to producer surplus.)

Total surplus under monopoly is therefore areas 1 + 2 + 4: a smaller surplus than under perfect competition. 'Monopolisation' of the industry has resulted in a loss of total surplus of areas 3 + 5. The producers' gain has been more than offset by the consumers' loss. This loss of surplus is known as the **deadweight welfare loss** of monopoly.

Conclusions

The firm with market power uses fewer factors and produces less output than the Pareto optimum. It also causes deadweight welfare loss. To the extent, however, that the firm seeks aims *other* than profit maximisation and thus may produce more than the profit-maximising output, so these criticisms must be relaxed.

As was shown in Chapter 6, there are possible social advantages from powerful firms: advantages such as economies of scale and more research and development. These advantages may outweigh the lack of Pareto optimality. It can be argued that an ideal situation would be where firms are large enough to gain economies of scale and yet are somehow persuaded or compelled to produce where $P = MC$ (assuming no externalities).

DEFINITION

Deadweight welfare loss The loss of consumer plus producer surplus in imperfect markets (when compared with perfect competition).

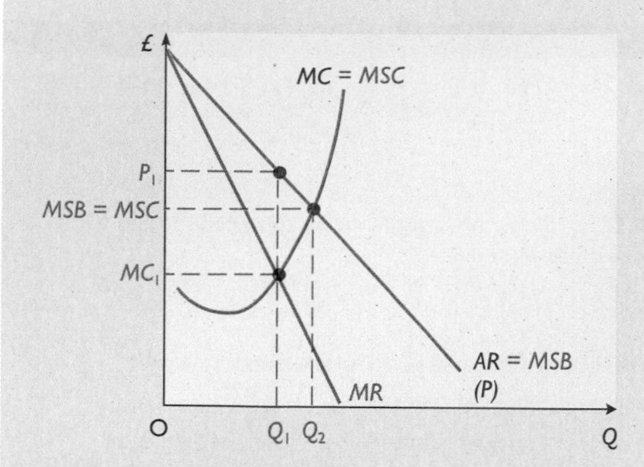

Figure 11.6 The monopolist producing less than the Pareto optimum

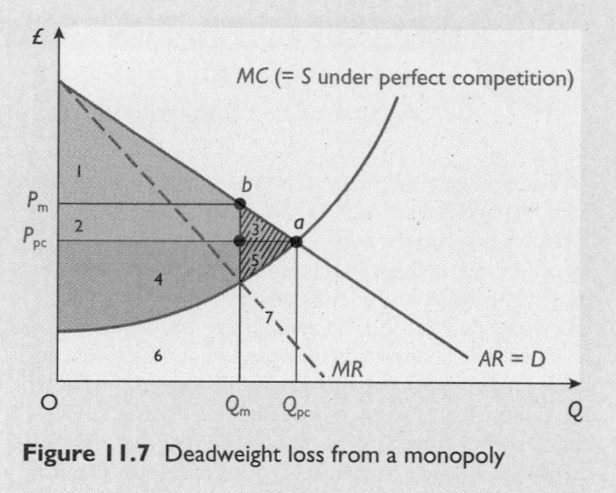

Figure 11.7 Deadweight loss from a monopoly

With oligopoly and monopolistic competition further wastes may occur because of possibly substantial resources involved in non-price competition. Advertising is the major example. It is difficult to predict just how much oligopolists will diverge from the Pareto optimum, since their pricing and output depends on their interpretation of the activities of their rivals.

?? Why will Pareto optimality not be achieved in markets where there are substantial economies of scale in production?

Ignorance and uncertainty

Perfect competition assumes that consumers, firms and factor suppliers have perfect knowledge of costs and benefits. In the real world there is often a great deal of ignorance and uncertainty. Thus people are unable to equate marginal benefit with marginal cost.

Consumers purchase many goods only once or a few times in a lifetime. Cars, washing machines, televisions and other consumer durables fall into this category. Consumers may not be aware of the quality of such goods until they have purchased them, by which time it is too late. Advertising may contribute to people's ignorance by misleading them as to the benefits of a good.

Firms are often ignorant of market opportunities, prices, costs, the productivity of factors (especially white-collar workers), the activity of rivals, etc.

Many economic decisions are based on expected future conditions. Since the future can never be known for certain, many decisions are taken that in retrospect will be seen to have been wrong.

In some cases it may be possible to obtain the information through the market. There may be an agency which will sell you the information or a newspaper or magazine that contains the information. In this case you will have to decide whether the cost to you of buying the information is worth the benefit it will provide you. A problem here is that you may not have sufficient information to judge how reliable the information is that you are buying!

??

1. Assume that you wanted the following information. In which cases might you (i) buy perfect information, (ii) buy imperfect information, (iii) be able to obtain information without paying for it, (iv) not be able to obtain information?
   (a) Which washing machine is the most reliable?
   (b) Which of two jobs that are vacant is the more satisfying?
   (c) Which builder will repair my roof most cheaply?
   (d) Which builder will make the best job of repairing my roof?
   (e) Which builder is best value for money?
   (f) How big a mortgage would it be wise for me to take out?
   (g) What course of higher education should I follow?
   (h) What brand of washing powder washes whiter?
   In which cases are there non-monetary costs to you of finding out the information? How can you know whether the information you acquire is accurate or not?
2. Make a list of pieces of information that a firm might want to know, and consider whether it could buy the information and how reliable that information might be.

Public goods

There is a category of goods that the free market, whether perfect or imperfect, will underproduce or may not produce at all. They are called **public goods**. Examples

DEFINITION

Public good A good or service which has the features of non-rivalry and non-excludability and as a result would not be provided by the free market.

CASE STUDIES

SHOULD HEALTH CARE PROVISION BE LEFT TO THE MARKET?

A case of multiple market failures

When you go shopping you may well pay a visit to the chemist and buy a bottle of paracetamol, some sticking plasters or a tube of ointment. These health-care products are being sold through the market system in much the same way as other everyday goods and services such as food, household items and petrol.

But many health-care services and products are not allocated through the market in this way. In the UK, the National Health Service provides free hospital treatment, a free general practitioner service and free prescriptions for certain categories of people (such as pensioners and children). Their marginal cost to the patient is thus zero. Of course, these services use resources and they thus have to be paid for out of taxes. In this sense they are not free. (Have you heard the famous saying, 'There's no such thing as a free lunch'?)

But why are these services not sold directly to the patient, thereby saving the taxpayer money? Why is it considered that certain types of health care should be provided free, whereas food should not? After all, they could both be considered as basic necessities of life.

The advocates of free health-care provision argue that there are a number of fundamental objections to relying on a market system of allocation of health care, many of which do not apply in the case of food, clothing, etc. So what are the reasons why a free market would fail to provide the optimum amount of health care?

People may not be able to afford treatment

This is a problem connected with the distribution of income. Because income is unequally distributed, some people will be able to afford better treatment than others, and the poorest people may not be able to afford treatment at all. On grounds of equity, therefore, it is argued that health care should be provided free – at least for poor people.

The concept of equity that is usually applied to health care is that of treatment according to medical need rather than according to the ability to pay.

?? Does this argument also apply to food and other basic goods?

Difficulty for people in predicting their future medical needs

If you were suddenly taken ill and required a major operation, or maybe even several, it could be very expensive indeed for you if you had to pay. On the other hand, you may go through life requiring very little if any medical treatment. In other words, there is great uncertainty about your future medical needs. As a result it would be very difficult to plan your finances and budget for possible future medical expenses if you had to pay for treatment. Medical insurance is a possible solution to his problem, but there is still a problem of equity. Would the chronically sick or very old be able to obtain cover, and if so, would the premiums be very high? Would the poor be able to afford the premiums? Also would insurance cover be comprehensive?

Externalities

Health care generates a number of benefits *external* to the patient. If you are cured of an infectious disease, for example, it is not just you who benefits but also others, since you will not infect them. Also your family and friends benefit from seeing you well; and if you have a job you will be able to get back to work, thus reducing the disruption there. These external benefits of health care could be quite large.

If the sick have to pay the cost of their treatment, they may decide not to be treated – especially if they are poor. They may not take into account the effect that their illness has on other people. The market, by equating *private* benefits and costs, would produce too little health care.

include lighthouses, pavements, flood-control dams, public drainage, public services such as the police and even government itself.

Public goods have two important characteristics: *non-rivalry* and *non-excludability*.

- If I consume a bar of chocolate, it cannot then be consumed by someone else. If, however, I walk along a pavement or enjoy the benefits of street lighting, it does not prevent you or anyone else doing the same. There is thus what we call **non-rivalry** in the consumption of such goods. If these goods were sold privately, they would have large external benefits relative to private benefits. This makes them socially desirable, but privately unprofitable. No one person alone would pay to

DEFINITION

Non-rivalry Where the consumption of a good or service by one person will not prevent others from enjoying it.

BOX 11.4

Patient ignorance

Markets only function well to serve consumer wishes if the consumer has the information to make informed decisions. If you are to buy the right things, you must know what you want and whether the goods you buy meet these wants. In practice, consumers do have pretty good knowledge about the things they buy. For example, when you go to the supermarket you will already have tried most of the items that you buy, and will therefore know how much you like them. Even with new products, provided they are the sort you buy more than once, you can learn from any mistakes.

In the case of health care, 'consumers' (i.e. patients) may have very poor knowledge. If you have a pain in your chest, it may be simple muscular strain, or it may be a symptom of heart disease. You rely on the doctor (the *supplier* of the treatment) to give you the information: to diagnose your condition. Two problems could arise here if there were a market system of allocating health care.

The first is that unscrupulous doctors might advise more expensive treatment than is necessary, or drugs companies might try to persuade you to buy a more expensive branded product rather than an identical cheaper version.

The second is that patients suffering from the early stages of a serious disease might not consult their doctor until the symptoms become acute, by which time it might be too late to treat the disease, or very expensive to do so. With a free health service, however, there is likely to be an earlier diagnosis of serious conditions. On the other hand, some patients may consult their doctors over trivial complaints.

Oligopoly

If doctors and hospitals operated in the free market as profit maximisers, it is unlikely that competition would drive down their prices. Instead it is possible that they would collude to fix standard prices for treatment, so as to protect their incomes.

Even if doctors did compete openly, it is unlikely that consumers would have the information to enable them to 'shop around' for the best value. Doctor A may charge less than doctor B, but is the quality of service the same? Simple bedside manner – the thing that may most influence a patient's choice – may be a poor indicator of the doctor's skill and judgment.

To argue that the market system will fail to provide an optimal allocation of health-care resources does not in itself prove that *free provision* is the best alternative. In the USA there is much more reliance on *private medical insurance*. Only the very poor get free treatment. Alternatively, the government may simply *subsidise* the provision of health care, so as to make it cheaper rather than free. This is the case with prescriptions and dental treatment in the UK, where many people have to pay part of the cost of treatment. Also the government can *regulate* the behaviour of the providers of health care, so as to prevent exploitation of the patient. Thus only people with certain qualifications are allowed to operate as doctors, nurses, pharmacists, etc.

??

1. Does the presence of external benefits from health care suggest that health care should be provided free?
2. If health care is provided free, the demand is likely to be high. How is this high demand dealt with? Is this a good way of dealing with it?
3. Go through each of the market failings identified in this box. In each case consider what alternative policies are open to a government to tackle them. What are the advantages and disadvantages of these alternatives?

have a pavement built along his or her street. The private benefit would be too small relative to the cost. And yet the social benefit to all the other people using the pavement may far outweigh the cost.

??

Which of the following have the property of non-rivalry: (a) a can of drink; (b) public transport; (c) a commercial radio broadcast; (d) the sight of flowers in a public park?

- If I spend money erecting a flood control dam to protect my house, my neighbours will also be protected by the dam. I cannot prevent them enjoying the benefits of my expenditure. This feature of **non-excludability**

DEFINITION

Non-excludability Where it is not possible to provide a good or service to one person without it thereby being available for others to enjoy.

means that they would get the benefits free, and would therefore have no incentive to pay themselves. This is known as the **free-rider problem**.

When goods have these two features the free market will simply not provide them. Thus these public goods can be provided only by the government or by the government subsidising private firms. (Note that not all goods produced by the public sector are public goods.)

??

1. Give some other examples of public goods. Does the provider of these goods (the government or local authority) charge for their use? If so, is the method of charging based on the amount of the good that people use? Is it a good method of charging? Could you suggest a better method?
2. Name some goods or services provided by the government or local authorities that are not public goods.

Immobility of factors and time lags in response

The *long-run* equilibrium under perfect competition with no externalities can be said to be socially optimal. $MSB = MSC$; there is maximum consumer plus producer surplus; all firms are producing at the bottom of their $LRAC$ curves; no firm is making supernormal profits.

Even under perfect competition, however, factors may be very slow to respond to changes in demand or supply conditions. Labour, for example, may be highly immobile both occupationally and geographically. This can lead to large price changes and hence to large supernormal profits and high wages for those in the sectors of rising demand or falling costs. The long run may be a very long time coming!

In the meantime, there will be further changes in the conditions of demand and supply. Thus the economy is in a constant state of disequilibrium and the long run never comes. The social optimum is never achieved. It is a bit like chasing rainbows. As you move towards the rainbow's end, so the rainbow moves. Likewise as firms and consumers respond to market signals and move towards equilibrium, so the equilibrium position moves.

Whenever monopoly/monopsony power exists, the problem is made worse as firms or unions put up barriers to the entry of new firms or factors.

Protecting people's interests

Dependants

People do not always make their own economic decisions. They are often dependent on decisions made by others. Parents make decisions on behalf of their children; spouses on each other's behalf; younger adults on behalf of old people; managers on behalf of shareholders; etc. This is the principal–agent issue that we looked at in section 8.1.

A free market will respond to these decisions, however good or bad they may be, and whether or not they are in the interests of the dependant. Thus the government may feel it necessary to protect dependants.

?? Give examples of how the government intervenes to protect the interests of dependants from bad economic decisions taken on their behalf.

Poor economic decision making by individuals on their own behalf

The government may feel that people need protecting from poor economic decisions that they make on their *own* behalf. It may feel that in a free market people will consume too many harmful things. Thus if the government wants to discourage smoking and drinking, it can put taxes on tobacco and alcohol. In more extreme cases it could make various activities illegal: activities such as prostitution, certain types of gambling, and the sale and consumption of drugs.

On the other hand, the government may feel that people consume too little of things that are good for them: things such as education, preventative health care and sports facilities. When the government feels that it knows better than individuals that certain items are good for them, such goods are known as **merit goods**. The government could either provide them free or subsidise their production.

?? How do merit goods differ from public goods?

Other objectives

As we saw in Chapter 10, one of the major criticisms of the free market is the problem of *inequality*. The Pareto criterion gives no guidance, however, as to the most

DEFINITIONS

Free-rider problem When it is not possible to exclude other people from consuming a good that someone has bought.

Merit goods Goods which the government feels that people will underconsume and which therefore ought to be subsidised or provided free.

desirable distribution of income. A redistribution of income will benefit some and make others worse off. Thus Pareto optimality can be achieved for *any* distribution of income. Pareto optimality merely represents the efficient allocation of resources for any *given* distribution of income.

Social efficiency is one possible social goal. Greater equality is another. Other possible social goals also can be identified: goals such as moral behaviour (however defined), enlightenment, social consciousness, co-operation, the development of more refined tastes, fulfilment, freedom from exploitation, and freedom to own, purchase and inherit property. The unfettered free market may not be very successful in achieving social efficiency. It may be even less successful in achieving many other social goals.

Finally, the free market is unlikely to achieve simultaneously the *macroeconomic objectives* of rapid economic growth, full employment, stable prices and a balance of international payments. These problems and the methods of government intervention to deal with them are examined in later chapters.

Conclusions

It is not within the scope of economics to make judgements as to the relative importance of social goals. Economics can only consider means to achieving stated goals. First, therefore, the goals have to be clearly stated by the policy makers. Second, they have to be quantifiable so that different policies can be compared as to their relative effectiveness in achieving the particular goal. Certain goals, such as growth in national income, changes in the distribution of income and greater efficiency, are relatively easy to quantify. Others, such as enlightenment, are virtually impossible to quantify. For this reason, economics tends to concentrate on the means to achieving a relatively narrow range of goals. The danger is that, by economists concentrating on a limited number of goals, they may well influence the policy makers – the government, local authorities, various pressure groups, etc. – into doing the same, and thus into neglecting other perhaps important social goals.

Different objectives are likely to conflict. For example, economic growth may conflict with greater equality. In the case of such 'trade-offs', all the economist can do is to demonstrate the effects of a given policy, and leave the policy makers to decide whether the benefits in terms of one goal outweigh the costs in terms of another goal.

Where there are two or more alternative policies, economists can go further than this. They may be asked to consider the relative effectiveness of the various policies or even themselves to suggest alternative policies. In such cases it may be possible to say that policy A is preferable to policy B because its benefits are greater or its costs lower in terms of all stated goals. On the other hand, if policy A better achieves one goal and policy B better achieves another, once more all the economist can do is to point this out and leave the policy makers to decide.

If people's interests conflict, the economist cannot say who is the more deserving. That is a normative issue.

?? Summarise the economic policies of the major political parties. (If it is near an election, you could refer to their manifestos.) How far can an economist go in assessing these policies?

SECTION SUMMARY

1. Real-world markets will fail to achieve Pareto optimality. What is more, there are objectives other than social efficiency, and real-world markets may fail to achieve these too.
2. Externalities are spillover costs or benefits. Whenever there are external costs, the market will (other things being equal) lead to a level of production and consumption *above* the socially efficient level. Whenever there are external benefits, the market will (other things being equal) lead to a level of production and consumption *below* the socially efficient level.
3. Monopoly power will (other things being equal) lead to a level of output below the socially efficient level. It will lead to a deadweight welfare loss: a loss of consumer plus producer surplus.
4. Ignorance and uncertainty may prevent people from consuming or producing at the levels they would otherwise choose. Information may sometimes be provided (at a price) by the market, but it may be imperfect; in some cases it may not be available at all.
5. Public goods will be underprovided by the market. The problem is that they have large external benefits relative to private benefits, and without government intervention it would not be possible to prevent people having a 'free ride' and thereby escaping contributing to their cost of production.
6. Markets may respond sluggishly to changes in demand and supply. The time lags in adjustment can lead to a permanent state of disequilibrium and to problems of instability.

continued

7. In a free market there may be inadequate provision for dependants and an inadequate output of merit goods; there are likely to be macroeconomic problems (which we shall look at in later chapters); there are likely to be problems of inequality and poverty (which we looked at in Chapter 10); finally, there may be a whole series of social, moral, attitudinal and aesthetic problems arising from a market system.
8. These being normative questions, the economist cannot make ultimate pronouncements on the rights and wrongs of the market. The economist can, however, point out the consequences of the market and of various government policies, and also the trade-offs that exist between different objectives.

11.3 Forms of government intervention

Faced with all the problems of the free market, what is a government to do?

There are several policy instruments that the government can use. At one extreme it can totally replace the market by providing goods and services itself. At the other extreme it can merely seek to persuade producers, consumers or workers to act differently. Between the two extremes the government has a number of weapons that it can use to change the way markets operate: weapons such as taxes, subsidies, laws and regulatory bodies. The following sections examine the different forms of government intervention.

Before looking at different forms of government intervention and their relative merits, it is first necessary to look at a general problem concerned with all forms of intervention. This is known as the **problem of the second best**.

In an ideal free market, where there are no market failures of any sort (the 'first-best' world), there would be no need for government intervention at all. If in this world there did then arise just one failure, in theory its correction would be simple. Say a monopoly arose, or some externality (e.g. pollution) was produced by a particular firm, with the result that the marginal social cost was no longer equal to the marginal social benefit. In theory the government should simply intervene to restore production to the point where $MSC = MSB$. This is known as the **first-best solution**.

Of course, the real world is not like this. It is riddled with imperfections. What this means is that, if one imperfection is 'corrected' (i.e. by making $MSB = MSC$), it might aggravate problems elsewhere. For example, if an airport like Gatwick banned night-time flights so as not to disturb the sleep of local residents, the airlines might simply use Heathrow instead. This simply passes the buck. It now imposes an additional cost on those people living near Heathrow.

?? Give some examples of how correcting problems in one part of the economy will create problems elsewhere.

As the first-best solution of a perfectly efficient, distortion-free world is obviously not possible, the **second-best solution** needs to be adopted. Essentially this involves seeking the best compromises. This means attempting to minimise the *overall* distortionary effects of the policy measure. Some second-best *rules* can be applied in certain cases. We will examine these in the following sections as we look at specific policy measures.

Taxes and subsidies

A policy instrument particularly favoured by many economists is that of taxes and subsidies. They can be used for two main microeconomic purposes: (a) to promote greater social efficiency by altering the composition of production and consumption: and (b) to redistribute incomes. We examined their use for the second purpose in

DEFINITIONS

Problem of the second best The difficulty of working out the best way of correcting a specific market distortion if distortions in other parts of the market continue to exist.

First-best solution The solution of correcting a specific market distortion by ensuring that the whole economy operates under conditions of social efficiency (Pareto optimality).

Second-best solution The solution to a specific market distortion that recognises distortions elsewhere and seeks to minimise the overall distortionary effects to the economy of tackling this specific distortion.

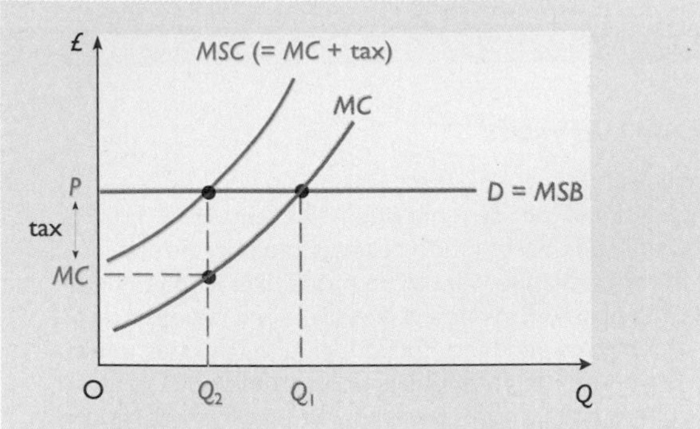

Figure 11.8 Using taxes to correct a distortion: the first-best world

the last chapter. Here we examine their use to achieve greater social efficiency.

When there are imperfections in the market (such as externalities or monopoly power), Pareto optimality will not be achieved. Taxes and subsidies can be used to correct these imperfections. Essentially the approach is to tax those goods or activities where the market produces too much, and subsidise those where the market produces too little.

Taxes to correct externalities

Assume that a chemical works emits smoke from a chimney and thus pollutes the atmosphere. This creates external costs for the people who breathe in the smoke. The marginal social cost of producing the chemicals thus exceeds the marginal private cost to the firm: $MSC > MC$.

The first-best world. In Figure 11.8 the firm is producing in an otherwise perfect world. It produces Q_1 where $P = MC$ (its profit-maximising output), but in doing so takes no account of the external pollution costs it imposes on society. If the government imposes a tax on production equal to the marginal pollution cost, it will effectively internalise the externality. The firm will now maximise profits at Q_2, which is the socially optimum output where $MSB = MSC$. In the first-best world, then, the optimum tax is equal to the marginal external cost.

By analogy, if a firm produced an external benefit, then in the first-best world it ought to be given a subsidy equal to that marginal external benefit.

Note that a tax or subsidy ought to be directed as closely as possible to the source of the externality. For example, if a firm trains labour, and that creates a benefit to society, then ideally it ought to be given a subsidy for each person trained, rather than a general output subsidy. After all, an output subsidy is not only encouraging the firm to train more people (the desired effect), but it is also encouraging it to use more capital and raw materials (an undesired side-effect). This is a general maxim of welfare economics: *a distortion should be corrected at source if side-effect problems are to be avoided.*

Second-best tax and subsidy policies. In reality, the government must tackle imperfections in a world that has many other imperfections. Figure 11.9 shows a firm which both produces an external cost ($MSC > MC$) and *also* has monopoly power. It will maximise profits at Q_1 where $MC = MR$ (point x).

The socially efficient level of output in this case is Q_2, where MSB equals MSC. To persuade the monopolist to produce at this level, a tax of $a - b$ must be imposed (since at point a, $MR = MC +$ tax). This tax is *less* than

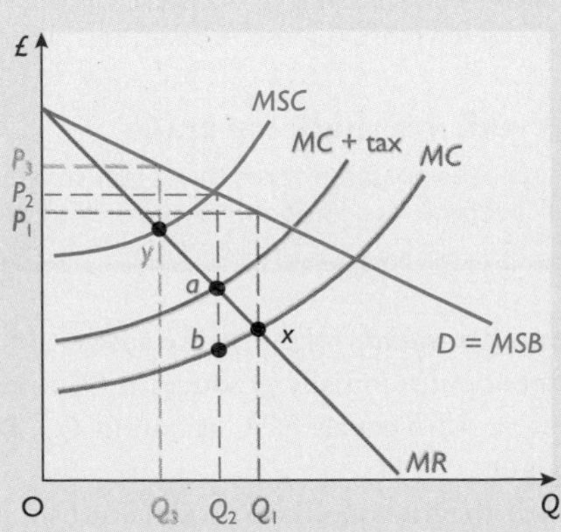

Figure 11.9 Using taxes to correct for externalities when firms have monopoly power

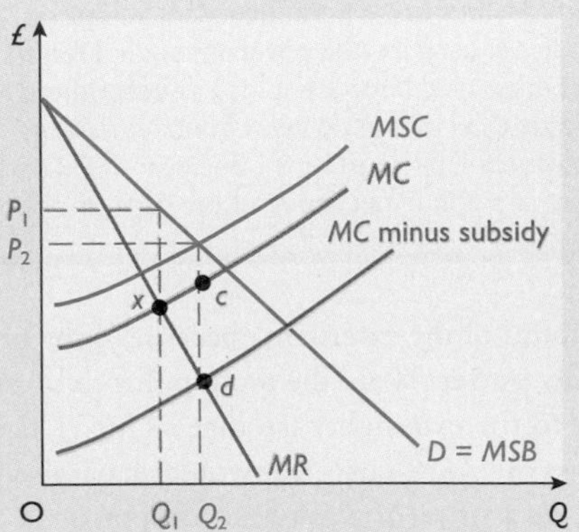

Figure 11.10 Correcting for externalities when firms have substantial monopoly power

CASE STUDIES

GREEN TAXES

Their growing popularity in the industrialised world

Growing concerns over acid rain, the depletion of the ozone layer, industrial and domestic waste, traffic fumes and other forms of pollution have made the protection of the environment a major political issue. Governments round the world have responded in different ways, but increasingly it is the tax weapon that is being used to control polluting activities.

Taxes have the advantage of relating the size of the penalty to the amount of pollution. This means that there is a continuous pressure to cut down on production or consumption of polluting products or activities in order to save tax.

One approach is to modify *existing* taxes. In most developed countries, there are now higher taxes on leaded than unleaded petrol, and lower taxes on low–emission cars. Tax regimes can also be modified which currently *encourage* environmental degradation. For example, lower taxes on diesel could be abolished (given the higher pollution from diesel engines), as could tax relief for commuting expenses. Tax benefits which encourage the use of fertilisers and pesticides in farming, or the felling of trees or hedgerows, could also be abolished.

Increasingly, however, countries are introducing new 'green' taxes in order to discourage pollution as goods are produced, consumed or disposed of. The table shows the range of green taxes in use in 1995 in eight countries. As you can see, the Scandinavian countries have gone the furthest, reflecting the strength of environmental concerns in these countries.

There are various problems, however, with using the tax weapon in the fight against pollution.

Conflicts with revenue objectives

As we saw in the case of tobacco taxes in Box 3.3, the more successful a tax is in reducing consumption, the less revenue it will earn for the government. In Denmark, where energy used in households has been taxed at higher rates than in most other countries, energy consumption fell by 25 per cent between 1973 and 1989. In Sweden, a sulphur tax reduced the sulphur content of fuel oils by 40 per cent between 1990 and 1992. Clearly, the reduced consumption reduces the tax revenue.

But the revenue will still be more than if no tax had been imposed! Provided green taxes are imposed on a wide range of products and at high enough rates, their revenue-earning potential can be considerable. After all, the aim is not to reduce the consumption of energy and many other potentially polluting activities to *zero*. If it were, it would be simplest just to ban the activity.

Redistributive effects

The poor spend a higher proportion of their income on domestic fuel than the rich. A 'carbon tax' on such fuel will, therefore, have the effect of redistributing incomes away from the poor. Thus, when the UK Conservative government in 1995 attempted to increase the rate of VAT on domestic fuel from 8 per cent to 17½ per cent (albeit primarily as a revenue-raising measure rather than as an environmental one), there was an outcry from groups representing the poor.

The poor also spend a larger proportion of their income on food than do the rich. Taxes on agriculture, designed to reduce intensive use of fertilisers and pesticides, will again tend to hit the poor proportionately more than the rich.

Not all green taxes, however, are regressive. The rich spend a higher proportion of their income on motoring than the poor (see Figure 12.1 on page 358). Thus petrol and other motoring taxes could have a progressive effect. Also, other taxes, such as those on packaging, batteries and disposable items, are likely to be neutral in their impact, since their prime purpose is to encourage people to switch to non-polluting alternatives.

Where adverse redistribution does occur, a solution would be to make compensating payments to the poor, or to reduce other even more regressive taxes, such as VAT.

Problems with international trade

If a country imposes pollution taxes on its industries, its products will become less competitive in world trade.

the full amount of the externality because of the problem of monopoly power. Were the monopolist to be charged a tax *equal* to the externality (so that its MC + tax curve was equal to the MSC curve), it would maximise profits at point y, at a price of P_3 and an output of Q_3. This would not be socially efficient, since MSB would now be *above MSC*.

If the monopoly power were large enough and external costs were small or non-existent, a tax would no longer be suitable. Instead a *subsidy* might be the answer. In Figure 11.10, the monopolist initially produces at Q_1, where MR = MC (point x). MSB equals MSC at output Q_2. But this is *higher* than Q_1.

To persuade the monopolist to produce at Q_2 a subsidy of $c - d$ must be paid, since at point d, $MR = MC$ minus the subsidy.

But should a monopolist be subsidised?! Two points arise here:

BOX 11.5

Taxes and charges with beneficial environmental effects: 1995

	Australia	Belgium	Denmark	Japan	Norway	Sweden	UK	USA
Motor fuel								
Leaded unleaded	•	•	•		•	•	•	•
Carbon/energy tax			•		•	•		
Sulphur tax				•	•	•		
Other excise duties	•	•	•		•	•	•	•
Other energy products								
Carbon/energy taxes			•		•	•		
Sulphur tax			•		•	•		
NO_2 charge						•		
Other excise duties	•	•	•	•	•	•	•	•
Vehicle-related								
Large cars>small cars		•	•	•	•	•		•
Agricultural inputs								
Fertilisers					•	•		
Pesticides			•		•	•		
Other goods								
Batteries		•	•			•		
Plastic carrier bags			•					
Disposable containers		•			•			
Tyres			•					•
CFCs	•		•					•
Disposable razors/cameras		•						

	Australia	Belgium	Denmark	Japan	Norway	Sweden	UK	USA
Lubricant oil charge					•			
Oil pollution charge	•							
Air transport								
Noise charges	•	•			•			
Other taxes					•	•		•
Water charges and taxes								
Water charges	•		•		•		•	•
Sewerage charges	•		•		•	•	•	•
Water effluent charges	•							
Waste disposal								
Municipal waste	•		•		•	•	•	•
Waste-disposal charge	•	•	•		•		•	
Hazardous-waste charge	•	•			•			•
Direct tax provisions								
Tax relief on green investment	•		•		•			•
Employer-paid commuting expenses taxable	•		•			•		•
Employer-paid parking expenses taxable	•							•
Commuter use of public transport tax deductible								•

Source: J-P. Barde and J. Owens, 'The evolution of eco-taxes', *OECD Economic Observer* (Feb./March 1996).

To compensate for this, the industries may need to be given tax rebates for exports. Also taxes would need to be imposed on imports of competitors' products from countries where there is no equivalent green tax.

Effects on employment

One of the worries about pollution taxes is that reduced output in the industries affected will lead to a reduction in employment. If, however, the effect was to encourage investment in new cleaner technology, employment might not fall. Where it did, there could be employment opportunities generated elsewhere if the extra revenues from the green taxes allowed reductions in taxes on labour (e.g. employers' national insurance contributions).

Given that much of the incidence of green taxes would fall on the consumer (e.g. the motorist), a reduction in employers' national insurance contributions would help to make industry *more* competitive. There could be a net *increase* in employment and exports.

?? Is it a good idea to use the revenues from green taxes to subsidise green alternatives (e.g. using petrol taxes for subsidising rail transport)?

- Subsidising the monopoly gives it even bigger supernormal profits. This could be seen as *unfair* even if the resulting level of output it produced was now the desirable level.
- In the second-best world, it is not necessarily desirable for firms to charge a price equal to *MSC* anyway! If other firms were charging a price, say, 20 per cent above *MSC*, and if this firm charged a price *equal* to *MSC*, this would *itself* be a distortion: causing a reallocation of consumption to it and away from other firms. It is better for the firm to have the same percentage difference between price and *MSC* as the average of other firms. This minimises the firm's *relative* distortion.

Taxes to correct for monopoly

So far we have considered the use of taxes to correct for externalities. Taxes can also be used to regulate the behaviour of monopolies and oligopolies.

If the government wishes to tackle the problem of excessive monopoly profits, it can impose a *lump-sum* tax on the monopolist. This is illustrated in Figure 11.11.

Being of a fixed amount, a lump-sum tax is a fixed cost to the firm. It does not affect the firm's marginal cost. It shifts the *AC* curve upwards.

Profits continue to be maximised where $MC = MR$, at an output of Q_1 and a price of P_1. But profits are reduced from areas 1 + 2 to area 1 alone. Area 2 now represents the amount of tax paid to the government. If the lump-sum tax were large enough to make the *AC* + lump-sum tax curve cross the demand curve at point *a*, *all* the supernormal profits would be taken as tax.

If the government also wants to increase the monopolist's output to the socially efficient level of Q_2, and wants it to charge a price of P_2, it could do this with a careful combination of a per-unit subsidy (which will shift both the *AC* and the *MC* curves downwards) and a lump-sum tax. The required level of subsidy will be that which shifts the *MC* curve downwards to the point where it intersects *MR* at output Q_2. Then a lump-sum tax would be imposed that would be big enough to shift the *AC* curve back up again so that it crosses the demand curve at point *b*.

?? What could we say about the necessary subsidy if the *MR* curve crossed the horizontal axis to the left of point *b*?

Advantages of taxes and subsidies

Many economists favour the tax/subsidy solution to market imperfections (especially the problem of externalities) because it still allows the market to operate. It forces firms to take on board the full social costs and benefits of their actions. It is also adjustable according to the magnitude of the problem.

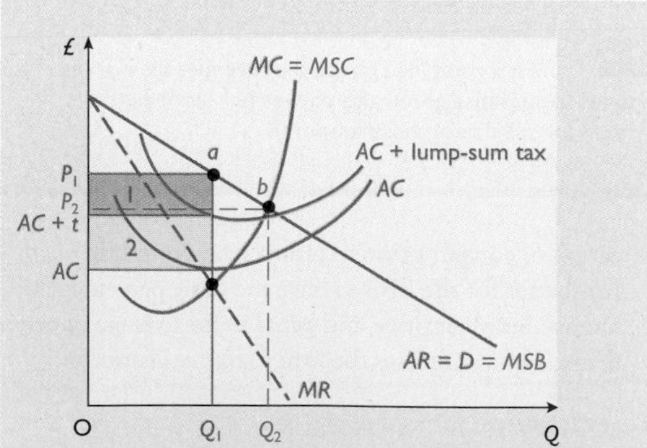

Figure 11.11 Using a lump-sum tax to reduce monopoly profits

Moreover, if firms are taxed for polluting they are encouraged to find cleaner ways of producing. The tax acts as an incentive over the longer run to reduce pollution. Likewise, by subsidising *good* practices, firms are given the incentive to adopt more good practices.

It might be argued that taxes are a bad way of dealing with pollution, because they still allow the pollution to continue. Advocates of the tax solution, however, argue that just because a firm pollutes, it does not mean that it should be shut down. The benefits to society of having the product may considerably outweigh the costs of its production, *including* the costs of the pollution.

The most suitable situation for imposing a pollution tax is when there is a clearly measurable emission, like a particular chemical waste. The government can then impose a tax per litre or per tonne of that waste.

Disadvantages of taxes and subsidies

Infeasible to use different tax and subsidy rates. Each firm produces different levels and types of externality and operates under different degrees of imperfect competition. It would be administratively very difficult and expensive to charge every offending firm its own particular tax rate (or grant every relevant firm its own particular rate of subsidy). Even in the case of pollution where it is possible to measure a firm's emissions, there would still have to be a different tax rate for each pollutant and even for each environment, depending on its ability to absorb the pollutant.

Using combinations of lump-sum taxes and per-unit subsidies to correct monopoly distortions to price, output and profit would also probably be totally impractical. Given that cost and revenue curves differ substantially from one firm to another, separate tax and subsidy rates would be needed for each firm. An army of tax inspectors would be necessary to adminster the system!

Lack of knowledge. Even if a government did decide to charge a tax equal to each offending firm's marginal external costs, it would still have the problem of measuring those costs and apportioning blame. The damage to lakes and forests from acid rain has been a major concern since the beginning of the 1980s. But just how serious is that damage? What is its current monetary cost? How long lasting is the damage? Just what and who are to blame? These questions cannot be answered precisely. It is thus impossible to fix the 'correct' pollution tax on, say, a particular coal-fired power station.

??

1. Why is it easier to use taxes and subsidies to tackle the problem of car exhaust pollution than to tackle the problem of peak-time traffic congestion in cities?
2. If the precise environmental costs of CFCs in fridges were known, would the tax solution be a suitable remedy for the problem?

Changes in property rights

One cause of market failure is the limited nature of property rights. If someone dumps a load of rubble in your garden, you can insist that it is removed. If, however, someone dumps a load of rubble in their *own* garden, which is next door to yours, what can you do? You can still see it from your window. It is still an eyesore. But you have no property rights over the next-door garden. Similarly the air you breathe is not your property. You cannot insist that it is clean air. Likewise the skies over your head. Noisy aircraft may disturb you, but it is not *your* airspace! You cannot insist that the aircraft fly elsewhere.

One solution, then, to the problem of market failure (again especially in the case of externalities) is to extend property rights. Property rights define who owns property, to what uses it can be put, the rights other people have over it and how it may be transferred. By extending these rights, individuals may be able to prevent other people from imposing costs on them.

Ultimately property rights could be extended so completely that everyone would have the right to prevent people imposing any costs on them whatsoever, or to charge them for the privilege. For example, if I were disturbed by noisy lorries outside my home, I would have the right to prohibit them from coming down my street, or to charge them. The charge would be negotiated between me and the lorry firm.

The socially efficient level of charge would be one that was equal to the marginal external cost (and would have the same effect as the government charging a tax on the firm of that amount: see Figure 11.8). The **Coase theorem**[4] states that in an otherwise perfectly competitive market, the socially efficient charge *will* be levied. But why? If sufferers charged *less* than the marginal external cost, they would suffer more from the last unit than they were being compensated. If they charged *more*, and thereby caused the firm to cut back its output below the socially efficient level, they would be sacrificing receiving charges which would be greater than the marginal suffering. It will be in the sufferers' best interests, therefore, to charge an amount *equal* to the marginal externality.

??

If the sufferers had no property rights, show how it would still be in their interests to 'bribe' the firm to produce the socially efficient level of output.

In most instances, however, this type of solution is totally impractical. It is impractical when *many* people are *slightly* inconvenienced, especially if there are many culprits imposing the costs. The case of the lorries is an example. How could I negotiate with every lorry firm? What if I wanted to ban the lorries from the street but my next-door neighbour wanted to charge them 10p per journey? Who gets their way? Likewise it would be totally impractical for me to negotiate with various airlines about diverting their aircraft because of my loss of sleep!

The extension of private property rights becomes more practical where the culprits are few in number, are easily identifiable and impose clearly defined costs. Thus a noise abatement Act could be passed which allowed me to prevent my neighbours from playing noisy radios, having noisy parties or otherwise disturbing the peace in my home. The onus would be on me to report them. Or I could agree not to report them if they paid me adequate compensation.

But even in cases where only a few people are involved, there may still be the problem of litigation. Justice may not be free, and thus there is a conflict with equity. The rich can afford 'better' justice. They can employ top lawyers. Thus even if I have a right to sue a large company for dumping toxic waste near me, I may not have the legal muscle to win.

Finally, the extension of private property rights may favour the rich at the expense of the poor. Ramblers may get great pleasure from strolling across a great country estate, along public rights of way. If the owner's property rights were now extended to exclude the ramblers, would this be a social gain?

Of course, equity considerations can also be dealt with by altering property rights, but in a different way. *Public* property, like parks, open spaces, libraries and historic buildings, could be extended. Also the property of the rich could be redistributed to the poor. Here it is less a ques-

[4] Named after Ronald Coase, who developed the theory. See his 'The problem of social cost', *Journal of Law and Economics* (1960).

DEFINITION

Coase theorem By sufferers from externalities doing deals with perpetrators (by levying charges or offering bribes), the externality will be 'internalised' and the socially efficient level of output will be achieved.

tion of the rights that ownership confers, and more a question of altering the ownership itself.

??

1. To what extent could property rights (either public or private) be successfully extended and invoked to curb the problem of industrial pollution (a) of the atmosphere; (b) of rivers; (c) by the dumping of toxic waste; (d) by the erection of ugly buildings; (e) by the creation of high levels of noise?
2. What protection do private property rights in the real world give to sufferers of noise (a) from neighbours; (b) from traffic; (c) from transistor radios at the seaside?

Laws prohibiting or regulating undesirable structures or behaviour

Laws are frequently used to correct market imperfections. This section examines three of the most common cases.

Laws prohibiting or regulating behaviour that imposes external costs

Laws can be applied both to individuals and to firms. In the case of individuals it is illegal to drive when drunk. Drunk driving imposes costs on others in the form of accidents and death. Another example is the banning of smoking in public places.

In the case of firms, various polluting activities can be banned or restricted; safety standards can be imposed in the place of work; building houses or factories may be prohibited in green-belt areas.

Advantages of legal restrictions

- They are simple and clear to understand and are often relatively easy to administer. Inspectors or the police can conduct spot checks to see that the law is being obeyed.
- When the danger is very great, it might be much safer to ban various practices altogether rather than to rely on taxes or on individuals attempting to assert their property rights through the civil courts. For example, if the dangers to the ozone layer from the use of certain aerosol cans are as serious as some scientists suggest, the offending propellant ought to be banned, not merely taxed.
- When a decision needs to be taken quickly it might be possible to invoke emergency action. For example, in a city like Athens or Los Angeles it would be simpler to ban or restrict the use of private cars during a chemical smog emergency than to tax their use (see Box 12.2).

Disadvantages of legal restrictions. The main problem is that legal restrictions tend to be a rather blunt weapon. If, for example, a firm were required to reduce the effluent of a toxic chemical to 20 tonnes per week, there would be no incentive for the firm to reduce it further. With a tax on the effluent, however, the more the firm reduced the effluent, the less tax it would pay. Thus with a system of taxes there is a *continuing* incentive to cut pollution.

The other problem is that in practice inspections may be few and/or penalties small. In such cases the pollution would simply continue.

Laws to prevent or regulate monopolies and oligopolies

Laws affecting structure. Various mergers or takeovers could be made illegal. The criterion would probably have to be the level of market concentration that results. For example, the law could set a limit of 60 per cent of the market to be controlled by the five largest firms. Or it could require that merging firms have less than a certain percentage share of the market.

Laws affecting behaviour. Firms could be prohibited from engaging in various types of oligopolistic collusion, or various monopolistic practices. For example, manufacturers could be prevented from fixing the prices that retailers must charge, or from refusing to supply certain retailers.

Use of the law to regulate monopolies and oligopolies in the UK and the EU is examined in section 12.2.

??

How suitable are legal restrictions in the following cases?
(a) Ensuring adequate vehicle safety.
(b) Reducing traffic congestion.
(c) Preventing the abuse of monopoly power.
(d) Ensuring that mergers are in the public interest.
(e) Ensuring that firms charge a price equal to marginal cost.

Laws to prevent firms from exploiting people's ignorance

Given that consumers have imperfect information, firms could sometimes take advantage of this by making false claims for their products or by producing poor-quality or unsafe goods.

Consumer protection laws can make it illegal for firms to sell shoddy or dangerous goods, or to make false or misleading claims about their products. The problem is that the firms most likely to exploit the consumer are often the ones that are most elusive when it comes to prosecuting them. Also it may be very difficult to frame the legislation tightly enough to prevent firms from getting around it.

Regulatory bodies

A more subtle approach than banning or restricting various activities involves the use of regulatory bodies. These could have the following functions:

- To seek out potential cases for investigation: e.g. potential cases of pollution, or the abuse of monopoly power.
- To conduct an investigation to decide whether certain activities should be permitted, reduced, modified or banned. They would obviously have to make their decisions according to stated criteria. Such criteria could be embodied in the legislation establishing the regulatory body.
- To take action themselves to enforce their decisions, or report to some higher authority which would decide whether to take action on the recommendation.

An example of such a body is the Monopolies and Mergers Commission (MMC), the work of which is examined in section 12.2. Other examples are the bodies set up to regulate the privatised utilities: e.g. OFGAS, the Office of Gas Supply. These are examined in section 12.3.

The advantage of this approach is that a case-by-case method can be used, and, as a result, the most appropriate solution adopted. However, investigations may be expensive and time consuming, only a few cases may be examined, and offending firms may make various promises of good behaviour which, owing to a lack of follow-up by the regulatory body, may not in fact be carried out.

?? What other forms of intervention are likely to be necessary to back up the work of regulatory bodies?

Price controls

Price controls could be used to prevent a monopoly or oligopoly from charging excessive prices. Currently, various privatised industries such as telecommunications, gas and electricity are not allowed to raise their prices by more than a certain percentage below the rate of inflation (see section 12.3).

Price controls could also be used with the objective of redistributing incomes. Prices could be fixed either above or below equilibrium. Thus (high) minimum farm prices can be used to protect the incomes of farmers, and minimum wage legislation can help those on low incomes. On the consumption side, (low) maximum rents can help poor people afford housing, and price ceilings on food or other essentials during a war or other emergency can allow poor people to afford such items. However, as was argued in section 3.1, the problem with price controls is that they cause shortages (in the case of low prices) or surpluses (high prices).

Provision of information

When ignorance is a reason for market failure, the direct provision of information by the government may help to correct that failure. Some examples would be the following:

- The provision of job centres. These provide information on jobs to those looking for work, and put firms in touch with possibly suitable labour. They thus help the labour market to work better and increase the elasticity of supply of labour.
- The provision of consumer information: for example, on the effects of smoking, or the dangers of inflammable furniture.
- The provision of government statistics on prices, costs, employment, sales trends, etc. This enables firms to plan with greater certainty.

The provision of information may also put pressure on firms to reduce external costs. For example, if the government advertises the effect of dumping toxic chemicals, offending firms may stop doing it, perhaps because of the fear of a hostile public reaction and a resulting loss of sales.

?? Information may not be provided by the private sector if it can be used by those who do not pay: if it is a public good (service). Do all the examples above come into the category of public goods? Give some other examples of information which is a public good. (Clue: do not confuse a public good with something merely provided by the government, which *could* also be provided by the private sector.)

The direct provision of goods and services

In the case of public goods and services, such as streets, pavements, seaside illumination and national defence, the market may completely fail to provide. In this case the government must take over the role of provision. Central government, local government or some other public agency could provide these goods and services directly. Alternatively, they could pay private firms to do so.

But just what quantity of the public good should be provided? How can the level of public demand or public 'need' be identified? Should any charge at all be made to consumers for each unit consumed?

With a pure public good, once it is provided the marginal cost of supplying one more consumer is zero. Take the case of a lighthouse. Once it is constructed and in operation, there is no extra cost of providing the service to additional passing ships. Even it were *possible* to charge ships each time they make use of it, it would not be socially desirable. Assuming no external costs, *MSC* is zero. Thus *MSB* = *MSC* at a price of zero. Zero is thus the socially efficient price.

But what about the construction of a new public good, like a new road or a new lighthouse? How can a rational decision be made by the government as to whether it should go ahead? This time the marginal cost is not zero: extra roads and lighthouses cost money to build. The solution is to identify all the costs and benefits to society from the project, and to weigh them up. This is where cost–benefit analysis comes in – the subject of section 11.4.

The government could also provide goods and services directly which are *not* public goods. Examples include health and education. There are four reasons why such things are provided free or at well below cost.

Social justice. Society may feel that these things should not be provided according to ability to pay. Rather, as *merit goods*, they should be provided according to need.

Large positive externalities. People other than the consumer may benefit substantially. If a person decides to get treatment for an infectious disease, other people benefit by not being infected. A free health service thus helps to combat the spread of disease.

Dependants. If education were not free, and if the quality of education depended on the amount spent, and if parents could choose how much or little to buy, then the quality of children's education would depend not just on their parents' income, but also on how much they cared. A government may choose to provide such things free in order to protect children from 'bad' parents. A similar argument is used for providing free prescriptions and dental treatment for all children.

Ignorance. Consumers may not realise how much they will benefit. If they had to pay, they might choose (unwisely) to go without. Providing health care free may persuade people to consult their doctors before a complaint becomes serious.

Public ownership

This is different from direct provision, in that the goods and services produced by publicly owned (nationalised) industries are sold in the market. The costs and benefits of public ownership are examined in detail in section 12.3.

SECTION SUMMARY

1. If there were a distortion in just one part of the economy, the 'first-best' solution would be possible. This would be to correct that one distortion. In the real world, where there are many distortions, the first-best solution will not be possible. The second-best solution will be to seek the best compromise that minimises the *relative* distortions between the industry in question and other parts of the economy.
2. Taxes and subsidies are one means of correcting market distortions. In the first-best world, externalities can be corrected by imposing tax rates equal to the size of marginal external costs, and granting rates of subsidy equal to marginal external benefits. In the second-best world, taxes and subsidies can be used to correct externalities that create *relative* distortions between this industry and others, or externalities that exist along with other distortions within this industry.
3. Taxes and subsidies can also be used to affect monopoly price, output and profit. Subsidies can be used to persuade a monopolist to increase output to the competitive level. Lump-sum taxes can be used to reduce monopoly profits without affecting price or output.
4. Taxes and subsidies have the advantages of 'internalising' externalities and of providing incentives to reduce external costs. On the other hand, they may be impractical to use when different rates are required for each case, or when it is impossible to know the full effects of the activities that the taxes or subsidies are being used to correct.
5. An extension of property rights may allow individuals to prevent others from imposing costs on them. This is not practical, however, when many people are affected to a small degree, or where several people are affected but differ in their attitudes towards what they want doing about the 'problem'.
6. Laws can be used to regulate activities that impose external costs, to regulate monopolies and oligopolies, and to provide consumer protection. Legal controls are often simpler and easier to operate than taxes, and are safer when the danger is potentially great. However, they tend to be rather a blunt weapon.
7. Regulatory bodies can be set up to monitor and control activities that are against the public interest (e.g. anti-competitive behaviour of oligopolists). They can conduct investigations of specific cases, but these may be expensive and time consuming, and may not be acted on by the authorities.
8. The government may provide information in cases where the private sector fails to provide an adequate level. It may also provide goods and services directly. These could be either public goods or other goods where the government feels that provision by the market is inadequate. The government could also influence production in publicly owned industries.

*11.4

Cost–benefit analysis

If the market produces the wrong amount of various goods and services, how is the government to determine the right amount? This is obviously a highly normative question because it depends on social goals. Nevertheless economists have developed a technique known as **cost–benefit analysis** (CBA). It is used to help governments decide whether to go ahead with various projects such as a new motorway, a bypass, an underground line, a hospital, a health-care programme, a dam, and so on. The analysis seeks to establish whether the benefits to society from the project outweigh the costs, in which case the project should go ahead; or whether the costs outweigh the benefits, in which case it should not.

CBAs are usually commissioned either by a government department or by a local authority. Unlike the techniques of project evaluation used by private firms, which only take into account *private monetary* costs and benefits, CBA takes into account *externalities* and private *non-monetary* costs and benefits as well. Thus the cost–benefit study on the siting of a third London airport attempted to assess the external costs of noise to local residents as well as the direct costs and benefits to the travellers.

The procedure

The procedure at first sight seems fairly straightforward.

- All costs and benefits are identified. These include all private monetary and non-monetary costs and benefits and all externalities.
- A monetary value is assigned to each cost and benefit. This is essential if costs and benefits are to be added up: a common unit of measurement must be used. As might be expected, assigning monetary values to externalities like noise, pollution and the quality of life is fraught with difficulties!
- Account is taken of the likelihood of a cost or benefit occurring. The simplest way of doing this is to multiply the monetary value of a cost or benefit by the probability of its occurrence. So if there were a 60 per cent chance of a cost of £100 occurring, it would be valued at £60.
- Account is taken of the timing of the costs and benefits. £100 of benefits received today would be regarded as more desirable than having to wait, say, ten years to receive the £100. Likewise it is a greater sacrifice to pay £100 today than being able to wait ten years to pay it. Thus future costs and benefits must be reduced in value to take this into account. *Discounting techniques* (similar to those we examined in section 9.4) are used for this purpose.
- Some account may also be taken of the distribution of the costs and benefits. Is it considered fair that, although some people will gain from the project, others will lose? Will the losers be compensated in any way?
- A recommendation is then made by weighing up the costs and benefits. In simplest terms, if the benefits exceed the costs, it will be recommended that the project goes ahead.

Each of these stages involves a number of difficulties. These are examined in the following sections.

Identifying the costs and benefits

Identifying costs and benefits is relatively easy, although there are some problems in predicting what types of external effect are likely to occur.

Costs

Direct (private) monetary costs. These are easy to identify. They simply include all the construction costs and the operating and maintenance costs.

External costs. These fall into two categories:

- *Monetary costs*, such as the loss of profits to competitors. Thus in the case of a CBA of a tunnel under a river, external monetary costs would include the loss of profits to ferry operators.
- *Non-monetary costs*, such as pollution, spoiling the landscape, noise and various other forms of inconvenience to local residents. In some projects like a tunnel, these costs will be largely confined to the construction phase. With other projects, however, like a new airport, there may be considerable externalities resulting from its operation (e.g. noise). These non-monetary externalities are usually the most difficult costs to identify.

DEFINITION

Cost–benefit analysis The identification, measurement and weighing-up of the costs and benefits of a project in order to decide whether or not it should go ahead.

Benefits

Direct (private) monetary benefits. These are also easy to identify. They consist of the revenues received from the users of the project. The direct monetary benefits of a toll bridge, for example, are the tolls paid.

Private non-monetary benefits. These are the benefits to consumers over and above what they actually pay: in other words, the consumer surplus. For example, if a bridge had a toll of 50p, and yet a person was prepared to pay £2 if necessary to avoid the long trip round the estuary, then the person's consumer surplus is £1.50. Total consumer surplus is thus the area between the demand curve (which shows what people are willing to pay) and the price charged. This is illustrated in Figure 11.12.

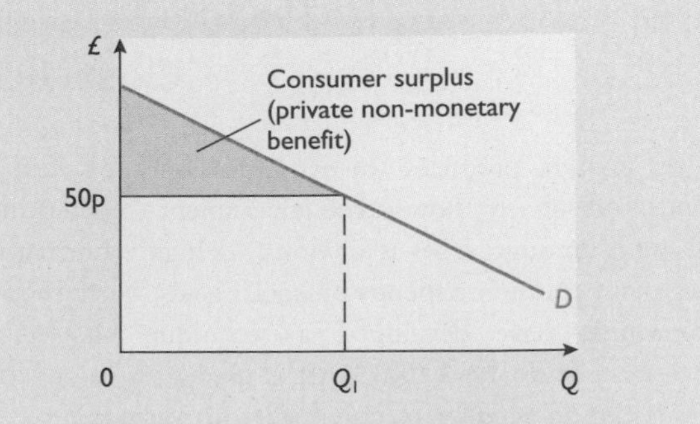

Figure 11.12 Private non-monetary benefits (consumer surplus)

External benefits. These are the benefits to the non-users of the project. For example, the Victoria Underground line CBA identified external benefits to road users in central London. The roads would become less congested as people used the new Underground line. Usually these benefits are non-monetary benefits, but sometimes they may result in direct financial gain (e.g. higher profits to companies from reduced transport costs on less crowded roads).

Measuring the costs and benefits

Identifying costs and benefits may be relatively easy: measuring them is another matter. Difficulties in measurement depend on the type of cost and benefit. There are four types.

Direct private monetary costs and benefits

These would seem to be the simplest to measure. Normally the simple financial costs and revenues are used. In the case of a new Underground line, for example, such costs would include excavation, construction and capital costs (such as new rolling stock) and the operating costs (such as labour, electricity and maintenance). Revenues would be the fares paid by travellers. There are two problems, nevertheless:

- What *will* these financial costs and revenues be? It is all very well using current prices, but prices rise over time, and at different and unpredictable rates. Also it is difficult to forecast demand and hence revenues. There is thus a large element of *uncertainty*.
- The prices will often be distorted by the existence of monopoly power. Should this be taken into account? Should, for example, fuel costs be estimated at prices that *would* be charged under perfect competition? In an otherwise perfect world (the first-best situation), the answer would be yes. But in the real world these price distortions exist throughout the economy. If a rational choice is to be made about whether to build a new Underground line, say, then generally speaking, actual market prices should be used. After all, these are the prices that have to be paid by car drivers and taxi and bus users (the alternatives to using the Underground). Thus the second-best solution is to use actual market prices *unless* there is a price distortion that applies *only* to the specific project.

?? What price should be used when there is such a distortion?

Non-monetary private benefits: consumer surplus

Consumer surplus is a private benefit – it accrues to the users of the project – but is not part of the money earned from the project. There are two ways of estimating it.

The first way is to estimate the demand curve and then estimate the shaded area in Figure 11.12. Estimating demand is very difficult, since it depends on the price and availability of substitutes. The demand for the Channel Tunnel depends on the price, frequency and convenience of ferry crossings. It also depends on the overall level of activity in the economy and perhaps the world generally. Thus estimates of air traffic (an essential piece of information when deciding whether to build a new airport) have often been proved wrong as the world economy has grown more rapidly or less rapidly than previously forecast.

Another problem is that the consumer surplus gained from this project (e.g. the Channel Tunnel) may replace the albeit smaller consumer surplus from a competing service (e.g. cross-Channel ferries). In this case the non-monetary private benefit is merely the *additional* consumer surplus of those who switch, but still the *full* consumer surplus of those who would not otherwise have crossed the Channel. This makes calculation less straightforward.

An alternative approach is to focus on specific non-monetary benefits to consumers. This approach is more useful when the service is to be provided free and thus no estimate of a demand curve can be made. Assume that a new motorway saves 20 000 hours of travelling time per week. (This, of course, will first have to be estimated, and again a prediction will have to be made of the number of people using the motorway.) How is this 20 000 hours to be evaluated? In the case of businesspeople and lorry drivers, the average hourly wage rate will be used to estimate the value of each labour hour saved. In the case of leisure time there is less agreement on how to value an hour saved. Usually it is simply assumed to be some fraction of the average hourly wage. This method is somewhat arbitrary, however, and a better approach, though probably impractical, would be to attempt to measure how the travellers themselves evaluate their time.

Another way of measuring time saved would be to see how much money people would be prepared to spend to save travelling time. For example, how much extra would people be prepared to pay for a taxi which saved, say, ten minutes over the bus journey? This method, however, has to take account of the fact that taxis may be more desirable for other reasons too, such as comfort.

> **??** How would you attempt to value time that you yourself save (a) getting to work; (b) going on holiday; (c) going out in the evening?

Similar calculations would need to be made for fuel saved by the traveller. This calculation is relatively easy to make. A much more difficult type of private benefit to estimate, however, would be the pleasure of travelling along that road (due, say, to the scenery). Note that, although some of these benefits do involve *money* savings to the consumer, they do not earn *revenue* for the project. It is in this sense that they are non-monetary benefits.

Monetary externalities

These would normally be counted at face value. Thus the external monetary costs of a new Underground would include the loss of profits to taxi and bus companies. The external monetary benefits of a new motorway would include the profits to be made by the owners of the motorway service stations.

Non-monetary externalities

These are likely to be the hardest to measure. The general principle employed is to try to find out how much people would be prepared to pay to obtain the benefits or avoid the costs, if they were able to do so. There are two approaches here.

Ask people (questionnaires). Take the case of noise from an airport or motorway. People could be asked how much they would need to be compensated. There are two problems with this:

- Ignorance. People will not know just how much they will suffer *until* the airport or motorway is built.
- Dishonesty. People will tend to exaggerate the compensation they would need. After all, if compensation is actually going to be paid, people will want to get as much as possible. But even if it is not, the more people exaggerate the costs to themselves, the more likely it is they can get the project stopped.

These problems can be lessened if people are questioned who have already experienced a similar project elsewhere. They have less to gain from being dishonest.

Make inferences from people's behaviour. Take the case of noise again. In similar projects elswhere, how have people actually reacted? How much have they spent on double glazing or other noise insulation? How much financial loss have they been prepared to suffer to move somewhere quieter? What needs to be measured, however, is not just the financial cost, but also the loss of consumer surplus. The Roskill Commission in 1968 examined the siting of a third London airport. It attempted to evaluate noise costs, and looked at the difference in value of house prices round Gatwick compared with elsewhere. A problem with this approach is in finding cases elswhere that are directly comparable. Were the four potential sites for the third London airport directly comparable with Gatwick?

Another example of externalities would be a reduction in accidents from a safer road. How is this to be measured? Obviously there are the monetary benefits from reduced medical expenditures. But how would you value a life saved? This question is examined in Box 11.6.

> **??** How would you evaluate (a) the external effects of building a reservoir in an area of outstanding natural beauty; (b) the external effects of acid rain pollution from a power station?

Risk and uncertainty

Taking account of *risk* is relatively straightforward. The value of a cost or benefit is simply multiplied by the probability of its occurrence.

ISSUES AND APPLICATIONS BOX 11.6

WHAT PRICE A HUMAN LIFE?

A difficult question for cost–benefit analysis

Many projects involve saving lives, whether they be new hospitals or new transport systems. This is obviously a major benefit, but how is a life to be evaluated?

Some people argue, 'You can't put a price on a human life: life is priceless.' But just what are they saying here? Are they saying that life has an *infinite* value? If so, this project must be carried out *whatever* the costs, and even if other benefits from it were zero! Clearly, when evaluating lives saved from the project a value less than infinity must be given.

Other people might argue that human life cannot be treated like other costs and benefits and put into mathematical calculations. But what are these people saying? That the question of lives saved should be excluded from the cost–benefit study? If so, the implication is that life has a *zero* value! Again this is clearly not the case.

So if a value somewhere between zero and infinity should be used, what should it be?

Some economists have suggested that a life be valued in terms of a person's future earning potential. But this implies that the only value of a person is as a factor of production! Would the life of a disabled person, for example, who is unable to work and draws state benefit be given a *negative* value? Again this is clearly not the solution.

Can any inferences be drawn from people's behaviour? How much are people prepared to spend on safety: on making their car roadworthy, on buying crash helmets, etc.? This approach too has serious drawbacks. People are wishful thinkers. They obviously do not want to be killed, but simply believe that accidents happen to other people, not to them.

Then again, there are the problems of estimating the effects on other people: on family and friends. Can the amount that people are willing to spend on life assurance be a guide here? Again people are wishful thinkers. Also it is not the family and friends who buy the assurance; it is the victim, who may not take the effect on others fully into account.

In the mid-1990s, the UK Department of Transport put a value of £786 500 on a life saved. This was based on an individual's willingness to pay to reduce risks. It thus ignored benefits to family, friends and the economy, let alone the benefits from safer roads to people now being able to cycle or let their children walk to school, etc. If these are taken into account, it is easy to arrive at a value closer to £2 million.

??

1. Can you think of any other ways of getting a more 'rational' evaluation of human life? Would the person's age make any difference?
2. If you had to decide whether more money from a hospital's budget were to be spent on hip replacements (which do not save lives, but do dramatically improve the quality of the patient's life), or on heart transplants (which do save lives, but are expensive), how would you set about making a rational decision?

The problem is that *risk* is less frequent than *uncertainty*. As was explained in Chapter 4, in the case of risk at least the probability of various outcomes is known. In the case of uncertainty all that is known is that an outcome *might* occur. The likelihood of its occurring, however, is uncertain.

How then can uncertainty be taken into account? The best approach is to use **sensitivity analysis**. Let us consider two cases.

Individual uncertain outcomes

A range of possible values can be given to an uncertain item in the CBA: for example, damage from pollution. Table 11.1 illustrates two possible cases.

The lowest estimate for pollution damage is £10 million; the highest is £50 million. In case A, given a very high margin of benefits over *other* costs, the project's desirability is *not* sensitive to different values for pollution damage. Even with the highest value (£50 million), the project still yields a net benefit.

In case B, however, the project's desirability *is* sensitive to pollution damage. If the damage exceeds £20 million, the project becomes undesirable. In this case the government will have to decide whether it is prepared to take the gamble.

A number of uncertain outcomes

When there are several uncertain outcomes the typical approach is to do three cost–benefit calculations: the most

DEFINITION

Sensitivity analysis Where a range of possible values of uncertain costs and benefits are given to see whether the project's desirability is sensitive to these different values.

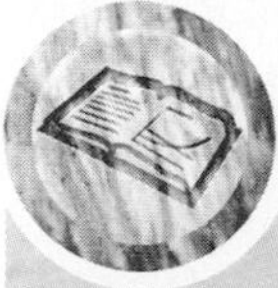

EXPLORING THE THEORY — BOX 11.7

CALCULATING NET PRESENT VALUE
The use of discounting techniques in CBA

The formula for calculating the net present value (*NPV*) of a project is as follows:

$$NPV = (B-C)_0 + \frac{(B-C)_1}{(1+d)} + \frac{(B-C)_2}{(1+d)^2} + \frac{(B-C)_3}{(1+d)^3} \ldots + \frac{(B-C)_n}{(1+d)^n}$$

where: $B_{1,2,3}$, etc. are the benefits in years 1, 2, 3, etc.; $C_{1,2,3}$, etc. are the costs in years 1, 2, 3, etc.; *n* is the life of the project in years; and *d* is the rate of discount expressed as a decimal (i.e. 10% = 0.1).

Now assume the following:

- A project has an initial construction cost of £30 000 (in year 0).
- It has a life of 4 years.
- It yields a net benefit of £10 000 each year in years 1–4.
- The rate of discount is 10 per cent.

Given these assumptions, the *NPV* can be worked out as follows:

$$NPV = -£30\,000 + \frac{£10\,000}{1.1} + \frac{£10\,000}{1.21} + \frac{£10\,000}{1.331} + \frac{£10\,000}{1.4641}$$

$$= -£30\,000 + £9090.91 + £8264.46 + £7513.15 + £6830.13$$

$$= -£30\,000 + £31\,698.65$$

$$= £1698.65$$

This is a positive figure. The project would thus be judged as desirable.

If, however, the rate of discount were 15 per cent, the figures would be:

$$NPV = -£30\,000 + £28\,549.78$$

$$= -£1450.22$$

This is negative. Thus at a 15 per cent discount rate the project would be judged as undesirable. This particular project's desirability, therefore, is relatively sensitive to a change in the discount rate.

?? Assume that a project has an initial construction cost of £10 000, takes a year to come into operation and then has a life of three years. Assume that it yields £5000 per year in each of these three years. Is the *NPV* positive at (a) a 10 per cent discount rate; (b) a 15 per cent discount rate?

optimistic (where all the best possible outcomes are estimated), the most pessimistic (where all the worst possible outcomes are estimated), and the most likely (where all the middle-of-the-range outcomes are estimated). This approach can give a good guide to just how 'borderline' the project is.

Discounting future costs and benefits

As we saw in section 9.4, discounting is a procedure for giving a present value to costs and benefits that will not occur until some time in the future.

Discounting in cost–benefit analysis

The procedure is as follows:

- Work out the costs and benefits for each year of the life of the project.
- Subtract the costs from the benefits for each year, to give a net benefit for each year.
- Discount each year's net benefit to give it a present value.
- Add up all of these present values. This gives a *net present value (NPV)*.
- If the *NPV* is greater than zero, the benefits exceed the costs: the project is worthwhile.

Table 11.1 Effect of different estimates of the costs of pollution on the viability of a project

	Total costs other than pollution (£m)	Total pollution cost (£m)	Total benefits (£m)	Net benefits (total benefits – total costs) (£m)
	100	10	200	90
Case A	100	20	200	80
	100	50	200	50
	140	10	160	10
Case B	140	20	160	0
	140	50	160	–30

CASE STUDIES

CBA OF THE GLASGOW CANAL PROJECT
Restoring the past

Opened in 1790, linking Glasgow to both the Atlantic and the North Sea, the Forth and Clyde Canal became a major trading route. By the early 1960s, however, such trade had largely ceased and the maintenance cost of the canal far outweighed the revenue raised from its use. By the mid-1980s, with only the statutory minimum of funds being spent on maintenance, the canal was in a poor state of repair. Buildings that flanked the canal had become derelict and it was seen as a major safety hazard to the local community, with a high number of drownings per mile. Along with the environmental and social problems linked with the canal, the need for an employment stimulus for the depressed local economy led to a review of the policy towards the canal in the mid-1980s.

The options identified in the review ranged from a policy of doing nothing, to a policy of partial regeneration in the worst affected areas, to a full refurbishment of the entire waterway.

The benefits from such an infrastructure project (whether from a partial or a total restoration) are not only difficult to quantify and evaluate, but also not straightforward to identify, given that a large number of people will be affected in different ways, and that those commissioning the study will not necessarily want to take into account the effects on absolutely everyone. Within the context of a policy of *urban renewal* the following categories of benefit were identified:

- The direct effects from the restoration work and the subsequent, long-term employment it creates.
- Environmental improvements that attract additional investment as the area becomes more attractive to new business.
- More intangible benefits associated with the enhanced welfare of those living in the immediate vicinity of the project, whether from appearance, leisure possibilities or reduced hazard.
- National benefits derived from the wider use of the restored facility, such as leisure activities and a wider appreciation that a symbol of national heritage has been restored.

The table shows the costs and benefits from the *full refurbishment* scheme.

On the cost side, 'total investment' is the total cost borne by all the investing agencies. 'Net recurrent' costs are the costs of maintenance less the (higher) maintenance costs of the do-nothing option. 'Net accidents' figures are based on a life being valued at £252 000 and assume a fall in the number of drownings by 0.5 per year up to the completion of the restoration and 0.7 per year thereafter.

On the benefit side, 'national output' is calculated as the value of the output of each job minus the marginal social costs of employment. A net employment benefit of £5365 per job was arrived at. The 'increase in residential property values' is used as an indicator for environmental improvement. The 'non-internalised consumer surplus' and 'other effects' account for benefits derived from recreational use and the wider benefits of saved heritage. Without an analysis of the demand curves for these features, it was not possible to place a value on them.

Using those items that were valued, and on the basis of a 5 per cent discount rate over a 25-year period, the NPV of restoration was estimated to be £11.2 million at 1986 prices. The do-nothing option, however, would result in a loss of £5.6 million.

Choosing the discount rate

Apart from the problems of measuring the costs and benefits, there is the problem of choosing the rate of interest/discount.

If it were a private-sector project, the firm would probably choose the market rate of interest as its rate of discount. This is the rate it would have to pay to borrow money to finance the project.

In the case of CBA, however, it is argued that the government ought to use a **social rate of discount**. This rate should reflect society's preference for present benefits over future benefits. But just what is this rate? If a high rate is chosen, then future net benefits will be discounted more, and projects with a long life will appear less attractive than projects yielding a quick return. Since the government has a responsibility to future generations and not just to the present one, it is argued that a relatively low discount rate should be chosen.

?? Imagine that a public project yields a return of 13 per cent (after taking into account all social costs and benefits), whereas a 15 per cent private return could typically be earned in the private sector. How would you justify diverting resources from the private sector to this project?

DEFINITION

Social rate of discount A rate of discount that reflects *society's* preferences for present benefits over future ones.

BOX 11.8

Costs and benefits of the 'Full Restoration Scheme'

Items	1987/8	1988/9	1989/90	1990/1	1991/2	1992/3	1993/4	1994/5	–	2012/13
Costs (£000):										
Total investment	29	1671	800	0	0	0	0	0	–	0
Net recurrent[1]	0	–6	–10	–10	–10	–10	–10	–10	–	–10
Net accidents[1]	–126	–126	–126	–176	–176	–176	–176	–176	–	–176
Benefits (£000):										
National output[2]	37	2146	188	644	778	778	778	778	–	778
Increase in residential property values	0	0	0	599	0	0	0	0	–	0
Non-internalised consumer surplus[3]	+	+	+	+	+	+	+	+	–	+
Other effects[4]	+	+	+	+	+	+	+	+	–	+

1 Net of the do-nothing option.
2 Marginal product is approximated by wage plus supplementary employer contributions. Average wage for a full-time adult in 1986 was £9422 p.a. Adding 10% for supplementary payments gives £10 365 (see *Employment Gazette*). In the absence of a detailed shadow price study, the shadow price of labour is taken to be £5000 p.a., giving a net employment benefit of £5365 per job.
3 Ideally analysis is required on the demand behaviour of recreationalists in response to time costs, licences, fees, etc. to evaluate these benefits.
4 There are probable positive valuations relating to future potential use, and to appreciation of improved environmental amenity unrelated to any use motive.

Source: *Urban Studies*, vol. 26 (1989).

Clearly on these figures the restoration project was desirable. Such a conclusion is reached, however, without a full assessment of the benefits. If the non-measured items had been included, the net benefit would have been even greater.

??

1. How sensitive is this conclusion to the valuation placed on a human life? Would the conclusion have been the same if (a) a life was valued at £100 000; (b) no account was taken of lives saved?
2. The maintenance costs of the do-nothing option were met by the British Waterways Board. Would it have been privately profitable for the BWB to have paid for the project itself?

Inevitably the choice of discount rate is arbitrary. As a result the analysis will normally be done using two or three alternative discount rates to see whether the outcome is sensitive to the choice of discount rate. If it is, then again the project will be seen as borderline.

CBA and the distribution of costs and benefits

Virtually all projects involve gainers and losers. For example, the majority may gain from the construction of a new motorway, but not those whose homes lie alongside it. So how is the distribution of costs and benefits to be taken into account?

The strict Pareto criterion

According to the strict Pareto criterion, a project is unequivocally desirable only if there are some gains and *no one* is made worse off. According to this, then, a project would be accepted only if the gainers *fully* compensated the losers, with the gainers still being better off after doing so.

In practice this never happens. Often compensation is simply not paid. Even when it is, the recipients rarely feel as well off as before, and there will still be many who do not get compensation. Also the compensation is usually paid not by the project users, but by the general taxpayer (who will thus be *worse* off).

The Hicks–Kaldor criterion

To get round this problem J. R. Hicks and N. Kaldor suggested an alternative criterion. This states that a project is desirable if it leads to a *potential* Pareto improvement: in other words, if the gainers could *in*

ISSUES AND APPLICATIONS

BOX 11.9

CATASTROPHIC RISK

Thinking the unthinkable

Some projects involve the remote chance that a total catastrophe might occur. A tunnel might collapse; a bridge might fall down; or, perhaps worst of all, a nuclear power station might explode. This last possibility was dramatically brought home to people with the Chernobyl disaster in the former USSR in 1986.

How are such disasters to be evaluated in a cost–benefit study? This is the subject of catastrophic risk.

First of all, a mathematical conundrum. What do you get when you multiply a number by zero? The answer is zero. What do you get when you multiply a number by infinity? The answer is infinity. What, then, do you get when you multiply infinity by zero? The answer is . . .? In fact there is no sensible answer to this question other than 'It can't be done', or 'Something between zero and infinity'.

A similar problem is raised in the measurement of catastrophic risk. Remember that the simplest way of measuring a risky outcome is to multiply its value (its cost or benefit) by the probability of its occurring. For example, if there is a 20 per cent chance of a benefit of £100 occurring, then the simplest way of valuing it is at £20. But what happens if you use a similar approach to measuring the cost of a nuclear disaster?

The power companies argue that the chance of such a disaster occurring is so remote that its probability can be regarded as zero. Many environmentalists argue that the costs to life, health and the environment generally, if such a disaster did occur, are so horrendous that the costs are virtually infinite.

So here is the conundrum. If both sides are right, then we have to multiply a cost that is virtually infinite by a probability that is virtually zero.

Of course, the costs are not *actually* infinite. But they are exceedingly large, and there may be long-term consequences (e.g. slowly developing cancers) which nobody can estimate. Likewise the probability may not actually be zero. There may be a very remote possibility of a disaster occurring, due, say, to human error or sabotage. But if you multiply a very very large number by a very very small fraction, the result is still highly suspect.

?? Assume that a disaster is estimated to cost society £1000bn (£1 000 000 000 000). The chances of the disaster occurring are said to be minute, however. Estimates vary from a probability of one in a million to one in a billion. What estimate of this cost would you include in a cost–benefit analysis?

Are there any solutions to the problem of measuring catastrophic risk? Pessimists would argue that uncertainty of the risks ought to make us cautious. They might quote Murphy's law: 'If anything can go wrong, it eventually will.'

Advocates of the project will argue that life is full of dangers. We could be run over or even struck by lightning (both of which may have a higher probability than the disaster). But we don't stay locked indoors. Thus rather than being 'negative' we ought to focus on ways of increasing safety and eliminating the possibilities of a disaster.

But what all this says is that there is no real solution to the conundrum. There are also other questions raised by the possibility of disaster:

- What discount rate would be used for measuring the long-term effects of, say, radiation?
- Which is worse, a thousand small disasters, or one disaster a thousand times bigger? (How is this relevant to the issue?)
- Should the effects on the rest of the world be included in a cost–benefit study, or just the effects on the UK?

?? Why are many developing countries apparently prepared to accept riskier projects than are industrialised countries?

---

principle fully compensate the losers and still have a net gain, even though in practice they do not pay any compensation at all.

This criterion is what lies behind conventional CBA. If the benefits of a project are greater than the costs, then in principle the losers could be fully compensated with some net benefits left over.

But what is the justification for using this test? The losers, after all, will still lose. Its advocates argue that questions of *efficiency* should be kept separate from questions of *equity*. Projects, they argue, should be judged on efficiency grounds. They are efficient if their benefits exceed their costs. Questions of fairness in distribution, on the other hand, should be dealt with through the general system of taxation and welfare.

This is a 'useful' argument because it lets the proponents of the project off the hook. Nevertheless the problem still remains that some people will lose. People do not like living near a new motorway, airport or power station. These people cannot expect to receive special welfare benefits from general taxation.

Thus other economists have argued that a more specific account should be taken of distributional effects when *measuring* costs and benefits.

Taking specific account of distributional consequences

The way this could be done would be to give a higher weighting to the costs of individual (as opposed to corporate) losers. The justification is simple. Most people would argue that the pain of losing £1000 is greater than the pleasure of gaining £1000. Just how much higher this weighting should be, however, is a matter of judgement, not of precise calculation.

Another way distribution can be taken into account is to give a higher weighting to the costs incurred by poor people than to those incurred by rich people. For example, assume that a new airport is built. As a result house prices nearby fall by 10 per cent. A rich person's house falls from £200 000 to £180 000 – a loss of £20 000. A poor person's house falls from £50 000 to £45 000 – a loss of £5000. Is the loss to the rich person four times as painful as that to the poor person? Probably not. It is argued, therefore, that the poorer people are, the higher the weighting that should be given to each £1 lost. Just what this weighting should be, however, is controversial.

SECTION SUMMARY

1. Cost–benefit analysis (CBA) can help a government decide whether or not to go ahead with a particular public project, or which of alternative projects to choose. CBA involves a number of stages.
2. All costs and benefits must be identified. These include the direct costs of constructing and operating the project, the direct monetary benefits to the operators and the consumer surplus of the users. They also include external costs and benefits to non-users.
3. Direct monetary costs and benefits are relatively easy to measure. Nevertheless there is still the uncertainty of how much these will be in the *future*. Also there is the problem that prices are distorted, although the theory of the second best would suggest that this is a problem only if the distortions are *different* for this project.
4. Non-monetary private benefit (consumer surplus) is difficult to estimate because of the difficulty of estimating the shape and position of the demand curve. The alternative approach is to focus on specific non-monetary benefits, such as journey time saved, and then to evaluate how much people would be prepared to pay for them if they could.
5. Monetary externalities would normally be counted at face value. Non-monetary externalities are much more difficult to estimate. The approach is to try to estimate the value that consumers would put on them in a market environment. Questionnaire techniques could be used, or inferences could be drawn from people's actual behaviour elsewhere.
6. Figures would then have to be adjusted for risk and uncertainty.
7. Discounting techniques would then have to be used to reduce future benefits and costs to a present value.
8. The study may also take distributional questions into account. The Hicks–Kaldor criterion suggests a compensation test for deciding whether a project is desirable. But given that in practice full compensation would be unlikely, the distributional questions may need to be taken into account more specifically.
9. Having adjusted the costs and benefits for risk and uncertainty, timing and distributional effects, a recommendation to go ahead with the project will probably be given if its net present value (*NPV*) is positive: in other words, if the discounted social benefits exceed the discounted social costs.

11.5 The case for *laissez-faire*

Government intervention in the market can itself lead to problems. The case for non-intervention (*laissez-faire*) or very limited intervention is not that the market is the *perfect* means of achieving given social goals, but rather that the problems created by intervention are greater than the problems overcome by that intervention. The proponents of *laissez-faire*, therefore, concentrate on (a) criticising government intervention and (b) demonstrating that the problems of the free market are relatively minor.

Drawbacks of government intervention

Shortages and surpluses

If the government intervenes by fixing prices at levels other than the equilibrium, this will create either shortages or surpluses.

If the price is fixed *below* the equilibrium, there will be a shortage. For example, if the rent of council houses is fixed below the equilibrium in order to provide cheap housing for poor people, demand will exceed supply. In the case of shortages resulting from fixing prices below the equilibrium, either the government will have to adopt a system of waiting lists, or rationing, or giving certain people preferential treatment, or alternatively it will have to allow allocation to be on a first-come, first-served basis or allow queues to develop. Black markets are also likely to develop. People unable to obtain the good or service at the fixed price may be prepared to pay considerably more. Their marginal utility may be well above the price. This could lead to very high profits for black marketeers (see pages 80–2 and Box 3.2).

If the price is fixed *above* the equilibrium price, there will be a surplus. For example, if the price of food is fixed above the equilibrium in order to support farmers' incomes, supply will exceed demand. Government will have to purchase such surpluses and then perhaps store them, throw them away or sell them cheaply in another market, or ration suppliers by allowing them to produce only a certain quota, or allow suppliers to sell to whom they can. Such surpluses are obviously wasteful. High prices may protect inefficient producers. (The problem of food surpluses in the European Union was examined in section 3.3.)

?? What are the possible arguments in favour of fixing prices (a) below and (b) above the equilibrium? Are there any means of achieving the same social goals without fixing prices?

Poor information

The government may not know the full costs and benefits of its policies. It may genuinely wish to pursue the interests of consumers or any other group, and yet may be unaware of people's wishes or misinterpret their behaviour. It may be poorly informed of the consequences of its policies, particularly if there is a considerable range of possible outcomes and if the factors influencing such outcomes are themselves uncertain.

Bureaucracy and inefficiency

Government intervention involves administrative costs. The more wide reaching and detailed the intervention, the greater the number of people and material resources that will be involved. These resources may be used wastefully. Civil servants and local authority officials may not be as accountable as employees of private industry. Government decision-making processes may be highly inflexible and bureaucratic, and may involve considerable duplication and red tape.

Lack of market incentives

If government intervention removes market forces or cushions their effect (by the use of subsidies, welfare provisions, guaranteed prices or wages, etc.), it may remove certain useful incentives. Subsidies may allow inefficient firms to survive. Welfare payments may discourage effort. The market may be imperfect, but it does tend to encourage efficiency by allowing the efficient to receive greater rewards. It also encourages factor mobility into those sectors of the economy offering higher rewards.

Shifts in government policy

The economic efficiency of industry may suffer if government intervention changes too frequently. It makes it difficult for firms to plan if they cannot predict tax rates, subsidies, price and wage controls, etc. Government policy is likely to change with a change in government, but even existing governments may change policies as they succumb to various political pressures or as a general election approaches.

Voters' ignorance

The economic issues before the electorate are often highly complex. The average voter is unlikely to appreciate the costs and benefits of the programmes of alternative political parties. Voters may be highly susceptible to political propaganda and deceit. Thus a government's programme may not really represent the 'will of the people'.

Unrepresentative government

Once elected, those in power may pursue their *own* interests rather than those of the people. Governments may not follow through the programmes on which they were elected. Also, the government may have a majority of seats, but have been elected by only a minority of the population.

Lack of freedom for the individual

One of the major arguments put forward by those advocating *laissez-faire* is that government intervention involves a loss of freedom for individuals to make economic choices. The argument is not just that the pursuit of individual gain is seen to lead to the social good, but that it is desirable in itself that individuals should be as free as possible to pursue their own interests with the minimum of government interference: that minimum being largely confined to the maintenance of laws consistent with the protection of life, liberty and property.

??

Go through the above arguments and give a reply to the criticisms made of government intervention.

Advantages of the free market

Although markets in the real world are not perfect, even imperfect markets can be argued to have positive advantages over government provision or even government regulation.

Automatic adjustments

Government intervention requires administration. A free-market economy, on the other hand, leads to the automatic, albeit imperfect, adjustment of demand to supply changes and supply to demand changes. If, therefore, the costs of correcting imperfections in a market outweigh the costs of those imperfections themselves, then a case has been made out for *laissez-faire*.

The advocates of *laissez-faire* argue that the costs of such imperfections are relatively small. Even under oligopoly, it is claimed, the competition between firms will be enough to encourage firms to produce goods that are desirable to consumers and at not excessively high prices, and will encourage more efficient production methods. Cases of pure monopoly with total barriers to entry are extremely rare. On the other hand, they argue that the costs of intervention are relatively high.

Dynamic advantages of capitalism

The chances of making high monopoly/oligopoly profits will encourage capitalists to invest in new products and new techniques. The benefits of growth from such innovations may considerably outweigh any problem of resource misallocation. Given time, the high profits will be so attractive to potential competitors that they will find some way of breaking into the industry even with substantial barriers to entry. If the government tries to correct the misallocation of resources under monopoly/oligopoly either by regulating monopoly power or by nationalisation, any resulting benefits could be outweighed by a loss in innovation and growth. This is one of the major arguments put forward by the neo-Austrian libertarian school – a school that passionately advocates the free market (see Box 11.10).

??

Are there any features of free-market capitalism which would *discourage* innovation?

A high degree of competition even under monopoly/oligopoly

Even though an industry at first sight may seem to be highly monopolistic, competitive forces may still work for the following reasons.

Fear of competition. Firms may fear that the possibility of high profits will encourage firms to attempt to break into an industry. Existing firms will therefore need to remain relatively efficient and not charge excessively high prices if they are to avoid such competition. These arguments have been developed into the theory of contestable markets which we examined in section 6.4.

Even if a small firm cannot overcome the barriers to entry of a monopolistic industry, a large powerful firm from another industry may well have the power to do so. Thus the possible diversification of firms from other industries is an important source of potential competition.

Competition from closely related industries. There are relatively close substitutes for many products. If, for example, a firm had a monopoly over the supply of tin cans to food producers, food could always be packed in glass or plastic containers instead, if the price of tin cans was too high.

Foreign competition. Even if a firm is the only producer in the country of a certain product, it may still face stiff competition from foreign producers, especially if the government does not intervene by imposing customs duties on imports. Additional competition was one of the main purposes behind the Single European Act which led to the abolition of barriers to trade within the EC in 1993 (see section 23.4).

Countervailing powers. Large powerful producers often sell to large powerful buyers. Powerful producers of raw materials may sell to powerful manufacturers. Powerful manufacturers may sell to powerful department stores or supermarket chains. Thus there are often countervailing powers. The power of detergent manufacturers to drive up the price of washing powder is countered by the power of supermarket chains to drive down the price at which they purchase it. Thus power is to some extent neutralised.

Should there be more or less intervention in the market?

No firm conclusions can be drawn in the debate between those who favour more and those who favour less government intervention, for the following reasons:

- Many normative issues are involved which cannot be settled by economic analysis. For example, it could be argued that freedom to set up in business and freedom from government regulation are desirable *for their own sake*. As a fundamental ethical point of view this can be disputed, but not disproved.

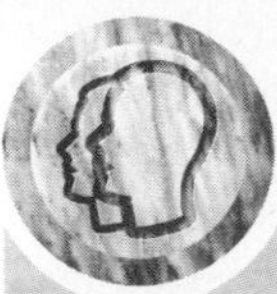

DEVELOPMENT OF IDEAS

MISES, HAYEK AND THE MONT PELERIN SOCIETY

The birth of post-war libertarianism

After the Second World War, governments in the Western world were anxious to avoid a return to the high levels of unemployment and poverty experienced in the 1930s. The free market was seen to have failed. Governments, it was therefore argued, should take on the responsibility for correcting or counteracting these failings. This would involve various measures such as planning, nationalisation, the restriction of monopoly power, controls on prices, the macroeconomic management of the economy and the provision of a welfare state.

But this new spirit of intervention deeply troubled a group of economists and other social scientists who saw it leading to an erosion of freedom. In 1947 this group met in an hotel in the Swiss Alps. There they formed the Mont Pelerin Society: a society pledged to warn against the dangers of socialism and to advocate the freedom for individuals to make their own economic choices.

Two of the most influential figures in the society were the Austrians Ludwig von Mises (1881–1973) and Friedrich von Hayek (1899–1992). They were the intellectual descendants of the nineteenth-century 'Austrian school'. Carl Menger, the originator of the school, had (along with Jevons and Walras (see Box 4.2)) emphasised the importance of individuals' marginal utility as the basis of demand. The Austrian school of economists was famous for its stress on individual choice as the basis for rational economic calculation and also for its advocacy of the free market.

Mises and Hayek (the 'neo-Austrians' as they became known) developed these ideas, both before and after the Second World War. Although both were born in Austria and both taught at the University of Vienna, both left for professorships in the English-speaking world. In 1932 Hayek became a professor at the London School of Economics and then in 1950 at the University of Chicago. Mises emigrated to the USA in 1940 to take up a chair in economics at New York University.

Mises and Hayek provided both a critique of socialism and an advocacy of the free market. There were two main strands to their arguments.

The impossibility of rational calculation under socialism

In his famous book *Socialism* (1922) Mises argued that centrally planned socialism was logically incapable of achieving a rational allocation of resources. Given that scarcity is the fundamental economic problem, all societies, whether capitalist or socialist, will have to make choices. But rational choices must involve weighing up the costs and benefits of alternatives. Mises argued that this cannot be done in a centrally planned economy. The reason is that costs and benefits can be measured only in terms of money prices, prices which reflect demand and supply. But such prices can be established only in a market economy.

In a centrally planned economy, prices will be set by the state and no state will have sufficient information on demand and supply to set rational prices. Prices under centrally planned socialism will thus inevitably be arbitrary. Also with no market for land or capital these factors may not be given a price at all. The use of land and capital, therefore, may be highly wasteful.

Many democratic socialists criticised Mises' arguments that rational prices *logically* cannot be established under socialism. In a centrally planned economy the state can in theory, if it chooses, set prices so as to balance supply and demand. It can, if it chooses, set an interest rate for capital and a rent for land, even if capital and land are owned by the state. And certainly in a mixed-market socialist economy, prices will merely reflect the forces of demand and supply that have been modified by the state in accordance with its various social goals.

Hayek modified Mises' arguments somewhat. He conceded that some imperfect form of pricing system could be established under socialism, even under centrally planned socialism. Hayek's point was that such a system would inevitably be inferior to capitalism. The problem was one of imperfect information under socialism.

Calculation of costs and benefits requires knowledge. But that knowledge is dispersed amongst the millions of consumers and producers throughout the economy. Each consumer possesses unique information about his or her own tastes; each manager or worker possesses unique information about his or her own job. No government could hope to have this knowledge.

- In principle, the issue of whether a government ought to intervene in any situation could be settled by weighing up the costs and benefits of that intervention. Such costs and benefits, however, even if they could be identified, are extremely difficult, if not impossible, to measure, especially when the costs are borne by different people from those who receive the benefits and when externalities are involved.

BOX 11.10

Planning will inevitably, therefore, be based on highly imperfect information.

The market, by contrast, is a way of co-ordinating this dispersed information: it co-ordinates all the individual decisions of suppliers and demanders, decisions based on individuals' own information. And it does it all without the need for an army of bureaucrats.

> The economic problem of society is thus not merely a problem of how to allocate 'given' resources – if 'given' is taken to mean given to a single mind which deliberately solves the problem set by these 'data'. It is rather a problem of how to secure the best use of resources known to any of the members of society, for ends whose relative importance only these individuals know. Or, to put it briefly, it is a problem of the utilization of knowledge not given to anyone in its totality.[5]

Lack of dynamic incentives under socialism

A planned socialist economy will, according to Mises and Hayek, lack the incentives for people to take risks. Even a 'market socialist' society, where prices are set so as to equate demand and supply, will still lack the crucial motivating force of the possibility of large personal economic gains. Under capitalism, by contrast, a firm which becomes more efficient or launches a new or improved product can gain huge profits. The prospect of such profits is a powerful motivator.

> The motive force of the whole process which gives rise to market prices for the factors of production is the ceaseless search on the part of capitalists and the entrepreneurs to maximize their profits by serving the consumers' wishes. Without the striving of entrepreneurs (including the shareholders) for profit, of the landlords for rent, of the capitalists for interest and the labourers for wages, the successful functioning of the whole mechanism is not to be thought of. It is only the prospect of profit which directs production into those channels in which the demands of the consumer are best satisfied at least cost. If the prospect of profit disappears the mechanism of the market loses its mainspring, for it is only this prospect which sets it in motion and maintains it in operation. The market is thus the focal point of the capitalist order of society; it is the essence of capitalism. Only under capitalism, therefore, is it possible; it cannot be 'artificially' imitated under socialism.[6]

In addition to these economic criticisms of socialism, Mises and Hayek saw government intervention as leading down the road towards totalitarianism. The more governments intervened to correct the 'failings' of the market, the more this tended to erode people's liberties. But the more people saw the government intervening to help one group of people, the more help they would demand from the government for themselves. Thus inexorably the role of the state would grow and grow, and with it the size of the state bureaucracy.

In the early years after the war, the Mont Pelerin Society had little influence on government policy. Government intervention and the welfare state were politically popular.

In the late 1970s, however, the society, along with other similar libertarian groups, gained increasing influence as a new breed of politicians emerged who were wedded to the free market and were looking for an intellectual backing for their beliefs.

Libertarian thinkers such as Hayek and Milton Friedman (see Box 15.8) have had a profound effect on many right-wing politicians, and considerably influenced the economic programmes of the Thatcher, Reagan and Bush administrations. Hayek right until his death at the age of 92 was still giving advice on putting free-market policies into action, and had become very much the 'elder statesman' of the libertarian movement.

?? Do the arguments of Mises and Hayek necessarily infer that a *free* market is the most desirable alternative to centrally planned socialism?

[5] F. von Hayek, 'The price system as a mechanism for using knowledge', *American Economic Review*, September 1945, p. 519.

[6] L. von Mises, *Socialism: An economic and sociological analysis* (Jonathan Cape, 1936), p. 138.

- Often the effect of more or less intervention simply cannot be predicted: there are too many uncertainties.

Nevertheless, economists can make a considerable contribution to analysing problems of the market and the effects of government intervention. Chapter 12 illustrates this by examining specific problem areas.

SECTION SUMMARY

1. Government intervention in the market may lead to shortages or surpluses; it may be based on poor information; it may be costly in terms of administration; it may stifle incentives; it may be disruptive if government policies change too frequently; it may not represent the majority of voters' interests if the government is elected by a minority, or if voters did not fully understand the issues at election time, or if the policies were not in the government's manifesto; it may remove certain liberties.
2. By contrast, a free market leads to automatic adjustments to changes in economic conditions; the prospect of monopoly/oligopoly profits may stimulate risk taking and hence research and development and innovation, and this advantage may outweigh any problems of resource misallocation; there may still be a high degree of actual or potential competition under monopoly and oligopoly.
3. It is impossible to draw firm conclusions about the 'optimum' level of government intervention. This is partly due to the normative nature of the question, partly due to the difficulties of measuring costs and benefits of intervention/non-intervention, and partly due to the difficulties of predicting the effects of government policies, especially over the longer term.

??? END-OF-CHAPTER QUESTIONS ???

1. Assume that a firm discharges waste into a river. As a result, the marginal social costs (*MSC*) are greater than the firm's marginal (private) costs (*MC*). The following table shows how *MC*, *MSC*, *AR* and *MR* vary with output.

Output	1	2	3	4	5	6	7	8
MC£	23	21	23	25	27	30	35	42
MSC£	35	34	38	42	46	52	60	72
TR£	60	102	138	168	195	219	238	252
AR£	60	51	46	42	39	36.5	34	31.5
MR£	60	42	36	30	27	24	19	14

   (a) How much will the firm produce if it seeks to maximise profits?
   (b) What is the socially efficient level of output (assuming no externalities on the demand side)?
   (c) How much is the marginal external cost at this level of output?
   (d) What size tax would be necessary for the firm to reduce its output to the socially efficient level?
   (e) Why is the tax less than the marginal externality?
   (f) Why might it be equitable to impose a lump-sum tax on this firm?
   (g) Why will a lump-sum tax not affect the firm's output (assuming that in the long-run the firm can still make at least normal profit)?
2. Why might it be argued that a redistribution of consumption, whilst not involving a Pareto improvement, could still be desirable?
3. Assume that a country had no state education at all. For what reasons might the private education system not provide the optimal allocation of resources to and within education?
4. Why might it be better to ban certain activities that cause environmental damage rather than to tax them?
5. Distinguish between publicly provided goods, public goods and merit goods.
6. Consider the advantages and disadvantages of extending property rights so that everyone would have the right to prevent people imposing any costs on them whatsoever (or charging them to do so).
7. Should all investment be subject to a social cost–benefit appraisal?
8. Make out a case for (a) increasing and (b) decreasing the role of the government in the allocation of resources.

12

Applied microeconomics

Just how far should things be left to the market in practice? Just how much should a government intervene? These are clearly normative questions, and the answers to them will depend on a person's politics.

Conservative politicians tend to favour the absolute minimum degree of intervention, to ensure the 'efficient' working of the market. Socialist politicians, on the other hand, prefer a much greater degree of intervention, to ensure not only that the inefficiencies of the market are corrected, but also that questions of 'fairness' and 'equality' are taken into account.

This chapter examines three topics which illustrate well the possible strengths and weaknesses of both the market and government intervention. Ultimately, you the reader must be left to judge where the correct balance lies, according to your political and ethical beliefs.

12.1 Traffic congestion and urban transport policies

The first topic is traffic congestion. This is a problem that faces all countries, especially in the large cities and at certain peak times: a problem that has grown at an alarming rate as our lives have become increasingly dominated by the motor car. Sitting in a traffic jam is both time wasting and frustrating. It adds considerably to the costs and the stress of modern living.

And it is not only the motorist that suffers. Congested streets make life less pleasant for the pedestrian, and increased traffic leads to increased accidents. What is more, the inexorable growth of traffic has led to significant problems of pollution. Traffic is noisy and car fumes are unpleasant and lead to substantial environmental damage. It is true that the move to unleaded petrol has reduced the problem of lead pollution, but the growing emissions of carbon dioxide and nitrogen dioxide have aggravated the problem of global warming and acid rain.

Between 1983 and 1996 road traffic in Great Britain rose by 55 per cent, whereas the length of public roads rose by only 6 per cent (albeit some roads were widened). Most passenger and freight transport is by road. In 1996, 94 per cent of passenger kilometres and 82 per cent of freight tonnage in Great Britain were by road, whereas rail accounted for a mere 5 per cent of both passenger traffic and freight tonnage. Of road passenger kilometres, 92 per cent was by car in 1996, and, as Table 12.1 shows, this proportion has been growing. Motoring costs now amount to some 13 per cent of household expenditure.

But should the government do anything about the problem? Is traffic congestion a price worth paying for the benefits we gain from using cars? Or are there things that can be done to ease the problem without greatly inconveniencing the traveller? And if something is to be done, should the government seek to extend the role of the market, for example by encouraging the building of private toll roads; or merely to amend market forces, for example by subsidising public transport; or to replace the market, for example by banning cars in certain areas?

Table 12.1 Passenger transport in Great Britain: percentage of passenger kilometres by road

	Cars	Motor cycles	Buses and coaches	Bicycles
1981	86.1	2.2	10.6	1.1
1987	89.3	1.3	8.4	1.0
1996	92.3	0.6	6.5	0.6

Source: *Annual Abstract of Statistics* (ONS, 1998).

We will look at various schemes later in this section and at their relative costs and benefits. But first it is necessary to examine the existing system of allocating road space to see the extent to which it meets or fails to meet society's transport objectives. This will enable us to identify the problems that the government must address. (Our discussion will focus on the motor car and passenger transport, but clearly lorries are another major source of congestion, and any comprehensive policy to deal with traffic congestion must also examine freight transport.)

The existing system of allocating road space

The allocation of road space depends on both demand and supply. Demand is by individuals who base their decisions on largely private considerations. Supply, by contrast, is usually by the central government or local authorities. Let us examine each in turn.

Demand for road space (by car users)

The demand for road space can be seen largely as a *derived* demand. What people want is not the car journey for its own sake, but to get to their destination. The greater the benefit they gain at their destination, the greater the benefit they gain from using their car to get there.

The demand for road space, like the demand for other goods and services, has a number of determinants. If congestion is to be reduced, it is important to know how responsive demand is to a change in any of these: it is important to consider the various elasticities of demand.

Price. This is the *marginal cost* to the motorist of a journey. It includes petrol, oil, maintenance, depreciation and any toll charges.

> **??** Are there any costs associated with motoring that would *not* be included as marginal costs? Explain why.

The price elasticity of demand for motoring tends to be relatively low. There can be a substantial rise in the price of petrol, for example, and there will be only a modest fall in traffic. After the 1973/4 oil crisis, the price of petrol doubled, but traffic in London fell by only 4 per cent.

> **??** What does this evidence suggest was the figure for the price elasticity of demand for petrol in London?

The low price elasticity of demand suggests that schemes to tackle traffic congestion that merely involve raising the costs of motoring will have only limited success.

In addition to monetary costs, there are also the time costs of travel. The opportunity cost of sitting in your car is the next best alternative activity you could have been pursuing – relaxing, working, sleeping or whatever. Congestion, by increasing the duration of the journey, increases the opportunity cost.

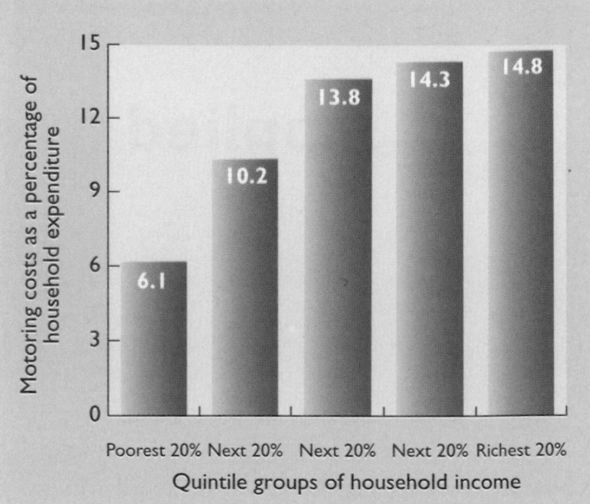

Figure 12.1 Motoring costs as a percentage of household expenditure in the UK by quintile groups of household income: 1996/7

Source: *Family Spending* (ONS, 1997).

Income. As incomes rise, car ownership and usage increase substantially. Demand for road space is elastic with respect to income.

Figure 12.1 shows motoring costs as a percentage of UK household expenditure by quintile groups of household income. The higher the household income, the higher the percentage of income spent on motoring. Clearly, the income elasticity of demand is significantly greater than 1 for all but the highest income groups.

This is also reflected in international statistics of car ownership. Figure 12.2 shows the growth of car ownership between 1980 and 1994 in selected countries. As national incomes have risen, so has the proportion of car ownership. People see car transport as a 'luxury good' compared with alternatives such as public transport, walking or cycling. Also the growth of suburbs has meant that many people travel longer distances to work.

The implication of this is that, if countries continue to experience economic growth, car ownership and usage is likely to increase substantially: a conclusion in line with most forecasts.

Price of substitutes. If bus and train fares came down, people might switch from travelling by car. The cross-price elasticity, however, is likely to be relatively low,

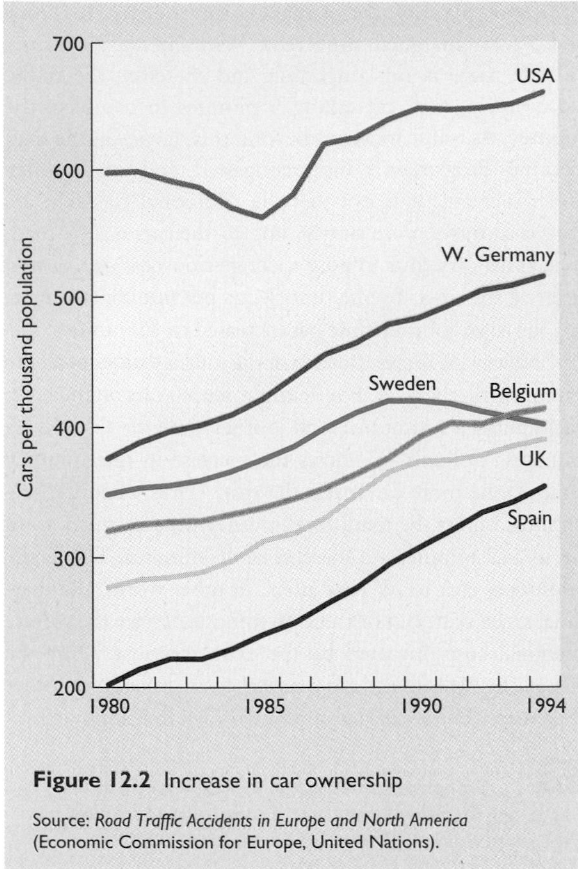

Figure 12.2 Increase in car ownership

Source: *Road Traffic Accidents in Europe and North America* (Economic Commission for Europe, United Nations).

given that most people regard these alternatives as a poor substitute for travelling in their own car. Cars are seen as more comfortable and convenient.

The 'price' of substitutes also includes the time taken to travel by these alternatives. The quicker a train journey is compared with a car journey, the lower will be its time cost to the traveller and thus the more people will switch from car to rail.

Price of complements. Demand for road space will depend on the price of cars. The higher the price of cars, the fewer people will own cars and thus the fewer cars there will be on the road.

> **??** Is the cross-price elasticity of demand for road space with respect to the price of cars likely to be high or low?

Demand will also depend on the price of complementary services, such as parking. A rise in car parking charges will reduce the demand for car journeys. But here again the cross elasticity is likely to be relatively low. In most cases, the motorist will either pay the higher charge or park elsewhere, such as in side streets.

> **??** Go through each of the determinants we have identified so far and show how the respective elasticity of demand makes the problem of traffic congestion difficult to tackle.

Tastes/utility. Another factor explaining the preference of many people for travelling by car is the pleasure they gain from it compared with alternative modes of transport. Car ownership is regarded by many people as highly desirable, and once accustomed to travelling in their own car, most people are highly reluctant to give it up.

One important feature of the demand for road space is that it fluctuates. There will be periods of peak demand, such as during the rush hour or at holiday weekends. At such times roads can get totally jammed. At other times, however, the same roads may be virtually empty. The problem is that supply cannot fluctuate to match demand. Empty road space available in the middle of the night cannot be 'stored' and then transferred as additional space during periods of peak demand!

Supply of road space

The supply of road space can be examined in two contexts: the short run and the long run.

The short run. In the short run, the supply of road space is constant. When there is no congestion, supply is more than enough to satisfy demand. There is spare road capacity. At times of congestion, there is pressure on this fixed supply. Maximum supply for any given road is reached at the point where there is the maximum flow of vehicles per minute along the road.

The long run. In the long run, the authorities can build new roads or improve existing ones. This will require an assessment of the costs and benefits of such schemes.

Identifying a socially efficient level of road usage (short run)

The existing system of *government* provision of roads and *private* ownership of cars is unlikely to lead to an optimum allocation of road space. So how do we set about identifying just what the social optimum is?

In the short run, the supply of road space is fixed. The question of the short-run optimum allocation of road space, therefore, is one of the optimum *usage* of existing road space. It is a question therefore of *consumption* rather than supply. For this reason we must focus on the road user, rather than on road provision.

A socially efficient level of consumption occurs where the marginal social benefit of consumption equals its marginal social cost ($MSB = MSC$). So what are the marginal social benefits and costs of using a car?

Marginal social benefit of road usage

Marginal social benefit equals marginal private benefit plus externalities.

Marginal private benefit is the direct benefit to the car user and is reflected in the demand for car journeys, the determinants of which we examined above. For example, the benefit from using your car depends on its relative comfort and convenience compared with alternative modes of transport.

External benefits are few. The one major exception occurs when drivers give lifts to other people.

Marginal social cost of road usage

Marginal social cost equals marginal private cost plus externalities.

Marginal private costs to the motorist include the costs of petrol, wear and tear, tolls, etc. They also include the time costs of travel.

There may also be substantial external costs. These include the following.

Congestion costs: time. When a person uses a car on a congested road, it will add to the congestion. This will therefore slow down the traffic even more and increase the journey time of other car users.

This is illustrated in Table 12.2 (which uses imaginary figures). Column (1) shows the number of cars travelling along a given road per minute. Column (2) shows the time taken for each car and thus can be seen as the marginal time cost to a motorist of making this journey. It is thus the *private* marginal time cost. With up to 3 cars per minute there is no congestion and therefore the traffic flows freely, each car taking 5 minutes to complete the journey. As traffic increases beyond this, however, the road becomes progressively more congested, and thus journey times increase. It is not just the additional cars that are forced to travel more slowly, but *all* the cars on the road. The extra cars thus impose a congestion cost on existing users of the road. By the time 7 cars per minute are entering the road, journey time has increased to 16 minutes.

Column (3) shows the sum of the journey times of all the motorists on the road. For example, with 6 cars on the road, each taking 11 minutes, total journey time for all six is 66 minutes. Column (4) shows the increase in total journey time as one more car enters the road. Thus when the seventh car enters the road, total journey time increases from 66 to 112 minutes: an increase of 46 minutes. This is the additional cost to *all* road users: in other words, the marginal *social* cost. But of these 46 minutes, 16 are the private marginal costs incurred by the extra motorist. Only the remaining 30 minutes are *external* costs imposed on other road users. These external costs are shown in column (5).

?? Complete Table 12.2 up to 9 cars per minute, assuming that the journey time increases to 24 minutes for the eighth car and 35 minutes for the ninth car.

Time costs can be converted into money costs if we know the value of people's time. If time were valued at 10p per minute, then the congestion costs (external costs) for the seventh car would be £3.00 (i.e. 30 minutes × 10p per minute). Box 12.1 examines the method used in the UK of estimating the value of time (in the context of evaluating new road schemes).

Table 12.2 Time taken to travel between two points along a given road

Traffic density (cars entering road per minute) (1)	Journey time per car (marginal private time cost: in minutes) (2)	Total journey time for all cars (total time cost: in minutes) (3) = (1) × (2)	Extra total journey time as traffic increases by one more car (marginal social time cost: in minutes) (4) = Δ(3)	Additional time cost imposed on other road users by one more car (marginal external time cost: in minutes) (5) = (4) – (2)
1	5	5	5	0
2	5	10	5	0
3	5	15	5	0
4	6	24	9	3
5	8	40	16	8
6	11	66	26	15
7	16	112	46	30

Congestion costs: monetary. Congestion increases fuel consumption, and the stopping and starting increases the costs of wear and tear. When a motorist adds to congestion, therefore, there will be additional monetary costs imposed on other motorists. A table similar to Table 12.2 could be drawn to illustrate this.

Environmental costs. When motorists use a road they reduce the quality of the environment for others. Cars emit fumes and create noise. This is bad enough for pedestrians and other car users, but can be particularly distressing for people living along the road. Driving can cause accidents, a problem that increases as drivers become more impatient as a result of delays.

Exhaust gases cause long-term environmental damage and are one of the main causes of the greenhouse effect, the increased acidity of lakes and rivers, and the poisoning of forests. The marginal pollution costs tend to grow as traffic increases: the environment can cope with low levels of pollution, but beyond certain levels damage begins to occur and can then accelerate rapidly.

The socially efficient level of road usage

The point where the marginal social benefit of car use is equal to the marginal social cost can be illustrated on a diagram. In Figure 12.3 costs and benefits are shown on the vertical axis and are measured in money terms. Thus any non-monetary costs or benefits (such as time costs) must be given a monetary value. The horizontal axis measures road usage in terms of cars per minute passing a specified point on the road.

For simplicity it is assumed that there are no external benefits from car use and that therefore marginal private and marginal social benefits are the same. The *MSB* curve is shown as downward sloping. The reason for this is that different road users put a different value on this particular journey. If the marginal (private) cost of making the journey were high, only those for whom the journey had a high marginal benefit would travel along the road. If the marginal cost of making the journey fell, more people would make the journey: people choosing to make the journey at the point at which the marginal cost of using their car had fallen to the level of their marginal benefit. Thus the greater the number of cars, the lower the marginal benefit.

The marginal (private) cost curve (*MC*) is likely to be constant up to the level of traffic flow at which congestion begins to occur. This is shown as point *a* in Figure 12.3. Beyond this point, marginal cost is likely to rise as time costs increase and as fuel consumption rises.

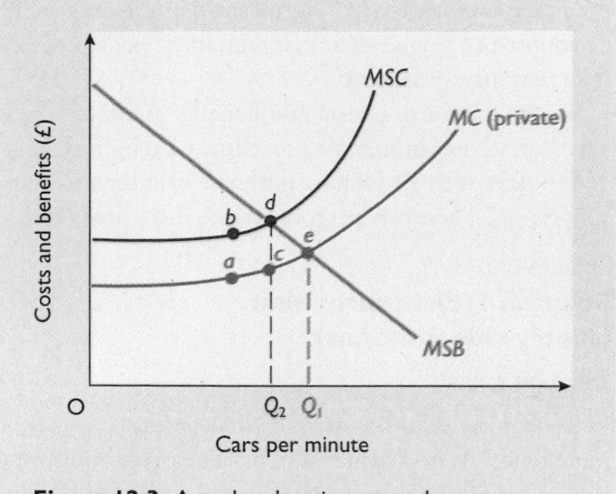

Figure 12.3 Actual and optimum road usage

The marginal *social* cost curve (*MSC*) is drawn above the marginal private cost curve. The vertical difference between the two represents the external costs. Up to point *b*, external costs are simply the environmental costs. Beyond point *b*, there are also external congestion costs, since additional road users slow down the journey of *other* road users. These external costs get progressively greater as the level of traffic increases (as column (5) of Table 12.2 illustrated).

The actual level of traffic flow will be at Q_1, where marginal private costs and benefits are equal (point *e*). The socially efficient level of traffic flow, however, will be at the lower level of Q_2, where marginal social costs and benefits are equal (point *d*). In other words, the existing system of allocating road space is likely to lead to an excessive level of road usage.

In addition to the problem of externalities, there is also the problem of poor information held by the traveller. Because congestion varies from day to day and at different times of the day, travellers may be unaware of the level of congestion on a particular road until they join the road and possibly find themselves in a traffic jam. Better information could have enabled them to delay or cancel their journey, or to take a diversion to avoid the congested stretch of road.

Identifying a socially optimum level of road space (long run)

In the long run the supply of road space is not fixed. The authorities must therefore assess what new road schemes (if any) to adopt. This will involve the use of some form of *cost–benefit analysis* (see section 11.4).

The socially efficient level of construction will be where the marginal social benefit from construction is equal to the marginal social cost. This means that schemes should be adopted as long as their marginal social benefit exceeds their marginal social cost.

But how are these costs and benefits assessed in practice? Box 12.1 examines the procedure used in the UK.

We now turn to look at different solutions to traffic congestion. These can be grouped into three broad types.

Solution 1: direct provision (supply-side solutions)

The road solution

One obvious solution to traffic congestion is to build more roads. At first sight this may seem an optimum strategy, provided the costs and benefits of road-building schemes are carefully assessed and only those schemes are adopted where the benefits exceed the costs.

There are serious problems, however, with this approach.

The objective of equity. The first problem concerns that of *equity*. After all, social efficiency is not the only possible economic objective. For example, when an urban motorway is built, those living beside it will suffer from noise and fumes. Motorway users gain, but the local residents lose. The question is whether this is fair.

The more the government tries to appeal to the car user by building more and better roads, the fewer will be the people who use public transport, and thus the more will public transport decline. Those without cars lose, and these tend to be from the most vulnerable groups – the poor, the elderly, children and the disabled. Even if public transport cannot make a profit, it may be regarded as desirable on grounds of equity that it should be made available and at a 'reasonable' price. This will involve such services being provided directly by the government or local authorities, or subsidies being paid to private bus or train companies.

Building more roads may lead to a *potential* Pareto improvement: in other words, if the gainers had fully to compensate the losers (e.g. through taxes or tolls), they would still have a net gain. The problem is that such compensation is rarely if ever paid. There is thus no actual Pareto improvement.

Congestion may not be solved. Increasing the amount of road space may encourage more people to use cars. Apart from the adverse effects of this on the profitability of public transport, it may mean that the problem of congestion persists. The government's forecasts have often underestimated the growth in traffic on new or improved roads.

A good example is the London orbital motorway, the M25. In planning the motorway, not only did the government underestimate the rate of economic growth and overestimate the level of fuel prices (and thus the demand for road space generally), but it also underestimated the direct effect it would have on encouraging people to use the motorway rather than some alternative route, or some alternative means of transport, or even not to make the journey at all. It also underestimated the effect it would have on encouraging people to live further from their place of work and to commute along the motorway. The result is that there is now serious congestion on the motorway, and the government is under pressure to build additional lanes.

Thus new roads may simply generate extra traffic, with little overall effect on congestion.

The environmental impact of new roads. New roads lead to the loss of agricultural land, the destruction of many natural habitats, noise, the splitting of communities and disruption to local residents. To the extent that they encourage a growth in traffic, they add to atmospheric pollution and a depletion of oil reserves. It is thus important to take account of these costs when assessing new road schemes. The problem, however, is that these environmental costs are frequently ignored, or only considered as an afterthought and not taken seriously. Part of the problem is that they are difficult to assess, and part is that there is often a strong road lobby which persuades politicians to ignore or play down environmental considerations.

Government or local authority provision of public transport

An alternative supply-side solution is to increase the provision of public transport. If, for example, a local authority ran a local bus service and decided to invest in additional buses, open up new routes and operate a low fare policy, these services might encourage people to switch from using their cars.

To be effective, this would have to be an attractive alternative. Many people would only switch if the buses were frequent, cheap, comfortable and reliable, and if there were enough routes to take people close to where they wanted to go.

> **??** What other types of transport could be directly provided by the government or a local authority?

A policy that has proved popular with many local authorities is to adopt park-and-ride schemes. Here the authority provides free or cheap out-of-town parking and cheap bus services from the car park to the town centre.

ISSUES AND APPLICATIONS *BOX 12.1

EVALUATING NEW ROAD SCHEMES

The system used in the UK[1]

In the UK, the Department of Transport uses the following procedure to evaluate new road schemes, a procedure very similar to that used in many countries.

Estimating demand

The first thing to be done is to estimate likely future traffic flows. These are based on the government's National Road Traffic Forecast. This makes two predictions: a 'low-growth case', based on the assumption of low economic growth and high fuel prices, and a 'high-growth case', based on the assumption of high economic growth and low fuel prices. The actual growth in traffic, therefore, is likely to lie between the two.

Identifying possible schemes

Various road construction and improvement schemes are constantly under examination by the government, especially in parts of the network where traffic growth is predicted to be high and where congestion is likely to occur. In each case forecasts are then made of the likely use of the new roads and the diversion of traffic away from existing parts of the network. Again, two forecasts are made in each case: a 'low-growth' and a 'high-growth' one.

The use of cost–benefit analysis

The costs and benefits of each scheme are assigned monetary values and are compared with those of merely maintaining the existing network. The government uses a computer program known as COBA to assist it in the calculations.

Estimating the benefits of a scheme (relative to the existing network)

Three types of benefit are included in the analysis:

- Time saved. This is broken down into two categories: working time and non-working time (including travelling to and from work).

  The evaluation of working time is based on average national wage rates, while that of non-working time is based on surveys and the examination of traveller behaviour (the aim being to assess the value placed by the traveller on time saved). This results in non-working time per minute being given a value of approximately a quarter of that given to working time.
- Reductions in vehicle operating costs. These include: fuel, oil, tyres, maintenance and depreciation from usage. There will be savings if the scheme reduces the distance of journeys or allows a more economical speed to be maintained.
- Reductions in accidents. There are two types of benefit here: (a) the reduction in casualties (divided into three categories – fatal, serious non-fatal, and slight); and (b) the reduction in monetary costs, such as vehicle repair or replacement, medical costs and police, fire service and ambulance costs.

  The reductions in monetary costs are relatively easy to estimate. The benefits from the reduction in casualties are more difficult. The current method of evaluating them is based on the amount people are prepared to pay to reduce the risks of accidents. This clearly has the drawback that people are often unaware of the risks of accidents or of the extent of the resulting pain and suffering (see Box 11.6).

?? Up to 1988 a different method was used. This was based on the 'human capital' approach, which involved estimating the contribution of the victim to the economy, plus an allowance for pain, grief and suffering. In the late 1980s this resulted in the following estimates: a death, £608 580; a serious casualty, £18 450; a slight casualty, £380. What are the drawbacks of this approach?

Estimating the costs of the scheme (relative to the existing network)

There are two main categories of cost: construction costs and additional road maintenance costs. If the new scheme results in a saving in road maintenance compared with merely retaining the existing network, then the maintenance costs will be negative.

The analysis

The costs and benefits of the scheme are assessed for the period of construction and for a standard life (in the UK this is 30 years). The costs and benefits are discounted back to a present value. The rate of discount used in the UK is 8 per cent. If the discounted benefits exceed the discounted costs, there is a positive net present value, and the scheme is regarded as justified on economic grounds. If there is more than one scheme, then their net present values will be compared so as to identify the preferable scheme.

It is only at this final stage that environmental considerations are taken into account. In other words, they are not included in the calculation of costs and benefits, but may have some influence in determining the choice between schemes. Clearly, if a *socially* efficient allocation of road space is to be determined, such externalities need to be included in the cost and benefit calculations.

[1] This box is based on *Assessing the Environmental Impact of Road Schemes* (Dept of Transport, 1992).

CASE STUDIES — BOX 12.2

RESTRICTING CAR ACCESS TO ATHENS

A solution to local atmospheric pollution?

Athens lies in a bowl-shaped valley. When there are light winds, a humid atmosphere and sunshine, the levels of atmospheric pollution can soar to dangerous heights. The major cause of this chemical smog is the emission of exhaust fumes.

The solution that the Greeks have adopted is one of restricting the use of vehicles in the city. The restrictions are of two levels of severity. The more severe ones apply on Mondays to Fridays when there is a chemical smog emergency, typically two or three times a month; the less severe ones apply on all other Mondays to Fridays.

The city is divided into an inner zone and an outer zone. The levels of various pollutants (such as nitrogen dioxide and ozone) are constantly monitored by the city authorities, and when they reach certain critical levels a smog emergency is declared on radio, on television and in the press.

During an emergency, all cars and half the taxis are banned from use in the inner zone. On even-numbered dates only taxis with an even-numbered registration can operate in the inner zone; on odd-numbered dates only those with an odd-numbered registration can operate. In the outer zone, all taxis can operate, but only cars with an even-numbered registration can be driven on even-numbered dates and those with an odd-numbered registration on odd-numbered dates. The police check on cars entering the zones and turn away those not allowed. The drivers of cars being used illegally in the zones can be fined.

When an emergency is not in force, restrictions only apply to the inner zone. The even-numbered/odd-numbered registration restrictions apply to cars, but not to taxis.

The measures are successful in one respect: very few cars are driven illegally in the zones (and it is not possible to have two numberplates for the same car!). But many commuters have resorted to owning two cars: one with an even-numbered plate and one with an odd-numbered one. The authorities even help in this by allowing people to request an even- or odd-numbered registration.

?? Compare the relative advantages and disadvantages of these measures with those of charging people to come into the zones.

Solution 2: regulation and legislation

An alternative strategy is to restrict car use by various forms of regulation and legislation.

Restricting car access

One approach involves reducing car access to areas that are subject to high levels of congestion. The following three measures are widely used:

- Bus and cycle lanes. The idea here is to give priority to alternative means of transport, thereby making them more attractive. Cycle lanes make cycling safer and more pleasant. Bus lanes both speed up the flow of buses and reduce the flow of cars. They can also be used flexibly by applying only at times of peak traffic.

  A version of this type of measure is to have 'car-sharing lanes'. This measure is used on many freeways in the USA. Here certain lanes can only be used by cars with three or more occupants. The aim is to encourage car sharing.
- No entry to side streets. Many people try to avoid congested main roads by diverting down side streets. The result is congestion on both the main road and the side streets, with the added risk of accidents and nuisance to local residents. Restricting access to side streets will confine the congestion to the main roads and may force people to take an alternative form of transport.
- Pedestrian-only areas. Many city centres have banned traffic, or all traffic except buses. This clearly makes it much more pleasant for pedestrians.

There is a serious problem, however, with these measures. They tend not to solve the problem of congestion, but merely to divert it. Bus lanes tend to make the car lanes more congested; no entry to side streets tends to make the main roads more congested; and pedestrian-only areas often make the roads round these areas more congested.

Parking restrictions

An alternative to restricting road access is to restrict parking. If cars are not allowed to park along congested streets, this will improve the traffic flow. Also, if parking is difficult, this will discourage people from using their cars to come into city centres.

Apart from being unpopular with people who want to park, there are some serious drawbacks with parking restrictions:

CASE STUDIES — BOX 12.3

ROAD PRICING IN SINGAPORE

Part of an integrated transport policy

It takes only one hour to drive from one end of Singapore to the other. Yet the average Singaporean driver travels an estimated 18 600 km per year, more than the average US driver, and over 50 per cent more than the average Japanese driver. In Singapore in 1996 there were a little over 300 000 cars, giving a vehicle density of 200 motor vehicles per kilometre of road. This compares with a vehicle density in the USA of only 27 motor vehicles per kilometre. It is hardly surprising that traffic congestion has become a major focus of public debate, particularly as the demand for cars is set to increase as consumer affluence grows.

In contrast to its neighbours, many of which are suffering more acute urban traffic congestion problems, Singapore has an integrated transport policy. This includes the following:

- Restricting the number of new car licences, and allowing their price to rise to the corresponding equilibrium. This makes cars in Singapore among the most expensive in the world.
- Investment in a mass rail transit (MRT) system with subsidised fares. Trains are comfortable, clean and frequent. Stations are air-conditioned.
- A programme of building new estates near MRT stations.
- Cheap, frequent buses, serving all parts of the island.

In addition, a 1996 White Paper proposed the following measures:

- Building an extra 56 km of MRT lines running parallel to busy commuter routes.
- A light rail system to serve as feeders to the MRT.
- Private bus companies to operate all routes, including unprofitable ones, with prescribed fares and frequencies.
- 'Premium' buses offering greater comfort and service at higher fares.
- The construction of an extra 225 lane-km of motorways by 2001.
- The possible construction of underground roads in the city centre.

But it is in respect to road usage that the Singaporean authorities have been most innovative.

The first innovation was to make the city centre a restricted zone. Motorists who wish to enter this zone must buy a ticket (an 'area licence') at any one of 33 entry points. Police are stationed at these entry points and check that cars have paid and displayed.

With traffic congestion steadily worsening, however, it was realised that the Area Licensing Scheme had either to be widened, or to be replaced with some more flexible alternative. The decision was taken to introduce electronic road pricing. This alternative would not only save on police labour costs, but enable charge rates to be varied according to levels of congestion, times of the day, and locality.

Under this system it is anticipated that all vehicles in Singapore will be fitted with an in-vehicle unit (IU). Every journey made will require the driver to insert a smart card into the IU. On specified roads, overhead gantries will first read the IU, deducting the road use charge, and at the same time take a photograph of the car's number plate. So long as there are no problems with the deduction from the smart card, the photograph is automatically overwritten. If a car does not have a smart card or the smart card has insufficient funds on it, the car's details will then be relayed to a control centre, and the necessary legal penalties imposed.

One of the major fears is that, if the system is abused, there will be no labour saving, with the police having to spend time tracking down motorists who have not paid.

In addition, the system is very expensive, given the need to avoid *creating* congestion. Several cheaper existing schemes, such as in Norway and parts of the United States, operate by funnelling traffic into a single lane in order to register the car. In Singapore the intention is to have the system operating on three-lane highways and not requiring the speed of traffic to slow. But despite the high set-up and running costs of the system, the Singapore government is quick to argue that the full social costs of doing nothing would be significantly greater, as would the direct cost of meeting all the potential extra demand by building new roads.

?? Explain how, by varying the charge debited from the smart card according to the time of day or level of congestion, a socially optimal level of road use can be achieved.

- People may well 'park in orbit', driving round and round looking for a parking space, and in the meantime adding to congestion.
- People may park illegally. This may add to rather than reduce congestion, and may create a safety hazard.
- People may feel forced to park down side streets in residential areas, thereby causing a nuisance for residents.

Solution 3: changing market signals

The solution favoured by many economists is to use the price mechanism. As we have seen, one of the causes of traffic congestion is that road users do not pay the full marginal social costs of using the roads. If they could be forced to do so, a social optimum usage of road space could be achieved.

CASE STUDIES

THE RIGHT TRACK TO REFORM?

Reorganising the railways in the UK

Over the past 25 years, freight transported by road in Europe has risen by 240 per cent, whereas freight transported by rail has fallen by 8 per cent. While there has been a modest growth in passenger traffic on the railways, it is tiny compared with the growth in journeys by private car. Today more than 70 per cent of all passengers and freight use road transport. The result is that European railways generally operate at a loss, except for a few high-speed routes.

But why has rail transport performed so poorly? Losses on freight are partly the result of the decline in heavy manufacturing industries. A large proportion of freight trains carried coal, iron ore, steel and chemicals. In addition there is the competition from long-distance road haulage, made more competitive with the growth of the motorway network and the long hours worked by lorry drivers.

In the case of passenger services, railways have not managed to match the flexibility of car transport, made increasingly available with the growth in car ownership. Then there is the problem that many road costs are not marginal costs to the motorist. This gives road transport a cost advantage to the traveller. Finally, railways have often been forced to keep unprofitable routes open to meet public-service obligations.

Such has been the strain placed upon public finances that European governments in recent years have been looking for ways of reforming their railways. The most radical approach has been adopted in the UK, which has sought to divide up the rail system and privatise its various parts.

The UK government stated that the aim of rail privatisation was to 'improve the quality of rail services for the travelling public and for freight customers'. The 1993 Railways Act detailed the privatisation programme. The management of rail infrastructure, such as track, signalling and stations, was to be separated from the responsibility for running trains. There would be 25 passenger train operating companies, each having a franchise lasting between seven and fifteen years. These companies would have few assets, being forced to rent track and lease stations from the infrastructure owner (Railtrack), and to lease trains and rolling stock from three new rolling-stock companies. There would be three freight companies, which would also pay Railtrack for the use of track and signalling.

Railtrack would be responsible for maintaining and improving the rail infrastructure, but rather than providing this itself, it would be required to purchase the necessary services from private contractors.

To oversee the new rail network, two new posts were created. The first was a rail franchising director, who would be responsible for specifying the length and cost of franchises, as well as for outlining passenger service requirements, including minimum train frequency, stations served and weekend provision. The second post created was that of the rail regulator, who would be responsible both for promoting competition and for protecting consumer interests, which might include specifying maximum permitted fares.

Although the individual train operators generally have

In Figure 12.3 (page 361) this would involve imposing a charge on motorists of $d-c$. By 'internalising' the congestion and environmental externalities in this way, traffic flow will be reduced to the social optimum of Q_2.

So how can these external costs be charged to the motorist? There are several possible ways.

Extending existing taxes

Three major types of tax are levied on the motorist: fuel tax, taxes on new cars and car licences. Could increasing these taxes lead to the optimum level of road use being achieved?

Increasing the rates of new car tax and car licences may have *some* effect on reducing the total level of car ownership, but will probably have little effect on car use. The problem is that these taxes do not increase the *marginal* cost of car use. They are fixed costs. Once you have paid these taxes, there is no extra to pay for each extra journey you make. They do not discourage you from using your car.

Unlike the other two, fuel taxes are a marginal cost of car use. The more you use your car, the more fuel you use and the more fuel tax you pay. They are also mildly related to the level of congestion, since fuel consumption tends to increase as congestion increases. Nevertheless, they are not ideal. The problem is that *all* motorists would pay an increase in fuel tax, even those travelling on uncongested roads. To have a significant effect on congestion, there would have to be a very large increase in fuel taxes and this would be very unfair on those who are not causing congestion, especially those who have to travel long distances.

?? Would a tax on car tyres be a good way of restricting car usage?

Road pricing

Taxes are inevitably an indirect means of tackling congestion. Charging people for using roads, on the other hand,

BOX 12.4

a monopoly over a given route, many see themselves directly competing with coaches and private cars. Several have expressed the intention to replace or refurbish rolling stock and to run additional services.

Despite these apparent benefits, considerable costs have been associated with this privatisation programme. Huge subsidies have had to be paid in order to make various parts of the system saleable. The size of the subsidies is determined by the competitive bidding process for the franchises.

It is estimated that total government subsidies will amount to £10 billion in the first ten years. These include fixed subsidies paid to train operating companies over the entire length of their franchise; the writing-off of all but £600 million of Railtrack's £1.5 billion debt prior to its sale in 1996; the payment of a dividend to Railtrack shareholders out of the revenues from the last year of British Rail's operation as a nationalised industry; and, most expensive of all, subsidies for fares. This last concession involves the government compensating companies for pegging two-thirds of their fares at or below the rate of inflation for the first three years after privatisation, and at 1 per cent below the rate of inflation for the following four years. Critics argue that, with such financial backing, the rail companies cannot fail to do well and improve upon British Rail's performance in the days of nationalisation.

Critics also argue that the new system is likely to create bureaucracy and a fragmenting of responsibility, with highly complex transactions between the individual companies. There are also problems associated with the provision of timetable information for other rail companies, and problems of through ticketing and the use of concessionary cards.

Other countries, such as Japan and Germany, have rejected the UK model in favour of maintaining a vertically integrated rail network, where rail infrastructure and train services are managed by the same company. It is suggested that a single management would be far more capable of successfully co-ordinating infrastructure and train service activities than two. As separate bodies, with each management team pursuing its own goals, the best interest of passengers and business might not be served.

Nevertheless, some aspects of the UK model have been adopted under EC Directive 91/440, which allows European train operators access to the rail networks of other companies. This means that several companies (say, from different EU countries) can offer competing services on the same international route.

But whatever system is adopted, the optimum use of rail transport is unlikely to be achieved unless road transport pays the full marginal *social* costs, and subsidies are paid to the railways to reflect their external benefits.

?? Why are subsidies more likely to be needed for commuter services than for medium-to-long-distance passenger services?

where the size of the charge reflects the marginal social cost, is a direct means of achieving an efficient use of road space. The higher the congestion, the higher should be the charge. This would not only encourage people to look for alternative means of transport, but would also encourage them to travel, wherever possible, at off-peak times.

Variable tolls. Tolls are used in many countries, and could be adapted to reflect marginal social costs. In the USA, many commuter routes charge tolls, but in general the charge does not vary with the time of day. The motive for collecting them is primarily to raise revenues rather than reduce congestion. Nevertheless, it would not be difficult in most cases to introduce peak and off-peak rates, or even to have rates that vary from day to day with the level of congestion. Indeed, many authorities throughout the world are considering introducing peak-time tolls on main routes into cities.

In many cases, however, there are problems with tolls. One obvious problem is that, even with automatic tolls, there can be considerable tail-backs from the booths at peak times. Another problem is that they may simply encourage people to use minor roads into cities, thereby causing congestion on these roads. Cities have networks of streets and thus in most cases it is not difficult to avoid the tolls. Finally, if the tolls are charged to people *entering* the city, they will not affect *local* commuters. But it is these short-distance commuters *within* the city that are most likely to be able to find some alternative means of transport (including walking!), and who thus could make a substantial contribution to reducing congestion.

Supplementary licences. One simple and practical means of charging people to use congested streets is the supplementary licence. Under this scheme, people have to purchase and display a special licence if they are to use their cars in specific areas at specific times. To be successful, there have to be substantial penalties for offenders and it must be simple to obtain the licences. The main problem with this scheme is that the price of the licences has to be set in advance and thus cannot reflect the variations in congestion from day to day. Nevertheless it can be an effective means of reducing congestion, as has been found in Singapore, where such a scheme has been in operation for many years (see Box 12.3).

Electronic road pricing. The scheme most favoured by many economists and traffic planners is that of electronic road pricing. It is the scheme that can most directly relate the price charged to the motorist to the specific level of marginal social cost. It involves having sensors attached to cars, perhaps in the numberplate. When the car passes a recording device in the road, a charge is registered to that car on a central computer. The car owner then receives a bill at periodic intervals, in much the same way as a telephone bill. The charge rate can easily be varied electronically according to the level of congestion (and pollution too). The rates could be in bands and the current bands displayed by the roadside so that motorists knew what they were being charged. Several cities around the world are already operating such schemes, including Barcelona, Dallas, Orlando, Lisbon, Oklahoma City and Oslo.

An alternative scheme involves having a device fitted to your car that deactivates the car unless a 'smart card' (like a telephone or photocopying card) is inserted. The cards have to be purchased and contain a certain number of units. The device deducts units from the card when the average speed of your car over a specified distance falls below a certain level, or when more than a certain number of stops are made within a specified distance. (Either would be the result of congestion.) Such a system has been tried in Cambridge. Alternatively, beacons or overhead gantries could deduct units from the smart cards at times of congestion. Such a system was introduced in 1997 on Stockholm's ring road. When empty, a new card must be purchased or the old one recharged.

The most sophisticated scheme, still under development, involves equipping all cars with a receiver. Their position is located by satellites, which then send this information to a dashboard unit, which deducts charges according to location, distance travelled, time of day and type of vehicle. The charges can operate through either smart cards or central computerised billing.

Despite the enthusiasm for such schemes amongst economists, there are nevertheless various problems associated with them:

- Estimates of the level of external costs are difficult to make.
- Motorists will have to be informed in advance what the charges will be, so that they can plan the timing of their journeys.
- There may be political resistance. Politicians may therefore be reluctant to introduce road pricing for fear of losing popular support.
- If demand is relatively inelastic, the charges might have to be very high to have a significant effect on congestion.
- The costs of installing road-pricing equipment could be very high.
- A new industry in electronic evasion may spring up!

Subsidising alternative means of transport

An alternative to charging for the use of cars is to subsidise the price of alternatives, such as buses and trains. But cheaper fares alone may not be enough. The government may also have to invest directly in or subsidise an *improved* public transport service: more frequent services, more routes, more comfortable buses and trains.

Subsidising public transport need not be seen as an alternative to road pricing: it can be seen as complementary. If road pricing is to persuade people not to travel by car, the alternatives must be attractive. Unless public transport can be made to be seen by the traveller as a close substitute for cars, the elasticity of demand for car use is likely to remain low.

Subsidising public transport can also be justified on grounds of equity. It benefits poorer members of society who cannot afford to travel by car.

?? Which is preferable: general subsidies for public transport, or cheap fare policies for specific groups (such as children, students and pensioners)?

Conclusions

It is unlikely that any one policy can provide the complete solution. Certain policies or mixes of policies are better suited to some situations than others. It is important for governments to learn from experiences both within their own country and in others, in order to find the optimum solution to each specific problem.

SECTION SUMMARY

1. Increased car ownership and car usage have led to a growing problem of traffic congestion.
2. The allocation of road space depends on demand and supply. Demand is derived from the demand by travellers to get to their destination. Demand depends on the price to motorists of using their cars, incomes, the cost of alternative means of transport, the price of cars and complementary services (such as parking), and the comfort and convenience of car transport. The price and cross-price elasticities of demand for car usage tend to be low: many people are unwilling to switch to alternative modes of transport. The income elasticity, on the other hand, is high. The demand for cars and car usage grows rapidly as incomes grow.
3. The short-run supply of road space is fixed. The long-run supply depends on government road construction programmes.
4. The existing system of government provision of roads and private ownership of cars is unlikely to lead to the optimum allocation of road space.
5. In the short run, with road space fixed, allocation depends on the private decisions of motorists. The problem is that motorists create two types of external cost: pollution costs and congestion costs. Thus $MSC > MC$. Because of these externalities, the actual use of road space (where $MB = MC$) is likely to be greater than the optimum (where $MSB = MSC$).
6. In the long run, the social optimum amount of road space will be where $LRMSB = LRMSC$. New road schemes should be adopted as long as their $LRMSB > LRMSC$. Governments must therefore conduct some form of cost–benefit analysis in order to estimate these costs and benefits. This will include measuring such externalities as reductions in the time taken to make a journey.
7. There are various types of solution to traffic congestion. These include direct provision by the government or local authorities (of additional road space or better public transport); regulation and legislation (such as restricting car access – by the use of bus and cycle lanes, no entry to side streets and pedestrian-only areas – and various forms of parking restrictions); changing market signals (by the use of taxes, by road pricing, and by subsidising alternative means of transport).
8. Problems associated with building additional roads include the decline of public transport, attracting additional traffic on to the roads and environmental costs.
9. The main problem with restricting car access is that it tends merely to divert congestion elsewhere. The main problem with parking restrictions is that they may actually increase congestion.
10. Increasing taxes is effective in reducing congestion only if it increases the *marginal* cost of motoring. Even when it does, as in the case of additional fuel tax, the additional cost is only indirectly related to congestion costs, since it applies to all motorists and not just those causing congestion.
11. Road pricing is the preferred solution of many economists. By the use of electronic devices, motorists can be charged whenever they add to congestion. This should encourage less essential road users to travel at off-peak times or to use alternative modes of transport, while those who gain a high utility from car transport can still use their cars, but at a price. Variable tolls and supplementary licences are alternative forms of congestion pricing, but are generally less effective than the use of electronic road pricing.
12. If road pricing is to be effective, there must be attractive substitutes available. A comprehensive policy, therefore, should include subsidising efficient public transport. The revenues required for this could be obtained from road pricing.

12.2 Policies towards monopolies and oligopolies

Competition, monopoly and the public interest

Most markets in the real world are imperfect, with firms having varying degrees of market power. But will this power be against the public interest? This is the question that has been addressed by successive governments in framing legislation to deal with monopolies and oligopolies.

It might be thought that market power is always 'a bad thing', certainly as far as the consumer is concerned. After all, it enables firms to make supernormal profit, thereby 'exploiting' the consumer. The greater the firm's power, the higher will prices be relative to the costs of production. Also a lack of competition removes the incentive to become more efficient.

But market power is not necessarily a bad thing. Firms may not fully exploit their position of power – perhaps for fear that very high profits would eventually lead to other firms overcoming entry barriers, or perhaps because they are not aggressive profit maximisers. Even if they do make large supernormal profits, they may still charge a lower price than more competitive sectors of the industry because of their economies of scale. Finally, they may use their profits for research and development and for capital investment. The consumer might then benefit from improved products at lower prices.

Competition policy could seek to *ban* various structures or activities. For example, it could ban mergers leading to market share of more than a certain amount, or it could ban price-fixing arrangements between oligopolists. However, most countries prefer to adopt a more flexible approach and examine each case on its merits. Such an approach does not presume that the mere *possession* of power is against the public interest, but rather that certain uses of that power may be.

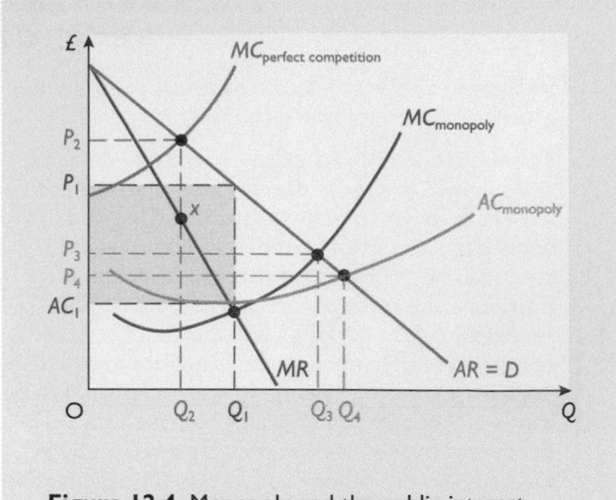

Figure 12.4 Monopoly and the public interest

?? Try to formulate a definition of 'the public interest'.

The targets of competition policy

There are three possible targets of competition policy.

The existing power of monopolies and oligopolies: monopoly policy

Monopoly policy seeks to prevent firms from abusing their economic power. Although it is referred to as 'monopoly' policy, it also applies to many larger oligopolists. The approach has been to weigh up the gains and losses to the public of individual firms' behaviour.

Figure 12.4 compares a monopoly with the same industry under perfect competition. Assuming that the monopoly wishes to maximise profits, it will produce an output Q_1 where marginal cost (MC) equals marginal revenue (MR). Its supernormal profits are shown by the shaded rectangle. Being large, this particular monopoly is able to produce with a lower MC curve than if the industry were perfectly competitive.

On the plus side, if the MC curve is a lot lower (as in Figure 12.4), the industry will operate with a lower price and higher output than it would under perfect competition. The monopoly price and output are P_1 and Q_1, whereas the perfectly competitive price and output are P_2 and Q_2. Also, the supernormal profits may be ploughed back into research and development: part of the reason, perhaps, why it has achieved a lower MC curve.

On the negative side, the MC curve may not be low enough to give a lower price and higher output. This would be the case if the monopolist's MC curve lay above point x in Figure 12.4. Even if it lay below point x (as illustrated), the monopoly could still have produced at an even lower price and higher output. At P_3 it would be equating MC and P, and thus producing at the Pareto optimal level. At P_4, a lower price still, it would still be making normal profits.

Thus the government has to work out, if it insisted on a reduction in price, whether research and development and investment would thereby suffer, and whether the consumer would lose in the long run.

The growth of power through mergers and acquisitions: merger policy

The aim of merger policy is to monitor mergers and prevent those that are considered to be against the public interest. The gains and losses to the public must be weighed up, and the government must then decide whether or not a prospective merger should be allowed to proceed.

On the plus side, the merged firms may be able to *rationalise*. Horizontal mergers particularly may allow economies of scale to be gained. Production may be able to be concentrated on fewer sites, with a more intensive utilisation of capital and labour. Also a more efficient use may be made of transport fleets, with distribution in greater bulk. Savings may be made in warehousing costs too.

There may also be some scope for rationalisation with vertical mergers. Various stages in the production process may be able to be concentrated on one site, with consequent savings in transport and handling costs.

Then there are cost savings that apply to all types of merger: horizontal, vertical and conglomerate. One of the two head offices may be closed down. Greater financial strength may allow the merged firm to drive down the prices charged by its suppliers. The combined profits may allow larger-scale investment and R & D. Finally, if two relatively small firms merge, their increased market power may allow them to compete more effectively against large firms.

On the negative side, mergers lead to a greater concentration of economic power, which could be used against the consumer's interests. This is particularly true of horizontal mergers, which will result in fewer firms for the consumer to choose from. But even conglomerate mergers can lead to certain anti-competitive activities. In particular, a conglomerate can use large profits gained in one market where it already has monopoly power to **cross-subsidise** prices in a competitive market, thereby driving out competitors.

?? What are the possible disadvantages of *vertical* mergers?

What is more, rationalisation may lead to redundancies. While this may be a potential Pareto gain, it is unlikely that the redundant will be fully compensated by the gainers.

In deciding how tough to be with mergers, the government must consider how this will affect firms' behaviour. It is not just actual mergers that will determine firms' price, output, investment, etc. It is also the *prospect* of mergers: either of an agreed merger, or of taking over another firm or of being taken over.

If the government has a liberal policy towards mergers, the competition for ownership and control of other companies may force firms to be more efficient. If the managers of a firm are afraid that it will be taken over, they will need to ensure that the firm is economically strong. Strength is not just a question of making profits at present: it is a question of being seen by shareholders as better able to make profits than an alternative ownership or control. This **competition for corporate control** may lead to lower costs and thereby benefit the consumer. It may, however, make firms even more keen to exploit any monopoly power they have, either in their battle for other firms, or in the battle to persuade shareholders not to vote for being taken over.

Government policy towards this market for corporate control will need to ensure that mergers and the possibility of mergers encourage competition rather than reducing it.

Oligopolistic collusion: restrictive practice policy

The approach towards **restrictive practices** tends to be tougher. After all, the firms are combining to exploit their joint power to make bigger profits. They could do this by jointly trying to keep out new entrants; or they could agree to keep prices high and/or restrict output; or they could divide up the market between them, agreeing not to 'poach' on each other's territory. For example, two or more supermarket chains could agree to open only one supermarket in each district.

Normally, therefore, governments aim to prevent collusion unless, perhaps, firms can prove that they are acting in the public interest – that the resulting higher profits are going to be used for investment or product development.

Banning formal cartels is easy. Preventing tacit collusion is another matter. It may be very difficult to prove that firms are making informal agreements behind closed doors.

UK policy towards monopolies and mergers

There are two main bodies involved with the operation of monopoly and merger policy: the Office of Fair Trading (OFT) and the Monopolies and Mergers Commission (MMC). Both bodies report to the government trade minister (the President of the Board of Trade).

The role of the OFT and its Director-General (DGFT) is to monitor firms which appear to be behaving uncompetitively or acting against the interests of consumers. The DGFT is also responsible for advising the minister on the administration of monopoly and merger policy, and for recommending which cases should be referred to the MMC.

The MMC is a purely advisory body whose role is to investigate cases of suspected abuse of monopoly power or proposed mergers. The following could be referred to the MMC:

- Any single firm whose current market share is 25 per cent or more of the national or local market. Alternatively, any two or more firms whose joint share is 25 per cent or more, if it is suspected that they are informally colluding to restrict competition. (As we shall see below, *formal* collusion is covered by restrictive practice legislation.)

DEFINITIONS

Cross-subsidise To use profits in one market to subsidise prices in another.

Competition for corporate control The competition for controlling companies through takeovers.

Restrictive practice Where two or more firms agree to adopt common practices to restrict competition.

- Any proposed merger that would result in a firm with assets over £30 million, or in a firm with a market share of 25 per cent or more (either national or local).

The MMC prepares a report in which it makes various recommendations to the minister, who then decides what action needs to be taken.

Suspected abuse of monopoly power

The OFT investigates and reports on suspected cases of anti-competitive practice, but only where the firm controls over 25 per cent of the national or local market. The DGFT may initiate the investigations itself, or at the request of the President of the Board of Trade.

The *1980 Competition Act* specified various types of anti-competitive practice. These include the following:

- Price discrimination.
- Predatory pricing: selling below cost to drive competitors from the market.
- Vertical price squeezing: where a vertically integrated firm, which controls the supply of an input, charges a high price for that input to competitors so that they cannot compete with it in selling the finished good.
- Tie-in sales: where a firm controlling the supply of a first product insists that its customers also buy a second product from it rather than its rivals.
- Selective distribution: where a firm is prepared to supply only certain selected retail outlets.
- Rental-only contracts: where a firm is prepared only to rent equipment (e.g. a photocopier) rather than to sell it.

If the OFT considers that firms are engaging in any of these anti-competitive practices, it will first try to get them to comply voluntarily with its recommendations. Failing this, it will refer them to the MMC.

When a case has been referred to the MMC, it will carry out a detailed investigation, often taking many months, in an attempt to establish whether or not the firm(s) are acting competitively. Do the firms promote the interests of the consumers – in terms of price, quality, variety and service? Is there sufficient competition to promote lower costs and technical progress?

Sometimes the MMC will recommend price cuts: for example, in 1966 it recommended that Kodak reduce the price of its films, and in 1973 that Hoffman LaRoche, the pharmaceutical company, reduce the price of its drugs, Librium and Valium. Sometimes it will recommend actions to reduce barriers to entry: for example, in 1966 it recommended that Unilever and Procter and Gamble, the two major detergent manufacturers, cut their advertising as well as their prices, and in 1995 that Sega and Nintendo reduce the licensing charges on competitor firms supplying software for their games consoles (see Box 12.5). Occasionally it will recommend altering the structure of an industry so as to reduce monopoly power: for example, in 1989 it recommended that no brewer should be allowed to own more than 2000 public houses (see Box 7.5).

Frequently, however, the MMC simply accepts the firms' arguments and makes no recommendations: for example, in 1993 it accepted perfume manufacturers' arguments that if they supplied discount chains, such as

Table 12.3 UK competition legislation

Year	Act	Provisions
1948	Monopolies and Restrictive Practices Act	Set up Monopolies and Restrictive Practices Commission (MRC) to investigate suspected cases of abuse by a firm or group of firms of a dominant market position.
1956, 1968, 1976	Restrictive Trade Practices Acts	Set up Restrictive Practices Court (RPC). All restrictive practices had to be registered. These would then have to be justified to the RPC. MRC renamed Monopolies Commission.
1964, 1976	Resale Prices Acts	Resale price maintenance banned unless firm could demonstrate to the RPC that it was in the public interest.
1965	Monopolies and Mergers Act	Role of Monopolies Commission now extended to examine mergers that would lead to a dominant market position.
1973	Fair Trading Act	Office of Fair Trading established. Its Director-General (DGFT) is responsible for referrals to the RPC or the renamed Monopolies and Mergers Commission (MMC).
1980	Competition Act	Various types of anti-competitive practice were specified. OFT would investigate alleged cases of such practices and possibly refer to MMC.
1989	Companies Act	Simplified and speeded-up mergers investigation procedures.

CASE STUDIES BOX 12.5

SONIC AND MARIO MEET THEIR MATCH

In March 1995, the Monopolies and Mergers Commission, after a fourteen-month investigation, ruled that Sega and Nintendo were guilty of operating monopolistic practices and practising discriminatory pricing, and that if prices failed to fall then some form of price control might be required.

The dominance of the computer games market by Sega and Nintendo is very significant. Sega controls 38 per cent and Nintendo 25 per cent of the combined console/games software sales. If the market is defined on more narrow criteria, then jointly they supply 99 per cent of all games consoles. The total value of the UK market was £550 million in 1993.

The charges levelled at Sega and Nintendo were as follows:

- Both businesses had been widely practising discriminatory pricing. In particular, both companies had been charging excessively high prices for software as opposed to hardware. The MMC argued that hardware prices had been deliberately held down so as to deter potential competitors in the hardware market, and to lock consumers into buying the companies' own software.
- Games software, supplied by third parties, had been controlled through strict licensing agreements. Software developers were forced to buy minimum numbers of software cartridges, and to pay a manufacturing charge and a royalty on each cartridge sold. Sega's gross profit margin on each single cartridge was estimated to be about 45 per cent.
- Both companies attempted to restrict the rental and part exchange of software products.

The main recommendation of the MMC was to change the licensing conditions of software as they currently stood. It argued that it was imperative that Sega's and Nintendo's control over software development and manufacturing be diminished, if there was to be any prospect that prices would fall.

??

1. What would be the likely effect of a reduction in software prices on the price of the hardware?
2. Could any 'consumer interest' justification be made out for the practices of Sega and Nintendo?

Superdrug, the perfumes would lose the appeal of 'exclusivity' that their high prices gave them.

Mergers

Companies must give details of any proposed merger to the OFT. These details can be used by the DGFT in making recommendations to the minister, who might then require the firms to sell off some of their assets, so as to reduce the power that would result from the merger. Alternatively the minister could refer the merger to the MMC. While investigations are proceeding, companies involved may not acquire each other's shares. If no reference is made within twenty days of the receipt of the details, the merger may proceed.

If reference is made to the MMC, then, as with the case of monopolies, there is no presumption that mergers are against the public interest. There are potential costs of greater market power in terms of higher prices and less choice, but also potential benefits from economies of scale, greater research and development, greater investment and greater power to compete internationally. After weighing up the evidence, the MMC will recommend to the minister whether or not the merger, or parts of it, should be allowed to proceed.

Assessing UK monopoly and mergers policy

Monopoly policy

It is not presumed that the mere possession of power is detrimental. Instead, the OFT and the MMC are concerned with how that power is *used*. But although it may be desirable to judge each case on its own merits, this can make the recommendations and decisions somewhat arbitrary. Very often the MMC has been only too ready to accept firms' assurances, and there has often been too little follow-up to ensure that firms have stuck to their word. For most companies, then, referral to the MMC is not a serious worry, except for the time and expense that an MMC investigation will incur.

There is also the problem that the minister can reject or amend the MMC's findings, and has done so on many occasions. What is more, of the thousands of possible cases for investigation, only some 160 have been referred to the MMC since an earlier version of it was formed in 1948 (see Table 12.4). Nevertheless, many firms have agreed with the OFT to modify their behaviour without the need for reference to the MMC.

So is the policy a success? Many on the political right argue that there is little need for intervention at all. Many large firms, who on the surface may seem very powerful,

Table 12.4 Monopolies and Mergers Commission reports

	Monopolies and competition inquiries	Merger inquiries	Public sector inquiries	Privatised industry inquiries	Total inquiries
1950–9	23	–	–	–	23
1960–9	20	12	–	–	32
1970–9	39	27	–	–	66
1980–9	42	69	29	2	142
1990–7[1]	37	76	6	21	140
Total	161	184	35	23	403

[1] up to Aug 1997

Sources: *The Role of the Commission*, 4th edition (Monopolies and Mergers Commission, 1992); information supplied by MMC.

do face substantial competition, often from abroad (especially since the abolition by 1993 of barriers to trade in the EU). This, they argue, will usually be enough to prevent the abuse of apparent market power. Then there is the argument about contestability. If entry and exit costs are relatively low, monopolistic and oligopolistic firms will need to have regard to potential competition. Even if firms do use their power to gain substantial profits, the consumer may still benefit in the long run from improved products at a lower cost and eventually lower price.

Critics of the UK legislation argue that it is too weak. Certain anti-competitive *practices*, they argue, ought to be made illegal. This is more the approach adopted by the EU (see below).

Merger policy

The vast majority (over 97 per cent) of proposed mergers have not been referred to the MMC. Of the 180 or so that have been referred since 1965 (the year when mergers were first investigated by the MMC), most have been abandoned or, after the MMC investigation, ruled against by the minister.

This suggests that the policy has not been tough enough, with many mergers not referred which should have been. Indeed, studies have shown that mergers have generally *not* been in the public interest. Significant benefits from cost reduction and research have not occurred, and yet mergers have contributed to a growing degree of market concentration in the UK. Several commentators have argued that the burden of proof ought to be changed so that the companies would have to demonstrate the *benefits* to the public of the merger if it were to be allowed to proceed.[2]

The other major criticism of the policy is that it has been too arbitrary. The references to the MMC, the MMC recommendations and the decisions of the minister have frequently, it is alleged, been decided according to political criteria. Although such allegations are difficult to prove, there does seem to have been a degree of inconsistency in decision making.

UK policy towards restrictive practices

Oligopolistic collusion

Whereas the policy towards monopolies and mergers seeks to judge each case on its merits, restrictive practice policy seeks to *ban* all open oligopolistic collusion unless it can be proved by the participants to be in the public interest. The procedure for dealing with restrictive practices is as follows:

- All agreements between firms over prices, quantity, product specifications, the markets to be supplied, or any other aspect that limits competition within the UK (including merely keeping each other informed of their plans), must be registered with the Office of Fair Trading.
- If the OFT considers that there is indeed collusion, the firms will then be required to appear before the *Restrictive Practices Court* to justify the agreement (unless they are prepared to end it voluntarily).
- The Court will automatically terminate the agreement unless the firms can prove that they serve the public interest under at least one of eight headings (or 'gateways'). These gateways are that the agreement would:

1. Protect the public against injury.
2. Provide specific benefits to the public.
3. Help prevent other restrictive practices.
4. Help secure fairer terms from the firms' suppliers or purchasers.
5. Help protect jobs.

[2] See, for example, M. Fleming and D. Swann, 'Competition policy: the pace quickens and 1992 approaches', *Royal Bank of Scotland Review*, June 1989.

6. Promote exports.
7. Support another agreement already found to be acceptable by the Court.
8. Not restrict competition.

- There is a final hurdle for the firms. The Court will still terminate the agreement if it feels on balance that the public interest is not served, even if it satisfies one or more gateways.

Since restrictive practices legislation was introduced in 1956, several thousand cases have been registered. In principle all these agreements should have been referred to the Restrictive Practices Court. Given the toughness of the legislation, however, most were abandoned before reference could be made. But even with those that were not, the OFT tries to avoid reference to the Court. If the agreement has little effect on competition, the DGFT can ask the minister to rule that no reference is warranted. In other cases the OFT offers businesses the opportunity to amend the agreements so as to remove anti-competitive practices. As a result only a few cases come before the Restrictive Practices Court each year: less than 1 per cent of all registered agreements.

The cases that are referred tend to be those where the issues are most complex. For example, in 1996 the OFT referred football's Premier League, accusing the individual clubs of acting as a cartel in bidding up the price to be paid by the BBC and Sky for broadcasting matches. The clubs argued that, if they were forced into price competition with each other for broadcasts, this would lead to the break-up of the League.

Resale price maintenance (RPM)

Resale price maintenance is where a manufacturer or distributor insists that retailers charge a set price for its products. It is a way of keeping prices high to the consumer and thereby discouraging firms from forcing down the price they pay to the manufacturer.

Any firm wishing to conduct RPM must register it with the OFT and then appear before the Restrictive Practices Court to justify it under at least one of five gateways. These are that without RPM:

1. The quality and variety of goods would be substantially reduced.
2. The number of retail outlets would be substantially reduced.
3. The retail price would increase.
4. There could be damage to health or safety.
5. There would be a substantial reduction in necessary services connected with the good.

The Court must also be satisfied that the overall benefits of the RPM outweigh the costs.

Assessing UK restrictive practice policy

The policy has virtually eliminated open formal collusion. In this sense it would seem to have been very tough and to contrast markedly with policy towards monopolies and mergers. Nevertheless, oligopolistic collusion remains.

Such collusion could be open, but involve no *formal* agreement. It would thus fall outside the scope of the Restrictive Practices Court. However, if firms' joint actions result in any of the anti-competitive practices specified in the 1980 Competition Act, they can be investigated by the Office of Fair Trading and if necessary referred to the MMC.

A more serious problem is that of collusion 'behind closed doors'. If firms are careful, they may well be able to keep their price-fixing or other collusive actions secret. Some cases have come to light, however. For example, one of the most widespread practices is that of collusive tendering, where two or more firms put in a tender for a contract at secretly agreed (high) prices. A well-known case is that of firms supplying ready-mixed concrete agreeing on prices they would tender to local authorities. But provided the firms do not tender at exactly the same price, it is very difficult to spot when such collusion is taking place. The cases that have been discovered may well, then, be simply the tip of an iceberg.

What is more, the *dis*incentive for such collusion is very small. The worst that is likely to happen is an OFT investigation and a court injunction to prevent *further* price fixing. Only then would heavy fines be imposed if the firms continued, for then they would be in contempt of court.

Another problem is that, if firms are prevented from colluding, they may simply merge instead!

Assessing policy towards resale price maintenance

As with oligopolistic collusion, the Restrictive Practices Court has been very tough. Until recently, RPM was allowed to continue only in the case of books (the Net Book Agreement) and certain medicines. But in 1995, the Net Book Agreement was finally ended, amid fears that supermarkets and chain stores would sell popular books at a discount, making it very difficult for smaller bookshops

DEFINITION

Resale (or retail) price maintenance Where the manufacturer of a product (legally) insists that the product should be sold at a specified retail price.

to survive, and thereby reducing the outlets for more specialised books.

> **??** What are the arguments in favour of having abandoned RPM for books?

Competition policy in the European Union

EU legislation is contained in Articles 85 and 86 of the Treaty of Rome and, since 1990, in additional regulations covering mergers.

Article 85 is concerned with restrictive practices and Article 86 with monopolies and mergers. The Articles are largely confined to firms trading between EU countries and thus do not cover monopolies or oligopolies operating solely within a member country. The policy is implemented by the European Commission. If any firm appears to be breaking the provisions of either of the Articles, the Commission can refer it to the European Court of Justice.

EU policy towards restrictive practices

Article 85 covers *agreements* between firms, *joint decisions* and concerted *practices* which prevent, restrict or distort competition. It is so worded as to include all types of oligopolistic collusion. On the surface, Article 85 appears to be similar to UK restrictive practice legislation: the presumption in both cases is that collusion is against the public interest; both allow for exemptions in specific cases.

But in other respects they are quite different. The UK legislation is designed to prevent oligopolistic *structures*: i.e. formal collusive agreements. Article 85, by contrast, focuses on collusive *behaviour*. No matter what form collusion takes, if the European Commission finds that firms are committing anti-competitive *practices*, they will be banned from doing so and possibly fined (up to 10 per cent of annual turnover), although firms do have the right of appeal to the European Court of Justice. Practices considered anti-competitive include firms jointly fixing prices, limiting output, charging discriminatory prices and sharing out markets between them. In recent years the Commission has adopted a tough stance and has fined many firms (see Box 12.6).

The other major difference between UK restrictive practice legislation and Article 85 is that there is little power of enforcement in the UK. If firms do not register agreements and are subsequently found to be operating a restrictive practice, they will merely be told to stop it. Only if they continue will they be fined, and even then the fines are not very heavy. By contrast, the European Commission has much greater powers to ban collusive behaviour.

EU policy towards monopolies

Article 86 relates to the abuse of monopoly power and has also been extended to cover mergers. As with Article 85, it is the *behaviour* of firms that is the target of the legislation: for example, charging unfair prices or restricting output to the disadvantage of consumers. Under Article 86, such practices can be banned and firms can be fined where they are found to have abused a dominant position.

In contrast to UK legislation, a firm does not have to have some specified minimum market share before Article 86 can be invoked. This is sensible given the difficulties of identifying the boundaries of a market, either in terms of geography or in terms of type of product.

EU policy towards mergers

The 1990 merger control measures tightened up the legislation in Article 86. They cover mergers where combined worldwide sales exceed ECU5 billion (approximately £4 billion); where EU sales of at least two of the companies exceed ECU250 million; and where at least one of the companies conducts no more than two-thirds of its EU-wide business in a single member state. (Less than 4 per cent of mergers involving European companies meet these conditions.)

Such mergers must be notified to the European Commission within one week of their announcement. The merger will then normally be suspended for three weeks. Within one month of the notification, the Commission, on the basis of preliminary investigations (Phase 1), must decide whether to conduct a formal investigation (Phase 2) or to let the merger proceed.

The 1990 measures have made the process of EU merger control very rapid and administratively inexpensive. Also, it would appear that the EU legislation is tougher than in the UK, albeit more limited in scope (being confined to companies operating in more than one member country). Nevertheless several criticisms have been made of the system.[3]

- The decisions of the Commission are often based on limited and poorly presented analysis and are inconsistent between different cases.
- The Commission, in being willing to show flexibility, can easily be persuaded by firms, and the conditions imposed on them are often very lax and rely on the firms' co-operation.
- Not enough emphasis is placed on possible cost reductions from mergers. The stress is almost exclusively on questions of competition.

[3] See D. Neven, R. Nuttall and P. Seabright, *Merger in Daylight* (Centre for Economic Policy Research, 1993).

CASE STUDIES BOX 12.6

CARTELS SET IN CONCRETE, STEEL AND CARDBOARD

Experiences in the UK and other European countries

> A concrete supplier who attended cartel meetings ... was the key witness in last year's contempt case in which three Oxfordshire firms were fined a total of £56 000 plus costs and two employees were told they had narrowly escaped gaol sentences.
>
> The witness told the Restrictive Practices Court in September that he had occasionally attended meetings between RMC (Thames Valley), Smiths Concrete, Hartigan Readymix, and Pioneer Concrete in 1983 and 1984. During these meetings, held at monthly intervals in pubs in Aylesbury, representatives of the four companies agreed market shares which were recorded in an allocation book. He kept a copy and sent it to the OFT in 1988...
>
> At each meeting representatives would state new jobs they were aware of, discuss prices and decide which firm should get the contract. The other cartel members would then agree to tender higher prices.[4]

When it comes to restrictive practices, few industries can match the poor record of the building materials industry. Firms in many parts of the industry, from glass suppliers to concrete makers, have admitted to operating market share agreements, price rings and other forms of price fixing. The OFT alleges that, in the concrete industry alone, at least 29 producers ran over 65 cartels throughout the UK from the late 1970s to the early 1990s. The cost to the consumer is estimated to have been in the region of £65 million.

Such extensive collusion is not confined to the UK. There are many cases throughout Europe and the rest of the world.

The Directorate General IV (DGIV) of the European Competition Department has extensive powers to deal with anti-competitive practices. These powers include raiding companies, seizing documents and levying huge fines (up to 10 per cent of turnover).

In December 1994 record fines of ECU248 million were imposed on 33 European cement producers and eight national cement associations. It was found that the European Cement Association, by exchanging price information, had managed to reduce price differences between producers in different countries, removing any incentive to export cement overseas, and thereby ensuring that prices remained high. Those producers which did export were encouraged to set their prices at the same level as those of local producers.

Collusion has also been rife in the steel industry, but it is only in recent years that the EU has taken a tough stance against steel cartels. Indeed, in the 1970s the EC even encouraged collusion to help ease the effects of a depression in the steel market. Eurofer, the European steel producers association, was established in 1976 and policed this collusion. What followed was a series of formal agreements between the main steel producers. Quotas were set; fines were imposed on members for quota violations; and committees were established to consider market forecasting and pricing.

However, the EC became increasingly unhappy with this collusion. Following a series of large Europe-wide price rises in steel, the Z Club, as it became known, was investigated in 1986, and members were fined.

Then in 1993 the DGIV investigated an alleged cartel between Europe's main steel producers in the supply of steel sections and heavy beams used in the construction industry. With a downturn in construction in the early 1990s, there should have been a fall in the price of steel. In fact, prices did not change. This led to claims that a price ring was in operation. For example, when European steel producers bid for UK contracts, they all tendered prices much the same as British Steel's, even though they could have offered prices some 20–30 per cent lower. In February 1994 the sixteen-strong European and Scandinavian cartel was found guilty by the Commission and fined ECU104 million. The largest single fine (ECU32 million) was imposed on British Steel.

In 1991, the same year as the investigation into the European steel industry, carton-board producers were subject to a 'dawn raid' by the Competition Department. Like the steel producers, the carton-board producers were found guilty of extensive price fixing and market manipulation. Operating in an association known as Product Group Paperboard, the cartel of nineteen producers met twelve times a year, most frequently in Zurich, but also in Nice and Barcelona. Behind the façade of a carton-board manufacturers' 'social gathering', the cartel members co-ordinated Europe-wide price rises. This was in part achieved by regulating the supply of carton-board (the largest producers in the cartel frequently engineered plant stoppages in order to keep production levels under control), and by the operation of a strict market-sharing arrangement.

The Commission found that, by controlling supply in this way and creating a shortage of board, the cartel managed to increase prices by 6–10 per cent twice each year from 1987 to 1990. This was in spite of a fall in raw material costs. In 1994 fines totalling ECU132 million were imposed on the nineteen-member cartel.

?? If formal collusive arrangements can be discovered by 'dawn raids' and the seizing of incriminating paperwork, why do cartel members not rely on a much looser informal arrangement, with nothing in writing?

[4] *Building*, 27 September 1991.

- In the first six years of the merger control measures, 398 mergers were notified, but only 27 proceeded to Phase 2. In many cases (too many, claim critics) the Commission accepted the undertakings of firms. By 1996, only five mergers had been prohibited.

  The next three were in the television, cable and media sector: one (in 1994) between three German companies, one (in 1995) between three Scandinavian companies, and one (again in 1995) between one Luxembourg and two Dutch companies. In each case the proposal was to set up a joint venture (MSG, NSD and HMG respectively), and in each case the Commission argued that the respective company, through both vertical and horizontal integration, would have a virtual monopoly and could use its power to obstruct competition.

  In 1996, the Commission blocked a fifth merger – the platinum operations of Lonrho (UK) and Gencor (South Africa). The Commission maintained that this would create a virtual duopoly (with the Anglo-American Corporation), with the threat of rigged prices in the world market. This was a particular problem, given the lack of substitutes for platinum in various industrial operations and hence a highly price-inelastic demand.

There is considerable conflict within the EU between those who want to encourage competition *within* the EU and those who want to see European companies being world leaders. For them, the ability to compete in *world* markets normally requires that companies are large, which may well imply having monopoly power within the EU.

One of the main problems with EU monopoly and merger legislation is its relationship with domestic legislation. EU competition law applies only to companies with a substantial proportion of their business in more than one EU country. By careful planning of takeovers and concentrating the location of their business, firms can avoid EU regulation. Moreover, they can choose to locate in countries with the most lax competition policy. There is thus an incentive for countries, if they want to attract inward investment, to reduce their regulation.

?? In what way does this competition between countries to minimise regulation impose harmful externalities on other countries?

Proposals for reform of UK competition policy

There has been considerable debate over the future direction of competition policy. The bulk of opinion has favoured changes to bring UK policy more in line with that of the EU and many of its other member states. This would mean shifting the target of policy from monopolistic/oligopolistic *structures* to anti-competitive *behaviour*. Collusive activities such as price fixing, collusive tendering and sharing out the market should be made illegal; so too should anti-competitive activities of single firms – activities such as predatory pricing and various types of price discrimination.

Such activities have become more prevalent. In 1993 News International reduced the price of *The Times* from 45p to 30p. This meant that the newspaper was now being sold at a loss. However, News International was able to cover the loss by using profits from B Sky B, its satellite broadcasting operation. The hope was that the price reduction would force competitors such as *The Independent* out of business, at which point the price of *The Times* could be raised once more. The resulting price war did, in fact, lead to the closure of one of the tabloid newspapers, *Today*. In contrast, under Article 86, the European Court fined the Dutch chemical company Akzo ECU7.5m in 1991 for pricing below average variable cost in order to eliminate a competitor.

In 1995 the all-party House of Commons trade and industry select committee published a report on competition policy. It supported making various anti-competitive activities illegal, with heavy fines for offending firms. It argued that the current system was too vague and open to personal interpretation by the minister, the OFT and the MMC. This had led to inconsistency and unpredictability. What is more, restrictive practices were allowed to flourish because the firms involved knew that, until the OFT or Restrictive Practices Court had ruled against them, there were no penalties. These arguments had been recognised by the government in a 1992 Green Paper, but no moves had been made to implement them.

The select committee also recommended replacing the OFT and the MMC by a single competition authority staffed by full-time experts, which would investigate breaches of the new laws. This proposal was endorsed by the Labour opposition and the outgoing head of the OFT, Sir Bryan Carsberg.

The government promised a reform of competition policy, but ruled out banning various anti-competitive activities, and merging the OFT and the MMC.

??

1. Are there any disadvantages in a policy of making certain 'anti-competitive' practices illegal?
2. Should a body like the OFT be given the legal authority to decide whether a breach of the law has occurred, or should it be a matter solely for the courts?

SECTION SUMMARY

1. Competition policy needs to recognise that monopolies, mergers and restrictive practices can bring both costs and benefits to the consumer. Generally, though, restrictive practices tend to be more damaging to consumer interests than simple monopoly power or mergers.
2. In the UK, monopolies and other dominant firms (with more than one-quarter of the market) can be referred to the Monopolies and Mergers Commission by the President of the Board of Trade. The MMC prepares a report and the government decides on what action, if any, to take. The same procedure applies to mergers. Mergers can be held up while the investigation takes place. The criterion for judging whether a monopoly or merger is in the public interest has become largely that of whether or not it damages competition.
3. Restrictive practices must be registered with the Office of Fair Trading. If firms want to continue their agreement, it will be referred to the Restrictive Practices Court. The onus is on firms to prove that their agreement is in the public interest. To do so they must 'pass through' (satisfy) at least one of eight gateways and demonstrate to the satisfaction of the Court that the public interest on balance is served by the agreement.
4. European Union legislation applies to firms trading between EU countries. Article 85 applies to restrictive practices. Article 86 applies to monopolies and dominant firms, but can also be used against mergers. These Articles focus on specific practices that are against the public interest. They can be banned unless exemption can be claimed.
5. Various commentators have suggested that the UK should adopt the EU approach to competition policy: to focus on anti-competitive behaviour rather than anti-competitive structures.

12.3 Privatisation and regulation

From the early 1980s, the Thatcher and Major governments engaged in extensive programmes of 'privatisation', returning most of the nationalised industries to the private sector. Nationalised industries, they claimed, were bureaucratic, inefficient, unresponsive to consumer wishes and often a burden on the taxpayer.

Other countries have followed similar programmes of privatisation in what has become a world-wide phenomenon. Privatisation has been seen by many governments as a means of revitalising ailing industries and raising revenues to ease budgetary problems.

However, privatisation has brought its own problems. Consumers have complained of poor service and high prices. The result is that governments have been increasingly concerned to *regulate* the behaviour of these industries, many of which are monopolies.

We will examine the nature and effectiveness of this regulation later. We begin, however, by examining the experience of nationalisation, which laid the foundations for the debate over privatisation.

The old nationalised industries

Nationalised industries are **public corporations** owned by the state, which produce goods or services that are sold on the market. Not all public corporations are classed as nationalised industries. For example, the BBC and the Bank of England are not, as they are not primarily concerned with producing goods or services directly for sale.

Most nationalisation in the UK took place during the Labour government of 1945–51, when coal, railways, gas and steel were nationalised. By the early 1990s, the only wholly nationalised industry remaining in the UK was the Post Office. Table 12.5 shows when the major nationalisations took place.

Nationalised industries were officially separate from government. Their boards of directors were appointed by

DEFINITIONS

Nationalised industries State-owned industries that produce goods or services that are sold in the market.

Public corporations State-owned organisations set up by statute and technically free to manage their own affairs within broad ministerial or parliamentary guidelines. They include nationalised industries and other organisations such as the BBC.

Table 12.5 The major nationalised industries in the UK

Industry	Date and form of nationalisation	Date and form of privatisation
Utilities/fuel		
Electricity	1926 Central Electricity Board (generation and transmission) 1948 Area Electricity Boards (supply to customers) 1958 Reorganised into Central Electricity Generating Board (CEGB) and 12 Area Electricity Boards	1990 Area Electricity Boards 1991 Non-nuclear generation 1996 Nuclear generation
Coal	1947 National Coal Board	1994– Mines sold off individually
Gas	1949 Gas Council and Area Boards 1973 Re-established as British Gas Corporation (later called British Gas)	1986 British Gas 1996 Split into TransCo and BG Energy
Water	1973 Regional Water Authorities (10) took over from local government	1989 10 separate companies
Oil	1976 British National Oil Corporation (BNOC) (part of industry)	1982 Privatised as Britoil
Transport and communications		
Posts and telecoms	1961 (Previously a government department) 1981 Split into the Post Office and British Telecom (BT)	1994 Privatised as BT
Railways	1948 British Transport Commission 1963 Split into British Railways and London Transport 1995 BR split into Railtrack and separate train operating divisions	1996– Train operating companies sold individually 1996 Railtrack privatised
Buses	1969 National Bus Company	1986 Privatised
Road haulage	1947 Later named National Freight Corporation	1982 Management/worker buyout
Airlines	1940 British Overseas Airways Corporation (non-European) 1946 British European Airways (European) 1974 BOAC and BEA combined to form British Airways	1987 Privatised as BA
Manufacturing, etc.		
Steel	1951 Iron and Steel Corporation 1967 Renationalised as British Steel Corporation	1953 Privatised 1988 Privatised as BSC
Shipbuilding	1977 British Shipbuilders	1985–6 Sold as separate companies
Aero engines	1971 Rolls-Royce nationalised	1987 Privatised
Aerospace	1977 British Aerospace (part of industry only)	1981 Privatised as BAe
Vehicles	1976 British Leyland (part of industry only)	1984 Jaguar division of BL privatised 1988 Rover group (part of old BL) privatised

the appropriate government minister, but were theoretically independent. In practice, however, there was often considerable government interference in their running.

The firms involved were generally monopolies, such as gas and electricity: these were true nationalised *industries*. Others were publicly owned but still competed with private-sector firms. Thus Rolls-Royce and British Airways before they were privatised were nationalised *firms*, but not nationalised *industries*. Even where a whole industry was nationalised, it often competed with the private sector or with other nationalised industries. Thus British Gas had to compete with electricity, coal and oil in many markets.

?? The National Health Service and state education are not counted as nationalised industries. Do you think that they should be?

Arguments for public ownership: ideological

Many on the political left argue that it is morally desirable to have the means of production in public ownership. Private ownership not only is highly unequal, but also involves the division of society into classes: a class of workers who only have their own labour to earn them money and a class of capitalists whose income is largely derived not from their own toil, but from the capital they own – capital that is often inherited. Such a social division is seen as unjust.

The political right argue that it is morally desirable for people to be free to own property and to pass it on to their children.

Economists cannot make a fundamental moral judgement as to the desirability of capitalism and socialism. All we can do is to note that ideological questions often play a major role in the nationalisation/privatisation debate.

Arguments for public ownership: market failure

If the market fails to achieve various objectives such as efficiency, growth and equality, then nationalisation may be a suitable means of correcting these failures. The arguments based on market failure are as follows.

Natural monopoly

Some industries have such great economies of scale that there is room for only one firm in the industry.

The cost of providing a national electricity grid or a national gas pipe network is a relatively high proportion of the total cost of providing electricity or gas. The more intensively these grids are used, however, the lower their cost will become per unit of fuel supplied. Similarly with railways: the relatively high costs of providing track and signalling, etc. will become smaller per passenger, the more passengers use the railway.

In the short run, these costs are fixed. Average fixed costs must necessarily decline as more is produced: overheads are being spread over a greater output.

In the long run, when new lines can be built (electricity, gas, railway), these costs become variable. It is still likely, however, that they will decline per unit of output, the higher the output becomes. A pylon carrying ten lines does not cost five times as much as one carrying two. This means that long-run average costs fall as more is produced.

In Figure 12.5, assume initially that the firm just seeks to cover long-run average costs ($P = LRAC$) and that, therefore, if it is in the private sector it does not exploit its monopoly power to earn supernormal profits. Q_1 will be sold at a price of P_1 and at a cost of $LRAC_1$.

Now assume that the industry is shared between two equal-sized producers. The average cost of each supplier would be considerably higher than that of a single supplier. In Figure 12.5, continuing with the assumption that a price is charged that just covers $LRAC$, the market price will have to rise to P_2, with total consumption of Q_2. This is divided equally between the two suppliers, which each supply Q_3 at a cost of $LRAC_2$ ($= P_2$).

It is potentially more efficient therefore to have a single monopoly supplier whenever there is a natural monopoly. It avoids wasteful duplication.

The problem is that the monopoly producer in a free market could use its power to drive up prices. The long-run profit-maximising position is illustrated in Figure 12.6. The monopolist produces Q_m at a price P_m and at a cost of $LRAC_m$. There is a misallocation of resources.

If the industry is nationalised, it can be run as a monopoly and thus achieve the full economies of scale. And yet it can choose a price where it just covers costs (including normal profits), and thus makes no more profit than a highly competitive industry. In Figure 12.6 it would produce Q_n at a price of P_n.

It may, however, be possible to achieve the same result without nationalisation. A private monopoly supplier could be ordered by the government or some regulatory agency to charge a price that just earns normal or 'reasonable' profits. This has been the recent approach in the UK and other European countries, where regulatory agencies have been set up to control the behaviour of privatised companies.

High capital costs and barriers to entry

A related problem is that of industries with high capital costs. Once established, a monopoly will have an effective barrier to the entry of competitors if it is very capital intensive. Potential entrants may be unable or unwilling to raise sufficient capital to break into the market. The market is not contestable, since the entry and exit costs are too high. Such industries are therefore likely to remain monopolies.

High capital costs and a lack of investment

Certain industries may require investment on such a large scale that they would find it difficult to raise the necessary capital from financial markets. This was one of the main arguments used to support the renationalisation of the steel industry in 1967 (it had been privatised in 1953).

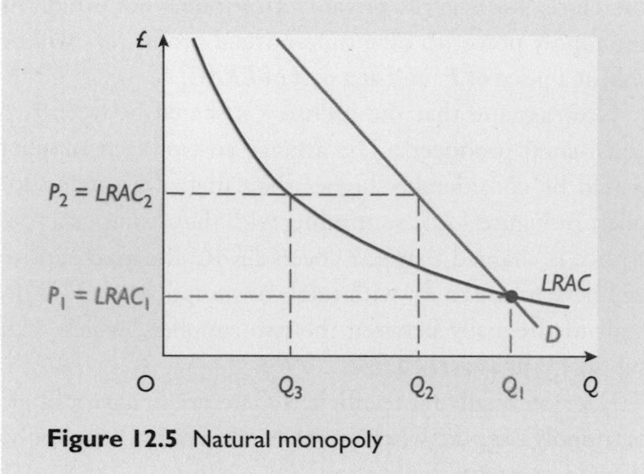

Figure 12.5 Natural monopoly

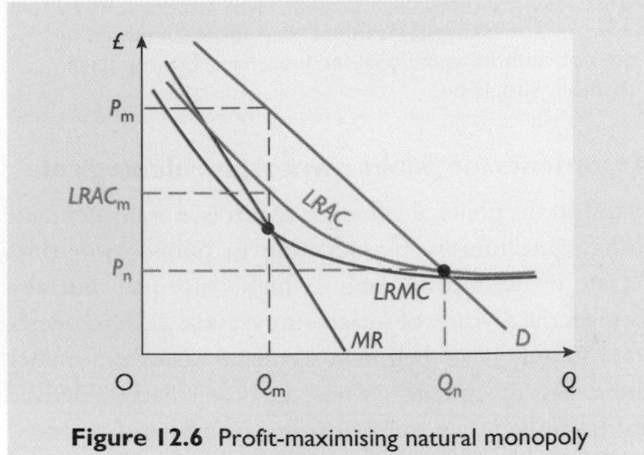

Figure 12.6 Profit-maximising natural monopoly

The problem is made worse if large amounts of money are required for research and development, or if the investment is risky.

Planning and the co-ordination of industry

Road use and road construction affect the demand for railways and vice versa. Decisions in the coal, electricity, gas and oil industries (and to a large extent in the steel industry) all affect each other. Nationalisation of these industries should make their decisions easier to co-ordinate in the public interest. It could also help the sensible planning of the nation's infrastructure. If these industries were under private enterprise, however, either there would be little co-ordination, or co-ordination might degenerate into oligopolistic collusion.

Externalities

Various industries may create substantial external benefits and yet may be privately unprofitable. A railway or an Underground line, for example, may ease congestion considerably on the roads, thus benefiting road as well as rail users. If nationalised, these industries could be run at a loss and subsidised by the taxpayer.

Other industries may cause substantial external costs. Nuclear power stations may produce nuclear waste that is costly to dispose of safely, and/or provides hazards for future generations. Coal-fired power stations may pollute the atmosphere and cause acid rain. If these various industries were nationalised, their statutory objectives could, it is argued, include taking account of these externalities.

Ailing firms

If a major firm is about to go bankrupt, then nationalisation may be a means of rescuing it. Jobs will be saved not only in the firm itself, but also in other firms servicing it and in the local community.

What is more, nationalisation of these firms may allow substantial investment to take place, which will eventually return them to solvency. At that stage they could then be privatised. Examples of the nationalisation of ailing firms/industries were Rolls-Royce in 1971, BL in 1976 and British Shipbuilders in 1977.

Fair provision of services

For reasons of equity, certain services could be cross-subsidised in order to keep them going and/or to keep their prices down. For instance, it can be argued that rural bus services should be kept operating at cross-subsidised prices and that certain needy people (e.g. pensioners) should be charged lower prices. This is easier to achieve, it is argued, under nationalisation.

Industrial relations

The early advocates of nationalisation in the 1930s and 1940s hoped that it would improve industrial relations. In theory this is possible, provided there is genuine industrial democracy in the nationalised industries. In practice the divide between workers and management has often been as deep as in the private sector, as the bitter dispute between the management of British Coal and the National Union of Mineworkers in 1985–6 over pit closures illustrates.

Management of the economy

Governments may wish to have certain key industries under nationalisation in order to make it easier to manage the economy. For instance, governments could attempt to restrain wages in the nationalised industries and keep their price increases small as a way of controlling inflation; and nationalised industry investment could be directed to regions of high unemployment.

Strategic

If certain industries such as aerospace and weapons manufacture were nationalised, it might be easier for the government to ensure that they were operated in the defence interests of the country.

> ?? The critics of nationalisation would claim that not one of these arguments is conclusive. All of the ten problem areas could be dealt with by other means. Try going through each of the arguments and think of other ways of dealing with the problems. Do you think that nationalisation is the best way of tackling each one?

Assessing the performance of nationalised industries

One of the major arguments for privatisation is the relatively poor performance of the nationalised industries. Assessing this performance, however, is fraught with difficulties.

Nationalised industries were often criticised for having had a poor *profit* record. But using profits as a means of assessment has very little validity for the following reasons:

- Many industries or firms were nationalised *because* they were having difficulty making profits.
- Loss-making parts of the nationalised industries were sometimes kept operating for *social* reasons.
- The industries were sometimes instructed to break even rather than maximise profits.
- The government often deliberately kept nationalised industry prices low to restrain inflation.
- High profits in the private sector are often an indication of firms' monopoly power rather than their efficiency.

An alternative is to try to assess nationalised industry *costs*. The problem here is to compare like with like. What is the nationalised industry to be compared with?

- If the whole industry were nationalised, it would have to be compared with another *industry*. But the conditions in another industry may be quite different. What meaningful comparison can be made of the costs of extracting a tonne of coal and those of obtaining a barrel of oil?
- An industry could be compared with the same industry abroad. For example, cost per passenger mile of British Rail could be compared with that of French Railways (SNCF). But SNCF has a higher proportion of freight traffic and a smaller proportion of commuter passengers than BR. The level and spread of subsidies differs between the two countries. SNCF has a much higher rate of investment per mile in track and rolling stock than BR. How then is any meaningful comparison to be made?
- Another possibility is to compare the costs of those parts of the nationalised sector that did compete with the private sector: for example, Parcelforce (Royal Mail parcels) with private parcel carriers. Again, however, the problem is whether ownership is the *only* thing that causes differences in efficiency. The Royal Mail has to carry parcels to any part of the country. Private carriers may confine themselves to certain high-density routes, and are thus able to carry full loads and operate with a lower cost per tonne/mile.
- The final possibility is to compare an industry's costs before and after privatisation (or nationalisation). The problem here is that the quality and quantity of output may have changed. For example, when local authorities began employing private firms to collect rubbish, rather than using their own (public-sector) workers, the costs of refuse collection fell. Many complaints were received, however, about a declining standard of service.

Even if meaningful comparisons of costs could be made, low costs are not the only objective of a nationalised industry. For instance, high-cost railway lines and bus routes may be kept open to provide a service to local communities. If any judgement is to be made about performance, the objectives must be clearly stated first.

> ?? Can you think of any test which would allow a fair assessment of the performance of nationalised industries?

Privatisation in the UK

Table 12.6 illustrates the history of privatisation in the UK.

When it came to power in 1979, the Conservative government gave a low priority to privatisation. The firms that were privatised in the first few years were companies that were already competing in the market, and where a change in ownership would make a relatively small difference to their operation. Some had only been partly owned by the government anyway, such as ICL, Ferranti and British Sugar.

After a few years, however, the government began to see the political advantages in privatisation:

- It was proving increasingly popular with the electorate, as more and more people became first-time share owners. There was often a substantial capital gain to be made as the share prices quickly rose after flotation.

Table 12.6 UK privatisations: 1979–

Year	Company	Business	Proceeds (£m)
1979	British Petroleum (1st part)[1]	Oil	276
	ICL[1]	Computers	37
1980	Fairey	Construction	22
	Ferranti[1,2]	Hi-tech industrial	55
	Motorway service stations (Dept of Transport)[2]	Motorway services	28
1981	British Aerospace (1st part)	Aerospace	149
	British Sugar Corporation[1]	Sugar refining	44
	Cable and Wireless (1st part)	Telecommunications systems	224
1982	Amersham International	Radio-chemicals	64
	National Freight Corporation[3]	Road haulage	54
	Britoil (1st part)	Oil	548
1983	Associated British Ports (1st part)[1,2]	Seaports	–34
	International Aeradio[2]	Aviation communications	60
	British Rail Hotels[2]	Hotels	51
	British Petroleum (2nd part)[1]	Oil	543
	Cable and Wireless (2nd part)	Telecommunications systems	275
1984	British Gas (onshore)[2]	Oil	82
	Associated British Ports (2nd part)[1,2]	Seaports	48
	Enterprise Oil	Oil	380
	Sealink[2]	Ferries	66
	Jaguar	Cars	297
	British Telecom (1st part)	Telecommunications	3916
	Inmos[2]	Computer systems	95
1985	British Aerospace (2nd part)	Aerospace	363
	British Shipbuilders (1st part)[2,3]	Various shipyards	220
	Britoil (2nd part)	Oil	449
	Cable and Wireless (3rd part)	Telecommunications systems	900
1986	British Shipbuilders (2nd part)[3]	Various shipyards	67
	Royal Ordnance (1st part)[2]	Weapons manufacture	11
	National Bus Company	Bus and coach carriers	260
	BA Helicopters[2]	Helicopter carriers	135
	British Gas	Gas	5400
1987	Unipart[3]	Car parts	30
	Leyland Bus[3]	Bus manufacture	4
	British Airways	Airline	900
	Royal Ordnance (2nd part)[2]	Weapons manufacture	190
	British Rail Doncaster Wagon Works[3]	Rolling stock manufacture	7
	Rolls-Royce	Aero engines	1080
	British Airports Authority (BAA)	Airports	1281
	British Petroleum (3rd part)[1]	Oil	7200
1988	British Steel	Steel	2500
	Rover Group (sold to British Aerospace)[2]	Car manufacture	–435
1989	Water companies (10)	Water supply and sewage treatment	3500
1990	Regional electricity companies (12)	Electricity supply and national grid	5300
1991	National Power and PowerGen (1st part)	Electricity generation	3200
	Scottish Electric	Electricity generation and supply	2200
	British Telecom (2nd part)	Telecommunications	11100
1994	British Coal (part)	Mines	800
1995	National Power and PowerGen (2nd part)	Electricity generation	1800
1996	Various train operating companies[4]	Trains	0
	Railtrack	Railway infrastructure	1930
	British Energy	8 nuclear power stations	2500
	Total privatisation proceeds		64 000

[1] In these cases the companies were only partly government owned in the first place.
[2] These were private sales to other companies.
[3] These were management and/or worker buyouts.
[4] Subsidies paid.

Sources: *Financial Statistics* (ONS); various newspaper articles.

- The revenues earned for the government were a convenient way of financing tax cuts.
- It was seen as the 'flagship' in the whole policy of 'rolling back the frontiers of the state' and establishing an 'enterprise culture'.

On being re-elected in 1983 the government embarked on a much more ambitious programme of privatisation. Over the next thirteen years, virtually all the major state monopolies such as telecommunications, gas, water, steel and electricity were sold. By the end of 1996, only the Post Office and parts of British Rail and British Coal remained in the public sector.

Forms of privatisation

Privatisation can take different forms:

- The introduction of private contractors to supply goods and services to parts of the public sector: e.g. private agencies supplying cleaners to hospitals or schools.
- The introduction into the public sector of firms selling directly to the public: e.g. private caterers on trains or in public-sector canteens.
- Selling various public-sector assets: e.g. the sale of council houses.
- Selling part or all of the public sector's shareholdings in otherwise private companies: e.g. the sale of BP shares.
- Selling a state-owned corporation by the sale of shares to the public (e.g. British Gas) or by selling it to another firm (e.g. the Rover Group to British Aerospace) or by selling it to the managers or workers in the firm (e.g. the National Freight Corporation).

All five forms of privatisation have been pursued since 1979, but we will concentrate on the last of these forms – the denationalising of nationalised industries/firms.

The arguments for privatisation

The arguments in favour of privatisation are to a large extent the same as the arguments *against* nationalisation.

Market forces

The first argument is that privatisation will expose these industries to market forces, from which will flow the benefits of greater efficiency, faster growth and greater responsiveness to the wishes of the consumer. There are three parts to this argument.

Greater competition in the goods market. If a privatised industry were previously a monopoly under nationalisation and were now split into competing parts (for example, separate power stations competing to sell electricity to different electricity distribution companies), then supernormal profits may be competed down. This will force the competing firms to keep their costs as low as possible in order to stay in business. It may also reduce the power of unions to increase wages unrelated to productivity, or to continue with inefficient working practices. Of course, if the privatised companies colluded with each other, the consumer might not benefit at all.

Even when a nationalised company was competing with other companies, it may still have been *cushioned* by government subsidies or by various barriers to competition (for example, when British Airways or the National Bus Company was granted sole licences to operate a particular route). If privatisation also involves **deregulation**, such that the newly privatised firm is forced to compete on *equal* terms with other firms, then again the consumer might gain from increased competition.

Greater competition for finance. After privatisation a company has to finance investment through the market: it must issue shares or borrow from financial institutions. In doing so, it will be competing for funds with other companies, and thus must be seen as capable of using these funds profitably.

Accountability to shareholders. Shareholders want a good return on their shares and will thus put pressure on the privatised company to perform well. If the company does not make sufficient profits, the share price will fall, and the company will be in danger of being taken over. The market for corporate control thus provides incentives for private firms to be efficient. There has been considerable takeover activity in the water and electricity industries, with most of the twelve regional electricity companies and several of the water companies being taken over, often by non-UK companies. The market for control of these regional monopolies is highly contestable.

Ultimately there is the threat of bankruptcy. A nationalised industry can always rely on the government to bale it out. A privatised company, so the argument goes, cannot.

Reduced government interference

In nationalised industries, managers may frequently be required to adjust their targets for political reasons. At one

DEFINITION

Deregulation Where the government removes official barriers to competition (e.g. licences and minimum quality standards).

time they may have to keep prices low as part of a government drive against inflation. At another they may have to raise their prices substantially in order to raise extra revenue for the government and help finance tax cuts. At another they may find their investment programmes cut as part of a government economy drive.

Privatisation frees the company from these constraints and allows it to make more rational economic decisions and plan future investments with greater certainty.

Reducing the public-sector borrowing requirement (PSBR)

The PSBR is the amount of money the public sector has to borrow each year to make up the shortfall between public-sector expenditure and public-sector receipts. Selling shares in privatised industries directly earns money for the government and thus reduces the amount it needs to borrow. Effectively, then, the government can use the proceeds of privatisation to finance tax cuts. Cuts in taxation not only are popular politically, but also are seen as a means of increasing incentives to work and invest, and thus as a means of stimulating increased output in the economy.

Increased share ownership

This is largely a political/ideological argument. The Conservative Party believes that 'true' public ownership is not state ownership. Although in theory the nationalised industries were owned by everyone in the UK, people did not feel a sense of ownership or participation. Instead the industries were run by 'bureaucrats'. This was not so after privatisation. Shares are now owned by members of the public, who thus feel a much greater sense of involvement. In this sense, then, the Conservatives argue that privatisation is really a return of industries to the public. It is a form of 'popular capitalism'.

By 1996 there were just over 9 million direct shareholders in Britain, some three times the number in 1979.[5] A large proportion of these new shareholders, however, only hold a very small number of shares in one or two of the privatised companies. Over half hold shares in only one company, and only around 100 000 hold shares in more than three companies. What is more, since 1990, when the number of shareholders peaked at over 11 million, the number has been falling.

The arguments against privatisation

The arguments against privatisation are in part a rebuttal of the arguments for, and in part a restatement of the arguments in favour of nationalisation.

Natural monopolies

The market forces argument for privatisation largely breaks down if a public monopoly is simply replaced by a private monopoly, as in the case of the water companies, which each have a monopoly in their own area. Critics of privatisation argue that at least a public-sector monopoly is not out to maximise profits and thereby exploit the consumer.

But will not competition for finance and pressure from shareholders force the privatised company to be more efficient? The problem here is that the monopoly has less need to rely on efficiency to make profits. It can make large profits for its shareholders simply by raising prices. In such cases the interests of the shareholders will be in conflict with the interests of customers.

Likewise monopoly profits can be used to finance investment. A monopoly has less need to rely on the capital market and is thus not put in competition with other firms for finance. Even if it were, it could simply use its promise of monopoly profits to attract new shareholders or bank loans.

Critics also dismiss the ultimate sanction of bankruptcy. In highly profitable industries like telecommunications and electricity, there *is* no fear of bankruptcy. Even in industries like the railways and coal, the stimulus to efficiency from the threat of loss of jobs for both managers and workers may be no greater than under nationalisation, which saw the closure of many unprofitable pits, steelworks and railway lines.

The public interest

Will the questions of externalities and social justice not be ignored after privatisation? The advocates of privatisation argue that externalities are a relatively minor problem, and anyway can be dealt with by appropriate taxes, subsidies and regulations even if the industry is privatised. Likewise questions of fairness and social justice can be dealt with by subsidies or regulations. A loss-making bus service can be subsidised so that it can be run profitably by a private bus company.

Critics argue that only the most glaring examples of externalities and injustice can be taken into account, given that the whole ethos of a private company is different from a nationalised one: private profit is the goal rather than public service. Externalities, they argue, are extremely widespread and need to be taken into account by the industry itself and not just by an occasionally intervening government.

[5] There are many more than this if people's indirect shareholdings via pension funds and insurance companies are counted. Only one-sixth of shares are held by individuals; this compares with just over one-half in the mid-1960s.

In assessing these arguments, a lot depends on the toughness of government legislation and the attitudes and powers of regulatory agencies after privatisation. For example, in the case of water and the environment, it depends on how tough the government's anti-pollution legislation is and on the vigour of the Environment Agency in insisting that environmental standards are maintained or improved.

The PSBR

The privatisation issue of shares will directly reduce the PSBR, it is true, but there are problems here:

- The nation's *capital* assets are being sold to finance *current* expenditure. This is what ex-prime minister Harold Macmillan called 'selling off the family silver'.
- The profits of nationalised industries also help to reduce the PSBR. Once sold, there will be no further profits accruing to the state from these industries. Of course, if these industries were made *much* more profitable by privatisation, the extra corporation tax they would pay would go some way towards offsetting this.
- Reducing the PSBR by privatisation does not increase the level of finance available to the private sector, since the money released is simply being used to buy the privatisation shares and is *not* being diverted to the rest of industry.
- There is a conflict between reducing the PSBR and avoiding monopoly exploitation. In order to earn the maximum revenue for the government from the privatisation issue, the industry must have the greatest possible potential for earning profit. This will be so if the industry is sold as a monopoly. But this directly conflicts with the aims of efficiency and the interests of the consumer, which are best served by splitting the industry up and selling it as competing parts.

Problems in the valuation of shares

It is very difficult for the government to predict the market price of shares in advance of their sale. If the price of the privatisation issue is set too high, the shares may be unattractive to shareholders. To guard against this eventuality, the government pays large fees to underwriters, who guarantee to buy up unsold shares. Thus when the sale of BP shares came just after the stock market collapse in October 1987, the underwriters had to buy up the vast bulk of these shares.

In practice, the government normally sets the offer price *below* the expected market price, in order to give purchasers a windfall gain and encourage them to buy future issues. This, however, means that the government has sacrificed revenue.

Just five years after privatisation, shares in the regional electricity companies were being sold for six times their flotation price.

Ideological objections

Critics argue that people are being sold shares in industries they already own, whereas those who do not buy them are actually being dispossessed. Privatisation, they claim, far from making ownership more widespread, actually further concentrates ownership. After privatisation, many shareholders sell their shares for a quick profit, and the industries end up with relatively few shareholders.

One radical alternative to privatisation would have been to issue everyone with an (equal) share certificate in the nationalised industries, on which was paid a dividend. The bigger the profit, the bigger the dividend. This, it is claimed, would have made the nationalised industries more accountable and given people a greater sense of ownership and involvement.

Ownership and the public interest

The debate about nationalisation and privatisation is so bound up with ideology that it is difficult to draw any firm conclusions. Nevertheless the following generalisations can be made:

- Ownership is only a minor determinant of an industry's efficiency. Both private- and public-sector monopolies can be inefficient. Both can be made much more efficient if they face effective competition. The issue, then, is much more one of liberalisation and deregulation than one of simple ownership.
- The functioning of both private- and public-sector industries depends on the attitudes of the government. Industries in both sectors can be given an 'easy ride' by government if it is prepared to provide subsidies or if it chooses not to regulate their behaviour. Alternatively, the government can be tough with both sectors. Nationalised industries can be forced to become more efficient through the imposition of cash limits on their expenditure; privatised industries can be forced to be more efficient through tough and rigorous price regulation.
- Externalities and questions of the public interest generally can be taken into account in both sectors. It is probably easier to impose a 'public-minded' regime in nationalised industries, but privatised firms too can be forced to behave in the public interest if the government is rigorous enough in its intervention.

Regulation: identifying the short-run optimum price and output

Privatised industries, if left free to operate in the market, will have monopoly power; they will create externalities; and they will be unlikely to take into account questions of fairness. An answer to these problems is for the government or some independent agency to regulate their behaviour so that they produce at the socially optimum price and output.

Exactly what this optimum is depends on what problems need to be taken into account. Take three cases. In the first, the privatised industry is a monopoly (perhaps it is a natural monopoly), but there are no other problems. In the second case there are also externalities to be considered, and in the third, questions of fairness too.

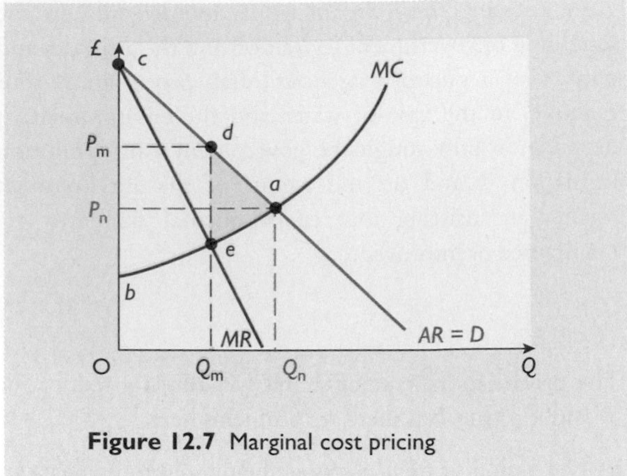

Figure 12.7 Marginal cost pricing

The privatised industry is a monopoly

The 'first-best' situation: P = MC. Assume that all other firms in the economy are operating under perfect competition, and thus producing where $P = MC$. This is the imaginary 'first-best' situation. If this were so, the privatised company should be required to follow the same pricing rule: $P = MC$. In Figure 12.7 this gives a price of P_n and an output of Q_n. But why should this be the rule?

If price (given by the demand curve) measures the marginal social benefit, and if the marginal social cost is given by the MC curve (remember that we are assuming no externalities), then net social gain from this industry is the area between these two curves. In Figure 12.7 this area is maximised with production at point *a*, giving an area *abc*. Pareto optimality is achieved.

If the company had instead been allowed to maximise profits, it would have produced only Q_m at a price P_m: where $MC = MR$. The social gain from production would have been only *bcde*: a *deadweight welfare loss* of the shaded area *aed*.

The theory of the 'second best': P = MC + Z. Now let us drop the assumption that the rest of the economy operates under perfect competition. If other industries on average are charging a price, say, 10 per cent above MC, then the theory of the second best suggests that the privatised company should also charge a price 10 per cent above MC. At least that way it will not cause a diversion of consumption away from relatively low-cost industries (at the margin) to a relatively high-cost one. The second-best rule is therefore to set $P = MC + Z$, where Z in this case is 10 per cent.

The privatised industry produces externalities

In the first-best situation the privatised industry should produce where price equals marginal *social* (not private) cost: $P = MSC$. The second-best solution is to produce where $P = MSC + Z$ (where Z is the average of other industries' price above their MSC).

The difficulty for the regulator in applying these rules in practice is to identify and measure the externalities: not an easy task! (See section 11.4.)

The behaviour of the privatised industry involves questions of fairness

If the government wishes the regulator to insist on a price below MC because it wishes to help certain groups (e.g. pensioners, children, rural dwellers, those below certain incomes), then what should this price be?

In practice, one of two simple rules could be followed. Either the industry could be required to charge uniform prices, despite higher costs for supplying certain categories of people (this could apply, for example, to rural customers of a privatised postal service); or a simple formula could be used (e.g. half price for pensioners and children). These are often the only practical solutions given the impossibility of identifying the specific needs of individual consumers.

Two further questions arise:

- Should the lower price be subsidised by central or local *government*, or by the privatised company and hence by *other users* of the service (i.e. by them paying *higher* prices)? Justice would suggest that support should come from the community as a whole – the taxpayer – and not just from other users of the service.
- If people require help, should they not be given *general* tax relief or benefits, rather than specifically subsidised services? For example, should pensioners not be paid better pensions, rather than be charged reduced fares on buses?

??

1. In the case of buses, subsidies are often paid by local authorities to support various loss-making routes. Is this the best way of supporting these services?
2. In the case of postal services, profitable parts of the service cross-subsidise the unprofitable parts. Should this continue if the industry is privatised?

Regulation: identifying the long-run optimum price and output

In the short run certain factors of production are fixed in supply. For example, electricity output can be increased by using *existing* power stations more fully, but the *number* of power stations is fixed. There will thus be a limit to the amount of electricity that can be generated in the short run. As that limit is approached, the marginal cost of electricity is likely to rise rapidly. For example, oil-fired power stations, which are more costly to operate will have to be brought on line.

In the long run all factors are variable. New power stations can be built. The *long*-run marginal costs therefore will probably not rise as more is produced. In fact they may even fall due to economies of scale.

Long-run marginal costs, however, unlike short-run marginal costs, will include the extra capital costs of increasing output. The long-run marginal cost of electricity will thus be all the extra costs of producing one more unit: namely, the extra operating costs (fuel, labour, etc.) *plus* the extra capital costs (power stations, pylons, etc.).

The rule for the optimum long-run price and output is simple. The regulator should require the industry to produce where price equals *long-run* marginal social cost (*LRMSC*). This is illustrated in Figure 12.8.

In the short run, optimum price and output are P_s and Q_s: where P = (short-run) *MSC*. This might mean that production is at quite a high cost: existing capital equipment is being stretched and diminishing returns have become serious.

In the long run, then, it will be desirable to increase capacity if *LRMSC* < *MSC*. Optimum long-run price and output are thus at P_L and Q_L: where P = *LRMSC*.

This is the rule for the first-best situation. In the second-best situation, the industry should produce where P = *LRMSC* + Z (where Z is the average of other industries' price above their *LRMSC*).

??

If the regulator imposed such rules, would they cause the firm to make a loss if it faced a downward-sloping *LRMSC* curve? (Clues: Where would the *LRAC* curve be relative to the *LRMC* curve? What would be the effect of externalities and the addition of the *Z* factor on the price?)

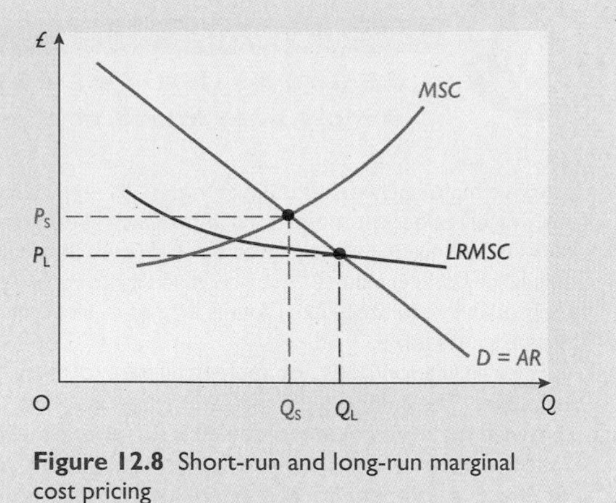

Figure 12.8 Short-run and long-run marginal cost pricing

Regulation in practice

To some extent the behaviour of privatised industries may be governed by general monopoly and restrictive practice legislation. For example, in the UK, privatised firms could be investigated by the Office of Fair Trading and if necessary referred to the Monopolies and Mergers Commission. If they engaged in any restrictive agreements, they could be referred to the Restrictive Practices Court.

In most cases, the problem is likely to be one of abuse of monopoly power rather than one of oligopolistic collusion. But it is this part of UK legislation that is weakest. It was increasingly realised by both government and commentators that specific regulation was required for the major privatised utilities, such as gas, electricity, water, telecommunications and railways.

In each of these five cases, plus airports, a separate regulatory office was established at the time of privatisation (see Box 12.7). Their legal authority is contained in the Act of privatisation, but their real power lies in the terms of their licences and price-setting formulae. These can be reviewed by negotiation between the regulator and the industry. If agreement cannot be reached, the MMC acts as an appeal court and its decision is binding.

The price-setting formulae are essentially of the '*RPI* minus *X*' variety. What this means is that the industries can raise their prices by the rate of increase in the retail price index (i.e. by the rate of inflation) *minus* a certain percentage (*X*) to take account of expected increases in efficiency. The idea is that this will force the industry to pass cost savings on to the consumer. Whether this will result in marginal cost pricing depends on what the price was in the first place. If the price was equal to marginal cost, and if the *X* factor is the amount by which the regulator expects the *MC* curve to shift downward (after

CASE STUDIES **BOX 12.7**

REGULATING THE PRIVATISED UTILITIES IN THE UK

A move away from 'free enterprise'?

The five major privatised utilities in the UK – electricity, gas, water, telecommunications and railways – all have certain of their prices regulated by their own particular regulatory office. Four of the privatised airports have their prices regulated too. Details of the regulation are shown in the table.

Price regulation does not apply to all parts of these industries. The parts where regulation *does* apply are shown in the third column of the table. In general these are the parts of the businesses where there is little chance for effective competition, and where, therefore, there is a risk of consumers being charged monopoly prices.

The price-setting formula adopted for each of these industries involves restricting percentage price increases to the percentage increase in the retail price index (*RPI*) plus or minus certain other percentages. These other percentages are known as *X*, *Y* and *K*. Their meanings are as follows:

X This is the negative figure in each of the formulae in the fourth column of the table. This *X* factor is an amount chosen by the regulator to reflect reductions in costs that can be expected in the industry through increases in productivity (e.g. through new technology or new working practices). It is thus a requirement that these cost reductions are passed on to the consumer.

Y This is an amount to reflect *increases* in costs that cannot be avoided by the producers (e.g. increases in the costs of gas supplies to British Gas, fuel costs of generating electricity, metering charges for water, extra security costs at airports to meet government requirements). The value of *Y* is not determined in advance, but will vary as costs change.

K This is an amount that water companies can add to cover the costs of environmental measures (e.g. improved sewage treatment). These environmental measures may be required of the industry by other agencies, such as the Environment Agency or the EU.

??

1. Under what circumstances would the formulae entail the industry having to *reduce* its prices?
2. Look through each of the parts of the industries in the final column and consider in what forms competition is likely to occur, and why, therefore, it is felt unnecessary for there to be price regulation. (For the electricity industry, see Box 12.9.)

Regulation of UK privatised utilities

Industry	Regulatory body	Parts regulated	Formula		Parts unregulated
Telecoms (British Telecom, Mercury, cable operators)	Office of Telecommunications (OFTEL)	Switched calls (national and international), line rentals	$RPI-3$ $RPI-4\frac{1}{2}$ $RPI-6\frac{1}{4}$ $RPI-7\frac{1}{2}$ $RPI-4\frac{1}{2}$	(1984–9) (1989–91) (1991–3) (1993–8) (1997–2000)	Payphone calls, customer premises equipment, telex, mobile radio, leased lines, etc.
Gas (British Gas/TransCo, independent gas producers and suppliers)	Office of Gas Supply (OFGAS)	Gas supplied to domestic users (up to 25K therms per annum to 1994 and 2.5K therms per annum from 1994 to 1998) Pipeline charges by TransCo to suppliers	*Supply* $RPI-2+Y$ $RPI-5+Y$ $RPI-4+Y$[2] *Pipeline charges* $RPI-5$ $RPI-6\frac{1}{2}$	 (1987–92) (1992–7) (1994–7) (1995–7) (1997–2001)	Price of gas supplied to industrial and commercial users (>25K therms to 1994, >2.5K therms from 1994); all supply from 1998 connection charges, appliance sales
Electricity (*Generators*: National Power, PowerGen, Nuclear Electric. *Distributors*: 12 regional companies. *Grid*: National Grid Company.)	Office of Electricity Regulation (OFFER)	Prices for transmission, distribution and supply <1 megawatt per annum up to 1994 < 0.1 megawatt per annum from 1994 to 1998	*Distribution* $RPI-0$ to $2\frac{1}{2}+Y$[1] $RPI-11$ to $17+Y$[1] $RPI-10$ to $13+Y$[1] $RPI-3+Y$ *Supply* $RPI-0+Y$ $RPI-2+Y$	 (1991–4) (1995/6) (1996/7) (1997–2000) (1991–4) (1994–8)	Generation; Supply: overall prices to customers consuming >1 megawatt per annum up to 1994 >0.1 megawatt per annum from 1994, electrical contracting appliances, etc.
Water (29 water and sewerage companies)	Office of Water Services (OFWAT) (pricing) Environment Agency (environmental control)	Standard domestic and non-domestic supply	$RPI+Y+K$ $RPI+1$[1] (includes *K* factor)	(1989–94) (1995–2005)	Bulk supplies to other users, water infrastructure charges (sewers, reservoirs, etc.)
Airports (BAA and Manchester Airport)	Civil Aviation Authority (CAA)	Airport charges at Heathrow, Gatwick, Manchester and Stansted	$RPI-4+Y$ $RPI-8$[3] $RPI-4$[3] $RPI-1$[3] $RPI-3$[4]	(1987–96) (1992–4) (1994/5) (1995–7) (1992–7)	Airport charges at other airports, commercial activities (e.g. shops, bars)
Railways (Railtrack plus train operating companies)	Office of the Rail Regulator (ORR) Office of Passenger Rail Franchising (OPRAF)	Charges by Railtrack to train operating companies	$RPI-8$ $RPI-2$	(1995/6) (1996–2001)	Charges by rail companies (but size of subsidy set at time of franchise)

Sources: various newspaper articles; regulatory offices.

[1] Depending on company. [2] Based on the Gas Cost Index (i.e. an index of North Sea gas prices) reduced by an efficiency factor. [3] Excluding Manchester Airport. [4] Manchester Airport.

CASE STUDIES BOX 12.8

REGULATION US-STYLE

The use of rate-of-return regulation

In the USA, utilities such as electricity, gas, water and telecommunications have for the most part always been private companies (although a few are state owned). To prevent the abuse of monopoly power, the utilities are regulated by federal or state governments through *regulatory commissions*. Unlike in the UK, where prices are regulated according to an '*RPI* minus *X*' formula (see Box 12.7), the prime focus of US regulation is the company's 'rate of return' (i.e. its rate of *profit*).

The system involves limiting prices to a level which will give a normal rate of profit. In other words, the company will be allowed to charge a price equal to the average cost of production, where average cost includes a 'fair rate of return on capital'. The actual calculations are normally done using total revenue and total cost according to the following formula:

$$TR^* = TVC + \pi K$$

where TR^* is the maximum permitted total revenue for that year (known as the 'revenue requirement'), TVC is total variable costs (known as 'operating expenses'), K is the total replacement cost of capital (known as the 'rate base') and π is the permitted annual rate of return, as a percentage of the rate base.

To give an example: if a firm's variable costs (TVC) were \$4 million, the rate base (K) were \$20 million and a normal rate of return (π) were judged by the regulatory commission to be 10 per cent, then according to the formula, the firm would be permitted to charge a price that would yield a revenue requirement (TR^*) of:

$$\$4\text{m} + 0.1(\$20\text{m}) = \$6\text{m}$$

Problems with rate-of-return regulation

There has been growing concern in the USA over the effects of using rate-of-return regulation. The argument is that it encourages inefficiency.

First there is the problem of *allocative inefficiency*. The US system will entail the company setting a price equal to long-run *average* cost. The socially efficient position, however, is where price equals long-run *marginal* cost.

Then there is the potentially more serious problem of *productive or technical inefficiency* (not using factors in the way that maximises output) and *X inefficiency* (lack of motivation to cut wasteful expenditure and to introduce cost-cutting measures). What is the incentive for a regulated firm to produce at a lower cost? If it introduces new technology or improved working practices that have the effect of increasing profit, the regulator would insist on a lower revenue requirement and hence a lower price. The extra profit would simply be taken away.

In fact, there is an incentive for the firms to let costs *rise*. The costs of higher salaries and more luxurious offices, for example, can simply be passed on to the consumer in higher prices!

With *unregulated* monopolies, at least there is pressure from shareholders for the firms to be efficient. There is also competition in the market for corporate control: managers are afraid that if their firm is inefficient, other firms may mount a takeover bid. With the regulated utilities in the USA, however, these pressures are absent. Shareholders have nothing to gain from increased efficiency if profits are not allowed to increase as a result. Also there is no benefit to other firms in mounting a takeover bid. If they were successful, they would merely find themselves the subject of regulation.

Then there is the problem of *regulatory lag*. In periods of rapidly rising costs, it may take some time before the regulatory commission sanctions a price increase (through a higher revenue requirement). In the meantime the firm may be forced to operate at a loss.

?? Do these arguments against rate-of-return regulation help support the case for *deregulation* (see Box 6.5)?

taking inflation into account), then the formula could result in marginal cost pricing.

?? Why might it equally result in average cost pricing?

The licence also permits the regulator to monitor other aspects of the behaviour of the industry and to require it to take various measures. For example, OFGAS (the gas industry regulator) has required the industry to allow other gas suppliers to use its pipelines and not to refuse to supply customers. Generally, however, the approach has been one of negotiation with the industry. The sanction has been the threat of appeal to the MMC, which could then alter the licence, if it so chose, to force the industry to behave in a certain way.

Appeal to the MMC to alter the licence or the price formula is time consuming, expensive and unpredictable. Both regulator and the industry, therefore, would rather come to an agreement. Regulation in the UK thus tends to involve bargaining and negotiation rather than the application of strict rules. In one way this weakens the power of the regulator. There is not the same backing of

CASE STUDIES

SELLING POWER TO THE PEOPLE

Attempts to introduce competition into the electricity industry

Regulation is generally seen to be less effective than competition in protecting the interests of the consumer. But with the privatisations prior to electricity, there had been little attempt to break up the industries being sold. The political pressure on the government for quick sales, and the desire to maximise the revenue from the sales, persuaded the relevant ministers to sell the industries as monopolies, or virtual monopolies. With electricity, however, there was considerable debate on ways in which competition could be introduced.

The industry before privatisation

Under nationalisation the industry in England and Wales was organised as a monopoly with the Central Electricity Generating Board (CEGB) supplying 99 per cent of all electricity. It operated the power stations and transmitted the electricity round the country via the national grid. However, the CEGB did not sell electricity directly to the consumer; rather it sold it to twelve regional boards, which in turn supplied it to the consumer.

Privatisation of the industry

Various methods of privatising the industry were proposed. At one extreme it was proposed to leave the industry as it was, simply transferring the public monopoly into the private sector. It was suggested by the CEGB that this was the simplest and best way to ensure the existing level of service and retain the full economies of scale. Predictably, this view was seen by most observers to be quite at odds with the desire for greater competition.

At the other extreme it was proposed to split the CEGB into five companies, each in competition. The national grid would be a separate company and would buy from the cheapest source. This structure was seen as the most desirable if competition was the principal aim of the sale. But even so there would be the possibility of oligopolistic collusion between the generating companies.

What transpired in 1990 and 1991 was a compromise between these two positions. Generation in England and Wales was split into three main companies. Two of these were privatised: National Power (with just over 50 per cent) and PowerGen (with nearly 30 per cent). The third, Nuclear Electric, which contained all the nuclear power stations, remained nationalised. The government was advised that this could not be privatised, given the limited life span of the nuclear stations and the very high decommissioning costs at the end of their life (they nevertheless have very low running costs). Nevertheless, in 1996, the eight most modern nuclear power stations of Nuclear Electric and Scottish Nuclear were privatised as British Energy. The eight were sold at a price equal to that of building just one!

The twelve regional boards were privatised in 1991 as separate regional electricity companies (RECs), which were responsible for local distribution and supply to consumers. They would also be permitted to build their own power stations if they chose. The RECs jointly owned the national grid, but it was run independently. This was eventually sold as a separate company in 1996.

An Office of Electricity Regulation (OFFER) was set up to control prices in parts of the industry where there was no competition, but it was hoped that the new structure would allow a growth in competition which would make regulation increasingly unnecessary. So what was the nature of this competition? After all, National Power had over half of the generating capacity; the National Grid Company had a natural monopoly of electricity transmission; and the twelve RECs had a natural monopoly of distribution in each of their areas.

At the centre of the privatised system is a new wholesale market in electricity.

The wholesale market for electricity

The wholesale market for electricity involves sales into and purchases from what is known as the 'electricity pool'. The various parts of the electricity industry and their relationship to the pool are shown in the diagram.

Electricity is produced by the *generators* (the power stations). The electricity is *transmitted* along the power lines of the National Grid Company plc (NGC) to different parts of the country. It is then transmitted locally by the *distributors* (the twelve distribution companies), which in most cases are also the *suppliers* of electricity to the customers (homes, local authorities and businesses).

The diagram also shows how the pool system works. Customers buy their electricity from suppliers, normally at fixed tariffs. The suppliers buy their electricity wholesale from the electricity pool, while the generators sell electricity to the pool. The pool is operated by NGC. It is the job of NGC in managing the pool to balance demand and supply, by ensuring that an equilibrium price is set, and that generators are always brought on line to meet any unexpected demand. NGC is thus responsible for setting the price (through its subsidiary NGC Settlements Ltd (NGCS)), and for bringing additional power stations on line as required.

In addition to the pool price, the suppliers also pay transmission charges to the distributors (often themselves) and to NGC. The generators also pay transmission charges to NGC. Because transmission is a natural monopoly, both nationally and locally, these charges are regulated by OFFER.

BOX 12.9

Setting the pool price

NGCS sets a pool purchase price (the price to be paid to the generators) and a pool selling price (the price to be charged to the purchasing suppliers). The selling price will generally be slightly higher than the purchase price to cover the various administrative costs of the system.

A separate purchase price and selling price is set for each half-hour of the day. Thus in any 24 hours, there will be 48 purchase and 48 selling prices. Provisional prices for the whole 24-hour period are made available by NGCS to generators and purchasers by about 16:00 on the day before. Final prices are published 24 days after the day in question, with settlement due 28 days after. The table illustrates this. It gives provisional prices for 16 November 1995 published on that day in the *Financial Times*, and final prices for the date 28 days previously.

To set the prices, NGC first works out the likely demand for electricity throughout the day. To do this its experts will need to examine the weather forecast, since the colder the weather, the greater the demand for electricity. It will also need to examine the TV schedules. For example, when a popular soap opera ends, the demand for electricity soars as people get up and put the kettle on for a cup of tea or coffee!

Having estimated demand, NGC will now need to ensure that there is sufficient supply to meet it. By 10:00 each day, each generator makes an offer bid for the day ahead for each of its power stations. This will state how much electricity it is prepared to supply and at what price. NGCS then arranges these bids from the lowest price upwards until all anticipated demand is met. The highest-price bid which is necessary to accept, known as the *system marginal price* (SMP), then becomes the price on which the pool purchase price is based. In other words, the highest accepted bid price is the price paid to *all* the generating stations in use.

Prices for electricity determined for the purposes of the electricity pooling and settlement arrangements in England and Wales

	Provisional price for trading on 16.11.95	Final prices for trading on 19.10.95	
1/2 hour period ending	Pool purchase price (£/MWh)	Pool purchase price (£/MWh)	Pool selling price (£/MWh)
0030	9.07	8.97	8.97
0100	34.53	8.90	8.90
0130	34.53	8.90	8.90
0200	34.53	8.94	8.94
0230	34.53	8.94	8.94
0300	9.04	8.90	8.90
0330	9.02	8.90	8.90
0400	9.02	8.90	8.90
0430	9.02	8.90	8.90
0500	8.98	8.90	8.90
0530	8.97	9.00	9.00
0600	8.98	8.97	8.97
0630	9.07	9.02	9.02
0700	19.74	15.85	17.26
0730	20.71	16.76	18.19
0800	20.96	29.11	30.62
0830	34.84	32.99	34.51
0900	34.86	33.04	34.58
0930	34.87	16.96	18.46
1000	35.86	16.97	18.47
1030	35.86	16.97	18.47
1100	35.87	16.99	18.49
1130	45.15	20.09	21.61
1200	45.18	20.15	21.68
1230	45.18	32.98	34.50
1300	45.18	32.89	34.39
1330	38.78	16.83	18.29
1400	37.23	16.79	18.23
1430	35.86	16.76	18.19
1500	35.86	16.75	18.18
1530	14.87	9.20	9.20
1600	14.91	16.79	18.24
1630	83.07	19.05	20.53
1700	135.28	17.01	18.53
1730	156.24	19.24	20.78
1800	128.58	20.05	21.85
1830	77.98	31.57	34.01
1900	53.10	60.40	62.87
1930	44.29	59.60	61.87
2000	41.44	29.04	30.71
2030	35.93	16.84	18.29
2100	38.14	16.74	18.16
2130	33.69	16.71	18.13
2200	21.06	16.71	18.12
2230	20.71	16.71	18.12
2300	13.07	16.71	18.12
2330	13.07	13.27	14.69
2400	9.00	9.02	9.02

Prices are determined for every half-hour in each 24-hour period. Prices are in pounds per megawatt-hour, rounded to two decimal places.

Competition within the system

So how does this wholesale market encourage competition? In theory, competition can occur in two ways.

First, the individual generating stations are supposedly put in competition with each other in the daily bidding process, knowing that the NGC will always bring on line the cheapest power station not already in use when consumer demand rises, and turn off the most expensive one when demand falls. In practice, however, there is a danger of oligopolistic collusion. Given that the nuclear power stations have the lowest marginal costs, they *always* operate. This means that National Power and PowerGen between them own virtually all the power stations that determine the SMP and hence the actual

CASE STUDIES

SELLING POWER TO THE PEOPLE

Attempts to introduce competition into the electricity industry

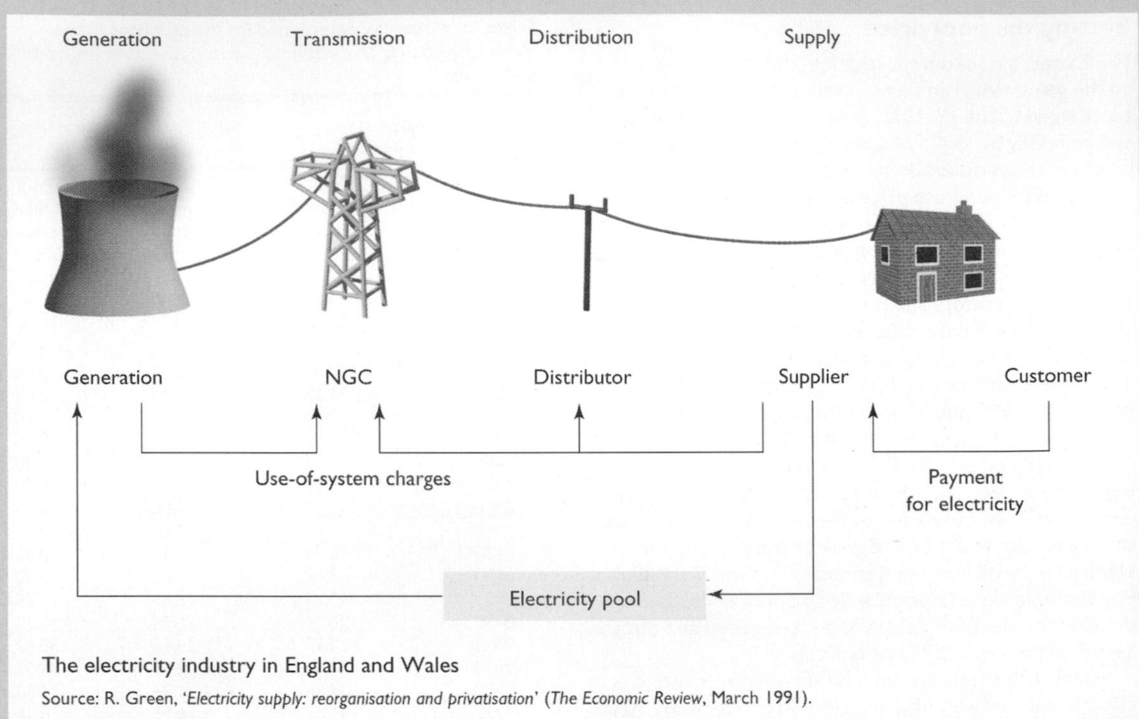

The electricity industry in England and Wales

Source: R. Green, '*Electricity supply: reorganisation and privatisation*' (*The Economic Review*, March 1991).

half-hourly price. Nevertheless, there has been a modest increase in competition in generation. For example, many of the distributors have built or are building their own gas-fired power stations.

Second, many customers are able to choose their suppliers. Since 1990 all customers consuming more than 1 megawatt (the electricity consumed by the equivalent of 1000 one-bar electric fires) have been able to buy from any supplier of their choice. These customers are typically medium-to-large firms or offices. The suppliers could be other distribution companies, or generators, or any other company obtaining a supply licence to bid from the pool. The local distribution company is obliged to transmit this electricity on behalf of other suppliers at the same (regulated) price that it charges itself. Since 1994 all customers consuming more than 0.1 MW have been able to choose their supplier, and from 1998 *any* customer, including you and I, can choose their supplier.

The development of new technology could increase competition further. So-called 'smart meters' could be installed in your home. These meters will be able to

law as in a more formal system. In another way, however, the informality strengthens the regulator. There is not the same accountability to Parliament or the courts. Instead, the regulator is given a virtually free hand to make demands of the industry, with the ultimate threat of going to the MMC for an alteration of the licence if the industry does not toe the line.

Assessing the system of regulation in the UK

The system that has evolved in the UK has various advantages over that employed in the USA and elsewhere (see Box 12.8):

- It is a *discretionary* system, with the regulator able to judge individual examples of the behaviour of the industry on their own merits. The regulator has a detailed knowledge of the industry which would not be available to government ministers or other bodies such as the Office of Fair Trading. The regulator could thus be argued to be the best person to decide on whether the industry is acting in the public interest.
- The system is *flexible*, since it allows for the licence and price formula to be changed as circumstances change.
- The '*RPI* minus *X*' formula provides an *incentive* for the privatised firms to be as efficient as possible. If they

communicate with suppliers via minute frequency modulations down the electricity cable. This will allow the meters to select electricity from the cheapest supplier and to display the current price, which can change half-hourly with the pool price. Appliances such as immersion heaters can be automatically switched on when the price falls below a certain level. The meters can display the current price, so that you can choose when to do your ironing!

The hope is that this will put suppliers in fierce competition with each other. They could still offer customers a fixed-price tariff, but they could now also offer one where the price varied with the pool price. Already many companies that use a significant amount of electricity are investing a lot of time and effort in rescheduling their production to times of the day when electricity is the cheapest.

Will competition replace regulation?

Regulation of supply is disappearing. As customers become able to choose their supplier, so there will no longer be regulation of supply. Thus between 1994 and 1998, only supply to customers consuming less than 0.1 MW has been regulated. From 1998 there is no regulation of supply at all. Regulation remains, however, for transmission and distribution charges. Here there is a natural monopoly.

What the electricity privatisation has demonstrated is that many industries are complex. Parts may be a natural monopoly. Here regulation is essential. But parts may be potentially competitive. Here it is up to the government or regulator to ensure that competition is allowed to flourish.

A significant step towards this objective was taken when the regulator insisted that National Power sell three of its largest power stations (4GW of plant) to independent generators during 1996. Similarly, PowerGen was required to divest itself of 2GW of plant. The net effect was a 10 per cent reduction in the combined capacity of the two companies. In addition to seeing their earnings fall, these two companies now had to face new competitors.

There is, however, a serious threat to competition. This is from the merging of generation and distribution. Examples include the takeover bids in 1995 by National Power and PowerGen for Southern Electric and Midlands Electricity respectively (the second and third largest RECs). Although these were blocked by the President of the Board of Trade, it was only after they had been cleared by the Monopolies and Mergers Commission. A similar threat comes from the fact that the new gas-fired power stations are mainly owned by the regional electricity companies, which may buy electricity from themselves at inflated prices which are then passed on to their customers. The regulator warned that a vertically integrated industry would be much harder to control – if contracts between separate companies were replaced by internal arrangements within a single company. These problems will become less, however, as consumers are increasingly able to choose between suppliers.

Nevertheless, by virtually controlling the pool, the generators have seen their profits soar. As a result, most of the benefits from reduced costs have gone to shareholders, not to consumers. In the first five years after privatisation, the share prices of the generators and RECs rose by nearly four times as much as the stock market average.

??

1. Examine the pool prices in the table. Account for the fluctuations in the price.
2. What effect will customers paying prices that vary with pool prices have on the amount that pool prices fluctuate?

can lower their costs by more than X, they will, in theory, be able to make larger profits and keep them. If, on the other hand, they do not succeed in reducing costs sufficiently, they will make a loss. There is thus a continuing pressure on them to cut costs. (In the US system, where *profits* rather than *prices* are regulated, there is little incentive to increase efficiency, since any cost reductions must be passed on to the consumer in lower prices, and do not, therefore, result in higher profits.)

There are, however, some inherent problems with the way in which regulation operates in the UK:

- The '*RPI* minus X' formula was designed to provide an incentive for the firms to cut costs. But if X is too low, the firm might make excessive profits. Frequently regulators have underestimated the scope for cost reductions resulting from new technology and reorganisation, and have thus initially set X too low. As a result, instead of X remaining constant for five years, as intended, new higher values for X have been set after only one or two years. But this then leads to the same problem as with the US system. The incentive for the industry to cut costs will be removed. What is the point of being more efficient if the regulator is merely going to insist on a higher value for *X* and thus take away the extra profits?

- A large amount of power is vested in a regulator who is unelected and largely unaccountable. What guarantee is there that the regulator's perception of the public interest is the same as that of the government?
- Regulation is becoming increasingly complex. This makes it difficult for the industries to plan and may lead to a growth of 'short-termism'. One of the claimed advantages of privatisation was to give greater independence to the industries from short-term government interference and allow them to plan for the longer term. In practice one type of interference may have been replaced by another.
- As regulation becomes more detailed and complex, and as the regulator becomes more and more involved in the detailed running of the industry, so managers and regulators will become increasingly involved in a game of strategy: each trying to outwit the other. Information will become distorted and time and energy will be wasted in playing this game of cat and mouse.
- Alternatively there is the danger of **regulatory capture**. As regulators become more and more involved in their industry and get to know the senior managers at a personal level, so they are increasingly likely to see the managers' point of view. They will begin to adopt the values and modes of thinking of the industry and will become less and less tough. Commentators do not believe that this has happened yet: the regulators are generally independently minded. But it is a danger for the future.

One way in which the dangers of ineffective or over-intrusive regulation can be avoided is to replace regulation with competition wherever this is possible. Indeed, one of the major concerns of the regulators has been to do just this. (See Boxes 6.4 and 12.9 for ways in which competition has been increased in the gas and electricity industries.)

Increasing competition in the privatised industries

Where natural monopoly exists, competition is impossible in a free market. Of course, the industry *could* be broken up by the government, with firms prohibited from owning more than a certain percentage of the industry. But this would lead to higher costs of production. Firms would be operating further back up a downward-sloping long-run average cost curve.

But many parts of the privatised industries are *not* natural monopolies. Generally it is only the *grid* that is a natural monopoly. In the case of gas and water, it is the pipelines. It would be wasteful to duplicate these. In the case of electricity, it is the power lines: the national grid and the local power lines. In the case of the railways, it is the track. *Other* parts of these industries are potentially competitive. There could be many generators of electricity, provided they had access to the national and local grids. There could be many producers of gas, provided they had access to the pipelines. There could be many operators of trains, provided they could all use the same track with central timetabling and signalling.

Even for the parts where there *is* a natural monopoly, they could be made *contestable* monopolies. One way of doing this is by granting operators a licence for a specific period of time. This is known as **franchising**. This has been the approach used for the independent television companies in the UK. Once a company has been granted the licence, it has the monopoly over independent television broadcasting in that area. But the awarding of the licences can be highly competitive, with rival companies putting in competitive bids, in terms of both price and quality of service.

?? How could the grids mentioned above be made contestable?

In those parts of the privatised industries which *are* potentially competitive, although many were privatised as monopolies or virtual monopolies, the regulators have been attempting to introduce competition. Examples include the following:

- Preventing or limiting access to parts of the market by the existing producer (e.g. British Gas had to limit its share of the industrial gas market to 40 per cent by 1995).
- Forcing owners of a grid to grant competitors access to it at competitive rates (e.g. alternative electricity suppliers being able to supply customers through the power lines of the local distribution company at the same rate that the local company charges; Mercury being allowed to use British Telecom telephone lines).

DEFINITIONS

Regulatory capture Where the regulator is persuaded to operate in the industry's interests rather than those of the consumer.

Franchising Where a firm is granted the licence to operate a given part of an industry for a specified length of time.

- Preventing restrictive practices by existing producers (e.g. preventing BT from refusing to supply telephone lines to customers not using BT telephones; British Gas not being allowed to charge discriminatory low prices to industrial customers where there is a threat of competition from alternative gas suppliers).
- Removing any legal barriers to the entry of new firms (e.g. removing the need for licences for all but natural monopolies; changing the original terms of privatisation to allow the entry of competitors).
- Removing the grid from the ownership of the major company (e.g. splitting British Gas into separate pipeline and supply companies (see Box 6.4); re-privatising the national electricity grid in 1996 as a separate company from the twelve regional electricity companies, which had previously owned it; privatising Railtrack as a separate company from British Rail, which continued to operate trains in most of the country).

But despite attempts to introduce competition into the privatised industries, they are still dominated by giant companies. Even if they are no longer strictly monopolies, they still have considerable market power. Competition is far from being perfect! The scope for price leadership or other forms of oligopolistic collusion is great. However, regulation through the price formula has been progressively abandoned as elements of competition have been introduced. The intention is ultimately to confine regulation to the operation of the grids: the parts that are natural monopolies. This assumes that competition really will be effective in protecting the public interest.

SECTION SUMMARY

1. The market failure arguments for nationalisation include the problems of monopoly power (due to industries being natural monopolies or there being high entry costs), lack of investment, lack of planning and co-ordination of key infrastructural industries, large external costs and benefits, and a lack of provision of non-profitable but socially desirable services. In addition 'lame duck', strategic and industrial relations arguments have been used to justify nationalisation.
2. From around 1983 the Conservative government in the UK embarked on a large programme of privatisation. The justification was partly ideological and partly to do with the perceived economic failures of the nationalised industries and their better prospects under private ownership.
3. The economic arguments for privatisation include: greater competition, not only in the goods market but in the market for finance and for corporate control; reduced government interference; reducing the PSBR; and making these industries more accountable to the public via share ownership.
4. The economic arguments against privatisation are largely the market failure arguments that were used to justify nationalisation. In reply the advocates of privatisation argue that these problems can be overcome through appropriate regulation and increasing the amount of competition.
5. Privatisation raises money for the government and thus in the short term the government can use these revenues to finance tax cuts. There is, however, a potential conflict between this objective and that of making the industry as competitive as possible. The more competition is introduced, the less profitable it is likely to be, and thus the less revenue is likely to be raised from the share flotation. There is also the problem of deciding the share issue price.
6. Assessing the performance of nationalised and privatised industries is difficult given the political constraints under which they have operated. It is possible for both or neither to be run in 'the public interest' (however defined): it depends crucially on the government's attitude towards them, the degree of competition they face and the regulatory framework within which they operate.
7. Whether under public or regulated private ownership, the question arises about the socially optimum price and output for these industries. In the first-best world it would be socially efficient to set price equal to marginal social cost. In the real world this is not the case given that prices elsewhere are not equal to marginal social costs. Ideally, prices should still *reflect* marginal social costs, but there are difficulties in identifying and measuring social costs.
8. In the long run, the optimum price and output will be where price equals long-run marginal social cost. If $LRMSC < MSC$ it will be desirable to invest in additional capacity.
9. Regulation in the UK has involved setting up regulatory offices for the major privatised utilities. These generally operate informally, using negotiation and bargaining to persuade the industries to behave in the public interest. As far as prices are concerned, the industries are required to abide by an '*RPI* minus *X*' formula. This forces them to pass potential cost reductions on to the consumer. At the same time they are allowed to retain any additional profits gained from cost reductions greater than X. This

continued

provides them with an incentive to achieve even greater increases in efficiency. The regulator can seek a revision of the industry's licence or price formula. If the firm does not agree, an appeal can be made to the MMC whose decision is binding.

10. Regulation in the UK has the advantages of giving the regulator discretion to judge the behaviour of the industry on its merits; of being flexible enough to take account of new circumstances as they arise; and potentially of providing incentives for the industry to be efficient.
11. It has the following problems, however: it *discourages* efficiency if cost reductions simply lead to the regulator demanding a higher value of X; the regulator may not act in the way the elected government would like; regulation may become excessively complex, which could lead to growing short-termism and game playing by both industry and regulator; the regulator may become 'captured' by the values of the industry and thus cease to look after the public interest.
12. Many parts of the privatised industries are not natural monopolies. In these parts, competition may be a more effective means of pursuing the public interest. Various attempts have been made to make the privatised industries more competitive, often at the instigation of the regulator. Nevertheless, considerable market power remains in the hands of many privatised firms, and thus the need for regulation will continue.

??? END-OF-CHAPTER QUESTIONS ???

1. Assume that as traffic density increases along a given stretch of road, there comes a point when traffic begins to slow down. The following table gives the times taken for a car to travel the stretch of road (in minutes) according to the number of cars entering the road per minute.

Cars entering the road	5	6	7	8	9	10	11
Journey time	10	10	11	13	16	22	30

   (a) Copy out the table and add the following rows: (i) total journey time for all cars; (ii) extra journey time as traffic increases by one more car (marginal social time cost); (iii) additional time cost imposed on other road users for each additional car entering the road (marginal external time cost). (See Table 12.2.)

   (b) Assume that time is valued at 1p per minute. On a graph, plot the marginal private time cost (journey time) and the marginal social time cost.

   (c) Assume that electronic road pricing is introduced. What charge should be levied when traffic density reaches (i) six cars per minute; (ii) eight cars per minute; (iii) eleven cars per minute?

   (d) What additional information would you need in order to work out the socially efficient traffic density on this particular stretch of road?

2. Compare the relative merits of increased road fuel taxes, electronic road pricing and tolls as means of reducing urban traffic congestion. Why is the price inelasticity of demand for private car transport a problem here, whichever of the three policies is adopted? What could be done to increase the price elasticity of demand?
3. How would you set about measuring the external costs of road transport?
4. Should governments or regulators always attempt to eliminate the supernormal profits of monopolists/oligopolists?
5. Compare the relative merits of banning certain types of market *structure* with banning certain types of market *behaviour*.
6. Consider the argument that whether an industry is in the public sector or private sector has far less bearing on its performance than the degree of competition it faces.
7. Should regulators of utilities that have been privatised into several separate companies allow (i) horizontal mergers (within the industry); (ii) vertical mergers; (iii) mergers with firms in other industries?
8. If an industry regulator adopts an RPI – X formula for price regulation, is it desirable that the value of X should be adjusted as soon as cost conditions change?

Macroeconomic issues I
Economic growth, unemployment and inflation

13.1 The scope of macroeconomics

The distinction between microeconomics and macroeconomics

We turn now to *macroeconomics*. This will be the subject for the second half of the book.

As we have already seen, *microeconomics* focuses on *individual* markets. It studies the demand for and supply of oranges, videos, petrol and haircuts; of bricklayers, doctors, office accommodation and blast furnaces. It examines the choices people make *between* goods, and what determines their relative prices and the relative quantities produced.

In macroeconomics we take a much loftier view. We examine the economy as a whole. We still examine demand and supply, but now it is the *total* level of spending in the economy and the *total* level of production. In other words, we examine *aggregate demand* and *aggregate supply*.

We still examine output, but now it is *national* output. What determines the size of national output? What causes it to grow? Why do growth rates fluctuate? These are typical macroeconomic questions to do with output.

We still examine employment, but now it is *national* employment. Here we will want answers to the question: what causes unemployment?

We still examine the determination of prices, but now it is the *general* level of prices. In particular we will want to know what causes prices to rise: what causes *inflation*.

In macroeconomics we will not just focus on a country in isolation. We will need to examine its economic relationships with the rest of the world. We will ask: what determines the level of its imports and exports? What determines the rate of exchange of its currency into other nations' currencies? How do these relationships with other countries affect the domestic economy?

These are all big issues: the sort of issues we constantly read about in the papers and hear about on radio and television; the sort of issues that the electorate is concerned about when deciding which way to vote in elections. In particular we will be focusing on four issues. These are the issues that seem of most concern to the electorate and hence to governments anxious to retain office.

The major macroeconomic issues

Economic growth

A growing economy means that there will be more goods and services for people to consume.

Some countries have grown more rapidly than others over the years. The UK has generally had a poor **economic growth** record compared with its major industrial rivals. The most spectacular growth rates have been seen in the newly industrialised countries (NICs): countries such as Brazil, South Korea, Singapore, Malaysia and Hong Kong. Table 13.1 shows the average annual growth in output between 1960 and 1998 for selected countries. As you can see the differences between countries are quite substantial. But why do countries grow at different rates? We will need to discover the causes of economic growth and what policies governments can pursue in order to achieve faster long-term growth.

But it is not just long-term growth with which governments are concerned: there is a short-term problem too. Growth fluctuates (see figure in Box 13.1, p. 404). In some years output may grow at 3 per cent or more. In other years, however, the economy may slide into recession with negative economic growth. By negative growth we mean a fall in output. (In the UK, the official definition of a recession is when negative economic growth occurs for more than two quarters.)

DEFINITION

Rate of economic growth The percentage increase in output over a twelve-month period.

Table 13.1 Economic growth (average % per annum), unemployment (average %) and inflation (average % per annum)

	France	Germany	Italy	Japan	UK	USA	EU (15)	OECD	Brazil	Malaysia	Singapore
Growth											
1960–9	7.5	4.4	5.3	10.9	2.9	4.3	3.5	4.6	5.4	6.5	8.8
1970–9	3.2	2.6	3.8	4.3	2.0	2.8	3.2	3.6	8.1	7.9	8.3
1980–9	2.2	1.8	2.4	4.0	2.4	2.5	2.2	2.6	3.0	5.8	6.1
1990–8	1.6	2.5	1.5	1.9	1.6	2.1	1.9	2.2	2.0	7.8	7.8
Unemployment											
1960–9	1.5	0.9	5.1	1.3	2.2	4.1	2.5	2.5	n.a.	n.a.	n.a.
1970–9	3.7	2.3	6.4	1.7	4.5	6.1	4.0	4.3	n.a.	n.a.	n.a.
1980–9	9.0	5.9	9.5	2.5	10.0	7.2	9.3	7.3	n.a.	6.2	3.6
1990–8	11.3	7.6	10.7	2.8	8.4	5.8	10.1	7.3	n.a.	3.4	2.6
Inflation											
1960–9	4.2	3.2	4.4	4.9	4.1	2.8	3.7	3.1	46.1	–0.3	1.1
1970–9	9.4	5.0	13.9	9.0	13.0	6.8	10.3	9.2	38.6	7.3	5.9
1980–9	7.3	2.9	11.2	2.5	7.4	5.5	7.4	8.9	227.8	2.2	2.5
1990–8	2.1	2.8	4.3	1.3	3.9	3.1	3.5	5.2	978.5	3.7	2.5

Governments, therefore, would like not only to achieve high long-run rates of growth, but also to achieve stable growth and avoid recessions.

Unemployment

In the 'Great Depression' of the inter-war period, mass unemployment was experienced in most industrialised countries. In the UK, unemployment reached 23 per cent of the working population by 1932. But after the Second World War, people believed that the problem of unemployment had been largely solved. In the 1950s and 1960s, unemployment throughout the industrialised world rarely exceeded 3 per cent.

In the 1970s, however, confidence in the ability of governments to prevent unemployment was gradually eroded again as unemployment began to rise. Then in the early 1980s, the world plunged into a recession. Unemployment soared. By 1983 the average unemployment in the OECD countries[1] had reached 8.5 per cent. In the UK it was 12.5 per cent. Then as countries' economies began to grow again in the mid-1980s, unemployment began to fall, only to rise once more with the recession of the early 1990s. As recovery followed this recession, so unemployment once more began to fall. But even by 1998, some five years after the end of the recession, the OECD unemployment rate remained over 7 per cent: some three times higher than the average of the 1950s and 1960s.

So, what causes unemployment? Why was it high in the 1930s, the early 1980s and the early 1990s, and so low in the 1950s and 1960s? Can the government do anything about unemployment, and if so, what? These are questions we shall need to explore.

Inflation

By **inflation** we mean a general rise in prices throughout the economy.

During the 1950s and 1960s, rates of inflation were generally low in the advanced industrialised economies. In the early 1970s, however, inflation rose dramatically (see Table 13.1). By the end of the decade, many governments regarded inflation as the most pressing of their economic problems. Mrs Thatcher, for example, declared inflation to be 'public enemy number one'. Then with the world recession of the early 1980s inflation began to fall, only to rise again with the boom of the late 1980s, but fall back with the recession of the early 1990s. As Table 13.1 shows, inflation has generally been less severe in the 1980s and 1990s than in the 1970s.

Just how serious a problem is inflation? What are its causes? What is the relationship between inflation and the other macroeconomic objectives? What can the government do to control inflation? Are there any undesirable

[1] The Organisation for Economic Co-operation and Development: the 29 major industrialised countries (excluding Russia but including Turkey and Mexico).

DEFINITION

Rate of inflation The percentage increase in prices over a twelve-month period.

side-effects of policies to control inflation? These are all questions we will be examining.

The balance of payments and the exchange rate

The final issue has to do with the country's foreign trade and its economic relationships with other countries.

A country's **balance of payments account** records all transactions between the residents of that country and the rest of the world. These transactions enter as either debit items or credit items. The debit items include all payments *to* other countries: these include the country's purchases of imports, the investments it makes abroad and the interest and dividends paid to foreigners who have invested in the country. The credit items include all receipts *from* other countries: these include the sales of exports, investments made by foreigners in the country and earnings of interest and dividends from abroad.

The sale of exports and any other receipts earn foreign currency. The purchase of imports or any other payments abroad use up foreign currency. If we start to spend more foreign currency than we earn, one of two things must happen. Both are likely to be a problem.

The balance of payments will go into deficit. In other words, there will be a shortfall of foreign currencies. The government will therefore have to borrow money from abroad, or draw on its foreign currency reserves to make up the shortfall. This is a problem because, if it goes on too long, overseas debts will mount, along with the interest that must be paid; and/or reserves will begin to run low.

The exchange rate will fall. The **exchange rate** is the rate at which one currency exchanges for another. For example, the exchange rate of the pound into the dollar might be £1 = $1.60.

If the government does nothing to correct the balance of payments deficit, then the exchange rate must fall. (We will show just why this is so in section 14.1.) A falling exchange rate is a problem because it pushes up the price of imports and may fuel inflation. Also if the exchange rate fluctuates, this can cause great uncertainty for traders and can damage international trade and economic growth.

What are the underlying causes of balance of payments problems? How do the balance of payments and the exchange rate relate to the other macroeconomic issues? What are the best policies for governments to adopt? These are the questions we must look at here.

Government macroeconomic policy

From the above four issues we can identify four macroeconomic policy objectives that governments typically pursue:

- High and stable economic growth.
- Low unemployment.
- Low inflation.
- The avoidance of balance of payments deficits and excessive exchange rate fluctuations.

Unfortunately, these policy objectives may conflict. For example, a policy designed to accelerate the rate of economic growth may result in a higher rate of inflation and a balance of payments deficit. We will be examining these policy conflicts in the following chapters.

The actual policies a government pursues will depend on two major factors.

Its order of priorities

If its economic goals conflict, the government must choose which is the most important. For example, if it makes the fight against inflation its major short-term objective, it may be prepared to accept, at least for the time being, a lower rate of economic growth and a higher level of unemployment. On the other hand, if it is anxious to reduce unemployment significantly in time for the next general election, it might be prepared to allow the rate of inflation to rise and the exchange rate to fall.

Which macroeconomic theories it believes to be the most accurate

There is not just one set of macroeconomic theories. If there were, it would make *your* life simpler – there would be less to learn! On the other hand, macroeconomics would be less controversial and hence less exciting.

DEFINITIONS

Balance of payments account A record of the country's transactions with the rest of the world. It shows the country's payments to or deposits in other countries (debits) and its receipts or deposits from other countries (credits). It also shows the balance between these debits and credits under various headings.

Exchange rate The rate at which one national currency exchanges for another. The rate is expressed as the amount of one currency that is necessary to purchase *one unit* of another currency (e.g. DM2.50 = £1).

One broad distinction between macroeconomic theories is between those that imply that the four policy objectives are generally best achieved through the free market, and those that imply that the market will probably fail to achieve some or all of them. Obviously a government that believes in the first set of theories is likely to pursue policies designed to 'free up' markets: policies that involve the minimum of government interference. In contrast, a government that believes in the second set of theories is likely to intervene much more actively in trying to steer the economy.

Macroeconomic theories are thus frequently associated with political parties: the non-interventionist, market-orientated theories are adopted by the political right; the interventionist theories are adopted by the political left.

It would be wrong to suggest that there are just two schools of macroeconomic thought. Just as there are many shades of political opinion about the success or otherwise of the market economy, so too there are many shades of economic opinion about how the market works or fails to work to achieve the macroeconomic goals. For the rest of this chapter and in the next, we will look at the range of *possible* causes of macroeconomic problems. Later we will see which schools of thought stress which causes, and what policy implications follow.

SECTION SUMMARY

1. Macroeconomics, like microeconomics, looks at issues such as output, employment and prices; but it looks at them in the context of the whole economy.
2. The four main macroeconomic goals that are generally of most concern to governments are economic growth, reducing unemployment, reducing inflation, and avoiding balance of payments and exchange rate problems.
3. Unfortunately these goals are likely to conflict. Which policies a government adopts, therefore, will depend on its order of priorities. It will also depend on which school of economic thought the government adheres to.

13.2 Economic growth

The distinction between actual and potential growth

Before examining the causes of economic growth, it is essential to distinguish between *actual* and *potential* economic growth. People frequently confuse the two.

Actual growth is the percentage annual increase in national output: the rate of growth in actual output. (See section 14.5 for alternative ways of measuring national output and income.) When statistics on growth rates are published, it is actual growth they are referring to.

Potential growth is the speed at which the economy *could* grow. It is the percentage annual increase in the economy's *capacity* to produce: the rate of growth in **potential output**. Two of the major factors contributing to potential economic growth are:

- An increase in resources – natural resources, labour or capital.
- An increase in the efficiency with which these resources are used, through advances in technology, improved labour skills or improved organisation.

If the potential growth rate exceeds the actual growth rate, there will be an increase in spare capacity and an increase in unemployment: there will be a growing gap between potential and actual output. To close this gap, the actual growth rate would temporarily have to exceed the potential growth rate. In the long run, however, the actual growth rate will be limited to the potential growth rate.

There are thus two major issues concerned with economic growth: the short-run issue of ensuring that actual growth is such as to keep actual output as close as possible

DEFINITIONS

Actual growth The percentage annual increase in national output actually produced.

Potential growth The percentage annual increase in the capacity of the economy to produce.

Potential output The output that could be produced in the economy if there were a full employment of resources (including labour).

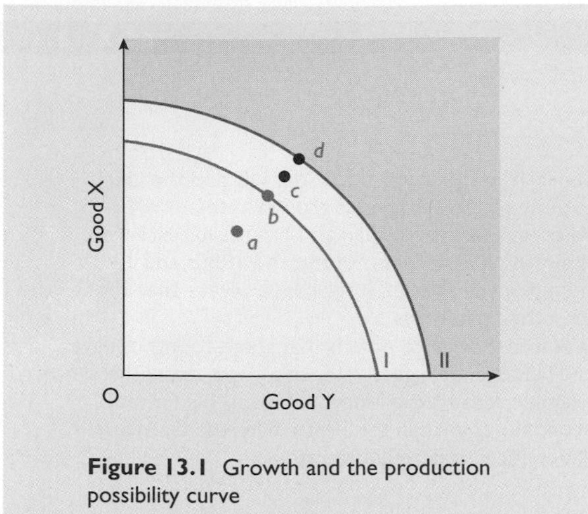

Figure 13.1 Growth and the production possibility curve

to potential output; and the long-run issue of what determines the rate of potential economic growth.

Growth and the production possibility curve

The distinction between actual and potential growth in output can be illustrated on a production possibility diagram. If you remember, a production possibility curve shows all the possible combinations of two goods that can be produced at any one time (see pages 7–11). For purposes of illustration we could lump all goods and services together into two categories: for example, agricultural goods (good X) and manufactured goods and services (good Y).

The production possibility curve itself shows potential *output*. Potential *growth*, then, is illustrated by a shift outward of the curve (e.g. curve I to curve II in Figure 13.1). Actual growth is represented by a movement outward of the production point (e.g. point *a* to point *b* to *c* to *d*).

In the short run, actual growth can arise from a fuller use of resources (e.g. a movement from point *a* to point *b*). This would involve taking up slack in the economy: using machinery more fully and reducing unemployment. For actual growth to be sustained over a number of years, however, there would also have to be an increase in potential output. In other words, to get beyond point *b* in Figure 13.1, the production possibility curve itself would have to shift outward beyond curve I.

Economic growth and the business cycle

Although growth in potential output will vary to some extent over the years – depending on the rate of advance of technology, the level of investment and the discovery of new raw materials – it will nevertheless tend to be much more steady than the growth in actual output.

Actual growth will tend to fluctuate. In some years, countries will experience high rates of economic growth: the country experiences a boom. In other years, economic growth will be low or even negative: the country experiences a slowdown or recession. This cycle of booms and recessions is known as the **business cycle** or **trade cycle**.

There are four 'phases' of the business cycle. They are illustrated in Figure 13.2.

1. The upturn. In this phase a stagnant economy begins to recover, and growth in actual output resumes.
2. The boom. During this phase there is rapid economic growth. A fuller use is made of resources, and the gap between actual and potential output narrows.

DEFINITION

Business cycle or **trade cycle** The periodic fluctuations of national output round its long-term trend.

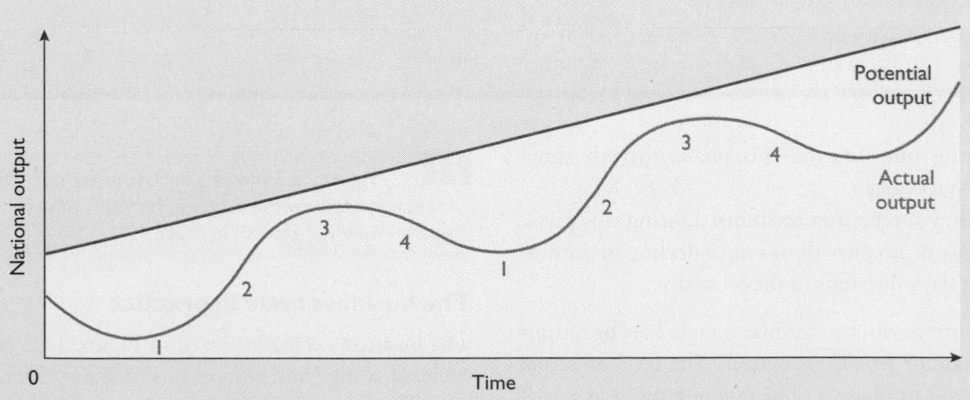

Figure 13.2 The business cycle

CASE STUDIES BOX 13.1

INTERNATIONAL FLUCTUATIONS

Countries throughout the world experience business cycles. The following diagram illustrates the cyclical fluctuations of five major industrial economies from 1971 to 1998. As you can see, all five economies suffered a recession or slowdown in the mid-1970s, the early 1980s and early 1990s and a boom in the early 1970s, the late 1970s and late 1980s.

But despite this broad similarity in their experience, there were nevertheless significant differences in the magnitude and timing of their individual cycles. For example, the UK plunged into recession in 1980, whereas it was not until 1982 or 1983 that the other countries experienced their lowest rate of growth.

Similarly in the early 1990s, the UK and the USA experienced their lowest growth rate in 1991, whereas Germany, Japan and France experienced theirs in 1993. What is more, the 1980s and 1990s recessions in the UK were more severe than those in the other countries.

Another point to note is that some countries have had persistently higher rates of growth than others. For example, Japan experienced relatively high rates of economic growth in the 1980s, whereas Germany experienced relatively low rates.

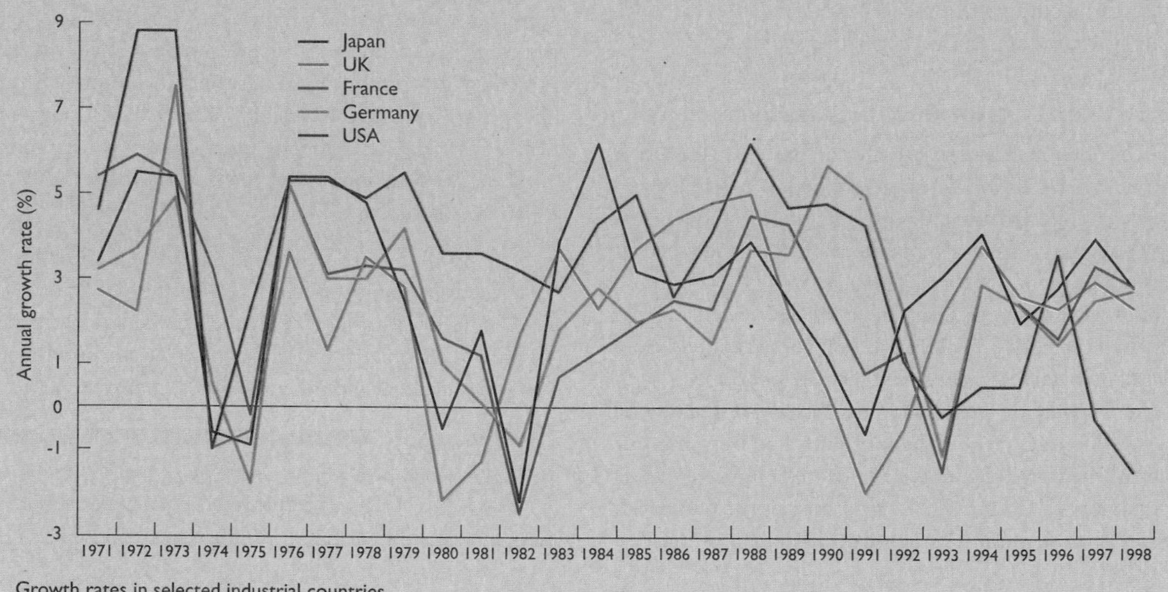

Growth rates in selected industrial countries

Source: *Economic Outlook* (OECD).

3. The peaking out. During this phase, growth slows down or even ceases.
4. The slowdown, recession or slump. During this phase there is little or no growth or even a decline in output. Increasing slack develops in the economy.

A word of caution: do not confuse a high *level* of output with a high rate of *growth* in output. The level of actual output is highest in phase 3. The rate of growth in actual output is highest in phase 2.

??

Figure 13.2 shows a decline in actual output in recession. Redraw the diagram, only this time show a mere slowing down of growth in phase 4.

The business cycle in practice

The business cycle illustrated in Figure 13.2 is a 'stylised' cycle. It is nice and smooth and regular. Drawing it this way allows us to make a clear distinction between each of the four phases. In practice, however, business cycles are highly irregular. They are irregular in two ways.

The length of the phases. Some booms are short lived, lasting only a few months or so. Others are much longer, lasting perhaps three or four years. Likewise some recessions are short while others are long.

The magnitude of the phases. Sometimes in phase 2 there is a very high rate of economic growth, perhaps 5 per cent per annum or more. On other occasions in phase 2 growth is much gentler. Sometimes in phase 4 there is a recession, with an actual decline in output. On other occasions phase 4 is merely a 'pause', with growth simply slowing down.

Nevertheless, despite the irregularity of the fluctuations, cycles are still clearly discernible, especially if we plot *growth* on the vertical axis rather than the *level* of output. This is done in Figure 13.3, which shows the UK business cycle from 1950 to 1998.

??
1. At what phases of the business cycle are points *w*, *x* and *y* in Figure 13.3?
2. How long was the average duration of the cycle from peak to peak between 1950 and 1998?

Causes of actual growth

The major determinants of variations in the rate of actual growth in the *short run* are variations in the growth of aggregate demand.

Aggregate demand (AD) is the total spending on goods and services made within the country. This spending consists of four elements: consumer spending (C), investment expenditure by firms (I), government spending (G), and the expenditure by foreign residents on the country's goods and services (i.e. their purchases of its exports and their new investments in the country) (X). From these four must be subtracted any expenditure that goes on imports (M), since this is expenditure that 'leaks' abroad, and is not therefore spent on domestic goods and services. Thus:

$$AD = C + I + G + X - M$$

Another way of saying the same thing is merely to count that element of consumption, investment, government expenditure and foreign expenditure that is spent on goods and services produced within the domestic economy. Thus:

$$AD = C_d + I_d + G_d + X_d$$

where 'd' stands for the part of each one that is spent on *domestically* produced goods and services.

?? Would you expect X to equal X_d? Explain.

A rapid rise in aggregate demand will create shortages. This will tend to stimulate firms to increase output, thus reducing slack in the economy. Likewise, a reduction in aggregate demand will leave firms with increased stocks of unsold goods. They will therefore tend to reduce output.

DEFINITION

Aggregate demand Total spending on goods and services made in the economy. It consists of four elements, consumer spending (C), investment (I), government spending (G) and the expenditure on exports (X), less any expenditure on foreign goods and services (M): $AD = C + I + G + X - M$.

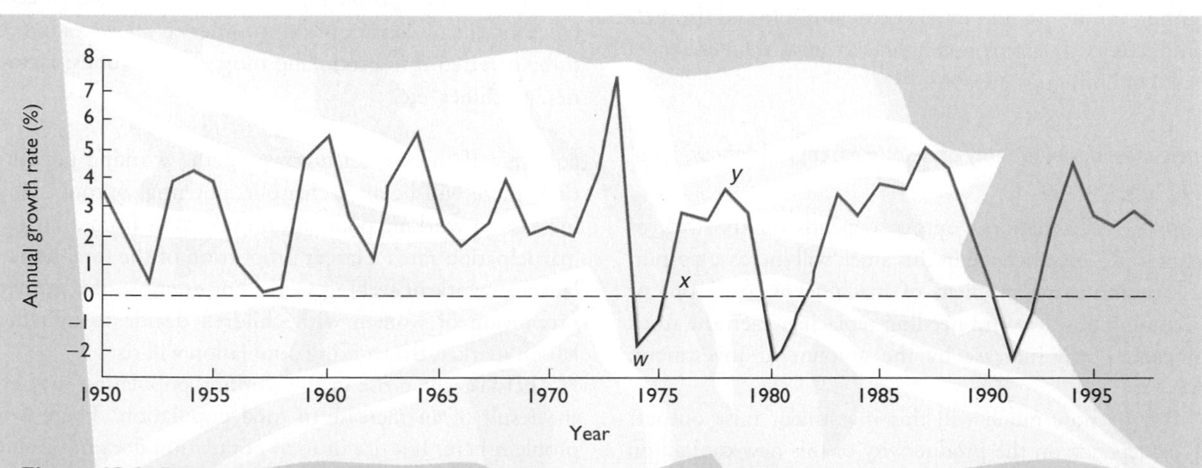

Figure 13.3 Fluctuations in UK growth

Source: *Economic Trends* (ONS, various issues).

Aggregate demand and actual output, therefore, fluctuate together in the short run. A boom is associated with a rapid rise in aggregate demand: the faster the rise in aggregate demand, the higher the short-run rate of actual growth. A recession, by contrast, is associated with a reduction in aggregate demand.

A rapid rise in aggregate demand, however, is not enough to ensure a continuing high level of growth over a *number* of years. Without an expansion of potential output too, rises in actual output must eventually come to an end. Once spare capacity has been used up, once there is full employment of labour and other resources, the rate of growth of actual output will be restricted to the rate of growth of potential output. This is illustrated in Figure 13.2 (page 403). As long as actual output is below potential output, the actual output curve can slope upward more steeply than the potential output curve. But once the gap between the two curves has been closed, the actual output curve can only slope as steeply as the potential output curve: the two curves cannot cross – actual output cannot be above potential output.

In the long run, therefore, there are two determinants of actual growth:

- The growth in aggregate demand. This determines whether potential output will be realised.
- The growth in potential output.

Causes of potential growth

We turn now to the *supply* side of the question. Here we are not concerned with the amount of *spending*, but rather with what determines the capacity of the economy to *produce*. There are two main determinants of this potential output: (a) the amount of resources available and (b) their productivity. If supply potential is to grow, then either (a) or (b) or both must grow.

Increases in the quantity of resources: capital, labour, land and raw materials

Capital. The nation's output depends on its stock of capital (K). An increase in this stock will increase output. If we ignore the problem of machines wearing out or becoming obsolete and needing replacing, then the stock of capital will increase by the amount of investment: $\Delta K = I$.

But by how much will this investment raise output? This depends on the productivity of this new capital: on the *marginal efficiency of capital* (see page 273). Let us define the nation's marginal efficiency of capital (MEC) as the annual extra income (ΔY) yielded by an increase in the capital stock, relative to the cost of that extra capital (ΔK).

$$MEC = \frac{\Delta Y}{\Delta K} = \frac{\Delta Y}{I}$$

Thus if £100 million of extra capital yielded an annual income of £25 million, the marginal efficiency of capital would be £25 million/£100 million = 1/4.

The rate of growth will depend on the fraction (i) of national income devoted to new investment (i.e. investment over and above what is necessary to replace worn-out equipment). The higher this rate of new investment, the higher will be the potential growth rate.

The relationship between the investment rate and the potential growth rate (g_p) is given by the simple formula:

$$g_p = i \times MEC$$

Thus if 20 per cent of national income went in new investment (i), and if each £1 of new investment yielded 25p of extra income per year (MEC = 1/4), then the growth rate would be 5 per cent. A simple example will demonstrate this. If national income is £100 billion, then £20 billion will be invested (i = 20 per cent). This will lead to extra annual output of £5 billion (MEC = 1/4). Thus national income grows to £105 billion: a growth of 5 per cent.

But what determines the rate of investment? There are a number of determinants. These include the confidence of businesspeople about the future demand for their products, the profitability of business, the tax regime, the rate of growth in the economy and the rate of interest. We will examine these determinants in section 16.1.

Over the long term, if investment is to increase, then *savings* must increase in order to finance that investment. Put another way, people must be prepared to forgo a certain amount of consumption in order to allow resources to be diverted into producing more capital goods: factories, machines, etc.

Labour. If there is an increase in the working population, there will be an increase in potential output. This increase in working population may result from a higher 'participation rate': a larger proportion of the total population in work or seeking work. For example, if a greater proportion of women with children decide to join the labour market, the working population will rise.

Alternatively, a rise in the working population may be the result of an increase in total population. There is a problem here. If a rise in total population does not result in a greater *proportion* of the population working, output per head may not rise at all. In practice, many developed countries are faced with a growing proportion of their population above retirement age, and thus a potential *fall* in output per head.

Land and raw materials. Land is virtually fixed in quantity. Land reclamation schemes and the opening-up of marginal land can only add tiny amounts to national output.

Whether new raw materials can be discovered is largely a matter of the luck of nature. A country might strike it lucky and discover vast new deposits of coal, oil or some other mineral. North Sea oil was one such bonanza. Such discoveries, however, are usually 'one-off' benefits. They simply provide short-term growth, while the rate of their exploitation is building up. Once their rate of extraction is at a maximum, growth will cease. Output will simply remain at the new higher level, until eventually the raw materials will begin to run out. This will cause output to fall.

The problem of diminishing returns. If a single factor of production increases in supply while others remain fixed, diminishing returns will set in. Remember the problem that Thomas Malthus referred to: the problem of a growing population with a fixed supply of land (see Box 5.2). As more and more workers crowd on to a fixed amount of land, so the marginal product of workers will fall.

The same argument applies to capital. If the quantity of capital increases with no increase in other factors of production, then diminishing returns to capital will set in. The rate of return on capital will fall.

Unless *all* factors of production increase, therefore, the rate of growth is likely to slow down. It is not enough that labour and capital increase if there is a limited supply of land and raw materials. This was the worry of the classical economists of the nineteenth century, who were pessimistic about the future prospects for growth (see Box 13.2).

Then there is the problem of the environment. If a rise in labour and capital lead to a more *intensive* use of land and natural resources, the resulting growth in output may be environmentally unsustainable.

The solution to the problem of diminishing returns is an increase in the *productivity* of resources.

Increases in the productivity of resources

Most economists of the twentieth century have not shared the pessimism of the classical economists. Although they do not deny the law of diminishing returns, they argue that the marginal productivity of factors can be increased in various ways.

Technological improvements can increase the marginal productivity of capital. Much of the investment in new machines is not just in extra machines, but in superior machines producing a higher rate of return. Consider the microchip revolution of recent years. Modern computers can do the work of many people and have replaced many machines which are cumbersome and expensive to build. Improved methods of transport have reduced the costs of moving goods and materials. Improved communications (such as fax machines and satellites) have reduced the costs of transmitting information. The high-tech world of today would seem a wonderland to a person of 100 years ago.

As a result of technical progress, the productivity of capital has tended to increase, not decrease, over time. Similarly, as a result of new skills, improved education and training, and better health, the productivity of labour has also tended to increase over time.

> **??** For what reasons might the productivity of land increase over time?

Although the main determinant of long-term growth is the rate of advance of technology, invention on its own is not enough. There must also be the institutions and attitudes that encourage *innovation*. In other words, the inventions must be exploited. One reason often cited for the UK's poor growth performance compared with other countries is its lack of innovation, despite a relatively good record of inventions.

The effects of actual growth on potential growth

Some economists argue that potential growth is not influenced by actual growth. It is dependent largely on growth in factor productivity, and that in turn depends on scientific and technical advance. Such advances, they argue, are independent of the state of the economy.

Other economists, however, argue that actual growth *stimulates* investment and the development of new technology. For these economists, therefore, it is vital for the achievement of high long-term growth rates that the economy continues to experience actual growth in the short run. Recessions breed pessimism and a lack of investment, a lack of research and a lack of innovation.

Policies to achieve growth

Can governments increase a country's growth rate? Most economists and politicians argue that they can, but just what policies should be adopted is a highly controversial issue. Policies differ in two ways.

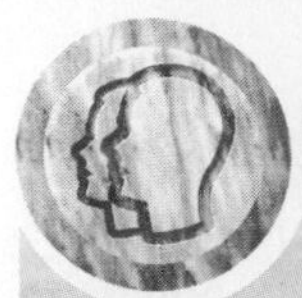

DEVELOPMENT OF IDEAS

THEORIES OF GROWTH

From dismal economics to the economics of optimism

The classical theory of growth

The classical economists of the nineteenth century were very pessimistic about the prospects for economic growth. They saw the rate of growth petering out as diminishing returns to both labour and capital led to low wages and a falling rate of profit. The only gainers would be landlords, who, given the fixed supply of land, would receive higher and higher rents as the demand for scarce land rose.

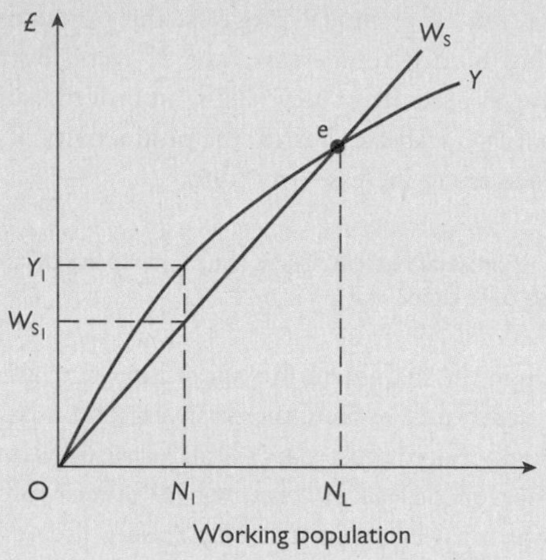

Long-run stationary state in the classical model

The classical position can be shown graphically. The size of the working population is plotted on the horizontal axis. If it is assumed that there is a basic minimum 'subsistence' wage that workers must earn in order to survive, then the line W_s traces out the total subsistence wage bill. It is a straight line because a doubling in the number of workers would lead to a doubling of the subsistence wage bill.

The line Y shows the total level of income that will be generated as more workers are employed, after subtracting rents to landlords. In other words, it is total wages plus profits. It gets less and less steep due to diminishing returns to labour and capital given the fixed supply of land.

As long as Y is above W_s (say, at a population of N_1), firms can make a profit. They will try to expand and will thus take on more labour.

Initially this will bid up the wage and will thus erode the level of profits. But the higher wages will encourage the population to expand. This increased supply of labour will compete wages back down to the subsistence level and will thus allow *some* recovery in profits. But profits will not be as high as they were before because, with an increase in workers, the gap between Y and W_s will have narrowed.

Firms will continue to expand and the population will continue to grow until point e is reached. At that point, even with wages at bare subsistence level, no profit can be made. Growth will cease. The economy will be in a long-run stationary state.

No wonder economics became dubbed 'the dismal science'.

New growth theory

Economists today are more optimistic about the prospects for economic growth. This is partly based on a

First, they may focus on the demand side or the supply side of the economy. In other words, they may attempt to create sufficient *aggregate demand* to ensure that firms wish to invest and that potential output is realised. Or alternatively they may seek to increase *aggregate supply* by concentrating on measures to increase potential output: measures to encourage research and development, innovation and training.

Second, they may be market-orientated or interventionist policies. Many economists and politicians, especially those on the political right, believe that the best environment for encouraging economic growth is one where private enterprise is allowed to flourish: where entrepreneurs are able to reap substantial rewards from investment in new techniques and new products. Such economists, therefore, advocate policies designed to free up the market. Others, however, argue that a free market will be subject to considerable cyclical fluctuations. The resulting uncertainty will discourage investment. These economists, therefore, tend to advocate active intervention by the government to reduce these fluctuations. Some go further and argue for economic planning and/or control of industry by the state. Only that way, they argue, can the high levels of investment necessary for high long-term rates of growth be sustained.

Throughout this second half of the book we will be looking at these various government policies. We will look at demand-side and supply-side policies. We will also look at market-orientated and interventionist policies.

*BOX 13.2

simple appeal to the evidence. Despite a rapid growth in world population, most countries have experienced sustained economic growth. Over the last hundred years the industrialised countries have seen per-capita growth rates averaging from just over 1 per cent to nearly 3 per cent per annum. This has resulted in per-capita real incomes many times higher than in the last century.

This world-wide experience of economic growth has stimulated the development of new growth theories. These stress two features:

- The development and spread of new technology. The rapid advances in science and technology have massively increased the productivity of factors of production. What is more, new inventions and innovations stimulate other people, often in other countries, to copy, adapt and improve on them in order to stay competitive. Growth through technical progress stimulates more growth.
- The positive externalities of investment. If one firm invests in training in order to raise labour productivity, other firms will benefit from the improved stock of 'human capital'. There will be better-trained labour that can now be hired by *other* firms. Similarly if one firm invests in research and development, the benefits can spill over to other firms (once any patents have expired). What is more, firms trade with other firms. If a firm that supplies components invests in better equipment, it might be able to supply better and/or cheaper components. The firms it supplies will thus benefit from the first firm's investment. These spillover benefits to other firms can be seen as the *positive externalities* of investment.

New growth theories seek to analyse the process of the spread of technology and how it can be influenced.

Given that technological progress allows the spectre of diminishing returns to be banished, or at least indefinitely postponed, it is no wonder that many economists are more optimistic about growth. Nevertheless, there are still serious grounds for concern.

- If the benefits of investment spill over to other firms (i.e. if there are positive externalities), the free market will lead to too little investment: firms considering investing will take into account only the benefits to themselves, not those to *other* firms. There is thus an important role for governments to encourage or provide training, research and capital investment. (We consider such policies in Chapter 22.)
- Potential growth may not translate into actual growth. A *potentially* growing economy may be languishing in a deep recession.
- There may be serious costs of economic growth: for those whose jobs are replaced by machines; for society, as new production and consumption patterns cause social upheavals; for the environment, as new production generates more waste and more pollution, and uses up scarce natural resources. (The costs of economic growth are examined in Box 13.3.)

?? Can growth go on *for ever*, given that certain resources are finite in supply?

Postscript: the role of investment

Investment plays a twin role in economic growth. It is a component of aggregate demand and thus helps determine the level of actual output. It is also probably the major determinant of potential output, since investment both increases the capital stock and also leads to the development of new technology.

There is a problem here, however: if investment rises, the resulting rise in aggregate demand may not match the resulting rise in aggregate supply.

If the rise in aggregate supply is greater than the rise in aggregate demand, potential growth will be greater than actual growth. Increased slack will develop in the economy, with a resulting rise in unemployment (of both labour and other resources). If, however, the rise in aggregate demand is greater than the rise in aggregate supply, slack will be taken up and unemployment will fall. Eventually, as firms approach full capacity, the economy will 'overheat'. Shortages will develop as supply cannot keep up with demand. Prices will rise.

Some economists argue that it will only be by chance that the supply effects and the demand effects of investment will match. This whole debate is examined in Chapter 15.

ISSUES AND APPLICATIONS

THE COSTS OF ECONOMIC GROWTH

Is more necessarily better?

For many Third World countries economic growth is a necessity if they are to remove mass poverty. When the majority of their population is underfed, poorly housed, with inadequate health care and little access to education, few would quarrel with the need for an increase in productive potential. The main query is whether the benefits of economic growth will flow to the mass of the population, or whether they will be confined to the few who are already relatively well off.

For developed countries the case for economic growth is less clear cut. Economic growth is usually measured in terms of the growth in national output valued in prices as given by the market (see section 14.5 for methods of measuring national output). The problem is that there are many 'goods' and 'bads' that are not included when measuring national output. Economic growth, therefore, is not the same as growth in a nation's *welfare*. True, there can be major advantages of economic growth, and certainly, other things being equal, the majority of the population wants higher levels of production and consumption. But it is important to recognise the costs of economic growth. Indeed, some people regard these costs as so serious that they advocate a policy of *zero economic growth*.

So, what are the benefits and costs of economic growth?

The benefits of growth

Increased levels of consumption
Provided economic growth outstrips population growth, it will lead to higher real income per head. This can lead to higher levels of consumption of goods and services. If human welfare is related to the level of consumption, then growth provides an obvious gain to society.

It can help avoid other macroeconomic problems
People have aspirations of rising living standards. Without a growth in productive potential, people's demands for rising incomes are likely to lead to higher inflation, balance of payments crises (as more imports are purchased), industrial disputes, etc. Growth in productive potential helps to meet these aspirations and avoid macroeconomic crises.

It can make it easier to redistribute incomes to the poor
If incomes rise, the government can redistribute incomes from the rich to the poor *without the rich losing*. For example, as people's incomes rise, they automatically pay more taxes. These extra revenues for the government can be spent on programmes to alleviate poverty.

Without a continuing rise in national income the scope for helping the poor is much more limited.

Society may feel that it can afford to care more for the environment
As people grow richer, they may become less preoccupied with their own private consumption and more concerned to live in a clean environment. The regulation of pollution tends to be tougher in developed countries than in the Third World.

The costs of growth

In practice, more consumption may not make people happier; economies may be no less crisis riven; income may not be redistributed more equally; the environment may not be better protected. More than this, some people argue that growth may worsen these problems and create additional problems besides.

The current opportunity cost of growth
To achieve faster growth, firms will probably need to invest more. This will require financing. The finance can come from higher savings or higher taxes. Either way, there must be a cut in consumption. In the short run, therefore, higher growth leads to *less* consumption, not more.

In the diagram, assume that consumption is currently at a level of C_1. Its growth over time is shown by the line out from C_1. Now assume that the government pursues a policy of higher growth. Consumption has to *fall* to finance the extra investment. Consumption falls to, say, C_2. The growth in consumption is now shown by the line out from C_2. Not until time t_1 is reached (which may be several years into the future) does consumption overtake the levels it would have reached with the previous lower growth rate.

Growth may simply generate extra demands
'The more people have, the more they want.' If this is so, more consumption may not increase people's utility at all. (Diagrammatically, indifference curves may move

BOX 13.3

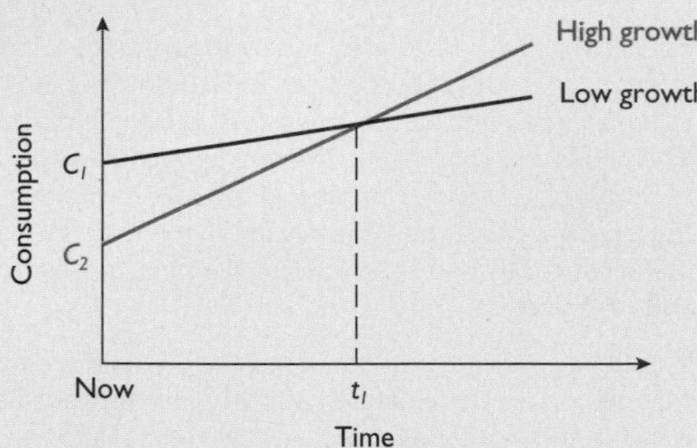

High and low growth paths

outward as fast as, or even faster than, consumers' budget lines: see section 4.2.) It is often observed that rich people tend to be miserable!

As people's incomes grow, they may become more materialistic and less fulfilled as human beings.

Social effects
Many people claim that an excessive pursuit of material growth by a country can lead to a more greedy, more selfish and less caring society. As society becomes more industrialised, violence, crime, loneliness, stress-related diseases, suicides, divorce and other social problems are likely to rise.

Environmental costs
A richer society may be more concerned for the environment, but it is also likely to do more damage to it. The higher the level of consumption, the higher is likely to be the level of pollution and waste. What is more, many of the environmental costs are likely to be underestimated due to a lack of scientific knowledge. Acid rain and the depletion of the ozone layer have been two examples.

Non-renewable resources
If growth involves using a greater amount of resources, rather than using the same amount of resources more efficiently, certain non-renewable resources will run out more rapidly. Unless viable alternatives can be found for various minerals and fossil fuels, present growth may lead to shortages for future generations.

Effects on the distribution of income
While some people may gain from a higher standard of living, others are likely to lose. If the means to higher growth are greater incentives (such as cuts in higher rates of income tax), then the rich might get richer, with little or no benefits 'trickling down' to the poor.

Growth involves changes in production: both in terms of the goods produced and in terms of the techniques used and the skills required. The more rapid the rate of growth, the more rapid the rate of change. People may find that their skills are no longer relevant. Their jobs may be replaced by machines. People may thus find themselves unemployed, or forced to take low-paid, unskilled work.

Conclusion

So should countries pursue growth? The answer depends on (a) just what costs and benefits are involved, (b) what weighting people attach to them, and (c) how opposing views are to be reconciled.

A problem is that the question of the desirability of economic growth is a normative one. It involves a judgement about what a 'desirable' society should look like.

A simpler point, however, is that the electorate seems to want economic growth. As long as that is so, governments will tend to pursue policies to achieve growth. That is why we need to study the causes of growth and the policies that governments can pursue.

One thing the government can do is to view the problem as one of *constrained optimisation*. It sets constraints: levels of environmental protection, minimum wages, maximum rates of depletion of non-renewable resources, etc. It then seeks policies that will maximise growth, while keeping within these constraints.

??

1. Is a constrained optimisation approach a *practical* solution to the possible costs of economic growth?
2. Are worries about the consequences of economic growth a 'luxury' that only rich countries can afford?

SECTION SUMMARY

1. Actual growth must be distinguished from potential growth. The actual growth rate is the percentage annual increase in the output that is actually produced, whereas potential growth is the percentage annual increase in the capacity of the economy to produce (whether or not it is actually produced).
2. Actual growth is represented by a movement outward of the production *point* on a production possibility diagram, whereas potential growth is represented by an outward shift of the whole curve.
3. Actual growth will fluctuate with the course of the trade cycle. The cycle can be broken down into four phases: the upturn, the boom, the peaking-out, and the slowdown or recession. In practice the length and magnitude of these phases will vary: the cycle is thus irregular.
4. Actual growth is determined by potential growth and by the level of aggregate demand. If actual output is below potential output, actual growth can temporarily exceed potential growth, if aggregate demand is rising sufficiently. In the long term, however, actual output can only grow as fast as potential output will permit.
5. Potential growth is determined by the rate of increase in the *quantity* of resources: capital, labour, land and raw materials; and by the *productivity* of resources. The productivity of capital can be increased by technological improvements and the more efficient use of the capital stock; the productivity of labour can be increased by better education, training, motivation and organisation.
6. Whether governments can best achieve rapid growth through market-orientated or interventionist policies is highly controversial.
7. Investment plays a key role in determining growth, since it affects both actual and potential growth: it affects both aggregate demand and aggregate supply. Whether investment leads to more or less slack developing in the economy depends on which of these effects is the larger.

13.3 Unemployment

In Europe, in North America, in Australasia, and in many developing countries too, the problem of unemployment rapidly worsened in the early 1980s as the world plunged into what was then the greatest recession since the Great Depression of the 1930s. But then, as the world economy recovered and sustained economic growth was experienced throughout the second half of the 1980s, so unemployment began to fall, only to rise again as the world once more experienced recession in the early 1990s. Then as the world slowly climbed out of recession in the mid-1990s, so unemployment rates once more began to fall. Figure 13.4 shows these cyclical movements in unemployment for selected countries.

As well as experiencing fluctuations in unemployment, most countries have experienced an increase in average unemployment rates from one cycle to another. This is illustrated in Table 13.2, which shows average unemployment in the UK, the OECD and the EU for four unemployment cycles (minimum to minimum). Average unemployment rates in the 1980s and 1990s have been higher than in the 1970s, and average rates in the 1970s were, in turn, higher than in the 1950s and 1960s.

In this section we will survey the problem of unemployment. We will first of all ask just what is meant by 'unemployment'. (The answer is not quite as obvious as it might at first seem.) Then we will ask what are the costs of unemployment: not just to the unemployed themselves, but to the whole economy. Then we will turn to the causes of unemployment. At this preliminary stage all we will do is to look at the range of *possible* causes. As the book progresses, however, we will see that different schools of thought put the major blame for unemployment on one or other specific cause. Finally, we will survey the possible policies that can be adopted to tackle unemployment.

Table 13.2 Average unemployment for given cycles (%)

Period	UK	EU	OECD
1964–73	3.0	2.7	3.0
1974–9	5.0	4.7	4.9
1980–9	10.0	9.3	7.3
1990–8	8.4	10.1	7.3

The meaning of 'unemployment'

Unemployment can be expressed either as a number (e.g. 2.5 million) or as a percentage (e.g. 8 per cent). But just who should be included in the statistics? Should it be everyone without a job? The answer is clearly no, since we would not want to include children and pensioners. We

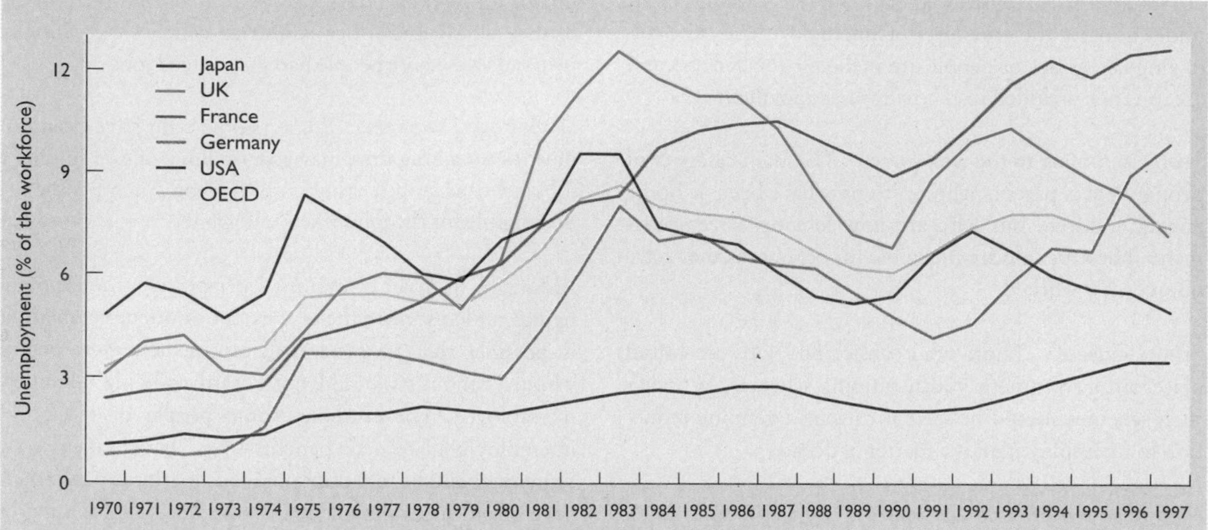

Figure 13.4 Unemployment in selected industrial countries: 1970–97
Source: *OECD Economic Outlook* (OECD).

would probably also want to exclude those who were not looking for work, such as parents choosing to stay at home to look after children.

The most usual definition that economists use for the **number unemployed** is: *those of working age who are without work, but who are available for work at current wage rates.* If the figure is to be expressed as a percentage, then it is a percentage of the total **labour force**. The labour force is defined as: *those in employment plus those unemployed.* Thus if 22.5 million people were employed and 2.5 million people were unemployed, the **unemployment rate** would be:

$$\frac{2.5}{22.5 + 2.5} \times 100 = 10\%$$

But how in practice is unemployment to be measured? This is a real problem because it is difficult to get politicians to agree on who should be classed as unemployed. Naturally a government wants the unemployment figures to be as low as possible. Equally naturally, opposition parties want the statistics to include everyone who could possibly be considered as unemployed. This lack of objectivity on the part of politicians makes it very difficult to get a clear, unbiased picture of the problem.

Official measures of unemployment

Claimant unemployment

There are two common measures of unemployment used in official statistics. The first is **claimant unemployment**. This is simply a measure of all those in receipt of unemployment-related benefits. This is the method used in the UK official statistics. Claimants receive the 'job-seeker's allowance'.

Claimant statistics have the advantage of being very easy to collect. However, they exclude all those of working age who are available for work at current wage rates, but who are *not* eligible for benefits. If the government changes the eligibility conditions so that fewer people are now eligible, this will reduce the number of claimants and hence the official number unemployed, even if there has been no change in the numbers with or without work. There have been some 30 changes to eligibility conditions since 1979, all but one of which have had the effect of reducing the claimant figures!

DEFINITIONS

Number unemployed (economist's definition) Those of working age who are without work, but who are available for work at current wage rates.

Labour force The number employed plus the number unemployed.

Unemployment rate The number unemployed expressed as a percentage of the labour force.

Claimant unemployment Those in receipt of unemployment-related benefits.

It is thus often argued that claimant statistics in the UK underestimate the true level of unemployment. The following categories of people are ineligible for benefits and are thus not included in claimant unemployment.

People returning to the workforce. The main category of people here is parents who up to now have been at home raising children, but who are now looking for employment. These people are ineligible for benefits as they have not recently worked.

School leavers. Those who cannot find jobs are found places on government youth training schemes. Whether such schemes should be seen as causing a genuine reduction in unemployment is a matter of debate.

Men between 60 and 65 who are seeking employment. Men in the UK are not entitled to state pensions until they are 65. Unemployed men of 60 and over, however, do not count in the claimant statistics, since they can receive benefits without having to register as being available for employment. The benefits they receive are not regarded as 'unemployment related'.

The temporarily unemployed. People temporarily out of work are not entitled to benefits. Whether they should be regarded as 'genuinely' unemployed is debatable. A lot depends on (a) how long is 'temporary' and (b) just why people are temporarily out of work. If people voluntarily quit their job and then spend two or three weeks looking for a better one, this is far less serious a problem for them than if they were made redundant and after two or three weeks settled for a much lower-paid job.

People seeking part-time work. Such people are not entitled to benefits and therefore do not count as unemployed, even though they cannot find employment.

Underemployment. Some people may want to work full time and yet are only able to find part-time work. They are thus 'underemployed'. They do not show up in the statistics – not even as a fraction of an unemployed person. Underemployment is a particular problem in developing countries (this is examined in Chapter 25).

Disguised unemployment. Some firms may be reluctant to shed labour even when they are clearly overstaffed. If four people are employed to do the work of three, then it can be said that there is 'disguised' unemployment of one person. Other examples of disguised unemployment are where skilled people are forced to take low-paid jobs that do not utilise their skills. This was a major problem in the former USSR and other countries which were centrally planned and where people had guaranteed jobs.

Discouraged workers. Some people who have been out of work for a long time may give up hope of ever finding a job and thus stop seeking employment. Such people are not eligible for the job seeker's allowance.

Although, from an economist's perspective, the claimant figures underestimate the true extent of unemployment, it is possible that they nevertheless include *some* people whom economists would not regard as being genuinely unemployed. For example, some people in receipt of unemployment-related benefits may have taken early retirement and be in receipt of an occupational pension, or have given up employment in order to raise a family, or would rather live on unemployment benefit than take a job. Other people may turn down several offers of employment in the hope of getting a better offer. Other people may already have a job but pretend that they are unemployed so as to be able to claim benefits.

The UK Department of Education and Employment has tightened up its checks on claimants in recent years in order to prevent fraudulent claims. It has also made the eligibility conditions for benefits tougher. Claimants have to be able to demonstrate that they are actively seeking work and are prepared to accept suitable work when it is offered. It is thus likely that there are very few people nowadays in the UK who receive the job seeker's allowance, and who thus appear in the official unemployment statistics, who are not (by the economist's definition) unemployed.

Standardised unemployment rates

Two international organisations that publish unemployment statistics for many countries are the International Labour Office (ILO) and the Organisation for Economic Co-operation and Development (OECD). They define the unemployed as persons of working age who are without work, available for work and *actively seeking employment* or waiting to take up an appointment. The figures are compiled from the results of labour force *surveys*.

?? How does the ILO/OECD definition differ from the economist's definition? What is the significance of the phrase 'available for work at current wage rates' in the economist's definition?

Because these international bodies use the same 'standardised' definition for all countries, it makes international

Table 13.3 UK claimant unemployment by duration

	Up to 26 weeks	Over 26 and up to 52 weeks	Over 52 weeks	Total
Oct. 1979 (thousands)	771.6	194.2	337.0	1302.8
(per cent)	59.2	14.9	25.9	100.0
Oct. 1981 (thousands)	1514.5	689.5	784.6	2988.6
(per cent)	50.7	23.1	26.2	100.0
Oct. 1988 (thousands)	873.0	360.4	885.5	2118.9
(per cent)	41.2	17.0	41.8	100.0
Oct. 1990 (thousands)	873.4	289.5	507.7	1670.6
(per cent)	52.3	17.3	30.4	100.0
Oct. 1992 (thousands)	1293.1	565.7	955.6	2814.4
(per cent)	46.0	20.0	34.0	100.0
Oct. 1994 (thousands)	1057.7	440.9	956.5	2455.0
(per cent)	43.1	17.9	39.0	100.0
Oct. 1997 (thousands)	762.4	227.2	443.2	1432.8
(per cent)	53.2	15.9	30.9	100.0

Source: *Labour Market Trends* (ONS).

comparisons easier. But is the **standardised unemployment rate** likely to be higher or lower than the claimant unemployment rate? The standardised rate is likely to be higher to the extent that it includes people seeking work who are nevertheless not entitled to claim benefits, but lower to the extent that it excludes those who are claiming benefits and yet who are not actively seeking work. Clearly, the tougher the benefit regulations, the lower the claimant rate will be relative to the standardised rate.

The duration of unemployment

A few of the unemployed may never have had a job and maybe never will. For the rest, however, unemployment lasts only a period of time. For some it may be just a few days while they are between jobs. For others it may be a few months. For others – the long-term unemployed – it could be several years. Table 13.3 shows the composition of claimant unemployment by duration.

What determines the average duration of unemployment? There are three important factors here.

The number unemployed (the size of the stock of unemployment). Unemployment is a 'stock' concept (see Box 9.10). It measures a *quantity* (i.e. the number unemployed) at a particular *point in time*. Another example of a stock concept is a firm's stock of finished goods in the warehouse. The higher the stock of unemployment, the longer will tend to be the duration of unemployment. There will be more people competing for vacant jobs. Likewise, the bigger a firm's stock of finished goods, the longer they will tend to stay in the warehouse.

The rate of inflow and outflow from the stock of unemployment. The people making up the unemployment total are constantly changing. Each week some people are made redundant or quit their jobs. They represent an inflow to the stock of unemployment. Other people find jobs and thus represent an outflow from the stock of unemployment. The various inflows and outflows are shown in Figure 13.5.

Unemployment is often referred to as 'the pool of unemployment'. This is quite a good analogy. If the water flowing into a pool exceeds the water flowing out, the level of water in the pool will rise. Similarly, if the inflow of people into unemployment exceeds the outflow, the level of unemployment will rise.

The duration of unemployment will depend on the *rate* of inflow and outflow. The rate is expressed as the number of people per period of time. Table 13.4 shows the inflows and outflows in selected years.

Note the magnitude of the flows. In each of the years, the outflows (and inflows) exceed the total number unemployed. The bigger the flows are relative to the total number unemployed, the less will be the average duration of unemployment. This is because people move into and out of the pool more quickly, and hence their average stay will be shorter.

DEFINITION

Standardised unemployment rate The measure of the unemployment rate used by the ILO and OECD. The unemployed are defined as persons of working age who are without work, available for work and actively seeking employment.

Table 13.4 UK unemployment flows (millions)

	1980	1982	1984	1986	1990	1992	1994	1996	1997
Inflow	3.85	4.53	4.50	4.49	3.53	4.57	3.94	3.46	3.37
Outflow	3.21	4.24	4.40	4.88	2.82	4.15	4.34	3.78	3.84
Total level of unemployment	1.66	2.92	3.16	3.29	1.66	2.78	2.64	2.12	1.60

Source: *Labour Market Trends* (ONS).

??

1. If the number unemployed exceeded the total annual outflow, what could we conclude about the average duration of unemployment?
2. Make a list of the various inflows to and outflows from employment from and to (a) unemployment; (b) outside the workforce.

The phase of the business cycle. The duration of unemployment will also depend on the phase of the business cycle. At the onset of a recession, unemployment will rise, but as yet the average length of unemployment is likely to have been relatively short. Once a recession has lasted for a period of time, however, people on average will have been out of work longer, and this long-term unemployment is likely to persist even when the economy is pulling out of recession. This is illustrated in Table 13.3. In 1981, the UK had recently moved into recession, but as yet the percentage of claimants who had been out of work for more than a year was only 26.2 per cent. By 1988, however, even though the economy was expanding again and overall unemployment was falling, the figure had risen to 41.8 per cent.

The composition of unemployment

National unemployment statistics tell us nothing about the *distribution* of unemployment among various groups in society.

Geographical differences. Table 13.5 illustrates the considerable differences in unemployment rates between countries. Compare the unemployment rates in Japan and Spain! Countries have very different labour markets, very different policies on unemployment, training schemes, redundancy, etc., and very different attitudes of firms towards their workers. Also, countries may not be at precisely the same phase of their respective business cycles.

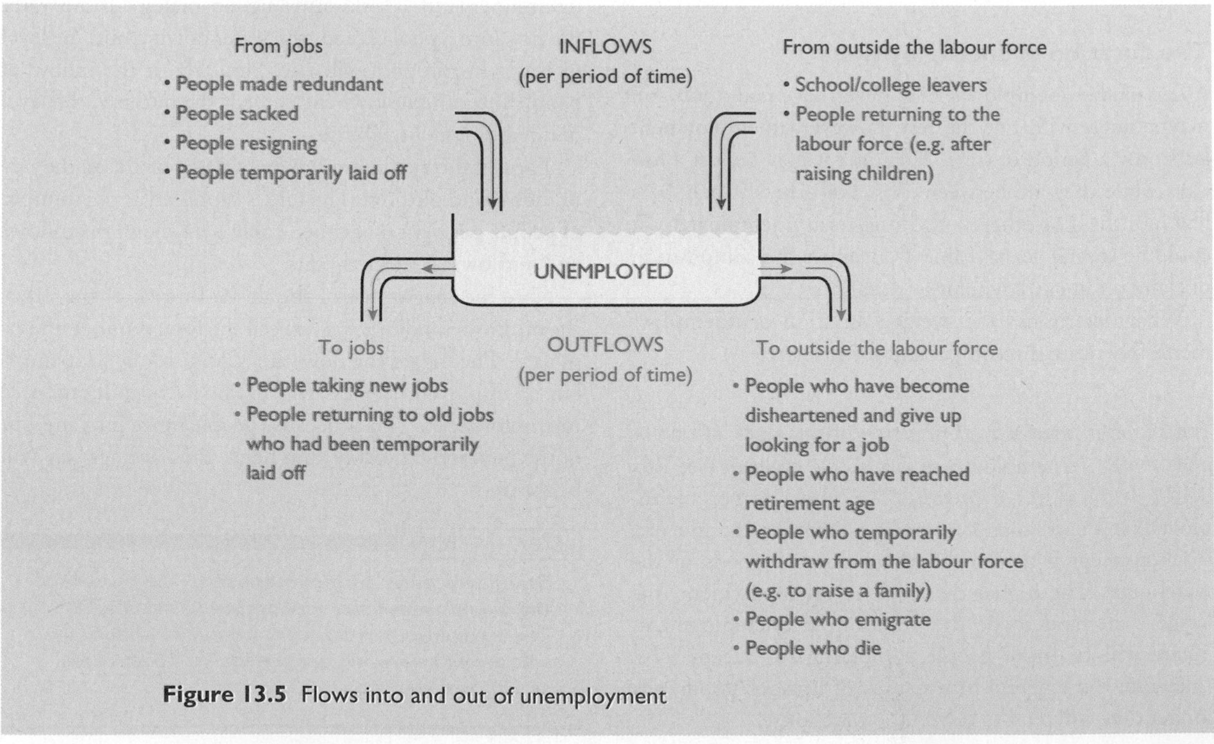

Figure 13.5 Flows into and out of unemployment

Table 13.5 Standardised unemployment rates in different sections of the labour market: March 1997

Country	Total (all ages)	Women (all ages)	Men (all ages)	Total under 25 years old	Women under 25 years old	Men under 25 years old
Belgium	9.6	12.5	7.5	22.4	26.7	18.9
Germany	9.7	10.7	8.9	9.7	8.8	10.6
France	12.5	14.7	10.6	28.2	31.3	25.3
Ireland	11.1	11.8	10.7	16.3	15.8	16.8
Japan	3.2	3.3	3.2	6.4	6.3	6.6
Netherlands	5.5	7.1	4.3	9.0	10.1	7.8
Spain	21.0	28.2	16.4	39.5	46.3	33.7
UK	7.2	6.1	8.2	14.8	12.6	16.7
USA	5.2	5.3	5.1	11.7	11.2	12.2
EU15	10.8	12.6	9.5	21.2	22.9	19.7

Source: *Eurostatistics* (Eurostat).

Unemployment also varies substantially within a country from one area to another. Most countries have some regions that are more prosperous than others. In the UK, unemployment in the north of England and in Northern Ireland is higher than in the south of England. For example, in 1997 claimant unemployment was 10.6 per cent in Merseyside and only 3.6 per cent in the south-east.

But geographical differences in unemployment are not just a regional problem. In many countries inner-city unemployment is very much higher than suburban or rural unemployment, and, as a result, most developed countries have schemes to attract employment to the inner cities.

Differences in unemployment rates between women and men. In virtually all developed countries, unemployment rates are higher for women than for men. This may reflect differences in education and training, discrimination by employers, more casual or seasonally related employment among women, or other social factors.

As can be seen from Table 13.5, the UK is the exception. Here the higher unemployment among men largely reflects the decline in many of the older industries, such as coal and steel, which employed mainly men. Given that fewer women who are unemployed are eligible for benefits in the UK, the gap is even bigger for claimant unemployment (8.3 per cent for men and 3.2 per cent for women in March 1997). Nevertheless the gap is closing. Explanations include: combinations of labour-saving technology in offices, equal-pay legislation, and the rise in unemployment in many service industries in the recession of the 1990s (industries where a high proportion of employees are women).

Differences in unemployment rates between different age groups. Table 13.5 also shows that unemployment rates in the under-25 age group are higher than the average, and substantially so in many countries. There are various explanations for this, including the suitability (or unsuitability) of the qualifications of school leavers, the attitudes of employers to young people and the greater willingness of young people to spend time unemployed looking for a better job or waiting to start a further or higher education course. The only exception in the table is Germany, which has a well-established apprenticeship system.

Differences in unemployment rates between different ethnic groups. In many countries, members of ethnic minorities suffer from higher unemployment rates than the average. In the UK, the unemployment rate for Afro-Caribbeans is $2^1/_2$ times greater than that for whites. For those of Pakistani and Bangladeshi origin, it is three times greater. Explanations are complex, but include differences in educational opportunities, a higher proportion of younger people, a greater sense of alienation among the unemployed, and the attitudes and prejudices of employers.

The costs of unemployment

The most obvious cost of unemployment is to the *unemployed themselves*. There is the direct financial cost of the loss in their earnings, measured as the difference between their previous wage and any unemployment benefit. Then there are the personal costs of being unemployed. The longer people are unemployed, the more dispirited they may become. Their self-esteem is likely to fall, and they are more likely to succumb to stress-related illness.

Then there are the costs to the *family and friends* of the unemployed. Personal relations can become strained, and there may be an increase in domestic violence and the number of families splitting up.

Then there are the *broader costs to the economy*. Unemployment represents a loss of output. In other words, actual output is below potential output. Apart from the lack of income to the unemployed themselves, this under-utilisation of resources leads to lower incomes for other people too:

- The government loses tax revenues, since the unemployed pay no income tax and national insurance, and, given that the unemployed spend less, they pay less VAT and excise duties. The government also incurs administrative costs associated with the running of benefit offices. It may also have to spend extra on health care, the social services and the police.
- Firms lose the profits that could have been made, had there been full employment.
- Other workers lose any additional wages they could have earned from higher national output.

What is more, the longer people remain unemployed, the more deskilled they tend to become, thereby reducing *potential* as well as actual income.

?? Why have the costs to the government of unemployment benefits not been included as a cost to the economy?

Finally, there is some evidence that higher unemployment leads to increased *crime and vandalism*. This obviously imposes a cost on the sufferers.

The costs of unemployment are to some extent offset by benefits. If workers voluntarily quit their jobs to look for a better one, then they must reckon that the benefits of a better job more than compensate for their temporary loss of income. From the nation's point of view, a workforce that is prepared to quit jobs and spend a short time unemployed will be a more adaptable, more mobile workforce – one that is responsive to changing economic circumstances. Such a workforce will lead to greater allocative efficiency in the short run and more rapid economic growth over the longer run.

Long-term involuntary unemployment is quite another matter. The costs clearly outweigh any benefits, both for the individuals involved and for the economy as a whole. A demotivated, deskilled pool of long-term unemployed is a serious economic and social problem.

Unemployment and the labour market

We now turn to the causes of unemployment. These causes fall into two broad categories: *equilibrium* unemployment and *disequilibrium* unemployment. To make clear the distinction between the two, it is necessary to look at the working of the labour market.

Figure 13.6 shows the **aggregate demand** for labour and **aggregate supply** of labour: that is, the total demand and supply of labour in the whole economy. The *real* average wage rate is plotted on the vertical axis. This is the average wage rate expressed in terms of its purchasing power: in other words, after taking prices into account.

The aggregate supply of labour curve (AS_L) shows the number of workers *willing to accept jobs* at each wage rate. This curve is relatively inelastic, since the size of the labour force at any one time cannot change significantly. Nevertheless it is not totally inelastic because (a) a higher wage rate will encourage some people to enter the labour market (e.g. parents raising children), and (b) the unemployed will be more willing to accept job offers rather than continuing to search for a better-paid job.

The aggregate demand for labour curve (AD_L) slopes downward. The higher the wage rate, the more firms will attempt to economise on labour. They will be encouraged to substitute other factors of production for labour.

The labour market is in equilibrium at a wage of W_e – where the demand for labour equals the supply.

If the wage rate were above W_e, the labour market would be in a state of disequilibrium. At a wage rate of W_1, there is an excess supply of labour of $A - B$. This is called **disequilibrium unemployment**.

For disequilibrium unemployment to occur, two conditions must hold:

- The aggregate supply of labour must exceed the aggregate demand.
- There must be a 'stickiness' in wages. In other words, the wage rate must not immediately fall to W_e.

DEFINITIONS

Aggregate demand for labour curve A curve showing the total demand for labour in the economy at different average real wage rates.

Aggregate supply of labour curve A curve showing the total number of people willing and able to work at different average real wage rates.

Disequilibrium unemployment Unemployment resulting from real wages in the economy being above the equilibrium level.

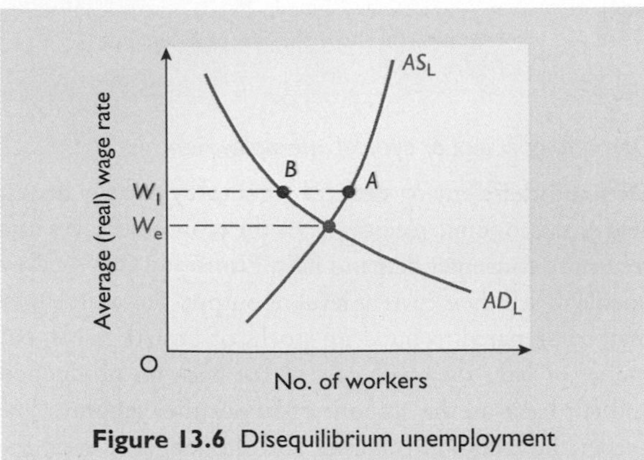

Figure 13.6 Disequilibrium unemployment

Even when the labour market *is* in equilibrium, however, not everyone looking for work will be employed. Some people will hold out, hoping to find a better job. This is illustrated in Figure 13.7.

The curve N shows the total number in the labour force. The horizontal difference between it and the aggregate supply of labour curve (AS_L) represents the excess of people looking for work over those actually willing to accept jobs. Q_e represents the equilibrium level of employment and the distance $D - E$ represents the **equilibrium level of unemployment**. This is sometimes known as the *natural level of unemployment*.

Note that the AS_L curve gets closer to the N curve at higher wages. The reason for this is that the unemployed will be more willing to accept jobs, the higher the wages they are offered.

Figure 13.8 shows both equilibrium *and* disequilibrium unemployment. At a wage of W_1, disequilibrium unemployment is $A - B$; equilibrium unemployment is $C - A$; thus total unemployment is $C - B$.

But what are the causes of disequilibrium unemployment? What are the causes of equilibrium unemployment? We will examine each in turn.

Disequilibrium unemployment

What causes the actual average wage rate to be above the market equilibrium wage rate? There are three possible reasons:

- The wage rate is pushed up above the equilibrium.
- There is a fall in the aggregate demand for labour with no corresponding fall in the wage rate.
- There is an increase in the aggregate supply of labour with no corresponding fall in the wage rate.

Each of these three causes gives rise to a distinct type of disequilibrium unemployment.

Real-wage or classical unemployment

Real-wage or **classical unemployment** is where trade unions use their monopoly power to drive wages above the market-clearing level. It could also be caused by governments introducing minimum wage legislation, or

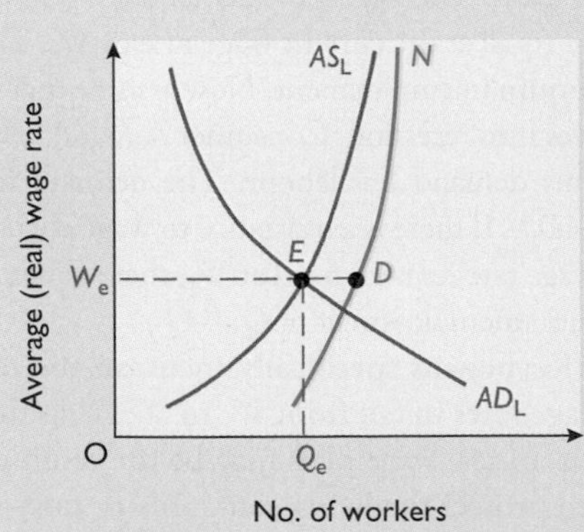

Figure 13.7 Equilibrium unemployment

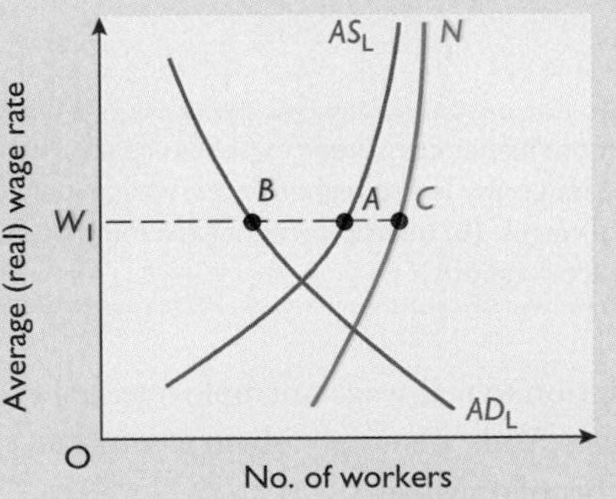

Figure 13.8 Equilibrium and disequilibrium unemployment

DEFINITIONS

Equilibrium ('natural') unemployment The difference between those who would like employment at the current wage rate and those willing and able to take a job.

Real wage or **classical unemployment** Disequilibrium unemployment caused by real wages being driven up above the market-clearing level.

operating a 'prices and incomes policy' where one of the provisions is for workers automatically to get wage increases above the rate of inflation.

In Figure 13.9, if the average wage rate is pushed up from W_e to W_1, the supply of labour will rise to Q_1 as higher wages encourage more people to join the labour force and to accept job offers. The demand for labour will fall to Q_2 as firms, faced by higher labour costs, cut back on production and attempt to substitute other factors of production for labour. (Their ability to do this will depend on the time scale. In the short run, some of the non-labour factors will be fixed. In the longer-run, however, firms will have greater flexibility. For example, they may replace workers by robots on assembly lines.)

The 'classical' economists in the 1920s and 1930s blamed the mass unemployment of that period on real wages being too high (hence the alternative name 'classical unemployment'). Excessive real wages have also been blamed by Conservative governments for the high unemployment of recent years (see Box 13.4).

Disequilibrium unemployment will thus be $Q_1 - Q_2$ (i.e. the amount $A - B$).

One effect of high real wages, however, may help to reduce real-wage unemployment. (This was an effect not recognised by classical economists.) The extra wages paid to those who are still employed could lead to extra *consumer* expenditure. This addition to aggregate demand would in turn lead to firms demanding more labour, as they attempted to increase output to meet the extra demand. If the effect of this is to shift the demand for labour to AD_{L_2}, real-wage unemployment will fall to $A - B'$.

?? If the higher consumer expenditure and higher wages subsequently led to higher *prices*, what would happen to: (a) real wages; (b) unemployment (assuming no further response from unions)?

The solution to real-wage unemployment is a reduction in real wages. This seemingly obvious solution, however, has a number of drawbacks:

- If the government reduces minimum wages, it will be the poorest workers who will suffer. It will not affect the wages or employment of those already on above-minimum wages.
- It may be very difficult to reduce the power of unions to push up wages.
- Even if the government succeeds in reducing the average real wage, there will then be a problem of reduced consumer expenditure and a reduced demand for labour.

?? How would you show this last problem in a diagram like Figure 13.9?

Demand-deficient or cyclical unemployment

Demand-deficient or **cyclical unemployment** is associated with economic recessions. As the economy moves into recession, consumer demand falls. Firms find that they are unable to sell their current level of output. For a time they may be prepared to build up stocks of unsold goods, but sooner or later they will start to cut back on production and cut back on the amount of labour they employ. The deeper the recession becomes and the longer it lasts, the higher will demand-deficient unemployment become.

As the economy recovers and begins to grow again, so demand-deficient unemployment will start to fall again. Because demand-deficient unemployment fluctuates with the business cycle, it is sometimes referred to as 'cyclical unemployment'.

Demand-deficient unemployment is also referred to as 'Keynesian unemployment', after John Maynard Keynes (see Box 15.6 for a person profile), who saw a deficiency of aggregate demand as the cause of the high unemployment between the two world wars. Today, many economists are known as 'Keynesian'. Although there are many strands of Keynesian thinking, these economists all see aggregate demand as important in determining a nation's output and employment.

Demand-deficient unemployment is illustrated in Figure 13.10. Assume initially that the economy is at the peak of the trade cycle. The aggregate demand for and supply of labour are equal at the current wage rate of W_1. There is no disequilibrium unemployment. Now assume that the economy moves into recession. Consumer demand falls and as a result firms demand less labour. The demand for labour shifts to AD_{L_2}. If there is a resistance to wage cuts, such that the real wage rate remains fixed at W_1, there will now be disequilibrium unemployment of $Q_1 - Q_2$.

Some Keynesians specifically focus on the reluctance of real wage rates to fall from W_1 to W_2. This downward 'stickiness' in real wage rates may be the result of unions seeking to protect the living standards of their members (even though there are non-union members out of work), or of firms worried about the demotivating effects

DEFINITION

Demand-deficient or **cyclical unemployment** Disequilibrium unemployment caused by a fall in aggregate demand with no corresponding fall in the real wage rate.

CASE STUDIES BOX 13.4

THE CONSERVATIVE PARTY'S ANALYSIS OF UNEMPLOYMENT

In his speech to the Conservative Party conference in 1985, the then Chancellor of the Exchequer, Nigel Lawson, made the following statement about unemployment:

> You won't reduce unemployment by increasing what government spends, or what government borrows, nor by printing more money. That approach has already been tested to destruction during the 1970s and unemployment went on rising . . .
>
> The main cause of high unemployment in Britain today, and it's much the same in the rest of Europe, is the determination of monopolistic trade unions to insist on levels of pay that price men out of work altogether.

On 13 December 1990, the Prime Minister, John Major, commenting on a dramatic rise in unemployment, said:

> Everyone regrets the rise in unemployment that we have seen, but I have been warning for some months that if wage rises stay high, that will have a necessary effect on jobs.

In his speech to the Conservative Party conference in 1993, the new Chancellor, Kenneth Clarke, put the blame for high unemployment in Europe on restrictive labour practices:

> Unemployment is a European problem, not just a British one. European labour markets are paralysed by restrictive practices, by social security systems that encourage dependency and by social laws that pile up costs on business. I promise British business that we will not go the way of France, where it costs an employer a minimum of £11 000 a year to employ a qualified 16-year-old school leaver. No wonder France has one of the highest unemployment rates in Europe.
>
> Labour's answer is simple. They want to sign up to the European Socialist Chapter; buying off the unions with a national minimum wage; pricing working people out of their jobs and on to the dole. It has been tried and it has failed. There are now 17 million unemployed people in Europe. And the numbers are rising.

?? What type of unemployment is being referred to in each of these three quotes?

of cutting the real wages of their workers. For such economists, the problem of demand-deficient unemployment would be solved if there could somehow be a fall in real wage rates.

For other Keynesian economists, however, the problem is much more fundamental than a downward stickiness in real wages. For them the problem is that the low level of aggregate demand causes an *equilibrium* in the *goods* market at an output that is too low to generate full employment. Firms' supply is low (below the full-employment level of supply) because aggregate demand is low.

This low-level equilibrium in the goods market, and the corresponding disequilibrium in the labour market, may *persist*. This is the result of a lack of confidence on the part of firms. After all, why should firms produce more and take on more workers, if they believe that the recession will persist and that they will therefore not sell any more? The economy remains trapped in a low-output equilibrium.

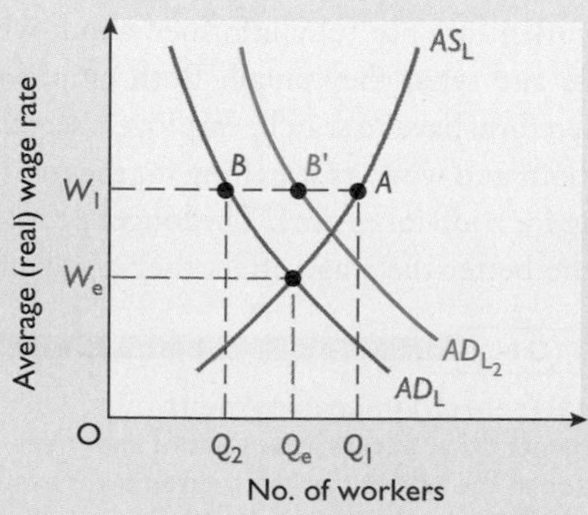

Figure 13.9 Real-wage unemployment

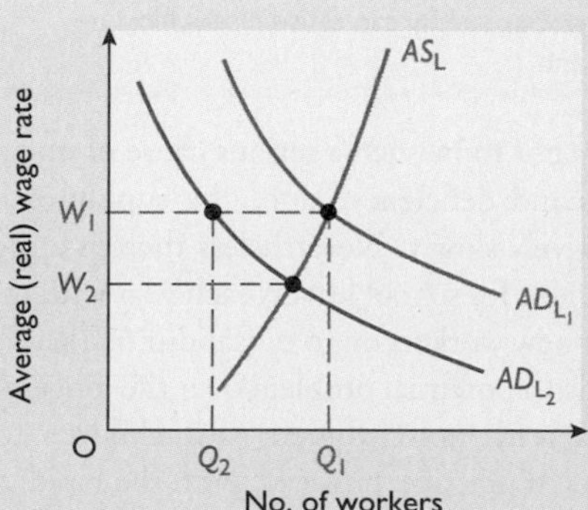

Figure 13.10 Demand-deficient unemployment

In such cases a fall in real wages would not cure the unemployment. In fact, it may even make the problem worse. In Figure 13.10, even if the average wage rate were to fall to W_2, demand-deficient unemployment would still persist. The reason is that this general cut in wages throughout the economy would reduce workers' incomes and hence reduce their *consumption of goods*. As the aggregate demand for goods fell, there would be a further reduction in demand for labour: the aggregate demand for labour curve would shift to the left of AD_{L_2}. By the time the wage had fallen to W_2, W_2 would no longer be the equilibrium wage. There would still be demand-deficient unemployment.

?? If this analysis is correct, namely that a reduction in wages will reduce the aggregate demand for goods, what assumption must we make about the relative proportions of wages and *profits* that are spent (given that a reduction in real wage rates will lead to a corresponding increase in rates of profit)?

Demand-deficient unemployment can also exist in the longer term if the economy is constantly run at below full capacity and labour markets continue not to be in equilibrium. Even at the peak of the business cycle, actual output may be considerably below potential output.

In an attempt to reduce demand-deficient unemployment, governments have sought to ensure that aggregate demand is high enough. Policies that raise aggregate demand may, however, worsen inflation and balance of payments deficits. (We will look at these effects later.)

Growth in the labour supply

If labour supply rises with no corresponding increase in the demand for labour, the equilibrium real wage rate will fall. If the real wage rate is 'sticky' downward, disequilibrium unemployment will occur.

?? On a diagram similar to Figure 13.10, illustrate how a growth in labour supply can cause disequilibrium unemployment.

This tends not to be such a serious cause of unemployment as demand deficiency, since the supply of labour changes relatively slowly. Nevertheless there is a problem of providing jobs for school leavers each year with the sudden influx of new workers on to the labour market.

There is also a potential problem over the longer term if social trends lead more women with children to seek employment. In practice, however, with the rapid growth of part-time employment, and the lower average wage rate paid to women, this has not been a major cause of excess labour supply.

Equilibrium unemployment (or natural unemployment)

Even when there is no general disequilibrium in the economy at the current wage levels – even when there are as many job vacancies as people unemployed – there will still be some unemployment. For various reasons, not all vacancies will be filled. The problem is one of mismatching. There may be excess demand for labour (vacancies) in some markets and excess supply (unemployment) in others. There may be vacancies for computer technicians and unemployment in the steel industry, but unemployed steel workers cannot immediately become computer technicians. There may even be vacancies *and* unemployment in the same market, but the unemployed may be unable, unwilling or unsuitable to take up the vacancies, or simply unaware of their existence.

Although there may be overall *macro*economic equilibrium, with the *aggregate* demand for labour equal to the *aggregate* supply, and thus no disequilibrium unemployment, at a *micro*economic level supply and demand may not match. This is when equilibrium unemployment will occur.

There are various types of equilibrium unemployment.

Frictional (search) unemployment

Frictional (search) unemployment occurs when people leave their jobs, either voluntarily or because they are sacked or made redundant, and are unemployed for a period of time while they are looking for a new job. They may not get the first job they apply for, despite a vacancy existing. The employer may continue searching, hoping to find a better-qualified person. Likewise unemployed people may choose not to take the first job they are offered. Instead they may continue searching, hoping that a better one will turn up.

The problem is that information is imperfect. Employers are not fully informed about what labour is available; workers are not fully informed about what jobs are available and what they entail. Both employers and workers, therefore, have to search: employers searching for the right labour and workers searching for the right jobs.

Searching for a job takes time. The longer people search for a job, the better the wage offers they are likely to be

DEFINITION

Frictional (search) unemployment
Unemployment that occurs as a result of imperfect information in the labour market. It often takes time for workers to find jobs (even though there *are* vacancies) and in the meantime they are unemployed.

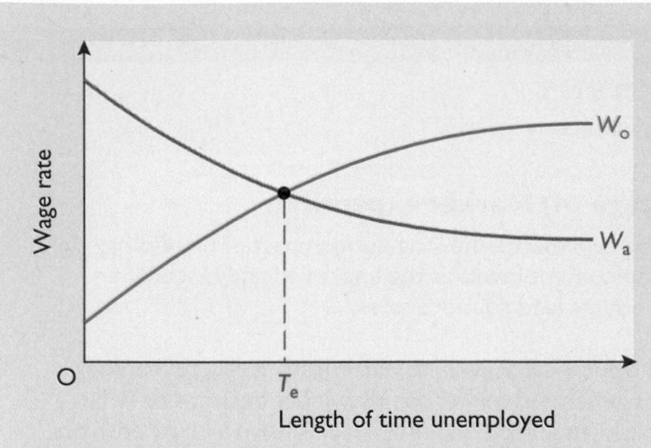

Figure 13.11 Average duration of unemployment

made. This is illustrated in Figure 13.11 by the curve W_o. It shows the highest wage offer that the typical worker will have received since being unemployed.

When they first start looking for a job, people may have high expectations of getting a good wage. The longer they are unemployed, however, the more anxious they are likely to be to get a job, and therefore the lower will be the wage they will be prepared to accept. The curve W_a shows the wage that is acceptable to the typical worker.

?? Why are W_o and W_a curves rather than straight lines?

The average duration of unemployment will be T_e. That is, workers will remain unemployed until they find a job at an acceptable wage.

One obvious remedy for frictional unemployment is for there to be better job information. This could be provided by government job centres, by private employment agencies, or by local and national newspapers. This would have the effect of making the curve W_o reach its peak earlier, and thus of shifting the intersection of W_o and W_a to the left.

Another much more controversial remedy is for the government to reduce the level of unemployment benefit. This will make the unemployed more desperate to get a job and thus prepared to accept a lower wage. It will therefore have the effect of shifting the W_a curve downwards and again of shifting the intersection of W_o and W_a to the left.

Structural unemployment

Structural unemployment is where the structure of the economy changes. Employment in some industries may expand while in others it contracts. There are two main reasons for this.

A change in the pattern of demand. Some industries experience declining demand. This may be due to a change in consumer tastes. Certain goods may go out of fashion. Or it may be due to competition from other industries. For example, consumer demand may shift away from coal and to other fuels. This will lead to structural unemployment in mining areas.

A change in the methods of production (technological unemployment). New techniques of production often allow the same level of output to be produced with fewer workers. This is known as 'labour-saving technical progress'. Unless output expands sufficiently to absorb the surplus labour, people will be made redundant. This creates **technological unemployment.**

Structural unemployment often occurs in particular regions of the country. When it does, it is referred to as **regional unemployment**. Regional unemployment is due to the concentration of particular industries in particular areas. For example, the decline in the South Wales coal-mining industry led to high unemployment in the Welsh valleys.

The level of structural unemployment will depend on three factors:

- The degree of regional concentration of industry. The more diversified is a region's economy, the less it will be affected by the decline of one particular industry.
- The speed of change of demand and supply in the economy. The more rapid the rate of technological change or the shift in consumer tastes, the more rapid will be the rate of redundancies.
- The immobility of labour. The less able or willing workers are to move to a new job, the higher will be the level of structural unemployment. Remember from Chapter 9 the distinction we made between geographical and occupational immobility. Geographical

DEFINITIONS

Structural unemployment Unemployment that arises from changes in the pattern of demand or supply in the economy. People made redundant in one part of the economy cannot immediately take up jobs in other parts (even though there are vacancies).

Technological unemployment Structural unemployment that occurs as a result of the introduction of labour-saving technology.

Regional unemployment Structural unemployment occurring in specific regions of the country.

ISSUES AND APPLICATIONS BOX 13.5

TECHNOLOGY AND EMPLOYMENT

Does technological progress create or destroy jobs?

Does technological progress destroy jobs? The obvious answer may seem to be yes. After all, new technology often involves machines taking over jobs that were previously done by people.

There is another view, however. This argues that a failure to introduce new technology and ultimately to remain competitive will offer an even worse long-term employment problem. Markets, and hence employment, will be lost to more efficient competitors.

The relative merits of each of these views are difficult to assess, since they depend greatly upon the type of technology, its organisation in the workplace and the market within which it is located. The diagram isolates four stages in the effects of new technology on jobs.

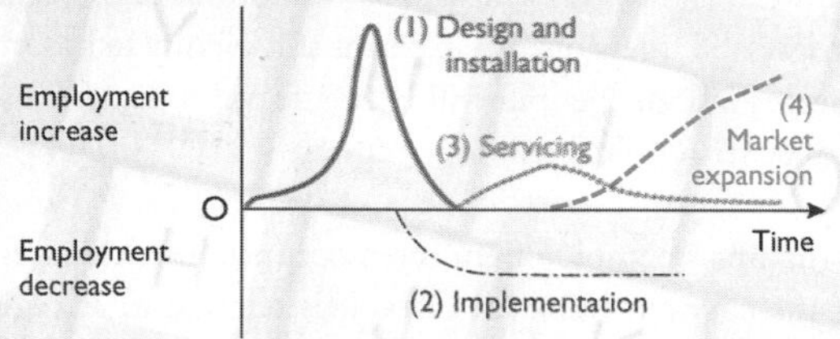

Four effects of new technology on employment

Source: A. Rajan and G. Cooke, 'The impact of IT on employment', (*National Westminster Bank Quarterly Review*, August 1986).

Stage (1) Design and installation

Here labour requirements grow as first designers and then construction workers are employed. As construction/installation is completed, employment from this source will then disappear.

Stage (2) Implementation

Here labour requirements decline, especially if the technology is concerned with improving existing processes rather than creating new products.

Stage (3) Servicing

Maintenance and repair may have positive employment effects. This may gradually decrease over time as 'teething troubles' are eliminated, or it may increase as the stock of initially new machines begins to grow older.

Stage (4) Market expansion

This represents the long-term impact of technology on employment levels as the improved and/or cheaper products lead to more sales.

The *optimistic* view holds that, historically, technology has generated more jobs than it has destroyed. Total employment today is much higher than a hundred years ago, and yet technological progress has allowed many goods and services to be produced with far fewer workers. What has happened is that increased output has more than compensated for the growth in labour productivity. There is no reason, say the optimists, why this process should not continue.

The *pessimists*, however, are less certain about the potential employment benefits of new technology. Even in growth industries, such as pharmaceuticals, electronics, optical technology and high-value plastics, there has been a decline in employment. Except in a few parts of the world where a rapid growth in exports has allowed a huge expansion of output (e.g. certain south-east Asian countries), output growth in high-tech industries has *not* kept pace with the growth in labour productivity.

But can workers who are displaced from high-tech industries not simply find jobs in other parts of the economy? There are two problems here. The first is that of structural unemployment. Displaced workers may not have the skills to take up work elsewhere. Clearly what is needed is a system of retraining that enables workers to move to alternative jobs. The second is that of income distribution. If the only alternative jobs are relatively low-skilled ones in the service sector (cleaners, porters, shelf packers, checkout assistants, etc.), the displaced workers may have to accept a considerable cut in wages.

??

1. In what areas of the economy are jobs growing most rapidly? Is this due to a lack of technological innovation in these areas?
2. Why have rural areas generally seen a smaller decline in high-tech employment than urban areas, and in some cases seen an increase?

EXPLORING THE THEORY — BOX 13.6

DO PEOPLE VOLUNTEER TO BE UNEMPLOYED?
The distinction between voluntary and involuntary unemployment

A distinction made by some economists is that between *voluntary* and *involuntary* unemployment. Many economists would regard equilibrium unemployment as voluntary. If people choose not to accept a job at the going wage, even though there are jobs available, then in a sense they could be said to have voluntarily chosen to be unemployed. Disequilibrium unemployment, according to these economists, would be classed as involuntary. Workers want to work at the current wage, but there are not enough jobs available.

Some economists would also include classical unemployment as voluntary. If people, through their unions, have chosen to demand a higher wage than the equilibrium wage, then they could be said to have collectively 'volunteered' to make themselves unemployed. According to these economists, then, only demand-deficient unemployment would be classed as involuntary.

Some economists go even further and argue that *all* unemployment should be classed as voluntary. If the cause of disequilibrium unemployment is a downward stickiness in real wage rates, then workers, either individually or collectively, are *choosing* not to accept work at a lower wage.

Other economists would go to the other extreme and claim that all disequilibrium unemployment and most equilibrium unemployment is involuntary. Structural unemployment, for example, results from changes in demand and/or supply patterns in the economy and a resulting mismatching of unemployed workers' skills to the person specifications of vacant jobs. Workers can hardly be said to have volunteered for these changes in demand. True, people can be retrained, but retraining takes time, and in the meantime they will be unemployed. Similarly with frictional unemployment, if the cause of some people being unemployed is initial ignorance of job opportunities and hence the time it takes to search for a job, they cannot be said to have volunteered to be initially poorly informed.

The terms 'voluntary' and 'involuntary' unemployment are not only ambiguous, they are also unfortunate because they have strong normative overtones. 'Voluntary' unemployment tends to imply that the *blame* for unemployment lies with the unemployed person and not with 'market forces' or with inadequate government policies. While in one sense, at a low enough wage rate there would probably be a job for virtually any unemployed person, the unemployed cannot be said to be voluntarily unemployed if they are choosing to turn down jobs at pitifully low wages.

Although the concepts of voluntary and involuntary unemployment are commonly used, for the above reasons we shall avoid them.

?? If I offered a job to someone to clean my house at 1p per hour, and unemployed people chose not to take the job, should they be classed as 'voluntarily' unemployed?

immobility is a particular problem with regional unemployment. Occupational immobility is a particular problem with technological unemployment where old skills are no longer required.

There are two broad approaches to tackling structural unemployment: *market orientated* and *interventionist*.

A market-orientated approach involves encouraging people to look more actively for jobs, if necessary in other parts of the country. It involves encouraging people to adopt a more willing attitude towards retraining, and if necessary to accept some reduction in wages.

An interventionist approach involves direct government action to match jobs to the unemployed. Two examples are providing grants to firms to set up in areas of high unemployment (regional policy), and government-funded training schemes.

Policies to tackle structural unemployment are examined in detail in sections 22.3 and 22.4.

Seasonal unemployment

Seasonal unemployment occurs when the demand for certain types of labour fluctuates with the seasons of the year. This problem is particularly severe in holiday areas such as Cornwall, where unemployment can reach very high levels in the winter months. Policies for tackling seasonal unemployment are similar to those for structural unemployment.

DEFINITION

Seasonal unemployment Unemployment associated with industries or regions where the demand for labour is lower at certain times of the year.

SECTION SUMMARY

1. Who should be counted as 'unemployed' is a matter for some disagreement. The two most common measures of unemployment are claimant unemployment (those claiming unemployment-related benefits) and ILO/OECD standardised unemployment (those available for work and actively seeking work or waiting to take up an appointment).
2. The 'stock' of unemployment will grow if the inflow of people into unemployment exceeds the outflow (to jobs or out of the labour market altogether). The more rapid these flows, the shorter the average duration of unemployment.
3. The costs of unemployment include the financial and other personal costs to the unemployed person, the costs to relatives and friends, and the costs to society at large in terms of lost tax revenues, lost profits and lost wages to other workers, and in terms of social disruption.
4. Unemployment can be divided into disequilibrium and equilibrium unemployment.
5. Disequilibrium unemployment occurs when real wages are above the level that will equate the aggregate demand and supply of labour. It can be caused by unions or government pushing up wages (classical or real-wage unemployment), by a fall in aggregate demand but a downward 'stickiness' in real wages (demand-deficient unemployment), or by an increase in the supply of labour with again a downward stickiness in wages.
6. In the case of demand-deficient unemployment, the disequilibrium in the labour market may correspond to a low-output *equilibrium* in the goods market. A fall in real wage rates may be insufficient to remove the deficiency of demand in the labour market.
7. Equilibrium unemployment occurs when there are people unable or unwilling to fill job vacancies. This may be due to poor information in the labour market and hence a time lag before people find suitable jobs (frictional unemployment), to a changing pattern of demand or supply in the economy and hence a mismatching of labour with jobs (structural unemployment – specific types being technological and regional unemployment), or to seasonal fluctuations in the demand for labour.

13.4 Inflation

The rate of inflation measures the annual percentage increase in prices. The most usual measure is that of *retail* prices. The government publishes an index of retail prices each month, and the rate of inflation is the percentage increase in that index over the previous twelve months.

Figure 13.12 shows the rates of inflation for the USA, Japan, the UK, the EU and the OECD. As you can see, inflation was particularly severe between 1973 and 1983, and relatively low in the late 1980s and mid-1990s. Although most countries have followed a similar pattern over time, the average rates of inflation have differed substantially from one country to another. This is shown in Table 13.6. The table also shows that inflation rates in the major industrialised economies have tended to converge as barriers to international trade and capital movements have been reduced.

It is also possible to give the rates of inflation for other prices. For example, indices are published for commodity prices, for food prices, for house prices, for import prices, for prices after taking taxes into account and so on. Their respective rates of inflation are simply their annual percentage increases. Likewise it is possible to give the rate of inflation of wage rates ('wage inflation').

A word on terminology: if prices rise, we refer to that as 'inflation'. If prices fall, however, this is normally referred to as 'negative inflation' rather than 'deflation'. The word 'deflation' is normally used to refer to a government policy of reducing aggregate demand – a policy designed to reduce excessive spending in the economy.

Finally, before we proceed, a word of caution: be careful not to confuse a rise or fall in *inflation* with a rise or fall in *prices*. A rise in inflation means a *faster* increase in prices. A fall in inflation means a *slower* increase in prices (but still an increase as long as inflation is positive). (See Box A1.1 on page 36.)

The costs of inflation

A lack of growth is obviously a problem if people want higher living standards. Unemployment is obviously a problem, both for the unemployed themselves and also for society, which suffers a loss in output and has to support the unemployed. But why is inflation a problem? If prices go up by 10 per cent, does it really matter? Provided your wages kept up with prices, you would have no cut in your living standards.

Table 13.6 Inflation rates for selected countries (average % per annum)

Country	1979–89	1990–98
USA	5.5	3.1
Japan	2.5	1.3
Germany	2.9	2.8
France	7.3	2.1
Italy	11.2	4.3
UK	7.4	3.9
Sweden	7.9	4.0
Netherlands	2.8	2.5
Belgium	4.8	2.4
EU15	7.4	3.5
OECD	8.9	5.2

Source: *OECD Economic Outlook* (OECD).

If people could correctly anticipate the rate of inflation and fully adjust prices and incomes to take account of it, then the costs of inflation would indeed be relatively small. For us as consumers, they would simply be the relatively minor inconvenience of having to adjust our notions of what a 'fair' price is for each item when we go shopping. For firms, they would again be the relatively minor costs of having to change price labels, or prices in catalogues or on menus, or adjust slot machines. These are known as **menu costs**.

In reality, people frequently make mistakes when predicting the rate of inflation and are not able to adapt fully to it. This leads to the following problems, which are likely to be more serious the higher the rate of inflation becomes and the more the rate fluctuates.

Redistribution. Inflation redistributes income away from those on fixed incomes and those in a weak bargaining position, to those who can use their economic power to gain large pay, rent or profit increases. It redistributes wealth to those with assets (e.g. property) which rise in value particularly rapidly during periods of inflation, and away from those with types of savings which pay rates of interest below the rate of inflation and hence whose value is eroded by inflation. Pensioners may be particularly badly hit by rapid inflation.

??

1. Do you personally gain or lose from inflation? Why?
2. Make a list of those who are most likely to gain and those who are most likely to lose from inflation.

DEFINITION

Menu costs of inflation The costs associated with having to adjust price lists or labels.

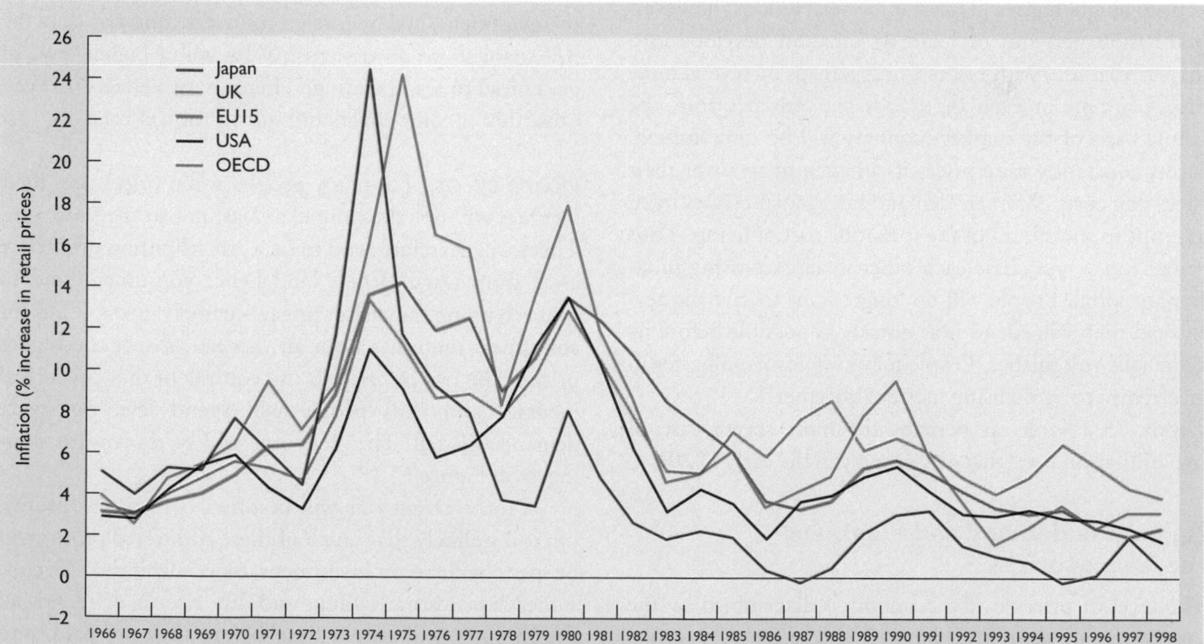

Figure 13.12 Inflation rates in selected industrial countries and groups of countries: 1966–98

Source: *Datastream*.

Uncertainty and lack of investment. Inflation tends to cause uncertainty among the business community, especially when the rate of inflation fluctuates. (Generally, the higher the rate of inflation, the more it fluctuates.) If it is difficult for firms to predict their costs and revenues, they may be discouarged from investing. This will reduce the rate of economic growth. On the other hand, as will be explained below, policies to reduce the rate of inflation may themselves reduce the rate of economic growth, especially in the short run. This may then provide the government with a policy dilemma.

Balance of payments. Inflation is likely to worsen the balance of payments. If a country suffers from relatively high inflation, its exports will become less competitive in world markets. At the same time, imports will become relatively cheaper than home-produced goods. Thus exports will fall and imports will rise. As a result the balance of payments will deteriorate and/or the exchange rate will fall. Both of these effects can cause problems. This is examined in more detail in section 14.1.

Resources. Extra resources are likely to be used to cope with the effects of inflation. Accountants and other financial experts may have to be employed by companies to help them cope with the uncertainties caused by inflation. The costs of inflation may be relatively mild if inflation is kept to single figures. They can be very serious, however, if inflation gets out of hand. If inflation develops into 'hyperinflation', with prices rising perhaps by several hundred per cent or even thousands per cent per year, the whole basis of the market economy will be undermined. Firms constantly raise prices in an attempt to cover their rocketing costs. Workers demand huge pay increases in an attempt to stay ahead of the rocketing cost of living. Thus prices and wages chase each other in an ever-rising inflationary spiral. People will no longer want to save money. Instead they will spend it as quickly as possible before its value falls any further. People may even resort to barter in an attempt to avoid using money altogether.

Box 13.7 looks at perhaps the most severe case of hyperinflation ever: that of Germany in the early 1920s.

Aggregate demand and supply and the level of prices

The level of prices in the economy is determined by the interaction of aggregate demand and aggregate supply. The analysis is similar to that of demand and supply in individual markets, although as we shall see in later chapters there are some crucial differences. Figure 13.13 shows an aggregate demand and an aggregate supply curve. As with demand and supply curves for individual goods, we plot price on the vertical axis, except that now it is the *general* price level; and we plot quantity on the horizontal axis, except that now it is the *total quantity of national output*.

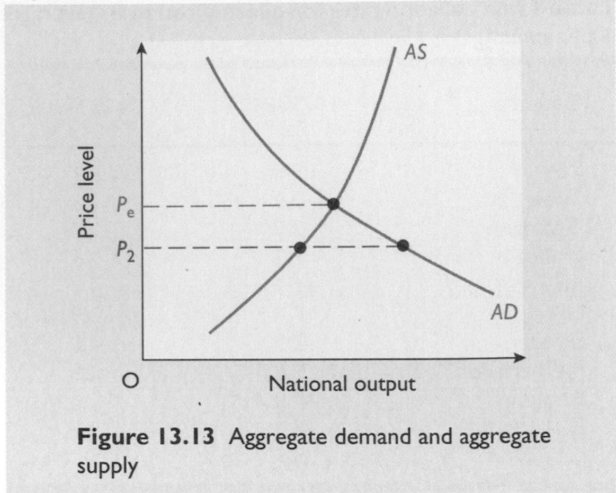

Figure 13.13 Aggregate demand and aggregate supply

Let us examine each curve in turn.

Aggregate demand curve

Remember what we said about aggregate demand earlier in the chapter. It is the total level of spending in the economy: that is, by consumers, by the government, by firms on investment, and by foreign residents. But why does the *AD* curve slope downwards? Why will a higher level of prices lead to less spending? There are two effects that can cause this: income effects and substitution effects.

Income effects. For many people, when prices rise, their incomes will not rise in line, at least not in the short run. There will therefore tend to be a redistribution of income away from wage earners (and hence consumers) and to those charging the higher prices – namely, firms. Thus for consumers there has been an *income effect* of the higher prices. The rise in prices is the equivalent of a cut in real incomes and thus people will spend less. Aggregate demand will fall. The *AD* curve will be downward sloping, as in Figure 13.13.

To some extent this will be offset by a rise in profits, but it is unlikely that much of these additional profits will be spent by firms on investment, especially if they see consumer expenditure falling; and any rise in dividends to shareholders will take a time before they are paid, and again may simply be saved rather than spent.

Clearly, this income effect will not operate if wages rise in line with prices. Real incomes of wage earners will be unaffected.

CASE STUDIES — BOX 13.7

HYPERINFLATION IN GERMANY: 1923

When prices went crazy

In recent years in the UK we have come to expect relatively stable prices. If the rate of inflation were to rise to anywhere near the levels reached in the mid-1970s (24 per cent) or the early 1980s (18 per cent), it would be looked upon as a clear sign of economic failure.

But such rates are mild compared with those experienced by many other countries in the past, or in some cases the present. In 1993 the rate of inflation in Ukraine was 500 per cent and in Brazil it was 1200 per cent. But even these cases of hyperinflation are mild compared with those experienced by several countries in the early 1920s!

In Austria and Hungary prices were several thousand times their pre-war level. In Poland they were over 2 million times higher, and in the USSR several billion times higher. But even these staggering rates of inflation seem insignificant beside those of Germany.

Following the chaos of the First World War, the German government resorted to printing money, not only to meet its domestic spending requirements in rebuilding a war-ravaged economy, but also to finance the crippling war reparations imposed on it by the allies in the Treaty of Versailles.

In 1919 the currency in circulation increased by a massive 80 per cent and prices increased by 91 per cent. At the end of 1919, however, a new socialist government attempted to slow this inflationary spiral. New taxes were imposed and government revenues increased. But public debt continued to grow, and by mid-1921 the government once more resorted to the printing presses to finance its expenditure.

Inflation now really began to take off, and by autumn 1923 the annual rate of inflation had reached a mind-boggling 7 000 000 000 000 per cent!

The table charts the rise in money supply and inflation from 1921 to 1923. (Note that the figures for inflation are *quarterly*.)

		Currency[1]	Prices[1]	Unemployment[2]	Real wages[3]
1921	I	−1.5	−7.1		
	II	5.6	2.1	2.8	18.1
	III	11.8	51.3		
	IV	29.5	68.7		
1922	I	14.3	55.8		
	II	28.6	29.4	1.5	−53.6
	III	84.0	308.3		
	IV	289.5	413.9		
1923	I	331.1	231.1		
	II	213.8	297.0	10.2	49.3
	III	1622.9	1234.4		
	IV	17 580.7	52 678.8		

[1] Percentage change from previous quarter.
[2] Percentage of the labour force.
[3] Percentage annual rate of change.

Source: A. Sommariva and G. Tullio, *German Macroeconomic History 1880–1979* (Macmillan, 1987).

As price increases accelerated, people became reluctant to accept money: before they knew it, the money would be worthless. People thus rushed to spend their money as quickly as possible. But this in turn further drove up prices.

For many Germans the effect was devastating. People's life savings were wiped out. Others whose wages were not quickly adjusted found their real incomes plummeting. Many were thrown out of work as businesses, especially those with *money* assets, went bankrupt. Poverty and destitution were widespread.

By the end of 1923 the German currency was literally worthless. In 1924, therefore, it was replaced by a new currency – one whose supply was kept tightly controlled by the government.

An income effect is also likely to occur as a result of the tax system. As prices and incomes rise, so people will find that they are paying a larger proportion of their incomes in taxes. As a result they cannot afford to buy so much.

Substitution effects. If, in the *micro*economic situation, the price of one good rises, people will switch to alternative goods. This is the substitution effect of that price rise and helps to explain why the demand curve for a particular good will be downward sloping. But how can there be a substitution effect at a *macro*economic level? If prices in general go up, what can people substitute for spending? There are in fact three ways in which people can switch to alternatives.

The first, and most obvious, concerns *imports and exports*. Higher prices for our country's goods will discourage foreign residents from buying our exports (which are part of aggregate demand) and encourage domestic residents to buy imports (which are *not* part of aggregate demand). Thus higher domestic prices will lead to a fall in aggregate demand (i.e. cause the *AD* curve to be downward sloping).

The second is known as the **real balance effect**. If prices rise, the value (i.e. the purchasing power) of people's balances in their bank and building society accounts will fall. But many people will be reluctant to reduce the real value of their balances too much, and will thus probably cut back on their spending also. This desire by people to protect the real value of their balances will thus also cause aggregate demand to fall.

The third reason why people may switch away from spending concerns changes in *interest rates*. With higher prices to pay by consumers, and higher wages to pay by firms, there will tend to be a greater demand for *money*. With a given supply of money in the economy, there will now be a shortage of money. As a result, banks will tend to raise interest rates. These higher rates of interest will have a dampening effect on spending: after all, the higher the interest rates people have to pay, the more expensive it is to buy things on credit. Again aggregate demand is likely to fall.

Aggregate supply curve

The aggregate supply curve slopes upwards – at least in the short run.[1] In other words, the higher the level of prices, the more will be produced. The reason is simple: provided that factor prices (and in particular wage rates) do not rise as rapidly as product prices, firms' profitability at each level of output will be higher than before. This will encourage them to produce more.

This is merely an extension of the microeconomic theory of the firm. If the rightward shift in the demand curve for a firm's product is less than fully offset by any leftward (upward) shifts in the firm's costs curves, its profit-maximising output will increase.

But what *limits* the increase in aggregate supply in response to an increase in prices? In other words, why is the aggregate supply curve not horizontal? There are two main reasons.

Diminishing returns. With some factors of production fixed in supply, firms will experience a diminishing marginal physical product from their variable factors, and hence will have an upward-sloping marginal cost curve. Any increase in demand would cause a movement up along this curve.

Growing shortages of certain variable factors. As firms produce more, even factors that can be varied may increasingly become in short supply. Skilled labour may be harder to find; certain raw materials may be harder to obtain; monopoly suppliers of component parts may raise their price to take advantage of the higher level of demand. (In a microeconomic diagram this would have the effect of shifting a firm's *MC* curve upwards.)

Thus rising costs explain the upward sloping aggregate supply curve. The more steeply costs rise, the less elastic will the curve be. In the extreme case, where wage rates and other costs rise by the full amount of any rise in prices, the aggregate supply curve will be vertical: i.e. totally inelastic. (In a microeconomic diagram the upward shift in the *MC* curve would fully offset the rightward shift in the demand curve.)

Equilibrium

The equilibrium price level will be where aggregate demand equals aggregate supply. To demonstrate this, consider what would happen if aggregate demand exceeded aggregate supply: for example, at P_2 in Figure 13.13. The resulting shortages throughout the economy would drive up prices. This would encourage firms to produce more: there would be a movement up *along* the *AS* curve. At the same time, for a given level of money income, people would not purchase so much: there would be a movement back up *along* the *AD* curve. The shortage would be eliminated when price had risen to P_e.

This explains how inflation occurs. An excess of aggregate demand over aggregate supply drives up prices. This excess can be caused by a rightward shift in *AD*, or a leftward shift in *AS*, or a combination of the two. When these shifts occur persistently, such as to give persistent rises in prices, then there is a problem of inflation. The faster the curves shift, the more rapidly prices rise and therefore the higher is the rate of inflation.

When inflation results from rightward shifts in aggregate demand it is known as **demand-pull inflation** (or 'demand-side' inflation). When it originates from leftward

[1] We will be looking at the distinction between short- and long-run aggregate supply curves in Chapters 15 and 21.

DEFINITIONS

Real balance effect As the price level rises, so the value of people's money balances will fall. They will therefore *spend* less in order to increase their money balances and go some way to protecting their real value.

Demand-pull inflation Inflation caused by persistent rises in aggregate demand.

shifts in aggregate supply it is known as **cost-push inflation** (or 'supply-side' inflation). Let us examine each in turn.

Demand-pull inflation

This is caused by rises in aggregate demand (i.e. persistent rightward shifts in the *AD* curve). These rises in aggregate demand may be due to rises in consumer demand, in the level of government expenditure, in investment by firms, or in foreign residents' demand for the country's exports, or any combination of these four.

Just what causes rises in aggregate demand is a matter of considerable debate among economists. Some economists attribute rises in aggregate demand entirely (or virtually so) to an increase in money supply. If there is more money in the economy, there will be more spending. These economists, called **monetarists**, therefore see the cure for inflation to lie in the government curbing the growth in supply of money in the economy.

Other economists see a much more tenuous link between money and spending. They argue that there can be an autonomous rise in spending with no increase in money supply. For example, consumer spending could rise substantially if the government cut the rate of income tax by 2 or 3 per cent, or if there were an upsurge in business confidence and hence investment.

Thus a distinction is frequently made between *monetary* and *non-monetary* explanations of demand-pull inflation.

So just what will happen if aggregate demand rises? Firms will respond to a rise in demand partly by raising prices and partly by increasing output. Just how much they raise prices depends on how much their costs rise as a result of increasing output. In other words, it will depend on the shape of the *AS* curve.

The effect is illustrated in Figure 13.14. The rise in aggregate demand is illustrated by a rightward shift in the aggregate demand curve, from AD_1 to AD_2. Prices rise from P_1 to P_2, and output rises from Q_1 to Q_2. The steeper the aggregate supply curve, the more prices will rise and the less output will increase.

The aggregate supply curve will tend to become steeper as the economy approaches the peak of the business cycle. In other words, the closer actual output gets to potential output, and the less slack there is in the economy, the more will firms respond to a rise in demand by raising their prices.

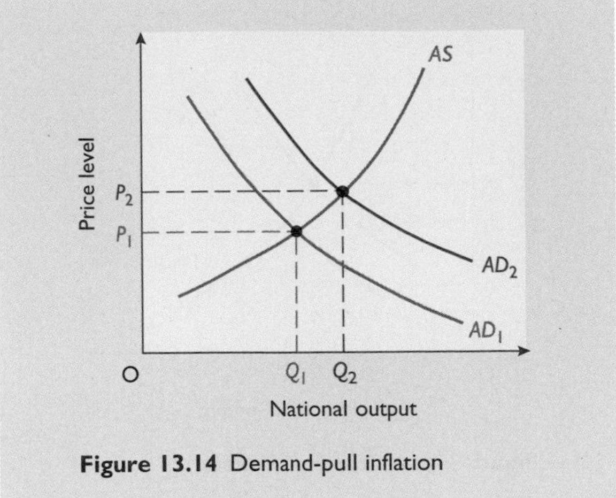

Figure 13.14 Demand-pull inflation

What we have illustrated so far is a *single* increase in demand (or a 'demand shock'). This could be due, for example, to an increased level of government expenditure. The effect is to give a *single* rise in the price level. Although this causes inflation in the short run, once the effect has taken place inflation will fall back to zero. For inflation to persist there must be *continuing* rightward shifts in the *AD* curve, and thus continuing rises in the price level. If *inflation* is to rise, these rightward shifts must get *faster*.

Demand-pull inflation is typically associated with a booming economy. Many economists therefore argue that it is the counterpart of demand-deficient unemployment. When the economy is in recession, demand-deficient unemployment will be high, but demand-pull inflation will be low. When, on the other hand, the economy is near the peak of the business cycle, demand-pull inflation will be high, but demand-deficient unemployment will be low.

Cost-push inflation

Cost-push inflation is associated with leftward (upward) shifts in the aggregate supply curve. Such shifts occur when costs of production rise *independently* of aggregate demand.

If firms face a rise in costs, they will respond partly by raising prices and passing the costs on to the consumer, and partly by cutting back on production. This is illustrated in Figure 13.15. There is a leftward shift in the aggregate supply curve: from AS_1 to AS_2. This causes the price level to rise to P_3 and the level of output to *fall* to Q_3.

DEFINITIONS

Cost-push inflation Inflation caused by persistent rises in costs of production (independently of demand).

Monetarists Those who attribute inflation solely to rises in money supply.

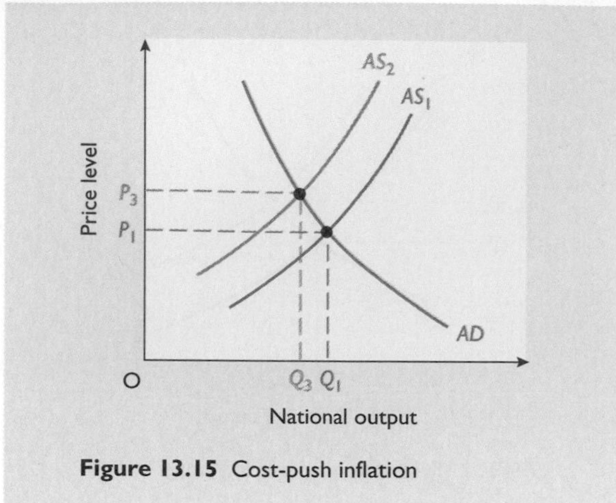

Figure 13.15 Cost-push inflation

Just how much firms raise prices and cut back on production depends on the shape of the aggregate demand curve. The less elastic the *AD* curve, the less will sales fall as a result of any price rise, and hence the more will firms be able to pass on the rise in their costs to consumers as higher prices.

Note that the effect on output and employment will be the opposite of demand-pull inflation. With demand-pull inflation, output and hence employment will tend to rise.

As with demand-pull inflation, we must distinguish between *single* shifts in the aggregate supply curve (known as 'supply shocks') and *continuing* shifts. If there is a single leftward shift in aggregate supply, there will be a single rise in the price level. For example, if the government raises the excise duty on oil, there will be a single rise in oil prices and hence in industry's fuel costs. This will cause *temporary* inflation while the price rise is passed on through the economy. Once this has occurred, prices will stabilise at the new level and the rate of inflation will thus fall back to zero again. If cost-push inflation is to continue over a number of years, therefore, the aggregate supply curve must *continually* shift to the left. If cost-push inflation is to *rise*, these shifts must get *faster*.

The rise in costs may originate from a number of different sources. As a result we can distinguish various types of cost-push inflation:

- Wage-push inflation. This is where trade unions push up wages independently of the demand for labour.
- Profit-push inflation. This is where firms use their monopoly power to make bigger profits by pushing up prices independently of consumer demand.
- Import-price-push inflation. This is where import prices rise independently of the level of aggregate demand. An example is when OPEC quadrupled the price of oil in 1973/4.

In all these cases, inflation occurs because one or more groups are exercising economic power. The problem is likely to get worse, therefore, if there is an increasing concentration of economic power over time (for example, if firms or unions get bigger and bigger, and more monopolistic) or if groups become more militant.

These causes are likely to interact. Firms and unions may compete with each other for a larger share of national income. This can lead to wages and prices chasing each other upwards.

Additional causes of cost-push inflation include the following:

- Tax-push inflation. This is where increased taxation adds to the cost of living. For example, when VAT in the UK was raised from 8 per cent to 15 per cent in 1979, prices rose as a result.
- The exhaustion of natural resources. If major natural resources become depleted, the *AS* curve will shift to the left. Examples include the gradual running-down of North Sea oil, pollution of the seas and hence a decline in incomes for nations with large fishing industries, and, perhaps the most devastating of all, the problem of 'desertification' in sub-Saharan Africa. Temporary inflationary problems could also arise due to short-run supply problems, such as a bad harvest.

The interaction of demand-pull and cost-push inflation

Demand-pull and cost-push inflation can occur together, since wage and price rises can be caused both by increases in aggregate demand and by independent causes pushing up costs. Even when an inflationary process *starts* as either demand-pull or cost-push, it is often difficult to separate the two. An initial cost-push inflation may encourage the government to expand aggregate demand to offset rises in unemployment. Alternatively, an initial demand-pull inflation may strengthen the power of certain groups which then use this power to drive up costs.

The interaction of the two causes is illustrated in Figure 13.16. Assume that powerful groups are constantly pushing up the costs of production. The *AS* curve is constantly shifting to the left. At the same time assume that the government, in order to prevent a rise in unemployment, is constantly boosting the level of aggregate demand (say, by cutting taxes). The *AD* curve is constantly shifting to the right. The net effect on output and employment may be very small, but prices may rise substantially.

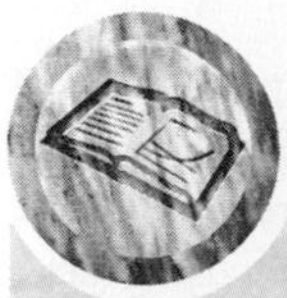

EXPLORING THE THEORY — BOX 13.8

COST-PUSH ILLUSION

When rising costs are *not* cost-push inflation

It is easy to get confused between demand-pull and cost-push inflation.

Frequently, inflationary pressures *seem* to come from the cost side. Shopkeepers blame their price rises on the rise in their costs – the wholesale prices they have to pay. The wholesalers blame their price rises on a rise in *their* costs – the prices they are charged by the various manufacturers. The manufacturers in turn blame rising raw material costs, rising wage rates, rising rents and so on. Everyone blames their price rises on the rise in their costs.

But why have these costs risen?

It could well be due to a rise in aggregate *demand*! Wages may go up because of falling unemployment and a shortage of labour. Firms *have* to pay higher wages in order to recruit or maintain enough labour. Rents may rise because of the upsurge in demand. So too with raw materials: higher demand may pull up their prices too.

What we have then is a 'cost-push illusion'. Costs rise, it is true, but they rise because of an increase in *demand*.

So when does genuine cost-push inflation occur? This occurs when costs of production rise *independently* of demand. This will normally involve an increased use of monopoly power: unions becoming more powerful or militant and thus driving up wages; firms using their monopoly/oligopoly power to push up prices; commodity producers such as the OPEC countries forming cartels to push up their prices; the government using its power to raise indirect taxes (such as VAT).

??

If consumer demand rises and firms respond by raising prices, is this necessarily an example of demand-pull inflation? Could there be such a thing as demand-pull illusion? (Clue: why might consumer demand have risen?)

If these shifts get more and more rapid, a **wage–price spiral** will result. Unions demand higher and higher wages to cover higher and higher costs of living. Firms put up their prices to higher and higher levels to cover the higher and higher costs of production. The government, in an attempt to avoid a recession, accommodates these price and wage rises by printing more and more money. Wage and price rises accelerate as these shifts get faster and faster. Inflation goes on rising.

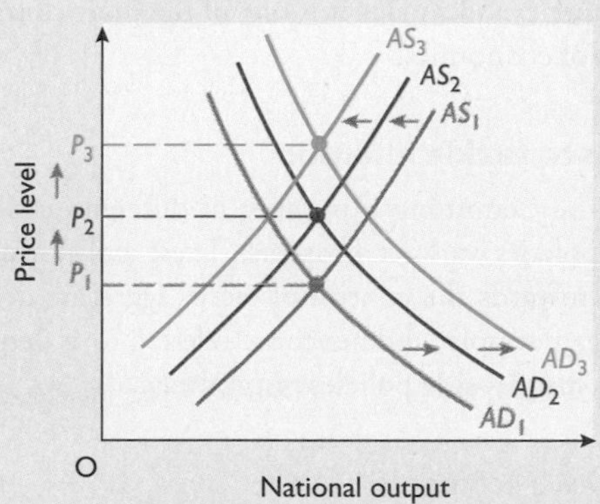

Figure 13.16 The interaction of demand-pull and cost-push inflation

Structural (demand-shift) inflation

When the *pattern* of demand (or supply) changes in the economy, certain industries will experience increased demand and others decreased demand. If prices and wages are inflexible downwards in the contracting industries, and prices and wages rise in the expanding industries, the overall price and wage level will rise. The problem will be made worse, the less elastic is supply to these shifts.

Thus a more rapid structural change in the economy can lead to both increased structural unemployment and increased structural inflation. An example of this problem was the so-called north–south divide in the UK during the boom of the second half of the 1980s. The north experienced high structural unemployment as old industries declined, while the south experienced excess demand. This excess demand in the south, among other things, led to rapid house price inflation, and rapid increases in incomes for various groups of workers and firms. With many prices and wages being set *nationally*, the inflation in the south then 'spilt over' into the north.

Expectations and inflation

Workers and firms take account of the *expected* rate of inflation when making decisions.

DEFINITION

Wage–price spiral Wages and prices chasing each other as aggregate demand continually shifts to the right and aggregate supply continually shifts to the left.

Imagine that a union and an employer are negotiating a wage increase.

Let us assume that both sides expect a rate of inflation of 10 per cent. The union will be happy to receive a wage rise somewhat above 10 per cent. That way the members would be getting a *real* rise in incomes. The employers will be happy to pay a wage rise somewhat below 10 per cent. After all, they can put their price up by 10 per cent, knowing that their rivals will do approximately the same. The actual wage rise that the two sides agree on will thus be somewhere around 10 per cent.

Now let us assume that the expected rate of inflation is 20 per cent. Both sides will now negotiate around this benchmark, with the outcome being somewhere round about 20 per cent.

Thus the higher the expected rate of inflation, the higher will be the level of pay settlements and price rises, and hence the higher will be the resulting actual rate of inflation.

The importance of expectations in explaining the actual rate of inflation has been increasingly recognised by economists in recent years. As a result economists have been concerned to discover just what determines people's expectations. As you might expect, there is considerable disagreement, and in fact it is one of the most controversial areas of economics.

Policies to tackle inflation

We will be examining a number of different anti-inflationary policies in later chapters. These policies can be directed towards the control of either aggregate demand or aggregate supply, and hence are referred to as **demand-side** and **supply-side** policies respectively.

Demand-side policies

There are two types of demand-side policy:

Fiscal policy. **Fiscal policy** involves altering government expenditure and/or taxation. Aggregate demand can be reduced by cutting government expenditure (one of the four elements in aggregate demand) or by raising taxes and hence reducing consumer expenditure. These are both examples of **deflationary** fiscal policy.

(Fiscal policy could also be used to *boost* aggregate demand if there were a problem of demand-deficient unemployment. In this case the government would raise government expenditure and/or cut taxes. This is called **reflationary** fiscal policy.)

Monetary policy. **Monetary policy** involves altering the supply of money in the economy or manipulating the rate of interest. The government can reduce aggregate demand (a *deflationary* monetary policy) by reducing the money supply, thereby making less money available for spending, or by putting up interest rates and thus making borrowing more expensive. If people borrow less, they will spend less.

Supply-side policies

The aim here is to reduce the rate of increase in costs. This will help reduce leftward shifts in the aggregate supply curve. This can be done either by restraining monopoly influences on prices and incomes (e.g. by various forms of wage and price control, policies to restrict the activities of trade unions, or policies to restrict mergers and takeovers), or by designing policies to increase productivity (e.g. giving various tax incentives, encouraging various types of research and development, giving grants to firms to invest in up-to-date equipment or in the training of labour).

We will examine all these various policies as the book progresses. As we shall see, just as economists cannot agree on the causes of inflation, so too they cannot agree on the most appropriate cures.

DEFINITIONS

Demand-side policies Policies designed to affect aggregate demand: fiscal policy and monetary policy.

Supply-side policies Policies designed to affect aggregate supply. Policies to affect costs or productivity.

Fiscal policy Policy to affect aggregate demand by altering the balance between government expenditure and taxation.

Deflationary policy Fiscal or monetary policy designed to reduce the rate of growth of aggregate demand.

Reflationary policy Fiscal or monetary policy designed to increase the rate of growth of aggregate demand.

Monetary policy Policy to affect aggregate demand by altering the supply or cost of money (rate of interest).

SECTION SUMMARY

1. Inflation redistributes incomes from the economically weak to the economically powerful; it causes uncertainty in the business community and as a result reduces investment; it tends to lead to balance of payments problems and/or a fall in the exchange rate; it leads to resources being used to offset its effects. The costs of inflation can be very great indeed in the case of hyperinflation.
2. Equilibrium in the economy occurs when aggregate demand equals aggregate supply. Inflation can occur if there is a rightward shift in the aggregate demand curve or an upward (leftward) shift in the aggregate supply curve.
3. Demand-pull inflation occurs as a result of increases in aggregate demand. This can be due to monetary or non-monetary causes.
4. Cost-push inflation occurs when there are increases in the costs of production independent of rises in aggregate demand. Cost-push inflation can be of a number of different varieties: wage-push, profit-push, import-price-push, tax-push or that stemming from reductions in potential output.
5. Cost-push and demand-pull inflation can interact to form spiralling inflation.
6. Inflation can also be caused by shifts in the pattern of demand in the economy, with prices rising in sectors of increasing demand but being reluctant to fall in sectors of declining demand.
7. Expectations play a crucial role in determining the level of inflation. The higher people expect inflation to be, the higher it will be.
8. Policies to tackle inflation can be either demand-side policies (fiscal or monetary) or supply-side policies (to reduce monopoly power or increase productivity).

??? END-OF-CHAPTER QUESTIONS ???

1. The following table shows index numbers for real GDP (national output) for various countries (1990 = 100).

	1987	1988	1989	1990	1991	1992	1993	1994	1995	1996	1997
USA	92.7	96.4	98.8	100.0	99.4	101.7	104.8	109.1	112.7	115.1	117.6
Japan	85.5	90.8	95.2	100.0	104.0	105.1	105.2	105.7	106.5	109.1	111.6
Germany (W)	87.9	91.1	94.4	100.0	104.6	105.8	103.8	107.4	108.5	109.4	112.1
France	89.5	93.8	97.6	100.0	100.8	102.1	100.6	103.5	106.0	107.4	110.3
UK	92.8	97.5	99.6	100.0	98.0	97.5	99.7	103.5	106.0	108.4	111.7

1997 figures are projected.

Source: *Economic Trends* (ONS); *OECD Economic Outlook* (OECD); *The Economist.*

(a) Work out the growth rate for each country for each year from 1988 to 1997.

(b) Plot the figures on a graph. Describe the pattern that emerges.

2. Will the rate of actual growth have any effect on the rate of potential growth?
3. For what possible reasons may one country experience a persistently faster rate of economic growth than another?
4. At what phase of the trade cycle is the average duration of unemployment likely to be the highest?
5. Would it be desirable to have zero unemployment?
6. What would be the benefits and costs of increasing the rate of unemployment benefit?
7. Consider the most appropriate policy for tackling each of the different types of unemployment.
8. Do any groups of people gain from inflation?
9. If everyone's incomes rose in line with inflation, would it matter if inflation were 100 per cent or even 1000 per cent per annum?
10. Imagine that you had to determine whether a particular period of inflation was demand pull, or cost push, or a combination of the two. What information would you require in order to conduct your analysis?

14

Macroeconomic issues II

The open economy

In the last chapter we looked at the three macroeconomic objectives of economic growth, low unemployment and low inflation. A country's ability to achieve these objectives will be influenced by its relationships with the rest of the world. We must now therefore look at the **open economy**, and examine a country's *international* economic relationships.

First we shall look at the flows of money from one country to another, as countries trade with each other and invest in each other's economies. We shall see how these flows are recorded in a *balance of payments account* (section 14.1), and then see how these flows affect the *exchange rate* (section 14.2). The balance of payments and the exchange rate constitute the fourth macroeconomic issue that we identified at the beginning of the last chapter.

Having looked at all four macroeconomic issues, we next examine how the four are related, and in particular how they are affected by aggregate demand and how they fluctuate over the course of the business cycle (section 14.3). This allows us then to develop a simple model (the circular flow of income) to show how national income is related to aggregate demand (section 14.4).

Central to all four macroeconomic issues is the level of national income. The chapter closes by examining how in practice national income is measured (section 14.5).

14.1 The balance of payments

The balance of payments account

A country's balance of payments account records all the flows of money between residents of that country and the rest of the world. *Receipts* of money from abroad are regarded as *credits* and are entered in the accounts with a positive sign. *Outflows* of money from the country are regarded as *debits* and are entered with a negative sign.

There are two main parts of the balance of payments account: the *current account* and the *capital account*. Each part is then subdivided. We shall look at each part in turn, and take the UK as an example. Table 14.1 gives a summary of the UK balance of payments for 1981, 1989 and 1997.

The current account

The **current account** records payments for imports and exports of goods and services, plus incomes from property flowing into and out of the country, plus net transfers of money into and out of the country. It is normally divided into three subdivisions.

The trade in goods account. This records imports and exports of physical goods (previously known as 'visibles'). Exports result in an inflow of money and are therefore a credit item. Imports result in an outflow of money and are therefore a debit item. The balance of these is called the **balance of trade in goods** or **balance of visible trade** or

DEFINITIONS

Open economy One that trades with and has financial dealings with other countries.

Current account of the balance of payments The record of a country's imports and exports of goods and services, plus incomes and transfers of money to and from abroad.

Balance of trade in goods or **balance of visible trade** or **merchandise balance** Exports of goods minus imports of goods.

Table 14.1 UK balance of payments (£ millions)

	1981		1989		1997	
CURRENT ACCOUNT						
1. Trade in goods						
a) Exports	+50 668		+92 154		+170 145	
b) Imports	−47 416		−116 837		−183 124	
Balance on trade in goods	+3 252		−24 683		−12 979	
2. Trade in services						
a) Exports	+16 764		+29 332		+53 299	
b) Imports	−12 972		−25 971		−44 015	
Balance on trade in services	+3 792		+3 361		+9 284	
Balance on trade in goods and services		+7 044		−21 322		−3 695
3. Other income flows						
Investment income balance		+1 251		+3 502		+12 166
Transfers balance		−1 547		−4 578		−3 968
Current account balance		**+6 748**		**−22 398**		**+4 503**
CAPITAL ACCOUNT						
(Transactions in UK external assets and liabilities)						
3. Long-term capital transactions						
a) Net investment in UK from abroad	+3 190		+34 646		+44 775	
b) Net UK investment abroad	−10 473		−58 027		−78 073	
Long-term capital balance		−7 283		−23 381		−33 298
4. Short-term capital flows						
a) Net deposits in UK from abroad and borrowing from abroad by UK residents	+40 143		+75 627		+205 772	
b) Net deposits abroad by UK residents and UK lending to overseas residents	−42 715		−38 081		−183 479	
Short-term capital balance		−2 572		+37 546		+22 293
5. Reserves (drawing on + adding to −)		+2 577		+5 440		+2 357
Net transactions in external assets and liabilities (capital account balance)		**−7 278**		**+19 605**		**−8 648**
TOTAL CURRENT + CAPITAL ACCOUNTS		−530		−2 793		−4 145
6. (Balancing item)		+530		+2 793		+4 145
		0		**0**		**0**

Source: *Economic Trends* (ONS); *Financial Statistics* (ONS).

merchandise balance. A *surplus* is when exports exceed imports. A *deficit* is when imports exceed exports.

The trade in services account. This records imports and exports of services (such as transport, tourism and insurance). Thus the purchase of a foreign holiday would be a debit, whereas the purchase by an overseas resident of a UK insurance policy would be a credit to the UK services account. The balance of these is called the *services balance*.

The balance of both the goods and services accounts together is known as the **balance on trade in goods and services** or simply the **balance of trade**.

Other current flows. There are two items here:

- Investment incomes. These consist of interest, profit and dividends flowing into and out of the country. For example, interest earned by a foreign resident from shares in a UK company would be an outlfow of money (a debit item).

DEFINITION

Balance of trade in goods and services or **balance of trade** Exports of goods and services minus imports of goods and services.

- Transfers of money. These include government grants to developing countries (aid), government contributions to the EU budget and to international organisations, and international transfers of money by private individuals and firms. For example, a birthday gift of money received by a British student from an aunt in Australia would be a credit item.

The **current account balance** is the overall balance of all the above three subdivisions. A *current account surplus* is where credits exceed debits. A *current account deficit* is where debits exceed credits. The record of the UK's balance of payments on current account since 1970 is shown in Figure 14.1. Note that the figures are given in 1985 prices.

> ?? Why does the use of constant prices allow better comparison of the figures over time?

The capital account

The official title for the **capital account** of the balance of payments is the *transactions in external assets and liabilities*. It records cross-border changes in the holding of shares, property, bank deposits and loans, government securities, etc. In other words, unlike the current account which is concerned with money incomes, the capital account is concerned with the purchase and sale of assets. There are three main sections in this part of the balance of payments.

The long-term capital account. This records capital investments. There are two categories here.

- Direct investment. If a foreign company invests in the UK (e.g. acquires a new factory), this represents an inflow of money when the investment is made and is thus a credit item. (Any subsequent profit from this investment that flows abroad will be recorded as an investment income outflow on the current account.) UK investment abroad represents an outflow of money when the investment is made. It is thus a debit item.

  Note that what we are talking about here is the acquisition or sale of assets: e.g. a factory or land, or the takeover of a whole firm, *not* the imports or exports of equipment.
- Portfolio investment. This is changes in the holding of paper assets, such as company shares. Thus if a UK resident buys shares in an overseas company, this is a debit item.

> ?? Is it a 'bad thing' to have a deficit on the long-term capital account?

Short-term capital flows. These consist of various types of short-term monetary movement between the UK and the rest of the world. Deposits by overseas residents in banks in the UK and loans to the UK from abroad are

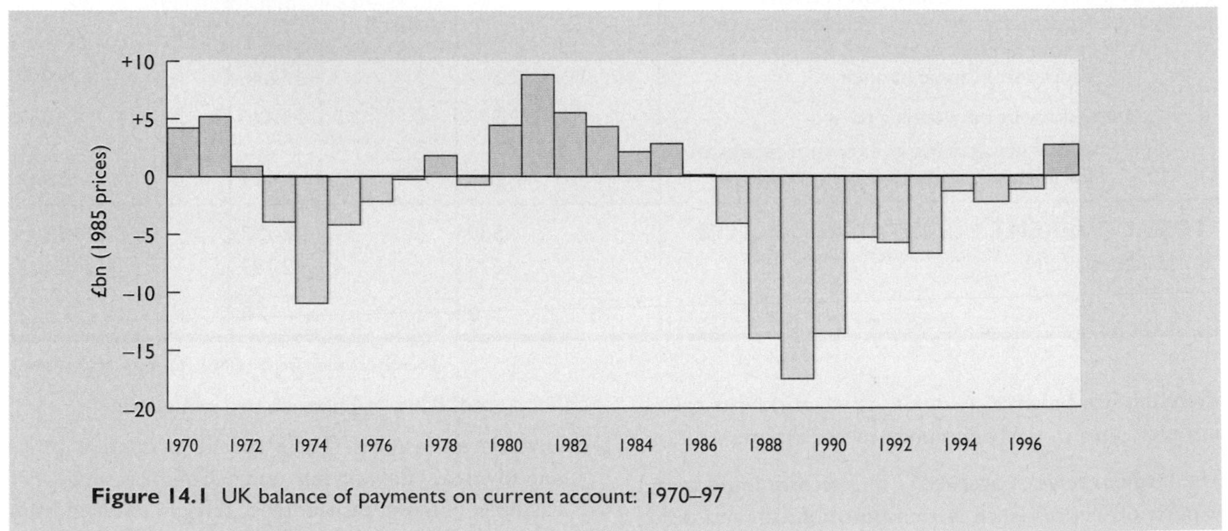

Figure 14.1 UK balance of payments on current account: 1970–97

DEFINITIONS

Balance of payments on current account The balance of trade in goods and services plus net investment incomes and transfers.

Capital account of the balance of payments (or transactions in external assets and liabilities) The record of all changes in the country's ownership of foreign assets and foreign ownership of this country's assets.

credit items, since they represent an inflow of money. Deposits by UK residents in overseas banks and loans by UK banks to overseas residents are debit items. They represent an outflow of money.

Short-term monetary flows are common between international financial centres to take advantage of differences in countries' interest rates and changes in exchange rates.

??

1. Why may inflows of short-term deposits create a problem?
2. Where would interest payments on short-term foreign deposits in UK banks be entered on the balance of payments account?

Note that in the case of both long- and short-term capital flows, credits and debits are recorded *net*. For example, UK investment abroad consists of the net acquisition of assets abroad (i.e. the purchase less the sale of assets abroad). Similarly foreign investment in the UK consists of the purchase less the sale of UK assets by foreign residents. Note that in either case the flow could be in the opposite direction. For example, if UK residents purchased less assets abroad than they sold, this item would be a net credit, not a debit (there would be a net return of money to the UK). This was the case in 1994.

By recording capital account items net, the flows seem misleadingly modest. For example, if UK residents deposited an extra £100bn in banks abroad but drew out £99bn, this would be recorded as a mere £1bn net outflow on the short-term capital account. In fact, *total* capital account flows vastly exceed current account flows.

Flows to and from the reserves. The UK, like all other countries, holds reserves of gold and foreign currencies. From time to time the Bank of England (acting as the government's agent) will sell some of these reserves to purchase sterling on the foreign exchange market. It does this normally as a means of supporting the rate of exchange (see below). Drawing on reserves represents a *credit* item in the balance of payments accounts: money drawn from the reserves represents an *inflow* to the balance of payments (albeit an outflow from the reserves account). The reserves can thus be used to support a deficit elsewhere in the balance of payments. Conversely, if there is a surplus elsewhere in the balance of payments, the Bank of England can use it to build up the reserves. Building up the reserves counts as a debit item in the balance of payments, since it represents an outflow from it (to the reserves).

When all the components of the balance of payments account are taken together, the balance of payments should exactly balance: credits should equal debits. As we shall see below, if they were not equal, the rate of exchange would have to adjust until they were, or the government would have to intervene to make them equal.

When the statistics are compiled, however, a number of errors are likely to occur. As a result there will not be a balance. To 'correct' for this a **balancing item** is included in the accounts. This ensures that there will be an exact balance. The main reason for the errors is that the statistics are obtained from a number of sources, and there are often delays before items are recorded and sometimes omissions too.

Assessing the balance of payments figures

It is often regarded as being undesirable for the combined current and long-term capital accounts to be in deficit. If they were in deficit, this would have to be covered by borrowing from abroad or attracting deposits from abroad. This might necessitate paying high rates of interest. It also leads to the danger that people abroad might at some time in the future suddenly withdraw their money from the UK and cause a 'run on the pound'. An alternative would be to draw on reserves. But this too causes problems. If the reserves are run down too rapidly, it may cause a crisis of confidence, and again a run on the pound. Also, of course, reserves are limited and hence there is a limit to which they can be used to pay for a balance of payments deficit.

It is also often regarded as undesirable for a country to have a *current account* deficit, even if it is matched by a long-term capital account surplus. Although this will bring the short-term benefit of a greater level of consumption through imports, and hence a temporarily higher living standard, the excess of imports over exports is being financed by foreign investment in the UK. This represents a greater claim on UK assets by foreigners. For example, the current account deficits of Western oil-importing countries after the oil price increases of the 1970s were partly offset by the purchase of large quantities of assets in the West by OPEC countries. On the other hand, investment by foreigners may lead to increased production and hence possibly increased incomes for UK residents.

??

With reference to the above, provide an assessment of the UK balance of payments in each of the three years illustrated in Table 14.1.

DEFINITION

Balancing item A statistical adjustment to ensure that the two sides of the balance of payments account balance. It is necessary because of errors in compiling the statistics.

CASE STUDIES BOX 14.1

WORLD TRADE IMBALANCE: JAPAN AND THE USA

Mirror images in the balance of payments

The old saying that one person's gain is another person's loss is nicely illustrated by the trade imbalance between the USA and its trading partners, most notably Japan.

In recent years the United States has run a huge current account deficit. This has been funded by a massive inflow of capital, causing a correspondingly huge capital account surplus. The major proportion of this capital is supplied by Japan, which has a huge current account surplus and uses this surplus to invest and lend abroad.

To rephrase the old saying, one person's surplus is another person's deficit!

??

1. What are the costs and benefits of this imbalance to the two countries?
2. The long-term capital account imbalances between the two countries are not a precise mirror image of the current account imbalances. What explanations can you offer for this?

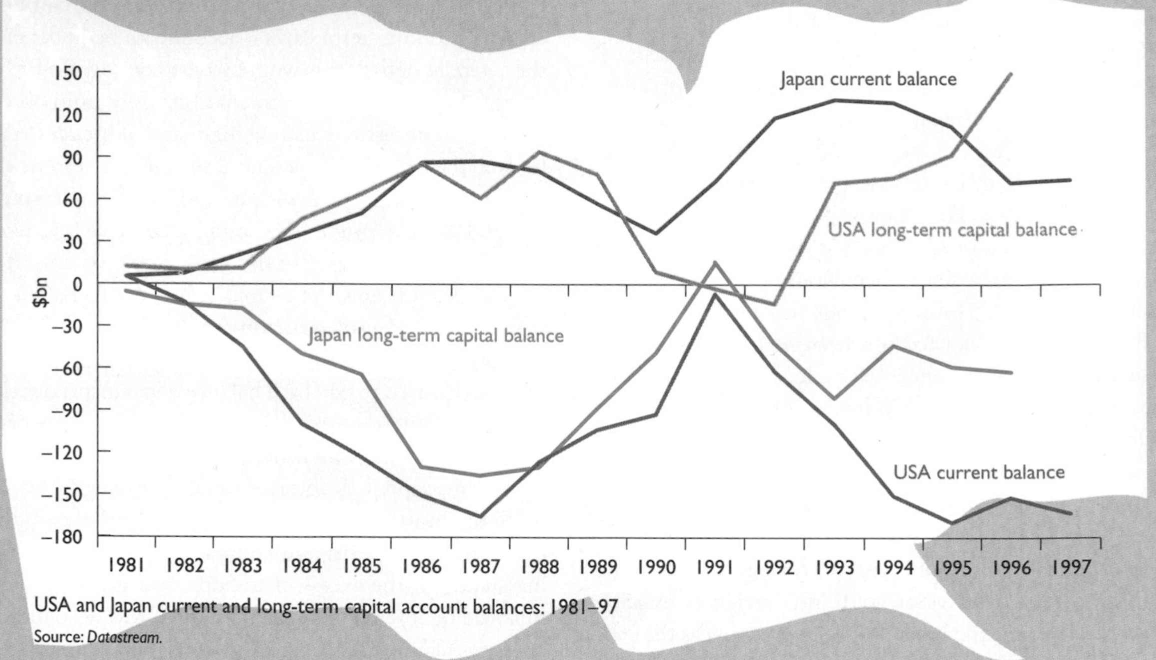

USA and Japan current and long-term capital account balances: 1981–97

Source: *Datastream.*

What causes deficits to occur on the various parts of the balance of payments? The answer has to do with the demand for and supply of sterling on the foreign exchange market. Thus before we can answer the question, we must examine this market and in particular the role of the rate of exchange.

SECTION SUMMARY

1. The balance of payments account records all payments to and receipts from foreign countries. The current account records payments for imports and exports, plus property incomes and transfers of money to and from abroad. The capital account records changes in foreign ownership of domestic assets and domestic ownership of foreign assets; it also includes dealings in the country's foreign exchange reserves.
2. The whole account must balance, but surpluses or deficits can be recorded on any specific part of the account. Thus the current account could be in deficit but it would have to be matched by an equal and opposite capital account surplus.
3. It is generally regarded as undesirable to have persistent current account deficits, since these lead to increased foreign ownership of domestic assets.

14.2 Exchange rates

The meaning of exchange rates

An exchange rate is the rate at which one currency trades for another on the foreign exchange market.

If you want to go abroad, you will need to exchange your pounds into francs, dollars, pesetas or whatever. To do this you will go to a bank. The bank will quote you that day's exchange rates: for example, 8 francs to the pound, or $1.50 to the pound. It is similar for firms. If an importer wants to buy, say, some machinery from Japan, it will require yen to pay the Japanese supplier. It will thus ask the foreign exchange section of a bank to quote it a rate of exchange of the pound into yen. Similarly if you want to buy some foreign stocks and shares, or if companies based in the UK want to invest abroad, sterling will have to be exchanged into the appropriate foreign currency.

Likewise, if Americans want to come on holiday to the UK or to buy UK assets, or American firms want to import UK goods or to invest in the UK, they will require sterling. They will be quoted an exchange rate for the pound in the USA: say £1 = $1.54. This means that they will have to pay $1.54 to obtain £1 worth of UK goods or assets.

Exchange rates are quoted between each of the major currencies of the world. These exchange rates are constantly changing. Minute by minute dealers in the foreign exchange dealing rooms of the banks are adjusting the rates of exchange. They charge commission when they exchange currencies. It is important for them, therefore, to ensure that they are not left with a large amount of any currency unsold. What they need to do is to balance the supply and demand of each currency: to balance the amount they purchase to the amount they sell. To do this they will need to adjust the price of each currency, namely the exchange rate, in line with changes in supply and demand.

Not only are there day-to-day fluctuations in exchange rates, but also there are long-term changes in them. Table 14.2 shows the average exchange rate between the pound and various currencies for each of the years 1980–98 (including each of the quarters in 1992).

One of the problems in assessing what is happening to a particular currency is that its rate of exchange may rise against some currencies (weak currencies) and fall against others (strong currencies). In order to gain an overall picture of its fluctuations, therefore, it is best to look at a weighted average exchange rate against all other currencies.

Table 14.2 Sterling exchange rates: 1980–98

	US dollar	French franc	Japanese yen	German mark	Italian lira	Sterling exchange rate index (1990 = 100)
1980	2.33	9.83	526	4.23	1992	124.4
1981	2.03	10.94	445	4.56	2287	127.9
1982	1.75	11.48	435	4.24	2364	123.2
1983	1.52	11.55	360	3.87	2302	115.6
1984	1.34	11.63	317	3.79	2339	111.4
1985	1.30	11.55	307	3.78	2463	111.3
1986	1.47	10.16	247	3.18	2186	101.4
1987	1.64	9.84	237	2.94	2123	99.3
1988	1.78	10.60	228	3.12	2315	105.4
1989	1.64	10.45	226	3.08	2247	102.3
1990	1.79	9.69	257	2.88	2133	100.0
1991	1.77	9.95	238	2.93	2187	100.8
1992 Q1	1.77	9.75	228	2.87	2155	99.4
Q2	1.81	9.83	235	2.92	2198	101.2
Q3	1.90	9.45	238	2.79	2154	99.4
Q4	1.58	8.30	194	2.45	2145	87.7
1993	1.50	8.51	167	2.48	2360	88.9
1994	1.53	8.49	156	2.48	2467	89.2
1995	1.58	7.87	148	2.26	2571	84.8
1996	1.56	7.99	170	2.35	2408	86.3
1997	1.64	9.56	198	2.84	2789	100.6
1998 Q1	1.65	10.04	217	3.04	2951	105.4

Source: *Economic Trends* (ONS).

This is known as the **exchange rate index**. The weight given to each currency in the index depends on the proportion of transactions done with that country. The last column in Table 14.2 shows the sterling exchange rate index based on 1990 = 100. Box 14.2 looks at the different weightings attached to each of the currencies in the index.

Note that all the exchange rates must be consistent with each other. For example, if £1 exchanged for $1.50 or 165 yen, then $1.50 would have to exchange for 165 yen directly (i.e. $1 = 110 yen), otherwise people could make money by moving around in a circle between the three currencies.

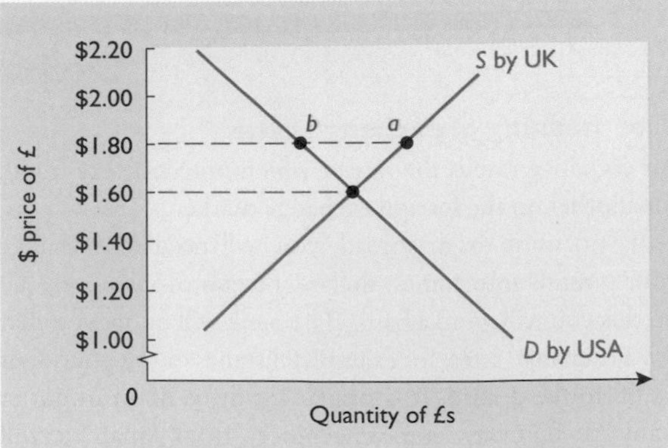

Figure 14.2 Determination of the rate of exchange

?? How did the pound 'fare' compared with the dollar, the lira and the yen from 1980 to 1998? What conclusions can be drawn about the relative movements of these three currencies?

The determination of the rate of exchange in a free market

In a free foreign exchange market the rate of exchange is determined by demand and supply. Thus the sterling exchange rate is determined by the demand and supply of pounds. This is illustrated in Figure 14.2.

For simplicity, assume that there are just two countries: the UK and the USA. When UK importers wish to buy goods from the USA, or when UK residents wish to invest in the USA, they will *supply* pounds on the foreign exchange market in order to obtain dollars. The higher the exchange rate, the more dollars they will obtain for their pounds. This will effectively make American goods cheaper to buy, and investment more profitable. Thus the *higher* the exchange rate, the *more* pounds will be supplied. The supply curve of pounds will therefore typically slope upwards.

When US residents wish to purchase UK goods or to invest in the UK, they will require pounds. They *demand* pounds by selling dollars on the foreign exchange market. The lower the $ price of the pound (the exchange rate), the cheaper it will be for them to obtain UK goods and assets, and hence the more pounds they are likely to demand. The demand curve for pounds, therefore, will typically slope downwards.

The equilibrium exchange rate will be where the demand for pounds equals the supply. In Figure 14.2 this will be at an exchange rate of £1 = $1.60. But what is the mechanism that equates demand and supply?

If the current exchange rate were above the equilibrium, the supply of pounds being offered to the banks would exceed the demand. For example, in Figure 14.2 if the exchange rate were $1.80, there would be an excess supply of pounds of *a* – *b*. The banks, wishing to make money by *exchanging* currency, would have to lower the exchange rate in order to encourage a greater demand for pounds and reduce the excessive supply. They would continue lowering the rate until demand equalled supply.

Similarly, if the rate were below the equilibrium, say at $1.40, there would be a shortage of pounds. The banks would find themselves with too few pounds to meet all the demand. At the same time they would have an excess supply of dollars. The banks would thus raise the exchange rate until demand equalled supply.

In practice the process of reaching equilibrium is extremely rapid. The foreign exchange dealers in the banks are continually adjusting the rate as new customers make new demands for currencies. What is more, the banks have to watch closely what each other is doing. Banks are constantly in competition with each other and thus have to keep their rates in line. The dealers receive minute-by-minute updates on their computer screens of the rates being offered round the world.

Exchange rates and the balance of payments: no government intervention

In a free foreign exchange market the balance of payments will *automatically* balance. But why?

The credit side of the balance of payments constitutes the demand for sterling. For example, when foreigners buy UK exports they will demand sterling in order to pay for them. The debit side constitutes the supply of sterling. For example, when UK residents buy foreign goods, the

DEFINITION

Exchange rate index A weighted average exchange rate expressed as an index, where the value of the index is 100 in a given base year. The weights of the different currencies in the index add up to 1.

ISSUES AND APPLICATIONS BOX 14.2

THE STERLING INDEX
What goes into the basket?

The UK's *effective* exchange rate measures the value of the pound against a group or 'basket' of other currencies. Each currency's exchange rate with the pound enters with a weight somewhere between 0 and 1. The size of each currency's weight depends on the relative importance of that country as a competitor to the UK. The more important it is, the bigger its weight. All the weights must add up to 1.

The effective exchange rate is expressed as an index with the base year equal to 100. The effective increase or decrease in the value of the pound can thus be expressed in terms of the percentage increase or decrease in this index.

The current official sterling index was introduced in February 1995. It is a weighted average of the sterling exchange rates with twenty other currencies. The weights are chosen to reflect the importance of UK trade with the various countries. The table shows the current and previous weights. The changes in these weights reflect the changing pattern of the UK's international trade and are based on 1989–91 trade flows.

The weights of foreign currencies in the sterling exchange rate index

	Previous	Current		Previous	Current
Germany	0.2001	0.2249	Ireland	0.0242	0.0308
USA	0.2044	0.1649	Finland	0.0145	0.0141
France	0.1175	0.1259	Canada	0.0190	0.0138
Italy	0.0766	0.0827	Denmark	0.0145	0.0138
Japan	0.0883	0.0700	Norway	0.0131	0.0119
Netherlands	0.0500	0.0571	Austria	0.0124	0.0119
Belgium	0.0525	0.0539	Portugal	–	0.0084
Spain	0.0202	0.0385	Australia	–	0.0048
Sweden	0.0379	0.0345	Greece	–	0.0031
Switzerland	0.0548	0.0327	New Zealand	–	0.0021

?? What are the current and previous total weights of the EU countries? Comment.

importers of these goods will require foreign currency to pay for them. They will thus supply pounds. A floating exchange rate will ensure that the demand for pounds is equal to the supply. It will thus also ensure that the credits on the balance of payments are equal to the debits: that the balance of payments balances.

This does not mean that each part of the balance of payments account will separately balance, but simply that any current account deficit must be matched by a capital account surplus and vice versa.

For example, suppose initially that each part of the balance of payments *did* separately balance. Then let us assume that aggregate demand expanded rapidly (the economy was experiencing a boom). Consumers would buy more goods and services, including more imports. The current account would begin to move into deficit. The supply of sterling would shift to the right. The exchange rate would fall.

As the exchange rate fell, so there would be a movement down along the demand curve for sterling. This would help to correct the current account deficit. The lower exchange rate would make UK exports cheaper for foreigners and thus more would be sold. It would also make imports into the UK more expensive and thus less would be purchased. But there would also be an effect on the capital account. Among other things, the lower exchange rate would attract long-term foreign investment into the UK. Also, as we shall see in later chapters, the higher aggregate demand is likely to drive up UK interest rates. This will encourage short-term capital inflows as foreigners deposit money in the UK to take advantage of the higher UK interest rates.[1] There is a resulting rightward shift in the demand curve for sterling. The capital account would thus move into surplus and would exactly offset any remaining deficit on the current account.

Floating exchange rates

If the government does not intervene in the foreign exchange market, the exchange rate will move up and down according to demand and supply. This is known as a system of **floating exchange rates**.

1 Under certain circumstances, a rise in aggregate demand may lead to such a large rise in interest rates, and such a large resulting surplus on the capital account, that this more than offsets the current account deficit. Under these circumstances the exchange rate will *rise*. The rightward shift in demand would have more than offset the initial rightward shift in supply. We examine this issue in detail in Chapter 24.

DEFINITION

Floating exchange rate When the government does not intervene in the foreign exchange markets, but simply allows the exchange rate to be freely determined by demand and supply.

ISSUES AND APPLICATIONS — BOX 14.3

DEALING IN FOREIGN EXCHANGE

A daily juggling act

Imagine that a large car importer in the UK wants to import 5000 cars from Germany costing DM75 million. What does it do?

It will probably contact a number of banks' foreign exchange dealing rooms in London and ask them for exchange rate quotes. It thus puts all the banks in competition with each other. Each bank will want to get the business and thereby obtain the commission on the deal. To do this it must offer a higher rate than the other banks, since the higher the DM/£ exchange rate, the more D-Marks the firm will get for its money. (For an importer a rate of, say, DM2.22 to £1 is better than a rate of, say, DM2.20.)

Now it is highly unlikely that any of the banks will have a spare DM75 million. But a bank cannot say to the importer 'Sorry, you will have to wait before we can agree to sell them to you.' Instead the bank will offer a deal and then, if the firm agrees, the bank will have to set about obtaining the DM75 million. To do this it must offer Germans who are *supplying* D-Marks to obtain pounds at a sufficiently *low* DM/£ exchange rate. (The lower the DM/£ exchange rate, the fewer D-Marks the Germans will have to pay to obtain pounds.)

The banks' dealers thus find themselves in the delicate position of wanting to offer a *high* enough exchange rate to the car importer in order to gain its business, but a *low* enough exchange rate in order to obtain the required amount of D-Marks. The dealers are thus constantly having to adjust the rates of exchange in order to balance the demand and supply of each currency.

In general, the more of any foreign currency that dealers are asked to supply (by being offered sterling), the lower will be the exchange rate they will offer. In other words, a higher supply of sterling pushes down the foreign currency price of sterling.

?? Assume that an American firm wants to import Rolls-Royces from the UK. Describe how foreign exchange dealers will respond.

If the demand or supply curves of sterling shift, the exchange rate will alter. This is illustrated in Figure 14.3. This time let us look at the Deutschmark/sterling exchange rate.

Assume, for example, that the supply curve shifts to the right from S_1 to S_2, and the demand curve to the left from D_1 to D_2. The rate of exchange will simply fall from the old equilibrium of £1 = DM2.50 to the new equilibrium of £1 = DM2.25. (Dealers mark the rate down in order to balance their books.)

But why should the demand and supply curves shift in this way? The following are the major reasons.

Changes in UK prices relative to foreign prices. If, for example, the UK inflation rate is higher than abroad, UK exports will become less competitive. The demand for sterling will fall. At the same time, imports will become relatively cheaper for UK consumers. The supply of sterling will rise.

Changes in relative incomes. If UK incomes rise, the demand for imports, and hence the supply of sterling, will rise. If foreign incomes fall, the demand for UK exports, and hence the demand for sterling, will fall.

Changes in relative interest rates. If UK interest rates fall relative to those abroad, UK residents will be more likely to deposit their money abroad, since they will earn a higher return there. The supply of sterling will rise. At the same time overseas residents will be less likely to put their money in the UK. The demand for sterling will fall.

Changes in relative investment prospects. If investment prospects become brighter abroad than in the UK, perhaps because of better incentives abroad, or because of worries about an impending recession in the UK, again the demand for sterling will fall and the supply of sterling will rise.

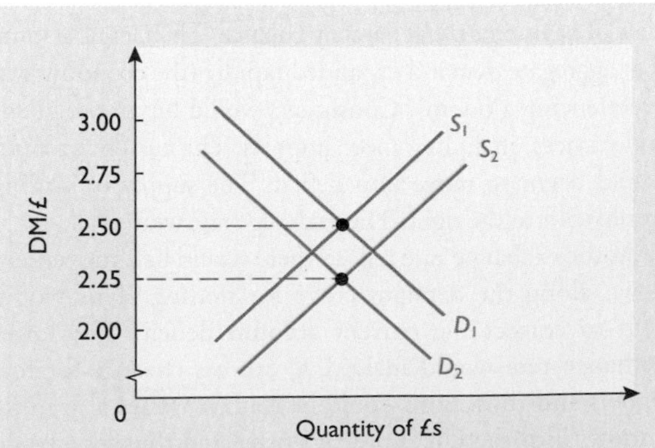

Figure 14.3 Floating exchange rates: movement to a new equilibrium

Speculators believe that the rate of exchange will change. By speculators we do not just mean people who make a living by financial dealing. We also include importers and exporters who want to choose the most favourable time to buy or sell currency. If they think that the exchange rate is about to fall, they will sell pounds *now* before the rate does fall. The supply of sterling will thus rise. At the same time people requiring pounds will *wait* until the rate has fallen before they purchase them. Thus the demand for sterling will fall.

Longer-term changes in international trading patterns. Over time the pattern of imports and exports is likely to change as (a) consumer tastes change, (b) the nature and quality of goods change and (c) the costs of production change. If as a result British goods become less competitive than, say, German or Japanese goods, the demand for sterling will fall and the supply will rise. These shifts, of course, are gradual, taking place over many years.

In each of the above cases the exchange rate will fall. We call this a **depreciation** of the pound. If the exchange rate rises, we call this an **appreciation**.

> **??** Go through each of the above reasons for shifts in the demand for and supply of sterling and consider what would cause an *appreciation* of the pound.

Government intervention in the foreign exchange market

The government may be unwilling to let the pound float freely. Frequent shifts in the demand and supply curves would cause frequent changes in the exchange rate. This, in turn, might cause uncertainty for businesses, which might curtail their trade and investment.

The government may thus intervene in the foreign exchange market. But what can it do? The answer to this will depend on its objectives. It may simply want to reduce the day-to-day fluctuations in the exchange rate, or it may want to prevent longer-term, more fundamental shifts in the rate.

Reducing short-term fluctuations

Assume in Figure 14.3 that the government believes that an exchange rate of DM2.50 to the pound is approximately the long-term equilibrium rate. It thus decides to intervene to prevent excessive fluctuations from that level. Assume now that the demand and supply curves shift to D_2 and S_2 respectively, albeit temporarily. There are three things that the government can do to prevent the rate falling to DM2.25.

Using reserves. The Bank of England can sell gold and foreign currencies from the reserves to buy pounds. This will shift the demand for sterling to the right.

Borrowing from abroad. The government can negotiate a foreign currency loan from other countries or from an international agency such as the International Monetary Fund. It can then use these moneys to buy pounds on the foreign exchange market, thus again shifting the demand for sterling to the right.

Raising interest rates. If the government raises interest rates, it will encourage people to deposit money in the UK and encourage UK residents to keep their money in the country. The demand for sterling will increase and the supply of sterling will decrease.

Maintaining a fixed rate of exchange over the longer term

Governments may choose to maintain a fixed rate over a number of months or even years. Indeed from 1945 to 1972 the whole world operated under such a system. Countries used to 'peg' (i.e. fix) their currencies against the US dollar. This meant, therefore, that every currency was fixed with respect to every other currency.

But how can a government maintain an exchange rate that is persistently above the equilibrium? How can it resist the downward pressure on the exchange rate? After all, it cannot *order* dealers to keep the rate up: the dealers would run out of foreign currency. Also it cannot go on and on using its reserves to support the rate: the reserves would begin to run out. Also it will probably not want to go on borrowing from abroad and building up large international debts.

So what can it do? It must attempt to shift the demand and supply curves back again so that they once more intersect at the fixed exchange rate. The following are possible methods it can use.

DEFINITIONS

Depreciation A fall in the free-market exchange rate of the domestic currency with foreign currencies.

Appreciation A rise in the free-market exchange rate of the domestic currency with foreign currencies.

Deflation. This is where the government deliberately curtails aggregate demand by either fiscal policy or monetary policy or both.

Deflationary fiscal policy will involve raising taxes and/or reducing government expenditure. Deflationary monetary policy will involve reducing the supply of money and raising interest rates. Note that in this case we are not just talking about the temporary raising of interest rates to prevent a short-term outflow of money from the country, but the use of higher interest rates to reduce borrowing and hence dampen aggregate demand.

A reduction in aggregate demand will work in two ways:

- It will reduce the level of consumer spending. This will directly cut imports, since there will be reduced spending on Japanese videos, German cars, Spanish holidays and so on. It will also indirectly cut imports when UK firms, themselves facing a reduction in demand, cut back on their purchases of raw materials and equipment, part of which comes from abroad. The supply of sterling coming on to the foreign exchange market thus decreases.
- It will reduce the rate of inflation. This will make UK goods more competitive abroad, thus increasing the demand for sterling. It will also cut back on imports as UK consumers switch to the now more competitive home-produced goods. The supply of sterling falls.

Supply-side policies. This is where the government attempts to increase the long-term competitiveness of UK goods by encouraging reductions in the costs of production and/or improvements in the quality of UK goods. For example, the government may give grants or tax incentives to encourage firms to engage in research and development. Or it may attempt to improve the quantity and quality of education and training.

Controls on imports and or foreign exchange dealing. This is where the government restricts the outflow of money, either by restricting people's access to foreign exchange, or by the use of tariffs and quotas. Tariffs are another word for customs duties. As taxes on imports, they raise their price and hence reduce their consumption. Quotas are quantitative restrictions on various imports.

?? What problems might arise if the government were to adopt this third method of maintaining a fixed exchange rate?

The exchange rate mechanism (ERM) of the European Monetary System

Both fixed exchange rates and freely floating exchange rates create problems. (These problems are examined in detail in Chapter 24.) To avoid these problems, various compromises have been tried between the two extremes of totally fixed and totally free exchange rates. One such example is that of the **exchange rate mechanism (ERM)** between the majority of European Union currencies, a mechanism set up in 1979. The member currencies are only allowed to fluctuate against each other within a specified band, but they jointly float against other currencies, such as the dollar and the yen.

Each of the member currencies of the ERM is assigned a central rate against the **ECU (European Currency Unit)**. The ECU is a weighted average of EU currencies, and is used as a reserve currency and increasingly for international trade. The central rate for each currency is not a fixed rate because fluctuations are allowed by a certain percentage (originally 2.25 per cent) either side of any other member currency. If the rate diverges by more than the agreed percentage from another ERM currency, the central banks of the two countries must intervene, selling the strong currency and purchasing the weak one.

There is also an agreement whereby, if a country's exchange rate diverges by more than a certain amount from its central rate against the ECU, the government concerned will take appropriate measures to stabilise its currency: measures such as raising interest rates.

If the currency persistently runs up against the limits of its band, then the member countries will consider whether the central rates should be changed: a 'realignment'. There were several of these realignments in the early years, but after 1987 it was hoped that further realignments would prove unnecessary as greater currency stability between the ERM currencies seemed to be occurring.

The UK was reluctant to join its fellow European Community partners in the exchange rate mechanism. Until Greece and then Spain and Portugal joined the EC,

DEFINITIONS

ERM (the exchange rate mechanism) A semi-fixed system whereby participating EU countries allow fluctuations against each other's currencies only within agreed bands. Collectively they float freely against all other currencies.

ECU (European Currency Unit) A weighted average of EU currencies used as a reserve currency and increasingly for international trade.

the UK was alone in staying outside the ERM. Spain joined the mechanism in 1989. The UK eventually joined in 1990. Portugal joined in 1991. The three new members were allowed a broader ±6 per cent band for fluctuations (as had been Italy until 1990).

But then in September 1992, with huge turmoil on the foreign exchange markets and massive speculation against sterling and the lira, both the UK and Italy were forced to withdraw from the ERM. Then, with further speculation, this time against the French franc and in favour of the German mark, the bands were widened to ±15 per cent in August 1993. In practice, however, the remaining members have tried to keep their exchange rates within much narrower limits.

We will be examining the advantages and disadvantages of the ERM and other exchange rate regimes in Chapter 24.

SECTION SUMMARY

1. The rate of exchange is the rate at which one currency exchanges for another. Rates of exchange are determined by demand and supply in the foreign exchange market. Demand for the domestic currency consists of all the credit items in the balance of payments account. Supply consists of all the debit items.
2. The exchange rate will depreciate (fall) if the demand for the domestic currency falls or the supply increases. These shifts can be caused by increases in domestic prices or incomes relative to foreign ones, reductions in domestic interest rates relative to foreign ones, worsening investment prospects at home compared with abroad, or the belief by speculators that the exchange rate will fall. The opposite in each case would cause an appreciation (rise).
3. The government can attempt to prevent the rate of exchange from falling by central bank purchases of the domestic currency in the foreign exchange market, either by selling foreign currency reserves or by using foreign loans. Alternatively, the government can raise interest rates. The reverse actions can be taken if it wants to prevent the rate from rising.
4. In the longer term it can prevent the rate from falling by pursuing deflationary policies, protectionist policies, or supply-side policies to increase the competitiveness of the country's exports.
5. Both fixed and floating exchange rates can cause problems. Various compromises have therefore been sought between these two extremes. One such example is the ERM. This is a system whereby participating EU countries permit their exchange rates to fluctuate against each other only within an agreed band, but jointly float freely against all other currencies.
6. The UK joined the ERM in October 1990, but was forced to leave in September 1992 by massive speculation against the pound. Since then it has been floating against all other currencies – both EU and non-EU.

14.3 The relationship between the four objectives

Aggregate demand and the short-term relationship between the four objectives

In the short term (up to about two years), the four objectives of faster growth in output, lower unemployment, lower inflation and the avoidance of balance of payments deficits (either current account or basic) are all related. They all depend on aggregate demand, and all vary with the course of the business cycle. This is illustrated in Figure 14.4.

In the expansionary phase of the business cycle (phase 2), aggregate demand grows rapidly. The gap between actual and potential output will narrow. There will be relatively rapid growth in output, and (demand-deficient) unemployment will fall. Thus two of the problems are getting better. On the other hand, the other two problems will be getting worse. The growing shortages lead to higher (demand-pull) inflation and current account balance of payments deficits as the extra demand 'sucks in' more imports and as higher prices make UK goods less competitive internationally. As a result, unless there is a compensating rise in interest rates, the equilibrium exchange rate is likely to fall, which will raise the price of imports, thus further stoking up inflation. This will probably increase inflationary expectations.

At the peak of the cycle (phase 3), unemployment is probably at its lowest and output at its highest (for the time being). But growth has already ceased or at least slowed down. Inflation and balance of payments problems are probably acute.

As the economy moves into phase 4, the recession, the reverse will happen to that of phase 2. Falling aggregate demand will make growth negative and demand-deficient

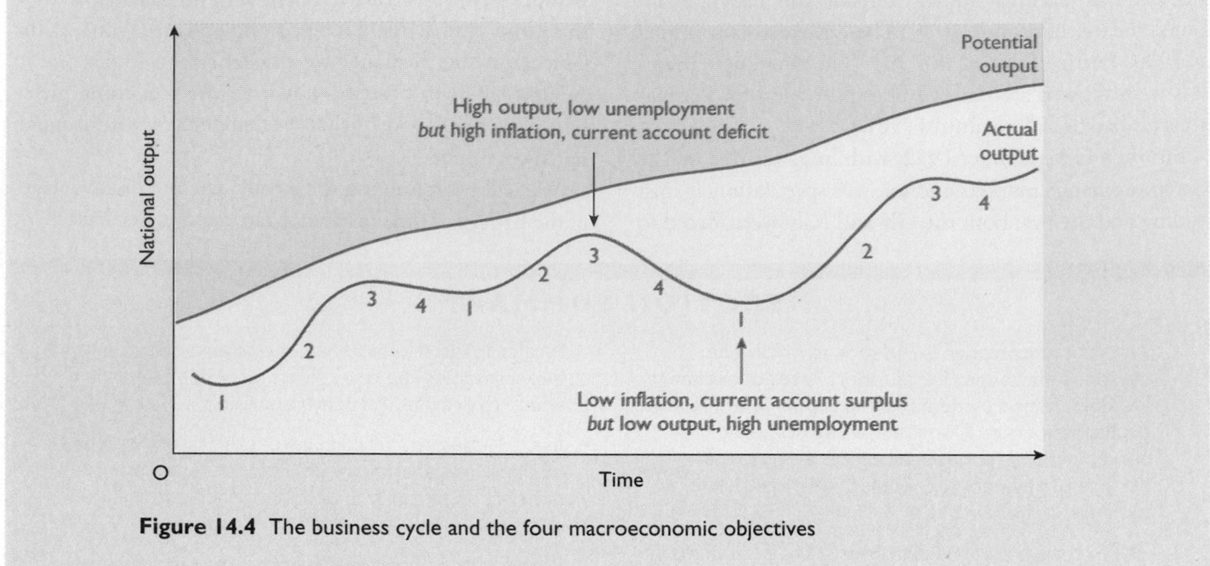

Figure 14.4 The business cycle and the four macroeconomic objectives

unemployment higher, but inflation is likely to slow down and the current account balance of payments will improve. These two improvements may take some time to occur, however.

Governments are thus faced with a dilemma. If they reflate the economy, they will make two of the objectives better (growth and unemployment), but the other two worse (inflation and the current account of the balance of payments). If they deflate the economy, it is the other way round: inflation and the current account of the balance of payments will improve, but unemployment will rise and growth or even output will fall.

Is there any point in the business cycle where all four objectives are looking reasonable? If so, that would be the time when it would be wise for a government to call a general election! (See Box 14.4.)

> **??** What is likely to happen to the exchange rate during phase 2 if the government (a) seeks to maintain a stable rate of interest; (b) raises the rate of interest in order to dampen the growth in aggregate demand?

The Phillips curve: the relationship between inflation and unemployment

The analysis of the last section suggests that in the short run governments are faced with a simple trade-off between the objectives. One such trade-off, namely that between inflation and unemployment, was illustrated by the famous **Phillips curve**.

A. W. Phillips in 1958 showed the statistical relationship between wage inflation and unemployment in the UK from 1861 to 1957. With wage inflation ($\dot{W}$) on the vertical axis and the unemployment rate (U) on the horizontal axis, a scatter of points was obtained. Each point represented the observation for a particular year. The curve that best fitted the scatter has become known as the 'Phillips curve'. It is illustrated in Figure 14.5 and shows an inverse relationship between inflation and unemployment.[2]

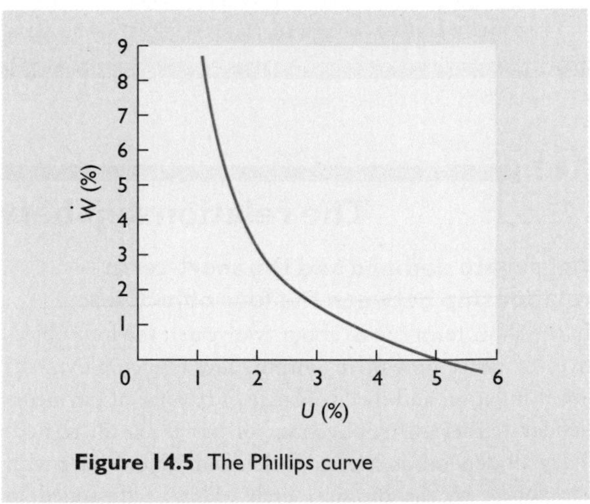

Figure 14.5 The Phillips curve

[2] Phillips' estimated equation was $\dot{W} = -0.9 + 9.638U^{-1.394}$

DEFINITION

Phillips curve A curve showing the relationship between (price) inflation and unemployment. The original Phillips curve plotted *wage* inflation against unemployment for the years 1861–1957.

ISSUES AND APPLICATIONS BOX 14.4

THE POLITICAL BUSINESS CYCLE (PART I)[3]

Getting things looking right on the night

Any government standing for re-election would like the economy to look as healthy as possible. It can then claim to the electorate that its economic policies have been a success.

Governments are able to engineer booms and recessions by the use of demand-side policies (fiscal and monetary). For example, by cutting taxes and/or increasing government expenditure, and by cutting interest rates, they can generate a period of economic expansion.

But how is this of any use politically, if the improvement in two of the objectives is at the cost of a deterioration in the other two? That would not help the government's election prospects.

The answer is that there is one point in the business cycle where *all four* objectives are likely to be looking good. This 'window of opportunity' for the government is in the middle of phase 2 – the period of rapid expansion. At this point, growth is at its highest and unemployment is *falling* most rapidly. In fact, falling unemployment is probably more popular with the electorate than simply a *low level* of unemployment. Three million unemployed but falling will win more votes than one million and rising rapidly!

But what about the other two objectives? Surely, in the middle of phase 2, inflation and the balance of payments will be deteriorating? The answer is that they will probably not yet have become a serious problem. Inflation takes a time to build up. It will probably only really start to rise rapidly as the peak of the business cycle is approached and shortages and bottlenecks occur. As far as the balance of payments is concerned, this tends only to become a serious *political issue* when the current account deficit gets really severe, or if the exchange rate starts to plummet. In the middle of phase 2, it is unlikely that this stage will yet have been reached.

By careful economic management, then, the government can get the four objectives to look good at the time of the election. Of course, economic management is not perfect and policies may take longer (or shorter) to work than the government had anticipated. Things are made easier for governments in countries like the UK, however, where the government can choose when to call an election. It is less easy in countries like the USA where elections are at fixed times.

Once a government has won an election it can then deflate the economy in order to remove inflationary pressures and improve the balance of payments. A recession is likely to follow. This will probably be highly unpopular with the electorate. But no matter: the government, having created sufficient slack in the economy, can then reflate the economy again in time for the next general election!

It is thus possible to observe a *political* business cycle. Recessions follow elections. Rapid growth precedes elections.

[3] See Box 21.3 on page 645 for part II.

Given that wage increases over the period were approximately 2 per cent above price increases (made possible because of increases in labour productivity), a similar-shaped, but lower curve could be plotted showing the relationship between *price* inflation and unemployment.

The curve has often been used to illustrate the effects of changes in aggregate demand. When aggregate demand rose (relative to potential output), inflation rose and unemployment fell: there was an upward movement along the curve. When aggregate demand fell, there was a downward movement along the curve.

There was also a second reason given for the inverse relationship. If wages rose, the unemployed may have believed that the higher wages they were offered represented a *real* wage increase. That is, they did not realise that the higher wages would be 'eaten up' by price increases: they suffered from **money illusion**. They would thus accept jobs more readily. The average duration of unemployment therefore fell. This is a reduction in *frictional* unemployment and is illustrated by an upward shift in the W_0 curve in Figure 13.11 (on page 423).

The Phillips curve was bowed in to the origin. The usual explanation for this is that, as aggregate demand expanded, at first there would be plenty of surplus labour, which could meet the extra demand without the need to raise wages very much. But as labour became increasingly scarce, firms would find they had to offer increasingly higher wages to obtain the labour they required, and the position of trade unions would be increasingly strengthened.

The *position* of the Phillips curve depended on *non*-demand factors causing inflation and unemployment: frictional and structural unemployment; and cost-push,

DEFINITION

Money illusion When people believe that a money wage or price increase represents a *real* increase: in other words, they ignore or underestimate inflation.

Table 14.3 UK macroeconomic indicators: 1959–98

	Inflation[1]	Unemployment[2]	Growth[3]	Current account balance[4]
1959–63	2.3	1.9	3.5	+302
1964–8	4.1	1.9	3.2	−1078
1969–73	8.7	3.0	3.4	+1784
1974–8	22.1	4.3	1.2	−2963
1979–83	14.0	8.1	0.8	+4241
1984–8	4.7	10.2	3.6	−3292
1989–93	5.7	8.7	0.4	−10 360
1994–8[5]	2.9	7.9	3.1	−835

[1] Average annual percentage increase in retail prices.
[2] Average percentage unemployed (excluding school leavers).
[3] Average annual growth rate in real GDP at market prices.
[4] Average annual current account deficit (–) or surplus (+) (£m) at 1985 prices.
[5] 1998 figures based on forecasts

Sources: *Economic Trends Annual Supplement* (ONS); *OECD Economic Outlook* (OECD).

structural and expectations-generated inflation. If any of these non-demand factors changed so as to raise inflation or unemployment, the curve would shift outward to the right. The relative stability of the curve over the 100 years or so observed by Phillips suggested that these non-demand factors had changed little.

The Phillips curve seemed to present governments with a simple policy choice. They could trade off inflation against unemployment. Lower unemployment could be bought at the cost of higher inflation, and vice versa. Unfortunately, the experience since the late 1960s has suggested that no such simple relationship exists beyond the short run.

The breakdown of the Phillips curve

From about 1966 the Phillips curve relationship seemed to break down. The UK, and many other countries in the Western world too, began to experience growing unemployment *and* higher rates of inflation as well.

Figure 14.6 shows price inflation and (ILO) unemployment in the UK from 1955 to 1997. From 1955 to 1966 a curve similar to the Phillips curve can be fitted through the data (diagram (a)). From 1967 to 1997, however, no simple picture emerges. Certainly the original Phillips curve can no longer fit the data; but whether the curve has been shifting to the right (the broken red lines), or whether the relationship has broken down completely, or whether there is some quite different relationship between inflation and unemployment, is not clear. There is much controversy among economists on this issue. The controversy will be examined in later chapters and particularly in Chapter 21.

Not only have inflation and unemployment generally been worse in the 1970s, 1980s and 1990s than in the 1950s and 1960s, but also growth has slowed down – except for a period in the second half of the 1980s. Table 14.3 illustrates the problem in the UK. If you look back to

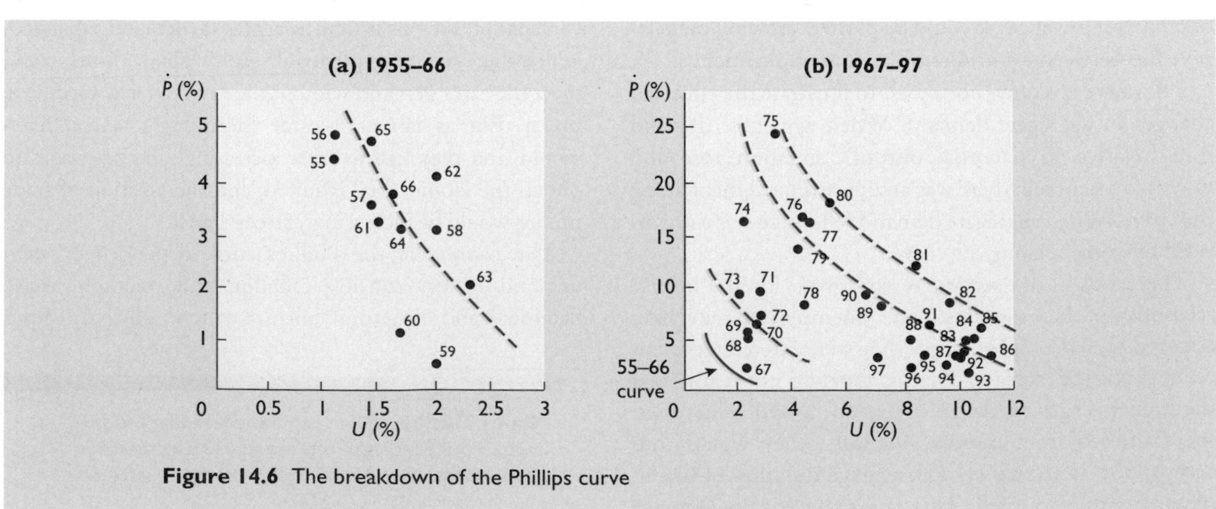

Figure 14.6 The breakdown of the Phillips curve

Table 13.1 on page 400 you will see that a similar deterioration in macroeconomic performance has been experienced by many other developed countries since the 1960s.

??

1. Which macroeconomic problem has generally been less severe in the 1990s than in the 1980s?
2. Why could the world as a whole not experience the problem of a current account balance of payments deficit?

Conclusions

Today the relationship between the four objectives seems far less simple than it did back in the 1950s.

In the short run, they still do seem to fluctuate with the business cycle. This does not necessarily make short-run prediction easy, however, since the course of the business cycle is irregular. Both booms and slumps can be long lived or short lived, lasting anything from a few months to a few years. What is more, even if accurate forecasts could be made, short-term management of the economy is still very difficult. We will be examining these difficulties as the book progresses.

In the long run, the relationship between the objectives is at the heart of the debate between the various schools of macroeconomic thought. These schools of thought are described in Chapter 15.

SECTION SUMMARY

1. In the short run, the four macroeconomic objectives are related to aggregate demand and the business cycle. In the boom phase, growth is high and unemployment is falling, but inflation is rising and the current account of the balance of payments is moving into deficit. In the recession, the reverse is the case.
2. The Phillips curve showed the trade-off between two of the problems: inflation and unemployment. There seemed to be a simple inverse relationship between the two.
3. After 1966 the relationship broke down as inflation *and* unemployment rose.
4. Although economists recognise that the relationships between the four objectives are more complex than was thought back in the 1950s, there is considerable disagreement as to precisely what these relationships are.

14.4 The circular flow of income

Another way of understanding the relationship between the four objectives is to use a simple model of the economy. This is an extension of the circular flow model that we looked at back in Chapter 1 (page 12) and Chapter 9 (page 237). This extended circular flow model is shown in Figure 14.7. In the diagram, the economy is divided into two major groups: *firms* and *households*. Each group has two roles. Firms are producers of goods and services; they are also the employers of labour and other factors of production. Households (which is the word we use for individuals) are the consumers of goods and services; they are also the suppliers of labour and various other factors of production. In the diagram there is an inner flow and various outer flows of incomes between these two groups.

Before we look at the various parts of the diagram, a word of warning. Do not confuse *money* and *income*. Money is a stock concept. At any given time there is a certain quantity of money in the economy (e.g. £1 billion). But that does not tell us the level of national *income*. Income is a flow concept (as is expenditure). It is measured as so much *per period of time*. The relationship between money and income depends on how rapidly the money *circulates*: its 'velocity of circulation'. (We will examine this concept in detail later on.) If there is £1 billion of money in the economy and each £1 on average is paid out as income five times per year, then annual national income will be £5 billion.

The inner flow, withdrawals and injections

The inner flow

Firms pay money to households in the form of wages and salaries, dividends on shares, interest and rent. These payments are in return for the services of the factors of production – labour, capital and land – that are supplied by households. Thus on the left-hand side of the diagram, money flows directly from firms to households as 'factor payments'.

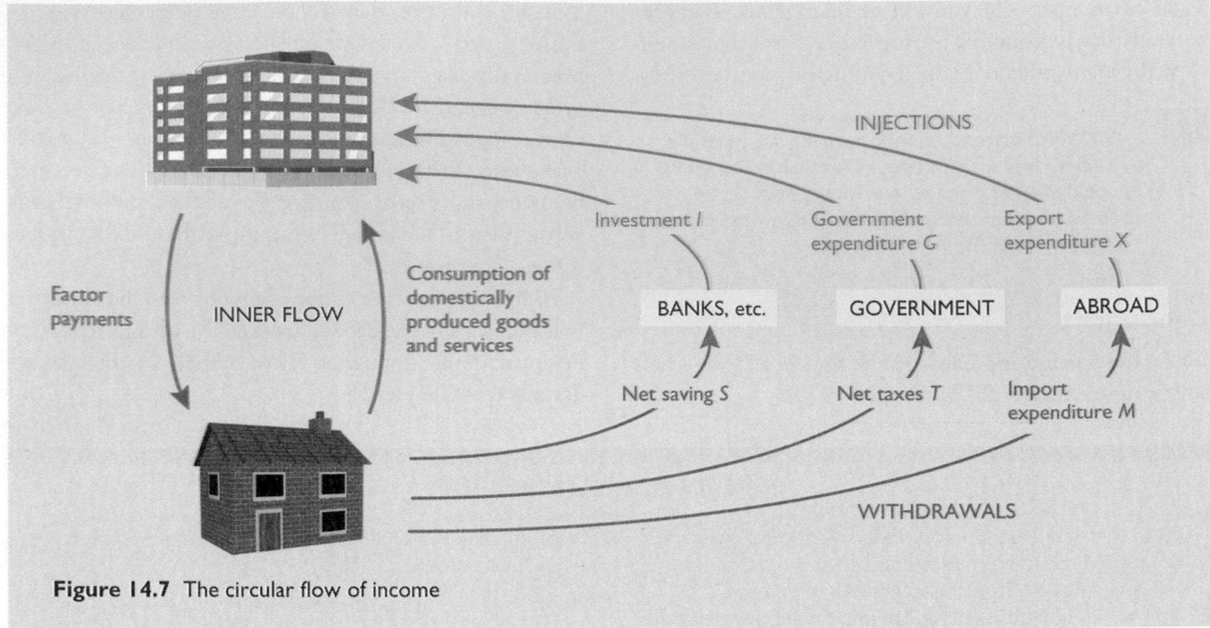

Figure 14.7 The circular flow of income

Households, in turn, pay money to UK firms when they **consume domestically produced goods and services (C_d)**. This is shown on the right-hand side of the inner flow. There is thus a circular flow of payments from firms to households to firms and so on.

If households spend *all* their incomes on buying domestic goods and services, and if firms pay out *all* this income they receive as factor payments to domestic households, and if the velocity of circulation does not change, the flow will continue at the same level indefinitely. The money just goes round and round at the same speed and incomes remain unchanged.

?? Would this argument still hold if prices rose?

In the real world, of course, it is not as simple as this. Not all income gets passed on round the inner flow; some is *withdrawn*. At the same time, incomes are injected into the flow from outside. Let us examine these withdrawals and injections.

Withdrawals (W)

Only part of the incomes received by households will be spent on the goods and services of domestic firms. The remainder will be withdrawn from the inner flow. Likewise only part of the incomes generated by firms will be paid to UK households. The remainder of this will also be withdrawn. There are three forms of **withdrawals** (or 'leakages' as they are sometimes called).

Net saving (S). Saving is income that households choose not to spend but to put aside for the future. Savings will normally be deposited in financial institutions such as banks and building societies. This is shown in the bottom right of the diagram. Money flows from households to 'banks, etc.'. What we are seeking to measure here, however, is the net flow from households to the banking sector. We therefore have to subtract from saving any borrowing or drawing on past savings by households in order to get the *net* saving flow. Of course, if household borrowing exceeded saving, the net flow would be in the other direction: it would be negative.

Net taxes (T). When people pay taxes (to either central or local government), this represents a withdrawal of money from the inner flow in much the same way as saving: only in this case people have no choice. Some taxes, such as income tax and employees' national insurance

DEFINITIONS

The consumption of domestically produced goods and services (C_d) The direct flow of money payments from households to firms.

Withdrawals (W) (or leakages) Incomes of households or firms that are not passed on round the inner flow. Withdrawals equal net savings (S) plus net taxes (T) plus import expenditure (M): $W = S + T + M$.

contributions, are paid out of household incomes. Others, such as VAT and excise duties, are paid out of consumer expenditure. Others, such as corporation tax, are paid out of firms' incomes before being received by households as dividends on shares. (For simplicity, however, taxes are shown in Figure 14.7 as leaving the circular flow at just one point.)

When, however, people receive *benefits* from the government, such as unemployment benefits, child benefit and pensions, the money flows the other way. Benefits are thus equivalent to a 'negative tax'. These benefits are known as **transfer payments**. They transfer money from one group of people (taxpayers) to others (the recipients).

In the model, 'net taxes' (T) represent the *net* flow to the government from households and firms. It consists of total taxes minus benefits.

Import expenditure (M). Not all consumption is of totally home-produced goods. Households spend some of their incomes on imported goods and services, or on goods and services using imported components. Although the money that consumers spend on such goods initially flows to domestic retailers, it will eventually find its way abroad, either when the retailers or wholesalers themselves buy the imports from abroad, or when domestic manufacturers purchase imported inputs to make their products. This expenditure on imports constitutes the third withdrawal from the inner flow. This money flows abroad.[4]

Total withdrawals are simply the sum of net saving, net taxes and the expenditure on imports:

$$W = S + T + M$$

Injections (J)

Only part of the demand for firms' output arises from consumers' expenditure. The remainder comes from other sources outside the inner flow. These additional components of aggregate demand are known as **injections** (J). There are three types of injection.

Investment (I). This is the money that firms spend which they obtain from various financial institutions – either past savings or loans, or through a new issue of shares. They may invest in plant and equipment or may simply spend the money on building up stocks of inputs, semi-finished or finished goods.

Government expenditure (G). When the government spends money on goods and services produced by firms, this counts as an injection. Examples of such government expenditure include spending on roads, hospitals and schools. (Note that government expenditure in this model does not include state benefits. These transfer payments, as we saw above, are the equivalent of negative taxes and have the effect of reducing the T component of withdrawals.)

Export expenditure (X). Money flows into the circular flow from abroad when foreign residents buy our exports of goods and services.[5]

Total injections are thus the sum of investment, government expenditure and exports:

$$J = I + G + X$$

The relationship between withdrawals and injections

There are indirect links between saving and investment, taxation and government expenditure, and imports and exports, via financial institutions, the government (central and local) and foreign countries respectively. If more money is saved, there will be more available for banks and

[4] There are other flows between the household sector and abroad, arising from the property incomes or transfers part of the current account, or from the capital account of the balance of payments. For example, households may purchase shares in foreign companies and make deposits in banks abroad. These constitute a withdrawal from the household sector (and a debit on the balance of payments). At the same time, households may *receive* money from abroad in the form of dividends on foreign shares or loans from foreign banks. As these represent an inflow into the household sector (a credit item on the balance of payments), they have to be subtracted to get the net withdrawal. Whether withdrawals to the financial sector abroad are included as part of M or part of S does not really matter, so long as they are only counted the once.

[5] Note that X would not include investment in the UK by foreign companies (i.e. credits on the long-term capital account of the balance of payments). Foreign 'investment' involves the acquisition of UK assets and thus represents an income to the previous owners of these assets. It therefore represents an inflow from abroad to the household sector and thus has the effect of reducing M.

DEFINITIONS

Transfer payments Moneys transferred from one person or group to another (e.g. from the government to individuals) without production taking place.

Injections (J) Expenditure on the production of domestic firms coming from outside the inner flow of the circular flow of income. Injections equal investment (I) plus government expenditure (G) plus expenditure on exports (X).

other financial institutions to lend out. If tax receipts are higher, the government may be more keen to increase its expenditure. Finally, if imports increase, incomes of people abroad will increase, which will enable them to purchase more of our exports.

These links, however, do not guarantee that $S = I$ or $G = T$ or $M = X$. For a period of time, financial institutions can lend out (I) more than they receive from depositors (S) or vice versa; governments can spend (G) more than they receive in taxes (T) or vice versa; and exports (X) can exceed imports (M) or vice versa.

A major point here is that the decisions to save and invest are made by different people, and thus they plan to save and invest different amounts. Likewise the demand for imports may not equal the demand for exports. As far as the government is concerned, it may choose not to make $T = G$. It may choose not to spend all its tax revenues: to run a 'budget surplus' ($T > G$). Or it may choose to spend more than it receives in taxes – to run a budget deficit ($G > T$) – by borrowing or printing money to make up the difference.

Thus planned injections (J) may not equal planned withdrawals (W).

?? Are the following net injections, net withdrawals or neither? If there is uncertainty, explain your assumptions.

(a) Firms are forced to take a cut in profits in order to give a pay rise.
(b) Firms spend money on research.
(c) The government increases personal tax allowances.
(d) The general public invests more money in building societies.
(e) UK investors earn higher dividends on overseas investments.
(f) The government purchases US military aircraft.
(g) People draw on their savings to finance holidays abroad.
(h) People draw on their savings to finance holidays in the UK.
(i) The government runs a budget deficit (spends more than it receives in tax revenues) and finances it by borrowing from the public.
(j) The government runs a budget deficit and finances it by printing more money.

The circular flow of income and the four macroeconomic objectives

If planned injections are not equal to planned withdrawals, what will be the consequences? To understand what will happen, it is useful to picture the circular flow of income as a flow of water through a series of pipes. Water flows round and round the inner system. Then there are inflows of water into the system (the injections) and outflows from it (the withdrawals). If the inflows exceed the outflows ($J > W$), the volume of water flowing round the system will increase. Likewise, if outflows exceed inflows, the volume of water flowing round the system will decrease.

To return to the circular flow of income: if injections exceed withdrawals, the level of expenditure will rise. This extra aggregate demand will generate extra incomes. In other words, *actual* national income will rise. If this rise in actual income exceeds any rise there may have been in potential income, there will be the following effects on the four macroeconomic objectives:

- There will be economic growth. The greater the initial excess of injections over withdrawals, the bigger will be the rise in national income.
- Unemployment will fall as firms take on more workers in order to meet the extra demand for output.
- Inflation will tend to rise. The more the gap is closed between actual and potential income, the more will firms find it difficult to meet the extra demand, and the more likely they will be to raise prices.
- The current account of the balance of payments will tend to deteriorate. The higher demand sucks more imports into the country, and higher domestic inflation makes exports less competitive and imports relatively cheaper compared with home-produced goods. Thus imports will tend to rise and exports will tend to fall.

?? What effect will there be on the four objectives of an initial excess of withdrawals over injections?

Equilibrium in the circular flow

When injections do not equal withdrawals, a state of disequilibrium will exist. This will set in train a process to bring the economy back to a state of equilibrium where injections are equal to withdrawals.

To illustrate this, let us consider the situation again where injections exceed withdrawals. Perhaps there has been a rise in business confidence so that investment has risen. Or perhaps the government has decided to spend more on health or education. Or perhaps there has been a rise in foreign demand for the country's exports. Or perhaps one or more of the three withdrawals has fallen (e.g. a tax cut). As we have seen, the excess of injections over withdrawals will lead to a rise in national income. But as national income rises, so households will not only spend more on domestic goods (C_d), but also save more (S), pay more taxes (T) and buy more imports (M). In other words, withdrawals will rise. This will continue until they have risen to equal injections. At that point, national income will stop rising, and so will withdrawals. Equilibrium has been reached.

SECTION SUMMARY

1. The circular flow of income model depicts the flows of money round the economy. The inner flow shows the direct flows between firms and households. Money flows from firms to households in the form of factor payments, and back again as consumer expenditure on domestically produced goods and services.
2. Not all incomes get passed on directly round the inner flow. Some is withdrawn in the form of saving, some is paid in taxes, and some goes abroad as expenditure on imports, etc.
3. Likewise not all expenditure on domestic firms is by domestic consumers. Some is injected from outside the inner flow in the form of investment expenditure, government expenditure and expenditure on the country's exports.
4. Planned injections and withdrawals are unlikely to be the same. What happens when they are not is a major area of debate among macroeconomists.
5. If injections exceed withdrawals, national income will rise, unemployment will tend to fall, inflation will tend to rise and the current account of the balance of payments will tend to deteriorate. The reverse will happen if withdrawals exceed injections.
6. If injections exceed withdrawals, the rise in national income will lead to a rise in withdrawals. This will continue until $W = J$. At this point the circular flow will be in equilibrium.

14.5

Measuring national income and output[6]

The circular flow of income is very useful as a model for understanding the working of an economy. It shows how national income can increase or decrease as a result of changes in the various flows. If, however, we want to have a precise measurement of national income, there are various qualifications that have to be made. This section shows the methods that are actually used to measure national income.

Comparing national incomes

- How does UK national income compare with that of other countries? Does the UK have a higher or lower national income than Germany or France or Spain or Portugal or ...?
- How much has the economy grown over the last five years?
- Are we better off than we were ten years ago?
- Which country in the world has the highest living standard?

These are typical questions that economists will be asked on the subject of national output and its growth. They are also at the forefront of political debate: after all, economic growth is a major objective of governments. When a government stands for re-election, voters will consider how much their living standards have improved over the government's term of office. Voters will also consider whether the opposition parties might do better. Voters will also look at how our growth performance compares with that of other countries.

To assess how fast the economy has grown we must have a means of *measuring* the value of the nation's output. The measure we use is called **gross domestic product** (GDP).

This section shows how GDP is calculated. It looks at some alternative ways of measuring national output, and at various complications that arise in the measurement process. It also looks at difficulties in interpreting GDP statistics. Does GDP give a good indication of human welfare? Can the figures be meaningfully used to compare one country's standard of living with another? Can they be used to show how living standards have changed?

The three ways of calculating GDP

GDP can be calculated in three different ways, which should all result in the same figure. These three methods are illustrated in the simplified circular flow of income shown in Figure 14.8.

The first method of measuring GDP is to add up the value of all the goods and services produced in the

[6] Although this section is not more difficult than other sections, it may be omitted without loss of continuity.

DEFINITION

Gross domestic product (GDP) The value of output produced within the country over a twelve-month period.

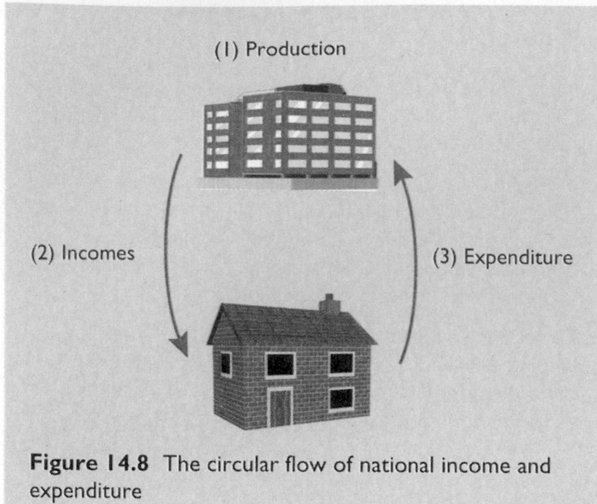

Figure 14.8 The circular flow of national income and expenditure

country, industry by industry. In other words, we focus on firms and add up all their production. This first method is known as the *product method*.

The production of goods and services generates incomes for households in the form of wages and salaries, profits, rent and interest. The second method of measuring GDP, therefore, is to add up all these incomes. This is known as the *income method*.

The third method focuses on the expenditures necessary to purchase the nation's production. In this simple model of the circular flow of income, with no injections or withdrawals, whatever is produced is sold. The value of what is sold must therefore be the value of what is produced. The *expenditure method* measures this sales value.

Because of the way the calculations are made, the three methods of calculating GDP *must* yield the same result. In other words:

National product ≡ National income ≡ National expenditure

We will look at each of the three methods in turn, and examine the various factors that have to be taken into account to ensure that the figures are accurate.

The product method of measuring GDP

This approach simply involves adding up the value of everything produced in the country during the year: the output of cars, timber, lollipops, shirts, etc.; and all the myriad of services such as football matches, haircuts, bus rides and insurance services. In the national accounts these figures are grouped together into broad categories such as manufacturing, construction and distribution. The figures for the UK economy for 1996 are shown in Figure 14.9.

The problem of double counting

When we add up the output of various firms we must be careful to avoid *double counting*. For example, if a manufacturer sells a television to a retailer for £200 and the retailer sells it to the consumer for £300, how much has this television contributed to GDP? The answer is *not* £500. We do not add the £200 received by the manufacturer to the £300 received by the retailer: that would be double counting.

There are two ways of estimating the true value of the output and avoiding double counting. The first is just to count the *final* value of the output. Thus in the case of the television set we would just count the £300 when the set is sold to the consumer. This is the approach we adopt in the *expenditure* method of calculating GDP (see page 459). The alternative is just to include the *extra* value that each firm adds to an item: this is known as *value added*.

The measurement of value added

In our complex modern economy, virtually every item goes through several stages of production and distribution. Take an item as simple as a pad of writing paper. A forestry company will grow trees from which the paper is made. The logs are sold to a timber merchant, which then sells the timber to the paper manufacturer. Another firm may then cut the paper and form it into pads. The pads will then be sold to wholesalers, which in turn will sell them to retailers. At each stage, transport companies may be involved in the distribution process. Each firm involved in production and distribution adds value to the product.

To arrive at the final value of a product, we must add up all the values added at each stage. For example, consider the following imaginary product that passes through just three stages.

Stage 1. Firm A produces the necessary raw materials and sells them for £1000 to firm B.

Stage 2. Firm B manufactures them into finished products and sells them to a retailer, firm C, for £1800.

Stage 3. Finally, firm C sells them to households for £2500.

How much has been contributed to GDP? We could simply look at the final sales value: £2500. But we will get the same answer by counting up the *values added* at each stage. Firm A does not make any purchases from other firms. Its value added is thus the full value of its sales of raw materials to the manufacturer: i.e. £1000. Firm B buys these materials for £1000 and sells the finished products to firm C for £1800. It thus adds £800 of value to the products. Finally, firm C sells the products to consumers

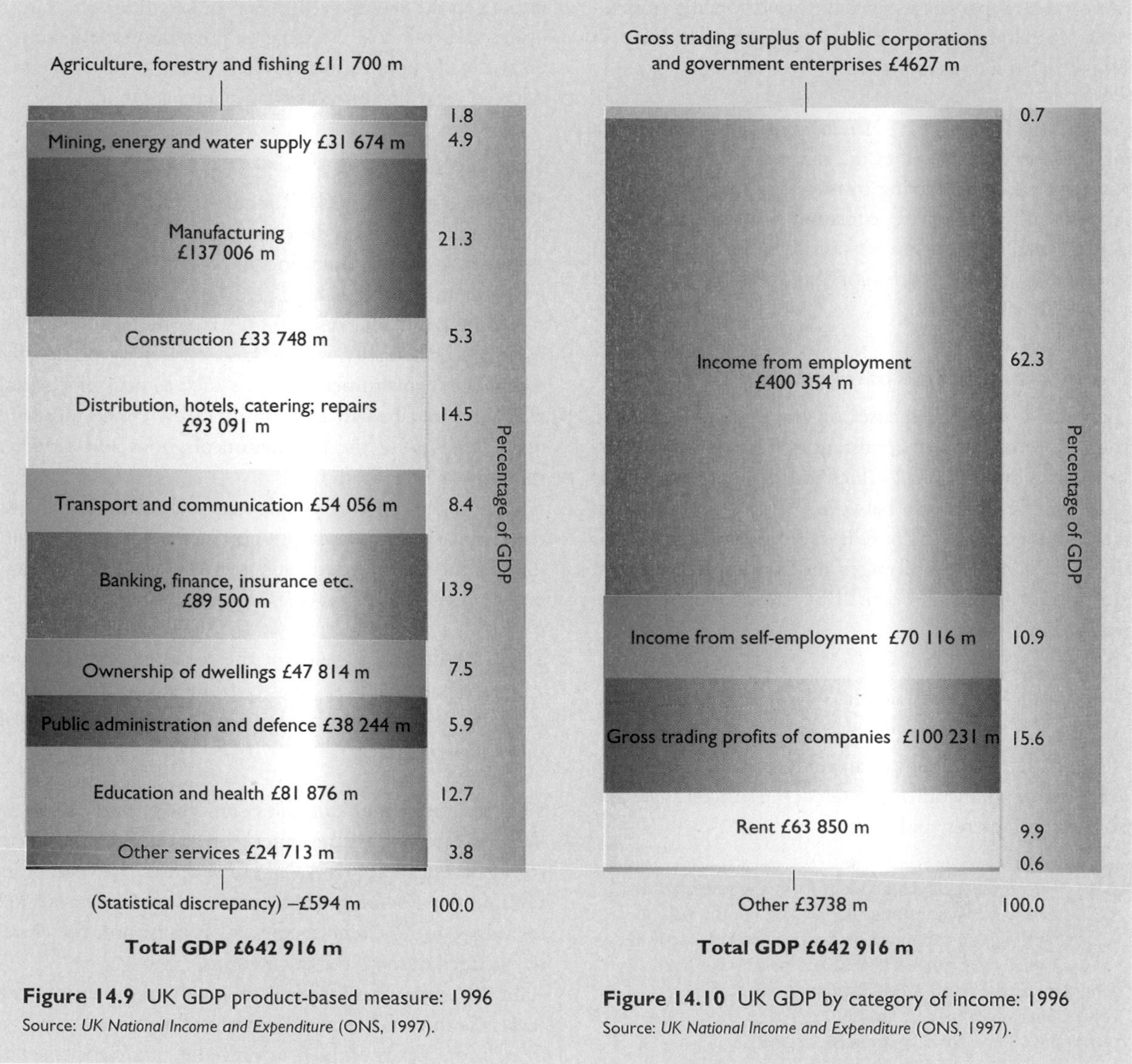

Figure 14.9 UK GDP product-based measure: 1996
Source: *UK National Income and Expenditure* (ONS, 1997).

Figure 14.10 UK GDP by category of income: 1996
Source: *UK National Income and Expenditure* (ONS, 1997).

for £2500 and thus adds £700 of value. Total value added is therefore £1000 + £800 + £700 = £2500.

Some qualifications

Stocks. We must be careful only to include the values added in the *particular year in question*. A problem here is that some goods start being produced *before* the year begins. Thus when we come to work out GDP we must ignore the values that had previously been added to stocks of raw materials and goods. Similarly, other goods are only sold to the consumer *after* the end of the year. Nevertheless we must still count the values that have been added during *this* year to these stocks of partially finished goods.

A final problem concerned with stocks is that they may increase in value simply due to increased prices. This is known as **stock appreciation**. Since there has been no real increase in output, stock appreciation must be deducted from value added.

Government services. The output of private industry is sold on the market and can thus be easily valued. This is not the case with most of the services provided by

DEFINITION

Stock appreciation The increase in monetary value of stocks due to increased prices. Since this does not represent increased output, it is not included in GDP.

government departments. For example, when a government official gives you free advice, it must be valued in terms of what it costs to provide.

Ownership of dwellings. When a landlord rents out a flat, this service is valued as the rent that the tenant pays. But owner occupiers living in their own property do not pay rent and yet they are 'consuming' a similar 'service'. Here a rental value for owner occupation is 'imputed'. In other words, a figure corresponding to a rent is included in the GDP statistics.

The income method of measuring GDP

The second approach focuses on the incomes generated from the production of goods and services. This must be the same as the sum of all values added, since value added is simply the difference between a firm's revenue from sales and the costs of its purchases from other firms. This difference is made up of wages and salaries, rent, interest and profit: the incomes earned by those involved in the production process.

Value added
= Wages and salaries + Rent + Interest + Profit
= Factor incomes

Since GDP is the sum of all values added, it must also be the sum of all incomes generated: the sum of wages and salaries, rent, interest and profit.

> **??** If a retailer buys a product from a wholesaler for £80 and sells it to a consumer for £100, then the £20 of value that has been added will go partly in wages, partly in rent and partly in profits. Thus £20 of income has been generated at the retail stage. But the good actually contributes a total of £100 to GDP. Where, then, is the remaining £80 worth of income recorded?

Figure 14.10 shows how these incomes are grouped together in the official statistics. By far the largest category is income from employment: in other words, wages and salaries. The next largest category is that of profit and interest, which is broken down into: the gross trading profits of companies; the income from self-employment; and the gross trading surplus of public corporations and government enterprises. Next comes income from rent, which includes an element of imputed rent for owner-occupied dwellings. The final category, 'other', includes an adjustment for statistical errors and also an imputed profit on capital in non-market parts of the economy (e.g. education, health and public administration) where there are no actual profits.

The total in Figure 14.10 is the same as in Figure 14.9, although the components are quite different. Gross domestic product is the same as 'gross domestic income', or put in the more usual way, GDP is the same whether calculated by the product or the income method.

Some qualifications

Transfer payments. GDP includes only those incomes that arise from the production of goods and services. We would not, for example, include a gift that one person makes to another. If an aunt gives you £50, this transfer of income has not increased GDP! It is the same with all *transfer payments*. By far the largest category of transfer payments is government benefits such as pensions, social security, child benefit and family credit. Since these are not payments for the production of goods and services, they are excluded from GDP.

Conversely, part of people's gross income is paid in taxes. Since it is this *gross* (pre-tax) income that arises from the production of goods and services, we count wages, profits, interest and rent *before* the deduction of taxes.

Stock appreciation. As in the case of the product approach, any gain in profits from stock appreciation must be deducted, since they do not arise from a real increase in output.

Indirect taxes and subsidies on goods and services. When a firm receives revenues from its sales, it may have to pay part of these as VAT or excise duties. The part of its revenues it pays in these indirect taxes will *not* be available for wages, profits, rent or interest. It must not, therefore, be included in the GDP calculations.

In the case of subsidies on goods and services the reverse is true. When the government pays a subsidy to a firm, it forms part of the firm's revenues and hence part of the incomes earned by factors. Subsidies must therefore be *added* to the revenues gained from consumers when calculating GDP.

If we do *not* make these adjustments for taxes and subsidies, and just look at the prices consumers pay – i.e. at the gross incomes of firms before they pay the taxes or obtain the subsidies – the figure we get is called **GDP at market prices**. The figure, however, that represents the true income to factors of production (i.e. after the *deduction* of

> **DEFINITION**
>
> **GDP at market prices** The value of output in terms of the price paid by consumers. These prices will reflect any indirect taxes and subsidies on the goods and services.

indirect taxes from and the *addition* of subsidies to the market value of sales) is called **GDP at factor cost.** Thus:

GDP at factor cost = GDP at market prices – Indirect taxes + Subsidies

Figures 14.9 and 14.10 showed GDP at *factor cost*.

> **??** GDP at factor cost represents the payments made to factors of production. To get this figure we have to deduct indirect taxes from firms' sales revenues. Why do we not also deduct income taxes?

The expenditure method of measuring GDP

The final approach is to add up all expenditure on final output. Again this will give us a figure for GDP at factor cost. To arrive at this figure, however, we have to go through a number of stages. Table 14.4 shows each of these stages in the calculation of the 1996 UK GDP at factor cost.

We start by measuring **total domestic expenditure (*TDE*) at market prices.**

Total domestic expenditure (TDE) (at market prices). This consists of the total expenditure on final goods and services by the residents of the country, whether these goods and services were produced at home or abroad. It consists of three elements:

- Consumer expenditure (C).
- Government expenditure on final goods and services (G). Note that this includes non-marketed services provided by government departments, but it excludes transfer payments such as pensions and social security payments.
- Investment expenditure (I). This includes investment in fixed capital, such as buildings and machinery. It also includes the value of any increases in stocks, whether of raw materials, semi-finished goods or finished goods. If there has been a net decline in stocks during the year, stock investment will be negative. Investment also includes expenditure on *new* housing. We count the expenditure on new housing as investment rather than consumption because houses yield benefits over many years to their owners.

Table 14.4 UK GDP at market prices by category of expenditure: 1996

	£million
Consumers' expenditure	473 509
Government final consumption	155 732
Gross domestic fixed capital formation (including new housing)	114 623
Value of physical increase in stocks and work in progress	2917
Total domestic expenditure	**746 781**
Plus Exports of goods and services	217 147
Total final expenditure	**963 928**
Less Imports of goods and services	–222 603
Statistical discrepancy	975
GDP at market prices	**742 300**
Less Taxes on expenditure	–108 484
Plus Subsidies	9100
GDP at factor cost	**642 916**

Source: *UK National Income and Expenditure* (ONS, 1997).

> **??** Should the sale of houses that are not new be included in the GDP statistics?

Note that total domestic expenditure excludes exports and includes imports.

$$TDE = C + G + I$$

Total final expenditure (TFE) (at market prices). The next step is to add in exports. This gives **total final expenditure at market prices**, which is the total expenditure that takes place within the country, whether by domestic residents or by people abroad. (Note that it includes *both* imports *and* exports.)

$$TFE = TDE + X$$
$$= C + G + I + X$$

Gross domestic product at market prices. The next step is to subtract imports. This gives us **gross domestic product at market prices.** In other words, we exclude that

DEFINITIONS

GDP at factor cost The value of output in terms of the resources used to produce it. It is thus GDP at market prices *less* indirect taxes and *plus* subsidies on goods and services.

Total domestic expenditure at market prices (*TDE*) The total annual expenditure on final goods and services by *domestic residents*. It includes expenditure on both domestic goods and services *and* imports (at prices that *include* indirect taxes and subsidies).

Total final expenditure at market prices (*TFE*) Total expenditure within the country: i.e. *TDE* plus exports.

Gross domestic product at market prices (second definition) The expenditure on final domestically produced goods (at prices that include indirect taxes and subsidies): i.e. *TFE* – imports.

component of consumption, government expenditure and investment that goes on imports. We also exclude any imported component (e.g. raw materials) from exports. What we are left with is the total expenditure on *domestically* produced goods at market prices.

$$GDP \text{ at market prices} = TFE - M$$
$$= C + G + I + X - M$$

Gross domestic product at factor cost. So far we have been using market prices: prices that have been increased by indirect taxes and reduced by any subsidies. To obtain a true measure of the expenditure on actual *output*, we must correct for these taxes and subsidies. The final step to get to GDP at factor cost is thus to subtract indirect taxes (T_i) and add subsidies (Sb). This gives us the formula we used above when looking at the income method of calculating GDP:

$$GDP \text{ at factor cost}$$
$$= GDP \text{ at market prices} - \text{Indirect taxes} + \text{Subsidies}$$
$$= C + G + I + X - M - T_i + Sb$$

Another way of expressing this is just to include the component of *C*, *G*, *I* and *X* that is spent on domestic output: i.e. after correcting for any imports and indirect taxes and subsidies. We show this by using the subscript 'd' after each term.

$$GDP \text{ at factor cost} = C_d + G_d + I_d + X_d$$

Gross national product

Some of the incomes earned in this country will go to shareholders abroad, or people with bank deposits in this country, but residing abroad. On the other hand, some of the incomes earned by domestic residents will come from shareholdings or accounts abroad. Gross *domestic* product, however, is concerned only with incomes generated *within* the country, irrespective of ownership. If, then, we are to take 'net property incomes' into account (i.e. these inflows minus outflows of dividends and interest), we need a new measure. This is **gross national product** (GNP). It is defined as follows:

$$GNP \text{ at factor cost} = GDP \text{ at factor cost} + \text{Net property income from abroad}$$

Thus *GDP* focuses on the value of domestic production, whereas *GNP* focuses on the value of incomes earned by domestic residents.

> **??** If a country persistently runs a long-term capital account deficit on the balance of payments, would you expect GNP to be bigger or smaller than GDP? (Clue: if there is a long-term capital account deficit, what is the balance between the country's investment abroad and foreign investment within the country?)

Net national product ('national income')

The measures we have used so far ignore the fact that each year some of the country's capital equipment will wear out or become obsolete: in other words, they ignore capital depreciation. If we subtract from gross investment an allowance for **depreciation** (or 'capital consumption' as it is called in the official statistics), we are left with **net investment**:

$$\text{Net investment} = \text{Gross investment} - \text{Depreciation}$$

GNP is calculated using gross investment figures (as is GDP). If we deduct depreciation from these figures, we get *net* national product (NNP), or **national income** as it is sometimes called:

$$NNP \text{ at factor cost (national income)} = GNP \text{ at factor cost} - \text{Depreciation}$$

Table 14.5 shows the 1996 GDP, GNP and NNP figures for the UK.

Although NNP gives a truer picture of the nation's income than GNP, economists tend to use the gross figures because depreciation is hard to estimate accurately.

Personal disposable income

Finally, we come to a measure that is useful for analysing consumer behaviour. If we are to examine how consumption responds to changes in households' disposable income, the measure we require is called **personal disposable income**.

GNP at factor cost measures the incomes generated by production. To get from this to personal disposable income we must first subtract company incomes that are

DEFINITIONS

Gross national product (GNP) GDP plus net property income from abroad.

Depreciation The decline in value of capital equipment due to age or wear and tear.

Net investment Total investment minus depreciation.

Net national product (NNP) or national income GNP minus depreciation.

Personal disposable income The income available for households to spend: i.e. personal incomes after deducting taxes on incomes and adding benefits.

Table 14.5 UK GDP, GNP and NNP at factor cost: 1996

	£million
Gross domestic product	**642 916**
Plus Net property income from abroad	9652
Gross national product	**652 568**
Less Capital consumption (depreciation)	–77 372
Net national product (national income)	**575 196**

Source: *UK National Income and Expenditure* (ONS, 1997).

not paid to households: namely, company taxes, allowances for depreciation and undistributed profits. This gives us the incomes received by households from firms. To get from this to what is available for households to spend we must subtract the money that households pay in income taxes and national insurance contributions, but add all benefits to households, such as pensions and family credit: in other words, we must *include* transfer payments.

Personal disposable income =
GNP at factor cost – Company taxes – Depreciation
– Undistributed profits – Personal taxes + Benefits

Taking account of inflation

If we are to make a sensible comparison of one year's national income with another, we must take inflation into account. For example, if this year national income is 10 per cent higher than last year, but at the same time prices are also 10 per cent higher, then the average person will be no better off at all. There has been no *real* increase in income.

An important distinction here is between **nominal national income** and **real national income**. *Nominal* national income, sometimes called 'money national income', measures national income in the prices ruling at the time and thus takes no account of inflation. *Real* national income, however, measures national income in the prices that ruled in some particular year – the *base year*. Thus we could measure each year's national income in, say, 1985 prices. This would enable us to see how much *real* income had changed from one year to another. In other words, it would eliminate increases in money national income that were merely due to an increase in prices.

The official statistics give both nominal and real figures for all the measures: GDP, GNP, NNP, etc. Box 14.5 shows in more detail how real national income figures are calculated.

Taking account of population: the use of per-capita measures

The figures we have been looking at up to now are *total* GDP or GNP figures. Although they are useful for showing how big the total output or income of one country is compared with another, we are often more interested in output or income *per head*. Luxembourg obviously has a much lower total national income than the UK, but it has a higher GDP per head.

Other per-capita measures are sometimes useful. For example, measuring GDP per head of the *employed* population allows us to compare how much the average worker produces. A country may have a relatively high GDP per head of population, but also have a large proportion of people at work. Its output per worker will therefore not be so high.

?? By what would we need to divide GDP in order to get a measure of labour productivity per hour?

Taking account of exchange rates: the use of PPP measures

There is a big problem with comparing GDP figures of different countries. They are measured in the local currency and thus have to be converted into a common currency (e.g. dollars or ECUs) at the current exchange rate. But the exchange rate may be a poor indicator of the purchasing power of the currency at home. For example, £1 may exchange for, say, 2500 Italian lire. But will £1 in the UK buy the same amount of goods as L2500 in Italy? The answer is almost certainly no.

To compensate for this, GDP can be converted into a common currency at a 'purchasing-power parity rate'. This is a rate of exchange that would allow a given amount of money in one country to buy the same amount of goods in another country after exchanging it into the currency of the other country. The European Commission publishes PPP rates against the ECU for all EU currencies and for the US dollar and Japanese yen. The OECD also

DEFINITIONS

Nominal national income National income measured at current prices.

Real national income National income after allowing for inflation: i.e. national income measured in constant prices: i.e. in terms of the prices ruling in some base year.

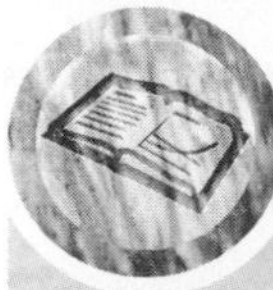

EXPLORING THE THEORY *BOX 14.5

THE GDP DEFLATOR
Taking account of inflation

In 1992 the UK's GDP was £515 billion. In 1979 it was £172 billion. Does this mean that the average Briton in 1992 was three times better off than in 1979? It's obvious that the answer is no. Prices rise over time and thus a pound in 1992 would not be worth as much as a pound in 1979.

To get a true picture of how a country's output has changed we must correct the figures for inflation. The *uncorrected* figures are known as the *nominal* figures. Thus in 1992 the UK's nominal GDP was £515 billion. The *corrected* figures are known as *real* GDP.

But how do we convert nominal GDP into real GDP? The answer is to measure each year's GDP at the prices that ruled in one particular year: the *base year*. Thus if 1985 were chosen as the base year, each year's GDP would be measured in 1985 prices. So if we wanted to measure the 1994 statistics in 1985 prices, we would need to know how much prices had risen between the two years. If prices had increased by 50 per cent then *nominal* GDP in 1994 would be 50 per cent higher than the *real* 1994 GDP measured in 1985 prices. To get the figures for real GDP, then, we must reduce the nominal figures by an appropriate amount.

The calculations are done by expressing average prices each year as an index, with the index for the base year being set at 100. If average prices are 20 per cent higher this year than in the base year, the index this year will be 120.

The price of each item which is entering into the average must be given a weight which reflects its proportion of GDP. Thus if the value of cars produced is twice that of bread, then car prices will have twice the weighting of bread prices. The weights of all items entering into the index must add up to 1.

The formula for calculating real GDP is as follows:

$$\text{Real } GDP_{\text{year a}} = \text{Nominal } GDP_{\text{year a}} \times \frac{\text{Index}_{\text{base year}}}{\text{Index}_{\text{year a}}}$$

Let's look at an example. Assume that Ruritania's nominal GDP was $150 billion in 1985 and $300 billion in 1994. Let us also assume that prices have risen by 50 per cent over the period. Thus if the index was 100 in 1985, it would be 150 in 1994. What is *real* GDP in 1994 measured in 1985 prices? Applying the formula we get:

Real 1994 GDP = $300 billion × 100/150 = $200bn

The figures are given in the table.

Ruritania's nominal and real GDP

Year	Nominal GDP	Price Index	Real GDP
1985	$150bn	100	$150bn
1994	$300bn	150	$200bn

Which prices should we use in calculating the index? The most usual index of prices is the *retail price index* (RPI). This shows the average prices of goods and services bought by consumers: in other words, prices *in the shops*. The RPI is the index used in calculating the rate of inflation. If the current rate of inflation is 6 per cent, this means that the RPI has risen by 6 per cent over the last twelve months.

When calculating real GDP, however, we must use a slightly different index. This is called the *GDP deflator*. It is an index of the average prices of *all* the components of GDP. Thus it includes not just consumer goods prices, but also the prices of investment goods, goods and services consumed by the government, and exports; it excludes the price of imported goods.

?? The following table shows UK (nominal) GDP at factor cost for the years 1979, 1981, 1985, 1990 and 1992. It also shows the GDP deflator with 1985 = 100. Work out the real GDP for each year based on 1985 prices. How much did *real* GDP grow between 1979 and 1981, between 1981 and 1990, and between 1990 and 1992?

	1979	1981	1985	1990	1992
Nominal GDP at factor cost (£bn at current prices)	172.4	217.8	307.9	479.5	514.6
GDP deflator (1985 = 100)	61.0	79.7	100.0	133.6	147.9

publishes PPP rates against the US dollar for all OECD currencies. Using such rates to measure GDP gives the 'purchasing-power standard' (PPS) GDP.

Box 14.6 compares GDP with PPS GDP for various countries.

Do national income statistics give a good indication of a country's standard of living?

If we take into account both inflation and the size of the population, and use figures for *real* per-capita PPS GNP, will this give us a good indication of a country's standard of living? The figures *do* give quite a good indication of

CASE STUDIES BOX 14.6

WHICH COUNTRY IS BETTER OFF?
Comparing national income statistics

Using PPS GDP figures can give a quite different picture of the relative incomes in different countries than using simple GDP figures. The table shows the GDP per head and PPS GDP per head in various countries. The figures are expressed as a percentage of the EU average. Thus in 1997 Japan had a GDP per head 48.6 per cent higher than the EU average. But, because of higher Japanese prices, the average person in Japan could only buy 18.1 per cent more goods and services. GDP per head in Portugal was only 46.3 per cent of the EU average, but the average person in Portugal could buy 69.0 per cent as much as the average EU citizen.

?? Referring to the figures in the table, which countries' actual exchange rates would seem to understate the purchasing power of their currency?

GDP per head as a percentage of the EU average: 1997

	GDP per head	GDP (PPS) per head
Luxembourg	175.4	168.0
Japan	148.6	118.1
Denmark	142.3	116.3
USA	129.7	142.1
Germany	120.3	109.9
Sweden	118.4	99.8
Austria	113.7	106.2
France	111.7	106.6
Belgium	109.0	111.3
Netherlands	106.8	108.1
Finland	104.8	99.1
UK	97.6	96.3
Ireland	93.8	102.6
Italy	92.4	102.7
Spain	62.7	77.5
Greece	52.6	66.3
Portugal	46.3	69.0

Source: *European Economy*.

the level of production of goods and the incomes generated from it, provided we are clear about the distinctions between the different measures. But when we come to ask the more general question of whether the figures give a good indication of the welfare or happiness of the country's citizens, then there are serious problems in relying exclusively on national income statistics.

Problems of measuring national output

The main problem here is that the output of some goods and services goes unrecorded and thus the GNP figures will understate the nation's output. There are two reasons why these items are not recorded.

Non-marketed items. If you employ a decorator to paint your living room, this will be recorded in the GNP statistics. If, however, you paint the room yourself, it will not. Similarly, if a farmer grows cabbages and sells them, this output will form part of GNP. If, however, you grow cabbages on your allotment, it will not. The exclusion of these 'do-it-yourself' activities means that the GNP statistics understate the true level of production in the economy. If over time there is an *increase* in the amount of do-it-yourself activities that people perform, the figures will also understate the *rate of growth* of national output. On the other hand, if in more and more families both partners go out to work and employ people to do the housework, this will overstate the rate of growth in output. The housework which was previously unrecorded now enters into the GNP statistics.

The 'underground' economy. The underground economy consists of illegal and hence undeclared transactions. These could be transactions where the goods and services are themselves illegal, such as drugs and prostitution. Alternatively, they could be transactions that are illegal only in that they are not declared for tax purposes. For example, to avoid paying VAT, a garage may be prepared to repair your car slightly more cheaply if you pay cash. Another example is that of 'moonlighting', where people do extra work outside their normal job and do not declare the income for tax purposes. For example, an electrician employed by a building contractor during the day may rewire people's houses in the evenings, again for cash. Unemployed people may do casual jobs which again they do not declare, this time for fear of losing benefits.

Problems of using national income statistics to measure welfare

GNP is essentially an indicator of a nation's *production*. But production may be a poor indicator of the well-being of society for the following reasons.

ISSUES AND APPLICATIONS BOX 14.7

HOW BIG IS THE UNDERGROUND ECONOMY?

The factors that determine its size

Estimates for the size of the underground economy vary enormously from country to country. Clearly it is impossible to get precise estimates because, by their very nature, the details are largely hidden from the authorities. Nevertheless economists have tried to identify the factors that determine the size of the underground economy.

The first determinant is the level of taxes and regulations. The greater their level, the greater the incentive for people to evade the system and 'go underground'.

The second is the determination of the authorities to catch up with evaders, and the severity of the punishments for those found out.

A third is the size of the service sector relative to the manufacturing sector. It is harder for the authorities to detect the illicit activities of motor mechanics, gardeners and window cleaners than the output of cars, bricks and soap.

Another determinant is the proportion of the population that is self-employed. It is much easier for the self-employed to evade taxes than it is for people receiving a wage where taxes are deducted at source.

Some indication of the size of the underground economy is given by the demand for cash in the economy, since most underground transactions are conducted in cash. In some parts of the USA which have witnessed a large rise in drug use, the banks have reported an increased demand for cash.

??

1. Is the size of the underground economy likely to increase or decrease as the level of unemployment rises?
2. If the amount of cash used in the economy falls, does this mean that the size of the underground economy must have fallen?

Production does not equal consumption. Production is desirable only to the extent that it enables us to *consume* more. If GNP rises as a result of a rise in *investment*, this will not lead to an increase in *current* living standards. It will, of course, help to raise *future* consumption.

The same applies if GNP rises as a result of an increase in exports. Unless there is a resulting increase in imports, it will be foreign consumers that benefit, not domestic consumers.

The human costs of production. If production increases, this may be due to technological advance. If, however, it increases as a result of people having to work harder or longer hours, its net benefit will be less. Leisure is a desirable good, and so too are pleasant working conditions, but these items are not included in the GNP figures.

GNP ignores externalities. The rapid growth in industrial society is recorded in GNP statistics. What the statistics do not record are the environmental side effects: the polluted air and rivers, the ozone depletion, the problem of global warming. If these external costs were taken into account, the *net* benefits of industrial production might be much less.

?? Name some external *benefits* that are not included in GNP statistics.

The production of certain 'bads' leads to an increase in GNP. As we have seen, external costs are not deducted from GNP. In some cases the production of undesirable things can actually count as an *increase* in GNP. If you have to travel a long distance to work, this will be a personal *cost* to you, in both money and lost leisure. Yet the provision of these transport services counts as part of GNP. The further people have to travel to work, the bigger this will make GNP!

Total GNP figures ignore the distribution of income. If some people gain and others lose, we cannot say that there has been an unambiguous increase in welfare. A typical feature of many rapidly growing countries is that some people grow very rich while others are left behind. The result is a growing inequality. If this is seen as undesirable, then clearly total GNP statistics are an inadequate measure of welfare.

A related point is that a given percentage growth in a rich person's income will add much more to GNP than the same percentage growth in a poor person's income. Yet the marginal utility of an extra £1 is greater for a poor person who has very little than it is for a rich person who already has a great deal. A way of dealing with this problem is to put a greater weighting on the growth in incomes of poor people than rich people.

Conclusions

If a country's citizens put a high priority on a clean environment, a relaxed way of life, greater self-sufficiency, a

DEVELOPMENT OF IDEAS — BOX 14.8

A MEASURE OF ECONOMIC WELFARE
MEW: an alternative to GNP?

GNP is not a complete measure of economic welfare; nor is it meant to be. So is there any alternative that takes other factors into account and gives a more complete picture of the level of human well-being?

In 1972 two economists, William Nordhaus and the subsequent Nobel prize winner James Tobin, introduced what they called a *measure of economic welfare* (MEW). This started with GNP and NNP. To this was added an allowance for leisure, for various non-marketed goods and services such as housework and underground activities, for the services of various public amenities such as parks and roads, and for private durable goods such as furniture and jewellery.

On the other hand, various items were subtracted. These included 'regrettables' such as expenditure on defence and commuting to work, and various 'bads' or 'disamenities' such as pollution. Also various intermediate items such as the benefits of education were subtracted. The logic for excluding these was that the benefits show up later in increased labour productivity and earnings, and to include them now would be to double count. Finally, amounts have to be deducted for the extra capital and extra current output required to meet any growth in population: after all, the objective is per-capita welfare and not merely some gross figure.

The table shows how Nordhaus and Tobin reworked the US GNP for 1965 to produce a value for MEW.

MEW has been growing at a slower pace than GNP. The reason for this is that, although leisure has been increasing, it has increased less quickly than the output of goods and services, whereas the output of 'bads' and 'regrettables' has increased more rapidly than the output of goods and services.

The big problem with using MEW is in obtaining reliable estimates of all the additional items it includes. As a result it has not been adopted by governmental statistical agencies around the world.

US GNP and MEW: 1965

Item	$bn
GNP	617.8
Capital consumption	–54.7
NNP	563.1
Regrettables and intermediates	
Government	–63.2
Private	–30.9
Items not included in GNP	
Leisure	626.9
Non-market activity	295.4
Disamenities	–34.6
Services of public and private capital	78.9
Additional capital consumption	–92.7
Growth requirement	–101.8
Sustainable MEW	1241.1

Source: W. Nordhaus and J. Tobin, 'Is growth obsolete?' in *Economic Growth* (National Bureau of Economic Research, Columbia University Press, 1972).

?? If defence should be excluded as a 'regrettable', should we also exclude expenditure on health, heating and double glazing?

less materialistic outlook, more giving rather than selling, and greater equality, then such a country will probably have a lower GNP than a similarly endowed country where the pursuit of wealth is given high priority. Clearly, we cannot conclude that the first country will have a lower level of well-being. However, this does not mean that we should reject GNP statistics as a means of judging economic performance. GNP statistics are not meant to be a measure of economic welfare. They are a measure of *output* or *income*, and should be seen in that context.

SECTION SUMMARY

1. National income is usually expressed in terms of gross domestic product. This is simply the value of domestic production over the course of the year. It can be measured by the product, expenditure or income methods.
2. The product method measures the values added in all parts of the economy. Care must be taken in the evaluation of stocks, government services and the ownership of dwellings.
3. The income method measures all the incomes generated from domestic production: wages and salaries, rent, interest and profit. Transfer payments are not included, nor is stock appreciation.

continued

4. The expenditure method adds up all the categories of expenditure: consumer expenditure, government expenditure and investment. If imports are included as well, this gives total domestic expenditure. If in addition exports are included, this gives total final expenditure. If imports are then deducted from total final expenditure, this gives GDP. Thus $GDP = C + G + I + X - M$.
5. GDP at *market prices* measures what consumers pay for output (including taxes and subsidies on what they buy). GDP at *factor cost* measures what factors receive. GDP at factor cost is thus GDP at market prices minus indirect taxes plus subsidies on goods and services.
6. Gross *national* product (GNP) takes account of incomes earned on assets held overseas and payments made to foreigners who hold assets in the country. Thus *GNP* = *GDP* plus net property income from abroad.
7. Net national product (NNP) takes account of depreciation of capital. Thus $NNP = GNP -$ depreciation.
8. Personal disposable income is a measure of household income after the deduction of income taxes and the addition of benefits.
9. *Real* national income takes account of inflation by being expressed in the prices of some base year.
10. In order to compare living standards of different countries, national income has to be expressed per capita and at purchasing-power parity exchange rates. Even if it is, there are still problems in using national income statistics for comparative purposes. Certain items will not be included: items such as non-marketed products, services in the family and activities in the underground economy. Moreover, the statistics include certain 'bads' and ignore externalities, and they also ignore questions of the distribution of income.

??? END-OF-CHAPTER QUESTIONS ???

1. The following are the items in the UK's 1994 balance of payments:

	£ billions
Exports of goods	134.7
Imports of goods	145.5
Net services	+4.7
Net investment income	+8.7
Net transfers	–5.0
Overseas investment in UK	39.4
UK investment overseas	0.4
Other capital inflows	–6.9
Other capital outflows	33.7
Reserves	–1.0

Calculate the following: (i) the balance of trade in goods; (ii) the balance of trade; (iii) the balance of payments on current account; (iv) the long-term capital account balance; (v) net transactions in external assets and liabilities (the capital account balance); (vi) the balancing item.

2. The following table shows UK National Income Accounts for 1994 by category of expenditure:

	£ millions
Consumers' expenditure	428 084
General government final consumption	144 084
Gross domestic fixed capital formation	100 075
Value of physical increase in stocks and work in progress	3 303
Exports of goods and services	173 925
Imports of goods and services	180 729
Statistical discrepancy	124
Taxes on expenditure	96 950
Subsidies	7 224
Net property income from abroad	10 519
Capital consumption	68 150

Calculate the following: (i) *TDE*; (ii) *TFE*; (iii) *GDP* at market prices; (iv) *GDP* at factor cost; (v) *GNP* at factor cost; (vi) Net National Product at factor cost; (vii) National income.

3. Explain how the current account of the balance of payments is likely to vary with the course of the business cycle.
4. List some factors that could cause an increase in the credit items of the balance of payments and a decrease in the debit items. What would be the effect on the exchange rate (assuming that it is freely floating)? What effect would these exchange rate movements have on the balance of payments?
5. What policy measures could the government adopt to prevent the exchange rate movements in question 4?
6. Assume that there is a trade-off between unemployment and inflation, traced out by a 'Phillips curve'. What could cause a leftward shift in this curve?
7. Explain how equilibrium would be restored in the circular flow of income if there were a fall in investment.
8. For what reasons might GDP be a poor indicator of (i) the level of development of a country; (ii) its rate of economic development?

15 Macroeconomic ideas

15.1 Macroeconomic controversies

Macroeconomics and politics

Macroeconomics is highly controversial. There is no universal agreement among economists as to how the economy functions at a macroeconomic level. Instead there are various schools of thought.

These schools of thought see very different roles for the government in managing the economy. Some economists argue that the economy is more likely to achieve the various macroeconomic objectives if the capitalist market economy is allowed to function pretty well freely, without hindrance from the government. Other economists argue that the government must intervene if macroeconomic objectives are to be met. There is further division among those who argue in favour of government intervention over the appropriate amount and type of intervention.

These divisions among economists tend to parallel political divisions. Politicians have tended to embrace schools of economic thought whose vision of the economy and the role of government is the same as their own. There is a big danger here, however. When economics is made to serve the political purposes of politicians, objectivity can fly out of the window. Economic analysis can become economic dogma. Evidence which is uncomfortable to a politician's point of view may be rejected, ignored or twisted. Evidence which supports the point of view may be given undue weight or accepted uncritically.

In this chapter we will examine the development of macroeconomic ideas over the last 60 years or so. We will identify various schools of macroeconomic thought, along with the political factions that have embraced them.

First, however, we need to identify those areas where debate takes place. Most of the debate centres on the working of the market mechanism: just how well or how badly it will achieve the various macroeconomic objectives. There are three major areas of disagreement: (a) how flexible are wages and prices, (b) how flexible is aggregate supply and (c) what is the role of expectations? We examine each in turn.

Issue 1: The flexibility of prices and wages

Generally, the political right tends to ally with those economists who argue that prices and wages are relatively flexible. Markets tend to clear, they say, and clear fairly quickly.

Disequilibrium unemployment is likely to be fairly small, according to their view, and normally only a temporary, short-run phenomenon. Any long-term unemployment, therefore, will be equilibrium (or 'natural') unemployment. To cure this, they argue, encouragement must be given to the free play of market forces: to a rapid response of both firms and labour to changes in market demand and supply, to a more rapid dissemination of information on job vacancies, and generally to greater labour mobility, both geographical and occupational.

There are some on the political right, however, who argue that in the short run wages may not be perfectly flexible. This occurs when unions attempt to keep wages above the equilibrium (see Box 13.4). In this case, disequilibrium unemployment may continue for a while. The solution here, they argue, is to curb the power of unions so that wage flexibility can be restored and disequilibrium unemployment cured.

The political centre and left tend to ally with economists who reject the assumption of highly flexible wages and prices. Generally, as one moves leftwards along the political spectrum, a greater degree of inflexibility of wages and prices is assumed. If there is a deficiency of demand for labour in the economy, during a recession say, there will be a resistance from unions to cuts in real wages and certainly to cuts in money wages. Any cuts that do occur will be insufficient to eliminate the disequilibrium, and will anyway only serve further to reduce aggregate demand so that workers have less money to spend. The demand curve in Figure 13.10 (see page 421) would shift further to the left.

The prices of goods may also be inflexible in response to changes in demand. As industry has become more concentrated and more monopolistic over the years, firms, it is argued, have become less likely to respond to a general fall in demand by cutting prices. Instead, they are likely to build up stocks if they think the recession is temporary, or cut production and hence employment if they think the recession will persist. It is also argued that firms typically use cost-plus methods of pricing. If wages are inflexible downwards, and if they form a major element of costs, prices will also be inflexible downwards.

Thus according to those who criticise the right, markets cannot be relied upon automatically to correct disequilibria and hence cure disequilibrium unemployment.

?? Why are *real* wages likely to be more flexible downwards than *money* wages?

Issue 2: The flexibility of aggregate supply

The question here is, how responsive is national output (i.e. aggregate supply), and hence also employment, to a change in aggregate demand?

The right tends to argue that aggregate supply does not respond, except perhaps in the short run, to changes in aggregate demand. Aggregate supply is determined *independently* of demand. It depends on the quantity and productivity of factors of production, *not* on the level of aggregate demand. An expansion of aggregate demand will merely lead to (demand-pull) inflation. It cannot lead to a long-term growth in output and employment. Likewise a contraction in aggregate demand will not lead to a long-term fall in output and a rise in unemployment. It will merely lead to a fall in prices.

If the government, therefore, wants to expand aggregate supply and get more rapid economic growth, it is no good, they argue, concentrating on demand. Instead, governments should concentrate directly on supply by encouraging enterprise and competition, and generally by encouraging markets to operate more freely. For this reason, this approach is often labelled **supply-side economics**.

Other economists and other politicians disagree – from the left of the Conservative Party leftwards. They argue that rises in aggregate demand *will* cause aggregate supply to rise, and if the rise in aggregate demand is sufficient, unemployment will fall. This rise in output and employment can persist into the long run if governments maintain a high and expanding level of aggregate demand. Buoyant and expanding markets for their products will encourage firms to produce up to capacity, to employ more people and to invest for the future, thus increasing capacity further.

However, these conditions will not be achieved, they argue, if the government pursues a non-interventionist, *laissez-faire* policy. The government instead must seek to control aggregate demand, to ensure that it continues to grow, and at a steady, non-fluctuating rate.

These arguments centre on the nature of the aggregate supply curve (*AS*). Three different *AS* curves are shown in Figure 15.1. The *AD* curves are drawn as downward sloping, showing that the higher the level of prices, the less will people purchase for a given level of money supply in the economy. In each of the three cases, it is assumed that the government now raises aggregate demand, by, say, increasing the amount of money in the economy. Aggregate demand shifts from AD_1 to AD_2. The effect on prices and output will depend on the shape of the *AS* curve.

The political right argues that there will be little or no effect on output. Instead, the rise in aggregate demand will simply lead to a rise in prices. They therefore envisage an *AS* curve like that in diagram (a).

Their critics, however, argue that a rise in aggregate demand will lead to a rise in output. In the extreme case, prices will not rise at all. In this case the *AS* curve is like that in diagram (b). Output will rise to Y_2 with the price level remaining at *P*.

Others argue that both prices and output will rise. In this case, the short-term curve will be like that in diagram (c). If there is plenty of slack in the economy – idle machines, unemployed labour, etc. – output will rise a lot and prices only a little. But as slack is taken up, the *AS* curve becomes steeper. Firms, finding it increasingly difficult to raise output in the short run, simply respond to a rise in demand by raising prices. In the longer term, if increased demand leads to more investment and increased capacity (potential output), the short-run *AS* curve will shift to the right. A long-term *AS* curve, in this view, therefore, would be more elastic than the short-term one.

?? Would it be possible for a short-run AS curve to be horizontal (as in diagram (b)) at *all* levels of output?

Issue 3: The role of expectations in the working of the market

How quickly and how fully will individuals and firms anticipate changes in prices and changes in output? How are their expectations formed, and how accurate are they?

DEFINITION

Supply-side economics An approach which focuses directly on aggregate supply and how to shift the aggregate supply curve outwards.

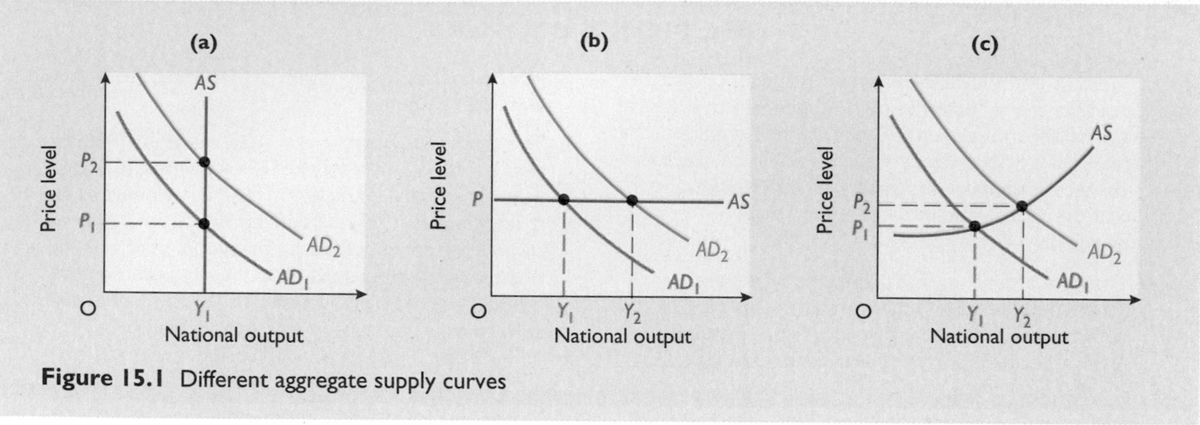

Figure 15.1 Different aggregate supply curves

What effect do these expectations have? This is the third major controversial topic.

The political right tends to ally with those economists who argue that people's expectations adjust rapidly and fully to changing economic circumstances. They emphasise the role of expectations of *price* changes.

If aggregate demand expands, they argue, people will expect higher prices. Workers will realise that the apparently higher wages they are offered are an illusion. The higher wages are 'eaten up' by higher prices. Thus workers are not encouraged to work longer hours, and unemployed workers are not encouraged to take on employment more readily. Likewise firms realise that any increased demand for their products is an illusion. Very soon all firms will raise their prices in response to the demand increase, and given that firms' costs are rising due to higher wages and the higher prices of raw materials, machinery, etc., their price rises will fully choke off the extra demand. There will be no increase in sales, and hence no increase in output and employment.

Thus, they argue, increased aggregate demand merely fuels inflation and can do no more than give a very temporary boost to output and employment. If anything, the higher inflation could damage business confidence and thus worsen long-term output and employment growth by discouraging investment.

Those who crticise the right argue that the formation of expectations is more complex than this, and that whether people expect an increase in demand to be fully matched by inflation depends on the current state of the economy and how any increase in demand is introduced.

If there is a lot of slack in the economy – if unemployment is very high and there are many idle resources – and if an increase in demand is in the form, say, of direct government spending on production – on roads, hospitals, sewers and other infrastructure – then output and employment may quickly rise. Here the effect of expectations may be beneficial. Rather than expecting inflation from the increased demand, firms may expect faster growth and an expansion of markets. As a result they may choose to invest, and this in turn will produce further growth in output and employment.

Views on expectations, therefore, parallel views on aggregate supply. The right argues that a boost to demand will not produce extra output and employment: aggregate supply is inelastic (as in Figure 15.1(a)) and therefore the higher demand will merely fuel expectations of inflation. Their critics argue that a boost to demand will increase aggregate supply and employment. Firms will expect this and therefore produce more.

?? If firms believe the aggregate supply curve to be moderately elastic, what effect will this belief have on the outcome of an increase in aggregate demand?

Policy implications

Generally, then, the economists supported by the political right tend to favour a policy of *laissez-faire*. At most, governments should intervene to remove hindrances to the free and efficient operation of markets: for example, by legislation to reduce the power of trade unions. This way, they argue, disequilibrium unemployment will be removed and the greatest opportunity will be given for long-term growth in output and the reduction in equilibrium unemployment. Any intervention by government to boost demand will merely be inflationary and will thus damage long-term growth and employment.

Economists supported by the political centre and left argue that disequilibrium unemployment may persist for many years and may be very great. The answer is to boost demand, thereby increasing aggregate supply and employment.

SECTION SUMMARY

1. There is considerable debate among economists and politicians over how the market mechanism works at a macroeconomic level. Those on the right argue that markets work relatively well and adjust quickly to changes in demand and supply. Their critics argue that there are various rigidities and that disequilibrium may persist.
2. The right argues (a) that prices and wages are relatively flexible, (b) that aggregate supply is determined independently of aggregate demand and (c) that people's price and wage expectations adjust rapidly to shifts in aggregate demand so as to wipe out any output effect.
3. The centre and left to varying degrees argue (a) that prices and wages are inflexible downwards, (b) that output depends on the level of aggregate demand and that aggregate supply is relatively elastic when there is slack in the economy and (c) that people's expectations of prices and wages depend on their expectations of output and employment, and anyway may be relatively slow to adjust to shifts in aggregate demand.

15.2 Classical macroeconomics

The classical economists of the early nineteenth century held a pessimistic view of the long-term prospects for economic growth (see Boxes 5.2, 13.2 and 15.1). Population growth combined with the law of diminishing returns would undermine any benefits from improved technology or the discovery of new sources of raw materials. What is more, there was little the government could do to improve these prospects. In fact governments, they argued, by interfering with competition and the functioning of the market would be likely to make things worse. They therefore advocated a policy of *laissez-faire* and free trade.

The classical school continued into the twentieth century. By then, its predictions about economic growth had become less pessimistic. After all, the Victorian years had been ones of rapid industrialisation and growth, with a massive expansion of Britain's overseas trade. This growing optimism had, if anything, strengthened the advocacy of *laissez-faire*. In the early years of this century, then, most economists, most politicians and virtually all bankers and businesspeople were relatively confident in the power of the free market to provide growing output and low unemployment.

The main role for the government was to provide 'sound finance' (i.e. not to print too much money), so as to maintain stable prices.

The classical analysis of output and employment

The classical theory predicted that, in the long run, equilibrium in the economy would be at virtually full employment. In the long run, any unemployment would be merely *frictional* unemployment: namely, people in the process of changing jobs.

There were two important elements in the classical theory.

The free-market economy works to equate demand and supply in all markets

This element of classical theory assumes flexible prices: of goods and services, of labour (i.e. wages) and of money (i.e. the rate of interest).

The classical economists argued that flexible prices would ensure that saving equalled investment ($S = I$) and that imports equalled exports ($M = X$). From this it follows that, if the government were to 'balance its budget' and make taxation equal to government expenditure ($T = G$), then total withdrawals would equal total injections ($W = J$).

$$\left.\begin{array}{l} S = I \\ M = X \\ T = G \end{array}\right\} \rightarrow W = J^1$$

But why should flexible prices ensure that $S = I$ and $M = X$? The reasoning of the classical economists was as follows.

S = I. This would be brought about by flexible rates of interest (r) in the **market for loanable funds**. When firms want to invest in new plant and equipment they will

[1] The classical economists did not use the terms 'withdrawals' and 'injections': these are modern terms. Nevertheless, their analysis implied an automatic equation of W and J if markets cleared and the government balanced its budget.

DEFINITION

Market for loanable funds The market for loans from and deposits into the banking system.

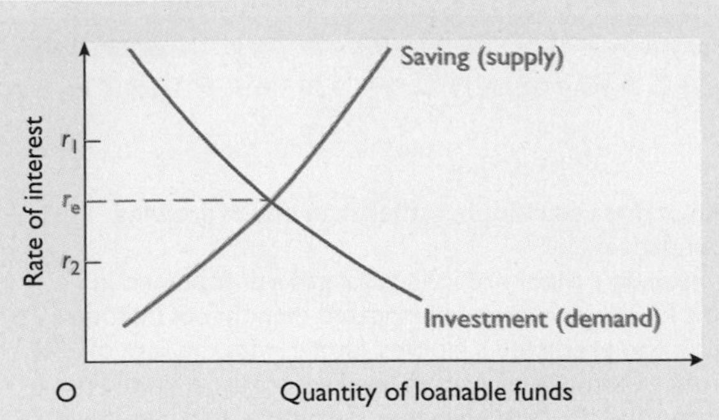

Figure 15.2 The market for loanable funds

require finance. Investment demand, therefore, represents a demand for loanable funds from financial institutions. The higher the rate of interest, the more expensive will borrowing be, and hence the less will be the demand for investment. The investment schedule will therefore be downward sloping with respect to *r*. This is illustrated in Figure 15.2.

Saving represents a supply of loanable funds. The saving schedule will be upward sloping. The higher the rate of interest, the more people will save: that is, the more they will deposit in financial institutions.

Equilibrium will be at r_e, where $S = I$. If the rate of interest were above r_e, say at r_1, financial institutions would have surplus funds. They would have to lower the rate of interest to attract sufficient borrowers. If the rate of interest were below r_e, say at r_2, financial institutions would be short of funds. They would raise the rate of interest.

> ?? Assuming that rates of interest are initially above the equilibrium and that one particular financial institution chooses *not* to reduce its rate of interest, what will happen? What will be the elasticity of supply of loanable funds to an *individual* institution?

$M = X$. This would be brought about by flexible UK prices and wages. Before 1914, and from 1925 to 1931, the UK was on the **gold standard**. This was a *fixed* exchange rate system in which each participating country's currency was valued at a certain fixed amount of gold.

If a country had a balance of payments deficit ($M > X$), this had to be paid in gold from its reserves. A country was then supposed to respond to this outflow of gold by reducing the amount of money in the economy and hence reducing total expenditure. This would create surpluses in the goods and labour markets, which would, in turn, lead to a fall in prices and wages. This fall in the prices of UK goods would increase the sale of exports and reduce the consumption of the now relatively expensive imports. This whole process would continue until the balance of payments deficit was eliminated: until $M = X$.

> ?? What would have happened if countries in deficit had not responded to an outflow of gold by reducing total expenditure?

(Note that, under a system of freely floating exchange rates, it is the flexibility in exchange rates, rather than the prices of goods and factors, that will ensure $M = X$.)

Provided the government balanced its budget ($T = G$), therefore, flexibility in the various markets would ensure that withdrawals equal injections.

Say's law

J.-B. Say was a French economist of the early nineteenth century (see Box 15.1). **Say's law** states that: *supply creates its own demand*. What this means is that the production of goods and services will generate expenditures sufficient to ensure that they are sold. There will be no deficiency of demand and no need to lay off workers. There will be full employment. The justification for the law is as follows.

When firms produce goods, they pay out money either directly to other firms, or as factor payments to households. The income that households receive is then partly paid back to firms in the form of consumption expenditure (C_d): the inner flow of the circular flow of income.

But any withdrawals by firms or households are also fully paid back to firms in the form of injections, since $S = I$, $M = X$ and $T = G$. Thus all the incomes generated by firms' supply will be transformed into demand for their products, either directly in the form of consumption, or indirectly via withdrawals and then injections. There will thus be no deficiency of demand.

Of course, although aggregate demand might equal aggregate supply, consumers may shift their demand away from some industries in favour of others. Unemployment

DEFINITIONS

Gold standard The system whereby countries' exchange rates were fixed in terms of a certain amount of gold and whereby balance of payments deficits were paid in gold.

Say's law Supply creates its own demand. In other words, the production of goods will generate sufficient demand to ensure that they are sold.

DEVELOPMENT OF IDEAS

THOMAS MALTHUS, DAVID RICARDO AND JEAN-BAPTISTE SAY

How gloomy was classical economics?

Thomas Robert Malthus (1766–1834) and David Ricardo (1772–1823) were probably the two most famous economists of the early nineteenth century. They were in fact close friends and spent much of their time in discussion, in correspondence and also in social gatherings – both men loving to entertain.

The two men came from quite different backgrounds and pursued very different careers.

Malthus, the gifted son of a gifted and eccentric father, with whom he would debate for hours, gained a degree in mathematics from Cambridge, took holy orders and became a rector (but left two curates to run the parish while he continued his academic research), and in 1804 became England's first professor of political economy.

While Malthus pursued an academic career, Ricardo was making a fortune in the world of finance. He was the third of seventeen children born to Jewish parents who had migrated to London from Holland. His father was a wealthy merchant banker, and at the age of 14 David went to work for him. But then when he was 21, against the wishes of his parents, he married a Quaker. Disinherited by his father, he set up in business on his own as a stockbroker. He was so successful that in 1814, when he was still only 42, he retired from the world of business to concentrate on writing and politics. Representing an Irish constituency in Parliament, he strongly advocated liberal reforms.

Malthus and Ricardo agreed on one thing: there was a gloomy long-term prospect for the human race.

As we saw back in Chapter 5, Malthus argued that population growth would outstrip the growth in food supplies. The future of the planet, therefore, was to be one of mass starvation, rather than one of growing abundance.

Ricardo's theory of long-term growth (outlined in Box 13.2) was more sophisticated than that of Malthus, but it too predicted a gloomy future, with the rate of profit eventually falling to a level where firms would no longer find it worth investing. Growth would ultimately grind to a halt.

But while Malthus and Ricardo agreed about the fate of the world in the distant future, that was about all they did agree on!

Malthus was also pessimistic about the more immediate future. Malthus saw the capitalist system as inherently unstable. He looked around him at a world in recession following the Napoleonic wars. Yet this recession with its high level of unemployment was not due to a lack of productive capacity. Quite the opposite: the warehouses were full; there was a general 'glut'. The problem according to Malthus was one of underconsumption, of a lack of 'effectual demand'. If consumers would not buy, firms would not produce.

Ricardo was totally dismissive of Malthus's ideas. Ignoring the evidence around him, Ricardo denied the possibility of a general glut. He denied the possibility of mass unemployment. If wages were too high to clear the labour market, they would simply fall until the disequilibrium was eliminated. In reply to Malthus he wrote:

> You say 'we know from repeated experience that the money price of labour never falls till many workmen have been for some time out of work.' I know no such

may then temporarily occur. But then wages would fall in the declining industries and rise in the expanding industries. Equilibrium would be restored. Unemployment would be eliminated.

The restoration of equilibrium, and thus the correction of this temporary unemployment, will be quicker (a) the more flexible are wages and (b) the more willing and able are workers to move to industries and towns where jobs are available (labour mobility). In other words, the better markets work, the sooner will full employment be restored.

The classical analysis of prices and inflation

The classical economists based their analysis of inflation on the **quantity theory of money**. In its simplest form it states that the general level of prices (P) in the economy depends on the supply of money (M):[2]

$$P = f(M)$$

The greater the quantity of money, the higher the level of prices. Under this theory inflation is simply caused by a rise in money supply.

[2] In the quantity theory of money the letter M is used to refer to money supply, whereas in the circular flow of income it is used to refer to the expenditure on imports. Naturally this is potentially confusing, but unfortunately it is normal practice to use the letter M in both ways. To avoid any such confusion we will always specify which is being referred to. Elsewhere, however, you will just have to judge from the context! (There is the same problem with the letter P, which can refer either to price or to product.)

DEFINITION

Quantity theory of money The price level (P) is directly related to the quantity of money in the economy (M).

BOX 15.1

thing, and if wages were previously high, I can see no reason whatever why they should not fall before many labourers are thrown out of work.[3]

Ricardo's more optimistic view about short-term growth and employment, even though it flew in the face of the evidence, carried public opinion with it. Ricardo was held in great respect, if not awe. A persuasive public speaker, a highly successful businessman, a writer of very difficult to understand economics: his ideas must be correct!

Jean-Baptiste Say (1776–1832) was a French economist and industrialist who was greatly influenced by both Adam Smith and David Ricardo. He was largely responsible for introducing to the continent Smith's ideas on the workings of markets and the 'invisible hand', and for a time fell out of favour with Napoleon for advocating a policy of extreme *laissez-faire*.

Say, who was a good friend of Malthus and Ricardo and visited England many times, was more optimistic than either of them. Himself a capitalist – he owned a cotton mill – he believed that free-market capitalism would provide both short-term and long-term prosperity. In the debate between Malthus and Ricardo, he sided with Ricardo, and claimed that a problem of general overproduction and unemployment is impossible. In what became known as Say's law of markets, or more simply Say's law, he argued:

[A] product is no sooner created, than it, from that instant, affords a market for other products to the full extent of its own value. When the producer has put the finishing hand to his product, he is most anxious to sell it immediately, lest its value should vanish in his hands. Nor is he less anxious to dispose of the money he may get for it; for the value of money is also perishable. But the only way of getting rid of money is in the purchase of some product or other. Thus the mere circumstance of the creation of one product immediately opens a vent for other products.[4]

Thus, according to Say, the production of goods would generate sufficient incomes to ensure that these goods were sold. Prolonged unemployment would be impossible.

This optimism about the free market, despite the criticisms of Karl Marx and others, was to dominate the thinking of mainstream economists right up to the 1930s. Even the *long*-run gloomy prognostications of Ricardo and Malthus were eventually dismissed, as the prospect of sustained technological progress seemed to allow economic growth to go on indefinitely. The attention of economists thus became increasingly focused on microeconomic considerations: on questions of efficiency and distribution.

It was not until the 1920s and 1930s, with the UK and then the rest of the world plunged into recession, with all the horrors of mass unemployment and poverty, that Say's law was seriously questioned and the possibility of deficient aggregate demand was once more entertained – this time by Keynes.

[3] P. Sraffa (ed.), *The Works and Correspondence of David Ricardo* (Cambridge University Press, 1951), p. 24.

[4] J. -B. Say, *Treatise on Political Economy* (1803), p. 167.

To understand the reasoning behind the quantity theory of money we need to examine the **equation of exchange**. This comes in various versions (see Box 15.2), but the one most useful for our purposes is the simple identity between national expenditure and national income. This identity may be expressed as follows:

$$MV = PY$$

M, as we have already seen, is the supply of money in the economy. V is the **velocity of circulation**. This is the number of times per year a pound is spent on buying goods and services that make up GDP. Suppose that each pound's worth of money is typically spent 5 times per year on such goods and services, and that money supply was £20 billion. This would mean that total expenditure on GDP ($M \times V$) was £100 billion.

P, again as we have already seen, is the general level of prices. Let us define it more precisely as the price index based on some specific year (e.g. 1995), where the index in the base year is assumed to be 1.00 (not 100) (see page 30). Y is the real value of national income (i.e. GDP expressed in the prices of the base year). $P \times Y$, therefore, is simply

DEFINITIONS

The equation of exchange *MV* = *PY*. The total level of spending on GDP (*MV*) equals the total value of goods and services produced (*PY*) that go to make up GDP.

Velocity of circulation The number of times annually that money on average is spent on goods and services that make up GDP.

the 'nominal' value of GDP (i.e. GDP expressed in *current* prices, rather than those of the base year). Thus if GDP in real terms (Y) (i.e. measured in base-year prices) were £80 billion and if the current price index (P) were 1.25, then nominal GDP ($P \times Y$) would be £100 billion.

Thus both MV and PY are equal to GDP and must, therefore, by definition be equal to each other.

The classical economists argued that both V and Y were determined independently of the money supply: i.e. a change in the money supply would *not* be expected to lead to a change in V or Y. The velocity of circulation (V), they claimed, was determined by the frequency with which people were paid (e.g. weekly or monthly), the nature of the banking system and other institutional arrangements for holding money. As far as Y was concerned, Say's law would ensure that the real value of output (Y) was maintained at the full-employment level.

With V and Y as 'constants' with respect to M, therefore, the quantity theory must hold:

$$P = f(M)$$

Increases in money supply simply lead to inflation.

?? Assuming that Y rises each year as a result of increases in productivity, can money supply rise without causing inflation? Would this destroy the validity of the quantity theory?

The Great Depression and the return to the gold standard

The classical economists had predicted that there would be virtual full employment. Any unemployment would simply be the frictional unemployment of people being 'between jobs'. Before the First World War their predictions were not far from the truth. Between the wars, however, Britain experienced a prolonged recession of unparalleled severity. Throughout this 'Great Depression' unemployment was very much higher than before the war, reaching over 22 per cent in the winter of 1932–3 with 3 million people unemployed. However, the depression eliminated inflation. In every year from 1921 to 1934 prices either were constant or fell (see Figure 15.3).

While in Britain output slumped and unemployment soared, most of the rest of the industrialised world was experiencing a boom. But in 1929, after a decade of rapid growth and a huge rise in share values, Wall Street crashed. This sent the US economy plunging into deep recession, with the rest of the world following suit. As the world economy slumped, so did international trade. With a collapse of its exports, Britain dived even deeper into depression.

The Great Depression was closely associated with Britain's return to the gold standard, a system that it had left in 1914 at the outbreak of the war. From 1918 to 1925 Britain adopted a flexible exchange rate system, a system felt necessary because of the disruption to foreign trade following the war and the monetary chaos in Europe. In 1925, however, Britain returned to the gold standard.

Britain's prosperity before the First World War was crucially dependent on its international trade and its position as provider of international financial services. Classical economists and bankers in the 1920s believed that free trade must be encouraged, and that the best way of doing this was to return to the gold standard. Moreover, the experience of international inflation in the years after the war made many people anxious to return to a system that forced countries to keep inflation under control.

The government and the Treasury felt it was important to return at the old rate to create confidence in the strength of sterling and to protect the value of sterling reserves held by various countries round the world. In

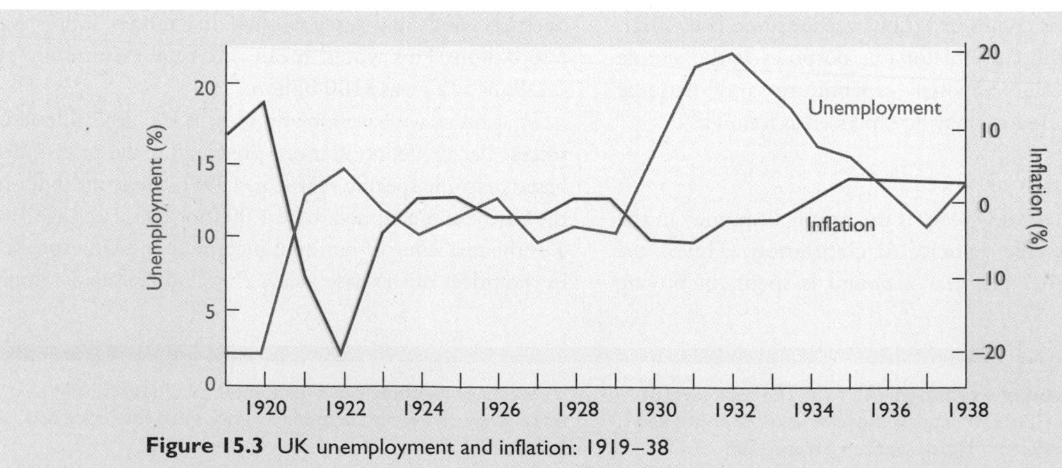

Figure 15.3 UK unemployment and inflation: 1919–38

EXPLORING THE THEORY BOX 15.2

THE EQUATION OF EXCHANGE
Two more versions

The Fisher version

Perhaps the most well-known version of the equation of exchange is the original one developed by the American, Irving Fisher. Fisher was born in New York State in 1867 and obtained a BA in mathematics from Yale and a Ph.D. in economics. He became a highly respected economist, as both a teacher and a writer. His works covered a wide range of topics and were renowned for their clarity and impeccable logic, and his theoretical works, unlike those of many other famous economists, have stood well the test of time.

He expounded his famous equation of exchange in his book *The Purchasing Power of Money* (1911). The equation is as follows:

$$MV = PT$$

where M is the supply of money; T is the total number of transactions taking place per year (whether on final or on intermediate goods and services); P is the average price of all these transactions; and V is the 'transactions' velocity – the number of times per year that money on average is spent on any transaction. MV can thus be seen as total spending, and PT as the total value of all transactions – which must be the same as total spending.

This version differs from the one we looked at in the main text in that T is a *physical* quantity, whereas in the other version Y was a *value* (expressed in base-year prices); Fisher's P is a value, whereas in the other version P was an index number; Fisher's V is the transactions velocity, whereas in the other version V was the 'income' or 'GDP' velocity. The implications, however, are very similar. If the quantity theory of money is to hold, then both V and T must be determined independently of the money supply. Only then will a given percentage change in M be guaranteed to lead to the same percentage change in P. The classical economists made these very assumptions.

Fisher's works were not just confined to economics. He wrote about and campaigned for world peace, methods of improving the physical and mental qualities of future generations, healthy eating, and the benefits of fresh air and a healthy lifestyle generally. In 1915 he wrote a best seller, *How to Live: Rules for healthful living based on modern science*. His fellow economists, suspicious of this populist image, began to brand him as an eccentric, and his influence waned dramatically towards the end of his life. This was not helped by his failure to predict the 1929 Wall Street crash and subsequent Great Depression, and by his subsequent insistence that the depression would soon end.

The Cambridge version

An alternative version was developed in Cambridge in the early 1900s. In this version, the *demand* for money (M_d) depends on national income (Y). The higher the level of national income, the more money balances people will require to hold in order to finance their transactions. When we refer to 'money balances' we are not talking about people's savings, but rather the amount of money they *currently* feel the need to hold. Obviously, the higher people's incomes are, the bigger the total money balances they will choose to hold.

The Cambridge version of the quantity equation is expressed as follows:

$$M_d = kY_n$$

where k is the proportion of national income that people desire to hold in money balances. Assume, for example, that for every £100 of annual income, people wish to hold £20 in money balances. In this case $k = 0.2$. Thus if national income were £100 billion, the demand for money balances (M_d) would be £20 billion.

Nominal national income (Y_n) is the money *value* of the nation's output, i.e. the physical level of national output (Q) times the average price (P) of that output. Thus:

$$M_d = kPQ$$

(Note that Y_n in this version is the equivalent of PY in the version we studied on page 473. There Y was defined as *real* national income (i.e. after correcting for inflation), and P was defined as the price index. Here Y_n is *not* corrected for inflation and P is defined as the average price of goods and services produced.)

Assuming flexible interest rates, and therefore that the money market will clear, the demand for money will equal the supply of money (M_s):

$$M_d = M_s$$

Thus:

$$M_s = kPQ$$

and:

$$P = M_s/kQ$$

The classical position was that k and Q were determined independently of the money supply. With k and Q as constants with respect to M, therefore, the quantity theory must hold:

$$P = f(M_s)$$

?? What is the relationship between the k term in this version and the V terms in the other two versions?

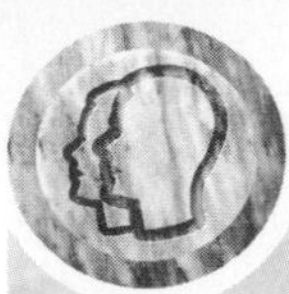

DEVELOPMENT OF IDEAS BOX 15.3

BALANCE THE BUDGET AT ALL COSTS
Fiscal policy in the early 1930s

The budget must be balanced. All government expenditure should be financed from taxation. This was orthodox opinion in the 1920s.

But as unemployment increased during the Great Depression, spending on unemployment benefits (the most rapidly growing item of government expenditure) threatened the balanced budget principle. Other spending had to be cut to restore balance. The result was more unemployment, and hence the payment of more unemployment benefits.

Treasury officials and classical economists called for cuts in unemployment benefits. The May Committee, set up to investigate the budgetary problem, recommended a 20 per cent reduction. Even the Labour government, elected on a mandate to tackle the unemployment problem, proposed a 10 per cent reduction in 1931. This contributed to its subsequent collapse.

Philip Snowdon, Labour's Chancellor of the Exchequer, remarked in 1931 how pensioners had returned their pension books and children sent in their savings to help the nation balance its budget. And yet, as Keynes argued, it was not savings that were necessary to cure the unemployment, but spending (see Box 15.6). Government deficits were *desirable*. Attempts to balance the budget merely deflated the economy further and deepened the problem of unemployment.

1925 Winston Churchill, who was Chancellor of the Exchequer at the time, made the fateful announcement: Britain was returning to the gold standard and at the pre-war rate of £1 = $4.86.

But this was way above the equilibrium rate. Britain had developed a large balance of payments deficit. Export markets had been lost during the war and industries had been diverted away from exporting to producing for the war effort. Imports were high, as post-war reconstruction took place. Also high inflation immediately after the war had reduced the competitiveness of Britain's exports.

Returning to the gold standard at the old rate therefore required harshly deflationary policies: to lower wages and prices, and to restore Britain's competitiveness. There followed a period of great pain. The balance of payments remained in severe deficit. At such a high exchange rate, prices and wages could not be forced downwards rapidly enough to restore the competitiveness of exports or to stem the flood of imports. The result was that gold poured out of the country.

Other countries made Britain's problem worse. The rules of the gold standard required not only that deficit countries should deflate, but also that surplus countries should *reflate*, increasing their money supply and reducing their interest rates, thereby expanding aggregate demand and raising prices. The result would be higher imports and lower exports in surplus countries and the reverse in deficit countries.

The problem was that the surplus countries did not reflate. They were quite happy simply to build up their stock of gold. Britain and other deficit countries had to deflate that much harder. Eventually, with the collapse of world trade following the Wall Street crash of 1929, and a resulting further decline in Britain's exports, there was simply not enough gold left in the Bank of England to support the exchange rate. Britain left the gold standard in 1931. The pound was allowed to depreciate.

The classical response to the Great Depression

The deflationary policies of the 1920s seemed to be directly responsible for increasing unemployment. Many critics argued that the government ought deliberately to *expand* aggregate demand. However, the Treasury and other classical economists rejected the analysis that unemployment was caused by a lack of demand; also they rejected policies of reflation (e.g. increased government expenditure).

The classical Treasury view on unemployment

Would deflation of demand not lead to unemployment? According to the Treasury view, unemployment would occur only if labour markets *failed to clear*: if real wage costs did not fall sufficiently.

In Figure 15.4, if aggregate demand for labour falls from AD_{L_1} to AD_{L_2}, then real wages (i.e. wage costs (W) as a proportion of the price (P) the employer receives for the good) must fall from W_1 to W_2 if equilibrium is to be restored in the labour market.

The Treasury concluded that people should be encouraged to take wage cuts. This would help to reduce prices and restore export demand, thus correcting the balance of payments. Moreover, it would help to reduce unemployment, if money wages fell faster than prices and hence *real* wages fell. People should also be encouraged to save. This would, via flexible interest rates, lead to more investment and hence a growth in output and demand for labour.

ISSUES AND APPLICATIONS

BOX 15.4

THE CROWDING-OUT EFFECT
When public expenditure replaces private

Critics of the use of government expenditure to stimulate output and employment often refer to the problem of *crowding out*. In its starkest form the argument goes like this.

There is no point in the government embarking on a programme of public works to bring the economy out of recession. If it attempts to spend more, it can do so only by reducing private expenditure. The effect on total spending will be zero. This crowding out can take two main forms.

Resource crowding out

This is when the government uses resources such as labour and raw materials that would otherwise be used by the private sector. If the economy is operating near full capacity, then if resources are used by the government, they cannot at the same time be used by private companies.

The argument is far less convincing, however, if there is slack in the economy. If the government merely mobilises otherwise *idle* resources, there need be no reduction in private-sector output. In fact, if private-sector firms have spare capacity, they will respond to the higher demand by producing more themselves: aggregate demand will stimulate extra production.

Financial crowding out

This occurs when extra government spending diverts *funds* from private-sector firms and thus deprives them of the finance necessary for investment.

If the government spends more (without raising taxes or printing more money), it will have to borrow more and will therefore have to offer higher rates of interest. Private companies will then have to offer higher rates of interest themselves in order to attract funds. Alternatively, if they borrow from banks, and banks have less funds, the banks will charge them higher interest rates. Higher interest rates will discourage firms from borrowing and hence discourage investment.

The weakness with this argument is that it assumes that the supply of money is fixed. If the government spends more but *increases* the amount of money in the economy, it need not deprive the private sector of finance. Interest rates will not be bid up.

But would that not be inflationary? Not if there are idle resources and hence the extra money can be spent on extra output. Only if *resource* crowding out takes place would it be inflationary.

?? Could resource crowding out take place at less than full employment?

The classical Treasury view on public works

In the 1920s and 1930s some politicians and economists argued that unemployment could be reduced if the government pursued a programme of public works: building roads, hospitals, houses, etc. The Treasury view was that this would not work and could have costly side-effects.

A programme of public works could be funded in three ways: from extra taxation, from extra government borrowing or by printing extra money. *None* of these three ways would, according to the classical Treasury view, solve the unemployment problem.

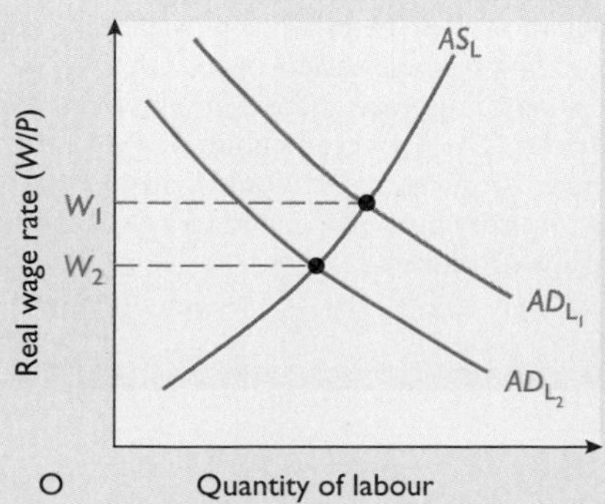

Figure 15.4 The labour market

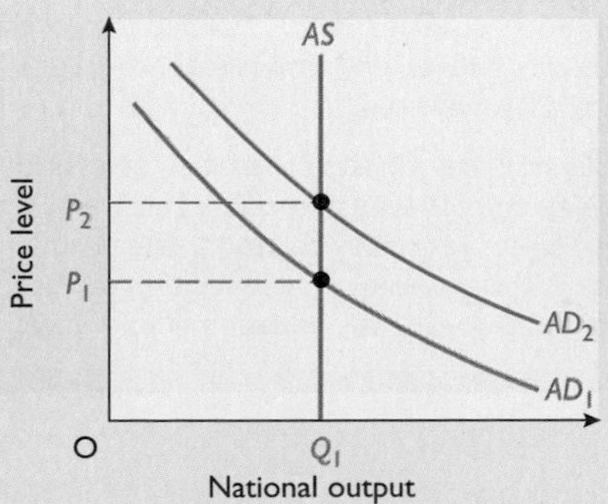

Figure 15.5 The effect of printing extra money: the classical analysis

- *Extra taxation* would merely have the effect of reducing the money that consumers would spend on private industry. Extra public-sector demand would thus be offset by a fall in private-sector demand.
- If the government *borrowed more*, it would have to offer higher interest rates in order to persuade people to buy the additional government securities. The private sector would then have to offer higher interest rates, to compete for funds. As interest rates went up, private borrowing would go down. Thus public investment would **crowd out** private investment (see Box 15.4).
- According to the quantity theory of money, *printing extra money* would simply lead to inflation. The assumption here is that the aggregate supply 'curve' is vertical. In Figure 15.5 a rise in aggregate demand from AD_1 to AD_2 (as a result of the extra money supply) would simply lead to a rise in the price level from P_1 to P_2. National output (and hence employment) would not increase. It would remain constant at Q_1. A re-emergence of inflation, which had been eliminated in the early 1920s, would further erode the competitiveness of British goods, jeopardising the return to the gold standard at the pre-war exchange rate.

Treasury orthodoxy insisted, therefore, that government should attempt to balance its budget, even if this meant cutting welfare benefits to the rising numbers of unemployed (see Box 15.3). The governments of the 1920s and early 1930s followed these classical recommendations. They attempted to balance their budgets and rejected policies of reflation. Yet mass unemployment persisted.

DEFINITION

Crowding out Where increased public expenditure diverts money or resources away from the private sector.

SECTION SUMMARY

1. The classical analysis of output and employment is based on the assumption that markets clear. More specifically, it assumes that there are flexible wages, flexible prices and flexible rates of interest. The result will be that demand and supply are equated in the labour market, in the goods market and in the market for loanable funds.
2. Given that markets will clear, Say's law will operate. This law states that supply creates its own demand. In other words, the production of goods and services will generate incomes for households, which in turn will generate consumption expenditure, ensuring that the goods are sold. If any incomes are not directly spent on domestic goods, flexible prices will help to ensure that any money withdrawn is reinjected. Flexible interest rates will ensure that investment equals saving, and flexible prices and wages will ensure that exports equal imports. Provided the government balances its budget, withdrawals will equal injections and Say's law will hold.
3. The classical economists based their analysis of prices on the quantity theory of money. This states that the level of prices is directly related to the quantity of money in the economy. Their position can be demonstrated using the equation of exchange:

   $$MV = PY$$

   where V is the velocity of circulation, P is the price index and Y is real national income expressed in the prices of the base year. The classical economists assumed that V and Y were not affected by changes in the money supply and could thus be regarded as 'constants'. From this it follows that:

   $$P = f(M)$$

   Increases in the money supply simply lead to inflation.
4. In 1925 Britain returned to the gold standard system of fixed exchange rates at the pre-war rate. But given the massive balance of payments deficit at this rate, it had to pursue tough deflationary policies. The result was mass unemployment.
5. The classical economists saw the remedy to the problem to lie in reductions in wages and prices. According to the classical theory this would allow Say's law to operate and full employment to be restored. They rejected public works as the solution, arguing that it would lead to crowding out if financed by borrowing, and to inflation if financed by printing money.

15.3

The Keynesian revolution

Keynes' rejection of classical macroeconomics

The main critic of classical macroeconomics was John Maynard Keynes. In his major work, *The General Theory of Employment, Interest and Money* (1936), he rejected the classical assumption that markets would clear. Disequilibrium could persist and mass unemployment could continue. There are two crucial markets in which disequilibrium could persist.

The labour market

Workers would resist wage cuts. Wages were thus 'sticky' downwards. In a recession, when the demand for labour is low, wages might not fall far or fast enough to clear the labour market.

In Figure 15.6 the recession has caused the aggregate demand for labour to shift to AD_{L_2}. If the real wage rate were to remain at W_1, the supply and demand for labour would no longer be in equilibrium. There would exist disequilibrium (demand-deficient) unemployment. But even if wage cuts could be introduced, as advocated by classical economists, Keynes rejected that as the solution to demand deficiency. Workers are also consumers. A cut in workers' wages would mean less consumer spending. Firms would respond to this by reducing their demand for labour. Thus a lowering of wage rates below W_1 would lead to a leftward shift in the AD_L curve, and this would more than offset the reduction in wages. Wage rates would not fall fast enough to clear the market. Disequilibrium would worsen. The recession would deepen.

Employers might well find that labour was cheaper to employ, but if demand for their product was falling, they would hardly be likely to take on more labour.

The market for loanable funds

Keynes also rejected the classical solution of increased savings as a means of stimulating investment and growth. Again the problem was one of market disequilibrium.

An increase in savings will cause a disequilibrium in the market for loanable funds. The rate of interest will fall from r_1 to r_2 in Figure 15.7. But an increase in saving means a fall in consumption. As a result, firms will sell less and will thus be discouraged from investing. The investment demand curve will shift to the left. The rate of interest will have to fall *below* r_2 to clear the market.

The demand for investment, according to Keynes, depends very much on business confidence in the future. A slide into recession could shatter such confidence. The resulting fall in investment would deepen the recession.

The problem of disequilibrium in the market for loanable funds is made worse, according to Keynes, because neither saving nor investment is very responsive to changes in interest rates, and thus very large changes in interest rates would be necessary if ever equilibrium were to be restored after any shift in the saving or investment curves.

Keynes also rejected the simple quantity theory of money. Increases in money supply will not necessarily lead merely to rises in prices. There are two reasons for this. First, not all extra money will be spent. Some of it may simply stay in people's bank accounts. The average speed at which money circulates, the velocity of circulation (V), may slow down. Thus in the equation $MV = PY$, V may vary. Second, and more important, increases in money supply may lead to increases in *real output*. If there is a lot of slack in the economy, with high unemployment, idle machines and idle resources, an increased spending of money may

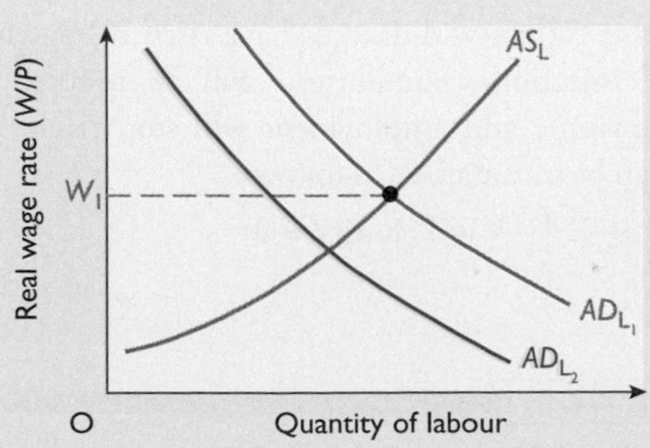

Figure 15.6 The problem of demand deficiency in the labour market

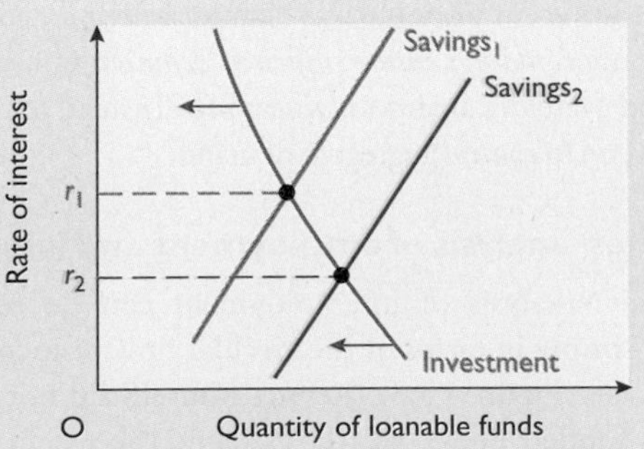

Figure 15.7 Disequilibrium in the market for loanable funds

ISSUES AND APPLICATIONS BOX 15.5

WILL WAGE CUTS CURE UNEMPLOYMENT?

Keynes' dismissal of the classical remedy

In *The General Theory of Employment, Interest and Money*, Keynes rejects the classical argument that unemployment is due to excessive wages. In Chapter 2 he argues:

> [T]he contention that the unemployment which characterises a depression is due to a refusal by labour to accept a reduction of money wages is not clearly supported by the facts. It is not very plausible to assert that unemployment in the United States in 1932 was due either to labour obstinately refusing to accept a reduction of money wages or to its obstinately demanding a real wage beyond what the productivity of the economic machine was capable of furnishing. Wide variations are experienced in the volume of employment without any apparent change either in the minimum real demands of labour or in its productivity. Labour is not more truculent in the depression than in the boom – far from it. Nor is its physical productivity less. These facts from experience are a *prima facie* ground for questioning the classical analysis . . .
>
> . . . A classical economist may sympathise with labour in refusing to accept a cut in its money-wage, and he will admit that it may not be wise to make it to meet conditions which are temporary; but scientific integrity forces him to declare that this refusal is, nevertheless, at the bottom of the trouble.[5]

[5] J. M. Keynes, *The General Theory of Employment, Interest and Money* (Macmillan, 1967), p. 9.

lead to substantial increases in real income (Y) and leave prices (P) little affected.

> **??** Demonstrate this argument on an aggregate demand and supply diagram.

If the government were to cut money supply in an attempt to reduce prices, the major effect might be to reduce output and employment instead. In terms of the quantity equation, a reduction in M may lead to a reduction in output and hence real income Y rather than a reduction in P.

All these arguments meant a rejection of Say's law. Far from supply creating demand and thus ensuring full employment, Keynes argued that it was *demand that created supply*. If aggregate demand rose, firms would respond to the extra demand by producing more and employing more people. But a fall in demand would lead to less output and rising unemployment.

Keynes' central point was that an unregulated market economy *could not ensure sufficient demand*. Governments should therefore abandon *laissez-faire*. Instead they should intervene to *control* aggregate demand.

Keynes' analysis of employment and inflation

Keynes' analysis of unemployment can be explained most simply in terms of the circular flow of income diagram (see Figure 15.8). Keynes himself did not use this exact model, but it clearly explains the essence of his argument.

If injections (J) do not equal withdrawals (W), a state of disequilibrium exists. What will bring them back into equilibrium, however, is not a change in prices (of labour or of loanable funds), but rather a change in *national income* and *employment*.

Start with a state of equilibrium, where injections equal withdrawals. If there is now a rise in injections – say, firms decide to invest more – aggregate demand ($C_d + J$) will be higher. Firms will respond to this increased demand by using more labour and other resources and thus paying out more incomes (Y) to households. Household consumption will rise and so firms will sell more.

Firms will respond by producing more, and thus using more labour and other resources. Household incomes will rise again. Consumption and hence production will rise again, and so on. There will thus be a multiplied rise in incomes and employment. This is known as the **multiplier effect**.

The process, however, does not go on for ever. Each time household incomes rise, households save more, pay more taxes and buy more imports. In other words, withdrawals rise. When withdrawals have risen to match the increased injections, equilibrium will be restored and national income and employment will stop rising. The process can be summarised as follows:

$$J > W \rightarrow Y\uparrow \rightarrow W\uparrow \text{ until } J = W$$

DEFINITION

Multiplier effect An initial increase in aggregate demand of £xm leads to an eventual rise in national income that is greater than £xm.

Similarly, an initial fall in injections (or rise in withdrawals) will lead to a multiplied fall in national income and employment:

$$J < W \rightarrow Y\downarrow \rightarrow W\downarrow \text{ until } J = W$$

Thus equilibrium in the circular flow of income can be at *any* level of output and employment.

If aggregate demand is too low, there will be a recession and high unemployment. In Figure 15.9 it is assumed that there is some potential level of national income and output (Y_p) at which there would be full employment of resources. This represents a limit to output. If aggregate demand were initially at AD_1, equilibrium would be at Y_1, considerably below the full-employment potential.

In this case, argued Keynes, governments should intervene to boost aggregate demand. There are two policy weapons they can use.

Fiscal policy

Remember how we defined this in Chapter 13. It is where the government alters the balance between government expenditure (G) and taxation (T), and thereby alters the balance between injections and withdrawals. In this way it controls aggregate demand. Faced with a recession, it should raise G and/or lower T. In other words, the government should run a budget deficit rather than a balanced budget. There will then be a multiplier effect:

$$G\uparrow \text{ or } T\downarrow \rightarrow J > W \rightarrow Y\uparrow \rightarrow W\uparrow \text{ until } J = W$$

If the eventual rise in aggregate demand were to, say, AD_2 in Figure 15.9, output would rise to Y_2.

Monetary policy

This is where the government alters the supply of money in the economy or manipulates interest rates. If it were to raise money supply, there would be more available in the economy for spending, interest rates would fall and aggregate demand would rise. Keynes argued that this was a less reliable policy than fiscal policy, since some of the extra money could be used for speculating in paper assets rather than spending on real goods and services. The details of how money supply is controlled and the effects it has on the economy are examined in later chapters.

It is most effective if both policies are used simultaneously. For example, if the government were to undertake a programme of public works (fiscal policy) and finance it through increases in money supply (monetary policy), there would be no crowding out. There would be a significant rise in output and employment.

> **??** What would be the classical economists' criticisms of this argument?

If aggregate demand rises too much, however, inflation becomes a problem. (This was the case during the Second World War, with the high expenditure on the war effort.) As Y_p is approached, with more and more firms reaching full capacity and with fewer and fewer idle resources, so additional increases in aggregate demand lead more and more to higher prices rather than higher output. This can be seen in Figure 15.9 as aggregate demand rises from AD_2 to AD_3 to AD_4.

> **??** Might the *AS* curve shift to the right in the meantime? If it did, how would this influence the effects of the rises in aggregate demand?

Governments faced with the resulting demand-pull inflation should, according to Keynes, use *contractionary* fiscal and monetary policies to reduce demand. Contractionary fiscal policy would involve reducing

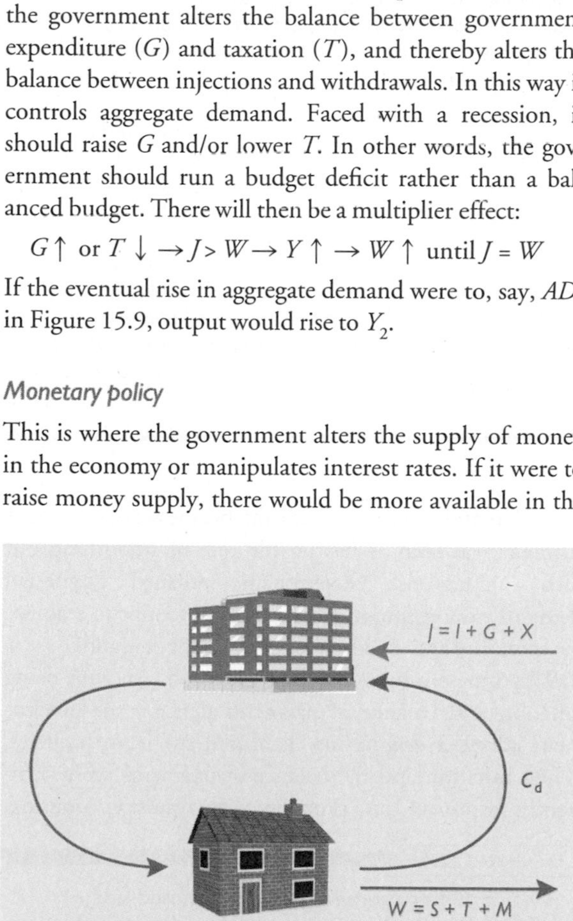

$J = I + G + X$

C_d

$W = S + T + M$

Figure 15.8 The circular flow of income

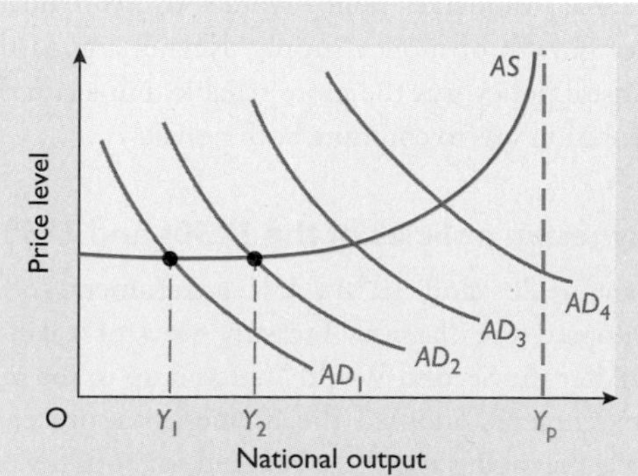

Figure 15.9 The effects of increases in aggregate demand on national output

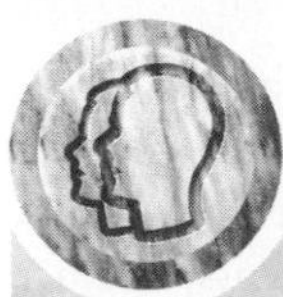

DEVELOPMENT OF IDEAS

JOHN MAYNARD KEYNES (1883–1946)
Person profile

Modern macroeconomics had its birth in 1936. That was when Keynes' *General Theory of Employment, Interest and Money* was published. Probably no other economist and no other book has ever had such a profound influence on the subject and on the policies pursued by governments. Indeed, throughout the 1950s and 1960s, governments in the UK and the USA, and many other countries too, considered themselves to be 'Keynesian'.

John Maynard Keynes came from an intellectual family. His father, John Neville Keynes, himself an economist and logician, spent his whole career at Cambridge first as a fellow and then as university registrar. His mother was a justice of the peace and at one time mayor of Cambridge.

Maynard (as he was called) won a scholarship to Eton. After a brilliant school career he progressed to King's College, Cambridge, to study classics and mathematics. There he made a profound impression on his tutors, who included the two great economists Alfred Marshall and Arthur Pigou. Marshall wanted him to become a full-time economist, but Keynes' interests were much broader. He loved debating and was elected secretary of the Cambridge Union and president of its famous debating society; he loved writing on all kinds of public issues; he loved climbing mountains; he loved socialising and mixing with famous literary and artistic figures – in fact he became one of the members of the 'Bloomsbury group', which included such famous literary people as Virginia Woolf, E. M. Forster and Bertrand Russell.

After leaving Cambridge, Keynes became a civil servant and worked in the Indian Office – a job he thoroughly disliked. But two years later, in 1908, he returned to King's College as a fellow, and in 1911 was made editor of the *Economic Journal*, Britain's foremost economics publication. He was to retain the editorship for 33 years.

With the outbreak of war in 1914, he left Cambridge temporarily and joined the Treasury. He gained rapid promotion, and was one of the major advisers to the government at the Versailles peace conference at the end of the war. Disgusted at the terms of the peace treaty, which was more concerned with making Germany pay than paving the way for the reconstruction of Europe, he resigned from the Treasury and wrote a damning critique of the treaty. *The Economic Consequences of the Peace* became a bestseller and rocketed him to international fame.

He returned to Cambridge. But he did not just teach and write. He began to speculate in international commodity and exchange markets. At first he had little success and just avoided going broke, but soon he was making huge amounts of money. He eventually built a fortune worth several million pounds at today's prices. Like Ricardo, he was not just a *theoretical* economist!

He made money for other people too. He acted as economic adviser to several companies, and then later became bursar of King's College. Through speculation he made the college very rich. A well-known story recounts how one day Keynes was walking across the quad with a friend, when he looked up at the famous King's College chapel and muttered to himself, 'Too small. Far too small.' 'Too small for what?' enquired his friend. 'If I have to take delivery of all the corn I have just bought for the college,' replied Keynes, 'it will never all go in there!'

government expenditure and/or raising taxes. Contractionary monetary policy would involve reducing the rate of growth of money supply. Keynes argued that here too fiscal policy was the more reliable, but again that the best solution was to combine both policies.

The Keynesian policies of the 1950s and 1960s

During the 1920s and 1930s, UK governments of all parties adopted the classical Treasury view of balanced budgets. After the Second World War and up to the mid-1970, governments adopted the Keynesian approach of deliberately managing aggregate demand. In both periods, therefore, there was a high degree of agreement between the political parties as to the way the economy worked and therefore the appropriate macroeconomic policies.

As demand fluctuated with the business cycle, so government was seen as having the role of smoothing out such fluctuations. Governments pursued Keynesian **demand management policies** in an attempt to stabilise the economy and avoid excess or deficient demand.

When the economy began to grow too fast, with rising inflation and balance of payments deficits, the government adopted *deflationary* fiscal and monetary policies. When inflation and the balance of payments were sufficiently improved, but probably with recession looming,

DEFINITION

Demand management policies Demand-side policies (fiscal and/or monetary) designed to smooth out the fluctuations in the trade cycle.

BOX 15.6

He also continued his association with the artistic world, including the ballet. He married Lydia Lopokova, a popular Russian ballerina. On marrying Keynes she gave up her career in the ballet, but later became a Shakespearean actress and on one occasion was leading lady in a new Cambridge theatre with which Keynes was closely associated – another of his ventures.

Throughout the 1920s he wrote many pamphlets and articles critical of the *laissez-faire*, balanced-budget policies of successive governments. Full employment, maintained Keynes, was not a natural state of affairs. To achieve full employment, the government would have to intervene actively in the economy to ensure a sufficient level of aggregate demand. This might well mean running a budget deficit: in other words, the government spending more than it receives in taxes.

His views gradually became more and more influential, but for years were steadfastly resisted by the Treasury and the Bank of England, which were steeped in balanced-budget orthodoxy.

Then in 1936 the *General Theory* was published. Although this is a difficult and rather dry work, it took the economic world by storm. It caused a revolution – the Keynesian revolution. Gone was the economist's cosy view of the world where unemployment was a mere temporary aberration. In its place was adopted a new orthodox view, that an economy could slide into a slump – *and stay there*. This, however, was not the long-term pessimistic picture painted by Malthus and Ricardo. A slump was essentially a short-term problem, a problem that a government could cure. Keynes was not particularly interested in the long-run future of the world. 'Take care of the short run and the long run will look after itself' might have been Keynes' maxim. Keynes himself put it more succinctly: 'In the long run we are all dead.'

By the outbreak of the Second World War, Keynes and the Treasury were reconciled. He was recruited as an adviser to the government on its wartime finances. But his health was ailing. He had suffered a heart attack in 1937, and never fully recovered. Despite his ill health, however, he made a major contribution to the management of the wartime economy and was made a baron in 1942.

He made several trips to the USA, with Lydia at his side as nurse, to negotiate wartime financial assistance. He was also concerned to map out with the Americans a new post-war economic order. This culminated in 1944 in an international conference at Bretton Woods, New Hampshire, at which Lord Keynes was the chief British negotiator. The system devised at that conference (albeit not entirely to Keynes' liking) was to last 27 years and was to provide the framework for the international post-war recovery.

Keynes died in 1946, an untimely end for someone who undoubtedly would have had much to contribute toward the shaping of the post-war world.

It might have been expected that the economic revolution which overthrew classical theory would have come from the left. But Keynes, stern critic of *laissez-faire* and advocate of government intervention though he was, was no socialist. His was a centrist revolution: not one that advocated the overthrow of capitalism, but one that advocated measures to support it – not by leaving it alone, but by intervening to make up for its shortcomings.

threatening rising unemployment and little or no growth, governments adopted *expansionary* fiscal and monetary policies. This succession of deflationary and reflationary policies to counteract the effect of the trade cycle became known as **stop–go policies**.

During the 1950s and 1960s, inflation in the UK averaged just 3.8 per cent and unemployment a mere 1.7 per cent. Similarly low rates of inflation and unemployment were experienced in other industrialised countries. Nevertheless, from the mid-1960s onwards there was increasing criticism of short-term demand management policies. Criticisms included the following:

- The policies were not very successful in stabilising the economy. Fluctuations still existed. Some economists even claimed that demand management policies made fluctuations worse. The main reason given was the time it took for policies to be adopted and to work. If time lags are long enough, a deflationary policy may only begin to work when the economy has already turned down into recession. Likewise a reflationary policy may only begin to work when the economy is already booming, thus further fuelling inflation.
- The UK's long-term growth at around 2.8 per cent per annum was appreciably lower than that of other industrialised countries. Some of the blame for this was

DEFINITION

Stop–go policies Alternate deflationary and reflationary policies to tackle the currently most pressing of the four problems which fluctuate with the trade cycle.

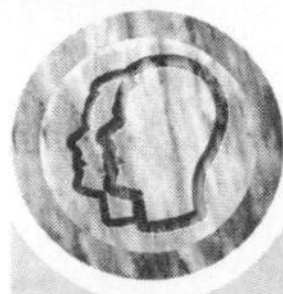

DEVELOPMENT OF IDEAS — BOX 15.7

'YOU'VE NEVER HAD IT SO GOOD'
Prosperity in the late 1950s

By the late 1950s people had come to expect rising living standards and the absence of economic depressions. True, the economy still fluctuated, and for short periods there would be only low rates of economic growth, but generally there was optimism that the government could ensure growing prosperity over the longer term.

Harold Macmillan was Prime Minister from 1957 to 1963, and his attitude epitomised this optimism (or complacency!). In a famous speech at Bedford in July 1957 he said:

> Indeed let us be frank about it: most of our people have never had it so good. Go round the country, go to the industrial towns, go to the farms and you will see a state of prosperity such as we have never had in my lifetime – nor indeed ever in the history of this country.

A few days later in the Commons he expanded on this claim:

> I confess that I find it rather a strange experience to sit here day after day and listen to the arguments and problems presented by high prices and over-full employment. When I first stood for the House of Commons in 1923, soon after the post-war boom broke, and for the next twelve or fifteen years, including four general elections, one problem and one problem only held the political field. It was the problem of deflation, violently and rapidly falling prices, and massive unemployment. We debated it, as many of the older members here remember, week by week and day by day. We put forward all kinds of rival views as to how it should be solved . . .
>
> Today, it has somehow solved itself, but this new trouble has come which seems to dog our footsteps. Having solved one problem we have now the one we are discussing, that of rising prices. Every honourable Member knows, and every man and woman in the country knows, that for the mass of the people – I would say for the great mass of the people – there has never been such a good time or such a high standard of living as at the present day. I repeat what I said at Bedford, that they have 'never had it so good' . . .
>
> I can only repeat that I have been grateful to see the change. I believe that all of us in the House, certainly the older members, feel grateful that there has been this great change. When I am told by some people, some rather academic writers, that inflation can be cured or arrested only by returning to substantial or even massive unemployment, I reject that utterly.

Not everyone in the country was this 'grateful'. Although the UK's economic performance was vastly better than in the inter-war period, the rate of growth was nevertheless poor compared with countries like France and West Germany.

attributed to an over-concentration on short-term policies of stabilisation, and a neglect of underlying structural problems in the economy.

- Persistent balance of payments problems meant that governments often had to pursue deflationary policies even when the economy was running below capacity and unemployment was rising.
- The simple Phillips curve relationship between inflation and unemployment was breaking down. If reflationary policies were the cure for unemployment and deflationary policies were the cure for inflation, what policies should be pursued when both inflation *and* unemployment were rising?
- The most fundamental criticism of all came from monetarists. They rejected Keynesianism as a whole, with its concentration on demand. They returned to the earlier classical analysis, with its concentration on supply, and extended it to take account of the increasingly important role of price expectations in explaining 'stagflation' (see the next section).

From the mid-1970s onwards the Keynesian/monetarist split between economists was reflected in the political parties. The Conservative leadership embraced monetarism, whereas the other political parties continued to embrace variants of Keynesianism.

SECTION SUMMARY

1. Keynes rejected the classical assumption that all markets would clear. Disequilibrium could persist in the labour market. A fall in aggregate demand would not simply lead to a fall in wages and prices and a restoration of the full-employment equilibrium. Instead there would be demand-deficient unemployment: as demand fell there would be less demand for labour.

continued

2. Disequilibrium could also persist in the market for loanable funds. As aggregate demand fell, and with it business confidence, so the demand for loanable funds for investment would shrink. Reductions in interest rates would be insufficient to clear the market for loanable funds.

3. Keynes also rejected the simple quantity theory. If there is slack in the economy, an expansion of the money supply can lead to an increase in *output* rather than an increase in prices.

4. Keynes argued that there would be a multiplier effect from changes in injections or withdrawals. A rise in investment, for example, would cause a multiplied rise in national income, as additional expenditures flowed round and round the circular flow stimulating more and more production and thus generating more and more real incomes.

5. If the economy is operating below full employment, the government can use fiscal and/or monetary policies to boost aggregate demand and thereby take up the slack in the economy. Excessive aggregate demand, however, causes inflation. Here deflationary fiscal and monetary policies can be used to remove this excess demand.

6. Keynesianism became the orthodoxy of the 1950s and 1960s. Governments used fiscal (and to a lesser extent monetary) policies to manage the level of aggregate demand.

7. After the mid-1960s, however, there was growing criticism of Keynesian demand management. The economy still fluctuated and the various macroeconomic problems seemed to be getting worse. Monetarists argued that Keynesian analysis was fundamentally flawed, and instead returned to the classical analysis.

15.4 Modern developments

The monetarist counter-revolution

The most powerful criticisms of the Keynesian conventional wisdom came from monetarists, whose chief advocate was Milton Friedman, Professor of Economics at Chicago University. Monetarists returned to the old classical theory as the basis for their analysis, and extended it to take account of the growing problem of **stagflation**.

At the heart of monetarism is the quantity theory of money. Friedman examined the historical relationship between money supply and prices, and concluded that inflation was 'always and everywhere a monetary phenomenon'. If money supply over the long run rises faster than the potential output of the economy, inflation will be the inevitable result.

Monetarists argue that over the long run, in the equation $MV = PY$, *both* V and Y are independently determined and are not, therefore, affected by changes in M. Any change in money supply (M), therefore, will only affect prices (P). Whether or not monetarists are correct in arguing that V and Y are not affected by changes in M will be examined in later chapters.

Monetarists draw two important conclusions from their analysis.

- The rising inflation from 1967 onwards was entirely due to the growth in money supply increasingly outstripping the growth in output. If money supply rises, they argue, then the resulting rise in aggregate demand will lead not only to rising prices but also, for a few months, to higher output and employment. But soon people's expectations will adjust. Workers and firms come to expect higher wages and prices. Their actions then ensure that wages and prices *are* higher. Thus after 1–2 years the extra demand is fully taken up in inflation, and so output and employment fall back again. Then governments are tempted to raise money supply and aggregate demand again in a further attempt to get unemployment down. The effect of this over a number of years is for inflation simply to get higher and higher.
- Reducing the rate of growth of money supply will reduce inflation without leading to long-run increases in unemployment. It *will* lead to temporary increases in unemployment, they argue, as the demand for goods and labour fall. But once price and wage inflation have adjusted down to this new level of demand, disequilibrium unemployment will be eliminated. This process will be hindered and high unemployment is likely to persist if workers persist in demanding excessive wage increases, or if firms and workers continue to expect high inflation rates.

DEFINITION

Stagflation A term used in the 1970s to refer to the combination of stagnation (low growth and high unemployment) and high inflation.

Monetarists argue that inflation is damaging to the economy because it creates uncertainty for businesspeople and therefore reduces investment, and also because it is damaging to the country's competitiveness in international trade. They see it as essential, therefore, for governments to keep a tight control over money supply and advocate the setting of money supply *targets*. Modest and well-publicised targets should help to reduce the *expected* rate of inflation. The UK government from the late 1970s to the mid-1980s set targets for the growth of money supply, and such targets were central to the Thatcher government's 'medium-term financial strategy'.

Apart from controlling the money supply, governments, according to monetarists, should intervene in the economy as little as possible, save to remove hindrances to the efficient functioning of the market (like various restrictive practices of unions). This way, they argue, aggregate supply will be encouraged to grow as firms and workers respond to market incentives. Monetarist 'supply-side policy', therefore, is essentially one of encouraging free enterprise.

Monetarist reappraisal of the Phillips curve

The monetarist position on inflation and unemployment can best be summarised by referring to their version of the long-run Phillips curve.

Unemployment

Unemployment may be temporarily reduced by raising aggregate demand, or increased by lowering aggregate demand, but in the long run it will tend to a 'natural' level (U_n). This is the equilibrium level of unemployment and is independent of aggregate demand. Disequilibrium unemployment will not exist in the long run. Equilibrium unemployment (U_n) consists of frictional, structural and technological unemployment. It can be reduced by increasing the mobility of labour by improved retraining, for example, or by reducing social security benefits. This should encourage a quicker matching of workers to jobs.

Inflation

Inflation is entirely dependent on aggregate demand, which in turn is entirely dependent on money supply. Inflation is thus of the demand-pull variety. Higher demand in the long run simply leads to more inflation. In the short run, higher demand will reduce unemployment below the natural level, but in the long run, once expectations have adjusted, unemployment rises back to the natural level. Thus the long-run Phillips curve is vertical (see Figure 15.10). A change in demand will lead in the long run to a move up or down this 'curve'. A shift in the 'curve' will be caused by a change in the level of equilibrium unemployment (U_n), *not* by a change in demand.

> **??** What effects, according to monetarists, would successful supply-side policies have on the Phillips curve?

Stagflation

Over time the vertical Phillips curve had moved to the right both in the UK and throughout the developed world. Natural (equilibrium) unemployment had increased, in the UK from around $1^1/_2$ per cent of the labour force in the 1960s to around 6–8 per cent in the 1980s. This was due to increased frictional and structural problems caused by the growth of union power and generous unemployment benefits which reduce the incentive to get a job.

Governments up to the late 1970s responded to rising unemployment by boosting aggregate demand (the balance of payments permitting). This, however, only led to more inflation fuelled by rising expectations of inflation.

When governments eventually did curb the growth in aggregate demand, as the Thatcher government did after 1979, it took a time for expectations to adjust downwards. In the meantime, there was a further temporary rise in unemployment (due to wage rises being slow to adjust downward) over and above that corresponding to the rightward shift of the long-run Phillips curve. Nevertheless the pursuit of these policies did, according to monetarists, lead to a dramatic fall in the rate of inflation, and eventually the growth in unemployment was reversed.

Modern-day Keynesians

Keynesians agreed with monetarists on one point. If demand is expanded too fast and for too long, inflation will result – and there will be a certain amount of unemployment of labour (and other resources too) that cannot be eliminated simply by expanding aggregate demand.

In Figure 15.11(a) there is a maximum level of output (Y_{max}) that can be achieved at any one time simply by expanding aggregate demand. This is below the potential output (Y_p) that could be achieved if all resources were used to the full.

Likewise in Figure 15.11(b) there is a minimum level of unemployment (U_{min}) that can be achieved by expanding aggregate demand. The Phillips curve becomes vertical at this point. Keynesians and monetarists alike argue that reductions in unemployment below U_{min} (or U_n in the

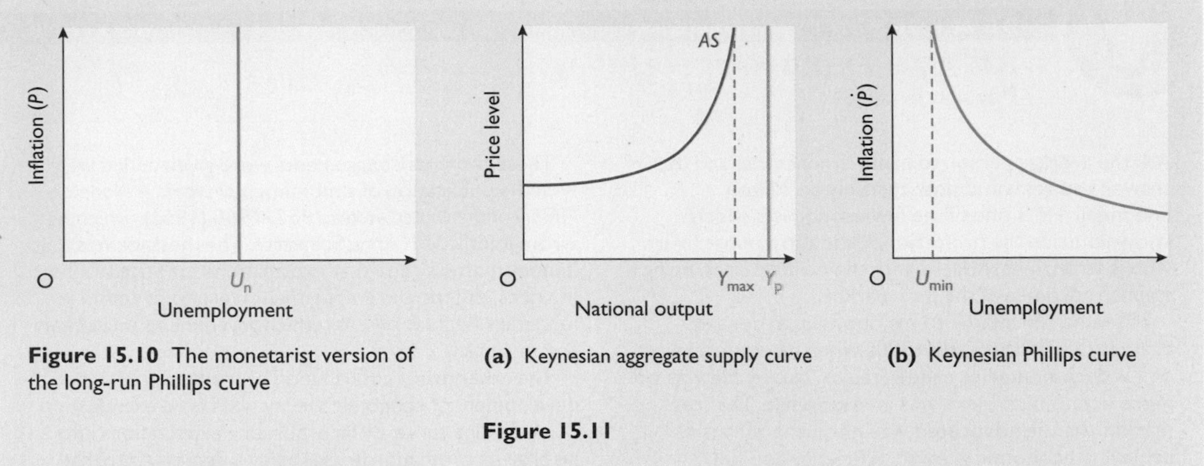

Figure 15.10 The monetarist version of the long-run Phillips curve

(a) Keynesian aggregate supply curve

(b) Keynesian Phillips curve

Figure 15.11

case of monetarists) can only be brought about by improved factor mobility or other structural policies. In other words, supply-side policies will be needed.

In other respects, Keynesians differ markedly from monetarists.

Inflation

Inflation may in the past have been caused by excess demand feeding into higher and higher expectations of inflation. But from the mid-1970s onwards there ceased to be a problem of general excess demand. Instead, excess demand was confined to certain sectors. The inflationary pressures here, however, were not offset by the deflationary pressures in sectors with excess supply because of the 'stickiness' downward of wages and prices. Demand-shift inflation was the result.

Inflation in the 1970s was also caused by increased cost-push pressures: the increasing concentration of economic power in large multinational companies and large trade unions, and the large oil price increases of 1973/4 and 1978/9.

Finally, workers had come to expect real wage increases each year which could simply not be met from real increases in national income. The problem here for the long term was not so much the expectations of price increases, but rather the expectations of increases in real living standards.

Unemployment

Keynesians blame a deficiency of aggregate demand for the massive rise in unemployment in the 1980s. Aggregate supply is highly elastic downwards in response to a reduction in aggregate demand. Firms respond to falling demand by producing less and employing fewer people. This may be further aggravated by firms running down stocks to try to reduce costs and maintain profits.

Expectations are relevant here. But it is not so much the expectation of lower inflation that reduces inflation (as monetarists claim); rather it is the expectation of lower sales that reduces production, investment and employment. The problem is not merely a short-term difficulty that markets will soon correct. Unless the government adopts a deliberate policy of reflation, the problem may continue. Business confidence may not return. Mass unemployment and recession may persist.

But why, when the world economy boomed in the late 1980s, did unemployment not return to the levels of the 1970s? In the late 1980s there was little or no deficiency of demand, and yet unemployment fell relatively slightly. Now the problem was not one of stagflation: a stagnant economy with high inflation. Now the problem was one of a booming economy but with persistently high unemployment. Keynesians typically offer two explanations of the persistence of unemployment.

Structural problems. The 1980s saw an acceleration in the decline of certain industries, a large-scale shift away from labour-intensive processes in manufacturing, an information technology revolution, a programme of privatisation, a more openly competitive world economy and campaigns by both governments and firms against overstaffing. The result was a large increase in equilibrium (structural) unemployment.

Hysteresis. The huge rise in unemployment in the early 1980s throughout the industrialised world, although largely caused by a lack of demand, could not simply be reversed by a rise in demand again. The recession had

DEVELOPMENT OF IDEAS — BOX 15.8

MILTON FRIEDMAN (1912–)
Person profile

Ask the average person to name a monetarist and the answer you get will almost certainly be 'Milton Friedman'. He is one of the few economists widely known outside the profession. He is also a public figure who is strongly associated with the political right, being a staunch advocate of the free market.

His fame (or infamy to his opponents) spread dramatically in the early 1980s when he made a series of TV documentaries called *Free to Choose*. He was no mere economist. Here was an evangelist. The free market that he advocated was not just a means to achieving economic growth, efficiency and full employment. Far more, it was the guarantor of human liberty; it was the best environment in which humans could develop their talents and their creative energies; it was a system which encouraged individuals to be responsible.

To economists he is much more than a TV personality. He is associated with a number of major developments in monetary theory, the theory of expectations and economic methodology.

Milton Friedman was born in New York in 1912. After teaching for many years at Columbia University, he became Professor of Economics at Chicago University in 1948 – a post he retained until his retirement in 1979. He was one of the leading lights of the 'Chicago school' of monetarist economics.

In his *Studies in the Quantity Theory of Money* (1956), Friedman developed his thesis that 'inflation is always and everywhere a monetary phenomenon'. This was a return to the classical belief in the quantity theory of money: that the level of prices depends on the quantity of money in the economy. The policy implications were simple. If the government wishes to control inflation, it must restrain the growth in the money supply.

These monetarist arguments were given added weight with the publication of a monumental work, *A Monetary History of the United States 1867–1960* (1963), which he wrote jointly with Anna Schwartz. The message was that 'money matters', and that explanations for fluctuations in prices, output and employment were to be found in monetary fluctuations, for which *governments* must bear responsibility.

The other major contribution he made to the development of economic theory was his re-examination of the Phillips curve. By incorporating expectations into his analysis of inflation he was able to demonstrate that the Phillips curve would be *vertical* in the long run.

The policy implications of this were profound. If he was correct, governments could not trade off lower unemployment against higher inflation. This seemed to run directly counter to orthodox Keynesian analysis, which had argued that a policy of expanding aggregate demand would reduce unemployment (albeit at a cost of somewhat higher inflation). What Friedman was saying was that a policy of expanding aggregate demand would, in the long run, lead merely to inflation. Unemployment would be unaffected. It would remain at its 'natural' level.

So how could this 'natural' level be reduced? Do we simply have to put up with it? No, says Friedman – and this is where we come back full circle to Friedman the apostle of the free market – the answer lies in incentives. The labour market must be freed up. Wages must be flexible and workers must be mobile. In other words, workers must respond to market signals. Excessive government welfare schemes and monolithic trade unions only stifle this process.

And so we return to Friedman, darling of the right and bogeyman of the left – skilled debater, media personality and populariser of *laissez-faire* economics.

---

itself *caused* higher levels of unemployment to become embedded in the economy. This is the problem known as **hysteresis**. This term, used in physics, refers to the lagging or persistence of an effect, even when the initial cause has been removed. In our context it refers to the persistence of unemployment even when the initial demand deficiency no longer exists. But why did the recession cause unemployment to persist, even when the economy was once more booming? Various explanations have been offered.

- Low capital stock. During the recession, many firms did not replace equipment. Thus when the boom came, such firms quickly reached full-capacity working, despite the surplus of labour in the economy. Full employment of capital was now being reached before full employment of labour.
- Deskilling. Many people who were out of work for long periods became deskilled and demotivated, and thus firms were less willing to employ them.

DEFINITION

Hysteresis The persistence of an effect even when the initial cause has ceased to operate. In economics it refers to the persistence of unemployment even when the demand deficiency that caused it no longer exists.

- Insiders and outsiders. People who remained employed (the **insiders**) were often able, through their unions or close relationships with their employers, or because of the possession of specific skills, to secure wage increases for themselves, and prevent the unemployed (the **outsiders**) from competing wages down. The insiders preferred to secure higher wages for themselves, rather than to have a larger number employed but with everyone on lower wages.
- Firms took the opportunity to reduce their workforce. In the recession, many firms persuaded their workers that the only way of avoiding bankruptcy was to slim down the workforce. The people who remained employed had to work *harder*. When the boom came, they were often required to work harder still, with the firm taking on few if any extra workers. Since the 1980s it has become commonplace for people in employment to have to work harder and often longer hours, while large numbers are without work or only able to secure part-time employment.
- Caution of firms. Once firms had experienced a deep recession, they were less optimistic about the future. Why take on extra workers, with the associated training costs, if they would only have to be made redundant again, with the associated redundancy costs, when the next recession came?

Keynesian criticisms of monetarism

Keynesians criticise monetarists for putting too much reliance on markets. The problems of inflation, unemployment and industrial declines are much too deep seated and complex to be rectified by a simple reliance on controlling the money supply and then leaving private enterprise and labour to respond to unregulated market forces.

Free markets are often highly imperfect and will not lead to an optimum allocation of resources. What is more, markets frequently reflect short-term speculative movements of demand and supply, and do not give a clear indication of long-term costs and benefits. In particular, the stock market, the money market and the foreign exchange market can respond quite violently to short-term pressures. Such fluctuations can be very damaging to investment. For example, violent swings in exchange rates, as experienced in the early 1980s, can dissuade firms from making long-term investment decisions to develop export markets. A sudden rise in exchange rates may make it impossible to compete abroad, even though at a lower exchange rate an exporter could have made a large profit.

The fluctuations inherent in free markets cause uncertainty about future demand, supply and prices. This uncertainty reduces investment and hence reduces growth. Government, therefore, should intervene much more to stimulate growth and investment. Keynesians frequently refer to the cases of Japan, France and Germany, where there is a much closer collaboration between government and industry than there is in the UK and the USA.

Keynesian policy proposals

Keynesians generally favour a much more interventionist approach to policy than do monetarists. The following policies are typical of those favoured by Keynesians.

Maintaining a high and stable level of aggregate demand. A substantial increase in demand may be necessary initially if unemployment levels are very high. The best way of achieving this is for the government to increase its expenditure on public works such as roads and housing, since these projects have a relatively low import content and therefore increased expenditure does not lead to balance of payments problems. Thereafter the government should maintain a high and stable demand, by appropriate demand management policies. This should keep unemployment down and set the environment for long-term investment and growth.

Balance of payments constraints would be further eased if there were an internationally co-ordinated reflation. Each country's exports would then rise roughly in line with imports. Some Keynesians go further and argue for a reduction in imports through the use of measures such as tariffs (customs duties) and restricting people's access to foreign exchange.

Control of exchange rates and interest rates. To reduce uncertainties, the government should intervene in foreign exchange and money markets to prevent excessive short-term fluctuations in exchange rates and interest rates. More stable rates will encourage investment and growth.

Greater co-operation between government and industry. To promote long-term growth and to avoid the uncertainties of the market, the government should work much more

DEFINITIONS

Insiders Those in employment who can use their privileged position (either as members of unions or because of specific skills) to secure pay rises despite an excess supply of labour (unemployment).

Outsiders Those out of work or employed on a casual, part-time or short-term basis, who have little or no power to influence wages or employment.

closely with industry. The government should help to coordinate the plans of interdependent sectors of industry and should channel finance to the more promising industries.

Structural policies. To reduce structural unemployment the government should pursue regional and urban policies to encourage firms to move to areas of high unemployment, and retraining policies to encourage greater occupational mobility of labour.

The current range of views

Not all monetarists agree with each other. Not all Keynesians agree with each other. What is more, many economists would not want to be classified as either monetarist or Keynesian, preferring to draw from elements of each.

One simple way of classifying these differing views is to see them falling along a spectrum. At the one end are those who see the free market as working well and who generally blame macroeconomic problems on excessive government intervention. At the other are those who see the free market as fundamentally flawed. Let us identify different views along this spectrum, starting with the pro-free market end.

The new classical/rational expectations school

The **new classical school** is like an extreme form of monetarism. New classicists maintain that markets clear very quickly and expectations adjust virtually instantaneously to new situations. These expectations are based on firms' and workers' rational assessment of what is happening in the economy and in their particular sector of it. They may be wrong, but they are as likely to overpredict as to underpredict the rate of inflation and hence the equilibrium price in their particular market. On average they will guess it about right.

Expanding money supply will virtually instantaneously lead to higher expectations of inflation. Therefore it can only cause inflation; it cannot reduce unemployment. The short-run Phillips curve is vertical, as well as the long-run. Likewise tight monetary policy reduces inflation; it does not increase unemployment. Rising unemployment is entirely due to a rise in the natural level of unemployment.

This school favours *laissez-faire* policies and is part of what is often called the 'radical right'.

Moderate monetarists

Moderate monetarists maintain that markets adjust fairly quickly – perhaps within one or two years.

A rise in money supply and hence aggregate demand will lead to a temporary reduction in unemployment, but as expectations of inflation (and hence of wage increases) adjust upwards, so eventually the whole of the rise in aggregate demand will be swallowed up in higher prices. *Real* aggregate demand falls back to its original level and hence the level of unemployment rises back to its original level too. Thus the short-run Phillips curve is downward sloping, but the long-run curve is vertical.

If the economy is faced with high inflation, a sudden tight monetary policy may temporarily lead to a recession. Thus sudden extreme policies should be avoided. Instead there should be a gradual reduction in the growth of the money supply.

Any temporary demand-deficient unemployment will be reduced if workers can be encouraged to take reductions in real wages. Ultimately, though, any policies to make long-term reductions in unemployment must be aimed at the supply side of the economy: reducing natural unemployment by increasing labour mobility.

Moderate Keynesians

Moderate Keynesians argue that economies will probably eventually pull out of recession even if governments do not boost demand. There will be a natural upturn in the business cycle. Firms' confidence will begin to return and investment will start to increase. Nevertheless a recession can be deep and long lived and the recovery slow and faltering. Thus moderate Keynesians argue for active intervention by government to boost demand.

Once the economy is back to near full employment, the government must continue to control aggregate demand to prevent fluctuations in output and employment. Keynesians generally advocate the use of anti-cyclical demand management policy.

Most moderate Keynesians blame the persistence of recessions on the reluctance of real wages to fall so as to clear the labour market and eliminate demand-deficient unemployment. In recent years **new Keynesians**, as they are called, have attempted to discover the reasons for the

DEFINITIONS

New classical school A body of economists who believe that markets are highly competitive and clear very rapidly; any expansion of demand will feed through virtually instantaneously into higher prices, giving a vertical *short*-run as well as a vertical long-run Phillips curve.

New Keynesians Economists who seek to explain the downward stickiness of real wages and the resulting persistence of unemployment.

downward stickiness in real wages during a recession. These include the following:

- The worry of employers about demotivating their workforce, and thus causing efficiency to suffer. This is known as the *efficiency wage theory*.
- The power of *insiders* to resist real wage cuts.
- Firms under *imperfect competition* have the power to maintain their prices. They may prefer to respond to a fall in demand by cutting output rather than cutting (real) prices, especially if they believe that their rivals will do the same. In such cases, they are not under the same pressure to cut real wage rates.

Extreme Keynesians

Extreme Keynesians argue that there is no automatic mechanism to eliminate demand-deficient unemployment even in the long run.

Not only are real wage rates sticky downwards, but also any reductions in real wage rates that do take place will further reduce consumer demand. Money circulating will automatically fall as banks lend out less and less in response to falling demand. Firms are unlikely to borrow for investment, since they have no confidence in their market. Expectations are likely to remain pessimistic.

Under these circumstances, government must intervene to expand demand. By raising government expenditure and cutting taxes, the nation must spend its way out of recession. It may be necessary to use import controls to prevent any resulting balance of payments problems.

After the economy has pulled out of recession, it is still important for the government to maintain a high level of demand. Not only will this maintain low unemployment and keep actual national income close to potential national income, but also it will provide the most favourable environment for research and development, innovations and investment generally. Thus *potential* national income will grow more rapidly.

Some Keynesians in this group are known as **post-Keynesians**. They highlight some of the key features of Keynes' *General Theory* to explain why economies are not self-correcting. In particular they stress the importance of what Keynes called 'animal spirits', or what is today known as business expectations or business confidence. The mood of the country's business community is fundamental in determining investment and output. Without appropriate demand management policy, this mood can remain depressed into the long term.

Post-Keynesians also challenge most of the microeconomic assumptions on which other more 'mainstream' macroeconomic theories are based. Firms are not cold, rational profit maximisers, making calm calculations based on marginal analysis. Instead, firms make output decisions largely in response to anticipated demand, again based on their *confidence* of their market. The result is that anticipated demand changes are likely to lead to *output* and *employment* changes, not price changes.

Finally, post-Keynesians tend to focus on a country's *institutions* and *culture* to explain how firms and consumers respond to economic stimuli. In other words, they try to base their explanations and policies on real-world institutional and behavioural information rather than on abstract models.

The radical left

Some economists make a far more fundamental attack on the market economy. Most Keynesians, although they see a *free* market leading to serious problems, nevertheless argue that government intervention can rectify these problems. Those on the radical left disagree. They see the market economy as so flawed that mere intervention will not solve its problems. Instead the market economy needs to be *replaced* by some alternative system such as state planning and/or worker control of industry. Marxist economists see the problem of capitalism to be so severe that ultimately there will be a revolution and it will be overthrown.

The fact that there are so many different views as to how the macroeconomy functions makes it impossible to do justice to them all in an introductory book. Nevertheless it is hoped that you will get some insight into the major schools of thought and why they advocate the policies they do. If nothing else, you will probably begin to see why economists never seem to be able to agree: why, as Bernard Shaw once said, 'If you laid all the economists of the world end to end, they would still never reach a conclusion.'

?? Two economists disagree over the best way of tackling the problem of unemployment. For what reasons might they disagree? Are these reasons positive or normative?

DEFINITION

Post-Keynesians Economists who stress the importance of institutional and behavioural factors, and the role of business confidence in explaining the state of the economy. They argue that firms are more likely to respond to changes in demand by changing output rather than prices.

SECTION SUMMARY

1. Monetarists argue that there is a close correlation between the rate of growth of the money supply and the rate of inflation. Increases in money supply cause increases in aggregate demand, which in turn cause inflation. Along with the classical economists, they argue that output and employment are determined independently of money supply (at least in the long run). This means that a deflationary policy to cure inflation will *not* in the long run cause a fall in output or a rise in unemployment.
2. Monetarists thus argue that the long-run Phillips curve is vertical. Its position along the horizontal axis will depend on the level of equilibrium or 'natural' unemployment.
3. According to monetarists, the simultaneously higher inflation and higher unemployment since the early 1970s has been caused by a combination of (a) rightward shifts in the vertical Phillips 'curve' due to increased frictional and structural problems in the economy, and (b) governments attempting to reduce unemployment by continuously expanding the money supply.
4. Modern-day Keynesians reject the notion of a totally vertical Phillips curve, but do accept that demand-side policies alone cannot cure unemployment completely. Keynesians blame the combination of high inflation and high unemployment on a number of factors, each of which has the effect of shifting the Phillips curve to the right. These factors include cost-push and demand-shift pressures on inflation, and government attempts to cure inflation by continually pursuing deflationary policies.
5. Unemployment caused initially by a recession (a deficiency of demand) may persist even when the economy is recovering. This 'hysteresis' may be due to the deskilling of labour, a decline in firms' capacity, insiders preventing outsiders from bidding down the wage rate, or firms being cautious about taking on extra labour when the recovery does come.
6. Keynesians argue that markets do not clear rapidly and that in the meantime expectations of output and employment changes can have major effects on investment plans.
7. Whereas monetarists generally favour policies of freeing up markets (within the framework of strict government control over money supply), Keynesians favour a much more interventionist approach by the government. Central to this is the control of aggregate demand so as to retain actual income as close as possible to its potential level. From time to time they also advocate such policies as controls over prices and incomes, import controls and controls over the exchange rate and interest rates. At the same time they advocate greater co-operation, planning and consultation both domestically and internationally so as to achieve co-ordinated and sustained economic growth.
8. There are many shades of opinion among the different groups of economists, from extreme new classical economists who advocate almost complete *laissez-faire* to the extreme left where economists advocate the virtual abandonment of markets. In between comes a whole spectrum of opinions and theories about the relative effectiveness of markets and the government in achieving the various macroeconomic goals.

??? END-OF-CHAPTER QUESTIONS ???

1. In a given economy, the supply of money is £10 billion; the velocity of circulation of money (spend on final goods and services) is 3; and the price index is 2.00.
   (a) What is the level of real national income?
   (b) How much have prices risen (in percentage terms) since the base year?
   (c) Assume that money supply increases by 10 per cent and that the velocity of circulation remains constant. What will be the rate of inflation if (i) there is no increase in real national income; (ii) real national income increases by 10 per cent; (iii) real national income increases by 5 per cent?
2. In what way will the nature of aggregate supply influence the effect of a change in aggregate demand on prices and real national income?
3. Criticise the classical theory that higher government spending will necessarily crowd out private spending.
4. Criticise the use of increasing government expenditure as a means of reducing unemployment.
5. In what way may short-term demand management policies help to stabilise the economy? What problems occur in the use of such policies?
6. What explanations can you give for the increase in *both* unemployment and inflation in the 1970s?
7. What is meant by *hysteresis* when applied to unemployment? How do you account for this phenomenon in the 1980s?
8. What will cause people to expect higher rates of inflation? How will expectations of inflation affect the actual rate of inflation?

16

The simple Keynesian analysis of national income, employment and inflation

16.1 Background to the theory

Keynesians argue that aggregate demand determines the level of economic activity in the economy. In other words, the nation's production and employment depend on the amount of spending. Too little spending will lead to unemployment. More spending will stimulate firms to produce more and employ more people. Too much spending, however, will cause inflation.

This chapter examines this relationship between aggregate demand and national income, production, employment and inflation.

One important simplifying assumption is made throughout the chapter: *the rate of interest is fixed*. This allows us for the time being to ignore what is happening to the amount of money in the economy. Our assumption of fixed interest rates effectively means that the supply of money will passively rise or fall as aggregate demand rises or falls. In other words, if there is an increase in spending and hence an increase in demand for money from the banking system, there will be a corresponding increase in the amount of money made available and hence no need for interest rates to rise. In subsequent chapters we will drop this assumption and take specific notice of the role of money in the economy.

The relationship between aggregate demand and national income

In the simple Keynesian theory, the consumption of domestically produced goods (C_d) and the three withdrawals (W) – net saving (S), net taxes (T) and spending on imports (M) – all depend on the level of national income (Y) (see Figure 16.1). In fact, in the model, national income must always equal consumption of domestic goods plus withdrawals: there is nothing else people can do with their incomes!

$$Y \equiv C_d + W$$

Total spending in the economy on the goods and services of domestic firms is what we have already defined as aggregate demand (AD). It is also referred to as **national expenditure on domestic product (E)**. It consists of C_d plus the three injections (J): investment in the domestic economy (I), government expenditure in the domestic economy (G) and expenditure from abroad on the country's exports (X).

$$AD \equiv E \equiv C_d + J$$

In equilibrium, withdrawals equal injections. (We demonstrated this in Chapter 14.) Since national income (Y) is simply withdrawals plus C_d, and national expenditure on domestic product (E) is simply injections plus C_d, it follows that in equilibrium national income must equal national expenditure on domestic product (aggregate demand). To summarise:

$$W = J$$

$$\therefore C_d + W = C_d + J$$

$$\therefore Y = E (= AD)$$

The level of national income is *determined* by aggregate demand. If aggregate demand exceeds current national income, firms will respond to the extra demand by producing more and hence employing more factors of production (assuming there are unemployed resources available). National income will thus rise.

How long will national income go on rising? Until a new equilibrium is reached where withdrawals equal injections and national income equals expenditure.

The process of reaching a new equilibrium is as follows. Whenever national expenditure ($C_d + J$) exceeds national income ($C_d + W$), injections will exceed withdrawals. National income will rise. But as national income rises, so

DEFINITION

National expenditure on domestic product (E)
Aggregate demand in the Keynesian model: i.e. $C_d + J$.

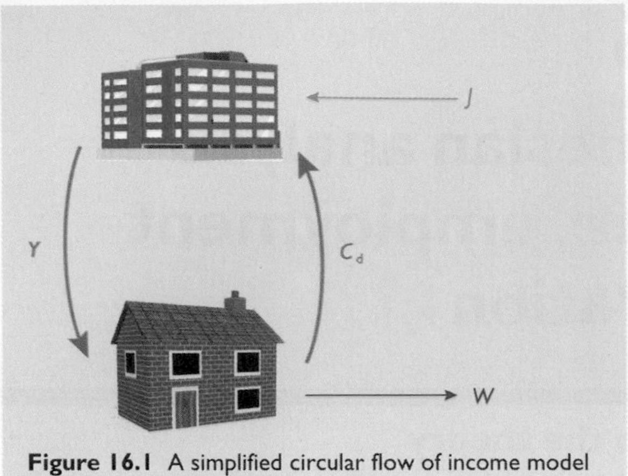

Figure 16.1 A simplified circular flow of income model

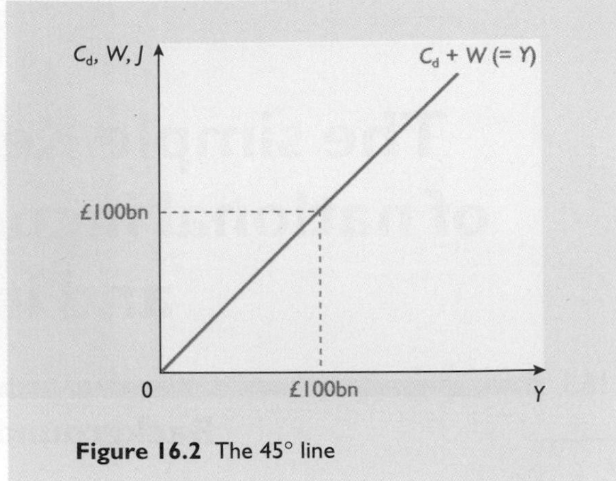

Figure 16.2 The 45° line

too will saving, imports and the amount paid in taxes: in other words, withdrawals will rise. Withdrawals will go on rising until they equal injections: until a new equilibrium has been reached.

$$J > W \rightarrow Y\uparrow \rightarrow W\uparrow \text{ until } W = J$$

But *how much* will income rise when aggregate demand (expenditure) rises? What will the new equilibrium level of national income be? To answer this question we must examine the relationship between national income and the component parts of the circular flow of income: consumption, withdrawals and injections. This relationship is shown in the Keynesian '45° line diagram'.

Introducing the Keynesian 45° line diagram

In this model it is assumed that the levels of consumption and withdrawals are determined by the level of national income. Since national income is part of the model, we say that consumption and withdrawals are **endogenous**. This means that they vary with one of the other components of the model (i.e. income). Injections, however, are assumed to be **exogenous**: they are determined independently of what is going on in the model; they do *not* depend on the level of national income.

We will justify these assumptions later. First we must look at how the diagram is constructed, and at the significance of the 45° line.

We plot real national income (i.e. national income matched by output) on the horizontal axis, and the various component parts of the circular flow (C_d, W and J) on the vertical axis. The 45° line out from the origin plots $C_d + W$ against Y. It is a 45° line because by definition $Y = C_d + W$. For example, if Y were £100 billion, then $C_d + W$ must also be £100 billion (see Figure 16.2).

We turn now to look at each of the components of the circular flow and see how they fit into the 45° line diagram.

Consumption

We will need to distinguish total consumption (C) from that part of consumption that goes purely on the output of domestically produced goods (C_d). C_d excludes expenditure taxes (e.g. VAT) and expenditure on imports. We start by looking at *total* consumption.

The consumption function

As national income increases, so does consumption. The reason is simple: if people earn more, they can afford to spend more. The relationship between consumption and income is expressed by the **consumption function**:

$$C = f(Y)$$

It can be shown graphically on the 45° line diagram (see Figure 16.3). The consumption function slopes upwards. This illustrates that, as national income rises, so does consumption. To keep the analysis simple the consumption function is drawn as a straight line.

DEFINITIONS

Endogenous variable A variable whose value is determined by the model of which it is part.

Exogenous variable A variable whose value is determined independently of the model of which it is part.

Consumption function The relationship between consumption and national income. It can be expressed algebraically or graphically.

Table 16.1

National income (£bn)	Consumption (£bn)
0	10
10	18
20	26
30	34
40	42
50	50
60	58
70	66
80	74
90	82
100	90
110	98
.	.

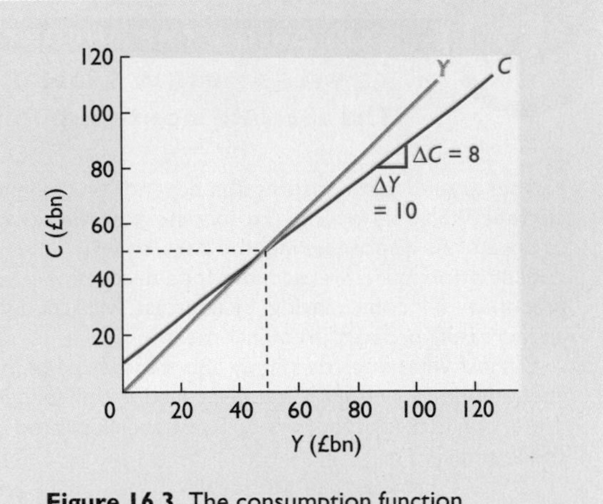

Figure 16.3 The consumption function

The following points should be noted about the consumption function:

- At very low levels of national income, it will lie above the 45° line. This is because when people are very poor they may be forced to spend more than they earn merely to survive. They will do this by borrowing or drawing on savings. A nation on this portion of its consumption function would be accumulating international debts: this is a problem that many developing countries have faced since the early 1970s. For developed countries, however, such low levels of income would be inconceivable. For them, this part of the diagram is merely an extrapolation backwards down the consumption function.
- At a certain point the consumption function will cross the 45° line. In Figure 16.3 this is at an income of £50 billion. At this point consumption equals income. The nation spends exactly what it earns.
- Above this point consumption is less than income. This means that some of people's incomes will go towards savings and the payment of income taxes. The higher the level of income, the smaller the proportion that will be consumed.
- It follows from these observations that the slope of the consumption function is less than 45°. The slope of the function is given by the 'marginal propensity to consume'.

The marginal propensity to consume (mpc)

The **marginal propensity to consume** is the proportion of any increase in national income that goes on consumption. In Table 16.1 for each £10 billion rise in national income there is an £8 billion rise in consumption. Thus the marginal propensity to consume is £8 billion/£10 billion = 8/10 or 4/5 or 0.8. The formula is:

$$mpc = \Delta C / \Delta Y$$

In Figure 16.3, it can be seen that the *mpc* is given by the slope of the consumption function. Being a straight line, the consumption function has a *constant* slope, and hence the *mpc* is also constant.

> **??** It is possible that as people get richer they will spend a smaller and smaller fraction of each rise in income (and save a larger fraction). Why might this be so? What effect will it have on the shape of the consumption function?

The average propensity to consume (apc)

The **average propensity to consume** is the proportion of *total* national income that is consumed. The formula is:

$$apc = C / Y$$

In Table 16.1, at a national income of £100 billion, £90 billion goes on consumption. The *apc* is 90/100 = 0.9.

> **??**
> 1. Referring to Table 16.1 what is the *apc* at a national income of (a) £50 billion; (b) £20 billion?
> 2. What happens to the *apc* as national income rises?
> 3. Would the *apc* ever equal the *mpc* in Table 16.1 if it were continued to a high enough income?

DEFINITIONS

Marginal propensity to consume The proportion of a rise in national income that goes on consumption: $mpc = \Delta C / \Delta Y$.

Average propensity to consume The proportion of total national income that goes on consumption: $apc = C / Y$.

EXPLORING THE THEORY BOX 16.1

KEYNES' VIEWS ON THE CONSUMPTION FUNCTION
The absolute income hypothesis

Keynes argued that consumption depends on the level of current *disposable* income (i.e. income after the payment of taxes).[1] As disposable income rises, so will consumption, but it will account for a decreasing *proportion* of income. Saving, by contrast, will account for an increasing proportion of income.

But just what does this imply about the shape of the consumption function? Typically, consumption functions are drawn in one of four ways. These are illustrated in the four diagrams.

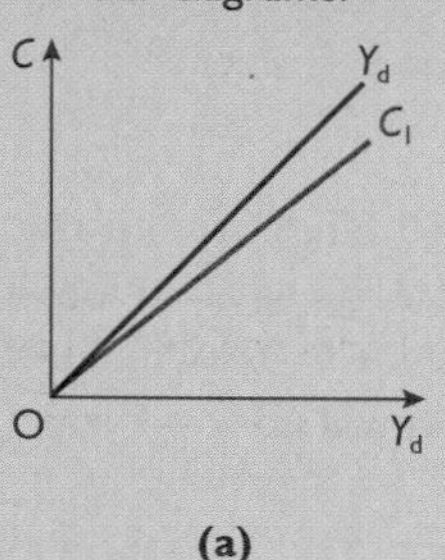

(a)

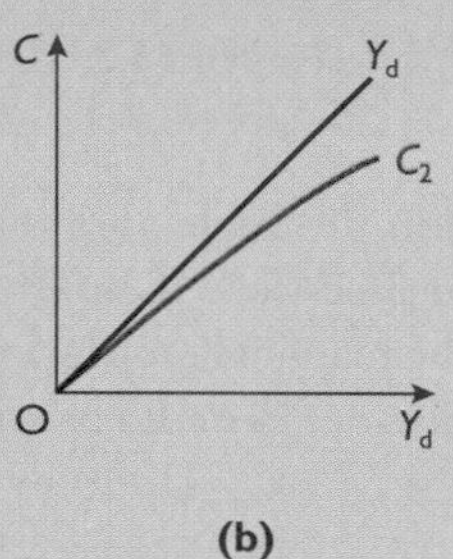

(b)

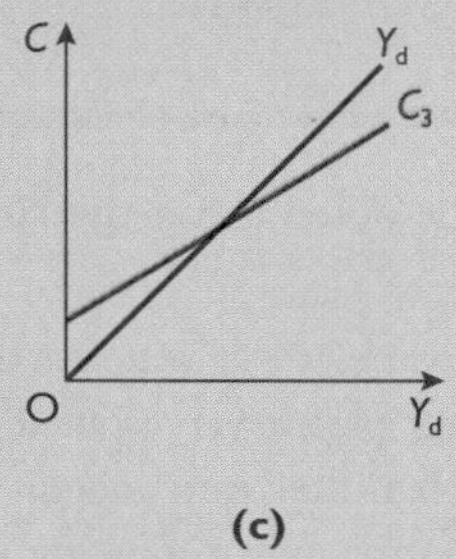

(c)

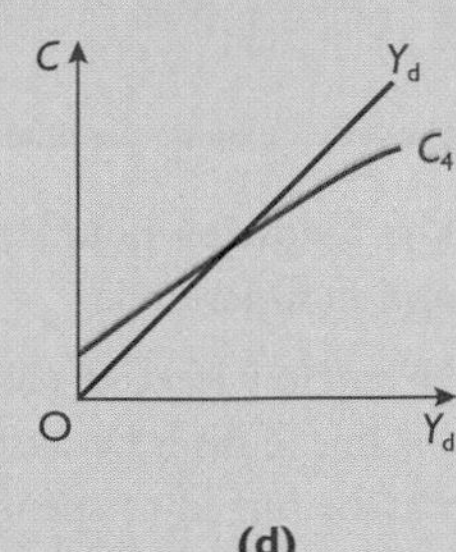

(d)

Different consumption functions

Consumption function C_1 has the form:

$C = bY_d$

When income is zero, consumption is zero too. As income rises, so does consumption, but at a constant rate: the *mpc* is constant. Consumption also always accounts for a constant *proportion* of income: the *apc* is constant too. However, Keynes assumed a decreasing *apc* as income rises.

Consumption function C_2 has the form:

$C = bY_d - cY_d^2$

This does give a decreasing *apc*, since consumption accounts for a declining proportion of income. It also gives a decreasing *mpc*, since the slope of the curve gets flatter.

But this diagram is not consistent with another assumption of Keynes, that if income falls far enough, consumption may even exceed income.

Consumption function C_3 has the form:

$C = a + bY_d$

and consumption function C_4 the form:

$C = a + bY_d - cY_d^2$

In both cases, provided the term *a* is a positive figure, consumption will exceed income at very low levels of income: the consumption function will cross the 45° line.

?? Using these two equations, what will be the level of consumption when national income is zero?

Keynes' argument that people's consumption depends on the level of their current income, irrespective of what their previous incomes were or what their future incomes are expected to be, and irrespective of what other people's incomes are, has led economists to call this the '*absolute income* theory of consumption' (see Box 16.3).

?? What will happen to the shape of the consumption function in diagram (d) in each of the following cases?
(a) When the value of term a increases.
(b) When the value of term b decreases.
(c) When the value of term c decreases.

[1] The theory we are developing in this chapter relates consumption to *gross* income (*Y*). If we relate consumption to *disposable* income (Y_d), as we are doing in this box, we must remember that the consumption function we get is not the one we will be using later on in the chapter.

The other determinants of consumption

Of course, people's incomes are not the only determinants of the amount they consume. There are several other determinants.

Assets held. The more wealth people have, whether as savings, as shares or as property, the more they are likely to spend out of current income.

Taxation. The higher the level of taxes, the less will people have left to spend out of their gross income: consumption depends on **disposable income**. If taxes are raised,

DEFINITION

Disposable income Household income after the deduction of taxes and the addition of benefits.

EXPLORING THE THEORY *BOX 16.2

USING CALCULUS TO DERIVE THE MPC

The consumption function can be expressed as an equation. For example, the consumption function of Table 16.1 and Figure 16.3 is given by the equation:

$$C = 10 + 0.8Y \quad (1)$$

?? Try using this equation to derive the figures in Table 16.1.

From this equation we can derive an equation for *apc* and *mpc*.

The *apc*

Remember how we defined *apc*.

$$apc = C/Y \quad (2)$$

Substituting (1) into (2) gives:

$$apc = \frac{10 + 0.8Y}{Y} \quad (3)$$

$$= 0.8 + 10/Y \quad (4)$$

?? Check out a few of the figures from Table 16.1 first by dividing consumption by income and then by substituting the figures into equation (4). The answer should be the same!

The *mpc*

The *mpc* is found by differentiating the consumption function. Remember from previous calculus boxes what it is we are doing when we differentiate an equation. We are finding its rate of change. Thus by differentiating the consumption function we are finding the rate of change of consumption with respect to income. But this is what we mean by the *mpc*.

The difference between using differentiation and the formula $\Delta C/\Delta Y$ is that with the former we are looking at the *mpc* at a single point on the consumption function. With the $\Delta C/\Delta Y$ formula we were looking at the *mpc* between two points.

Differentiating equation (1) gives:

$$mpc = dC/dY = 0.8 \quad (5)$$

Note that, since the consumption function is a straight line in this case, the *mpc* (which measures the slope of the consumption function) is constant.

Finding the *apc* and *mpc* of a non-linear consumption function

What would we do to find the *apc* and *mpc* of a curved consumption function? The procedures are the same.

Assume that the consumption function is given by the following equation:

$$C = 20 + 0.9Y - 0.001Y^2 \quad (6)$$

?? First of all try constructing a table like Table 16.1 and then graph the consumption function that it gives. What is it about equation (6) that gives the graph its particular shape?

The apc

The *apc* is given by C/Y:

$$apc = \frac{20 + 0.9Y - 0.001Y^2}{Y}$$

$$= 0.9 + 20/Y - 0.001Y$$

The mpc

The *mpc* is given by dC/dY:

$$mpc = 0.9 - 0.002Y$$

??
1. What are the values of *apc* and *mpc* at incomes of (a) 20; (b) 100?
2. What happens to the value of *mpc* as national income increases? Is this what you would expect by examining the shape of the consumption function?

how much will consumption fall? This depends on the marginal propensity to consume. The bigger the *mpc*, the more will consumption fall.

Expectations of future prices and incomes. If people expect rapid price rises in the future, they will tend to buy durable goods such as furniture and cars *now* before prices do rise.

If people expect a rise in their incomes in the future, they are likely to spend more now. If, on the other hand, they are uncertain about their future income prospects, or fear unemployment, they are likely to be cautious in their spending.

The distribution of income. The poor have a higher *mpc* and *apc* than the rich. A redistribution of national income from the poor to the rich will therefore tend to reduce the total level of consumption in the economy.

Tastes and attitudes. If people have a 'buy now, pay later' mentality, or a craving for consumer goods, they are likely to have a higher level of consumption than if their

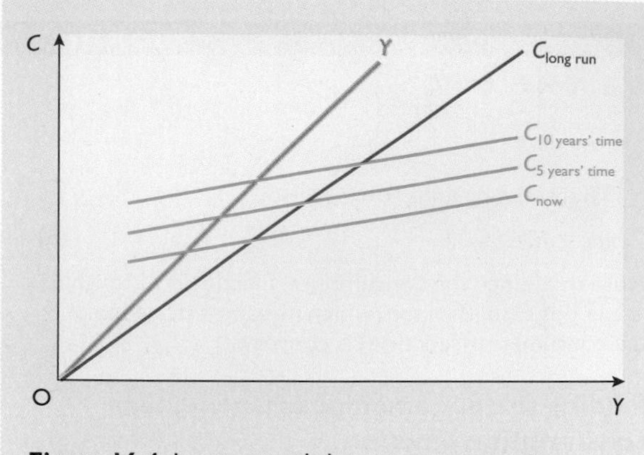

Figure 16.4 Long-run and short-run consumption functions

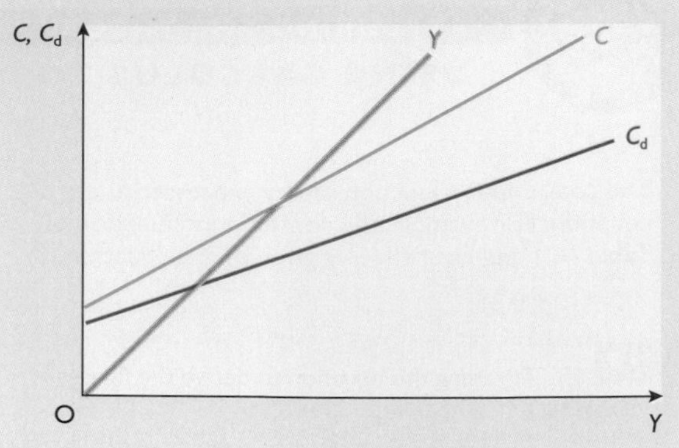

Figure 16.5 The consumption of domestic product

tastes are more frugal. The more 'consumerist' and materialistic a nation becomes, the higher will its consumption be for any given level of income.

The age of durables. If people's car, carpets, clothes, etc. are getting old, they will tend to have a high level of 'replacement' consumption. This is particularly likely after a period of recession during which people had cut back on their consumption of durables. Conversely, as the economy reaches the peak of the boom, people will probably spend less on durables as they will have already bought the items they wanted.

Movements along and shifts in the consumption function

The effect on consumption of a change in national income is shown by a movement *along* the consumption function. A change in any of the other determinants is shown by a *shift* in the consumption function.

> ?? What effect will the following have on (1) the *apc* and (2) the *mpc*:
> (a) a rise in the rate of income tax; (b) the economy begins to recover from recession; (c) people anticipate that the rate of inflation is about to rise; (d) the government redistributes income from the rich to the poor? In each case sketch what would happen to the consumption function.

Long-run and short-run consumption functions

The long-run consumption function is likely to be steeper than the short-run one (see Figure 16.4).

In the short run, people may be slow to respond to a rise in income. Perhaps they are cautious about whether their higher income will last, or are slow to change their consumption habits. In the short run, then, people may have a relatively low *mpc*. In the long run, however, people have time to adjust their consumption patterns.

Assuming that national income rises over time, the long-run consumption function will be intersected by a series of short-run ones. Each year's short-run function will be above the previous year's.

> ?? Which is likely to show the greater variation from one person to another at any given level of income: the short-run *mpc* or the long-run *mpc*?

Consumption of domestically produced goods (Cd)

The parts of consumption that go on imports and indirect taxes constitute withdrawals from the circular flow of income and thus do not contribute to aggregate demand. We shall concentrate on the part of consumption that *does*: namely, the consumption of domestic product (C_d). The C_d function lies below the C function, as in Figure 16.5. The gap between them constitutes imports of consumer goods and indirect taxes.

Withdrawals

All three withdrawals – net saving, net taxes and import expenditure – depend on the level of national income. They are thus all *endogenously* determined within the model.

Net saving

The net saving function. As with consumption, the major determinant of net saving (i.e. saving minus consumer borrowing and drawing on past savings) is income. Figure 16.6 illustrates two saving functions. In diagram (a) the net saving function is linear; in (b) it is curved. But in both cases, as income increases, and a

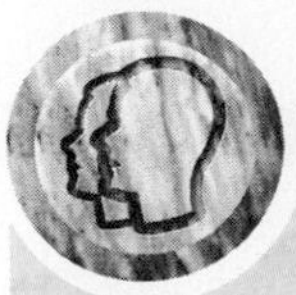

DEVELOPMENT OF IDEAS — BOX 16.3

THE RELATIONSHIP BETWEEN INCOME AND CONSUMPTION

Three alternative theories of the consumption function

The absolute income hypothesis

This is the title of the Keynesian theory of consumption that we have been looking at so far. It assumes that people's consumption depends on their *current* disposable income. It assumes a declining *apc*.

This theory fits quite well with the evidence on *short-run* consumption behaviour. Unfortunately, it fits much less well with *long-run* consumption behaviour. The evidence suggests that, over the long term, the *apc* is roughly constant as income rises, and that the *apc* is approximately equal to the *mpc*. This gives a long-run consumption function that is a straight line out from the origin, as in Figure 16.4.

How can we explain short-run consumption that tails off as income rises, but long-run consumption that rises proportionately with income? There are two alternative theories of consumption which provide such an explanation.

The relative income hypothesis

This theory was put forward by J. S. Duesenberry in 1947.[2] It assumes that people's consumption behaviour is influenced by others. If your friends have videos or CDs or a second car, then you will probably buy these items too, even if you are poorer. Your *apc* will be high. If, on the other hand, your income is *high* relative to others, you will not need to spend such a large proportion of your income. Your *apc* will be lower.

This explains the discrepancy between the short-run and long-run consumption functions. In the short run, if people have a rise in their incomes, they will feel *relatively* better off compared with others. They will therefore increase their consumption by only a modest amount.

In the long run, if national income increases, people will not feel better off *relative* to others. As average incomes increase, people generally consume more as they see others consuming more.

The permanent income hypothesis

This was put forward by Milton Friedman in 1957.[3] Friedman divided a person's income into two types: permanent and transitory.

Permanent income is the average (discounted) income a person expects to receive over his or her lifetime. To estimate this, people look at their current wages and what they are likely to be earning in the future. It is on this that people base their normal planned spending.

The permanent income hypothesis has been extended by various economists who have looked at the typical *patterns* of income that people earn over their life span. (These are known as 'life cycle theories'.)

Transitory income is defined as temporary, unexpected income. People do not base their consumption plans on this. If people have an unexpected rise in income, they are likely to save most, if not all of it.

How can this distinction be used to explain the difference between short- and long-run consumption functions?

In the short run, a rise in national income may well lead to *unexpected* rises in individuals' incomes. For example, a boom in the trade cycle can lead to unexpected overtime for many workers. Since this is transitory income, it is largely saved. Consumption only rises slightly and the *apc* falls.

In the long run, if higher incomes persist, people are likely to adjust their expectations of their permanent income upwards. They will thus adjust their standard of living upwards. Their *apc* will not fall.

?? Is it a reasonable assumption that consumption does not depend on transitory income? If it did, what would this do to the shape of the short-run consumption function?

[2] J. S. Duesenberry, *Income, Saving and the Theory of Consumer Behaviour* (Harvard University Press, 1947).
[3] M. Friedman, *A Theory of the Consumption Function* (Princeton University Press, 1957).

decreasing fraction of it goes on consumption, so an increasing fraction of it will be saved. The rich can afford to save a larger proportion of their income than the poor.

Average and marginal propensities to save. Just as we did with consumption, we can distinguish between the average and marginal propensities to save. The **average propensity to save** (*aps*) is the proportion of total income saved:

$$aps = S/Y$$

In *both* parts of Figure 16.6 the *aps* increases as national income increases.

DEFINITION

Average propensity to save The proportion of national income saved: $aps = S/Y$.

CASE STUDIES

CONSUMPTION AND SAVING IN PRACTICE

Consumer spending follows a regular cyclical pattern each year, reaching its peak in the fourth quarter as Christmas approaches. The graph shows the levels of UK personal disposable income and total consumer expenditure (i.e. consumption before indirect taxes and imports have been deducted) from 1984 Q2 to 1997 Q4.

The annual cyclical pattern can clearly be seen, with consumption actually falling in quarter 1 of each year. The area between consumer expenditure and disposable income represents that fraction of disposable income that is saved.

£bn
150
140
130
120
110
100
90
80
70
60
50
40

Disposable income
Consumers' expenditure
Saving

1984 1985 1986 1987 1988 1989 1990 1991 1992 1993 1994 1995 1996 1997

Quarterly data

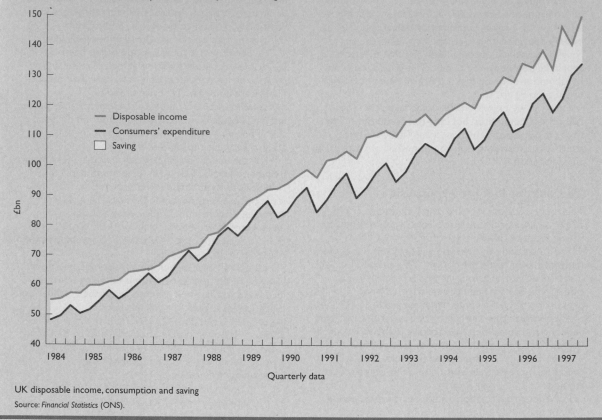

UK disposable income, consumption and saving

Source: *Financial Statistics* (ONS).

The **marginal propensity to save** (*mps*) is the proportion of an *increase* in income that is saved:

$$mps = \Delta S / \Delta Y$$

The *mps* is given by the slope of the net saving function. The *aps* is given by the slope of the line from the origin to the relevant point on the net saving function.

Other determinants of saving. To a large extent these are the same as the other determinants of consumption, since most things that encourage people to spend more will thereby encourage them to save less.

It might be easy to get the impression that saving is merely what is left over after consumption has taken place. In fact for many people the decision to save is a very positive one. They might be saving up for something they are eager to buy but cannot afford at the moment, or saving for retirement. Thus factors which affect people's attitudes towards saving (such as changes in pension provisions, or new government-sponsored saving schemes) could shift the net saving function. However, saving and consumption are still closely linked, and what determines the one will usually determine the other.

DEFINITION

Marginal propensity to save The proportion of an increase in national income saved: $mps = \Delta S / \Delta Y$.

BOX 16.4

As well as there being a clear annual pattern for consumption and saving, patterns can also be observed over the years. For example, saving ratios tend to fluctuate with the business cycle. In booms, especially if real interest rates are low and people are keen to spend, perhaps anticipating rising inflation, the saving ratio tends to fall. In 1988 the world economy was booming and consequently most countries experienced a relatively low saving ratio. This is illustrated in the table. In a recession, by contrast, with worries over job security and high levels of personal debt accumulated during the previous boom, people often attempt to reduce borrowing and increase saving. This was clearly seen in the UK in the early 1990s.

The table also shows that there are marked differences in saving ratios between countries. This is partly a reflection of national attitudes towards saving and spending, and partly a reflection of the encouragement given to saving by government and financial institutions.

Some of the changes in saving ratios reflect long-term trends. For example, Italy's saving ratio has shown a long-term decline, as traditional beliefs in the 'virtues' of saving have gradually been eroded. Other changes reflect changes in government policy. For example, Sweden after 1990 was concerned to 'shadow' the ECU: to prevent its exchange rate falling relative to the ECU. This involved pursuing a policy of high interest rates, which had the effect of encouraging saving and discouraging borrowing (negative saving).

??

Comparing the saving ratios in Belgium and the Netherlands, what do the differences imply for the balance between government expenditure and taxation if both countries want to achieve similar rates of investment and want to maintain a balance between imports and exports?

Ratio of household saving to personal disposable income

	1978	1980	1982	1984	1986	1988	1990	1992	1994	1996	1998[1]
Belgium	18.3	18.3	15.8	15.1	14.6	14.4	16.3	18.8	18.4	16.3	16.3
France	20.4	17.6	17.3	14.5	12.9	11.0	12.2	13.6	13.6	12.8	13.4
Germany	12.1	12.8	12.7	11.4	12.3	12.8	13.8	12.9	11.6	11.4	11.0
Italy	26.9	23.4	20.8	21.5	19.0	17.3	17.4	17.3	15.1	12.9	11.3
Japan	20.8	17.9	16.7	15.8	15.6	13.0	12.1	13.1	13.3	11.9	11.1
Netherlands	3.1	1.8	3.4	−0.6	2.8	2.2	5.8	2.3	1.0	1.2	1.2
Sweden	4.5	6.7	1.7	2.1	1.3	−4.8	−0.6	7.7	8.0	4.7	2.4
UK	10.9	13.4	11.3	11.1	8.7	6.0	8.1	12.0	10.4	11.9	10.1
USA	7.1	8.8	9.3	9.0	6.7	5.7	5.5	6.0	4.5	4.4	4.2

[1] Forecast

Source: *OECD Economic Outlook* (OECD).

??

Go through each of the determinants of consumption that were listed in the previous section and consider how they will affect saving. Are there any determinants of consumption which will *not* cause saving to rise if consumption is caused to fall?

Net taxes

Marginal and average tax propensities. The **average tax propensity** (*apt*) is the proportion of national income paid in taxes:

$$apt = T/Y$$

The **marginal tax propensity** (*mpt*) is the proportion of an *increase* in national income paid in taxes:[4]

[4] We have defined net taxes as taxes minus benefits (i.e. the net flow from the household sector to the government). For our purposes, then, the *apt* is the proportion of total income going in taxes minus benefits, and the *mpt* is the proportion of any rise in income going in taxes and reduced benefits.

DEFINITIONS

Average tax propensity The proportion of national income paid in taxes: $apt = T/Y$.

Marginal tax propensity The proportion of an increase in national income paid in tax: $mpt = \Delta T/\Delta Y$.

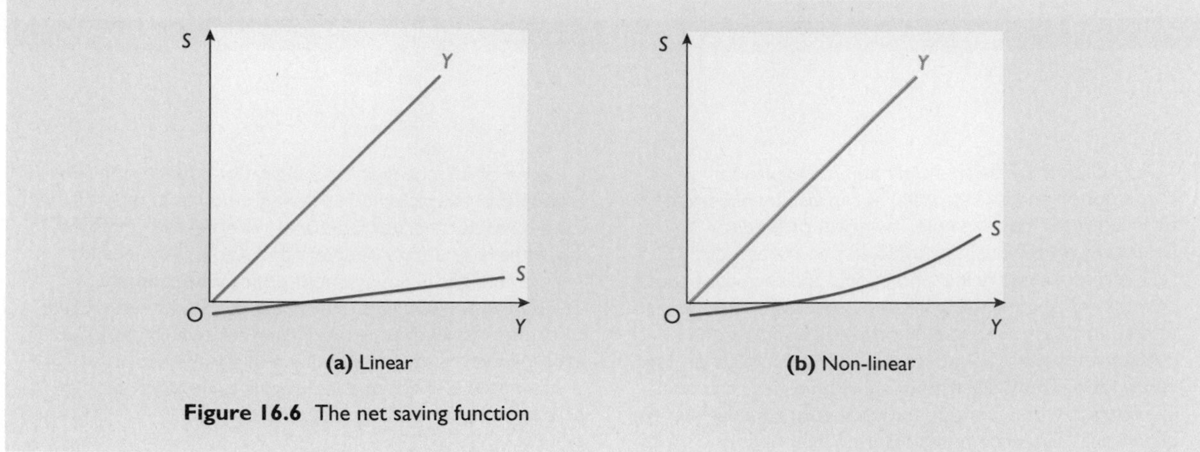

Figure 16.6 The net saving function

$$mpt = \Delta T / \Delta Y$$

The *mpt* depends on tax rates. In a simple world where there were only one type of tax, which was charged at a constant rate – for example, an income tax of 22 per cent – the *mpt* would be given directly by the tax rate. In this example, for each extra pound earned, 22p would be paid in income tax. The $mpt = \Delta T/\Delta Y = 22/100 = 0.22$. In practice, of course, there are many types of tax charged at many different rates, and thus working out the *mpt* is more complicated.

The aggregate net tax function. This shows the relationship between total tax payments (less benefits) and national income. Figure 16.7 shows a typical aggregate net tax function. It is *progressive*: i.e. the proportion of national income flowing to the government as tax revenues net of benefits (the *apt*) rises as national income rises. In practice the aggregate net tax function in the UK and many other countries has become much *less* progressive in the 1980s and 1990s.

> ?? What would cause (a) a movement along the net tax function; (b) a parallel downward shift in the net tax function; (c) a steepening of the net tax function and an increase in its curvature?

Imports

The marginal and average propensities to import. The **average propensity to import** (*apm*) is the proportion of national income that goes on imports from the country:

$$apm = M/Y$$

The **marginal propensity to import** (*mpm*) is the proportion of a *rise* in national income that goes on imports:

$$mpm = \Delta M/\Delta Y$$

Notice that we only count that part of the expenditure on imports that actually goes abroad. Amounts retained by the retailer, the wholesaler and the importer, and amounts paid in indirect taxes are excluded.

The import function. The higher the level of national income, the higher will be the level of imports. The import function, like all the others we have considered, is thus upward sloping. Two possible import functions are illustrated in Figure 16.8.

Curve (a) would be the function for a country which imported predominantly basic goods, which have a relatively low income elasticity of demand. The rate of increase in the consumption of such goods tails off rapidly as incomes increase. The *mpm* for such a country would thus also rapidly decrease.

Curve (b) would be the function for a country whose imports were mainly of luxury goods. Here imports account for an increasing proportion of any rise in national income.

> ?? If a country imports a whole range of goods whose average income elasticity of demand is the same as for home-produced goods, what will the import function look like?

DEFINITIONS

Average propensity to import The proportion of total national income that goes on imports: $apm = M/Y$.

Marginal propensity to import The proportion of an increase in national income that goes abroad: $mpm = \Delta M/\Delta Y$.

EXPLORING THE THEORY — BOX 16.5

NATIONAL INCOME AND TAX REVENUE

Various tax functions

Generally, as income increases so does the amount paid in taxes. The pattern, however, varies enormously from one type of tax to another. The four diagrams illustrate the possible different types of tax function.

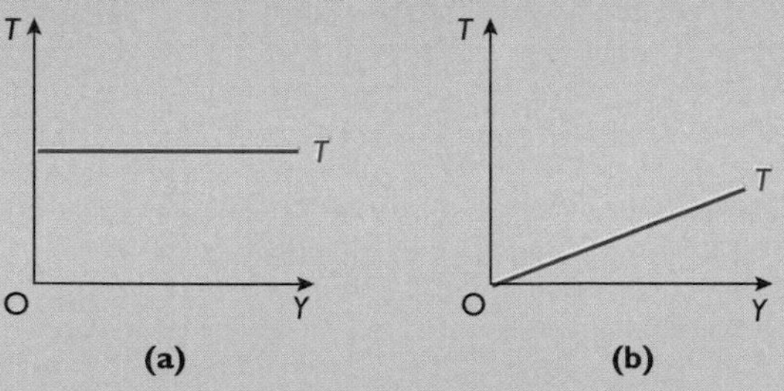

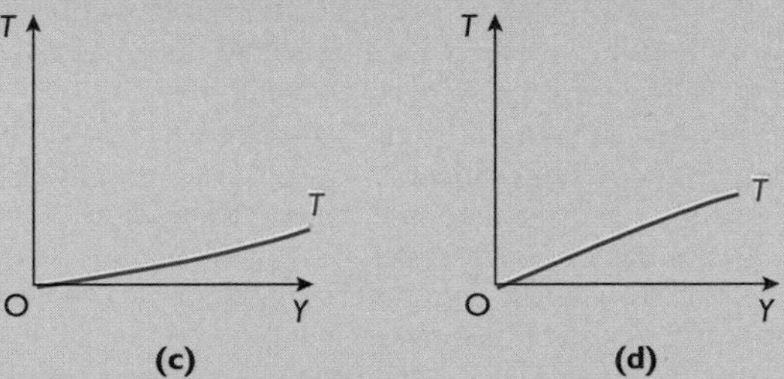

Diagram (a) shows the tax function for a *lump-sum* tax. This is one that does *not* vary with income. An example of a lump-sum tax was the community charge (the poll tax). With the exception of the very poor, everyone in a given local authority paid the same. The *mpt* for such a tax is zero. The *apt* declines as income increases.

Diagram (b) shows a *proportional* tax. It is a constant fraction of income: the *apt* is constant. The way it is drawn in the diagram, the *mpt* is constant too.

Diagram (c) shows a *progressive* tax. The proportion paid in this type of tax increases as income increases. The *apt* increases as income increases. In diagram (c), the *mpt* (i.e. the marginal tax rate) also increases as income increases. Nevertheless it would still be possible to have a progressive tax even with a constant *mpt* and hence a straight-line tax function, provided that the tax function intersected the horizontal axis to the right of the origin. This would be the case if people started paying the tax only when their income had reached a certain level (as with income tax, where people are given tax-free personal allowances).

Diagram (d) shows a *regressive* tax. This accounts for a smaller proportion of income as income rises: the *apt* falls.

There are more complicated tax functions than these, where marginal rates are constant over a large range of income but then suddenly rise. The most obvious example is income tax.

?? With a progressive tax, which is higher: the *mpt* or the *apt*?

The determinants of the level of imports. Apart from national income, there are a number of other determinants of the level of imports:

- *Relative prices.* If the prices of home-produced goods go up relative to the prices of imports, the level of imports will rise. The rate of exchange is a major influence here. The higher the rate of exchange, the cheaper will imports be and hence the more will be spent on them.
- *Tastes.* If consumer tastes shift towards foreign goods and services, imports will rise. For example, it might become more popular to go abroad for your holidays.
- *Relative quality.* If the quality of foreign goods and services increases relative to that of UK goods and services, imports will rise.
- *The determinants of consumption.* Since imports of goods and services are part of *total* consumption (as

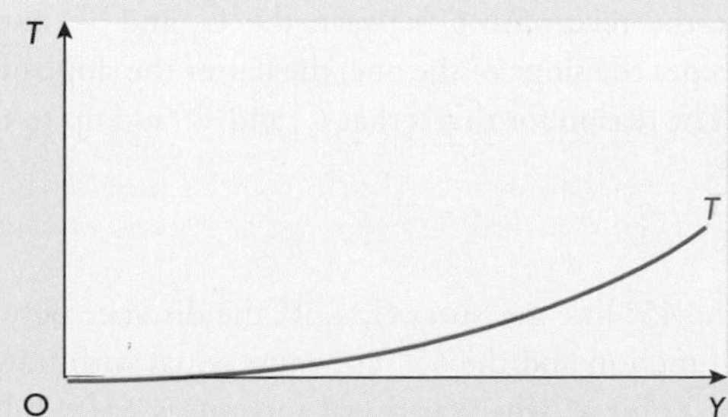

Figure 16.7 The aggregate net tax function

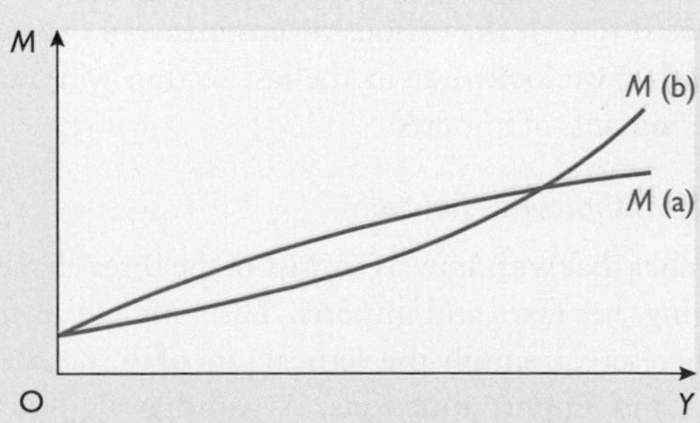

Figure 16.8 Import functions

CASE STUDIES

BUSINESS EXPECTATIONS AND THEIR EFFECT ON INVESTMENT

Recent European experience

In the boom years of the late 1980s, business optimism was widespread throughout Europe. Investment was correspondingly high, and with it there was a high rate of economic growth.

Surveys of European business expectations in the early 1990s, however, told a very different story. Pessimism was rife. Europe was in the grip of a recession, and output was falling (see table (a)). Along with this decline in output and deteriorating levels of business and consumer confidence, there was a significant fall in investment.

Not only was the total level of investment falling, but the proportion of that investment used to expand capacity was also falling (see figure (a)). By contrast, the proportion of investment devoted to rationalisation schemes had risen. Firms were increasingly having to look for ways of cutting their costs through restructuring their operations. One of the consequences of this was a growth in structural unemployment (as well as in demand-deficient unemployment).

But whereas these reductions in costs, and corresponding increases in labour productivity, provided a partial solution to the short-run difficulties faced by firms during the recession, in the long run productivity gains became increasingly difficult to achieve without investment in new capacity. This suggested that it was vital for firms to have confidence that their market *would* expand.

So were there any signs that confidence would pick up? As table (b) and figure (b) show, pessimism began to decrease after 1993, but it was not until the last quarter of 1994 that the average industrial confidence indicator for the EU as a whole became positive. (The figures in

(b) Industrial confidence indicator

Country	Trough 1991–3	Peak 1988–90	1989	1991	1993	1995	1996	1997
Belgium	−33	2	0	−15	−29	−9	−18	−3
Denmark	−20	5	4	−8	−12	6	−8	5
France	−40	12	8	−20	−35	−2	−18	−5
Germany	−36	11	5	0	−34	−3	−19	−6
Ireland	−22	14	10	−9	−13	7	−1	3
Italy	−22	13	8	−13	−17	6	−12	0
Netherlands	−12	3	1	−5	−10	2	−2	3
UK	−40	21	−2	−32	−11	3	−5	−1
EU	−28	6	4	−14	−26	0	−14	−3

Source: *European Economy Supplement B* (Commission of the European Communities).

(a) Macroeconomic indicators for the EU countries

	1989	1990	1991	1992	1993	1994	1995	1996	1997
GDP growth (%)	3.5	2.9	1.5	0.9	−0.6	2.8	2.5	1.6	2.4
Investment (% change)	7.2	3.8	−0.5	−0.9	−6.6	2.4	3.7	1.1	3.0
Unemployment (%)	9.0	8.4	8.8	9.4	10.7	11.4	10.9	11.0	10.6
Inflation (%)	5.2	5.7	5.1	4.5	3.6	3.1	3.0	2.7	2.2
Net government borrowing (−) (% of GDP)	−2.9	−4.1	−4.3	−5.1	−6.2	−5.5	−5.0	−4.4	−3.0
Current account balance (% of GDP)	−0.3	−0.5	−1.3	−1.2	0.0	0.0	0.5	0.7	0.9

Source: *European Economy Annual Report* (Commission of the European Communities).

opposed to C_d), the various determinants of consumption that we looked at in the last section will also be determinants of imports.

The total withdrawals function

Remember that withdrawals consist of the three elements: net saving, net taxes and imports. The withdrawals function, therefore, is simply the vertical sum of the net saving, net tax and import functions. A withdrawals function along with the corresponding consumption of domestic goods function is shown in Figure 16.9.

Note the relationship between the C_d and W curves. The steeper the slope of the one, the flatter the slope of the other. The reason for this is that C_d and W add up to total income:

$$Y = C_d + W$$

Since the 45° line measures $C_d + W$, the distance between the C_d function and the 45° line must equal withdrawals. Thus at point x, where national income is £100 billion and C_d is £70 billion, W must be £30 billion – the gap between C_d and the 45° line.

BOX 16.6

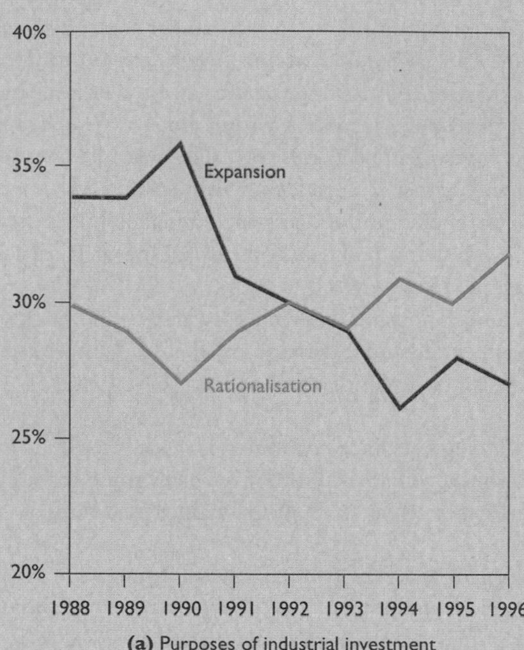

(a) Purposes of industrial investment (% of total investment)

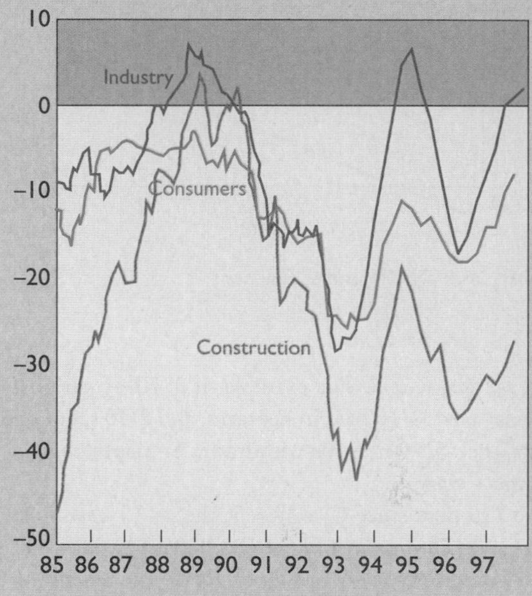

(b) Confidence indicators in the EU

Source: *European Economy* (Commission of the European Communities).

the table show the percentage excess of confident over pessimistic replies to business questionnaires: a negative figure meaning that there was a higher percentage of pessimistic responses.) Indeed, after mid-1995, the recovery in Europe began to slow down, and as a result industrial confidence waned, becoming negative once more.

As far as consumers were concerned, even with the recovery in Europe, which began in late 1993, the average EU consumer confidence indicator, although rising, remained negative. This was hardly the basis for a sustained rise in consumer expenditure and hence investment. From mid-1995 consumer confidence began falling again (see figure (b)).

??

1. How is the existence of surveys of business confidence likely to affect firms' expectations and actions?
2. Why, if the growth in output slows down (but is still positive), is investment likely to *fall* (i.e. the growth in investment be *negative*)? If you look at table (a) you will see that this happened in 1991 and 1992. (We will examine this question in section 16.4 when we look at the accelerator theory.)

Average and marginal propensities to withdraw

The formulae for the **average propensity to withdraw** (*apw*) and the **marginal propensity to withdraw** (*mpw*) are as we would expect:

$$apw = W/Y$$

$$mpw = \Delta W/\Delta Y$$

The *mpw* is the slope of the withdrawals function. The *apw* is the slope of the line from the origin to the withdrawals function.

Note that, since $W = S + T + M$, the *apw* must equal

DEFINITIONS

Average propensity to withdraw The proportion of national income that is withdrawn from the circular flow of income: $apw = W/Y$, where $apw = aps + apt + apm$.

Marginal propensity to withdraw The proportion of an increase in national income that is withdrawn from the circular flow: $mpw = \Delta W/\Delta Y$, where $mpw = mps + mpt + mpm$.

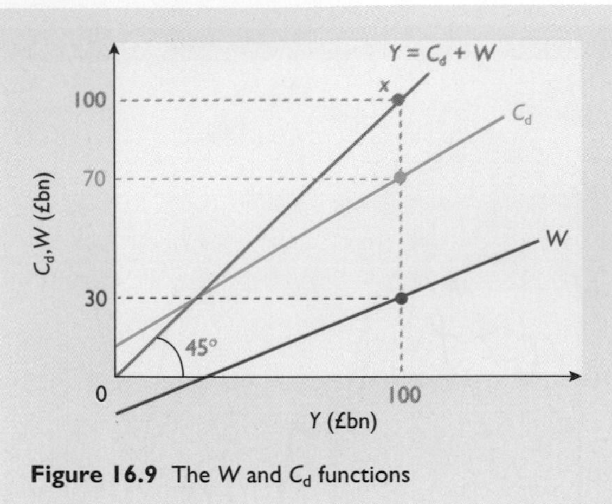

Figure 16.9 The W and C_d functions

the *aps* + *apt* + *apm*. For example, if 1/10 of national income is saved, 2/10 paid in net taxes, and 2/10 spent on imports, then 5/10 must be withdrawn. Similarly, *mpw* = *mps* + *mpt* + *mpm*.

Note also that, since $C_d + W = Y$, the apc_d + *apw* must add up to 1. If your income is £20 000 and you spend £13 000 on domestically produced goods, the remaining £7000 must go in withdrawals. Your apc_d is 13/20 and your *apw* is 7/20. But 13/20 + 7/20 = 1. Likewise, mpc_d + *mpw* = 1. If you spend, say, 3/5 of any rise in income on domestically produced goods, the remaining 2/5 must go in withdrawals.

?? If the slope of the C_d function is 3/4, what is the slope of the W function?

Injections

In simple Keynesian theory, injections are assumed not to depend on the level of national income: they are *exogenously* determined. This means that the injections function will be a horizontal straight line. Injections will be at a given level irrespective of the level of national income. The injections function is the vertical addition of the investment, government expenditure and export functions, each of which is a horizontal straight line.

The assumption that injections are independent of national income makes the theory simpler. (It is possible to drop this assumption, however, without destroying the theory.) But is the assumption sufficiently realistic? Let us examine each of the injections in turn.

Investment

There are four major determinants of investment.

Increased consumer demand. Investment is to provide extra capacity. This will only be necessary, therefore, if consumer demand increases. The bigger the increase in consumer demand, the more the investment that will be needed.

You might think that, since consumer demand depends on the level of national income, investment must too, and that therefore our assumption that investment is independent of national income is wrong. But we are not saying that investment depends on the *level* of consumer demand; rather it depends on *how much it has risen.* If income and consumer demand are high but *constant*, there will be no point in firms expanding their capacity: no point in investing.

The relationship between investment and increased consumer demand is examined by the 'accelerator theory'. We will look at this theory in section 16.4.

Expectations. Since investment is made in order to produce output for the future, investment must depend on firms' expectations about future market conditions.

The cost and efficiency of capital equipment. If the cost of capital equipment goes down or machines become more efficient, the return on investment will increase. Firms will invest more. Technological progress is an important determinant here.

The rate of interest. The higher the rate of interest, the more expensive will it be for firms to finance investment, and hence the less profitable will the investment be. Just how responsive total investment in the economy is to changes in interest rates is a highly controversial issue and we will return to it later.

So if these are the main determinants of investment, does it mean that investment is totally independent of the level of national income? Not quite. Replacement of worn-out or outdated equipment *will* depend on the level of national income. The higher the current level of national income, the greater will be the stock of capital and therefore the more will need replacing each year. It is also possible that, if the level of national income is high and firms' profits are high, they will be able to *afford* more investment. However, it is not a gross distortion of reality to assume that investment and the level of national income are independent.

Government expenditure

To some extent, especially over the longer term, government expenditure *will* depend on national income. The higher the level of national income, the higher is the amount of tax revenue that the government receives, and hence the more it can afford to spend. The governments of richer nations clearly spend much more than those of developing countries.

Nevertheless governments can run a budget deficit or surplus. Moreover, the government can always raise or lower taxes if it wants to. Certainly then, in the short run at least, government expenditure can be regarded as independent of national income.

Exports

The amount that foreigners spend on UK exports depends largely on *their* national incomes. Nevertheless there are two indirect links between UK incomes and exports:

- Via foreign countries' circular flows of income. If UK incomes rise, more will be spent on imports. But this will cause a rise in other countries' incomes and lead them to buy more imports, part of which will be UK exports.
- Via the exchange rate. A rise in UK incomes will lead to a rise in imports. Other things being equal, this will lead to a depreciation in the exchange rate. This will make it cheaper for foreigners to buy UK exports. Export sales will rise.

However, it is useful in simple Keynesian models to assume that exports are determined independently of domestic national income.

Note that, although the injections function is assumed to be constant with respect to income and is drawn as a horizontal straight line, this does not mean that it will be constant *over time*. Investment can suddenly rise or virtually collapse as the confidence of businesspeople changes. Exports can change dramatically too with shifts in the exchange rate or with speculation. The injections line, then, is constantly shifting up and down.

SECTION SUMMARY

1. In the simple Keynesian model, equilibrium national income is where withdrawals equal injections, and where national income equals the total expenditure on domestic products: where $W = J$ and where $Y = E$.
2. The relationships between national income and the various components of the circular flow of income can be shown on a 45° line diagram. In the diagram, C, C_d and W are endogenous variables. Each one rises as income rises. The relationships can also be expressed in terms of average and marginal propensities. The average propensity of each variable is given by V/Y (where V is the variable in question). The marginal propensity is given by $\Delta V/\Delta Y$.
3. Apart from being determined by national income, consumption is determined by wealth, taxation, the availability and cost of credit, expectations about future prices and incomes, the distribution of income, tastes and attitudes, and the average age of durables. Consumption of domestic product (C_d) is total consumption minus imports of goods and services and minus indirect taxes and plus subsidies on goods and services.
4. Like consumption, withdrawals (S, T and M) vary with national income. Net saving is also determined by the various factors that determine consumption: if these factors cause consumption to rise, then except in the case of a cut in income taxes they will cause saving to fall and vice versa. Net tax revenues, apart from being dependent on incomes, will depend on the rates of tax and benefits the government sets and how progressive or regressive they are. Imports will depend on the relative prices and quality of domestic and foreign goods, total consumption and tastes.
5. In the simple Keynesian model, injections are assumed to be exogenous variables. They are therefore drawn as a horizontal straight line in the 45° line diagram. In practice there will be *some* relationship between injections and national income. Replacement investment depends to some extent on the level of output; government expenditure depends to some extent on the level of tax revenues; and exports depend on exchange rates and foreign incomes, both of which will depend on the level of imports. Nevertheless in the short run it is reasonable to assume that injections are independent of national income.
6. The determinants of investment include the rate of interest, the size of increases in consumer demand, the cost and efficiency of capital equipment, and expectations about prices, consumer demand, interest rates and other costs.

16.2

The determination of national income

Equilibrium national income

We can now put the various functions together on one diagram. This is done in Figure 16.10. Note that there is a new line on the diagram that we have not looked at so far. This is the national expenditure (i.e. the aggregate demand) function. We defined national expenditure as $C_d + J$. Graphically, then, the E function is simply the C_d function shifted upward by the amount of J.

Equilibrium national income can be found in either of two ways.

$W = J$

Withdrawals equal injections at point x in the diagram. Equilibrium national income is thus Y_e. If national income were below this level, say at Y_1, injections would exceed withdrawals (by an amount $a - b$). This additional net expenditure injected into the economy would encourage firms to produce more and hence cause national income to rise. But as people's incomes rose, so they would save more, pay more taxes and buy more imports. In other words, withdrawals would rise. There would be a movement up along the W function. This process would continue until $W = J$ at point x.

If, on the other hand, national income were at Y_2, withdrawals would exceed injections (by an amount $c - d$). This deficiency of demand would cause production and hence national income to fall. As it did so, there would be a movement down along the W function until again point x was reached.

$Y = E$

If $W = J$, then $C_d + W = C_d + J$. In other words, another way of describing equilibrium is where national income ($Y \equiv C_d + W$) equals national expenditure ($E \equiv C_d + J$). This is shown at point z in Figure 16.10. This is where the expenditure function ($C_d + J$) crosses the 45° line ($C_d + W$).

If national expenditure exceeded national income, say at Y_1, there would be excess demand in the economy (of $e - f$). In other words, people would be buying more than was currently being produced. Firms would find their stocks dwindling and would therefore increase their level of production. In doing so they would employ more factors of production. National income would thus rise. As it did so, consumption and hence national expenditure would rise. There would be a movement up along the expenditure function. But because not all the extra income would be consumed (i.e. some would be withdrawn), expenditure would rise less quickly than income (the E line is flatter than the Y line). As income rises towards Y_e, the gap between Y and E gets smaller. Once point z is reached, $Y = E$. There is then no further tendency for income to rise.

If national income exceeded national expenditure, at say Y_2, there would be insufficient demand for the goods and services currently being produced. Firms would find their stocks of unsold goods building up. They would thus respond by producing less and employing fewer factors of production. National income would thus fall and go on falling until Y_e was reached.

?? Why do $a - b = e - f$, and $c - d = g - h$?

The multiplier: the withdrawals and injections approach

When injections rise this will cause national income to rise. But by how much?

In fact, national income will rise by *more* than injections: Y rises by a *multiple* of the rise in J.

$$\Delta Y > \Delta J$$

The number of times that the increase in income (ΔY) is greater than the increase in injections (ΔJ) is known as the **multiplier** (k).

$$k = \Delta Y / \Delta J$$

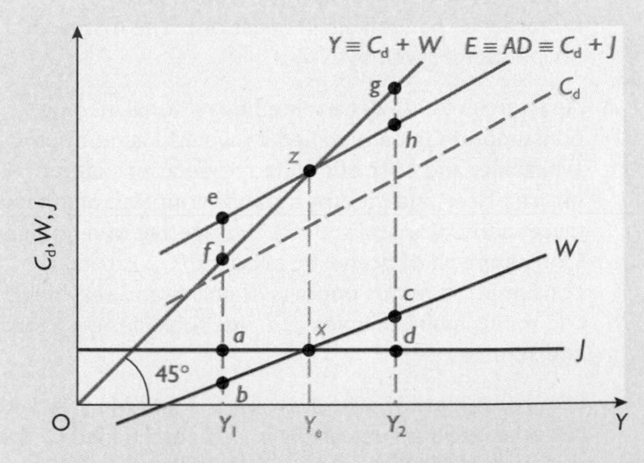

Figure 16.10 Equilibrium national income

DEFINITION

(Injections) multiplier The number of times by which a rise in income exceeds the rise in injections that caused it: $k = \Delta Y/\Delta J$.

Thus if a £10 billion rise in injections caused a £30 billion rise in national income, the multiplier would be 3.

What causes the multiplier effect? The answer is that, when extra spending is injected into the economy, it will then stimulate further spending, which in turn will stimulate yet more spending and so on. For example, if firms decide to invest more, this will lead to more people being employed and hence more incomes being paid to households. Households will then spend part of this increased income on domestically produced goods (the remainder will be withdrawn). This increased consumption will encourage firms to produce more goods to meet the demand. Firms will thus employ more people and other factors of production. This leads to even more incomes being paid out to households. Consumption will thus increase yet again. And so the process continues.

Note that in this simple Keynesian theory we are assuming that prices are constant (i.e. that there is no inflation) and hence that any increase in income is a *real* increase in income matched by extra production. So when we talk about extra injections into the economy causing extra spending, it is the extra *output* that this spending generates that we are concerned with. If the multiplier were 3, for example, this would mean that an injection of £1 of expenditure into the economy would lead to an increase in *output* of £3.

But even if there were limitless resources, an increase in injections would not cause national income to go on rising for ever: the multiplier is not infinite. Each time people receive extra income they will save some of it, pay some of it in taxes and spend some of it on imports. Eventually, as income goes on rising, all the extra injections will have leaked away into the three withdrawals. At that point the multiplier process will have ceased; a new equilibrium will have been reached.

What determines the size of the multiplier? This can be shown graphically using either withdrawals and injections or income and expenditure. The income/expenditure approach will be examined shortly. For now we will use the withdrawals/injections approach. This is illustrated in Figure 16.11.

Assume that injections rise from J_1 to J_2. Equilibrium will move from point *a* to point *b*. Income will thus rise from Y_{e1} to Y_{e2}. The multiplier is therefore:

$$\frac{Y_{e2} - Y_{e1}}{J_2 - J_1} \quad \left(\text{i.e. } \frac{\Delta Y}{\Delta J}\right)$$

It can be seen that the size of the multiplier depends on the *slope of the W function*. Remember that the slope of the *W* function is given by the marginal propensity to withdraw ($\Delta W/\Delta Y$). The flatter the line (and hence the lower the *mpw*), the bigger will be the rise in national income: the bigger will be the multiplier.

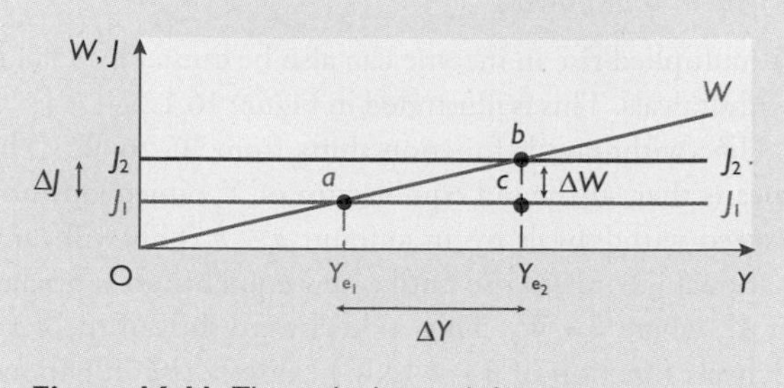

Figure 16.11 The multiplier: a shift in injections

?? Try this simple test of the above argument. Draw a series of *W* lines of different slopes all crossing the *J* line at the same point. Now draw a second *J* line above the first. Mark the original equilibrium and all the new ones corresponding to each of the *W* lines. It should be quite obvious that the flatter the *W* line is, the more *Y* will have increased.

The point here is that the less is withdrawn each time money circulates, the more will be recirculated and hence the bigger will be the rise in national income. The size of the multiplier thus varies inversely with the size of the *mpw*. The bigger the *mpw*, the smaller the multiplier; the smaller the *mpw*, the bigger the multiplier. In fact the **multiplier formula** simply gives the multiplier as the inverse of the *mpw*:

$$k = 1/mpw$$

or alternatively, since $mpw + mpc_d = 1$ and thus $mpw = 1 - mpc_d$:

$$k = 1/(1 - mpc_d)$$

Thus if the *mpw* were ¼ (and hence the mpc_d were 3/4), the multiplier would be 4. So if *J* increased by £10 billion, *Y* would increase by £40 billion.

But why is the multiplier given by the formula 1/*mpw*? This can be illustrated by referring to Figure 16.11. The *mpw* is the slope of the *W* line. In the diagram this is given by the amount $(b - c)/(c - a)$. The multiplier is defined as $\Delta Y/\Delta J$. In the diagram this is the amount $(c - a)/(b - c)$. But this is merely the inverse of the *mpw*. Thus the multiplier equals 1/*mpw*.[5]

[5] In some elementary textbooks, the formula for the multiplier is given as 1/*mps*. The reason for this is that it is assumed (for simplicity) that there is only one withdrawal, namely savings, and only one injection, namely investment. As soon as this assumption is dropped, 1/*mps* becomes the wrong formula.

DEFINITION

(Injections) multiplier formula The formula for the multiplier is $k = 1/mpw$ or $1/(1 - mpc_d)$.

A shift in withdrawals

A multiplied rise in income can also be caused by a fall in withdrawals. This is illustrated in Figure 16.12.

The withdrawals function shifts from W_1 to W_2. This means that, at the old equilibrium of Y_{e1}, injections now exceed withdrawals by an amount $a - b$. This will cause national income to rise until a new equilibrium is reached at Y_{e2} where $J = W_2$. Thus a downward shift of the withdrawals function of $a - b$ (ΔW) causes a rise in national income of $c - a$ (ΔY). The multiplier in this case is given by $\Delta Y/\Delta W$: in other words, $(c - a)/(a - b)$.

> **??** Why is the 'withdrawals multiplier' strictly speaking a negative figure?

The multiplier: a numerical illustration

The multiplier effect does not work instantaneously. When there is an initial increase in injections, it takes time before this brings about the full multiplied rise in national income.

Consider the following example. Let us assume for simplicity that the *mpw* is ½. This will give an mpc_d of ½ also. Let us also assume that there is an increase in injections into the economy of £160 million. Table 16.2 shows what will happen.

The initial injection of £160 million will generate an immediate increase in national income of £160 million. When this income is received by households, half will be withdrawn (*mpw* = ½) and half will be spent on the goods and services of domestic firms. This increase in consumption thus generates additional incomes for firms of £80 million over and above the initial £160 million. When this additional £80 million of incomes is received by households (period 2), again half will be withdrawn and half will go on consumption of domestic product. This increases national income by a further £40 million (period 3). And so each time we go around the circular flow of income, national income increases, but by only half as much as the previous time (mpc_d = ½).

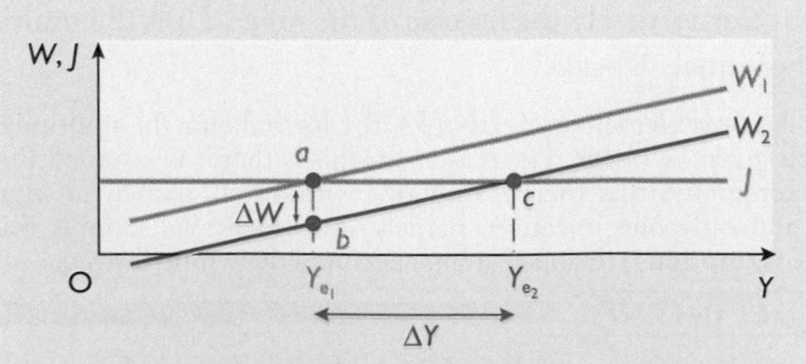

Figure 16.12 The multiplier: a shift in withdrawals

Table 16.2 The multiplier 'round'

Period	ΔJ (£m)	ΔY (£m)	ΔC_d (£m)	ΔW (£m)
1	160	160	80	80
2	–	80	40	40
3	–	40	20	20
4	–	20	10	10
5	–	10	5	5
6	–	5	.	.
.		.	.	.
.		.	.	.
.		.	.	.
$1 \rightarrow \infty$		320	160	160

If we add up the additional income generated in each period (assuming the process goes on indefinitely), the total will be £320 million: twice the initial injection. The multiplier is 2.

The bigger the mpc_d (and hence the smaller the *mpw*), the more will expenditure rise each time national income rises, and hence the bigger will be the multiplier.

The multiplier: the income and expenditure approach

The multiplier can also be demonstrated using the income/expenditure approach. Assume in Figure 16.13 that the expenditure function shifts to E_2. This could be due either to a rise in one or more of the three injections, or to a rise in the consumption of domestically produced goods (and hence a fall in withdrawals). Equilibrium national income will rise from Y_{e1} to Y_{e2}. What is the size of the multiplier? The initial rise in expenditure was $b - a$. The resulting rise in income is $c - a$. The multiplier is thus $(c - a)/(b - a)$.

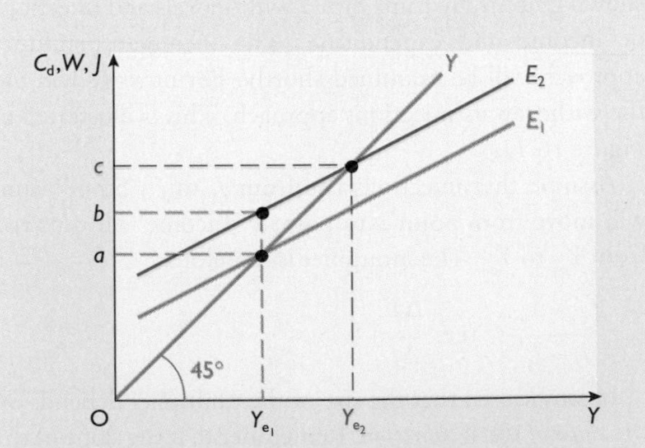

Figure 16.13 A shift in the expenditure function

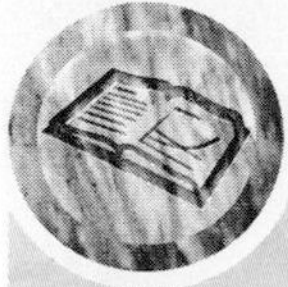

EXPLORING THE THEORY BOX 16.7

DERIVING THE MULTIPLIER FORMULA
An algebraic proof

The formula for the multiplier can be derived using simple algebra. First of all remember how we defined the multiplier:

$$k \equiv \Delta Y/\Delta J \quad (1)$$

and the marginal propensity to withdraw:

$$mpw \equiv \Delta W/\Delta Y \quad (2)$$

If we now take the inverse of equation (2) we get:

$$1/mpw \equiv \Delta Y/\Delta W \quad (3)$$

But in equilibrium we know that $W = J$. Hence any change in injections must be matched by a change in withdrawals and vice versa, to ensure that withdrawals and injections remain equal. Thus:

$$\Delta W = \Delta J \quad (4)$$

Substituting equation (4) in equation (3) gives:

$$1/mpw = \Delta Y/\Delta J \ (= k)$$

i.e. the multiplier equals $1/mpw$.

??

1. What determines the slope of the E function?
2. How does the slope of the E function affect the size of the multiplier? (Try drawing diagrams with E functions of different slopes and see what happens when they shift.)

*The multiplier: some qualifications

There are some possible errors that can easily be made in calculating the value of the multiplier. These often arise from a confusion over the meaning of terms.

The marginal propensity to consume domestic product

Remember the formula for the multiplier:

$$k = 1/(1 - mpc_d)$$

It is important to realise just what is meant by the mpc_d. It is the proportion of a rise in households' gross (i.e. pre-tax-and-benefit) income that actually accrues to domestic firms. It thus excludes that part of consumption that is spent on imports and that part which is paid to the government in VAT and other indirect taxes.

Up to now we have also been basing the *mpc* on gross income. As we saw in Box 16.1, however, the *mpc* is often based on *disposable* (i.e. post-tax-and-benefit) income. After all, when consumers decide how much to spend, it is their disposable income rather than their gross income that they will consider. So how do we derive the mpc_d (based on gross income) from the *mpc* based on disposable income? To do this we must use the following formula:

$$mpc_d = mpc\,(1 - t_E)(1 - t_Y) - mpm$$

where t_Y is the marginal rate of income tax, and t_E is the marginal rate of expenditure tax.

To illustrate this formula consider the following effects of an increase in national income of £100 million. It is assumed that T_Y = 20 per cent, T_E = 10 per cent and *mpc* = 7/8. It is also assumed that the *mps* = 1/10 and the *mpm* = 13/100. Table 16.3 sets out the figures.

Gross income rises by £100 million. Of this, £20 million is taken in income tax (t_Y = 20 per cent). This leaves a rise in disposable income of £80 million. Of this, £10 million is saved (*mps* = 1/10) and £70 million is spent. Of this, £7 million goes in expenditure taxes (t_E = 10 per cent) and £13 million leaks abroad (*mpm* = 13/100). This leaves £50 million that goes on the consumption of domestic product (mpc_d = 50/100) = ½). Substituting these figures in the above formula gives:

$$mpc_d = mpc\,(1 - t_E)(1 - t_Y) - mpm$$
$$= 7/8(1 - 1/10)(1 - 2/10) - 13/100$$
$$= 7/8 \,.\, 9/10 \,.\, 8/10 - 13/100$$
$$= 63/100 - 13/100 = 50/100 = 1/2$$

Note that the mpc_d, *mps*, *mpm* and *mpt* are all based on the rise in *gross* income, not disposable income. They are 50/100, 10/100, 13/100 and 27/100 respectively.

??

Assume that the rate of income tax is 15 per cent, the rate of expenditure tax is 12½ per cent, the *mps* is 1/20, the *mpm* is 1/8 and the *mpc* (from disposable income) is 16/17. What is the mpc_d? Construct a table like Table 16.3 assuming again that national income rises by £100 million.

Table 16.3

	ΔY	–	ΔT_Y	=	ΔY_{dis}		
(£m)	100		20		80		
	ΔY_{dis}	–	ΔS	=	ΔC		
(£m)	80		10		70		
	ΔC	–	ΔT_E	–	ΔM	=	ΔC_d
(£m)	70		7		13		50

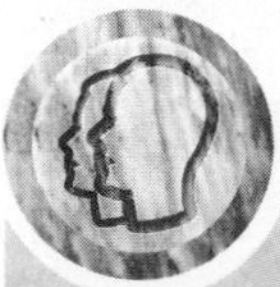

DEVELOPMENT OF IDEAS

BOX 16.8

THE PARADOX OF THRIFT

When prudence is folly

The classical economists argued that saving was a national virtue. More saving would lead via lower interest rates to more investment and faster growth. Keynes was at pains to show the opposite. Saving, far from being a national virtue, could be a national vice.

Remember the fallacy of composition (see Box 3.5). Just because something is good for an individual, it does not follow that it is good for society as a whole. This fallacy applies to saving. If individuals save more, they will increase their consumption possibilities in the future. If society saves more, however, this may *reduce* its future income and consumption. As people save more, they will spend less. Firms will thus produce less. There will thus be a multiplied *fall* in income (see Figure 16.13). The phenomenon of higher saving leading to *lower* national income is known as 'the paradox of thrift'.

But this is not all. Far from the extra savings encouraging more investment, the lower consumption will *discourage* firms from investing. If investment falls, the *J* line will shift downwards. There will then be a further multiplied fall in national income. (This response of investment to changes in consumer demand is examined in section 16.4 under the 'accelerator theory'.)

The paradox of thrift had in fact been recognised before Keynes, and Keynes himself referred to various complaints about 'underconsumption' that had been made back in the sixteenth and seventeenth centuries:

> In 1598 Laffemas . . . denounced the objectors to the use of French silks on the grounds that all purchasers of French luxury goods created a livelihood for the poor, whereas the miser caused them to die in distress. In 1662 Petty justified 'entertainments, magnificent shews, triumphal arches, etc.', on the ground that their costs flowed back into the pockets of brewers, bakers, tailors, shoemakers and so forth . . . In 1695 Cary argued that if everybody spent more, all would obtain larger incomes 'and might then live more plentifully'.[6]

But despite these early recognitions of the danger of underconsumption, the belief that saving would increase the prosperity of the nation was central to classical economic thought.

?? Is an increase in saving ever desirable?

[6] J. M. Keynes, *The General Theory of Employment, Interest and Money* (Macmillan, 1967), pp. 358–9.

The effects of changes in injections and withdrawals on other injections and withdrawals

In order to work out the size of a multiplied rise or fall in income it is necessary to know first the size of the initial *total* change in injections and/or withdrawals. The trouble is that a change in one injection or withdrawal can affect others. For example, a rise in income taxes will reduce not only consumption, but also saving, imports and the revenue from indirect taxes. Thus the total rise in withdrawals will be *less* than the rise in income taxes.

?? Give some other examples of changes in one injection or withdrawal that can affect others.

The relationship between the 45° line diagram and the aggregate demand and supply diagram

We have used two diagrams to show the determination of equilibrium national income: the aggregate demand and supply diagram and the 45° line diagram. The first shows aggregate demand dependent on the price level. The second shows aggregate demand (E) dependent on the level of national income. Figure 16.14 shows the multiplier effect simultaneously on the two diagrams. Initially equilibrium is at Y_{e_1} where aggregate demand equals aggregate supply and where the expenditure function crosses the 45° line.

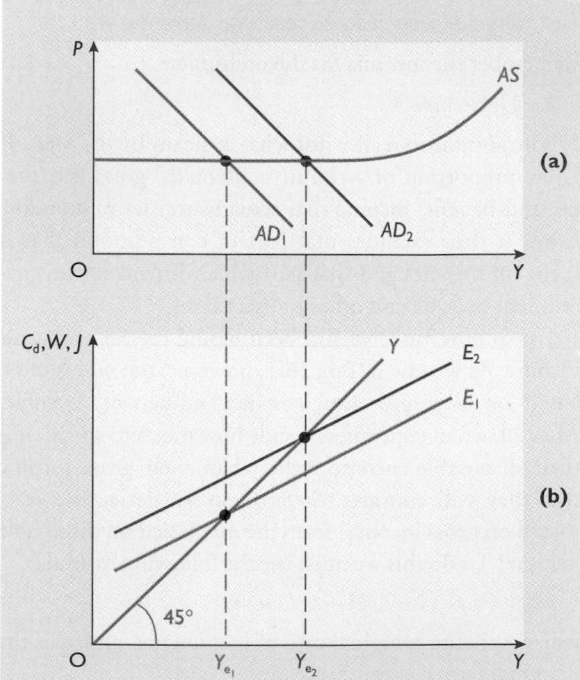

Figure 16.14 Showing the multiplier effect on the 45° line and AD/AS diagrams

Now assume that there is an autonomous increase in expenditure. For example, increased business confidence results in increased investment. In diagram (b) the E line shifts to E_2. There is a multiplied rise in income to Y_{e_2}. In diagram (a) the aggregate supply curve is drawn as a horizontal straight line between Y_{e_1} and Y_{e_2}. This means that an increase in aggregate demand from AD_1 to AD_2 will raise income to Y_{e_2} with no increase in prices.

But what if the economy is approaching full employment? Surely we cannot expect the multiplier process to work in the same way as when there is plenty of slack in the economy? In this case the aggregate supply curve will be upward sloping. This means that an increase in aggregate demand will raise prices and not just output. How do we analyse this with the 45° line diagram? We examine this in the next section.

SECTION SUMMARY

1. Equilibrium national income can be shown on the 45° line diagram at the point where $W = J$ and $Y = E$.
2. If there is an increase in injections (or a reduction in withdrawals), there will be a multiplied rise in national income. The multiplier is defined as $\Delta Y/\Delta J$.
3. The size of the multiplier depends on the marginal propensity to withdraw (*mpw*). The smaller the *mpw*, the less will be withdrawn each time incomes are generated round the circular flow, and thus the more will go round again as *additional* demand for domestic product. The multiplier formula is $k = 1/mpw$ or $1/(1 - mpc_d)$.

*4. When working out the size of the multiplier you must be careful to identify clearly the mpc_d (which is based on *gross* income and only includes expenditure that actually accrues to domestic firms) and not to confuse it with the *mpc* based on *disposable* income (which includes consumption of imports and the payment of indirect taxes). It is also necessary to identify the *full* changes in injections and withdrawals on which any multiplier effect is based.

5. The multiplier effect can also be illustrated on an aggregate demand and supply diagram.

16.3 The simple Keynesian analysis of unemployment and inflation

'Full-employment' national income

In the simple Keynesian theory it is assumed that there will be a maximum level of national output, and hence real income, that can be obtained at any one time. If the equilibrium level of income is at this level, there will be no deficiency of aggregate demand and hence no disequilibrium unemployment. This level of income is referred to as the **full-employment level of national income**. (In practice there would still be some unemployment at this level because of the existence of equilibrium unemployment – structural, frictional and seasonal.)

Post-war governments of the 1950s, 1960s and early 1970s aimed to achieve this full employment income (Y_f), if inflation and the balance of payments permitted. To do this they attempted to manipulate the level of aggregate demand.

The deflationary gap

If the equilibrium level of income (Y_e) is below the full-employment level (Y_f), there will be excess capacity in the economy and hence demand-deficient unemployment.

There will be what is known as a **deflationary gap**. This is illustrated in Figure 16.15.

The gap is $a - b$: namely, the amount that the E line is below the 45° line at the full-employment level of income (Y_f). It is also $c - d$: the amount that injections fall short of withdrawals at the full-employment level of income.

Note that the size of the deflationary gap is *less* than the amount by which Y_e falls short of Y_f. This is another illustration of the multiplier. If injections are raised by $c - d$, income will rise by $Y_f - Y_e$. The multiplier is thus given by:

$$\frac{Y_f - Y_e}{c - d}$$

DEFINITIONS

Full-employment level of national income The level of national income at which there is no deficiency of demand.

Deflationary gap The shortfall of national expenditure below national income (and injections below withdrawals) at the full-employment level of national income.

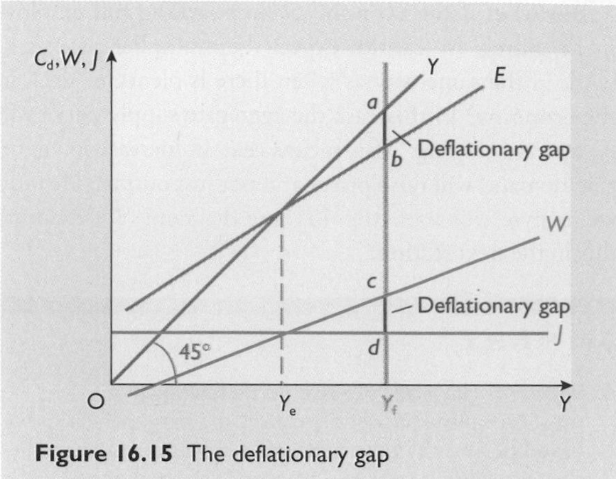

Figure 16.15 The deflationary gap

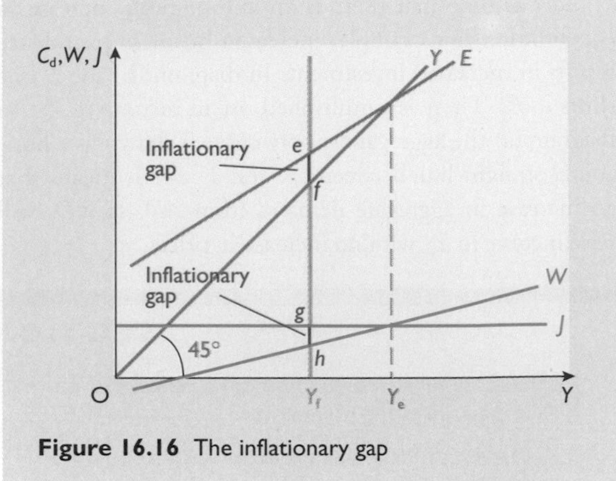

Figure 16.16 The inflationary gap

In this simple Keynesian model, then, the cure for demand-deficient unemployment is to close the deflationary gap. Doing so, by fiscal or monetary policy, will lead to a multiplied rise in income of $Y_f - Y_e$. Equilibrium national income will be restored to the full-employment level.

The inflationary gap

If at the full-employment level of income national expenditure exceeds national income, there will be a problem of *excess* demand. Y_e will be above Y_f. The problem is that Y_f represents a real ceiling to output. In the short run, real national income *cannot* expand beyond this point. Y_e cannot be reached. The result will therefore be demand-pull inflation.[7]

This situation involves an **inflationary gap**. This is the amount by which expenditure exceeds income or injections exceed withdrawals at the full-employment level of national income. This is illustrated by the gaps $e - f$ and $g - h$ in Figure 16.16.

To eliminate this inflation, the inflationary gap must be closed by either raising withdrawals or lowering injections or some combination of the two until Y_e equals Y_f. This can be done by a deliberate government policy of deflation. This could be either a deflationary *fiscal* policy of lowering government expenditure or raising taxes, or a deflationary *monetary* policy of reducing the amount of money in the economy and/or deliberately raising interest rates.

Even if the government does not actively pursue a deflationary policy, the inflationary gap may still close automatically. If the rich are better able to defend themselves against inflation than the poor, there will be a redistribution from the poor to the rich. But the rich tend to have a higher marginal propensity to save than the poor. Thus savings will rise and consumption will fall. This will shift the *W* line up and the *E* line down, thus narrowing the inflationary gap.

Inflation will also tend to worsen the balance of payments. Higher money incomes at home will lead to more imports being purchased. Higher domestic prices will lead to fewer exports being sold and more imports being bought in preference to the now dearer home-produced goods. The effect of this will be to shift the *W* line up and the *J* and *E* lines down, thus helping to close the inflationary gap.

Finally, as money incomes go up, people will tend to find themselves paying higher rates of tax (unless the government increases tax bands and allowances in line with inflation). This will shift the *W* line up and the *E* line down.

?? The present level of a country's exports is £12 billion; investment is £2 billion; government expenditure is £4 billion; *total* consumer spending (not C_d) is £36 billion; imports are £12 billion; and expenditure taxes are £2 billion. The economy is currently in equilibrium. It is estimated that an income of £50 billion is necessary to generate full employment. The *mps* is 0.1, the *mpt* is 0.05 and the *mpm* is 0.1.

(a) Is there an inflationary or deflationary gap in this situation?
(b) What is the size of the gap? (Don't confuse this with the difference between Y_e and Y_f.)
(c) What would be the appropriate government policies to close this gap?

[7] Note that the horizontal axis in the 45° line diagram represents *real* national income. If incomes were to rise by, say, 10 per cent but prices also rose by 10 per cent, real income would not have risen at all. People could not buy any more than before. In such a case there will have been no rightward movement along the horizontal axis.

DEFINITION

Inflationary gap The excess of national expenditure over income (and injections over withdrawals) at the full-employment level of national income.

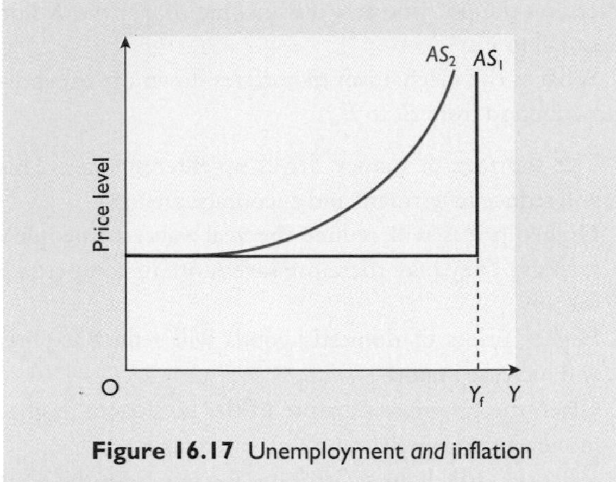

Figure 16.17 Unemployment *and* inflation

Unemployment and inflation at the same time

The simple analysis of the preceding pages implies that the aggregate supply curve looks like AS_1 in Figure 16.17. Up to Y_f, output and employment can rise with no rise in prices at all. The deflationary gap is being closed. At Y_f no further rises in output are possible. Any further rise in aggregate demand is entirely reflected in higher prices. An inflationary gap opens. In other words, this implies that either inflation *or* unemployment can occur, but not both simultaneously.

Keynesians make two important qualifications to this analysis to explain the occurrence of both unemployment *and* inflation at the same time.

First, there are *other* types of inflation and unemployment not caused by an excess or deficiency of aggregate demand: for example, cost-push and expectations-generated inflation; frictional and structural unemployment.

Thus, even if a government could manipulate national income so as to get Y_e and Y_f to coincide, this would not eliminate all inflation and unemployment – only demand-pull inflation and demand-deficient unemployment. Keynesians argue, therefore, that governments should use a whole package of policies, each tailored to the specific type of problem. But certainly one of the most important of these policies will be the management of aggregate demand.

Second, not all firms operate with the same degree of slack. Thus a rise in aggregate demand can lead to *both* a reduction in unemployment *and* a rise in prices: some firms responding to the rise in demand by taking up slack and hence increasing output; other firms, having little or no slack, responding by raising prices; others doing both. Similarly, labour markets have different degrees of slack and therefore the rise in demand will lead to various mixes of higher wages and lower unemployment.

Thus the AS curve will look like AS_2 in Figure 16.17.

> ?? How does the above argument about firms' responses to a rise in demand relate to the shape of their marginal cost curves?

It was these types of argument that were used to justify a belief in a downward-sloping Phillips curve by the majority of economists and politicians in the 1960s and into the 1970s. A modified version of these arguments is still used today by Keynesian economists. This is examined in more detail in Chapter 21.

The problem is that if there is a trade-off between unemployment and inflation, demand management policies used to make one of the objectives better will only succeed in making the other one worse. It then becomes a matter of political judgement as to which of the objectives is the right one to direct demand management policies towards. Is *inflation* public enemy number one, or is it *unemployment*?

The relationship between the *AD*/*AS* diagram and the 45° line diagram

Now that we have introduced the argument that inflation can begin to occur *before* the full-employment level of income is reached, how does this affect the relationship between our two models: the *AD*/*AS* model and the 45° line model? This is examined in Figure 16.18. Initial equilibrium is at Y_{e_1} in both parts of the diagram, where $AD_1 = AS$ and where E_1 crosses the 45° line.

Now let us assume that there is a rise in aggregate demand. The E line shifts initially to E_2 in diagram (b). If this rise in demand were to lead to a full multiplied rise in real income, equilibrium income would rise to Y_{e_2}. But we are now assuming that inflation can occur *before* the full-employment level of income is reached. In other words, we are assuming that the AS curve is upward sloping (not horizontal as it was in Figure 16.14).

In diagram (a) the rise in aggregate demand has shifted the AD curve from AD_1 to AD_2. Part of this increase in demand is reflected in higher prices – the price level rises to P_2 – and only *part* is reflected in higher output. Equilibrium real income therefore rises only to Y_{e_3} and not Y_{e_2}.

In diagram (b) the effect of the higher prices is to reduce the real value of expenditure (E). In other words, a given amount of money buys fewer goods. If there is no compensating increase in money supply by the government (which would shift the AD curve further to the right in diagram (a)), the E line must fall to the point where it

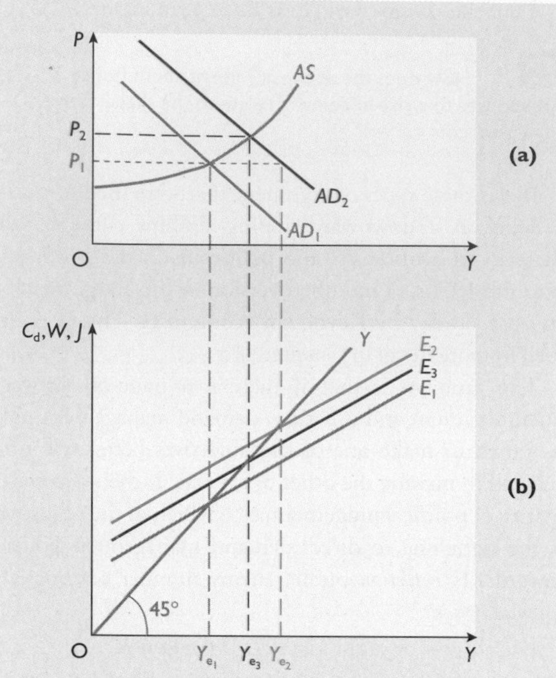

Figure 16.18 Allowing for inflation in the 45° line and AD/AS diagrams

intersects the 45° line at a real income of Y_{e_3}: the E line must fall to E_3.

What is the mechanism that drives down the expenditure function from E_2 to E_3?

- The shortage of money drives up interest rates. This will reduce investment and encourage savings.
- Higher prices will reduce the real value of people's savings. They may therefore save more to compensate for this.
- Higher prices of domestic goods will reduce exports and increase imports.
- Given the progressive nature of the tax system, higher money incomes will lead to increased taxes.
- Inflation is likely to redistribute income from the poor to the rich, who have a higher *mps*.

?? If money supply *did* increase sufficiently for the E line to remain at E_2, what would be the position of the new *AD* curve?

SECTION SUMMARY

1. If equilibrium national income (Y_e) is below the full-employment level of national income (Y_f), there will be a deflationary gap. This gap is equal to $Y - E$ or $W - J$ at Y_f. This gap can be closed by reflationary fiscal or monetary policy, which will then cause a multiplied rise in national income (up to a level of Y_f) and will eliminate demand-deficient unemployment.
2. If equilibrium national income exceeds the full-employment level of income, the inability of output to expand to meet this excess demand will lead to demand-pull inflation. This excess demand gives an inflationary gap, which is equal to $E - Y$ or $J - W$ at Y_f. This gap can be closed by deflationary policies.
3. This simple analysis tends to imply that the *AS* curve will be horizontal up to Y_f and then vertical. If allowance is made for other types of inflation and unemployment, the *AS* curve will be upward sloping but getting steeper as full employment is approached and as bottlenecks increasingly occur.
4. An initial rise in aggregate demand (and an upward shift in the *E* curve) will be eroded to the extent that inflation reduces the real value of this demand: the *E* curve will shift back downwards again somewhat, unless there is a further boost to demand.

16.4 The Keynesian analysis of the business cycle

Keynesians blame fluctuations in output and employment on fluctuations in aggregate demand. Theirs is therefore a 'demand-side' explanation of the business cycle. In the upturn (phase 1), aggregate demand starts to rise. It rises rapidly in the expansionary phase (phase 2). It then slows down and may start to fall in the peaking-out phase (phase 3). It then falls or remains relatively stagnant in the recession (phase 4) (see Figure 13.2 on page 403).

Keynesians seek to explain why aggregate demand fluctuates, and then to devise appropriate stabilisation policies to iron out these fluctuations. A more stable economy, they argue, will provide a better climate for investment.

With more investment, *potential* output will grow more rapidly. This, given appropriate demand management policy, will then allow a faster growth in actual output to be maintained.

A demand-side theory of the business cycle must explain the following:

- Why does aggregate demand *continue* to rise (or fall) once it has started to rise (or fall)?
- Why does a boom break or a recession end? In other words, why does aggregate demand stop moving in one direction and start moving in the other?
- What determines the length of each phase? Why do some recessions last several years, whereas others last only a few weeks?
- What determines the magnitude of each phase? Why are some recessions really severe, whereas others are merely 'pauses' before rapid growth resumes?

A comprehensive theory will seek to answer all these questions. Here we will simply identify the range of possible causes and show how they can contribute to the instability of aggregate demand.

Instability of investment: the accelerator

One of the major factors contributing to the ups and downs of the business cycle is the instability of investment.

When an economy begins to recover from a slump, investment can rise very rapidly. When the growth of the economy slows down, however, investment can fall dramatically, and during a recession it can all but disappear. Since investment is an injection into the circular flow of income, these changes in investment will cause multiplied changes in income and thus heighten a boom or deepen a recession.

The theory that relates investment to *changes* in national income is called the **accelerator theory**. The term 'accelerator' is used because a relatively modest rise in national income can cause a much larger percentage rise in investment.

When there is no change in income and hence no change in consumption, the only investment needed is a relatively small amount of replacement investment for machines that are wearing out or have become obsolete. When income and consumption increase, however, there will have to be *new* investment in order to increase production capacity. This is called **induced investment** (I_i). Once this has taken place, investment will fall back to mere replacement investment (I_r) unless there is a further rise in income and consumption.

Thus induced investment depends on *changes* in income (ΔY):

$$I_i = \alpha\Delta Y$$

where α is the amount by which induced investment depends on changes in national income. α is known as the **accelerator coefficient**. Thus if a £1 million *rise* in national income caused the *level* of induced investment to be £2 million, the accelerator coefficient would be 2.

The size of α will depend on the economy's **marginal capital/output ratio** ($\Delta K/\Delta Y$). This is the cost of extra capital required to produce a £1 increase in national output. Thus if an increase in the country's capital stock of £2 million (i.e. an investment of £2 million) is required to produce £1 million extra national output, the marginal capital/output ratio would be 2. Other things being equal, the accelerator coefficient and the marginal capital/output ratio will therefore be the same.

?? How is it that the cost of an investment to a firm will exceed the value of the output that the investment will yield? Surely that would make the investment unprofitable? (Clue: the increase in output refers to output over a specific time period, usually a year.)

The following example (see Table 16.4) illustrates some important features of the accelerator. It looks at the investment decisions made by a firm in response to changes in the demand for its product. The firm is taken as representative of firms throughout the economy. The example is based on various assumptions:

- The firm's machines last exactly 10 years and then need replacing.
- At the start of the example, the firm has 10 machines in place, one 10 years old, one 9 years old, one 8 years old, one 7, one 6 and so on. Thus one machine needs replacing each year.

DEFINITIONS

Accelerator theory The *level* of investment depends on the *rate of change* of national income, and as result tends to be subject to substantial fluctuations.

Induced investment Investment that firms make to enable them to meet extra consumer demand.

Accelerator coefficient The level of induced investment as a proportion of a rise in national income: $\alpha = I_i/\Delta Y$.

Marginal capital/output ratio The amount of extra capital (in money terms) required to produce a £1 increase in national output. Since $I_i = \Delta K$, the marginal capital/output ratio $\Delta K/\Delta Y$ equals the accelerator coefficient (α).

Table 16.4 The accelerator effect

	Year						
	0	1	2	3	4	5	6
Quantity demanded by consumers (sales)	1000	1000	2000	3000	3500	3500	3400
Number of machines required	10	10	20	30	35	35	34
Induced investment (I_i) (extra machines)		0	10	10	5	0	0
Replacement investment (I_r)		1	1	1	1	1	0
Total investment ($I_i + I_r$)		1	11	11	6	1	0

- Machines produce exactly 100 units of output per year. This figure cannot be varied.
- The firm always adjusts its output and its stock of machinery to match consumer demand.

The example shows what happens to the firm's investment over a six-year period when there is first a substantial rise in consumer demand, then a levelling off and then a slight fall. In year 2 consumer demand shoots up from 1000 units to 2000 units. In year 3 it goes up by a further 1000 units to 3000 units. In year 4 the rise begins to slow down: demand goes up by 500 units to 3500 units. In year 5 demand is constant at 3500 units. In year 6 it falls slightly to 3400 units. This example illustrates the following features of the accelerator.

Investment will rise when the growth of national income (and hence consumer demand) is rising ($\Delta Y_{t+1} > \Delta Y_t$). The rise in consumer demand is zero in year 1 and 1000 units in year 2. Investment rises from 1 to 11 machines. The growth in investment may be considerably greater than the growth in consumer demand, giving a large accelerator effect. Between years 1 and 2, consumer demand doubles but investment goes up by a massive *eleven* times!

Investment will be constant even when national income is growing, if the increase in income this year is the same as last year ($\Delta Y_{t+1} = \Delta Y_t$). In years 2 to 3, consumer demand continues to rise by 1000 units, but investment is constant at 11 machines.

Investment will fall even if national income is still growing, if the rate of growth is slowing down ($\Delta Y_{t+1} < \Delta Y_t$). In years 3 to 4, consumer demand rises by 500 units (rather than the 1000 units last year). Investment falls from 11 to 6 machines.

If national income is constant, investment will be confined to replacement investment only. In years 4 to 5, investment falls to the one machine requiring replacement.

If national income falls, even if only slightly, investment can be wiped out altogether. In years 5 to 6, even though demand has only fallen by 1/35, investment will fall to zero. Not even the machine that is wearing out will be replaced.

In practice the accelerator will not be as dramatic and clear cut as this. The effect will be extremely difficult to predict for the following reasons:

- Many firms may have spare capacity and/or carry stocks. This will enable them to meet extra demand without having to invest.
- The willingness of firms to invest will depend on their confidence in *future* demand. Firms are not going to rush out and spend large amounts of money on machines that will last many years if it is quite likely that next year demand will fall back again.
- Firms may make their investment plans a long time in advance and may be unable to change them quickly.
- Even if firms do decide to invest more, the producer goods industries may not have the capacity to meet a sudden surge in demand for machines.
- Machines do not as a rule suddenly wear out. A firm could thus delay replacing machines and keep the old ones for a bit longer if it was uncertain about its future level of demand.

All these points tend to reduce the magnitude of the accelerator and to make it very difficult to predict. Nevertheless the effect still exists. Firms still take note of changes in consumer demand when deciding how much to invest.

Box 16.9 shows how, from 1978 to 1996, fluctuations in investment were far more severe than fluctuations in national income. This tends to suggest that there was a substantial accelerator effect operating during the period.

The multiplier/accelerator interaction

If there is an initial change in injections or withdrawals, then theoretically this will set off a chain reaction between

CASE STUDIES BOX 16.9

HAS THERE BEEN AN ACCELERATOR EFFECT SINCE 1978?

Investment is highly volatile. It is subject to far more violent swings than national income. If we look at the period from 1978 to 1998, the maximum annual rise in GDP was 5.6 per cent and the maximum fall was 3.8 per cent. By contrast, the maximum annual rise in investment was 19.4 per cent and the maximum fall was 11.7 per cent.

If we focus on *manufacturing* investment, the swings were even greater. The maximum annual rise in manufacturing investment in plant and machinery was 20 per cent and the maximum fall was 28 per cent, and in new buildings and works the maximum annual rise was a massive 59 per cent and the maximum fall was 39 per cent.

These figures are consistent with the accelerator theory, which argues that the *level* of investment depends on the *rate of change* of national income. A relatively small percentage change in national income can give a much bigger percentage change in investment. The graph shows this pattern from 1978 to 1998.

The ups and downs in GDP and investment do not completely match because there are additional factors that determine investment other than simple changes in national income. These factors include interest rates, exchange rates and business expectations of future demand.

??

1. Can you identify any time lags in the graph? Why might there be time lags?
2. Why does investment in construction and producer goods industries tend to fluctuate more than investment in retailing and the service industries?

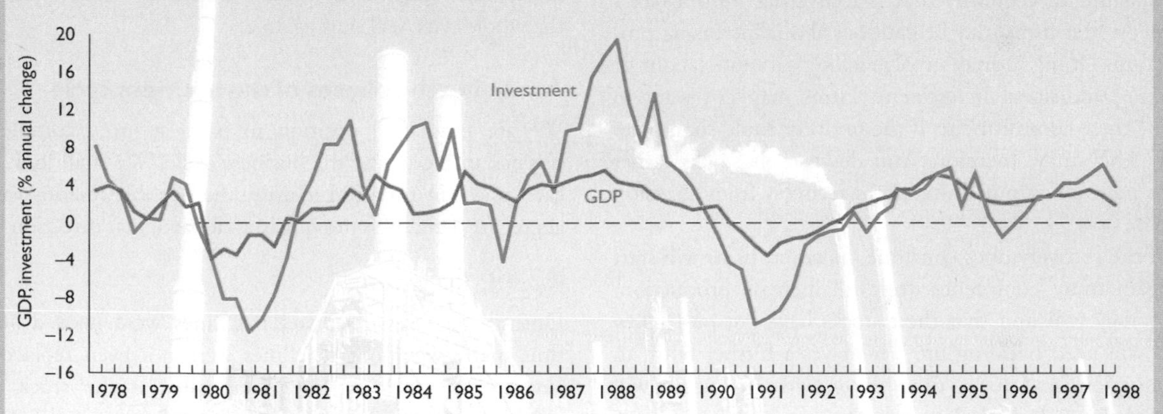

Fluctuations in real GDP and investment: 1978–98

Source: *Economic Trends* (ONS, various issues)

the multiplier and accelerator. For example, if there is a rise in government expenditure, this will lead to a multiplied rise in national income. But this *rise* in national income will set off an accelerator effect: firms will respond to the rise in income and the resulting rise in consumer demand by investing more. But this rise in investment constitutes a further rise in injections and thus will lead to a second multiplied rise in income. If this rise in income is larger than the first, there will then be a second rise in investment (the accelerator), which in turn will cause a third rise in income (the multiplier). And so the process continues indefinitely.

But does this lead to an exploding rise in national income? Will a single injection cause national income to go on rising for ever? The answer is no, for two reasons. The first is that national income, in real terms, cannot go on rising faster than the growth in potential output. It will bump up against the ceiling of full employment, whether of labour or of other resources.

A second reason is that, if investment is to go on rising, it is not enough that national income should merely go on *rising*: instead, national income must *rise faster and faster*. Once the growth in national income slows down, investment will begin to fall, and then the whole process will be reversed. A fall in investment will lead to a fall in national income, which will lead to a massive fall in investment. The multiplier/accelerator interaction is shown more formally in Table 16.5.

Table 16.5 The multiplier/accelerator interaction

Period t	$J\uparrow \rightarrow Y\uparrow$	(Multiplier)
Period $t+1$	$Y\uparrow \rightarrow I\uparrow$	(Accelerator)
	$I\uparrow \rightarrow Y\uparrow$	(Multiplier)
Period $t+2$	If $\uparrow Y_{t+1} > \uparrow Y_t$ then $I\uparrow$ If $\uparrow Y_{t+1} = \uparrow Y_t$ then I stays the same If $\uparrow Y_{t+1} < \uparrow Y_t$ then $I\downarrow$ This in turn will have a multiplied upward effect, no effect, or a multiplied downward effect respectively on national income.	} (Accelerator)
Period $t+3$	This will then lead to a further accelerator effect and so on . . .	

Fluctuations in stocks

Firms hold stocks of finished goods. These stocks tend to fluctuate with the course of the business cycle, and these fluctuations in stocks themselves contribute to fluctuations in output.

Imagine an economy that is recovering from a recession. At first firms may be cautious about increasing production. Doing so may involve taking on more labour or making additional investment. Firms may not want to make these commitments if the recovery could soon peter out. They may, therefore, run down their stocks rather than increase output. Initially the recovery from recession will be slow.

If the recovery does continue, however, firms will start to gain more confidence and will increase production. Also they will find that their stocks have got rather low and will need building up. This gives a further boost to production, and for a time the growth in output will exceed the growth in demand. This extra growth in output will then, via the multiplier, lead to a further increase in demand.

Once stocks have been built up again, the growth in output will slow down to match the growth in demand. This slowing down in output will, via the accelerator and multiplier, contribute to the ending of the expansionary phase of the business cycle.

As the economy slows down, retailers will find themselves with unsold goods on their shelves. They will thus order less from the wholesalers, who in turn will order less from the manufacturers, who, unless they cut back production immediately, will find their stocks building up too. This increase in stocks cushions the effect of falling demand on output and employment.

If the recession continues, however, firms will be unwilling to go on building up stocks. But as firms attempt to reduce their stocks back to the desired level, production will fall *below* the level of sales, despite the fact that sales themselves are lower. This could lead to a dramatic fall in output and, via the multiplier, to an even bigger fall in sales.

Eventually, once stocks have been run down to the minimum, production will have to rise again to match the level of sales. This will contribute to a recovery and the whole cycle will start again.

Analysing the phases of the business cycle

We are now in a position to paint a more complete Keynesian picture of the business cycle. We shall look at each phase in turn and identify the possible reasons why aggregate demand is moving in that particular direction.

Phase 1: The upturn

During the recession fewer machines were needed and thus many worn-out machines were not even replaced. Investment was very low. Gradually, as the stock of machines is reduced, replacement investment re-emerges. This can be more dramatic if many machines were purchased during the previous expansionary phase and now need replacing. This is an 'echo' effect of the previous expansion. $I\uparrow \rightarrow AD\uparrow$

Consumer durables (cars, televisions, washing machines, etc.) that were bought in the previous period of expansion will start needing to be replaced. This is another echo effect. $C_d\uparrow \rightarrow AD\uparrow$

Firms during the recession initially found that their stocks of finished goods increased as sales fell. They therefore cut back on production while drawing on these surplus stocks. Once stocks are back down to the desirable level again, production will increase. $AD\uparrow$

As the rate of inflation falls during the recession, and there may be a time lag before this occurs, so exports should rise as they become relatively less expensive for foreigners to buy. At the same time imports should fall as home-produced substitutes become relatively cheaper.

However, consumers may be slow to respond to changing relative prices. The effects on aggregate demand may therefore become significant only after the recession has continued for some time. $X\uparrow, M\downarrow \rightarrow AD\uparrow$

Eventually, people may begin to believe that a recovery will soon be on the way. The experience of previous cycles shows that recessions have never lasted for ever. Anticipation of recovery may encourage firms to start investing again and consumers to start buying more durables. $I\uparrow, C_d\uparrow \rightarrow AD\uparrow$

Consumption and investment are low during the recession. Borrowing from banks is therefore likely to be low. Banks will thus have surplus funds and interest rates (r) will be low. This stimulates borrowing, especially if people begin to anticipate recovery. $r\downarrow \rightarrow C_d\uparrow, I\uparrow \rightarrow AD\uparrow$

As the balance of payments improves during the recession and the rate of inflation falls, the government may adopt reflationary fiscal and/or monetary policy to tackle the growing unemployment and falling or stagnant output. It will therefore use some combination of lower taxes, higher government expenditure and lower interest rates. $T\downarrow, G\uparrow, r\downarrow \rightarrow AD\uparrow$

Firms and consumers may anticipate such government policy and spend more even before the measures are announced. $I\uparrow, C_d\uparrow \rightarrow AD\uparrow$

Random events may stimulate demand: for example, the settling of a major international dispute or a fall in the world oil price. These 'random shocks' can occur at any point in the business cycle, and if large enough can have a significant effect on its course.

Phase 2: The expansion

Most of the factors that caused the recovery are likely to go on stimulating the economy for some time. Initial increases in aggregate demand will cause a *multiplied* rise in income and hence demand. Rises in income will lead, via the *accelerator*, to increases in investment. This accelerator effect will be large at first, given that there had been little or no rise in consumer demand during the recession. The multiplier and accelerator will interact.

Firms, finding that stocks are beginning to run low, will increase production not only to meet extra sales but also to rebuild stocks. People begin to anticipate rising prices. Thus both firms and consumers stock up now while prices are still relatively low. Firms anticipate further rises in demand and hence invest now in both capital and stock.

Phase 3: The peaking out

Many firms reach capacity and hence cannot increase output further. The consumer spending boom levels out. People have now purchased all the consumer durables they can currently afford. $C_d\downarrow \rightarrow AD\downarrow$

According to the accelerator theory, a levelling-out of consumption will lead to a fall in investment. Firms anticipate the impending recession and invest less. $I\downarrow \rightarrow AD\downarrow$

The growing demand for bank loans during the period of expansion has driven up interest rates. This will help to curtail further growth in consumption and investment. $r\uparrow \rightarrow C_d\downarrow, I\downarrow \rightarrow AD\downarrow$

Inflation has been rising during the latter part of the expansionary phase. The government is likely to take counter-inflationary measures, involving some combination of lower government expenditure, higher taxes or higher interest rates. $G\downarrow, T\uparrow \rightarrow AD\downarrow; r\uparrow \rightarrow C_d\downarrow, I\downarrow \rightarrow AD\downarrow$

Higher inflation makes exports less competitive abroad and imports relatively cheaper than home-produced goods. Exports thus fall and imports rise. $X\downarrow, M\uparrow \rightarrow AD\downarrow$

Various random shocks may bring a boom to an abrupt end: e.g. a war, a sudden oil price rise or a stock market crash.

Phase 4: The recession

Many of the factors that led to a downturn in aggregate demand in the previous phase are still operative. Some work with a time lag and their effect is still building up.

Business prospects are poor. Confidence is low. Investment remains very low. The effects on the capital goods industries may thus be very severe. Firms, finding their stocks of unsold goods rising, cut back on production. They may even attempt to reduce stocks to the bare minimum in order to save costs. In such cases the cuts in production may be very large indeed. If aggregate demand actually falls (as opposed to merely being stagnant), there will be a resulting multiplied fall in income.

The government may be unwilling to stimulate the economy as long as the inflation rate remains high and/or the balance of payments current account remains in deficit.

Conclusions

Let us return to two of the questions we posed at the beginning of this section.

Why do booms and recessions last for several months or even years?

Time lags. It takes time for changes in injections and withdrawals to be fully reflected in changes in national income, output and employment. The multiplier process takes time. Moreover, consumers, firms and government may not all respond immediately to new situations.

'Bandwagon' effects. Once the economy starts expanding, expectations become buoyant. People think ahead and adjust their expenditure behaviour: they consume and invest more *now*. Likewise in a recession a mood of pessimism may set in. The effect is cumulative. The multiplier and accelerator interact: they feed on each other.

Why do booms and recessions come to an end? What determines the turning points?

Ceilings and floors. Actual output can go on growing more rapidly than potential output only as long as there is slack in the economy. As full employment is approached and as more and more firms reach full capacity, so a ceiling to output will be reached.

There is a basic minimum level of consumption that people will maintain. During a recession people may not buy many luxury and durable goods, but they will continue to buy food and other basic goods. There is thus a floor to consumption.

The industries supplying these basic goods will need to maintain their level of replacement investment. Also there will always be some minimum investment demand as firms feel the need to install the latest equipment. There is thus a floor to investment too.

Echo effects. Durable consumer goods and capital equipment may last several years, but eventually they will need replacing. The replacement of goods and capital purchased in a previous boom may help to bring a recession to an end.

The accelerator. For investment to continue rising, consumer demand must rise at a *faster and faster* rate. If this does not happen, investment will fall back and the boom will break.

Random shocks. National or international political, social or natural events can affect the mood and attitudes of firms, governments and consumers, and thus affect aggregate demand.

Changes in government policy. In a boom, a government may become most worried by inflation and balance of payments deficits and thus pursue deflationary policies. In a recession, it may become most worried by unemployment and lack of growth and thus pursue reflationary policies. These government policies, if successful, will bring about a turning point in the cycle.

Keynesians argue that governments should attempt to reduce cyclical fluctuations by using active stabilisation policies. A more stable economy will encourage investment and allow a faster growth in output to be maintained. The policy most favoured by Keynesians is *fiscal policy*. This is the subject of Chapter 17.

SECTION SUMMARY

1. Keynesians explain cyclical fluctuations in the economy by examining the causes of fluctuations in the level of *demand*.
2. A major part of the Keynesian explanation of the business cycle is the instability of investment. The accelerator theory explains this instability. It relates the level of investment to *changes* in national income and consumer demand. An initial increase in consumer demand can result in a very large percentage increase in investment; but as soon as the rise in consumer demand begins to level off investment will fall; and even a slight fall in consumer demand can reduce investment to virtually zero.
3. The accelerator effect will be dampened by the carrying of stocks, the cautiousness of firms, forward planning by firms and the inability of producer goods industries to supply the capital equipment.
4. The interaction of the multiplier and accelerator will cause cycles.
5. Keynesians identify other causes of cyclical fluctuations, such as cycles in the holding of stocks, time lags, 'bandwagon' effects, ceilings and floors to output, echo effects, swings in government policy and random shocks.

??? END-OF-CHAPTER QUESTIONS ???

1. An economy is currently in equilibrium. The following figures refer to elements in its national income accounts.

	£ billions
Consumption (total)	60
Investment	5
Government expenditure	8
Imports	10
Exports	7

   (a) What is the current equilibrium level of national income?

   (b) What is the level of injections?

   (c) What is the level of withdrawals?

   (d) Assuming that tax revenues are £7 billion, how much is the level of saving?

   (e) If national income now rose to £80 billion and, as a result, the consumption of domestically produced goods rose to £58 billion, what is the mpc_d?

   (f) What is the value of the multiplier?

   (g) Given an initial level of national income of £80 billion, now assume that spending on exports rises by £4 billion, spending on investment rises by £1 billion, whilst government expenditure falls by £2 billion. By how much will national income change?

   (h) Given this new level of national income, assume that full employment is achieved at a national income of £100 billion. Is there an inflationary or a deflationary gap?

   (i) What is the size of this gap?

2. What is the relationship between the *mpc*, the mpc_d and the *mpw*?

3. Why will the short-run consumption function be different from the long-run consumption function?

4. Construct a table similar to Table 16.2 (on page 510), only this time assume that the mpc_d is 3/4. Show that national income will increase by £640 million.

5. Assume that the multiplier has a value of 3. Now assume that the government decides to increase aggregate demand in an attempt to reduce unemployment. It raises government expenditure by £100 million with no increase in taxes. Firms, anticipating a rise in their sales, increase investment by £200 million, of which £50 million consists of purchases of foreign machinery. How much will national income rise? (Assume *ceteris paribus*.)

6. What factors could explain why some countries have a higher multiplier than others?

7. How can the interaction of the multiplier and accelerator explain cyclical fluctuations in national income?

8. Why is it difficult to predict the size of the accelerator?

17 Fiscal policy

17.1 The nature of fiscal policy

For most of the 1950s and 1960s fiscal policy was seen as the major way of controlling the economy. It was seen to have two main roles. The first was to remove any severe deflationary or inflationary gaps. In other words, expansionary fiscal policy could be used to prevent a recurrence of the mass unemployment that was experienced between the wars, and deflationary fiscal policy could be used to prevent rampant inflation. This first role was to prevent the occurrence of *fundamental* disequilibrium in the economy. Keynesian economists today still argue that fiscal policy has this role.

The second role was to smooth out the fluctuations in the economy associated with the business cycle. This would involve reducing government expenditure or raising taxes during phase 2 of the cycle. This would dampen down the expansion and prevent 'overheating' of the economy with its attendant rising inflation and deteriorating balance of payments. Conversely, during phase 4, as the problems of unemployment and low or negative growth get worse, the government should cut taxes or raise government expenditure in order to boost the economy. If these stabilisation policies are successful, they will amount merely to **fine tuning**. Problems of excess or deficient demand will never be allowed to get severe. Any movement of aggregate demand away from a steady growth path would be immediately 'nipped in the bud'. Virtually no economist argued then or now that perfect fine tuning is possible. There will always be some fluctuations in aggregate demand. Nevertheless many Keynesians argue that the careful use of fiscal policy can make the economy much *more* stable than it would otherwise be.

Government finances: some terminology

Budget deficits and surpluses

An expansionary fiscal policy will involve raising government expenditure and/or lowering taxes. This will have the effect of either increasing the budget deficit or reducing the budget surplus. A **budget deficit** in any one year is where central government's expenditure (both on goods and services and on transfer payments) exceeds its revenue from taxation. A **budget surplus** is where tax revenues exceed central government expenditure.

With the exception of short periods in 1969–70 and 1987–90, governments in the UK, like most governments round the world, have run budget deficits.

Financing a deficit

If the government spends more than it receives in taxes, how is it to finance this deficit? The answer is that it will have to borrow the money. It can do this either by borrowing from the Bank of England, or by issuing National Savings certificates or by selling government securities. There are two types of government security: Treasury bills and government bonds. Treasury bills are short-term loans to the government (three months). Bonds are long-term loans (several years). At the end of the loan period, the government redeems the securities at their face value.

DEFINITIONS

Fine tuning The use of demand management policy (fiscal or monetary) to smooth out cyclical fluctuations in the economy.

Budget deficit The excess of central government's spending over its tax receipts.

Budget surplus The excess of central government's tax receipts over its spending.

Table 17.1 UK public-sector deficits/surpluses: 1968–97

Year	1968	1969	1970	1971	1972	1973	1974	1975	1976	1977
PSBR (£m)	1252			1320	1950	4093	6452	10 161	9000	5466
PSDR (£m)		534	51							
% of GDP	–3.3	+1.3	+0.1	–2.6	–3.4	–6.2	–8.6	–10.7	–8.0	–4.2
Year	1978	1979	1980	1981	1982	1983	1984	1985	1986	1987
PSBR (£m)	8195	12 551	11 786	10 507	4880	11 605	10 281	7476	2418	
PSDR (£m)										1432
% of GDP	–5.5	–7.3	–5.9	–4.8	–2.1	–4.5	–3.7	–2.4	–0.7	+0.4
Year	1988	1989	1990	1991	1992	1993	1994	1995	1996	1997
PSBR (£m)				7661	28 664	42 503	37 891	35 120	25 010	12 454
PSDR (£m)	11 611	9276	2125							
% of GDP	+2.9	+2.1	+0.4	–1.5	–5.5	–7.8	–6.5	–5.8	–3.9	–1.8

Source: *Economic Trends* (ONS).

To persuade people to buy these securities the government has to pay interest or, what amounts to the same thing, sell them below their redemption value.

Details of the two types of security and how their rates of interest are determined are given in Chapters 18 and 19, but for now we will simply observe that, if the government wants to sell more of these securities, it will have to sell them at a lower price or offer a higher rate of interest.

The national debt

The budget deficit refers to the debt that the government incurs in one year. If the government runs persistent deficits over many years, these debts will accumulate. The accumulated debt is known as the **national debt**. Note that the national debt is *not* the same thing as the country's overseas debt. Only a relatively small fraction of the UK national debt is owed overseas. The bulk of it is owed to UK citizens. In other words, the government finances its budget deficits largely by borrowing at home and not from abroad.

The PSBR and PSDR

So far we have looked at merely the *central* government deficit or surplus. To get a more complete view of the overall 'stance' of fiscal policy – just how expansionary or contractionary it is – we would need to look at the deficit or surplus of the entire public sector: namely, central government, local government and public corporations. If the public sector spends more than it earns (through taxes and the revenues of public corporations, etc.), the amount of this deficit is known as the **public-sector borrowing requirement (PSBR)**. It is defined as public-sector expenditure minus public-sector receipts.

The reason for the name 'public-sector borrowing requirement' is simple. If the public sector runs a deficit in the current year of, say, £1 billion, then it will have to borrow £1 billion this year in order to finance it.

If the public sector runs a surplus, it will be able to repay some of the public-sector debts that have accumulated from previous years. In 1987, when for the first time since 1970 the UK ran a public-sector surplus, this was given the name **public-sector debt repayment (PSDR)** by the then Chancellor, Nigel Lawson. His hope was that over the years these surpluses would allow the whole of the national debt to be paid off. But with the public-sector finances diving into deficit again after 1990 such a hope was dashed. Table 17.1 shows the PSBR/PSDR from 1968 to 1997.

The public-sector debt

Just as the national debt was the total outstanding debt of central government, so the public-sector debt is the total outstanding debt of the entire public sector. Table 17.2 shows the level of UK public-sector debt since 1977. As

DEFINITIONS

National debt The accumulated budget deficits (less surpluses) over the years: the total amount of government borrowing.

Public-sector borrowing requirement (PSBR) The (annual) deficit of the public sector (central government, local government and public corporations), and thus the amount that the public sector must borrow.

Public-sector debt repayment (PSDR) The (annual) surplus of the public sector, and thus the amount of debt that can be repaid.

Table 17.2 UK national and public-sector debt

Year	National debt (£m)	Public-sector debt (£m)	Public-sector debt as a percentage of GDP	Public-sector debt held overseas as a percentage of GDP
1977	52 748	88 287	60.5	9.4
1982	104 108	147 161	52.7	6.0
1987	169 341	204 094	48.2	6.2
1990	160 407	189 470	36.0	5.6
1994	274 653	306 665	47.9	9.3
1997	369 332	400 962	53.3	8.1

Source: *Financial Statistics* (ONS).

can be seen from the figures, although the total debt increased up until 1987 (due to persistent annual deficits) the size of the debt as a proportion of national income fell. Then with the public sector running a surplus between 1987 and 1990, the total level of public-sector debt fell. Since 1991, however, with the public sector moving sharply back into deficit, the public-sector debt has risen again, both absolutely and as a percentage of GDP.

Note from the table the relatively small proportion of UK public-sector debt owed abroad.

General government

A final category is 'general government'. This includes central and local government, but excludes public corporations. Thus we can refer to **general government deficits and surpluses** and **general government debt**. Table 17.3 shows average government deficits/surpluses and debt for selected countries for the years 1987 to 1996. They are expressed as a proportion of GDP. As you can see, all of them except Japan have experienced deficits.

Public-sector deficits and surpluses and the government's 'fiscal stance'

The government's **fiscal stance** refers to whether it is pursuing an expansionary or contractionary fiscal policy. Does the fact that there was a public-sector deficit right from 1971 to 1986 mean that the government's fiscal stance was reflationary throughout this period? Would the mere existence of a *surplus* mean that the stance was deflationary? The answer is no.

Table 17.3 General government deficits/surpluses and debt as percentage of GDP

Country	General government deficits (–) / surpluses (+) Average annual 1987–96	General government debt Average 1987–96
Belgium	–5.9	135.3
France	–3.4	47.9
Germany	–2.3	49.6
Italy	–9.6	108.7
Japan	+1.0	76.9
Netherlands	–3.8	77.2
Sweden	–3.1	65.4
UK	–3.1	44.6
USA	–2.5	59.1
OECD	–2.9	64.3

DEFINITIONS

General government deficit (or surplus) The combined deficit (or surplus) of central and local government.

General government debt The combined accumulated debt of central and local government.

Fiscal stance How deflationary or reflationary the Budget is.

What we need to discover is whether the current *size* of the public-sector deficit or surplus is causing aggregate demand to expand or contract (and by how much). This will depend on two things:

- The previous level of the deficit (or surplus). If the deficit this year is lower than last year, then (*ceteris paribus*) aggregate demand will be lower this year than last. The reason is that either government expenditure (an injection) must have fallen, or tax revenues (a withdrawal) must have increased, or a combination of the two.
- Changes in other components of aggregate demand. Government expenditure is only one of the three injections into the circular flow of income. Taxation is only one of three withdrawals. If one of the *other* injections or withdrawals changes, then this will affect the size of the public-sector deficit or surplus required to achieve any given level of national income. For example, if business optimism were low and as a result investment had fallen by £2 million, then even if the level of government expenditure were increased, with a consequent increase in the public-sector deficit, the increase in government expenditure would have to be *more* than £2 million if there were to be an increase in national income.

The mere existence of a deficit or surplus therefore tells us very little about whether the economy will expand or contract.

Another problem is that the size of the deficit or surplus is not entirely due to deliberate government policy. It may not give a very good guide, therefore, to government intentions. The size of the deficit or surplus will depend on the state of the economy. If the economy is booming with people earning high incomes, the amount paid in taxes will be high. In a booming economy the level of unemployment will be low. Thus the amount paid out in unemployment benefits will also be low. The combined effect of increased tax revenues and reduced benefits is to give a public-sector surplus (or a reduced deficit). By contrast, if the economy were depressed, tax revenues would be low and government expenditure on benefits would be high. The public-sector deficit would thus be high.

This relationship between the budget deficit or surplus and the state of the economy is illustrated in Figure 17.1. The tax revenue function is upward sloping. Its slope depends on tax rates. The government expenditure function is drawn as downward sloping, showing that at higher levels of income and employment less is paid out in benefits. As can be clearly seen, there is only one level of income (Y_1) where there is a public-sector financial balance. Below this level of income there will be a public-sector deficit. Above this level there will be a surplus. The further income is from Y_1, the bigger will be the deficit or surplus.

To conclude, the size of the deficit or surplus is a poor guide to the stance of fiscal policy. A large deficit *may* be due to a deliberate policy of reflation, but it may be due simply to the fact that the economy is depressed.

Automatic fiscal stabilisers

We saw from Figure 17.1 that the size of the public-sector surplus or deficit will automatically vary according to the level of national income. The effect of this will be to reduce the level of fluctuations in national income without the government having to take any deliberate action.

Taxes whose revenues rise as national income rises and benefits that fall as national income rises are called **automatic stabilisers**. They have the effect of reducing the size of the multiplier. They therefore reduce both upward movements and downward movements of national income. Thus, in theory, the business cycle should be dampened by such built-in stabilisers. The more taxes rise or benefits fall, the bigger will be the *mpt* (the net marginal tax propensity). Remember that we defined this as the proportion of any rise in income going in taxes and reduced benefits. The bigger the *mpt*, the smaller will be the multiplier and the greater will be the stabilising effect.

Figure 17.2 looks at two economies. Economy 1 has a low marginal rate of net taxation (a low *mpt*). As a result its withdrawals function is relatively gently sloping. Economy 2 has a much higher marginal rate of net tax. Its withdrawals function is relatively steep. As we shall see, taxes and benefits act as a bigger automatic stabiliser in economy 2 than in economy 1.

Assume that the two economies both have the same initial level of injection J_1 and that the withdrawals functions of the two economies both intersect J_1 at an equilibrium national income of Y_0. Now assume that there is an autonomous rise in injections – perhaps the level of business confidence has risen with a corresponding rise in investment. The effect in economy 1 is for national income to rise to Y_1. The relatively shallow W line (i.e. a low *mpw*) gives a large multiplier effect. In economy 2, however, national income only rises to Y_2. The relatively steep W line (i.e. a high *mpw*), caused by a high *mpt*, gives a smaller multiplier effect.

DEFINITION

Automatic fiscal stabilisers Tax revenues that rise and government expenditure that falls as national income rises. The more they change with income, the bigger the stabilising effect on national income.

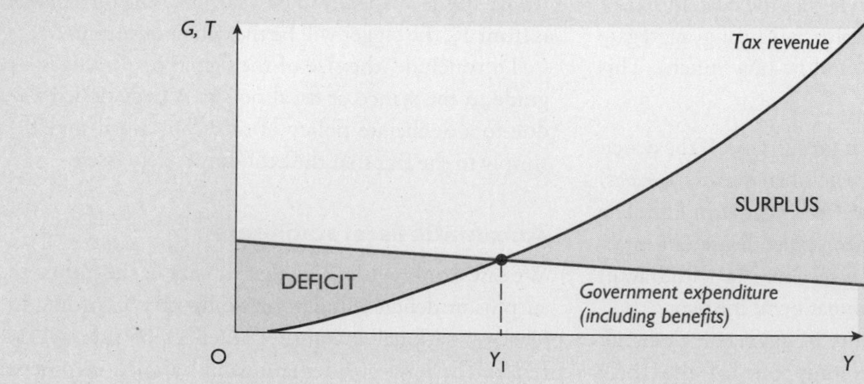

Figure 17.1 National income and the size of the public-sector deficit or surplus

To summarise: the higher the *mpt*, the higher the *mpw* and hence the smaller the multiplier, and hence the bigger the stabilising effect of the taxes and benefits.

> **??** The withdrawals functions in Figure 17.2 were based on the assumption that the marginal rate of tax, although higher in economy 2, was nevertheless constant in each case. Redraw the diagram, only this time assume that the marginal rate of tax in economy 2 increases. How will this affect the stabilising properties of the tax?

Discretionary fiscal policy

Automatic stabilisers cannot prevent fluctuations. They merely reduce their magnitude. If there is a fundamental disequilibrium in the economy or substantial fluctuations in other injections and withdrawals, the government may choose to *alter* the level of government expenditure or the rates of taxation. This is known as **discretionary fiscal policy**. It involves *shifting* the *J* and *W* lines.

In the UK, changes in government expenditure and taxation for the next financial year (April to March) are announced by the Chancellor of the Exchequer in the Budget. Since 1993 this takes place in the late autumn.

In the past, governments sometimes felt it necessary to have more than one Budget a year in order to be able to respond more quickly to changing economic circumstances. These additional Budgets were known as 'mini Budgets'. Nowadays, however, Budgets are held only once a year. 'Fine tuning' aggregate demand on a week-by-week or month by month basis is left to monetary policy – to changes in interest rates (see Chapter 19).

Discretionary changes in taxation or government expenditure, as well as being used to alter the level of aggregate demand, are also used for other purposes, including the following:

- Altering aggregate supply. The tax system may be altered so as to provide more incentives (e.g. by cutting the top rates of income tax). This, it is argued, will encourage more investment, more initiative and more risk taking. Government expenditure may be directed

> **DEFINITION**
>
> **Discretionary fiscal policy** Deliberate changes in tax rates or the level of government expenditure in order to influence the level of aggregate demand.

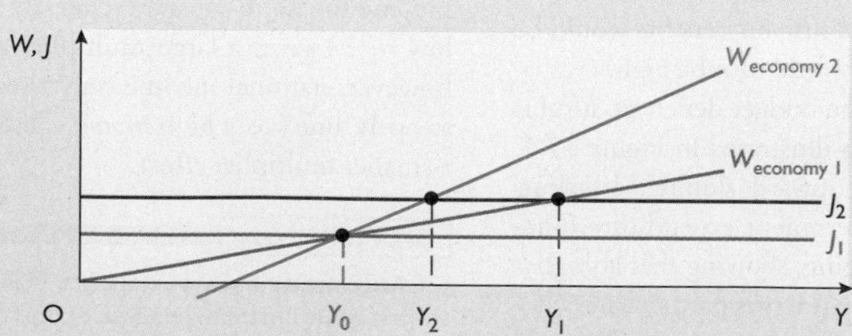

Figure 17.2 Economies with different marginal rates of taxation

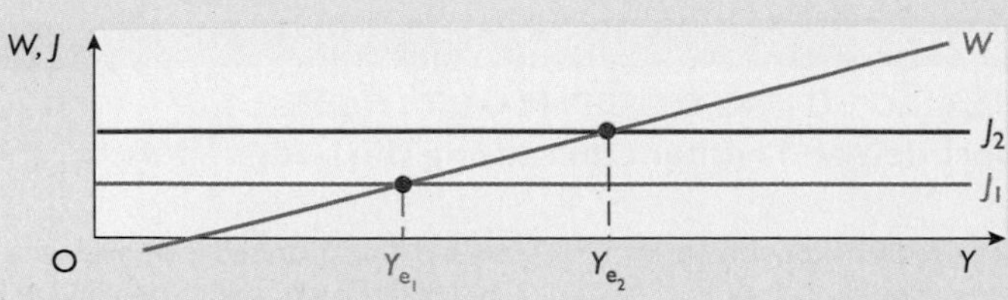

Figure 17.3 A discretionary rise in government expenditure

into building up the infrastructure of the economy (e.g. new roads) or into providing grants for research and development or the training of labour.

- Altering the distribution of income. As Chapter 10 explained, government transfer payments and taxation are major weapons in redistributing incomes from the rich to the poor.
- Altering the degree of state ownership and intervention. For ideological reasons governments may want a larger or smaller amount of state ownership and intervention in industry.

When we refer to 'fiscal policy', however, we are normally referring to the use of government expenditure and taxation specifically to control aggregate demand. Of course, changes in G or T can be made for more than one purpose. For example, if an expansionary fiscal policy were required, taxes could be reduced so as to boost aggregate demand, but at the same time bigger tax cuts could be given to the poor than to the rich so as to redistribute incomes more equally.

Let us now compare the relative effects of changing government expenditure and changing taxes. Will a £1 million increase in government expenditure have the same effect as a £1 million cut in taxes? Will the multiplier be the same in each case?

Discretionary fiscal policy: changing G

If government expenditure on goods and services (roads, health care, education, etc.) is raised, this will create a full multiplied rise in national income. The reason is that all the money gets spent and thus all of it goes to boosting aggregate demand.

Diagrammatically, it has the effect of shifting the J line upward by the full amount of the increase in government expenditure. In Figure 17.3 this is shown as a shift in the J line from J_1 to J_2. This gives a full multiplied rise in income from Y_{e1} to Y_{e2}. The size of the multiplier (as you should know by now!) is given by $1/mpw$.

?? Show the effect of an increase in government expenditure by using the income/expenditure diagram.

Discretionary fiscal policy: changing T

Cutting taxes by £1 million will have a smaller effect on national income than raising government expenditure on goods and services by £1 million. The reason is that cutting taxes increases people's *disposable* incomes, of which only *part* will be spent. Part will be withdrawn into extra savings, imports and other taxes. In other words, not all the tax cuts will be passed on round the circular flow of income as extra expenditure.

The proportion of the cut in taxes that will be withdrawn is given by the mpw, and the proportion that will circulate round the flow is given by the mpc_d. Thus if the mpc_d were 4/5, the tax multiplier would only be 4/5 of the normal multiplier. If the mpc_d were 2/3, the tax multiplier would only be 2/3 of the normal multiplier, and so on. The formula for the tax multiplier (k_t) becomes:[1]

$$k_t = mpc_d \times k$$

Thus if the normal multiplier was 5 (given an mpc_d of 4/5), the tax multiplier would be $4/5 \times 5 = 4$. If the normal multiplier was 4 (given an mpc_d of 3/4), the tax multiplier would be $3/4 \times 4 = 3$, and so on. It should be obvious from this that the tax multiplier is always 1 less than the normal multiplier:

$$k_t = k - 1$$

The effect of cutting taxes is to shift the W line down, but not by the *full* cut in taxes. The fall in withdrawals is given by:[2]

$$\Delta W = \Delta T \times mpc_d$$

For example, if taxes were cut by £100 and the mpc_d was 3/4 and the mpw was 1/4, the consumption of domestic goods would rise by £75 and other withdrawals would rise

[1] Strictly speaking, the tax multiplier is negative, since a *rise* in taxes causes a *fall* in national income.

[2] To be accurate, the cut in taxes (ΔT) should be given as the *gross* income equivalent. Thus if the rate of income tax were cut to 20 per cent, and as a result a person paid £80 less income tax per year, this would be equivalent to a gross income increase of £100: i.e. disposable income would rise by £80. The mpc_d and mpw terms are based on gross income, not disposable income.

CASE STUDIES BOX 17.1

THE BALANCED-BUDGET MULTIPLIER

How to boost demand without increasing the budget deficit

Suppose that the government raised its expenditure by £1 million and at the same time raised taxes by £1 million in order to finance it. What would happen to aggregate demand?

At first sight the answer would seem to be 'nothing'. After all, injections have been raised by £1 million but withdrawals would seem also to have been raised by £1 million.

But this is not so. Although taxes have risen by £1 million, *net* withdrawals have risen by *less* than £1 million. The reason is that part of the extra taxes is met by reductions in savings and imports. Consumption of domestic product therefore does not fall by the full £1 million that government expenditure has risen. There is thus a net boost to the economy given by the amount that the net withdrawals fall short of the increase in government expenditure. This boost will then be multiplied by the size of the full multiplier.

How much will national income rise? The answer is £1 million. In other words, the *balanced-budget multiplier* has a value of 1. But why?

If the *mpw* is 1/5, for example, the full multiplier is 5. If *G* and *T* both rise by £1 million, one-fifth of the rise in taxes will be financed from reduced withdrawals: i.e. £200 000. This boost to demand will then be multiplied by the full multiplier of 5, giving a total rise in income of £200 000 × 5 = £1 million.

Algebraically, the formula for the balanced-budget multiplier (k_b) is:

$$k_b = mpw \times k$$
$$= mpw \times 1/mpw$$
$$= 1$$

Thus it is possible for a government committed to maintaining a balanced budget to boost demand without unbalancing its budget. The problem is that, with such a small multiplier, it would need a much larger increase in *G* and *T* to achieve the same result as by increasing *G* alone.

?? Suppose that the economy is in recession and that the government wishes to maintain a balanced budget and not to increase the size of the public sector. Is it possible for it to use fiscal policy to reflate the economy?

by £25. The *net* fall in withdrawals would thus be £100 – £25 = £75:

$$£75(\Delta W) = £100(\Delta T) \times 3/4(mpc_d)$$

The effect is illustrated in Figures 17.4 and 17.5.

Figure 17.4 shows the effect of a cut in lump-sum taxes (i.e. taxes like the community charge, which do not depend on income). There is a parallel shift downward of the *W* line by an amount $\Delta T \times mpc_d$.

Figure 17.5 shows the effect of a cut in taxes that vary with income (e.g. income tax). If the income tax rate is cut, it will have the effect of making the *W* line less steep. The vertical difference between W_1 and W_2 is still given by the formula $\Delta T \times mpc_d$, only in this case ΔT will vary with the level of income: the higher the level of income, the bigger the absolute cut in tax revenues for a given cut in the tax rate.

The tax multiplier is smaller than the government expenditure multiplier. To achieve a given rise in income through tax cuts would therefore require a bigger budget deficit than if it were achieved through increased government expenditure. In other words, the required tax cut would be bigger than the required government expenditure increase. This poses a dilemma for a government which at one and the

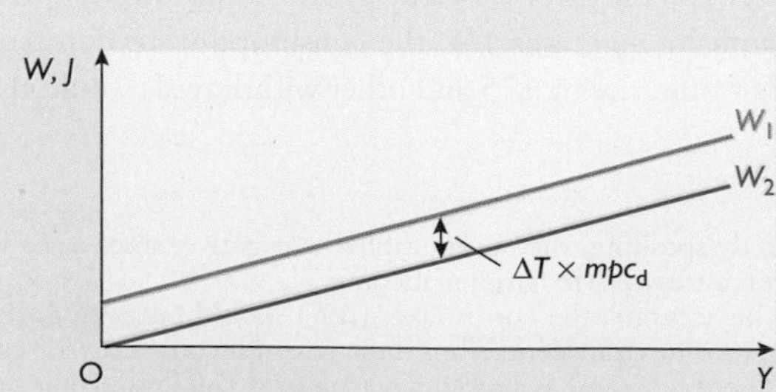

Figure 17.4 A cut in lump-sum taxes

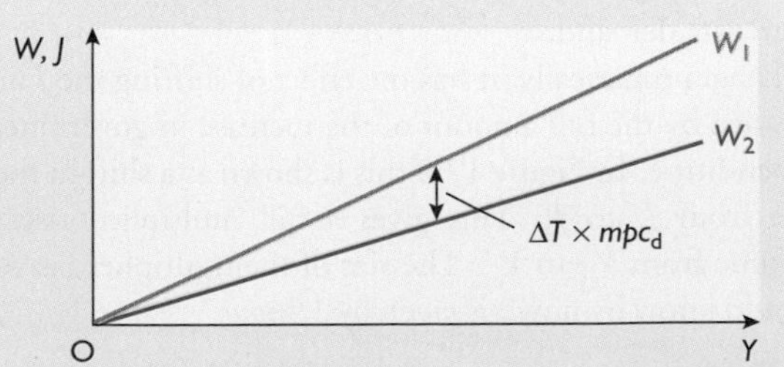

Figure 17.5 A cut in tax rates

same time wants to boost aggregate demand and yet to minimise the size of the budget deficit and the size of the public sector. Wishing to minimise the size of the public sector, it would prefer to achieve the rise in aggregate demand by cutting taxes. But this would require a bigger rise in the budget deficit than if the government had used increased government expenditure instead.

?? Why will the multiplier effect of government transfer payments such as child benefit, pensions and social security be less than the *full* multiplier effect given by government expenditure on goods and services? Will this 'transfer payments multiplier' be the same as the tax multiplier? (Clue: will the recipients of such benefits have the same mpc_d as the average person?)

SECTION SUMMARY

1. The government's fiscal policy will determine the size of the budget deficit or surplus and the size of the PSBR or PSDR. The size of these alone, however, is a poor guide to the government's fiscal stance. A large deficit, for example, may simply be due to the fact that the economy is in recession and therefore tax receipts are low. A better guide is whether the change in the deficit or surplus will be reflationary or deflationary.
2. Automatic fiscal stabilisers are tax revenues that rise and benefits that fall as national income rises. They have the effect of reducing the size of the multiplier and thus reducing cyclical upswings and downswings.
3. Discretionary fiscal policy is where the government deliberately changes taxes or government expenditure in order to alter the level of aggregate demand. Changes in government expenditure on goods and services will have a full multiplier effect. Changes in taxes and benefits will have a smaller multiplier effect as some of the tax/benefit changes will merely affect other withdrawals and thus have a smaller net effect on consumption of domestic product. The tax multiplier will have a value 1 less than the full multiplier.

17.2 The effectiveness of fiscal policy

How successful will fiscal policy be? Will it be able to 'fine tune' demand? Will it be able to achieve the level of national income that the government would like it to achieve? Will it be able to give full employment without inflation? Will the government know just how much to change taxes and/or government expenditure?

The effectiveness of fiscal policy will depend on a number of factors, including the following:

- The accuracy of forecasting. Governments would obviously like to act as swiftly as possible to prevent a problem of excess or deficient demand. The more reliable are the forecasts of what is likely to happen to aggregate demand, the more able will the government be to intervene quickly.
- The extent to which changes in government expenditure and taxation will affect total injections and withdrawals. Will changes in G or T be partly offset by changes in *other* injections and withdrawals? If so, are these changes predictable?
- The extent to which changes in injections and withdrawals affect national income. Will it be possible to predict the size of the multiplier and accelerator effects?
- The timing of the effects. It is no good simply being able to predict the *magnitude* of the effects of fiscal policy. It is also necessary to predict how long they will take. If there are long time lags with fiscal policy, it will be far less successful as a means of reducing fluctuations.
- The extent to which changes in aggregate demand will have the desired effects on output, employment, inflation and the balance of payments.
- The extent to which fiscal policy has undesirable side-effects, such as higher taxes reducing incentives.

The effectiveness of automatic stabilisers

Automatic stabilisers have the obvious advantage that they act instantly as soon as aggregate demand fluctuates. By contrast, it may take some time before the government can institute discretionary changes in taxes or government expenditure, especially if forecasting is unreliable.

Nevertheless automatic stabilisers can never be the complete answer to the problem of fluctuations. Their effect is merely to reduce the multiplier – to reduce the severity of fluctuations, not to eliminate them altogether.

In addition they tend to suffer two specific drawbacks: adverse effects on aggregate supply and the problem of 'fiscal drag'. Let us examine each in turn.

Adverse supply-side effects

High tax rates may discourage effort and initiative. The higher the *mpt*, the greater the stability provided by the tax system. But the higher tax rates are, the more likely they are to create a disincentive to work and to invest. For example, steeply progressive income taxes may discourage workers from doing overtime or seeking promotion. A higher marginal rate of income tax is equivalent to a higher marginal cost of working. People may prefer to work less and substitute leisure for income. The substitution effect of more progressive taxes may thus outweigh the income effect. These issues were examined in detail in section 10.2 (see pages 304–7).

High unemployment benefits may increase equilibrium unemployment. High unemployment benefits, by reducing the hardship of being unemployed, may encourage people to spend longer looking for the 'right' job rather than taking the first job offered. This has the effect of increasing unemployment and thus of shifting the Phillips curve to the right. This is because a longer average period of job search represents a higher level of *friction* in the economy and thus a higher *natural* (or *equilibrium*) level of unemployment.

To the extent, however, that such unemployment is *voluntary* (people choosing not to take the first job offered), rather than involuntary (lack of jobs available due to insufficient demand), the unemployment *problem* can be said to have been eased.

High income-related benefits may create a poverty trap. The higher the level of income-related benefits and the more steeply they taper off, the greater will be the problem of the 'poverty trap'. What is the point in unemployed people seeking jobs, or people in very low-paid jobs seeking better ones, if as a result they lose their benefits and end up being little or no better off than before? The more that people are discouraged in this way, the lower will be the level of aggregate supply. (The question of the poverty trap was also examined in Chapter 10 (see pages 312–14).)

The problem of fiscal drag

Automatic stabilisers help to reduce upward and downward movements in national income. This is fine if the current level of income is the *desirable* level. But suppose that there is currently a deep recession in the economy, with mass unemployment. Who would want to stabilise the economy at this level?

In these circumstances, if the economy began to recover, the automatic stabilisers would act as a drag on the expansion. This is known as **fiscal drag**. By reducing the size of the multiplier, the automatic stabilisers reduce the magnitude of the recovery. Similarly, they act as a drag on discretionary policy: the more powerful the automatic stabilisers are, the bigger the change in *G* or *T* that would be necessary to achieve a given change in national income.

Discretionary fiscal policy: problems of magnitude

Before changing government expenditure or taxation the government will need to calculate the effect of any such change on national income, employment and inflation. The magnitude of these effects will depend on (a) the extent to which changes in *G* or *T* will affect *net* injections and withdrawals and (b) the extent to which the changes in injections and withdrawals will affect final national income. If the magnitude of these effects could be forecast with relative accuracy, then fiscal policy could be a relatively powerful tool for controlling the economy. Forecasting, however, is often very unreliable for a number of reasons.

First, a rise in government expenditure of £*x* may lead to a rise in injections (relative to withdrawals) that is smaller or larger than £*x*. The rise in injections will be *smaller* than £*x* if the rise in government expenditure *replaces* a certain amount of private expenditure. Examples include the following:

- A rise in government expenditure on social services could lead to a fall in private consumer spending. For example, a rise in expenditure on state education may dissuade some parents from sending their children to private schools. Similarly, an improvement in the National Health Service may lead to fewer people paying for private treatment.
- An increase in government expenditure on research and development or training may make firms feel less need to invest in these areas themselves.
- Crowding out. If the government relies on **pure fiscal policy** – that is, if it does not finance an increase in the budget deficit by increasing the money supply, it will

DEFINITIONS

Fiscal drag The tendency of automatic fiscal stabilisers to reduce the recovery of an economy from recession.

Pure fiscal policy Fiscal policy which does not involve any change in money supply.

CASE STUDIES — BOX 17.2

FISCAL DRAG IN THE LATE 1980S
Tax cuts and budget surpluses

In the March 1988 Budget the Chancellor at the time, Nigel Lawson, made substantial cuts in taxes. The standard rate of income tax was cut from 27 per cent to 25 per cent. The top rate of income tax was cut from 60 per cent to 40 per cent. Personal allowances were increased by more than the rate of inflation. At the same time government expenditure was planned to increase in real terms.

With a seemingly reflationary Budget like this, it might be thought that the Chancellor was planning for a massive public-sector deficit.

In fact he was planning for a public-sector surplus of £3.2 billion. So how was this so? The answer is that he anticipated rapid economic growth in national income: growth that would bring in extra tax revenues despite the cut in tax rates. In his Budget speech he said:

> We have secured an enviable virtuous circle in public finance: lower borrowing and lower tax rates create both the scope and incentive for the private sector to expand. And the private sector then generates higher revenues which permit further reductions in borrowing or tax.

In the event, the public-sector debt repayment (the public-sector *surplus*) for 1988/9 turned out to be over £14 billion!

So how was this possible? The answer is 'fiscal drag'. Although the Chancellor was making discretionary cuts in tax *rates*, the growth in the economy was so strong that tax revenues actually increased. At the same time unemployment was falling rapidly and hence government spending on unemployment benefits also fell. With such a strong growth in the economy, however, the dragging effect of these automatic stabilisers was far too small to prevent the overheating in the economy that subsequently occurred.

A word of caution. The cuts in tax rates alone would not have been sufficient to increase tax revenues. The reduced tax rates only stimulated an *already* strongly growing economy.

??

1. If the Chancellor had foreseen how rapidly aggregate demand would grow, and the inflation and balance of payments problems that would follow, what should he have done? What would this have done to the PSDR?
2. In his 1988 Budget statement he also argued: 'A balanced budget is a valuable discipline for the medium term. It represents security for the present and an investment for the future. Having achieved it, I intend to stick to it. In other words, henceforth a zero PSBR will be the norm.' Assuming that he had adjusted taxes and government expenditure throughout the year by whatever was necessary to keep a balanced budget, would this have had a stabilising or a destabilising effect?

have to borrow the money from individuals and firms. It will thus be competing with the private sector for finance and will have to offer higher interest rates. This will force the private sector also to offer higher interest rates, which may discourage firms from investing and individuals from buying on credit. Thus government borrowing *crowds out* private borrowing. In the extreme case, the fall in consumption and investment may completely offset the rise in government expenditure, with the result that aggregate demand does not rise at all. (This issue is examined in detail in section 20.2.)

The problem in each of these three cases is not whether the rise in government expenditure will or will not simply replace private expenditure. The problem is in predicting the extent to which this will happen.

?? How do people's expectations influence the outcome?

The second problem in forecasting the effects of fiscal policy is that a change in taxes, by changing people's real disposable income, will change not only the amount they spend but also the amount they save. (This is why the tax multiplier is less than the full multiplier.) The problem is that it is not easy to predict just how much people will cut down on their spending and how much on their saving. In part it will depend on whether people feel that the rise in tax is only temporary, in which case they may well cut savings in order to maintain their level of consumption, or permanent, in which case they may well reduce their consumption.

?? Do theories of the long-run and short-run consumption functions help us to understand consumer reactions to a change in taxes?

Third, even if the government *could* predict the net initial effect on injections and withdrawals, the extent to

CASE STUDIES

DISCRETIONARY FISCAL POLICY IN JAPAN

An emergency package to stimulate the economy

Tokyo: 31 March 1992
The Japanese government early today approved a package of emergency economic measures that will increase public spending by at least ¥4000 billion (£17 billion) in the first half of the fiscal year, which begins tomorrow. The measures . . . are a response to rising concern at the slowdown of the Japanese economy. Industrial output is falling sharply and money supply growth is at an historic low.

Mr Masaru Yoshitomi, director-general of the Economic Planning Agency's co-ordination bureau, said the measures would give a strong stimulus to the economy, arrest further decline, and allow the government to reach its economic growth target of 3.5 per cent in 1992.[3]

In previous decades a fiscal expansion of this magnitude would have proved to be more than successful in getting the Japanese economy moving. Yet after an average growth rate of 5.0 per cent in the previous four years, growth in 1992 turned out to be a mere 1.1 per cent, and was followed by a decline of 0.3 per cent in 1993 and growth of only 0.5 and 0.8 per cent in 1994 and 1995. This proved to be the longest recession experienced by the Japanese economy since the Second World War.

Yet over the four-year period 1992–5, the Japanese government had injected into the economy five public spending packages totalling ¥59 500 billion (£330 billion): an average increase in government spending of 7 per cent a year in real terms. There were also substantial cuts in taxes. This, combined with the economic slowdown, moved the public-sector finances massively into deficit. A public-sector surplus of 3 per cent of GDP in 1991 was transformed into a public-sector deficit of nearly 5 per cent of GDP by 1996 (see figure (a)). Japan's national debt rose from 63 per cent of GDP in 1991 to over 90 per cent by 1996.

In addition to this fiscal stimulus, the government reduced interest rates nine times, to a record low of 0.5 per cent by 1996. It also pursued a policy of business deregulation, especially within the service and financial sectors. Yet despite all these measures, the Ministry of International Trade and Industry feared that the Japanese economy might be unable to grow faster than 1 per cent per year for the rest of the decade.

Why did such an expansionary fiscal (and monetary) policy prove to be so ineffective? With a rise in G and a fall in T, why did the economy not expand? The answer can be found in the behaviour of the other components of aggregate demand.

Exports

In previous decades the prosperity of Japanese business was built upon an export-led growth strategy. If there was a lack of demand at home, surplus capacity in the economy could simply be exported. But this option was no longer so easy. Since 1985, as the graph shows, there had been a massive appreciation of the exchange rate: the yen rose by over 150 per cent against the US dollar in the ten years up to 1995 (the reasons are explored in Box 24.4). This, plus growing competition from other Asian exporters, meant that Japanese firms were finding it harder to export. The result was that by 1995 less than 70 per cent of productive capacity was being used.

Investment

The recession and the slowdown in export sales, plus high levels of debt from the expansion of the late 1980s, reduced profits to near record lows and created a climate of business pessimism. After increases in investment averaging 10 per cent per year from 1987 to 1990, investment fell for three successive years after 1991.

Consumption

Consumers too were in a pessimistic mood. The salaries of many Japanese workers are heavily reliant upon

which national income will change is still hard to predict for the following reasons:

- The size of the multiplier may be difficult to predict. This is because the mpc_d and mpw may fluctuate. For example, the amount of a rise in income that households save or consume will depend on their expectations about future price and income changes.
- Induced investment through the accelerator is also extremely difficult to predict. It may be that a relatively small fiscal stimulus will be all that is necessary to restore business confidence, and that induced investment will rise substantially. In such a case fiscal policy can be seen as a 'pump primer'. It is used to *start* the process of recovery, and then the *continuation* of the recovery is left to the market. But for pump priming to work, business people must *believe* that it will work. If they are cautious and fear that the recovery will falter, they may hold back from investing. This lack of investment will probably mean that the recovery *will* falter, and that the effects of the fiscal expansion are therefore very modest. The problem is in predicting just how the business community will react. Business confidence can change very rapidly and in ways that could not have been foreseen a few months earlier.

BOX 17.3

bonuses and overtime payments. Such performance-related rewards can be as much as 50 per cent of total pay. The low profitability of Japanese business hit consumers hard. Even with a ¥5000 billion cut in taxation in 1994, consumer spending on domestic goods and services grew only marginally, whereas *saving* increased sharply, as did *imports*. Encouraged by the high yen, imports grew in real terms by an average of over 7 per cent per year between 1992 and 1995.

As deflationary pressure mounted (inflation became *negative* after 1994), so the criticisms of the Japanese government's fiscal policy grew stronger. The policy, said the critics, had been too little and too late. Even though the total fiscal stimulus over the years since 1992 had been large, the incremental nature of the government's action had failed on each occasion to stimulate business and consumer activity to any significant degree. What was needed, they claimed, was a more aggressive reflation to kick-start the economy, coupled with measures to support the banking sector and the further deregulation of industry.

?? Would there have been any adverse consequences if the Japanese government had adopted a more reflationary fiscal policy?

[3] Steven Butler, *Financial Times*, 31 March 1992.

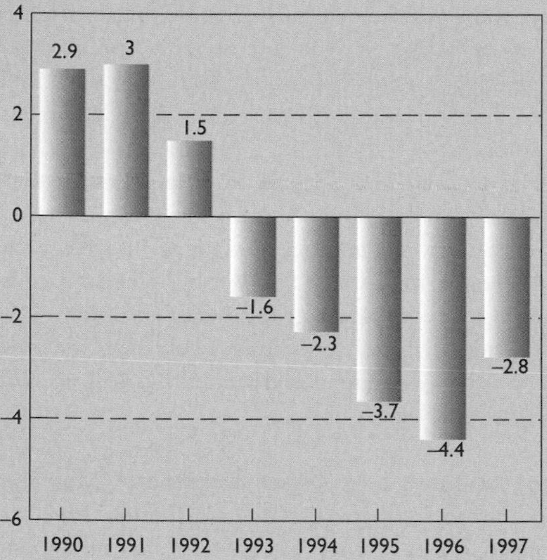

(a) Japan's general government budget balance as % of GDP

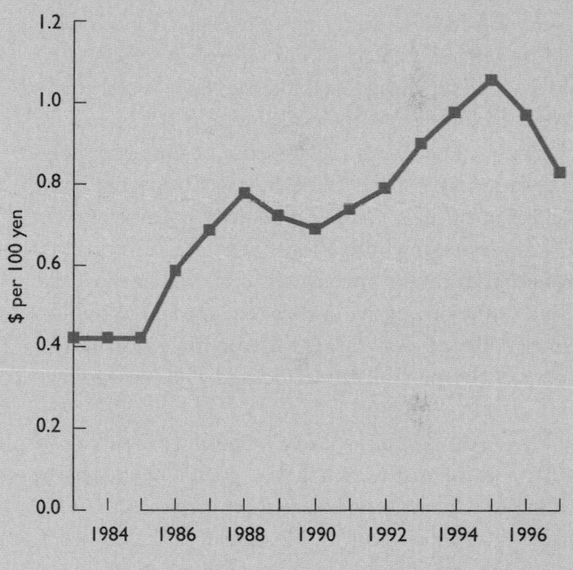

(b) The US dollar/Japanese yen exchange rate

Source: *OECD Economic Outlook* (OECD).

- Multiplier/accelerator interactions. If the initial multiplier and accelerator effects are difficult to estimate, their interaction will be virtually impossible to estimate. Small divergences in investment from what was initially predicted will become magnified as time progresses.

Fourth, there is the problem of random shocks. Forecasts cannot take into account the unpredictable. Unfortunately, unpredictable events do occur and may seriously undermine the government's fiscal policy.

?? Give some examples of these random shocks.

Discretionary fiscal policy: problems of timing

Fiscal policy can involve considerable time lags. If these are long enough, fiscal policy could even be *de*stabilising. Reflationary policies that are taken to cure a recession may only come into effect once the economy has *already* recovered and is experiencing a boom. Under these circumstances reflationary policies will be quite inappropriate: they will simply worsen the problems of overheating. Similarly, deflationary policies that are taken to prevent excessive expansion may only start taking effect once the economy has peaked and is already plunging into recession. The deflationary policies will only deepen the recession.

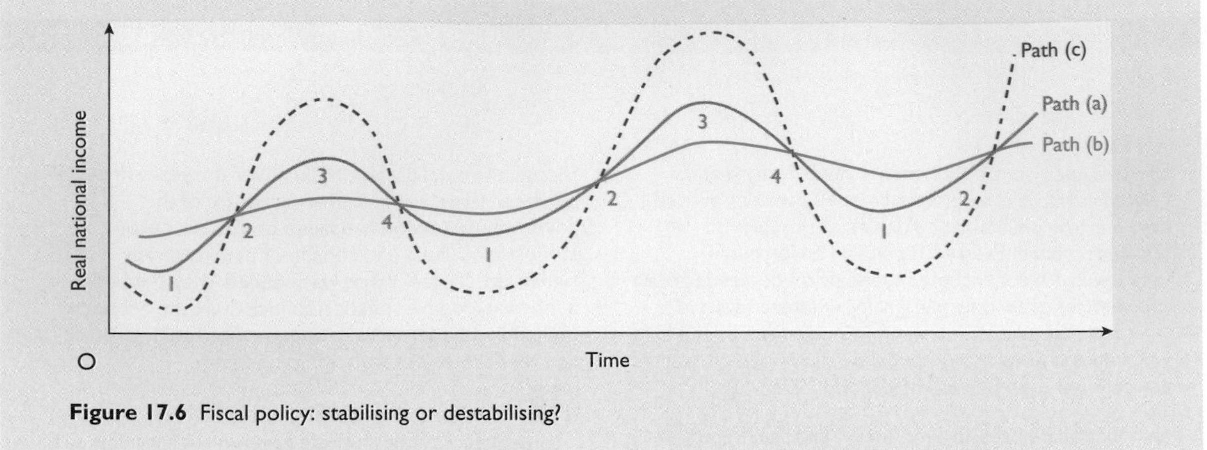

Figure 17.6 Fiscal policy: stabilising or destabilising?

This problem is illustrated in Figure 17.6. Path (a) shows the course of the business cycle without government intervention. Ideally, with no time lags, the economy should be deflated in stage 2 and reflated in stage 4. This would make the resulting course of the business cycle more like path (b), or even, if the policy were perfectly stabilising, a straight line. With the presence of time lags, however, deflationary policies taken in stage 2 may not come into effect until stage 4, and reflationary policies taken in stage 4 may not come into effect until stage 2. In this case the resulting course of the business cycle will be more like path (c). Quite obviously, in these circumstances 'stabilising' fiscal policy actually makes the economy less stable.

There are five possible lags associated with fiscal policy.

Time lag to recognition. Since the business cycle can be irregular and forecasting unreliable, governments may be unwilling to take action until they are convinced that the problem is serious. This is illustrated in Figure 17.7, which shows an imaginary cycle with no government intervention.

Let us compare points *a* and *b*. In both cases the level of output is falling. In the first case this is only temporary. If the government pursues a reflationary fiscal policy at this stage, it will end up only stimulating the impending renewed expansion. As a result the economy will quickly overheat. So what does the government do at point *b*?

Having learned the lesson from last time, it may be reluctant to reflate the economy before it is convinced that this time the economy really is going into recession. It thus chooses to wait and see. But in doing so it ends up allowing the economy to go into a deep recession!

Obviously, better forecasting would help the government to be less cautious and would thus help to remove this first time lag.

Time lag between recognition and action. Most significant changes in government expenditure have to be planned well in advance. The government cannot increase spending on motorways overnight or suddenly start building new hospitals.

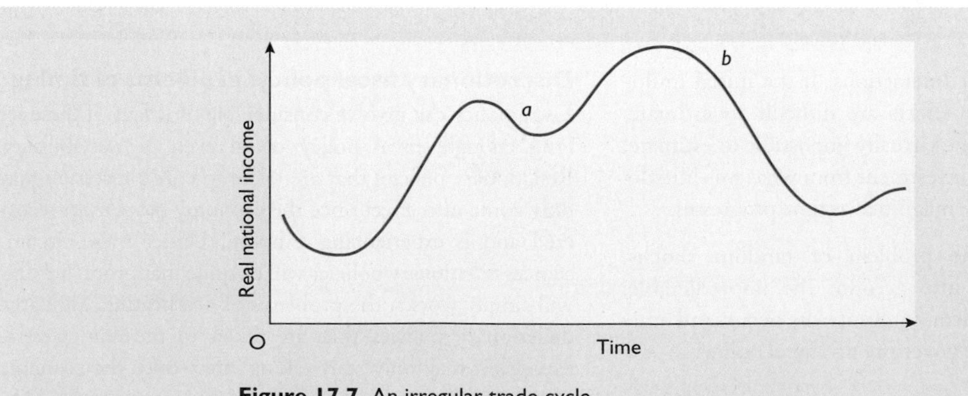

Figure 17.7 An irregular trade cycle

ISSUES AND APPLICATIONS — BOX 17.4

RIDING A SWITCHBACK

A parable for Chancellors

Imagine that you are driving a car along a straight but undulating road. These undulations are not regular: some of the hills are steep, some are gentle; some are long, some are short.

You are given the instruction that you must keep the car going at a constant speed. To do this you will need to accelerate going up the hills and brake going down them.

There is a serious problem, however. The car is no ordinary car. It has the following distinctly unusual features:

- The front windscreen and side windows are blacked out, so you cannot see where you are going! All you can see is where you have *been* by looking in your rearview mirror.
- The brake and accelerator pedals both work with a considerable and unpredictable delay.
- The car's suspension is so good that you cannot feel whether you are going up or downhill. You can only judge this by looking in your mirror and seeing whether the road behind you is higher or lower than you are.
- Finally (you are relieved to know), the car has a special sensor and automatic steering that keep it in the correct lane.

As you are going along, you see that the road behind you is higher, and you realise that you are going downhill. The car gets faster and faster. You brake – but nothing happens. In your zeal to slow the car down, you put your foot down on the brake as hard as you can.

When the brake eventually does come on, it comes on very strongly. By this time the car has already reached the bottom of the hill. As yet, however, you do not realise this and are still braking.

Now the car is going up the hill the other side, but the brakes are still on. Looking in your mirror, you eventually realise this. You take your foot off the brake and start accelerating. But the pedals do not respond. The car is still slowing down rapidly, and you only just manage to reach the top of the hill.

Then, as you start going down the other side, the brakes eventually come off and the accelerator comes on . . .

This famous parable – first told by Frank Paish, Professor of Economics at the LSE, over twenty years ago – demonstrates how 'stabilising' activity can in fact be destabilising. When applied to fiscal policy, long and uncertain time lags can mean that the government can end up stimulating the economy in a boom and contracting it in a slump.

So what should be done? One alternative, of course, would be to try to reduce the time lags and to improve forecasting. But failing this, the best policy may be to do nothing: to take a 'steady as you go' or 'fixed throttle' approach to running the economy. Going back to the car analogy, a fixed throttle will not prevent the car from going faster downhill and slower uphill, but at least it will not make the speed even *more* irregular.

??

1. Could you drive the car at a steady speed if you knew that all the hills were the same length and height, and if there were a constant 30 second delay on the pedals?
2. What would a fixed throttle approach to fiscal policy involve?

Changes in taxes and benefits cannot be introduced overnight either. They normally have to wait to be announced in the Budget, and will not be instituted until the new financial year or at some other point in the future. As Budgets normally occur annually, there could be a considerable time lag if the problems are recognised a long time before the Budget.

Time lag between action and changes taking effect. A change in tax rates may not immediately affect tax payments. Income tax PAYE codings take two or three months to be changed by the Inland Revenue. A change in corporation tax will not affect payments until the *end* of the financial year – a full twelve months' delay. Not all taxes suffer this delay, however. New rates of excise duty on petrol, for example, come into effect immediately they are announced in the Budget.

Time lag between changes in government expenditure and taxation and the resulting change in national income, prices and employment. The multiplier round takes time. Accelerator effects take time. The multiplier and accelerator go on interacting. It all takes time.

Consumption may respond slowly to changes in taxation. The short-run consumption function tends to be flatter than the long-run function.

If the fluctuations in aggregate demand can be forecast, and if the lengths of the time lags are known, then all is not lost. At least the fiscal measures can be taken early and their delayed effects can be taken into account. Keynesians admit that problems of magnitude and time lags make stabilisation less than perfect: a completely stable growth in demand could never be achieved. But at least, they argue, intervention is better than doing nothing. Fiscal policy will go *some* way to reducing fluctuations, especially if forecasting techniques are improved and measures are used which involve the minimum of time lags.

Side-effects of discretionary fiscal policy

The purpose of fiscal policy is to control aggregate demand. In doing so, however, it may create certain undesirable side-effects.

Cost inflation. If the economy is overheating and inflation is rising, the government may raise taxes. Although this will lower aggregate demand, a rise in expenditure taxes and corporation taxes will usually be passed on in full or in part to the consumer in higher prices. This in turn could lead to higher wage claims, as could a rise in income tax.

Welfare and distributive justice. The use of fiscal policy may conflict with various social programmes. The government may want to introduce cuts in public expenditure in order to reduce inflation. But where are the cuts to be made? Cuts will often fall on people who are relatively disadvantaged. After all, it is these people who are the most reliant on the welfare state and other public provision (such as state education).

Incentives. As with automatic stabilisers in the form of steeply progressive income taxes, discretionary rises in taxes could be a disincentive to effort. People may substitute leisure for income – the substitution effect may outweigh the income effect. On the other hand, it could work the other way: people may work harder or longer in an attempt to maintain their previous level of disposable income – the income effect may outweigh the substitution effect.

Postscript: the relative merits of changing government expenditure and changing taxes

Let us assume that despite all the problems of fiscal policy the government still wants to go ahead and use it to control aggregate demand. Which should it change: government expenditure, taxation or some combination of the two? There are various things it will need to take into account in making this decision.

The first consideration will probably be in its overall political objectives. Does it generally favour a larger or smaller public sector?

The political left tends to argue that market economies like the UK suffer from too little public expenditure. While private expenditure by the relatively wealthy on fast cars, designer jeans, junk food and home security continues to grow rapidly, the public sector is deprived of resources. State education is squeezed; the streets are dirty; the environment is threatened; crime increases; the lot of the poor and homeless deteriorates. Private affluence goes side by side with public poverty.

The political right argues that the solution to social and economic problems does not lie in a growth of the 'nanny state', which stifles individual initiative. It is better, so the argument goes, to encourage attitudes where people take responsibility for the social consequences of their own actions, rather than leaving it up to the state.

Even if left and right agree on how much to deflate or reflate the economy by fiscal policy, they will disagree over the means. The left will tend to favour increasing government expenditure as the means of stimulating demand, and increasing taxes as the means of reducing it. The right, by contrast, will tend to favour cutting taxes as the means of stimulating aggregate demand, and cutting government expenditure as the means of reducing it.

Apart from ideological considerations, there are the practical questions of which policies are the most effective and which suffer the fewer drawbacks.

Changing government expenditure has the advantage that it affects aggregate demand directly and has a bigger multiplier effect. Changes in government expenditure can be more specifically targeted than changes in taxation. For example, government expenditure can be directed to regions of high unemployment or to specific industries that either need government support to prevent them going bankrupt or have potential for growth that could be more easily exploited with government aid. Taxes cannot be used so selectively.

Nevertheless the government can alter the balance between income and expenditure tax, or between personal income tax and corporation tax. Also the government can use taxes to alter the distribution of income. What is more, changes in taxes can usually be brought about more speedily than changes in government expenditure, and are thus more suitable for stabilising the economy.

SECTION SUMMARY

1. The effectiveness of fiscal policy depends on the accuracy of forecasting. It also depends on the predictability of the outcome of the fiscal measures: the effect of changes in *G* and *T* on other injections and withdrawals, the size and timing of the multiplier and accelerator effects, the relative effects of changes in aggregate demand on the various macroeconomic objectives, and whether there are any side-effects. It also depends on whether there are any random shocks.
2. Automatic stabilisers take effect as soon as aggregate demand fluctuates, but they can never remove fluctuations completely. They also create disincentives and act as a drag on recovery from recession.
3. There are problems in predicting the magnitude of the effects of discretionary fiscal policy. Expansionary fiscal policy can act as a pump primer and stimulate increased private expenditure, or it can crowd out private expenditure. The extent to which it acts as a pump primer depends crucially on business confidence – something that is very difficult to predict beyond a few weeks or months. The extent of crowding out depends on monetary conditions and the government's monetary policy.
4. There are five possible time lags involved with fiscal policy: the time lag before the problem is diagnosed, the lag between diagnosis and new measures being announced, the lag between announcement and implementation, the lag while the multiplier and accelerator work themselves out, and the lag before consumption fully responds to new economic circumstances.
5. Discretionary fiscal policy can involve side-effects, such as disincentives, higher costs and adverse effects on social programmes.
6. The choice of which to change – government expenditure, taxation or a bit of both – depends partly on the government's political objectives: whether it wants to increase or decrease the size of the public sector. It also depends on their relative effectiveness in changing aggregate demand. Changes in *G* tend to have a bigger multiplier effect than changes in *T*. Changes in *T*, however, can usually be implemented more quickly than changes in *G*.

??? END-OF-CHAPTER QUESTIONS ???

1. The following table shows part of a country's national expenditure schedule (in £ billions):

National income (Y)	100	120	140	160	180	200	220
National expenditure (E)	115	130	145	160	175	190	205

   (a) What is the government expenditure multiplier?

   (b) What is the tax multiplier?

   Assume that full employment is achieved at a level of national income of £200 billion.

   (c) Is there an inflationary or a deflationary gap, and what is its size?

   (d) By how much would government expenditure have to be changed in order to close this gap (assuming no shift in other injections or withdrawals)?

   (e) Alternatively, by how much would taxes have to be changed in order to close the gap (again assuming no shift in other injections or withdrawals)?

   (f) Alternatively, assuming that there were initially a balanced budget, and that the government wanted to maintain a balanced budget, by how much would both government expenditure and taxes have to be changed in order to close the gap?
2. Will a highly progressive tax system have as strong an effect on reducing slumps as it does on reducing booms? (Draw a diagram showing the effect of an equal-sized fall and rise in injections.)
3. What are the problems on relying on automatic fiscal stabilisers to ensure a stable economy at full employment?
4. Does it matter if a country has a large national debt as a proportion of its national income?
5. If the government is running a budget deficit, does this mean that national income will increase?
6. What factors determine the effectiveness of discretionary fiscal policy?
7. Why is it difficult to use fiscal policy to 'fine tune' the economy?
8. Compare the benefits of using changes in government expenditure on goods and services with those of using changes in government transfer payments as means of stabilising aggregate demand.

18

Money and interest rates

In this chapter and the next we are going to look at the special role that *money* plays in the economy. We begin here by considering the relationship between the amount of money in the economy and the level of economic activity. What effect do changes in the amount of money have on the four macroeconomic objectives? We shall see that there is considerable disagreement between economists about just what the effects are.

Before going any further we must define precisely what we mean by 'money'. Money is more than just notes and coin. In fact the main component of a country's money supply is not cash but deposits in banks and other financial institutions. In section 18.2 we examine the key institutions and their role in the UK financial system.

This enables us in section 18.3 to understand the definitions of money that are officially used in the UK and other countries. We will then consider what causes the supply of money to rise or fall.

In section 18.4 we turn to why people demand money. We are not asking why people want to obtain money: that is obvious. What we are asking is what determines the amount of money people want to *hold*, whether in cash or in some form of account. If people choose to hold money, they are thereby choosing *not* to spend it on goods and services or on acquiring some other form of asset such as shares or property.

Having looked at what determines the supply and demand for money, in section 18.5 we put them together and see what determines equilibrium in money markets.

Chapter 19 then looks at how the government alters the supply of money in the economy and influences the money market.

18.1 The role of money in the economy

The way in which changes in money supply influence the economy is a fiercely debated subject in macroeconomics.

Monetarists argue that changes in money supply have a large effect on aggregate demand. This in turn has a large effect on inflation and the balance of payments, but in the long run little or no effect on output and employment.

Keynesians argue that changes in money supply have a rather uncertain effect on aggregate demand. Any changes in aggregate demand that do occur, however, will affect output and employment as well as inflation and the balance of payments, depending on the amount of slack in the economy. Because of the rather uncertain link between money supply and aggregate demand, Keynesians argue that the government should try to influence aggregate demand directly through *fiscal* policy.

Money supply and aggregate demand

Keynesians argue that changes in money supply will affect aggregate demand only indirectly, and that these effects are uncertain. Monetary policy is therefore both weak and unreliable. Monetarists, on the other hand, argue that changes in money supply will have a strong effect on aggregate demand, directly as well as indirectly. Let us examine these direct and indirect transmission mechanisms between changes in money supply and changes in aggregate demand.

The direct transmission mechanism

People desire to hold a certain proportion of their assets in money form. This creates a demand for money (M_d). If

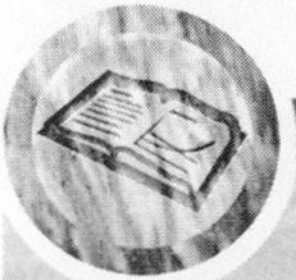

EXPLORING THE THEORY — BOX 18.1

MONEY SUPPLY, NATIONAL INCOME AND NATIONAL WEALTH

Don't confuse the supply of money with the money value of national income. National income is a *flow* concept. It measures the value of the nation's output per year. Money supply, by contrast, is a *stock* concept. At any one point in time there is a given amount of money in the economy.

But what if the money supply increases? Will the national income increase by that amount? No, because the extra money will usually be spent more than once on final goods and services. The rise in national income would thus be greater than the rise in money supply. On the other hand, some of the extra spending may simply result in higher prices. *Real* national income will rise by less than national income measured at current prices.

So if money supply is not the same as national *income*, is it the same as national *wealth*? After all, wealth is a stock concept. Again the answer is no. The nation's wealth consists of its *real* assets: land, buildings, capital equipment, works of art, etc. People may well hold part of their wealth in the form of money, it is true, but this is not wealth as far as the nation is concerned: if it were, the government could make us all wealthier by simply printing more money! Money only represents wealth to the individual to the extent that it represents a claim on *real* goods and services. It has nothing to do with national wealth.

the supply of money in the economy (M_s) increases, there will be more money available than people require to hold ($M_s > M_d$). They will therefore spend the surplus, thereby increasing aggregate demand:

$$M_s \uparrow \rightarrow M_s > M_d \rightarrow AD \uparrow$$

There is thus a **direct transmission mechanism** from an increase in money supply to an increase in aggregate demand.

Indirect transmission mechanisms

An **indirect transmission mechanism** is where a change in money supply first affects some intermediate variable, which then affects aggregate demand. There are two main intermediate variables: interest rates and the exchange rate.

Changes in interest rates. An alternative to spending money on goods and services is to purchase securities (e.g. government bonds, company shares). Thus when money supply increases, the demand for securities will rise. This will cause their price to rise.

Securities yield a given interest or dividend which is payable on the *original face value* of the security, not on its current market price. For example, the government may issue some **bonds** today with a face value of £100 which pay £10 interest per year. (The interest paid will reflect the market rate of interest at the time when the bonds are issued.) These bonds will be redeemed by the government at their face value at some specified date in the future, say in twenty years' time (the 'maturity date'). In the meantime, of course, the holders of the bonds may want to sell them. This they can do through a stockbroker, who will sell them via the stock market to people who want to buy such bonds. The current market price of such bonds will be determined by demand and supply. It may be above or below the face value. But whatever the current price of the bond, the government will pay the same fixed sum every year. The higher the current market rate of interest, the lower will be the market price of existing bonds. This has to be so otherwise no one would be willing to buy old bonds. For example, if the current rate of interest were 20 per cent, no one would be willing to pay £100 for a bond that only yielded £10 per year. The bond's market value would have to fall to around £50. At that price an annual payment of £10 would be equivalent to a 20 per cent rate of interest. Table 18.1 shows how the market price and the market rate of interest vary with each other for a bond yielding £5 per year.

DEFINITIONS

Direct monetary transmission mechanism A change in money supply having a direct effect on aggregate demand.

Indirect monetary transmission mechanism A change in money supply affecting aggregate demand indirectly via some other variable.

Government bonds or 'gilt-edged securities' A government security paying a fixed sum of money each year. It is redeemed by the government on its maturity date at its face value.

Table 18.1 The relationship between bond prices and market rates of interest

Face value	Annual interest payment (nominal 5%)	Current market rate of interest	Market price
£100	£5	5%	£100
£100	£5	4%	£125
£100	£5	10%	£50

?? Complete a similar table showing the market price for a bond yielding £6 per year when current market rates of interest are 6 per cent, 4 per cent and 8 per cent.

When money supply rises, people will buy more securities. This will drive up the price of securities and hence will drive *down* their current market rate of interest. It is the same with company shares (or **equities** as they are called). A rise in money supply causes more shares to be purchased. This drives up share prices. But given that companies pay a dividend (based on current profit) *per share*, the higher the price of the shares, the lower the dividend will be as a percentage of that price.

Thus an increase in money supply will lower interest rates, thereby making it cheaper for firms and individuals to borrow. Borrowing and hence spending will thus increase:

$$M_s \uparrow \rightarrow M_s > M_d \rightarrow r \downarrow \rightarrow I \uparrow, C_d \uparrow \rightarrow AD \uparrow$$

Will there be a relatively large or small increase in aggregate demand? Keynesians and monetarists do not agree on this. We will examine their disagreement in Chapter 20.

Changes in the exchange rate. The exchange rate is an important indirect transmission mechanism if a country (a) has a high proportion of imports and exports and/or capital account flows to national income and (b) operates under a system of floating exchange rates.

A rise in money supply will cause an increase in the demand for imports and for foreign assets. What is more, the fall in interest rates we saw above will also lead to a rise in demand for foreign assets (as domestic assets now earn a lower rate of interest). There will thus be an increase in the supply of pounds coming on to the foreign exchange market. This will cause a fall in the exchange rate (a depreciation). This will make exports (X) more competitive. At the same time imports will now be more expensive and thus some consumers will switch from imports to domestic goods (C_d). The overall effect will be to increase aggregate demand:

$$M_s \uparrow \rightarrow er \downarrow \rightarrow X \uparrow, C_d \uparrow \rightarrow AD \uparrow$$

where *er* is the exchange rate.

Whether in the long term this will lead to a permanent increase in output, or simply to higher prices, is again a fiercely debated question. Certainly prices can be expected to rise somewhat because of the higher price of imports, and any rise in wages as workers seek to maintain their standard of living.

We will examine this mechanism in detail in Chapter 24.

The functions of money

If changes in money supply have a major effect on the economy, and if the government therefore attempts to control the supply of money, it is important to have a clear understanding of (a) the purposes of money and (b) the definition of money.

The main purpose of money is as a 'medium of exchange'. It also has three other important functions.

A medium of exchange

In a subsistence economy where individuals make their own clothes, grow their own food, provide their own entertainments, etc., people do not need money. If people want to exchange any goods, they will do so by barter. In other words, they will do swaps with other people.

The complexities of a modern developed economy make barter totally impractical for most purposes. Someone may have something you want, but they may not want what you have to offer them in return. What is more, under a system of capitalism where people are employed by others to do a specialist task, it would be totally impractical for people to be paid in food, clothes, cars, electrical goods, etc. What is necessary is a **medium of exchange** which is

DEFINITIONS

Equities Company shares. Holders of equities are owners of the company and share in its profits by receiving dividends.

Medium of exchange Something that is acceptable in exchange for goods and services.

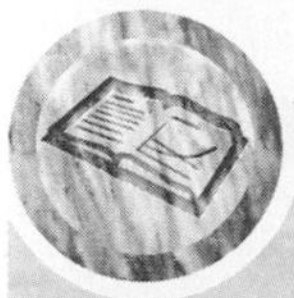

EXPLORING THE THEORY — BOX 18.2

THE ATTRIBUTES OF MONEY

Money has come in many forms. Pigs, cattle, jewels, ornaments and shells are just a few examples. On the South Pacific island of Yap, giant stone wheels are the local currency – hardly suitable as 'small' change! In times of war or rampant inflation, cigarettes, nylon stockings, sugar, coffee and various other commodities have been used.

With the possible exception of Yapese stones, these items are all examples of *commodity money*. That is, they have value in themselves. Animals can be slaughtered for food; jewellery can be worn; coffee can be drunk. But although they can all be used as a medium of exchange, in most cases they are far from ideal. So what are the features of an ideal form of money?

Acceptability

If money is to act as a medium of exchange, it must be generally acceptable as a means of payment. If commodity money is to be generally acceptable, it must have a recognised intrinsic value.

Durability

Money must last a reasonable length of time before deteriorating, certainly if it is to be used as a means of storing wealth. Stone wheels are very good in this respect. Fresh fish aren't.

Convenience

It must be easy to use. In the case of money that physically changes hands, this means that it must be light and small to carry around. In the case of bank accounts (or Yapese stone wheels), it must be easy to transfer ownership, by the use of cheques, standing orders, etc.

Divisibility

Money must come in different denominations so as to be able to pay for an item of any value, however large or small. Thus there is use for a 1p coin, for £20 notes and for the ability to transfer any amount from a bank account. In this respect, animals are a poor form of money. You could not exchange half a (live) pig.

Uniformity

Money of the same value must be of uniform quality. This applies particularly to the case where money has intrinsic value. People would be unwilling to part with a young fat cow as payment if it only had the same value as an old thin one.

Hard for individuals to produce themselves

This is an obvious requirement of paper money. It must be hard to forge.

In terms of commodity money, there would only be a problem of individuals producing it themselves if the monetary value of the item exceeded its intrinsic value.

Stability of value

If money is to fulfil its various functions (especially as a store of wealth and as a means of evaluating future payments), it must retain its value. In terms of money produced by the state, the requirement here is that the government keeps its supply under control. In terms of commodity money, it must not be subject to violent fluctuations in supply. Animals would be a poor form of money in countries subject to drought.

??

1. Would it matter if it was easy to forge a £10 note but cost £15 to do so?
2. How well do each of the following meet the seven requirements listed above: grain, strawberries, strawberry jam, gold, diamonds, luncheon vouchers, ICI share certificates, a savings account requiring one month's notice of withdrawal, notes and coin?

---

generally acceptable as a means of payment for goods and services and as a means of payment for labour and other factor services. 'Money' is any such medium.

To be a suitable physical means of exchange, money must be light enough to carry around, must come in a number of denominations, large and small, and must not be easy to forge (see Box 18.2). Alternatively, money must be in a form that enables it to be transferred *indirectly* through some acceptable mechanism. For example, money in the form of bookkeeping entries in bank accounts can be transferred by the use of cheques, debit cards, standing orders and direct debits.

A means of storing wealth

People need a means whereby the fruits of *today's* labour can be used to purchase goods and services in the *future*. People need to be able to store their wealth: they want a means of saving. Money is one such medium in which to hold wealth. It can be saved.

DEVELOPMENT OF IDEAS BOX 18.3

FROM COINS TO BANK DEPOSIT MONEY

Precious metals have been used as money for thousands of years. Even as lumps of metal carried around in sacks they still functioned quite well as money.

Coins made from these precious metals were an early improvement introduced by many societies including the Greeks and Romans. Coins had the clear advantage that they did not have to be weighed out each time they were used. But the use of coins enabled many rulers to increase their spending by adding base metals to the coins and thereby increasing the number of coins. This debasement frequently led to problems of inflation as money supply increased too rapidly.

Paper money has a much more recent origin. The first paper money was issued by goldsmiths. Wealthy merchants and individuals would deposit their gold with goldsmiths, whose businesses required them to have safe storage facilities. The goldsmith would issue a receipt for the gold.

It was soon realised that it was much easier to use these receipts to buy goods than for the purchaser to withdraw gold, pay it to the seller of the goods, and for the seller then to redeposit it with the goldsmith. It was easier still if these receipts were issued in fixed denominations. Thus goldsmiths' receipts became very much like modern banknotes.

The alternative was for a purchaser to write a note instructing the goldsmith to transfer a certain amount of gold to the seller. These notes were very much like modern cheques.

Goldsmiths also realised that only a small fraction of the gold in their vaults would be withdrawn at any one time, and even then there would be other people who were making new deposits. So they found they could *lend out* some of the gold and make money by charging interest. When these loans of gold were redeposited back with goldsmiths, *new* notes were issued in addition to the original ones.

Soon the total value of the notes issued considerably exceeded the total value of the gold! The notes were only *partly* backed by gold. This is known as a system of *fractional backing*.

It was a short step from goldsmiths' notes to banknotes and bank loans. Banks, often originally operating as goldsmiths, issued their own banknotes in excess of the gold in their vaults, just as the goldsmiths had done.

Today banks in England and most other countries do not issue their own notes, but their loans still exceed their deposits of cash. This process of *credit creation* is examined in section 18.3. Today it is bank deposits that form the bulk of money supply. Only a fraction of these deposits are in cash. The rest are simply bookkeeping entries created by the banks.

Modern banknotes are not backed by gold. The amount of gold in the Bank of England is only a tiny fraction of the total amount of currency in circulation.

A currency not backed by gold (and no currencies in the world today are) is known as a *fiat* currency: a currency whose supply depends on the will of government. The issuing of currency not backed by gold is known as *fiduciary issue*. This means currency issued on trust. If the government is prepared and able to match the supply of currency to the requirements of the economy, then this will be adequate to ensure the stability of the currency. The backing of gold will be unnecessary.

??

1. If money is not backed by gold, what gives it its value?
2. If the money that banks have created vastly exceeds the amount of cash in the economy, does this mean that there is too much money in the economy?

A means of evaluation

Money allows the value of goods, services or assets to be compared. The value of goods is expressed in terms of prices, and prices are expressed in money terms. Money also allows dissimilar things, such as a person's wealth or a company's assets, to be added up. Similarly, a country's national income is expressed in money terms.

?? Why may money prices give a poor indication of the value of goods and services?

A means of establishing the value of future claims and payments

People often want to agree *today* the price of some *future* payment. For example, workers and managers will want to agree the wage rate for the coming year. Firms will want to sign contracts with their suppliers specifying the price of raw materials and other supplies. Money prices are the most convenient means of measuring future claims.

What should count as money?

What items, then, should be included in the definition of money? Unfortunately, there is no sharp borderline between money and non-money.

Cash (notes and coin) obviously counts as money. It readily meets all the functions of money. Goods (fridges, cars and cabbages) do not count as money.

But what about various financial assets, such as bank accounts, building society accounts and stocks and shares? Do they count as money? The answer is 'It depends': it depends on how narrowly money is defined.

Narrow definitions of money include only items that can be spent directly, such as cash and current accounts in banks (since they can be spent directly by using cheques or debit cards). Note that cheques, debit cards and credit cards, although they are used to pay for goods directly, do not themselves count as money. Rather it is the balance in the account on which they are drawn that counts as money.

Broad definitions of money also include various items such as deposit accounts in banks that cannot be spent directly but which can nevertheless be readily converted into cash.

?? In terms of the broad definition of money, would a deposit account passbook count as money?

In the UK there are several different measures of money supply. In order to understand their significance and the ways in which money supply can be controlled, it is first necessary to look at the various types of account in which money can be held and at the various financial institutions involved.

SECTION SUMMARY

1. How changes in money supply affect aggregate demand is a highly controversial issue. Monetarists argue that changes in money supply have a direct and powerful effect. Keynesians argue that they have an indirect and uncertain effect.
2. The direct mechanism is where an increase in money supply leads people directly to spend the resulting excess of money supply over money demand.
3. The indirect mechanism operates via interest rates or exchange rates. In the former, a rise in money supply leads to a fall in interest rates, which in turn leads to an increase in consumption and investment. In the latter, a rise in money supply leads to a fall in the exchange rate, which leads to a rise in exports and a fall in imports.
4. Money's main function is as a medium of exchange. In addition it is a means of storing wealth, a means of evaluation and a means of establishing the value of future claims and payments.
5. Narrow definitions of money include items that can be directly spent: cash and money in cheque-book and debit-card accounts. Broad definitions of money also include items that cannot be directly spent but can, nevertheless, be readily converted into cash.

18.2 The financial system in the UK

The role of the financial sector

Many different types of institution make up the financial sector, from banks to building societies to various institutions in the City of London. They are jointly known as **financial intermediaries**. They all have the common function of providing a link between those who wish to lend and those who wish to borrow. In other words, they act as the mechanism whereby the supply of funds is matched to the demand for funds.

As financial intermediaries these institutions provide four important services.

Expert advice

Financial intermediaries can advise their customers on financial matters: on the best way of investing their funds and on alternative ways of obtaining finance. This should help to encourage the flow of savings and the efficient use of them.

DEFINITIONS

Narrow definitions of money Items of money that can be spent directly (cash and money in cheque-book/debit-card accounts).

Broad definitions of money Items in narrow definitions plus other items that can be readily converted into cash.

Financial intermediaries The general name for financial institutions (banks, building societies, etc.) which act as a means of channelling funds from depositors to borrowers.

Expertise in channelling funds

Financial intermediaries have the specialist knowledge to be able to channel funds to those areas that yield the highest return. This too encourages the flow of savings as it gives savers the confidence that their savings will earn a good rate of interest. Financial intermediaries also help to ensure that projects that are potentially profitable will be able to obtain finance. They help to increase allocative efficiency.

Maturity transformation

Many people and firms want to borrow money for long periods of time, and yet many depositors want to be able to withdraw their deposits on demand or at short notice. If people had to rely on borrowing directly from other people, there would be a problem here: the lenders would not be prepared to lend for a long enough period. If you had £100 000 of savings, would you be prepared to lend it to a friend to buy a house if the friend was going to take 25 years to pay it back? Even if there was no risk whatsoever of your friend defaulting, most people would be totally unwilling to tie up their savings for so long. This is where a building society comes in. It borrows money from a vast number of small savers, who are able to withdraw their money on demand or at short notice. It then lends the money to house purchasers for a long period of time by granting mortgages (typically these are paid back over 20 to 30 years). This process whereby financial intermediaries lend for longer periods of time than they borrow is known as **maturity transformation**. They are able to do this because with a large number of depositors it is highly unlikely that they would all want to withdraw their deposits at the same time. On any one day, although some people will be withdrawing money, others will be making new deposits.

Risk transformation

You may be unwilling to lend money directly to another person in case they do not pay up. You are unwilling to take the risk. Financial intermediaries, however, by lending to large numbers of people, are willing to risk the odd case of default. They can absorb the loss because of the interest they earn on all the other loans. This spreading of risks is known as **risk transformation**. What is more, financial intermediaries may have the expertise to be able to assess just how risky a loan is.

?? Which of the above are examples of economies of scale?

In addition to channelling funds from depositors to borrowers, certain financial institutions have another important function. This is to provide a means of transmitting payments. Thus by the use of cheques, debit cards, credit cards, standing orders, etc., money can be transferred from one person or institution to another without having to rely on cash.

Financial institutions in the UK

The different financial intermediaries can be grouped according to the types of deposit taking and lending in which they specialise.

Retail banks

Retail banks include the 'big four' (Barclays, Lloyds, Midland and National Westminster) and the other familiar high street banks, such as the Abbey National and the Scottish banks. They specialise in providing branch banking or postal banking facilities to individuals. They operate current (cheque-book) accounts, on most of which overdraft facilities can be arranged, and deposit accounts, which by offering a higher interest rate but no cheque book are designed to encourage savers. They also provide personal loan facilities and financial advice to their customers. Unlike most other financial institutions, they are involved in operating the *payments* system: the transmission of money through cheques, standing orders, direct debits, etc.

Wholesale banks

Wholesale banks deal primarily in receiving large deposits from and making large loans to industry and other financial institutions. One category of wholesale banks is the *merchant banks*. These often act as 'brokers', arranging loans for companies from a number of different sources. They also offer financial advice to industry and

DEFINITIONS

Maturity transformation The transformation of deposits into loans of a longer maturity.

Risk transformation The process whereby banks can spread the risks of lending by having a large number of borrowers.

Retail banks 'High street banks'. Banks operating extensive branch networks and dealing directly with the general public with published interest rates and charges.

Wholesale banks Banks specialising in large-scale deposits and loans and dealing mainly with companies.

'accept' *bills of exchange* (see page 554). They provide assistance to firms in raising new capital through the issue of new shares. Examples of merchant banks are Rothschilds and Hambros.

Wholesale banks also include many overseas banks, especially Japanese and American. They have expanded their business in the UK enormously in recent years, especially since the abolition of foreign exchange controls in 1979. Their major specialism is the finance of international trade and capital movements, and they deal extensively in the foreign exchange market. Most of their deposits are in foreign currencies.

Building societies

These specialise in granting loans (mortgages) for house purchase. They compete for the savings of the general public through a network of high street branches. Unlike retail banks they are not public limited companies, their 'shares' being the deposits made by their investors.

Finance houses

These specialise in providing hire-purchase finance for the purchase of consumer durables such as cars and electrical goods. This is normally arranged through the retailer, which will offer credit to its customers. Finance houses also lease out capital equipment to firms. Their main sources of funds are banks, but they do also receive deposits from the general public. Several finance houses are subsidiaries of retail banks.

Discount houses

These institutions, unique to the UK, play an absolutely central role in the monetary system. Their specialism is in lending and borrowing for very short periods of time – from one day to up to about three months. There are eight discount houses, all members of the London Discount Market Association. Despite their importance they are not household names as they do not deal with the general public. (Have you heard of King & Shaxson or Gerrard & National?)

We will examine these various institutions in more detail later, as we see just how the financial system operates. At this stage, however, it is worth noting an important trend in recent years. Increasingly, the boundaries between the different financial institutions are becoming less clear cut. For example, in the past there was a clear distinction between banks and building societies. Today, however, they have become much more similar, with building societies now offering current account facilities and cash machines, and commercial banks granting mortgages. In fact, in 1989 the Abbey National Building Society became a public limited company and thereby ceased to be a building society, becoming instead a retail bank. It was followed in the second half of the 1990s by several others, including the Halifax and the Woolwich.

This is all part of a trend away from the narrow specialisation of the past and towards the offering of a wider and wider range of services. Inevitably, as this trend continues the services offered by the various institutions will increasingly overlap.

At the heart of the financial system of a country is the **central bank**. In the case of the UK this is the Bank of England. Its role is to oversee and regulate the activities of the different financial institutions. It has the task of ensuring the stability and efficiency of the financial system. It also has the task of carrying out the government's monetary policy.

In order to understand how these various institutions affect the economy and the part they play in the operation of monetary policy, we need to examine some of their activities and functions in more detail.

Deposit taking and lending

Liabilities

Customers' deposits in banks and other deposit-taking institutions such as building societies are **liabilities** to these institutions. This means simply that the customers have the claim on these deposits and thus the institutions are liable to meet the claims.

There are two major types of deposit: *sight deposits* and *time deposits*.

Sight deposits. **Sight deposits** are any deposits that can be withdrawn on demand by the depositor without penalty. They are sometimes called 'demand deposits'. In the past, sight deposits did not pay interest. In recent years,

DEFINITIONS

Central bank Banker to the banks and the government.

Liabilities All legal claims for payment that outsiders have on an institution.

Sight deposits Deposits that can be withdrawn on demand without penalty.

however, banks have introduced various types of interest-bearing sight account.

The most familiar form of sight deposit are current accounts at banks. Depositors are issued with cheque books which enable them to spend the money directly without first having to go to the bank and draw the money out in cash. Cheque guarantee cards facilitate the process. A recent development with current accounts has been the introduction of **debit cards**. You hand them to the shop assistant when making a purchase and your current account is automatically debited by the amount of your purchase. This process is usually done electronically via a machine at the shop's cash till (see Box 18.4). Banks hope that in time the use of these cards will substantially reduce the number of cheques that are written, since debit-card transactions are much cheaper for the banks to process than transactions by cheque.

An important feature of current accounts is that banks often allow customers to be overdrawn. That is, they can draw on their account and make payments to other people in excess of the amount of money they have deposited. This facility is a crucial ingredient in the process whereby the money supply expands. If person A is given an overdraft and then draws a cheque on the account and pays it to person B, person B's bank account has been credited and he or she can draw this money even though person A never deposited the money in the first place.

Time deposits. **Time deposits** require notice of withdrawal. They pay interest. With some types of account a depositor can withdraw a certain amount of money on demand, but will have to pay a penalty of so many days' interest. They are not cheque-book accounts. The most familiar form of time deposits are the deposit and savings accounts in banks and the various savings accounts in building societies. No overdraft facilities exist with time deposits.

The distinction between sight and time deposits has become increasingly blurred in recent years, with interest being paid on current accounts and with instant-access, no-penalty, high-interest accounts.

Assets

A financial institution's **assets** are items it owns and its claims on others.

Banks and certain other financial institutions, such as building societies, need to hold a certain amount of their assets as notes and coin. This is largely used as 'till money' to meet the day-to-day demands by customers for cash.

Cash, however, earns no interest for banks. The vast majority of banks' assets are therefore in the form of various types of loan – to individuals and firms, to other financial institutions and to the government. These are 'assets' since they represent claims that the banks have on other people. Some of these loans are for short periods. Overdrafts to customers are often granted for a few days or weeks. Some loans to other financial institutions may be loans 'at call'. These are loans that the banks can reclaim on demand. Some institutions, such as building societies, have few if any short-term assets. Others, such as the discount houses (as we shall see later), have assets that are almost entirely short term.

Other loans are for much longer periods. For example, banks grant personal loans to customers to be repaid in instalments over a set number of years (typically six months to five years). Building societies' major assets are mortgage loans. These are very long term and are typically paid back over 25 years.

Retail and wholesale deposits and loans

An important distinction is that made between *retail* and *wholesale* deposits and loans.

Retail deposit taking and lending are the familiar type done by the high street banks and the building societies, through their various branches. The terms of deposits and loans are published and are at standard rates of interest for each category. Interest rates are adjusted from time to time to reflect market conditions, and will be chosen to balance long-term inflows of deposits with the demand for loans; higher interest rates attracting more deposits and reducing the demand for loans.

Wholesale deposits and loans are those by and to firms which want to deposit or borrow large sums of

DEFINITIONS

Debit card A card that has the same use as a cheque. Its use directly debits the person's current account.

Time deposits Deposits that require notice of withdrawal or where a penalty is charged for withdrawals on demand.

Assets Possessions, or claims held on others.

Retail deposits and loans Deposits and loans made through bank/building society branches at published interest rates.

Wholesale deposits and loans Large-scale deposits and loans made by and to firms at negotiated interest rates.

ISSUES AND APPLICATIONS — BOX 18.4

ARE THE DAYS OF CASH NUMBERED?

EFTPOS versus ATMs

Banking is becoming increasingly automated, with computer debiting and crediting of accounts replacing the moving around of pieces of paper. What was once done by a bank clerk is often now done by computer.

One possible outcome of this replacement of labour by computers is the gradual elimination of cash from the economy – or so some commentators have claimed.

The most dramatic example of computerisation in recent years has been EFTPOS (electronic funds transfer at the point of sale). This is where you pay for goods in the shops by means of a card – either a credit card (like Access or Visa) or a debit card (like Switch or Connect). The card is simply 'swiped' across a machine at the till which may then require you to enter your PIN (personal identification number). The details of the transaction (the amount, the retailer and your card number) are then transmitted down the line to the EFTPOS UK processing centre. If necessary, the information is then directed down the line to the card issuer for authorisation. If the card is valid and the transaction acceptable, then within seconds the machine will issue a slip for you to sign and the purchase is complete. Subsequently your account will be automatically debited and the retailer's account automatically credited.

The advantage of this system is that it does away with the processing by hand of pieces of paper. In particular it does away with the need for (a) credit-card slips when used in conjunction with credit cards and (b) cheques. Both cheques and credit-card slips have to be physically moved around and then read and processed by *people*. If this EFTPOS system were to become widely used for *small* transactions, it could well reduce the need for cash. But reducing the need for cash is *not* the prime purpose of EFTPOS. Its prime purpose is to do away with cheques and credit-card slips.

So are we moving towards a cashless society? Probably not. Cash is still the simplest and most efficient way of paying for a host of items, from your bus ticket to a newspaper to a packet of mints. What is more, another technical innovation is moving us in the direction of using *more* cash, not less! This is the cash machine – or *ATM* (automated teller machine), to give it its official title. The spread of cash machines to virtually every bank and building society branch and to many larger stores has been rapid in recent years. The sheer simplicity of obtaining cash at all hours from these machines, not only from your current account but also on your credit card, is obviously a huge encouragement to the use of cash.

So are we using more cash or less cash? The evidence suggests a gradual decline in cash in circulation as a proportion of GDP. It fell from just over 5 per cent of GDP in 1980 to just over $2^1/_2$ per cent in 1996.

But although the effects of EFTPOS and ATMs may be quite different in terms of the use of cash, they both have the same advantage to banks: they reduce the need for bank staff and thereby reduce costs.

?? Under what circumstances are cheques more efficient than cash and vice versa? Would you get the same answer from everyone involved in transactions: individuals, firms and banks?

money. These may be for short periods of time to account for the non-matching of the firm's payments and receipts from its business. They may be for longer periods of time, for various investment purposes. These wholesale deposits and loans are very large sums of money. Banks thus compete against each other for them and negotiate individual terms with the firm to suit the firm's particular requirements. The rates of interest negotiated will reflect the current market rates of interest and the terms of the particular loan/deposit. Very large loans to firms are often divided ('syndicated') between several banks.

Banks also lend and borrow wholesale funds to and from each other. This inter-bank lending has grown enormously in recent years and it is now the largest of the wholesale markets. Banks short of funds borrow large sums from others with surplus funds, thus ensuring that the banking sector as a whole does not have funds surplus to its requirements. The rate at which they lend to each other is known as the London Inter-Bank Offer Rate (LIBOR). LIBOR has a major influence on the other rates banks charge.

Liquidity and profitability

Financial institutions keep a range of liabilities and assets. The balance of items in this range is influenced by two important considerations: profitability and liquidity.

Profitability. Profits are made by lending money out at a higher rate of interest than that paid to depositors.

Liquidity. The **liquidity** of an asset is the ease with which it can be converted into cash without loss. Cash itself, by definition, is perfectly liquid.

Some assets, such as money lent at call to other financial institutions, are highly liquid. Although not actually cash, these assets can be converted into cash on demand with no financial penalty.

Other assets, however, are much less liquid. Personal loans to the general public or mortgages for house purchase can only be redeemed by the bank as each instalment is paid. Other advances for fixed periods are only repaid at the end of that period.

Other assets, such as government bonds – i.e. loans to government for a fixed number of years – are somewhere in the middle. They can be sold quickly on the Stock Exchange if banks are short of cash. But their price fluctuates with market conditions and the banks may be unwilling to sell them if their current market price is too low. In other words, they can easily be converted into cash but may involve some loss.

Financial institutions must maintain sufficient liquidity in their assets to meet the demands of depositors.

Profitability is the major aim of banks and most other financial institutions. However, the aims of profitability and liquidity tend to conflict. In general, the more liquid an asset, the less profitable it is, and vice versa. Advances to customers are profitable to banks but highly illiquid. Cash is totally liquid, but earns no profit. Thus financial institutions like to hold a range of assets with varying degrees of liquidity and profitability.

To economise on cash holdings (which earn no interest), financial institutions hold other highly liquid assets which act as reserves, but which nevertheless earn them some interest (see pages 552–4). The greater the liquidity of its liabilities, and the more volatile the demands of depositors are for cash, the greater the proportion of liquid assets the institution must hold.

The ratio of an institution's liquid assets to total assets is known as its **liquidity ratio**. For example, if a bank had £100 million of assets, of which £10 million were liquid and £90 million were illiquid, the bank would have a 10 per cent liquidity ratio. If a financial institution's liquidity ratio is too high, it will make too little profit. If the ratio is too low, there will be the risk that customers' demands may not be able to be met: this would cause a crisis of confidence and possible closure. Institutions thus have to make a judgement as to what liquidity ratio is best – one that is neither too high nor too low. They are guided and persuaded in this process by the Bank of England.

The key role of banks in the monetary system

By far the largest element of money supply is bank deposits. It is not surprising, then, that banks play an absolutely crucial role in the monetary system.

The 1979 and 1987 Banking Acts defined a UK **monetary sector** (or UK **banking sector** as the Bank of England now prefers to call it). This consists of a series of financial institutions, known as **authorised institutions**, whose activities are supervised by the Bank of England. The largest group of institutions in the banking sector are the **recognised banks**. (Also included are the discount houses and the banking department at the Bank of England.) To be a recognised bank, a bank must be granted a licence by the Bank of England. This requires it to have paid-up capital of at least £5 million and to meet other requirements about its asset structure and the range of banking services it offers. If a bank is not recognised, it cannot use the word 'bank' in its title (unless it is an overseas bank operating in the UK and it is made clear that it is using the title 'bank' because it is entitled to do so in its country of origin). All the major banks in the UK and most of the larger foreign ones are in fact recognised by the Bank of England.

The most important of the recognised banks in the UK for the functioning of the economy and for the implementation of monetary policy are the **clearing banks**. These are the main retail banks in the UK and include the familiar high street names: Barclays, Lloyds, Midland, National Westminster, Co-operative Bank, Abbey National, Royal Bank of Scotland, TSB, Bank of Scotland, Clydesdale Bank and Standard Chartered.

DEFINITIONS

Liquidity The ease with which an asset can be converted into cash without loss.

Liquidity ratio The proportion of a bank's total assets held in liquid form.

Monetary sector or banking sector Those financial institutions whose activities are supervised by the Bank of England.

Authorised institutions The institutions comprising the monetary (or banking) sector.

Recognised banks Those commercial banks whose activities are supervised by the Bank of England.

Clearing banks The main UK retail banks: members of the Clearing House Association.

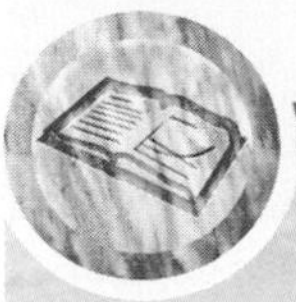

EXPLORING THE THEORY BOX 18.5

SECONDARY MARKETING
Or how to make illiquid assets liquid

Banks have the two conflicting aims of liquidity and profitability. They must hold sufficient liquid assets to be able to meet any demands from their customers and avoid a crisis of confidence. But they want to hold illiquid assets in order to make a profit – after all, the less liquid the asset, the greater the interest the bank is likely to be able to charge. The greater their ratio of illiquid assets to liquid ones, the greater their profit.

This conflict can be put another way. This is in terms of the size of the gap between the average maturity of a bank's assets and liabilities.

For reasons of profitability, the banks will want to 'borrow short' and 'lend long'. In other words, they will want to receive deposits that can be withdrawn instantly (like current accounts) or at only short notice. The benefits of liquidity to their customers will involve banks only having to pay out low rates of interest (or in the case of certain types of current account, none at all). But banks will want to grant *loans* with a much longer maturity (e.g. two-year personal loans), since these are charged at much higher interest rates than banks have to pay to their depositors. The difference in the average maturity of loans and deposits is known as the *maturity gap*.

For reasons of *profitability*, the banks will want a large maturity gap between loans and deposits. For reasons of *liquidity*, however, banks will want a relatively small gap: if there is a sudden withdrawal of deposits, banks will need to be able to call in enough loans.

The obvious way of reconciling the two conflicting aims of liquidity and profitability is by compromise: to hold a mixture of liquid and illiquid assets – to have a 'reasonable' maturity gap.

There is another way, however, whereby banks can reconcile these aims, whereby they can close the gap for *liquidity* purposes, but maintain the gap for *profitability* purposes. This is by the *secondary marketing* of assets.

Certificates of deposit (CDs) are a good example of secondary marketing. CDs are issued for fixed-period deposits in a bank (e.g. one year) at an agreed interest rate. The bank does not have to repay the deposit until the year is up. CDs are thus illiquid liabilities for the bank, and they allow it to increase the proportion of illiquid assets without having a dangerously high maturity gap. But the holder of the CD in the meantime can sell it to someone else (through a broker). It is thus liquid to the holder.

Because CDs are liquid to the holder, they can be issued at a relatively *low* rate of interest and thus allow the bank to increase its profitability.

Another example is when a bank sells some of its assets to another bank. The advantage to the first bank is that it gains liquidity. The advantage to the second bank is that it gains profitable assets (assuming that it has spare liquidity).

The effect of secondary marketing is to reduce the liquidity ratio that banks feel they need to keep. It has the effect of increasing their maturity gap.

There are dangers to the banking system, however, from secondary marketing. To the extent that banks individually feel that they can operate with a lower liquidity ratio, so this will lead to a lower *national* liquidity ratio. This may lead to an excessive expansion of credit (illiquid assets) in times of economic boom. Also there is an increased danger of banking collapse. If one bank fails, this will have a knock-on effect on those banks which have purchased its assets.

??

Is it possible to argue that secondary marketing allows a lower safe average liquidity ratio? (Clue: the answer has to do with risk transformation.)

Banks and the transmission of payments: the clearing system

The clearing banks are so called because they operate a central **clearing system**. This is a means of settling banks' debts with each other on a daily basis. It enables cheques, standing orders and other means of payment to be cleared rapidly. But how does it work?

Let us examine the case of just two banks, say Lloyds and Midland. Each day all the cheques written by Midland customers that Lloyds customers have deposited in their accounts represent money owed by Midland to Lloyds. Likewise all the cheques that Lloyds customers have written and have been deposited in Midland accounts represent money owed by Lloyds to Midland. At the end of the day these two sets of debts are compared. If Midland customers have paid, say, £1 million more to Lloyds customers than Lloyds customers have to Midland customers, Midland makes a *single* payment of £1 million to Lloyds, drawn on Midland's account in the Bank of England. A simple bookkeeping entry adjustment is made. (As we shall see, all recognised banks keep accounts with the Bank of England.) The debt has been settled.

DEFINITION

Clearing system An institution where inter-bank debts are settled.

This procedure is carried out for each pair of banks. When customers of one branch deposit cheques from customers of a different branch of the *same* bank, the central clearing system is not involved. Clearing simply takes place within the bank.

Increasingly, the process of clearing is done electronically rather than manually, the information to debit or credit individuals' accounts being sent down the line to the various branches by computer. Direct debits, standing orders and debit-card payments are cleared entirely by computer.

Banks and the transformation of maturity: liabilities and assets

Apart from providing a mechanism for the transmission of payments, banks also provide financial intermediation. As we have seen, this involves maturity transformation: borrowing relatively short and lending relatively long.

To understand this process in more detail and to prepare the way for showing how money supply expands or contracts, we must examine the different types of deposit and loan (of liability and asset). The balance sheet in Table 18.2 shows the total liabilities and assets of UK recognised banks at the end of May 1997.

Sterling liabilities

Time deposits form the largest item, accounting for around 42 per cent of the total. *Sight deposits* are the other major item, accounting for around 30 per cent.

Most sight deposits are from the *private sector*: individuals and firms. In the case of time deposits, although private-sector deposits are the largest component, a substantial proportion are from the *banking sector*: i.e. other banks and other financial institutions. Inter-bank lending has grown over the years as money markets have become deregulated and as deposits are moved from one currency to another to take advantage of different rates of interest between different countries. A large proportion of overseas deposits are from foreign banks.

Certificates of deposit (CDs) are certificates issued by banks to customers (usually firms) for large deposits of a fixed term (e.g. £100 000 for eighteen months). They can be sold by one customer to another, and are thus relatively liquid to the depositor but illiquid to the bank issuing them (see Box 18.5). The use of CDs has grown rapidly in recent years. Their use by firms has meant that, at a wholesale level, sight accounts have become *less* popular.

Sale and repurchase agreements ('repos'). If banks have a temporary shortage of funds, they can sell some of their financial assets to other banks or to the Bank of England (see below), and later repurchase them on some agreed date, often about a fortnight later. These **sale and repurchase agreements (repos)** are in effect a form of loan, the bank borrowing for a period of time using some of its financial assets as the security for the loan. The most usual assets to use in this way are government bonds, normally called 'gilt-edged securities' or simple 'gilts' (see below). Sale and repurchase agreements involving gilts are known at *gilt repos*. As we shall see, gilt repos play a vital role in the operation of monetary policy.

Items in suspense and transmission are funds in the process of being transferred from one customer's account to another.

Capital and other funds include shareholders' funds and internal funds of the banks themselves.

The Bank of England must ensure that the banking system is stable and that banks have adequate liquidity. It also has the responsibility for controlling the money supply, which largely consists of bank deposits. Hence the Bank of England will need to monitor and if necessary influence the level of bank deposits. The deposits which the Bank of England considers important for this are known as **eligible liabilities**. These are total sterling deposits less (a) those having an original maturity in excess of two years, (b) various inter-bank deposits, since to count these would essentially be double counting, and (c) 40 per cent of items in transit.

Sterling assets

Banks hold a whole range of assets of varying degrees of liquidity and profitability. The balance sheet in Table 18.2 shows the various sterling assets of the recognised banks in descending order of liquidity.

Notes and coin by definition are totally liquid. This is the money that banks keep in their safes or tills for everyday use.

DEFINITIONS

Certificates of deposit Certificates issued by banks for fixed-term interest-bearing deposits. They can be resold by the owner to another party.

Sale and repurchase agreements (repos) An agreement between two financial institutions whereby one in effect borrows from another by selling its assets, agreeing to buy them back (repurchase them) at a fixed price and on a fixed date

Eligible liabilities The sterling liabilities of banks that the Bank of England monitors for purposes of monetary policy.

Table 18.2 Balance sheet of UK banks: May 1997

Sterling liabilities	£bn	%	Sterling assets	£bn	%
Sight deposits		(30.0)	Notes and coin	4.8	(0.5)
UK banks	34.0		Balances with Bank of England		(0.2)
UK public sector	3.0		Operational deposits	0.2	
UK private sector	232.5		Cash ratio deposits	2.1	
Overseas	17.3		Market loans		(25.7)
			UK banks	129.5	
Time deposits		(42.2)	UK banks CDs	49.9	
UK banks	103.2		Building Society CDs etc.	5.4	
UK public sector	6.9		UK Local authorities	1.1	
UK private sector	226.8		Overseas	60.1	
Overseas	67.6		Bills of exchange		(1.8)
			Treasury	1.7	
Certificates of			Local authority	0.0	
deposit, etc.	100.6	(10.5)	Commercial	15.4	
			Sales and repurchase		
Sale and repurchase			agreements (repos)	56.5	(5.9)
agreements (repos)	55.4	(5.8)	Investments		(8.4)
			Public sector	19.2	
Items in suspense			Building societies	4.1	
and transmission	11.6	(1.2)	Other	57.1	
			Advances		(53.9)
Capital and other funds	95.4	(10.0)	UK public sector	2.9	
			UK private sector	496.2	
Notes outstanding	2.5	(0.3)	Overseas	16.7	
			Miscellaneous	33.8	(3.5)
Total sterling liabilities	**956.9**	(100.0)	**Total sterling assets**	**956.7**	(100.0)
(of which: eligible liabilities)	(615.0)	(64.3)	Assets in other currencies	1135.5	
Liabilities in other currencies	1135.3		Total assets	2092.2	
Total liabilities	2092.2				

Source: *Financial Statistics* (ONS).

Operational balances in the Bank of England are the banks' own current accounts and are used for clearing purposes. They can be withdrawn in cash on demand and are thus also totally liquid. They do not earn interest.

The amount that banks hold in cash and operational balances depends on the demand for cash that they expect from their customers. Since they earn no interest, the banks like to keep as little as possible of their assets in these two forms. As you can see from Table 18.2, they account for a tiny fraction of total assets.

All recognised banks are *required* to keep cash balances in the Bank of England to the value of 0.35 per cent of their eligible liabilities. These *cash ratio deposits* are non-operational: the banks cannot withdraw them.

Banks hold only very small amounts of cash, but they hold a large amount of other relatively liquid assets which act as reserves and also earn interest. The largest category of these is market loans.

Market loans are short-term loans made mainly to other banks or financial institutions. The market for such loans and deposits is known as the **money market**.

The most liquid of the market loans are **money at call and short notice** lent to the discount houses. Money at call can be withdrawn at only a few hours' notice. It is

DEFINITIONS

Money market The market for short-term loans and deposits.

Money at call and short notice Money lent by the banks to the discount houses from overnight to fourteen days.

sometimes referred to as 'overnight money'. Money at short notice is money lent for up to fourteen days. Money at call is the main reserve that banks draw on if they are short of cash. An important form of market loans are loans to, or assets in, other banks. Certificates of deposit are also important. A bank with surplus cash could buy CDs issued by another bank.

Market loans account for some 26 per cent of banks' sterling assets and are thus a major source of liquidity to individual banks. Note, however, that they do not provide the banking system *as a whole* with liquidity.

?? Suppose there were a sudden surge in demand for cash from the general public. Would the existence of inter-bank market loans help to meet the demand in any way?

Bills of exchange are of three types: Treasury bills, local authority bills and commercial bills. They are certificates whereby the issuer (the borrower) promises to pay a certain amount of money on some specified future date. The purchaser of the bill is thus giving the issuer of the bill a loan from the date of purchase until the date of maturity.

Bills pay no interest, so they must be sold below their face value (i.e. at a *discount*). The discount price will depend on current short-term rates of interest on comparable investments in other assets. The higher the rates of interest on other assets, the lower will be the price that people will be prepared to pay for bills (and hence the higher their *rate of discount*).

Treasury bills are issued by the Bank of England on behalf of the government. They are, in effect, loans to the government. They are issued for three months (91 days) at a weekly tender (an auction where bids are submitted in writing). The price that they are sold for, and hence their rate of discount, will depend on demand and supply and will reflect market rates of interest. But the Bank of England can influence the rate of discount by altering the amount of Treasury bills it sells. In fact this is the major way in which the government seeks to *alter* market rates of interest (see Chapter 19). They are thus of great importance in the management of the economy.

Commercial bills are issued by firms. They have grown in importance in recent years as a way of financing trade, and in particular of improving cash flow. They are issued for anything from one month to twelve, but three months is typical.

Some of the main purchasers of bills are the discount houses, which then sell many of them at a slightly higher price, to the banks. Bills can be very easily bought and sold, and their market price steadily rises throughout the three months, until the face value is reached at maturity. They therefore provide a secure and highly liquid asset for the banks.

?? If a discount house buys a £50 000 Treasury bill for £48 000, at roughly what price will it sell it to a bank after six weeks?

Investments are of two major types. *Investments in public-sector stock* are mainly in short-dated government bonds. Since a rise in interest rates can cause quite a severe fall in the price of bonds (see section 18.1), banks could make a considerable capital loss if they were forced to sell them at such times. Thus although they can *easily* be sold, they are not very *liquid*. If, however, a bond only has a short time left to maturity, it will be much more liquid: its market price will be near its face value. Banks normally do not hold bonds with more than five years to maturity and a large proportion of their bonds have less than one year to maturity. *Other investments* are largely in subsidiary banks in the UK or abroad. Banks do not invest in company shares (equities) or company bonds (debentures).

Advances are the major profit-earning asset for the banks and account for over 60 per cent of their sterling assets. Advances include all the various forms of loan to households and firms. The three major categories at retail level are overdrafts, personal loans for fixed periods, and mortgages.

Miscellaneous assets largely consist of payments owed but not yet received from other banks.

As we have seen, it is important for banks to maintain adequate liquidity. They must hold enough cash and assets that can be readily turned into cash to be able to meet any demands from their customers. The Bank of England regards the following assets as liquid:

- Operational balances with the Bank of England.

DEFINITIONS

Bill of exchange A certificate promising to repay a stated amount on a certain date, typically three months from the issue of the bill. Bills pay no interest as such, but are sold at a discount and redeemed at face value, thereby earning a rate of discount for the purchaser.

Treasury bills Bills of exchange issued by the Bank of England on behalf of the government. They are a means whereby the government raises short-term finance.

Commercial bills Bills of exchange issued by firms.

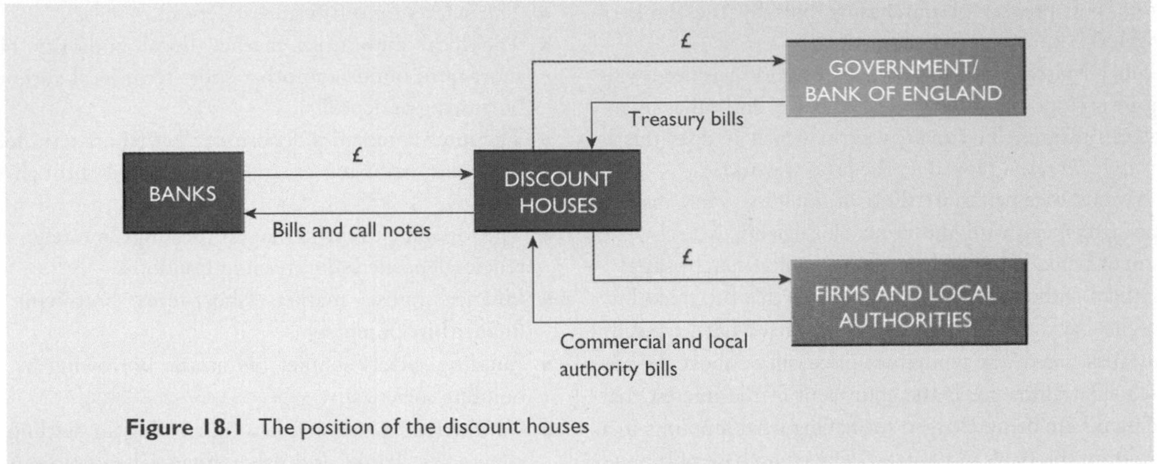

Figure 18.1 The position of the discount houses

- Money at call and short notice with the discount houses and various other money market loans.
- Bills of exchange: Treasury, local authority and certain commercial bills.
- Government bonds with less than a year to maturity.

Before 1981, these assets were known as 'reserve assets' and banks were required to hold a $12^1/_2$ per cent 'reserve assets ratio': reserve assets had to be at least $12^1/_2$ per cent of eligible liabilities. Today the only *statutory* requirements are that banks keep a 0.35 per cent cash ratio with the Bank of England, and that very-short-term market loans in total should be a minimum of 5 per cent of eligible liabilities. It is largely up to the banks themselves to decide on the liquidity ratio that they consider to be 'prudent': i.e. the ratio that provides them with enough liquid assets to meet any demands for cash.

?? Why are government bonds which still have eleven months to run regarded as liquid, whereas overdrafts granted for a few weeks are not?

The role of the London money market

It is through the London money market that the Bank of England exercises its control of the economy. The market deals in short-term lending and borrowing. It is normally divided into the 'discount' and 'repo' markets and the 'parallel' or 'complementary' market.

The discount and repo markets

Traditionally this was simply the *discount market*, and in this market the discount houses played a central role. As we have seen, their specialism is in the 'short end' of the market: i.e. they specialise in borrowing and lending for very short periods of time. They lend money short term to the government (through the Bank of England), to local authorities and to firms by buying bills of exchange. To do this they obtain money from the banks by borrowing money at call and short notice and by selling them bills. This relationship is illustrated in Figure 18.1.

The discount houses provide an important service to the banks by allowing them to hold extremely liquid assets (money at call) which nevertheless earn interest. They also provide an important service to issuers of bills by offering a specialist market for such bills. In recent years the discount houses have not only borrowed from banks, but also lent to them by purchasing certificates of deposit.

Like banks, the discount houses make their profit by a process of maturity transformation: by borrowing short and lending long – or to be more precise, by borrowing very short indeed and lending slightly less short. They borrow from the banks for as little as a few hours' notice of recall by the banks (money at call), and lend to the government, local authorities and firms for typically three months (bills of exchange). They pay a slightly lower rate of interest on money at call than they earn by discounting bills.

If banks were short of cash they could call in loans from the discount houses. But then the discount houses in turn would probably be short of liquid assets to meet this demand. What could they do?

In such circumstances (known as 'the last resort') the Bank of England would always step in and lend to the discount houses, or purchase bills of exchange from them before the bills had reached maturity. The preferred method in the recent past was to purchase commercial bills. (The Bank of England is normally only prepared to buy commercial bills if they have been accepted, i.e. insured against default ('underwritten') by an acceptance house or other recognised bank. These are called *fine bills*.) The process of purchasing bills by the Bank of England is known as **rediscounting**.

Since March 1997, the Bank of England has been willing to provide liquidity *directly* to banks and other financial institutions. The main way in which it does this is through *gilt repos*. How does the process work?

Assume that banks are short of liquidity. They make a repo agreement with the Bank of England, whereby the Bank of England buys gilts from the banks (thereby supplying them with money) on the condition that the banks buy the gilts back at a fixed price and on a fixed date, typically two weeks later. The repurchase price will be above the sale price. The difference is the equivalent of the interest that the banks are being charged for having what amounts to a loan from the Bank of England. The repurchase price (and hence the 'repo rate') will be set by the Bank of England to reflect its chosen rate of interest: i.e. the rate of interest chosen by the Bank of England's Monetary Policy Committee. This committee, consisting of eight experts, with the Governor in the chair, meets once per month.

In being prepared to rediscount bills or provide money through gilt repos, the Bank of England is thus the ultimate guarantor of sufficient liquidity in the monetary system and is known as **lender of last resort**.

The need for banks to acquire liquidity in this way is not uncommon: the 'last resort' occurs on most days! It is generally a deliberate policy of the Bank of England to create a shortage of liquidity in the economy to force banks to obtain liquidity from it. But why should the Bank of England do this? It does it as a means of controlling interest rates. If the banks are forced to obtain liquidity from the Bank of England, they will be borrowing at the Bank of England's *chosen rate* (i.e. the repo rate). The banks will then have to gear their other rates to it, and other institutions will gear their rates to those of the banks.

The way in which the Bank of England creates a shortage of liquidity and the way in which it forces through changes in interest rates are examined in Chapter 19. The day-to-day operations of the Bank of England in the discount and gilt repo markets is examined in Box 19.2.

The parallel money markets

The parallel money markets include the following:

- The inter-bank market (wholesale loans from one bank to another from one day to up to several months).
- The market for certificates of deposit.
- The local authorities market (local authority bills, short-term bonds and other short-term local authority borrowing or deposits).
- The inter-companies deposit market (short-term loans from one company to another arranged through the market).
- The foreign currencies market (dealings in foreign currencies deposited short term in London).
- Finance house market (short-term borrowing to finance hire purchase).
- Building society market (wholesale borrowing by the building societies).
- Commercial paper market (borrowing in sterling by companies, banks and other financial institutions by the issue of short-term (less than one year) 'promissory notes'. These, like bills of exchange, are sold at a discount and redeemed at their face value.)

The parallel markets have grown in size and importance in recent years. The main reasons for this have been (a) the opening-up of markets to international dealing, given the abolition of exchange controls in 1979, (b) the deregulation of banking and money market dealing and (c) the volatility of interest rates and exchange rates, and thus the desire of banks to keep funds in a form that can be readily switched from one form of deposit to another, or from one currency to another. The main areas of growth have been in inter-bank deposits, certificates of deposit and the foreign currency markets.

Although the Bank of England does not deal directly in the parallel markets and does not provide 'last resort' lending facilities, it nevertheless closely monitors the various money market rates of interest and if necessary seeks to influence them, either by its dealings in the discount market or by 'indicating' the direction it would like to see interest rates move.

??

1. Why should Bank of England intervention to influence rates of interest in the discount market also influence rates of interest in the parallel markets?
2. If the Bank of England indicates that it would like to see interest rates rise, why should dealers in the parallel markets take any notice?

DEFINITIONS

Rediscounting bills of exchange Buying bills before they reach maturity.

Lender of last resort The role of the Bank of England as the guarantor of sufficient liquidity in the monetary system.

The Bank of England

We end this section by having a closer look at the Bank of England, the UK's central bank. All countries have a central bank and they fulfil two vital roles in the economy. The first is to oversee the whole monetary system and ensure that banks and other financial institutions operate as stably and as efficiently as possible. The second is to act as the government's agent, both as its banker and in carrying out monetary policy. Just how closely a central bank works with the government will vary from country to country. In the UK the Bank of England works in very close liaison with the Treasury, and although it may disagree with Treasury policy it is always obliged to carry it out. In some other countries central banks are more independent of the government and can take much more initiative in deciding monetary policy.

Within these two broad roles the Bank of England has a number of different functions.

It issues notes

The Bank of England is the sole issuer of banknotes in England and Wales. (In Scotland the clearing banks issue notes.) The issue of notes is done through the Issue Department, which organises their printing. This is one of two departments of the Bank of England. The other is the Banking Department. Table 18.4 shows the balance sheets of these two departments on 17 January 1996. As you can see from the balance sheet for the Issue Department, the note issue is backed by government and other securities (such as fine bills purchased from the discount houses).

The amount of banknotes issued by the Bank of England depends largely on the demand for notes from the general public. If people draw more cash from their bank accounts, the banks will have to draw more cash from their balances in the Bank of England. These balances are held in the Banking Department. The Banking Department will thus have to acquire more notes from the Issue Department, which will simply print more in exchange for extra government or other securities supplied by the Banking Department. Thus the amount of notes in circulation is always more at Christmas time.

It acts as a bank

To the government. It keeps the two major government accounts: the 'Exchequer' and the 'National Loans Fund'. Taxation and government spending pass through the Exchequer. Government borrowing and lending pass through the National Loans Fund. The government tends to keep its deposits in the Bank of England (the *public deposits* item in the balance sheet) to a minimum. If the deposits begin to build up (from taxation), the government will probably spend them on paying back government debt. If, on the other hand, it runs short of money, it will simply borrow more.

To the recognised banks. The *bankers' deposits* item in the balance sheet refers to the cash ratio and operational balances of the banks. As we have seen, the operational balances are used for clearing purposes between the banks and to provide them with a source of liquidity.

To overseas central banks. These are deposits of sterling held by overseas authorities as part of their official reserves and/or for purposes of intervening in the foreign exchange market in order to influence the exchange rate of their currency.

Table 18.3 Balance sheet of the Bank of England: 21 January 1998

Liabilities	£m	Assets	£m
Issue Department			
Notes in circulation	21 995	Government securities	12 763
Notes in Banking Department	5	Other securities	9 237
	22 000		22 000
Banking Department			
Public deposits	889	Government securities	1 369
Bankers' deposits	2 729	Advances and other accounts	6 837
Reserves and other accounts	5 047	Premises, equipment, etc.	454
		Notes and coin from Issue Department	5
	8 665		8 665

Source: *Financial Statistics* (ONS).

It manages the government's borrowing programme

Whenever the government runs a budget deficit, it will have to finance that deficit by borrowing. It can borrow by issuing either gilt-edged securities (government bonds) or Treasury bills. The Bank of England organises this borrowing. Even when the government runs a budget surplus the Bank of England will still have to manage the national debt (the accumulated borrowing from the past). The reason is that old bonds will be maturing and new issues of bonds will probably be necessary to replace them.

When an old issue of bonds is approaching maturity, the Bank of England will probably enter the market to buy them back over a number of weeks or months, rather than waiting to the maturity date and then suddenly releasing a large amount of liquidity into the economy.

When a new issue of bonds is made, the Bank of England will set a minimum price somewhat below the £100 face value and then invite tenders for these bonds above or at the minimum price. It will allocate them in descending order from the highest-priced bid to the lowest. Any unsold bonds (known as 'tap stock') will then be released on to the market in an orderly way at a price set by the Bank of England. Any temporary shortfall of money for the government is met by issuing Treasury bills.

The issuing of bonds and bills will also depend on the government's monetary policy. This is examined in Chapter 19.

It oversees the activities of banks and other financial institutions

It advises banks on good banking practice. It discusses government policy with them and reports back to the government. It requires all recognised banks to maintain adequate *liquidity*: this is called **prudential control**. Since May 1997, the Bank of England has ceased to be responsible for the detailed supervision of banks' activities. This responsibility has passed to the Securities and Investment Board.

It provides liquidity, as necessary, to banks

As lender of last resort to the discount houses, it ensures that there is always an adequate supply of liquidity to meet the legitimate demands of depositors in recognised banks. It may also come to the rescue of ailing banks. Of course, if the Bank of England's supervision were perfect, rescue packages would be unnecessary.

It operates the government's monetary and exchange rate policy

Monetary policy. By careful management of the issue and purchase/rediscounting of government bonds and Treasury bills, the Bank of England can manipulate interest rates and influence the size of the money supply. Details of this are given in Chapter 19.

Exchange rate policy. The Bank of England manages the country's gold and foreign currency reserves. This is done through the **exchange equalisation account**. By buying and selling foreign currencies on the foreign exchange market, the Bank of England can affect the exchange rate. For example, if there were a sudden selling of sterling (due, say, to bad trade figures and a resulting fear that the pound would depreciate), the Bank of England could help to prevent the pound from falling by using reserves to buy up pounds on the foreign exchange market. Intervention in the foreign exchange market is examined in detail in Chapter 24.

??

1. Would it be possible for an economy to function without (a) a central bank; (b) discount houses?
2. What effect would a substantial increase in the sale of government bonds and Treasury bills have on interest rates?

DEFINITIONS

Prudential control The insistence by the Bank of England that recognised banks maintain adequate liquidity.

Exchange equalisation account The gold and foreign exchange reserves account in the Bank of England.

SECTION SUMMARY

1. Financial intermediaries include retail and wholesale banks, building societies, finance houses and discount houses. Between them they provide the following important functions: giving expert advice, channelling capital to areas of highest return, maturity transformation, risk transformation and the transmission of payments.
2. Banks aim to make profits, but they must also maintain sufficient liquidity. Liquid assets, however, tend to be unprofitable and profitable assets tend to be illiquid. Banks therefore hold a range of assets of varying degrees of profitability and liquidity.
3. Commercial banks' liabilities include both sight and time deposits. They also include certificates of deposit. Their assets include in descending order of liquidity: notes and coin, balances with the Bank of England, market loans (including money at call with the discount houses), bills of exchange (Treasury, commercial and local authority), investments (government bonds and inter-bank investments) and advances to customers (the biggest item, including overdrafts, personal loans and mortgages).
4. The money market is the market in short-term deposits and loans. It consists of the discount market and the parallel money markets. The discount market centres on the activities of the discount houses. The Bank of England operates in the discount market by buying (rediscounting) and selling bills. It thereby seeks to manipulate interest rates. It is always prepared to lend to the discount houses in the *last resort* in order to ensure adequate liquidity in the economy.
5. The parallel money markets consist of various markets in short-term finance between various financial institutions.
6. The Bank of England is the UK's central bank. It issues notes; it acts as banker to the government, to the commercial banks, to various overseas central banks and to certain private customers; it manages the government's borrowing programme; it supervises the activities of banks and other financial institutions; it provides support to prevent banks getting into difficulties; it operates the government's monetary and exchange rate policy.

18.3 The supply of money

Definitions of the money supply

If money supply is to be monitored and possibly controlled, it is obviously necessary to measure it. But what should be included in the measure? Here we need to distinguish between the *monetary base* and *broad money*.

The **monetary base** (or 'high-powered money') consists of cash (notes and coin) in circulation outside the central bank. It is sometimes referred to as the 'narrow monetary base' to distinguish it from the **wide monetary base**, which also includes banks' balances with the central bank. In the UK, the wide monetary base is known as *M0*.

But the monetary base gives us a very poor indication of the effective money supply, since it excludes the most important source of liquidity for spending: namely, bank deposits. The problem is which deposits to include. We need to answer three questions:

- Should we include just sight deposits, or time deposits as well?
- Should we include just retail deposits, or wholesale deposits as well?
- Should we include just bank deposits, or building society deposits as well?

In the past there has been a whole range of measures, each including different combinations of these accounts. However, financial deregulation, the abolition of foreign exchange controls and the development of computer technology have led to huge changes in the financial sector throughout the world. This has led to a blurring of the distinctions between different types of account. It has also made it very easy to switch deposits from one type of account to another. For these reasons, the most usual measure that countries use for money supply is **broad money**, which in most cases includes

DEFINITIONS

Monetary base Notes and coin outside the central bank.

Wide monetary base (M0) Notes and coin outside the central bank plus banks' operational deposits with the central bank.

Broad money Cash in circulation plus retail and wholesale bank and building society deposits.

CASE STUDIES

UK MONETARY AGGREGATES

How long is a piece of string?

In the recent past, measures of 'money supply' in the UK have included M0, non-interest-bearing M1, M1, M2, M3, M3H, M3c, M4, M4c, M5. This confusing array of measures reflected the many different types of deposit that might be considered to be part of money.

Today, there are just four official measures: M0, M2, M4 and M3H. The government regards M0 and M4 as the most important. M0 is referred to as the 'wide monetary base' and M4 is referred to as 'broad money' or simply as 'the money supply'. The definitions of these four aggregates are:

M0. Cash in circulation with the public and cash held by banks and building societies, plus banks' operational balances with the Bank of England.

M2. Cash in circulation with the public (but not cash in banks and building societies), plus private-sector *retail* sterling deposits in banks and building societies.

M4. M2 plus private-sector wholesale sterling deposits in banks and building societies, plus sterling certificates of deposit.

M3H. M4 plus private-sector foreign currency deposits in banks and building societies (in the UK), plus public corporations' sterling and foreign currency deposits in UK banks and building societies. (This measure of broad money is that adopted by the EU to allow comparisons between member countries.)

In addition, the Bank of England publishes figures for 'Divisia money'. This is M4 adjusted so that it gives a better measure of money held for *transactions* purposes, rather than as a form of savings. Each item is given a weight according to the interest it earns relative to the interest rate on equivalent assets used for savings. Thus components of M4 that earn no interest, and are thus held purely for transactions purposes (i.e. cash and most current accounts), have a weight of 1 and are entered at their full value. Components that earn the full savings rate of interest, and would not therefore normally be used for transactions purposes, have a weight of 0 and do not count at all. The value of other components will have a lower weight (i.e. be reduced more), the higher the interest rate they pay.

The table gives the figures for all these aggregates for the end of March 1996.

But what of all the other measures that have been used? You may well come across references to them.

M1 included cash and bank sight deposits (both retail and wholesale). M3 was M1 plus bank time deposits (again, both retail and wholesale). Neither M1 nor M3 included building society deposits. In the 1980s, the business of banks and building societies became more and more similar, as banks increasingly became a source of mortgages, and building societies offered cheque-book accounts and cash machines. Those measures of money supply that included bank deposits, but not building society deposits (M1 and M3), therefore ceased to provide a useful measure of liquidity in the economy. They were dropped as official measures in 1989 when the Abbey National Building Society changed its status to a bank, thereby increasing M1 and M3 at a stroke!

M3c and M4c were M3 and M4 plus private-sector foreign currency deposits in the UK. They have been replaced by M3H.

M5 was M4 plus various other holdings of liquid assets, such as bills of exchange. It was designed to give a

both time and sight deposits, retail and wholesale deposits, and bank and building society (savings institution) deposits.

In the UK this measure of broad money is known as *M4*. In most other European countries and the USA it is known as *M3*. There are, however, minor differences between countries in what is included. (Official UK measures of money supply are given in Box 18.6.)

As we have seen, bank deposits of one form or another constitute by far the largest component of (broad) money supply. To understand how money supply expands and contracts, and how it can be controlled, it is thus necessary to understand what determines the size of bank deposits. Banks can themselves expand the amount of bank deposits, and hence the money supply, by a process known as 'credit creation'.

The creation of credit: the simplest case

To illustrate this process in its simplest form, assume that banks have just one type of liability – deposits – and two types of asset – balances with the Bank of England (to achieve liquidity) and advances to customers (to earn profit).

Banks want to achieve profitability while maintaining sufficient liquidity. Assume that they believe that sufficient liquidity will be achieved if 10 per cent of their assets are held as balances with the Bank of England. The remaining 90 per cent will then be in advances to customers. In other words, the banks operate a 10 per cent liquidity ratio.

BOX 18.6

UK monetary aggregates, end December 1997

		£ million
	Cash outside Bank of England	27 662
+	Banks' operational deposits with Bank of England	155
=	**M0**	**27 817**
	Cash outside banks (i.e. in circulation with the public and non-bank firms)	22 248
+	Private-sector retail bank and building society deposits	462 373
=	**M2**	**484 621**
+	Private-sector wholesale bank and building society deposits + CDs	236 651
=	**M4**	**721 272**
+	Private-sector foreign currency bank and building society deposits	107 869
+	Public corporations' sterling and foreign currency bank and building society deposits	2 662
=	**M3H**	**831 803**
	M4	721 272
–	Element not held for transactions purposes	28 918
=	**Divisia money**	**692 354**

broad measure of liquidity in the economy. The problem was that the list of liquid assets included in it was felt to be too arbitrary to give a true indication of general liquidity in the economy. As a result it is no longer published. It is possible that the authorities may devise a new measure that takes into account some of the newer instruments, such as sterling commercial paper, and which includes various foreign currency assets, given their growing importance in international finance. In the meantime, figures for 'liquid assets outside M4' are published in official statistics.

??

1. Why would the inclusion in any of the definitions of money deposited at call with the discount houses be a case of double counting?
2. Why is cash in banks and building societies included in M0 but not in the other measures?

Assume initially that the combined balance sheet of the banks is as shown in Table 18.4. Total deposits are £100 billion, of which £10 billion (10 per cent) are kept in balances with the Bank of England. The remaining £90 billion (90 per cent) are lent to customers.

Now assume that the government spends more money – £10 billion, say, on roads or the National Health Service. It pays for this with cheques drawn on its account with the Bank of England. The people receiving the cheques deposit them in their banks. Banks return these cheques to the Bank of England and their balances correspondingly increase by £10 billion. The combined banks' balance sheet now is shown in Table 18.5.

But this is not the end of the story. Banks now have surplus liquidity. With their balances in the Bank of England having increased to £20 billion, they now have a liquidity ratio of 20/110. If they are to return to a 10 per cent liquidity ratio, they need only retain £11 billion as balances at the Bank of England (£11 billion/£110 billion = 10 per cent). The remaining £9 billion they can lend to customers.

Assume now that customers spend this £9 billion in shops and the shopkeepers deposit the cheques in *their* bank accounts.[1] When the cheques are cleared, the

[1] It is assumed for simplicity that the customers and shopkeepers use different banks. The process works just the same if they use the same bank. In this case, when the cheques are cleared the bank's balances at the Bank of England are unaltered. It still has the excess balances on which it can base further loans.

Table 18.4 Banks' original balance sheet

Liabilities	£bn	Assets	£bn
Deposits	100	Balances with the B. of E. Advances	10 90
Total	100	Total	100

balances in the Bank of England of the customers' banks will duly be debited by £9 billion, but the balances in the Bank of England of the shopkeepers' banks will be credited by £9 billion: leaving *overall balances in the Bank of England unaltered.* There is still a surplus of £9 billion over what is required to maintain the 10 per cent liquidity ratio. The new deposits of £9 billion in the shopkeepers' banks, backed by balances in the Bank of England, can thus be used as the basis for *further* loans: 10 per cent (i.e. £0.9 billion) must be kept back in the Bank of England, but the remaining 90 per cent (i.e. £8.1 billion) can be lent out again. When the money is spent and the cheques are cleared, this £8.1 billion will still remain as surplus Bank of England balances and can therefore be used as the basis for yet more loans. Again, 10 per cent must be retained and the remaining 90 per cent can be lent out. This process goes on and on until eventually the position is as shown in Table 18.6.

The initial increase in balances with the Bank of England of £10 billion has allowed banks to create new advances (and hence deposits) of £90 billion, making a total increase in money supply of £100 billion.

This effect is known as the **bank (or deposits) multiplier**. In this simple example with a liquidity ratio of 1/10 (i.e. 10 per cent), the bank multiplier is 10. An initial increase in deposits of £10 billion allowed total deposits to rise by £100 billion. In this simple world, therefore, the bank multiplier is the inverse of the liquidity ratio (L).

$$\text{Bank multiplier} = 1/L$$

?? If banks choose to operate a 20 per cent liquidity ratio and receive extra cash deposits of £10 million:
(a) How much credit will ultimately be created?
(b) By how much will total deposits have expanded?
(c) What is the size of the bank multiplier?

The creation of credit: the real world

In practice the creation of credit is not as simple as this. There are three major complications.

Banks' liquidity ratio may vary

Banks may choose a different liquidity ratio. At certain times, banks may decide that it is prudent to hold a bigger proportion of liquid assets. If Christmas or the summer holidays are approaching and people are likely to make bigger cash withdrawals, banks may decide to hold more liquid assets. They may also do so if they anticipate that their liquid assets may soon be squeezed by government monetary policy.

Customers may not want to take up the credit on offer. Banks may wish to make additional loans, but customers may not want to borrow. There may be insufficient demand. But will the banks not then lower their interest rates, thus encouraging people to borrow? Possibly, but it

DEFINITION

Bank (or deposits) multiplier The number of times greater the expansion of bank deposits is than the additional liquidity in banks that causes it: $1/L$ (the inverse of the liquidity ratio).

Table 18.5 The initial effect of an additional deposit of £10 billion

Liabilities	£bn	Assets	£bn
Deposits (old) Deposits (new)	100 10	Balances with the B. of E. (old) Balances with the B. of E. (new) Advances	10 10 90
Total	110	Total	110

Table 18.6 The full effect of an additional deposit of £10 billion

Liabilities	£bn	Assets	£bn
Deposits (old)	100	Balances with the B. of E. (old)	10
Deposits (new: initial)	10	Balances with the B. of E. (new)	10
(new: subsequent)	90	Advances (old)	90
		Advances (new)	90
Total	200	Total	200

is not as simple as this. Banks must keep all their interest rates in line with other financial institutions in order to remain competitive. If banks lower the interest rates they charge to borrowers, they must also lower the rate they pay to depositors. But then depositors may switch to other institutions such as building societies.

Thus, just because banks have acquired additional liquid assets, it does not automatically follow that they will create credit on the basis of it.

Just as a change in liquid assets may lead to little or no change in credit, so a change in credit may occur with little or no change in liquid assets. For example, if there is an upsurge in consumer demand for credit, banks may be very keen to grant additional loans and thus make more profits, even though they have acquired no additional liquid assets. They may simply go ahead and expand credit, and accept a lower liquidity ratio. Obviously they will be much more willing to do this if they already have plenty of spare liquidity.

?? Why might a bank with a given amount of liquid assets be more willing to expand its mortgage loans for house purchase than to expand its personal loans for the purchase of consumer goods?

Banks may not operate a simple liquidity ratio

The fact that banks hold a number of fairly liquid assets, such as money at call, bills of exchange and short-dated bonds, makes it difficult to identify a simple liquidity ratio. Which items should count as liquid?

To illustrate the problem consider the following case. Assume (a) that banks hold just three types of asset: cash, bills and advances; (b) that they operate a 10 per cent liquidity ratio; and (c) that they acquire additional cash deposits of £1 million.

If bills are counted as liquid, then the banks can purchase up to £1 million of extra bills and *still* create the full £9 million of credit. The bills are equivalent to cash. If, however, bills are not counted as liquid, then for each extra £1 worth of bills they purchase, they can grant £10 worth less credit (£9 less created, and £1 displaced by the (non-liquid) bills).

Thus whether **near money** assets such as call money, bills and short-dated bonds count as liquid may affect the amount of credit created.

Of course, banks still have to maintain adequate liquidity, but in practice they do not see a clear-cut dividing line between liquid and non-liquid assets. They try to maintain a rough balance across the liquidity range, but the precise composition of assets will vary as interest rates on the various assets vary, and as the demands for liquidity vary.

In practice, therefore, the size of the bank multiplier will vary and is thus difficult to predict in advance.

?? Is the following statement true: 'The greater the number of types of asset that are counted as being liquid, the smaller will be the bank multiplier'?

Some of the extra cash may be withdrawn by the public

If extra cash comes into the banking system, and as a result extra deposits are created, part of them may be held by the public as cash *outside* the banks. In other words, some of the extra cash leaks out of the banking system. This will result in an overall multiplier effect that is smaller than the full bank multiplier. This overall multiplier is known as the **money multiplier**. It is defined as the rise in total money supply expressed as a proportion of the rise in the monetary base that caused it: $\Delta Ms/\Delta Mb$ (where Ms is total money supply and Mb is the monetary base). In the UK, the money multiplier is given by $\Delta M4/\Delta M0$. Box 18.7 shows how the money multiplier is calculated.

DEFINITIONS

Near money Highly liquid assets (other than cash).

Money multiplier The number of times greater the expansion of money supply is than the expansion of the monetary base that caused it: $\Delta Ms/\Delta Mb$.

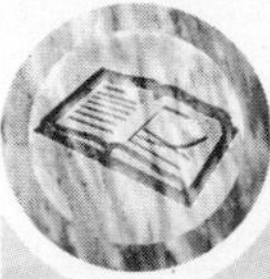

EXPLORING THE THEORY *BOX 18.7

CALCULATING THE MONEY MULTIPLIER

The money multiplier (m) is the rise in total money supply ($\Delta M4$) divided by the rise in the monetary base ($\Delta M0$):

$$m = \Delta M4/\Delta M0 \quad (1)$$

The total money supply ($M4$) consists of deposits in banks and building societies (D) plus cash held by the public (C). Thus a rise in money supply would be given by:

$$\Delta M4 = \Delta D + \Delta C \quad (2)$$

The monetary base ($M0$) consists of bank and building society reserves (R) plus cash held by the public (C). Thus a rise in the monetary base would be given by:

$$\Delta M0 = \Delta R + \Delta C \quad (3)$$

Thus, by substituting equations (2) and (3) into equation (1), the money multiplier is given by:

$$m = \frac{\Delta D + \Delta C}{\Delta R + \Delta C} \quad (4)$$

Assume now that banks wish to hold a given fraction (r) of any rise in deposits in the form of reserves, i.e.

$$r = \Delta R/\Delta D \quad (5)$$

and that the public wishes to hold a given fraction (c) of any rise in its deposits as cash, i.e.

$$c = \Delta C/\Delta D \quad (6)$$

If we now divide the top and bottom of equation (4) by ΔD we get:

$$m = \frac{\Delta D/\Delta D + \Delta C/\Delta D}{\Delta R/\Delta D + \Delta C/\Delta D} = \frac{1 + c}{r + c} \quad (7)$$

Thus if c were 0.2 and r were 0.1, the money multiplier would be:

$$(1 + 0.2)/(0.1 + 0.2) = 1.2/0.3 = 4$$

i.e. $\Delta M4 = 4 \times \Delta M0$.

??

1. If c were 0.1 and r were 0.01, by how much would M4 expand if the monetary base rose by £1 million?
2. M4 includes wholesale as well as retail deposits. Given that firms will wish to keep only a very small fraction of a rise in wholesale deposits in cash (if any at all), how will a change in the balance of wholesale and retail deposits affect the value of c and hence of the money multiplier?

What causes money supply to rise?

There are four sets of circumstances in which the money supply can rise.

Banks choose to hold a lower liquidity ratio

If banks choose to hold a lower liquidity ratio, they will have surplus liquidity. The banks have tended to choose a lower liquidity ratio over time because of the increasing use of cheque and credit-card transactions.

Surplus liquidity can be used to expand advances, which will lead to a multiplied rise in money supply. The impetus to expand advances may come from the banks themselves. The aggressive promotion of credit cards and the advertising of personal loans are familiar examples. The impetus may also come from the customer. As an economy pulls out of recession, the demand for loans is likely to rise.

An important trend in recent years has been the growth in *inter-bank lending*. Table 18.2 showed that short-term loans to other banks (including overseas banks) and CDs are now the two largest elements in banks' liquid assets. These assets may be used by a bank as the basis for expanding loans and thereby starting a chain of credit creation. But although these assets are liquid to an *individual bank*, they do not add to the liquidity of the banking system *as a whole*. By using them for credit creation, the banking system is operating with a lower *overall* liquidity ratio.

??

What effects do EFTPOS and ATMs (see Box 18.4) have on (a) banks' prudent liquidity ratios; (b) the size of the bank multiplier?

An inflow of funds from abroad

If the government intervenes in the foreign exchange market to maintain a rate of exchange below the equilibrium, there will be an excess demand for sterling. To maintain the exchange rate at this level the Bank of England has to buy up the excess foreign currencies on offer with *extra* pounds, thereby building up the foreign currency reserves. When this sterling is used to pay for UK exports and is then deposited back in the banks by the exporters, credit will be created on the basis of it, leading to a *multiplied* increase in money supply.

ISSUES AND APPLICATIONS — BOX 18.8

MAKING MONEY GROW
A touch of banking magic

Let us examine in a bit more detail the way banks create money. First, it is worth noting that most bank managers would claim that they do no such thing. Their business is to balance their books; to lend out money that has *already* been deposited, not to create things out of thin air. But, unbeknown to them perhaps, the creation of money is precisely what they *initiate* when they grant a loan.

This time, rather than assuming that the government spends extra money and issues cheques drawn on its account in the Bank of England, let us do some magic of our own. Let us assume that while digging your garden you unearth a chest containing £1000. Delighted, you rush down to your bank (Lloyds) and deposit it before it gets stolen or the police start asking awkward questions.

Your Lloyds bank manager, only slightly less delighted than you, realises that most of it can be lent to other customers and hence earn interest for the bank (more than the bank pays you!). First, though, the bank deposits the bulk of the cash with the Bank of England, thus swelling its operational balances there. Assuming, for simplicity, that all banks operate a 10 per cent liquidity ratio, the bank will only need to retain £100 in cash for any withdrawals you are likely to make. But the bank now has £900 worth of balances in the Bank of England above what it needs to maintain. It thus grants loans of £900.

Assume that the £900 is lent to Amanda to buy a set of golf clubs. The sports shop, on receiving her cheque for £900, deposits it in its account in, say, the Midland. When the cheque is cleared, the Midland's balances in the Bank of England will have risen by £900. The Midland bank can now use this increased liquidity to make additional loans itself. Duly keeping 10 per cent back (i.e. £90), it grants a loan of £810 to Jason to buy a luxury hamster cage and a pair of very rare Mongolian crested hamsters from the local pet shop.

The pet shop banks Jason's cheque in its branch of Barclays. When it is cleared, Barclays lends 90 per cent (i.e. £729) of it to Charlene to buy a mountain bike. The bike shop deposits Charlene's cheque in its branch of the National Westminster, which duly makes a loan (or loans totalling) £656.10. And so on and so on ...

This process is shown in the table.

Bank	New deposits	Extra balances required at Bank of England	New loans granted
Your bank (Lloyds)	£1000.00	£100.00	£900.00
Amanda's bank (Midland)	£900.00	£90.00	£810.00
Jason's bank (Barclays)	£810.00	£81.00	£729.00
Charlene's bank (Nat. West.)	£729.00	£72.90	£656.10
.	.	.	.
.	.	.	.
Totals	£10 000.00	£1000.00	£9000.00

?? 'Surely, when people deposit money in bank accounts, they often demand all or nearly all of it out in cash. Isn't it very dangerous, then, for banks to keep only a small percentage of it in cash or in their operational balances in the Bank of England?' How would you answer this worry?

What we have been describing here is a **total currency flow** surplus: a net surplus on all elements of the balance of payments (current plus capital) but excluding the reserves.

Under a totally free floating rate, total currency flow surpluses will be eliminated by an appreciation of the exchange rate: there will be no expansion of the money supply. If, however, the Bank of England attempts to maintain an exchange rate below the equilibrium, it must continue to supply extra sterling to meet the shortfall and thus continue to expand the money supply. Eventually, however, the rise in money supply will eliminate the surplus because it will raise aggregate demand, which will lead to more imports and, via higher prices, to fewer exports. Once the total currency flow surplus has been eliminated, money supply will stop rising.

A similar effect will be experienced if depositors in foreign currencies wish to switch their deposits into sterling in the UK – in response, say, to higher UK interest rates. If the exchange rate is not allowed to appreciate, the demand for sterling will increase.

The money supply will also expand if depositors of *sterling* in banks overseas redeposit their sterling in the UK. This is a direct increase in the money supply. In an open economy like the UK, movements of sterling and other

DEFINITION

Total currency flow on the balance of payments The current plus capital account balance but excluding the reserves.

currencies into and out of the country can be very large, leading to large fluctuations in the money supply.

?? Describe the process whereby a currency flow deficit will lead to a fall in the money supply.

The government can take deliberate steps to offset the monetary effects of currency flow surpluses or deficits. This process is known as *sterilisation*. It is examined in Chapter 24.

A public-sector deficit: a PSBR

The public-sector borrowing requirement is the difference between public-sector expenditure and public-sector receipts. To meet this deficit the government has to borrow money. In general, the bigger the PSBR, the greater will be the growth in the money supply. Just how the money supply will be affected, however, depends on the form the borrowing takes. There are six possible forms. Assume in each case a PSBR of £1 billion.

1. The government sells securities to the Bank of England. The Bank of England purchases £1 billion of government securities, and credits the government's account at the Bank of England by £1 billion. The government, when it spends this £1 billion, pays with cheques drawn on its account at the Bank of England. When the recipients of these cheques pay them into their banks, the banks will present the cheques to the Bank of England, and their own balances at the Bank of England will rise by £1 billion. Thus banks' liabilities (customers' deposits of government payments) and assets (balances with the Bank of England) have both increased by £1 billion. Money supply has therefore increased by £1 billion.

Since banks' balances with the Bank of England are liquid assets, credit will probably be created. This will lead to an eventual rise in money supply considerably greater than £1 billion.

2. The government sells securities to overseas purchasers. This will lead to an inflow of foreign currency. If the government does not allow the exchange rate to appreciate, a multiplied process of money expansion will occur.

3. The Bank of England, on behalf of the government, sells Treasury bills to the banking sector. If £1 billion of Treasury bills are sold to the discount houses, the discount houses will borrow money at call from the banks, or sell bills to the banks, to pay for these Treasury bills. Banks will thus acquire £1 billion of extra call notes and bills, but their cash or balances at the Bank of England will be reduced by £1 billion.

When, however, the government spends the £1 billion and the money finds its way back to the banks, the banks' balances at the Bank of England will rise back again by £1 billion.

There has thus been no overall change in balances at the Bank of England, but banks' holdings of call notes and bills have risen. To the extent that these are regarded as liquid assets, they can be used as the liquidity base for additional loans to customers. A multiplied process of money expansion will occur: money supply will expand by more than £1 billion.

4. The government sells bonds to the banks. If £1 billion of bonds are sold to the banks, the banks' balances at the Bank of England will be reduced by £1 billion. When the government spends the money and it is deposited in the banks, the banks' balances at the Bank of England will be restored. Banks have thus had an increase of £1 billion deposits (new money) on their liabilities side, and £1 billion of government bonds on their assets side.

The liquidity ratio, however, has been reduced, since bonds (except for very short-dated ones) are regarded as illiquid. If banks are already operating at their minimum prudent liquidity ratio, they must reduce advances (and hence deposits) by £1 billion, which will exactly match the £1 billion increase in deposits from the PSBR. In this case there will have been *no* expansion of the money supply at all.

5. The government sells bonds and Treasury bills to the general public and non-bank firms (ultimately known as the 'non-bank private sector'). When the public buy the bonds or bills they will draw money from their banks. When the government spends the money it will be redeposited in banks. There is no increase in money supply. It is just a case of existing money changing hands.

6. The government borrows foreign currency, thereby directly financing government imports. This will not affect money supply, since it involves no *sterling* transactions and hence will not affect banks' sterling deposits.

Financing the PSBR by methods 1, 2 and 3 will lead to a multiple growth in money supply (assuming sufficient demand for credit). Financing it by method 4 will lead to little or no growth in the money supply. Financing it by methods 5 and 6 will lead to no growth in the money supply at all.

Note that if there is a public-sector *surplus* (public-sector debt repayment or PSDR), this will either reduce the money supply or have no effect, depending on what the government does with the surplus. The fact that there is a surplus means that the public sector is spending less than it receives in taxes, etc. The initial effect, therefore, is to reduce the money in the economy: it is being 'retired' in the Bank of England.

If the government then uses this money to buy back securities from the non-bank private sector, the money will merely return to the economy, and there will be no net effect on money supply. If, however, the government uses it to buy back Treasury bills from banks, banks' liquidity will not be restored: the return of money to the banks will be offset by a fall in bills. There will thus be a multiple contraction of credit. Similarly if the government reduces its borrowing from the Bank of England, the money will remain 'retired'. There will be a multiple contraction of credit.

A change in the method of financing the national debt

The rate of growth of money supply will be affected by the way in which government finance is raised. If there is a switch to methods 1, 2 or 3 (on page 566) from methods 4, 5 or 6, money supply will increase. How the government raises finance depends on its monetary policy (see Chapter 19). In practice the government's choice is somewhat limited. It can choose whether to sell bonds or Treasury bills, but it cannot decide just who is to purchase them – banks/discount houses, the general public or foreigners.

?? If the government borrows *but does not spend the proceeds*, what effect will this have on the money supply if it borrows from (a) the banking sector; (b) the non-bank private sector?

The flow-of-funds equation

All these effects on money supply can be summarised using a **flow-of-funds equation**. This shows the components of a *change* in money supply. A change in money supply is a flow into (increase) or out of (decrease) the money stock. (Remember the distinction between stocks and flows.) In other words, if we want to compare the size of the money stock at one point in time (M_{s_t}) with that of a previous point in time ($M_{s_{t-1}}$), we have to look at the flow (change) of money between those two points (ΔM_s).

$$M_{s_t} = M_{s_{t-1}} + \Delta M_s$$

So what does ΔM_s consist of? The answer is given in the flow-of-funds equation, which consists of four major items (or 'counterparts' as they are known). The following flow-of-funds equation is the one most commonly used, that for M4:

ΔM_s	*equals*	PSBR	(Item 1)
	minus	Sales of public-sector debt to (or *plus* purchases of public-sector debt from) the non-bank private sector	(Item 2)
	plus	Banks' and building societies' sterling lending to the UK private sector	(Item 3)
	plus	External effect	(Item 4)

Public-sector borrowing (item 1) will lead to a direct increase in the money supply, but not if it is funded by selling bonds and bills to the non-bank private sector. Such sales (item 2) have therefore to be subtracted from the PSBR. But conversely, if the government buys back old bonds from the non-bank private sector, this will further increase the money supply.

The initial increase in liquidity from the sale of government securities to the banking sector is given by item 1. This increase in their liquidity will enable banks to create credit. To the extent that this extra lending is to the UK private sector (item 3), money supply will increase, and by a multiple of the initial increase in liquidity (item 1). Bank lending may also increase (item 3) even if there is no increase in liquidity or even a reduction in liquidity (item 1 is zero or negative), if banks respond to increases in the demand for loans by accepting a lower liquidity ratio.

Finally, if there is a currency flow surplus and hence a net inflow of funds from abroad (item 4), this too will increase the money supply. A currency flow deficit will appear as a negative figure. Also included in item 4 is that part of the PSBR that is funded by borrowing in *foreign* currency. Since, as we saw when looking at the financing of the PSBR, such borrowing does not increase the money supply, it reduces the otherwise expansionary effect on the money supply of the PSBR. It thus enters item 4 with a negative value.

The flow-of-funds equation we have just described is a simplified version of the one actually used in official statistics to analyse the components of changes in M4. The equation can easily be modified to show changes in M2.

Table 18.7 shows the components of changes in M4 for 1989 and 1996. It is interesting to compare the two years. In 1996 there was a large public-sector deficit (PSBR),

DEFINITION

Flow-of-funds equation The various items making up an increase (or decrease) in money supply.

Table 18.7 Counterparts to changes in M4 (£m)

	PSBR(+) PSDR (−) (1)	Sales (−)/purchases (+) of public-sector debt to/from non-bank private sector (2)	Banks' and building societies' sterling lending to UK private sector (less increases in banks' capital) (3)	External effect: inflows (+) outflows (−) (4)	Total ΔM4
1989	−9082	+12 974	+76 385	−15 318	= +64 959
1996	+24 919	−19 222	+47 070	+6 607	= +59 374

Source: *Financial Statistics* (ONS).

which therefore had the effect of increasing the money supply. The effect was limited, however, by substantial sales of government stock (item 2) and there was only a moderately large amount of credit created by the banking sector (item 3). In 1989, however, there was a public-sector surplus (PSDR), which, other things being equal, would have reduced the money supply. But as you can see quite clearly from the table, other things were not equal: there was a massive release of liquidity to the private sector from the repayment of public debt (item 2) and an even more massive increase in bank lending (item 3), although this was to some extent offset by a large currency flow deficit (an outflow of funds under item 4).

The relationship between money supply and the rate of interest

Simple monetary theory often assumes that the supply of money is totally independent of interest rates. This is illustrated in Figure 18.2. The money supply is 'exogenous'. The supply of money is assumed to be determined by government: what the government chooses it to be, or what it allows it to be by its choice of the level and method of financing the PSBR.

More complex models, and especially Keynesian models, assume that higher interest rates will lead to higher levels of money supply, as in Figure 18.3. The reasons for this are as follows:

- Increases in money supply may occur as a result of banks expanding credit in response to the demand for credit. This assumes that banks have surplus liquidity in the first place. Higher demand for credit will drive up interest rates, making it more profitable for banks to supply more credit.
- Higher interest rates may encourage depositors to switch their deposits from sight accounts (earning little or no interest) to time accounts. Since money is less likely to be withdrawn quickly from time accounts, banks may feel the need to hold less liquidity, and therefore may decide to increase credit, thus expanding the money supply.
- Higher interest rates attract deposits from overseas. This increases the money supply in the same way as does a balance of payments surplus.

An upward-sloping supply curve assumes that interest rates are determined by the market: by the interaction of supply and demand for money. An increase in demand for money raises interest rates, which in turn increases the supply of money (see sections 18.4 and 18.5). Supply is merely reflecting demand and is thus *endogenously* determined.

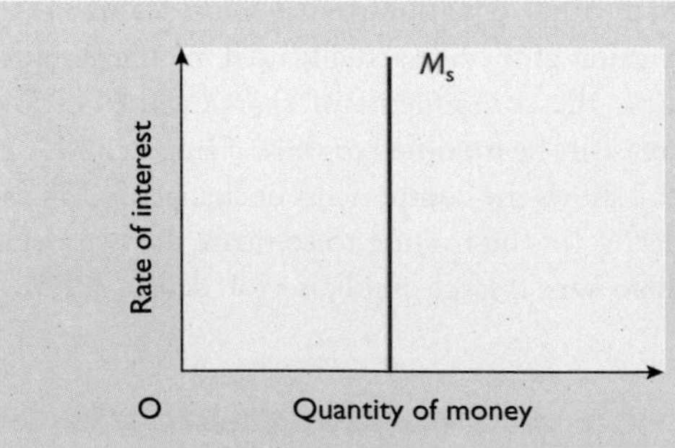

Figure 18.2 The supply of money curve: exogenous money supply

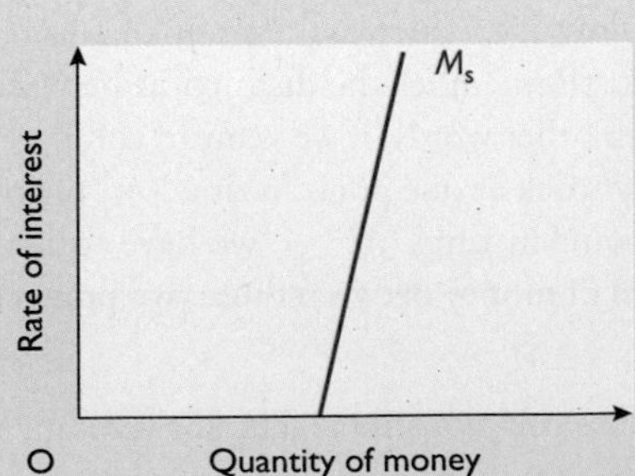

Figure 18.3 The supply of money curve: endogenous money supply

SECTION SUMMARY

1. Money supply can be defined in a number of different ways, depending on what items are included. M0, the narrowest definition, only includes cash and banks' operational balances in the Bank of England. M2 is cash in circulation plus all retail deposits (including time deposits and building society deposits). M4 is M2 plus all wholesale bank and building society deposits. M3H is M4 plus public corporations' deposits and all foreign currency deposits.
2. Bank deposits are a major proportion of money supply (except M0). The expansion of bank deposits is the major element in the expansion of the money supply.
3. Bank deposits expand through a process of credit creation. If banks' liquid assets increase, they can be used as a base for increasing loans. When the loans are redeposited in banks, they form the base for yet more loans, and thus takes place a process of multiple credit expansion. The ratio of the increase of deposits to an expansion of banks' liquidity base is called the 'bank multiplier'. It is the inverse of the liquidity ratio.
4. In practice it is difficult to predict the precise amount by which money supply will expand if there is an increase in cash. The reasons are that banks may choose to hold a different liquidity ratio; customers may not take up all the credit on offer; there may be no simple liquidity ratio given the range of near money assets; and some of the extra cash may leak away into extra cash holdings by the public.
5. Money supply will rise if (a) banks choose to hold a lower liquidity ratio and thus create more credit for an existing amount of liquidity; (b) there is a total currency flow surplus; (c) the government runs a PSBR and finances it by borrowing from the banking sector or from abroad; (d) an increased proportion of the national debt is financed by borrowing from the banking sector or from abroad.
6. The flow-of-funds equation shows the components of any change in money supply. A rise in money supply equals the PSBR *minus* sales of public-sector debt to the non-bank private sector, *plus* banks' lending to the private sector (less increases in banks' capital), *plus* inflows of money from abroad.
7. Simple monetary theory assumes that the supply of money is independent of interest rates. In practice, a rise in interest rates will often lead to an increase in money supply. But conversely if the government raises interest rates, the supply of money may fall in response to a lower demand for money.

18.4 The demand for money

The motives for holding money

The demand for money refers to the desire to *hold* money: to keep your wealth in the form of money, rather than spending it on goods and services or using it to purchase financial assets such as bonds or shares. It is usual to distinguish three reasons why people want to hold their assets in the form of money.

The transactions motive. Since money is a medium of exchange, it is required for conducting transactions. But since people receive money only at intervals (e.g. weekly or monthly) and not continuously, they require to hold balances of money in cash or in sight accounts.

The precautionary motive. Unforeseen circumstances can arise, such as a car breakdown. Thus individuals often hold some additional money as a precaution. Firms too keep precautionary balances because of uncertainties about the timing of their receipts and payments. If a large customer is late in making payment, a firm may be unable to pay its suppliers unless it has spare liquidity.

The speculative or assets motive. Certain firms and individuals who wish to purchase financial assets such as bonds, shares or other securities, may prefer to wait if they feel that their price is likely to fall. In the meantime they will hold idle money balances instead. This speculative demand can be quite high when the price of securities is considered certain to fall. Money when used for this purpose is a means of temporarily storing wealth.

Similarly, people who at some time in the future will require foreign currency (people such as importers, holiday makers, or those thinking of investing abroad or in foreign securities) may prefer to wait before exchanging pounds into the relevant foreign currencies if they believe that the sterling price of these currencies is likely to fall (the pound is likely to *appreciate*).

The transactions and precautionary demand for money: L_1

The transactions plus precautionary demand for money is termed L_1. 'L' stands for **liquidity preference**: that is, the desire to hold assets in liquid form. Money balances held for these two purposes are called **active balances**: money to be used as a medium of exchange. What determines the size of L_1?

The major determinant of L_1 is *national income* (Y). The bigger people's income, the more their purchases and the bigger their demand for active balances.

The *frequency with which people are paid* also affects L_1. The less frequently they are paid, the greater the level of money balances they will tend to hold. For example, people paid £100 per week, whose expenditure is spread evenly over the week and who spend all the £100 by the end of the week, will have roughly £50 (in the bank or in cash) on average: that is, midway between pay days. People paid £400 per month will have roughly £200 on average: that is, mid-month. Income is the same in both cases, but monthly paid people will have a much higher demand for active balances.

> **??** Will students in receipt of a grant or an allowance who are paid once per term have a high or a low transactions demand for money relative to their income?

The *rate of interest* has some effect on L_1, albeit rather small (see Figure 18.4). At high rates of interest, people may choose to spend less and save more of their income, e.g. by buying shares. The effect is likely to be bigger on the precautionary demand: a higher interest rate may encourage people to risk tying up their money. Firms' active balances are more likely to be sensitive to changes in r than those of individuals.

The elasticity of L_1 with respect to changes in the rate of interest will also depend on how money is defined. The demand for M0 is likely to be more elastic than the demand for M2 or M4. A rise in the rate of interest may encourage people to switch from holding cash to keeping more money in an instant-access, but interest-bearing account. The demand for M0 will fall, but the demand for M2 and M4 (which include both cash and deposits) will remain the same.

Other determinants of L_1 include the season of the year: people require more money balances at Christmas, for example. Also, any other factors that affect consumption will affect L_1.

The increased use of credit cards in recent years has reduced both the transactions and precautionary demands. Paying once a month for goods requires less money on average than paying separately for each item purchased. Also the possession of a credit card reduces or even eliminates the need to hold precautionary balances for many people.

The speculative (or assets) demand for money: L_2

The speculative demand for money balances is termed L_2. Money balances held for this purpose are called **idle balances**.

People who possess wealth, whether it be wealthy people or simply small savers, have to decide the best form in which to hold that wealth. Do they keep it in cash in a piggy bank, or in a current account in a real bank; or do they put it in some interest-bearing time account; or do they buy stocks and shares or government bonds; or do they buy some physical asset such as a car or property?

In making these decisions, people will have to weigh up the relative advantages and disadvantages of the various alternative assets. Assets can be compared according to two criteria: *liquidity* and the *possibility of earning income*. Just as we saw in the case of a bank's assets, these two criteria tend to conflict. The more liquid an asset is, the lower is likely to be the income earned from holding it. Thus cash is totally liquid to the holder: it can be used to buy other assets (or spent on goods) instantly, but it earns no interest. Stocks and shares, on the other hand, are not very liquid since they cannot be sold instantly *at a guaranteed price*. (They *can* be sold pretty well instantly, but if share prices are depressed, a considerable loss may be incurred in so doing.) But stocks and shares have the *potential* of earning quite a high income for the holder, not only in terms of the dividends paid out of the firms' profits, but also in terms of the capital gain from any increase in the shares' prices.

DEFINITIONS

Liquidity preference The demand for holding assets in the form of money.

Active balances Money held for transactions and precautionary purposes.

Idle balances Money held for speculative purposes: money held in anticipation of a fall in asset prices.

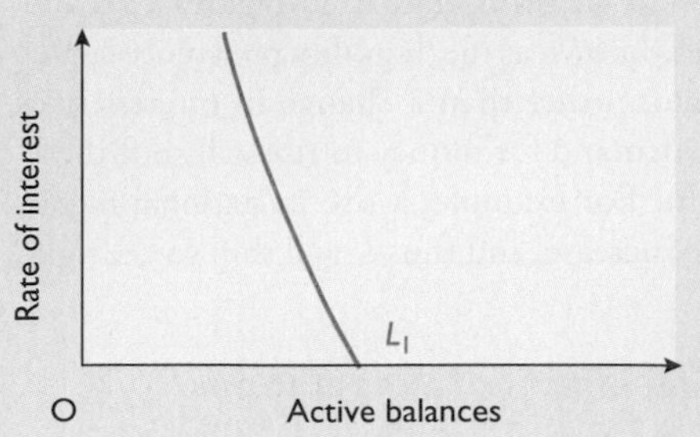

Figure 18.4 The transactions-plus-precautionary demand for money: L_1

??
Buying something like a car is at the other end of the spectrum from holding cash. A car is highly illiquid, but yields a high return to the owner. In what form is this 'return'?

The major determinant of L_2 is expectations of changes in the earning potential of securities and other assets. If the earning potential of an asset goes up, people will be likely to switch to that asset from others with a lower earning potential. Thus, for example, if people believe that the stock market is about to go through a period of 'boom' with share prices going up rapidly, they will switch some of their wealth into stocks and shares. Thus the greater the earning potential of non-money assets, the less will be the demand for money (with its zero earning potential in the case of M0, and with only a relatively low earning potential in the case of M2 and M4).

The major determinants of expectations of assets' earning potential are (a) expectations about changes in security prices and interest rates, and (b) expectations about changes in the exchange rate.

Security prices and interest rates

If the market price of securities is high, the rate of interest (i.e. the rate of return) on these securities will be low (see section 18.1). Potential purchasers of these securities will probably wait until their prices fall and the rate of interest rises. Similarly, existing holders of securities will probably sell them while the price is high, hoping to buy them back again when the price falls, thus making a capital gain. *In the meantime, therefore, large speculative balances of money will be held.* L_2 is high.

If, on the other hand, the rate of interest is high, then L_2 is likely to be low. To take advantage of the high rate of return on securities, people buy them now instead of holding on to their money.

??
Would the demand for securities be low if their price was high, but was expected to go on *rising*?

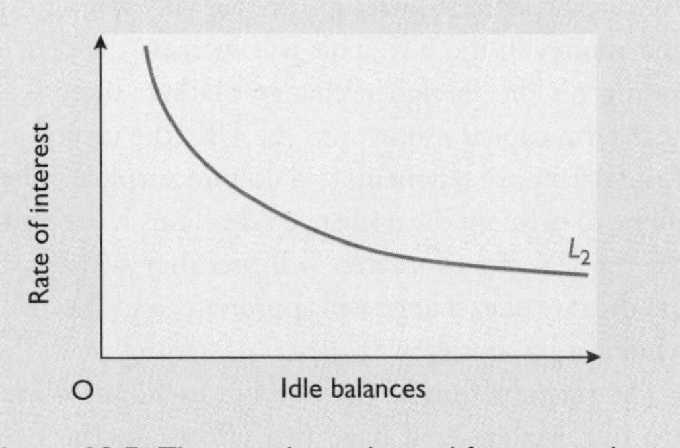

Figure 18.5 The speculative demand for money: L_2

The relationship between L_2 and the rate of interest (r) is shown in Figure 18.5. The inverse relationship between r and L_2 gives a downward-sloping curve.

As with L_1, the elasticity of L_2 depends on how money is defined. Only this time it is the other way round. Only very short-term speculative balances will be held in cash: they will be held mainly in deposits which earn some interest, but which are still totally risk free. Thus it is the demand for broad money, rather than the monetary base (M0), that varies with speculative demand and hence interest rates.

Speculative demand and the exchange rate

In an open economy like the UK where large-scale movements of currencies across the foreign exchanges take place, expectations about changes in the exchange rate are a major determinant of the speculative demand for money.

If people believe that the pound is likely to appreciate, they will want to hold sterling until it does appreciate. For example, if the current exchange rate is £1 = $1.50 and speculators believe that it will shortly rise to £1 = $1.75, then if they are correct they will make a 25c per £1 profit by holding sterling. The more quickly is the exchange rate expected to rise, the more will people want to hold sterling (as money). If, however, people believe that it will be a slow rise over time, they will want to buy sterling assets (such as UK government bonds) rather than money, since such assets will also earn the holder a rate of interest.

Conversely, if people believe that the exchange rate is likely to fall in the near future, they will economise on their holdings of sterling, preferring to hold their liquid assets in some other currency – the one most likely to appreciate against other currencies.

Graphically, changes in expectations about the exchange rate will have the effect of shifting the L_2 curve in Figure 18.5.

There is a further complication here. Expectations about changes in the exchange rate will themselves be influenced by the interest rate (relative to overseas interest rates). If the

UK rate of interest goes up, people will want to deposit their money in the UK. This will increase the demand for sterling on the foreign exchange market: there will be a short-term capital inflow into the UK (the capital account of the balance of payments will go into surplus). The effect will be to drive up the exchange rate. Thus if people believe that the UK rate of interest will rise, they will *also* believe that the rate of exchange will appreciate, and they will want to hold larger speculative balances of sterling.

The introduction of the 'foreign exchange dimension' into our analysis will have two effects on the L_2 curve. First, the curve will become more elastic. If the rate of interest is low and is thought likely to rise, the speculative demand is likely to be *very* high. Not only will people hold money in anticipation of a fall in security prices, but they will also hold money (sterling) in anticipation of an appreciation of the exchange rate.

Second, the curve will become more unstable. Expectations of changes in the exchange rate do not just depend on current domestic interest rates. They depend on the current and anticipated future state of the balance of trade, the rate of inflation, the current and anticipated levels of interest rates in other major trading countries, the price of oil, and so on. If any of these cause people to expect a lower exchange rate, the speculative demand for money will fall: L_2 will shift to the left.

?? Which way is the L_2 curve likely to shift in the following cases?

(a) The balance of trade moves into deficit.
(b) People anticipate that foreign interest rates are likely to rise substantially relative to domestic ones.
(c) The domestic rate of inflation falls below that of other major trading countries.
(d) People believe that the pound is about to depreciate.

The total demand for money: $L_1 + L_2$

Figure 18.6 shows the total demand for money (L) plotted against the rate of interest (r). This is found by the horizontal addition of curves L_1 and L_2 in Figures 18.4 and 18.5. This curve is known as the 'liquidity preference curve'.

Any factor, other than a change in interest rates, that causes the demand for money to rise will shift the L curve to the right. For example, a rise in national income will cause L_1 to increase, and thus L will shift to the right.

Additional effects of expectations

We have talked about expectations and their importance in determining the speculative demand for money. In particular we have looked at (a) the effect of interest rates on people's anticipations of future security prices and (b) the effect of expectations about exchange rate movements. There are two other ways in which expectations can influence the demand for money, and make it more unstable.

Expectations about prices. If people expect prices to rise, they may reduce their money balances and purchase goods and assets now, before prices do rise. This will tend to shift L to the left. (Note, though, that once prices *have* risen, people will need more money to conduct the same amount of transactions.)

Expectations of interest rate levels over the longer term. If people come to expect that interest rates will normally be higher than they used to be, then any given interest rate will seem lower relative to the 'normal' rate than it used to be. People will be more inclined to hold speculative balances of money in anticipation of a rise in interest rates. This will tend to shift L upwards.

In an era of uncertainty about inflation and interest rates, people's expectations will be hard to predict. They will be volatile and susceptible to rumours and political events. In such circumstances, the L curve itself will be hard to predict and will be subject to considerable shifts. Generally, it is likely that the greater the uncertainty, the greater will be

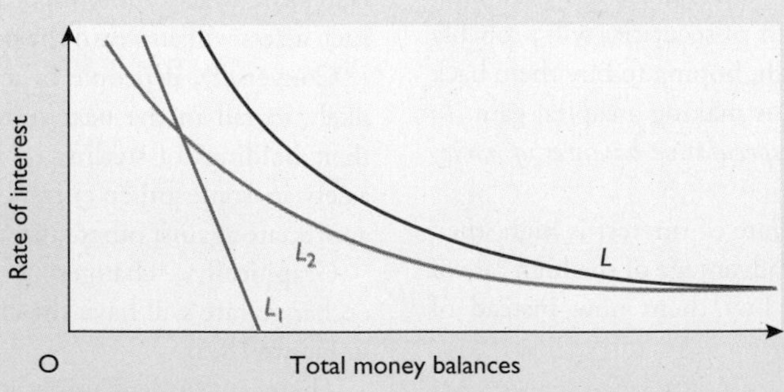

Figure 18.6 The total demand for money curve: L (= L_1 + L_2)

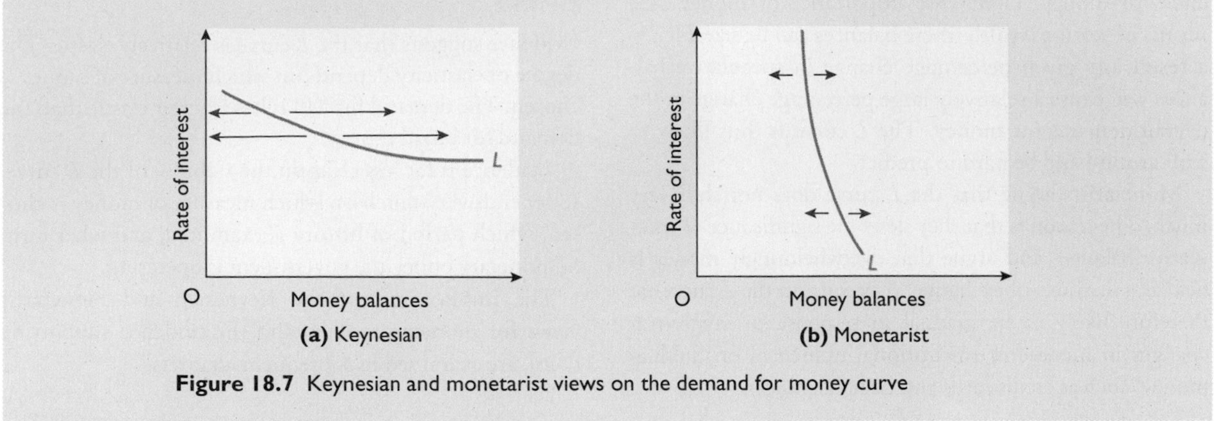

Figure 18.7 Keynesian and monetarist views on the demand for money curve

the preference for liquidity, and the greater the risk of tying money up in illiquid assets.

Keynesian and monetarist views on the demand for money

Keynesians and monetarists disagree over the shape and stability of the liquidity preference curve (the demand for money curve). In fact this is one of the most crucial areas of disagreement between them. Keynesians argue that the *L* curve is relatively elastic and unstable, as in Figure 18.7(a). Monetarists argue that it is relatively inelastic and stable, as in Figure 18.7(b).

The shape of the demand for money curve

The disagreement here is over the substitutability of assets. Are other assets a close substitute for money? Are non-money assets such as stocks and shares, bonds and property close substitutes for each other?

To understand the debate we must introduce the concept of **portfolio balance**. People hold a whole range (or 'portfolio') of assets, from money at one end of the spectrum of liquidity to physical assets such as property and consumer durables at the other. Between the two extremes come the various financial assets such as bonds and shares. The balance of assets in people's portfolios will depend on the relative returns on these assets. If the return on one type of asset goes up, people will switch to holding more of that asset in their portfolios. The more substitutable one asset is for another, the more readily people will switch.

For simplicity let us group assets into just three types: money, financial assets and physical goods.

Keynesians. Keynesians argue that money and financial assets are relatively close substitutes for each other. They are alternative means of holding wealth. Money has the advantage of liquidity and hence lack of risk. Financial assets have the advantage of earning income. People thus switch between them as the balance of advantage changes. As interest rates go up, the balance of advantage shifts towards holding financial assets which earn these higher interest rates. People thus hold less of their wealth in the form of money. The demand for money falls significantly. *The L curve is elastic.*

Physical goods, by contrast, are not seen by Keynesians as being close substitutes for financial assets (and certainly not for money). They are far too illiquid.

Thus the stress on money as a *means of storing wealth* and the close substitutability of money and other financial assets give an elastic liquidity preference curve.

Monetarists. Monetarists stress the function of money as a *medium of exchange* and play down its role as a store of wealth. It is thus not a close substitute for financial assets. If the rate of interest changes, there will be relatively little shifting between money and financial assets. *The L curve is inelastic.*

At the same time monetarists argue that physical goods *are* a relatively close substitute for financial assets. If, therefore, the rate of interest falls on financial assets, then people, rather than shifting away from financial assets towards money, will buy more physical goods instead.

The stability of the demand for money curve

Keynesians argue that expectations about inflation, exchange rates and interest rates frequently change and have significant effects on the holding of speculative bal-

DEFINITION

Portfolio balance The balance of assets, according to their liquidity, that people choose to hold in their portfolios.

ances of money. Given the importance of money as a means of storing wealth, these balances can be sizeable. As a result any given percentage change in speculative balances will cause a relatively large percentage change in the overall demand for money. The L curve is thus likely to shift around and be hard to predict.

Monetarists argue that the L curve does not shift very much. The reason is that they deny the significance of speculative balances and argue that overwhelmingly money is held as a medium of exchange. Any shifts in the L curve are therefore likely to be gradual in response to longer-run changes in income or institutional influences on holding money (such as credit cards and cash machines).

Evidence

Evidence suggests that the L curve is relatively elastic. The degree of elasticity depends on which measure of money is chosen. The demand for M0 is less interest elastic than the demand for broad money.

Evidence is far less clear on the stability of the L curve. It depends very much on which measure of money is chosen, which period of history is examined, and what form of monetary policy the government is operating.

The implications of the Keynesian and monetarist views for monetary policy, and the evidence supporting them, are examined in subsequent chapters.

SECTION SUMMARY

1. The three motives for holding money are the transactions, precautionary and speculative (or assets) motives.
2. The transactions-plus-precautionary demand for money (L_1) depends primarily on the level of national income, the frequency with which people are paid and institutional arrangements (such as the use of credit or debit cards). It also depends to some degree on the rate of interest. The transactions-plus-precautionary demand for very narrow money is more interest elastic than for broader money.
3. The speculative demand for money (L_2) depends primarily on anticipations about future movements in security prices (and hence their rate of return) and future movements in exchange rates. If security prices are anticipated to fall or the exchange rate to rise, people will hold more money balances.
4. The demand for money is also influenced by expectations of price changes and the levels of interest rates over the longer term.
5. Keynesians argue that the demand for money is elastic with respect to interest rates and also unstable. They stress the importance of money as a means of storing wealth, and argue that (broad) money is a close substitute for financial assets. Thus people will readily switch back and forth from money to other assets.
6. Monetarists argue that the demand for money is inelastic with respect to interest rates and also fairly stable over time. They stress the importance of money as a medium of exchange, and argue that money is not a close substitute for financial assets. Thus people will not switch back and forth, but will hold a relatively constant amount of money.

18.5 Equilibrium

Equilibrium in the money market

Equilibrium in the money market will be where the demand for money (L) is equal to the supply of money (M_s). This equilibrium will be achieved through changes in the rate of interest and the exchange rate. For the moment let us ignore the exchange rate and concentrate on changes in the rate of interest.

In Figure 18.8, equilibrium is achieved with a rate of interest r_e and a quantity of money M_e. If the rate of interest were above r_e, people would have money balances surplus to their needs. They would use these to buy securities and other assets. This would drive up the price of securities and drive down the rate of interest. As the rate of interest fell, so there would be a contraction of the money supply (a movement down along the M_s curve) and an increase in the demand for money balances – especially speculative balances, since people would increasingly judge with lower interest rates that now was not the time to buy securities (there is a movement down along the liquidity preference curve). The interest rate would go on falling until it reached r_e. Equilibrium would then be achieved.

Similarly, if the rate of interest were below r_e, people would have insufficient money balances. They would sell securities, thus lowering their prices and raising the rate of interest until it reached r_e.

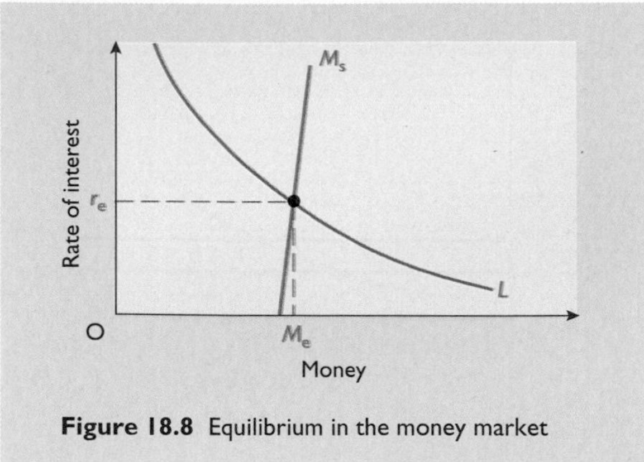

Figure 18.8 Equilibrium in the money market

A shift in either M_s or L will lead to a new equilibrium quantity of money and rate of interest at the new intersection of the curves.

In practice there is no *one* single rate of interest. Different assets have different rates of interest. Table 18.8 gives examples of the rates of interest on various assets in February 1998.

Equilibrium in the money markets, therefore, will be first where the *total* demand for and supply of money are equal. This is achieved by adjustments in the average rate of interest. Second, it will be where demand and supply of *each type* of financial asset separately balance. If, for example, there were excess demand for short-term loans (like money at call) and excess supply of money to invest in long-term assets (like bonds), short-term rates of interest would rise relative to long-term rates.

Equilibrium in both the money market and national income

Changes in money supply (or demand) will affect national income via changes in the rate of interest. It is a three-stage process. This is illustrated in Figure 18.9:

- In diagram (a) a rise in money supply (M_s) will lead to a fall in the rate of interest (r): this is necessary to restore equilibrium in the money market.
- In diagram (b) the fall in r will lead to a rise in investment and other forms of borrowing (I). Since borrowing money will be cheaper, investment will cost less.
- In diagram (c) the rise in investment (being an injection) will lead to a multiplied rise in national income (Y) and aggregate demand (AD).

The rise in income will be less than that shown in diagram (c), however, since any rise in income will lead to a rise in the transactions demand for money, L_1. L will shift to the right in diagram (a), and thus r will not fall as much as illustrated. Thus investment (diagram (b)) and income (diagram (c)) will not rise as much as illustrated either.

?? Trace through the effect of a rise in the demand for money.

How big will the effect of changes in money supply be on output, employment and prices?

The effect on national income will be bigger:

- The less elastic the liquidity preference curve: this will cause a bigger change in the rate of interest.
- The more interest elastic the investment curve: this will cause a bigger change in investment.
- The lower the marginal propensity to withdraw (*mpw*), and hence the flatter the withdrawals function: this will cause a bigger multiplied change in national income and aggregate demand.

The change in aggregate demand will have a bigger effect on output and employment, the more elastic is the aggregate supply curve. This is illustrated in Figure 18.10. Aggregate demand rises from AD to AD'. With the more

Table 18.8 Selected rates of interest: end February 1998

Asset	Period of loan	Rate of interest (% per annum)
Call money	Overnight	7.38
Treasury bills	3 months	7.09
Inter-bank loans	1 month	7.44
Certificates of deposit	3 months	7.44
Long-dated government bonds	20 years	6.11
Building society mortgage	Variable (25 years typical)	8.20
Ordinary shares (dividend yield)	≃	2.96
(Banks' base rate)	≃	7.25

Source: *Financial Statistics* (ONS).

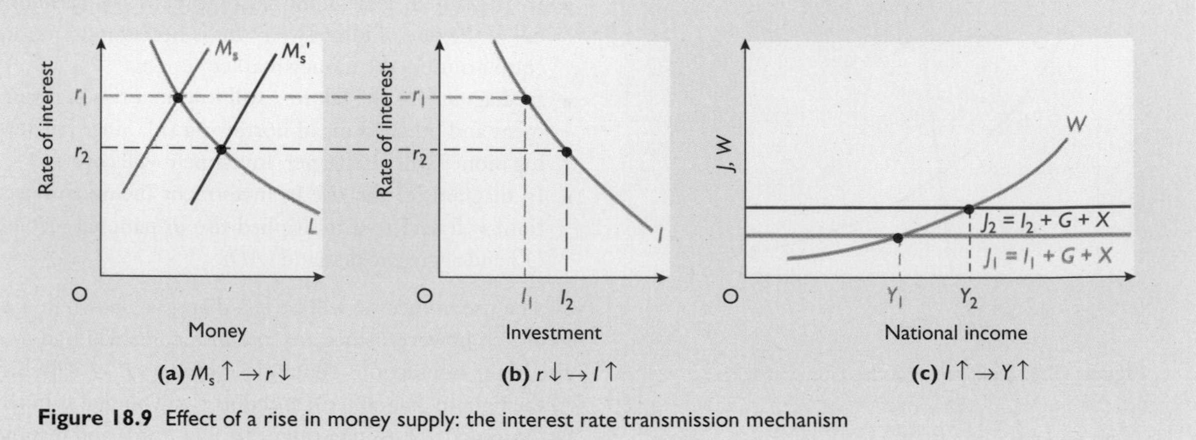

Figure 18.9 Effect of a rise in money supply: the interest rate transmission mechanism

elastic aggregate supply curve AS_2, national output rises to Y_2. With the less elastic curve, AS_1, output only rises to Y_1.

All these issues – the shape and stability of the *L* curve, the shape and stability of the *I* curve and the shape of the *AS* curve – are highly controversial.

Generally, Keynesians argue that increases in money supply have a small and uncertain effect on aggregate demand because the *L* curve is elastic and unstable and because investment is not very responsive to changes in interest rates; but that any increase that does occur in aggregate demand is likely to affect output and employment if there is demand-deficient unemployment: *AS* is relatively elastic until full employment is approached.

Monetarists argue that increases in money supply have a large effect on aggregate demand (certainly in the long run) because the *L* curve is inelastic and investment is responsive to changes in interest rates; but that this increase in aggregate demand will simply be reflected in the long run in higher prices: the *AS* curve is vertical.

These arguments will be examined in Chapters 20 and 21.

Equilibrium in an open economy

Finally let us see what happens when money supply changes in an open economy with floating exchange rates. Assume that the money supply increases. This has three direct effects:

- *Part* of the excess balances will be used to purchase foreign assets. This will therefore lead to an increase in the supply of pounds coming on to the foreign exchange markets.
- The excess supply of money in the domestic money market will push down the rate of interest. This will reduce the return on UK assets below that on foreign assets. This, like the first effect, will lead to an increased demand for foreign assets and thus an increased supply of pounds on the foreign exchange market.
- Speculators will anticipate that the higher supply of sterling will cause the exchange rate to depreciate. They will therefore sell sterling and buy foreign currencies.

The effect of all three is to cause the exchange rate to depreciate. This will have two effects on aggregate demand:

- Imports will be more expensive relative to home-produced goods. People will thus buy fewer imports and more home-produced goods. Withdrawals (*W*) will thus fall and consumption of domestic goods (C_d) will rise.
- The initial effect on exporters depends on how exports are priced. If they are priced in dollars, D-Marks or some other foreign currency, they will now earn more pounds and will therefore be more profitable for exporters. Exporters will thus increase their production. If exports are priced in *pounds*, they will now be

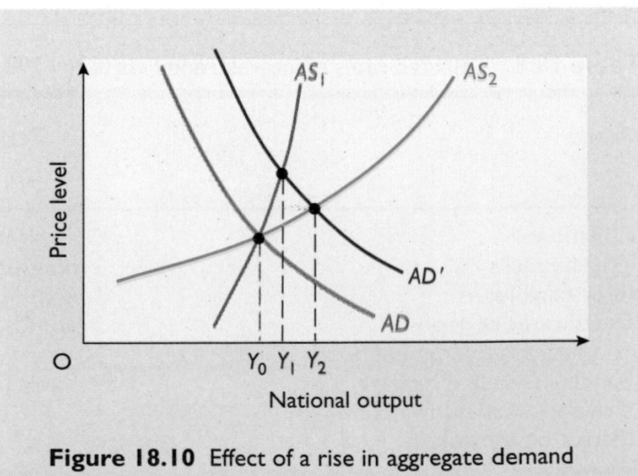

Figure 18.10 Effect of a rise in aggregate demand

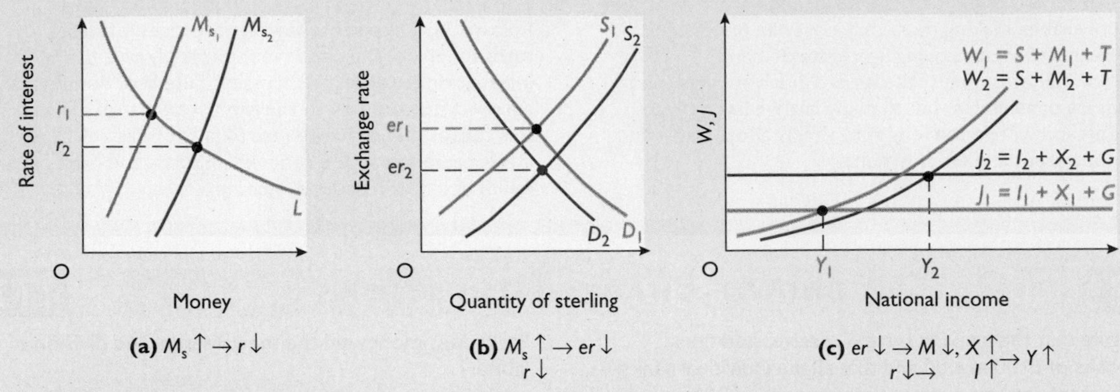

Figure 18.11 Effect of a rise in the money supply: the exchange rate transmission mechanism

cheaper in foreign currency terms for foreigners to buy. The demand for UK exports will thus increase. Either way, a rise in exports, being an injection into the circular flow of income, will raise aggregate demand and hence lead to a multiplied rise in income.

The various effects are illustrated in Figure 18.11.

- In diagram (a) a rise in money supply will cause the rate of interest to fall from r_1 to r_2.
- In diagram (b) the rise in money supply plus the fall in the rate of interest will cause the exchange rate to depreciate from er_1 to er_2.
- In diagram (c) the fall in the exchange rate will cause a fall in imports and a rise in exports. This, coupled with the effect on investment of a fall in interest rates, will cause a multiplied rise in national income from Y_1 to Y_2.

Note that the lower interest rate causes a capital account deficit on the balance of payments as people buy foreign assets. This is matched (as it must be if the government does not use the reserves to support the pound) by a current account surplus as exports rise and imports fall.

The full effect will not be as large as that illustrated. This is because the increased national income will cause an increased *transactions* demand for money. This will shift the *L* curve to the right in diagram (a), and thus lead to a smaller fall in the rate of interest than that illustrated.

?? Trace through the effects of a *fall* in the supply of money.

In the extreme case where the aggregate supply curve is vertical, the increased money supply will simply lead to higher prices. In such a case the rise in the transactions demand for money will match the rise in the supply of money. Interest rates will rise back up to the original level. The exchange rate depreciation will then simply match the rise in prices.

Monetarists take this extreme view. Any increase in the money supply, they argue, will simply lead to higher prices and a lower exchange rate. A 10 per cent rise in money supply will lead to a 10 per cent rise in prices and a 10 per cent depreciation of the exchange rate (assuming no potential economic growth at home and no inflation abroad).

?? If foreign prices rose on average by 4 per cent and UK prices rose by 10 per cent, how much would the pound have to depreciate?

We will examine the relationship between money and exchange rates in more detail in Chapter 24.

SECTION SUMMARY

1. Equilibrium in the money market is where the supply of money is equal to the demand. Equilibrium is achieved through changes in the interest rate and the exchange rate.
2. The interest rate transmission mechanism works as follows: (a) a rise in money supply causes money supply to exceed money demand; interest rates fall; (b) this causes investment to rise; (c) this causes a multiplied rise in national income; but (d) as national income rises so the transactions demand for money will rise, thus preventing quite such a large fall in interest rates.

continued

3. Keynesians argue that effects (a) and (b) are weak and unreliable, making monetary policy an unreliable weapon for controlling aggregate demand. Monetarists argue that they are much stronger and more predictable, but that any change in aggregate demand will (in the long run) simply affect prices and not output and employment.
4. The exchange rate transmission mechanism works as follows: (a) a rise in money supply causes interest rates to fall; (b) the rise in money supply plus the fall in interest rates causes an increased supply of domestic currency to come on to the foreign exchange market; this causes the exchange rate to fall; (c) this will cause increased exports and reduced imports, and hence a multiplied rise in national income.

??? END-OF-CHAPTER QUESTIONS ???

1. Imagine that the banking system receives additional deposits of £100 million and that all the individual banks wish to retain their current liquidity ratio of 20 per cent.
   (a) How much will banks choose to lend out initially?
   (b) What will happen to banks' liabilities when the money that is lent out is spent and the recipients of it deposit it in their bank accounts?
   (c) How much of these latest deposits will be lent out by the banks?
   (d) By how much will *total* deposits (liabilities) eventually have risen, assuming that none of the additional liquidity is held outside the banking sector?
   (e) How much of these are matched by (i) liquid assets; (ii) illiquid assets?
   (f) What is the size of the bank multiplier?
   (g) If one half of any additional liquidity is held *outside* the banking sector, by how much less will deposits have risen compared with (d) above?
2. What is meant by the terms *narrow money* and *broad money*? Does broad money fulfil all the functions of money?
3. How does money aid the specialisation and division of labour?
4. What enables banks safely to engage in both maturity transformation and risk transformation?
5. Why do banks hold a range of assets of varying degrees of liquidity and profitability?
6. If the government reduces the size of its public-sector borrowing requirement, why might the money supply nevertheless increase more rapidly?
7. Why might the relationship between the demand for money and the rate of interest be an unstable one?
8. What effects will the following have on the equilibrium rate of interest? (You should consider which way the demand and/or supply curves of money shift.)
   (a) Banks find that they have a higher liquidity ratio than they need.
   (b) A rise in incomes.
   (c) A growing belief that interest rates will rise from their current level.

19 Monetary policy

19.1 Attitudes towards monetary policy

Monetary policy is the deliberate attempt by the authorities (a) to control the supply of money, or (b) to control interest rates, or (c) to ration the amount of credit granted by banks.

Monetary policy is highly controversial. Economists (and politicians) are not agreed on how effective it has been or can be, or on what form it should take.

Government attitudes towards monetary policy have undergone enormous changes since 1945. In the Keynesian era from 1945 to the end of the 1960s, *fiscal* policy was seen as the major weapon for controlling the economy. Monetary policy was relegated to the fairly minor role of preventing excessive fluctuations in interest rates. For most of this period, this simply meant allowing money supply to expand to accommodate increases in aggregate demand associated with expansionary fiscal policy. It also meant allowing money supply to contract, or grow less rapidly, when deflationary fiscal policies were pursued.

During the 1970s there was a major swing in the attitudes of many economists and politicians. The rise of monetarism was accompanied by increased importance being attached to monetary policy. The main reasons were as follows:

- The failure of Keynesianism to account for and provide solutions to the growing problem of stagflation.
- Increased academic interest in monetary economics, and increased evidence, most notably from Milton Friedman and Anna Schwartz in their *Monetary History of the United States*, that there is a direct causal link between growth in the money supply and inflation.
- The growth of the radical right in politics, and the subsequent elections of Reagan, Thatcher, Kohl and others. The radical right is committed to *laissez-faire* policies, with the main economic role of the government reduced to that of providing 'sound money'. This means controlling the money supply to control inflation. Stable prices will then allow the market mechanism to give clear, unambiguous signals of relative scarcities. This will help enterprise to flourish, and output and employment should grow.

The high point of monetarism came in the early 1980s. Governments round the world made the control of inflation the number one short-term macroeconomic objective. To achieve this they pursued tight monetary policies, which in many cases involved setting targets for the growth in money supply. In the UK the Conservative government adopted a **medium-term financial strategy** (MTFS). This involved setting targets each year for the growth of money supply over the following four years: the targets got progressively tighter over the four years, thus 'putting the squeeze on inflation'. The MTFS also included targets for cutting the public-sector borrowing requirement.

From the mid-1980s the UK, along with several other countries, began to adopt a more pragmatic approach to monetary policy. It had been found difficult to control money supply and to keep it within target ranges. Anyway, as elections approached it was not always politically desirable to have a tight monetary policy. But perhaps one of the main reasons for abandoning monetary targets was the desire to prevent exchange rate fluctuations, and the use of changes in interest rates to achieve this. As we shall see, if the interest rate is used to control exchange rates, it cannot at the same time be used to achieve money supply targets. Once the UK had joined the ERM in 1990, the role of monetary policy was almost entirely confined to maintaining the value of the exchange

DEFINITION

Medium-term financial strategy The policy of the Conservative government in the UK during the 1980s of setting targets for the PSBR and the growth of money supply for the following four years.

rate within the permitted band. With the withdrawal from the ERM in 1992, however, monetary policy was able to be used once more to influence the level of activity in the economy. Then from 1993 monetary policy was used primarily to keep inflation within target bands.

What form should monetary policy take?

In framing its monetary policy, a government must address a number of important questions:

- What are the goals of monetary policy? Is the aim simply to control inflation, or does the government wish also to affect output and employment, or does it want to control the exchange rate?
- Where does monetary policy fit into the total package of macroeconomic policies? Is it seen as the major or even sole macroeconomic policy weapon, or is it merely one of several policy weapons, and possibly a minor one at that?
- What element of the monetary system should the government seek to control? Should it be the supply of money, and if so which measure? Should it be the demand for money, and if so how should that be measured? Or should it be the rate of interest, and if so at what level?
- Should the government take a long-term or short-term perspective? Should it adopt a target for money supply growth, and stick to it come what may? Or should it adjust its policy as circumstances change and attempt to 'fine tune' the economy?
- Just how reliable is monetary policy in controlling monetary variables such as money supply and interest rates?

Keynesian and monetarist attitudes towards monetary policy

Keynesians and monetarists give very different answers to these questions. Keynesians see the prime role of demand-side policy as stabilising aggregate demand at or near 'full-employment' income. The prime weapon for managing demand is discretionary *fiscal* policy, with monetary policy being used merely as a back-up to this.

They see monetary policy on its own as rather ineffective, for three reasons:

- It is difficult to control money supply, and impossible to control it precisely.
- The link between money supply and aggregate demand is weak and unpredictable. Thus if aggregate demand requires controlling, monetary policy is a poor weapon.
- Monetary policy affects aggregate demand through interest rate changes. It is best to control interest rates directly, rather than relying on changes in money supply to affect them.

Monetarists reject the Keynesian approach to monetary and fiscal policies, which sees them as discretionary, essentially short-term, demand management policies. Both policies, monetarists argue, involve considerable time lags, which can make them destabilising. Instead a much longer-term perspective should be taken. Long-run price stability requires long-run control over the money supply. This involves setting targets for money supply into the future, and then using monetary policy to ensure that these targets are met. Monetary policy, they argue, providing it is carefully designed and executed, *can* control the money supply.

SECTION SUMMARY

1. During the 1970s and 1980s, governments around the world attached increasing importance to monetary policy and less importance to fiscal policy. This was due to an increased acceptance of monetarist arguments and a rejection of Keynesian ones.
2. Keynesians argue that monetary policy is an unreliable means of controlling aggregate demand. Instead governments should use fiscal policy combined with a policy of relatively stable interest rates.
3. Monetarists argue that monetary policy is a powerful weapon. A stable economy is best achieved by ensuring a steady and low rate of growth in the money supply.
4. In framing its monetary policy a government must have a clear idea of what the goals of the policy are, which monetary variable it is going to attempt to control and by what means, whether to take a long-term or short-term perspective, and how the policy fits in with other policies.

19.2 Varieties of monetary policy

Control of the money supply over the medium and long term

As explained in Chapter 18, there are four possible sources of monetary growth: (a) banks choosing to hold a lower liquidity ratio; (b) a balance of payments surplus; (c) public-sector borrowing; and (d) a change in the method of financing the national debt. If the government wishes to restrict monetary growth over the longer term, it could in theory attempt to control any of these four.

Banks' liquidity ratio

The government, operating through the Bank of England, could impose statutory minimum reserve requirements on the banks to prevent them reducing their liquidity ratio and creating more credit.

A major problem is that banks may find ways of getting round such restrictions. After all, banks would like to lend and customers would like to borrow. It would be very difficult for the Bank of England to regulate and police every single part of the UK's complex financial system. If it succeeds merely in regulating *part* of the system, then **Goodhart's law** is likely to come into operation. This law (named after Charles Goodhart, formerly of the Bank of England) states that attempts to regulate *one* part of the financial system will merely divert business to *other* parts which are unregulated (see Box 19.1). Total borrowing may thus continue to increase.

Monetarists are opposed to this form of monetary control, arguing that banks, like any firm, ought to be free from government restrictions. Imposing reserve requirements on banks is 'anti-market' and could lead to banks becoming inefficient.

So how else can the government discourage banks from increasing their lending? The answer is to curb the long-run *demand* for money, which will normally involve keeping interest rates high. However, this will drive up the exchange rate and thus make it harder for firms to export.

A total currency flow surplus

Total currency flow surpluses will occur only if the government keeps the exchange rate below the equilibrium by continuing to sell the domestic currency on the foreign exchange market. Since governments are unlikely to do this over the long term, this will not be a long-term source of excessive monetary growth.

The PSBR and its method of financing

Government borrowing will tend to lead to an increase in money supply. To prevent this, the PSBR must be financed by selling *bonds* (as opposed to bills, which could well be taken up by the banking sector, thereby increasing money supply). However, to sell extra bonds the government will have to offer higher interest rates. This will have a knock-on effect on private-sector interest rates. The government borrowing will thus 'crowd out' private-sector borrowing and investment.

This **financial crowding out** could be partially offset by an increase in the speed at which money circulates – the *velocity of circulation*. If existing money circulates faster, there will be less shortage of money and less upward pressure on interest rates. The velocity of circulation will rise if there is a reduction in idle balances. But why should idle balances fall? This is simply the result of a downward-sloping liquidity preference curve. As interest rates begin to rise, so people choose to hold less idle balances. The more elastic the liquidity preference curve, the more idle balances will fall. Nevertheless, unless the liquidity preference curve is totally elastic, *some* financial crowding out will occur. (Crowding out is examined in detail in Chapter 20.)

If governments wish to reduce monetary growth and yet avoid financial crowding out, they must therefore reduce the level of the PSBR. Monetarists argue that governments should make reductions in the PSBR (as a proportion of national income) the central part of their medium- and longer-term monetary strategy. Not only is this desirable as a means of restricting monetary growth, but, if it involves cutting government expenditure (as opposed to increasing taxes), it will also increase the size of the private sector relative to the public sector – and it is the private sector that monetarists see as the main source of long-term growth in output and employment.

DEFINITIONS

Goodhart's law Controlling a symptom of a problem or only one part of the problem will not *cure* the problem: it will simply mean that the part that is being controlled now becomes a poor indicator of the problem.

Financial crowding out Where an increase in government borrowing diverts money away from the private sector.

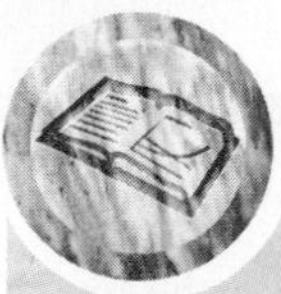

EXPLORING THE THEORY — BOX 19.1

GOODHART'S LAW

'To control is to distort'

'If you want to tackle a problem, it's best to get to the root of it.'

This is a message that economists are constantly preaching. If you merely treat the *symptoms* of a problem rather than its *underlying causes*, the problem may simply manifest itself in some other form. What is more, the symptoms (or lack of them, if the treatment makes them go away) will now be a poor indicator of the problem. Let's illustrate this with a medical example.

Assume that you suffer from deteriorating eyesight. As a result you get increasingly bad headaches. The worse the headaches become, the worse it suggests your eyesight is getting. The headaches are thus a symptom of the problem and an indicator of the problem's magnitude. So what do you do? One approach is to treat the symptoms. As a result you regularly take aspirins and the headaches go away. But you haven't treated the underlying problem – by getting stronger glasses, or perhaps even having eye surgery – all you have done is to treat the symptoms. As a result, headaches (or rather the lack of them) are now a poor indicator of your eyesight.

If you control the indicator rather than the underlying problem, the indicator ceases to be a good indicator. 'To control [the indicator] is to distort [its use as an indicator].' This is Goodhart's law and it has many applications in economics, especially in the field of monetary policy.

Money as an indicator of aggregate demand

Monetarists argue that the level of money supply determines the level of aggregate demand and prices. They therefore argue in favour of setting targets for the growth of money supply. Critics, however, argue that the level of money supply is only an *indicator* of the level of aggregate demand (and a poor one at that). As soon as you start to *control* money supply, they say, the relationship between them breaks down. If, for example, you restrict the amount of money and yet people still want to borrow, money will simply circulate faster, and hence aggregate demand may not decline.

The choice of money supply target

If targets for the growth of money supply are to be set, which measure of money supply should be chosen? Goodhart's law suggests that whichever measure is chosen it will, by virtue of its choice, become a poor indicator. If the government targets M0 and directs its policy to reducing the amount of notes and coin in the economy, banks may try to reduce their customers' demand for cash by, say, increasing the charges for cash advances on credit cards. As a result, M0 may well be constrained, but all the other measures of money supply are likely to go on rising.

The choice of institutions

If bank advances are a good indicator of aggregate demand, the government may choose to control bank lending. But as soon as it does so, bank lending will become a poor indicator. If people's demand for loans is still high and *bank* loans are becoming difficult to obtain, people will simply go elsewhere to borrow money. If you regulate *part* of the financial system, you are likely to end up merely diverting business to other parts which are unregulated.

?? Give some everyday examples of Goodhart's law.

In the UK, the Conservative government's medium-term financial strategy introduced in 1980 attempted to do just this. As well as setting targets for the growth of money supply, it also gave targets for the PSBR as a percentage of GDP.

?? How could long-term monetary growth come about if the government persistently ran a public-sector surplus (public-sector debt repayment, PSDR)?

Control of the money supply in the short term

Monetary policy may be off target. Alternatively, the government may wish to alter its monetary policy. Assume, for example, that the government wishes to operate a tighter monetary policy in order to reduce aggregate demand. What can it do?

For any given supply of money (M_s) there will be a particular equilibrium rate of interest at any one time: where the supply of money (M_s) equals the demand for money (L). This is shown as r_1 in Figure 19.1.

Thus to operate a tighter monetary policy the authorities can do the following:

- Reduce money supply and accept whatever equilibrium interest rate results. Thus if money supply is reduced to Q_2 in Figure 19.1, a new higher rate of interest, r_2, will result.
- First raise interest rates to r_2 and then manipulate the money supply to reduce it to Q_2.

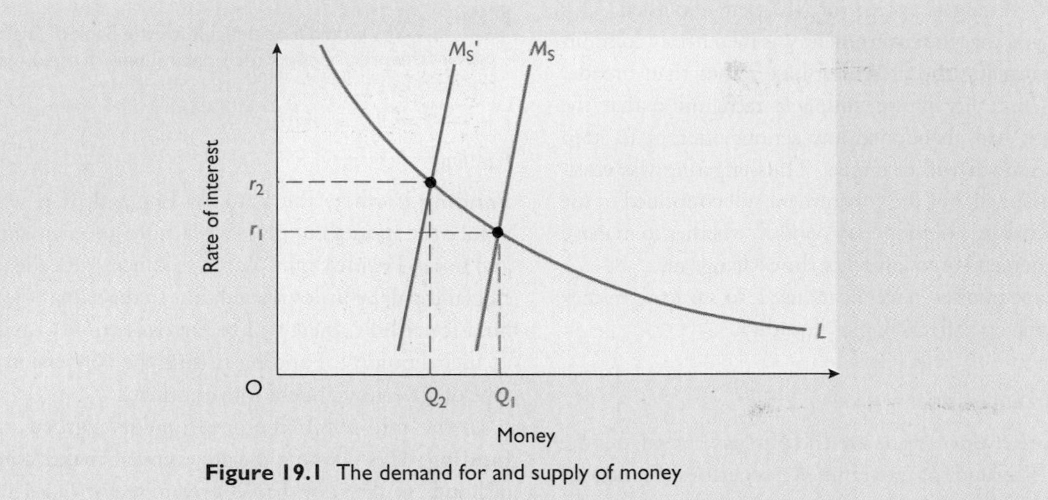

Figure 19.1 The demand for and supply of money

- Keep interest rates low (at r_1) in order, say, to keep down the costs of investment, but also reduce money supply to a level of Q_2. The trouble here is that the government cannot both control the money supply *and* keep interest rates down without running into the problem of disequilibrium. Since the demand for money now exceeds the supply by $Q_1 - Q_2$, some form of credit rationing will have to be applied.

There is a fourth possibility, but this is not primarily monetary policy. This would be to reduce the demand for money (i.e. *shift* the demand for money curve (L) to the left). A contractionary fiscal policy is probably necessary here. This would reduce aggregate demand directly and thus reduce the transactions demand for money. Money supply could be reduced without raising interest rates or having to ration credit.

The following sections look at various techniques of monetary policy in each of the three categories: (a) controlling the money supply, (b) controlling interest rates and (c) rationing credit.

Techniques to control the money supply

To control the money supply, the authorities will seek to manipulate the liquid assets of the banking system. The aim is to influence the money supply by affecting the amount of credit that banks can create.

Suppose that banks operate a rigid 10 per cent cash ratio and just have two types of asset: cash and advances. Suppose also that the government is able to reduce cash by £1 million. With a bank multiplier of 10 (= 1/cash ratio), advances must be reduced by £9 million, and hence money supply by £10 million (see Table 19.1).

??

- If banks operated a rigid 12½ per cent cash ratio and the government reduced the supply of cash by £1 million, how much must *credit* contract? What is the bank multiplier?

Before they can actually apply techniques of monetary control, the authorities must make two preliminary decisions:

- Should a statutory liquidity ratio be imposed on the banks, or should the banks be allowed to choose whatever ratio they consider to be prudent?
- Should the authorities attempt to control a range of liquid assets, or should they focus on controlling just the monetary base?

In the UK, before 1981 statutory liquidity ratios were imposed on the banks. Since 1981, however, banks have been left to decide their own prudent liquidity ratios. Many other countries too have abandoned statutory liquidity ratios as part of a worldwide trend towards financial deregulation.

Before 1981 the authorities concentrated on a whole range of liquid assets and on broad measures of money supply, like M3: the argument being that it is broad liquidity that determines credit creation. After 1981 government opinion shifted in favour of focusing on the monetary base, as this is more easily controlled by the authorities.

Table 19.1

Liabilities		Assets	
Deposits	£10m ↓	Cash Advances	£1m ↓ £9m ↓

In 1985 all targets except for M0 were abolished. This might suggest that the government was then firmly committed to controlling the monetary base rather than broader liquidity. In reality it was simply a recognition that the government had abandoned any serious attempt to keep monetary growth within targets. Thus targeting was effectively abandoned, but the government still continued to use various techniques of monetary control, whether to manage aggregate demand or to influence the exchange rate.

Three techniques have been used to control money supply. Each one affects banks' liquidity.

Open-market operations

Open-market operations are the purchase or sale by the Bank of England of government securities (bonds or Treasury bills) in the open market. These purchases or sales are *not* in response to changes in the PSBR or PSDR, and are best understood in the context of an unchanged PSBR or PSDR.

If the government wishes to *reduce* the money supply, the Bank of England sells more securities. When people buy these securities, they pay for them with cheques drawn on banks. Thus banks' balances with the Bank of England are reduced. If this brings bank reserves below their prudent ratio (or statutory ratio, if one is in force), banks will reduce advances. There will be a multiple contraction of credit and hence of money supply.

The effect will be limited if the extra securities are Treasury bills (as opposed to bonds) and if some are purchased by discount houses and banks. The reduction in one liquid asset (balances with the Bank of England) will be offset to some extent by an increase in another liquid asset (Treasury bills). Open-market operations are more likely to be effective in reducing the money supply, therefore, when conducted in the bond market.

If the government wishes to *increase* the money supply, the Bank of England purchases back securities. When people pay the Bank of England cheques into their banks, the banks' balances with the Bank of England will rise. Credit creation can take place.

?? Why would it be difficult for the Bank of England to predict the precise effect on money supply of open-market operations?

Funding

Funding is where the Bank of England, if it wishes to reduce the money supply, issues more government bonds and fewer Treasury bills. Banks' balances with the Bank of England will be little affected, but to the extent that banks hold fewer bills, there will be (*ceteris paribus*) a reduction in their liquidity. Funding is thus the conversion of one type of government debt into another.

In the mid-1980s the government engaged in **overfunding**. This is where the government makes a net issue of bonds to the (non-bank) private sector *in excess* of the total PSBR. The sale of securities to the private sector leads to a squeeze on banks' balances at the Bank of England. As a result banks may have to call in money from the discount houses, which, in turn being short of liquidity, have to sell bills back to the Bank of England (acting as lender of last resort). If there are insufficient Treasury bills to be rediscounted by the Bank of England, the discount houses will have to sell other bills, such as commercial bills that have been accepted by an acceptance house or bank. In 1984 the Bank of England built up a 'commercial bill mountain' through overfunding.

Special deposits

Banks can be required to deposit a given percentage of their deposits in a special account at the Bank of England. These **special deposits** are frozen, and cannot be drawn on until the authorities choose to release them. They provide a simple means of reducing banks' liquidity and hence their ability to create credit. Releasing special deposits allows banks to create more credit.

A particular variant of special deposits, used on and off during the 1970s, were **supplementary special deposits ('the corset')**. The authorities set limits to the expansion of bank deposits. Whenever these limits were exceeded,

DEFINITIONS

Open-market operations The sale (or purchase) by the authorities of government securities in the open market in order to reduce (or increase) money supply.

Funding Where the authorities alter the balance of bills and bonds for any given level of government borrowing.

Overfunding Where the issue of bonds (minus those maturing) exceeds the PSBR.

Special deposits Deposits that the banks can be required to make in the Bank of England. They remain frozen there until the Bank of England chooses to release them.

Supplementary special deposits ('the corset') Where banks were automatically required to place a proportion of an increase in customers' deposits above a specified limit in special deposits (frozen deposits) in the Bank of England.

banks were required to place a proportion of them in special deposits. The more the limits were exceeded, the bigger was this proportion. This was a form of automatic, as opposed to discretionary, monetary policy. In theory it was a very simple way of keeping money supply within limits: within a corset. The more that deposits expanded, the tighter would become the corset.

Although all three techniques have been used in the past, they have not been used as the prime form of monetary policy. In fact special deposits have not been used at all as an instrument of control since 1981, being seen by the government as too 'interventionist' in banks' affairs. The government today prefers to rely on controlling interest rates, backed up, as we shall see, by open-market operations.

Techniques to control interest rates

If in Figure 19.1 the authorities wished to reduce the demand for money from Q_1 to Q_2, they would raise interest rates from r_1 to r_2. How, then, can the authorities control interest rates? Interest rates are controlled by the Bank of England, through its operations in the discount market.

The Bank of England ('the Bank') is the lender of the last resort. If commercial banks are short of liquid assets, they will call in money from the discount houses. The discount houses, as a result, may themselves become short of liquid assets. They will be forced to borrow from the Bank, as lender of last resort, or get the Bank to rediscount (buy) bills of exchange. The Bank can *choose what rate of interest or rediscount to charge the discount houses.* This in turn will affect interest rates generally throughout the economy.

Until 1972 this rate of interest was called *Bank rate.* The clearing banks used to change their interest rates on advances and deposits *automatically* by the same amount that Bank rate changed. Thus by changing Bank rate the authorities could directly change banks' interest rates. This would stimulate other institutions to change their rates too, in order to remain competitive with the clearing banks.

From 1972 to 1981 Bank rate was replaced by *minimum lending rate* (MLR). This too was the rate at which the Bank of England would lend to the discount houses in the last resort. Unlike with Bank rate the clearing banks were not obliged to change their rates when MLR changed. But they usually did, for two reasons.

First, the Bank of England would usually back up any change in MLR with *open-market operations* in the bond or more likely the bill market. If, for example, the authorities wished to pursue a tighter monetary policy, they would raise MLR and at the same time sell more government bonds and Treasury bills. These open-market sales would lower the price of bonds and bills, and hence raise their rate of interest to match the rise in MLR.

Further, purchases of these securities by the general public would reduce banks' liquidity, as people paid with cheques drawn on their bank accounts. The banks might then be obliged to call in money from the discount houses. This would reduce the liquidity of the discount houses, which then would be forced to borrow from the Bank of England at the new higher MLR.

To avoid the resulting loss, the discount houses would tender a lower price for bills, in order to get a higher rate of discount. Higher rates of discount on bills would in turn drive up interest rates on other types of borrowing and lending that compete with bills (e.g. short-term bank loans). In other words, a rise in MLR had a knock-on effect on interest rates throughout the economy.

Second, MLR was seen as a *signal of government intention.* A rise in MLR was a sign that the authorities wanted to pursue a tighter monetary policy. As a result banks would tend to raise their rates in anticipation of a general rise in rates.

After 1981 a formally announced MLR was abandoned. Nevertheless the Bank still actively intervened to affect interest rates. It did this by conducting *open-market operations* in the bill market.

Assume that the Bank of England wished to raise interest rates. Assume first that the discount houses had *surplus* liquidity and therefore used it to buy bills, including Treasury bills. The greater the supply of Treasury bills on offer by the Bank, the lower the price the discount houses would be prepared to pay for them, and hence the higher the rate of discount (r) they would receive. This is illustrated in Figure 19.2(a). It gives an upward-sloping demand curve for bills with respect to their rate of discount: the higher the rate of discount, the more bills would discount houses be prepared to buy. A rise in Treasury bill issue from S_1 to S_2 would raise the discount rate from r_1 to r_2. Thus the Bank of England could alter the discount rate by altering the supply of Treasury bills. The more it supplied, the more it would drive up the rate of discount.

Now assume that discount houses had *insufficient* liquidity and were forced to borrow from the Bank of England. After 1981 the Bank preferred not to lend as such, but rather to purchase ('rediscount') bills from the discount houses. The Bank did not announce its rediscount rate, but instead invited the discount houses to offer it bills. If the price asked by the discount houses was thought to be too high, the Bank would refuse to purchase them. This would drive down the price and hence drive up the rate of rediscount (r). The discount houses would thus try to economise

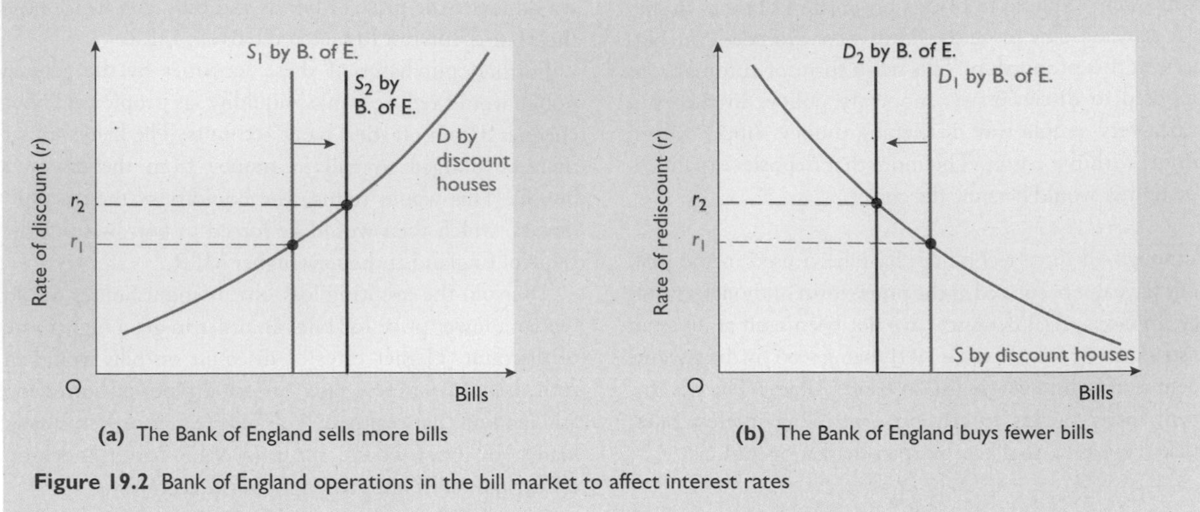

Figure 19.2 Bank of England operations in the bill market to affect interest rates

on the bills they offered to the Bank by, say, offering a higher rate of interest on money at call, and thus encouraging further such deposits from the banks. Thus in Figure 19.2(b), the supply of bills on offer by the discount houses to the Bank falls as the rate of rediscount rises. The Bank, by rejecting offers at r_1, would, in effect, be reducing its demand for bills (D_1 to D_2), and thereby driving up the rediscount rate to r_2.

In either case (the Bank selling more or buying fewer bills), there would be a knock-on effect on interest rates throughout the economy, just as there used to be with MLR.

In recent years there has been a return to announcing interest rate changes. Before May 1997, these changes were decided by the government. Since then, however, with the Bank of England being made independent of government, interest rate changes have been decided by the Bank of England's Monetary Policy Committee. The Bank then ensures that this new interest rate is the *equilibrium* rate by its operations in the discount and gilt repo markets. Thus, although the current approach to monetary policy focuses on the rate of interest in order to affect the demand for money, this approach is still backed up by measures to control the money *supply*. In Figure 19.1, if the Bank of England wants to raise the rate of interest from r_1 to r_2, its actions in the discount and gilt repo markets will reduce money supply from Q_1 to Q_2, to ensure that r_2 is an equilibrium rate of interest.

Techniques to ration credit

In the past, and particularly in the late 1960s, governments attempted to keep interest rates low so as not to discourage investment. This frequently meant that the demand for money exceeded the supply of money that the authorities were prepared to permit. Thus in Figure 19.1, if the authorities keep interest rates at r_1, and yet do not allow money supply to expand beyond Q_2, there will be excess demand for money of $Q_1 - Q_2$. Faced with this excess demand, the authorities had to ration credit.

There were two main ways in which credit was rationed. First, the Bank of England could ask banks to restrict their total lending to a certain amount, or to reduce lending to more risky customers or for non-essential purchases. The Bank of England had the power to order banks to obey, but in practice it always relied on persuasion. This was known as *suggestion and request* (or 'moral suasion'). Second, the authorities could restrict *hire-purchase credit*, by specifying minimum deposits or maximum repayment periods.

Table 19.2 Effect of raising the minimum reserve ratio from 20% to 25%

Initial position: 20% reserve ratio				New position: 25% reserve ratio			
Liabilities		Assets		Liabilities		Assets	
Deposits	£50bn	Reserve assets Advances, etc.	£10bn £40bn	Deposits	£40bn	Reserve assets Advances, etc.	£10bn £30bn
Total	£50bn	Total	£50bn	Total	£40bn	Total	£40bn

CASE STUDIES BOX 19.2

THE DAILY OPERATION OF MONETARY POLICY

What goes on at Threadneedle Street?

The Bank of England does not attempt to control money supply directly. Instead it seeks to control short-term interest rates by conducting open-market operations in the discount and gilt 'repo' markets (see page 552). These operations as we shall see, will determine short-term interest rates, which will then have a knock-on effect on longer-term rates, as returns on different forms of assets must remain competitive with each other.

Let us assume that the Monetary Policy Committee of the Bank of England is worried that inflation is set to rise, perhaps because there is excessive growth in the money supply. At its monthly meeting, therefore, it decides to raise interest rates. What does the Bank do?

The first thing is that it will *announce* a rise in interest rates. But it must do more than this. It must back up the announcement by using open market operations to ensure that its announced interest rate is the *equilibrium rate*. In fact, it has to conduct open market operations every day to keep interest rates at the level it chooses.

How do these open market operations work? In general, the Bank of England seeks to keep banks short of liquidity. This will happen automatically on any day when tax payments by banks' customers exceed the money they receive from government expenditure. This excess is effectively withdrawn from banks and ends up in the government's account at the Bank of England. Even when this does not occur, weekly sales of Treasury bills by the Bank of England to the banks, discount houses and other financial institutions (collectively known as the Bank's 'counterparties') will be used to keep the banking system short of liquidity.

The counterparties will thus have to borrow from the Bank of England. They do this by entering into repurchase agreements (repos). This entails them selling gilts or bills to the Bank, with an agreement that they will repurchase them from the Bank at a fixed date in the future (typically about two weeks). The difference between the sale and repurchase prices will be set by the Bank of England to reflect its chosen rate of interest. By the Bank determining the repo rate in this way, there will then be a knock-on effect on other interest rates throughout the banking system.

Each morning at 9.45 the Bank of England forecasts that day's shortage (forecasts that are updated during the day). It then contacts its counterparties to offer them assistance. The assistance is provided at the published rate in two rounds of open market operations: at 12.00 noon and at 2.30 pm, with an additional 'early round' at 9.45 am if the predicted shortage of liquidity is large.

At about 3.45 pm the Bank publishes a final update for the day's liquidity shortage. If it is greater than was forecasted earlier in the day, the Bank may make a further repo facility available, for which banks must apply by 3.55 pm.

Although there is usually a shortage of liquidity in the banking system, on some days there may be a *surplus*. To prevent this driving market interest rates down, the Bank will invite its counterparties to bid for outright purchase of short-dated Treasury bills (i.e. ones part-way through their life) at prices set by the Bank to reflect its current (above equilibrium) interest rate: i.e. at prices lower than the market would otherwise set. At such prices, the Bank has no difficulty in selling them and hence in 'mopping up' the surplus liquidity.

?? Assume that the Bank of England wants to reduce interest rates. Trace through the process during the day by which it achieves this.

One technique of monetary control, which amounts to a form of credit rationing, is to vary the statutory reserve ratio that banks must adhere to. Clearly this policy option will not be open in the UK as long as there are effectively no statutory reserve requirements and it is up to banks to decide their own prudent ratio.

If, however, the central bank sets the reserve ratio, then by simply increasing it, it can force banks to reduce their non-reserve assets (mainly credit). Table 19.2 illustrates the effect of raising the ratio from 20 per cent to 25 per cent. Initially the banks have reserve assets of £10 billion and advances, etc. of £40 billion, giving total assets of £50 billion (of which £10 billion is 20 per cent). Increasing the reserve ratio to 25 per cent forces banks to reduce their advances, etc. to £30 billion, giving total assets of £40 billion (of which £10 billion is 25 per cent). This is equivalent to credit rationing because banks would *like* to continue lending the £40 billion (or even more), but are being prevented from doing so by the authorities.

Minimum reserve ratios have been widely used around the world to restrict credit, including in the USA, Japan, Canada and several of the EU countries (see Box 19.4).

SECTION SUMMARY

1. In the medium and long term, the major sources of monetary growth are banks choosing to operate with a lower liquidity ratio and government borrowing.
2. Banks choosing to operate with a lower liquidity ratio could be prevented by the authorities imposing statutory reserve requirements on banks. This practice is commonplace throughout the world, but the authorities in the UK regard it as 'anti-market'. Instead they have chosen to rely on using interest rates to curb the *demand* for credit.
3. In the UK, the government has tried to limit the size of the PSBR, or even to run a PSDR, in order to keep monetary growth in check.
4. In the short term, the government can use monetary policy to restrict the growth in aggregate demand in one of three ways: (a) reducing money supply direct, (b) reducing the demand for money by raising interest rates, or (c) rationing credit.
5. The money supply can be reduced directly by using open-market operations. This involves selling more government securities and thereby reducing banks' reserves when their customers pay for them from their bank accounts. Alternatively, funding can be used. This is where the government increases the ratio of bonds to bills. Finally, banks' liquidity can be reduced directly by techniques such as special deposits.
6. Interest rates can be controlled by order of the central bank. In the UK banks used to have to set their interest rates in line with Bank rate. Today the Bank of England influences interest rates by its operations in the discount market. By selling more bills or buying back fewer, it can force down their price and hence force up the rate of discount. This then has a knock-on effect on interest rates throughout the economy.
7. Credit rationing in the UK has not been used in the 1980s and 1990s. In the past, rationing took the form of requests to the banks by the Bank of England, and hire-purchase controls. The manipulation of statutory reserve requirements is a form of credit rationing which is used in many countries.

19.3 Problems of monetary policy

Medium- and long-term control over the money supply

A government committed to a sustained reduction in the growth of the money supply over a number of years will find this very difficult unless it restricts the size of the public-sector deficit. The Thatcher government in the 1980s made reducing the PSBR the central feature of its medium-term financial strategy. There are serious problems, however, in attempting to reduce the PSBR.

Automatic fiscal stabilisers

Reducing the PSBR must involve either reducing government expenditure or raising taxes, or some combination of the two. This is deflationary and may lead to a recession. But in a recession automatic fiscal stabilisers come into force which will tend to push the PSBR back up again. Lower incomes and lower expenditure will mean that less taxes are paid. At the same time, higher unemployment will involve increased government expenditure on unemployment benefits. This was a major problem in the early 1980s, and again in the early 1990s, when the severe recession turned a public-sector surplus of £12 billion in 1988 into a massive deficit of £43 billion by 1993. Attempts to cut the size of the PSBR by tax increases (e.g. VAT on domestic fuel) and cuts in government expenditure served only to prolong the recession.

The desire to cut taxes

Governments gain popularity by cutting taxes, not by increasing them. The Thatcher government repeatedly committed itself to cutting the burden of taxation, and thereby to increasing incentives and encouraging enterprise. But cutting taxes raises the PSBR. Thus governments, faced with a large PSBR, may be forced to *raise* taxes, as did the Major government in Budgets after 1992. This cost it a great deal of public support.

The difficulty in cutting government expenditure

Cuts in government expenditure are politically unpopular. The Thatcher government as soon as it came into office met considerable opposition in Parliament, from public opinion, from local authorities and from various pressure groups, to 'cuts'. Moreover, much of government expenditure is committed a long time in advance and cannot easily be cut. As a result the government may find itself forced into refusing to sanction *new* expenditure. But this will mean cuts in capital projects such as roads, housing, schools and sewers, with a resulting decline in the country's infrastructure and long-term damage to the economy.

The less successful a government is in controlling the PSBR, the more it will have to borrow through bond issue to prevent money supply from growing too fast. This will mean high interest rates and the problem of crowding out.

Successive American presidents have found it difficult to reduce the US budget deficit for the same reasons. As a result US interest rates have often had to be kept at a high level. This has tended to crowd out investment in the rest of the world, as other countries have raised their interest rates too to prevent an excessive outflow of money to the USA and the resulting depreciation of their currency against the US dollar.

There is a further reason why it is difficult to restrain the growth of the money supply over the longer term. Over the years, individuals have increasingly used cheques and credit cards for transactions, and firms have increasingly used various forms of trade credit. Thus people's cash requirements have proportionately reduced (see Box 18.4). Banks therefore require to hold a lower liquidity ratio, and can create more credit. Thus, over time, for any given PSBR, the money supply will tend to rise.

In the mid-1980s, as the UK pulled out of recession, automatic stabilisers worked in reverse. The fall in unemployment meant a fall in government expenditure on unemployment benefits. The rapid rise in incomes meant a substantial rise in tax revenues, despite cuts in tax *rates*. The effect on the PSBR was dramatic. It disappeared and from 1987 was replaced by a public-sector surplus (PSDR). This should have made it easier to restrain the growth of the money supply. But the demand for credit was high and banks, being prepared to operate with a lower liquidity ratio, were only too pleased to supply the credit being demanded.

The conclusion is that the state of the economy will have a crucial effect on the demand for and supply of money. If, therefore, the government wishes to *control* the demand for and supply of money, it must actively intervene in money markets. For the remainder of this section we will look at the problems associated with such intervention.

Practical difficulties in controlling money supply in the short run

The authorities may experience considerable difficulties in controlling the money supply. Difficulties occur whether they focus on the monetary base or on a wider range of liquid assets, and whether they impose statutory ratios or allow banks to determine their own prudent ratios.

Problems with monetary base control

Assume that the authorities seek to control M0, the broad monetary base. This could be done by imposing a statutory 'cash' ratio on banks (where 'cash' is notes and coin and banks' balances with the Bank of England). Assume that a statutory ratio of 10 per cent is imposed. Then provided the authorities control the supply of 'cash' by, say, open-market operations, it would seem that they can thereby control the creation of credit and hence deposits. There would be a bank multiplier of 10. For every £1 million decrease in cash held by the banks, money supply would fall by £10 million. There are serious problems, however, with this form of **monetary base control**:

- Banks could hold cash in excess of the statutory minimum. For a time, therefore, they could respond to any restriction of cash by the authorities by simply reducing their cash ratio towards the minimum, rather than having to reduce credit.
- Goodhart's law. Unless cash ratios were imposed on every single financial institution, the control of certain institutions' lending would merely shift business to other uncontrolled institutions.
- Alternatively, if those banks subject to statutory cash requirements were short of cash, they could attract cash away from the uncontrolled institutions.
- Similarly, banks could encourage the general public to withdraw less cash: for example, by making time deposits more attractive than sight deposits or by encouraging a greater use of credit cards.

These problems could be eased by (a) bringing as many institutions as possible under control and (b) backing up open-market operations with a rigorous use of special deposits applied across the range of financial institutions.

The switching of business away from the banks is known as **disintermediation**. To avoid this problem and to allow the greatest freedom of competition between financial institutions, the alternative is to use monetary base control with no *statutory* cash ratio. But this too has problems.

- Banks may vary their prudential ratio. For example, when the base is squeezed by open-market operations etc., the banks may be able to economise on cash

DEFINITIONS

Monetary base control Monetary policy that focuses on controlling the monetary base (as opposed to broad liquidity).

Disintermediation The diversion of business away from financial institutions which are subject to controls.

CASE STUDIES **BOX 19.3**

THE CREDIT BOOM OF THE 1980s AND DECLINE OF THE EARLY 1990s

The abandonment of all forms of credit rationing in the early 1980s contributed to a subsequent boom in consumer credit.

Between 1981 and 1989 consumer credit increased by some 17 per cent per year. Average (nominal) earnings grew by only 8 per cent per year over the same period. By 1989 £48 billion was owed. This amounted to 14 per cent of total personal disposable income (compared with 7.5 per cent in 1981). The table highlights the massive credit expansion.

As the economy pulled out of the recession of the early 1980s, so this rapid rise in credit helped to fuel the recovery. But there were two macroeconomic problems with this credit boom. The first was that spending was going ahead of the ability to produce, and so inflation began to rise after 1986. The second was that a large proportion of the goods bought on credit were imported. Consequently, the balance of payments on current account began to 'dive into the red' (see Figure 14.1 on page 438).

The credit boom was a problem not only for the nation as a whole, but also for those individuals who, tempted by easy credit and the promise of instant consumption, found that they could not afford the repayments. Their problem was compounded in 1988 when there were substantial rises in the rate of interest. Many people were forced into borrowing more in order to pay the interest on existing loans, thus getting even deeper into debt.

Mortgages too were readily available, with various schemes to tempt the first-time buyer to enter the housing market. This fuelled the demand for houses, and hence drove up their prices. People had to take out bigger and bigger mortgages, and when mortgage interest rates were raised in 1988, many people had real difficulties in making ends meet.

But just as the boom in credit fuelled the expansion of the 1980s, so the recession of the early 1990s was aggravated by a *decline* in credit and hence a decline in spending.

So why was there a decline in credit? Households were faced with falling property prices, which for many people meant that their mortgages were now bigger than the value of their house (they had 'negative equity'). Many found themselves in mortgage arrears and were forced to sell their houses. What is more, as real incomes fell and unemployment rose, many people found they could not afford to take on new personal loans or build up their credit-card debts. As a result, rather than spending, people felt the need to pay off debts and to save as much as possible (see Box 16.4 on pages 500–1).

After 1993 consumer credit began to grow rapidly again, contributing to the recovery of the mid 1990s.

?? How does the easy availability of credit affect the problem of inequality?

The rapid growth in credit (1981–9), slowdown and decline (1990–3), and growth again (1994–7)

	1981	1982	1983	1984	1985	1986	1987	1988	1989	1990	1991	1992	1993	1994	1995	1996	1997
Outstanding credit (£bn)	13.4	16.0	18.9	22.3	26.1	30.2	36.2	42.5	48.4	52.6	54.0	53.2	53.0	57.6	67.6	76.8	87.4
Growth of credit (%)	21.2	19.4	18.1	18.0	17.0	15.7	13.2	17.4	13.9	8.7	2.7	−1.6	−0.4	8.7	17.4	13.6	13.8
Disposable income growth (%)	10.6	7.9	7.8	8.7	8.9	8.6	8.3	11.1	10.6	7.9	6.4	7.2	5.2	3.2	5.6	6.1	6.2
Price inflation (%)	11.9	8.6	4.6	5.0	6.1	3.4	4.2	4.9	7.8	9.5	5.9	3.7	1.6	2.4	3.5	2.4	3.1

Sources: *Financial Statistics* and *Economic Trends* (ONS).

balances by encouraging customers to switch to time accounts which have less risk of large cash withdrawals.

- Banks may keep cash balances surplus to their requirements in times of 'easy' money to enable them later to resist open-market operations when the authorities are attempting to squeeze the base.
- Goodhart's law may still apply. There may still be disintermediation. For example, banks may encourage business customers to take a loan in a foreign currency from one of their overseas branches and then convert the currency into sterling. With an absence of foreign exchange controls this is not difficult.

The most serious problem with monetary base control, with or without a statutory cash ratio, is that the Bank of England, as lender of the last resort, *is always prepared to lend cash if it is demanded*. This makes it virtually impossible to have a precise control of the monetary base.

Thus despite the fact that the Thatcher government in the early 1980s was committed to a tight control of money supply and set targets for the broad monetary base M0, and despite the fact that the authorities have expressed interest in monetary base control, this has not been the form of policy pursued.

??

1. Trace through the effects of a squeeze on the monetary base from an initial reduction in cash to banks' liquidity being restored by the rediscounting of bills. Will this restoration of liquidity by the Bank of England totally nullify the initial effect of reducing the supply of cash? (Clue: what is likely to happen to the rate of interest?)
2. Given the difficulties of monetary base control, would you expect M0 and broader measures of the money supply, such as M4, to rise and fall by the same percentage as each other?

Problems with controlling broad liquidity

One solution to the problems of monetary base control would be for the authorities to attempt to control *broader* measures of liquidity. Targets for M3 were an important part of monetary policy from 1976 to 1985, and for part of the time a measure similar to M5 was targeted.

How would such a policy work? Assume that the authorities want to operate a tight monetary policy. They sell bonds on the open market. Banks, now short of cash, call in money from the discount houses, which are in turn forced to borrow from the Bank of England. The Bank of England lends by rediscounting bills. Thus, although the Bank of England has been obliged to restore the amount of cash it had withdrawn from the system, there has been an equal and opposite decrease in bills plus money at call held by the banks. Banks' *overall* liquidity has thus been reduced.

Open-market operations should therefore be much more effective in reducing general liquidity than in reducing the monetary base. Note here that open-market operations must be conducted in the bond market not the bill market, since selling Treasury bills would merely exchange one liquid asset for another!

Focusing on the control of broad liquidity also allows another method of control, namely funding, to be used. By merely converting short-term debt (Treasury bills) into long-term debt (bonds), the authorities can reduce liquidity without increasing the size of the national debt.

Just as with a cash ratio, the authorities could impose a statutory liquidity ratio or they could merely allow banks to set their own prudent liquidity ratio. An example of a statutory liquidity ratio was the minimum 12½ per cent reserve assets ratio imposed on banks from 1971 to 1981. These reserves included balances with the Bank of England, money at call, bills of exchange and government bonds with less than one year to maturity.

But despite the advantages of focusing on broad liquidity, there were considerable problems in operating statutory reserve requirements:

- As with cash ratios, banks could hold reserve assets above the statutory minimum, thus helping them to resist a squeeze on reserves (but not indefinitely).
- Goodhart's law again! Business could switch to uncontrolled institutions.
- Not all reserve assets were under government control. If, for example, the authorities attempted to reduce Treasury bills through funding, the banks could increase their holdings of *other* types of bill instead.
- Even those assets whose supply *was* controlled by the authorities were not all held by the controlled institutions. Thus if more bonds and fewer Treasury bills were issued, the banks could still obtain the same amount of bills as before (by paying a higher price), with other buyers getting less. Similarly, they can persuade other holders of bills to exchange them for time deposits in banks, by offering a higher rate of interest on time deposits.

Even with no statutory reserve ratio, it is still difficult to control the money supply by seeking to control broad liquidity, especially if banks are prepared to reduce their liquidity ratio. This is likely if they already have surplus liquidity, or if their customers are prepared to switch from sight to time accounts (for which banks require fewer cash reserves). This will involve offering higher interest rates on time accounts, and hence charging higher interest rates on bank loans. But if the demand for loans is relatively insensitive to interest rate changes, this will have little effect on credit and hence overall deposits. What is more, disintermediation may still occur as customers turn from institutions short of liquidity to those which feel that they have sufficient liquidity to increase their lending.

The effect on interest rates

A policy of controlling money supply can lead to severe fluctuations in interest rates. This can cause great uncertainty for business and can be very damaging to long-term investment and growth.

The problem is more acute if the overall demand for money is inelastic and is subject to fluctuations. In Figure 19.3, with money supply controlled at M_s, even a fairly moderate increase in demand from L to L' leads to a large rise in interest rates from r to r_1.

And yet, if the authorities are committed to controlling money supply, they will have to accept that equilibrium interest rates may well fluctuate in this way.

CASE STUDIES

VIEWS ON CREDIT CONTROL

A comparison of German and UK attitudes

The following are extracts from an article appearing in the *Guardian* on 11 April 1990.

The view of the Bundesbank (the German central bank)

'Minimum reserves, or closely related arrangements, have long been an integral part of the monetary armoury of Western industrialised countries.'

Reserve ratios are different between countries, and there is a host of factors, not least the globalisation of financial markets and varying legal regimes, that account for the variations; but, says the Bundesbank, 'it would be wrong to infer that the minimum reserve instrument is increasingly being abandoned. No major country in which this instrument is available has abolished the right to maintain minimum reserves...'

The Bundesbank recognises that there has been a worldwide trend towards more free market monetary management systems, and that changing reserve ratios has become less popular as a means of managing the financial systems' liquidity than open market operations . . . But in a key passage the Germans insist that even in these circumstances minimum reserve requirements 'ensure the effectiveness of monetary policy'.

For if the banks are given a completely free hand, then they will lend as much as they can, converting all their former deposits with the central bank into interest-bearing assets.

In this case 'the central bank would then be faced with the problem of having to refuse to provide liquidity assistance if pressure was building up in the monetary market – which in all probability would give rise to extreme interest rate swings in the money market or, conversely, the central bank would run the risk of being "dragged along" by excessive funding requests from banks and thus losing control over monetary expansion.

'Hence most central banks still regard the minimum reserve instrument as an integral part of their monetary management system. Any proposals drastically to lower minimum reserve requirements or to lift them altogether that are based solely on the grounds of the side-effects on interest rates or the potential competitive impact of the instrument therefore miss the point.'

The view of the UK Treasury

In his Budget speech [20 March 1990], the Chancellor John Major said: 'It is extremely unlikely that credit controls would work in the modern world in anything other than the very short term.

'They were becoming less and less effective even before exchange controls were abolished over 10 years ago. Their main impact now would be to replace domestic borrowing. These days it would, for example, be a simple matter for any High Street bank to arrange its lending through an overseas branch . . .

'It is for this reason that governments of all persuasions throughout the Western world are

Difficulties in selling bonds

The use of open-market operations or funding to reduce money supply involves selling more bonds. But if potential purchasers believe interest rates will rise in the future (highly likely when the government is attempting to operate a tighter monetary policy), they will hold off buying bonds now and may even attempt to sell bonds before bond prices fall. Thus the authorities may be forced into a large immediate increase in bond interest rates.

Problems with credit rationing

To overcome many of the above problems, governments in the past, and particularly in the late 1960s, resorted to various forms of credit rationing, such as ceilings on bank lending, requests to banks to discriminate between customers, and hire-purchase controls. Credit rationing has three potential advantages:

- It allows interest rates to be kept lower. In Figure 19.4, if the government wants money supply to be reduced from Q_1 to Q_2, but wants to keep interest rates at r_1 rather than raising them to r_2, the excess demand for money $Q_1 - Q_2$ can be eliminated by rationing.
- It affects lending *directly*. It thus tackles head on the problem of excess or deficient aggregate demand. Altering banks' liquidity or the rate of interest are *indirect* methods of controlling spending.
- It allows the authorities to discriminate between loans for productive investment and loans merely for consumption or speculation.

However, the problems of credit rationing can be serious:

- Given that there is surplus liquidity that banks are prevented from using to grant loans, Goodhart's law may apply quite severely. Credit rationing is unlikely to

BOX 19.4

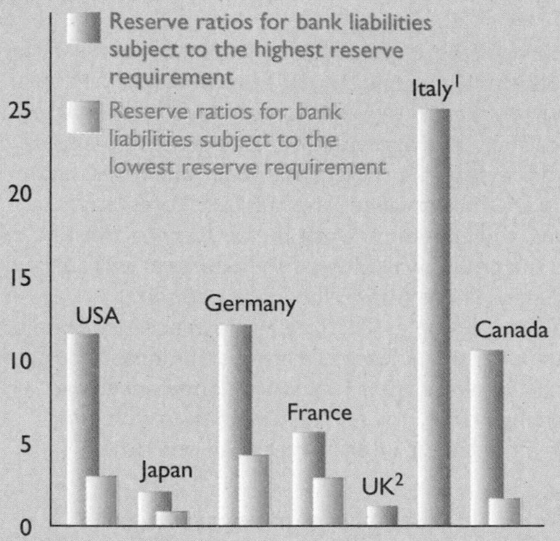

Notes: [1] Uniform incremental reserve ratio: in Italy minimum reserves carry interest.

[2] Uniform reserve ratio: in the UK the minimum reserve instrument does not serve monetary policy purposes.

Minimum reserve ratios in major countries

abolishing credit controls and are relying on interest rates to control money – and thus inflation.'

The Treasury's 'Red Book' published on Budget day explained the government's view that reserve ratios are no more than a means of ensuring that the State's chosen interest rate percolates efficiently through the monetary system; they are not, in the Treasury's view, a means of controlling credit in their own right.

'Because interest rates are the essential instrument of monetary policy, the monetary authorities must be in a position to exercise a high degree of influence over their movements…

'To achieve this result, a number of other countries – France and Germany for example – impose minimum reserve assets ratios on their banks. The operation of the ratio increases the banking system's need for funds from the central bank, and thereby helps to ensure that market rates will reflect the rate of interest at which the central bank provides the supply. Only the central bank can meet these needs. It is thus mistaken to see reserve requirements as an alternative monetary instrument to interest rates.

'In particular, reserve requirements do not serve as a direct credit control. Rather, they provide a means whereby official influence on interest rates is made effective.'

??

1. On what points do the UK and German authorities agree and disagree concerning the role of minimum reserve ratios?
2. 'It is not the mere existence of minimum reserve ratios that constitutes a form of credit rationing, rather it is the deliberate *increasing* of the ratios.' Do you agree?

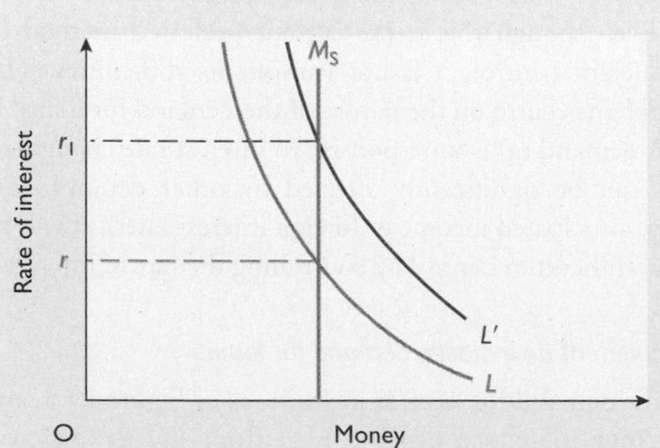

Figure 19.3 The effect on interest rates of a change in demand for money when money supply is kept under control

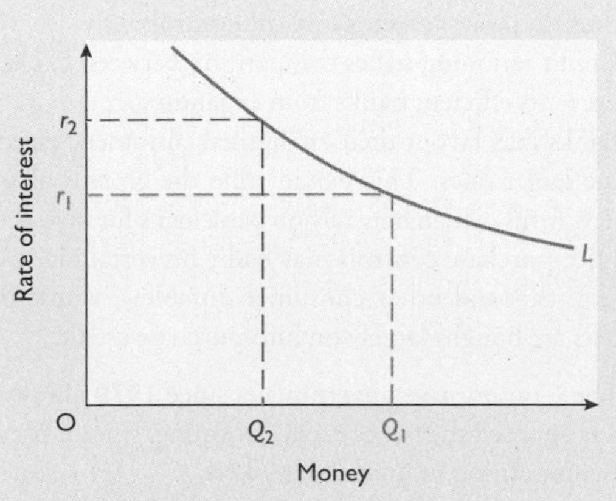

Figure 19.4 The effects of credit rationing

ISSUES AND APPLICATIONS BOX 19.5

USING INTEREST RATES TO CONTROL BOTH AGGREGATE DEMAND AND THE EXCHANGE RATE

A problem of one instrument and two targets

Assume that the government is worried about excessive growth in the money supply and rising inflation. It thus decides to raise interest rates. One effect of these higher interest rates is to attract foreign capital into the country (causing a capital account surplus) and thus drive up the exchange rate. This makes imports cheaper and exports less competitive. This will result in a current account deficit, which will match the capital account surplus.

Now let us assume that the government becomes worried about the damaging effect on exports and wants to reduce the exchange rate. If it uses interest rates as the means of achieving this, it will have to *lower* them: lower interest rates will cause capital to flow out of the UK, and this will cause the rate of exchange to depreciate.

But there is a dilemma here. The government wants *high* interest rates to contain inflation, but *low* interest rates to help exporters. If interest rates are the government's only weapon, one objective will have to be sacrificed for the other.

Another example, but this time the reverse case, was when the UK was forced out of the ERM in September 1992. In its attempt to stay in the ERM at a central rate of DM2.95 and prevent speculation driving down the exchange rate, it had to keep interest rates at very high levels. But the economy was deep in recession and a lower interest rate would have helped to stimulate investment and aggregate demand generally. On this occasion the government wanted *high* interest rates to support the exchange rate, but *low* interest rates to revive the economy. Once the country had left the ERM and the pound was allowed to float, interest rates were reduced. There was no longer any conflict.

These examples illustrate a rule in economic policy: you must have at least as many instruments as targets. If you have two targets (e.g. low inflation and a low exchange rate), you must have at least two policy instruments (e.g. interest rates and one other).

??

1. Give some other examples of the impossibility of using one policy instrument to achieve two policy objectives simultaneously.
2. If the government wanted to achieve a lower rate of inflation and also a *higher* exchange rate, could it under these circumstances rely simply on the one policy instrument of interest rates?

apply to *all* financial institutions. In the late 1960s it applied only to the clearing banks, and so other financial institutions expanded their activities. To avoid this, credit rationing would have to extend to all institutions. The more complex the banking system, the more difficult it is to do this.

- Banks may resist the attempts at rationing. They would *like* to lend and have the liquidity to do so. They may thus find ways to get round the controls.
- Credit rationing stifles competition between banks and prevents efficient banks from expanding.
- Banks may favour their established customers, especially the larger ones. This would stifle the growth of small, new firms, which may rely on bank loans for investment.
- Hire-purchase controls may badly hit certain industries (e.g. cars and other consumer durables), whose products are bought largely on hire-purchase credit.

The Conservative governments since 1979 always very much opposed the use of credit rationing, since it prevents free competition in financial markets.

?? Is credit rationing easier to implement if banks operate as a cartel or if they are highly competitive?

Problems with controlling interest rates

As long as people want to borrow, banks and other financial institutions will normally try to find ways of meeting the demand. In the short run at least, the supply of money is to a large extent demand determined. For this reason the authorities prefer to control the demand for money, and to do this the Bank of England, as lender of the last resort, alters its lending rate to the discount houses.

Even though this is the current preferred method of monetary control, it is not without its difficulties. The problems centre on the nature of the demand for loans. If this demand (a) is unresponsive to interest rate changes or (b) can be significantly affected by other determinants (e.g. anticipated income or foreign interest rates), it will be very difficult to control by controlling the rate of interest.

Problem of an inelastic demand for loans

If the demand for loans is inelastic, as in Figure 19.5, any attempt to reduce demand (e.g. from Q_1 to Q_2) will involve large rises in interest rates (r_1 to r_2). The problem will be compounded if the demand curve shifts to the right, due, say, to a consumer spending boom. High interest rates lead to the following problems:

ISSUES AND APPLICATIONS

BOX 19.6

EFFECTIVE MONETARY POLICY VERSUS BANKING STABILITY AND EFFICIENCY

A problem for the Bank of England?

Three of the principal aims of the Bank of England are as follows:

- To maintain a stable banking system and avoid bank failure.
- To encourage efficient banking by increased competition.
- To carry out the government's monetary policy efficiently and effectively.

In practice, these aims are likely to conflict.

Conflicts between stability and efficiency

The more the competition between the banks, the greater will be the risk of bank failure. Supernormal profits will be eroded; banks may feel forced to grant riskier loans in order to retain market share; a failure of one bank could more easily lead to failures of other banks once public confidence was shaken.

Putting it the other way round, if the Bank of England guarantees the stability of the system, it may make banks more complacent and less concerned to be efficient.

Conflicts between stability and the operation of monetary policy

If monetary policy is to be effective, banks must fear the risk of failure. If they do, then any squeeze on their liquidity by the Bank of England will force them to cut back on their lending. If, by contrast, there is little competition between the banks and they thus operate with high profit margins and plenty of surplus liquidity, it will be harder for the Bank of England to engineer a liquidity shortage.

More important, if the Bank of England acts as lender of last resort, this will remove altogether the fear of a liquidity shortage. The Bank of England will have to rely much more on high interest rates to deter the *demand* for credit.

To summarise: the aim of stability requires banks to be invulnerable; an effective monetary policy requires banks to be vulnerable.

Conflicts between efficiency and the operation of monetary policy

Competition between banks makes it more difficult for the Bank of England to impose credit controls on the banks. If it tries to impose ceilings on clearing bank credit, this will simply encourage the growth of credit through non-clearing banks.

A lack of competition between banks makes it easier for the Bank of England. It is easier to deal with a cartel and to impose rules on its behaviour than it is to influence a highly diverse and competitive banking sector that is open to international movements of capital.

?? Does increased bank competition necessarily make it harder for the Bank of England to force through changes in interest rates (a) by decree; (b) by dealings in the money market?

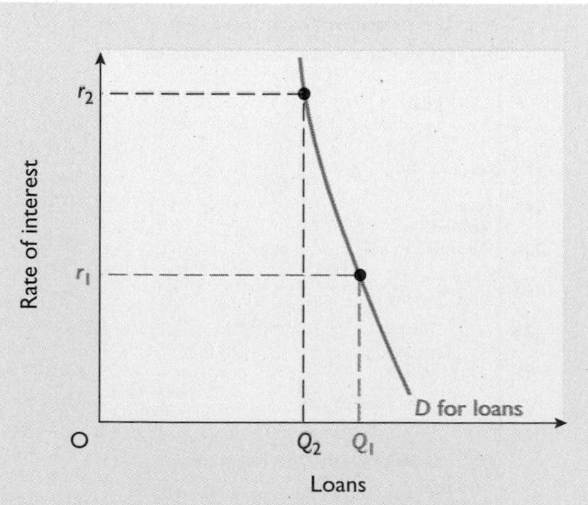

Figure 19.5 An inelastic demand for loans

- They may discourage investment plans and hence long-term growth.
- They add to the costs of production, to the costs of house purchase and generally to the cost of living. They are thus cost inflationary.
- They are politically unpopular, since the general public do not like paying higher interest rates on overdrafts, credit cards and mortgages.
- The necessary bond issue to restrain liquidity will commit the government to paying high rates on these bonds for the next twenty years or so.
- High interest rates encourage inflows of money from abroad. This makes it even more difficult to restrain bank lending.
- Inflows of money from abroad drive up the exchange rate. This can be very damaging for export industries and industries competing with imports. Many firms

ISSUES AND APPLICATIONS BOX 19.7

SHOULD CENTRAL BANKS BE INDEPENDENT OF GOVERNMENT?

In recent times there has been much discussion among both economists and politicians as to whether the Bank of England should be independent. The Conservative governments under Margaret Thatcher and John Major felt that it was important for the government to retain control over monetary policy, if it was to achieve its macroeconomic objectives: a view also held by many on the left of the Labour party.

In contrast to these views, the advocates of independence frequently cited the experience of Germany. The Bundesbank, Germany's central bank, is fiercely independent, and is credited with being instrumental in Germany's economic success. The Bundesbank's philosophy is simple: monetary and price stability are of overriding importance in the pursuit of growth. Inflation should be tightly controlled at all times.

The arguments in favour of an independent central bank are strong.

- An independent central bank is free from political manipulation. It can devote itself to attaining long-run economic goals, rather than to helping politicians achieve short-run economic success in time for the next election.
- Independence may strengthen the *credibility* of monetary policy. This may then play an important part in shaping expectations: workers may put in moderate wage demands and businesses may be more willing to invest.
- An independent central bank like the Bundesbank, has a clear legal status and set of responsibilities. It is the 'protector of the currency' and as such it is not subordinate to government. This is important given the political nature of economic policy making in both a domestic and an international context.

The diagram clearly illustrates that the greater the independence of a country's central bank, the lower and more stable is its rate of inflation. If this is the goal of economic policy, it would seem that more rather than less independence is desirable.

Certainly the incoming Labour government in 1997 was convinced of these arguments. Indeed, granting independence to the Bank of England was the very first act of the Chancellor, Gordon Brown. The decision could also have been affected by two other arguments.

The first was a political one: any blame for rises in interest rates would be deflected from the government.

The second was concerned with moves towards economic and monetary union (EMU) in the European Union. EMU will involve an independent European central bank to manage a single European currency (the euro) and to set the interest rates of the member states that adopt the single currency. The transition to a European central bank would be easier if the Bank of England was already independent: if the government had already relinquished control over monetary policy. We will examine the issues surrounding EMU in section 24.8.

One of the major arguments *against* having an independent central bank is that it makes it more difficult to integrate monetary management into wider economic policy objectives. On some occasions, for example, it might be desirable to accept a *higher* rate of inflation – if this were the consequence of a growth stimulus aimed at reducing unemployment. But with an independent central bank committed to monetary stability, it may be difficult for the government to achieve such economic policy goals. As Kenneth Clarke, the Chancellor in the outgoing Conservative government, argued: 'What you are going to see is tighter monetary policy than you might otherwise have got from a perfectly responsible Chancellor of the Exchequer.'

?? Is there any case for an independent body to determine fiscal policy? If so, what would its role be?

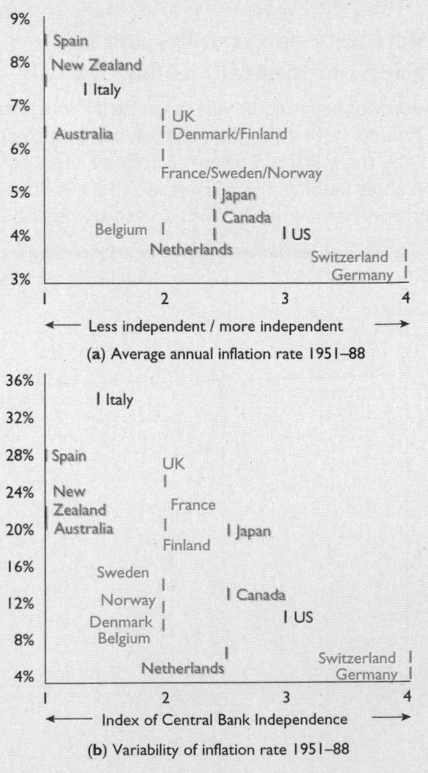

(a) Average annual inflation rate 1951–88

(b) Variability of inflation rate 1951–88

Source: *Financial Times*, 25 September 1992.

suffered badly in 1980 when the exchange rate soared, partly as a result of a high interest rate policy.

Evidence suggests that the demand for loans may indeed be quite inelastic. The reasons include the following:

- A rise in interest rates, particularly if it deepens a recession, may force many firms and individuals into borrowing merely to survive. This increase in 'distress borrowing' may largely offset any decline in borrowing by other firms or individuals.
- Although investment *plans* may be curtailed by high interest rates, *current* borrowing by many firms cannot easily be curtailed. Similarly, householders may be discouraged from taking on new mortgages, but existing mortgages are unlikely to be reduced.
- High interest rates may discourage many firms from taking out long-term fixed-interest loans. But instead of reducing their total borrowing, some firms may merely switch to shorter-term variable-interest loans. This will reduce the overall fall in demand for bank loans, thus making the demand less elastic.

Problem of an unstable demand

Accurate monetary control requires the authorities to be able to predict the demand curve for money. Only then can they set the appropriate level of interest rates. Unfortunately, the demand curve may shift unpredictably, making control very difficult. The major reason is *speculation*:

- If people think interest rates will rise and bond prices fall, in the meantime they will demand to hold their assets in liquid form. The demand for money will rise.
- If people think exchange rates will rise, they will demand sterling while it is still relatively cheap. The demand for money will rise.
- If people think inflation will rise, the transactions demand for money may rise. People spend now while prices are still relatively low.
- If people think the economy is going to grow faster, the demand for loans will increase as firms seek to increase their investment.

It is very difficult for the authorities to predict what people's speculation will be. Speculation depends largely on world political events, rumour and 'random shocks'.

If the demand curve shifts very much, and if it is inelastic, monetary control will be very difficult. Furthermore, the authorities will have to make frequent and sizeable adjustments to interest rates. These fluctuations can be very damaging to business confidence and may discourage long-term investment.

> **??** Why does an unstable demand for money make it difficult to control the *supply* of money?

Conclusions

It is impossible to use monetary policy as a precise means of controlling aggregate demand. It is especially weak when it is pulling against the expectations of firms and consumers, and when it is implemented too late. If the authorities operate a tight monetary policy firmly enough and long enough, they should eventually be able to reduce lending and aggregate demand. But there will inevitably be time lags and imprecision in the process.

An expansionary monetary policy is even less reliable. If the economy is in recession, no matter how low interest rates are driven, people cannot be forced to borrow if they do not wish to.

Few economists, therefore, argue that monetary policy can be used to 'fine tune' the economy. Even monetarists accept that monetary policy is best regarded as the means of keeping monetary growth within fairly broad medium- or long-term target ranges. This was very much the approach of the Thatcher government's medium-term financial strategy in the early and mid-1980s.

SECTION SUMMARY

1. It is difficult to control the growth of the money supply over the longer term without controlling the growth of the PSBR. This will be difficult in a recession, when automatic fiscal stabilisers will cause a growth in government expenditure and a cut in tax revenues. What is more, tax increases or cuts in government expenditure are politically unpopular. Even if the PSBR *is* reduced, this may be insufficient to prevent the growth of credit, especially if banks are prepared to operate with a lower liquidity ratio.
2. All forms of short-term monetary policy involve problems. Controlling either the monetary base or broad liquidity is difficult given that the Bank of England is always prepared to provide liquidity to the discount houses as lender of last resort. Also there are the problems of disintermediation, as customers switch their borrowing away from those banks short of liquidity, and the problem of banks resisting the squeeze on liquidity by operating with a lower liquidity ratio. If the government is successful in

continued

controlling the money supply, there then arises the problem of severe fluctuations in interest rates if the demand for money fluctuates and is relatively inelastic.

3. Credit rationing is a means of directly reducing aggregate demand without having to raise interest rates. It stifles competition between banks, however, and encourages banks to discriminate (perhaps unfairly) between customers. Banks may also try to evade the controls, and disintermediation is likely to occur towards those institutions that are not controlled.
4. The form of monetary policy that has been favoured in recent years is the control of interest rates. Higher interest rates, by reducing the demand for money, effectively also reduce the supply. However, with an inelastic demand for loans, interest rates may have to rise to very high levels in order to bring the required reduction in monetary growth. They are politically unpopular and discriminate against those with high borrowing commitments. They also drive up the exchange rate, which can damage exports. Controlling aggregate demand through interest rates is made even more difficult by fluctuations in the demand for money. These fluctuations are made more severe by speculation against changes in interest rates, exchange rates, the rate of inflation, etc.
5. It is impossible to use monetary policy as a precise means of controlling aggregate demand in the short term. Nevertheless in the long term, if the policy is pursued rigorously enough, many economists argue that it is the most effective way of keeping inflation under control.

??? END-OF-CHAPTER QUESTIONS ???

1. Assume that a bank has the following simplified balance sheet, and is operating at its desired liquidity ratio:

Liabilities	(£m)	Assets	(£m)
Deposits	100	Balances with central bank	10
		Advances	90
	100		100

Now assume that the central bank repurchases £5 million of government bonds on the open market. Assume that the people who sell the bonds all have their accounts with this bank.

(a) Draw up the new balance sheet directly after the purchase of the bonds.

(b) Now draw up the eventual balance sheet after all credit creation has taken place.

(c) Would there be a similar effect if the central bank rediscounted £5 billion of Treasury bills?

(d) How would such open market operations affect the rate of interest?

2. Distinguish between the Keynesian and monetarist attitudes towards monetary policy. What is the significance of the demand for money in their respective analyses?
3. Is it possible for the government to target the money supply over the longer term without targeting the PSBR?
4. What are the mechanics whereby the government raises the rate of interest?
5. What is Goodhart's Law? How is it relevant to (i) monetary policy; (ii) using assignment grades to assess a student's ability; (iii) paying workers according to the amount of output they produce; (iv) awarding local authority contracts to cleaning or refuse disposal companies on the basis of tendered prices?
6. What are the advantages and disadvantages of the government imposing statutory reserve ratios on banks?
7. How might the central bank being prepared to offer last resort facilities to the banking system have an adverse effect on the behaviour of banks?
8. 'It is easier to control the monetary base than broader money, but it is less relevant to do so.' Do you agree with this statement?

20

Macroeconomic controversies I

The control of aggregate demand

There is no current orthodoxy in macroeconomics. The debates between Keynesians (of various types), monetarists and new classicists show no signs of being settled. At their centre are the key questions of how well does a free-market economy meet the various macroeconomic objectives, and to what extent can government intervention improve things?

The debates fall into two main categories. The first concerns the control of aggregate demand. How effectively can the government use either fiscal or monetary policy to achieve a given level of aggregate demand? The second concerns aggregate supply. What determines output and employment, and what is the relationship between aggregate supply and the level of prices?

We will consider aggregate supply and supply-side policies in Chapters 21 and 22. This chapter looks at the debate over aggregate demand and draws together several of the threads of the last three chapters.

20.1 Monetary policy and aggregate demand

The quantity theory of money

A simple illustration of the controversy over the effects of monetary policy on aggregate demand is provided by the *quantity theory of money* (see pages 472–5). One version of this theory is expressed in the following equation:[1]

$$MV = PQ$$

where M is the supply of money; Q is the quantity of national output sold in a year; P is the average level of prices; and V is the income velocity of circulation (the number of times money is spent on national output in a year).

PQ is thus the money value of national output sold. MV is the total spending on national output, and therefore must equal PQ. The quantity *equation* is true by definition. MV is *necessarily* equal to PQ because of the way the terms are defined. What a change in M does to P, however, is a matter of debate. The controversy centres on whether and how V and Q are affected by changes in the money supply (M).

?? Refer back to the Cambridge version of the quantity equation we looked at in Box 15.2 (page 475). What is the relationship between the term k in that version and the term V in the version we have just looked at?

The velocity of circulation (V)

Monetarists argue that in the long run V is determined *totally independently* of the money supply (M). Thus a change in money supply (M) leaves V unaffected and brings a corresponding change in expenditure (MV):

$$M\uparrow, \bar{V} \rightarrow MV\uparrow$$

where the bar over the V term means that it is exogenously determined: i.e. determined *independently* of M.

Monetarists therefore claim that monetary policy over the longer term is an extremely powerful weapon for controlling (nominal) aggregate demand (PQ).

?? If V is constant, will (a) a £10 million rise in M give a £10 million rise in MV: (b) a 10 per cent rise in M give a 10 per cent rise in MV?

Keynesians argue that V tends to vary inversely with M, but rather unpredictably. An increase in money supply will not necessarily have much effect on spending; instead

[1] This differs from the version we looked at on page 472 in that Q is a *physical* measure of national output, i.e. the total number of units of goods and services produced, and P is their average value.

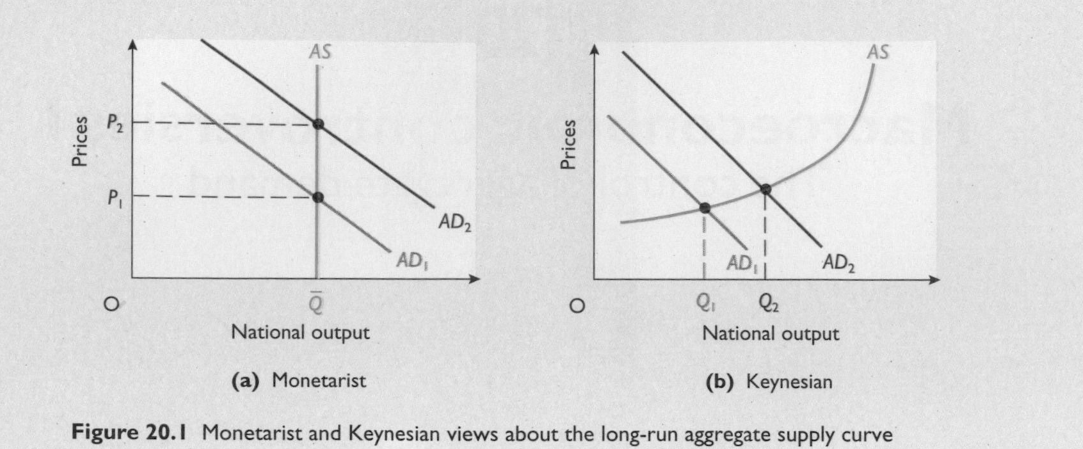

Figure 20.1 Monetarist and Keynesian views about the long-run aggregate supply curve

people may simply increase their holdings of idle speculative balances, with a corresponding decline in the speed with which money circulates (V). How much extra idle balances people will hold will depend on their expectations of changes in interest rates, prices and exchange rates. Since expectations are difficult to predict, the amount by which V will fall is also difficult to predict:

$$M\uparrow \rightarrow V\downarrow \ (?) \rightarrow MV?$$

Keynesians therefore claim that monetary policy is an extremely unreliable weapon for controlling aggregate demand.

The quantity of national output (Q)

Monetarists argue that aggregate supply is inelastic in the long run (see Figure 20.1(a)), and therefore output (Q) is determined independently of aggregate demand. Any rise in MV will be totally reflected in a rise in prices (P):

$$MV\uparrow \rightarrow P\uparrow, \bar{Q}$$

The stock of money therefore determines the price level, and the rate of increase in money supply determines the rate of inflation. In the long run, control of the money supply will not affect output (Q) and employment.

?? If both V and Q are constant, will (a) a £10 million rise in M lead to a £10 million rise in P; (b) a 10 per cent rise in M lead to a 10 per cent rise in P?

Keynesians argue that aggregate supply is relatively elastic except when full employment is approached (see Figure 20.1(b)). Thus Q is variable. A tight monetary policy therefore, to the extent that it does affect aggregate demand, is likely to reduce Q as well as P, especially when there is resistance from monopolistic firms and unions to price and wage cuts:

$$MV\downarrow \rightarrow P\downarrow \text{ and } Q\downarrow$$

If monetary policy is successful in reducing aggregate demand, it can lead to a lasting recession.

The variability of V is the subject of this section. The variability of Q is the subject of Chapter 21.

Monetary policy's effect on aggregate demand: the traditional Keynesian transmission mechanism

In order to assess the arguments over the variability of V it is necessary to see just how a change in money supply is transmitted through to a change in aggregate demand.

Keynesians stress that transmission mechanisms are indirect: changes in money supply affect aggregate demand *indirectly* via changes in interest rates or exchange rates. We will look first at the interest rate mechanism (see Figure 20.2). Changes in money supply affect aggregate demand in three stages:

1. A rise in money supply from M to M' leads to a fall in the rate of interest from r_1 to r_2.[2]
2. A fall in the rate of interest leads to more investment and any other interest-sensitive expenditures (from I_1 to I_2).
3. A rise in investment leads to a multiplied rise in national income (from Y_1 to Y_2).

However, according to Keynesians, stages 1 and 2 are unpredictable and perhaps rather weak.

[2] We are assuming here that the money supply curve is upward sloping (see page 568).

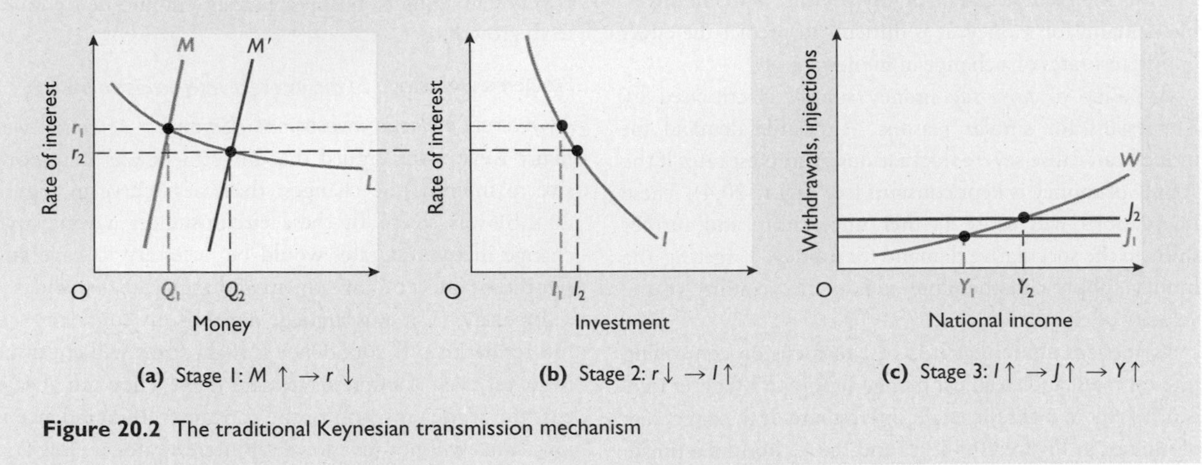

Figure 20.2 The traditional Keynesian transmission mechanism

Problems with stage 1: the money–interest link

An interest-elastic demand for money. According to Keynesians, the speculative demand for money is highly responsive to changes in interest rates. If people believe the rate of interest will rise, and thus the price of bonds and other securities will fall, few people will want to buy them. Instead there will be a very high demand for liquid assets (money and near money). The demand for money will therefore be very elastic in response to changes in interest rates. The demand for money curve (the liquidity preference curve, *L*) will be shallow and may even be infinitely elastic at some minimum interest rate. This is the point where everyone believes interest rates will rise, and therefore no one wants to buy bonds. Everyone wants to hold their assets in liquid form.

With a very shallow *L* curve (as in Figure 20.3), a rise in money supply from *M* to *M′* will lead to only a small fall in the rate of interest from r_1 to r_2. Once people believe that the rate of interest will not go any lower, any further rise in money supply will have no effect on *r*. The additional money will be lost in what Keynes called the **liquidity trap**. People simply hold the additional money as idle balances.

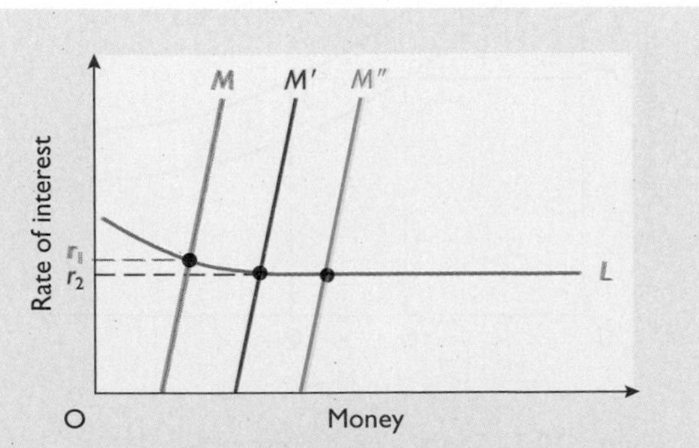

Figure 20.3 An elastic liquidity preference curve

Keynes himself saw the liquidity trap as merely a special case: the case where the economy is in deep recession. In such a case, an expansion of money supply would have no effect on the economy. In more normal times, an expansion of money supply would be likely to have some effect on interest rates.

An unstable demand for money. A more serious problem is that the liquidity preference curve (*L*) is *unstable*. People hold speculative balances when they anticipate that interest rates will rise (security prices will fall). But it is not just the current interest rate that affects people's expectations of the future direction of interest rates. Many factors could affect such expectations:

- Changes in foreign interest rates. UK interest rates would have to follow suit if the authorities wished to maintain a stable exchange rate.
- Changes in exchange rates. With a falling exchange rate, the authorities may raise interest rates to protect sterling.
- Statements of government intentions on economic policy.
- Good or bad industrial news. With good news, people tend to buy shares.
- Newly published figures on inflation or money supply. If inflation or the growth in money supply is higher than anticipated, people will expect a rise in interest rates in anticipation of a tighter monetary policy.

DEFINITION

Liquidity trap The absorption of any additional money supply into idle balances at very low rates of interest, leaving aggregate demand unchanged.

Thus the L curve can be highly volatile. With an unstable demand for money, it is difficult to predict the effect on interest rates of a change in money supply.

A policy of *targeting* money supply is criticised by Keynesians for similar reasons. A volatile demand for money can cause severe fluctuations in interest rates if the supply of money is kept constant (see Figure 20.4). These fluctuations will cause further uncertainty and further shifts in the speculative demand for money. Targeting the money supply can therefore add to the volatility of the velocity of circulation (V).

Keynesians argue that it is best to focus on controlling interest rates, and to adjust money supply to whatever level is necessary to meet the target interest rate. If the target rate of interest in Figure 20.5 is r^*, and the authorities estimate the demand for money to be L, they should allow the money supply to be Q_1. If demand increases to L', then the authorities should allow the money supply to rise to Q_2.

Controlling interest rates is likely to cause a more stable demand for money, with fewer shifts in the speculative demand. This in turn will aid the control of interest rates.

Although the authorities in the UK have sought to control interest rates by their operations in the discount market, this relates much more to Figure 20.4 than Figure 20.5, especially during the first part of the 1980s. For any given demand for money, they sought to adjust interest rates so as to make the demand for money equal to the target money supply. Thus in Figure 20.4, if the demand for money increased to L', and the money supply target was Q_1, the authorities would raise interest rates to r_2.

Keynesians are critical of this policy, arguing that uncertainty over interest rates, combined with a generally too restrictive monetary policy and a correspondingly too high average interest rate, causes a 'deflationary bias' and is very damaging to business investment and hence long-term growth.

Problems with stage 2: the interest rate–investment link

An interest-inelastic investment demand. After the war many Keynesians argued that investment was unresponsive to interest rate changes: that the I curve in Figure 20.2(b) was steep. In these circumstances a very large change in interest rates would be necessary to have any significant effect on investment and aggregate demand.

Investment, it was argued, depends on confidence of future markets. If confidence is high, firms will continue to invest even if interest rates are high. They can always pass the higher costs on to the consumer. If confidence is low, firms will not invest even if interest rates are low and borrowing is cheap. Evidence seemed to confirm the interest inelasticity of investment demand.

Few Keynesians hold this extreme position today. The evidence for an inelastic investment demand has been challenged. Just because investment was not significantly lower on occasions when interest rates were high, it does not follow that investment is unresponsive to interest rate changes. There may have been changes in *other* factors that helped to *maintain* investment: in other words, the I curve shifted to the right. For example, a rise in consumer demand would both cause the high interest rate *and* encourage higher investment.

?? Figure 20.6 shows a steep investment demand curve. If the rate of interest rises from r_1 to r_2, there is only a small fall in investment from I_1 to I_2. Now draw a much more elastic I curve passing through point a. Assume that this is the true I curve. Show how the rate of interest could still rise to r_2 and investment still only fall to I_2 if this curve were to shift.

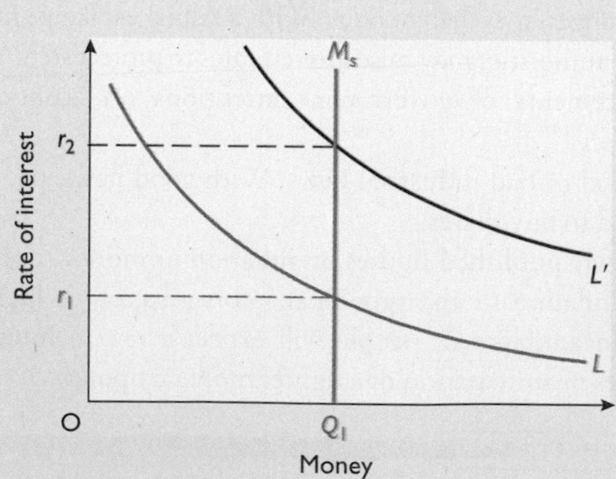

Figure 20.4 The effects on interest rates of a fluctuating demand for money

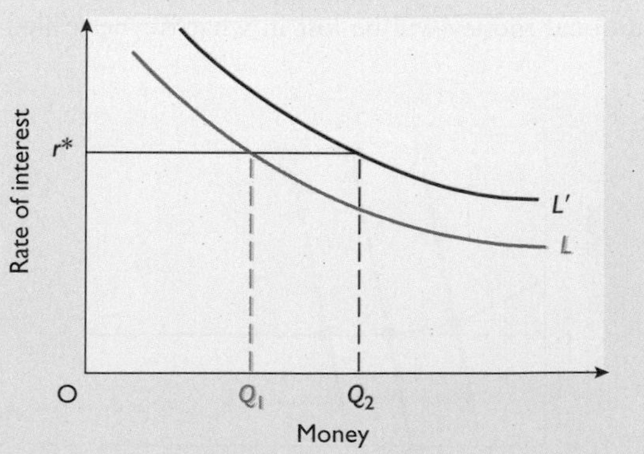

Figure 20.5 Controlling interest rates

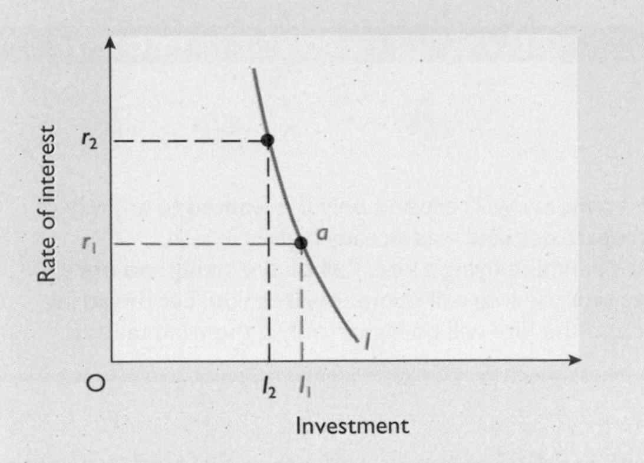

Figure 20.6 Does a rise in interest rates cause only a small fall in investment?

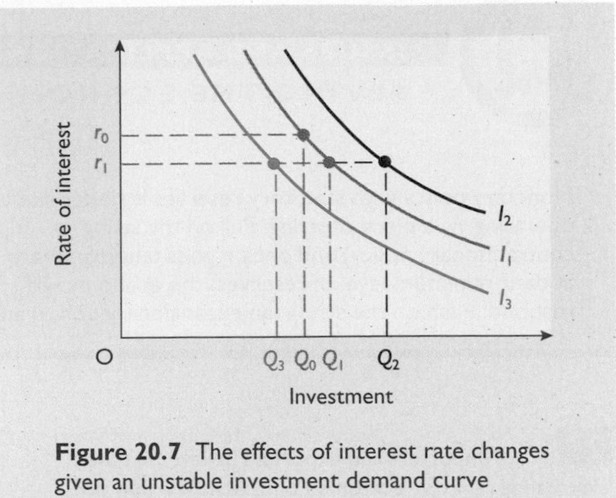

Figure 20.7 The effects of interest rate changes given an unstable investment demand curve

Even if fixed investment in plant and machinery is not very interest sensitive, other components of aggregate demand may well be: for example, investment in stocks, consumer demand financed through credit cards, bank loans or hire purchase, and the demand for houses financed through mortgages.

An unstable investment demand. Today the major worry about the interest–investment link is not that the investment curve is inelastic, but rather that it shifts erratically with the confidence of investors.

Assume in Figure 20.7 that the authorities reduce interest rates from r_0 to r_1. Other things being equal, the level of investment will rise from Q_0 to Q_1. If, however, firms believe that the economy will now pull out of recession, their confidence will increase. The investment curve will shift to I_2 and investment will increase quite markedly to Q_2. If, on the other hand, firms believe that inflation will now rise, which in turn will later force the authorities to pursue a tighter monetary policy, their confidence may well decrease. The investment curve will shift to I_3 and the level of investment will actually fall to Q_3.

Monetary policy is likely to be effective, therefore, only if people have confidence in its effectiveness. This *psychological* effect can be quite powerful. It demands considerable *political* skill, however, to manipulate it.

Keynesian analysis of the exchange rate transmission mechanism

The traditional Keynesian mechanism can be extended to an open economy to take into account international capital flows and movements in the exchange rate. The mechanism now includes the exchange rate as an intermediate variable between changes in the money supply and changes in aggregate demand. There are four stages in the mechanism (see Figure 20.8):

1. A rise in money supply will cause a fall in interest rates.
2. A fall in interest rates will lead to an outflow of short-term capital from the country. This will cause a depreciation of the exchange rate (assuming the authorities allow it).
3. This will cause a rise in demand for exports and a fall in demand for imports.
4. This will cause a multiplied rise in national income.

Stage 1 will tend to be more powerful than in a closed economy. The liquidity preference curve will tend to be less elastic because, as interest rates fall, people may fear a depreciation of sterling and switch to holding other currencies. Just how strong stage 1 will be depends on *how much* people think the exchange rate will depreciate.

Stage 2 is likely to be very strong indeed. Given the openness of international financial markets, international capital flows can be enormous in response to interest rate changes. Only a relatively small change in interest rates is necessary to cause a relatively large capital flow.

Stage 3 may be quite strong in the long run. Given time, the demand by consumers abroad for UK exports and demand in the UK for imports may be quite elastic. In the short run, the effect may be rather limited. However, the size of the effect depends on people's expectations of exchange rate movements. If people think that the exchange rate will fall further, importers will buy *now* before the rate does fall. Exporters, on the other hand, will hold back as long as possible before shipping their exports. These actions will tend to push the exchange rate down. But such speculation is very difficult to predict as it depends on often highly volatile expectations.

ISSUES AND APPLICATIONS — BOX 20.1

FLYING THE ECONOMIC KITE

Monetary policy with statutory reserves is rather like operating via a piece of string. Pull on the string (a contractionary policy) and once it goes taut (banks are at their minimum level of reserves) the economy will respond. Push on the string (an expansionary policy) and the economy will respond only if it wanted to anyway (if aggregate demand was already high).

It's a bit like flying a kite. Pull on the string and once it goes taut the kite will come towards you. Let the string out and the kite will go higher only if the wind takes it.

?? If importers and exporters believe that the exchange rate has 'bottomed out', what will they do?

Stage 4 is the familiar multiplier, only this time triggered off by a change in imports and exports.

To summarise: the effects of a change in the money supply might be quite strong, but their precise magnitude is usually highly unpredictable.

The effects of changes in money supply will depend also on just how free the exchange rate is. If the government intervenes to 'peg' (i.e. fix) the exchange rate or to prevent excessive fluctuations, the transmission mechanism will not work in the way described. Alternative exchange rate systems (or 'regimes', as they are called) are examined in Chapter 24.

Monetary policy's effect on aggregate demand: the monetarist transmission mechanism

The direct mechanism

Monetarists stress the direct transmission mechanism. If money supply increases, people will have more money than they require to hold. They will spend this surplus. Much of this spending will go on goods and services, thereby directly increasing aggregate demand:

$$M_s \uparrow \rightarrow M_s > M_d \rightarrow AD \uparrow$$

The theoretical underpinning for this is given by the *theory of portfolio balance*. People have a number of ways of holding their wealth: as money, or as financial assets such as bills, bonds and shares, or as physical assets such as houses, cars and televisions. In other words, people hold a whole portfolio of assets of varying degrees of liquidity – from cash to central heating.

If money supply expands, people will find themselves holding more money than they require: their portfolios are unnecessarily liquid. Some of this money will be used to purchase financial assets, and some to purchase *goods and services*. As more assets are purchased, this will drive up their price. This will effectively reduce their 'yield'. For bonds and other financial assets, this means a reduction in their rate of interest. For goods and services, this means a reduction in their marginal utility/price ratio: a higher level of consumption will reduce their marginal utility and drive up their price. The process will stop when a balance has been restored in people's portfolios. In the meantime, there will have been extra consumption and hence a rise in aggregate demand.

?? Do you think that this is an accurate description of how people behave when they acquire extra money?

This mechanism has been criticised by Keynesians. Just how is the extra money injected into people's portfolios in the first place? There are two possible means in the short term.

An expansionary fiscal policy financed by an increased money supply. In this case, people receive the extra money through tax cuts or increased government expenditure. But in these circumstances, claim Keynesians, it is *fiscal* policy that is causing the resulting increase in aggregate demand through its effect on people's real incomes.

The use of monetary techniques. Assume that there is an expansionary open-market operation. This will involve people exchanging bonds and bills for money. Therefore the resulting extra money in their portfolios has not involved any increase in wealth. People have more money but fewer bonds and bills. Any increase in the ratio of shares and physical assets in people's portfolios will be due simply to the new lower interest rates on bonds. In the *short run*, therefore, the direct mechanism may be weak. The subsequent effects, however, when the banks use their newly acquired balances to grant loans and hence initiate a process of credit creation, will be stronger.

EXPLORING THE THEORY BOX 20.2

CHOOSING THE EXCHANGE RATE OR THE MONEY SUPPLY

You can't choose both

If the government expands the money supply, then interest rates will fall and aggregate demand will tend to rise. With a floating exchange rate this will cause the currency to depreciate.

But what if the government attempts to maintain a fixed exchange rate? To do this it must keep interest rates comparable with world rates. This means that it is no longer free to choose the level of money supply. The money supply has become endogenous.

The government can't have it both ways. It can choose the level of the money supply (providing it has the techniques to do so) and let interest rates and the exchange rate be what they will. Or it can choose the exchange rate, but this will then determine the necessary rate of interest and hence the supply of money. These issues are explored in Chapter 24.

?? Can the government choose both the exchange rate *and* the money supply if it is prepared to use the reserves to support the exchange rate?

The indirect mechanisms

Monetarists also see monetary policy operating through the indirect mechanisms.

The traditional interest rate mechanism. This, they argue, is more powerful than in traditional Keynesian theory, because stages 1 and 2 are much stronger. The liquidity preference curve (L) (Figure 20.2(a)) is relatively inelastic. This is because of the much smaller role played by speculative balances. The investment demand curve (I) (Figure 20.2(b)), on the other hand, is relatively elastic. (See pages 600–1 above.) With a steep L curve and a shallow I curve, the effect on aggregate demand will be much greater.

?? Redraw the three diagrams of Figure 20.2 with a steeper L curve and a shallower I curve. Show how an increase in money supply will have a larger effect on national income.

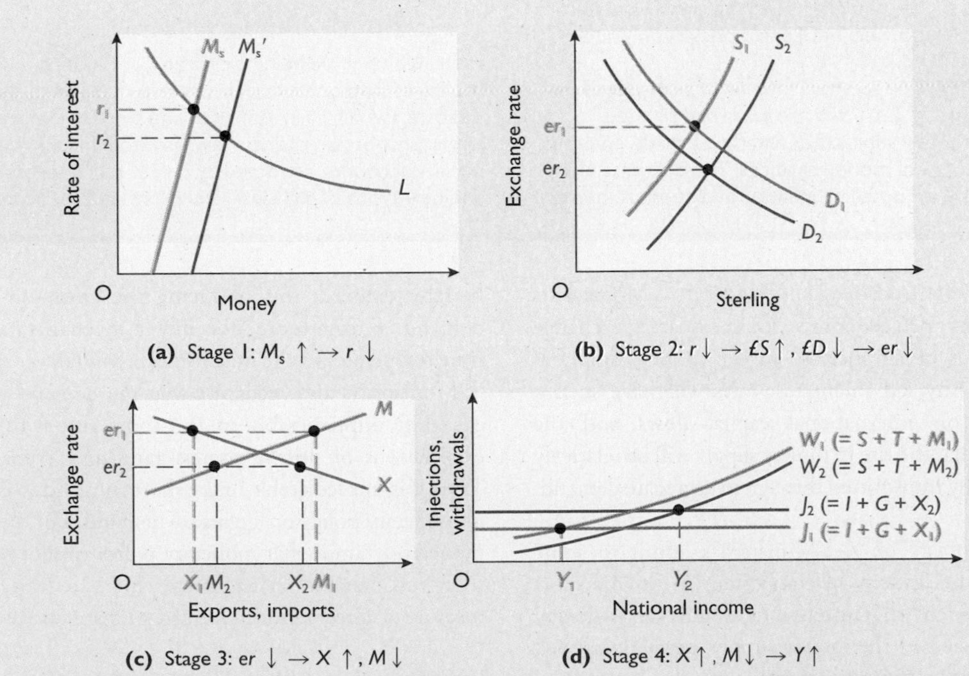

Figure 20.8 The exchange rate transmission mechanism

CASE STUDIES

THE STABILITY OF THE VELOCITY OF CIRCULATION
Who are right: Keynesians or monetarists?

Both Keynesian and monetarist theories of money are logically consistent with their assumptions. Who then is right? Are the Keynesians right that the velocity of circulation of money (V) is highly unstable, and that therefore a change in the level of money supply has an uncertain effect on national expenditure? Or are the monetarists right that V is relatively stable, especially in the longer run, and that therefore changes in money supply have a relatively predictable effect on expenditure?

Not surprisingly, the facts do not unequivocally support either side. Both sides tend to interpret the facts in ways that suit their particular case.

The evidence

How has V behaved over time? To answer this we need to measure V. A simple way of doing this is to use the formula $V = PQ/M$ (rearranging the terms in the quantity equation $MV = PQ$). Thus we need to measure PQ and M. PQ is simply the money value of national output: in other words, GDP. The value of M (and hence V) will depend on which measure of the money supply we use.

The diagram shows how the velocities of circulation of both M4 and M0 have changed over the years.

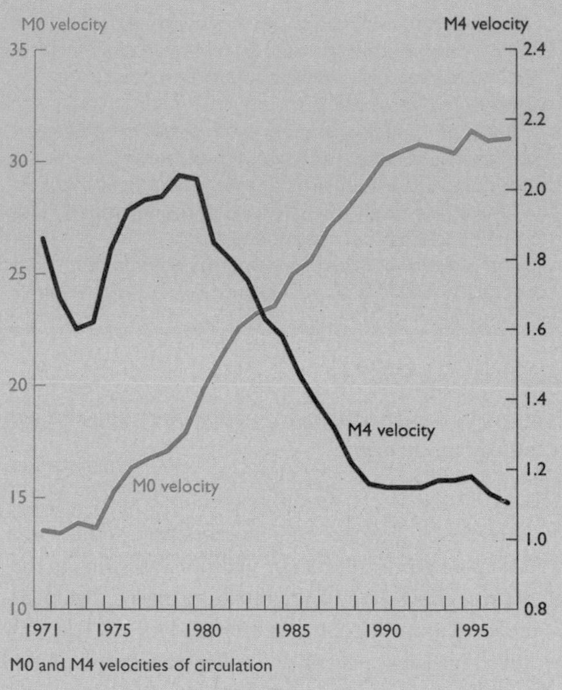

M0 and M4 velocities of circulation

The monetarist case

Monetarists argue that V has been sufficiently stable to give a close relationship between money supply and aggregate demand.

As far as M4 is concerned, long-term increases in its velocity from 1973 to 1979 are explained by the increase in money substitutes and credit cards, and thus smaller holdings of money balances. The decrease after 1980 is explained by falling inflation and nominal interest rates, with people being increasingly prepared to hold money in sight accounts; by the growth in wholesale deposits (which earn interest); and by people putting a larger proportion of their savings into bank and building society accounts, attracted by higher *real* interest rates and new types of high-interest instant-access account.

The exchange rate transmission mechanism. Monetarists argue that, in an open economy with free-floating exchange rates, the effect of an increase in the money supply is stronger still. Any fall in interest rates will have such a strong effect on international capital flows and the exchange rate that the rise in money supply will be relatively quickly and fully transmitted through to aggregate demand.

Short-run variability of V. Monetarists admit to some variability of the velocity of circulation (V) in the short run. To the extent that interest rates and yields do fall with an expansion of the money supply, people may well hold larger money balances: after all, the interest sacrificed by not holding bonds, etc. has been reduced. If people hold relatively more money, the velocity of circulation is thereby reduced, thus reducing the effect on aggregate demand. Furthermore, the direct mechanism may take time to operate. In the meantime V will fall.

Monetarists also recognise that the demand for money can shift unpredictably in the short run with changing expectations of prices, interest rates and exchange rates. Thus V is unpredictable in the short run, and so is the effect of monetary policy on aggregate demand. For these reasons monetarists argue that monetary policy cannot be used for short-run demand management. Here at least there is a measure of agreement between Keynesians and monetarists.

Long-run stability of V. The main claim of monetarists is that the velocity of circulation (V) is relatively stable over the longer run, and any changes that do occur are the pre-

BOX 20.3

As the pace of these changes slowed down, so the fall in velocity ceased after 1990.

As far as M0 is concerned, its velocity more than doubled between 1974 and 1991. One reason for this is the increased use of credit and debit cards, which has reduced the amount of cash people need to hold. The growth of cash machines has also reduced the need to hold so much cash, given that people can easily obtain more 24 hours per day. The relatively smaller amount of cash thus circulates faster. But, as with M4, these changes in M0's velocity ceased in the 1990s. Part of the reason has been a slowing down in the growth of credit and debit cards, and part has been lower inflation, which has reduced the opportunity cost of holding cash.

The point made by monetarists is that these changes are predictable and do not, therefore, undermine the close relationship between *M* and *PQ*.

Keynesian criticisms

1. Not all measures of money supply (M0, M2, M4, etc.) have moved together. Thus the variability of *V* depends on the choice of definition of *M*.
2. How long is the long run? Instability can always be explained away by saying that it is merely a short-run effect. But if the time lag with monetary policy is very long, there is a case for using some alternative policy in the meantime. Keynesians favour fiscal policy here.
3. Monetary and fiscal policy often work together – especially in the long run. An expansionary fiscal policy over a number of years will increase the PSBR, which in turn will lead to an increase in money supply (*M*). If the fiscal policy increases the money value of national output (*PQ*), *V* may well as a result remain constant. But it does not follow from this that it was the growth in *M* that *caused* the growth in *PQ*. On the few occasions when fiscal and monetary policy work in opposite directions the evidence is unclear as to which has the bigger effect – especially as the time period is rarely long enough for the full effects to be identified.
4. The changes in the velocity of circulation over the short-to-medium term may seem relatively small (44 per cent), but the change in the *marginal* velocity of circulation (the *rise* in GDP divided by the *rise* in money supply) will be much bigger.

   Thus from 1978 to 1979 a *rise* in M4 of £12.1 billion was associated with a rise in GDP of £29.6 billion, giving a marginal velocity of circulation of 2.5. But from 1980 to 1981 M4 rose by £23.8 billion and yet GDP only rose by £23.2 billion, giving a marginal velocity over the period of 0.97. In other words, a given rise in money supply over this later time period was associated with a rise in GDP *less than half* that of the earlier period.
5. Finally there is perhaps the most serious problem of all. In which direction does the causality lie? Changes in aggregate demand may go together with changes in money supply. But is it higher money supply causing higher aggregate demand, or the other way round?

   Keynesians argue that higher aggregate demand causes an increased demand for bank loans, and banks are only too happy to create the necessary credit, thus expanding the money supply.

   This fifth issue is the issue of whether money supply is 'exogenous' or 'endogenous'.

?? How would a monetarist answer the five Keynesian criticisms given above?

dictable outcome of institutional changes, such as the increased use of credit cards.

One reason why *V* remains relatively stable in the long run, despite an increase in money supply, is that sufficient time has elapsed for the direct mechanism to have worked fully through. The other reason is the effect on inflation and consequently on interest rates. This works as follows.

Assume an initial increase in money supply. Interest rates fall. *V* falls. But if money supply goes on rising and hence expenditure goes on rising, inflation will rise. This will drive up *nominal* interest rates (even though *real* interest rates will stay low). But in choosing whether to hold money or to buy assets, it is the *nominal* rate of interest that people look at, since that is the opportunity cost of holding money. Thus people economise on money balances and *V* rises back again.

(Note that in extreme cases *V* will even rise to levels higher than before. This is likely if people start speculating that prices will rise further. People will rush to buy goods and assets before their prices rise further. This action will help to push the prices up even more. This form of destabilising speculation took place in the hyperinflation of Germany in the 1920s, as people spent their money as quickly as possible.)

With a predictable *V* in the longer run, monetary policy becomes the essential means of controlling long-term aggregate demand. For this reason monetarists favour a longer-term approach to monetary policy, including targets for the growth of the money supply (see pages 579–82).

Is money supply exogenous or endogenous?

Money supply is **exogenous** (independently determined) if it can be fixed by the authorities and if it does not vary with aggregate demand and interest rates. In Figure 20.2(a) the M 'curve' would be vertical. It would shift only if the government *chose* to alter the money supply. Money supply is **endogenous** (determined within the model) if it is determined by aggregate demand and hence the demand for money: banks simply expanding or contracting credit in response to customer demand.

The extreme monetarist position is that money supply is wholly exogenous. The extreme Keynesian position is that money supply is wholly endogenous.

In reality, money supply is partly exogenous and partly endogenous. The authorities are able to influence money supply, but banks and other financial institutions have considerable scope for creating credit in response to demand. If monetarism is adopted as the basis for policy, the authorities must reduce the endogenous element to a minimum.

One approach is to impose statutory reserve or cash requirements on *all* financial institutions, and then engage in tough open-market operations, possibly backing them up with special deposits. Many monetarists reject statutory ratios as being anti-market. Relying on banks' prudent ratios, however, which can vary considerably, makes precise control of the money supply very difficult indeed.

As we saw in Chapter 19, the authorities in the UK recognise the difficulties in controlling the money supply directly. They therefore influence the supply of money indirectly by controlling interest rates and hence the demand for money.

SECTION SUMMARY

1. The quantity equation $MV = PQ$ can be used to analyse the possible relationship between money and prices. Monetarists argue that the velocity of circulation (V) and the level of output (Q) are independent of money supply (M), and that therefore increases in money supply will simply raise prices (P).
2. Keynesians argue that V varies inversely, but unpredictably, with M and that Q will depend on aggregate demand (MV) according to the degree of slack in the economy.
3. Keynesians argue that the interest rate transmission mechanism between changes in money and changes in national income is unreliable and possibly weak. The reasons are (a) an unstable and possibly elastic demand for money and (b) an unstable and possibly inelastic investment demand.
4. They argue that the exchange rate transmission mechanism is stronger but still very unpredictable.
5. Monetarists argue that the transmission mechanisms are strong and relatively stable in the long run. If people have an increase in money in their portfolios, they will attempt to restore portfolio balance by purchasing assets, including goods. Thus an increase in money supply is transmitted directly into an increase in aggregate demand. The interest rate and exchange rate mechanisms are also argued to be strong. The demand for money is seen to be stable in the long run. This leads to a long-run stability in V (unless it changes as a result of other factors, such as institutional arrangements for the handling of money).
6. Money supply is exogenous if it is wholly determined by the authorities. In practice it is in part endogenously determined by aggregate demand. This makes it difficult to have precise control over the money supply.

20.2 Fiscal policy and aggregate demand

Fiscal policy is favoured by Keynesians as the prime means of controlling aggregate demand. Monetarists argue that, at best, fiscal policy can have a lasting effect only if it is accompanied by monetary policy; in which case, it is really the monetary policy that is affecting aggregate demand. At worst, fiscal policy is positively damaging, causing greater fluctuations in demand than would otherwise have occurred. Possible problems of controlling aggregate demand through fiscal policy were examined in Chapter 17. The most important are as follows:

DEFINITIONS

Exogenous money supply Money supply that does not depend on the demand for money but is set by the authorities.

Endogenous money supply Money supply that is determined (at least in part) by the demand for money.

- Predicting the extent to which changes in government expenditure or taxation will affect other injections and withdrawals.
- Predicting the size of the multiplier and accelerator.
- The time lags involved.

Monetarists argue that these problems are so severe as to rule out the use of fiscal policy. Keynesians argue that the problems can to a large extent be overcome.

The Keynesian view: fiscal policy to cure fundamental disequilibria

Fiscal policy can be used either to shift aggregate demand to cure a sizeable and persistent deflationary or inflationary gap; or to 'fine tune' the economy, by smoothing out cyclical fluctuations. First we look at the use of fiscal policy in the former context.

Persistent deflationary gap

If the economy is in a deep and lasting recession, aggregate demand can be boosted either by tax cuts or by increased government expenditure.

Advantages of tax cuts and benefit increases. Tax cuts and benefit increases (pensions, child benefit, social security, etc.) can provide a quick and general boost to the economy. There are only small time lags between tax or benefit changes being announced in the Budget and the measures actually being implemented. Tax cuts that lower the marginal rate of taxation also have the advantage of increasing incentives. This in turn can stimulate output, investment and growth. These *supply-side* effects are considered in Chapter 22.

Problems with tax cuts and benefit increases. It may be difficult to estimate exactly how much of the tax cuts or benefit increases will be spent. However, the exact size of the effect may be of secondary importance to 'getting the economy moving'.

There may be a large resulting increase in imports. If there is a high marginal propensity to import, the multiplier effect will be lower and there may be a significant deterioration in the current account of the balance of payments.

?? Will there be any difference in the size of the multiplier effect from a change in taxes and a change in benefits? Will all types of tax change have the same-size multiplier?

Advantages of increased government expenditure. Government expenditure directly increases aggregate demand, and there is therefore the full multiplier effect. Government expenditure can be used more selectively than tax cuts. For example, money can be put into infrastructural projects, which will lead not only to higher demand but also to higher productive potential for the economy. Projects can be chosen which bring the maximum desired effect, such as labour-intensive projects (to reduce unemployment as much as possible), projects with a low import content, and projects in particularly depressed regions.

Problems with increased government expenditure. The main problem is the time lag involved. Infrastructure projects may take a long time to plan and execute. However, in dealing with a *long-term* recession, this problem may not be too serious.

The main monetarist objection to fiscal policy as a cure for recession is that it simply will not work to increase *output*, and to the extent that it does increase demand (because of a simultaneous expansion of the money supply), inflation will be the sole long-term result. This is especially likely in the context of a floating exchange rate: the expansion of demand will simply lead to a depreciation of the exchange rate. This will directly fuel inflation by raising the price of imported goods and materials.

Moreover, in a recession there is likely to be a high PSBR. An expansionary fiscal policy will make the PSBR even higher and could lead to a crisis of confidence. Interest rates may have to be raised to very high levels, and this would have the effect of cancelling out the expansionary fiscal policy.

Persistent inflationary gap

If the economy experiences persistent demand-pull inflation accompanied by near full employment, Keynesians argue that *deflationary* fiscal policy should be used.

Only during the two world wars have there been persistent inflationary gaps, due to the high level of wartime government spending. There have been no periods since the war when such a situation has existed, other than on a temporary basis. The persistently high inflation of the 1970s was accompanied by rising unemployment. Keynesians explain this stagflation in terms of a leftward shift in the aggregate supply curve (from AS_1 to AS_2 in Figure 20.9). A contraction in aggregate demand under these circumstances (from AD_1 to AD_2) may offset the inflationary effect, but there will be a further decline in output (to Y_3) and a corresponding rise in unemployment.

One of the major problems with tough deflationary policies is their political unpopularity: no one likes paying higher taxes; few people like substantial cuts in public services.

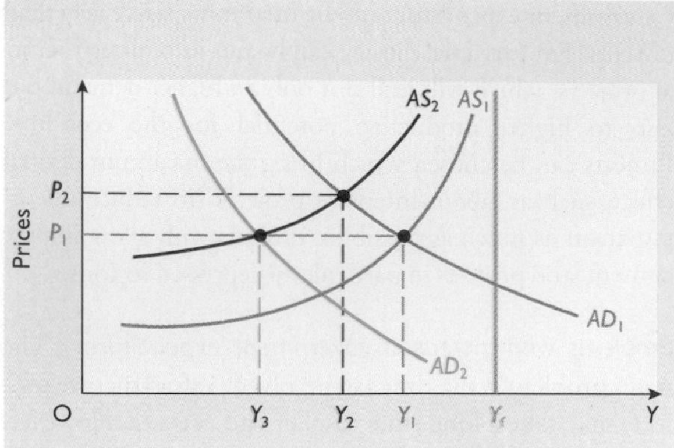

Figure 20.9 Keynesian explanation of stagflation

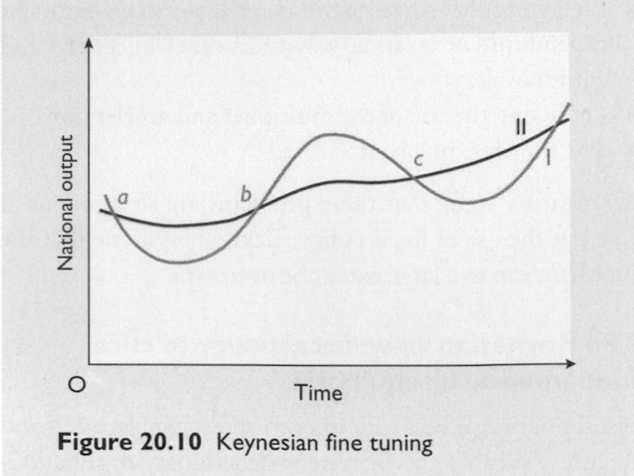

Figure 20.10 Keynesian fine tuning

What is more, there may be adverse supply-side effects. Tax increases may reduce incentives. They may also stimulate cost-push inflation. Cuts in government expenditure can have serious effects on particular sections of the economy – health, education, public transport, etc. Damage to the infrastructure may damage long-term growth. In addition, persistent deflationary policy is likely to reduce private investment. The effect of all these will be a reduction in the capacity of the economy to produce: the Y_f line and the *AS* curve will shift to the left.

Perhaps the most serious question is whether deflation can squeeze out the inflation from the economy without causing a severe recession. This depends on the shape of the aggregate supply curve and people's expectations of prices and markets. These are the subject of Chapter 21.

The Keynesian view: fine tuning

During the 1950s and 1960s, governments and most economists believed that business cycle fluctuations could be considerably lessened by demand management policy. This involved both fiscal and monetary policy, but fiscal policy was regarded as the more important.

By reflating the economy when in recession and deflating when in boom, economists believed that the growth path of the economy could be stabilised. Between points *a* and *b* in Figure 20.10, the government would pursue a reflationary fiscal policy. Between points *b* and *c* it would pursue a deflationary one. Instead of being like path I, therefore, the growth path would become more like path II. No one, however, claimed that fluctuations could be removed completely.

Stabilisation policy was helped by automatic fiscal stabilisers. These reduce the size of the multiplier and thus help to reduce the severity of the fluctuations. The main weapons, however, were discretionary changes in taxation and benefits announced each year in the Budget, or sometimes more frequently; and to a lesser extent changes in other forms of government expenditure.

?? Why are automatic fiscal stabilisers rather limited in their effect? (Refer back to Chapter 17.)

The advantages claimed for stabilisation policy were as follows:

- The avoidance of alternating periods of unemployment and stagnation followed by periods of inflation and balance of payments deficits.
- The creation of a more stable and certain environment for businesses to plan and invest, thereby encouraging faster long-term growth in both actual and potential output.

The main problems with fine tuning the economy centred on timing. If time lags are long enough, 'stabilisation' policy can actually be *destabilising* (see pages 535–7). The following are therefore the main requirements for successful stabilisation:

- Accurate forecasting, so that appropriate policies can be introduced early.
- Policies that can be introduced quickly. Government expenditure programmes often take a long time to plan, but taxes and benefits can be changed simply and quickly.
- Policies that have a predictable effect on aggregate demand.
- Policies that can be readily reversed. Here again, taxes are far easier to increase or decrease than government expenditure.

Keynesians argue that, although fiscal policy can never remove all fluctuations, combinations of good forecasting, appropriately designed measures and swift action can go a long way to creating relatively stable growth.

?? Do you think it is more difficult to stabilise an open economy like the UK's than one that engages far less in international trade?

The monetarist view

Monetarists make a clear distinction between *pure* fiscal policy, where fiscal policy operates with *no* change in the money supply, and fiscal policy operating *alongside* a change in money supply. The latter could be due either to active fiscal and monetary policies being pursued at the same time, or to a passive expansion (contraction) of money supply to accommodate an expansionary (contractionary) fiscal policy.

Monetarists argue that pure fiscal policy may have some short-term effects on demand, but due to time lags, the difficulties in predicting people's reactions to the policy, and the problem of random unexpected shocks to the economy, it cannot be used to control demand with any precision, and certainly cannot be used for fine tuning. In the long run, pure fiscal policy is totally ineffective: it will simply lead to *crowding out*. Increases in government expenditure will lead to corresponding decreases in private expenditure.

Fiscal policy operating alongside a change in money supply *will* affect demand. But here it is the change in the money supply, not the fiscal policy, that is having the effect.

To assess these arguments, it is necessary to examine the monetary effects of fiscal policy.

The monetary effects of fiscal policy

Fiscal and monetary policy are closely interrelated. Any fiscal policy that a government adopts will have monetary implications. Likewise any specific monetary policy will have implications for the conduct of the government's fiscal policy.

Assume that previously the government has had a balanced budget, but that now it chooses to adopt a reflationary fiscal policy. As a result it runs a budget deficit ($G > T$). But this deficit will have to be financed by borrowing. The resulting public-sector borrowing requirement will lead to an increase in the money supply if it is financed by borrowing from the Bank of England or by the sale of Treasury bills to the banking sector. Alternatively, if it is financed by selling bills or bonds outside the banking sector or by selling bonds to the banks, there will be no increase in the money supply.

At the same time, the increase in aggregate demand that results from the budget deficit will lead to an increased transactions demand for money.

These effects are illustrated in Figure 20.11. Assume that the budget deficit arises from an increase in government expenditure. In Figure 20.11(a), injections will rise to J_2 and, other things being equal, national income will rise to Y_2. But this increase in national income will lead to a rise in the demand for money. In Figure 20.11(b) the demand for money curve shifts from L to L'. If the PSBR is financed in such a way as to allow money supply to expand to M_s', there will be no change in the interest rate and no crowding-out effect. If, however, the money supply is not allowed to expand, interest rates will rise to r_2. This in turn will reduce investment: crowding out will occur. Injections will fall back again below J_2. In the extreme case, injections could even fall back to J_1 and thus national income return to Y_1.

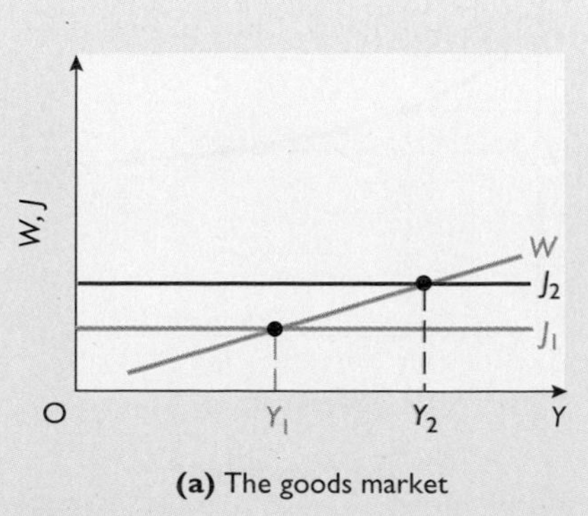

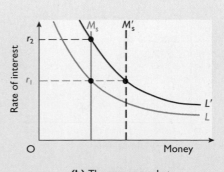

(a) The goods market

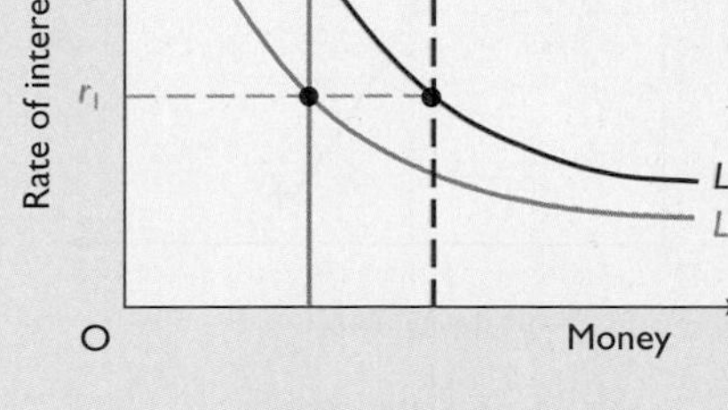

(b) The money market

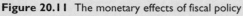

Figure 20.11 The monetary effects of fiscal policy

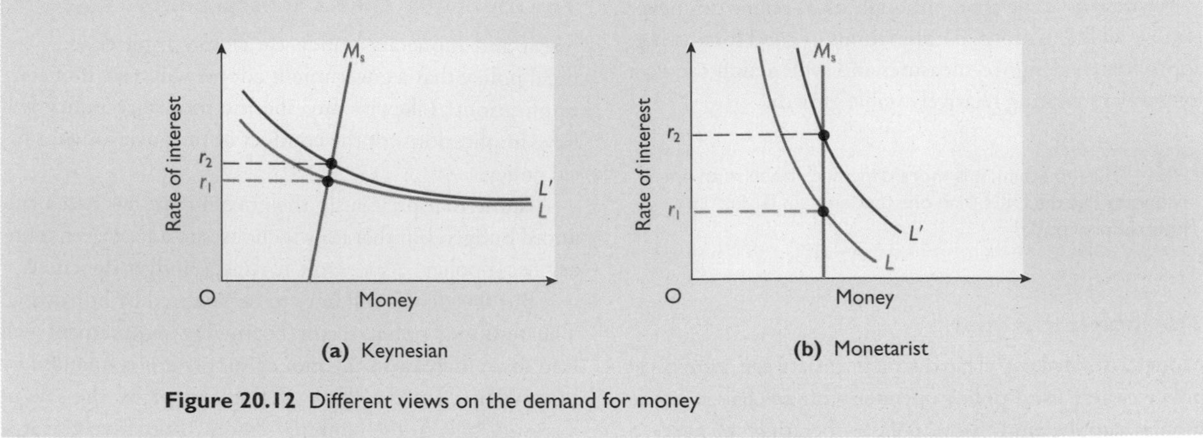

Figure 20.12 Different views on the demand for money

?? Assume that the government cuts its expenditure and thereby runs a public-sector surplus.

(a) What will this do initially to equilibrium national income?
(b) What will it do to the demand for money and initially to interest rates?
(c) Under what circumstances will it lead to (i) a decrease in money supply; (ii) no change in money supply?
(d) What effect will (i) and (ii) have on the rate of interest compared with its original level?

Keynesian and monetarist analyses of crowding out

Just how much crowding out will occur when there is an expansionary fiscal policy, but when money supply is *not* allowed to expand, depends on two things.

The responsiveness (elasticity) of the demand for money to a change in interest rates. Keynesians argue that the demand is relatively *elastic* (as in Figure 20.12(a)). In this case the increase in demand, represented by a *horizontal* shift in the liquidity preference curve from L to L', will lead to only a small rise in interest rates. Monetarists argue that the demand is relatively *inelastic* (as in Figure 20.12(b)), in which case the same horizontal shift will lead to a bigger rise in interest rates.

The responsiveness (elasticity) of investment to a change in interest rates. Keynesians argue that investment is relatively *unresponsive* to changes in interest rates. Businesspeople are much more likely to be affected by the state of the market for their product rather than by interest rates. Thus in Figure 20.13(a), there is only a small fall in investment. Monetarists argue that investment is relatively *responsive* to changes in interest rates. Thus in Figure 20.13(b), there is a bigger fall in investment.

In the Keynesian case, therefore, the rise in demand for money arising from an expansionary fiscal policy will have only a small effect on interest rates and an even smaller effect on investment. Little or no crowding out takes

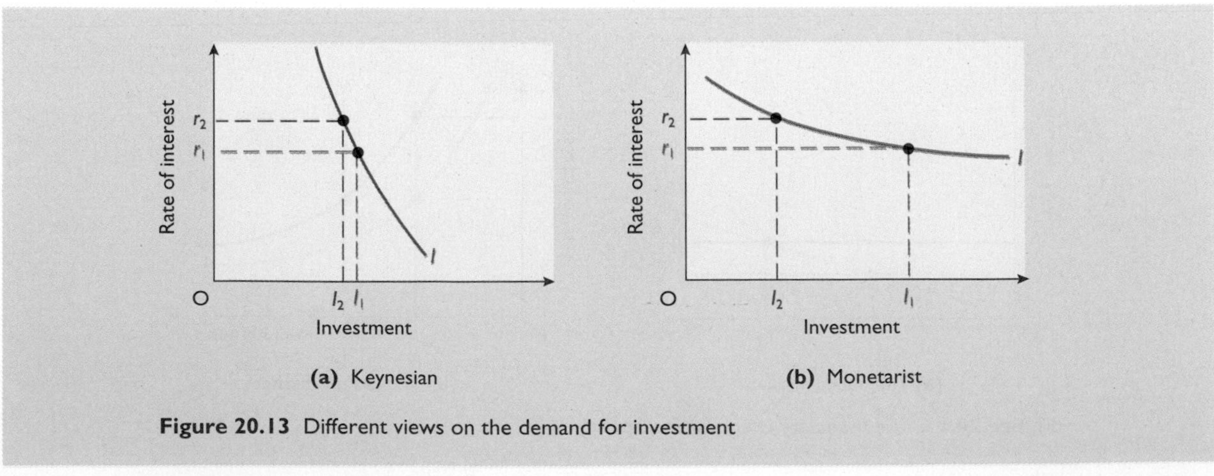

Figure 20.13 Different views on the demand for investment

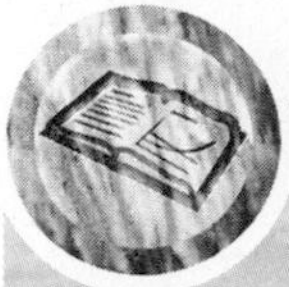

EXPLORING THE THEORY BOX 20.4

CROWDING OUT IN AN OPEN ECONOMY
Taking exchange rate effects into account

Will fiscal policy be crowded out in an open economy with floating exchange rates? Assume that the government increases its expenditure but does not allow the money supply to expand: a case of pure fiscal policy. What will happen?

- The increased government expenditure will increase the demand for money (see Figure 20.12).
- This will drive up interest rates – the amount depending on the elasticity of the liquidity preference curve.
- This will lead to an inflow of capital from abroad, which in turn will lead to an appreciation of the exchange rate.
- The higher exchange rate will reduce the level of exports (an injection) and increase the level of imports (a withdrawal). This will add to the degree of crowding out.

Thus in an open economy with floating exchange rates an expansionary fiscal policy will be crowded out not only by higher interest rates, but also by a higher exchange rate.

?? We have argued that the short-term capital inflow following a rise in the rate of interest will drive up the exchange rate. Are there any effects of expansionary fiscal policy on the demand for imports (and hence on the current account) which will go some way to *offsetting* this?

place. In fact, the expansion of demand might cause an increase in investment through the accelerator effect.

Monetarists argue that interest rates will rise significantly and that there will be a severe effect on investment. Crowding out is substantial. For this reason they argue that it is vital for governments to reduce the size of their budget deficit. They argue that in the long run crowding out is total, given the long-run stability of the velocity of circulation.

SECTION SUMMARY

1. Keynesians argue that persistent inflationary or deflationary gaps can be closed by fiscal policy. Monetarists argue that, if there is a significant change in aggregate demand as a result of the policy, it will only be because money supply has changed, in which case the policy is really monetary policy.
2. Many Keynesians also argue that fiscal policy can help to reduce (but not eliminate) cyclical fluctuations, provided that forecasting is reasonably accurate and that the appropriate changes in *G* or *T* can be made swiftly and with predictable effects.
3. Any fiscal changes will have monetary implications. If there is a fiscal expansion and *no* change in the money supply, the increased demand for money will drive up the interest rate and drive down the exchange rate. This will to some extent crowd out private expenditure and thus reduce the effectiveness of the fiscal policy.
4. The extent of crowding out will depend on the shape of the liquidity preference curve and the investment demand curve. The less elastic the demand for money, and the more elastic the investment demand, the more crowding out will take place, and the less effective will fiscal policy be.
5. With a floating exchange rate, the higher interest rates from an expansionary fiscal policy will drive up the exchange rate and lead to fewer exports and more imports, thereby leading to additional crowding out.

*20.3 ISLM analysis: the integration of the goods and money market models

The goods and money markets

In this chapter we have shown that there are two key markets through which both fiscal and monetary policy operate. The first is the goods market; the second is the money market. Each of these two markets has been analysed by using a model.

In the case of the goods market, the model is the Keynesian injections/withdrawals model. Fiscal policy operates directly in this market. For example, a rise in government expenditure shifts the *J* line upwards and causes a rise in equilibrium national income. In other words, an increase in the demand for goods causes a (multiplied) rise in the output of goods (assuming that there are sufficient idle resources).

In the case of the money market, the model is the one showing the demand for money (L) and the supply of money (M) and their effect on the rate of interest. Monetary policy operates directly in this market, either by affecting the supply of money or by operating on interest rates.

What we have shown in this chapter is that the two markets *interact*: that changes in one market cause changes in the other. Take the case of an expansionary fiscal policy: it has a direct effect in the goods markets, but also an indirect effect in money markets. We illustrated this in Figure 20.11. The goods market effect was shown in Figure 20.11(a). The rise in injections led to a multiplied rise in income to Y_2. The money market effect was shown in Figure 20.11(b). The rise in income led to a rise in the transactions demand for money and a resulting rise in interest rates to r_2. This in turn had an effect back in the goods market, with a higher interest rate dampening investment somewhat and reducing the final rise in income.

The effect of monetary policy in the two markets was shown in Figures 20.2 and 20.8. An expansionary monetary policy, by increasing the money supply, will reduce interest rates. This will then, via an increase in investment (or a reduction in the exchange rate and a resulting increase in exports and a reduction in imports), lead to a multiplied rise in income in the goods market. This in turn has an effect back in the money market, with a higher income leading to a higher demand for money, thus limiting the fall in interest rates.

The trouble with our analysis so far is that we have needed at least two diagrams. What we are going to look at in this section is a model which *combines* these two markets, which means that we will need only one diagram. The model is known as the **ISLM model**.

The model allows us to examine the effects of fiscal and monetary policy on both national income *and* interest rates: it shows what the equilibrium will be in both the goods and the money markets simultaneously. The model, as its name suggests, consists of two curves: an *IS* curve and an *LM* curve. The *IS* curve is based on equilibrium in the goods market; the *LM* curve is based on equilibrium in the money market.

Let us examine these two curves in turn.

The *IS* curve

Deriving the IS curve

To explain how the *IS* curve is derived let us examine Figure 20.14, which as you can see is in two parts. The top part shows the familiar Keynesian injections and withdrawals diagram, only in this case, for simplicity, we are assuming that savings are the only withdrawal from the circular flow of income, and investment the only injection. Thus in equilibrium $I = S$ (i.e. $J = W$). The bottom part of the diagram shows the *IS* curve. This shows all the various combinations of interest rates (r) and national income (Y) at which $I = S$.

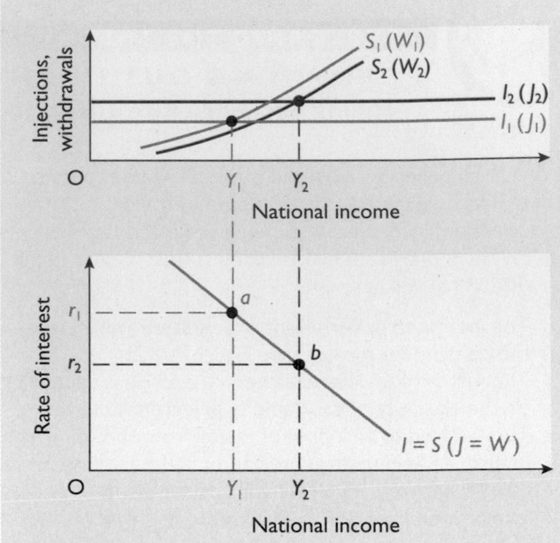

Figure 20.14 Goods market equilibrium: deriving the *IS* curve

Let us assume that initially interest rates are at r_1. Both investment and savings are affected by interest rates, and thus, other things being equal, an interest rate of r_1 will give particular investment and savings schedules. Let us say that in the top part of the diagram these are shown by the curves I_1 and S_1. Equilibrium national income will be where $I = S$, i.e. at Y_1. Thus in the lower part of the diagram, an interest rate of r_1 will give a level of national income of Y_1. Thus point *a* is one point on the *IS* curve. At an interest rate of r_1 the goods market will be in equilibrium at an income of Y_1.

Now what will happen if the rate of interest changes? Let us assume that it falls to r_2. This will cause a rise in investment and a fall in savings. A rise in investment is shown in the top part of Figure 20.14 by a shift in the investment line to I_2. Likewise a fall in savings is shown by

DEFINITION

ISLM model A model showing simultaneous equilibrium in the goods market ($I = S$) and the money market ($L = M$).

a shift in the savings curve to S_2. This will lead to a multiplied rise in income to Y_2 (where $I_2 = S_2$). This corresponds to point *b* in the lower diagram, which therefore gives a second point on the *IS* curve.

Thus *lower* interest rates are associated with *higher* national income, if equilibrium is to be maintained in the goods market ($I = S$).

The elasticity of the IS curve

The elasticity of the *IS* curve (i.e. the responsiveness of national income to changes in interest rates) depends on two factors.[3]

The responsiveness of investment and savings to interest rate changes. The more investment and savings respond, the bigger will be the vertical shift in the *I* and *S* curves in the top part of the diagram, and thus the bigger will be the effect on national income. The bigger the effect on national income, the more elastic will be the *IS* curve.

The size of the multiplier. This is given by the *mps* (i.e. the *mpw*). The larger the value of the multiplier, the bigger will be the effect on national income of any rise in investment and fall in savings, and the more elastic therefore will be the *IS* curve.

> **??** In a complete model where there were three injections (*I*, *G* and *X*) and three withdrawals (*S*, *T* and *M*), what else would determine the shape of the '*JW*' curve?

Keynesians argue that the *IS* curve is likely to be fairly inelastic. The reason they give is that investment is unresponsive to changes in interest rates: the demand for investment curve in Figure 20.2(b) on page 601 is relatively inelastic. Savings also, claim Keynesians, are unresponsive to interest rate changes. The effect of this is that there will only be a relatively small shift in the *I* and *S* curves in response to a change in interest rates, and thus only a relatively small change in national income.

Monetarists, by contrast, argue that investment and savings are relatively responsive to changes in interest rates and that therefore the *IS* curve is relatively elastic.

Shifts in the IS curve

A change in interest rates will cause a movement *along* the *IS* curve. As we saw in Figure 20.14, a reduction in interest rates from r_1 to r_2 causes a movement *along* the *IS* curve from point *a* to point *b*.

A change in any *other* determinant of investment or savings, however, will *shift* the whole curve. The reason is that it will change the equilibrium level of national income at any given rate of interest.

An increase in investment, other than as a result of a fall in interest rates, will shift the *IS* curve to the *right*. This could happen, for example, if there were an increase in business confidence. A rise in business confidence *at the current interest rate* will cause an upward shift of the *I* curve in the top diagram of Figure 20.14, which will cause a multiplied rise in income. Thus in the lower part of the diagram a higher equilibrium income is now associated with each level of the interest rate: the *IS* curve has shifted to the right. Likewise, for any given interest rate, a fall in savings, and hence a rise in consumption, would also shift the *IS* curve to the right.

In a complete model (with three injections and three withdrawals), where the *IS* curve was a '$J = W$' curve rather than a simple '$I = S$' curve, similar shifts would result from changes in other injections or withdrawals. Thus an expansionary fiscal policy that increased government expenditure (*G*) or cut taxes (*T*) would shift the '*IS*' curve (i.e. the *JW* curve) to the right.

> **??** In a complete *JW* model, what else would cause the *JW* curve (a) to shift to the right; (b) to shift to the left?

The LM curve

The *IS* curve is concerned with equilibrium in the goods market. The *LM* curve is concerned with equilibrium in the money market. The *LM* curve shows all the various combinations of interest rates and national income at which the demand for money equals the supply ($L = M$).

Deriving the LM curve

To explain how the *LM* curve is derived we again use a diagram in two parts, only this time they are side by side (the reason being that we use the same *vertical* axis (*r*) this time, whereas in Figure 20.14 we used the same horizontal axis (*Y*)). The left-hand part of the diagram is the familiar money market diagram, showing a liquidity preference (demand for money) curve (*L*) and a supply of money curve (*M*).

At any given level of national income there will be a particular level of transactions-plus-precautionary demand for money, and hence a given overall demand for money curve (*L*). Let us assume that, when national income is at a level of Y_1 in the right-hand diagram of Figure 20.15, the demand for money curve is L'. With the given money supply curve M_s, the equilibrium rate of interest will be r_1. Thus point *c* is one point on the *LM*

[3] Note that, as with demand and supply curves, the elasticity of the *IS* curve will vary along its length. Therefore we should really talk about the elasticity at a particular point on the curve, or between two points.

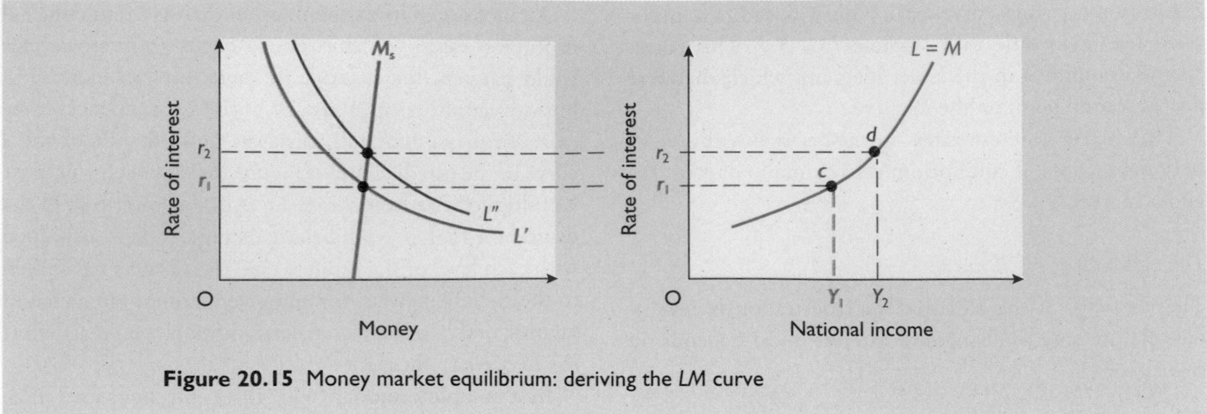

Figure 20.15 Money market equilibrium: deriving the *LM* curve

curve. At a level of national income Y_1, the money market will be in equilibrium at a rate of interest of r_1.

Now what will happen if the level of national income changes? Let us assume that national income rises to Y_2. The effect is to increase the transactions-plus-precautionary demand for money. The *L* curve shifts to the right: to, say, *L*″. This will cause the rate of interest to rise to the new equilibrium level of r_2. This therefore gives us a second point on the *LM* curve (point *d*).

Thus *higher* national income will lead to a greater demand for money and hence *higher* interest rates if equilibrium is to be maintained in the money market. The *LM* curve will therefore be upward sloping.

The elasticity of the LM curve

The elasticity of the *LM* curve (i.e. the responsiveness of interest rate changes to a change in national income)[4] again depends on two factors.

The responsiveness of the demand for money to changes in national income. The greater the marginal propensity to consume, the more will the transactions demand for money rise as national income rises, and thus the more will the *L* curve shift to the right. Hence the more will the equilibrium interest rate rise, and the steeper will be the *LM* curve.

The responsiveness of the demand for money to changes in interest rates. The more the demand for money responds to a change in interest rates, the flatter will be the liquidity preference curve in the left-hand diagram. The flatter the *L* curve, the less will the equilibrium interest rate change for any given horizontal shift in the *L* curve (arising from a change in *Y*). The less the equilibrium interest rate changes, the flatter will be the *LM* curve.

The Keynesian and monetarist views on the shape of the *LM* curve reflect their views on the elasticity of the *L* curve. Keynesians argue that the *L* curve is likely to be relatively flat given the responsiveness of the speculative demand for money to changes in interest rates. They thus argue that the *LM* curve is correspondingly flat (depending, of course, on the scales of the axes). Monetarists, on the other hand, argue that the *LM* curve is relatively steep. This is because they see the demand for money as insensitive to changes in interest rates.

Shifts in the LM curve

A change in national income will cause a movement *along* the *LM* curve to a new interest rate. Thus in Figure 20.15 a rise in national income from Y_1 to Y_2 leads to a rise in the rate of interest from r_1 to r_2.

A change in any *other* determinant of the demand and supply of money will *shift* the whole curve. The reason is that it will change the equilibrium level of interest associated with any given level of national income.

An increase in the demand for money, other than as a result of a rise in income, will shift the *L* curve to the *right*. This could be due to people being paid less frequently, or a greater use of cash machines, or increased speculation that the price of securities will fall. This increased demand for money will raise the equilibrium rate of interest at the current level of national income. The *LM* curve will shift upwards.

An increased supply of money will shift the M_s curve to the right. This will lower the rate of interest (in the left-hand part of Figure 20.15). This will shift the *LM* curve downwards: a lower rate of interest will be associated with any given level of national income.

[4] Note this time that the rate of interest is the dependent variable and the level of national income is the independent variable. Thus the more elastic is the *LM* curve (i.e. the more responsive interest rates are to changes in national income), the *steeper* will it be.

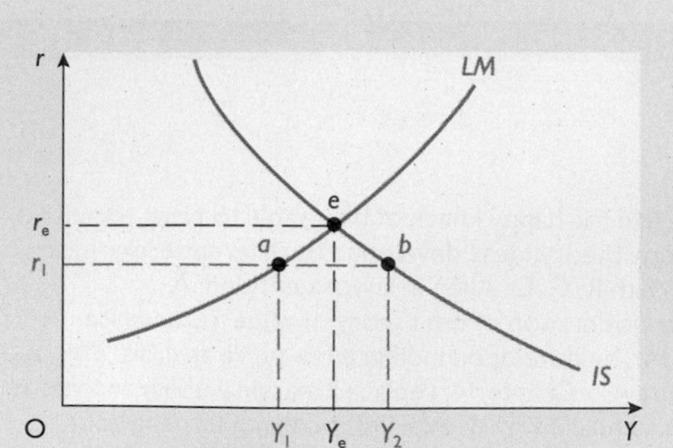

Figure 20.16 Equilibrium in both the goods and money markets

> **??** Draw a diagram like Figure 20.15, only with just one *L* curve. Assume that the current level of national income is Y_1. Now assume that the supply of money decreases. Show the effect on (a) the rate of interest; (b) the position of the *LM* curve.

Equilibrium

The *IS* curve shows all the combinations of the rate of interest (*r*) and national income (*Y*) at which the *goods* market is in equilibrium. The *LM* curve shows all the combinations of *r* and *Y* at which the *money* market is in equilibrium. *Both* markets will be in equilibrium where the curves intersect. This is at r_e and Y_e in Figure 20.16.

But what would happen if both markets were not simultaneously in equilibrium? How would equilibrium be achieved?

Let us suppose that the current level of national income is Y_1. This will create a demand for money which will lead to an equilibrium interest rate of r_1 (point *a* on the *LM* curve). But at this low interest rate the desired level of investment and savings would generate an income of Y_2 (point *b* on the *IS* curve). Thus national income will rise. But as national income rises, there will be a movement up along the *LM* curve from point *a*, since the higher income will generate a higher demand for money and hence push up interest rates. And as interest rates rise, so the desired level of investment will fall and the desired level of savings will rise so as to reduce the equilibrium level of national income below Y_2. There will be a movement back up along the *IS* curve from point *b*. Once the interest rate has risen to r_e, the actual level of income will be at the equilibrium level (i.e. *on* the *IS* curve). Both markets will now be in equilibrium.

> **??**
> 1. Assume that national income is initially at Y_2 in Figure 20.16. Describe the process whereby equilibrium in both markets will be achieved.
> 2. Assume that business confidence rises and firms decide to increase their investment. Trace through the effects of this in the ISLM model. (One of the curves shifts.)

Fiscal and monetary policy

ISLM analysis can be used to examine the effects of fiscal and monetary policy. Assume that the economy is in recession and that the government wishes to raise the level of national income. Figure 20.17 illustrates the policy alternatives.

Figure 20.17(a) shows the effect of an increase in government expenditure (*G*) or a cut in taxes (*T*), but with no increase in money supply. The *IS* curve shifts to the right. Income rises to Y_2, but interest rates also rise (to r_2). Thus some crowding out occurs.

Figure 20.17(b) shows the effect of an increase in money supply. The *LM* curve shifts to the right. Interest

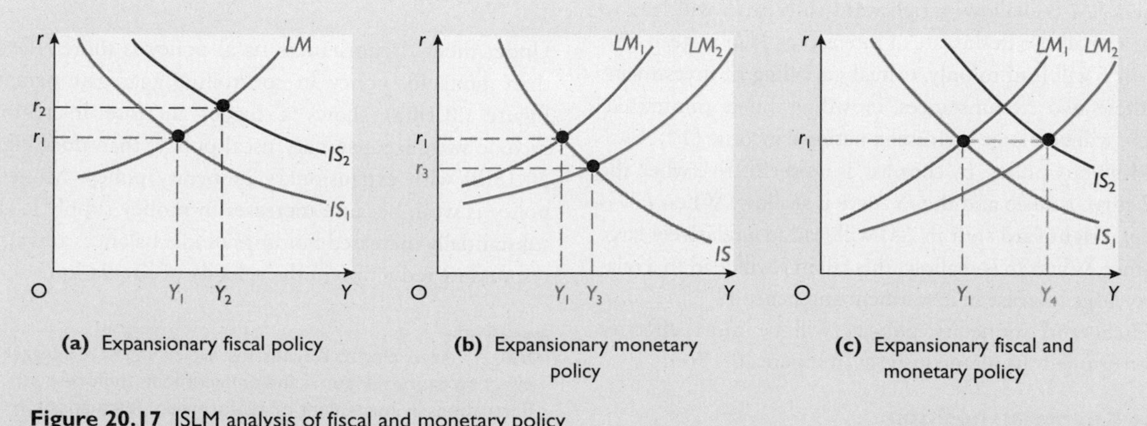

Figure 20.17 ISLM analysis of fiscal and monetary policy

DEVELOPMENT OF IDEAS BOX 20.5

SIR JOHN HICKS (1906–89)
Person profile

With more than twenty books and fifty articles to his credit, John Hicks ranks high in the list of 'great economists'. His first book, *The Theory of Wages*, was published in 1932, but he was still writing actively up to his death 57 years later.

He was born in Warwick in 1906 and entered Oxford as a student in 1922. Shortly after graduating he became a lecturer at the London School of Economics, where he stayed until 1935. After three years as a fellow at the University of Cambridge, he became Professor of Economics at Manchester University. He then moved to Nuffield College, Oxford, in 1946, where he remained for the rest of his career.

He was knighted in 1966, and then in 1972 he received perhaps the highest recognition the economics world can bestow: the Nobel prize in economics. The award was for his outstanding contribution to the development of economic theory in both the micro and macro fields. This says a lot about Hicks' place in the history of economics. His contributions were not confined to just one area, but covered a whole range of issues.

Perhaps his major contribution was as a synthesiser. He had the happy knack of being able to bring together in one theory ideas developed by different economists.

With R. G. D. Allen in a work entitled 'A reconsideration of the theory of value' (*Economica*, 1934), he developed indifference curve analysis. This, as we saw in Chapter 4, replaced marginal utility analysis as the standard way of explaining consumer behaviour.

His most famous contribution to the field of macroeconomics came in his article 'Mr Keynes and the classics' (*Econometrica*, 1937). It was in this work that ISLM analysis was born. The analysis was used by Hicks to provide a graphical interpretation of Keynes' *General Theory*, and to show how Keynes' policy prescriptions differed from his predecessors'. Subsequently, Hicks' ISLM approach became widely adopted throughout the economics profession, and it is now a core element in macroeconomic theory.

It is these contributions to fundamental economic theory, contributions which have changed the way the subject is taught, which set Hicks apart from his contemporaries and ensure that his work will have a lasting impression on all those who study the discipline of economics.

rates fall to r_3 and this encourages an increase in investment. As a result of this, income rises to Y_3.

Figure 20.17(c) shows what happens when the government finances higher government expenditure or lower taxes by increasing the money supply. There is no rise in interest rates, and thus no crowding out. National income rises by a greater amount than in (a) or (b), to Y_4.

The effectiveness of fiscal and monetary policy depends on the slope of the two curves. Fiscal policy is most effective when the *LM* curve is shallow and the *IS* curve is steep. When *LM* is shallow, a rightward shift in *IS* will lead to only a small rise in the rate of interest (r). If *IS* is steep, this rise in r will lead to only a small curtailing of investment. In these two circumstances, crowding out is minimised. There will be a large increase in national income (Y).

Monetary policy, by contrast, is most effective when the *LM* curve is steep and the *IS* curve is shallow. When *LM* is steep, a rightward shift in *LM* will lead to a relatively large fall in r. When *IS* is shallow, this fall in r will lead to a relatively large increase in investment and hence Y.

Fiscal and monetary policies will be most effective when applied simultaneously, as in Figure 20.17(c).

The Keynesian position

The Keynesian analysis makes the following assumptions.

The LM curve is relatively shallow. This is because the liquidity preference curve (L) is relatively shallow, due to the important role of the speculative demand for money (see Figure 20.2(a) on page 601).

The IS curve is relatively steep. This is because the investment demand curve is relatively inelastic, due to the unresponsiveness of investment to changes in interest rates (see Figure 20.2(b)). Also savings are relatively unresponsive to interest rate changes.

Under these circumstances fiscal policy is more effective than monetary policy in controlling aggregate demand. Figure 20.18(a) shows a bigger increase in national income with expansionary fiscal policy, than does Figure 20.18(b) with expansionary monetary policy. Monetary policy is weak because increases in money supply lead to substantially increased holdings of idle balances and a corresponding reduction in the velocity of circulation.

?? According to Keynesians, which will have a bigger effect on national income and employment: (unforeseen) fluctuations in investment or (unforeseen) fluctuations in the money supply?

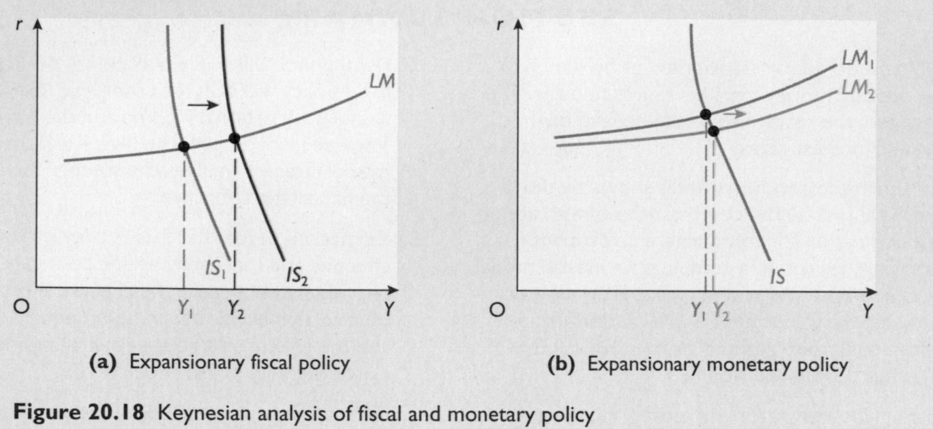

(a) Expansionary fiscal policy

(b) Expansionary monetary policy

Figure 20.18 Keynesian analysis of fiscal and monetary policy

If money supply is endogenous, fiscal policy will be more effective still. A relatively elastic supply of money curve in the left-hand diagram of Figure 20.15 will give an even shallower *LM* curve.

Keynesians also stress that the *IS* curve tends to be *unstable* (for example, as investment fluctuates with business confidence). Fluctuations in a steep *IS* curve will lead to substantial fluctuations in national income (*Y*). To avoid this, argue Keynesians, active demand management (fiscal) policy will be required.

The monetarist position

The monetarist analysis makes the following assumptions.

The LM curve is relatively steep. This is because the *L* curve is relatively steep, due to the relatively small role of speculative balances of money, and the general interest inelasticity of the demand for money.

The IS curve is relatively shallow. This is because the *I* curve is relatively shallow, due to the wide range of interest-sensitive expenditures.

Under these circumstances monetary policy is more effective than fiscal policy. Figure 20.19(b) shows a bigger increase in income with expansionary monetary policy than does Figure 20.19(a) with expansionary fiscal policy.

According to monetarists, fiscal policy is weak because of crowding out. This is illustrated in Figure 20.19(a) by the steepness of the *LM* curve. The increased transactions demand resulting from a rise in income will lead to a large rise in interest rates. The reason is that there are few speculative holdings of money, and therefore a large rise in interest rates will be necessary to release sufficient money balances to meet the new higher transactions demand.

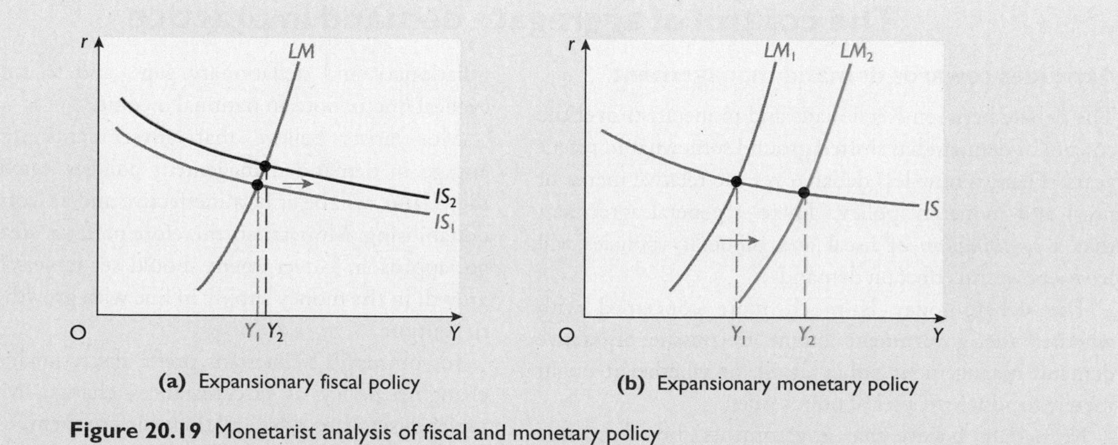

(a) Expansionary fiscal policy

(b) Expansionary monetary policy

Figure 20.19 Monetarist analysis of fiscal and monetary policy

SECTION SUMMARY

1. The ISLM model allows equilibrium to be shown in both goods and money markets simultaneously. The model shows the relationship between national income and interest rates.
2. Equilibrium in the goods market is shown by the *IS* curve. This shows all the combinations of the rate of interest and national income where investment (*I*) equals savings (*S*) (or, in a complete Keynesian model, where injections equal withdrawals). As the rate of interest rises, so investment will fall and savings will rise: thus equilibrium national income will fall. The *IS* curve is thus downward sloping.
3. A change in interest rates will cause a movement along the *IS* curve. A change in anything else that affects national income (i.e. a change in injections or withdrawals other than as a result of a change in interest rates) will cause a shift in the *IS* curve.
4. Equilibrium in the money market is shown by the *LM* curve. This shows all the combinations of national income and the rate of interest where the demand for money (*L*) equals the supply (*M*). As national income rises, so the demand for money will rise: thus the equilibrium rate of interest in the money market will rise. The *LM* curve is thus upward sloping.
5. A change in national income will cause a movement along the *LM* curve. A change in anything else that affects interest rates (i.e. a change in the demand or supply of money other than as a result of a change in national income) will shift the *LM* curve.
6. Simultaneous equilibrium in both goods and money markets (i.e. the equilibrium national income *and* the equilibrium rate of interest) is where $IS = LM$.
7. Fiscal policy will shift the *IS* curve. An expansionary fiscal policy will shift it to the right. This will cause a rise in both national income and the rate of interest. The rise in income will be bigger and the rise in the rate of interest smaller, the steeper the *IS* curve and the flatter the *LM* curve.
8. Keynesians argue that fiscal policy is relatively effective and that there will be relatively little crowding out because the *IS* curve is relatively steep (due to an inelastic investment demand schedule) and the *LM* curve is relatively shallow (due to an elastic liquidity preference curve).
9. Monetarists argue the opposite: that fiscal policy is relatively ineffective and that there will be substantial crowding out because the *IS* curve is relatively shallow (due to the wide range of interest-sensitive expenditures) and the *LM* curve is relatively steep (due to the small role of speculative balances).
10. Monetary policy will shift the *LM* curve. An expansionary monetary policy will shift it to the right. This will cause a fall in interest rates and a rise in national income. The rise in national income will be larger, the steeper the *LM* curve and the flatter the *IS* curve. This means that monetarists argue that monetary policy is relatively effective, whereas Keynesians argue that it is relatively ineffective.
11. Fiscal and monetary policy operating together will have the most powerful effect. An expansionary fiscal policy accompanied by a rise in money supply can lead to an increase in national income with no rise in interest rates and thus no crowding out irrespective of the shapes of the *IS* and *LM* curves.

20.4 The control of aggregate demand in practice

Attitudes towards demand management

The debate between Keynesians and monetarists over the control of demand has shifted ground somewhat in recent years. There is now less debate over the relative merits of fiscal and monetary policy. There is general agreement that a *combination* of fiscal and monetary policies will have a powerful effect on demand.

The debate today is much more concerned with whether the government ought to pursue an active demand management policy at all, or whether it ought merely to adhere to a set of policy rules.

Keynesians believe that governments should manage the level of aggregate demand, both to remove persistent inflationary and deflationary gaps, and to smooth out cyclical fluctuations in national income.

Monetarists believe that governments should not engage in demand management policies. Such policies, they claim, will be at best ineffective and at worst actually destabilising. Monetarists therefore prefer a 'steady as you go' approach. Government should set targets for steady growth in the money supply in line with growth in potential output.

In summary: Keynesians prefer discretionary policy – changing policy as circumstances change. Monetarists prefer to set firms rules and then stick to them.

Keynesian demand management in the 1950s and 1960s

During the 1950s and 1960s both Labour and Conservative governments in the UK embraced Keynesian ideas. They pursued active demand management policies in an attempt to smooth out cyclical fluctuations and to keep national income as close as possible to the full-employment level.

The main weapon was changes in tax rates. But use was also made of government expenditure changes. Monetary policy was generally thought to be ineffective, because of both the insensitivity of demand to interest rate changes, and the difficulties in controlling overall liquidity through open-market operations. In the 1960s, however, increasing use was made of credit rationing to back up fiscal policy and to keep interest rates down.

The overall performance of the economy

Economic performance during the 1950s and 1960s compares very favourably with the periods both before and after (see Figure 20.20 and Table 20.1).

Unemployment was considerably lower in the 1950s and 1960s than either before or after. *Inflation*, although averaging 4 per cent, and thus above the negative rates of the inter-war years, was nevertheless very modest by recent standards. Only in the deep recession of the early 1990s has inflation fallen below this average. *Growth* in the 1950s and 1960s was at a higher level than in the periods before or up to the mid-1980s. Also there was no deep or prolonged recession like those of the early 1920s, the early 1930s, 1979–82 and 1990–3.

Table 20.1 UK macroeconomic performance: 1921–98

	Unemployment (% of labour force)[1]	Inflation (% increase in RPI)[2]	Growth (% increase in real GDP)[2]
1921–38	13.4	−1.5	2.1
1950–69	1.6	4.0	2.8
1970–98	6.9	7.8	2.1

[1] Average.
[2] Average annual.

However, there were still fluctuations in the economy, albeit of shorter duration and lower intensity than before or since. Also, although growth was relatively high by UK standards, it was significantly lower than in West Germany, France and Japan.

The balance of payments

Throughout the 1950s and 1960s, the UK was operating on a fixed exchange rate system. The exchange rate was pegged at $2.80 to the pound from 1949 until 1967 when it was devalued to $2.40. A fixed exchange rate constrained the government in its demand management policy. If the economy expanded too fast, the balance of payments went into deficit. The government would then pursue a deflationary policy, both to reduce the demand for imports directly, and to reduce inflation in order to increase the competitiveness of UK goods. If the balance of payments went into surplus, the government would reflate the economy. As a result of this, demand management was often

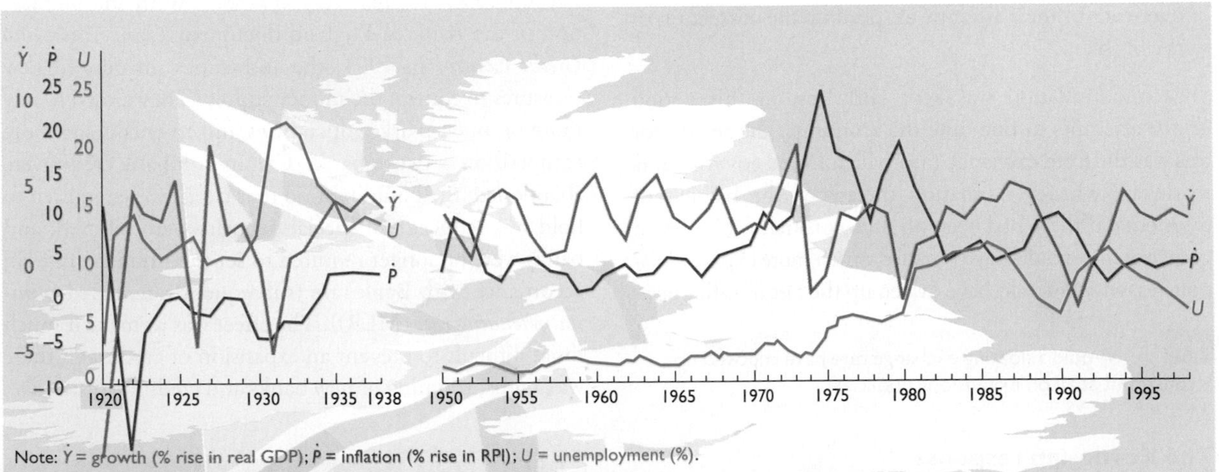

Note: $\dot{Y}$ = growth (% rise in real GDP); $\dot{P}$ = inflation (% rise in RPI); U = unemployment (%).

Figure 20.20 UK growth, inflation and unemployment: 1920–98

Sources: *British Economy Key Statistics in 1900–1964* (Time Publishing Co.); *Economic Trends* (ONS, various issues).

referred to as **stop–go policy**. The most common weapon used in times of balance of payments crisis was Bank rate, which rose quite steeply on several occasions.

During the 1960s, however, the maintenance of balance of payments equilibrium and of growth at full employment became increasingly incompatible objectives. Stop–go policy was thus perceived as swinging from one objective (correction of balance of payments deficits with 'stop' policy) to the other (stimulating growth and employment with 'go' policy). The underlying problem was that UK goods were becoming increasingly uncompetitive in world markets, due to a decline in the relative quality of UK goods and their higher relative prices.

Under a fixed exchange rate system there was therefore a long-term tendency for the balance of payments to deteriorate, and for governments to deflate. Eventually in 1967, with mounting pressure on sterling, the UK was forced to devalue the pound.

Monetarist criticisms of the policies of the 1950s and 1960s

Monetarists make two major criticisms of the Keynesian policies pursued during the 1950s and 1960s. First, they actually served to make the economy more unstable for the following reasons:

- Forecasting was bad. Frequently the forecasters failed to foresee exogenous changes to demand, or wrongly predicted the magnitude and timing of their effects.
- Governments as a result were hesitant to take action until the economy was clearly either booming (or in balance of payments crisis) or in recession.
- When governments did take action, they tended to overreact in their attempt to speed up the correction of the problem.

Second, inflation was kept fairly low in this period *despite* attempts to fine tune the economy. The reason for this was the fixed exchange rate, which forced governments to deflate whenever inflation threatened the balance of payments. If there had been no such constraint, Keynesian governments would have pursued much more expansionist policies, which would have driven up the rate of inflation.

> **??** Would a floating exchange rate have imposed no constraint at all on expansionist policies?

The Keynesian response

Keynesians argue that the economy was relatively stable, and that there was a good record of achieving the various macroeconomic objectives.

However, they admit that if there had been more flexibility in the exchange rate, or at least an earlier devaluation, this would have reduced the need for stop–go measures. There could then have been a more sustained expansion of the economy. This in turn would have boosted business confidence, increased investment and thereby increased long-term growth potential.

Provided demand was prevented from expanding too rapidly, any tendency for inflation to increase would be more due to cost-push or structural factors. These would be much better dealt with by using interventionist supply-side policies, such as prices and incomes policy to prevent cost-push inflation, and selective investment grants and infrastructure projects to relieve bottlenecks.

Finally, improvements in forecasting techniques and the swifter implementation of policies would help to reduce time lags and allow finer tuning.

> **??** Answer these points from a monetarist perspective.

The demise of fine tuning in the 1970s: the problem of stagflation

Fine tuning became impossible in the 1970s because of the rising problem of stagflation (see Figure 20.20). Demand management policies were still used, but they could no longer achieve an acceptable combination of inflation and unemployment. The Phillips curve had broken down.

Economists are not agreed on the causes of this stagflation, but there were a number of possible contributing factors.

The approach to monetary control. With the publication of the Bank of England document *Competition and Credit Control* in 1971, the authorities introduced new measures to control the money supply. They aimed to rely more on open-market operations and to encourage more competition between banks. Ceilings on bank credit were abandoned; the liquidity ratio that banks were required to hold was reduced; all special deposits were released; and banks were no longer required to set their interest rates in accordance with Bank rate (subsequently renamed *minimum lending rate* (MLR)). The effect was to make it much more difficult to prevent an expansion of credit and there was a mushrooming of new banks and credit institutions.

> **DEFINITION**
>
> **Stop–go policies** Alternate deflationary and reflationary policies.

Table 20.2 Selected monetary indicators: 1969–97

	Change in M4 (%) (1)	PSBR (£m) (2)	Inflation (% rise in RPI) (3)	Nominal interest rate (av. on 20-year bonds) (4)	Real interest rate (4) – (3) (5)
1969	5.1	–534	5.4	9.1	3.7
1970	11.5	–51	6.3	9.3	3.0
1971	16.0	1320	9.4	8.9	–0.5
1972	23.7	1950	7.3	9.0	1.7
1973	22.3	4093	9.1	10.8	1.7
1974	11.1	6452	16.0	14.8	–1.2
1975	12.4	10 161	24.2	14.4	–9.8
1976	11.2	9000	16.5	14.4	2.1
1977	14.7	5466	15.9	12.7	–3.2
1978	15.0	8195	8.3	12.5	4.2
1979	14.1	12 551	13.4	13.0	–0.4
1980	17.2	11 786	18.0	13.8	–4.2
1981	20.9	10 507	11.9	14.7	2.8
1982	12.1	4880	8.6	12.9	4.3
1983	13.2	11 605	4.6	10.8	6.2
1984	13.6	10 281	5.0	10.7	5.7
1985	13.1	7474	6.1	10.6	4.5
1986	15.4	2418	3.4	9.9	6.5
1987	16.3	–1432	4.2	9.5	5.3
1988	17.3	–11 611	4.9	9.4	4.5
1989	18.0	–9276	7.8	9.6	1.8
1990	12.1	–2125	9.5	11.1	1.6
1991	5.8	7661	5.9	9.8	3.9
1992	3.6	28 664	3.7	9.3	5.6
1993	4.6	42 503	1.6	7.9	6.3
1994	4.6	37 895	2.4	8.1	5.7
1995	9.9	35 120	3.5	8.3	4.8
1996	9.5	25 011	2.4	8.1	5.7
1997	11.6	12 476	3.1	7.1	4.0

Source: *Economic Trends Annual Supplement* (ONS).

Highly reflationary budgets in 1972 and 1973. The Heath government (1970–4) was committed to a rapid rate of economic growth. This was to be achieved by sharply expansionary fiscal policy. The effect was a rapid increase in the PSBR. This, combined with the 1971 monetary measures, led to a very rapid growth in money supply in 1972 and 1973 (see Table 20.2). Growth in aggregate demand could only in small part be met by increased output and employment.

Statutory controls over wages and prices, first introduced in November 1972, kept price rises in check for a while. But with a miners' strike being seen as a direct challenge to this prices and incomes policy, the government called an election in February 1974 and was defeated. The incoming Labour government abolished the prices and incomes policy, but this allowed the pent-up demand to feed straight through into price and wage increases. Inflation soared. By 1975 price inflation was nearly 25 per cent and wage inflation was over 30 per cent.

The adoption of floating exchange rates. In June 1972 a fixed exchange rate with the dollar was abandoned. A floating pound reduced the need to pursue deflationary policies in response to a balance of payments deficit. Instead the exchange rate could be allowed to depreciate. This removed a major constraint on the growth in money supply. This applied not just in the UK but throughout the world as countries moved over to floating exchange rates.

Oil prices. Between 1973 and 1974 the price of oil rose from \$3 to \$12 per barrel, and between 1978 and 1980 it rose from \$13 to \$31 per barrel. This not only raised costs and thus caused cost-push inflation, but also caused recessions in 1975 and 1979–81 as governments throughout the world deflated in response to the inflation and balance of payments crises.

Domestically generated cost-push pressures. Cost-push inflationary pressures increased as a result of the following:

growing union power and militancy; the desire for real wage increases each year in excess of the economy's real growth; the increasing monopoly power of firms, as increased mergers led to a growth in industrial concentration; and low productivity growth and hence a lack of price competitiveness of UK goods.

Increased import penetration and a decline in the UK's share of world exports. Increasing competition from foreign imports and a lack of quality of UK goods led to a poor balance of payments, low growth, structural unemployment, and inflation caused by a falling exchange rate (necessary to restore price competitiveness of UK exports).

Technological change. The microchip revolution and other labour-displacing technology created unemployment. There was insufficient aggregate demand to create new jobs elsewhere.

Expectations of inflation. High and volatile inflation rates fuelled expectations of high inflation, which then made inflation worse.

> **??** Go through each of the above causes of the stagflation of the 1970s and early 1980s and consider whether there were any policies that the government could realistically have adopted to deal with each one.

The response to stagflation

Several of these problems were problems of cost and supply, rather than excess or deficient demand. It was increasingly realised that in addition to fiscal and monetary policies there would have to be significant 'supply-side' policies.

The Keynesian response was to recommend supplementing demand management with interventionist supply-side policies, such as prices and incomes policy, regional policy, import restrictions and retraining policies.

The labour government of 1974–9 responded to the rise in both inflation and unemployment by reintroducing prices and incomes policy in the summer of 1975. Inflation began to fall in 1976 and growth re-emerged. The government let the exchange rate fall to help stimulate the demand for exports, but the falling pound caused speculation and a sterling crisis in late 1976. The government was forced to borrow from the International Monetary Fund to support the pound, and in return had to pursue tough monetary and fiscal policies, including setting targets for the growth in money supply.

This accorded with the views of monetarists, who recommended abandoning discretionary demand management of the stop–go variety altogether, and moving to a 'steady-as-you-go' policy of sticking to monetary targets. In addition they advocated the use of market-orientated supply-side policies such as tax reform, union reform, the abandonment of minimum wage rates, and lower unemployment benefits.

From 1976 to 1979 growth was steady at between 2½ and 3 per cent, unemployment was steady at between 5 and 5½ per cent, and inflation was falling. But growing resentment at incomes restraint led to the 'winter of discontent' of 1978–9, when several groups of workers attempted to defy the incomes policy. The government lost the 1979 election.

Monetarism under Thatcher

With the election of the Conservatives in 1979, the UK for the first time had a government committed to monetarist policies.

On the supply side, the government pursued policies to free up the market. The prices and incomes policy was abandoned; legislation was introduced to curb trade union power; foreign exchange controls were lifted; the standard rate of income tax was cut from 33 per cent to 30 per cent (with VAT being raised to compensate for the loss of revenue); the government made it clear that it would not bale out 'lame duck' industries; and later on it pursued a comprehensive policy of privatisation.

On the demand side, the cornerstone of the government's policy on inflation was the medium-term financial strategy (MTFS). Discretionary demand management in an attempt to fine tune the economy was totally abandoned. Instead progressively descending targets were adopted for money supply each year for the following four years. These, combined with statements that inflation was 'public enemy number one', were designed to reduce people's expectations of inflation, and hence the level of wage settlements. Money supply was to be kept on target in the short term by changes in interest rates, brought about by Bank of England operations in the discount market. All other forms of monetary control were abandoned. Foreign exchange controls were abolished in 1979 as were all forms of credit rationing; the corset was abandoned in 1980; statutory reserve requirements were abolished in 1981. The special deposits scheme was retained as an option, but from 1981 the banks were not required to make any.

In the medium term, the achieving of the targets would require a progressive reduction in the PSBR as a proportion of GDP (if crowding out was to be avoided). Thus tight monetary policy was backed up by tight fiscal policy.

In the public mind the government's monetarist policy became synonymous with 'cuts'.

Demand-side policies in the early 1980s

1979–81. The abandoning of incomes policy, the rise in oil prices from 1979 to 1981 and the rise in VAT from 7 per cent to 15 per cent led to a rise in inflation from 8.3 per cent in 1978 to 18 per cent in 1980. At the same time, fiscal and monetary policy had a highly deflationary effect. Interest rates rose rapidly, with MLR reaching 17 per cent in late 1979. The high interest rates, plus an improving balance of payments due to North Sea oil, led to a rapid rise in the exchange rate, fuelled by speculation of further rises.

The combination of low demand, high interest rates, a high exchange rate and rapidly rising costs led to a severe recession – the deepest since the 1930s. Unemployment rocketed from 4.7 per cent in 1979 to nearly 10 per cent in 1981.

1982–5. The continuing tight monetary policy with high real interest rates allowed only a slow recovery from recession. Recovery was, however, helped somewhat by a fall in the exchange rate between 1981 and 1985. This was in part a response to the strength of the dollar, which was due to high US interest rates resulting from the large and growing US budget deficit. Growth re-emerged from 1982 and inflation fell back to around 5 per cent. The growth in demand, however, was insufficient to prevent the continuing rise in unemployment.

Exogenous factors such as consumer and business expectations made it difficult to keep money supply on target, but there was a relatively consistent attempt to pursue a steady-as-you-go demand management policy. Rules had replaced discretion (see Section 20.5).

Assessing the monetarist experiment

Was the government able to carry through its monetarist intentions? On the plus side, after an initial upsurge (1979–81) the growth of money supply was reduced and inflation fell. But despite this there were a number of problems. Some of these are illustrated in Table 20.3.

- The PSBR proved very difficult to control and was above target in several years.
- From 1983 onwards the recorded level of the PSBR was artificially reduced by the sale of public-sector assets (British Telecom, British Gas, etc.). This allowed the government to pursue a more expansionary fiscal policy while *appearing* to maintain a tight monetary policy.
- The growth in M3 was also above target in several years despite a wide target range. The eventual reduction in its growth after 1981 was achieved at the cost of very high real interest rates.
- The government was forced to raise the target ranges in 1982, despite its commitment in the MTFS to a progressive lowering of them.
- In its search for the best measure of money supply – or the easiest to control – the government, in addition to M3 which it targeted throughout, first targeted M1

Table 20.3 Monetary targets:[1] 1979/80–1985/6

	1979/80	1980/1	1981/2	1982/3	1983/4	1984/5	1985/6
PSBR target (% of GDP)	–	3.25	4.25[2]	3.5	2.75	2.25	2.0
PSBR actual (% of GDP)	4.9	5.4	3.4	3.1	3.2	3.2	
M3 target (% growth)	–	7–11	6–10	8–12[2]	7–11	6–10	5–9
M3 actual (% growth)	15.2	19.4	12.8	11.2	9.5	9.7	13.6
M1 target (% growth)	–	–	6–10	8–12[2]	7–11	–	–
M1 actual (% growth)	5.3	11.9	7.2	12.3	14.0	14.6	17.4
M5 target (% growth)	–	–	6–10	8–12[2]	7–11	–	–
M5 actual (% growth)	12.5	14.8	12.0	11.5	12.6	15.2	14.6
M0 target (% growth)	–	–	–	–	–	4–8	3–7
M0 actual (% growth)	9.2	6.2	2.7	4.6	5.8	5.3	3.0
Sterling index (weighted average exchange rate)	89.9	98.3	92.3	87.9	83.5	76.3	79.8

[1] Targets were set each year for the following four years.
[2] Revised upwards from original target in previous years' MTFS.

Sources: *Midland Bank Review* (Autumn 1984); *Economic Trends* (ONS: various issues).

(cash held outside banks plus sight deposits in banks) and M5. It then abandoned targeting M1 and M5, and instead targeted M0. This makes it very difficult to assess the success of the policy.

- M3 was targeted and brought under control, but other measures of money supply went on growing – an example of Goodhart's law.
- Allowing sterling to float more freely brought problems. High interest rates and North Sea oil caused the pound to soar in 1980, with consequent damage to the export sector. But the government was afraid of intervening to lower the exchange rate because that would have increased the money supply (through reducing interest rates or running a total currency flow surplus).
- The opposite problem was faced in January/February 1985, when the pound fell dramatically against a strong US dollar. As the pound approached $1, the government felt obliged to intervene. Interest rates were raised dramatically, and on 14 January a formally announced MLR was reintroduced for one day to drive interest rates up by 2 per cent.

Despite all these difficulties, monetary policy was more consistent in the early 1980s than in most other periods. Inflation was seen as 'public enemy number one', and the means of getting it down was seen to be a tight monetary policy and adherence to monetary targets.

A return to discretionary policies after 1985

As the 1980s progressed, although monetary targets were almost being achieved, their importance was waning. With unemployment over 3 million, the government was putting less emphasis on the desirability of a generally tight monetary policy and instead was becoming more pragmatic. It wanted to allow monetary growth, and with it the growth of private-sector activity, to be as fast as possible without causing a resurgence of inflation or a run on the pound. Interest rate policy was thus becoming increasingly determined by short-run considerations of managing the exchange rate or responding to upward pressures on inflation.

With the effective abandonment of money supply targets after 1985, demand management policy reverted to a more traditional stop–go pattern. Discretion seemed to be replacing rules.

The period from 1985 to 1988 can be summarised as a period of unbalanced fiscal and monetary policy. Monetary policy was expansionary. With inflation still relatively low after the recession, interest rates were lowered to stimulate economic growth, reduce unemployment and prevent further rises in the exchange rate (and the consequent damage to exports). Fiscal policy, on the other hand, remained relatively tight. Although the government made several cuts in tax rates, the now rapid growth in incomes caused tax *revenues* to increase. At the same time the government continued to try to reduce its expenditure as a proportion of national income. The net result was that a PSBR of over £11 billion in 1983 was turned into a PSDR of over £11 billion by 1988.

This resulted in an imbalance in the impact of the policy. The extra money was spent largely on property and consumer durables (a large proportion of which were imported). House prices soared as mortgages were easy to obtain. Car sales boomed, as did the sales of electrical goods, furniture and foreign holidays.

Monetary policy was relatively expansionary throughout the world, and part of the extra money went into stocks and shares. The resulting increase in share prices was faster than the increase in profits and dividends. Eventually, in October 1987, 'the bubble burst' and share prices crashed. To avoid a collapse of confidence by firms and a plunge into recession, monetary policy was further relaxed. Aggregate demand grew more rapidly. Unemployment fell more rapidly and output grew more rapidly; but inflation began to rise and the balance of payments on current account plunged into a record deficit.

In response to this crisis, interest rates were raised several times in the last part of 1988 and during 1989. Banks' base rate rose from 7.5 per cent in May 1988 to 15 per cent by October 1989, and then remained at this level until October 1990 when the UK joined the exchange rate mechanism (ERM) of the European Monetary System (see section 24.7). It was clear that the government was pursuing a stop–go monetary policy, depending on how bad were the problems of inflation, the balance of payments and a depreciating exchange rate.

?? In what way was the stop–go policy of the late 1980s different from the stop–go policies pursued during the 1950s and 1960s?

Targeting the exchange rate

Shadowing the D-Mark

Targets were not completely abandoned after 1985. There was a growing belief that, with closer links being forged with Europe, and with the desirability of a stable exchange rate between the pound and other European currencies, the exchange rate ought to be targeted. But as we saw in Box 19.5, the problem with effectively having only one instrument (interest rates) was that the government could not use it at one and the same time to control both the level of aggregate demand (and hence inflation) *and* the rate of exchange. In 1988, high interest rates were required to control the rapidly expanding credit, but low interest rates were required to prevent the exchange rate from rising above its target level of around £1 = DM3.00: a rise that would be damaging to exports. The debate, however, resolved itself. With a *falling* pound in 1989, high interest rates were desirable for both exchange rate and counter-inflationary reasons.

> **??** Will targeting the exchange rate help to reduce inflation? Does it depend on the rate of inflation in the countries to whose currencies the pound is fixed?

Fiscal policy was largely confined to the role of improving the *supply* side of the economy. This would be achieved by reducing the size of the public sector (which was seen by the government to be less productive than the private sector), and by giving tax cuts to improve incentives. So did fiscal policy have no demand management role at all? It did, but only to the extent that the amount of tax cuts was influenced by demand considerations.

ERM membership: 1990–2

In October 1990 the UK joined the ERM. The requirement to keep the pound within an exchange rate band of approximately DM2.78–3.13 meant that there was now effectively an exchange rate target. But with essentially only one instrument of macroeconomic policy, namely the rate of interest, all other macroeconomic goals had to be subordinated to this target.

In a fixed exchange rate system, UK interest rates were largely governed by those of the other countries within the system. The reunification of Germany had involved a large expansion of German money supply. In response the Bundesbank (the German central bank), in order to prevent inflation rising, raised interest rates to 8.75 per cent. To maintain sterling's value within the ERM, the government therefore had to pursue a high interest rate policy. But since the German inflation rate was still only 2.8 per cent and the UK inflation rate was nearly 11 per cent, UK interest rates had to be considerably above the German level. UK money market rates were 13.5 per cent.

Within a few months it was clear that the UK was plunging into recession. On domestic grounds alone, lower interest rates would have been desirable. But by mid-1991 the pound was again under pressure in the ERM and so monetary policy had to be kept tight. Inflation was now falling rapidly, but interest rates were reduced only slightly. This meant that *real* interest rates had risen (see Table 20.2 on page 623). In the twelve months after joining the ERM, UK inflation fell by 7 percentage points whereas interest rates fell by only 3 percentage points. There was thus a growing policy conflict between the *external* requirement of maintaining the exchange rate and the internal requirement of reflating a depressed domestic economy.

Throughout 1991 and the first part of 1992 the government stuck resolutely to maintaining sterling's value in the ERM. Ministers justified this as being the best means of continuing the fight against inflation. But by September 1992, three factors were making continued membership of the ERM at a central parity of DM2.95 increasingly untenable:

- A growing uncertainty throughout Europe about the prospects for European Monetary Union given the Danish rejection in a referendum of the Maastricht Treaty, and thus growing worries about the possibilities of currency realignments.
- The weakness of the dollar. A growing US balance of trade deficit plus the uncertainties of an impending US election led to speculation against the dollar. Money flowed to stronger currencies such as the Deutschmark, which made sterling comparatively weaker.
- The weakness of the Italian economy. A huge Italian budget deficit plus a rate of inflation above the EC average made it uncertain whether the value of the lira could be maintained in the ERM.

Eventually after massive speculation against the lira, which initially forced its devaluation in the ERM, speculation against sterling became irresistible. On 'Black Wednesday', 16 September 1992, after a 5 per cent rise in interest rates was insufficient to stop the speculation, the UK left the ERM and the pound was allowed to float, as was the lira.

A return to domestic-orientated policies: targeting inflation

With the need to defend the value of the pound removed, the government could focus once more on the domestic situation. Within four months, interest rates had been reduced by 4 per cent. This loosening of monetary policy gave a welcome boost to the economy, which was still only just beginning to pull out of recession.

The government was not worried that this would lead to an unwelcome growth in money supply and inflation. Indeed, the control of inflation was now to be the main objective of monetary policy. An initial target rate of inflation of 1–4 per cent was set, to be backed up by 'monitoring ranges' of 0–4 per cent for M0 and 3–9 per cent for M4 until 1997, by which time inflation should be between 1 and $2^1/_2$ per cent.

Targeting inflation was based on the belief that monetary policy cannot influence *real* variables such as output and employment in the long run. It can only influence inflation. It is better, therefore, to focus on achieving low inflation in order to provide the best environment for businesses to thrive. But to achieve an inflation target meant doing two things.

First, given the time lags between changing interest rates and their effect on inflation, interest rates would have to be changed in response to inflation *forecasts*, rather than the current rate of inflation. Second, people would have to be made to believe that the government could and would achieve the target. To this end, a number of steps were taken:

- The Bank of England published inflation forecasts, which the government publicly used to assess whether policy was on target.
- The Chancellor and the Governor of the Bank of England met monthly to consider the necessary interest rate policy to keep inflation within the target range. The Bank would then determine the *timing* of any agreed changes.
- Minutes of these meetings were published six weeks later, in order to give transparency to the process.
- Each time interest rates were changed, a press notice would be issued explaining the reasons. The idea here was to show the government's commitment to keeping to the target.

Was the policy a success? Inflation remained within the target bands, and the government claimed that this was the result of the policy. In fact, the reduction in inflation from 1992 to 1994 was the lagged result of the tight monetary conditions during the previous two years when the UK was in the ERM. Indeed, the government *reduced* interest rates several times between September 1992 and February 1994. After 1994, however, the policy *did* help to keep inflation down, with the government raising interest rates whenever inflationary forecasts were adverse.

As far as fiscal policy was concerned, with the PSBR for the year ending March 1993 being a massive £36.3 billion, there was a serious problem that, if monetary growth was kept in check, government borrowing would crowd out private-sector growth. The government thus saw the need to get a 'better' balance between fiscal and monetary policy. It therefore announced a series of tax increases to be phased in over the coming years. It also stated its intention to examine ways of reducing government expenditure.

?? If tax increases are 'phased in' as an economy recovers from recession, how will this affect the magnitude and timing of the recovery?

In 1997, the incoming Labour government declared its commitment to stick to the previous government's expenditure targets and to continue bringing down the PSBR. That, plus a commitment not to raise taxes, prevented it from spending money on various social programmes advocated by many of its supporters.

As far as monetary policy was concerned, the government made the Bank of England independent. This allowed the Bank to focus on meeting inflation targets without political interference from the government (see Box 19.7).

SECTION SUMMARY

1. In the 1950s and 1960s, both Labour and Conservative governments pursued active demand management policies. The dominating constraints on these policies were the balance of payments and electoral considerations. Demand management was little more than stop–go policy dictated by the state of the balance of payments and the need to win elections.
2. The 1950s and 1960s was a period of relative economic success. But whether this was due to the pursuit of Keynesian demand management policies or to other factors such as a buoyant world economy and economic optimism is a matter of debate.
3. In the 1970s stagflation became a major problem due to a number of factors, including expansionary fiscal and monetary policies in the early 1970s, the adoption of floating exchange rates, a large rise in oil prices, growing domestically generated cost-push pressures, a decline in the competitiveness of UK exports, technological change and increasingly pessimistic expectations.
4. As a result of the dilemma of rising inflation *and* rising unemployment, government policy swung violently from a 'dash for growth' in the early 1970s, to two sets of prices and incomes policies, to a tight monetary policy towards the end of the decade.
5. The Conservative government in the 1980s initially pursued a tight monetary policy and targeted the PSBR and the growth in the money supply. The

continued

exchange rate rose and the economy plunged into a deep recession. The economy started to grow again after 1982, but for a time a tight monetary policy was retained (along with monetary targets) in order to keep a downward pressure on inflation.

6. Then, after 1985, targets for monetary growth were abandoned and for a time targeting the exchange rate become the main focus of monetary policy. But with only one instrument (interest rates) there was a conflict between keeping exchange rates down and controlling inflation. This conflict disappeared after 1988 when high interest rates were required both for keeping inflation down and for preventing a *fall* in the exchange rate.
7. The UK joined the ERM in October 1990 and the conflict between domestic and exchange rate policy soon re-emerged. The economy was moving rapidly into recession, but the government was unable to make substantial cuts in interest rates because of the need to defend the value of the pound. Eventually in September 1992, with huge speculation in favour of the Deutschmark and against sterling and the lira, the UK and Italy were forced to leave the ERM.
8. Since 1992, there has been a return to using interest rates to manage domestic demand in line with inflation targets. There was mounting concern, however, about the size of the PSBR, and fiscal policy was tightened until the PSBR had been sufficiently reduced.

20.5 Rules versus discretion

Central to the debate between Keynesians and monetarists over the control of demand is the question of rules versus discretion. Should monetary (and fiscal) rules be adhered to, or should governments exercise the discretion to change the policies as economic circumstances change? Monetarists favour rules. Keynesians favour discretion. We finish this chapter by having a look at the arguments on each side.

The monetarist case against discretion and in favour of rules

Monetarists are highly critical of discretionary policy, both fiscal and monetary. Such policy can involve long and variable time lags, which can make the policy at best ineffective and at worst destabilising. Taking the measures *before* the problem arises, and thus lessening the problem of lags, is no answer since forecasting tends to be unreliable.

By setting and sticking to rules, and then not interfering further, the government can provide a sound monetary framework in which there is maximum freedom for individual initiative and enterprise, and in which firms are not cushioned from market forces and are therefore encouraged to be efficient. By the government declaring medium-term targets for a steady reduction in the growth of money supply, and then resolutely sticking to them, people's expectations of inflation will be reduced. This will help further to reduce inflation. This sound and stable monetary environment, with no likelihood of sudden deflations or reflations, will encourage firms to take a longer-term perspective and to plan ahead. This could then lead to increased capital investment and long-term growth.

The optimum situation is for all the major countries to adhere to mutually consistent rules, so that their economies do not get out of line. This will create more stable exchange rates and provide the climate for world growth.

?? Would it be desirable for all countries to stick to the *same* money supply targets?

The Keynesian case against rules and in favour of discretion

Keynesians reject one of the central points of the monetarist argument: that rules provide the environment for high and stable growth. Demand, argue Keynesians, is subject to many and sometimes violent exogenous shocks: e.g. changes in expectations, political events (such as an impending election), world economic factors (such as a change in US interest rates) or world political events (such as a war). The resulting shifts in injections or withdrawals cause the economy to deviate from a stable full-employment growth path.

Any change in injections or withdrawals will lead to a cumulative effect on national income via the multiplier and accelerator and via changing expectations. These endogenous effects take time and interact with each other, and so a process of expansion or contraction can last many months before a turning point is eventually reached.

Since the exogenous changes in demand occur at irregular intervals and are of different magnitudes, the

EXPLORING THE THEORY

WHICH TARGET TO AIM FOR?

A choice of bull's-eyes

Money supply targets are not the only ones that governments can choose. There are several other possible targets, each having arguments to recommend it, but each having drawbacks.

Interest rate targets

A major problem with sticking to money supply targets is that interest rates will fluctuate with fluctuations in economic activity and hence in the demand for money. For this reason many economists have argued that it is best to target interest rates. Stable interest rates will provide an environment of certainty in which businesses can make long-term investment plans. In the Keynesian era of the 1950s and 1960s, governments were more concerned to achieve relatively stable interest rates than a stable growth in money supply.

The problem with targeting interest rates is that the money supply will fluctuate with demand and hence feed those fluctuations. For example, if aggregate demand grows rapidly and inflation begins to soar, then to keep interest rates down to the target level, money supply will have to be allowed to expand. But this will feed the inflation. People will come to expect higher and higher inflation, and prices and expectations will chase each other in an upward spiral. Discretionary fiscal policies or prices and incomes policies will then be needed to break the spiral.

Exchange rate targets

Provided the rest of the world is relatively stable, an exchange rate target can provide a useful brake on domestic policy. If the government were to allow the money supply to expand too fast and/or the interest rate to fall, the resulting increase in demand and outflow of capital would lead to a depreciation of the exchange rate. To get it back on target, therefore, the government would have to raise interest rates and reduce the growth in money supply.

In addition, an exchange rate target (a fixed exchange rate) is usually preferred by firms, which are thereby given the certainty to plan their imports and exports and investment abroad.

The main problem with exchange rate targets comes when major world economies are not pursuing policies that are consistent with domestic policy requirements. If world interest rates change, then domestic interest rates will have to follow suit in order to prevent capital flows and the resulting change in the exchange rate. But these changes in interest rates may have adverse consequences at home. For example, in 1992 the Germans were pursuing a high interest rate policy in order to dampen the inflationary consequences of reunification. The UK, being a member of the ERM at the time, and therefore having to pursue an exchange rate target, was obliged to maintain high interest rates too. But this ran directly counter to the need to stimulate the UK economy, which was deep in recession. After withdrawing from the ERM, UK interest rates were then able to fall, much to the relief of industry and house owners with large mortgages.

France experienced a similar problem in the spring and summer of 1993. Being still a member of the ERM, it was obliged to match German interest rates, which were still high. After the crisis of August 1993, when the ERM bands were widened to 15 per cent and the franc was able to depreciate against the mark, French interest rates were able to come down.

PSBR/PSDR targets

Part of the medium-term financial strategy of the UK government in the early 1980s consisted of setting PSBR targets (as a percentage of GDP). Even after the abandoning of money supply targets after 1986, the government still set targets for the PSBR, with the long-term aim of running a balanced public-sector budget (PSBR = 0).

To the extent that the size of the PSBR (or PSDR) determines the growth of the money supply, then a PSBR target can be seen as a form of money supply target.

The problem is that the correlation between the PSBR and money supply is not very close (as Chapter 18 showed): after 1987 there was a growing public-sector surplus accompanied by a rapid growth in the money supply.

economy is likely to experience cycles of irregular duration and of varying intensity.

Given that the economy is inherently unstable and is buffeted around by various exogenous shocks, Keynesians argue that the government needs actively to intervene to stabilise the economy. Otherwise, the uncertainty caused by unpredictable fluctuations will be very damaging to investment and hence to long-term growth in potential output (quite apart from the short-term effects of recessions on actual output and employment).

If demand fluctuates in the way Keynesians claim, and if the monetarist policy of having a money supply rule is adhered to, interest rates must fluctuate. But excessive fluctuations in interest rates will discourage long-term business planning and investment. What is more, the government may find it difficult to keep to its targets (see Table 20.3). This too may cause uncertainty and instability.

BOX 20.6

Inflation targets

	Inflation targets (%)		Actual inflation (1997) (%)
Primary targets			
Canada	1–3	1995–8	1.6
Finland	2	1995 onwards	1.2
New Zealand	0–2	medium term	1.1
Sweden	1–3	1995 onwards	0.9
UK	$1–2\frac{1}{2}$	by 1997	3.1
Secondary targets			
Australia	2–3	medium term	0.3
Denmark	2–3	medium term	2.1
France	max. 2	medium term	1.2
Germany	max. 2	medium term	1.7
Italy	2	by 1996	1.8
Spain	3	by 1997	2.0
Switzerland	0–1	medium term	0.6

Source: © *The Economist, London.*

Also if the government aims for a set PSBR/PSDR, this removes the automatic stabilising property of fiscal policy. If, for example, there is an economic recession, tax revenues will fall and benefit payments will rise. This will increase the PSBR. To bring it back to target, therefore, the government would have to raise taxes or cut government expenditure, either of which would deepen the recession.

Final goal targets

The problem with all the targets we have looked at so far – money supply, interest rate, exchange rate and PSBR targets – is that they are all *intermediate targets*: that is, they are not the ultimate goals of policy, but merely means of achieving them. Thus, for example, control of the money supply is not the ultimate goal of monetarist economic policy, but rather the *means* of achieving low inflation and an environment conducive to the flourishing of private enterprise.

Some economists argue that it is better to target the final goals themselves, given the problems we have looked at of targeting the means. For example, the government could target physical goals such as economic growth or unemployment, or financial goals such as inflation. Several countries now target inflation. Some, such as New Zealand, the UK and Sweden, have made it the prime target of monetary policy. Interest rates are adjusted as inflation forecasts diverge from the target. In other countries, inflation targets are secondary to exchange rate targets (see table).

?? Should low inflation be regarded as a final goal or merely an intermediate one?

The problem with final goals is that they may be inconsistent with each other. For example, low unemployment may be inconsistent with low inflation (the Phillips curve trade-off). Thus governments may swing from aiming for one target to aiming for another – and that is hardly consistent with the idea of targets being something you set and then stick to, come what may.

Also there is the problem of how you achieve the targets. The longer the transmission mechanism is from the 'levers' to the target, the more difficult it will be to achieve the target with any degree of accuracy. Thus it is relatively easy to achieve an interest rate target, since the Bank of England has direct control over interest rates. But to achieve an inflation target or an unemployment target may involve frequent *adjustments* to policy depending on how successful previous policies have been. Thus a final goal target relates less to the 'steady as you go', 'fixed throttle' policies of intermediate targets, and more to discretionary policies.

?? Make a list of other possible targets the government could aim for. Are they intermediate or final targets? What problems might the government have in achieving them? Would there be any other problems if the government did achieve them?

If the government is to adopt a rule, which rule should it choose? If a monetary measure is to be chosen, which one? They frequently do not grow at the same rate. What is more, the adoption of one measure as the target may lead to distortions as people switch the form of their holdings of liquidity and wealth (Goodhart's law).

Economic circumstances may change. The rules adopted in the past may no longer be relevant. For example, a faster growth in productivity or a large increase in oil revenues may increase potential growth and thus warrant a faster growth in money supply. The government must at least have the discretion to *change* the rules, even if only occasionally.

The short-term costs of sticking to previously set rules may be too high. If expectations are slow to adjust downward and inflation remains high, then adherence to a tight monetary rule may lead to a very deep and unacceptable recession. This was a criticism made by many economists of monetarist policies between 1979 and 1982.

But if rules should not be stuck to religiously, does this mean that the government can engage in fine tuning? Keynesians today recognise that fine tuning may not be possible; nevertheless, significant and persistent excess or deficient demand *can* be corrected by demand management policy. For example, the deep recession of 1980–1 could have been substantially relieved by a more expansionary fiscal and monetary policy.

Improvements in forecasting, a willingness of governments to act quickly and the use of quick-acting policies can all help to increase the effectiveness of discretionary demand management.

?? Under what circumstances would adherence to money supply targets lead to (a) more stable interest rates and (b) less stable interest rates than pursuing discretionary demand management policy?

Conclusions

The resolution of this debate will depend on the following factors:

- The confidence of people in the effectiveness of either discretionary policies or rules.
- The degree of self-stabilisation of the economy (in the case of rules), or conversely the degree of inherent instability of the economy (in the case of discretion).
- The size and frequency of exogenous shocks to demand.
- The ability and determination of governments to stick to rules.
- The ability of governments to adopt and execute appropriate discretionary policy, the speed with which such policies can be effected and the accuracy of forecasting.

SECTION SUMMARY

1. The monetarist case against discretionary policy is that it involves unpredictable time lags which can make the policy destabilising. Also the government may ignore the long-run adverse consequences of policies designed for short-run political gain.
2. The monetarist case in favour of rules is that they help to reduce inflationary expectations and thus create a stable environment for investment and growth.
3. The Keynesian case against sticking to money supply rules is that they may cause severe fluctuations in interest rates and thus create a less stable economic environment for business planning. Also, given Goodhart's law, it is not clear which rule should be chosen. Given the changing economic environment in which we live, rules adopted in the past may no longer be suitable for the present.
4. Although perfect fine tuning may not be possible, Keynesians argue that the government must have the discretion to change its policy as circumstances demand.

??? END-OF-CHAPTER QUESTIONS ???

1. Using one or more diagrams like Figures 20.2, 20.8, 20.11, 20.12 and 20.13, illustrate the following:

   (a) The effect of a contractionary monetary policy on national income from (i) a Keynesian perspective; (ii) a monetarist perspective. In each case refer to both the interest-rate and the exchange-rate transmission mechanisms.

   (b) The effect of a contractionary fiscal policy on national income from (i) a Keynesian perspective; (ii) a monetarist perspective. Specify your assumptions about the effects on the *supply* of money.
2. Compare Keynesian and monetarist assumptions about the V and Q terms in the quantity equation $MV = PQ$. What are the implications of these respective assumptions for the effectiveness of monetary policy to control inflation?
3. Imagine you are a Keynesian economist called in by the government to advise on whether it should adopt a policy of targeting the money supply. What advice would you give and how would you justify the advice?
4. Imagine you are a monetarist economist called in by the government to advise on whether it should attempt to prevent cyclical fluctuations by the use of fiscal policy. What advice would you give and how would you justify the advice?

*5. Using diagrams like Figures 20.18 and 20.19 compare Keynesian and monetarist analyses of contractionary fiscal and monetary policy.

6. In what ways does the evidence of post-war UK macroeconomics policy provide support for the monetarist critique of fine tuning?
7. Would you describe the policies pursued by the Conservative government in the UK since 1979 as strictly monetarist?
8. Is there a compromise between purely discretionary policy and adhering to strict targets?

21

Macroeconomic controversies II

Aggregate supply, unemployment and inflation

21.1 Aggregate supply

The effect of an increase in aggregate demand on output, employment and prices is a crucial issue in macroeconomic policy and is at the heart of the Keynesian/monetarist/new classical debate. The debate hinges on the shape of the aggregate supply curve.

The extreme Keynesian and extreme monetarist new classical positions are shown in Figure 21.1. Extreme Keynesians argue that up to full employment (Y_f), the aggregate supply (AS) curve is *horizontal*, at least in the short run. A rise in aggregate demand from AD_1 to AD_2 will raise output from Y_1 to Y_2, but there will be *no effect on prices* until full employment is reached. In this model, aggregate supply up to the full-employment level is determined entirely by the level of aggregate demand. But there is no guarantee that aggregate demand will intersect aggregate supply at full employment. Therefore governments should manage aggregate demand by appropriate fiscal and monetary policies to ensure production at Y_f.

Monetarists argue that the aggregate supply curve is *vertical*, at least in the long run. New classicists argue that it is vertical in the short run too. Any rise in aggregate demand will have *no effect on output and employment*. It will merely lead to higher prices. Thus it is essential to control demand if *prices* are to be kept under control. To raise output and employment, however, will require supply-side policies: to shift the AS curve to the right.

If AS is somewhere between these two extremes, an increase in AD will have some effect on prices and some effect on output and employment (see Figure 21.1(c)).

Just what is the shape of the AS curve in practice, and what implications follow for policies to cure inflation and unemployment? How do Keynesians and monetarists differ in their answers to these questions? These are the topics for this chapter. First we must distinguish between short-run and long-run aggregate supply curves.

??

1. In the extreme Keynesian model, is there any point in supply-side policies?
2. In the new classical model, is there any point in using supply-side policies as a weapon against *inflation*?

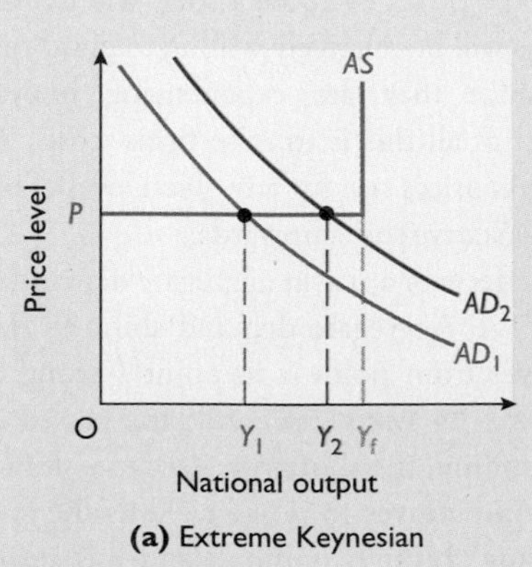

(a) Extreme Keynesian

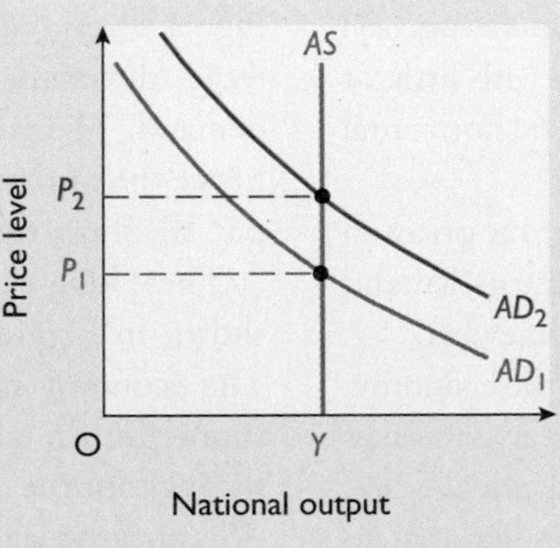

(b) Extreme monetarist/new classical

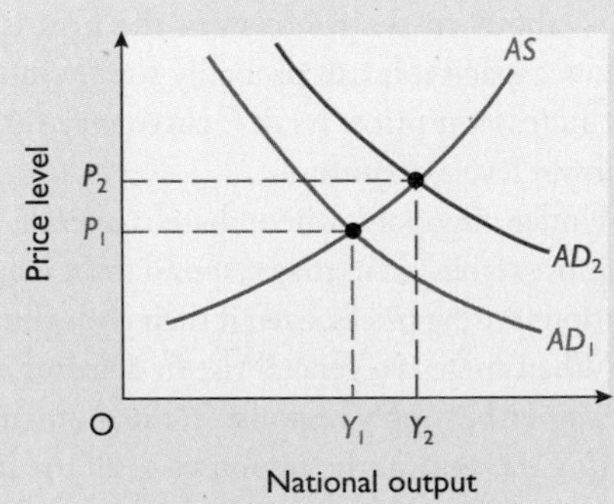

(c) A 'moderate' view of the aggregate supply curve

Figure 21.1 Contrasting views of the aggregate supply curve

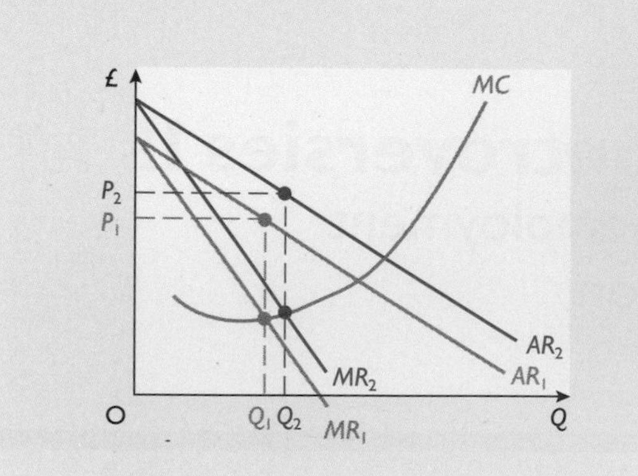

Figure 21.2 Short-run response of a profit-maximising firm to a rise in demand

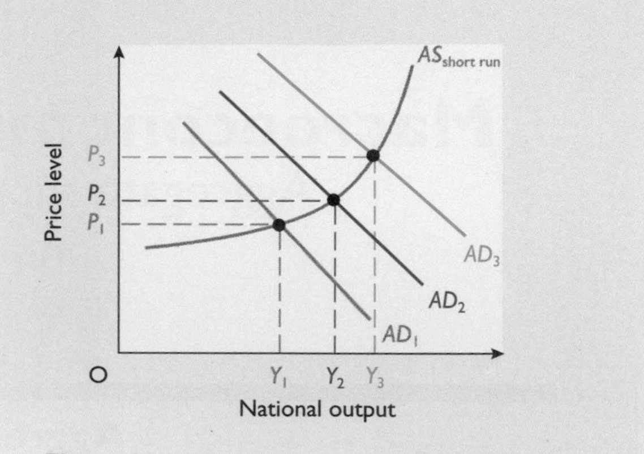

Figure 21.3 The short-run aggregate supply curve

Short-run aggregate supply

To understand the shape of the short-run *AS* curve, it is necessary to look at its microeconomic foundations. How will *individual* firms and industries respond to a rise in demand? What shape will their individual supply curves be?

In the short run, we assume that firms respond to the rise in demand for their product without considering the effects of a general rise in demand on their suppliers or on the economy as a whole. We also assume that the prices of inputs, including wage rates, are constant.

In the case of a profit-maximising firm under monopoly or monopolistic competition, there will be a rise in price and a rise in output. In Figure 21.2, profit-maximising output rises from where $MC = MR_1$ to where $MC = MR_2$. Just how much price changes compared with output depends on the slope of the marginal cost (*MC*) curve.

The nearer the firm is to full capacity, the steeper the *MC* curve is likely to be. Here the firm is likely to find diminishing returns setting in rapidly, and it is also likely to have to use more overtime with correspondingly higher unit labour costs. If, however, the firm is operating well below capacity, it can probably supply more with little or no increase in price. Its *MC* curve may thus be horizontal at lower levels of output.

Under oligopoly, where there is a tendency for prices to be more stable, firms may respond to an increase in demand without raising prices, even if their costs rise somewhat.

When there is a general rise in demand in the economy, the *aggregate* supply response in the short run can be seen as simply the sum of the responses of all the individual firms. The short-run *AS* curve will look something like that in Figure 21.3. If there is generally plenty of spare capacity, a rise in aggregate demand (e.g. from AD_1 to AD_2) will have a big effect on output and only a small effect on prices. However, as more and more firms find their costs rising as they get nearer to full capacity, so the *AS* curve becomes steeper. Further increases in aggregate demand (e.g. from AD_2 to AD_3) will have bigger effects on prices and smaller effects on output. A general rise in prices, of course, means that individual firms will have been mistaken when they assumed that a rise in price from P_1 to P_2 in Figure 21.2 was a *real* price rise (i.e. relative to prices elsewhere).

Long-run aggregate supply

Three important factors affect the *AS* curve in the long run.

The interdependence of firms

A rise in aggregate demand will lead firms throughout the economy to raise their prices (in accordance with the short-run *AS* curve). But as raw material and intermediate good producers raise their prices, this will raise the costs of production further up the line. A rise in the price of steel will raise the costs of producing cars and washing machines. At the same time, workers, experiencing a rise in demand for labour, and seeing the prices of goods rising, will demand higher wages. Firms will be relatively willing to grant these wage demands, since they are experiencing buoyant demand. The effect of all this is to raise firms' costs, and hence their prices. As prices rise for any given level of output, the short-run *AS* curve shifts upwards.

These long-run effects of a rise in aggregate demand are shown in Figure 21.4. Aggregate demand shifts to AD_1. The economy moves from point *a* to point *b* along the short-run *AS* curve. As costs rise and are passed on throughout the economy, the short-run *AS* curve shifts to AS_1, and the economy moves to point *c*. Thus the long-run *AS* curve passing through points *a* and *c* is steeper than the short-run *AS* curve. A rise in aggregate demand will therefore have a smaller effect on output and a bigger effect on prices in the long run than in the short run.

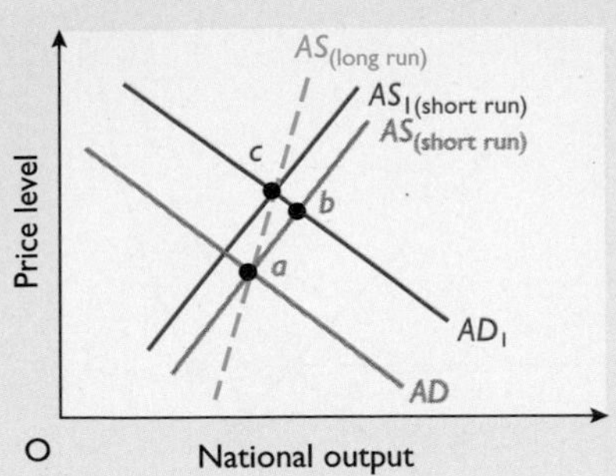

Figure 21.4 The long-run aggregate supply curve when firms are interdependent

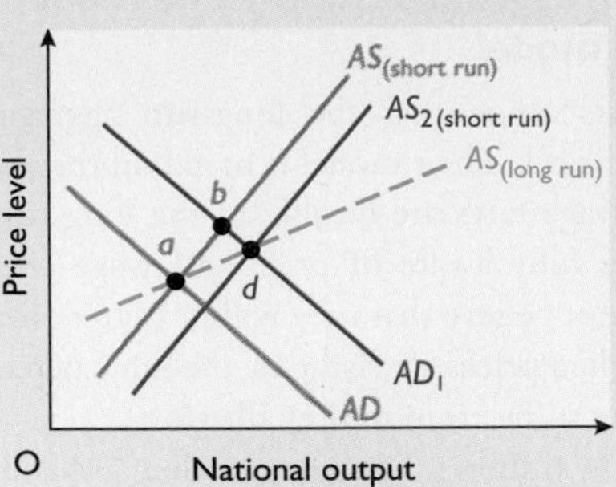

Figure 21.5 Effect of investment on the long-run aggregate supply curve

?? Under what circumstances would this interdependence of firms give a vertical long-run *AS* curve?

Investment

With a rise in demand, firms may be encouraged to invest in new plant and machinery (the accelerator effect). In so doing they may well be able to increase output significantly in the long run with little or no increase in their prices. Their long-run *MC* curves are much flatter than their short-run *MC* curves.

In Figure 21.5 the short-run *AS* curve shifts to the right. Equilibrium moves from point *a* to *b* to *d*. In this case the long-run *AS* curve joining points *a* and *d* is much more elastic than that in Figure 21.4. There is a relatively large increase in output and a relatively small increase in price.

The long-run *AS* curve will be flatter and possibly even downward sloping if the investment involves the introduction of new cost-reducing technology, or if firms generally experience economies of scale. It will be steeper if the extra investment causes significant shortages of materials, machinery or labour. This is more likely when the economy is already operating near its full potential.

??
1. Will the shape of the long-run *AS* curve here depend on just how the 'long' run is defined?
2. If a shift in the aggregate demand curve from *AD* to AD_1 in Figure 21.5 causes a movement from point *a* to point *d* in the long run, would a shift in aggregate demand from AD_1 to *AD* cause a movement from point *d* back to point *a* in the long run?

Expectations

The effect of a rise in aggregate demand on output and prices will depend crucially on what effect people *expect* it will have.

If firms believe that it will lead to rapid economic growth, they will invest. The short-run *AS* curve will shift to the right.

If, on the other hand, people expect that a rise in demand will simply lead to higher prices, firms will not invest. Workers will demand higher wages to compensate for the higher costs of living. Firms will grant wage rises, knowing that they can pass on the rise in labour costs to the consumer. In these circumstances the short-run *AS* curve will shift upwards (to the left).

If there is a fall in aggregate demand, the above three factors will operate in reverse; and again they will affect aggregate supply in different ways:

- The general reduction in costs will lead to the short-run *AS* curve shifting downwards (to the right).
- A fall in investment may lead to a decline in the capital stock and a leftward shift in the short-run *AS* curve.
- People may expect a recession and falling output (*AS* shifts to the left), or merely that prices will fall (*AS* shifts downwards to the right).

Depending on the relative strength of these three factors, the long-run *AS* curve could be shallow, steep or vertical. A fall in *AD* could thus lead to a deep recession with little effect on prices, or there could be little or no long-run reduction in output, but a significant reduction in prices. Keynesians and monetarists put very different emphases on the three factors, and as a result draw very different conclusions about the shape of the long-run *AS* curve. Central to the debate is their analysis of labour markets and the link between the aggregate demand and supply of goods and the aggregate demand and supply of labour.

Long-run aggregate supply: the monetarist/classical model

Monetarists argue that the long-run aggregate supply curve is vertical. Their model is based on the assumptions that real wage rates are flexible in the long run and that people are fully aware of price and wage changes, and hence do not believe that they will be better off with a pay increase when prices are rising by the same percentage (i.e. they do not suffer from **money illusion**).

Figure 21.6 shows the aggregate demand and supply of labour. It is the same diagram we looked at back on page 419. On the vertical axis we measure the average *real* wage rate (W/P): i.e. the wage rate after adjusting for prices. The aggregate demand for labour curve (AD_L) slopes downwards. This is merely an extension of the microeconomic demand for labour curve (see section 9.2) and is based on the assumption of diminishing returns to labour. For a given capital stock, the more people who are employed, the lower will be their marginal productivity. Thus firms will take on more labour only if there is a fall in the real wage rate to compensate them for the lower output produced by the additional workers.

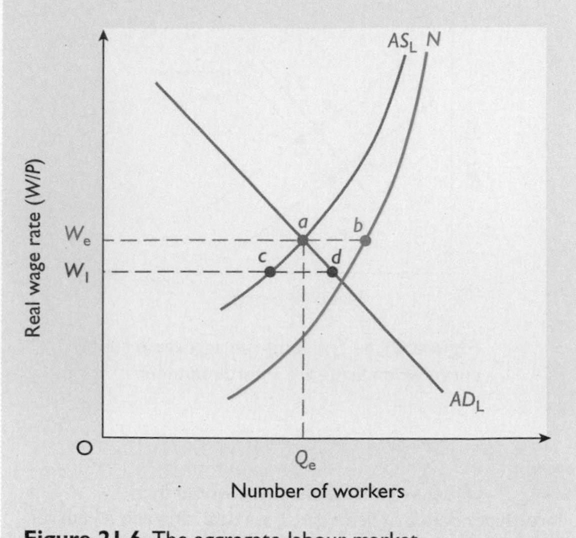

Figure 21.6 The aggregate labour market

A higher real wage rate will encourage more people to enter the labour market. For example, more married women may seek employment. The total number in the labour force (N) rises. The curve gets steeper as the limit of the potential labour force is reached.

There will, however, be some frictional and structural unemployment. Some workers will be searching for better jobs and others will have the wrong qualifications or live in the wrong location. The number of workers willing and able to accept jobs, therefore – the *effective aggregate supply of labour* (AS_L) – will be less than the total labour force.

The equilibrium real wage will be W_e, where $AD_L = AS_L$, with Q_e workers employed. There is no disequilibrium unemployment at this real wage rate, but there is some equilibrium or **natural unemployment** (i.e. frictional plus structural unemployment), shown by $(b - a)$.

With flexible prices and wage rates in the long run, *real* wage rates will also be flexible in the long run. This will ensure that long-run employment is kept at Q_e. Assume that aggregate demand (for goods) rises. Prices rise. This causes the real wage to fall below W_e, say to W_1 in Figure 21.6. But at this real wage rate there is an excess demand for labour of $d - c$. This will drive up the money wage rate until the *real* wage rate has returned to W_e. Thus equilibrium employment is at Q_e irrespective of changes in aggregate demand. Q_e would change only if there were some *exogenous* shift in the AD_L or AS_L curves (e.g. a growth in the working population would cause N and AS_L to shift to the right; a growth in labour productivity would cause AD_L to shift to the right).

> **??** Assume that there is a *fall* in aggregate demand (for goods). Trace through the short-run and long-run effect on employment.

With long-run employment being at Q_e (the natural rate) irrespective of what happens to prices and *money* wages, the long-run aggregate supply curve will be vertical at the **natural level of output**.

Long-run aggregate supply: Keynesian models

Keynesian models of long-run aggregate supply make one or more of four assumptions:

DEFINITIONS

Money illusion The belief that a *money* change in wages or prices represents a *real* change.

Natural level of unemployment The level of equilibrium unemployment in monetarist analysis measured as the difference between the (vertical) long-run gross labour supply (N) and the (vertical) long-run effective labour supply (AS_L).

Natural level of output The level of output in monetarist analysis where the vertical long-run aggregate supply curve cuts the horizontal axis.

- Wages and prices are not perfectly flexible even in the long run (unless the long run is defined as a very long time indeed).
- Hysteresis. This is where an equilibrium position depends on the path taken to arrive there (see page 488). In this context, hysteresis would be where long-run aggregate supply depends on what has been happening to aggregate demand and supply in the short run.
- Firms may expect changes in aggregate demand to affect the level of sales, not just prices. A reduction in aggregate demand will thus cause a reduction in investment.
- People may suffer from money illusion, even in the long run.

Many labour markets exhibit considerable wage inflexibility. Employers bargain with unions and set wage rates usually for a whole year. If there is a fall in consumer demand, firms usually respond *not* by cutting wages, but rather by laying off workers, or by instituting early retirement, or by not replacing workers when they leave. In the short run, therefore, wages in many sectors of the economy are insensitive to a fall in demand.

In Figure 21.7 assume initially that with aggregate demand for labour at AD_{L1}, the labour market is in equilibrium. The only unemployment is equilibrium unemployment of $b - a$. If there is a fall in the aggregate demand for goods, with prices sticky in the short run, the production of goods goes down, but real wage rates are little affected. The effect on the labour market is felt, therefore, not by a rise in the real wage, but by a fall in the aggregate demand for labour to AD_{L2}, reflecting the lower demand for goods. But with wages sticky downwards, the real wage rate does not fall either. Instead, firms reduce employment from Q_1 to Q_2. There is now demand-deficient unemployment of $a - c$. *Total* unemployment is $b - c$.

This will give a short-run aggregate supply (of goods) curve that is highly elastic below the current wage. A fall in aggregate demand will lead to a large fall in output and only a small fall in prices. The flatter are firms' marginal cost curves, the smaller will be the fall in prices.

But what about the *long* run? Clearly it depends on how long the long run is. Many Keynesians argue that prices and especially wages exhibit a degree of inflexibility over quite a long period of time, and over this period of time, therefore, the aggregate supply curve would not be vertical. What is more, Keynesians argue that the long-run *AS* curve is unlikely to be vertical for a number of other reasons.

Hysteresis. Assume that the economy goes into recession, with a corresponding rise in demand-deficient unemployment and a fall in output. In Figure 21.8, aggregate demand has fallen from AD_{L1} to AD_{L2}. Demand deficient unemployment is $a - b$.

As the recession persists, those previously laid off may not be readily re-employable, especially if they have been out of work for some time and have become deskilled and demoralised. The aggregate supply of labour curve has shifted to the left, perhaps as far as AS_{L2}. In such a case there would now no longer be an excess supply of labour that firms regard as 'employable' ($AD_{L2} = AS_{L2}$). There is no downward pressure on real wages: a long-run equilibrium has been reached. The implication of this is that the long-run aggregate supply (of goods) curve is *not* vertical. A leftward shift in aggregate demand has led to a long-run fall in output.

Assume now that the government pursues a reflationary policy, and that the aggregate demand for labour shifts back to AD_{L1}. There will be a move up along AS_{L2} to point *d*. Unemployment is now $e - d$, higher than the original level of $c - a$.

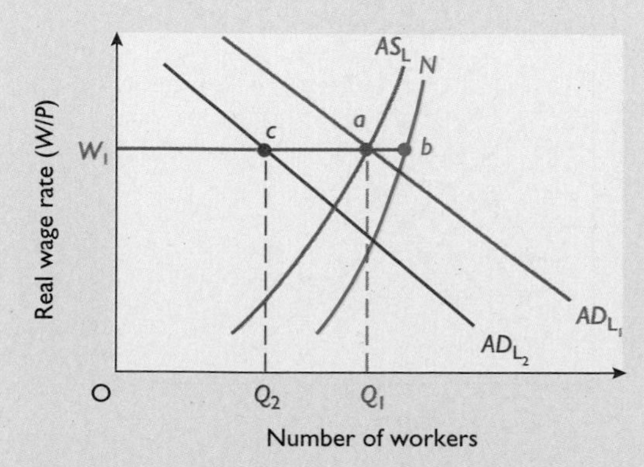

Figure 21.7 Short-run response to a fall in the aggregate demand for labour: sticky wages

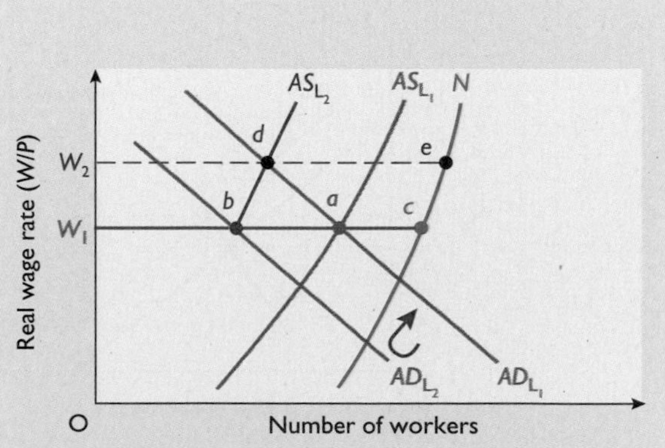

Figure 21.8 The effect on wages and employment of a recovery from recession

Expectations of output. If aggregate demand falls and the economy moves into recession, business confidence will fall and so will investment. The capital stock will therefore fall. This will reduce aggregate supply. Unless confidence quickly returns, and there is no guarantee that it will, the recession may be long lived. The reduction in aggregate supply will be *long* term.

The reduction in the capital stock will magnify the leftward shift in the aggregate demand for labour and increase the level of demand-deficient unemployment.

Long-run money illusion. The problem of demand deficiency will be compounded if there is long-run money illusion. Assume again that there is a fall in aggregate demand. Workers may be reluctant to accept a reduction in money wages, not appreciating that there is a corresponding fall in prices, thus leaving real wages unaffected. Thus real wages may be forced up, compounding the problem of disequilibrium unemployment.

Aggregate demand and supply, and inflation

Aggregate demand and supply analysis can be used to distinguish between demand-pull and cost-push inflation.

Demand-pull inflation

Assume that aggregate demand rises. In Figure 21.9(a), there is some increase in output, and the price level rises from P_0 to P_1. If demand goes on rising, so that the *AD* curve goes on shifting to the right, the price level will go on rising and there will be demand-pull inflation. There will be a movement from point *a* to *b* to *c* in Figure 21.9(b).

But sooner or later the short-run aggregate *supply* curve will start shifting. If the effects of rising costs and rising price expectations offset any stimulus to investment, the short-run *AS* curve will shift upward. This will lead to a falling back of output but a further rise in prices as the economy moves to point *d*. If the government responds by giving a further boost to demand in order to keep expansion going, there will be a movement outward again to point *e*, but a further rise in prices. Then the *AS* curve will probably continue shifting upward and the economy will move to point *f*.

If the government now makes the control of inflation its main policy objective, it may stop any further increases in aggregate demand. Aggregate supply may continue to rise for a while as cost increases and expectations feed through. The economy moves to point *g*. In the extreme case, point *g* may be vertically above point *a*. The only effect of the shift in *AD* to AD_3 has been inflation.

If, however, the increased aggregate demand has increased investment, which in turn has increased capacity sufficiently to absorb all the extra demand, there will be no demand-pull inflation: the long-run *AS* curve is horizontal, or even downward sloping.

Note that, although costs in Figure 21.9(b) have increased and hence the *AS* curves have shifted upward, this is not *cost-push* inflation because the rise in costs is the result of the rise in *demand*.

> **??** If point *g* is vertically above point *a*, does this mean that the long-run *AS* curve is vertical? Are there any circumstances where point *g* might be to the left of point *a*?

Cost-push inflation

Assume that there is some exogenous increase in costs: a sharp increase in world oil prices, or an increase in wages

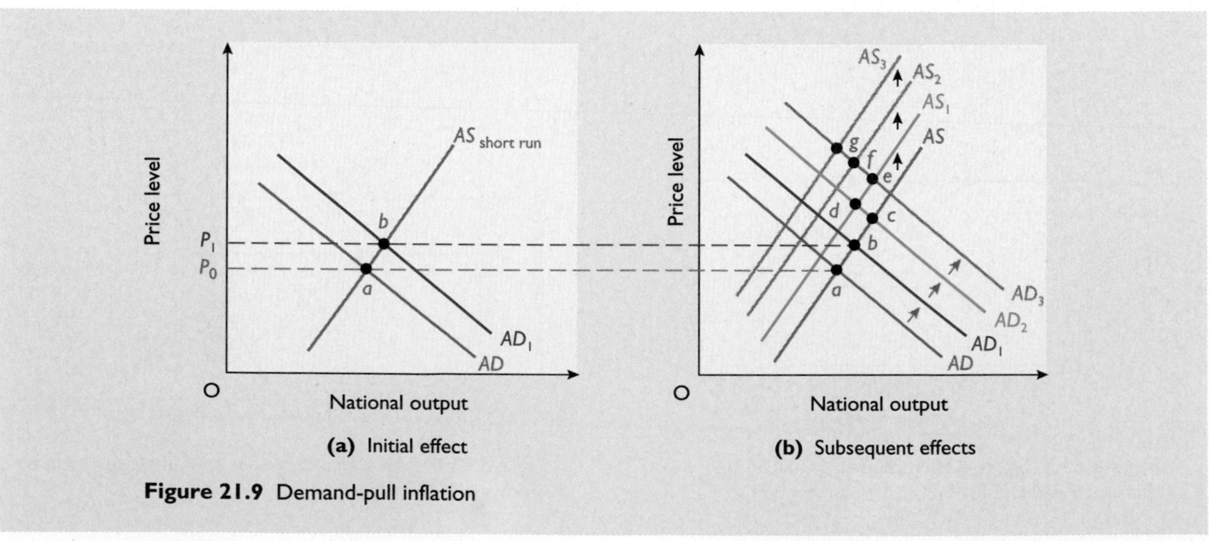

(a) Initial effect

(b) Subsequent effects

Figure 21.9 Demand-pull inflation

EXPLORING THE THEORY BOX 21.1

COST-PUSH INFLATION AND SUPPLY SHOCKS

It is important to distinguish a *single* supply shock, such as the rise in oil prices in 1973 and the increase in VAT from 15 per cent to $17^1/_2$ per cent in 1991, from a continuing upward pressure on costs, such as workers continually demanding increases in real wages above the level of labour productivity, or firms continually using their monopoly power to increase the real value of profits.

A single supply shock will give a *single* upward movement in the *AS* curve. Prices will move to a new higher equilibrium. Cost-push inflation in this case is a *temporary* phenomenon. Once the new higher price level has been reached, the cost-push inflation disappears. If, however, there is a continuous upward pressure on costs, cost-push inflation is likely to continue. It will get worse if the cost pressure intensifies.

due to increased trade union militancy, or firms raising prices to cover the costs of a rise in interest rates. In Figure 21.10(a), the short-run *AS* curve shifts to AS_1. Prices rise to P_1 and there is a fall in national output.

If these increases in costs continue for some time, the *AS* curve will go on shifting upwards. Price rises will continue and there is cost-push inflation. The economy will move from point *a* to *b* to *c* in Figure 21.10(b). Continuous upward shifts in the *AS* curve are particularly likely if there is a continuing struggle between different groups (e.g. unions and employers' organisations) for a larger share of national income.

After a time aggregate demand is likely to rise. This may be due to the government using expansionary fiscal and monetary policies to halt the falling output and employment. Or it may be due to money supply expanding endogenously as workers and firms need larger money balances to allow for increasingly costly transactions. Aggregate demand shifts to AD_1 and there is a movement to point *d*. There may be a further increase in costs and a movement to point *e*, and then a further increase in aggregate demand and so on.

Note again that, although demand has increased, this is not *demand-pull* inflation because the rise in demand is the result of the upward pressure on *costs*.

What causes inflation in practice?

Monetarists blame exogenous rises in money supply. For them inflation is of the demand-pull variety. Some Keynesians also blame rises in demand, but tend to focus on exogenous rises in consumer demand or excessive fiscal expansion rather than monetary expansion. Other Keynesians tend to highlight cost-push factors such as higher wage demands. Most Keynesians argue that there are a mixture of causes.

Unfortunately, the evidence is ambiguous. Probably inflation is a mixture of demand-pull and cost-push, since there are a number of factors that can cause exogenous rises in demand and a number that can cause

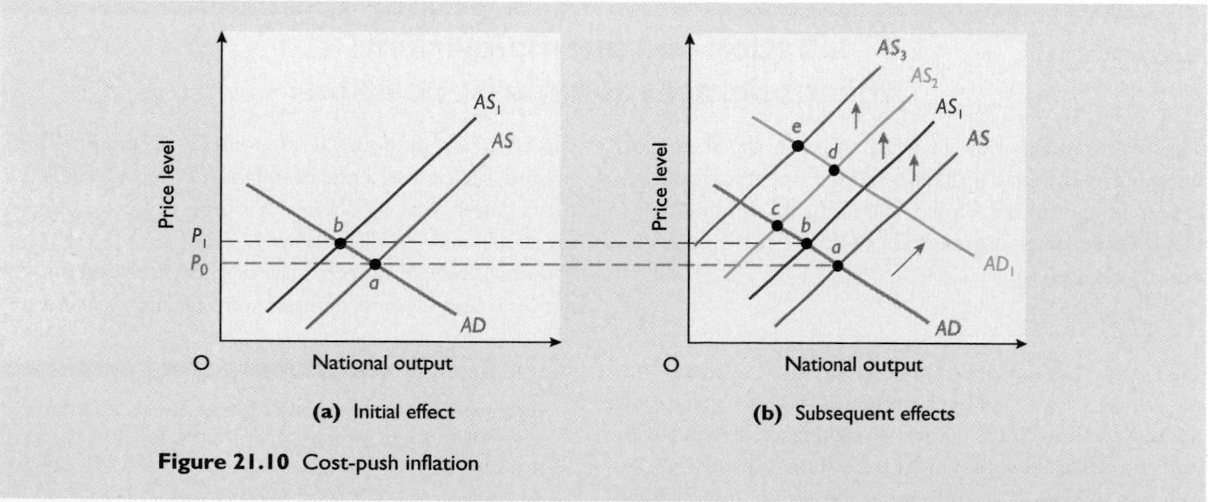

Figure 21.10 Cost-push inflation

exogenous rises in supply. These can occur either at different times or simultaneously.

Aggregate supply, unemployment and inflation

So far in this chapter we have looked at the relationship between aggregate supply, unemployment and the *level* of prices. The modern world, however, is not characterised by single rises in demand and single price rises, or by rising unemployment accompanied by actual falls in the price level. Instead there are the problems of both inflation (*continuously* rising prices) *and* unemployment.

How can the above analysis be extended to cope with the relationship between aggregate supply, unemployment and the *rate of inflation* (rather than the *level* of prices)? The answer lies in theories that develop the old Phillips curve.

The remainder of the chapter, therefore, looks at the ways in which the different schools of thought have modified the Phillips curve to fit in with their assumptions.

SECTION SUMMARY

1. Keynesians argue that the aggregate supply curve is relatively elastic up to the full-employment level of output. Monetarists argue that it is relatively inelastic, and that in the long run it is vertical.
2. The short-run aggregate supply curve depends on firms' short-run marginal cost curves. The more rapidly costs rise as output increases, the less elastic will the *AS* curve be.
3. The long-run *AS* curve will be less elastic (a) the more that cost increases are passed on from one part of the economy to another, (b) the less that increases in aggregate demand stimulate cost-reducing investment and (c) the more that people expect prices to rise as a result of the increase in demand.
4. Monetarists argue that the long-run aggregate supply curve is vertical. This follows from their assumptions of flexible prices and wages, and an absence of money illusion.
5. Keynesians argue that the long-run supply curve will not be vertical. It will be more elastic the greater the problem of hysteresis, the more that firms react to changes in aggregate demand by changing the level of investment and hence the size of the capital stock, and the greater the degree of long-run money illusion.
6. Demand-pull inflation occurs where there is a continuous rightward shift in the *AD* curve. There may also be (upward) shifts in the *AS* curve (e.g. as a result of higher wages), but if these are in response to the higher demand it still constitutes demand-pull inflation.
7. Cost-push inflation occurs where there is a continuous upward shift in the *AS* curve. There may also be rightward shifts in the *AD* curve (e.g. the government responding to higher costs and the resulting higher unemployment by increasing the money supply), but again if these are in response to the higher costs it still constitutes cost-push inflation.
8. In practice it is difficult to separate demand-pull and cost-push inflation as there are often exogenous and endogenous factors affecting both demand and costs simultaneously.

21.2 Inflation and unemployment: the moderate monetarist position

The main contribution of monetarists to the theory of unemployment and inflation is the incorporation of expectations into the Phillips curve. In its simplest form this **expectations-augmented Phillips curve** may be expressed as:

$$\dot{P} = f(1/U) + \dot{P}^e \qquad (1)$$

This states that the rate of price inflation ($\dot{P}$) depends on two things. First, it is a function (f) of the inverse of unemployment ($1/U$). A rise in aggregate demand will lead to a fall in unemployment (a rise in $1/U$) and a rise in inflation. There is a movement up along the Phillips curve, say from point *a* to point *b* in Figure 21.11. Second, the expected rate of inflation $\dot{P}^e$ must be added to the inflation that would result simply from the level of excess demand represented by ($1/U$).

Thus if people expected a 5 per cent inflation ($\dot{P}^e = 5$ per cent) and if excess demand were causing demand-pull

DEFINITION

Expectations-augmented Phillips curve A (short-run) Phillips curve whose position depends on the expected rate of inflation.

Table 21.1 The accelerationist theory of inflation and inflationary expectations

Year	Point on graph	$\dot{P}$	=	$f(1/U)$	+	$\dot{P}^e$
1	*a*	0	=	0	+	0
2	*b*	4	=	4	+	0
3	*c*	4	=	0	+	4
4	*d*	8	=	4	+	4
5	*e*	12	=	4	+	8
6	*f*	16	=	4	+	12

inflation of 3 per cent ($f(1/U) = 3$ per cent), actual inflation would be 8 per cent.

Monetarists develop their model in the framework of market clearing. Wages are not sticky downwards, at least not in the long run. There can be no long-run disequilibrium unemployment: no long-run deficiency of demand.

Adaptive expectations

What determines the expected rate of inflation ($\dot{P}^e$)? The moderate monetarist position is that it depends on inflation rates *in the past*. This is known as the **adaptive expectations hypothesis**. What this means is that people learn from experience. If last year they underpredicted the rate of inflation, then this year they will adapt: they will revise their expectations of inflation upwards.

In its simplest form the adaptive expectations hypothesis assumes that the expected rate of inflation this year ($\dot{P}^e_t$) will be the rate that inflation actually was last year ($\dot{P}_{t-1}$):

$$\dot{P}^e_t = \dot{P}_{t-1} \qquad (2)$$

To keep the analysis straightforward we will stick to this simple version of the adaptive expectations hypothesis.

Figure 21.11 A Phillips curve

Shifts in the short-run Phillips curve and the accelerationist theory

Let us trace the course of inflation and expectations over a number of years in an imaginary economy. To keep the analysis simple, assume there is no growth in the economy.

Year 1. Assume that at the outset, in year 1, there is no inflation of any sort; that none is expected; that $AD = AS$; and that equilibrium unemployment is 8 per cent. The economy will be at point *a* in Figure 21.12 and Table 21.1.

Year 2. Now assume that the government expands aggregate demand in order to reduce unemployment. Unemployment falls to 6 per cent. The economy moves to point *b* along curve I. Inflation has risen to 4 per cent, but people, basing their expectations of inflation on year

DEFINITION

Adaptive expectations hypothesis The theory that people base their expectations of inflation on past inflation rates.

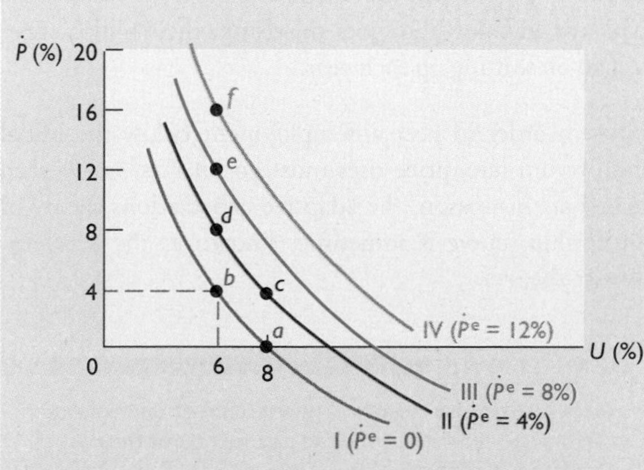

Figure 21.12 The accelerationist theory of inflation and inflationary expectations

1, still expect a zero inflation. There is therefore no shift as yet in the Phillips curve. Curve I corresponds to an expected rate of inflation of zero.

Year 3. People now revise their expectations of inflation to the level of year 2. The Phillips curve shifts up by 4 percentage points to position II. If aggregate *monetary* demand continues to rise at the same rate, the whole of the increase will now be absorbed in higher prices. *Real* aggregate demand will fall back to its previous level and the economy will move to point *c*. Unemployment will return to 8 per cent. There is no *demand-pull* inflation now, ($f(1/U) = 0$), but inflation is still 4 per cent due to expectations ($\dot{P}^e = 4$ per cent).

Year 4. Assume now that the government, not happy with the rise in unemployment back to 8 per cent, expands *real* aggregate demand again so as to reduce unemployment once more to 6 per cent. This time it must expand aggregate *monetary* demand by *more* than it did in year 2, because this time, as well as reducing unemployment, it also has to validate the 4 per cent expected inflation. The economy moves to point *d* along curve II. Inflation is now 8 per cent.

Year 5. *Expected* inflation is now 8 per cent (the level of actual inflation in year 4). The Phillips curve shifts up to position III. If at the same time the government now tries to keep unemployment at 6 per cent, it must expand aggregate monetary demand 4 per cent faster in order to validate the 8 per cent expected inflation. The economy moves to point *e* along curve III. Inflation is now 12 per cent.

Year 6. To keep unemployment at 6 per cent, the government must continue to increase aggregate monetary demand by 4 per cent more than the previous year. As the expected inflation rate goes on rising, the Phillips curve will go on shifting up each year.

Thus in order to keep unemployment below the initial equilibrium rate, price rises must go on *accelerating* each year. For this reason, the adaptive expectations theory of the Phillips curve is sometimes known as the **accelerationist theory**.

The more the government reduces unemployment, the greater the rise in inflation that year, and the more the rise in expectations the following year and each subsequent year; and hence the more rapidly will price rises accelerate. Thus the true longer-term trade-off is between unemployment and the rate of *increase* in inflation.

$$\Delta\dot{P} = f(1/U) \tag{3}$$

($\Delta\dot{P}$ may be written $\ddot{P}$.)

Note that the upward shift in the Phillips curve will be less rapid if expectations do not fully adjust to last year's inflation rate. The upward shift will be more rapid if expectations adjust to the rate of *increase* in inflation last year ($\Delta\dot{P}_{t-1}$).

?? Construct a table like Table 21.1, only this time assume that the government wishes to reduce unemployment to 5 per cent. Assume that every year from year 1 onwards the government is prepared to expand aggregate demand by whatever it takes to do this. If this expansion of demand gives $f(1/U) = 7$ per cent, fill in the table for the first six years. Do you think that after a couple of years people might begin to base their expectations differently?

The long-run Phillips curve and the natural rate of unemployment

As long as there are demand-pull pressures ($f(1/U) > 0$), inflation will rise as the expected rate of inflation ($\dot{P}^e$) rises. In the long run, therefore, the Phillips curve will be vertical (see Figure 21.13) at the rate of unemployment where real aggregate demand equals *real* aggregate supply. This is the rate of unemployment that monetarists call the *natural rate* (U_n). It is sometimes also known as the **non-accelerating-inflation rate of unemployment (NAIRU)**.[1]

The implication for government policy is that expansionary monetary and fiscal policy can only reduce unemployment below U_n in the *short* run. In the long run, the effect will be purely inflationary.

[1] Strictly speaking, the NAIRU is theoretically different from the natural rate in that it is based on the assumption of imperfect competition, price and wage stickiness and hysteresis: in other words, on Keynesian assumptions. The NAIRU is thus merely the rate of unemployment at which inflation is constant. We look at the NAIRU in section 21.4.

DEFINITIONS

Accelerationist theory The theory that unemployment can only be reduced below the natural rate at the cost of accelerating inflation.

Natural rate of unemployment or non-accelerating-inflation rate of unemployment (NAIRU) The rate of unemployment consistent with a constant rate of inflation: the rate of unemployment at which the vertical long-run Phillips curve cuts the horizontal axis.

EXPLORING THE THEORY *BOX 21.2

BASING EXPECTATIONS ON THE PAST
More sophisticated adaptive expectations models

More complex adaptive expectations models assume that $\dot{P}^e$ is a weighted average of past rates of inflation:

$$\dot{P}^e_t = a\dot{P}_{t-1} + b\dot{P}_{t-2} + c\dot{P}_{t-3} \ldots + m\dot{P}_{t-n} \quad (4)$$

where $a + b + c \ldots + m = 1$, and where $a > b > c$, etc.

In other words, people will base their expectations of inflation on the actual inflation rates over the last few years, but with last year's inflation having a bigger influence on people's expectations than the previous year's and so on.

In times of rapidly *accelerating* inflation, people may adjust their expectations of inflation upward by the amount that inflation *rose* last year (ΔP_{t-1}). This gives:

$$\Delta\dot{P}^e_t = \Delta\dot{P}_{t-1} \quad (5)$$

?? Under what circumstances will term *a* in equation (4) be large relative to terms *b*, *c*, etc.?

?? What will determine the speed at which inflation accelerates?

The effects of deflation

Let us now move on a few years from Table 21.1. Assume that the economy has returned to the natural rate of unemployment: $f(1/U) = 0$. The economy is therefore on the long-run Phillips curve. But, due to past excess demand, the expected rate of inflation is 20 per cent. The economy is thus at point *j* on short-run Phillips curve X in Figure 21.14.

The government now decides to make the control of inflation its main priority. It therefore reduces the growth of aggregate monetary demand *below* the rate of inflation. Real aggregate demand falls. Let us assume that there is a 2 per cent downward pressure on inflation: $f(1/U) = -2$. Inflation thus falls to 18%. But unemployment rises, let us assume, from 8 per cent to 13 per cent. The economy moves along curve X to point *k*.

Next year the expected rate of inflation will fall to 18 per cent to match, and if real demand is still being deflated by the same amount ($f(1/U) = -2$), actual inflation will fall to 16 per cent. The economy moves to point *l* on curve XI.

If the government maintains unemployment at 13 per cent, inflation will continue to fall by 2 per cent a year. After ten years of unemployment at 13 per cent the economy could return to point *a*, with unemployment falling back to U_n.

?? Construct a table like Table 21.1, only this time assume that in year 1 the economy is in recession with high unemployment, but also high inflation due to high inflationary expectations as a result of past excess demand. Assume that in year 1, $\dot{P}$ = 30 per cent, $f(1/U) = -6$ per cent and $\dot{P}^e$ = 36 per cent. Continue the table for as many years as it takes for inflation to be 'squeezed out' of the economy (assuming that the government keeps aggregate demand at a low enough level to maintain $f(1/U) = -6$ per cent throughout).

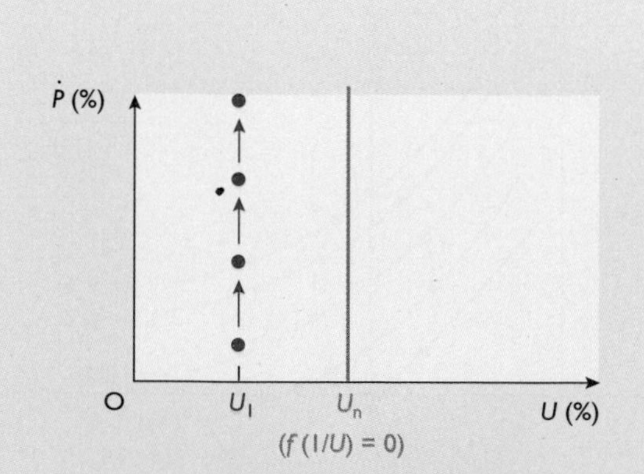

Figure 21.13 The long-run Phillips 'curve'

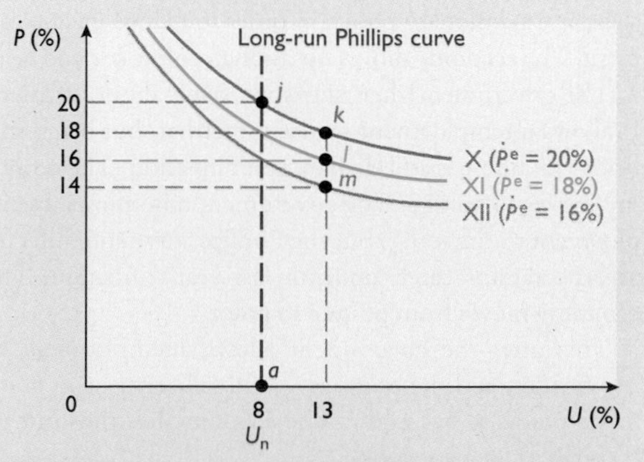

Figure 21.14 The effects of deflation

How quickly can inflation be eliminated?

The short-run Phillips curve may be relatively shallow to the right of U_n. The more sticky downwards wages and prices are in the short run, the shallower the curve will be. Thus to get a relatively rapid fall in inflation, unemployment may have to be very high indeed.

Moderate monetarists therefore present two alternative routes to eliminating inflation.

The quick route. This involves a *severe* deflation. Unemployment rises to very high rates and the economy is plunged into a deep recession. However, the short-run Phillips curve shifts down fairly rapidly as the expected rate of inflation ($\dot{P}^e$) falls quite quickly. Inflation may be squeezed out of the economy within two or three years. This approach could be called the 'short, sharp shock'.

The slow route. This involves a *mild* deflation. Unemployment rises perhaps one or two percentage points above the natural rate. Inflation falls only slightly in the first year, and thus $\dot{P}^e$ falls only slowly the next year and each subsequent year. Although less painful, this approach may take many years to eliminate inflation.

Explanations of stagflation

The moderate monetarist explanation of stagflation – the simultaneous rise in both unemployment and inflation – can now be presented quite simply. There are two possibilities: clockwise loops and rightward shifts in the long-run Phillips curve.

Clockwise Phillips loops

Consider a ten-year cycle. This is illustrated in Figure 21.15. The economy starts at position *a* in year 0. There is no inflation and the economy is at the natural rate of unemployment. The government over the next three years pursues an expansionary policy in order to reduce unemployment. The economy moves up through points *b*, *c* and *d*.

The government then starts worrying about inflation. It allows unemployment to rise somewhat, but being still below U_n, there is still demand-pull inflation. The economy moves to point *e*. The government now allows unemployment to rise to U_n, but the Phillips curve still shifts up as expectations catch up with last year's inflation. The economy moves from point *e* to point *f*.

Thereafter the government allows unemployment to rise further, and the economy eventually returns to point *a*, via points *g*, *h*, *i* and *j*. The economy has thus moved through a clockwise loop.

Stagflation is easy to see. From points *d* to *f*, both unemployment *and* inflation are rising. What is more, several points are to the 'north-east' of other earlier points. For example, point *g* is north-east of point *c*. In other words, inflation *and* unemployment in year 6 (point *g*) are worse than in year 2 (point *c*).

?? Under what circumstances would a Phillips loop be (a) tall and thin; (b) short and wide?

Rightward shifts in the long-run Phillips curve

If frictional or structural unemployment rises (due, say, to increased unemployment benefits), U_n will increase. The long-run Phillips curve will shift to the right.

Assume that the economy was initially on the long-run Phillips curve with U_n = 8 per cent and a stable inflation rate of 5 per cent. U_n now rises to 12 per cent. The government uses demand management policy to keep the rise in unemployment to only 10 per cent. But this is now *below* U_n and thus inflation will increase. Thus both inflation *and* unemployment have risen.

Evidence

The evidence for the UK since 1971 fits in with the above moderate monetarist explanation. (But note that it also fits in with other explanations too!) In Figure 21.16 loops can clearly be seen. At the same time, U_n would seem to be increasing from about 2.5 per cent in 1972/3 to about 4.4 per cent in 1978 to over 10 per cent in 1985, and then falling to about 8 per cent in the late 1980s and early 1990s.

Policy implications

Monetarists make a sharp distinction between demand-side policies (which for them means monetary policy) and supply-side policies.

Monetary policy in the long run can only be used to control inflation and not unemployment. It will merely move the economy up or down the long-run Phillips

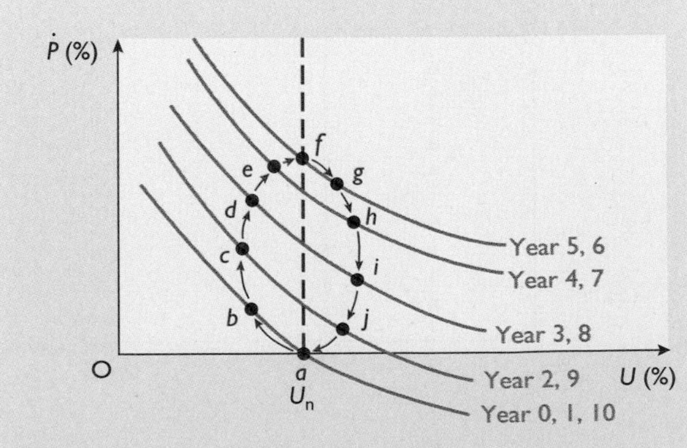

Figure 21.15 Clockwise Phillips loops

ISSUES AND APPLICATIONS — BOX 21.3

THE POLITICAL BUSINESS CYCLE (PART II)[2]

The art of looping the loop

Imagine that a politically naïve government has been fulfilling election promises to cure unemployment, cut taxes and increase welfare spending. In Figure 21.15 this is shown by a move from points *a* to *b* to *c*.

To its dismay, by the time the next election comes, inflation is accelerating and unemployment is rising again. The economy is moving from point *d* to *e* to *f*. You would hardly be surprised to learn that it loses the election!

But now suppose a much more politically adroit government is elected. What does it do? The answer is that it does politically unpopular things at first, so that before the next election it can do nice things and curry favour with the electorate.

The first thing it does is to have a tough Budget and to raise interest rates. 'We are having to clear up the economic mess left by the last government.' It thus engineers a recession and begins to squeeze down inflationary expectations. The economy moves from point *f* to *g* to *h*.

But people have very short memories (despite opposition attempts to remind them). After a couple of years of misery, the government announces that the economy has 'begun to turn the corner'. Things are looking up. Inflation has fallen and unemployment has stopped rising. The economy has moved from point *h* to *i* to *j*.

'Thanks to prudent management of the economy', claims the Chancellor, 'I am now in a position to reduce taxes and to allow modest increases in government expenditure.' Unemployment falls rapidly; the economy grows rapidly; the economy moves from point *j* to *a* to *b*.

The government's popularity soars; the pre-election 'give-away' Budget is swallowed by the electorate who trustingly believe that similar ones will follow if the government is returned to office. The government wins the election.

Then comes the nasty medicine again. But who will be blamed this time?

??

1. Why might a government sometimes 'get it wrong' and find itself at the wrong part of the Phillips loop at the time of an election?
2. Which electoral system would most favour a government being re-elected: the US fixed-term system with presidents being elected every four years, or the UK system where the government can choose to hold an election any time within five years of the last one?

[2] See Box 14.4 for part I.

curve. Given that inflation is undesirable, monetarists argue for a tight control over money supply. Expansionary monetary policy could only ever bring a *temporary* reduction in unemployment below U_n. But likewise a deflationary monetary policy will bring only a temporary rise in unemployment above U_n.

To reduce unemployment permanently, *supply-side* policies should be used. For monetarists this means policies to reduce impediments to the working of the free market (see section 22.2). By reducing frictional and/or structural unemployment, such policies will shift the long-run Phillips curve back to the left.

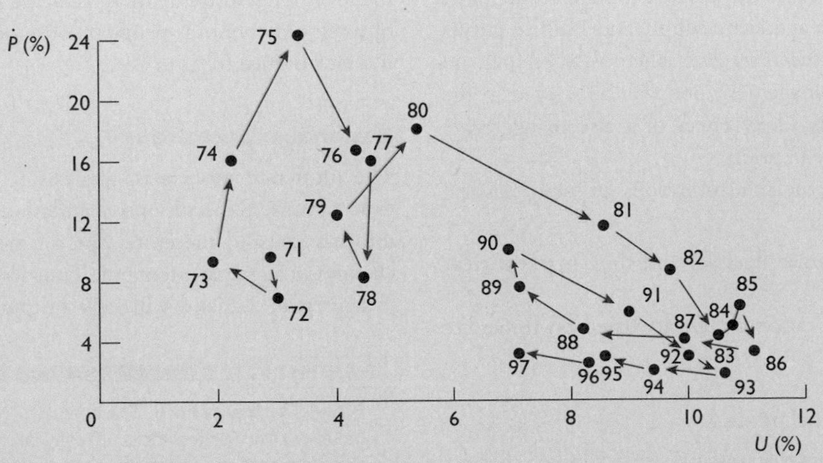

Figure 21.16 Phillips loops in the UK?

SECTION SUMMARY

1. The moderate monetarist analysis of the relationship between inflation and unemployment is based on the adaptive expectations hypothesis. In its simplest form the hypothesis states that the expected rate of inflation this year is what it actually was last year: $\dot{P}^e_t = \dot{P}_{t-1}$.
2. If there is excess demand in the economy, producing upward pressure on wages and prices, initially unemployment will fall. The reason is that workers and firms will believe that wage and price increases represent *real* wage and price increases. Thus workers are prepared to take jobs more readily and firms choose to produce more. But as people's expectations adapt upwards to these higher wages and prices, so ever increasing rises in aggregate monetary demand will be necessary to maintain unemployment below the natural rate. Price and wage rises will accelerate: i.e. inflation will rise.
3. The Phillips curve, according to monetarist analysis, is thus vertical at the natural rate of unemployment.
4. If an economy suffering from high inflation is deflated, initially unemployment will rise above the natural rate. But as expectations adapt downwards, so the short-run Phillips curve will shift downwards and inflation will fall. Eventually the economy will return to zero inflation at the natural rate of unemployment.
5. This position can be reached more quickly if the government deflates sharply, but then in the short run the rate of unemployment may rise substantially above the natural rate.
6. Stagflation can be explained in this model either by a movement from 9 o'clock to 12 o'clock round a clockwise Phillips loop, or by a rightward shift in the vertical Phillips curve combined with a mild reflationary policy.
7. The evidence since 1970 is consistent with clockwise Phillips loops.

21.3 Inflation and unemployment: the new classical position

Over the last twenty years or so the **new classical school** has gained a considerable following. Leading exponents of new classical macroeconomics include Robert Lucas and Thomas Sargent in the USA and Patrick Minford in the UK.

The *moderate* monetarists argue that the aggregate supply and Phillips curves are vertical in the long run. The policy implication of this is that demand management can have no effect on *long*-run output and employment.

The *new classical* economists take a more extreme view. They argue that the aggregate supply and Phillips curves are vertical also in the *short run*. There is, therefore, no role for demand management policy at all – even in the short run. The only likely effect of a rise in aggregate demand will be a rise in prices.

There are two crucial assumptions in new classical macroeconomics:

- Prices and wages are flexible, and thus markets clear very rapidly.
- Expectations are 'rational', but are based on imperfect information.

Flexible wages and prices

The moderate monetarists assume that markets have a tendency to clear. Prices and wages are fairly flexible, and therefore disequilibrium unemployment is merely a temporary phenomenon. This was also the position of the classical economists of the 1920s and 1930s.

The new classical economists take this further. They assume that markets clear virtually instantaneously. There is thus no disequilibrium unemployment, even in the short run. All unemployment, therefore, is *equilibrium* unemployment, or 'voluntary unemployment' as new classical economists tend to call it. Increases in unemployment are therefore due to an increase in the natural level of unemployment, as people choose not to take jobs due to a lack of incentives to do so.

Rational expectations

The moderate monetarist analysis is based on *adaptive* expectations. Expectations of inflation are based on *past* information and therefore take a time to catch up with changes in aggregate demand. Thus for a short time a rise in aggregate demand will raise output and employment

DEFINITION

New classical school The school of economists which believes that markets clear virtually instantaneously and that expectations are formed 'rationally'.

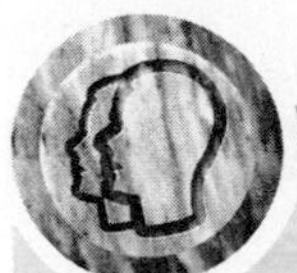

DEVELOPMENT OF IDEAS — BOX 21.4

THE RATIONAL EXPECTATIONS REVOLUTION

Trying to 'unfool' the economics profession

The rational expectations revolution swept through the economics profession in the 1970s in a way that no other set of ideas had done since Keynes. Although largely associated with the free-market, non-interventionist wing of economics, the rational expectations revolution has been far more wide reaching. Even economists implacably opposed to the free market have nevertheless incorporated rational expectations into their models.

The rational expectations revolution is founded on a very simple idea. People base their expectations of the future on the information they have available. They don't just look at the past, they also look at current information, including what the government is saying and doing and what various commentators have to say.

The new classical economists use rational expectations in the following context. If the *long-run* Phillips curve is vertical, so that an expansionary policy will in the end merely lead to inflation, it will be difficult for the government to fool people that this will not happen. If employers, unions, city financiers, economic advisers, journalists, etc. all expect this to happen, then it will do: and it will happen in the *short run*. Why should firms produce more in response to a rise in demand if their costs are going to rise by just as much? Why should higher wages attract workers to move jobs, if wages everywhere are going up? Why should firms and unions not seek price and wage rises fully in line with the expected inflation?

But can the government not surprise people? The point here is that 'surprising' people really only means 'fooling' them – making them believe that an expansionary policy really *will* reduce unemployment. But why should the public be fooled? Why should people believe smooth-talking government ministers rather than the whole host of critics of the government, from the opposition, to economic commentators, to the next-door neighbour?

The rational expectations school revised the old saying, 'You can't fool all the people all the time' to 'You can hardly fool the people at all.' And if that is so, argue the new classical economists, unemployment can only momentarily be brought below its natural level.

Two of the most famous rational expectations economists are Robert Lucas and Thomas Sargent. Robert Lucas, like Milton Friedman and many other famous conservative economists, has his academic base in the University of Chicago, where he has been a professor since 1974. In 1995, like Milton Friedman in 1976, Lucas was awarded the Nobel prize in economics. Tom Sargent was professor at the University of Minnesota but is now also at the University of Chicago.

Both Lucas and Sargent have written extensively on the subject and have developed highly complex models: complex in the way in which the expectations themselves are modelled, and complex in the way in which they are incorporated into the models of the economy. They have both undertaken extensive testing of their models, involving sophisticated econometric techniques – far too sophisticated (you will be relieved to know) for beginning students!

In recent years they have gone beyond the simple context of the new classical world of perfect markets with instant market clearing, and have considered the role of rational expectations when markets are distorted. In this context, government policy *can* be effective. For example, supply-side policies can be directed to removing market distortions.

above the natural level, while prices and wages are still relatively low.

The new classical analysis is based on **rational expectations**. Rational expectations are not based on past rates of inflation. Instead they are based on the current state of the economy and the current policies being pursued by the government. Workers and firms look at the information available to them – at the various forecasts that are published, at various economic indicators and the assessments of them by various commentators, at government pronouncements, etc. Then, on the basis of this information, they predict as well as they can what the rate of inflation will be. It is in this sense that the expectations are 'rational': people use their reason to assess the future on the basis of current information.

But forecasters frequently get it wrong, and so do economic commentators! And the government does not always do what it says it will. Thus workers and firms will be basing expectations on *imperfect information*. Some versions of rational expectations theory assume that workers and firms will make the best forecasts possible on the basis of this imperfect information. Other versions assume

DEFINITION

Rational expectations Expectations based on the *current* situation. These expectations are based on the information people have to hand. While this information may be imperfect and therefore people will make errors, these errors will be random.

ISSUES AND APPLICATIONS BOX 21.5

FORECASTING THE WEATHER: AN EXAMPLE OF RATIONAL EXPECTATIONS

'What's the weather going to be like tomorrow?' If you are thinking of having a picnic, you will want to know the answer before deciding.

So what do you do? You could base your assessment on past information. Yesterday was fine; so was the previous day. Today is glorious. So, you think to yourself, it's a good bet that tomorrow will be fine too. If, on the other hand, the weather has been very changeable recently, you may feel that it's wiser not to take the risk. These 'forecasts' are examples of *adaptive* expectations: your forecasts are based on the actual weather over the last few days.

But would you really base such a crucial decision as to whether or not to have a picnic on something so unreliable? Wouldn't you rather take on board more information to help you make up your mind?

The first thing that might come to mind is the old saying that a British summer is three fine days and a thunder storm. We've just had the three fine days, you think to yourself, so perhaps we'd better stay at home tomorrow.

Or, being a bit more scientific about it, you turn on the weather forecast. Seeing loads of sunshine symbols all over the map, you decide to take a chance.

Basing your expectations this way on current information (including even seeing whether there is a red sky that night) is an example of *rational* expectations.

So you go on your picnic, and, guess what, it rains!

'I bet if we had decided to stay at home it would have been fine', you grumble, as you eat your soggy sandwiches.

What you are acknowledging is that your decision was made on *imperfect* information. But the decision was still rational. It was still the best decision you could have made on the information available to you.

Weather forecasters make mistakes. But they are just as likely to get it wrong in predicting a sunny day as in predicting a wet day. It is still rational to base your decisions on their forecasts provided they are reasonably accurate.

?? Under what circumstances might weather forecasters have a tendency to err on the side of pessimism or optimism? If you knew this tendency, how would this affect your decisions about picnics, hanging out the washing or watering the garden?

that they may make very poor use of this information. But either way, people will frequently forecast incorrectly.

The crucial point about the rational expectations theory is that these errors in prediction are *random*. People's predictions of inflation are just as likely to be too high as too low.[3]

Aggregate supply and the Phillips curve when expectations are correct

If people are correct in their expectations, and if the long-run aggregate supply and Phillips curves are vertical, so too will be the short-run curves. In the moderate monetarist (adaptive expectations) model, the short-run *AS* curve is upward sloping (and the short-run Phillips curve downward sloping) only because expectations lag behind any changes in aggregate demand. Once expectations have adapted, the effect is felt purely in terms of price changes. Output and employment stay at the natural level in the long run.

In the new classical (rational expectations) model, there is *no* lag in expectations. If their information is correct, people will rationally predict that output and employment will stay at the natural level. They predict that any change in aggregate *monetary* demand will be reflected purely in terms of changes in prices, and that real aggregate demand will remain the same. If real aggregate demand remains the same, so will the demand for and supply of labour and the demand for and supply of goods. Thus, even in the *short* run, output and employment will stay at the natural level.

Let us see how the adaptive expectations and the rational expectations models analyse the effects of an increase in aggregate demand. Figure 21.17 uses simple aggregate demand and supply curves. Diagram (a) gives the adaptive expectations analysis. Diagram (b) gives the rational expectations analysis.

In both diagrams there is an initial equilibrium at point *a*. This is a long-run equilibrium, where aggregate demand (AD_1) equals long-run aggregate supply (*LRAS*). Price is stable and is at the level of P_1. The short-run sup-

[3] The rational expectations hypothesis can be stated as:

$$\dot{P}_t = \dot{P}^e_t + \epsilon_t \left(\sum_{t=1}^{t=\infty} \epsilon = 0 \right)$$

In other words, the rate of inflation for any time period ($\dot{P}_t$) will be the rate that people expected in that time period ($\dot{P}^e_t$) plus an error term (ϵ_t). This error term may be quite large but is equally likely to be positive or negative. Thus when you sum (Σ) the error terms over the years (strictly speaking to infinity) the positive and negative values will cancel each other out and the sum will therefore be zero.

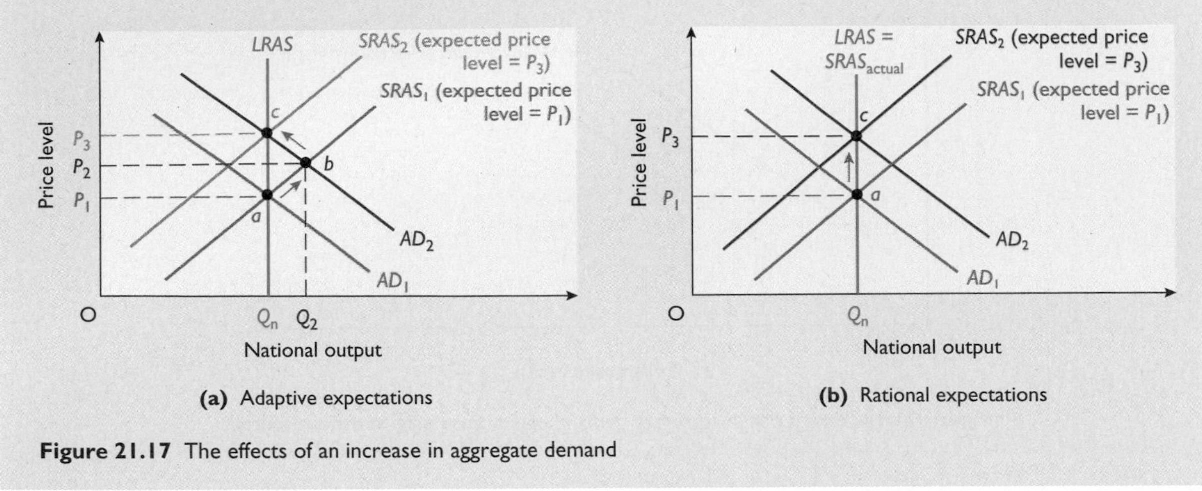

Figure 21.17 The effects of an increase in aggregate demand

ply curve with P_1 as the *expected* price level is given by $SRAS_1$. Note that this is upward sloping in *both* diagrams because it shows how much will be supplied *if* (and only if) people expect price to remain at P_1.

Now assume that the government raises aggregate demand to AD_2. What will happen to prices and output?

In Figure 21.17(a), people base their expectations of prices on the past. In other words, at first they expect the price level to stay at P_1. The economy thus moves to point *b*, where $AD_2 = SRAS_1$. Output rises to Q_2 and the price level rises to P_2. Then over time, as price expectations rise, the short-run aggregate supply curve shifts upwards, eventually reaching $SRAS_2$. Long-run equilibrium is thus at point *c*, where $AD_2 = LRAS$. In the short run, therefore, if the government expands aggregate demand there will be a rise in output and employment. It is only in the long run that the effect is confined to higher prices. The actual length of time it takes to reach point *c* will depend on how quickly expectations adjust upwards.

In Figure 21.17(b), people correctly anticipate the full price effects of any increase in aggregate demand. The short-run aggregate supply curve based on a particular price (e.g. $SRAS_1$ based on a price level P_1) cannot be moved along. The moment aggregate demand shifts to the right, people will correctly anticipate a rise in the price level. Thus the moment the economy begins to move up along $SRAS_1$ from point *a*, the whole *SRAS* curve will shift upwards. As a result the economy moves *directly* to point *c*. Thus the *actual* short-run supply curve is vertical and, assuming expectations are correct, will be identical to the long-run 'curve'.

?? Show these effects of an increase in aggregate demand from both the adaptive expectations and rational expectations points of view, only this time show the effects on Phillips curves.

Aggregate supply and the Phillips curve when expectations are incorrect

Although over the years people's expectations are assumed to be correct on average, it is more than likely that in any one year they will be wrong. What implication does this have for output and employment?

The goods market

Assume that aggregate demand increases but that firms *under*predict the resulting rate of inflation: $\dot{P}^e < \dot{P}$. Firms do not realise that the increased expenditure on their product will be offset by an increase in costs. As a result, as profit maximisers, they decide to produce more. Thus if the government catches people unawares and unexpectedly boosts demand, then output will rise as firms, underpredicting the rate of inflation, believe that *real* demand has risen.

But in a rational expectations framework, this is just luck on the government's side. Firms might just as well have thought the government would give an even bigger boost to aggregate demand than it actually did. In this case firms would have *over* predicted the rate of inflation, and as a result would have cut their output, believing that real demand had fallen.

This cut in output is illustrated in Figure 21.18. Aggregate demand is initially at AD_1 and the short-run aggregate supply curve based on an expected price of P_1 is given by $SRAS_1$. The long-run aggregate supply curve is vertical at the natural level of output. Firms predict that the government will boost aggregate demand to AD_2 and thus adjust their price expectations to P_2: the short-run aggregate supply curve shifts to $SRAS_2$. But this turns out to be an *over*prediction of price increases: aggregate demand rises only to AD_3, and thus the price level rises only to P_3. The result is that output *falls* to Q_3.

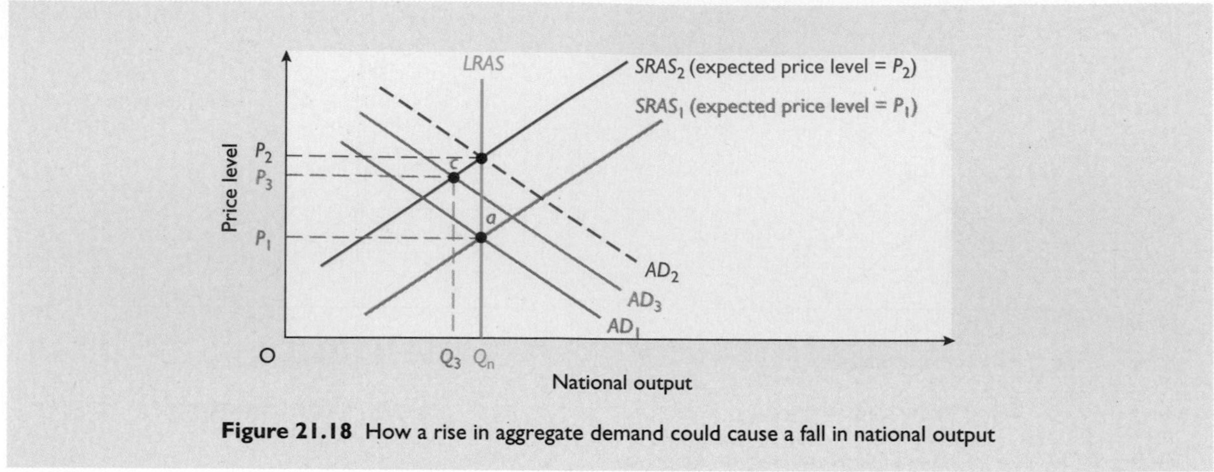

Figure 21.18 How a rise in aggregate demand could cause a fall in national output

?? Show diagrammatically how an *underprediction* of inflation would lead to a *rise* in output if the government raised aggregate demand.

The labour market

Let us assume that the government raises aggregate demand more than people expect so that people underpredict the rate of inflation: $\dot{P}^e < \dot{P}$.

This means that workers will believe that they are getting a higher real wage (W/P) than they really are: $(W/P)^e > W/P$. They will supply more labour. In Figure 21.19, the labour supply curve shifts from AS_{L1} to AS_{L2}. Employment rises above the natural level Q_1 (where expectations are correct), to Q_2. If only labour (and not firms) underpredict the rate of inflation, this rise in employment to Q_2 is the only short-run effect.

If, however, firms underpredict the rate of inflation too, the effect on employment will be more complicated. On the one level, as explained above, firms will want to produce more, and thus the demand for labour will tend to increase. For example, it might shift to AD_{L2} in Figure 21.19, and thus employment would rise to Q_3. On the other hand, given that they are underpredicting the rate of inflation, they will believe that any given level of money wages (W) represents a higher level of *real* wages $(W/P)^e$ than it really does (W/P). They will tend, therefore, to employ fewer people at each wage rate, and the demand curve will shift to the left. Thus, depending on which way the demand curve shifts, firms could employ more or less labour than Q_2.

If people *over*predict the rate of inflation, employment will fall as workers believe that their real wage is lower than it really is and therefore work less; and output may well fall as firms believe their product's relative price has fallen.

Thus output and employment can vary from their natural level when people make errors in their predictions of inflation. But the short-run *AS* and Phillips curves will still be vertical because these errors are random. Errors in prediction simply shift the curves. Underprediction of inflation shifts the short-run Phillips curve to the left (and the *AS* curve to the right) as unemployment temporarily falls below the natural level (and output rises above its natural level). Overprediction of inflation shifts the Phillips curve to the right (and the *AS* curve to the left). This is shown in Figure 21.20. The average position for the short-run Phillips curve will be at U_n.

?? Should the government therefore simply give up as far as curing unemployment is concerned? (For the answer, see below.)

Policy implications

If the new classical analysis is correct, anticipated changes in aggregate demand will have no effect on output and employment. *Un*anticipated changes in aggregate demand will have some effect, but only for as long as it takes people to realise their mistake and for their wages and prices to be corrected. Given rational expectations, people can be fooled in this way only by luck. There is no way that a government can *systematically* use demand management policy to keep output and employment above the natural level.

The new classical economists therefore totally reject Keynesian demand management policy, even in the short run. Monetary policy should be used to control inflation, but neither fiscal nor monetary policy can be used to increase output and employment. Similarly, there is no fear of a deflationary monetary policy reducing output

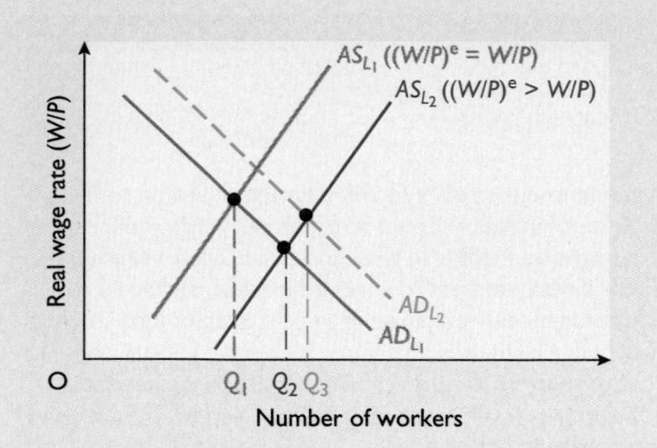

Figure 21.19 Effects in the labour market of an underprediction of inflation

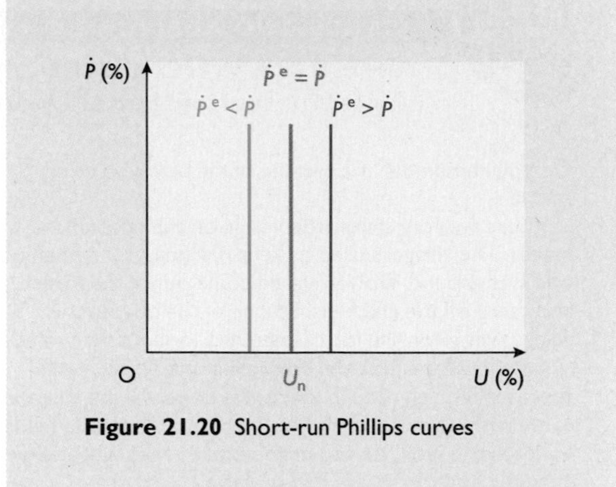

Figure 21.20 Short-run Phillips curves

and employment and leading to a recession. The reduction in aggregate demand will simply lead to lower inflation. Output and unemployment will remain at the natural level.

Thus for new classicists, the problems of inflation and unemployment are totally separate. Inflation is caused by excessive growth in the money supply and should be controlled by monetary policy. Unemployment will be at the natural rate and should be reduced by supply-side policies designed to increase the incentives to work.

To prevent unanticipated changes in aggregate demand and thus to prevent unemployment deviating from its natural level, new classical economists, like moderate monetarists, advocate the announcement of clear monetary rules and then sticking to them.

?? If the government announced that it would, come what may, reduce the growth of money supply to *zero* next year, what (according to new classical economists) would happen? How might their answer be criticised?

Real business cycles

If unemployment and output fluctuate only *randomly* from the natural level, and then only in the short run, how can the new classical economists explain booms and recessions? How can they explain the business cycle? Their answer, unlike Keynesians, lies not in fluctuations in aggregate demand. Rather it lies in shifts in aggregate *supply*. In a recession, the vertical short- and long-run aggregate supply curves will shift to the left (output falls) and the vertical short- and long-run Phillips curves will shift to the right (unemployment rises). The reverse happens in a boom. Since the new classical theory of cyclical fluctuations focuses on supply, it is known as **real business cycle theory**.

But what causes aggregate supply to shift in the first place, and why, once there has been an initial shift, will the aggregate supply curve *go on* shifting, causing a recession or boom to continue?

The initial shift in aggregate supply could come from a structural change: say, a shift in demand from older manufacturing industries to new service industries. Because of the immobility of labour, not all those laid off in the older industries will find work in the new industries. Structural unemployment (part of equilibrium unemployment) rises and output falls. *Aggregate* demand may be the same, but because of a change in its pattern, aggregate supply shifts to the left and the Phillips curve shifts to the right.

Alternatively the initial shift in aggregate supply could come from a change in technology. For example, a technological breakthrough in telecommunications could shift aggregate supply to the right. Or it could come from an oil price increase, shifting aggregate supply to the left.

But why, when a shift occurs, does the effect persist? Why is there not a single rise or fall in aggregate supply? There are two main reasons. The first is that several changes may take months to complete. For example, a decline in demand for certain older industries, perhaps caused by growing competition from abroad, does not

DEFINITION

Real business cycle theory The new classical theory which explains cyclical fluctuations in terms of shifts in aggregate supply, rather than aggregate demand.

ISSUES AND APPLICATIONS BOX 21.6

THE BOY WHO CRIED WOLF

A government had better mean what it says

Do you remember the parable of the boy who cried, 'Wolf!'?

There was once this little village on the edge of the forest. The villagers used to keep chickens, but, when no one was around, wolves would come out of the forest and carry off the chickens. So one of the boys in the village was given the job of keeping a lookout for wolves.

One day for a joke the boy called out, 'Wolf, wolf! I see a wolf!' even though there was none. All the villagers came rushing out of their houses or back from the fields to catch the wolf. As you might expect, they were very angry to find that it was a false alarm.

The next day, thinking that this was great fun, the boy played the same trick again. Everyone came rushing out, and they were even more angry to find that they had been fooled again. But the boy just grinned.

The next day, when everyone was away in the fields, a wolf stalked into the village. The boy, spotting the animal, cried out 'Wolf, wolf! I see a wolf!' But the people in the fields said to each other, 'We're not going to be fooled this time. We've had enough of his practical jokes.' And so they carried on working. Meanwhile, back in the village, the wolf was killing all the chickens.

You can probably guess what the villagers said when they returned in the evening to find just a large pile of feathers.

A government says, 'We will take tough action to bring the rate of inflation down to 2 per cent.' Now of course this might be a 'joke' in the sense that the government doesn't really expect to succeed or even seriously to try, but is merely attempting to persuade unions to curb their wage demands. But if unions *believe* in both the government's intentions and its ability to succeed, the 'joke' may pay off. Some unions may well moderate their pay demands.

But some may not. What is more, the government may decide to give tax cuts to boost its popularity and stimulate growth, knowing that union pay demands are generally quite moderate. As a result inflation soars.

But can the government get away with it a second or third time? It's like the boy who cried, 'Wolf!' After a time people will simply not believe the government. If they see the government boosting aggregate demand, they will say to themselves, 'Here comes inflation. We'd better demand higher wages to compensate.'

?? Does this parable support the adaptive or the rational expectations hypothesis?

take place overnight. Likewise, a technological breakthrough does not affect all industries simultaneously.

The second reason is that these changes will affect the profitability of investment. If investment rises, this will increase firms' capacity and aggregate supply will shift to the right. If investment falls (as a result, say, of the election of a government less sympathetic to industry), aggregate supply will shift to the left. In other words, investment is not causing changes in output through its effect on aggregate *demand* (through the multiplier), but rather through its effect on aggregate *supply*.

So far we have seen how the theory of real business cycles explains persistent rises or falls in aggregate supply. But how does it explain *turning points*? Why do recessions and booms come to an end? The most likely explanation is that once a shock has worked its way through, aggregate supply will stop shifting. If there is then any shock in the other direction, aggregate supply will start moving back again. For example, after a period of recession, an eventual rise in business confidence will cause investment to rise and hence aggregate supply to shift back to the right. Since these 'reverse shocks' are likely to occur at irregular intervals, they can help to explain why real-world business cycles are themselves irregular.

?? Assume that there are two shocks. The first causes aggregate supply to shift to the left. The second, occurring several months later, has the opposite effect on aggregate supply. Show that if both these effects persist over a period of time, but gradually fade away, the economy will experience a recession which will bottom out and be followed in smooth succession by a recovery.

SECTION SUMMARY

1. The new classical theory assumes flexible prices and wages in the short run as well as in the long run. It also assumes that people base their expectations of inflation on a rational assessment of the *current* situation.
2. People may predict wrongly, but they are equally likely to underpredict or to overpredict. On average over the years they will predict correctly.
3. The rational expectations theory implies that not only the long-run but also the short-run *AS* and Phillips curves will be vertical. If people correctly predict the rate of inflation, they will correctly predict that any increase in aggregate *monetary* demand will simply be reflected in higher prices. Total output and employment will remain the same: at the natural level.
4. If people underpredict the rate of inflation, they will believe that there has been a *real* increase in aggregate demand, and thus output and employment will increase. But they are just as likely to overpredict the rate of inflation, in which case they will believe that real aggregate demand has fallen. The result is that output and employment will fall.
5. When the government adopts fiscal and monetary policies, people will rationally predict their effects. Given that people's predictions are equally likely to err on either side, fiscal and monetary policies are useless as means of controlling output and employment.
6. With a vertical aggregate supply curve, cyclical fluctuations must arise from shifts in aggregate supply, not shifts in aggregate demand. Real business cycle theory thus focuses on aggregate supply shocks, which then persist for a period of time. Eventually their effect will peter out, and supply shocks in the other direction can lead to turning points in the cycle.

21.4 Inflation and unemployment: the modern Keynesian position

Keynesians in the 1950s and early 1960s looked to aggregate demand to explain inflation and unemployment. Their approach was typically that of the inflationary/deflationary gap model. Although they recognised the existence of some cost-push inflation and some equilibrium unemployment, these factors were seen as relatively constant. As a result there was thought to be a relatively stable inverse relationship between inflation and unemployment, as depicted by the Phillips curve. Governments could trade off inflation against unemployment by manipulating aggregate demand.

Modern developments of the Keynesian model

Keynesians still see aggregate demand as playing the crucial role in determining the level of inflation, output and employment. They still argue that the free market works inefficiently: it frequently does not clear; price signals are distorted by economic power; most wages and many prices are 'sticky'; and most important, the free market is unlikely to settle at full employment.

They still argue, therefore, that it is vital for governments to intervene actively to prevent either a slump in demand or an overexpansion of demand.

Nevertheless the Keynesian position has undergone four major modifications in recent years. This has been in response to the problem of a rise in both inflation and unemployment and the inability of the traditional Keynesian model to explain it. The four modifications are as follows:

- An increased importance attached to cost-push factors.
- An increased importance attached to equilibrium unemployment.
- The incorporation of the theory of expectations: either adaptive or rational.
- A rationale for the persistence of demand-deficient unemployment.

Cost-push explanations: growth in monopoly power

Most Keynesians argue that the Phillips curve has shifted to the right. A major explanation for this is the increased exercise of monopoly power at home and abroad.

The breakdown of the original Phillips curve in the late 1960s and early 1970s was accompanied by growing industrial unrest, with an increased number of strikes and other forms of industrial action. At the same time there was growing concentration of monopoly power in industry, with a large number of mergers and takeovers. Oil price and other commodity price increases provided a further supply shock.

Many economists saw these developments as the major cause of the stagflation of the 1970s and early 1980s.

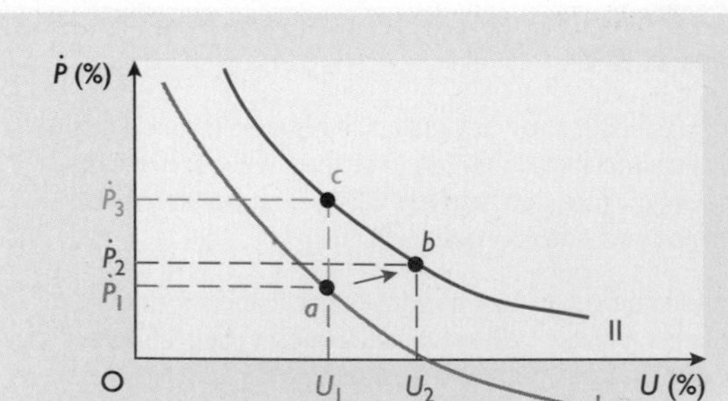

Figure 21.21 A cost-push shift in the Phillips curve

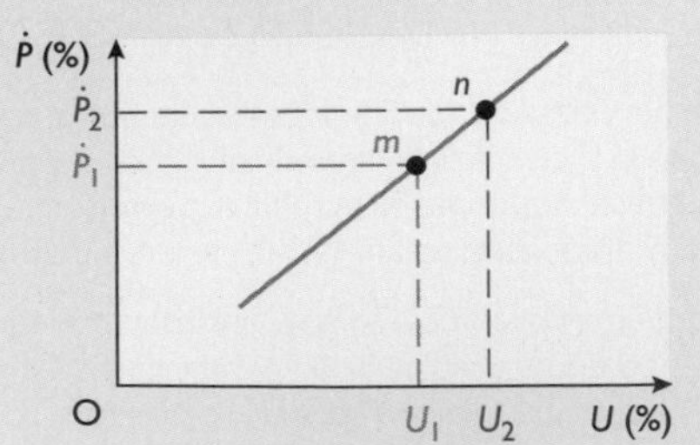

Figure 21.22 The target real wage explanation of stagflation

Governments, faced by higher inflation, attempted to deal with the problem by using (among other things) deflationary policies. This is illustrated in Figure 21.21.

Assume that the economy is initially at point *a* on Phillips curve I. There is a politically acceptable level of unemployment U_1 and inflation $\dot{P}_1$.

Now assume that, as a result of cost-push pressures, the Phillips curve shifts to position II. The government responds to the new cost inflation by pursuing mildly deflationary policies. Unemployment rises and the economy moves to point *b*. The movement from *a* to *b* represents stagflation. The growth in unemployment is due to the government's refusal to validate the increases in costs. The unemployment level *could* be reduced back to U_1 by expanding aggregate monetary demand sufficiently, but then the economy would move to point *c* with inflation of $\dot{P}_3$. If cost-push pressures persisted (i.e. were more than mere supply shocks), there would be further upward shifts in the Phillips curve.

The preferred solution to this stagflation would be to try to shift the Phillips curve back again. For this reason, many Keynesians in the 1970s advocated some form of prices and incomes policy. If such a policy succeeded in reducing cost inflation, aggregate demand could be expanded again, and the economy could move back from point *b* to point *a*.

The explanation given for the apparent leftward shift of the Phillips curve in recent years (see Figure 21.16) is that there has been a decline in union power.

??

Assume that the Phillips curve has shifted from position I to II in Figure 21.21. Assume that the government blames the cost-push inflation on a growth in the power and militancy of trade unions. Its long-term goal is to reduce this power by passing anti-union legislation, and hence to get the Phillips curve to shift back again. However, it believes that it will be able to do this only if it can weaken unions' resistance to the government in the short term by having a large rise in unemployment. Trace out the path from point *a* in the beginning and eventually back to point *a* at the end.

Cost-push explanations: target real wages

A major development in Keynesian theory in the 1970s was the theory of the **target real wage**. Evidence was used to show that unions bargain for a given *real* wage increase each year. If the growth in the economy is sufficient to pay this increase, there will be no cost inflation. But if workers start bargaining for a higher real wage increase (perhaps due to their increased monopoly power), or alternatively if the growth in the economy slows down, then there will be increased cost pressures as the demands for real wage increases cannot be met.

In its extreme form, this theory can give an upward-sloping Phillips curve. In Figure 21.22, the economy is initially at point *m*. Assume that real aggregate demand now falls. Output and employment fall. Unemployment rises from U_1 to U_2 and the growth in real wages falls. Unions use their monopoly power to attempt to maintain the target growth in their wages. But with no growth in output the effect is merely to fuel inflation. Inflation rises from $\dot{P}_1$ to $\dot{P}_2$ and the economy moves from point *m* to point *n*. This is a movement *along* the curve because the higher unemployment (and lower output) has caused the higher inflation.

??

1. If trade unions decide to bargain for higher real wage increases, what effect will this have on the curve?
2. What will determine the *slope* of the curve?

A more moderate version of this theory accepts that the power of unions to force through such wage increases is limited when they are faced with growing unemployment. The more moderate version, therefore, simply argues that

DEFINITION

Target real wage theory The theory that unions bargain for target real wage increases each year irrespective of the level of real growth in the economy.

the attempt to maintain target real wage increases will make the downward-sloping Phillips curve less steep.

The growth in equilibrium unemployment: higher structural unemployment

Most Keynesians include growth in equilibrium unemployment (NAIRU) as part of the explanation of a rightward shift in the Phillips curve. In particular, Keynesians highlight the considerable structural rigidities in the economy in a period of rapid industrial change. The changes include the following:

- Dramatic changes in technology. The microchip revolution, for example, had led to many traditional jobs becoming obsolete.
- Competition from abroad. The introduction of new products from abroad, often of superior quality to UK goods, or produced at lower costs, had led to the decline of many older industries: e.g. the textile industry.
- Shifts in demand away from the products of older labour-intensive industries to new capital-intensive products.

Keynesians argue that the free market simply cannot cope with these changes without a large rise in structural/technological unemployment. Labour is not sufficiently mobile – either geographically or occupationally – to move to areas where there are labour shortages or into jobs where there are skill shortages.

One of the worst manifestations of this problem is regional or local unemployment and regional decline or the decline of specific localities, especially in the inner cities: a problem made worse when the declining industries are concentrated in already depressed geographical regions or localities. Keynesians argue that the free market does not provide enough incentives for new firms to move into these regions.

??

1. What effect will these developments have had on (a) the Phillips curve; (b) the aggregate supply curve?
2. What policy implications follow from these arguments?

The growth in equilibrium unemployment: hysteresis

If a recession causes a rise in unemployment which is not then fully reversed when the economy recovers, there is a problem of hysteresis.

The recessions of the early 1980s and early 1990s created a growing number of people who were both deskilled and demotivated. Many in their forties and fifties who had lost their jobs were seen as too old by prospective employers. Many young people, unable to obtain jobs, became resigned to 'life on social security' or to doing no more than casual work. What is more, many firms, in an attempt to cut costs, cut down on training programmes. In these circumstances, a rise in aggregate demand again will not simply enable the long-term unemployed to be employed again. The effect has been a rightward shift in the Phillips curve: a rise in the NAIRU. To reverse this, argue Keynesians, the government should embark on a radical programme of retraining.

Recessions also cause a lack of investment. The reduction in their capital stock means that many firms cannot respond to a recovery in demand by making significant increases in output and taking on many more workers. Instead they are more likely to raise prices. Unemployment may thus fall only modestly and yet inflation may rise substantially. The NAIRU has increased: the Phillips curve has shifted to the right.

The incorporation of expectations

Some Keynesians incorporate adaptive expectations into their models. Others incorporate rational expectations. Either way their models differ from monetarist models in two important respects:

- Prices and wages are not perfectly flexible. Markets are characterised by various rigidities.
- Expectations influence *output* and *employment* decisions, not just pricing decisions.

Price and wage rigidities are likely to be greater downwards than upwards. It is thus necessary to separate the analysis of a decrease in aggregate demand from that of an increase.

Expansion of aggregate demand

Unless the economy is at full employment or very close to it, Keynesians argue that an expansion of demand *will* lead to an increase in output and employment, even in the long run after expectations have fully adjusted.

In Figure 21.23, assume that the economy is at the bottom of a recession, with high unemployment (U_1) but at the same time some cost inflation. Inflation is constant at $\dot{P}_1$, with expectations of inflation at $\dot{P}_1$ also. The economy is at point *a*.

Now assume that the economy begins to recover. Aggregate demand rises. As there is plenty of slack in the economy, output can rise and unemployment fall. The economy moves to point *b* on short-run Phillips curve I. The rise in inflation will feed through into expectations.

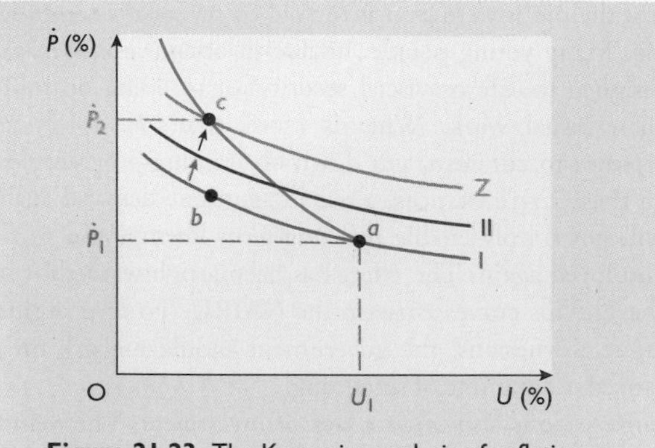

Figure 21.23 The Keynesian analysis of reflationary policies

The short-run Phillips curve will shift upwards. With adaptive expectations, it will initially shift up, say, to curve II.

But will the short-run Phillips curve not go on shifting upwards as long as there is any upward pressure on inflation, with this feeding through into higher and higher unemployment? Keynesians reject this argument for two reasons:

- If there is a gradual but sustained expansion of aggregate demand, firms, seeing the economy expanding and seeing their orders growing, will start to invest more and make longer-term plans for expanding their labour force. People will generally *expect* a higher level of output, and this optimism will cause that higher level of output to be produced. In other words, expectations will affect output and employment as well as prices. The Phillips curve will shift downwards to the left, offsetting (partially, wholly or more than wholly) the upward shift from higher inflationary expectations.
- If U_1 includes a considerable number of long-term unemployed, then the expansion of demand may be *initially* inflationary, since many of the newly employed will require some retraining (a costly exercise). But as these newly employed workers become more productive, their lower labour costs may offset any further upward pressure on wages from the expansion of demand. At the same time, the higher investment may embody new, more productive, techniques which will also help to prevent further acceleration in costs.

It is quite likely that these effects can prevent any further rises in inflation. Inflation can become stable at, say, $\dot{P}_2$, with the economy operating at point *c*. The short-run Phillips curve settles at position Z. There is thus a long-run downward-sloping Phillips curve passing through points *a* and *c*.

?? Would it in theory be possible for this long-run Phillips curve to be horizontal or even upward sloping over part of its length?

If expectations are formed rationally rather than adaptively, there will merely be a quicker movement to this long-run equilibrium. If people rationally predict that the effect of government policy will be to move the economy to point *c*, then their predictions will bring this about. All rational expectations do is to bring the long run about much sooner! The theory of rational expectations on its own does not provide support specifically for either the new classical or the Keynesian position.

Contraction of aggregate demand

Most Keynesians argue that the short-run Phillips curve is kinked at the current level of real aggregate demand. A reduction in real aggregate demand will have only a slight effect on inflation, since real wages are sticky downwards. Unions may well prefer to negotiate a reduction in employment levels, preferably by natural wastage (i.e. not replacing people when they leave), rather than accept a reduction in real wages. Thus in Figure 21.24, to the right of point *a*, the short-run Phillips curve is very shallow.

As long as this curve is not totally horizontal to the right of *a*, the introduction of expectations into the analysis will cause the short-run curve to shift downward over time (if unemployment is kept above U_1) as people come to expect a lower rate of inflation.

With *adaptive* expectations, however, the curve could shift downward very slowly indeed. If a movement from point *a* to point *d* causes only a 1 per cent reduction in inflation, and if it takes, say, two years for this to be fully reflected in expectations, then if unemployment is kept at U_2, inflation will reduce (i.e. the curve shift downward) by only 1/2 per cent a year. This may be totally unacceptable politically if inflation is already at very high levels, and if U_2 is also very high.

Even with *rational* expectations the response may be too slow. If there is a resistance from unions to receiving increases in wages below the current rate of inflation, or if they are attempting to 'catch up' with other workers, then even if they rationally predict the correct amount by which inflation will fall, inflation will fall only slowly. People will rationally predict the *resistance* to wage restraint, and sure enough, therefore, inflation will fall only slowly.

The worst scenario is when the government, in its attempt to eliminate inflation, keeps unemployment high for a number of years. As the core of long-term unem-

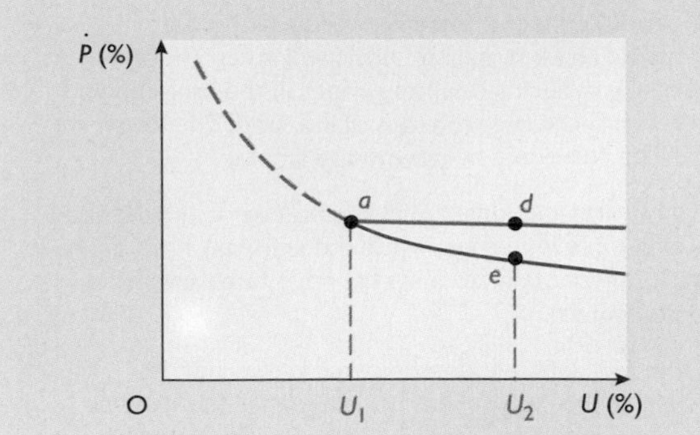

Figure 21.24 The Keynesian analysis of deflationary policies

ployed workers grows, there will be an increasing number of workers who become deskilled and therefore effectively unemployable. The effective labour supply is reduced, and firms no longer find there is a surplus of employable labour *despite* high unemployment. A long-term equilibrium is reached at, say, point *e* with still substantial inflation. The *long*-run Phillips curve too may thus be relatively shallow to the right of point *a*.

A rationale for the persistence of demand-deficient unemployment

If there is demand-deficient unemployment, why will there not be a long-run fall in real wage rates so as to eliminate the surplus labour? Keynesians give two major explanations for the persistence of real wage rates above equilibrium.

Efficiency wages. The argument here is that wage rates fulfil two functions. The first is the traditional one of balancing the demand and supply of labour. To this Keynesians add the function of motivating workers. If real wage rates are reduced when there is a surplus of labour (demand-deficient unemployment), then those workers already in employment may become dispirited and work less hard. If, on the other hand, firms keep wage rates up, then by maintaining a well-motivated workforce, by cutting down on labour turnover and by finding it easier to attract well-qualified labour, firms may find their costs are reduced: a higher real wage rate is thus more profitable for them. The maximum-profit real wage rate (the **efficiency wage rate**) is likely to be above the market-clearing real wage rate. Demand-deficient unemployment is likely to persist.

Insider power. If those still in employment (the insiders) are members of unions while those out of work (the outsiders) are not, or if the insiders have special skills or knowledge that give them bargaining power with employers while the outsiders have no influence, then there is no mechanism whereby the surplus labour – the outsiders – can drive down the real wage rate and eliminate the demand-deficient unemployment.

These two features help to explain why real wage rates did not fall during the recessions of the early 1980s and early 1990s.

The Keynesian criticisms of non-intervention

Keynesians are therefore highly critical of the new classical conclusion that governments should not intervene other than to restrain the growth of money supply. High unemployment may persist for many years and become deeply entrenched in the economy if there is no deliberate government policy of creating a steady expansion of demand.

?? Why is it important in the Keynesian analysis for there to be a *steady* expansion of demand?

DEFINITION

Efficiency wage rate The profit-maximising wage rate for the firm after taking into account the effects of wage rates on worker motivation, turnover and recruitment.

SECTION SUMMARY

1. Modern Keynesians incorporate expectations into their analysis of inflation and unemployment. They also see an important role for cost-push factors in inflation. Like the monetarists, they accept that equilibrium unemployment has increased since the 1950s and 1960s.
2. An increase in cost-push inflation will shift the Phillips curve upwards. A moderate deflation will then bring increased unemployment as well: i.e. stagflation.
3. If unions seek to maintain a target real wage rate irrespective of the real growth in the economy, this

continued

will lead to higher cost-push inflation the lower the rate of economic growth (and the higher the level of unemployment). The Phillips curve will slope upwards.

4. The growth in equilibrium unemployment has been caused by more rapid changes in technology, greater competition from abroad and more rapid changes in demand patterns. It is also due to the persistence of unemployment beyond the recessions of the early 1980s and early 1990s, because of a deskilling of labour during the recessions (an example of hysteresis). The effect of increased equilibrium unemployment is to shift the Phillips curve to the right.
5. If expectations are incorporated into Keynesian analysis, the Phillips curve will become steeper in the long run (and steeper in the short run too in the case of rational expectations). It will not become vertical, however, since people will expect changes in aggregate demand to affect output and employment as well as prices.
6. If people expect a more rapid rise in aggregate demand to be sustained, firms will invest more, thereby reducing unemployment in the long run and not just increasing the rate of inflation. The long-run Phillips curve will be downward sloping.
7. The short- and long-run Phillips curves may be kinked. Reductions in real aggregate demand may have only a slight effect on inflation if real wage rates are sticky downwards.
8. Demand-deficient unemployment may persist because real wage rates may be sticky downwards, even into the longer term. This stickiness may be the result of efficiency real wage rates being above market-clearing real wage rates and/or outsiders not being able to influence wage bargains struck between employers and insiders.

21.5 Postscript: the importance of expectations

Expectations are crucial in determining the success of government policy on unemployment and inflation. Whatever people expect to happen, their actions will tend to make it happen.

If people believe that an expansion of money supply will merely lead to inflation (the monetarist position), then it will. Firms and workers will adjust their prices and wage rates upwards. Firms will make no plans to expand output and will not take on any more labour. If, however, people believe that an expansion of demand will lead to higher output and employment (the Keynesian position), then, via the accelerator mechanism, it will.

Similarly, just how successful a deflationary policy is in curing inflation depends in large measure on people's expectations (but, as explained above, it also depends on the downward stickiness of real wages). If people believe that a deflationary policy will cause a recession, then firms will stop investing and will cut their workforce. If they believe that it will cure inflation and restore firms' competitiveness abroad, firms may increase investment.

To manage the economy successfully, therefore, the government must convince people that its policies will work. This is as much a job of public relations as of pulling the right economic levers.

??

1. If constant criticism of governments in the media makes people highly cynical about any government's ability to manage the economy, what effect will this have on the performance of the economy?
2. Suppose that, as part of the national curriculum, everyone in the country had to study economics up to the age of sixteen. Suppose also that the reporting of economic events by the media became more thorough (and interesting!). What effects would these developments have on the government's ability to manage the economy? How would your answer differ if you were a Keynesian from if you were a new classicist?

??? END-OF-CHAPTER QUESTIONS ???

1. Assume that inflation depends on two things: the level of aggregate demand, indicated by the inverse of unemployment ($1/U$), and the expected rate of inflation ($\dot{P}^e_t$). Assume that the rate of inflation ($\dot{P}_t$) is given by the equation:

$$\dot{P}_t = (48/U - 6) + \dot{P}^e_t$$

Assume initially (year 0) that the actual and expected rate of inflation is zero.

(a) What is the current (natural) rate of unemployment?

(b) Now assume in year 1 that the government wishes to reduce unemployment to 4 per cent and continues to expand aggregate demand by as much as is necessary to achieve this. Fill in the rows for years 0 to 4 in the following table. It is assumed for simplicity that the expected rate of inflation in a given year ($\dot{P}^e_t$) is equal to the actual rate of inflation in the previous year ($\dot{P}_{t-1}$).

Year	U	$48/U - 6$	+	$\dot{P}^e$	=	$\dot{P}$
0	...	...	+	...	=	...
1	...	...	+	...	=	...
2	...	...	+	...	=	...
3	...	...	+	...	=	...
4	...	...	+	...	=	...
5	...	...	+	...	=	...
6	...	...	+	...	=	...
7	...	...	+	...	=	...

(c) Now assume in year 5 that the government, worried about rising inflation, reduces aggregate demand sufficiently to reduce inflation by 3 per cent in that year. What must the rate of unemployment be raised to in that year?

(d) Assuming that unemployment stays at this high level, continue the table for years 5 to 7.

2. For what reasons might the long-run aggregate supply curve be (i) vertical; (ii) upward sloping; (iii) downward sloping?

3. How would you attempt to assess whether a particular period of inflation was the result of cost-push or demand-pull pressures?

4. What is the difference between adaptive expectations and rational expectations?

5. How can adaptive expectations of inflation result in clockwise Phillips loops? Why would these loops not be completely regular?

6. What implications would a vertical short-run aggregate supply curve have for the effects of demand management policy?

7. For what reasons may the NAIRU increase?

8. Given the Keynesian explanation for the persistence of high levels of unemployment after the 1980s recession, what policies would you advocate to reduce unemployment?

22 Supply-side policies

22.1 The supply-side problem

Lack of aggregate demand is only one of the causes of unemployment and lack of growth. Excess aggregate demand is only one of the causes of inflation and balance of payments deficits. Many of the causes of these problems lie on the supply side. This chapter examines various policies that can be adopted to influence aggregate supply.

Unemployment and supply-side policies

Equilibrium unemployment – frictional, structural, etc. – is caused by rigidities or imperfections in the market. There is a mismatching of aggregate supply and demand, and vacancies are not filled despite the existence of unemployment. The problem is that labour is not sufficiently mobile, either occupationally or geographically, to respond to changes in the job market. Labour supply for particular jobs is too inelastic.

Supply-side policies aim to influence labour supply by making workers more responsive to changes in job opportunities. They may also aim to make employers more adaptable and willing to operate within existing labour constraints. Alternatively they may seek to reduce the monopoly power of unions to drive real wages above the equilibrium.

Inflation and supply-side policies

If inflation is caused by cost-push pressures, supply-side policy can help to reduce it in three ways:

- By reducing the power of unions and/or firms (e.g. anti-monopoly legislation) and thereby encouraging more competition in the supply of labour and/or goods.
- By preventing people from exercising that power by some form of prices and incomes policy.
- By encouraging increases in productivity through the retraining of labour, or by investment grants to firms, or by tax incentives, etc.

Growth and supply-side policies

Traditional Keynesian economics tends to assume that there is a given potential national income. The actual level of national income is determined by aggregate demand. This focus, then, is a *demand-side* focus.

Supply-side economics focuses on *potential* income. Supply-side policies aim to shift the production possibility curve outwards, to shift the full-employment level of national income to the right in the Keynesian 45° line diagram (see page 514), and to shift the long-run *AS* curve to the right. Supply-side policies can be used to increase the total quantity of factors of production (e.g. policies designed to encourage the building of new factories) or they can be used to encourage greater productivity of factors of production (e.g. incentives for people to work harder).

?? Why do Keynesians argue that even in the long run demand-side policies will still be required?

The monetarist approach to supply-side policy

Monetarists argue that demand-side policy (by which they mean monetary policy) can only be used as a weapon against inflation, not to influence growth and employment in the long run. Supply-side policy is the appropriate policy to increase output and reduce the level of unemployment.

Supply-side policy can be used to shift the aggregate supply curve to the right: to increase the amount that firms wish to supply at any given price. In Figure 22.1, output rises to Q_2 and prices fall to P_2. In the labour market, it can also reduce the natural level of unemployment, and thus shift the vertical long-run Phillips curve to the left. In Figure 22.2, unemployment falls from U_{n_1} to U_{n_2}.

Monetarists advocate policies to 'free up' the market: policies that encourage private enterprise, or provide incentives and reward initiative. This part of monetarism,

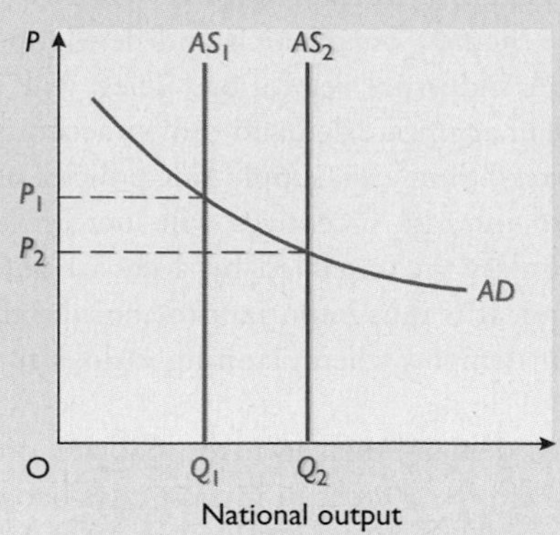

Figure 22.1 Aggregate demand and supply: monetarist analysis

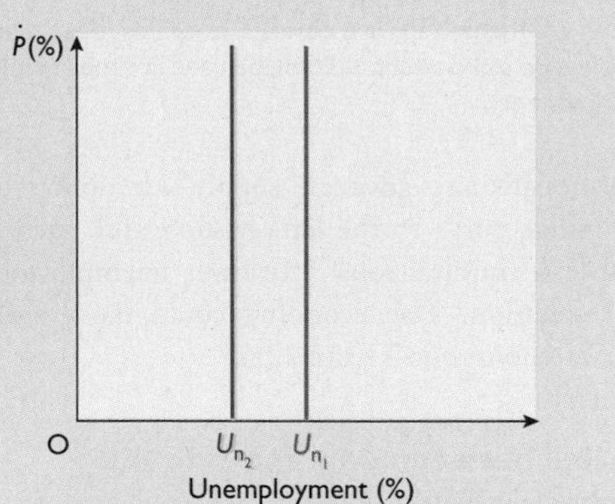

Figure 22.2 Long-run Phillips curve: monetarist analysis

more than any other, associates it with the political right. Section 22.2 examines these **market-orientated supply-side policies**.

The Keynesian approach to supply-side policy

Modern Keynesians do not just advocate the management of demand. They too advocate supply-side policies, but generally of a more **interventionist** nature (e.g. training schemes, or policies to encourage firms to set up in areas of high unemployment).

The appropriate balance between demand- and supply-side policies depends on the degree of slack in the economy. In Figure 22.3, if output is at Q_1 with aggregate demand at AD_1, the appropriate policy is to increase aggregate *demand* rather than aggregate supply. If, however, the economy is approaching full employment with aggregate demand at AD_2 and output at Q_2, the most appropriate policy to increase output is a supply-side policy. This will shift the AS curve to the right (e.g. to AS_2) and raise output (e.g. to Q_3).

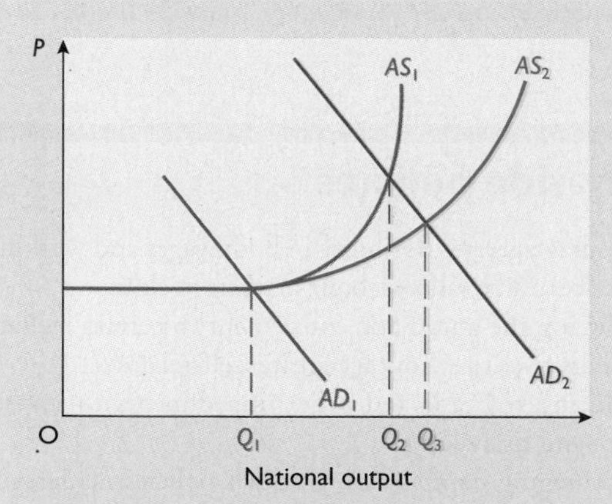

Figure 22.3 Aggregate demand and supply: Keynesian analysis

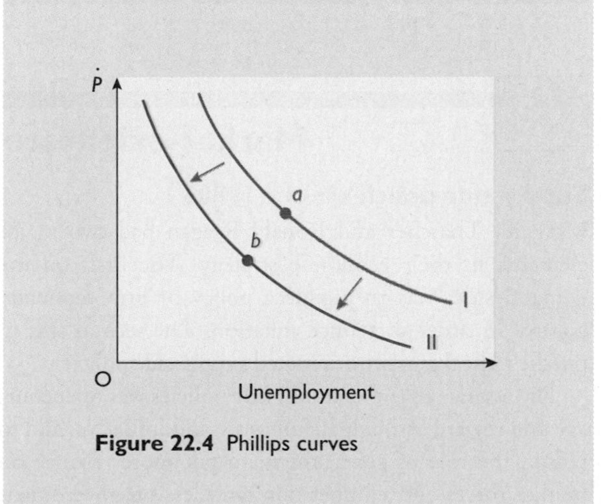

Figure 22.4 Phillips curves

DEFINITIONS

Market-orientated supply-side policies Policies to increase aggregate supply by freeing up the market.

Interventionist supply-side policies Policies to increase aggregate supply by government intervention to counteract the deficiencies of the market.

?? If Keynesians are correct, does this mean that supply-side policies should only be used at times of full employment?

Keynesians also advocate supply-side policies to shift the Phillips curve to the left. If successful, such policies could lead simultaneously to lower unemployment and lower inflation. The economy could move from, say, point *a* to point *b* in Figure 22.4.

The link between demand-side and supply-side policies

Policies can have both demand-side and supply-side effects. For example, many supply-side policies involve increased government expenditure: whether it be on retraining schemes, on research and development projects, or on industrial relocation. They will therefore cause a rise in aggregate demand (unless accompanied by a rise in taxes). Similarly, supply-side policies of tax cuts designed to increase incentives will increase aggregate demand (unless accompanied by a cut in government expenditure). It is thus important to consider the consequences for demand when planning various supply-side policies.

Likewise, demand management policies often have supply-side effects. If a cut in interest rates boosts investment, there will be a multiplied rise in national income: a demand-side effect. But that rise in investment will also create increased productive capacity: a supply-side effect.

SECTION SUMMARY

1. Demand-side policies (fiscal and monetary) may be suitable for controlling demand-pull inflation or demand-deficient unemployment, but supply-side policies will be needed to control the other types of inflation and unemployment.
2. Demand-side policies can be used to increase the actual rate of economic growth if there is slack in the economy. In the long term, however, economic growth can be increased only if there is an increase in the *potential* rate of economic growth. To achieve this the government will require supply-side policies.
3. Supply-side policies, if successful, will shift the aggregate supply curve to the right, and possibly the Phillips curve downwards/to the left.
4. Monetarists favour market-orientated supply-side policies. Keynesians tend to favour interventionist supply-side policies.
5. Supply-side policies often have demand-side effects, and demand-side policies often have supply-side effects. It is important for governments to take these secondary effects into account when working out their economic strategy.

22.2 Market-orientated supply-side policies

Supply-side policies in the 1980s

Margaret Thatcher and Ronald Reagan had two major elements in their economic strategy. The first, on the demand side, was to pursue a policy of firm monetary control in order to reduce inflation. The second was to pursue radical market-orientated supply-side policies.

The essence of these supply-side policies was to encourage and reward individual enterprise and initiative, and to reduce the role of government; to put more reliance on market forces and competition, and less on government intervention and regulation. The policies were thus associated with the following:

- Reducing government expenditure so as to release more resources for the private sector.
- Reducing taxes so as to increase incentives.
- Reducing the monopoly power of trade unions so as to encourage greater flexibility in both wages and working practices and to allow labour markets to clear.
- Reducing the automatic entitlement to certain welfare benefits so as to encourage greater self-reliance.
- Reducing red tape and other impediments to investment and risk taking.
- Encouraging competition through policies of deregulation and privatisation.
- Abolishing exchange controls and other impediments to the free movement of capital.

Seventeen years after Margaret Thatcher was elected, the government of John Major was still advocating deregulation and free-market policies. Similarly, governments throughout the industrialised world have reduced intervention and tried to create a climate in which private enterprise can flourish.

CASE STUDIES BOX 22.1

THE SUPPLY-SIDE REVOLUTION IN THE USA
'Reaganomics'

In both the UK and the USA, the 1980s proved to be years of radical political and economic change. Traditional economic and political practices were replaced by new and often controversial policies, although in theory many of the ideas advocated were based on old principles of *laissez-faire* capitalism.

In the USA, the era of 'Reaganomics' began in January 1981 when Ronald Reagan became President. With this new administration came a radical shift in policy aimed at directly tackling the supply side of the economy. This policy strategy involved four key strands:

- A reduction in the growth of Federal (central government) spending.
- A reduction in individual and corporate tax rates.
- A reduction in Federal regulations over private enterprise.
- A reduction in inflation through tight monetary policy.

On all four points President Reagan was to achieve a degree of success. Federal spending *growth* was reduced even though military spending rocketed. Tax rates fell dramatically. Deregulation was speeded up. Inflation at first was stabilised and then fell sharply.

These supply-side measures were hailed as a great success by Republicans, and followers in both the UK and the USA were quick to advocate an even bigger reduction in the government's role.

Critics remained sceptical and pointed to the costs of Reaganomics. Huge budget deficits plagued the Reagan administration and the Bush and Clinton administrations that followed. The massive tax cuts were not matched by an equivalent cut in public expenditure; nor did they produce a sufficiently high rate of economic growth, through which additional tax revenues were to balance the budget. In the 1980s, 'civilian' or welfare spending was cut repeatedly in preference to the huge military budget. This led to increasing social hardship.

Reducing government expenditure

Monetarism is often associated with 'cuts'. The desire of monetarists to cut government expenditure is not just to reduce the PSBR and hence reduce the growth of money supply; it is also an essential ingredient of their supply-side strategy.

In most countries the size of the public sector, relative to national income, had grown substantially since the 1950s (see Tables 22.1 and 22.2). A major aim of conservative governments throughout the industrialised world was to reverse this trend. The public sector was portrayed as more bureaucratic and less efficient than the private sector. What is more, it was claimed that a growing proportion of public money was being spent on administration and other 'non-productive' activities, rather than on the direct provision of goods and services.

Two things were needed: (a) a more efficient use of resources within the public sector and (b) a reduction in the size of the public sector. This would allow private investment to increase with no overall rise in aggregate demand. Thus the supply-side benefits of higher investment could be achieved without the demand-side costs of higher inflation. A number of measures were adopted. In the UK these included the following:

- Cash limits were imposed on various government departments and local authorities. It was hoped thereby to force them to become more efficient. Local authorities which planned to spend beyond their limits were prevented from raising additional rates to finance 'excess' expenditure. This process of rate capping was later changed to a system of Standard Spending Assessments (SSA). The government calculates an SSA for each local authority based on government estimates of how much the authority needs to spend in order to provide a 'standard' level of service. If a local authority's

Table 22.1 UK government expenditure (central plus local) as a percentage of GDP at market prices: 1950–97

	1950	1960	1970	1975	1979	1981	1983	1985	1987	1989	1991	1993	1995	1996	1997
Final consumption	16.5	16.4	17.6	21.8	19.8	21.9	21.9	21.1	20.4	19.7	21.6	21.8	21.2	20.9	20.1
Investment	3.4	3.3	4.8	4.7	2.6	1.8	2.0	2.0	1.6	1.8	2.1	1.9	1.8	1.3	1.0
Transfers, etc.	14.8	15.0	18.3	22.0	21.0	22.5	22.2	21.8	18.2	16.9	16.0	19.6	20.4	19.0	18.6
Total	34.7	34.7	40.7	48.5	43.4	46.2	46.1	44.9	40.2	38.4	39.7	43.3	43.4	41.2	39.7

Source: *Economic Trends* (ONS, various issues).

Table 22.2 General government expenditure as a percentage of GDP at market prices

	1961–70	1971–80	1981–5	1986–90	1991–8[1]
Belgium	33.7	50.6	62.6	57.1	53.9
Germany	37.0	45.3	48.2	46.0	48.5
France	38.3	42.3	51.5	51.0	53.7
Japan	–	26.8	33.2	32.3	34.3
Netherlands	39.9	49.8	59.5	45.4	51.9
UK	36.5	41.3	45.0	40.3	41.9
USA	29.1	32.3	35.9	36.5	33.0

[1] Forecast

Source: *OECD Economic Outlook*.

spending exceeds its SSA, then the council tax (previously the poll tax) will be increased by proportionately *more* than this, thus effectively imposing a penalty on 'high-spending' authorities.

- Grants and subsidies were reduced. The rate support grant from the government to local authorities was reduced from 61 per cent of local authority expenditure in 1979 to 47 per cent in 1989. (This process was reversed in 1991, however, when the government, worried about its low ratings in the opinion polls and the unpopularity of the poll tax, decided to increase the level of support. By 1992 the level of central government support had risen to 66 per cent.) The government also sought to reduce its expenditure on the nationalised industries. Subsidies (e.g. to British Rail) were reduced and many nationalised industries were forced to raise their prices.
- Tough managers were appointed in several nationalised industries, in order to bring about radical reorganisation and substantial increases in efficiency. In several cases this meant redundancies. The government was prepared to withstand lengthy industrial disputes in the pursuit of this policy, such as the bitter miners' dispute in 1984–5 over pit closures.
- Staffing in the civil service was cut by some 15 per cent between 1979 and 1990.
- The government pursued a tough line on public-sector pay. Here too it was prepared to withstand union action.

These policies were not without problems, however:

- In some sectors the effect was to cut services rather than increase efficiency.
- It was found much easier to cut long-term capital expenditure than current expenditure (e.g. wages). Thus there was a sharp decline in new roads, schools, public-sector housing, etc. Public investment was cut from 2.6 per cent of GDP in 1979 to 1.6 per cent in 1987 (see Table 22.1). Recognising the importance of infrastructure expenditure for the long-run growth of the economy, the Major government made some attempt to reverse this trend in the early 1990s, only to reduce it again to provide scope for tax cuts.
- Reducing the overall size of the public sector was very difficult when the government was also trying to reduce inflation by tight monetary policy. The dramatic rise in unemployment after 1979 led to large increases in expenditure on unemployment and other social security benefits. Up to 1982 government expenditure actually rose as a proportion of GDP. This problem re-emerged in the recession of the early 1990s.

?? Why might a recovering economy (and hence a fall in government expenditure on social security benefits) make the government feel even more concerned to make discretionary cuts in government expenditure?

Tax cuts: the effects on labour supply and employment

Cutting the marginal rate of income tax was a major objective of the Thatcher government (as it was of the Reagan administration). When the government came to office in 1979 the basic rate of income tax was 33 per cent, with higher rates rising to 83 per cent. By 1988 the basic rate had been cut to 25 per cent and the top rate to 40 per cent. Cuts in the marginal rate of income tax are claimed to have five beneficial effects: people work longer hours; more people wish to work; people work more enthusiastically; unemployment falls; employment rises. These are big claims. Are they true?

People work longer hours

A cut in the marginal rate of income tax has a *substitution effect* inducing people to work more and also an *income effect* causing people to work less. (At this point you should review the arguments about the incentive effects of tax cuts: see pages 305–9.). Evidence suggests that the two effects will roughly cancel each other out. Anyway, for many people there is no such choice in the short run.

There is no chance of doing overtime or working a shorter week. In the long run there may be some flexibility in that people can change jobs.

More people wish to work

This applies largely to second income earners in a family, mainly women. A rise in after-tax wages may encourage more women to look for jobs. It may now be worth the cost in terms of transport, child minders, family disruption, etc. The effects of a 1 or 2 per cent cut in income tax rates, however, are likely to be negligible. A more significant effect may be achieved by raising tax allowances. Part-time workers, especially, could end up paying no taxes. Of course, if unemployment is already high, the government will not want to increase the labour force.

People work more enthusiastically

There is little evidence to test this claim. The argument, however, is that people will be more conscientious and will work harder if they can keep more of their pay.

Employment rises

If wages are flexible, total employment will rise. This is illustrated in Figure 22.5. The N curve shows the total labour force. The AS_L curve shows the number of people who are actually qualified and willing to do the specific jobs they are offered at each (after-tax) wage rate. Equilibrium will be where the aggregate demand for labour (AD_L) is equal to the labour cost to the employer (i.e. the pre-tax wage rate). Assume an initial income tax per worker of $a - b$. The equilibrium employment will be Q_1. Workers receive an after-tax wage W_1 and thus supply Q_1 labour. Employers' labour cost is the pre-tax wage lc_1. At this wage they demand Q_1 labour.

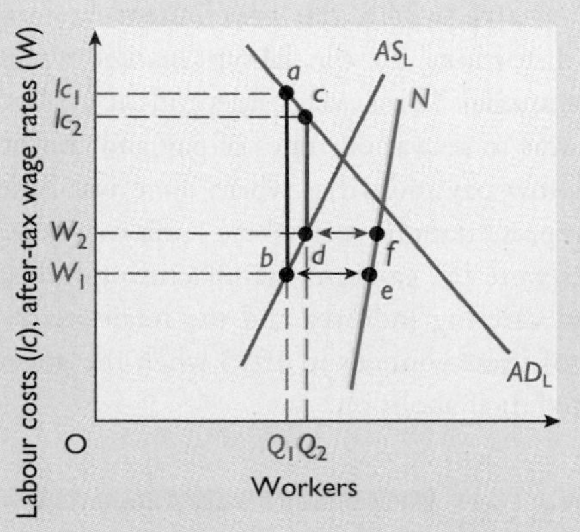

Figure 22.5 Effect of a tax cut on total unemployment

If the income tax per worker now falls to $c - d$, equilibrium employment will rise to Q_2. Firms will employ more workers because their labour costs have fallen to lc_2. More workers will take up jobs because their after-tax wages have risen to W_2.

Unemployment falls

One of the causes of natural (equilibrium) unemployment highlighted by monetarists is the cushioning provided by unemployment benefit. If income tax rates are cut, there will be a bigger difference between after-tax wage rates and unemployment benefit. More people will be motivated to 'get on their bikes' and look for work.

In Figure 22.5, the gap between N and AS_L represents equilibrium unemployment. With a cut in income tax per worker from $a - b$ to $c - d$, equilibrium unemployment will fall from $e - b$ to $f - d$.

?? What would happen to the AS_L curve and the level of unemployment if unemployment benefits were increased?

While marginal income tax rates were cut during the 1980s, these were offset by increases in VAT and national insurance contributions (see Box 10.5 on pages 300–1). Total taxes and national insurance contributions as a proportion of GDP rose from 34.2 per cent in 1979 to 39.5 per cent in 1984, and then fell back to 34.1 per cent in 1993. But with a PSBR rising to over £42 billion in 1993 (nearly 7 per cent of GDP), taxes were raised to over 36 per cent of GDP by 1996.

?? Does this mean that there were *no* positive incentive effects from the Conservative government's tax measures?

To the extent that tax cuts do succeed in increasing take-home pay, there is a danger of 'sucking in' imports. Consumers may have a high marginal propensity to import: spending their money on Japanese videos and hi-fi, foreign cars, holidays abroad and so on. Tax cuts can therefore have a serious effect on the balance of payments.

Tax cuts for business and other investment incentives

A number of financial incentives can be given to encourage investment. Selective intervention in the form of grants for specific industries or firms is best classified as an interventionist policy and will be examined later in this chapter. Market-orientated policies seek to reduce the general level of taxation on profits, or to give greater tax relief to investment.

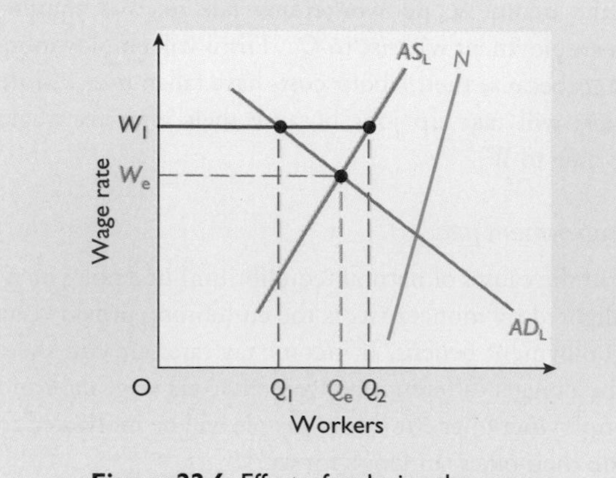

Figure 22.6 Effect of reducing the power of labour

A cut in corporation tax will increase after-tax profits. This means that more money will be available for ploughing back into investment and also that the higher after-tax return on investment will encourage more investment to take place. In 1984 the main rate of corporation tax in the UK was reduced from 52 per cent of profits, the amount of the reduction depending on the size of the company. In 1996 the rate of corporation tax was 33 per cent for large companies and 24 per cent for small.

An alternative policy would be to increase investment allowances. Investment allowances are the system whereby the cost of investment can be offset against pre-tax profit, thereby reducing a firm's tax liability.

Until 1984 the UK system of investment and other allowances for firms and various subsidies had been quite complex, and discriminated seemingly arbitrarily between different types of investment. After 1984 the whole system was simplified in order to reduce these distortions and allow investment to be more 'market determined'. Nevertheless, as previously, better allowances were given for plant and machinery than for industrial buildings, and no allowances were given for most commercial buildings. The overall level of allowances, however, was reduced.

Since 1979 various tax allowances and grants have been provided for small businesses. Since these amount to selective *intervention* rather than market-orientated policies, they are examined in section 22.4.

Reducing the power of labour

In Figure 22.6, if the power of unions to push wage rates up to W_1 were removed, then (assuming no change in the demand curve for labour) wage rates would fall to W_e. Disequilibrium unemployment $(Q_2 - Q_1)$ would disappear. Employment would rise from Q_1 to Q_e.

Equilibrium unemployment, however, will rise somewhat as the gap between gross and effective labour supply widens. With the reduction in wage rates, some people may now prefer to remain 'on the dole'.

If labour costs to employers are reduced, their profits will probably rise. This could encourage and enable more investment and hence economic growth. If the monopoly power of labour is reduced, then cost-push inflation will also be reduced.

But will a policy that reduced wages not also reduce aggregate demand? The answer depends on the government's demand management policy. If real aggregate demand is maintained by fiscal and/or monetary policies, demand-deficient unemployment need not arise.

The Thatcher government took a number of measures to weaken the power of labour. These included restrictions on union closed shops, restrictions on secondary picketing, financial assistance for union ballots, and enforced secret ballots on strike proposals (see Chapter 9). It set a lead in resisting strikes in the public sector. Unlike previous Labour governments, it did not consult with union leaders over questions of economic policy. It was publicly very critical of trade union militancy and blamed the unions for many of the UK's economic ills. As a result, unions lost a lot of political standing and influence.

Apart from the miners' strike in 1984–5 and the industrial action of teachers in 1986–7, most of the 1980s and early 1990s was a period of relative industrial calm. Despite the legislation, it can be argued that the main factor that weakened the power of unions was the very high level of unemployment during most of the period.

?? Is the number of working days lost through disputes a good indication of (a) union power; (b) union militancy?

Another area where the government attempted to reduce 'distortions' in the labour market was that of **wages councils**. These were independent bodies whose purpose was to set various rates of pay and conditions in generally low-pay industries where there was little or no union representation, or where unions were weak. Examples were the garment manufacturing industry, the hotel and catering industry and the retail sector. There were 26 of these councils in 1993 when the government announced their abolition.

DEFINITION

Wages councils Independent bodies which set rates of pay in certain low-pay industries.

Reducing welfare

Monetarists claim that a major cause of unemployment is the small difference between the welfare benefits of the unemployed and the take-home pay of the employed. This causes voluntary unemployment (i.e. frictional unemployment). People are caught in a 'poverty trap': if they take a job, they lose their benefits (see pages 312–14).

A dramatic solution to this problem would be to cut unemployment benefits. Unlike policies to encourage investment, this supply-side policy would have a very rapid effect. It would shift the effective labour supply curve to the right. In Figure 22.7, equilibrium unemployment would fall from $a - b$ to $c - d$ if real wage rates were flexible downwards; or from $a - b$ to $a - e$ if they were not flexible. In the case of non-flexible real wage rates, the reduction in equilibrium unemployment would be offset by a rise in disequilibrium unemployment $(e - b)$.

Because workers would now be prepared to accept a lower wage, the average length of job search by the unemployed would be reduced. In Figure 22.8, the average duration of unemployment would fall from T_1 to T_2 (see pages 422–3).

?? Would a cut in benefits affect the W_o curve? If so, with what effect?

In practice the gap between take-home pay and welfare benefits to the unemployed had actually widened up to 1979. This suggests that too high benefits were not a cause of the growing unemployment up to that time. After 1979 the gap continued to widen, but unemployment rose dramatically. Nevertheless, the claim that there was too little incentive for people to work was still a major part of the Thatcher government's explanation of growing unemployment.

With changing requirements for labour skills, many of the redundant workers from the older industries are simply not qualified for new jobs that are created. What is more, the longer people are unemployed, the more demoralised they become. Employers would probably be prepared to pay only very low wage rates to such workers. To persuade people to take these low-paid jobs, the welfare benefits would have to be slashed. A 'market' solution to the problem, therefore, may be a very cruel solution. A fairer solution would be an interventionist policy: a policy of retraining labour.

Policies to encourage competition

If the government can encourage more competition, this should have the effect of increasing national output and reducing inflation. There were four major types of policy pursued under this heading.

Privatisation

If privatisation simply involves the transfer of a natural monopoly to private hands (e.g. the water companies), the scope for increased competition is limited. However, where there is genuine scope for competition (e.g. in the sale of telephones), privatisation can lead to increased efficiency, more consumer choice and lower prices.

Alternatively, privatisation can involve the introduction of private services into the public sector (e.g. private contractors providing cleaning services in hospitals, or refuse collection for local authorities). Private contractors may compete against each other for the franchise. This may well lower the cost of provision of these services, but the quality of provision may also suffer unless closely monitored. The effects on unemployment are uncertain. Private contractors may offer lower wages and thus may

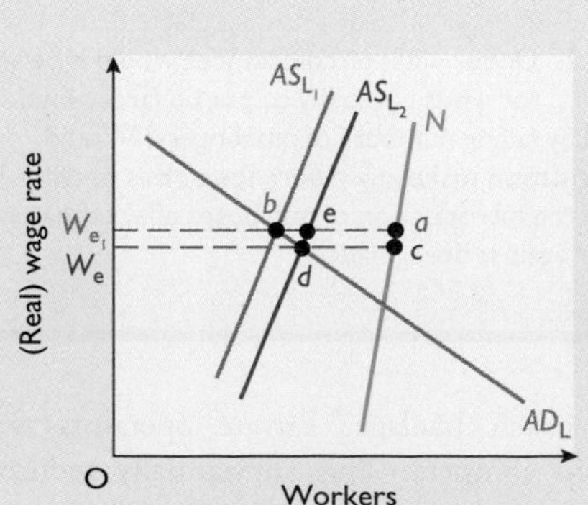

Figure 22.7 The effects of a cut in benefits on the number unemployed

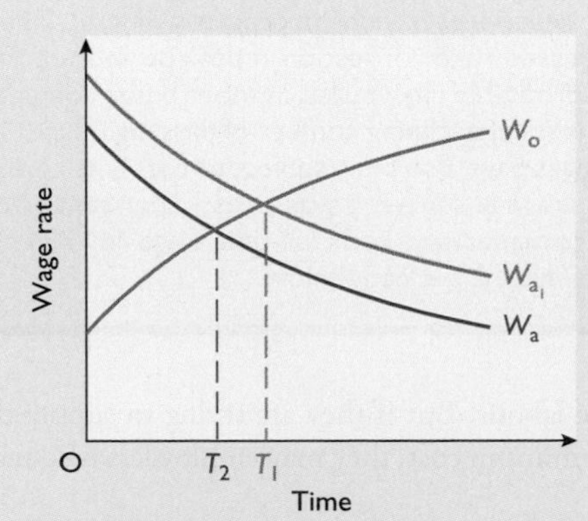

Figure 22.8 The effects of a cut in benefits on the average duration of unemployment

CASE STUDIES — BOX 22.2

DEREGULATING THE BUS INDUSTRY

Bus services were deregulated in the 1985 Transport Act, which came into effect on 26 October 1986. The Act privatised the National Bus Company and ended a system of strict route licensing which had been in existence for over 55 years.

For 30 years prior to deregulation the bus industry had been losing on average 4 per cent of its passengers per year. As a consequence the local authorities had been obliged to provide growing subsidies to the bus operators in order to keep loss-making services running. In 1985 such subsidies stood at £544 million at 1996 prices.

It was hoped that, following deregulation, greater competition in supply would lead to improved service efficiency, a growth in service provision and the number of passengers, lower fares, and the development of transport innovations, such as the new light-rail schemes (trams!) that had been proposed in many cities.

The impact of deregulation has, however, been mixed. On the positive side, the Department of Transport estimated that by 1993 operating costs per vehicle per mile had fallen by 36 per cent in real terms since deregulation, and that subsidies from local government to bus operators had fallen by over 50 per cent. Total bus mileage has increased since deregulation, along with the general frequency of service. Innovation in the form of minibuses has been significant. They now represent over 30 per cent of the total bus fleet.

However, many of the hoped-for benefits from deregulation have not materialised. Fares have increased by an average of 12 per cent in real terms. With direct income from fares falling by over 10 per cent from 1987 to 1993, the new bus operators have attempted to cut costs. Vehicles are being used more intensively and are not being replaced as frequently.

Other cost savings are being made by running services only on the busiest urban routes. Country routes and off-peak services have been progressively cut. The result is increased road congestion at peak periods on the most profitable city routes, as more buses compete for what is still a declining number of passengers.

Wages have also been subject to cost cutting. In 1993 the average bus driver's wage was 18 per cent below the average manual worker's full-time wage. In 1984 it had been a mere 2 per cent below.

Passenger information has been very poor in many towns and cities. Companies form and collapse with such frequency that no reliable bus timetable is possible. Not only this, but the duplication of services leads to a massive waste of resources as well as congestion.

In cities where competition is more limited, such as Birmingham and Bristol, some economies of scale are possible from which both passengers and bus operators benefit. Services appear superior, being more organised and with up-to-date timetable information.

When companies have a monopoly on routes, however, fares are likely to rise unless the market remains contestable. With the establishment of large bus companies such as Stagecoach Holdings and the Go-Ahead Group, contestability has tended to decline. Both companies were criticised by the Monopolies and Mergers Commission in August 1995 for their predatory behaviour. For example, when Stagecoach lost the bid to acquire the Darlington Transport Company (the town's former municipal bus company), Stagecoach decided to register a new bus service on all DTC routes. It announced that it would not wait the required six weeks before charging fares, but would offer a free service for the whole period. In addition it offered a £1000 signing-on fee to any qualified bus driver and wages 3 per cent higher than those at DTC. Predictably, DTC drivers left in droves to join the new bus company. Yorkshire Traction, the company that had won the DTC bid, subsequently pulled out as DTC faced the prospect of losing £30 000 per week for the six-week period. As a consequence, DTC went into liquidation.

Faced with aggressive business tactics like these, small operators would be unlikely to risk entering such a market: it would not be contestable. Responding to this situation, the MMC has suggested that it might become necessary to establish a bus regulator, OFBUS.

??

1. Under what circumstances would it be wise for a bus company to put up fares when faced by falling numbers of passengers? Would deregulation make any difference to this decision?
2. Does the introduction of minibuses affect the case for or against deregulation?

use more labour. But if they are trying to supply the service at minimum cost, they may employ less labour.

Deregulation

This involves the removal of monopoly rights. In 1979 the National Bus Corporation lost its monopoly of long-distance coach haulage. Private operators were now allowed to compete. This substantially reduced coach fares on a number of routes. In 1986 competition was allowed in providing local bus services (see Box 22.2).

An example in the private sector was the so-called 'Big Bang' on the Stock Exchange in 1986. Under this, the

CASE STUDIES BOX 22.3

THE MARKET FOR PATIENTS
The internal market in the NHS

The National Health Service was formed in 1948 and since then it has been the principal provider of health care in the UK, with the private sector contributing relatively little to the overall total. Criticisms, however, were frequently made of the 'wastage' and 'inefficiency' in the NHS.

The Thatcher government, anxious to reduce health costs, saw the NHS as ripe for supply-side reforms. In 1989 the government's white paper *Working for Patients* proposed a massive reform of the NHS, involving the introduction of an 'internal market'.

- Responsibility for the provision of health care would be devolved from regional health authorities to individual hospitals.
- NHS hospitals would be able to apply for trust status, which would allow them greater freedom over pay, the provision of medical services and access to finance.
- Hospitals would be able to offer their services to all district health authorities in the UK and to the private sector.
- General practitioners would be offered the opportunity to control their budgets. GP fundholders would purchase services directly from hospitals and have to cover their drugs bill.
- Management in the NHS was to adopt a more business-like ethos.

In the internal market, demand comes not from the patient, but from GPs, who exercise spending power on behalf of their patients. The size of GPs' budgets is determined by the number of patients they have on their list and by the 'needs' of the practice, given its geographical location and the structure of its patient group. GPs have the incentive to be efficient in the use of their budgets, since they can use any moneys left over at the end of the year to develop the practice. There are also financial rewards for meeting various targets, such as immunisations.

The supplier of treatment, the hospital, depends for much of its income on attracting the business of GP purchasers. Hospitals can do this by periodically adjusting the price of treatment to make it competitive with other hospitals. The price then remains fixed as a contract price for a given period of time. Hospitals also compete using non-price factors such as quality of care and the length of time patients must wait for treatment.

Advocates of the reforms argue that advantages will only be fully realised in the long run as the system's efficiency improves. Many GP practices have grown, resulting in economies of scale (e.g. in sharing the costs of operating health centres). These larger purchasers should provide countervailing power to the monopoly power of the large hospitals. However, patient choice is likely to be reduced as the number of practices declines.

Arguments concerning the length of waiting lists, the closure of hospitals and the problems faced by GPs who exhaust their budget are uncertain. It will probably be some time before it becomes clear whether the internal market has achieved an improvement in economic efficiency.

However, as NHS hospitals compete for private patients, there exists a real fear that the NHS, which was set up to offer everyone equal access to health care, may end up offering two very different types of service: those who can pay, or who are patients of a well-endowed fundholding practice, getting quicker access to medical facilities, better treatment and superior after care.

?? What effect is the type of competition introduced in the NHS reforms likely to have on the *quality* of health care provision?

monopoly power of jobbers to deal in stocks and shares on the Stock Exchange was abolished. In addition, stockbrokers now compete with each other in the commission rates they charge.

Introducing market relationships into the public sector

This is where the government tries to get different departments or elements within a particular part of the public sector to 'trade' with each other, so as to encourage competition and efficiency.

The process often involves 'devolved budgeting'. For example, under the locally managed schools scheme (LMS), schools have become self-financing. Rather than the local authority meeting the bill for teachers' salaries, the schools have to manage their own budgets. The hope is that it will encourage them to cut costs, thereby reducing the burden on council tax payers. However, one result is that schools have tended to appoint inexperienced (and hence cheaper) teachers rather than those who can bring the benefits of their years of teaching.

Perhaps the most comprehensive introduction of market relationships has been in the field of health (see Box 22.3).

Free trade and free capital movements

The opening-up of international trade and investment is central to a market-orientated supply-side policy. One of the first measures of the Thatcher government (in October 1979) was to remove all exchange controls, thereby permitting the free inflow and outflow of capital, both long term and short term. Most other industrialised countries also removed or relaxed exchange controls during the 1980s.

The Single European Act of 1986, which came into force in 1993, was another example of international liberalisation. It created a 'single market' in the EU: a market without barriers to the movement of goods, services, capital and labour. The arguments for and against free trade and the single market are examined in Chapter 23.

Conclusions

Although a number of supply-side measures have been taken in many countries during the last twenty years, many of the supply-side *effects* have been the result of changes in demand.

During the recession of the early 1980s, much of UK industrial capacity was lost for ever. Many of the redundant became deskilled and demoralised as they became long-term unemployed. On the other hand, many of those companies that survived were only able to do so by considerable increases in efficiency. Resistance from unions to the introduction of new labour-saving technology was weakened by high unemployment and the fear that without the new technology firms might be forced to close.

When demand was expanded in the late 1980s and unemployment began to fall, inflation rose and the balance of trade went into record deficit and remained in severe deficit even during the depth of the succeeding recession in 1991 and 1992. These events cast serious doubts on the ability of the economy to maintain sustained high economic growth and on whether the supply-side measures were as successful as the government maintained. The rate of increase in productivity has been higher in the 1980s and 1990s than in the 1960s and 1970s. But to what extent this is attributable to the government's supply-side measures rather than to other factors, such as international competition and a more rapid rate of technological advance, is not clear.

?? If supply-side measures led to a 'shake out' of labour and a resulting reduction in overstaffing, but also to a rightward shift in the Phillips curve, would you judge the policy as a success?

SECTION SUMMARY

1. Market-orientated supply-side policies aim to increase the rate of growth of aggregate supply by encouraging private enterprise and the freer play of market forces.
2. Reducing government expenditure as a proportion of GDP is a major element of such policies. This can involve the use of cash limits on government departments and local authorities, reducing grants and subsidies, reducing the number of civil servants and other public employees, resisting pay increases in the public sector, and reorganising public-sector industries and departments in order to achieve greater efficiency.
3. Tax cuts can be used to encourage more people to take up jobs, and people to work longer hours and more enthusiastically. They can be used to reduce equilibrium unemployment and encourage employers to take on more workers. Likewise tax cuts for businesses or increased investment allowances may encourage higher investment. The effects of tax cuts will depend on how people respond to incentives. For example, people will work longer hours only if the substitution effect outweighs the income effect.
4. Reducing the power of trade unions by legislation could reduce disequilibrium unemployment and cost-push inflation. It could also lead to a redistribution of income to profits, which could increase investment and growth (but possibly lead to greater inequality).
5. A reduction in welfare benefits, especially those related to unemployment, will encourage workers to accept jobs at lower wages and thus decrease equilibrium unemployment.
6. Privatisation and deregulation are two examples of policies that could be used to encourage greater competition. In practice, there will be little or no gain in competition from privatisation if industries are sold as monopolies.
7. A policy of free trade and free capital movements can be used to encourage greater competition from abroad.

22.3 Regional and urban policy

Regional disparities in unemployment in the UK increased substantially during the early and mid-1980s, with the recession hitting the north, with its traditional heavy industries, much harder than the south. Table 22.3 shows unemployment rates for the various UK regions.

Similarly, there are regional disparities in average incomes, rates of growth and levels of prices, as well as in health, crime, housing, etc. Many of these disparities too grew wider in the 1980s. The magnitude of these problems in many parts of the north led to the 'north–south divide' becoming a major political issue.

In recent years, however, concern has shifted away from the problems of broad regions. Regional disparities of income still exist, but they narrowed dramatically during the recession of the early 1990s. The recession hit service industries, which are more concentrated in the south, harder than manufacturing industries, which are more concentrated in the north. Moreover, many industries today have less need than in the past to be located in a specific region, and can therefore move to parts of the country where labour and other costs are lower. The problem today, therefore, is seen to be more one of specific *areas*, especially inner cities and urban localities subject to industrial decline.

Let us first, however, examine the causes of *regional* imbalance.

Causes of regional imbalance

The decline and/or rationalisation of many of the older industries (mining, textiles, steel, shipbuilding), and the concentration of many of the newer industries in the south, resulted in structural and technological unemployment and demand-shift inflation.

If the market functioned perfectly, there would be no regional problem. If wages were lower and unemployment were higher in the north, people would simply move to the south. This would reduce unemployment in the north and help to fill vacancies in the south. It would drive up wages in the north and reduce wages in the south. The process would continue until regional disparities were eliminated.

The capital market would function similarly. New investment would be located in the areas offering the highest rate of return. If land and labour were cheaper in the north, capital would be attracted there. This too would help to eliminate regional disparities.

In practice, labour may be geographically immobile. The regional pattern of industrial location may change more rapidly than the labour market can adjust to it. Thus jobs may be lost in the depressed areas more rapidly than people can migrate.

Similarly, existing capital stock is highly immobile. Buildings and most machinery cannot be moved to where the unemployed are! *New* capital is much more mobile. But there may be insufficient new investment, especially during a recession, to halt regional decline, even if some investors are attracted into the depressed areas by low wages and cheap land.

The continuing shift in demand may in part be due to **regional multiplier effects**. In the prosperous regions, the new industries and the new workers attracted there create additional demand. This creates additional output and jobs and hence more migration. There is a multiplied rise in income. In the depressed regions, the decline in demand and loss of jobs causes a multiplied downward effect. Loss of jobs in manufacturing leads to less money being spent in the local community; transport and other service industries lose custom. The whole region becomes more depressed.

There can be a similar process between countries. With the opening-up of the EU in 1993 to the free movement of capital, capital may flow to the more prosperous regions of the Union, such as Germany, the northern half of France and the Benelux countries, and away from the less prosperous regions, such as Portugal, Ireland, Greece and southern Italy.

Differences in regional unemployment and incomes cannot be eliminated by general demand management policies, since they reflect imbalances *between* markets that have not been corrected. In theory, regional policy could aim to increase consumer demand for the goods produced in the depressed regions, and reduce consumer demand for goods produced in the prosperous ones. In practice, however, regional policy concentrates on the supply side. It aims to encourage industries to move to the depressed regions.

DEFINITION

Regional multiplier effects When a change in injections into or withdrawals from a particular region causes a multiplied change in income in that region. The regional multiplier (k_r) is given by $1/mpw_r$, where the import component of mpw_r consists of imports into that region either from abroad or from other regions of the economy.

Table 22.3 Regional unemployment: selected years

Region	Unemployment (%)				
	January 1979	January 1987	January 1990	January 1993	January 1996
UK (average)	4.2	10.9	5.7	10.6	7.9
East Anglia	3.5	8.2	3.3	8.6	6.1
South-West	4.5	9.0	4.0	10.0	6.8
East Midlands	3.5	9.9	4.9	9.7	7.3
South-East	2.9	7.9	3.6	10.5	7.6
West Midlands	3.8	12.5	5.9	11.5	7.8
Scotland	5.8	13.8	8.4	9.9	7.8
Wales	5.6	13.1	6.5	10.3	8.1
North-West	5.3	13.4	7.7	10.9	8.2
Yorks & Humberside	4.1	12.3	6.7	10.6	8.4
North	6.2	15.1	8.8	12.2	10.0
Northern Ireland	7.9	17.6	13.7	14.6	11.4

Source: *Economic Trends* (ONS).

Causes of urban decay

Throughout the post-war period there has been a general movement of people from the inner areas of the big cities to the suburbs, to smaller towns and cities, and to rural areas within easy commuting distance of towns. This movement has been paralleled by a decline in employment in the inner cities. But with an increasing number of urban jobs being taken by people commuting into the cities, the unemployment problem for those living in these areas grew dramatically. Moreover, many of the older manufacturing industries were located in the inner cities and it was these industries that were hardest hit by the recession of the early 1980s. Now there are large differences in living standards and unemployment rates between the inner city areas and the rest of the country.

The run-down nature of many inner cities causes the more mobile members of the workforce to move away. Spending in these areas thus declines, causing a local multiplier effect. The jobs that poor people living in these areas do manage to find are often low-paid, unskilled jobs in the service sector (such as shops and the hotel and catering trade) or in petty manufacturing (like garment workshops).

Many of the newer industries prefer to locate away from the inner city areas on sites where land is cheaper, rates are lower and there is easy access to the motorway network. At the same time, for financial reasons local authorities have found it difficult to offer inducements to firms to move into the inner cities. Nor can they afford to spend large amounts on improving the infrastructure of the blighted areas. Their council taxes are also higher, which again provides an inducement for more mobile workers to move away as well as a disincentive for new firms to move into the area.

Radical-right policies

Since regional and urban problems are due to a failure of markets, the radical right advocates making the market more perfect. Maintaining that firms are the best judges of where they should locate, they favour removing impediments to the market achieving regional and local balance, and support the following.

Locally negotiated wage agreements. Nationally negotiated wage rates mean that wages are not driven down in the less prosperous areas and up in the more prosperous ones. This discourages firms from locating in the less prosperous areas. At the same time, firms find it difficult to recruit labour in the more prosperous ones, where wages are not high enough to compensate for the higher cost of living there.

Control of local authority taxes. Many Labour-led local authorities in depressed areas in the past sought to protect services by putting up local taxes (both to individuals and to businesses). This could discourage firms from moving into the area and might encourage others to leave. The radical right supports measures to prevent such increases and thereby to remove this impediment to regional and local balance.

Reducing unemployment benefits. A general reduction in unemployment and other benefits would encourage the unemployed in the areas of high unemployment to migrate to the more prosperous areas, or enable firms to offer lower wages in the areas of high unemployment.

The problem with these policies is that they attempt initially to *widen* the economic divide between workers in the different areas in order to encourage capital and labour to move. Such policies would hardly be welcomed by workers in the poorer areas!

> ??
> 1. Think of some other 'pro-market' solutions to the regional problem.
> 2. Do workers in the less prosperous areas benefit from pro-market solutions?

Interventionist policies

The political centre and left argue in favour of an *interventionist* approach. In theory, people could be given grants to move, or retraining programmes could be devised for potential migrants to enable them to take up jobs in the more prosperous areas. However, this approach might exacerbate the problem. The depressed areas could become more depressed; the prosperous areas more overcrowded. Interventionists therefore favour policies to encourage *firms* to move.

Subsidies and tax concessions in the depressed areas

These can have two beneficial effects: an *income* effect and a *substitution* effect. The income effect is where higher income for firms, as a result of subsidies, encourages them to produce more output and hence to employ more people. The substitution effect is where firms are encouraged to substitute labour for capital: i.e. to use more labour-intensive techniques.

General subsidies. Grants or concessions for buildings, reduced rates of corporation tax, grants for firms to move, etc. would lead to an income effect as firms were attracted into the region. But the firms would not thereby be encouraged to use more labour-intensive techniques. There would be no substitution effect.

Employment subsidies. Subsidies for employment, or reduced employers' national insurance contributions, would lead to both an income effect *and* a substitution effect. Firms would be attracted into the region and there would also be an encouragement to substitute (now cheaper) labour for capital.

Capital subsidies. Grants for investment or other measures which reduce the cost of capital would lead to a positive income effect. The substitution effect, however, would be *negative*. Firms attracted to the area would be encouraged to use capital-intensive techniques, and would thus provide little employment.

In the short run, employment subsidies will have the largest effect on employment. In the long run, however, it is not so clear cut. Capital-intensive industries may require the services of local *labour*-intensive industries. Also capital-intensive industries may be more profitable and have a higher rate of growth, thus generating more employment in the future.

> ??
> If a Japanese car manufacturer were attracted into an unemployment blackspot and opened up a highly capital-intensive 'robot-line' car assembly plant, in what other local industries might employment be stimulated?

The provision of facilities in the depressed areas

The government or local authorities could provide facilities such as land and buildings to incoming firms. Alternatively, government could improve the infrastructure of the area, such as roads and communications, and local technical colleges. Another alternative is for the government to move some of its own departments out of London and locate them in areas of high unemployment. The siting of the vehicle licensing centre in Swansea is an example.

Restrictions on the expansion of firms in prosperous areas

The government could restrict expansion of firms in prosperous areas, thereby encouraging firms to move to less prosperous ones. There are two ways this could be done.

Taxes. The government could tax company income, employment or new buildings at higher rates in prosperous areas. A tax on income or buildings is probably preferable to a tax on employment. If employment is taxed, it might simply encourage firms in prosperous areas to substitute capital for labour, rather than move to depressed areas. It depends on the elasticity of substitution of capital for labour. The more readily capital can be substituted, the less likely will the firms be to move.

Regulation. The government could simply prevent firms from setting up or expanding in the prosperous regions. Prior to their abolition in 1982, the government could refuse to grant an Industrial Development Certificate in prosperous regions, hoping to force firms to move to depressed regions. But if firms are prevented or discouraged from expanding in prosperous regions, they may not expand at all, or may go abroad.

It is important to distinguish interventionist policies that merely seek to *modify* the market by altering market signals, from those that *replace* the market.

Regulation replaces the market, and unless very carefully devised and monitored may lead to ill-thought-out decisions being made. *Subsidies* and *taxes* merely modify the market, leaving it to individual firms to make their final local decisions. Taxes and subsidies in theory can internalise external costs and benefits, and can make actual prices reflect opportunity costs rather than market power. But if there are uniform tax or subsidy rates throughout a region, they will be higher than necessary in some cases and lower in others.

??

1. If you were the government, how would you set about deciding the rate of subsidy to pay a firm thinking of moving to a less prosperous area?
2. Should firms already located in less prosperous areas be paid a subsidy?

Regional and urban policy in the UK

Regional policy

Certain areas are identified as requiring government financial assistance. These are known as **assisted areas** (AAs) and cover just over one-third of the UK population. Until recently these were divided into two types: *development areas* and *intermediate areas*. *Development areas* cover much of Scotland, South Wales, parts of North Wales, the north-east, north-west and far south-west of England, plus other smaller areas severely affected by industrial closures. *Intermediate areas* lie outside the development areas, often adjacent to them. They suffer problems similar to but less acute than the development areas, and therefore qualify for less assistance. The particularly acute economic problems of Northern Ireland qualify it for more generous assistance than the development areas.

In 1993, recognising that the problems were often highly localised, the government created more but smaller assisted areas. It also established new 'split areas' which were a mixture of development and intermediate areas or intermediate and non-assisted areas. For the first time parts of London, East Anglia and the south coast were given AA status.

Regional development grants (RDGs) were the major form of regional assistance for many years. They were *automatically* available to manufacturing firms and certain service-sector firms locating in development (but not intermediate) areas. RDGs were phased out from 1988.

Regional selective assistance (RSA) is in the form of *discretionary* grants given for certain projects. The main basis for their award is job creation. They are available in both development and intermediate areas. They can be capital-related grants, for the purchase of land, buildings or equipment; or job-related grants, for the employment or training of labour. The amount awarded is normally that judged to be the minimum necessary for the project to proceed (subject to certain maxima).

The largest amount of regional assistance comes from the *European regional development fund* (ERDF). Since 1985 it has provided grants up to 50 per cent for job-creating projects and projects to develop infrastructure. The money is available for use only in the assisted areas, and is intended to be *additional* to any supplied by member governments. However, some countries, including the UK, have tended to use ERDF grants to *replace* domestic assistance and have thus come into dispute with the EU. The bulk of ERDF grants are allocated to the four poorest members of the EU: Greece, Ireland, Portugal and Spain.

Regional enterprise grants (REGs) were introduced in 1988 to encourage the development of small businesses in assisted areas. They are of two types. *Investment grants* of 15 per cent of capital expenditure up to a maximum of £15 000 are available to firms employing fewer than 25 people. *Innovation grants* of 50 per cent of expenditure on product development up to a maximum of £25 000 are available to firms employing fewer than 50 people. In addition, *enterprise initiative consultancy grants* are available in assisted areas to encourage the launching of new enterprises.

Urban policy

During the 1980s, the thrust of policy shifted away from regional and towards urban policy. Several new schemes were introduced involving the creation of various new categories of deprived area.

Enterprise zones are very small districts in urban areas suffering acute industrial decline. Firms setting up in enterprise zones receive 100 per cent capital allowances on property, exemption from rates and land tax, fewer planning regulations and less bureaucratic intervention generally. By the mid-1990s there were 30 such zones.

Simplified planning zones (SPZs) were set up in 1990 to provide a cheaper means of encouraging firms to set up in deprived inner city areas. SPZs are similar to enterprise zones in having fewer planning regulations, but there are no financial incentives available to firms.

Urban Development Corporations (UDCs) were first established in the early 1980s. They were temporary bodies which had a pump-priming role: to stimulate private-

DEFINITION

Assisted areas Areas of high unemployment qualifying for government regional selective assistance (RSA) and grants from the European regional development fund (ERDF).

sector-led regeneration of inner city areas. They had considerable powers to enable them to do this, many of which overrode local authority powers. They could grant planning permission; acquire, hold and manage land and property (including making compulsory purchases); and provide grants and other assistance to firms. By the mid-1990s there were twelve UDCs in operation. They were all wound up between 1995 and 1998.

In 1994 the government established a *Single Regeneration Budget* (SRB), which is administered through ten regional offices. The aim is to encourage a partnership between government and the private sector (the Private Finance Initiative (PFI)) and to ensure that the maximum benefit is gained from European Structural Funds. Currently there are three major programmes under which new SRB moneys can be allocated:

- The *Challenge Fund* provides grants for schemes which meet various local objectives, such as increased employment, training, new businesses, housing, crime prevention and support for ethnic minorities. Partnerships drawn from local authorities, TECs and the private, community and voluntary sectors draw up the schemes and then bid for money from the Fund in an annual competition. Of the 329 bids for the 1996/7 grants, 172 were successful, receiving on average £1.5 million each.
- *English Partnerships*, originally the *Urban Regeneration Agency* (URA), aims to act as a partner with private firms, local authorities and the voluntary sector. It provides support in the form of grants, loans, guarantees and partnership investment, for local regeneration. It operates through six regional offices and supports projects which would not be privately profitable, but where the marginal *social* benefit exceeds the marginal social cost. Such projects include clearing and reclaiming derelict land, providing commercial/industrial premises where private development is not forthcoming (e.g. in severely depressed areas), and providing incentive grants for private companies to move into such areas.
- *Housing Action Trusts* (HATs) are public bodies dedicated to the regeneration of run-down housing estates. They repair and improve houses and improve the local environment and amenities. By 1996, six HATs had been established in different parts of the country.

In addition to the above schemes which continue to provide new funding, there are other SRB schemes which are being wound up, but which will continue to provide finance for some time:

- The *Urban Programme* provided grants to local authorities for urban regeneration projects, such as factory building or improving the local environment.
- *City Challenge* was a competitive scheme. Local authorities submitted proposals for improving specific inner city areas, and then the Department of the Environment selected those it considered to be the best. City Challenge grants were allocated up to 1998.
- *Estate Action* provided funds to help local authorities improve run-down housing estates. Although funding will continue into the late 1990s, no new projects were adopted after 1995.

The *Training and Enterprise Councils* (TECs) are independent companies responsible for providing various training schemes. They are supervised by the Department of Education and Employment, which provides various grants to them. In the inner city areas, the TECs are involved in arranging and funding 'compacts' between employers and schools, whereby the employers agree to provide jobs and training to school leavers who have achieved an agreed level of attainment at school.

The former Conservative government's attitude towards regional policy

There were substantial changes in UK regional policy under the Conservative government. There were two main elements in these changes.

Reducing the total amount of money spent on regional assistance

After considerable growth in government expenditure on regional policies in the late 1960s and mid-1970s, there were substantial cuts in regional assistance in the 1980s and 1990s, falling from 0.34 per cent of GDP in 1981 to 0.05 per cent in 1996.

In part this stemmed from the government's general desire to cut the size of public expenditure, in order to reduce the PSBR and give scope for tax cuts; and in part it stemmed from its desire to allow regional disparities to be corrected, wherever possible, by market forces.

Making regional assistance more cost-effective

The Thatcher government used the following arguments to justify its decision to abolish RDGs:

- Regional development grants were paid automatically to firms moving into development areas, even if they would have moved there anyway.
- RDGs were paid for replacement of plant and machinery, as well as for new investment. But replacement investment creates few if any jobs.

CASE STUDIES BOX 22.4

'WILL THE LAST ONE IN CONSETT PLEASE TURN OUT THE LIGHTS'[1]

When the steelworks in Consett finally stopped production in September 1980, making 3700 steelworkers redundant, this small town of 30 000 inhabitants was devastated. Over the following months a further twenty local firms closed down and by 1982 Consett had lost half its traditional manufacturing industry. Unemployment and despondency were high. But despite this, a wholesale exodus of Consett residents did not occur and the picture today presents a dramatic change in fortunes. Since 1980 over 5000 jobs have been created, reducing unemployment to well below its 1979 level. Of the 180 companies that invested in Consett between 1985 and 1996, 98 were new business start-ups, 51 were expansions of businesses that existed prior to the steelworks closing, and 31 were new inward investment.

Has this turnabout been due to the operation of the free market, or to government intervention?

Private enterprise certainly played a decisive role in the area's redevelopment, with capital being attracted by low costs and a relatively skilled pool of labour. But there were also key organisational, financial and infrastructural inputs from the public sector. Regional grants were co-ordinated by the Derwentside Development Agency, and British Steel helped in re-establishing the local economy by encouraging the setting-up of new businesses.

Consett seems to be a successful case of co-ordinated public and private enterprise.

??

1. Why is there not necessarily a mass exodus from towns experiencing exceptionally high rates of local unemployment?
2. What sort of industries would be most likely to be attracted into a town like Consett?

[1] Graffiti on a door of the derelict steelworks.

- RDGs were largely confined to manufacturing industry, even though service industries are generally more labour intensive.
- Some RDGs were paid automatically: they did not discriminate between efficient and inefficient firms.
- RDGs were essentially *capital* grants: they thus encouraged firms to become more capital intensive.

Henceforth government help would be mainly in the form of regional selective assistance. RSA is not automatic. It is given at the discretion of the Department of Trade and Industry. The government intended that it would be awarded only to projects that were cost-effective in creating jobs. But given the substantial reduction in total government expenditure on regional assistance, there would have to have been a huge increase in cost-effectiveness in the move from RDGs to RSA, if as many jobs were to have been created as before.

The effectiveness of regional policy

The following tentative conclusions can be reached about the effectiveness of regional policy:

- A carefully targeted policy, which focuses on job creation (subject to efficiency criteria), is likely to be more cost-effective than general investment grants. Similarly, a policy that does not discriminate against the service sector, or small firms, is likely to be more cost-effective than one that concentrates on large-scale manufacturing.
- The government could focus its *national* expenditure more specifically on the depressed regions. The relocation of more government offices might help, as would the deliberate location of government spending and the targeting of infrastructure construction in the depressed regions.

High regional unemployment in the 1980s was in part a manifestation of the much higher levels of *national* unemployment than in the past. An expansion of economic activity throughout the whole country can go a long way towards easing the problems of the depressed regions.

The effectiveness of urban policy

Despite the large number of initiatives, the effectiveness of urban policy is limited by several factors:

- Government attempts to reduce local authority taxes have drastically reduced the ability of local authorities to provide the infrastructure and other incentives necessary to attract industry into their areas. This has been a particular problem for inner city areas where the tax base has been low and the demands on expenditure have been high.
- The total amount of public money spent is relatively low compared with other areas of government expenditure. In 1995/6 the total spent on grants for urban regeneration was £1359 million (see Table 22.4). This amounted to only 0.44 per cent of total government

Table 22.4 Planned government expenditure (actual and planned) on urban policy: Single Regeneration Budget (£m)

<table>
<tr><th></th><th>1991/2</th><th>1992/3</th><th>1993/4</th><th>1994/5</th><th>1995/6</th><th>1996/7</th><th>1997/8</th><th>1998/9</th></tr>
<tr><td>Current schemes</td><td></td><td></td><td></td><td></td><td></td><td></td><td></td><td></td></tr>
<tr><td>Challenge Fund</td><td>–</td><td>–</td><td>–</td><td>–</td><td>125</td><td>265</td><td>483</td><td>600</td></tr>
<tr><td>English Partnerships (URA)</td><td>99</td><td>153</td><td>165</td><td>192</td><td>210</td><td>210</td><td>210</td><td>210</td></tr>
<tr><td>Housing Action Trusts</td><td>10</td><td>27</td><td>78</td><td>92</td><td>90</td><td>89</td><td>89</td><td>89</td></tr>
<tr><td>Previous schemes</td><td></td><td></td><td></td><td></td><td></td><td></td><td></td><td></td></tr>
<tr><td>UDCs</td><td>509</td><td>431</td><td>343</td><td>258</td><td>218</td><td>190</td><td>168</td><td>69</td></tr>
<tr><td>Estate Action</td><td>268</td><td>348</td><td>357</td><td>373</td><td>314</td><td>256</td><td>178</td><td>115</td></tr>
<tr><td>City Challenge</td><td>–</td><td>73</td><td>240</td><td>234</td><td>242</td><td>224</td><td>143</td><td>7</td></tr>
<tr><td>Urban Programme</td><td>238</td><td>236</td><td>167</td><td>68</td><td rowspan="2">160</td><td rowspan="2">84</td><td rowspan="2">57</td><td rowspan="2">43</td></tr>
<tr><td>Other</td><td>336</td><td>317</td><td>288</td><td>241</td></tr>
<tr><td>Total</td><td>1460</td><td>1585</td><td>1638</td><td>1458</td><td>1359</td><td>1318</td><td>1328</td><td>1133</td></tr>
</table>

Source: *Department of the Environment Report 1996* (HMSO).

expenditure and 1.24 per cent of total government grants and subsidies. What is more, the total amount allocated to urban programmes has declined. In 1996/7, real SRB expenditure was only just over 70 per cent of that in 1993/4.

- It is questionable whether the jobs created by the various projects are in fact *new* jobs, or whether they would have been created anyway, either in that particular area or in a neighbouring (and possibly only marginally less deprived) area.
- Some of the new jobs created are filled not by residents of the areas, but by people commuting into them. The local residents often do not have sufficient skills to compete with outsiders.

Clearly the needs of the inner cities are great, and there is the danger that many of the initiatives may do little more than tinker with the problem. Unless sufficiently large amounts of *extra* money are available, it is unlikely that the effects of the policies will be substantial.

SECTION SUMMARY

1. Regional and local disparities arise from a changing pattern of industrial production. With many of the older industries concentrated in certain parts of the country and especially in the inner cities, and with an acceleration in the rate of industrial change, so the gap between rich and poor areas has widened.
2. Regional disparities can in theory be corrected by the market, with capital being attracted to areas of low wages and workers being attracted to areas of high wages.
3. In practice, regional disparities persist because of capital and labour immobility and regional multiplier effects.
4. The radical-right solution is to remove impediments to the market achieving regional balance. They favour such policies as local, rather than national, pay bargaining, reducing unemployment benefits, adopting uniform business rates and limiting local authority expenditure.
5. Interventionist solutions focus on measures to encourage firms to move to areas of high unemployment. These measures might include subsidies or tax concessions for firms which move, the provision of facilities and improved infrastructure in the depressed area, the siting of government offices in the depressed areas and the prevention of firms expanding in the prosperous ones. Employment subsidies will create more jobs than general subsidies, which in turn will create more jobs than capital subsidies.
6. In the UK there has been a movement away from general grants towards discretionary grants based on job creation. There are also regional grants from the EU and grants and initiatives for the regeneration of the inner cities.
7. The success of regional and urban policies has been limited by the relatively low level of government grants and by the fact that some of the money has gone to projects which would have gone ahead anyway.

22.4 Industrial policy

The poor performance of UK industry

For decades, the UK has had a lower level of investment relative to national income than other industrialised countries (see Table 22.5). This low level of investment has been a major reason for the UK's poor growth performance. It has also meant that in many industries there has emerged a widening technological gap between the UK and its major competitors, such as Japan and Germany. This is reflected in the poor quality and high cost of many UK products.

As a result there has been a growing import penetration of the UK market. Imports of manufactured products have grown more rapidly than UK manufactured exports, and the UK in recent years has become a net importer of manufactured products (see Table 22.6).

Three vicious circles have existed:

- Low investment leads to low productivity, low quality and hence a lack of competitiveness of UK goods. This leads to balance of trade deficits. This leads to deflationary policies with higher interest rates. This leads to low investment.
- Low investment leads to low growth of profits. This leads to low investment.
- Low investment leads to low productivity growth. This leads to low growth in real wages. Unions, seeking to achieve an increase in living standards, demand higher real wages. This causes cost-push inflation. This may cause deflationary policies to be pursued, uncertainty for firms and an erosion of profits. This leads to low investment.

Deindustrialisation

Not only has the competitiveness of UK industry declined, but industrial production in the UK has grown much more slowly than in other industrialised countries. Manufacturing industry hardly grew at all until the end of the 1980s. Manufacturing output in the UK in 1986 was only 1 per cent higher than in 1970, whereas in the developed world as a whole it was 50 per cent higher. Then in the recession of the early 1990s, manufacturing suffered a bigger decline in the UK than in other industrialised countries (see Table 22.7).

?? Why, do you think, was the UK's performance in *industrial* production in the early 1980s better than in *manufacturing* production?

Policy alternatives

There are two approaches to increasing investment and halting or slowing down deindustrialisation: a demand-side approach and a supply-side approach.

On the *demand side,* we have already examined the Keynesian approach of trying to maintain a high level of activity in the economy by demand management. It is based on the premise that the major determinant of investment is consumer demand.

Supply-side approaches aim to provide more incentives to invest for any given level of aggregate demand. They also attempt to improve industrial efficiency and competitiveness for any given level of investment.

The advocates of such policies highlight a number of supply-side weaknesses of the UK economy: overstaffing, union restrictive practices, an outdated educational and training system insufficiently geared to industry's needs, too little research and development, misdirected research and development, and a poor management that is unwilling to go out into world markets and compete aggressively.

Supply-side policies to tackle these weaknesses can be interventionist or non-interventionist. Radical-right non-

Table 22.5 Gross fixed capital formation as a percentage of GDP: 1960–97

Year (average)	UK	W. Germany[1]	Japan	EU	OECD (total)
1960–7	17.7	25.2	31.0	22.8	21.0
1968–73	18.9	24.5	34.6	23.6	22.3
1974–80	19.2	21.0	31.8	22.2	22.2
1981–5	16.5	20.4	28.7	19.8	20.7
1986–90	18.9	19.9	29.8	20.1	20.8
1991–7	15.4	21.9	29.7	19.2	20.8

[1] All Germany from 1991.

Sources: *Historical Statistics 1960–87* (OECD, 1988); *Main Economic Indicators* (OECD).

Table 22.6 UK balance of trade in manufactures: selected years 1974–97

	1974	1978	1980	1982	1984	1986	1988	1989	1990	1992	1994	1995	1996	1997
Exports of manufactures (£bn)	13.3	28.0	34.8	37.3	46.7	54.5	66.0	76.0	82.4	87.7	111.7	127.8	139.8	144.0
Imports of manufactures (£bn)	11.7	24.4	31.2	37.1	53.0	62.8	83.3	95.6	94.1	94.8	119.2	135.8	147.9	152.9
Balance of trade in manufactures (£bn)	+1.6	+3.6	+3.6	+0.2	−6.3	−8.3	−17.3	−19.6	−11.7	−7.1	−7.5	−8.0	−8.1	−8.9

Sources: *Monthly Digest of Statistics* (ONS); *Annual Abstract of Statistics* (ONS).

interventionist supply-side policies were examined in section 22.2. The remainder of this chapter considers interventionist policies. In particular, it focuses on **industrial policies**: policies to reverse the relative decline of industry by providing government incentives or encouragement to invest.

The case against the market

The basis of the case for government intervention is that the free market is likely to provide too little research and development, training and investment.

There are potentially large external benefits from research and development. Firms investing in developing and improving products, and especially firms engaged in more general scientific research, may produce results that provide benefits to many other firms. Thus the social rate of return on investment may be much higher than the private rate of return. Investment that is privately unprofitable for a firm may therefore still be economically desirable for the nation.

Similarly, investment in training may continue yielding benefits to society which are lost to the firms providing the training when the workers leave.

Investment often involves risks. Firms may be unwilling to take those risks, since the costs of possible failure may be too high. When looked at nationally, however, the benefits of investment might well have substantially outweighed the costs, and thus it would have been socially desirable for firms to have taken the risk. Successes would have outweighed failures.

Markets in the real world may be highly monopolistic. This lack of competition may discourage investment. Monopoly profits may allow management and labour to continue to be inefficient without their firms being driven out of business – at least until there is an economic recession.

The *capital* market may be imperfect. This may result in even privately profitable investment not being financed. Banks in the UK, unlike banks in France, Germany and Japan, have been reluctant to lend to firms for long-term investment. Similarly, if firms rely on raising finance by the issue of new shares, this makes them very dependent on the stock market performance of their shares, which depends on current profitability and expected profitability in the near future, not on long-term profitability. Shareholders, who are mainly financial institutions, tend to demand too high a dividend rate from the companies in which they invest. This, in part, is due to

DEFINITION

Industrial policies Policies to encourage industrial investment and greater industrial efficiency.

Table 22.7 Industrial and manufacturing production in the UK and the OECD countries: selected years 1970–96

	Industrial production (1970 = 100)		Manufacturing production[1] (1970 = 100)	
	UK	OECD (total)	UK	OECD (total)
1970	100	100	100	100
1978	115	129	106	129
1982	109	131	91	128
1986	123	153	101	150
1989	132	171	120	172
1992	126	171	111	171
1994	135	178	117	179
1996	140	187	121	190

[1] Industrial production less mining, oil, energy and water.

Sources: *Indicators of Industrial Activity* (OECD); *Monthly Digest of Statistics* (ONS).

CASE STUDIES — BOX 22.5

OILING THE WHEELS OF BRITISH INDUSTRY?

Has North Sea oil been a supply-side bonanza?

When the UK oil production was at its peak in 1985, some 2½ million barrels a day were being pumped from the North Sea. This made the UK the world's sixth largest oil producer, accounting for some 5 per cent of total production.

Not surprisingly, this has had a major impact on the UK economy. The government raised £12.2 billion in revenue in 1985/6, and oil contributed £16 billion to the value of exports in 1985. This enabled the government to reduce the public-sector borrowing requirement, which in turn allowed the government to make substantial cuts in tax rates.

But has North Sea oil been an unmixed blessing? Or has the way in which the oil revenues have been used actually contributed to the country's economic problems?

From the late 1970s to the mid-1980s, the time when oil began to bring in substantial revenues, the government pursued strong anti-inflationary policies. These involved high interest rates and thus led to a high exchange rate. This made it difficult for UK exporters to compete abroad. Oil only compounded the problem. Oil revenues led to a current account surplus, and this drove up the exchange rate even further, thereby further squeezing UK industry's international competitiveness.

In the early part of the 1980s North Sea oil effectively *crowded out* traditional UK exports. Rather than being used to pay for more imports of capital goods to refurbish UK industry, it was used to soften the blow of deflationary policies by helping to keep taxes low.

By the late 1980s, when oil was selling for a much lower price and thus making a much smaller contribution to the balance of payments, the current account had moved into severe deficit (see Box 24.1). A consumer boom had sucked in vast quantities of imports. UK industry had simply not been able to meet this demand.

Critics of the Thatcher government argue that North Sea oil revenues should have been spent on long-term investment in the export and import-substituting industries and on improving the nation's infrastructure.

??

1. Would the UK have been better off without North Sea oil?
2. How could the crowding-out effect of North Sea oil have been avoided?

Contribution of oil to the UK balance of payments

Year 19...	78	79	80	81	82	83	84	85	86	87	88	89	90	91	92	93	94	95	96	97
Oil balance (£bn)	−2.3	−1.1	0.1	2.9	4.4	6.8	6.6	7.8	3.7	4.2	2.8	1.3	1.5	1.2	1.5	2.4	3.9	4.3	4.7	4.3

competition between financial institutions to attract savers to buy their savings packages. The result is that there is less profit left over for ploughing back into investment. The fear of takeovers (the competition for corporate control) again makes managers overconcerned to keep shareholders happy. Finally, floating successful companies on the stock exchange provides a large windfall gain to the original owners. This encourages entrepreneurs to *set up* companies, but discourages them from making *long-term* commitments to them. This all leads to the UK disease of 'short-termism': the obsession with short-term profits and the neglect of investment that yields profits only after a number of years.

Finally, in the case of ailing firms, if the government does not help finance a rescue investment programme, there may be substantial social costs from job losses. The avoidance of these social costs may make the investment socially profitable.

??

How would the radical right reply to these arguments?

The forms of intervention

Nationalisation. This is the most extreme form of intervention. As in the cases of Rolls-Royce in 1971 and British Leyland in 1975, nationalisation may initially be a means of rescuing firms in financial difficulties – firms that are probably considered to be of strategic importance. Once they are nationalised, however, the government may choose to invest public money in them with the aim of making them profitable in the long run. By the time it was privatised in 1987, BL had become profitable again, thanks largely to a major programme of investment in new models and new production-line techniques.

Grants. The government may sponsor research and development in certain industries (e.g. aerospace) or in specific fields (e.g. microprocessors). It may back investment programmes considered to benefit the economy as a whole.

Rationalisation. The government may encourage mergers or other forms of industrial reorganisation that will lead to greater efficiency and/or higher levels of investment. This could be done through government agencies (e.g. the IRC: see below) or government departments.

Advice and persuasion. The government may engage in discussions with private firms in order to find ways to improve efficiency and innovation. It may bring firms together to exchange information and create a climate of greater certainty. It may bring firms and unions together to try to create greater industrial harmony.

Information. The government may provide various information services to firms: technical assistance, the results of public research, information on markets, etc.

Direct provision. Improvements in infrastructure – such as a better motorway system – can be of direct benefit to industry. Alternatively, the government could provide factories or equipment to specific firms.

Policies designed to achieve other objectives may also affect industrial performance. For example, regional policy involves grants to firms and provision of infrastructure. Fiscal policies to stimulate demand may also involve increased government expenditure on infrastructure.

Planning

The most comprehensive approach to industrial policy is for the government to engage in national economic planning. This is not the 'command planning' of the former Soviet Union, where factories were issued with instructions on what to produce, what inputs to use and how much to invest. Rather, it is 'indicative planning'. Indicative planning works alongside the market. It does not replace it.

In a free market there are likely to be many uncertainties for firms. Firms are often highly interconnected. If the car industry plans to expand, there must be enough steel available to build the cars, and dealers must be willing to take extra cars. If more steel is to be produced, there must be enough coal available, and enough blast furnace capacity. If individual firms' and industries' plans do not match, there will be either bottlenecks or idle capacity. Unless firms can know the plans of other firms, they may be cautious about taking investment decisions.

Indicative planning is where the government consults with industrialists to find out their intentions. It then seeks to co-ordinate the plans of firms, industries and sectors, and to recommend realistic and mutually consistent targets for output and investment. If firms' plans do not match, the government hopes that, in the light of the information provided, the firms will adjust their plans. The government could also use persuasion or various financial incentives to obtain a consistent plan.

The nearest the UK came to full-scale indicative planning was the National Plan of 1965. This was strongly influenced by French experience. France had used national planning since shortly after the Second World War and, up to the late 1970s, it is generally considered to have been a success. Investment and growth were higher than in the UK and higher than the European average.

In 1962 the UK government set up the National Economic Development Council (NEDC or 'Neddy'). This was a body with representatives of employers, trade unions and the government. Also 21 Economic Development Committees (EDCs or 'Little Neddies') were set up, each for a specific industry. Their purpose was to exchange information on plans and priorities.

The National Plan of 1965 was the brainchild of the Department of Economic Affairs, set up by the newly elected Labour government to administer industrial policy. Both the earlier NEDC reports and the plan itself explored the implications for industry of a 4 per cent target growth rate.

However, the 4 per cent growth target was far too optimistic, and the plan was rapidly overtaken by a balance of payments crisis and the adoption of deflationary fiscal and monetary policy. Planning was abandoned, although the NEDC and the EDCs continued to provide reports and encouraged the exchange of information.

A modified form of planning was resurrected in the mid-1970s. When Labour returned to power in 1974, they stressed the role of the NEDC in implementing an 'industrial strategy'. Sector working parties (SWPs) were established (like the NEDC on a tripartite basis), to identify bottlenecks and obstacles to economic growth in specific industries. The SWPs produced reports and made recommendations on increasing efficiency, training, research and development, marketing, etc.; and grants were provided by the government to support their recommendations. For example, the Microprocessor Application Project (MAP) was set up to promote the understanding and use of computers in industry.

CASE STUDIES

ALTERNATIVE APPROACHES TO TRAINING AND EDUCATION

It is generally recognised by economists and politicians alike that improvements in training and education can yield significant supply-side gains. Indeed, the UK's failure to invest as much in training as many of its major competitors is seen as a key explanation for the country's poor economic performance since the early 1970s. In the UK some 62 per cent of the manufacturing labour force have no qualifications. In Germany the figure is less than 30 per cent.

Training and economic performance are linked in three main ways:

- *Labour productivity*. In various studies comparing the productivity of UK and German industry, education and training was seen as the principal reason for the productivity gap between the two countries. In 1992 this gap was estimated at 22 per cent, of which nearly half was due to the superior skills of German workers.
- *Innovation and change*. A key factor in shaping a firm's willingness to introduce new products or processes will be the adaptability and skills of its workforce. If the firm has to spend a lot of money on retraining, or on attracting skilled workers away from other firms, the costs may prove prohibitive.
- *Costs of production*. A shortage of skilled workers will quickly create labour bottlenecks and cause production costs to increase. This will stifle economic growth.

If training is left to the employer, the benefits will become an externality if the workers leave to work elsewhere. Society has benefited from the training, but the firm has not. The free market, therefore, will provide a less than optimal amount of training. The more mobile the labour force, and the more 'transferable' the skills acquired from training, the more likely it is that workers will leave, and the less willing firms will be to invest in training.

In the UK, there is a high level of labour turnover. What is more, wage differentials between skilled and unskilled workers are narrower than in many other countries, and so there is less incentive for workers to train.

How can increased training be achieved? There are three broad approaches:

- Workers could be encouraged to stay with their employer so that employers would be more willing to invest in training. Externalities would be reduced.
- The government could provide subsidies for training. Alternatively, the government or some other agency could provide education and training directly.
- Firms could co-operate to prevent 'poaching' and set up industry-wide training programmes, perhaps in partnership with the government and unions.

As far as the first approach is concerned, most countries have seen a movement towards *greater* labour mobility. The rise in the 'flexible firm' (see Box 9.9) has involved the employment of fewer permanent workers and more part-time and temporary workers. Some countries, such as Japan and Germany, however, have a generally lower rate of labour turnover than most. In Japan, in particular, it is common for workers to stay with one employer throughout their career. There the relationship between employer and employee extends well beyond a simple short-term economic arrangement. Workers give loyalty and commitment to their employer, which in return virtually guarantees long-term employment and provides various fringe benefits (such as housing, child care, holiday schemes and health care). It is not surprising that Japanese firms invest highly in training.

In the USA, labour turnover is very high and yet there is little in the way of industry-wide training. Instead, the US government hopes, by having a high percentage of young people in further and higher education, that sufficient numbers and quality of workers are available

The industrial strategy of the Labour government led also to the establishment of the National Enterprise Board (NEB) in 1975 as a state industrial holding company. In other words, the NEB provided financial assistance to firms in exchange for shares. This shareholding enabled it to take part in the decision making of the firms. Originally, it was intended that the NEB would have a wide share ownership and hence a wide influence across the country. As it turned out, it was mainly occupied with supervising British Leyland and Rolls-Royce, and the majority of its resources were used to finance these two companies.

When the Conservatives were elected in 1979, they abandoned completely the idea of national planning, preferring to rely on the market for the co-ordination of the various sectors of the economy. The NEB was wound up, and the NEDC (then called the National Economic Development Office) was virtually ignored and eventually abolished in 1992.

??

1. Are bodies like the SWPs better able to forecast a firm's markets than the firm itself? Explain why or why not.
2. What instruments might a government use to 'persuade' firms to abide by a national plan? What are their advantages and disadvantages?

BOX 22.6

for industry. Almost 30 per cent of the US population graduates, and only just over 0.2 per cent of GDP is spent on training. The problem with the US approach is that many non-graduates are unskilled and receive no training at all.

In Germany the proportion of graduates is considerably lower (less than 14 per cent), but expenditure on training accounts for nearly 1.6 per cent of GDP. Most young people who do not enter higher education embark on some form of apprenticeship. They attend school for part of the week, and receive work-based training for the rest. The state, unions and employers' associations work closely in determining training provision, and they have developed a set of vocational qualifications based around the apprenticeship system. Given that virtually all firms are involved in training, the 'free-rider' problem of firms poaching labour without themselves paying for training is virtually eliminated. The result is that the German workforce is highly skilled. Many of the skills, however, are highly specific. This is a problem when the demand for particular skills declines.

In the UK, the Conservative government's attitude towards training was initially influenced by its free-market approach to supply-side policy. Training was to be left largely to employers. Government schemes such as the Youth Training Scheme (YTS), first introduced in 1983, were seen mainly as a means of reducing youth unemployment, rather than as a means of improving labour productivity. The 'training' element was often very limited or non-existent.

However, with growing worries over the UK's 'productivity gap', the government set up Training and Enterprise Councils (TECs) in 1988. The TECs were to be government funded, and to be responsible for identifying regional skill needs and the manner in which training was to be conducted.

Then in 1991, the National Vocational Qualification (NVQ) was launched. Students work for an employer, and receive on-the-job training. They also attend college on an occasional basis. The NVQ is awarded when they have achieved sufficient experience. In addition the government launched General National Vocational Qualifications (GNVQs). These further-education qualifications were aimed to bridge the gap between education and work, by ensuring that education was more work relevant.

The GNVQ system was modelled on that in France, where a clear vocational educational route is seen as the key to reducing skills shortages. At the age of fourteen, French students can choose to pursue academic or vocational education routes. The vocational route provides high-level, broad-based skills (unlike in Germany, where skills tend to be more job specific).

Critics of the UK strategy argue that it fails to address fundamental problems of funding, co-ordination and labour market flexibility. Employers still face the threat of having newly trained labour poached; the regional activities of the TECs fail to account for national, long-term training issues; and NVQs often provide too narrow forms of training. Most important, the funding devoted to training (0.5 per cent of GDP) is still low compared with most other industrialised countries. Critics claim that the UK system has the worst features of both the US and the German systems: too little training and too specific training.

??

1. Governments and educationalists generally regard it as desirable that trainees acquire transferable skills. Why may many employers disagree?
2. There are externalities (benefits) when employers provide training. What externalities are there from the undergoing of training by the individual? Do they imply that individuals will choose to receive more or less than the socially optimal amount of training?

Selective intervention

Conservative governments have never favoured a comprehensive industrial strategy. Nevertheless, governments of both parties have intervened selectively in areas where they have felt that the market has provided inadequate investment.

Research and development

Slightly more than half of UK research and development is financed by the government, but this has been highly concentrated in the fields of defence, aerospace and the nuclear power industry. As a result, there has been little government sponsorship of research in the majority of industry. Since the mid-1970s, however, there have been a number of government initiatives in the field of information technology. Funds have been provided for various educational programmes in schools, higher education and industry, and for research into computers and their applications. Even so, the amount of government support in this field has been very small compared with Japan, France and the USA. What is more, the amount of support has declined since the mid-1980s.

CASE STUDIES BOX 22.7

INDUSTRIAL POLICY IN JAPAN
Helping the sunrise industries shine

Japan is now the world's largest manufacturer of steel, ships, cars and lorries, motor cycles, engines, cameras, calculators, big memory chips, televisions, video tape recorders and photocopiers. Between 1960 and 1995 investment averaged 31 per cent of GDP, industrial output grew by over 5 per cent per annum, real GDP grew by 5.7 per cent per annum and the rate of automation outpaced all Japan's economic rivals.

Part of the explanation for the rapid growth in industrial output in the 1960s and 1970s was the fact that Japan was starting from a low base and was copying and adapting technology developed in the West. But, despite a slowing down in growth after 1973 and particularly in the 1990s, investment remains higher than in Europe and North America (see Table 22.5) and the development of new products and processes is actively encouraged by the Japanese government.

Industrial policy in Japan is guided by the Ministry of International Trade and Industry (MITI), whose role is to encourage co-operation between private companies, to help stimulate investment in new technology and product development, and to help companies' position in international trade. Using a mixture of state aid and legislative power, MITI wields a considerable amount of influence.

MITI encourages older industries to close or to adapt, and provides grants for this purpose. But it is for its help to the 'sunrise' industries that MITI is best known. It provides subsidies and helps these industries to raise finance. It also uses tariffs and quotas (see section 23.2) to protect them from international competition while they are becoming established. It provided help in the 1950s to the steel, shipbuilding and electricity industries, and in the 1960s and 1970s to the chemical, car and electrical goods industries. In the 1980s and 1990s it has given substantial support to the computer industry.

The computer industry and MITI

The computer industry took off in Japan in the late 1970s, although MITI had been active in organising its structure as early as 1957. It established in 1961 a computer leasing firm, enabling firms to reduce their capital outlay on renting computers. This was superseded in 1971 by various research associations which were set up and partly financed by MITI. Companies were encouraged to work together on a set project (usually on different aspects) for a given period of time; then findings were pooled. The research would then be available to the participating firms, which would compete with each other in making use of it.

The extent of MITI's active role was highlighted in 1981 with the announcement of a ten-year project of research into 'next-generation computing technology'. This encompassed twelve distinct projects, covering investigations into new materials, bio-technology and semi-conductors.

Long-term industrial policy on this scale helps to give Japanese companies a competitive advantage and encourages them to adopt a long-term investment strategy.

?? Compare and contrast the Japanese attitude towards industrial policy with that of the current and previous UK governments.

Industrial reorganisation

Labour governments have been concerned with encouraging efficiency and investment via rationalisation. The Industrial Reorganisation Corporation (IRC) was set up in 1967 to provide loans to industry, and to arrange and finance mergers, where these were felt to lead to economies of scale and greater scope for investment. The Industrial Expansion Act of 1968 provided additional funds for encouraging industrial reorganisation and investment.

The 1970 Conservative government abolished the IRC, but its Industry Act of 1972 enabled the government to provide finance to firms for reorganisation and investment. This act was used extensively by the 1974 Labour government. It was used in particular to help ailing companies: e.g. British Leyland and Alfred Herbert (the machine-tool producer).

The main industrial reorganisation strategy pursued by the Conservative governments of the 1980s and 1990s has been privatisation (see section 12.3 and pages 667–9).

Assistance to small firms

Conservative governments have been concerned to assist small firms. The 1970 Conservative government set up small firms' advisory centres and introduced various forms of tax relief. The 1979 Conservative government extended this policy and introduced a number of new tax concessions. Current measures include the following.

Tax concessions. Small firms pay a 24 per cent rate of corporation tax compared with 33 per cent for larger companies. Also, under the *Enterprise Investment Scheme*, people investing by buying shares in small companies, not quoted on the Stock Exchange, are granted income tax relief of 20 per cent on investments of up to £100 000 per year. To qualify for the tax relief, investors must hold the shares for five years. Any gains made on shares held for more than five years are also exempt from capital gains tax. Companies are normally permitted to raise up to £1 million per year through the scheme.

Grants. The *Business Start-up Scheme*, administered by the ten government Regional Offices, provides up to £90 per week for up to 66 weeks for unemployed people wishing to start up their own business. The *Regional Enterprise Grants* scheme provides help for small firms in assisted areas (see page 674). The *small firms merit award for research and technology* (SMART) is a grant to firms with up to 50 employees to support the use of new technology.

Loans. Under the *Loans Guarantee Scheme*, the government guarantees 70 per cent of loans of up to £100 000 by banks to small businesses against default. This therefore encourages banks to lend to businesses it might otherwise regard as too risky.

Advice. Many people setting up small businesses have very little experience or training. *Business Links* are government-funded agencies established in 1993 to co-ordinate the work of other agencies, such as local authorities, Chambers of Commerce and *Local Enterprise Agencies*. Personal Business Advisers working for Business Links provide specialist advice in the fields of management skills, exporting, marketing, design, etc.

Reductions in 'red tape'. Small firms are subject to fewer planning and other bureaucratic controls than large companies.

Training

The UK invests little in training programmes compared with most of its industrial competitors (see Box 22.6). However, Training and Enterprise Councils, which are run by local business and funded by the government, attempt to meet local training needs by running various schemes such as Youth Training and Compacts between employers and schools (see page 675). The *Technical and Vocational Educational Initiative* (TVEI) is an attempt to gear the school and college curriculum to the requirements of industry.

The case against intervention

Although the Conservative government continued to intervene selectively, it substantially cut the overall level of industrial support, claiming that intervention weakens market forces and in the long run reduces industrial efficiency. The following arguments were used:

- A poor investment record may be due to managerial inertia and union restrictive practices. Forcing firms and unions to face up to competition in the market may be a better way of encouraging willingness to accept change. Government subsidies may simply allow firms to continue producing inefficiently.
- The government may not make an efficient use of taxpayers' money by giving investment grants. The money may well go to extravagant and unprofitable projects like Concorde.
- The low investment record of private industry may be due to a low potential return on investment. If market opportunities were good, firms would invest without the need of government support.
- UK investment has remained low in the past despite interventionist industrial policy.
- If the government is to help industry, it is best to reduce the tax burden generally, so as to increase the return on investment. The microeconomic allocation of investment resources will then still be provided by the market.

?? Provide a critique of these arguments.

SECTION SUMMARY

1. The UK has had a lower rate of investment than most other industrialised countries. This has contributed to a historically low rate of economic growth and a growing trade deficit in manufactures.
2. Those in favour of interventionist industrial policy point to failings of the market, such as the externalities involved in investment and training, the imperfections in the capital market and the short-term perspective of decision makers.
3. Intervention can take the form of grants, the encouragement of mergers and other forms of rationalisation, advice and persuasion, the provision of information and the direct provision of infrastructure.

continued

4. The government could engage in indicative planning, where the government seeks a partnership with industry to co-ordinate investment decisions throughout the economy. Such planning met with a great deal of success in France in the 1950s, 1960s and 1970s. The UK's one major attempt at national planning in 1965, however, was a failure.
5. Selective intervention in the UK has taken the form of grants for research and development, encouragement of reorganisation, assistance to small firms and help for training. Apart from the last two of these, the Conservative government has generally been against intervention, preferring to use market-orientated supply-side policies.

??? END-OF-CHAPTER QUESTIONS ???

1. Define *demand-side* and *supply-side* policies. Sometimes it is said that Keynesians advocate demand-side policies and monetarists advocate supply-side policies. Is there any accuracy in this statement?
2. What is the relationship between 'successful' supply-side policies and unemployment in (i) the short run and (ii) the long run, according to (a) Keynesian and (b) monetarist assumptions?
3. Why might market-orientated supply-side policies have undesirable side effects on aggregate demand?
4. What type of tax cuts are likely to create the greatest (i) incentives, (ii) disincentives to effort?
5. Compare the relative merits of pro-market and interventionist solutions to regional decline.
6. What are the arguments for and against relying entirely on *discretionary* regional and urban policy?
7. Is deindustrialisation necessarily undesirable?
8. In what ways can interventionist industrial policy work *with* the market, rather than against it? What are the arguments for and against such policy?

23 International trade

Without international trade we would all be much poorer. There would be some items like pineapples, coffee, cotton clothes, foreign holidays and uranium that we would simply have to go without. Then there would be other items like wine and spacecraft that we could only produce very inefficiently.

International trade has the potential to benefit *all* participating countries. This chapter explains why.

Totally free trade, however, may bring problems to countries or to groups of people within those countries. Many people argue strongly for restrictions on trade. Textile workers see their jobs threatened by cheap imported cloth. Car manufacturers worry about falling sales as customers switch to Japanese models or to cheap Eastern European ones. The chapter therefore also examines the arguments for restricting trade. Are people justified in fearing international competition, or are they merely trying to protect some vested interest at the expense of everyone else?

The third part of the chapter considers the arguments for a *partial* form of free trade. This is where a group of countries agree to have free trade between themselves, but still impose trade restrictions on the rest of the world. We will have a look at the general arguments for and against such arrangements, which go under the various titles of *customs unions*, *free trade areas* and *common markets*.

The most famous of common markets is that of the European Union, and the chapter finishes by looking at its arrangements and evolution, from its founding as the European Economic Community (EEC) in 1957 to the enactment in 1993 of the 1986 Single European Act and to the proposals in the Maastricht Treaty.

23.1 The advantages of trade

Specialisation as the basis for trade

Why do countries trade with each other, and what do they gain out of it? The reasons for international trade are really only an extension of the reasons for trade *within* a nation. Rather than people trying to be self-sufficient and do everything for themselves, it makes sense to specialise.

Individuals specialise in the jobs they do, and with the money they earn from selling their labour they buy the goods they need: goods that other people have specialised in producing.

Firms specialise in producing certain goods. This allows them to gain economies of scale and to exploit their entrepreneurial and management skills and the skills of their labour force. It also allows them to benefit from their particular location and from the ownership of any particular capital equipment or other assets they might possess. With the revenues firms earn, they buy in the inputs they need from other firms and the labour they require. Firms thus trade with each other.

Countries also specialise. They produce more than they need of certain goods. What is not consumed domestically is exported. The revenues earned from the exports are used to import goods which are not produced in sufficient amounts at home.

?? Why does the USA not specialise as much as General Motors or Texaco?
Why does the UK not specialise as much as ICI? Is the answer to these questions similar to the answer to the questions, 'Why does the USA not specialise as much as Luxembourg?', and 'Why does ICI or Unilever not specialise as much as the local butcher?'

But which goods should a country specialise in? What should it export and what should it import? The answer is that it should specialise in those goods in which it has a *comparative advantage*. Let us examine what this means.

The law of comparative advantage

Countries have different endowments of factors of production. They differ in population density, labour skills, climate, raw materials, capital equipment, etc. These differences tend to persist because factors are relatively immobile between countries. Obviously land and climate are totally immobile, but even with labour and capital there are more restrictions on their international movement than on their movement within countries. Thus the ability to supply goods differs between countries.

What this means is that the relative costs of producing goods will vary from country to country. For example, one country may be able to produce 1 fridge for the same cost as 6 tonnes of wheat or 3 compact disc players, whereas another country may be able to produce 1 fridge for the same cost as only 3 tonnes of wheat but 4 CD players. It is these differences in relative costs that form the basis of trade.

At this stage we need to distinguish between *absolute advantage* and *comparative advantage*.

Absolute advantage

When one country can produce a good with less resources than another country it is said to have an **absolute advantage** in that good. If France can produce wine with less resources than the UK, and the UK can produce gin with less resources than France, then France has an absolute advantage in wine and the UK an absolute advantage in gin. Production of both wine and gin will be maximised by each country specialising and then trading with the other country. Both will gain.

Comparative advantage

The above seems obvious, but trade between two countries can still be beneficial even if one country could produce *all* goods with less resources than the other, providing the *relative* efficiency with which goods can be produced differs between the two countries.

Take the case of a developed country that is absolutely more efficient than a less developed country at producing both wheat and cloth. Assume that with a given amount of resources (labour, land and capital) the alternatives shown in Table 23.1 can be produced in each country.

Despite the developed country having an absolute advantage in both wheat and cloth, the less developed country (LDC) has a **comparative advantage** in wheat, and the developed country has a comparative advantage in cloth.

This is because wheat is relatively cheaper in the LDC: only 1 metre of cloth has to be sacrificed to produce 2 kilos of wheat, whereas 8 metres of cloth would have to be sacrificed in the developed country to produce 4 kilos of wheat. In other words, the opportunity cost of wheat is four times higher in the developed country (8/4 compared with 1/2).

On the other hand, cloth is relatively cheaper in the developed country. Here the opportunity cost of producing 8 metres of cloth is only 4 kilos of wheat, whereas in the LDC 1 metre of cloth costs 2 kilos of wheat. Thus the opportunity cost of cloth is four times higher in the LDC (2/1 compared with 4/8).

?? Draw up a similar table to Table 23.1, only this time assume that the figures are: LDC 6 wheat or 2 cloth; DC 8 wheat or 20 cloth. What are the opportunity cost ratios now?

To summarise: countries have a comparative advantage in those goods that can be produced at a lower opportunity cost than in other countries.

If countries are to gain from trade, they should export those goods in which they have a comparative advantage and import those goods in which they have a comparative disadvantage. Given this we can state a **law of comparative advantage**: provided opportunity costs of various goods differ in two countries, both of them can gain from mutual trade if they specialise in producing (and exporting) those goods that have relatively low opportunity costs compared with the other country.

But why do they gain if they specialise according to this law? And just what will that gain be? We will consider these questions next.

DEFINITIONS

Absolute advantage A country has an absolute advantage over another in the production of a good if it can produce it with less resources than the other country.

Comparative advantage A country has a comparative advantage over another in the production of a good if it can produce it at a lower opportunity cost: i.e. if it has to forgo less of other goods in order to produce it.

The law of comparative advantage Trade can benefit all countries if they specialise in the goods in which they have a comparative advantage.

ISSUES AND APPLICATIONS

BOX 23.1

SHARING OUT THE JOBS

A parable of comparative advantage

Imagine that you and a group of friends are fed up with the rat race and decide to set up a self-sufficient community. So you club together and use all your savings to buy an old run-down farmhouse with 30 acres of land and a few farm animals.

You decide to produce all your own food, make your own clothes, renovate the farmhouse, make all the furniture, provide all your own entertainment and set up a little shop to sell the things you make. This should bring in enough income to buy the few items you cannot make yourselves.

The day comes to move in, and that evening everyone gathers to decide how all the jobs are going to be allocated. You quickly decide that it would be foolish for all of you to try to do all the jobs. Obviously it will be more efficient to specialise. This does not necessarily mean that everyone is confined to doing only one job, but it does mean that each of you can concentrate on just a few tasks.

But who is to do which job? The answer would seem to be obvious: you pick the best person for the job. So you go down the list of tasks. Who is to take charge of the renovations? Pat has already renovated a cottage, and is brilliant at bricklaying, plastering, wiring and plumbing. So Pat would seem to be the ideal person. Who is to do the cooking? Everyone agrees on this. Pat makes the best cakes, the best quiches and the best Irish stew. So Pat is everyone's choice for cook. And what about milking the sheep? 'Pat used to keep sheep', says Tarquin, 'and made wonderful feta cheese.' 'Good old Pat!' exclaims everyone.

It doesn't take long before it becomes obvious that 'clever-clogs' Pat is simply brilliant at everything, from planting winter wheat, to unblocking drains, to doing the accounts, to tie-dyeing. But it is soon realised that, if Pat has to do everything, nothing will get done. Even Chris, who has never done anything except market research, would be better employed milking the sheep than doing nothing at all.

So what's the best way of allocating the jobs so that the work gets done in the most efficient way? Sharon comes up with the solution. 'Everyone should make a list of all the jobs they could possibly do, and then put them in order from the one they are best at to the one they are worst at.'

So this is what everyone does. And then people are allocated the jobs they are *relatively* best at doing. Chris escapes milking the sheep and keeps the accounts instead. And Pat escapes with an eight-hour day!

?? If Pat took two minutes to milk the sheep and Tarquin took six, how could it ever be more efficient for Tarquin to do it?

The gains from trade based on comparative advantage

Before trade, unless markets are very imperfect, the prices of the two goods are likely to reflect their opportunity costs. For example, in Table 23.1, since the less developed country can produce 2 kilos of wheat for 1 metre of cloth, the *price* of 2 kilos of wheat will roughly equal the price of 1 metre of cloth.

Assume, then, that the pre-trade exchange ratios of wheat for cloth are as follows:

LDC	:	2 wheat for 1 cloth
Developed country	:	1 wheat for 2 cloth (i.e. 4 for 8)

Both countries will now gain from trade, provided the exchange ratio is somewhere between 2:1 and 1:2. Assume, for the sake of argument, that it is 1:1, that 1 wheat trades internationally for 1 cloth. How will each country gain?

The LDC gains by exporting wheat and importing cloth. At an exchange ratio of 1:1, it now only has to give up 1 kilo of wheat to obtain a metre of cloth, whereas before trade it had to give up 2 kilos of wheat.

The developed country gains by exporting cloth and importing wheat. Again at an exchange ratio of 1:1, it now has to give up only 1 metre of cloth to obtain 1 kilo of wheat, whereas before it had to give up 2 metres of cloth.

Thus both countries have gained from trade.

The actual exchange ratios will depend on the relative prices of wheat and cloth after trade takes place. These prices will depend on total demand for and supply of the two goods. It may be that the trade exchange ratio is nearer to the pre-trade exchange ratio of one country than the other. Thus the gains to the two countries need not be equal. (We will examine these issues below.)

Table 23.1 Production possibilities for two countries

		Kilos of wheat		Metres of cloth
Less developed country	Either	2	or	1
Developed country	Either	4	or	8

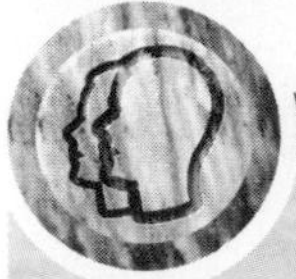

DEVELOPMENT OF IDEAS — BOX 23.2

DAVID RICARDO AND THE LAW OF COMPARATIVE ADVANTAGE

We came across David Ricardo in Chapter 15 (see Box 15.1). His most important work on economics is *On the Principles of Political Economy and Taxation* (1817). In expounding the advantages of free trade he gives the first clear analysis of the law of comparative advantage. In Chapter VII he writes:

> Under a system of perfectly free commerce, each country naturally devotes its capital and labour to such employments as are most beneficial to each. This pursuit of individual advantage is admirably connected with the universal good of the whole ... It is this principle which determines that wine shall be made in France and Portugal, that corn shall be grown in America and Poland, and that hardware and other goods shall be manufactured in England.
>
> If Portugal had no commercial connexion with other countries, instead of employing a great part of her capital and industry in the production of wines, with which she purchases for her own use the cloth and hardware of other countries, she would be obliged to devote a part of that capital to the manufacture of those commodities, which she would thus obtain probably inferior in quality as well as quantity ...
>
> England may be so circumstanced, that to produce the cloth may require the labour of 100 men for one year; and if she attempted to make the wine, it might take the labour of 120 men for the same time. England would therefore find it in her interest to import wine, and to purchase it by the exportation of cloth.
>
> To produce the wine in Portugal, might require only the labour of 90 men for the same time. It would therefore be advantageous for her to export wine in exchange for cloth. This exchange might even take place, notwithstanding that the commodity imported by Portugal could be produced with less labour than in England. Though she could make the cloth with the labour of 90 men, she would import it from a country where it required the labour of 100 men to produce it, because it would be advantageous to her rather to employ her capital in the production of wine, for which she would obtain more cloth from England, than she could by diverting a portion of her capital from the cultivation of vines to the manufacture of cloth.
>
> Thus England would give up the produce of labour of 100 men, for the produce of 90.[1]

?? In Ricardo's example, what is the opportunity cost of wine in terms of cloth in (a) Portugal; (b) England? (Assume that the only costs are labour costs.)

[1] P. Sraffa (ed.), *The Works and Correspondence of David Ricardo* (Cambridge University Press, 1951), volume I, pp. 133–5.

??

1. Show how each country could gain from trade if the LDC could produce (before trade) 3 wheat for 1 cloth and the developed country could produce (before trade) 2 wheat for 5 cloth, and if the exchange ratio (with trade) was 1 wheat for 2 cloth. Would they both still gain if the exchange ratio was (a) 1 wheat for 1 cloth; (b) 1 wheat for 3 cloth?
2. In question 1, which country gained the most from a trade exchange ratio of 1 wheat for 2 cloth?

Simple graphical analysis of comparative advantage and the gains from trade: constant opportunity cost

The gains from trade can be shown graphically using production possibility curves. Let us continue with the example of the developed and less developed countries that we looked at in Table 23.1, where both countries produce just two goods: wheat and cloth.

For simplicity, assume that the pre-trade opportunity costs of cloth in terms of wheat in the two countries do not vary with output: i.e. there are *constant opportunity costs* of cloth in terms of wheat of 2/1 in the LDC and 1/2 in the developed country. Let us assume that the pre-trade production possibilities are as shown in Table 23.2.

For each 100 extra metres of cloth that the LDC produces it has to sacrifice 200 kilos of wheat. For each extra 200 kilos of wheat that the developed country produces it has to sacrifice 400 metres of cloth. Straight-line pre-trade production possibility 'curves' can thus be drawn for the two countries with slopes of 2/1 and 1/2 respectively. These lines illustrate the various total combinations of the two goods that can be produced and hence consumed. They are shown as the blue lines in Figure 23.1.

Let us assume that before trade the LDC produces (and consumes) at point *e*: namely, 200 million kilos of wheat and 400 million metres of cloth; and that the developed country produces at point *k*: namely, 400 million kilos of wheat and 1600 million metres of cloth.

If they now trade, the LDC, having a comparative advantage in wheat, will specialise in it and produce at point *a*. It will produce 1000 million kilos of wheat and no cloth. The developed country will specialise in cloth and produce at point *m*. It will produce 2400 million metres of cloth and no wheat.

Table 23.2 Pre-trade production possibilities

	Less developed country			Developed country	
	Wheat (kilos m)	Cloth (metres m)		Wheat (kilos m)	Cloth (metres m)
a	1000	0	*g*	1200	0
b	800	100	*h*	1000	400
c	600	200	*i*	800	800
d	400	300	*j*	600	1200
e	200	400	*k*	400	1600
f	0	500	*l*	200	2000
			m	0	2400

For simplicity let us assume that trade between the two countries takes place at an exchange ratio of 1:1. This means that the two countries can now *consume* along the red lines in Figure 23.1: at, say, points *x* and *y* respectively. At point *x* the LDC consumes 400 million kilos of wheat (a gain of 200 million kilos over the pre-trade position) and 600 million metres of cloth (a gain of 200 million metres over the pre-trade position). At point *y* the developed country consumes 600 million kilos of wheat (a gain of 200 million kilos over the pre-trade position) and 1800 million metres of cloth (a gain of 200 million metres over the pre-trade position). Thus trade has allowed both countries to increase their consumption of both goods.

To summarise: before trade, the countries could only consume along their production possibility curves (the blue lines); after trade, they can consume along the higher red lines.

Note that in this simple two-country model the production and consumption of the two countries must match, since one country's exports are the other's imports. Thus if the LDC produces at point *a* and consumes at point *x*, the developed country, producing at point *m*, must consume at point *y*. The effects on trade of the two countries consuming at points *x* and *y* are shown in Table 23.3.

As complete specialisation has taken place in our example, the LDC now has to import all its cloth and the developed country has to import all its wheat. Thus, given the exchange ratio of 1:1, the LDC exports 600 million kilos of wheat in exchange for imports of 600 million metres of cloth. (These imports and exports are also shown in Figure 23.1.)

The final two columns of Table 23.3 show that trade has increased the total production and consumption of the two countries.

??

1. If the opportunity cost ratio of *wheat* for *cloth* is 1/2 in the LDC, why is the slope of the production possibility curve 2/1? Is the slope of the production possibility curve always the reciprocal of the opportunity cost ratio?
2. Show (graphically) that, if the (pre-trade) opportunity cost ratios of the two countries were the same, there would be no gain from trade – assuming that the production possibility curves were straight lines and did not shift as a result of trade.

International trade and its effect on factor prices

Countries will tend to have a comparative advantage in goods that are *intensive in their abundant factor*. Canada

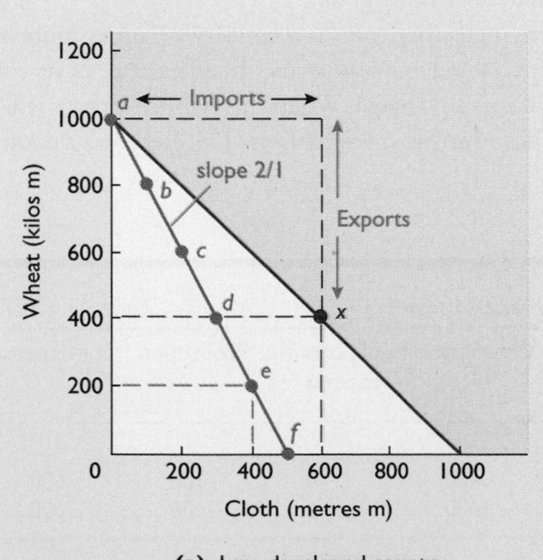

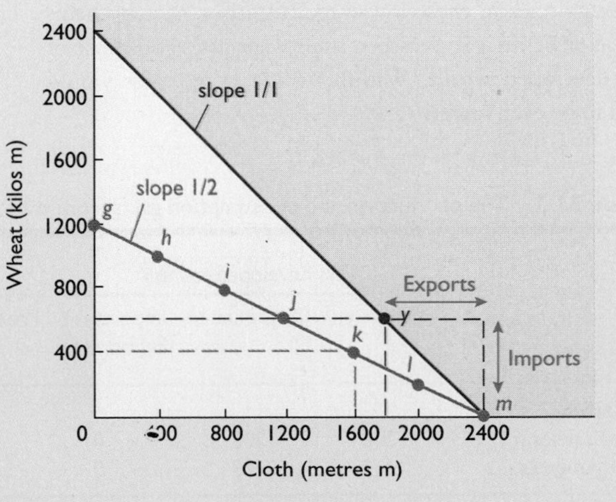

(a) Less developed country

(b) Developed country

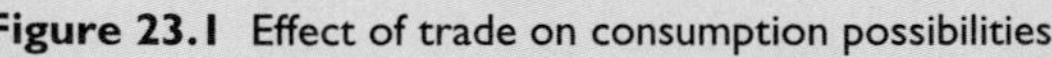

Figure 23.1 Effect of trade on consumption possibilities

ISSUES AND APPLICATIONS — BOX 23.3

TRADE AS EXPLOITATION?

People sometimes question the morality of buying imports from countries where workers are paid 'pittance' wages. 'Is it right', they ask, 'for us to support a system where workers are so exploited?' As is often the case with emotive issues, there is some truth and some misunderstanding in a point of view like this.

First the truth. If a country like the UK trades with a regime which denies human rights, and treats its workers very badly, then we may thereby be helping to sustain a corrupt system. We might also be seen to be lending it moral support. In this sense, therefore, trade may not help the cause of the workers in these countries. It is arguments like these that were used to support the imposition of trade sanctions against South Africa in the days of apartheid.

Now the misunderstanding. If we buy goods from countries that pay low wages, we are *not* as a result contributing to their low-wage problem. Quite the reverse. If countries like India export textiles to the West, this will help to *increase* the wages of Indian workers. If India has a comparative advantage in labour-intensive goods, these goods will earn a better price by being exported than by being sold entirely in the domestic Indian market. Provided *some* of the extra revenues go to the workers, they will gain from trade.

?? Under what circumstances would a gain in revenues by exporting firms *not* lead to an increase in wage rates?

has abundant land and hence it is cheap. Therefore Canada specialises in grain production since grains are land intensive. South Asian countries have abundant supplies of labour with low wage rates, and hence specialise in clothing and other labour-intensive goods. Europe, Japan and the USA have relatively abundant and cheap capital, and hence specialise in capital-intensive manufactured goods.

Trade between such countries will tend to lead to greater equality in factor prices. For example, the demand for labour will rise in labour-abundant countries like India if they specialise in labour-intensive goods. This will push up wage rates in these low-wage countries, thereby helping to close the gap between their wage rates and those of the developed world. Without trade, wage rates would tend to be even lower.

Increasing opportunity costs and the limits to specialisation and trade

In practice, countries are likely to experience increasing opportunity costs (and hence have bowed-out production possibility curves). The reason for this is that, as a country increasingly specialises in one good, it will have to use resources that are less and less suited to its production and which were more suited to the other good. Thus ever increasing amounts of the other good will have to be sacrificed. For example, as a country specialises more and more in grain production, it will have to use land that is less and less suited to growing grain.

These increasing costs as a country becomes more and more specialised will lead to the disappearance of its comparative cost advantage. When this happens, there will be no point in further specialisation. Thus whereas a country

Table 23.3 The production and consumption gains from trade

	Less developed country			Developed country			Total	
	Production	Consumption	Imports (–) Exports (+)	Production	Consumption	Imports (–) Exports (+)	Production	Consumption
No trade								
Wheat (kilos m)	200	200	0	400	400	0	600	600
Cloth (metres m)	400	400	0	1600	1600	0	2000	2000
With trade								
Wheat (kilos m)	1000	400	+600	0	600	–600	1000	1000
Cloth (metres m)	0	600	–600	2400	1800	+600	2400	2400

like Germany has a comparative advantage in capital-intensive manufactures, it does not produce only manufactures. It would make no sense not to use its fertile lands to produce food or its forests to produce timber. The opportunity costs of diverting all agricultural labour to industry would be very high.

Thus increasing opportunity costs limit the amount of a country's specialisation and hence the amount of its trade. There are also other limits to trade:

- Transport costs may outweigh any comparative advantage. A country may be able to produce bricks more cheaply than other countries, but their weight may make them too expensive to export.
- It may be the factors of production, rather than the goods, that move from country to country. Thus developed countries, rather than exporting finished goods to LDCs, may invest capital in LDCs to enable manufactures to be produced there. Labour may migrate from low-wage to high-wage countries.
- Governments may restrict trade (see section 23.2).

The terms of trade

What price will our exports fetch abroad? What will we have to pay for imports? The answer to these questions is given by the *terms of trade*.

To simplify matters, let us assume to start with that there is only one exported good and only one imported good. In this case the terms of trade are defined as P_x/P_m, where P_x is the price of the exported good and P_m is the price of the imported good. This is the reciprocal of the exchange ratio: for example, if 2x exchange for 1m (an exchange ratio of 2/1), the price of x will be half the price of m. The terms of trade will be 1/2.

> **??**
> 1. If 4x exchange for 3m, what are the terms of trade?
> 2. If the terms of trade are 3, how many units of the imported good could I buy for the money earned by the sale of 1 unit of the exported good? What is the exchange ratio?

In the real world where countries have *many* exports and imports, the **terms of trade** are given by:

$$\frac{\text{Average price of exports}}{\text{Average price of imports}}$$

expressed as an index, where price changes are measured against a base year in which the terms of trade are assumed to be 100.

If the terms of trade rise (export prices rising relative to import prices), they are said to have 'improved', since fewer exports need now be sold to purchase any given quantity of imports. Changes in the terms of trade are caused by changes in the demand for and supply of imports and exports, and by changes in the exchange rate.

The terms of trade and comparative advantage

Assuming there are two goods x and m, trade can be advantageous to a country as long as the terms of trade P_x/P_m are different from the opportunity cost ratios of the two goods, given by MC_x/MC_m. For example, if the terms of trade were greater than the opportunity cost ratio ($P_x/P_m > MC_x/MC_m$), it would benefit the country to produce more x for export in return for imports of m, since the relative value of producing x (P_x/P_m) is greater than the relative cost (MC_x/MC_m).

With increasing opportunity costs, however, increasing specialisation in x will lead to MC_x rising (and MC_m falling), until $P_x/P_m = MC_x/MC_m$. At this point there can be no more gain from further specialisation and trade: the maximum gain has been achieved and comparative cost advantages have been exhausted.

The determination of the terms of trade

When countries import and export many goods, the terms of trade will depend on the prices of all the various exports and imports. These prices will depend on the demand and supply of each traded good and their elasticities in the respective countries. Take the case of good g in which country A has a comparative advantage with respect to the rest of the world. This is illustrated in Figure 23.2.

Demand and supply curves of good g can be drawn for both country A and the rest of the world. (The upward-sloping supply curves imply increasing opportunity costs of production.) Before trade, country A has a low equilibrium price of P_1 and the rest of the world a high equilibrium price of P_2. After trade, price will settle at P_3 in both countries (assuming no transport costs), where total demand by both country A and the rest of the world together equals total supply, and thus where the imports of g into the rest of the world ($d - c$) equal the exports from country A ($b - a$). The position of P_3 relative to P_1 and P_2 will depend on the elasticities of demand and supply.

> **DEFINITION**
>
> **Terms of trade** The price index of exports divided by the price index of imports and then expressed as a percentage. This means that the terms of trade will be 100 in the base year.

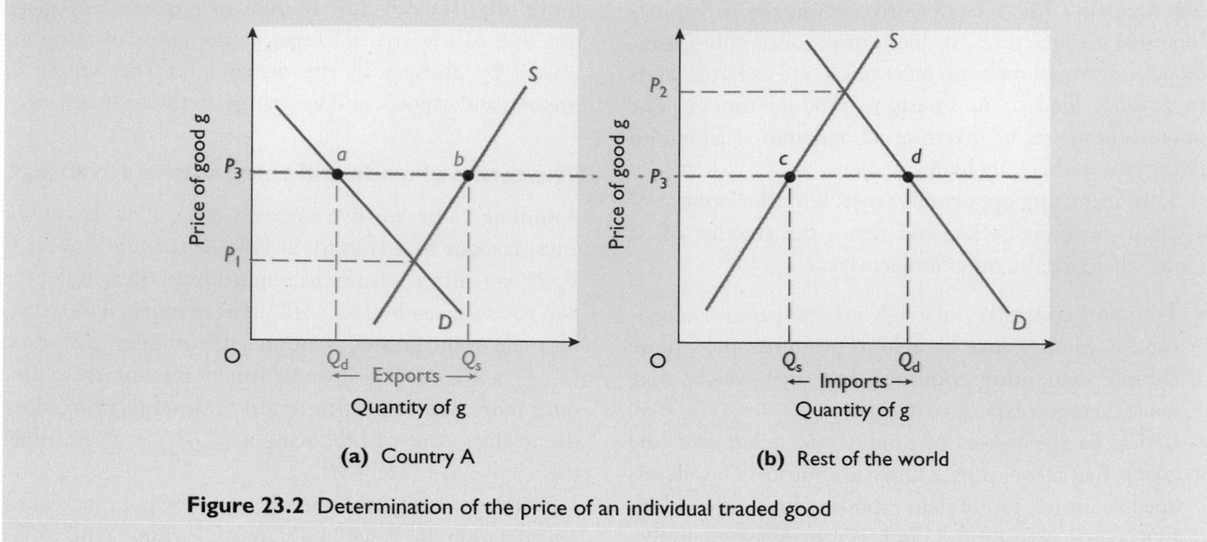

Figure 23.2 Determination of the price of an individual traded good

A similar analysis can be conducted for all the other traded goods – both exports and imports of country A. The resulting prices will allow country A's terms of trade to be calculated.

> **??** Draw a similar diagram to Figure 23.2 showing how the price of an individual good imported into country A is determined.

The analysis is complicated somewhat if different national currencies are involved, since the prices in each country will be expressed in its own currency. Thus to convert one country's prices to another currency will require knowledge of the rate of exchange: e.g. for the USA and the UK it might be $2 = £1. But under a floating exchange rate system the rate of exchange will depend in part on the demand for and supply of imports and exports. If the rate of exchange were to depreciate – say, from $2 = £1 to $1.50 = £1 – the UK's terms of trade will worsen. Exports will earn less foreign currency per pound: e.g. £1 worth of exports will now be worth only $1.50 rather than $2. Imports, on the other hand, will be more expensive: e.g. $6 worth of imports previously cost £3; they now cost £4.

> **??** Why will exporters probably welcome a 'deterioration' in the terms of trade?

In a world of many countries and many goods, an individual country's imports and exports may have little effect on world prices. In the extreme case it may face prices totally dictated by the external world demand and supply. The country in this case is similar to an individual firm under perfect competition. The country is too small to influence world prices, and thus faces a horizontal demand curve for its exports and a horizontal supply curve for its imports. In foreign currency terms, therefore, the terms of trade are outside its control. Nevertheless, these terms of trade will probably be to its benefit in the sense that the gains from trade will be virtually entirely received by this small country rather than the rest of the world. It is too small for its trade to depress the world price of its exports or drive up the price of its imports.

In general a country's gains from trade will be greater the less elastic its own domestic demand and supply of tradable goods, and the more elastic the demand and supply of other countries. You can see this by examining Figure 23.2. The less elastic the domestic demand and supply, the bigger will be the effect of trade on prices faced by that country. The more the trade price differs from the pre-trade price, the bigger the gain.

*Intermediate analysis of the gains from trade

The analysis of section 11.1 can be used to demonstrate the welfare gains from trade and the limits to specialisation under conditions of increasing opportunity cost. A simple two-good model is used, and the pre-trade position is compared with the position with trade.

Pre-trade

Let us make the following simplifying assumptions:

- There are two goods, x and m.
- Country A has a comparative advantage in the production of good x.

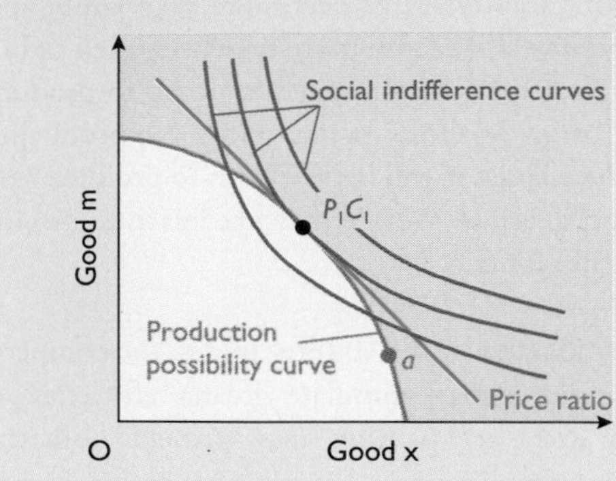

Figure 23.3 Equilibrium before trade

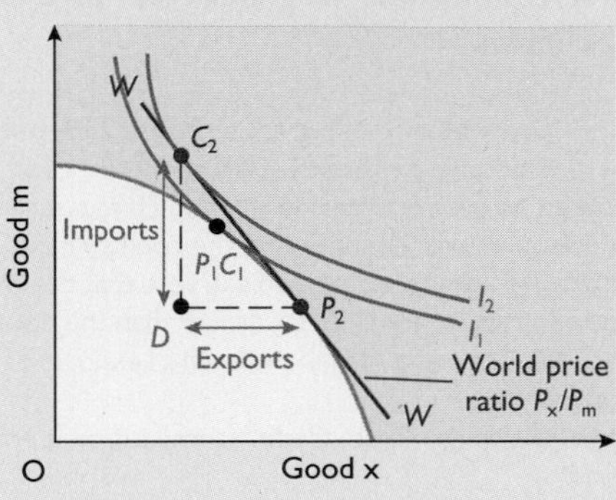

Figure 23.4 Equilibrium with trade

- There are increasing opportunity costs in the production of both x and m. Thus the production possibility curve is bowed out.
- Social indifference curves can be drawn, each one showing the various combinations of x and m that give society in country A a particular level of utility.

Figure 23.3 shows the pre-trade position in country A. Production and consumption at P_1C_1 will give the highest possible utility. (All other points on the production possibility curve intersect with lower indifference curves.)

If there is perfect competition, production will indeed be at P_1C_1. There are four steps in establishing this:

- The slope of the production possibility curve $(-\Delta m/\Delta x)$ is the marginal rate of transformation (*MRT*), and equals MC_x/MC_m. For example, if the opportunity cost of producing 1 extra unit of x (Δx) was a sacrifice of 2 units of m ($-\Delta m$), then an extra unit of x would cost twice as much as an extra unit of m: i.e. $MC_x/MC_m = 2/1$, which is the slope of the production possibility curve, $-\Delta m/\Delta x$.
- The slope of each indifference curve $(-\Delta m/\Delta x)$ is the marginal rate of substitution in consumption (*MRS*), and equals MU_x/MU_m. For example, if x had three times the marginal utility of m ($MU_x/MU_m = 3$), consumers would be willing to give up 3m for 1x ($-\Delta m/\Delta x = 3$).
- Under perfect competition:

$$\frac{MC_x}{MC_m} = \frac{P_x}{P_m} = \frac{MU_x}{MU_m}$$

- Thus the domestic pre-trade price ratio P_x/P_m under perfect competition must equal the slope of the production possibility curve (MC_x/MC_m) and the slope of the social indifference curve (MU_x/MU_m). This is the case at P_1C_1 in Figure 23.3.

??

1. If production were at point *a* in Figure 23.3, describe the process whereby equilibrium at point P_1C_1 would be restored under perfect competition.
2. Why would production be unlikely to take place at P_1C_1 if competition were not perfect?

With trade

If country A has a comparative advantage in good x, the price of x relative to m is likely to be higher in the rest of the world than in country A: i.e. world P_x/P_m > pre-trade domestic P_x/P_m. This is shown in Figure 23.4. The world price ratio is given by the slope of the line *WW*. With this new steeper world price ratio the optimum production point will be P_2 where *MRT* (the slope of the production possibility curve) = world P_x/P_m (the slope of *WW*).

With production at P_2, the country can by trading consume *anywhere* along this line *WW*. The optimum consumption point will be C_2 where *MRS* (the slope of the indifference curve) = world P_x/P_m (the slope of *WW*). Thus trade has allowed consumption to move from point C_1 on the lower indifference curve I_1 to point C_2 on the higher indifference cuve I_2. There has thus been a gain from trade. Perfect competition will ensure that this gain is realised, since production at P_2 and consumption at C_2 meet the equilibrium condition that:

$$\frac{MC_x}{MC_m} = \frac{P_x}{P_m} = \frac{MU_x}{MU_m}$$

How much will be imported and how much will be exported? With production at P_2 and consumption at C_2, country A will import $C_2 - D$ of good m in exchange for exports of $P_2 - D$ of good x.

Similar diagrams to Figure 23.4 can be drawn for other countries. Since they show equilibrium for both imports and exports on the *one* diagram, economists refer to them as **general equilibrium diagrams** (see page 323 for another example).

??

1. Draw a similar diagram to Figure 23.4, only this time assume that the two goods are good a measured on the vertical axis and good b measured on the horizontal axis. Assume that the country has a comparative advantage in good a. (Note that the world price ratio this time will be shallower than the domestic pre-trade price ratio.) Mark the level of exports of a and imports of b.
2. Is it possible to gain from trade if competition is not perfect?

Other reasons for gains from trade

Decreasing costs. Even if there are no initial comparative cost differences between two countries, it will still benefit both to specialise in industries where economies of scale (either internal or external) can be gained, and then to trade. Once the economies of scale begin to appear, comparative cost differences will also appear, and thus the countries will have gained a comparative advantage in these industries.

This reason for trade is particularly relevant for small countries where the domestic market is not large enough to support large-scale industries. Thus exports form a much higher percentage of GNP in small countries such as Luxembourg than in large countries such as the USA.

??

Would it be possible for a country with a comparative *dis*advantage in a given product at *pre*-trade levels of output to obtain a comparative advantage in it by specialising in its production and exporting it?

Differences in demand. Even with no comparative cost differences and no potential economies of scale, trade can benefit both countries if demand conditions differ.

If people in country A like beef more than lamb, and people in country B like lamb more than beef, then rather than A using resources better suited for lamb to produce beef and B using resources better suited for producing beef to produce lamb, it will benefit both to produce beef *and* lamb and to export the one they like less in return for the one they like more.

Increased competition. If a country trades, the competition from imports may stimulate greater efficiency at home. This extra competition may prevent domestic monopolies/oligopolies from charging high prices. It may stimulate greater research and development and the more rapid adoption of new technology. It may lead to a greater variety of products being made available to consumers.

Trade as an 'engine of growth'. In a growing world economy, the demand for a country's exports is likely to grow over time, expecially when these exports have a high income elasticity of demand. This increase in injections will provide a stimulus to aggregate demand and allow a country to purchase additional imports. This argument is particularly relevant when countries have an abundance of a certain commodity, such as oil or uranium.

Non-economic advantages. There may be political, social and cultural advantages to be gained by fostering trading links between countries.

DEFINITION

General equilibrium diagrams (in trade theory)
Indifference curve/production possibility curve diagrams that show a country's production and consumption of both imports and exports.

SECTION SUMMARY

1. Countries can gain from trade if they specialise in producing those goods in which they have a comparative advantage: i.e. those goods that can be produced at relatively low opportunity costs. This is merely an extension of the argument that gains can be made from the specialisation and division of labour.
2. If two countries trade, then, provided that the trade price ratio of exports and imports is between the pre-trade price ratios of these goods in the two countries, both countries can gain. They can both consume *beyond* their production possibility curves.
3. With increasing opportunity costs there will be a limit to specialisation and trade. As a country increasingly specialises, its (marginal) comparative advantage will eventually disappear. Trade can also be limited by transport costs, factor movements and government intervention.
4. The terms of trade give the price of exports relative to the price of imports. Additional trade can be beneficial if the terms of trade (P_x/P_m) are greater than the relative marginal costs of exports and imports (MC_x/MC_m).
5. A country's terms of trade are determined by the demand and supply of imports and exports and their

continued

respective elasticities. This will determine the prices at which goods are traded and affect the rate of exchange. A country's gains from trade will be greater the less elastic its own domestic demand and supply of tradable goods, and the more elastic the demand and supply of other countries.

*6. Trade allows countries to achieve a higher level of utility by consuming on a higher social indifference curve. The maximum gain from trade is achieved by consuming at the point where the world price ratio is tangential to both the production possibility curve and a social indifference curve. This would be achieved under perfect competition.

7. Gains from trade also arise from decreasing costs (economies of scale), differences in demand between countries, increased competition from trade and the transmission of growth from one country to another. There may also be non-economic advantages from trade.

23.2

Arguments for restricting trade

Most countries have not pursued a policy of free trade. Their politicians know that trade involves costs as well as benefits. In this section we will attempt to identify what these costs are, and whether they are genuine reasons for restricting trade.

Although countries may sometimes contemplate having completely free trade, typically countries limit their trade. However, they certainly do not ban it altogether. The sorts of questions that governments pose are (a) should they have freer or more restricted trade and (b) in which sectors should restrictions be tightened or relaxed? Ideally, countries should weigh up the marginal benefits against the marginal costs of altering restrictions.

Methods of restricting trade

Tariffs (customs duties). These are taxes on imports and are usually **ad valorem**: i.e. a percentage of the price of the import. Tariffs that are used to restrict imports will be most effective if demand is elastic (e.g. when there are close domestically produced substitutes). Tariffs can also be used as a means of raising revenue. Here they will be more effective if demand is inelastic. They can also be used to raise the price of imported goods to prevent 'unfair' competition for domestic producers. In this case the rate of tariff would have to rise if the world price fell and vice versa. Examples are the variable levies of the European Union on imported foodstuffs.

Quotas. This is where a limit is imposed on the quantity of a good that can be imported. The quotas can be imposed by the government, or negotiated with importing countries which agree 'voluntarily' to restrict the amount of imports (see Box 23.4).

Exchange controls. These include limits on the amount of foreign exchange made available to importers (financial quotas), or to citizens travelling abroad, or for investment. Alternatively, they can be in the form of charges made on people purchasing foreign currencies.

Import licensing. The imposition of exchange controls or quotas will often involve importers obtaining licences so that the government can better enforce its restrictions.

Embargoes. This is where the government completely bans certain imports (e.g. drugs) or exports to certain countries (e.g. to enemies during war).

Export taxes. These can be used to increase the price of exports when the country has monopoly power in their supply.

Subsidies. These can be given to domestic goods to prevent competition from otherwise lower-priced imports. They can also be given to exports in a process known as **dumping**. The goods are 'dumped' at artificially low prices in the foreign market.

DEFINITIONS

Ad valorem tariffs Tariffs levied as a percentage of the price of the import.

Dumping Where exports are sold at prices below marginal cost – often as a result of government subsidy.

CASE STUDIES — BOX 23.4

RELUCTANT VOLUNTEERS

The USA's use of 'voluntary restraint arrangements'

Much of US industry was having a hard time in the 1980s. With high interest rates causing a high exchange rate for the dollar against other currencies, US exporters found themselves unable to compete in overseas markets. In the home market too, European, Japanese and Korean imports were eroding US companies' market share. And it was not just a problem of the low price of foreign goods, it was also often a question of their superior quality.

Despite the free-trade rhetoric of Presidents Reagan and Bush, the huge and growing US balance of trade deficit prompted the government to take tough action to cut down on foreign imports, especially in key industries like automobiles, steel and computer chips. In particular there was a growth of special protective measures for politically sensitive industries.

One of the most widely used of these was the VRA – voluntary restraint arrangement. This is where an importing country such as Japan agrees to limit its imports to a quota. Two major examples of VRAs were in steel and automobiles.

Steel

In the early 1980s, US steel companies were making huge losses. A combination of gross inefficiency and intense foreign competition had seen the USA's share of the world steel market fall from over 50 per cent after the Second World War to under 10 per cent by the beginning of the 1980s.

In 1984, after intense lobbying by the industry, the US government decided to try to cut steel imports from 26 to 20 per cent of the home market. VRAs were negotiated for a five-year period with 29 other countries. The 20 per cent target was eventually reached in 1988, shortly before the VRAs were due to expire. By that time, however, the US steel industry had been transformed. Employment had fallen dramatically, old plant had been closed, productivity had increased and costs had fallen.

The steel companies claimed that the protection had enabled them to afford the investment necessary to transform the industry. Without a continuation of VRAs they would face unfair competition from countries which subsidised their steel industries. Critics claimed that an extension of VRAs would discourage further cost reductions and encourage other countries to protect *their* steel industries more heavily.

The advocates of continuing VRAs won the argument and the 20 per cent ceiling was extended until March 1992. US steel producers were relieved, especially given the fall in demand for steel that accompanied the recession of 1990–2.

With the ending of VRAs and the continuing slump in the world demand for steel, the USA became worried once more about cheap imports of steel. And so in January 1993 the US Commerce Department imposed large 'anti-dumping' duties on imported steel products from nineteen countries, including EC members. With an appeal pending by the EC to GATT (the international free-trade organisation: see page 706), the US International Trade Commission ruled against these and other anti-dumping duties. It would seem that VRAs were less controversial than tariffs!

Automobiles

With large increases in the sales of Japanese and European cars, the US car companies were also calling for protection in the early 1980s. VRAs were first 'negotiated' with Japan in 1981 and were successful to the extent that Japan accepted the arrangement and imports were cut. As with steel, the VRAs helped the US automobile industry to survive a very difficult period.

But critics claim that the costs to the US consumer have been high. Various studies have estimated that VRAs have pushed up the price of imported Japanese cars by between \$1000 and \$3000 per car, and that they have also, by reducing foreign competition, pushed up the price of US cars by between \$500 and \$1000 per car.

The EU too has used VRAs against Japanese car imports, and they have been the cause of considerable disagreement with Japan. In 1991 it was agreed to phase out such VRAs by the year 2000.

?? Might the US consumer gain any benefits from VRAs?

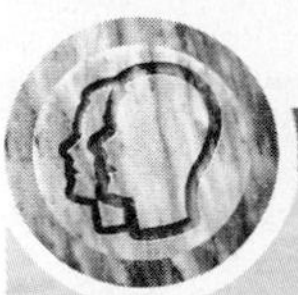

DEVELOPMENT OF IDEAS BOX 23.5

FRIEDRICH LIST (1789–1846)

Person profile

Friedrich List is probably the most famous representative of the *German historical school*, but is perhaps best known as the 'inventor' of the infant industry argument for protectionism.

The German historical school was fundamentally opposed to British classical economics with its stress on the benefits of the market and its advocacy of *laissez-faire* and free trade. List criticised Adam Smith and Jean-Baptiste Say for ignoring the political, institutional and social environment in which the economy functions.

Countries, he argued, go through a series of historical stages, and it is the function of economists to identify these stages and devise appropriate policies for each one. Classical theory might have been relevant to an industrially advanced country like Britain, but it was inapplicable to countries like Germany and the USA which had not yet reached that stage. These countries could not hope to compete internationally without some degree of protection.

After an illustrious early career in Germany, being made professor at the age of 31, he fled to the USA in 1825 to escape a gaol sentence for advocating reforms to the German legal and administrative system. In the USA his protectionist views were very popular among politicians and the business community alike. He is sometimes referred to in the USA as the 'father of American protectionism'. After lending support to Andrew Jackson's presidential election campaign in 1832, he returned to Germany as US consul.

In 1837 he once more had to flee Germany, this time because of a business scandal. After three years in Paris he returned to Germany, and in 1841 he published his best-known work, *The National System of Politicial Economy*, which was generally well received. Later, in 1846, being deeply depressed by serious business problems, he took his own life.

Administrative barriers. Regulations may be designed in such a way as to exclude imports. For example, in Germany all lagers not meeting certain purity standards could be banned. Taxes may be imposed which favour local products or ingredients.

Economic arguments having some general validity

The infant industry argument. There may be industries in a country that are in their infancy, but which have a potential comparative advantage. This is particularly likely in developing countries. These industries are too small yet to have gained economies of scale; workers are inexperienced; there is a lack of back-up facilities – communications networks, specialist suppliers, etc. They may have only limited access to finance for expansion. Without protection, these **infant industries** will not survive competition from abroad.

Protection from foreign competition, however, will allow them to expand and become more efficient. Once they have achieved a comparative advantage, the protection can then be removed to enable them to compete internationally.

The senile industry argument. This is where industries with a potential comparative advantage have been allowed to run down and can no longer compete effectively. They may have considerable potential, but be simply unable to make enough profit to afford the necessary investment without some temporary protection. This is one of the most powerful arguments used to justify the use of special protection for the automobile and steel industries in the USA (see Box 23.4).

?? How would you set about judging whether an industry had a genuine case for infant/senile industry protection?

Changing comparative advantage and the inflexibility of markets. Comparative advantage can change over time, either naturally (e.g. new raw materials may be discovered) or as a result of deliberate policies (e.g. in the field of education, capital investment or technological research). Due to factor immobility, production may respond fairly slowly to these changing conditions. Thus free trade may reflect *past* comparative advantage rather than present. These industries could be regarded as infants and thus warranting protection.

To prevent 'dumping' and other unfair trade practices. A country may engage in dumping by subsidising its

DEFINITION

Infant industry An industry which has a potential comparative advantage, but which is as yet too underdeveloped to be able to realise this potential.

exports. Alternatively, firms may practise price discrimination by selling at a higher price in home markets and a lower price in foreign markets in order to increase their profits. Either way, prices may no longer reflect comparative costs. Thus the world would benefit from tariffs being imposed to counteract the subsidy.

> ?? Does the consumer in the importing country gain or lose from dumping?

It can also be argued that there is a case for retaliating against countries which impose restrictions on your exports. In the *short* run, both countries are likely to be made worse off by a contraction in trade. But if the retaliation persuades the other country to remove its restrictions, it may have a longer-term benefit. In some cases, the mere threat of retaliation may be enough to get another country to remove its protection.

To prevent the establishment of a foreign-based monopoly. Competition from abroad, especially when it involves dumping, could drive domestic producers out of business. The foreign company, now having a monopoly of the market, could charge high prices with a resulting misallocation of resources.

To reduce reliance on goods with little dynamic potential. Many developing countries have traditionally exported primaries: foodstuffs and raw materials. The world demand for these, however, is fairly income inelastic, and thus grows relatively slowly. In such cases, free trade is not an engine of growth. Instead, if it encourages countries' economies to become locked into a pattern of primary production, it may prevent them from expanding in sectors like manufacturing which have a higher income elasticity of demand. There may thus be a valid argument for protecting or promoting manufacturing industry.

To spread the risks of fluctuating markets. A highly specialised economy – Zambia with copper, Cuba with sugar – will be highly susceptible to world market fluctuations. Greater diversity and greater self-sufficiency can reduce these risks.

To reduce the influence of trade on consumer tastes. The assumption of fixed consumer tastes dictating the pattern of production through trade is false. Multinational companies through their advertising and other forms of sales promotion may influence consumer tastes. Thus some restriction on trade may be justified in order to reduce this 'producer sovereignty'.

> ?? In what ways may free trade have harmful cultural effects on developing countries?

To prevent the importation of harmful goods. A country may want to ban or severely curtail the importation of things such as drugs, pornographic literature and live animals.

To take account of externalities. Free trade will tend to reflect private costs. Both imports and exports, however, can involve externalities. The mining of many minerals for export may adversely affect the health of miners; the production of chemicals for export may involve pollution; the importation of juggernaut lorries may lead to structural damage to houses.

Economic arguments having some validity for specific groups or countries

The following are arguments for restricting trade to enable some groups to benefit but at the expense of others. Whether there would be a *net* gain in welfare is difficult to assess.

To improve a country's terms of trade by exploiting its market power. If a country, or a group of countries, has market power in the supply of exports (e.g. South Africa with diamonds, OPEC with oil) or market power in the demand for imports (e.g. the USA or other large wealthy countries), it can exploit this power by intervening in trade.

Let us first take the case of a country, or a group of countries acting as a cartel, which has monopoly power in the sale of a particular export: for example, West African countries in the sale of cocoa. But let us assume that there are many individual producers which are therefore price takers and are thus not in a position to exploit the country's overall market power. In Figure 23.5, these price-taking firms will collectively produce at point *a* where $P = MC$. Market equilibrium will be at a trade price of P_1 and an output of Q_1.

The country's profit, however, would be maximised at point *b* where $MC = MR$, with output at the lower level of Q_2. By imposing an export tax of $P_2 - P_3$, therefore, the country can maximise its gain from this export. Producers will receive P_3 and will therefore supply Q_2. Market price will be P_2.

> ??
> 1. How much would be the total tax revenue for the government?
> 2. Will the individual producers gain from the export tax?

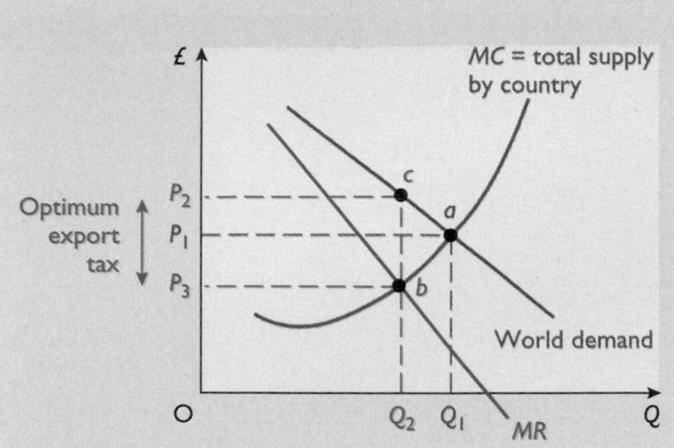

Figure 23.5 A country with a monopoly supply of an export

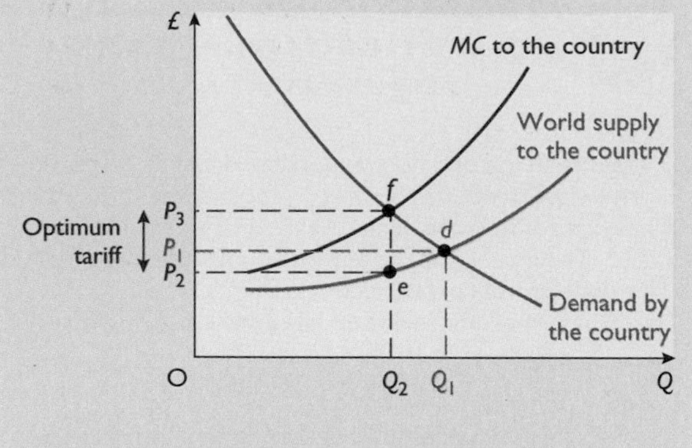

Figure 23.6 A country with a monopsony demand for an import

Now let us take the case of a country which has *monopsony* power in the demand for an import. This is illustrated in Figure 23.6. Without intervention, equilibrium will be at point *d* where demand equals supply. Q_1 would be purchased at a price of P_1.

But the marginal cost of imports curve will be *above* the supply curve because, given the country's size, the purchase of additional imports would drive up their price. This means that the cost of additional imports would be the new higher price (given by the supply curve) *plus* the rise in expenditure on the imports that would previously have been purchased at a lower price. The country will maximise its gain from trade at point *f* by importing Q_2, where demand equals marginal cost. Consumption can be reduced to Q_2 if the government imposes a tariff of $P_3 - P_2$. This is known as the **optimum tariff**. The country now only pays P_2 to importers. Consumers have to pay P_3, but $P_3 - P_2$ will be revenue to the government.

The country gains from such intervention, but only at the expense of the other countries with which it trades.

To protect declining industries. The human costs of sudden industrial closures can be very high. In such circumstances, temporary protection may be warranted to allow industries that have lost comparative advantage to decline more slowly. Such policies will be at the expense of the consumer, who will be denied access to cheaper foreign imports.

To improve the balance of payments. Under certain special circumstances, when other methods of balance of payments correction are unsuitable, there may be a case for resorting to tariffs (see Chapter 24).

'Non-economic' arguments

A country may be prepared to forgo the direct economic advantages of free trade – consumption at a lower opportunity cost – in order to achieve objectives that are often described as 'non-economic':

- It may wish to maintain a degree of self-sufficiency in case trade is cut off in times of war. This may apply particularly to the production of food and armaments.
- It may decide not to trade with certain countries with which it disagrees politically.
- It may wish to preserve traditional ways of life. Rural communities or communities built round old traditional industries may be destroyed by foreign competition.
- It may prefer to retain as diverse a society as possible, rather than one too narrowly based on certain industries.

Pursuing such objectives, however, will involve costs. Preserving a traditional way of life, for example, may mean that consumers are denied access to cheaper goods from abroad. Society must therefore weigh up the benefits against the costs of such policies.

?? If economics is the study of choices of how to use scarce resources, can these other objectives be legitimately described as 'non-economic'?

DEFINITION

Optimum tariff A tariff that reduces the level of imports to the point where marginal social cost equals marginal social benefit.

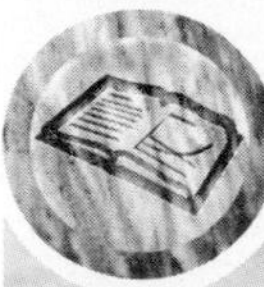

EXPLORING THE THEORY *BOX 23.6

THE OPTIMUM TARIFF OR EXPORT TAX
Using calculus

The size of the optimum export tax depends on the price elasticity of demand ($P\epsilon_d$). You can see this if you imagine rotating the demand and *MR* curves in Figure 23.5. The less elastic the demand curve, the bigger will be the optimum export tax.

The formula for the optimum export tax rate is:

$t = 1/P\epsilon_d$

The proof of this is as follows.

In Figure 23.5, the optimum tax rate is:

$$(P_2 - P_3) \div P_2 \qquad (1)$$

From the point of view of the country (as opposed to individual producers) this is simply:

$$(P - MR) \div P \qquad (2)$$

Remember from Box 2.6 that price elasticity of demand is given by:

$$P\epsilon_d = \frac{-dQ}{dP} \times \frac{P}{Q} \qquad (3)$$

Remember also, from Box 5.10, that:

$$MR = \frac{dTR}{dQ} = \frac{d(P.Q)}{dQ} \qquad (4)$$

From the rules of calculus:

$$\frac{d(P.Q)}{dQ} = \frac{dP.Q + dQ.P}{dQ} \qquad (5)$$

$$\therefore P - MR = P - \frac{(dP.Q + dQ.P)}{dQ} \qquad (6)$$

$$\text{and } \frac{P}{P - MR} = \frac{P}{P - \frac{(dP.Q + dQ.P)}{dQ}} \qquad (7)$$

$$= 1 - \frac{P}{\frac{(dP.Q + dQ.P)}{dQ}} \qquad (8)$$

Again from the rules of calculus:

$$= 1 - \left(\frac{dQ.P}{dP.Q} + \frac{dQ.P}{dQ.P}\right) \qquad (9)$$

$$= 1 - \frac{dQ.P}{dP.Q} - 1 \qquad (10)$$

$$= \frac{-dQ.P}{dP.Q} = P\epsilon_d \qquad (11)$$

$\therefore$ from equations (2) and (11):

$$\frac{P - MR}{P} = \text{optimum tax rate} = \frac{1}{P\epsilon_d}$$

?? See if you can devise a similar proof to show that the optimal import tariff, where a country has monopsony power, is $1/P\epsilon_s$ (where $P\epsilon_s$ is the price elasticity of supply of the import).

Fallacious arguments for restricting trade

The following arguments for protection simply do not stand up to close inspection.

'Imports should be reduced since they lower the standard of living. The money goes abroad rather than into the domestic economy.' Imports are consumed and thus add directly to consumer welfare. Also, provided they are matched by exports, there is no net outflow of money. Trade, because of the law of comparative advantage, allows countries to increase their standard of living: to consume beyond their production possibility curve (see Figures 23.1 and 23.4).

'Protection is needed from cheap foreign labour.' Importing cheap goods from, say, Hong Kong, allows more goods to be consumed. The UK uses less resources by buying these goods through the production and sale of exports than by producing them at home. However, there will be a cost to *certain* UK workers whose jobs are lost through foreign competition.

'Protection reduces unemployment.' At a microeconomic level, protecting industries from foreign competition may allow workers in those industries to retain their jobs. But if foreigners sell fewer goods to the UK, they will not be able to buy so many UK exports. Thus unemployment will rise in UK export industries. Overall unemployment, therefore, is little affected, and in the meantime the benefits from trade to consumers are reduced. *Temporary* protection given to declining industries, however, may help to reduce structural unemployment.

'Dumping is always a bad thing, and thus a country should restrict subsidised imports.' Dumping may well reduce world economic welfare: it goes against the law of comparative advantage. The importing country, however, may well *gain* from dumping. Provided the dumping is not used to drive domestic producers out of business and establish a foreign monopoly, the consumer gains from lower prices. The losers are the taxpayers in the foreign country and the workers in competing industries in the home country.

Problems with protection

Tariffs and other forms of protection impose a cost on society. This is illustrated in Figure 23.7. It illustrates the case of a good that is partly home produced and partly imported. Domestic demand and supply are given by D_{dom} and S_{dom}. It is assumed that firms in the country produce under perfect competition and that therefore the supply curve is the sum of the firms' marginal cost curves.

Let us assume that the country is too small to affect world prices: it is a price taker. The world price is given, at P_w, and world supply to the country (S_{world}) is perfectly elastic. At P_w, Q_2 is demanded, Q_1 is supplied by domestic suppliers and hence $Q_2 - Q_1$ is imported.

Now a tariff is imposed. This shifts up the world supply curve to the country by the amount of the tariff. Price rises to $P_w + t$. Domestic production increases to Q_3, consumption falls to Q_4, and hence imports fall to $Q_4 - Q_3$.

This imposes a cost on society. Consumers are having to pay a higher price, and hence consumer surplus falls from *ABC* to *ADE*. The cost to consumers in lost consumer surplus is thus *EDBC* (i.e. areas 1 + 2 + 3 + 4). *Part* of this cost, however, is redistributed as a *benefit* to other sections in society. *Firms* face a higher price, and thus gain extra profits (area 1): where profit is given by the area between the price and the *MC* curve. The *government* receives extra revenue from the tariff payments (area 3): i.e. $Q_4 - Q_3 \times$ tariff. These revenues can be used, for example, to reduce taxes.

But *part* of this cost is not recouped elsewhere. It is a net cost to society (areas 2 and 4).

Area 2 represents the extra costs of producing $Q_3 - Q_1$ at home, rather than importing it. If $Q_3 - Q_1$ were still imported, the country would only be paying S_{world}. By producing it at home, however, the costs are given by the domestic supply curve (= *MC*). The difference between *MC* and S_{world} (area 2) is thus the efficiency loss on the production side.

Area 4 represents the loss of consumer surplus by the reduction in consumption from Q_2 to Q_4. Consumers have saved area FBQ_2Q_4 of expenditure, but have sacrificed area DBQ_2Q_4 of utility in so doing – a net loss of area 4.

The government should ideally weigh up such costs against any benefits that are gained from protection.

?? In this model, where the country is a price taker and faces a horizontal supply curve (the small country assumption), is any of the cost of the tariff borne by the overseas suppliers?

There are other specific problems with protection.

Protection as 'second best'. Many of the arguments for protection amount merely to arguments for some type of government intervention in the economy. Protection, however, may not be the best way of dealing with the problem, since protection may have undesirable side-effects. There may be a more direct form of intervention that has no side-effects. In such a case, protection will be no more than a *second-best* solution.

For example, using tariffs to protect old inefficient industries from foreign competition may help prevent unemployment in those parts of the economy, but the consumer will suffer from higher prices. A better solution would be to subsidise retraining and investment in those areas of the country in *new efficient* industries – industries with a comparative advantage. In this way, unemployment is avoided, but the consumer does not suffer.

Even if the *existing* industries were to be supported, it would still be better to do this by paying them subsidies than by putting tariffs on imports. This argument can be expressed in terms of Figure 23.7. As we have seen, a tariff imposes costs on the consumer of areas 1 + 2 + 3 + 4. In the current example, area 2 may be a cost worth paying in

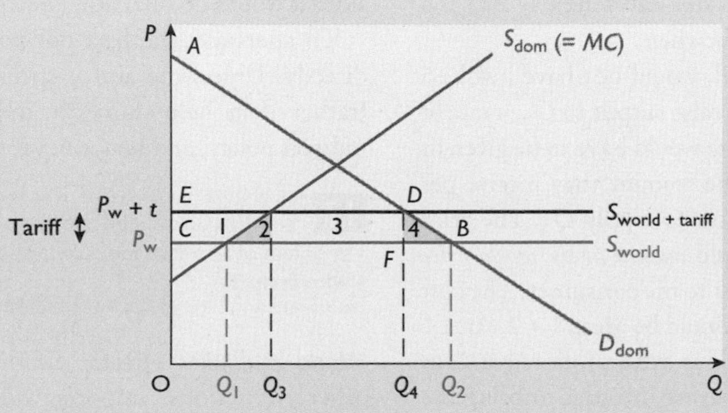

Figure 23.7 The cost of protection

CASE STUDIES

THE URUGUAY ROUND

The tortuous route to freer trade

In September 1986 in the town of Punta del Este, in Uruguay, the members of GATT, the General Agreement on Tariffs and Trade, began a new round of trade negotiations, but it was not until December 1993 that final agreement was reached between the 111 participating countries.

On the agenda was the extensive liberalisation of trade in virtually all goods and services. One means of achieving this was to reduce tariffs, but these had already been reduced substantially in previous rounds. By the end of the 1980s, the average tariff rate for developed countries was only around 6 per cent, compared with around 40 per cent back in 1947. Tariff rates in developing countries, however, were considerably higher.

Tariffs are the only form of trade restriction permitted under GATT and yet, as tariffs had fallen, so other forms of trade restriction, such as VRAs (see Box 23.4) had grown, in many cases quite dramatically. If there was to be a significant movement towards free trade, therefore, these non-tariff barriers would have to be substantially reduced.

The major goals set for the Uruguay round included: cutting tariffs on industrial products by one-third; substantially reducing non-tariff measures; liberalising trade in natural resources, textiles and tropical products; liberalising foreign investment; reducing agricultural support (such as that of the CAP); strengthening GATT rules and streamlining the procedure for settling disputes; strengthening voluntary codes against dumping and against technical and administrative barriers to trade; tightening the rules on the emergency protection of particular industries; agreements on fair trade in services; and the protection of intellectual property rights (copyright, patents, etc.).

These were an ambitious set of targets and it was soon clear that reaching agreement was not going to be easy. In particular, the USA and the EC were highly suspicious of each other and were unwilling to make concessions unilaterally without an equivalent concession from the other side. What is more, the USA was not prepared to liberalise its restrictions on imports while it saw other countries maintaining or increasing theirs. With the passing of the 1988 Trade Act, the USA was prepared to flout GATT rules and retaliate unilaterally against those countries it accused of unfair trade practices.

The biggest stumbling block to agreement in the Uruguay round was agriculture. In the eyes of the USA, the main problem was the unwillingness of the EC to make fundamental changes to the Common Agricultural Policy. As a result, despite considerable progress in many areas, such as services and textiles, the original December 1990 deadline passed with no final agreement.

It was agreed to continue with negotiations, but it was only with the signing in London of the 'Blair House accord' in November 1992 that a breakthrough came. Under this agreement, the EC agreed to cut subsidised farm exports by 21 per cent in volume and by 36 per cent in value within six years. Over the same period, support for domestic farmers would be cut by 20 per cent.

Despite worries of the French government over the implications for French farmers, and last-minute fears that a deal would lead to the demise of the European

order to increase domestic output to Q_3 (and hence reduce unemployment). Areas 1 and 3, as argued above, are merely *redistributed* elsewhere (to firms and the government respectively). But this still leaves area 4. This is a side-effect cost *not* recouped elsewhere.

A *subsidy*, on the other hand, would not have involved this side-effect cost. In order to raise output to Q_3, a rate of subsidy the same as the tariff rate would have to be given to producers. This would raise the amount they receive per unit to $P_w + t$. They would choose to supply Q_3. The price to the consumer, however, would *remain at the world price* P_w. There would thus be no cost to the consumer. The cost of the subsidy to the taxpayer would be areas 1 + 2. Area 1 would be redistributed to firms as extra profit. Area 2, as argued above, may be worth paying in order to bring the desirable output and employment consequences.

If the aim is to increase output, a *production* subsidy is the best policy. If the aim is to increase employment, an *employment* subsidy is the best policy. In either case, to use *protection* instead would be no more than second best, since it would involve side-effects.

To conclude: the best policy is to tackle the problem directly. Unless the aim is specifically to reduce imports (rather than help domestic industry), protection is an indirect policy, and hence never more than second best.

?? What would be the 'first-best' solution to the problem of an infant industry not being able to compete with imports?

World multiplier effects. If the UK imposes tariffs or other restrictions, imports will be reduced. But these imports are other countries' exports. A reduction in their exports will reduce the level of injections into the 'rest-of-

BOX 23.7

film industry and an erosion of European culture by Hollywood, a final GATT agreement was reached in December 1993 and signed in April 1994. The deal led to the setting up in 1995 of the World Trade Organisation (WTO) as a successor to GATT.

Was the Uruguay round a success? The answer must be a qualified yes: the net effect being to increase world GDP by about 1 per cent. The following are the main features of the agreement:

- Tariffs on industrial products cut by an average of 38 per cent (more than the original target) and eliminated entirely on certain products.
- Prohibition of export subsidies and voluntary restraint arrangements (VRAs) – alternatively known as 'voluntary export restraints' (VERs).
- Non-tariff measures to be converted to tariffs.
- The Multifibre Agreement, which protected industrialised countries against imports of textiles from developing countries, to be phased out over ten years.
- Tariffs on agricultural products reduced by 36 per cent over six years in industrialised countries and ten years in developing countries.
- Adoption of the Blair House measures.
- Protection of intellectual property rights strengthened (including patents, copyrights and trademarks).
- Adoption of rules limiting the power of countries to restrict the provision of services (e.g. banking and insurance) by foreign companies, and to restrict multinational investment (e.g. by forcing them to use a proportion of local inputs). Existing measures to be phased out within seven years.
- Adoption of voluntary codes limiting anti-dumping measures and the practice of government procurement favouring domestic suppliers.
- Stronger powers for the WTO than the old GATT to settle disputes and to enforce its rulings (e.g. against non-tariff barriers), with the new rules applying to *all* signatories, not just the industrialised countries, as was previously the case.
- Each country to have its trade policy periodically reviewed by the WTO.

But despite these successes, the cuts in agricultural protection were less than was originally hoped for. Although it was agreed to replace food import quotas into the EU and other industrialised countries by tariff equivalents, the degree of protection remains high, and the industrialised world continues to export food to many developing countries which have a comparative advantage in food production!

??

1. Why are food-importing developing countries likely to lose in the short run from a reduction in agricultural support in rich countries? (These issues are examined in Box 25.1.)
2. If rich countries stand to gain substantially from freer trade, why have they been so reluctant to reduce the levels of protection of agriculture?

the-world' economy, and thus lead to a multiplied fall in rest-of-the-world income. This in turn will lead to a reduction in demand for UK exports. This, therefore, tends to undo the benefits of the tariffs.

?? What determines the size of this world multiplier effect?

Retaliation. If the UK imposes restrictions on, say, Japan, then Japan may impose restrictions on the UK. Any gain to UK firms competing with Japanese imports is offset by a loss to UK exporters. What is more, UK consumers suffer, since the benefits from comparative advantage have been lost.

The increased use of tariffs and other restrictions can lead to a trade war: each country cutting back on imports from other countries. In the end, everyone loses.

Protection may allow firms to remain inefficient. By removing or reducing foreign competition, protection may reduce firms' incentive to reduce costs. Thus if protection is being given to an infant industry, the government must ensure that the lack of competition does not prevent it 'growing up'. Protection should not be excessive and should be removed as soon as possible.

Bureaucracy. If a government is to avoid giving excessive protection to firms, it should examine each case carefully. This can lead to large administrative costs.

Corruption. Some countries that have an extensive programme of protection suffer from corruption. Home producers want as much protection as possible. Importers want as much freedom as possible. It is very tempting for both groups to bribe officials to give them favourable treatment.

World attitudes towards trade and protection

Pre-war growth in protectionism

After the Wall Street crash of 1929, the world plunged into the Great Depression. Countries found their exports falling dramatically, and many suffered severe balance of payments difficulties. The response of many countries was to restrict imports by the use of tariffs and quotas. Of course, this reduced other countries' exports, which encouraged them to resort to even greater protectionism. The net effect of the Depression and the rise in protectionism was a dramatic fall in world trade. The volume of world trade in manufactures fell by more than a third in the three years following the Wall Street crash. Clearly there was a net economic loss to the world from this decline in trade.

On the other hand, the protectionism allowed countries to build up their own home industries behind the trade barriers. This helped to offset the effects of the Depression and lessened the fall in demand for imports. Nevertheless, world trade was still 14 per cent lower in real terms in 1937 than in 1929.

Post-war reduction in protectionism and the role of GATT

After the war there was a general desire to reduce trade restrictions, so that all countries could gain the maximum benefits from trade. There was no desire to return to the beggar-my-neighbour policies of the 1930s.

In 1947, 23 countries got together and signed the General Agreement on Tariffs and Trade (GATT): today there are some 120 members of its successor organisation, the World Trade Organisation, which was formed in 1995. Between them, the members of the WTO account for over 90 per cent of world trade. The aims of GATT, and now the WTO, have been to liberalise trade. Periodically, member countries have met to negotiate reductions in tariffs and other trade restrictions. There have been eight 'rounds' of such negotiations since 1947. The three major ones were the Kennedy round (1964–7), the Tokyo round (1973–9) and the Uruguay round (1986–93). The Kennedy round led to tariff reductions averaging 35 per cent. The Tokyo round involved agreements for tariff reductions of about 33 per cent, but many of the reductions in the event were less than those agreed.

In addition to the negotiated reductions in trade restrictions, GATT provided various rules governing trade:

- *Most favoured nation* clause. This required that any trade concession that a country makes to one member must then be granted to *all* signatories. There was an exception to this, however, in the case of free trade areas and customs unions. In such cases, trade restrictions could be eliminated between the countries involved and yet still be maintained with the rest of the world – provided this did not involve *raising* them with the rest of the world.
- *Reciprocity*. Any nation benefiting from a tariff reduction made by another country had to reciprocate by making similar tariff reductions itself.
- The general prohibition of quotas.
- The forbidding of any member from taking retaliatory action against countries it suspects of unfair trade practices.

The re-emergence of protectionist sentiments in the 1980s

The balance of payments problems that many countries experienced after the oil crisis of 1973 and the recession of the early 1980s led many politicians round the world to call for trade restrictions. Although a tariff war was averted, there was a gradual increase in non-tariff barriers, such as subsidies on domestic products, the prohibition of imports that did not meet precise safety or other specifications, administrative delays in customs clearance, limits on investment by foreign companies and governments favouring domestic firms when purchasing supplies.

Quotas were increasingly used, especially against Japanese imports. In most cases these were 'voluntary' agreements (see Box 23.4). Japan, on a number of occasions, agreed to restrict the number of cars it exported to various European countries. Similar restrictions applied to Japanese televisions and videos. Over 200 VRAs were in force around the world in 1990.

The Uruguay round and the World Trade Organisation

The problem of increasing protectionism was recognised in the Uruguay round of GATT negotiations. This was much more comprehensive than previous rounds. Unlike the others, it included negotiations on tariff reductions in agricultural products and in services (as well as in industrial products), and reductions in non-tariff barriers. Despite fears that an agreement would never be reached, negotiations were completed in December 1993 and a deal was signed in April 1994. This involved a programme of phasing in substantial reductions in tariffs and other restrictions up to the year 2002 (see Box 23.7).

Most of the old GATT rules still apply, but the WTO has additional powers. If there are disputes between member nations, these will be settled by the WTO, although there is provision for appeals, and the parties can agree to go to arbitration.

EXPLORING THE THEORY — BOX 23.8

STRATEGIC TRADE THEORY

An argument for protection?

Lester Thurow is Dean of the Sloan School of Management at the Massachusetts Institute of Technology (MIT). He is also one of the USA's best-known and most articulate advocates of 'managed trade'.

Thurow (and others) have been worried by the growing penetration of US markets by imports from Japan, Europe and many developing countries. Their response is to call for a carefully worked-out strategy of protection for US industries.

The *strategic trade theory* that they support argues that the real world is complex. It is wrong, they claim, to rely on free trade and existing comparative advantage. Particular industries will require particular policies of protection or promotion tailored to their particular needs:

- Some industries will require protection against unfair competition from abroad – not just to protect the industries themselves, but also to protect the consumer from the oligopolistic power that the foreign companies will gain if they succeed in driving the domestic producers out of business.
- Other industries will need special support in the form of subsidies to enable them to modernise and compete effectively with imports.
- New industries may require protection to enable them to get established – to achieve economies of scale and build a comparative advantage.
- If a particular foreign country protects or promotes its *own* industries, it may be desirable to retaliate in order to persuade the country to change its mind.

Thurow claims that Japan has been following a policy of managed trade for years – and look how successful it has been!

But, despite the enthusiasm of the strategic trade theorists, their views have come in for concerted criticism from economic liberals. If the USA is protected from cheap Japanese imports, they claim, all that will be achieved is a huge increase in consumer prices. The car, steel, telecommunications and electrical goods industries might find their profits bolstered, but this is hardly likely to encourage them to be more efficient.

Another criticism of managed trade is the difficulty of identifying just which industries need protection, and how much and for how long. Governments do not have perfect knowledge. What is more, the political lobbyists from various interested groups are likely to use all sorts of tactics – legal or illegal – to persuade the government to look favourably on them. In the face of such pressure will the government remain 'objective'? No, say the liberals.

So how do the strategic trade theorists reply? If it works for Japan, they say, it can work for the USA. What is needed is a change in attitudes. Rather than industry looking on the government as either an enemy to be outwitted or a potential benefactor to be wooed, and government looking on industry as a source of votes or tax revenues, both sides should try to develop a partnership – a partnership from which the whole country can gain.

But whether sensible, constructive managed trade is possible in the US democratic system, or the UK for that matter, is a highly debatable point. 'Sensible' managed trade, say the liberals, is just pie in the sky.

?? Airbus, a consortium based in four European countries, has received massive support from the four governments, in order to enable it to compete with Boeing, which until the rise of Airbus had dominated the world market for aircraft. To what extent are (a) air travellers; (b) citizens of the four countries likely to gain or lose from this protection?

SECTION SUMMARY

1. Countries use various methods to restrict trade, including tariffs, quotas, exchange controls, import licensing, export taxes, and legal and administrative barriers. Countries may also promote their own industries by subsidies.
2. Reasons for restricting trade that have some validity in a world context include the infant industry argument, the inflexibility of markets in responding to changing comparative advantage, dumping and other unfair trade practices, the danger of the establishment of a foreign-based monopoly, the problems of relying on exporting goods whose market is growing slowly or even declining, the need to spread the risks of fluctuating export prices, and the problems that free trade may adversely affect consumer tastes, may allow the importation of harmful goods and may not take account of externalities.
3. Often, however, the arguments for restricting trade are in the context of one country benefiting even though other countries may lose more. Countries may intervene in trade in order to exploit their

continued

monopoly/monopsony power. In the case of imports, the optimum tariff would be that which would reduce consumption to the level where price was equal to the country's marginal cost. In the case of exports, the optimum export tax would be that which reduced production to the level where the country's marginal revenue was equal to marginal cost. Other 'beggar-my-neighbour' arguments include the protection of declining industries and improving the balance of payments.

4. Finally, a country may have other objectives in restricting trade, such as remaining self-sufficient in certain strategic products, not trading with certain countries of which it disapproves, protecting traditional ways of life or simply retaining a non-specialised economy.
5. Arguments for restricting trade, however, are often fallacious. In general, trade brings benefits to countries, and protection to achieve one objective may be at a very high opportunity cost. Other things being equal, there will be a net loss in welfare from restricting trade, with any gain in government revenue or profits to firms being outweighed by a loss in consumer surplus. Even if government intervention to protect certain parts of the economy is desirable, restricting trade is unlikely to be a first-best solution to the problem, since it involves side-effect costs. What is more, restricting trade may have adverse world multiplier effects; it may encourage retaliation; it may allow inefficient firms to remain inefficient; it may involve considerable bureaucracy and possibly even corruption.
6. Most countries of the world are members of the WTO and in theory are in favour of moves towards freer trade. The Uruguay round brought significant reductions in trade restrictions, both tariff and non-tariff. Nevertheless, countries have been very unwilling to abandon restrictions if they believe that they can gain from them, even though they might be at the expense of other countries.

23.3 Preferential trading

Types of preferential trading arrangement

A partial move towards free trade is for a country to remove trade restrictions with selected other countries. There are three possible forms of such trading arrangements.

Free trade areas

A **free trade area** is where member countries remove tariffs and quotas between themselves, but retain whatever restrictions *each member chooses* with non-member countries. Some provision will have to be made to prevent imports from outside coming into the area via the country with the lowest external tariff.

Customs unions

A **customs union** is like a free trade area, but in addition members must adopt common external tariffs and quotas with non-member countries.

Common markets

A **common market** is where member countries operate as a *single* market. Like a customs union there are no tariffs and quotas between member countries and there are common external tariffs and quotas. But a common market goes further than this. A full common market includes the following features.

A common system of taxation. In the case of a *perfect* common market this will involve identical rates of tax in all member countries.

A common system of laws and regulations governing production, employment and trade. For example, in a perfect common market there would be a *single* set of laws governing the following:

- Product specification (e.g. permissible artificial additives to foods, or levels of exhaust emissions from cars).

DEFINITIONS

Free trade area A group of countries with no trade barriers between themselves.

Customs union A free trade area with common external tariffs and quotas.

Common market A customs union where the member countries act as a single market with free movement of labour and capital, common taxes and common trade laws.

- Industrial technology (e.g. standard sizes of equipment, or the composition of various inputs).
- Health and safety at work.
- The employment and dismissal of labour.
- The rights of trade unions and their members.
- Mergers and takeovers.
- Monopolies and restrictive practices.
- The setting-up of new companies.

Free movement of labour, capital and materials and of goods and services. In a perfect common market this will involve a total absence of border controls between member states, the freedom of workers to work in any member country, the freedom of firms to expand into any member state, and the absence of administrative barriers such as the requirement for firms to fill in separate forms for each country in the market to which it exports.

The absence of special treatment by member governments of their own domestic industries. For example, governments are large purchasers of goods and services. In a perfect common market they should buy from whichever companies within the market offer the most competitive deal and not show favouritism towards domestic suppliers: they should operate a *common procurement policy*.

The definition of a common market is sometimes extended to include the following two features of *economic and monetary union*.

A fixed exchange rate between the member countries' currencies. In the extreme case this would involve a *single currency* for the whole market.

Common macroeconomic policies. To some extent this must follow from a fixed exchange rate, but in the extreme case it will involve a single macroeconomic management of the whole market, and hence the abolition of separate fiscal or monetary intervention by individual member states.

The static effects of a customs union: trade creation and trade diversion

By joining a customs union (or free trade area), a country will find that its trade patterns change. Two such changes can be distinguished: trade creation and trade diversion.

Trade creation

Trade creation is where consumption shifts from a high-cost producer to a low-cost producer. The removal of trade barriers allows greater specialisation according to comparative advantage. Instead of consumers having to pay high prices for domestically produced goods in which the country has a comparative disadvantage, the goods can now be obtained more cheaply from other members of the customs union. In return, the country can export to them goods in which it has a comparative advantage.

For example, suppose that the most efficient producer in the world of good x is France. Assume that, before it joined the EC, the UK had to pay tariffs on good x from France. After joining the EC, however, it was then able to import good x from France without paying tariffs. There was a gain to UK consumers. This gain is illustrated in Figure 23.8. The diagram assumes for simplicity that the UK is a price taker as an importer of good x from France: the EC price is given.

The diagram shows that, before joining the EC, the UK had to pay the EC price *plus* the tariff (i.e. P_1). At P_1 the UK produced Q_2, consumed Q_1 and thus imported $Q_1 - Q_2$. With the removal of tariffs, the price falls to P_2. Consumption increases to Q_3 and production falls to Q_4. Imports have thus increased to $Q_3 - Q_4$. Trade has been created.

The gain in welfare from the removal of the tariff is also illustrated in Figure 23.8. A reduction in price from P_1 to P_2 leads to an increase in consumer surplus of areas 1 + 2 + 3 + 4. On the other hand, there is a loss in profits to domestic producers of good x of area 1 and a loss in tariff revenue to the government of area 3. There is still a net gain, however, of areas 2 + 4.

The increased consumption of wine in the UK after joining the EC may be seen as trade creation.

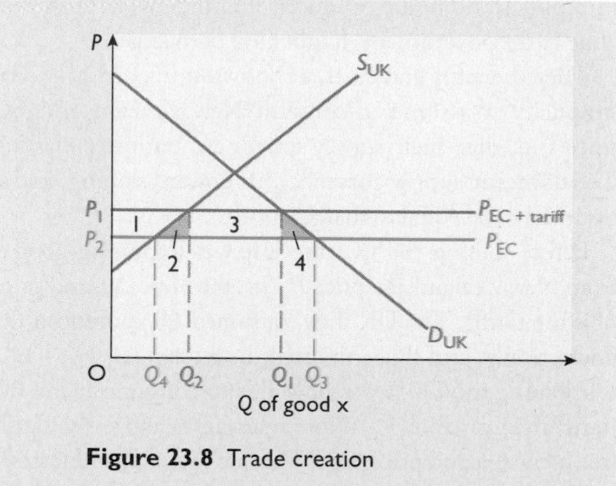

Figure 23.8 Trade creation

DEFINITION

Trade creation Where a customs union leads to greater specialisation according to comparative advantage and thus a shift in production from higher-cost to lower-cost sources.

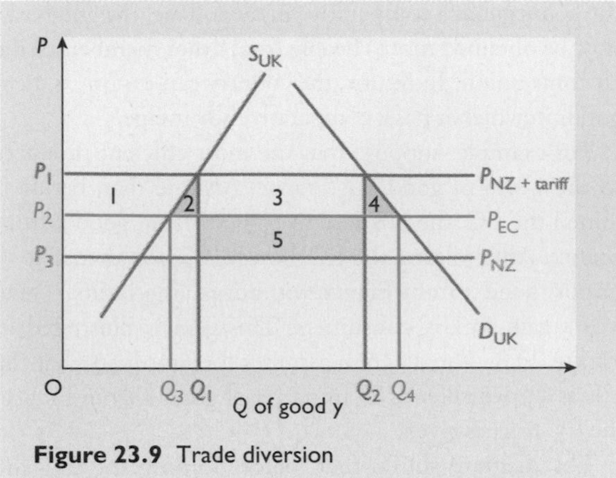

Figure 23.9 Trade diversion

Trade diversion

Trade diversion is where consumption shifts from a lower-cost producer outside the customs union to a higher-cost producer within the union.

Assume that the most efficient producer of good y in the world was New Zealand – outside the EC. Assume that, before membership, the UK paid a similar tariff on good y from any country, and thus imported the product from New Zealand rather than the EC.

After joining the EC, however, the removal of the tariff made the EC product cheaper, since the tariff remained on the New Zealand product. Consumption thus switched to a higher-cost producer. Consumers still gained, since they were paying a lower price than before, but this time the loss in profits to domestic producers and the loss in tariff revenue to the governments might have been larger.

These benefits and costs are shown in Figure 23.9. For simplicity it assumes a constant New Zealand and EC price (i.e. that their supply curves are infinitely elastic). The domestic supply curve (S_{UK}) is upward sloping, and is assumed to be equal to marginal cost.

Before joining the EC, the UK was importing good y from New Zealand at a price P_1 (i.e. the New Zealand price plus the tariff). The UK thus consumed Q_2, produced Q_1 domestically, and thus imported the remainder, $Q_2 - Q_1$. On joining the EC it was now able to consume at the EC (tariff-free) price of P_2. (Note that this is above the tariff-free New Zealand price, P_3). What are the gains and losses?

- Consumers' gain: consumer surplus rises by areas 1 + 2 + 3 + 4.
- Producers' loss: UK producer surplus (profit) falls by area 1.
- Government's loss: previously tariffs of areas 3 + 5 were paid. Now no tariffs are paid. The government thus loses this revenue.

There is thus a net gain of areas 1 + 2 + 3 + 4 minus areas 1 + 3 + 5, i.e. areas 2 + 4 minus area 5. If, however, area 5 is bigger than area 2 + 4, there is a net loss.

When trade *diversion* takes place, therefore, there may still be a net gain, but there may be a net loss. It depends on circumstances.

?? Under which of the following circumstances is there likely to be a net gain from trade diversion? (Refer to Figure 23.9.)

(a) A small difference between the EC price and the New Zealand pre-tariff price, and a large difference between the EC price and the New Zealand price with the tariff, or vice versa.
(b) Elastic or inelastic UK demand and supply curves.
(c) The UK demand and supply curves close together or far apart.

A customs union is more likely to lead to trade diversion rather than trade creation:

- When the union's external tariff is very high. Under these circumstances the abolition of the tariff within the union is likely to lead to a large reduction in the price of goods imported from other members of the union.
- When there is a relatively small cost difference between goods produced within and outside the union. Here the abolition of even relatively low tariffs within the union will lead to internally produced goods becoming cheaper than externally produced goods.

Dynamic effects of a customs union

The problem with the above analysis is that it assumes *static* demand and supply curves: in other words, supply and demand curves that are unaffected by changes in trading patterns. In reality, if a country joins a customs union, the curves are likely to shift. Membership itself affects demand and supply – perhaps beneficially, perhaps adversely.

Dynamic advantages (economic)

- *External economies of scale.* Increased trade may lead to improvements in the infrastructure of the members of

DEFINITION

Trade diversion Where a customs union diverts consumption from goods produced at a lower cost outside the union to goods produced at a higher cost (but tariff free) within the union.

the customs union (better roads, railways, financial services, etc.). This in turn could bring bigger long-term benefits from trade between members, and from external trade too, by making the transport and handling of imports and exports cheaper.

- The bargaining power of the whole customs union with the rest of the world may allow member countries to gain *better terms of trade*. This, of course, will necessarily involve a degree of political co-operation between the members.
- *Increased competition* between member countries may stimulate efficiency, encourage investment and reduce monopoly power. Of course, a similar advantage could be gained by the simple removal of tariffs with any competing country.
- Integration may encourage a *more rapid spread of technology*.

Dynamic disadvantages (economic)

- *Resources may flow from the country* to more efficient members of the customs union, or to the geographical centre of the union (so as to minimise transport costs). This can be a major problem for a *common market* (where there is free movement of labour and capital). The country could become a depressed 'region' of the community, with adverse regional multiplier effects.
- If integration encourages greater co-operation between firms in member countries, it may also encourage *greater oligopolistic collusion*, thus keeping prices higher to the consumer. It may also encourage mergers and takeovers which would increase monopoly power.
- *Diseconomies of scale*. If the union leads to the development of very large companies, they may become bureaucratic and inefficient.
- The *costs of administering* the customs union may be high. These costs may increase over time if the member countries have inadequate controls over the union's expenditure. This problem is likely to be worse the more the intervention in the affairs of individual members. This will encourage members to press for higher expenditure when it benefits them specifically, knowing that the costs will be met by the members collectively.

It is extremely difficult to assess these arguments. To decide whether membership has been beneficial to a country requires a prediction of what things would have been like if it had not joined. No *accurate* predictions of this sort can be made, and they can never be tested. Also, many of the advantages and disadvantages are very long term, and depend on future attitudes, institutions, policies and world events, which again cannot be predicted.

In addition, some of the advantages and disadvantages are distinctly political, such as 'greater political power' or 'loss of sovereignty'. Assessment of these arguments cannot be made by economists.

?? How would you set about assessing whether or not a country had made a net dynamic gain by joining a customs union? What sort of evidence would you look for?

Preferential trading in practice

There are several examples of preferential trading arrangements in different parts of the world. These are essentially regional trading blocs. Although they clearly encourage trade between their members, there was growing fear, especially when it seemed that the Uruguay round of negotiations would fail, that they would cause considerable trade diversion, and essentially become 'trade fortresses'. With a phased reduction in tariffs and other trade restrictions after 1993, these fears have waned somewhat. Nevertheless, many countries outside the blocs complain that they benefit the members at the expense of the rest of the world.

Preferential trading has the greatest potential to benefit countries whose domestic market is too small, taken on its own, to enable them to benefit from economies of scale, and where they face substantial barriers to their exports. Most developing countries fall into this category, and as a result many have attempted to form preferential trading arrangements.

Examples in Latin America include the Latin American Integration Association (LAIA), the Andean Pact and the Central American Common Market (CACM). A Southern Common Market (MerCoSur) was formed in 1995, consisting of Argentina, Brazil, Paraguay and Uruguay. It has a common external tariff and most of its internal trade is free of tariffs.

In 1993, the Asian Free Trade Area (AFTA) was formed. This plans to achieve a reduction in internal tariffs to a maximum of 5 per cent by 2008, with many products being tariff free. In Africa, the Economic Community of West African States (ECOWAS) has been attempting to create a common market between its members.

The two most powerful trading blocs are NAFTA and the EU. The North American Free Trade Association (NAFTA) was formed in 1993 and consists of the USA, Canada and Mexico. These three countries have agreed to abolish tariffs between themselves in the hope that increased trade and co-operation will follow. Tariffs between the USA and Canada will be phased out by 1999, and between Mexico and the other two countries by 2009. New non-tariff restrictions will not be permitted either, but many existing ones can remain in force, thus preventing the development of true free trade between the members. Indeed, some industries, such as textiles and agriculture, will continue to have major non-tariff restrictions.

NAFTA members hope that, with a market similar in size to the EU, they will be able to rival the EU's economic power in world trade. Other countries may join in the future, so NAFTA may eventually develop into a Western Hemisphere free trade association.

NAFTA is, however, at most only a free trade area and not a common market. Unlike the EU, it does not seek to harmonise laws and regulations. Member countries are permitted total legal independence, subject to the one proviso that they must treat firms of other member countries equally with their own firms. Nevertheless, NAFTA has encouraged a growth in trade between its members, most of which is trade creation rather than trade diversion.

The longest established and most comprehensive of preferential trading arrangements is the European Union (until November 1993 known as the European Community). Despite for years being referred to as 'The Common Market', it has not in fact been a true common market, but rather a customs union, and an imperfect one at that. For most of the 1970s and 1980s, the number and variety of non-tariff barriers increased. Member countries adopted all sorts of laws and administrative restrictions to prevent the free flow of goods and resources within the EU, and to favour their own domestic industries over those of other members.

By the mid-1980s, however, the tide of opinion was turning in the Community. Member governments were becoming much more wedded to the idea of free markets and free trade. In this atmosphere of encouraging competition the member countries signed the 'Single European Act'. This committed the twelve countries to the establishment of a true common market – 'the single market' as it is called – by the end of 1992.

Section 23.4 focuses on the EU as an example of a preferential trading system, and looks at the costs and benefits of its move towards being a full common market.

SECTION SUMMARY

1. Countries may make a partial movement towards free trade by the adoption of a preferential trading system. This involves free trade between the members, but restrictions on trade with the rest of the world. Such a system can be either a simple free trade area, or a customs union (where there are common restrictions with the rest of the world), or a common market (where in addition there is free movement of capital and labour, and common taxes and trade laws).
2. A preferential trading area can lead to trade creation where production shifts to low-cost producers within the area, or to trade diversion where trade shifts away from lower-cost producers outside the area to higher-cost producers within the area.
3. There is a net welfare gain from trade creation: the gain in consumer surplus outweighs the loss of tariff revenue and the loss of profit to domestic producers. With trade diversion, however, these two losses may outweigh the gains to consumers: whether they do depends on the size of the tariffs and on the demand for and supply of the traded goods.
4. Preferential trading may bring dynamic advantages of increased external economies of scale, improved terms of trade from increased bargaining power with the rest of the world, increased efficiency from greater competition between member countries, and a more rapid spread of technology. On the other hand, it can lead to increased regional problems for members, greater oligopolistic collusion and various diseconomies of scale. There may also be large costs of administering the system.
5. There have been several attempts around the world to form preferential trading systems. The two most powerful are the European Union and the North American Free Trade Association (NAFTA).

23.4 The European Union

Historical background

The European Economic Community was formed by the signing of the Treaty of Rome in 1957 and came into operation on 1 January 1958.

The original six member countries of the EEC (Belgium, France, Italy, Luxembourg, Netherlands and West Germany) had already made a move towards integration with the formation of the European Coal and Steel Community in 1952. This had removed all restrictions on trade in coal, steel and iron ore between the six countries. The aim had been to gain economies of scale and allow more effective competition with the USA and other foreign producers.

The European Economic Community extended this principle and aimed eventually to be a full common market with completely free trade between members in all products, and with completely free movement of labour, enterprise and capital. By uniting many of the countries of Western Europe it was hoped too that the conflicts of the two world wars would never be repeated, and that acting together the countries of the EEC could be an effective political and economic force in a world dominated by political giants such as the USA and the USSR, and by economic giants such as the USA (and later Japan).

All internal tariffs between the six members had been abolished and common external tariffs established by 1968. But this still only made the EEC a *customs union*, since a number of restrictions on internal trade remained (legal, administrative, fiscal, etc.). Nevertheless the aim was eventually to create a full common market.

In 1973 the UK, Denmark and Ireland joined the EEC. Greece joined in 1981, Spain and Portugal in 1986, and Sweden, Austria and Finland in 1995.

The institutions of the European Union

The goal of some politicians is for the European Union (as it is now called) to become a complete political union, with a central federal government: a 'United States of Europe'. Although this is unlikely in the foreseeable future, there are some political and legal institutions that affect life in member countries.

European Commission. This consists of twenty commissioners appointed by the member countries, two each from the five large countries, and one each from the small. The commissioners administer existing Union policy and propose new policies. They are backed up by a secretariat of some 3000 people in Brussels.

European Council of Ministers. This consists of twelve senior ministers, one from each country. It receives proposals from the Commission, and has the power to decide on all EU issues. Which ministers are represented on the Council depends on the purpose of the meeting. Thus finance ministers represent their country on economic issues, agricultural ministers on farm policy, etc.

European Parliament. Constituencies in the member countries elect MEPs to serve in the European Parliament in Strasbourg. Its powers are rather limited in practice, but in theory both the Commission and the Council are answerable to it.

The European Court of Justice. This meets in Luxembourg and decides on areas of legal dispute arising from the Rome Treaty, whether between governments, institutions or individuals.

Customs union or common market?

The European Union is clearly a customs union. It has common external tariffs and no internal tariffs. But is it also a common market? For years there have been *certain* common economic policies. In other respects the Community of the 1970s and 1980s was far from a true common market: there were all sorts of non-tariff barriers. The Single European Act sought to remove these barriers and to form a genuine common market by the end of 1992.

Four questions arise: (a) In what areas has the EU had common economic policies? (b) What were the non-tariff barriers preventing the operation of a single market? (c) How has the Single European Act changed things? Is the EU now a true common market? (d) What have been the benefits of these changes?

Common economic policies of the EU

There are six major areas where the EU has operated economic policies with at least some common element throughout the Union.

The Common Agricultural Policy (CAP). The Union sets common high prices for farm products. This involves charging variable import duties to bring foreign food imports up to EU prices and intervention to buy up surpluses of food produced within the EU (see section 3.3).

Regional policy. EU regional policy provides grants to firms and local authorities in depressed regions of the Union (see section 22.3).

Monopoly and restrictive practice policy. EU policy here has applied primarily to companies operating in more than one member state (see section 12.2). For example, Article 85 of the Treaty of Rome prohibits agreements between firms which will adversely affect competition in trade between member states. In practice, relatively few cases have been taken to the European Court of Justice.

Harmonisation of taxation. VAT is the standard form of indirect tax throughout the EU. However, there are substantial differences in VAT rates between member states (see Box 23.11), and rates of other types of indirect tax (such as excise duties) vary considerably between the members, as do rates of direct taxation.

CASE STUDIES

THE SOCIAL DIMENSION OF THE EU

In 1989 eleven of the twelve EC countries adopted a social charter. The UK did not participate. The social charter established twelve principles concerning workers' rights and social justice. The intention was that these should be progressively put into practice by means of EC legislation and other measures adopted by member states.

1. *Freedom of movement*: measures to ease free movement of labour between EC states, including recognition of qualifications and host country 'social protection' for employees from one EC state working in another.
2. *Employment and remuneration*: rights to 'decent' wages; freedom to pursue an occupation; access to placement services free of charge.
3. *Living and working conditions*: commitment to improvements, including establishment of maximum weekly hours of work and rights to annual paid leave and a weekly rest period; improvements relating to fixed-term contracts, temporary work, weekend work, night work and shift work.
4. *Social protection*: rights to a minimum income for those 'excluded from the labour market'.
5. *Freedom of association and collective bargaining*: the right to belong to any professional or union organisation of one's choice; to negotiate collective agreements; and to resort to collective action.
6. *Vocational training*: covers training opportunities, training and retraining systems and the freedom for every EC citizen to enrol for occupational training on the same terms as any national of the member state where the course is to take place.
7. *Equal treatment*: guarantees 'intensification' of measures to ensure equal treatment between men and women in matters such as remuneration, employment, training and career development.
8. *Information, consultation and participation of workers*: to be developed along lines that take practice in member states into account – particularly applicable to technological change; company restructuring and mergers; and 'transfrontier' employees.
9. *Health and safety*: covers further harmonisation in this area, with particular regard to public works.
10. *Children and adolescents*: covers minimum employment age (16), equitable remuneration, training and labour regulations.
11. *Elderly*: covers living standards, minimum income and social protection.
12. *Disabled*: covers integration into working life, including training, accessibility, transport and housing.[2]

The principles would seem to be very wide ranging, but they are also quite general. For example, there was no attempt to define a 'decent wage'.

Since the adoption of the social charter, there has been slow progress in putting the principles into practice. This is only to be expected, given the huge diversity of social and economic situations between the member states (see the table). Harmonisation is difficult where wage rates in the poorest countries are less than half of those in the richest ones.

Nevertheless progress has been made in the following areas:

- The right for EU citizens to live and work in another EU country for the same wages and under the same working conditions as workers of that country.
- The passing of various forms of equal opportunities legislation (e.g. child care for working parents).
- Working hours: a maximum 48-hour working week; a minimum daily rest period of 11 hours; at least one day per week off; four weeks' minimum annual holiday.
- The protection of pension and other social security rights of workers moving from one EU country to another.
- Health and safety in the workplace.
- The creation of *EurES* (European Employment Service), a European information network for job vacancies.

?? What would be the economic effects of (a) different rates of VAT, (b) different rates of personal income tax and (c) different rates of company taxation between member states if there were no other barriers to trade or factor movements?

Transport policy. Given that transport costs account for around 25 per cent of firms' costs, differences in taxes and subsidies on transport can considerably affect the pattern of trade. Articles 74–84 of the Treaty of Rome outline the features of a common transport policy. These include free competition between carriers of all Community countries, common regulations for crossing frontiers, and the regulation of state financial assistance to their domestic transport industries. After many years of negotiations, however, many different restrictions remained throughout the Community on all parts of the transport industry – road, rail, sea and air.

Social policy. Articles 117–28 refer to social policy, and include calls for collaboration between member states on

BOX 23.9

Different social situations 1994

	Employment			Gross hourly earnings of manual workers in industry	Social protection benefits	
	Agriculture (%)	Industry (%)	Services (%)	ECU (PPS)	% of GDP	ECU (PPS) per inhabitant
Austria	7	34	59	9.28	30.2	5611
Belgium	3	29	68	10.13	27.0	5052
Denmark	5	26	69	11.22	33.7	6374
Finland	8	27	65	8.45	34.8	5262
France	5	27	68	7.28	30.5	5500
Germany	3	38	59	10.86	30.7	5514
Greece	21	24	55	5.47	16.0	1645
Ireland	13	28	59	8.88	21.1	2873
Italy	8	32	60	n.a.	25.3	4312
Luxembourg	3	27	70	10.06	24.9	6674
Netherlands	4	24	72	9.70	32.3	5536
Portugal	12	32	56	3.53	19.5	2162
Spain	10	30	60	7.83	23.6	3020
Sweden	4	25	71	7.82	39.2	6832
UK	2	28	70	9.00	28.1	4649
EU(15)	5	30	64	n.a.	28.2	4675

- Requiring employers to inform workers of their conditions of employment.

The social chapter of the Maastricht Treaty (1991) has speeded the progress of social protection. Article 2.1 of the treaty states:

> The eleven countries agreed that they will have as their objectives the promotion of employment, improved living and working conditions, proper social protection, dialogue between management and labour, the development of human resources with a view to lasting high employment and the combating of social exclusion.

It was also agreed that for several types of measure, only a qualified majority in the Council of Ministers will be required.

?? Which of the elements of the social charter would be likely to affect employment and in what way?

[2] This summary is from *Industrial Relations* (11 July 1989).

laws relating to employment, health and safety at work and collective bargaining rights, and equal pay for men and women doing the same work.

In practice during the 1980s there was a little harmonisation of Community social policy. But in 1989 the European Commission presented a *social charter* to the EC heads of state. This represented the culmination of the Commission's efforts to tackle the social dimension of the single market. The social charter (see Box 23.9) spelt out a series of worker and social rights that should apply across the whole Community. However, the charter was only a recommendation and each element had to be approved separately by the Council.

The Conservative government in the UK was strongly opposed to the social charter, seeing it as an attempt to introduce 'socialism by the back door'. The government was particularly opposed to any attempt to introduce a minimum wage, arguing that it would increase unemployment (see Boxes 10.4 and 13.4).

Then in December 1991 the Maastricht Treaty was signed. This set out a timetable for economic and monetary union for the EC (see section 24.7), but also included a 'social chapter', which attempted to move the Community forward in implementing the details of the social charter. The UK government refused to sign this part of the Maastricht Treaty and will take no part in voting on the implementation of the elements of the social chapter. It maintained that such measures would increase costs of production and make EC goods less competitive in world trade. Critics of the UK position argue that the refusal to adopt minimum working conditions (and also a minimum wage) will make the UK the 'sweat-shop' of Europe.

?? Would the adoption of improved working conditions necessarily lead to higher labour costs per unit of output?

Non-tariff barriers

Tariffs were eliminated long ago between EU members. But the 1980s saw a proliferation of non-tariff barriers.

Quotas and other quantitative restrictions

From time to time quotas were imposed by *individual* members on imports from outside the EC (e.g. on cars and textiles). This then required customs checks at the borders with other EC countries to prevent the goods coming in via them.

Cost-increasing barriers

This is where the cost of importing goods from other member states was artificially increased. There were three major types of cost-increasing barrier.

Taxation. As long as different rates of VAT and excise duties are charged in the various member states, this will affect competition. In the mid-1980s Italy, Greece, Spain, Portugal and West Germany put no excise duty on wine. The UK, Denmark and Ireland (non-wine producers) in contrast had quite high duties on wine. Not surprisingly, wine-producing countries claimed that this was an unfair barrier to their exports.

Customs formalities. Different rates of VAT and excise duties necessarily involved customs checks and paperwork. These added to the costs of trade within the Community.

Regulations and norms. Regulations were often cleverly designed by countries to favour their domestic suppliers. For example, the Danes have a highly developed industry producing recycled containers. A Danish law required that all soft drinks in Denmark be sold in recycled containers. This added substantially to the costs of EC member companies exporting soft drinks to Denmark. In Spain, double inspection had to be made of imported spirits. This cost approximately 1 per cent of the value of these imports.

Barriers to entry

This was where entry to another member's market was blocked or restricted. These barriers were often more serious than cost barriers, since companies could at least attempt to overcome cost handicaps.

State procurement (government favouring domestic suppliers). National governments, local governments and nationalised industries between them spend over 20 per cent of the Union's GDP. But whether it be for defence equipment, power stations, office equipment, railway rolling stock or official cars, governments prefer to buy from their own national industries. In fact this government purchasing policy has kept many firms afloat.

Licensing and similar restrictions. In certain industries, firms may require a licence to operate. Governments often favoured domestic firms in granting such licences. National airlines were often granted sole right to operate a given domestic route (or pairs of airlines on routes between two countries).

Educational qualifications. Some professions only recognised their own national qualifications.

Financial barriers. Up to the mid-1980s there were many barriers to financial dealing in other members' countries: exchange controls, limited entry to stock markets, licensing of financial dealers, restrictions on the right to sell financial services across EC borders, restrictions on cross-country mergers and takeovers, government control over the allocation of credit, etc.

Regulations and norms. This category was often cited by businesses as being the most important single barrier. In some cases the regulations merely added to the costs of imports. But in the case of many mechanical engineering and telecommunications products, technical and health and safety regulations sometimes ruled out foreign imports altogether.

Market-distorting barriers. These are barriers that distort the market so as to give domestic producers an unfair

CASE STUDIES BOX 23.10

MUTUAL RECOGNITION: THE CASSIS DE DIJON CASE
Or when is a liqueur not a liqueur?

Crème de Cassis is an alcoholic blackcurrant drink made by the French firm Cassis de Dijon. Added to white wine it makes the drink kir. It is not just the French that like drinking kir; it is also, among others, the Germans. In this seemingly innocent fact lay the seeds for the dismantling of some of the most serious trade barriers in Europe!

The story starts back in 1978. The West German company Rewe Zentral AG wanted to import Cassis, but found that under West German law it could not. The problem was that Cassis does not contain enough alcohol to be classed as a liqueur, and it also fell outside any other category of alcoholic drink that was permitted by West German law.

But Rewe was not to be put off. It started legal proceedings in Europe to challenge the German law. The basis of Rewe's case was that this law discriminated against non-German companies. After much legal wrangling the European Court of Justice in Luxembourg ruled that Germany had no right to prevent the importation of a product that was legitimately on sale in another member country (i.e. France). The only exceptions to this ruling would be if the product was barred for reasons of consumer protection, health or fair trade. None of these applied to Cassis, so the Germans can now drink kir to their hearts' content without having to become smugglers.

But what of the implications of the case? These are enormous and were spelt out in the Single European Act: 'the Council may decide that provisions in force in a member state must be recognised as being equivalent to those applied by another'. In other words, individuals and firms can choose which country's sets of regulations suit them the best and then insist that they be applied in *all* member states.

'Mutual recognition' of each other's laws will tend to lead to deregulation, as people choose those countries' laws that give them the greatest freedom. This appeals to economic and political liberals. Equally it worries those who argue that regulations and laws on industrial standards have been instituted for a purpose, and should not be undone just because some other member country has not been wise enough to institute them itself.

?? How did the Cassis de Dijon ruling affect the balance of power in the Community between
(a) individual states and the whole Community;
(b) governments and the courts?

advantage. Examples included government subsidies or tax relief, price controls that favoured domestic suppliers and government connivance in restrictive practices operated by domestic firms.

Completing the internal market

Despite its agricultural and regional policies, the EC even after 25 years was still little more than a customs union. Extensive barriers remained in place, and in many cases increased, for most of the 1970s and 1980s. But ever since the Treaty of Rome was signed in 1957, politicians and economists had debated ways of moving towards a true common market.

In the mid-1980s, things were changing. There had been a general movement to the right in European politics and a growing belief in the merits of free markets and competition. Even President Mitterrand's Socialist government in France, after an early attempt at increased intervention and reflation (1981–3), began to relax controls.

In 1984 the French finance minister, Jacques Delors, had extensive discussions with other European leaders to find the best way forward for Europe. It quickly became clear that this could now be achieved not by greater intervention or by a major extension of the political powers of European institutions, but simply by the removal of barriers to internal trade – by 'completing the internal market'.

In 1985 Delors became President of the European Commission and asked Lord Cockfield (a newly appointed commissioner from the UK) to prepare a white paper on dismantling barriers. What resulted was a proposal for 300 measures. These became the basis for the Single European Act of 1986. The Act set a date of 31 December 1992 by which its proposals should be in place. The Act did not propose the removal of *all* barriers, but was a massive move in that direction.

One of the most crucial aspects of the Act was its acceptance of the principle of **mutual recognition**.

DEFINITION

Mutual recognition The EU principle that one country's rules and regulations must apply throughout the Community. If they conflict with those of another country, individuals and firms should be able to choose which to obey.

CASE STUDIES

FEATURES OF THE SINGLE MARKET

Since January 1 1993 trade within the EU has operated very much like trade within a country. In theory there should be no more difficulty for a firm in Birmingham to sell its goods in Paris than in London. At the same time, the single market allows free movement of labour and involves the use of common technical standards.

The features of the single market are summed up in two EC publications:[3]

- Elimination of border controls on goods within the EU: no more long waits.
- Free movement of people across borders.
- Common security arrangements.
- No import taxes on goods bought in other member states for personal use.
- The right for everyone to live in another member state.
- Recognition of vocational qualifications in other member states: engineers, accountants, medical practitioners, teachers and other professionals able to practise throughout Europe.
- Technical standards brought into line, and product tests and certification agreed across the whole EU.
- Common commercial laws – making it attractive to form Europe-wide companies and to start joint ventures.
- Public contracts to supply equipment and services to state organisations now open to tenders across the EU.

Of the 282 proposals in the Internal Market Programme established in the Single European Act of 1986, 91 per cent had been adopted by the beginning of 1993 and 96 per cent by the end of that year.

So what does the single market mean for individuals and for businesses?

Individuals

Before 1993, if you were travelling in Europe, you had a 'duty-free allowance'. This meant that you could only take goods up to the value of ECU600 across borders within the EC without having to pay VAT in the country into which you were importing them. Now you can take as many goods as you like from one EU country to another, provided they are for your own consumption. But to prevent fraud, member states may ask for evidence that the goods have been purchased for the traveller's own consumption if they exceed specified amounts (e.g. 800 cigarettes, 10 litres of spirits, 90 litres of wine, 110 litres of beer).

The one exception to the free import of goods for personal consumption is means of transport, such as cars, boats and planes. If a person imports a car from another member state which has been driven for less than 3000 km and is less than three months old, VAT must be paid in the person's home country. No VAT is levied on second-hand means of transport, however.

Individuals have the right to live and work in any other member state. Qualifications obtained in one member state must be recognised by other member states.

This is the principle whereby if a firm or individual is permitted to do something under the rules and regulations of *one* EU country, it must also be permitted to do it in all other EU countries. This means that firms and individuals can choose the country's rules that are least constraining. It also means that individual governments can no longer devise special rules and regulations that keep out competitors from other EU countries (see Box 23.11).

Another crucial aspect of the Single European Act was the institution of *majority* voting in questions of harmonisation of rules and regulations (Article 100 of the Treaty of Rome). Previously, unanimous approval had been necessary. This had meant that an individual country could veto the dismantling of barriers. This new system of majority voting, however, does not apply to the harmonisation of taxes.

The benefits and costs of the single market

When the Single European Act was passed it was very difficult to calculate its benefits and costs. There are two key reasons for this. The first is that it was not clear just how completely the barriers would be eliminated. The second is that removing barriers merely creates an opportunity. Just how far firms would exploit the opportunities of an open market and just how much one country's firms would benefit relative to another's could not be predicted with any precision.

Nevertheless many studies have been done to try and estimate the benefits and costs. These studies tend to group benefits into the following main categories.

Trade creation. Costs and prices are likely to fall from a greater exploitation of comparative advantage. Member

BOX 23.11

Firms

Before 1993 all goods traded in the EC were subject to VAT at every internal border. This involved some 60 million customs clearance documents at a cost of some ECU70 (about £50) per consignment.[4]

This has all now disappeared. Goods can cross from one member state to another without any border controls: in fact the concepts of 'importing' and 'exporting' within the EU no longer officially exist. All goods sent from one EU country to another will be charged VAT only in the country of destination. They are exempt from VAT in the country where they are produced.

One of the important requirements for fair competition in the single market is the convergence of tax rates. Although income tax rates, corporate tax rates and excise duties still differ between member states, there has been some narrowing in the range of VAT rates. There is now a lower limit of 15 per cent on the standard rate of VAT. What is more, the member states have agreed to abolish higher rates of VAT on luxury goods, and to have no more than two lower rates of at least 5 per cent on 'socially necessary' goods, such as food and water supply. The table shows VAT rates in 1988 and 1996.

?? In what ways would competition be 'unfair' if VAT rates differed widely between member states?

VAT rates (%) in the EC/EU: 1988 and 1996

	1988		1996
	Standard rate	High rates	Standard rate
Austria			20
Belgium	19	25, 33	20.5
Denmark	22	–	25
Finland			22
France	18.6	33.3	20.6
Germany	14	–	15
Greece	18	36	18
Ireland	25	–	21
Italy	18	38	19
Luxembourg	12	–	15
Netherlands	20	–	17.5
Portugal	16	30	17
Spain	12	33	16
Sweden			25
UK	15	–	17.5

[3] *A Single Market for Goods* (Commission of the European Communities, 1993); *10 Key Points about the Single European Market* (Commission of the European Communities, 1992).
[4] See *A Single Market for Goods* (Commission of the European Communities, 1993).

countries can now specialise further in those goods and services that they can produce at a comparatively low opportunity cost.

Reduction in the direct costs of barriers. This category includes administrative costs, border delays and technical regulations. Their abolition or harmonisation has led in many cases to substantial cost savings.

Economies of scale. With industries based on a Europe-wide scale, many firms can now be large enough, and their plants large enough, to gain the full potential economies of scale. Yet the whole European market is large enough for there still to be adequate competition. Such gains vary from industry to industry depending on the minimum efficient scale of a plant or firm.

Greater competition: short run. More effective competition from other EU countries can (a) squeeze profit margins and thus bring prices more in line with costs and (b) encourage more efficient use of resources and thus reduce costs.

Greater competition: long run. In the long run, greater competition can stimulate greater innovation, the greater flow of technical information and the rationalisation of production.

The single market has not received universal welcome within the Union. Its critics argue that, in a Europe of oligopolies, unequal ownership of resources, rapidly changing technologies and industrial practices, and factor immobility, the removal of internal barriers to trade has merely exaggerated the problems of inequality and

CASE STUDIES

THE BENEFITS OF COMPLETING THE INTERNAL MARKET

Predictions and outcomes

In March 1988 the European Commission's journal, *European Economy*, published a special edition entitled 'The economics of 1992'. It contained the following estimates of the benefits of the removal of all trade barriers in Europe:

- The removal of *frontier formalities* could save some 1.8 per cent of the value of goods traded in the Community (about £6 billion).
- The removal of *all industrial barriers* (including technical regulations as well as frontier formalities) was estimated in opinion surveys of industrialists to save some 2 per cent on industrial costs (about £26 billion). Other surveys supported these findings, with estimates ranging from a 1–2 per cent cost reduction in the food, construction materials and clothing industries to a 5 per cent reduction in the car industry.
- In addition to direct cost savings, *economies of scale* were likely to arise from a larger market. One study showed that, in more than half of all branches of industry, at least twenty firms of efficient size could exist in the Community market, whereas the largest national markets could only have an average of four firms each. With four firms there was likely to be a problem of oligopoly power. With twenty firms there was not. Only the European internal market could therefore combine the advantages of economies of scale with those of competition. The benefits of economies of scale and rationalisation could yield cost savings of between 1 and 7 per cent (some £40 billion).
- In branches of industry which were subject to *entry barriers*, the combined savings from increased competition and economies of scale could be much greater still. This was particularly so in industries supplying government departments under contract (e.g. energy generating, transport, and office and defence equipment). Here savings of some 10–20 per cent (about £13 billion) could be expected if governments ceased to favour domestic suppliers. Savings of a similar magnitude could be expected in the financial services industry.
- Gains from reductions in *X inefficiency* (see Box 6.4) were very hard to estimate, but they could be as high as those from economies of scale, and for several industries some 2–3 times higher than the direct cost savings from the removal of barriers.

There were likely to be some initial costs of market integration, the most serious of which would probably be the redundancies arising from a process of rationalisation. In the medium term, however, the total benefits could be substantial. Even with a passive macroeconomic policy, after 5–6 years the cumulative increase in GDP was estimated to be about $4^1/_2$ per cent and the decrease in prices about 6 per cent. Even employment would be likely to grow by some 2 million jobs (about 2 per cent). The overall EU budget balance and the balance of payments were both predicted to improve significantly.

With a more expansive macroeconomic policy, GDP after the 5–6 years could be some $2^1/_2$ per cent higher still (making a total of 7 per cent) without causing serious problems of inflation or balance of payments deficits. The report concluded that:

> The potential gains from a full, competitive integration of the internal market are not trivial in macroeconomic terms. They could be about large enough to make the

economic power. More specifically a number of criticisms are made.

Radical economic change is costly. Substantial economic change is necessary to achieve the full economies of scale and efficiency gains from a single European market. These changes necessarily involve redundancies – from bankruptcies, takeovers, rationalisation and the introduction of new technology. The severity of this structural and technological unemployment depends on (a) the pace of economic change and (b) the mobility of labour – both occupational and geographical.

Adverse regional multiplier effects. Firms are likely to locate as near as possible to the 'centre of gravity' of their markets and sources of supply. If, before barriers were removed, a firm's prime market was the UK, it might well have located in the Midlands or the north of England. If, however, with barriers now removed, its market has become Europe as a whole, it may choose to locate in the south of England or in France, Germany or the Benelux countries instead. The creation of a single European market thus tends to attract capital and jobs away from the edges of the Union to its geographical centre.

In an ideal market situation, areas like the west of Ireland, the south of Italy or Portugal should attract resources from other parts of the Union. Being relatively depressed areas, wages and land prices are lower. The resulting lower industrial costs should encourage firms to move into the areas. In practice, regional multiplier effects may worsen the problem. As capital and labour (and especially young and skilled workers) leave the extremities of the Union, so these regions are likely to become more

BOX 23.12

difference between a disappointing and very satisfactory economic performance for the Community economy as a whole.[5]

The benefits could eventually turn out to be even greater than those estimated. The reason is that the estimates left out the possible benefits from an increased rate of technical progress as a result of greater competition and economies of scale, the increased spread of skills and information, and the development of truly European companies with international economic power.

Any forecasts of the benefits and costs of a programme as large as that of completing the internal market can soon be overtaken by events. Before 1993, there were worries about whether all the proposals contained in the Single European Act would in fact be adopted. However, by the end of 1994 some 95 per cent of the 282 proposals had passed into European law. Many of the proposals, however, have yet to become part of national law in each of the fifteen member states.

Soon after the implementation of the Single European Act, clear evidence emerged that it was beginning to bring benefits. The narrowing of price differences between countries for many manufactured products, especially cars, was one of the first signs that the Single European Act was having an impact. The elimination of border controls for goods has reduced costs and shortened delivery times. The simplification of VAT arrangements on cross-border transactions has also reduced costs. Several national government contracts have been won by firms from other member states. Many of Europe's larger retailers, such as Marks & Spencer and Carrefour, are taking advantage of the single market by expanding across Europe, and hope to gain economies of scale from so doing. The financial services sector is also facing increased competition from other member states (and non-member states too, such as the USA and Japan).

Although the elimination of trade barriers has brought initial benefits, the development of the internal market is now seen as vital if the gains so far achieved are to be built upon. Although there has been some adoption of common technical standards, separate national standards still exist in several industries. There is no truly single market for labour, with differences in employment and remuneration regulations between countries. There are still significant differences in VAT rates across the EU (see Box 23.11). Government procurement contracts are still awarded predominantly to domestic companies. Environmental measures still differ substantially from one member country to another.

Probably the biggest barrier to the future development of the internal market has been the existence of multiple currencies – the costs of changing money and the uncertainties associated with currency fluctuations. Many have argued that, without greater monetary union and the advent of the single European currency, the single European market would remain incomplete. (We examine these issues in section 24.8.)

??

If the benefits of a single internal market are so great, why did individual member governments of the EC often fiercely resist the dismantling of particular internal barriers?

[5] *European Economy*, no. 35 (March 1988), pp. 19–20.

depressed. If, as a result, their infrastructure is neglected, they then become even less attractive to new investment.

??

Is the problem of adverse regional multiplier effects likely to be made better or worse by the adoption of a single European currency? (This issue is explored in Chapter 24.) (Clue: without a single currency how would the devaluation of the drachma affect a depressed Greek economy?)

The development of monopoly/oligopoly power. The free movement of capital is likely to lead to the development of giant 'Euro-firms' with substantial economic power. This can lead to higher, not lower prices, and less choice for the consumer. It all depends on just how effective competition is, and how effective EU competition policy is in preventing monopolistic and collusive practices.

Trade diversion. Just as increased trade creation has been a potential advantage from completing the internal market, so trade diversion has been a possibility too. This is more likely if *external* barriers remain high (or are even increased) and internal barriers are *completely* abolished.

??

Is trade diversion more likely or less likely in the following cases?

(a) European producers gain monopoly power in world trade.
(b) Modern developments in technology and communications reduce the differences in production costs associated with different locations.
(c) The development of the internal market produces substantial economies of scale in many industries.

Perhaps the biggest objection raised against the single European market is a political one: the loss of national sovereignty. Governments find it much more difficult to intervene at a microeconomic level in their own economies.

But what of Brussels? Has the completion of the internal market meant more intervention by the Union? Those worried about the *adverse* economic consequences of a single market argue that there will need to be much more effective regional, social and anti-monopoly policies. Large-scale increases in the various Union funds may be necessary to alleviate some of the inequalities and hardships associated with the single market.

?? Why may the newer members of the Union have the most to gain from the single market, but also the most to lose?

Postscript: the future of the European Union

A number of factors will have a major effect on the shape and performance of the Union and on the costs and benefits to the members. The first of these, as we have seen, is the extent to which the goals of the Single European Act will be realised. Over time will there in fact be a genuine single market, or will governments find ways of frustrating the goals of the Act by continuing to favour their own industries?

Another factor is the extent to which there will be a monetary union with not only fixed exchange rates, but also common monetary and fiscal policies or even a common currency. These issues are examined in section 24.8. An important issue here is whether there will be the development of a two-tier Union, with some countries entering wholeheartedly into an economic and political union, and other countries – such as the UK – remaining more independent.

A major issue into the next century is the question of new membership of the Union. With the enlargement of the Union to include various eastern European countries, or Mediterranean countries such as Cyprus, Turkey and Malta, there will be new pressures on the EU and calls upon its budget. The larger the EU becomes, the more difficult will be political union and full monetary union, and the more likely it will be that the European Union will remain primarily a single market.

To examine the arguments about full monetary union we need first to look at the whole question of exchange rate determination and alternative exchange rate systems. This is the subject of the next chapter.

SECTION SUMMARY

1. The European Union is a customs union in that it has common external tariffs and no internal ones. But virtually from the outset it has also had elements of a common market, particularly in the areas of agricultural policy, regional policy, monopoly and restrictive practice policy, and to some extent in the areas of tax harmonisation, transport policy and social policy.
2. Nevertheless, there were substantial non-tariff barriers to trade within the Community: these included cost-increasing barriers, such as different tax rates, customs formalities and various regulations over product quality; barriers to the entry of firms into other members' markets, through such practices as licensing, state procurement policies, educational qualification requirements, financial barriers and various regulations and norms; and market-distorting barriers, such as subsidies or tax relief to domestic producers and lax policies towards domestic restrictive practices.
3. The Single European Act of 1986 sought to sweep away these restrictions and to establish a genuine free market within the EC: to establish a full common market. Benefits from completing the internal market have included trade creation, cost savings from no longer having to administer barriers, economies of scale for firms now able to operate on a Europe-wide scale, and greater competition leading to reduced costs and prices, greater flows of technical information and more innovation.
4. Critics of the single market point to various changes in industrial structure that have resulted, bringing problems of redundancies and closures. They also point to adverse regional multiplier effects as resources are attracted to the geographical centre of the EU, to possible problems of market power with the development of giant 'Euro-firms', and to the possibilities of trade diversion.
5. The actual costs and benefits of EU membership to the various countries vary with their particular economic circumstances – for example, the extent to which they gain from trade creation, or lose from adverse regional multiplier effects – and with their contributions to and receipts from the EU budget.
6. These cost and benefits in the future will depend on just how completely the barriers to trade are abolished, on the extent of monetary union and on any enlargements to the Union.

??? END-OF-CHAPTER QUESTIONS ???

1. Imagine that two countries, Richland and Poorland, can produce just two goods, computers and coal. Assume that for a given amount of land and capital, the output of these two products requires the following constant amounts of labour:

	Richland	Poorland
1 computer	2	4
100 tonnes of coal	4	5

Assume that each country has 20 million workers.

(a) Draw the production possibility curves for the two countries (on two separate diagrams).

(b) If there is no trade, and in each country 12 million workers produce computers and 8 million workers produce coal, how many computers and tonnes of coal will each country produce? What will be the total production of each product?

(c) What is the opportunity cost of a computer in (i) Richland; (ii) Poorland?

(d) What is the opportunity cost of 100 tonnes of coal in (i) Richland: (ii) Poorland?

(e) Which country has a comparative advantage in which product?

(f) Assuming that price equals marginal cost, which of the following would represent possible exchange ratios?

(i) 1 computer for 40 tonnes of coal; (ii) 2 computers for 140 tonnes of coal; (iii) 1 computer for 100 tonnes of coal; (iv) 1 computer for 60 tonnes of coal; (v) 4 computers for 360 tonnes of coal.

(g) Assume that trade now takes place and that 1 computer exchanges for 65 tonnes of coal. Both countries specialise completely in the product in which they have a comparative advantage. How much does each country produce of its respective product?

(h) The country producing computers sells 6 million domestically. How many does it export to the other country?

(i) How much coal does the other country consume?

(j) Construct a table like Table 23.3 to show the no-trade and with-trade positions of each country.

(k) How much coal does the other country consume?

2. If capital moves from developed to less developed countries, and labour moves from less developed to developed countries, what effects will these factor movements have on wage rates and the return on capital in the two types of country?

3. What factors determine a country's terms of trade?

4. Go through each of the arguments for restricting trade (both those of general validity and those having some validity for specific countries) and provide a counter-argument for not restricting trade.

5. If countries are so keen to reduce the barriers to trade, why do many countries frequently attempt to erect barriers?

6. What factors will determine whether a country's joining a customs union will lead to trade creation or trade diversion?

7. Why is it difficult to estimate the magnitude of the benefits of completing the internal market of the EU?

8. Look through the costs and benefits that we identified from the completion of the internal market. Do the same costs and benefits arise from a substantially enlarged EU?

24

The balance of payments, exchange rates and international economic relationships

24.1 Alternative exchange rate regimes

Policy objectives: internal and external

A country is likely to have various **internal** and **external policy objectives**. *Internal* objectives include such things as economic growth, low unemployment and low inflation. *External* objectives include such things as achieving balance of payments equilibrium, encouraging international trade and preventing excessive exchange rate fluctuations. Internal and external objectives may come into conflict, however.

A simple illustration of potential conflict is with the objectives of *internal balance* and *external balance*.

Internal balance. **Internal balance** is the term used to refer to a Keynesian *full-employment* equilibrium: where Y_e (equilibrium national income) = Y_f (full-employment national income) (see Chapter 16).[1]

External balance. **External balance** is the term used to refer to a *balance of payments* equilibrium. Sometimes it is used in the narrow sense to refer to a current account balance, and therefore also a capital account balance. Sometimes it is used more loosely to refer merely to a *total currency flow balance* (where any current account deficit is matched by an identical capital account surplus, and vice versa, with *no need for intervention from the reserves*).

Internal and external balance are illustrated in Figure 24.1. In Figure 24.1(a) internal balance is achieved at Y_e, where $Y_e = Y_f$ (e.g. with curves W_1 and J_1). In Figure 24.1(b) external balance (in the loose sense) is achieved where the demand for and supply of the currency intersect at the current exchange rate (e.g. S_1 and D_1 intersecting at a current exchange rate of r_1).

It may, however, be difficult to achieve internal and external balance simultaneously. Assume, for example, that there was a recession and high unemployment, and thus a deflationary gap. Withdrawals and injections are now given by W_2 and J_2 in Figure 24.1(a). Equilibrium is at Y_{e_2} – below Y_f. There is no *internal* balance. Let us assume, however, that there is *external* balance in both the narrow and the loose sense. If the government expands aggregate demand to close the deflationary gap and restore internal balance, demand for imports will rise. The supply of sterling will shift to S_2 in Figure 24.1(b). There will now be a current account deficit, and external balance in the narrow sense will be destroyed. If the government maintains the exchange rate at r_1, external balance will have been destroyed in the loose sense too.

External balance in the loose sense could be restored if the exchange rate were allowed to depreciate, so that the demand and supply of sterling were equated at the new lower exchange rate. This, however, may conflict with internal objectives. For example, a falling exchange rate will increase the cost of imports. This can lead to higher

[1] Alternatively, within a monetarist analysis, internal balance could refer to employment being at the natural level: i.e. the economy being on the long-run Phillips curve.

DEFINITIONS

Internal policy objectives Objectives relating solely to the domestic economy.

External policy objectives Objectives relating to the economy's international economic relationships.

Internal balance Where the equilibrium level of national income is at the desired level.

External balance Narrow definition: where the current account of the balance of payments is in balance (and thus also the capital account). Loose definition: where there is a total currency flow balance at a given exchange rate.

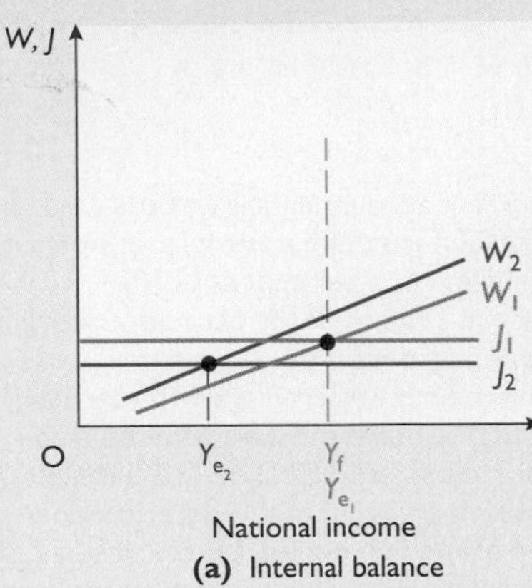

(a) Internal balance

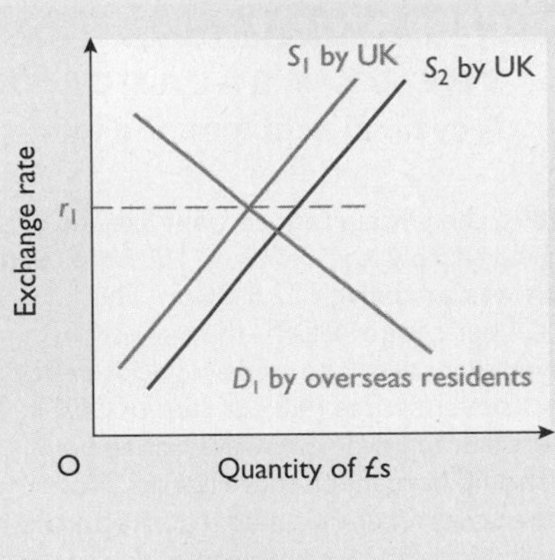

(b) External balance

Figure 24.1

inflation. A falling exchange rate may lead to currency speculation. People sell sterling before its dollar price drops any lower. But this leads to a further fall in the exchange rate. Finally, a falling exchange rate will boost exports (an injection) and reduce imports (a withdrawal), thus increasing aggregate demand. This will then destroy internal balance again (assuming that it had been restored).

There are a number of such potential conflicts between internal and external objectives. But in each case, the nature of the conflict depends on the **exchange rate regime**.

> **??** Imagine that there is an *inflationary* gap, but a balance of payments equilibrium. Describe what will happen if the government raises interest rates in order to close the inflationary gap. Assume first that there is a fixed exchange rate and then that there is a floating exchange rate.

Alternative exchange rate regimes

There are a number of possible exchange rate regimes. They all lie somewhere between two extremes. These two extreme regimes are a **totally fixed rate**, and a **freely floating rate**.

In the case of a *fixed rate*, the government will almost certainly have to intervene in the foreign exchange market in order to maintain that rate, and will probably have to take internal policy measures too.

In the case of a *freely floating rate*, there is no government intervention in the foreign exchange market. Exchange rates fluctuate according to market forces – according to changes in the demand for and supply of sterling. Changes in the exchange rate may well affect internal policy objectives, however, and thus cause the government to take various internal policy measures.

> **??** What adverse internal effects may follow from (a) a depreciation of the exchange rate; (b) an appreciation of the exchange rate?

Between these extremes there are a number of **intermediate regimes**, where exchange rates are partly left to the market, but where the government intervenes to influence the rate. These intermediate regimes differ according to the amount that the government intervenes, and thus according to how much flexibility of the exchange rate it is prepared to allow.

Correction under fixed exchange rates

Foreign exchange intervention

Unless the demand for and supply of sterling on the foreign exchange markets are equal at the fixed rate – unless,

DEFINITIONS

Exchange rate regime The system under which the government allows the exchange rate to be determined.

Totally fixed exchange rate Where the government takes whatever measures are necessary to maintain the exchange rate at some stated level.

Freely floating exchange rate Where the exchange rate is determined entirely by the forces of demand and supply in the foreign exchange market with no government intervention whatsoever.

Intermediate exchange rate regimes Where the government intervenes to influence movements in the exchange rate.

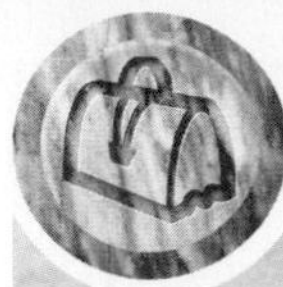

CASE STUDIES **BOX 24.1**

THE UK'S BALANCE OF PAYMENTS DEFICIT

A cyclical problem or a long-term trend?

In the late 1980s, the UK current account balance of payments moved sharply into deficit. In 1989 the current account deficit was a massive £22.5 billion. This represented 4.4 per cent of GDP – the highest percentage ever recorded. The trade in goods deficit at £24.7 billion was even worse (4.8 per cent of GDP). Opinions differed dramatically, however, as to how seriously we should have taken these figures. Not surprisingly, the government claimed that the problem was merely temporary and was not something to cause serious concern. The opposition parties (also not surprisingly) saw the figures as disastrous and a sign that the economy was badly off course.

So who was correct? In fact there was an element of truth in both these claims.

The government was correct to the extent that the severity of the deficit partly reflected the unprecedented boom of the late 1980s. An average growth rate of real GDP of 3.6 per cent between 1984 and 1988 had led to a huge increase in imports. Since the boom could not be sustained, the growth in imports was bound to slow down. Another factor contributing to the deficit was the fall in oil revenues caused by a fall in oil prices, a situation that would be reversed once oil prices began to rise again.

But the opposition parties were also correct. The severity of the deficit reflected an underlying weakness of the UK's trading position. If the deficit had been merely a cyclical problem associated with the boom phase of the trade cycle, the current account should have gone into surplus in the early 1990s as the economy moved into recession. But as the diagram clearly shows, although the deficit became smaller in the early 1990s, it was still substantial, despite the fact that the recession was the worst since the Great Depression of the 1920s and 1930s. Even at its lowest point in 1991, the current account deficit was still £8.0 billion (1.7 per cent of GDP) and the trade in goods deficit was still £10.3 billion (2.1 per cent of GDP).

Then in 1992, with the economy sliding further into recession (growth was –0.5 per cent), the current account deficit *worsened* again to reach £10.8 billion in 1993 (2.0 per cent of GDP) with the trade in goods deficit reaching £13.5 billion (2.5 per cent of GDP). The opposition argued that this deterioration could clearly not be blamed on cyclical factors. Instead, they blamed it on fundamental structural weaknesses in the UK economy and a long-term erosion of the industrial base. The government, however, sought to place a large portion of the blame on a falling demand for exports as the rest of the world began to move into recession.

Subsequent events seemed to support the government's interpretation. The world economy was recovering in 1994 and the current account deficit fell to a mere £1.7 billion. But the major explanation for this turnaround in the balance of payments was a substantial growth in earnings from overseas investment – a reflection, in part, of investors' lack of confidence in investment opportunities at home. Despite the eventual elimination of the current account deficit in 1997, the trade in goods deficit still stood at £13.0 billion. What little improvement had taken place in the trade account could be explained by the depreciation of sterling after 1992 and a rise in oil revenues (see pages 441 and 680). Then with the large appreciation of sterling from 1997, (see Table 14.2 on page 441) the current account started to deteriorate again.

So should we worry about balance of payments deficits? What effect do they have on exchange rates, inflation, growth, unemployment, etc? What should the government do? These are questions we shall look at in this chapter.

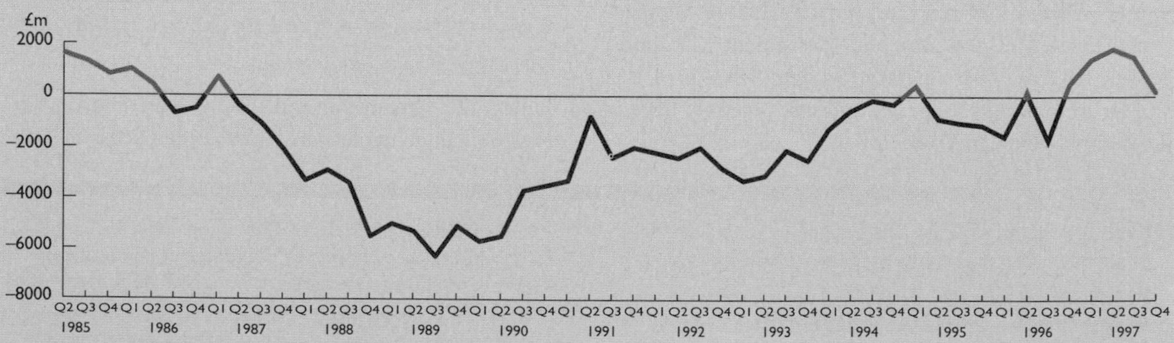

UK balance of payments current account (quarterly figures): 1985–97

Source: *Economic Trends* (ONS, various issues).

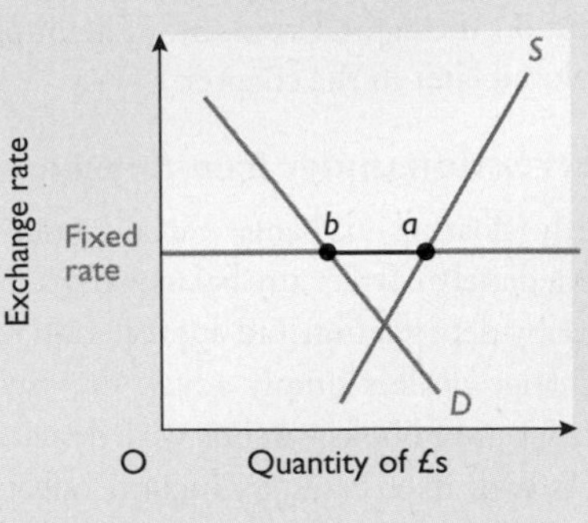

(a) Total currency flow deficit

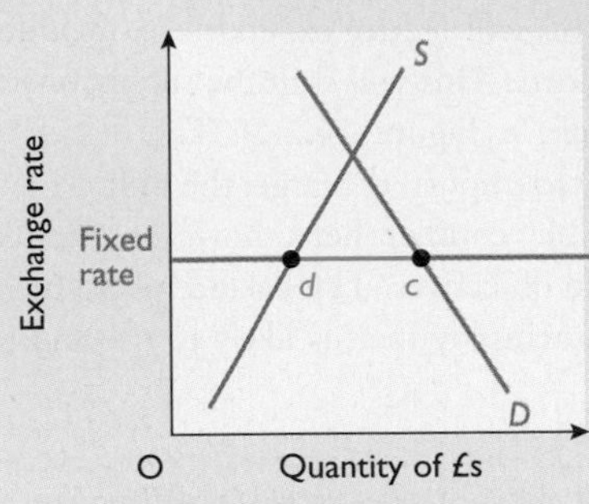

(b) Total currency flow surplus

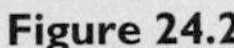

Figure 24.2

in other words, there is a total currency flow balance (i.e. a net current plus capital account balance) – the Bank of England will have to buy or sell sterling to make up the difference. This is illustrated in Figure 24.2.

Figure 24.2(a) shows the case of a currency flow deficit (an excess of pounds) of an amount $a - b$. The Bank of England thus has to purchase these excess pounds by drawing on its foreign exchange reserves, or by borrowing foreign currency from foreign banks.

In Figure 24.2(b) there is a currency flow surplus of $c - d$. In this case the Bank of England has to supply $c - d$ additional pounds on to the market, and will acquire foreign currencies in exchange. It can use these to build up reserves or to pay back foreign loans.

Foreign exchange market intervention and the money supply. Maintaining a fixed rate will cause changes in the money supply. If the rate is maintained *above* the equilibrium (Figure 24.2(a)), there is a total currency flow deficit. The Bank of England buys pounds. It thereby withdraws them from circulation and reduces the money supply.

If the rate is maintained *below* equilibrium (Figure 24.2(b)), there is a total currency flow surplus. The Bank of England supplies additional pounds (which are spent by foreigners on UK exports, etc. and are thus injected into the UK economy). It thereby increases the money supply.

If the Bank of England did not want the money supply to alter, it would have to counter these effects with other monetary measures: e.g. open-market operations. Thus when there is a deficit and money supply falls, the Bank of England could buy back government bonds from the general public, thereby restoring the money supply to its previous level.

This process of countering the effects on money supply of a balance of payments deficit or surplus is known as **sterilisation**.

> **??** Describe the open-market operations necessary to sterilise the monetary effects of a balance of payments surplus. Would this in turn have any effect on the current or capital accounts of the balance of payments?

Correcting the disequilibrium

If a balance of payments deficit persists, and reserves continue to dwindle or foreign debts mount, the government will have to tackle the underlying disequilibrium. If the exchange rate is to remain fixed, it must shift the demand and supply curves so that they intersect at the fixed exchange rate.

It can use deflationary fiscal and monetary policies for this purpose. Such policies have two main effects on the current account: an income effect (**expenditure reducing**) and a substitution effect between home and foreign goods (**expenditure switching**).

DEFINITIONS

Sterilisation Where the government uses open-market operations or other monetary measures to neutralise the effects of balance of payments deficits or surpluses on the money supply.

Expenditure changing (reducing) from deflation: the income effect Where deflationary policies lead to a reduction in national income and hence a reduction in the demand for imports.

Expenditure switching from deflation: the substitution effect Where deflationary policies lead to a reduction in inflation and thus cause a switch in expenditure away from imports and towards exports.

Expenditure reducing. Deflationary policy will reduce national income. This will reduce expenditure, including expenditure on imports. This will shift the supply of sterling curve to the left in Figure 24.2(a). The bigger the marginal propensity to import, the larger the shift.

There is a possible conflict here, however, between external and internal objectives. The balance of payments may improve, but unemployment is likely to rise and the rate of growth fall.

> **??** Under what circumstances would (a) deflationary and (b) reflationary policies cause *no* conflict between internal and external objectives?

Expenditure switching. If deflationary policies reduce the rate of inflation below that of foreign competitors, exports will become relatively cheaper compared with foreign competing goods and imports relatively more expensive compared with home-produced alternatives. Foreign consumers will switch to UK exports. The more elastic their demand, the bigger the switch. UK consumers will switch to home-produced goods. Again, the more elastic their demand, the bigger the switch. Demand in both cases will be more elastic the closer UK goods are as substitutes for foreign goods.

To the extent that deflation leads to expenditure switching rather than expenditure reducing, so this will reduce the conflict between balance of payments and employment objectives.

Expenditure switching could also be achieved by the use of restrictions on imports: tariffs and/or quotas, or the subsidising of exports. But this would conflict with the objective of free trade.

To the extent that fiscal and monetary policies affect interest rates, so this will affect the capital account of the balance of payments. Higher interest rates will increase the demand for sterling and will thus lead to an improvement on the capital account. (The implications of this are explored later in the chapter.)

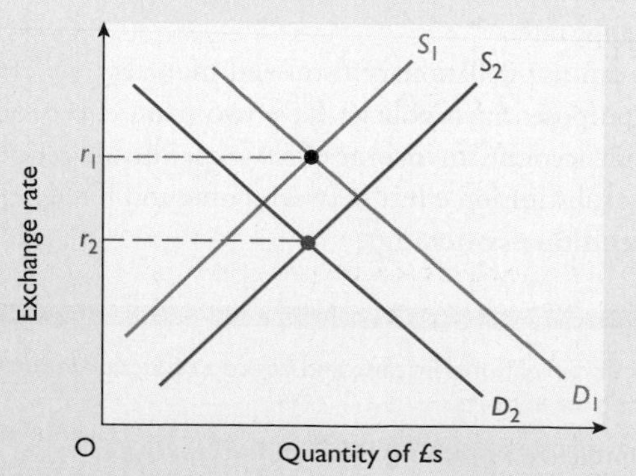

Figure 24.3 Adjustment of the exchange rate to a shift in demand and supply

Correction under free-floating exchange rates

Freely floating exchange rates should automatically and immediately correct any balance of payments deficit or surplus: by depreciation and appreciation respectively. Foreign exchange dealers simply adjust the exchange rate so as to balance their books – in line with demand and supply.

As with fixed rates, an income effect and a substitution effect of the correction process can be distinguished. But the nature of the income and substitution effects of depreciation/appreciation is quite different from that of deflation. It is only the substitution effect that corrects the disequilibrium. The income effect makes the problem *worse*! First the substitution effect: **expenditure switching**.

Expenditure switching (the substitution effect)

The process of adjustment. Assume a higher rate of inflation in the UK than abroad. As domestic prices rise relative to the price of imports, more imports will be purchased. The supply of pounds curve will shift to the right (to S_2 in Figure 24.3). UK exports will now be relatively more expensive for foreigners. Less will be sold. The demand for pounds curve will shift to the left (to D_2).

Foreign exchange dealers will now find themselves with a glut of unsold pounds. They will therefore lower the exchange rate (to r_2 in Figure 24.3). The amount that the exchange rate has to change will depend on:

- The amount that the curves shift. Thus large differences in international inflation rates or large differences in international interest rates will cause large shifts in the demand for and supply of currencies, and hence large movements in exchange rates.
- The elasticity of the curves. The less elastic the demand and supply curves of sterling, the greater the change in the exchange rate for any given shift in demand and supply.

The elasticity of *demand* for sterling depends on the elasticity of demand for UK *exports*.

If sterling depreciates, the foreign currency price of UK exports falls; thus more will be purchased by foreigners. The *sterling* price of these exports, however, has not

> **DEFINITION**
>
> **Expenditure switching from depreciation: the substitution effect** Where a lower exchange rate reduces the price of exports and increases the price of imports. This will increase the sale of exports and reduce the sale of imports.

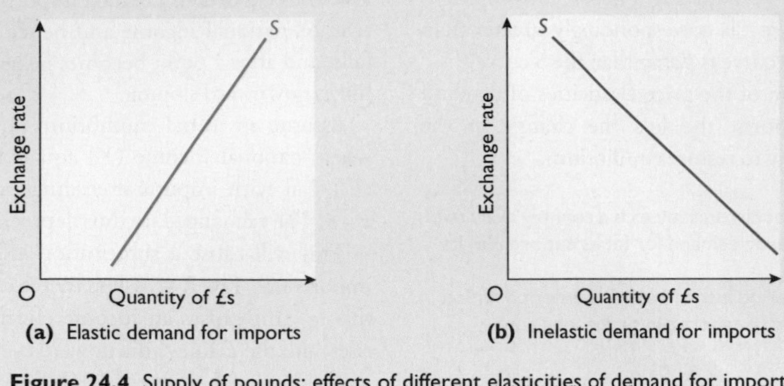

(a) Elastic demand for imports (b) Inelastic demand for imports

Figure 24.4 Supply of pounds: effects of different elasticities of demand for imports

changed. But since more exports are now being purchased, foreigners will require more pounds than before. Thus as long as demand is not totally inelastic the demand for sterling curve will be downward sloping. The lower the exchange rate, the more exports will be sold and the more pounds will be demanded.

The greater the elasticity of demand for exports, the more will be purchased as the exchange rate falls, and hence the more pounds will be demanded. Thus the greater the elasticity of demand for UK exports, the greater the elasticity of demand for sterling.

The elasticity of *supply* of sterling depends on the elasticity of demand for *imports*. The relationship, however, is different from that between the elasticity of demand for sterling and the elasticity of demand for exports.

If sterling depreciates, the sterling price of imports rises and hence less will be purchased. However, fewer pounds will be required only if total *expenditure* on imports falls. This will occur only if the demand for imports is elastic: if it has an elasticity greater than 1.

If the demand for imports *is* elastic, there will be a 'normal' upward-sloping supply of sterling curve (as in Figure 24.4(a)). A lower exchange rate (higher import prices) leads to a lower expenditure and hence a lower quantity of sterling supplied.

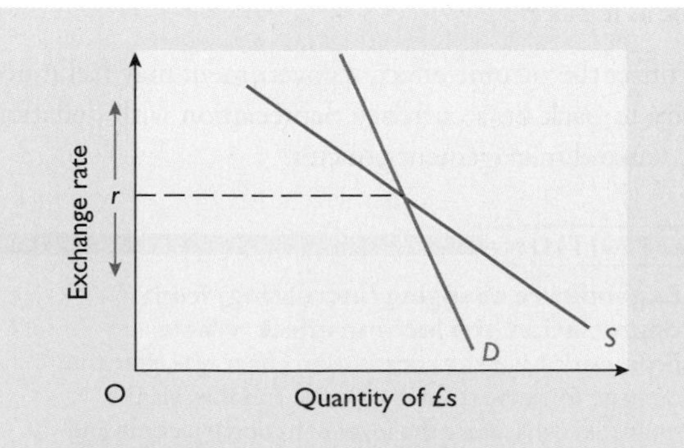

Figure 24.5 Unstable equilibrium

If, however, the demand for imports is *in*elastic, the rise in the price of imports from the depreciation will more than offset the fall in sales. More pounds will thus be spent as the exchange rate falls. The supply of sterling curve will be downward sloping (as in Figure 24.4(b)).

Unstable equilibrium. If the supply curve were downward sloping *and* flatter than the demand curve, exchange rates would be unstable. As soon as the exchange rate fell below r in Figure 24.5 (due to a shift in demand or supply), the supply of pounds would exceed the demand. The rate would fall further and further. Similarly, if the rate went above r, it would continue rising.

In order for the exchange rate to be stable, the supply curve must be steeper than the demand curve. This is known as the 'Marshall–Lerner condition' after the two economists who analysed it.

The Marshall–Lerner condition. We have already established that a depreciation will increase the *demand* for pounds if the demand for exports rises at all ($P\epsilon_{d_x} > 0$), and that it will reduce the *supply* of pounds if the demand for imports is elastic ($P\epsilon_{d_m} > 1$). Overall, therefore, a depreciation will improve the balance of payments such as to give a stable equilibrium if:

$$(P\epsilon_{d_x} + P\epsilon_{d_m}) > 1$$

This is the **Marshall–Lerner condition**. In other words, there can still be an improvement in the balance of

DEFINITION

Marshall–Lerner condition Depreciation will improve the balance of payments only if the sum of the price elasticities of demand for imports and exports is greater than 1.

payments *even* if $P\epsilon_{d_m} < 1$ (giving a *downward*-sloping S curve) *provided* that $P\epsilon_{d_x}$ is correspondingly greater than zero – such that the D curve is *flatter* than the S curve.

The greater the sum of the price elasticities of demand for imports and exports, the less the change in the exchange rate necessary to restore equilibrium.

??

1. Under what circumstances is a country likely to have an elastic demand for (a) its exports; (b) its imports?
2. Over which time period is the Marshall–Lerner condition less likely to be met: the short run or the long run?

Expenditure changing (the income effect)

Depreciation, as well as affecting relative prices, will affect national income. This will cause **expenditure changing**.

We have already established that, as the exchange rate falls, so more exports will be sold and less imports purchased: this was the substitution effect. But this is only an initial effect.

Exports are an injection into, and imports a withdrawal from, the circular flow of income. There will thus be a multiplied rise in national income. This income effect (expenditure *increasing*) will reduce the effectiveness of the depreciation. Two situations can be examined.

A rise in national income and employment, but no change in prices. Assume that there are substantial unemployed resources, so that an increase in aggregate demand will raise output and employment but not prices. As national income rises, so imports rise (thereby tending to offset the initial fall), but exports are unaffected.

This is illustrated by the line $(X - M)_1$ in Figure 24.6. At low levels of national income, spending on imports is low; thus exports (X) exceed imports (M). $X - M$ is positive. As national income and hence imports rise, $X - M$ falls, and after a point becomes negative. Thus the $X - M$ line is downward sloping.

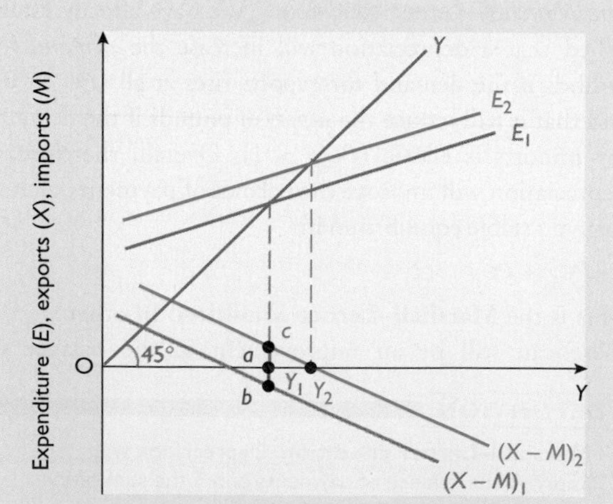

Figure 24.6 The income effect (stable prices)

Assume an initial equilibrium national income at Y_1, where national income (Y) equals national expenditure (E_1), but with imports exceeding exports by an amount $a - b$. The exchange rate thus depreciates.

This will cause a substitution effect: exports rise and imports fall. The $X - M$ line therefore shifts upwards. But this in turn causes an income effect. Aggregate demand rises, and the E line shifts upwards.

An eventual internal and external equilibrium is reached at Y_2, where $Y = E_2$ and $(X - M)_2 = 0$.

The positive substitution effect of this depreciation is $c - b$. The negative income effect is $c - a$. The net effect is thus only $a - b$, which is the size of the initial deficit. Had it not been for this negative income effect, a smaller depreciation would have been needed.

At least in this case the income effect is having a desirable *internal* consequence: reducing unemployment.

A rise in prices. If the economy is near full employment, the rise in aggregate demand from depreciation will make that depreciation even less effective. Not only will the higher demand lead directly to more imports, but it will also lead to higher inflation. There will thus be an adverse substitution effect too. This will partially offset the beneficial substitution effect of the depreciation. The higher inflation will have the effect of shifting the $X - M$ line back down again somewhat.

In the extreme case, where money supply expands to accommodate the rise in aggregate demand, $X - M$ may simply return to its original position. The depreciation will fail to correct the balance of payments disequilibrium. In Figure 24.3, the fall in the exchange rate to r_2 will simply lead to a further rightward shift in supply and a leftward shift in demand, until the gap between them is the same as it was at r_1.

To offset the income effect, a government may feel it necessary to back up a currency depreciation with deflationary demand management policies.

DEFINITION

Expenditure changing (increasing) from depreciation: the income effect Where depreciation, via the substitution effect, will alter the demand for imports and exports, and this, via the multiplier, will affect the level of national income and hence the demand for imports.

Intermediate exchange rate regimes

There are a number of possible intermediate systems between the two extremes of totally fixed and completely free-floating exchange rates.

Adjustable peg. The **adjustable peg** system is towards the fixed end of the spectrum. Exchange rates are fixed (or 'pegged') for a period of time – perhaps several years.

In the short and medium term, therefore, correction is the same as with a totally fixed system. Central banks have to intervene in the foreign exchange market to maintain the rate. If a deficit persists, then deflationary or other policies must be adopted to *shift* the currency demand and supply curves. This will be a problem, however, if there already exist substantial unemployed resources.

In the long term, however, if a fundamental disequilibrium occurs, the currency can be repegged at a lower or higher rate. Adjusting the peg downwards is known as **devaluation**. Adjusting it upwards is known as **revaluation**.

Alternatively, more frequent smaller adjustments could be made, thus moving the system away from the fixed end of the spectrum.

Dirty floating. The **dirty floating** system is towards the free-floating end of the spectrum. Exchange rates are not pegged: they are allowed to float. But the central bank intervenes from time to time to prevent excessive exchange rate fluctuations. It is thus a form of 'managed flexibility'.

Under such a system the central bank does not seek to maintain a long-term or even medium-term disequilibrium rate. Rather it tries to allow an 'orderly' exchange rate adjustment to major changes in demand and supply, while preventing the violent short-term swings that can occur with a totally free float (swings arising from currency speculation).

To back up the central bank's use of reserves, the government may also alter interest rates to prevent exchange rate fluctuations. If, for example, there were a large-scale selling of pounds, the government could raise interest rates to counter this effect and prevent the exchange rate from falling.

?? How would raising interest rates in this way affect the balance between the current and capital accounts of the balance of payments?

The degree of currency stability sought, and hence the degree of intervention required, will vary from country to country and from government to government. At one extreme, the government may intervene only if exchange rate fluctuations become very severe; at the other extreme, the government may try to maintain the exchange rate at some unofficial target level.

Crawling peg. The **crawling peg** system is midway between dirty floating and the adjustable peg system. Instead of making large and infrequent devaluations (or revaluations), the government adjusts the peg by small amounts, but frequently – say, once a month, as the equilibrium exchange rate changes.

Joint float. Under a **joint float** a group of countries have a fixed or adjustable peg system between their *own* currencies, but *jointly float* against all other currencies.

Exchange rate band. With an **exchange rate band** the government sets a lower and an upper limit to the exchange rate: say, £1 = $1.40 and £1 = $1.60. It will then allow the exchange rate to fluctuate freely within these limits. It will intervene, however, if the rate hits the floor or the ceiling. Exchange rate bands could be narrow (say ±1 per cent) or wide (say ±15 per cent).

Exchange rate bands can be incorporated in other systems – the band could be adjustable, crawling or fixed. For example, Figure 24.7 illustrates a crawling peg system with an exchange rate band. The exchange rate mechanism (ERM) of the European Monetary System (EMS) is an example of a joint float against non-member currencies

DEFINITIONS

Adjustable peg A system whereby exchange rates are fixed for a period of time, but may be devalued (or revalued) if a deficit (or surplus) becomes substantial.

Devaluation Where the government repegs the exchange rate at a lower level.

Revaluation Where the government repegs the exchange rate at a higher level.

Dirty floating (managed flexibility) A system of flexible exchange rates, but where the government intervenes to prevent excessive fluctuations or even to achieve an unofficial target exchange rate.

Crawling peg A system whereby the government allows a gradual adjustment of the exchange rate.

Joint float Where a group of currencies pegged to each other jointly float against other currencies.

Exchange rate band Where a currency is allowed to float between an upper and lower exchange rate but is not allowed to move outside this band.

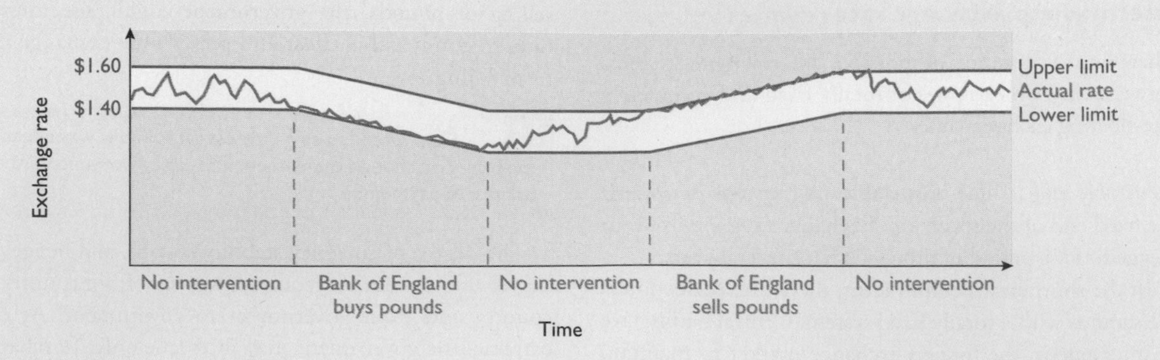

Figure 24.7 The crawling peg within exchange rate bands

and an adjustably pegged exchange rate band with member currencies (see section 24.7).

All these intermediate systems are attempts to achieve as many as possible of the advantages of both fixed and flexible exchange rates, with as few as possible of the attendant disadvantages. To assess any of these compromise systems, therefore, the advantages and disadvantages of fixed and flexible exchange rates must be examined. This is done in the next two sections.

SECTION SUMMARY

1. There may be a conflict in achieving both internal and external balance simultaneously. The nature of the conflict will depend on the exchange rate regime that the country adopts.
2. Under a fixed exchange rate system, the government will have to intervene whenever the equilibrium exchange rate ceases to coincide with the fixed rate. If the equilibrium rate falls below the fixed rate, the government will have to buy in the domestic currency on the foreign exchange market. This will have the effect of reducing the money supply. Likewise selling the domestic currency in order to prevent an appreciation will increase money supply. The government can prevent these changes in money supply by the use of appropriate open-market operations or other monetary measures. This is known as 'sterilisation'.
3. If a deficit (or surplus) persists under a fixed rate, the government can attempt to shift the currency demand and supply curves. To cure a deficit it can use deflationary fiscal or monetary policies. These will have two effects. Deflation leads to a fall in national income (the income effect) and hence a fall in the demand for imports. It also leads to a fall in inflation and hence a switch in demand from foreign goods to home-produced goods (the substitution effect).
4. Correction under free-floating exchange rates will also involve an income and a substitution effect. If there is a deficit, the exchange rate will depreciate. This will make imports more expensive and exports cheaper, and hence there will be a substitution effect as imports fall and exports rise. The balance of payments will only improve, however, if the Marshall–Lerner condition holds: namely, that the sum of the price elasticities of demand for imports and exports is greater than 1.
5. The income effect of a depreciation will reduce its effectiveness. The rise in exports and fall in imports (i.e. the substitution effect of a depreciation) will lead to a multiplied rise in national income, which will cause imports to rise back again somewhat. The bigger this income effect, the bigger will be the depreciation necessary to achieve equilibrium in the foreign exchange market. Correction is made more difficult if any depreciation leads to increases in domestic prices and hence to a second substitution effect – only this time an adverse one.
6. There are intermediate exchange rate regimes between the extremes of fixed rates and free-floating rates. The exchange rate may be fixed for a period of time (the adjustable peg); or it may be allowed to change gradually (the crawling peg); or the government may merely intervene to dampen exchange rate fluctuations (dirty floating); or the exchange rate may be allowed to fluctuate within a band, where the band in turn may be fixed, adjustable or crawling.

24.2 Fixed exchange rates

Under fixed exchange rates, it is unlikely that internal and external balance can persist for long without government intervention. Various shocks are likely to occur that will destroy either internal or external balance or both. Even with government intervention, it may still be very difficult, if not impossible, to restore both balances. Correction of balance of payments disequilibria will come into conflict with the other macroeconomic goals of growth, full employment and stable prices.

Monetarists and Keynesians differ in their analysis of how the economy responds to shocks under fixed exchange rates, and which policy measures are most effective in dealing with the resultant disequilibria.

Monetarist and new classical analysis

Monetarists assume price and wage flexibility. This will ensure that internal balance is maintained – at least in the long run. The long-run Phillips curve is vertical. But, with a fixed exchange rate, will it also ensure external balance?

Response to an internal shock

Let us assume that people decide to spend more and save less. This internal shock will have an effect on both the current and capital accounts.

The higher demand will push up wages and prices, and thus cause imports to rise and exports to fall. There will be a *current account* deficit.

There will be an opposite effect on the *capital account*. The increased transactions demand for money will put upward pressure on interest rates. This will cause a capital inflow and hence a capital account surplus.

But which will be larger: the current account deficit, or the capital account surplus? This depends on the marginal propensity to import (*mpm*) and the mobility of international capital. The higher the *mpm*, the bigger the current account deficit. The higher the international mobility of capital, the bigger will be the capital inflow and hence the bigger the capital account surplus. Monetarists and new classicists assume that international capital is highly, if not perfectly mobile, and that the capital account surplus will therefore exceed the current account deficit. There will be an overall currency flow surplus.

This will lead to an expansion in the money supply, which will ease the upward pressure on interest rates, thereby allowing the capital account surplus to fall to match the current account deficit. The currency flow surplus will be eliminated. *Overall* external balance will be restored.

There is no mechanism, however, to restore *current* account balance.

Response to an external shock

Let us assume that there is a fall in demand for exports. The *current account* will go into deficit.

The reduction in aggregate demand will reduce the transactions demand for money, putting downward pressure on interest rates. Initially there will be a capital outflow and hence a *capital account* deficit, making the overall currency flow deficit worse. This will cause a fall in the money supply.

Money supply will go on falling, until there is eventually an *upward* pressure on interest rates sufficient to restore overall external balance. This will be achieved by improvements on both the current and the capital accounts. Higher interest rates will dampen aggregate demand and hence the demand for imports, thereby reducing the current account deficit. At the same time, higher interest rates will encourage an inflow of capital again. With highly mobile capital, this effect is likely to be large. The capital account will move into surplus, offsetting any remaining deficit on the current account. Overall external balance has been restored.

But is there any mechanism for restoring current account balance? The fall in aggregate demand will reduce wages and prices. This will make exports more competitive and imports relatively more expensive. With sufficient wage and price flexibility, current account balance *could eventually be restored*. Indeed, under new classical assumptions of *short-run* wage and price flexibility, it will be restored quickly.

Keynesian analysis

Keynesians assume that prices and especially wages are inflexible downwards. They also assume that the money supply is endogenously determined, expanding passively to meet the demand for money.

Response to an internal shock

Let us again assume that there is a rise in consumer demand and a fall in savings.

As with the monetarist analysis, the higher demand will push up wages and prices, and thus cause imports to rise and exports to fall. There will be a *current account* deficit. The deficit will lead to a fall in the money supply, as the

Bank of England buys in pounds in order to maintain the exchange rate. But, under Keynesian assumptions, this will be more than offset by a passive expansion of the money supply as banks create more credit to meet the higher level of aggregate demand. This will allow the current account deficit to persist.

The expansion of the money supply will prevent upward pressure on interest rates. There will thus be no *capital account* surplus to match the current account deficit. Overall external imbalance will persist.

Response to an external shock

Assume again a fall in demand for UK exports.

The fall in exports will cause the *current account* to go into deficit. It also reduces aggregate demand, causing a multiplied fall in national income. This will reduce the demand for imports: the larger the *mpm*, the bigger the reduction in imports. Aggregate demand will go on falling until the lower injections are matched by lower withdrawals. But the current account deficit will not be eliminated, since the fall in withdrawals to match the fall in exports consists only partly of lower imports, but *partly* of lower savings and lower tax receipts.

The reduction in demand may also put downward pressure on UK prices and wages. The greater the downward rigidity of prices and wages, however, the less will prices fall of exports and import substitutes, and hence the less will the current account deficit be reduced.

It is unlikely that these combined effects will be sufficient to eliminate the deficit. Even if they did, *internal* balance would be destroyed. There would be a deflationary gap, with demand-deficient unemployment.

The effects on the *capital account* are likely to be relatively small because of contradictory forces operating on interest rates. The current account deficit will reduce the supply of money, but the fall in national income will reduce the demand for money. If there is little effect on interest rates, and hence on the capital account, the overall external imbalance is likely to persist.

?? Making first new classical, and then Keynesian assumptions, trace through the effects (under a fixed exchange rate) of (a) an increase in domestic savings; (b) a rise in the demand for exports.

Causes of balance of payments problems under fixed exchange rates

With moderately flexible prices, current account balance may eventually be restored after 'one-off' shocks. However, long-term continuing shifts in the demand and supply of imports and exports can make balance of payments problems persist. We will examine four causes of these long-term shifts.

Different rates of inflation between countries. If a country has persistently higher rates of inflation than the countries with which it trades, there will be a growing current account deficit. Exports and import substitutes will become less and less competitive.

Different rates of growth between countries. If a country grows faster than the countries with which it trades, its imports will tend to grow faster than its exports.

Income elasticity of demand for imports higher than for exports. If the income elasticity of demand for imports is relatively high, and the income elasticity of demand for exports is relatively low, then as world incomes grow, the country's imports will grow faster than its exports. This is a particular problem for many developing countries: they import manufactured goods and capital equipment, whose demand grows rapidly, and export primary products – food and raw materials – whose demand grows relatively slowly.

Long-term structural changes.

- Trading blocs may emerge, putting up tariff barriers to other countries. Australian and New Zealand exports were adversely affected when the UK joined the EC.
- Countries may exercise monopoly power to a greater extent than previously. The OPEC oil price increases of 1973/4 and 1978/9 are examples.
- Countries may develop import substitutes. Thus plastics and other synthetics have in many cases substituted for rubber and metals, thus worsening the balance of payments of traditional primary exporters.
- The nature and quality of a country's products may change. Thus Japan has shifted from producing low-quality simple manufactured goods in the 1950s to producing high-quality sophisticated manufactured goods today. This has helped increase its exports.

If a fixed exchange rate is to be maintained under such circumstances, governments will have to take measures to correct the disequilibria. They can use demand-side policies (fiscal and monetary), supply-side policies or protectionist policies (see Box 24.2).

Advantages of fixed exchange rates

Many economists are opposed to fixed exchange rates, for the reasons examined shortly. Nevertheless many businesspeople are in favour of relatively rigid exchange rates. The following arguments are used.

EXPLORING THE THEORY BOX 24.2

THE EFFECTIVENESS OF FISCAL AND MONETARY POLICIES UNDER FIXED EXCHANGE RATES

Monetary policy

Monetary policy will not be very effective under fixed exchange rates.

Assume a high rate of domestic inflation and a balance of payments deficit. The government now reduces money supply and raises interest rates in order to reduce aggregate demand and correct the deficit. The higher interest rates will simply encourage an inflow of capital. This capital account surplus will *increase* money supply again and reduce interest rates back towards the world level.

Overall external balance has been improved, but the rise in money supply again will cause inflation to continue and the current account to remain in deficit.

The greater the mobility of international capital, the more closely will domestic interest rates be pegged to world rates, and the less effective, therefore, will monetary policy be. In the extreme case of an infinitely elastic money supply curve, *monetary policy will be totally ineffective*.

Fiscal policy

Fiscal policy will be much more effective.

Assume a high rate of inflation and a resulting current account deficit. The government now raises taxes and/or reduces government expenditure. This will reduce aggregate demand and thereby help to reduce the current account deficit.

The reduction in aggregate demand will lower interest rates. This will lead to an outflow of capital and a capital account deficit. This will reduce the money supply, thereby *reinforcing* the deflationary fiscal policy. Inflation will fall, thus reducing the current account deficit further. Once money supply has fallen to match the reduced demand, interest rates can rise again, thus correcting the capital account deficit.

The greater the mobility of capital, the more will interest rates be pegged to world rates and the more, therefore, will the supply of money contract (or expand) to reinforce any contraction (or expansion) of demand through fiscal policy.

??

1. Suppose that under a *dirty floating system* the government is worried about high inflation and wants to keep the exchange rate up in order to prevent import prices rising. To tackle the problem of inflation it raises interest rates. (Similar policies have been pursued in recent years.) What will happen to the current and capital accounts of the balance of payments?
2. Why did many monetarists oppose the UK's entry to the ERM and welcome its departure from it?

Certainty. With fixed exchange rates, international trade and investment become much less risky, since profits are not affected by movements in the exchange rate.

Little or no speculation. Provided the rate is *absolutely* fixed – and people believe that it will remain so – there is no point in speculating.

?? When the UK joined the ERM in 1990, it was hoped that this would make speculation pointless. As it turned out, speculation forced the UK to leave the ERM in 1992. Can you reconcile this with the argument that fixed rates *discourage* speculation?

Automatic correction of monetary errors. If the government allows the money supply to expand too fast, the resulting extra demand and lower interest rates will lead to a balance of payments deficit. This will force the Bank of England to intervene to support the exchange rate. It must either buy pounds on the foreign exchange market, thereby causing money supply to fall again (unless it sterilises the effect), or it must raise interest rates. Either way this will have the effect of correcting the error.

Prevents governments pursuing 'irresponsible' macroeconomic policies. If a government deliberately and excessively expands aggregate demand – perhaps in an attempt to gain short-term popularity with the electorate – the resulting balance of payments deficit will force it to constrain demand again (unless it resorts to import controls).

Disadvantages of fixed exchange rates

The new classical view

As we explained earlier, in the new classical world of flexible prices and international capital mobility, the overall balance of payments will be corrected automatically if there are any shocks to the economy. Any deficit on the current account will be matched by an equal and opposite surplus on the capital account. Nevertheless, new classicists and monetarists make three crucial criticisms of fixed rates.

Fixed exchange rates make monetary policy ineffective. Interest rates are pegged to world levels, and thus money supply is infinitely elastic and will depend purely on the demand for money. As a result the government cannot control inflation by attempts to control money supply. Inflation will depend on world rates, which may be high and domestically unacceptable. If the government tries to reduce inflation by attempting to reduce money supply and raise interest rates, the current and capital account will go into surplus. Money supply will thus increase until domestic inflation rises back to world levels.

An imbalance between current and capital account may persist. As we explained before, although an *overall* external balance may be achieved automatically under fixed rates, a current account deficit may persist. The surplus on capital account required to finance this is likely to lead to an accumulation of overseas debt. This may become a burden for the future, in terms of interest payments.

Fixed rates contradict the objective of having free markets. Why fix the exchange rate, when a simple depreciation or appreciation can correct a disequilibrium? In the new classical world where markets clear, and supply and demand are relatively elastic, why not treat the foreign exchange market like any other, and simply leave it to supply and demand?

The Keynesian view

In the Keynesian world, wages and prices are relatively 'sticky', and demand-deficient unemployment and cost-push inflation may persist. In this world there is no guarantee of achieving both internal and external balance simultaneously when exchange rates are fixed. This leads to the following problems.

Balance of payments deficits can lead to a depression. A balance of payments deficit can occur even if there is no excess demand: even though there is internal balance. For example, there can be a fall in the demand for the country's exports as a result of an external shock or because of increased foreign competition. If protectionism is to be avoided, and if supply-side policies work only over the long run, the government will be forced to deflate the economy. If wages and prices are sticky downwards, the deflation may have to be severe if the deficit is to be corrected. Reliance will have to be placed largely on lower *incomes* reducing the demand for imports. A severe recession, with high unemployment, may thus result.

Even if the price level (or at least inflation) does fall, demand for exports may be relatively price inelastic, as may also be the domestic demand for substitutes for imports. Again, the deflation will thus have to be severe to bring the required adjustment.

The problem here is that, with fixed exchange rates, domestic policy is entirely constrained by the balance of payments. Any attempt to reflate and cure unemployment will simply lead to a balance of payments deficit and thus force governments to deflate again.

Competitive deflations leading to world depression. If deficit countries deflated, but surplus countries *reflated*, there would be no overall world deflation or reflation. Countries may be quite happy, however, to run a balance of payments surplus and build up reserves. Countries may thus competitively deflate – all trying to achieve a balance of payments surplus. But this is beggar-my-neighbour policy. Not all countries can have a surplus! Overall the world must be in balance. The result of these policies is to lead to general world deflation and a restriction in growth.

Problems of international liquidity. If trade is to expand, there must be an expansion in the supply of currencies acceptable for world trade (dollars, marks, gold, etc.): there must be adequate **international liquidity**. Countries' reserves of these currencies must grow if they are to be sufficient to maintain a fixed rate at times of balance of payments disequilibrium. Conversely, there must not be excessive international liquidity. Otherwise the extra demand that would result would lead to world inflation. It is important under fixed exchange rates, therefore, to avoid too much or too little international liquidity. The problem is whether there is adequate control of international liquidity. The supply of dollars, for example, depends largely on US policy, which may be dominated by its internal economic situation rather than by a concern for the well-being of the international community.

> **??** Why will excessive international liquidity lead to international inflation?

Inability to adjust to shocks. With sticky prices and wages, there is no swift mechanism for dealing with sudden balance of payments crises – like that caused by a sudden increase in oil prices. In the short run, countries will need huge reserves or loan facilities to support their currencies. There may be insufficient international liquidity to permit this. In the longer run, countries may be forced into a depression by having to deflate. The alternative may be to resort to protectionism, or to abandon the fixed rate and devalue.

DEFINITION

International liquidity The supply of currencies in the world acceptable for financing international trade and investment.

Speculation. If speculators believe that a fixed rate simply cannot be maintained, speculation is likely to be massive. If there is a huge deficit, there is no chance whatsoever of a *re*valuation. Either the rate will be devalued or it will remain the same. Speculators will thus sell the domestic currency. After all, it is a pretty good gamble: heads they win (devaluation); tails they stay the same (no devaluation). This speculative selling will worsen the deficit, and may itself force the devaluation.

?? To what extent do Keynesians and new classicists agree about the role of fixed exchange rates?

Postscript

An argument used in favour of fixed rates is that they prevent governments from pursuing inflationary policies. But if getting inflation down is desirable, why do governments not pursue an anti-inflationary policy directly? In 1979 when Mrs Thatcher was first elected, she declared inflation to be 'public enemy number one'. Yet the UK was under a floating exchange rate regime and was thus not *forced* to follow an anti-inflationary policy. If, however, elected governments choose *not* to pursue anti-inflationary policy, is it desirable that they should be forced to?

SECTION SUMMARY

1. The effects of internal and external shocks under fixed exchange rates are analysed differently by new classical and Keynesian economists.
2. New classical economists argue that an *internal* shock will not affect internal balance (because of price flexibility), nor will it affect the *overall* external balance. Any current account imbalance will, via pressure on interest rates, lead to an equal and opposite capital account imbalance. Keynesian economists, however, argue that an internal shock can cause a persistent imbalance, both internally and externally. Inflexible prices can cause a persistent recession, and an endogenous money supply will remove the pressure on interest rates that would be necessary for capital flows to counterbalance the current account imbalance.
3. New classical economists argue that an *external* shock will have a relatively small effect on both current and capital accounts. Flexible wages and prices will restore current account balance and ensure little pressure on interest rates and thus little effect on the capital account. Keynesian economists argue that an external shock will, via the multiplier, destroy internal balance and may lead to a persistent current account imbalance given the inflexibility of prices. The effects on the capital account will be relatively small given that endogenous changes in money supply result in little change in interest rates.
4. Under fixed exchange rates, monetary policy will not be very effective, but fiscal policy will be much more effective.
5. Fixed exchange rates bring the advantage of certainty for the business community, which encourages trade and foreign investment. They also help to prevent governments from pursuing irresponsible macroeconomic policies.
6. Both new classical and Keynesian economists, however, see important disadvantages in fixed exchange rate. New classical economists argue that they make monetary policy totally ineffective; that an imbalance between current and capital accounts may persist; and that they run counter to the efficiency objective of having free markets. Keynesians argue that fixed rates can lead to serious internal imbalance with perhaps a deep recession; that with competitive deflations a recession can be world-wide; that there may be problems of excessive or insufficient international liquidity; that there may be difficulty in adjusting to external shocks; and that speculation could be very severe if people came to believe that a fixed rate was about to break down.

24.3 Free-floating exchange rates

Floating exchange rates and the freeing of domestic policy

With a freely floating exchange rate there can be no overall balance of payments disequilibrium. Foreign exchange dealers will constantly adjust the exchange rate so as to balance their books: so that the demand for and supply of any currency are equal.

This, therefore, removes the balance of payments constraint on domestic policy that exists under a fixed exchange rate. No reserves are required, since there is no central bank intervention to support the exchange rate. The government, it would seem, is free to pursue whatever domestic policy it likes. Any resulting effects on the balance of payments are simply and automatically corrected by a depreciation or appreciation of the exchange rate.

CASE STUDIES

THE PRICE OF A BIG MAC

The Economist's guide to purchasing-power parity rates

Once a year *The Economist* publishes its 'hamburger standard' exchange rates for currencies. It is a lighthearted attempt to see if currencies are exchanging at their purchasing-power parity rates. The test is the price at which a 'Big Mac' McDonald's hamburger sells in different countries!

The following extract is from the 1998 Big Mac report (11/4/98).

The Big Mac index is based upon the theory of purchasing-power parity (PPP), the notion that a dollar should buy the same amount in all countries. Supporters of PPP argue that in the long run, the exchange rate between two currencies should move towards the rate that would equalise the prices of an identical basket of goods and services in each country.

Our "basket" is a McDonald's Big Mac, produced in 110 countries. The Big Mac PPP is the exchange rate that would leave hamburgers costing the same in America as abroad. Comparing actual rates with PPPs signals whether a currency is under- or overvalued.

The first column of the table shows local-currency prices of a Big Mac; the second converts the prices into dollars. The cheapest Big Macs are now in Indonesia and Malaysia, where they cost $1.16. At the other extreme, Big Mac fans in Switzerland have to pay $3.87. Given that Americans in four cities pay an average of $2.56, the rupiah and the ringgit look massively undervalued, the Swiss franc massively overvalued.

The third column calculates Big Mac PPPs. For example, dividing the Japanese by the American price

The hamburger standard

	Big Mac prices				
	in local currency	in Dollars	Implied PPP* of the dollar	Actual $ exchange rate 6/4/98	Under (–)/ over (+) valuation against dollar, (%)
USA†	**$2.56**	**2.56**	-	-	-
Argentina	Peso2.50	2.50	0.98	1.00	–2
Australia	A$2.65	1.75	1.04	1.51	–32
Belgium	BFr109	2.87	42.58	38.00	+12
Canada	C$2.79	1.97	1.09	1.42	–23
China	Yuan9.90	1.20	3.87	8.28	–53
Czech Republic	CKr54.0	1.57	21.10	34.4	–39
Denmark	DKr23.8	3.39	9.28	7.02	+32
France	FFr17.5	2.84	6.84	6.17	+11
Germany	DM4.95	2.69	1.93	1.84	+5
Hong Kong	HK$10.2	1.32	3.98	7.75	–49
Indonesia	Rupiah9,900	1.16	3,867	8,500	–55
Japan	¥280	2.08	109	135	–19
Malaysia	M$4.30	1.16	1.68	3.72	–55
Netherlands	Fl5.45	2.63	2.13	2.07	+3
Poland	Zloty5.30	1.53	2.07	3.46	–40
Russia	Rouble12,000	2.00	4,688	5,999	–22
Singapore	S$3.00	1.85	1.17	1.62	–28
South Africa	Rand8.00	1.59	3.13	5.04	–38
Spain	Pta375	2.40	146	156	–6
Sweden	SKr24.0	3.00	9.38	8.00	+17
Switzerland	SFr5.90	3.87	2.30	1.52	+51
Thailand	Baht52.0	1.30	20.3	40.0	–49
UK	£1.84	3.05	1.39‡	1.66‡	+19

* Purchasing-power parity: local price divided by price in United States.
† Average of New York, Chicago, San Francisco and Atlanta. ‡ Dollars per pound.
Source: McDonald's.

In reality, however, things are not quite so simple. Even under a totally free-floating exchange rate, there may be some constraints on domestic policy from the effects of these exchange rate movements. For example, a depreciation of the exchange rate increases the price of imports. If the demand for imports is relatively inelastic, this may lead to a higher rate of inflation.

Response to shocks under a floating exchange rate

Internal shocks

Let us assume that there is a rise in aggregate demand that causes inflation. For the moment, however, let us also assume that monetary policy maintains real interest rates at international levels. For simplicity, let us assume that there is no inflation abroad. How will a floating exchange rate system cope with this internal shock of a rise in aggregate demand? The exchange rate will simply depreciate to maintain the competitiveness of UK exports and import substitutes.

For example, assume an initial exchange rate of £1 = $2. A UK product costing $2 in the USA will earn £1 for the UK exporter. If UK inflation now causes prices to double, the exchange rate will roughly halve. If it falls to £1 = $1, then the same product costing $2 in the USA will now earn £2 for the UK exporter: which in *real* terms is the same amount as before. This is the **purchasing-power parity theory**. This states that domestic price changes will be offset by exchange rate changes, thereby maintaining the same relative prices between countries as before.

BOX 24.3

gives a dollar PPP of ¥109. On April 6th, the exchange rate was ¥135, implying that the yen is 19% undervalued against the dollar. Three years ago the index suggested that the yen was 100% overvalued against the dollar. Likewise, the D-mark is now only 5% overvalued, against 50% in April 1995.

Thanks to the dollar's rise – long predicted by burgernomics – it is now closer to its PPP against other big currencies than for many years. Indeed, only five currencies in the table are now significantly overvalued against the greenback, among them Britain's, Sweden's and Denmark's. All three countries have decided not to adopt Europe's single currency, the euro, next year. The pound is 19% overvalued against the dollar, which implies it is 14% overvalued against the D-mark. In contrast, the currencies of the euro-block countries are close to Mcparity against the D-mark.

The most dramatic changes in the index over the past year are in East Asia, where devaluations have left currencies significantly undervalued..

The article does not claim that the Big Mac PPP is an infallible guide to true PPPs. It goes on ...

The Big Mac index is not a perfect measure of PPP. Price differences may be distorted by trade barriers on beef, sales taxes, local competition and changes in the cost of non-traded inputs such as rents. But despite its flaws, the Big Mac index produces PPP estimates close to those derived by more sophisticated methods. A currency can deviate from PPP for long periods, but several studies have found that the Big Mac PPP is a useful predictor of future movements – enabling the hungry investor to get rich by putting his money where his mouth is.

However, even if movements in the Big Mac index give a pretty accurate guide to movements in true PPPs, PPPs still only reflect the influence of *trade* on the exchange rate. Exchange rate movements, especially over the short and medium terms, reflect factors influencing the capital account of the balance of payments: factors such as actual and expected interest-rate differentials, investment prospects and speculation about exchange-rate movements.

??

1. If the Malaysian ringgit is undervalued by 55 per cent in PPP terms against the US dollar and the Swiss franc overvalued by 51 per cent, what implications does this have for the interpretation of Malaysian, Swiss and US GDP statistics?
2. Why do developing countries' currencies tend to be undervalued relative to those of developed countries?

??

If this is the case, need firms worry about losing competitiveness in world markets if domestic inflation is higher than world inflation?

If we now drop the assumption that real interest rates are maintained at the same level as abroad, the purchasing-power parity theory will break down. Let us assume that the rise in aggregate demand causes a rise in UK real interest rates.

There are now two effects on the exchange rate. The higher aggregate demand and higher inflation will cause the current account to move into deficit, thereby putting downward pressure on the exchange rate. The higher real interest rates, however, will cause the capital account to move into surplus as depositors choose to hold their money in pounds. This will put upward pressure on the exchange rate. Whether the exchange rate actually falls or rises will depend on which of the two effects is the bigger.

But either way, the new equilibrium exchange rate will be above the purchasing-power parity rate. This will adversely affect export industries, since the exchange rate has not fallen sufficiently (if at all) to compensate for their higher sterling price. It will also adversely affect domestic industries that compete with imports, since again the

DEFINITION

Purchasing-power parity theory The theory that the exchange rate will adjust so as to offset differences in countries' inflation rates, with the result that the same quantity of internationally traded goods can be bought at home as abroad with a given amount of the domestic currency.

exchange rate has not fallen sufficiently to retain their competitiveness with imports. The current account thus remains in deficit, matched by an equal and opposite capital account surplus.

External shocks

Now let us assume that the rest of the world goes into recession (but with no change in international interest rates). The demand for UK exports will fall. This will lead to a depreciation of the exchange rate. This in turn will boost the demand for UK exports and substitutes for imports. This boost to demand again will help to offset the dampening effect of the world recession.

Floating exchange rates thus help to insulate the domestic economy from world economic fluctuations.

> **??** Will there be *any* cost to the UK economy from a decline in the demand for exports resulting from a world recession?

Speculation

Things are made more complicated, however, by the activities of speculators. As soon as any exchange rate change is anticipated, speculators will buy or sell the currency.

Assume, for example, that there is a rise in UK inflation above international rates. This causes a fall in the demand for exports and hence a fall in the demand for sterling (assuming a price elasticity of demand greater than 1), and a rise in imports and hence a rise in the supply of sterling. This is illustrated in Figures 24.8 and 24.9. The exchange rate depreciates from r_1 to r_2. Speculators seeing the exchange rate falling can react in one of two ways. The first is called *stabilising speculation*; the second is called *destabilising speculation* (see section 2.5).

Stabilising speculation

This occurs when speculators believe that any exchange rate change will be reversed.

In our example, speculators may anticipate that the government will raise interest rates or take some other measure to reduce inflation. They thus believe that the exchange rate will appreciate again. As a result, they buy more pounds and sell fewer. But this very act of speculation causes the appreciation they had anticipated.

This is illustrated in Figure 24.8. Inflation has caused the demand for and supply of pounds to shift from D_1 and S_1 to D_2 and S_2, and the exchange rate to fall from r_1 to r_2. Stabilising speculation then shifts the curves back again, to D_3 and S_3, and the exchange rate rises again to r_3.

The action of speculators in this case, therefore, prevents excessively large exchange rate changes. In general, stabilising speculation will occur whenever speculators believe that the exchange rate has 'overreacted' to the current economic situation.

> **??** Draw a similar diagram to Figure 24.8, showing how an initial *appreciation* of the exchange rate would similarly be reduced by stabilising speculation.

Destabilising speculation

This occurs when speculators believe that exchange rate movements will continue in the same direction.

In our example, speculators may believe that the government will not succeed in getting inflation under control. They anticipate a continuing fall in the exchange rate and thus sell *now* before the exchange rate falls any further. In Figure 24.9 this speculation causes the demand and supply curves to shift further, to D_3 and S_3; and causes the exchange rate to fall further, to r_3.

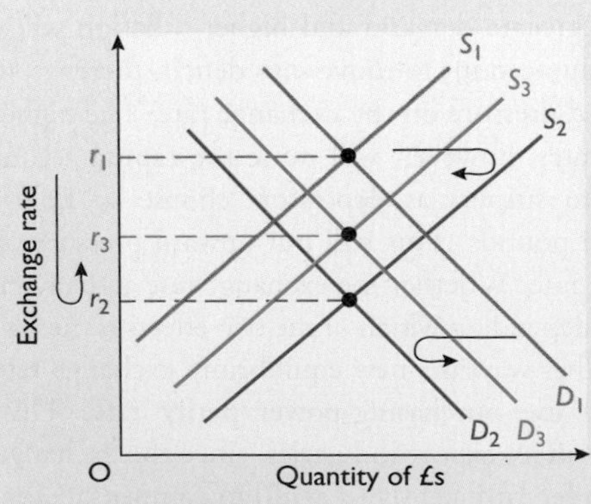

Figure 24.8 Stabilising speculation

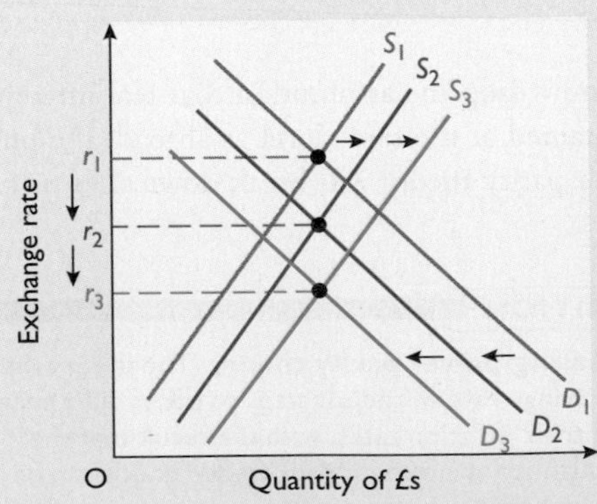

Figure 24.9 Destabilising speculation

CASE STUDIES

BOX 24.4

CURRENCY TURMOIL IN MARCH 1995

It may well have seemed in March 1995 that the currency crisis which had hit the ERM in September 1992 was returning with a vengeance. Only this time the currency turmoil extended way beyond Europe, involving as it did the US dollar, the yen and many other currencies, such as the Mexican peso.

On 6 March the dollar reached post-war lows against the D-Mark and the yen, standing at DM1.386 and ¥92.40 respectively. The fall in value against the yen represented a 32 per cent depreciation since 1992.

In Europe, the knock-on effect of the strong D-Mark was felt in some measure by all the currencies, especially those within the ERM. The Spanish peseta, under pressure prior to the D-Mark's rise, was devalued by 7 per cent, and the Portuguese escudo by 3.5 per cent. Both the French and Swedish governments, with their currencies reaching record lows against the D-Mark, were forced to put up interest rates to prevent further depreciation.

The high yen and mark proved to be equally problematic for the Japanese and German governments. The Japanese economy, which is highly dependent on the US economy for its export earnings (over a third of its foreign sales go to the USA, amounting to 15 per cent of its GDP), found its competitive position significantly eroded. On top of this, a surge in cheap imports reduced many Japanese companies' share of their home market and subsequently stifled the recovery of business growth. Such growth was also being undermined by the sustained high value of the yen, which was encouraging many Japanese businesses to shift production facilities overseas, reducing domestic investment still further.

In Germany, too, concern was being expressed about the high exchange rate and its impact upon the economy's faltering economic recovery. It was suggested that if the 13 per cent appreciation of the D-Mark since December 1994 were not reversed, economic growth could be reduced by as much as 1 per cent.

But why had there been such a large appreciation of the mark and yen? The speculative pressure on the dollar began in late December following an economic crisis in Mexico. Not only did the USA quickly arrange a $20 billion aid package, but more significantly, the prospect of a large decline in Mexican imports was seen by many speculators as a severe blow to the USA's export recovery. On top of this, market analysts were predicting that US interest rates, which had previously been rising, would now fall as US economic growth slowed. In contrast, interest rates in Germany looked set to rise, as the German authorities faced growing inflationary pressures. Faced by all this, many investors moved out of dollars and into the more stable D-Mark. This merely intensified a process that had been occurring throughout 1994, whereby US and Asian investors, seeking to diversify their portfolios and invest in non-US equities and bonds, sold dollars.

The US Federal Reserve seemed unconcerned about the falling dollar and took no steps to support it. This expression of total indifference led speculators to believe that the dollar's fall was not yet over, encouraging yet further selling of dollar balances.

Such was the strength of the speculative wave driving the dollar down that many investment banks began to argue that the dollar had significantly overshot its long-term equilibrium value. By early March the investment bank Goldman Sachs estimated that the real value of the dollar against the yen and D-Mark, using purchasing-power parities, was anywhere between 40 and 50 per cent undervalued. Such a view of an undervalued dollar was supported by the Economist's Big Mac Index (see Box 24.3), which at the time was showing that a McDonald's burger would cost only $2.30 in the USA, compared to $3.30 in Germany and $4.34 in Japan.

The currency crisis of March trailed on into April and was the main topic of discussion at the IMF summit held in Washington on the 26th of that month. Blame for the volatility in currency markets was squarely levelled at the USA for being far too slow to raise domestic interest rates to halt the dollar's slide. Both France and Japan (the one keen to push its currency up, the other down) argued that greater international co-operation was vital if the dollar's slide was to be halted and currency speculation stabilised.

However, critics were quick to point out that co-ordinated action between central banks, to buy the dollar and prevent its slide, was only a short-term solution. What was needed was greater international harmonisation in domestic fiscal and monetary policy in order to create exchange rate stability. As it turned out, the G7 economies – the USA, Japan, Germany, France, Italy, the UK and Canada (see Box 24.9) – were far from unanimous in their desire to enter into such an integrated strategy of exchange rate co-ordination, and no agreement was reached.

?? If the Japanese yen was already above its purchasing-power parity rate, and was therefore likely to depreciate over the longer term, why did speculators still continue to buy yen?

Eventually, however, this destabilising speculation could cause **overshooting**, with the exchange rate falling well below the purchasing-power parity rate. At this point speculators, believing that the rate will rise again, will start buying pounds again. This causes the exchange rate to rise.

Obviously, governments prefer stabilising to destabilising speculation. Destabilising speculation can cause severe exchange rate fluctuations. The resulting uncertainty is very damaging to trade. It is very important, therefore, that governments create a climate of confidence. People must believe that the government can prevent economic crises from occurring.

Conclusion

Whatever speculators anticipate will happen to the exchange rate, their actions will help to bring it about. If they think the rate will fall, they will sell pounds, hence causing it to fall. Thus speculators as a whole will gain. This applies to both stabilising and destabilising speculation.

?? If speculators on average gain from their speculation, who loses?

Advantages of a free-floating exchange rate

The advantages and disadvantages of free-floating rates are to a large extent the opposite of fixed rates.

Automatic correction. The government simply lets the exchange rate move freely to the equilibrium. In this way, balance of payments disequilibria are automatically and instantaneously corrected without the need for specific government policies – policies which under other systems can be mishandled.

No problem of international liquidity and reserves. Since there is no central bank intervention in the foreign exchange market, there is no need to hold reserves. A currency is automatically convertible at the current market exchange rate. International trade is thereby financed.

Insulation from external economic events. A country is not tied to a possibly unacceptably high world inflation rate, as it is under a fixed exchange rate. It is also to some extent protected against world economic fluctuations and shocks (see page 740).

Governments are free to choose their domestic policy. Under a fixed rate a government may have to deflate the economy even when there is high unemployment. Under a floating rate the government can choose whatever level of domestic demand it considers appropriate, and simply leave exchange rate movements to take care of any balance of payments effect. This is a major advantage, especially when the effectiveness of deflation is reduced by downward wage and price rigidity, and when competitive deflation between countries may end up causing a world recession.

Disadvantages of a free-floating exchange rate

Despite these advantages there are still a number of serious problems with free-floating exchange rates.

Unstable exchange rate. If the demands for imports and exports are highly inelastic, such that $(P\epsilon_{d_m} + P\epsilon_{d_x}) < 1$, equilibrium will tend to be unstable (see Figure 24.5). The Marshall–Lerner condition is not satisfied. If there is a deficit, a depreciation will *worsen* that deficit.

In the long run, in a competitive world with domestic substitutes for imports and foreign substitutes for exports, it is highly unlikely that the sum of the elasticities *will* be less than 1. Nevertheless, in the short run, given that many firms have contracts with specific overseas suppliers or distributors, the demands for imports and exports are less elastic. Even if the Marshall–Lerner condition is satisfied, the steepness of the short-run demand and supply curves of sterling may cause severe exchange rate fluctuations.

Speculation. Short-run instability can be lessened by stabilising speculation, thus making speculation advantageous. If, due to short-run inelasticity of demand, a deficit causes a very large depreciation, speculators will *buy* pounds, knowing that in the long run the exchange rate will appreciate again. This action of speculators will therefore help to lessen the short-run fall in the exchange rate.

Nevertheless, in an uncertain world where there are few restrictions on currency speculation, where the fortunes and policies of governments can change rapidly, and where large amounts of short-term deposits are internationally 'footloose', speculation can be highly destabilising in the short run. Considerable exchange rate overshooting can occur. As we shall see in section 24.6, there have been violent swings in exchange rates in recent years – even under a dirty floating exchange rate system where governments have attempted to dampen such fluctuations!

The continuance of exchange rate fluctuations over a number of years is likely to encourage the growth of spec-

DEFINITION

Exchange rate overshooting Where a fall (or rise) in the long-run equilibrium exchange rate causes the actual exchange rate to fall (or rise) by a greater amount before eventually moving back to the new long-run equilibrium level.

EXPLORING THE THEORY BOX 24.5

THE EFFECTIVENESS OF MONETARY AND FISCAL POLICY UNDER FLOATING EXCHANGE RATES

With a floating exchange rate, monetary policy is strong and fiscal policy is weak (the reverse of the case with fixed exchange rates).

Monetary policy

Assume that the government wishes to reduce aggregate demand. It reduces money supply. This pushes up interest rates. Three effects follow, each contributing to the effectiveness of the monetary policy:

1. *The tighter monetary policy directly reduces aggregate demand.* The size of the effect here depends on: the ability of the authorities to control money supply; the amount that interest rates change; and the elasticity of aggregate demand in response to these changes in interest rates.
2. *The exchange rate appreciates.* Lower aggregate demand reduces imports and (via lower prices) increases exports. This plus the higher interest rates increase the demand for and reduce the supply of sterling. The exchange rate thus appreciates (the purchasing power parity rate has increased).

   This reinforces the reduction in domestic demand. A higher exchange rate makes exports more expensive again and therefore reduces their demand (an injection). Imports become cheaper again and therefore their demand rises (a withdrawal). There is thus a *further* multiplied fall in income.
3. *Speculation causes initial exchange rate overshooting.* Higher UK interest rates cause speculative inflows of capital, in anticipation of the appreciation. This will cause the exchange rate to rise above its eventual rate – to overshoot, thus causing a further reduction in aggregate demand.

   This is only a short-term effect, since speculators will stop buying pounds when the rate has gone so high that they feel it must fall again (back towards the purchasing-power parity level) sufficiently fast to offset the higher interest rates they are now getting.

The new classical view of monetary policy
In the new classical world, prices and wages are flexible. A reduction in money supply will quickly lead to a reduction in prices. Effects 1 and 2 above are thus rapid and strong. Effect 3, however, is limited or non-existent, since the rapid fall in prices quickly eliminates the excess demand for money, and thus quickly removes the upward pressure on interest rates.

The Keynesian view of monetary policy
In the Keynesian world, prices and wages are inflexible downwards, and monetary policy is generally less effective (see Chapter 20). Effects 1 and 2 are therefore weaker. Nevertheless effect 3 will be relatively strong, since higher interest rates will persist.

Fiscal policy

Fiscal policy is relatively weak under a floating rate. Again let us assume that the government wishes to reduce aggregate demand. It thus raises taxes and/or lowers government expenditure. The reduction in aggregate demand will reduce imports and (via lower prices) increase exports. This effect on the current account of the balance of payments will put upward pressure on the exchange rate.

The lower aggregate demand, however, will lower the transactions demand for money and hence *reduce* interest rates. These lower interest rates will lead to an outflow of capital. This will put downward pressure on the exchange rate, which, if strong enough, could more than offset the upward pressure from the current account effect. In today's world, where international capital is very mobile and flows across the international exchanges can be very large indeed, it is likely that the capital account effect will be bigger than the current account effect, at least in the short run. There will therefore be a *depreciation* of the exchange rate. This will reduce imports and increase exports, thus raising aggregate demand again, and reducing the effectiveness of the fiscal contraction.

?? Compare the relative effectiveness of fiscal and monetary policies as means of *expanding* aggregate demand under a system of floating exchange rates.

ulative holdings of currency. This can then cause even larger and more rapid swings in exchange rates.

Uncertainty for traders and investors. The uncertainty caused by currency fluctuations can discourage international trade and investment. To some extent the problem can be overcome by using the **forward exchange market**. Here traders agree with a bank *today* the rate of exchange for some point in the *future* (say, six months' time). This

DEFINITION

Forward exchange market Where contracts are made today for the price at which a currency will be exchanged at some specified future date.

allows traders to plan future purchases of imports or sales of exports at a known rate of exchange. Of course, banks charge for this service, since they are taking on the risks themselves of adverse exchange rate fluctuations.

This will not help long-term investment, however. The possibility of exchange rate appreciation may well discourage firms from investing abroad.

?? Why would banks not be prepared to offer a forward exchange rate to a firm for, say, five years' time?

Lack of discipline on the domestic economy. Governments may pursue irresponsibly inflationary policies. Also unions and firms may well drive up wages and prices, without the same fear of losing overseas markets or of the government imposing deflationary policies. The depreciation resulting from this inflation will itself fuel the inflation by raising the price of imports.

Conclusion

Neither fixed nor free-floating exchange rates are free from problems. For this reason governments have sought a compromise between the two, the hope being that some intermediate system will gain the benefits of both, while avoiding most of their disadvantages.

One compromise was tried after the Second World War. This was the *adjustable peg*. We will examine this system in section 24.5. Another is the system that replaced the adjustable peg in the early 1970s and continues for much of the world today. This is the system of *dirty floating*. We will examine this in section 24.6.

SECTION SUMMARY

1. Under a free-floating exchange rate the balance of payments will automatically be kept in balance by movements in the exchange rate. This will remove the *balance of payments* constraint on domestic policy. It will not, however, remove external constraints entirely.
2. According to the purchasing-power parity theory, any changes in domestic prices will simply lead to equivalent changes in the exchange rate, leaving the international competitiveness of home-produced goods unaffected. If, however, internal shocks cause changes in interest rates, there will be a change in the *capital* account balance. This will influence exchange rates and destroy the purchasing-power parity theory. The current account will go out of balance (in an equal and opposite way to the capital account).
3. External shocks will be reflected in changes in exchange rates and will help to insulate the domestic economy from international economic fluctuations.
4. Exchange rate movements are highly influenced by speculation. If speculators believe that an appreciation or depreciation is merely temporary, their activities will help to stabilise the exchange rate. If, however, they believe that an exchange rate movement in either direction will continue, their activities will be destabilising and cause a bigger movement in the exchange rate.
5. The advantages of free-floating exchange rates are that they automatically correct balance of payments disequilibria; they eliminate the need for reserves; and they give governments a greater independence to pursue their chosen domestic policy.
6. On the other hand, a completely free exchange rate can be highly unstable, especially when the elasticities of demand for imports and exports are low; also speculation may be destabilising. This may discourage firms from trading and investing abroad. What is more, a flexible exchange rate, by removing the balance of payments constraint on domestic policy, may encourage governments to pursue irresponsible domestic policies for short-term political gain.

*24.4 The open economy and ISLM analysis

In this section we show how the ISLM analysis that we examined in section 20.3 can be extended to incorporate the open economy. We will first assume a fixed rate of exchange and then later a free-floating rate.

Analysis under a fixed exchange rate

The BP curve

We start by introducing a third curve, the *BP* (balance of payments) curve. This curve, like the *IS* and *LM* curves, plots a relationship between the rate of interest (r) and the level of national income (Y). All points along the *BP* curve represent a position of *balance of payments equilibrium*.

The curve slopes upwards from left to right (see Figure 24.10). Increases in the rate of interest (r) will cause the capital account to move into surplus as capital is attracted into the country. Increases in national income (Y), in contrast, will cause the current account to move into deficit as more imports are purchased. If the overall balance of pay-

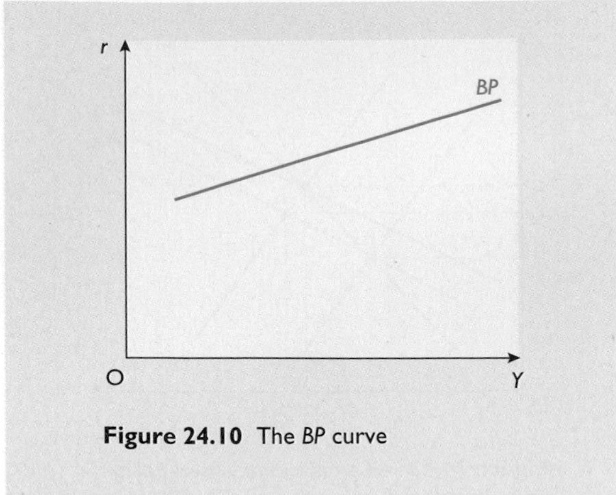

Figure 24.10 The *BP* curve

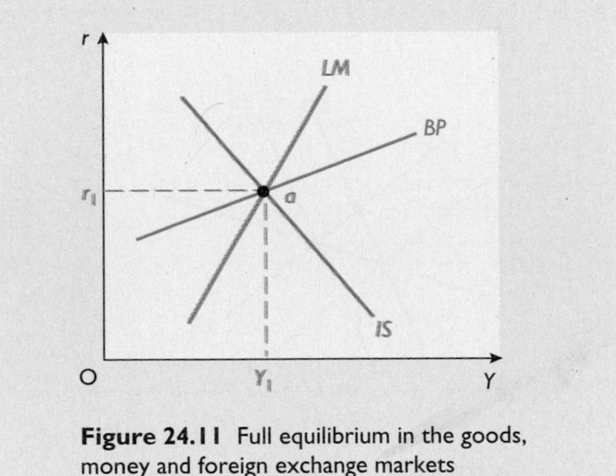

Figure 24.11 Full equilibrium in the goods, money and foreign exchange markets

ments is to stay in equilibrium, current account deficits must be matched by capital account surpluses and vice versa. Thus a rise in *Y* must be accompanied by a rise in *r*, and reductions in *Y* must be accompanied by reductions in *r*. The *BP* curve therefore slopes upwards. Any point below the *BP* line represents a position of overall deficit; any point above the line, a position of surplus.

The slope of the *BP* curve depends on two factors.

The marginal propensity to import (mpm = ΔM/ΔY). The higher the *mpm*, the steeper will be the *BP* curve. The reason is that with a high *mpm* there will be a correspondingly large rise in imports for any given rise in national income. This will cause a large current account deficit. To maintain an overall balance of payments equilibrium this will require a correspondingly large capital account surplus. This in turn will require a large rise in interest rates. Thus the bigger the *mpm*, the larger the rise in interest rates that will be necessary to restore balance of payments equilibrium, and hence the steeper will be the *BP* curve.

The elasticity of supply of international capital. The greater the elasticity of supply of international capital, the less will be the rise in interest rates necessary to attract an inflow of capital and thereby restore balance of payments equilibrium after a rise in national income, and hence the flatter will be the *BP* curve. In the case of a perfectly elastic supply of international capital, the *BP* curve will be horizontal at the world rate of interest.

Equilibrium in the model

If we now put the *BP* curve on an ISLM diagram, we have the position shown in Figure 24.11. Point *a* represents full equilibrium. At r_1 and Y_1, investment equals savings (point *a* is on the *IS* curve), the demand for money equals the supply (point *a* is also on the *LM* curve), and finally the balance of payments is in balance (point *a* is also on the *BP* curve).

But what is the mechanism that ensures that all three curves intersect at the same point? To answer this question, let us assume that the three curves just happen to intersect at the same point, and then let us examine the effects of changes in fiscal and monetary policies, which shift the *IS* and *LM* curves respectively. Will equilibrium be restored? The answer is yes, via a change in the money supply. Let us examine fiscal and monetary policy changes in turn.

Fiscal policy under fixed exchange rates

An expansionary fiscal policy, i.e. a rise in government spending and/or a reduction in tax, will have the effect of shifting the *IS* curve to the right (e.g. to IS_2 in Figure 24.12). The reason is that for any given rate of interest there will be a higher equilibrium level of national income than before.

This will increase national income, but the extra demand for money that results will drive up interest rates. In a *closed* economy, equilibrium would now be at point *b* (r_2, Y_2), where $IS_2 = LM_1$. But in our open economy model this equilibrium is *above the BP curve.* There is a balance of payments surplus. The reason for this is that the higher interest rates have caused a capital account surplus that is bigger than the current account deficit that results from the higher national income.

Such a surplus will cause the money supply to rise as funds flow into the country. This will in turn cause the *LM* curve to shift to the right. Equilibrium will finally be achieved at point *c* (r_3, Y_3), where $IS_2 = LM_2 = BP$. Thus under these conditions, the monetary effect of the change

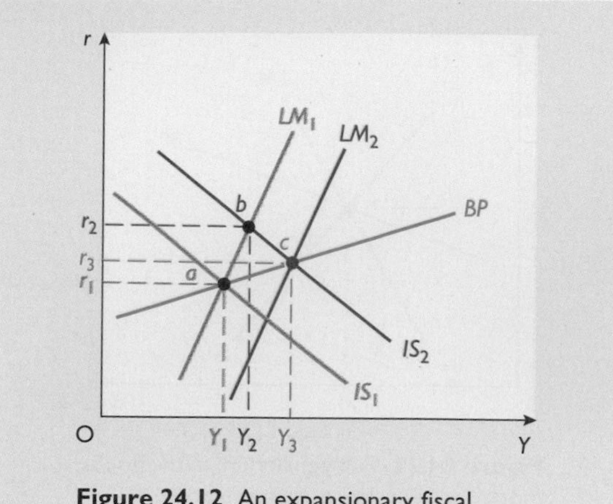

Figure 24.12 An expansionary fiscal policy under fixed exchange rates

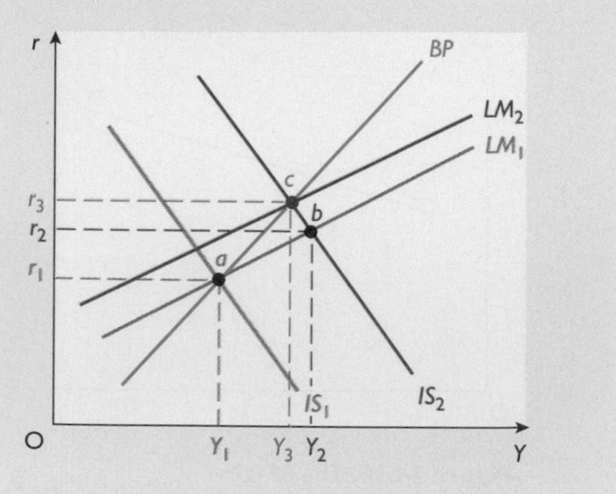

Figure 24.13 An expansionary fiscal policy under fixed exchange rates: a steep *BP* curve

in the balance of payments will *reinforce* the fiscal policy and lead to a bigger rise in national income.

> **??** What will be the effect of an expansionary fiscal policy on interest rates and national income if there is a perfectly elastic supply of international capital?

If the *BP* curve were steeper than the *LM* curve, the effect would be somewhat different. (Remember the *BP* curve will be steep if there is a high *mpm* and an inelastic supply of international capital.) This is illustrated in Figure 24.13.

Under these circumstances an initial rise in national income to Y_2 (where $IS_2 = LM_1$) will cause a balance of payments *deficit* (point *b* is *below the BP curve*). The reason is that this time the current account deficit is bigger than the capital account surplus (due to a large *mpm* and a small inflow of capital). This will reduce the money supply and cause the *LM* curve to shift to the left. Equilibrium will be achieved at point *c*, where $LM_2 = IS_2 = BP$.

When the *BP* curve is steeper than the *LM* curve, therefore, the monetary effect of the change in the balance of payments will *dampen* the effect of the fiscal policy and lead to a smaller rise in national income.

Monetary policy under fixed exchange rates

An expansionary monetary policy will cause the *LM* curve to shift to the right (e.g. to LM_2 in Figure 24.14). The increased supply of money will drive down the rate of interest and increase national income. In a closed economy, equilibrium would now be at point *b* (r_2, Y_2), where $LM_2 = IS$. But in an open economy, this extra demand will have sucked in extra imports, and the lower interest rate will have led to net capital outflows. There will be a balance of payments deficit: point *b* is below the *BP* curve.

The balance of payments deficit will cause the money stock to fall as money flows abroad. This will cause the *LM* curve to shift back again to its original position. The economy will return to its initial equilibrium at point *a*.

Thus under a fixed exchange rate regime, monetary policy alone will have *no long-term effect* on national income and employment. Only when accompanied by an expansion in aggregate demand (either through fiscal policy or through an autonomous rise in investment or a fall in savings) will an expansion of money supply lead to higher national income.

> **??**
> 1. Why does this conclusion remain the same if the *BP* curve is steeper than the *LM* curve?
> 2. Trace through the effects of a fall in exports (thereby shifting the *BP* curve).
> 3. Show what will happen if there is (a) a rise in business confidence and a resulting increase in investment; (b) a rise in the demand for money balance (say, for precautionary purposes).

Analysis under free-floating exchange rates

As the exchange rate changes, the *BP* curve will shift (see Figure 24.15). If the *IS* and *LM* curves intersect *above* the *BP* curve, there will be a balance of payments surplus. This will cause the exchange rate to appreciate. The appreciation will cause the surplus to disappear. This in turn will cause the *BP* curve to shift upwards.

Similarly, if the *IS* and *LM* curves intersect *below* the *BP* curve, the resulting balance of payments deficit will cause a depreciation and a downward shift of the *BP*

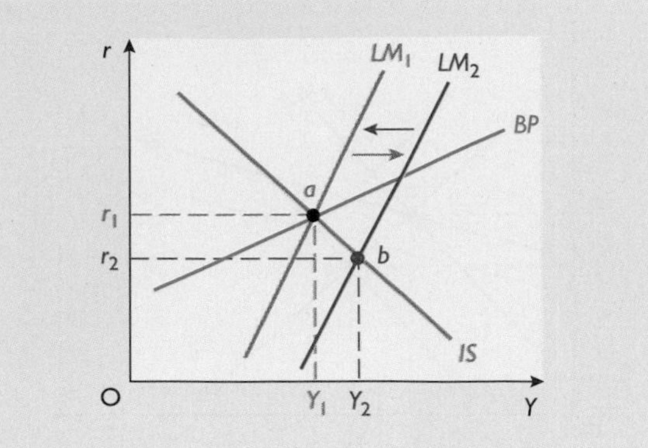

Figure 24.14 An expansionary monetary policy under fixed exchange rates

curve. Thus the *BP* curve will always shift so that it intersects where the *IS* and *LM* curves intersect.

Fiscal policy under floating exchange rates

Assume that the government pursues a reflationary fiscal policy. The *IS* curve shifts to IS_2 in Figure 24.16.

At point *b*, where the *LM* curve and the new *IS* curve intersect, there is a balance of payments surplus (due to higher capital inflows attracted by the higher rate of interest). This causes the exchange rate to appreciate and the *BP* curve to shift upwards.

But the higher exchange rate will cause a fall in exports and a rise in imports. This fall in aggregate demand will cause the *IS* curve to shift back towards the left. The new equilibrium will be at a point such as *c*. This represents only a modest change from point *a*. Thus under a floating exchange rate the effects of fiscal policy may be rather limited.

The effect will be stronger, however, the steeper the *BP* curve. In Figure 24.17, the *BP* curve is steeper than the *LM* curve. This time a rise in the *IS* curve from IS_1 to IS_2 will lead to a balance of payments *deficit* and hence a *depreciation* of the exchange rate. The *BP* curve will shift *downwards*. The depreciation will cause a rise in exports and a fall in imports. This *rise* in aggregate demand will cause the *IS* curve to shift to the *right*. The new equilibrium will be at point *c*, which is at a higher level of national income, Y_3. Under these circumstances the balance of payments effect makes fiscal policy stronger.

?? Under what circumstances would an expansionary fiscal policy have *no effect at all* on national income?

Monetary policy under floating exchange rates

An expansionary monetary policy will shift the *LM* curve to the right, to LM_2 in Figure 24.18. In a closed economy, equilibrium would now be at point *b*.

In an open economy under a floating exchange rate, the fall in the rate of interest will cause the exchange rate to depreciate and the *BP* curve to shift downwards. The depreciation will cause exports to rise and imports to fall. This increase in aggregate demand will shift the *IS* curve to the right. The new equilibrium will thus be at point *c*, where $LM_2 = IS_2 = BP_2$. This represents a large change from the initial point *a*.

Thus monetary policy can have a substantial effect on the level of national income under a system of floating exchange rates.

?? What will determine the size of the shift in the *BP* curve in each case?

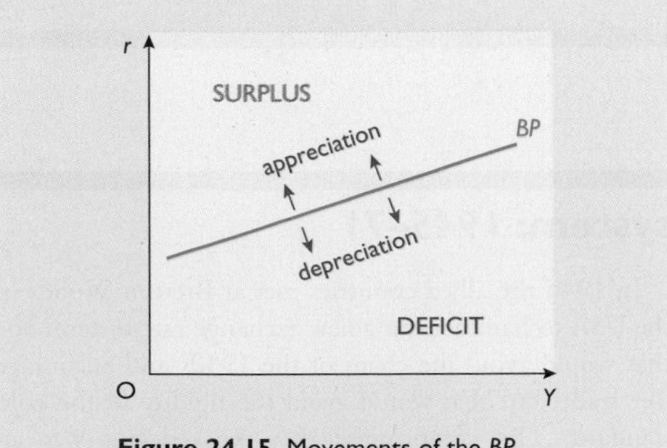

Figure 24.15 Movements of the *BP* curve under floating exchange rates

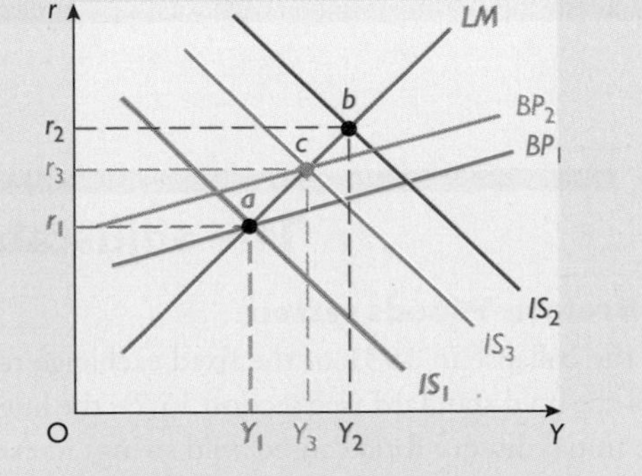

Figure 24.16 An expansionary fiscal policy under floating exchange rates

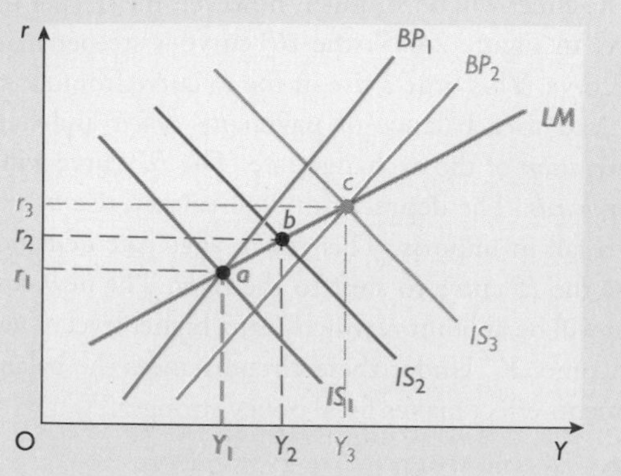

Figure 24.17 An expansionary fiscal policy under floating exchange rates: steep *BP* curve

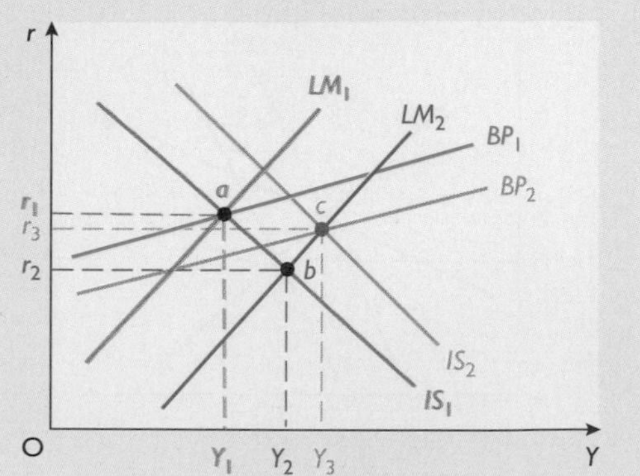

Figure 24.18 An expansionary monetary policy under floating exchange rates

SECTION SUMMARY

1. A *BP* curve can be added to an ISLM diagram. It shows all the combinations of national income and interest rates at which the balance of payments is in equilibrium. The curve is upward sloping, showing that a rise in national income (causing a current account deficit) will require a rise in interest rates to give a counterbalancing capital account surplus.
2. The higher the *mpm* and the less elastic the supply of international capital, the steeper will be the *BP* curve.
3. Under a fixed exchange rate, the flatter the *BP* curve, the larger will be the effect on national income of an expansionary fiscal policy. Provided the *BP* curve is flatter than the *LM* curve, an expansionary fiscal policy will cause a balance of payments surplus (via its effect of increasing interest rates). The resulting increase in money supply will strengthen the initial effect of the fiscal policy.
4. Monetary policy under fixed exchange rates will have no effect on national income. Any expansion of money supply will, by depressing interest rates, simply lead to a balance of payments deficit and thus a reduction in the money supply again.
5. Under a floating exchange rate an appreciation will shift the *BP* curve upwards and a depreciation will shift it downwards.
6. If the *BP* curve is flatter than the *LM* curve, fiscal policy under a floating exchange rate will be dampened by the resulting changes in the exchange rate. An expansionary fiscal policy will lead to an appreciation (due to the effects of higher interest rates), which in turn will dampen the rise in aggregate demand.
7. Monetary policy will have a relatively large effect on aggregate demand under floating rates. A rise in money supply will reduce interest rates and raise aggregate demand. This will cause a balance of payments deficit and thus a depreciation. This in turn will lead to a further expansion of aggregate demand.

24.5 The adjustable peg system: 1945–71

The Bretton Woods system

After the collapse in 1931 of the fixed exchange rate system of the gold standard (see section 15.2), the huge scale of the initial disequilibria caused wild swings in exchange rates. Many countries resorted to protectionism, given the great uncertainties associated with free trade under fluctuating exchange rates.

In 1944 the allied countries met at Bretton Woods in the USA to hammer out a new exchange rate system: one that would avoid the chaos of the 1930s and encourage free trade, but that would avoid the rigidity of the gold standard. The compromise they worked out was an adjustable peg system that lasted until 1971.

Under the **Bretton Woods system** there was a totally fixed dollar/gold exchange rate ($35 per ounce of gold). The USA guaranteed that it would freely convert dollars into gold. It was hoped thereby to encourage countries to hold dollars as their major reserve currency. After all, if dollars were freely convertible into gold, they were as good as gold. All other countries pegged their exchange rate to the dollar.

To prevent temporary, short-term fluctuations in the exchange rate, central banks *intervened* on the foreign exchange markets using their foreign reserves. This enabled them to maintain the pegged rate within a 1 per cent band.

If the disequilibrium became more serious, governments were supposed to pursue policies of *deflation* or *reflation*. In the meantime, in the case of a deficit, the central bank might have insufficient reserves to maintain the exchange rate. The International Monetary Fund was set up to provide such liquidity. All countries were required to deposit a quota of funds with the IMF, depending on the size of their trade. The IMF would then lend to countries in balance of payments deficit to enable them to maintain their exchange rate. The more a country had to borrow from the IMF, the more the IMF would insist that it pursued appropriate deflationary policies to correct the disequilibrium.

If the deficit (or surplus) became severe, countries could *devalue* (or *revalue*): the pegged rate could be adjusted (in consultation with the IMF).

?? Under this system how would you expect countries to respond to a balance of payments surplus? Would a revaluation benefit such countries?

Advocates of an adjustable peg system argue that the Bretton Woods arrangement made a significant contribution to the long boom of the 1950s and 1960s.

- Since rates were fixed for a long period of time – perhaps many years – uncertainty was reduced and trade was encouraged.
- Pegged rates, plus the overseeing role of the IMF, prevented governments from pursuing irresponsible policies, and helped to bring about an international harmonisation of policies. They kept world inflation in check.
- If a deficit became severe, countries could devalue. This prevented them being forced into a depression or into adopting protectionist policies. The IMF ensured an orderly process of devaluation.

However, there were two serious weaknesses with the system. These became more and more apparent during the 1960s, and eventually led to the system's downfall.

Problems of adjustment to balance of payments disequilibria

To avoid internal policy being governed by the balance of payments, and to avoid being forced into a depression, countries with a fundamental deficit were supposed to devalue. There were several difficulties here, however.

- Identifying whether a deficit was fundamental. Governments were frequently overoptimistic about the future balance of payments position.
- If devaluation did take place, it could be very disruptive to firms. A devaluation suddenly alters the costs and revenues of importers and exporters by a substantial amount. If a devaluation is felt to be imminent, it can cause great uncertainty and may make them reluctant to take on new trade commitments.

?? Will this uncertainty have a similar or a different effect on exporting companies and companies using imported inputs?

- At first a devaluation might make a deficit *worse*: the **J-curve effect**. The price elasticities of demand for imports and exports may be low in the short run. As a result the Marshall–Lerner condition may not be initially satisfied (see page 729 above). Directly after devaluation few extra exports may be sold, and more will have to be paid for imports that do not have immediate substitutes. There is thus an initial deterioration in the balance of trade before it eventually improves. In Figure 24.19, devaluation takes place at time t_1. As you can see, the diagram has a J shape.

For these reasons, countries in deficit tended to put off devaluing until they were forced to by a crisis. This applied particularly to the UK, given sterling's role as a reserve currency. Many countries held sterling as a major

DEFINITIONS

Bretton Woods system An adjustable peg system whereby currencies were pegged to the US dollar. The USA maintained convertibility of the dollar into gold at the rate of $35 to an ounce.

The J-curve effect Where a devaluation causes the balance of payments first to deteriorate and then to improve. The graph of the balance of payments over time thus looks like a letter J.

CASE STUDIES BOX 24.6

WAS THERE A J-CURVE EFFECT AFTER 1967?

The aftermath of the 1967 devaluation

Chronic balance of payments problems had bedevilled the UK economy for much of the 1950s and 1960s. Yet for nearly twenty years from 1949 the exchange rate was kept fixed at £1 = $2.80. Successive governments preferred *deflation* as the solution to a balance of payments crisis, rather than risking the uncertain reaction of overseas holders of sterling to a devaluation.

But finally in November 1967 the long-resisted devaluation came. The pound was devalued from $2.80 to $2.40. A current account deficit of £294 million in 1967 was transformed into a current account surplus of £463 million in 1969, £731 million in 1970 and £1111 million in 1971. The success of devaluation, however, was not immediate. It took many months before exports and imports adjusted fully to the new lower terms of trade.

But was there actually a J-curve effect? Did the balance of payments deteriorate before it improved? The facts are set out in the table.

UK balance of payments (£m): 1967–70

	Current account (1)	Capital account (excluding official transactions) (2)	Balance of payments (1) + (2) (3)	Terms of trade (1975 = 100) (4)
1967 Q1	+22	+487	+509	122.5
Q2	−38	+26	−12	124.2
Q3	−59	−447	−506	123.9
Q4	−219	−443	−662	devaluation
1968 Q1	−149	−370	−519	116.9
Q2	−55	−466	−521	118.6
Q3	−66	+42	−24	118.3
Q4	−16	−330	−346	117.7
1969 Q1	−18	+290	+272	119.9
Q2	+165	−103	+62	118.6
Q3	+154	−234	−80	117.7
Q4	+162	+595	+433	116.4
1970 Q1	+235	+680	+915	119.0
Q2	+166	+61	+227	119.4
Q3	+88	−290	−202	121.4
Q4	+242	+105	+347	122.0

Source: *Economic Trends* (ONS).

??

1. Draw a chart with time on the horizontal axis and the balance of payments on the vertical axis. Show (a) the current account balance, (b) the capital account balance (excluding official financing, i.e. government borrowing from abroad and drawing on reserves) and (c) the total balance: (a) + (b).
2. Was there a J curve in either the current account or the capital account?
3. Why does the capital account show greater short-term fluctuations than the current account?
4. How much did devaluation affect the terms of trade?
5. If traders had accurately *predicted* both the timing and the amount of the devaluation, how would this have affected a possible J-curve effect?
6. The UK was forced out of the ERM in September 1992 and sterling depreciated by 15 per cent within two months. The following table shows the balance of payments on current account from 1992 Q1 to 1994 Q4.

UK balance of payments, current account (seasonally adjusted) (£ billion)

1992				1993				1994			
Q1	Q2	Q3	Q4	Q1	Q2	Q3	Q4	Q1	Q2	Q3	Q4
−2.2	−2.4	−2.0	−2.8	−3.3	−3.1	−2.1	−2.5	−1.3	−0.3	+0.1	−0.5

Was there a J-curve effect? What other influences were there on the current account after 1992? (See Box 24.1.)

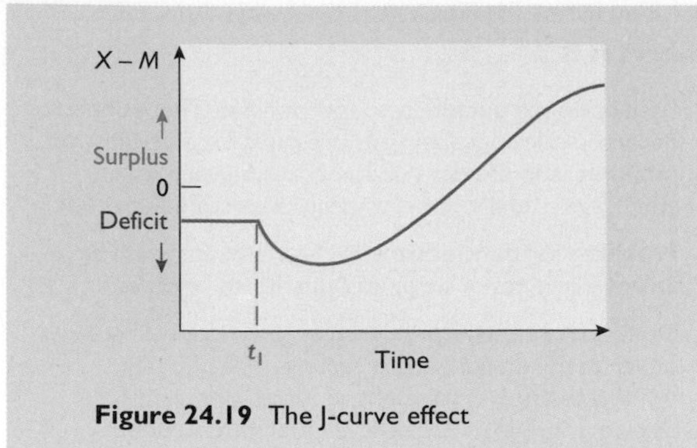

Figure 24.19 The J-curve effect

part of their reserves. A devaluation of sterling would reduce the value of these countries' reserves. They might then lose confidence in sterling. The UK, however, had insufficient gold and dollar reserves to buy back all these pounds if the countries decided to sell them. Such selling would cause a crisis, forcing further devaluation.

The reluctance of countries to devalue caused other problems.

Stop–go policies. Countries had to rely much more on *deflation* as a means of curing deficits. The UK in particular found that, whenever the economy started to grow, the balance of payments went into deficit. This forced the government to curb demand again through fiscal and/or monetary policies.

Speculation. If countries delayed devaluing until a deficit became really severe, an eventual large devaluation became inevitable. This provided a field day for speculators: they could not lose, and there was a high probability of a substantial gain.

Large-scale disruption. The delay in devaluing plus the build-up of speculative pressure could cause the devaluation to be very large when it eventually came. This could be highly disruptive.

Countries' balance of payments deficits could be reduced and adjustment made easier if surplus countries were willing to revalue. There was a reluctance to do this, however, by countries such as Japan. Revaluation was strongly opposed by exporters (and producers of import substitutes), who would find it suddenly more difficult to compete. What is more, there were not the same pressures for surplus countries to revalue as there were for deficit countries to devalue. A lack of reserves can force deficit countries to devalue. Surplus countries, however, may be quite happy to carry on building up reserves.

The USA was not allowed to devalue when in deficit. The onus was on other countries to revalue, which they were reluctant to do. Hence large US deficits persisted. The problem of these deficits was linked to the second major problem area: that of international liquidity.

Problems of international liquidity and the collapse of the system

International liquidity refers to the amount of reserves that are acceptable to central banks for intervention in the foreign exchange market. Under the Bretton Woods system there were three main sources of liquidity: gold, dollars and IMF quotas. But since IMF quotas were only in existing currencies, they were not a source of *additional* liquidity.

As world trade expanded, so deficits (and surpluses) were likely to be larger, and so more reserves were required. But the supply of gold was not expanding fast enough, so countries increasingly held dollars. After all, dollars earned interest. The willingness to hold dollars enabled the USA to run large balance of payments deficits. All the USA needed to do to pay for the deficits was to 'print' more dollars, which other countries were prepared to accept as reserves.

US balance of payments deficits in the 1960s got steadily worse. The financing of the Vietnam War, in particular, deepened the deficit. Dollars flooded out of the USA. World liquidity thus expanded rapidly, fuelling world inflation. Furthermore, the rapid growth in overseas dollar holdings meant that US gold reserves were increasingly inadequate to guarantee convertibility. Some countries, fearful that the USA might eventually be forced to suspend convertibility, chose to exchange dollars for gold. US gold reserves fell, creating a further imbalance and a deepening of the crises.

Despite various attempts to rescue the system with its overreliance on the dollar, it eventually collapsed. In June 1972 the pound was floated. Over the following year other countries followed suit, and despite a further dollar devaluation the system was finally abandoned in 1973.

?? Why would the adjustable peg system have been less suitable in the world of the mid-1970s than it was back in the 1950s?

SECTION SUMMARY

1. Under the Bretton Woods system (1945–71), currencies were pegged to the US dollar. The rate was supported from countries' reserves and if necessary with loans from the IMF. If there was a moderate disequilibrium, countries were supposed to use deflationary/reflationary policies. If the disequilibrium became severe, they were supposed to devalue/revalue.
2. The system was claimed to bring certainty for business and a constraint on governments pursuing irresponsible fiscal and monetary policies while avoiding the problem of recession if a balance of payments deficit became severe.
3. However, it was sometimes difficult to identify whether a deficit was severe enough to warrant a devaluation; a devaluation could be very disruptive for firms; and devaluation at first could make the deficit worse (the J-curve effect).
4. If a country was reluctant to devalue, as was the UK given sterling's role as a reserve currency, it could find itself having to pursue 'stop–go' policies. There could be large-scale speculation as pressure for a devaluation mounted; and the devaluation could be very large when it eventually came, causing large-scale disruption.
5. Problems for deficit countries were made worse by an unwillingness of surplus countries to revalue.
6. Dollars were the main source of international liquidity under the Bretton Woods system. The USA, by running balance of payments deficits, was therefore able to print world currency, which forced other countries, via their balance of payments surpluses, to do likewise if they were to maintain the pegged rate. The resulting excess liquidity caused world inflation and a growing lack of confidence in US ability to maintain the fixed dollar/gold rate.
7. Attempts to patch up the system failed to solve these problems and the system was replaced by dirty floating in the early 1970s.

24.6 Dirty floating: 1972 onwards

Forms of managed flexibility

The world has been on a floating exchange rate system since the breakdown of the Bretton Woods system in the early 1970s. Some minor currencies remain pegged (but adjustable) to a major currency such as the dollar, but float along with it against other currencies. Other currencies are pegged to each other, but jointly float with the rest of the world. The most notable example of this is the currencies of the exchange rate mechanism of the European Monetary System (see section 24.7).

Except for limited periods, no country has adopted a free float. All countries manage their exchange rate and are thus under a 'dirty' floating system. Nevertheless the extent and forms of this intervention vary.

Extent of intervention

Some countries intervene a great deal, attempting to maintain what amounts to a *crawling peg* system. They attempt to prevent short-term fluctuations in exchange rates, keeping their currency within fairly narrow bands, but allow the exchange rate to adjust gradually to long-term shifts in the demand for and supply of their currency. Other countries, such as the USA for most of the period, and the UK from late 1977 to late 1981 and since departing from the ERM in 1992, have intervened very little, except when there has been sudden large-scale buying, or more likely selling, of their currency.

Forms of intervention

The following can be used to prevent the exchange rate falling:

- Central bank purchases of the currency on the foreign exchange market using reserves or foreign loans.
- Raising interest rates to attract short-term capital inflows.
- Indirect methods: e.g. deflationary fiscal policy, or prices and incomes policy. These policies, although they will not affect imports and exports for some time, may nevertheless encourage stabilising speculation. If speculators believe that the measures will eventually work to prevent depreciation, they will purchase the currency.

?? What could be done to stop the exchange rate *appreciating?*

Justification of dirty floating

After the breakdown of the Bretton Woods system, countries felt they had no option but to float their currencies.

This was the only way at that time of achieving the following objectives:

- Allowing exchange rates to adjust to inevitable shifts in demand and supply, without the huge pressures that used to build up under the Bretton Woods system and all the attendant problems of speculation and disruption.
- Freeing the world from the need for large amounts of reserves, and the previous overreliance on US balance of payments deficits to provide adequate liquidity.
- Preventing domestic policy from being almost wholly determined by the balance of payments situation.

Some countries hoped eventually to return to an improved adjustable peg system, where less reliance needed to be placed on the dollar for liquidity purposes and where adjustments could be made more frequently and less painfully. In the meantime, however, floating exchange rates were felt to be a definite improvement. This was confirmed as the 1970s progressed and greater exchange rate adjustments were required, given the oil crises of 1973/4 and 1979/80, and the rapid change in world trading patterns.

But why not adopt a free float? The reason has largely to do with the potential volatility of short-term exchange rates. With various economic shocks, both domestically and in the international economy, there could be very large changes in the exchange rate, made worse by speculation. This would be very disruptive to trade and investment.

Over the longer term, if the exchange rate needs to change to reflect shifts in long-term trading patterns, or differences in the rate of inflation from world rates, then intervention can allow a gradual and orderly adjustment to the new equilibrium. Without such intervention, there may be a sudden and damaging change in exchange rates, made worse by destabilising speculation, overshooting and a possible J-curve effect.

Problems with dirty floating since 1972

Managing the exchange rate involved problems, however. Governments needed to know when to intervene, what exchange rate level they should aim to maintain, and how persistently they should try to maintain that rate in the face of speculative pressure.

Predicting the long-term equilibrium exchange rate

Differing inflation rates between countries will require exchange rate adjustments to maintain purchasing-power parity. It is not correct, however, for governments to assume that this will be the *only* cause of shifts in the long-term equilibrium exchange rate. The 1973/4 and 1979/80 oil crises caused fundamental and unpredictable changes in currency demand and supply. So too did other factors, such as UK membership of the EC and its effect on trading patterns, protectionist measures adopted in different parts of the world, changes in technology and changes in tastes.

It is therefore very difficult for the government to predict what the long-term equilibrium will be, and what proportion of any exchange rate movement is therefore due to long-term and what proportion merely to short-term phenomena.

The growth in speculative capital movements

The OPEC oil price increase in 1973/4 caused huge balance of payments deficits for oil importers. The OPEC countries could not spend all of these surpluses on additional imports since (a) they did not have the capacity to consume such a huge increase in imports and (b) the oil-importing countries did not have the capacity to supply such a huge increase in exports. The surpluses were thus largely invested in short-term dollar and to a lesser extent sterling and other western currency assets. This created a large capacity for short-term loans by western banks. These moneys could be rapidly shifted from one world financial centre to another, depending on which country had the most favourable interest rates and exchange rates.

This created a massive capacity for speculation, and thus made it difficult for countries to control exchange rates by currency sales alone. Reserves and access to foreign loans were simply inadequate to prevent concerted speculative selling. Governments therefore had to rely much more on using interest rates, which would enable them better to control these speculative flows.

Conflicts with internal policy

If the main weapon for controlling the exchange rate is interest rates, then interest rates cannot also be used to determine domestic money supply. The growth of monetarism in the late 1970s, and the setting of monetary targets, therefore made it far more difficult for government to control the exchange rate (see Box 19.5 and section 20.4).

Beggar-my-neighbour policies

The use of higher interest rates to prevent short-term capital outflows may cause other countries to raise their interest rates in competition. This could then lead to world deflation and world recession.

?? Would any of these problems be lessened by the world returning to an adjustable peg system? If so, what sort of adjustable peg system would you recommend?

ISSUES AND APPLICATIONS — BOX 24.7

THE IMPORTANCE OF CAPITAL MOVEMENTS

How a current account deficit can coincide with an appreciating exchange rate

The era of dirty floating exchange rates has seen a huge increase in short-term capital movements. Vast amounts of moneys transfer from country to country in search of higher interest rates or a currency that is likely to appreciate. This can have a bizarre effect on exchange rates.

If a country pursues a reflationary fiscal policy, the current account will tend to go into deficit as extra imports are 'sucked in'. What effect will this have on exchange rates? You might think that the answer is obvious: the higher demand for imports will create an extra supply of domestic currency on the foreign exchange market and hence drive down the exchange rate.

In fact the opposite is likely. The higher interest rates resulting from the higher domestic demand can lead to a massive inflow of short-term capital. The capital account can thus move sharply into surplus. This is likely to outweigh the current account deficit and cause an *appreciation* of the exchange rate.

Exchange rate movements, especially in the short term, are largely brought about by changes on the capital rather than the current account.

?? Why do high international capital mobility and an absence of exchange controls severely limit a country's ability to choose its interest rate?

The UK experience of dirty floating

Figure 24.20 shows the fluctuations in UK exchange rates since 1976, with respect to both the dollar and the more important trade-weighted average exchange rate with all other countries. As can be seen, the fluctuations have been large and often violent. Other countries have experienced similar fluctuations. Also there have been clear long-term trends, as Table 24.1 shows.

But why have exchange rates changed so much? Part of the explanation lies in differences in countries' rates of inflation. This is the purchasing-power parity theory (see page 738). If a country's prices went up by 10 per cent more than the weighted average of its trading partners, its exchange rate would need to depreciate by 10 per cent to compensate. But this provides only part of the explanation. Other causes of exchange rate movements include changes in relative interest rates, various international shocks, longer-term shifts in demand and supply for imports and exports, and speculation.

The first oil crisis and its aftermath: 1973–6

The 1973/4 oil crisis, which followed large world commodity price increases over the previous two years, caused a major shock to the world economy. What were the UK and other industrialised countries to do?

Depreciation could not provide the solution. The demand for oil is highly price inelastic. The price increase had thus already caused a major inflationary shock to the

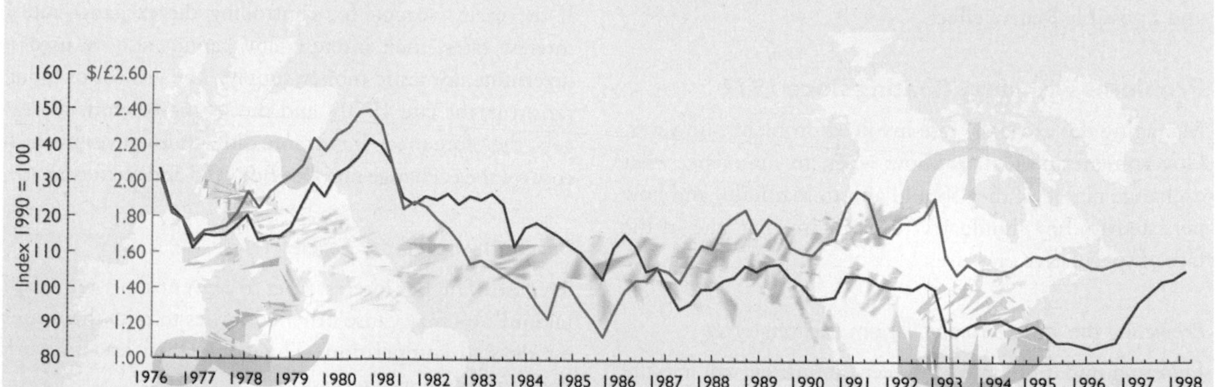

Figure 24.20 Dollar/sterling exchange rate and sterling exchange rate index: 1976–98

Source: *Economic Trends Annual Subblement* (ONS, various years).

Table 24.1 Exchange rate indices, averages for each period (1991 = 100)

	1970–3	1974–7	1978–81	1982–5	1986–9	1990–3	1994–7
USA	95	91	88	119	105	100	102
Japan	40	43	56	63	98	106	134
Germany	51	62	73	80	94	103	114
UK	154	116	114	111	100	96	86
Italy	254	213	130	105	100	95	74

Source: *OECD Economic Outlook* (OECD); *Datastream*.

world economy. Depreciation would probably have made things worse. What is more deflationary policies, or a growth in protectionism, would have caused a major world recession.

The solution seemed to be to borrow: (a) to 'recycle' the oil revenue so as to prevent excessive deflation, and (b) to attempt to maintain reasonably stable exchange rates and avoid competitive depreciation. Until 1975 the UK was reasonably successful in this policy. A substantial proportion of the OPEC surpluses were deposited in the UK, and the government undertook large-scale foreign borrowing. The exchange rate was thus kept up by these capital inflows, and also by using reserves.

From early 1975, however, the exchange rate began falling, despite continued intervention. In 1976 it began to plummet, even though by now inflation was falling and the balance of payments was improving. Destabilising speculation set in. Many of the short-term capital deposits were withdrawn from the UK.

In November 1976, a major loan had to be negotiated with the IMF. The resulting rescue package included an insistence on deflationary measures such as higher interest rates. The exchange rate bottomed out at the end of 1976.

The second oil crisis and the rise of monetarism: 1976–81

The measures of late 1976, helped by the growing importance of North Sea oil, caused renewed confidence in sterling. Until autumn 1977, the Bank of England intervened to prevent the exchange rate from rising too much. Vast amounts of sterling were sold, and the foreign exchange acquired was used to build up the reserves and to pay off some of the foreign loans of previous years.

Then, from autumn 1977 to autumn 1981, the pound was allowed to float relatively freely. The result was a massive 30 per cent appreciation of the exchange rate (a 53 per cent appreciation in the PPP rate!) from its low point in 1976.

The UK's growing oil surplus. North Sea oil was making an increasing contribution to the current account of the balance of payments.

The 1979/80 oil crisis. Oil rose in price from $13 to $19 per barrel during 1979 and to $31 during 1980. Since the UK was becoming a major oil exporter, and the pound was now a 'petrocurrency', OPEC surpluses were attracted to London.

The advent of monetarism. From 1977 the money supply was targeted. When the Thatcher government came to power in 1979, these monetarist policies were more rigorously applied. In order to keep to its monetary targets, the government drove up interest rates, with short-term interest rates reaching over 17 per cent in late 1979. Interest rates remained considerably higher than in competitor countries. But this simply encouraged further capital inflows. The exchange rate had to rise.

The recession of 1980–2. These highly deflationary monetary policies caused a deep recession. The resulting decline in the demand for imports further contributed to a rising exchange rate.

The huge appreciation of sterling devastated large parts of UK industry. Many exporters simply could not compete, while imports were so cheap that they drove many firms out of business.

Keynesian critics argue that the government should have adopted a less restrictive fiscal and monetary policy. As far as fiscal policy is concerned, they argue that taxation from oil revenues could have been directly invested in infrastructure. Alternatively, significant tax cuts could have been given. As for monetary policy, they argue that the government should have adopted higher monetary targets. This would have kept interest rates down and lowered the exchange rate.

Keynesians argue that these policies would not have been inflationary because North Sea oil gave the UK an increase in *potential* income. A rise in aggregate demand to match this would simply have prevented a deflationary gap from opening.

??

1. Were there any advantages of the high exchange rate?
2. Would there have been a danger of inflation rising if deflationary policies had not been used, even though there was a rise in potential income caused by North Sea oil?

'Reaganomics' and the US budget deficit: 1981–5

With the election of President Reagan in late 1980, the USA adopted 'Reaganomics'. This had two main features:

- Increasing incentives. The major element in this policy was tax cuts.
- Monetarism. Tight control was to be kept over the growth of the money supply.

Initially President Reagan had hoped to maintain a balanced budget, with tax cuts being matched by cuts in government expenditure. But his commitment to increasing defence expenditure led to a rapid increase in the overall level of government spending, and the budget deficit increased from $76 billion in 1980 to $212 billion in 1985. The US administration was unwilling to finance the budget deficit by significantly increasing the money supply. The deficit therefore had to be financed largely by borrowing. This pushed interest rates well above those of other countries.

High aggregate demand (from the tax cuts) led to a rise in imports and a current account deficit. High interest rates, however, attracted foreign capital to the USA and thus provided a capital account surplus. These capital movements were so large that they caused the dollar to appreciate, despite the current account deficit. This, in turn, worsened the current account deficit.

Other industrialised economies, and especially Japan, experienced the opposite effect. With its lower inflation and lower growth in domestic demand, Japan had a large current account surplus. This was more than offset, however, by a huge capital outflow, encouraged by low Japanese interest rates. The yen *depreciated* (see Table 24.2).

The high dollar caused grave problems for US exporting industries and industries competing with imports. Large numbers of bankruptcies were suffered in both industry and agriculture. There were growing demands for protectionism, but President Reagan resisted them.

Sterling was particularly vulnerable as many of the OPEC oil revenues deposited in the UK were switched to the USA. As the dollar rose, so the pound fell (see Figure 24.20). Crisis was reached in January/February 1985 with the exchange rate dipping as low as £1 = $1.05 (see Box 24.8).

To arrest this fall, the Bank of England sold large quantities of dollars and other reserves. Interest rates were raised dramatically. Minimum lending rate was even reintroduced on 14 January for one day to drive up interest rates by 2 per cent. Eventually the crisis was averted at the end of February by concerted action between European central banks and the Bank of Japan, which jointly sold $11 billion over a period of a few days.

Until early 1985, destabilising speculation had worked to drive the dollar up and other currencies, especially the pound, down. After February 1985, speculation went into reverse. The dollar was now falling. People therefore sold dollars and bought other currencies.

??

1. Why would the pound not have gone on falling indefinitely?
2. Could the UK have done anything to prevent the massive fall in the dollar/pound exchange rate from $2.40 in 1981 to only just above $1.00 in early 1985?

Mixed fortunes for the pound: 1985–8

After February 1985 the dollar fell and the yen rose. Although there were still considerable currency fluctuations after that, the dollar did not return to those record high levels. Reasons include: a rapid growth in the US money supply and a fall in US interest rates; a slowing down of US growth rates; and a belief by speculators that the dollar had been overvalued.

Sterling at first appreciated. This was encouraged by high interest rates in the UK. Interest rates had been dri-

Table 24.2 US and Japanese exchange rates: 1980–5 (1980 = 100)

	1980	1981	1982	1983	1984	1985
US effective exchange rate (trade weighted)	100.0	112.7	125.9	133.2	143.7	150.2
Japanese effective exchange rate (trade weighted)	100.0	102.6	91.0	95.1	95.2	95.4

Source: *International Finance Statistics* (IMF).

CASE STUDIES BOX 24.8

THE STERLING CRISIS OF JANUARY/FEBRUARY 1985

As Figure 24.20 shows, the period from 1981 to 1985 was one of a massive decline in the $/£ exchange rate. But this fall was not steady. It was greatly influenced by speculation. Whenever speculators believed that the rate would fall there would be a new wave of selling sterling (and buying dollars), and sure enough the rate would fall – and often quite dramatically.

In November 1984, at a time when the exchange rate was falling (from $1.26 to $1.22), the government *reduced* interest rates. The intention was to stimulate demand and prevent further rises in unemployment. This triggered off a massive selling of sterling, a problem aggravated by the growing attractiveness of the dollar. But it was not until January 1985, with the exchange rate down to $1.12, that the government eventually raised interest rates.

By this time speculation had reached fever pitch, and it was not just the pound that was coming under pressure. Unprecedented sales of sterling and other currencies took place as dealers rushed to buy the soaring dollar. The following is an extract from the *Financial Times* of 26 February 1985:

Banks powerless as dollar soars

Central banks stood by powerless yesterday as a remarkable surge in the dollar's value swept it to record highs against sterling and other European currencies ...

Sterling closed in New York at $1.0565 after finishing in London down 2.25 cents at an all time low of $1.054. The French franc, Italian lira and many other currencies were at their lowest ever against the dollar ...

Dealers cited as reasons for the latest surge ...the expectation of higher US interest rates and President Reagan's rejection of moves to depress the US currency. Central bankers acknowledged that intervention against such a strong trend would have been hopeless.

But then the following day the central banks fought back. The following extract is from the *Financial Times* of 28 February:

Dollar falls in chaotic trading after central bankers' intervention

Large-scale and concerted intervention by central banks sent the dollar plunging against other leading currencies in chaotic trading on foreign exchange markets yesterday.

The intervention, one of the largest ever and the first joint move for more than a month, triggered off what dealers called panic selling of the US currency ...

Over the next few days the fall of the dollar continued, and the pound consequently rose against it. Within a few weeks the exchange rate was around $1.25, and a few weeks after that it was around $1.40.

?? How in practice could central banks decide when to intervene?

ven up in an attempt to maintain monetary targets and to encourage the recovery of sterling.

In 1986, however, oil prices fell: from $28 per barrel in 1985 to $13.50 in 1986. This was due to an increasing oil glut, as individual producers, both within and outside OPEC, attempted to increase their share of the oil market. Oligopolistic collusion was breaking down. The pound, as a petrocurrency, therefore depreciated. Also, as 1986 wore on, and a general election drew closer, people began to believe that the government would engineer a pre-election boom. Certainly, money supply was being allowed to increase well above original targets. The prediction of a boom plus a relaxed monetary policy therefore led to expectations of a depreciation of the pound, which speculators then helped to bring about. The exchange rate index fell from over 96.6 in the spring of 1986 to 84.6 in October.

But then in 1987 the pound began to rise again. Oil prices were firmer; inflation had fallen to just over 3 per cent and interest rates were still very high relative to those of other countries. The Chancellor, Nigel Lawson, anxious to avoid repeating the damage to UK industry that was done by the high exchange rate of the early 1980s, was keen to prevent the pound rising. He was also keen to keep the exchange rate pegged as closely as possible to the German mark, hoping to pave the way for the UK joining the ERM (see section 24.7).

But how was he to keep the exchange rate from rising? The answer was to reduce interest rates. Between October 1986 and May 1988 interest rates fell from 11 per cent to $7^1/_2$ per cent. For several months the policy of shadowing the D-Mark seemed to work. The exchange rate was effectively pegged at around DM2.95; the economy grew and unemployment fell.

A deteriorating balance of payments: 1988–90

Keeping the exchange rate down through reductions in interest rates, plus a policy of reducing income taxes, was causing the economy to expand rapidly. The current account thus moved rapidly into deficit (see Box 24.1) and inflation began to rise sharply. In June 1988 the government was forced to raise interest rates again in order to dampen demand. But this had the effect of keeping up the exchange rate, and further worsening the current account deficit. Between 1985 and 1989 an annual current account surplus of £2.2 billion had been transformed into a deficit of £22.4 billion.

Nevertheless in mid-1989, with the current account still deteriorating, the exchange rate began to fall. The fear of the authorities was that with such a huge deficit, once the rate began to fall, speculation would cause the fall to be very severe. Thus the government was forced to maintain high interest rates, and the Bank of England frequently had to intervene in the foreign exchange markets to steady the rate.

The weakness of the pound and worries about rising inflation put growing pressure on the government to join the ERM. After all, the ERM countries had managed to secure much lower average rates of inflation than the UK, and there was a strong desire among the business community to be part of this 'low inflation club'. Eventually, in October 1990, Margaret Thatcher decided to join the ERM and sacrifice the monetary independence she had so long cherished. The era of a floating pound had apparently come to an end.

?? To what extent was there a conflict after 1988 between using interest rates to affect the rate of inflation and using them to maintain a given exchange rate? Explain under what circumstances there was and was not a conflict.

The volatility of exchange rates

Exchange rates have become extremely volatile. Currencies can gain or lose several percentage points in the space of a few days. These changes can then make all the difference between profit and loss for trading companies. There are a number of reasons for this volatility:

- Monetarist policies. Although few countries today follow strict monetarist policies, many are prepared to make considerable changes to interest rates in order to keep monetary growth moderately stable. These in turn cause exchange rate fluctuations.
- A huge growth in international financial markets. This has encouraged the international transfer of money and capital.
- The abolition of exchange controls in most industrialised countries.
- The growth in information technology. With the simple use of a computer and a VDU, capital can be transferred internationally in a matter of seconds.
- The preference for liquidity. With the danger of currency fluctuations, companies prefer to keep their financial capital as liquid as possible. They do not want to be locked into assets denominated in a declining currency.
- The growing speculative activities of trading companies. Many large companies will put together a team of dealers to help manage their liquid assets: to switch them from currency to currency in order to take advantage of market movements.
- The growing speculative activities of banks and other financial institutions.
- The growing belief that rumour and 'jumping on the bandwagon' are more important determinants of currency buying or selling than cool long-term appraisal. If people *believe* that speculation is likely to be destabilising, their actions will ensure that it is. Many companies involved in international trade and finance have developed a 'speculative mentality'.
- The growing belief that governments are powerless to prevent currency movements. As short-term capital (or 'hot money') grows relative to official reserves, it is increasingly difficult for central bank exchange market intervention to stabilise currencies.

Although most governments and firms dislike highly volatile exchange rates, few today advocate a return to fixed exchange rates, or a Bretton Woods type system. Nevertheless, suggestions have been made for reducing volatility. Two of these – international harmonisation of economic policies, and an adjustable peg system between a group of currencies (as in the European Monetary System) – are discussed in section 24.7.

SECTION SUMMARY

1. Since the early 1970s the world has largely been on a dirty floating exchange rate system. The degree of intervention varies from country to country and from time to time. Its forms include central bank purchases and sales of currencies, changes in interest rates, exchange controls and, over the longer term, demand management policies.

continued

2. With the collapse of the Bretton Woods system, dirty floating was felt to be the best compromise. It would give the necessary degree of exchange rate flexibility in a world where shifts in currency demand and supply were becoming much larger. It would also release domestic policy from being dominated by balance of payments considerations. At the same time, the intervention could (in theory) prevent violent exchange rate fluctuations and allow a more orderly adjustment to new equilibrium exchange rates.
3. Nevertheless there are problems under dirty floating of predicting long-term equilibrium exchange rates. What is more, with the massive growth in 'hot money' since the early 1970s, it has become increasingly difficult for countries on their own to counteract speculation. The main weapon of intervention has become the rate of interest. There may be a conflict, however, in using interest rates both to control exchange rates *and* as the weapon of domestic monetary policy.
4. Sterling exchange rates have shown considerable volatility over the years, with large divergences from the purchasing-power parity rate. For example, with the rise in the value of the dollar in the early 1980s – as a result of high US interest rates – the pound fell. There was massive speculation, leading to a crisis in early 1985.
5. In October 1990, with pressure from the business community for stable exchange rates with other EC countries, the UK abandoned floating exchange rates and joined the ERM.
6. The volatility of exchange rates around the world has tended to grow. There are many reasons for this, including a growth in international financial markets and a liberalisation of international financial movements combined with easier computer transfer of funds, a growth in speculative activities and a growing belief in the impotence of governments acting on their own to stabilise rates.

24.7 Concerted international action to stabilise exchange rates

International harmonisation of economic policies

One of the major causes of currency fluctuations is the very different conditions existing in different countries and the different policies they pursue. For example, an expansionary fiscal policy plus a tight monetary policy can lead to a huge currency appreciation if other countries do not follow suit. This is what happened to the dollar in 1983 and 1984. Conversely, a persistent current account deficit, plus a policy of interest rate reductions in order to stimulate the economy, can lead to large-scale currency depreciation. This happened to sterling after it left the ERM in 1992.

Changes in exchange rates that result from such imbalances are then often amplified by speculation. And this problem is becoming worse. Approximately one trillion dollars per day passes across the foreign exchange markets. The scale of such movements makes any significant speculation simply too great for individual countries to resist. And on some occasions even the concerted action of groups of countries cannot maintain exchange rate stability.

The four main underlying causes of exchange rate movements are divergences in *interest rates*, *growth rates*, *inflation rates* and *current account balance of payments*. Table 24.3 shows the levels of these and other indicators for the seven major industrial countries. As can be seen, the variations between countries have been considerable.

For many years now the leaders of these countries have met once a year at an economic summit conference (and more frequently if felt necessary). Top of the agenda in most of these 'Group of Seven' (G7) meetings has been how to generate world economic growth without major currency fluctuations. But to achieve this it is important that there is a **harmonisation** of economic policies between nations. In other words, it is important that all the major countries are pursuing consistent policies aiming at common international goals.

But how can policy harmonisation be achieved? As long as there are significant domestic differences between the major economies, there is likely to be conflict, not harmony. For example, if one country, say the USA, is worried about the size of its budget deficit, it may be unwilling to respond to world demands for a stimulus to aggregate demand to pull the world economy out of recession. What is more, speculators, seeing differences between countries, are likely to exaggerate them by their actions, causing large changes in exchange rates. The G7 countries

DEFINITION

International harmonisation of economic policies Where countries attempt to co-ordinate their macroeconomic policies so as to achieve common goals.

Table 24.3 Macroeconomic indicators for the G7 countries

	USA			Japan			Germany			France			Italy			UK			Canada		
	1991	1993	1996	1991	1993	1996	1991	1993	1996	1991	1993	1996	1991	1993	1996	1991	1993	1996	1991	1993	1996
Short-term interest rate (% average)	5.4	3.0	5.0	7.2	2.9	0.6	9.2	7.3	3.3	9.6	8.6	3.9	12.0	10.7	9.4	11.5	10.7	6.0	9.0	5.0	4.4
Economic growth (% change in real GDP)	−0.6	3.1	2.4	4.3	−0.2	3.7	5.0	−1.2	1.3	0.8	−1.5	1.3	1.2	−1.2	0.7	−2.0	2.3	2.1	−1.8	2.2	1.5
Inflation (%)	4.2	3.0	3.0	3.3	1.3	0.5	3.6	3.6	1.6	3.2	2.1	2.0	6.5	4.2	3.9	5.9	1.6	2.4	5.6	1.8	1.5
Current account (% of GDP)	−0.1	−1.6	−2.2	2.2	3.1	1.4	−1.1	−0.8	−0.7	−0.5	0.7	1.3	−2.1	1.2	3.5	−1.4	−1.9	0.0	−4.0	−4.0	−0.2
General government borrowing requirement (% of GDP)	−3.2	−3.4	−1.6	3.0	−1.4	−4.4	−3.3	−3.5	−3.8	−2.2	−6.1	−4.2	−10.2	−9.6	−6.7	−2.6	−7.8	−4.4	−6.6	−7.3	−1.8
National debt (% of GDP)	41.5	46.4	49.2	5.4	4.4	14.3	22.1	35.0	48.1	16.5	27.2	39.3	89.3	106.3	111.7	19.2	35.5	44.2	48.5	62.5	70.3
Effective exchange rate (1991 = 100)	100.0	100.7	107.6	100.0	126.5	125.5	100.0	107.4	115.0	100.0	106.5	112.3	100.0	82.0	79.3	100.0	88.3	87.3	100.0	88.8	84.8

have therefore sought to achieve greater **convergence** of their economies. But as Box 24.9 shows, convergence may be a goal of policy, but in practice it has proved elusive.

?? Referring to Table 24.3, is there any evidence that there was any greater convergence between the G7 countries in 1996 than in 1993 or 1991?

Because of a lack of convergence, there are serious difficulties in achieving international policy harmonisation:

- Countries' budget deficits and national debt differ substantially as a proportion of their national income. This puts very different pressures on the interest rates necessary to service these debts.
- Harmonising rates of monetary growth would involve letting interest rates fluctuate with the demand for money. Without convergence in the demand for money, interest rate fluctuations could be severe.
- Harmonising interest rates would involve abandoning both monetary targets and exchange rate targets (unless interest rate 'harmonisation' meant adjusting interest rates so as to maintain monetary targets or a fixed exchange rate).
- Countries have different internal structural relationships. A lack of convergence here means that countries with higher endemic *cost* inflation would require higher interest rates and higher unemployment if international inflation rates were to be harmonised, or higher inflation if interest rates were to be harmonised.
- Countries have different rates of productivity increase, product development, investment and market penetration. A lack of convergence here means that the growth in exports (relative to imports) will differ for any given level of inflation or growth.
- Countries may be very unwilling to change their domestic policies to fall in line with other countries. They may prefer the other countries to fall in line with them! Japan, for example, on several occasions has been reluctant to reflate. Likewise Germany, following the inflationary effects of reunification, was unwilling to reflate in the early 1990s and kept interest rates high. This forced other countries, despite being in recession, to keep their interest rates high if they were to maintain fixed exchange rates with the D-Mark.

If any one of the four – interest rates, growth rates, inflation rates or current account balance of payments – could be harmonised across countries, it is likely that the other three would then not be harmonised.

Total convergence and thus total harmonisation may not be possible. Nevertheless most governments favour some movement in that direction: some is better than none.

DEFINITION

Convergence of economies When countries achieve similar levels of growth, inflation, budget deficits as a percentage of GDP, balance of payments, etc.

CASE STUDIES BOX 24.9

'SEVEN MEN IN A BOAT'

Attempts at harmonisation

In recent years, governments of the major industrial nations have tried to come to terms with the ever-growing interdependence of their economies. Economic disruptions in one country (e.g. a worsening UK budget deficit or a unilateral decision by, say, Germany or Japan to raise interest rates) can have profound effects on the world economy.

As a result of the potentially highly unstable nature of economic relationships, finance ministers and heads of state of the *Group of Seven* (G7) countries – the USA, Japan, Germany, France, Italy, the UK and Canada – have met on a regular basis to try to harmonise their policies. But the key problem in this has been the nations' overriding self-interest.

For example, in early 1987 the G7 countries decided to try to stem the fall of the dollar caused by the huge US budget and balance of payments deficits and relatively low US interest rates at the time. Under the *Louvre Accord*, as it became known, the G7 countries would bring their interest rates closer together and would intervene on the foreign exchange market to achieve greater exchange rate stability. But although some intervention did take place, markets were not convinced that there was a real commitment on the part of the USA to tackle its twin deficits, or on the part of Japan or (West) Germany to support the dollar or to limit their trade surpluses. Then, with the world stock market crash in October 1987, the dollar fell sharply. The Louvre Accord collapsed.

There are two major problems with G7 agreements. The first is that they are not binding. If governments are not prepared to give up national sovereignty and submit to international control, they are always likely to put purely national interests first. For example, the USA may unilaterally cut interest rates in order to tackle domestic unemployment, or Germany may raise interest rates, as it did to tackle the inflationary effects of reunification. In such cases, the rest of the world may suffer.

The second problem is the lack of international convergence. Successful policy co-ordination requires that serious imbalances in world trade should be kept to a minimum. But such is the size of the US current account deficit and the Japanese surplus that huge pressures are placed on the foreign exchange market. The imbalances create massive capital flows and great uncertainty. As a result, speculation is likely to be a far more powerful determinant of events than any agreement made by finance ministers. Exchange rates can thus be highly volatile (see Box 24.4).

Such problems are unlikely to diminish in the future as international interdependence continues to grow. The G7 nations have responded to the problem of co-ordination by seeking to expand and reform the responsibilities of the world's leading international financial and trade institutions. For example, the key reform proposed at the 1995 G7 summit in Halifax, Canada was that the IMF, the WTO and the World Bank should work more closely together, offering advice to borrowing countries and help with economic adjustment and trade liberalisation.

The G7 nations hope that greater co-operation between these international institutions will enable the world economy to be more successfully managed in the future.

?? To what extent can international negotiations over economic policy be seen as a game of strategy? Are there any parallels between the behaviour of countries and the behaviour of oligopolists? (See the section on game theory in Chapter 7, pages 203–6.)

?? If total convergence were achieved, would harmonisation of policies follow automatically?

Greater exchange rate rigidity between groups of currencies: the European Monetary System

One means of achieving greater currency stability is for countries to group together into blocs, and to peg their exchange rates to each other, while floating against the rest of the world. This will have two potential advantages:

- Trade will be encouraged between the members of the bloc. The greater the harmonisation of policies within the bloc, and therefore the less frequent any adjustments of the pegged rates, the more will trade be encouraged.
- The combined reserves of all countries in the bloc can be used to prevent excessive fluctuations of the bloc's currencies with the rest of the world.

The *exchange rate mechanism* (ERM) of the *European Monetary System* (EMS) is an example of such an arrangement. The EMS came into existence in March 1979. Its aim was to create currency stability, monetary co-operation and the convergence of economic policies of the EC countries. The ERM involves participants pegging their exchange rate to each other within bands, and jointly floating with the rest of the world.

A similar system, known as the *snake in the tunnel*, had been tried by the six original EEC members in 1972, but with a lack of convergence between the six members'

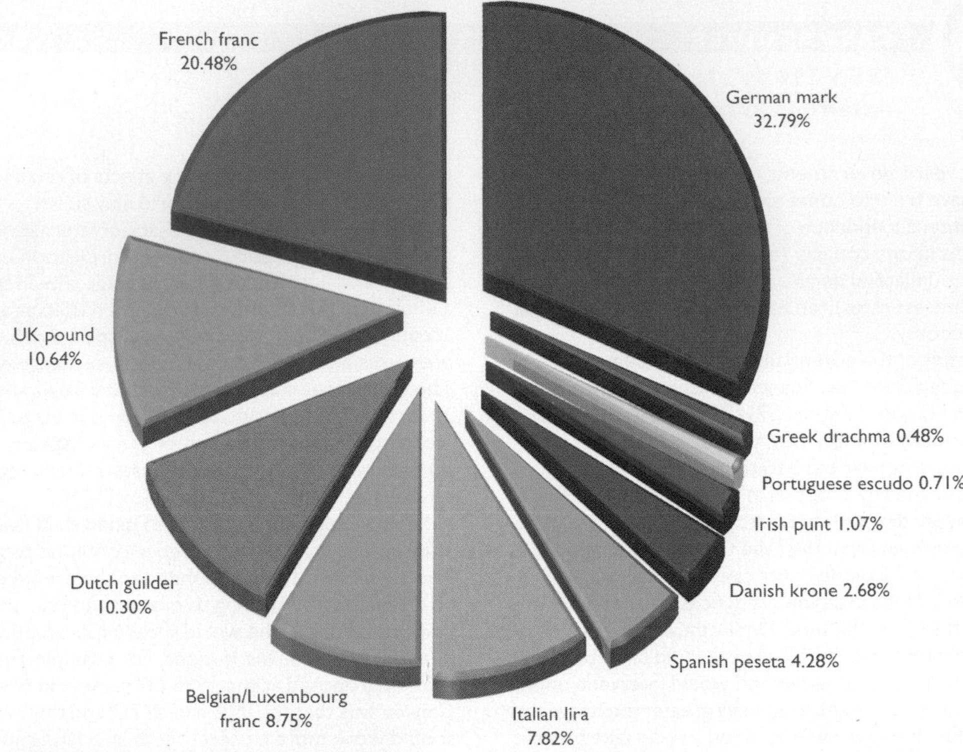

Figure 24.21 Composition of the ECU

economies, and the currency turmoil of the time (resulting from the world oil crisis, and high but differing rates of inflation round the world), the system collapsed.

Although the UK became a formal member of the EMS, it chose not to join the exchange rate mechanism. When Greece joined the EC in 1984, it too joined the EMS but stayed outside the ERM. Spain and Portugal joined the EC in 1986, but it was not until 1989 that Spain joined the ERM. The UK eventually joined in 1990. Finally Portugal joined in April 1992. Then in September 1992, the UK and Italy indefinitely suspended their membership of the ERM.

From the outset, all members of the EMS lent central bank support to each other's currencies, but only the members of the exchange rate mechanism pegged their exchange rates to each other (jointly floating against other currencies).

The features of the EMS

There are three main features of the European Monetary System:

- The European Currency Unit – the ECU.
- The exchange rate mechanism – the ERM.
- The European Monetary Co-operation Fund – the EMCF (later replaced by the European Monetary Institute, or EMI).

The European Currency Unit. Members' currencies are denominated in ECUs (European Currency Units). The ECU is a composite currency (or 'basket of currencies'). It consists of fixed amounts of the currencies of the twelve countries which were members of the EU before 1995. Thus the currencies of Sweden, Austria and Finland are not included in the basket, whereas those of Italy, the UK and Greece (which are outside the ERM) are.

The amount of each currency in the ECU depends on the size of the country's economy, its exchange rate and its proportion of intra-EU trade. The composition of the ECU was periodically reviewed, but has been frozen since November 1993. An ECU consists of 0.6242 D-Marks (approximately 33 per cent of the value of the ECU), 1.332 French francs (approximately 20 per cent), 0.08784 UK pounds (approximately $11^1/_2$ per cent), 151.8 Italian lire (approximately 8 per cent), and various amounts of the other currencies. Although the amount of each currency in the ECU is fixed, their percentages in the ECU vary with fluctuations in exchange rates. The percentages in August 1996 are shown in Figure 24.21.

The ECU is a unit of account for the exchange rate mechanism. But it is increasingly playing the role of a currency in its own right: it can be used for making payments in international trade, for making loans, for denominating assets, as a basis for travellers' cheques and as a reserve currency.

The exchange rate mechanism. This is a 'parity grid' system. Each currency is denominated in terms of the other ERM currencies in a grid. The grid specifies the central parity rates for each pair of currencies, and fluctuations from parity are allowed within specified limits. The parities can be adjusted from time to time by agreement, thus making the ERM an 'adjustable peg' system. All the currencies float jointly with currencies outside the ERM.

Two important rules govern fluctuations between member currencies.

1. Each currency's fluctuations are limited to a certain percentage either side of each other currency.

These bands were set at ±2¼ per cent in 1979 for all countries except Italy, which was given a ±6 per cent band. It moved to the narrow band in 1990. Spain, the UK and Portugal all joined at the ±6 per cent band. In 1993, the bands were widened for the countries remaining in the ERM to ±15 per cent (except for Germany and the Netherlands, which maintained the ±2¼ per cent band between their two currencies).

If a currency reaches the upper or lower limit against *any* other ERM currency, the two countries must intervene to maintain their currencies within the band. This can take the form of their central banks selling the stronger currency and buying the weaker one, or reducing interest rates in the case of the strong currency and raising interest rates in the case of the weak currency. Thus any currency's limit to appreciation is determined by the weakest currency in the band, and any currency's limit to depreciation is determined by the strongest currency in the band.

Before these limits are reached, however, the second rule is likely to come into effect.

2. Each country has a central parity against the ECU. But given that the value of the ECU will itself be influenced by changes in the exchange rate of any member currency, the ±15 per cent permitted band for fluctuations against other currencies will be narrower in the case of the ECU. The formula is $\pm 15(1 - w)$ per cent, where w is that currency's weight in the ECU basket. Thus the permitted fluctuation for the D-Mark against the ECU is $\pm 15(1 - 0.328)$ per cent from its central parity, i.e. ±10.082 per cent.

To provide an 'early warning' of currencies reaching their limit of divergence, the system specifies *divergence indicators* for each currency. A **divergence threshold** is reached when a currency reaches 75 per cent of its permitted divergence from its central parity against the ECU (i.e. in the case of the D-Mark, 75 per cent of ±10.082 per cent = ±7.561 per cent). The country in question is then supposed to take appropriate measures in consultation with other ERM countries (e.g. changing interest rates).

If it proves difficult to maintain a currency within its divergence threshold, the EMS members may decide that a *realignment* of the central parities is necessary: i.e. a devaluation or revaluation.

The European Monetary Co-operation Fund. This was intended to be a forerunner to an eventual European central bank (see section 24.8). Its prime purpose was to provide credit facilities to allow member countries to support their exchange rates. When it was created, all the EMS countries deposited 20 per cent of their dollar and gold reserves with the Fund, and in return received a credit in ECUs.

From 1989 the EMCF also provided a very-short-term financing facility (VSTF), whereby virtually unlimited funds would be available for up to a few weeks to support a currency in difficulties. Loans for longer periods remained much more limited. In 1994 the EMCF was replaced by the European Monetary Institute (EMI) (see Box 24.11).

The ERM in practice

The ERM in the 1980s

In a system of pegged exchange rates, countries should harmonise their policies to avoid excessive currency misalignments and the need for large devaluations or revaluations. In the early 1980s, however, French and Italian inflation rates were persistently higher than German rates. At first, there were approximately two realignments per year (see Table 24.4). This was frequent enough to prevent severe balance of payments disequilibria from building up, and thus helped to reduce speculation. It was also frequent enough to allow the realignments to be relatively small.

After 1983 realignments became less frequent, and then from 1987 to 1992 they ceased altogether. This was due to a growing convergence of members' internal policies. France, Italy and the other members increasingly adopted exchange rate stability as their major monetary goal. This disciplined them into adopting the lower inflation rates experienced in Germany, especially as it was the D-Mark exchange rate with their currencies that had become the major target.

DEFINITION

Divergence threshold The point of divergence from a currency's central parity with the ECU at which consultations will take place about action to prevent further divergence. The divergence threshold is $\pm 11.25(1 - w)$%.

Table 24.4 History of the ERM

	Mar 1979	Sept 1979	Nov 1979	Mar 1981	Oct 1981	Feb 1982	June 1982	Mar 1983	July 1985	Apr 1986	Aug 1986	Jan 1987	Jun 1989	Jan 1990	Oct 1990	Apr 1992	Sept 1992	Sept 1992	Nov 1992	Jan 1993	May 1993	Aug 1993	Jan 1995	Mar 1995	Oct 1996	Nov 1996	Mar 1998	Jan 1999
Belgian franc	En2¼%					–8.5		+1.5	+2.0	+1.0		+2.0										B15%						S
Danish krone	En2¼%	–2.9	–4.8			–3.0		+2.5	+2.0	+1.0												B15%						
German mark	En2¼%	+2.0			+5.5		+4.25	+5.5	+2.0	+3.0		+3.0										B15%						S
French franc	En2¼%				–3.0		–5.75	–2.5	+2.0	–3.0												B15%						S
Irish punt	En2¼%							–3.5	+2.0		–8.0									–10.0		B15%					+3.0	S
Italian lira	En6%			–6.0	–3.0		–2.75	–2.5	–6.0					B2¼%			–7.0	Ex	–	–	–	–	–	–	–	En15%		S
Dutch guilder	En2¼%				+5.5		+4.25	+3.5	+2.0	+3.0		+3.0										B15%						S
UK pound	–	–	–	–	–	–	–	–	–	–	–	–	–	–	En6%			Ex	–	–	–	–	–	–	–	–	–	
Spanish peseta	–	–	–	–	–	–	–	–	–	–	–	–	En6%				–5.0		–6.0		–8.0	B15%		–7.0				S
Portuguese escudo	–	–	–	–	–	–	–	–	–	–	–	–	–	–	–	En6%			–6.0		–6.5	B15%		–3.5				S
Austrian schilling	–	–	–	–	–	–	–	–	–	–	–	–	–	–	–	–	–	–	–	–	–	–	En15%					S
Finnish markka	–	–	–	–	–	–	–	–	–	–	–	–	–	–	–	–	–	–	–	–	–	–	–	–	En15%			S
Greek drachma	–	–	–	–	–	–	–	–	–	–	–	–	–	–	–	–	–	–	–	–	–	–	–	–	–	–	En15%	

– = % devaluation; + = % revaluation; B% = new band; En% = entry band; Ex = exit; S = join single currency

Source: *European Economy*.

By 1990, the ERM was generally seen by its existing members as being a great success. It had created a zone of currency stability in a world of highly unstable exchange rates, and had provided the environment for the establishment of a truly common market by the end of 1992.

> **??** Under what circumstances may a currency bloc like the ERM (a) help to prevent speculation; (b) aggravate the problem of speculation?

Background to UK membership of the ERM

Politicians and academics were generally against the UK joining the ERM in 1979:

- The UK had a higher 'endemic' inflation rate than the ERM countries (except Italy). This would soon cause a misalignment under fixed rates.
- The UK is an oil exporter whereas the EMS countries are oil importers. Changes in oil prices would thus cause misalignment.
- The UK's medium-term financial strategy included setting monetary targets. This involved allowing interest rates to fluctuate as necessary to keep within these targets. Interest rate fluctuations would have caused balance of payments disequilibria under a fixed exchange rate, and made that exchange rate unsustainable.

By the late 1980s, however, opinion had changed:

- There was general agreement that exchange rate volatility was undesirable.
- The UK inflation rate had come down and was similar to the European average (although by the end of the 1980s it had risen above the European average again).
- Oil prices had fallen, and oil was no longer such an important element in the UK's balance of payments.
- Targeting of the money supply had been abandoned.

From early 1987, the UK pursued a policy of 'shadowing' the D-Mark. Interest rates were geared to maintaining the exchange rate at around £1 = DM3. At first, given the relative strength of the pound and weakness of the D-Mark, this meant reducing interest rates. But this had the effect of boosting aggregate demand at a time when the economy was beginning to overheat, and when interest rates should ideally have been kept at a higher level.

Critics argued that this experience demonstrated that ERM membership would involve a loss of independence in monetary policy. In reply it was pointed out that, with an absence of exchange controls, the pursuit of an independent interest rate policy even outside the ERM had become virtually impossible. Any change in German interest rates forced the UK to make similar changes if massive capital flows and large swings in exchange rates were to be avoided.

By 1990 the government was committed to the UK's joining the ERM. The last obstacle was the UK's high rate of inflation compared with the other ERM members. By October, however, inflation appeared to have peaked. John Major, who was then the Chancellor, announced that the UK was joining the ERM at a central parity of DM2.95 and would adopt the ±6 per cent band for fluctuations against other ERM currencies.

Soon after joining, the economy moved sharply into recession and inflation fell rapidly. There were thus calls from industry for cuts in interest rates to arrest the decline in aggregate demand. But interest rates that fell too rapidly would push the pound towards the bottom of its band. The government thus felt unable to make substantial cuts in interest rates, with the result that the economy continued to plunge into recession. An exchange rate rule had replaced monetary discretion.

Crisis in the ERM

For most of the period 1990–2, there was optimism that convergence in the enlarged ERM would remove the need for realignments. After all, there had been no realignments since 1987, and there seemed a genuine collective commitment to defend the agreed parities. The anchor was the German economy, with its history of monetary stability and low inflation.

It might have been expected that, with the abolition of capital controls (achieved by 1991), there would have been the danger of increased speculation. But speculation will occur only if the speculators believe that realignments are likely – and they did not. This confidence in the stability of the ERM was reinforced by the introduction of the very-short-term financing facility (VSTF), whereby the EMCF could lend unlimited amounts on a very-short-term basis to defend currencies against speculative attacks.

In fact, so great was the conviction that currencies would not be realigned that a paradox arose: currencies of high-inflation economies such as Spain and Italy were pushed up to the top of their bands! The reason for this perverse effect was that they were pursuing a policy of high interest rates in order to reduce inflation. Normally, this would not have led to an increased demand for their currency because speculators would fear an impending devaluation (the inflation having worsened their current account deficit). But if there was believed to be no risk of a devaluation, people were keen to purchase currencies such as the peseta in order to benefit from the higher interest rate.

> **??** What problems would this have caused Spanish industry?

But despite the apparent strength of the ERM, it suffered from a number of underlying weaknesses:

- The removal of capital controls, even with the VSTF, had made the ERM currencies vulnerable to speculative attack, were such an attack ever to occur.
- The German economy was becoming subject to increasing strains from the reunification process. The finance of reconstruction in the East was causing a growing budget deficit. The Bundesbank thus felt obliged to maintain high interest rates in order to keep inflation in check.
- The UK had entered the ERM at a rate that many commentators felt was unsustainably high without considerable deflation. Indeed, with a massive current account deficit, and high German interest rates, the UK was obliged to keep interest rates up to protect the pound at a time when the economy was sliding rapidly into recession.
- The Franch franc was perceived to be overvalued, and there were the first signs of worries as to whether its exchange rate within the ERM could be retained. For much of the period 1990–3, it was the weakest of the ERM currencies.
- The US economy was moving into recession and, as a result, US interest rates were cut. This led to a large outflow of capital from the USA. With high German interest rates, much of this capital flowed to Germany. This pushed up the value of the D-Mark and with it the other ERM currencies.
- The likelihood of a successful move towards European economic and monetary union was diminishing with the rejection of the Maastricht Treaty by the Danes in the referendum of June 1992, and with the possibility that the French might also reject the treaty. Fears were expressed that exchange rate instability might re-emerge.

As the summer of 1992 progressed, these tensions increased (see Box 24.10). In September 1992, with a further fall in US interest rates and further buying of the D-Mark, things reached crisis point. First the lira was devalued. Then two days later, on 'Black Wednesday' (16 September), the UK and Italy were forced to suspend their membership of the ERM: the pound and the lira were floated. At the same time, the Spanish peseta was devalued by 5 per cent.

After this turmoil a period of relative calm ensued. Even so, the peseta and the escudo were devalued twice (in November 1992 and May 1993) and the Irish punt was devalued once in January 1993. Thus the ERM that had survived the departure of Italy and the UK was no longer one of fixed rates.

Turmoil returned in the summer of 1993. The French economy was moving into recession and there were calls for cuts in French interest rates. But this was only possible if Germany was prepared to cut its rates too, and it was not. Speculators began to sell francs and it became obvious that the existing franc/D-Mark parity could not be maintained. In an attempt to rescue the ERM, the EC finance ministers agreed to adopt wide ±15 per cent bands. The result was that the franc and the Danish krone depreciated against the mark.

An ERM with ±15 per cent bands is a quite different system from one with $\pm 2\frac{1}{4}$ per cent bands. There is considerable scope for fluctuations and much less need for intervention.

CASE STUDIES

THE END OF THE ERM?
The events of 1992/3

The following are extracts from *European Economy: Annual Report 1993*, charting the events surrounding the crisis in the ERM in 1992/3.

> 2 June 1992: Danish voters narrowly reject the Maastricht Treaty by referendum leading to the emergence of exchange-rate tensions within the ERM and rises in short-term interest rates in several Member States.
>
> 2 July 1992: The US Federal Reserve announces the seventh consecutive reduction in its discount rate to only 3%, accelerating the recent rapid depreciation of the dollar relative to Community currencies.
>
> 16 July 1992: The Bundesbank raises its discount rate by three-quarters of a percentage point.
>
> 25 August 1992: Publication of first polls suggesting a negative vote in the French referendum.
>
> 28 August 1992: Fuelled by growing fears over the unsustainability of the Italian budget deficit, the lira falls to its floor in the ERM.
>
> 3 September 1992: The UK, under growing pressure to increase interest rates in defence of sterling's weakness, chooses instead to arrange lending facilities for an amount equal to £7¼ billion to bolster its external reserves.
>
> 4 September 1992: The US further reduces the federal funds rate by a quarter of a percentage point to 3% and the dollar falls to a record low relative to the German mark. Italy raises interest levels sharply in an attempt to raise the lira above its ERM floor, and announces that it will be making use of the very-short-term financing facility.
>
> 6 September 1992: The informal Economic and Financial Council in Bath reaffirms its commitment to existing exchange-rate parities in the ERM. A succession of opinion polls point to the possibility of a rejection of the Maastricht Treaty in the French referendum.
>
> 8 September 1992: Finland floats the markka and Sweden increases its short-term rates.
>
> 14 September 1992: In an effort to relieve ever-mounting tensions within the ERM and to reduce massive speculative attacks on the lira, a 7% devaluation of the lira is agreed. The Bundesbank reduces the discount rate by half a percentage point.
>
> 16 September 1992: Notwithstanding massive central bank intervention and a cumulative 5-point increase in the minimum lending rate, sterling falls substantially and the Chancellor announces its suspension from the mechanism. The lira also suffers further massive speculative attacks and also falls to its new ERM floor. The Swedish Central Bank increases its marginal lending rate to 500%.
>
> 17 September 1992: Italy abandons attempts to maintain the lira within the ERM and temporarily suspends its participation in the mechanism. The Spanish peseta is devalued by 5%. The Danish krone, French franc and Irish punt are all subject to speculative attacks requiring central bank intervention and rises in interest rates.
>
> 23 September 1992: Joint statement by the French and German authorities that 'no change in the central rates is justified'.

The road to EMU

The EC countries were right to stress the importance of convergence of their economies. Certainly, if they were to progress from the ERM to eventual monetary union, with a single currency, then convergence was essential: not only between economic indicators, such as growth, interest rates, inflation rates and levels of government debt, but also between the policies of their governments and the structure of their economies and institutions.

As the 1990s progressed, so the economies of most of the EU countries were converging, and in May 1998 the decision was made that 11 of the 15 EU countries would proceed to economic and monetary union (EMU), with a single currency (the euro) in January 1999. EMU is the subject of the next section.

SECTION SUMMARY

1. Currency fluctuations can be lessened if countries harmonise their economic policies. Ideally this will involve achieving common growth rates, inflation rates, balance of payments (as a percentage of GDP) and interest rates. The attempt to harmonise one of these goals, however, may bring conflicts with one of the other goals.
2. Leaders of the G7 countries meet annually to discuss ways of harmonising their policies. Usually, however, domestic issues are more important to the leaders than international ones, and frequently they pursue policies that are not in the interests of the other countries.

BOX 24.10

19 November 1992: Following several weeks of relative calm and a gradual return to pre-September interest-rate levels within the ERM, tensions are revived following Sweden's decision to abandon its peg to the ECU.

22 November 1992: The Spanish peseta and the Portuguese escudo are both devalued by 6%, while pressure continues to mount against the French franc, the Danish krone and in particular the Irish punt. Conversely, short-term money market rates continue to fall in Germany, Belgium and the Netherlands.

10 December 1992: The Bundesbank increases its M3 monetary target for 1993 by 1 percentage point at both extremes to a range of 4½ to 6½%. Norway suspends its ECU peg, putting pressure on the Danish krone and the French franc.

Early January 1993: Tensions are again revived in the ERM ... and interest rates are raised in France and Ireland. The French and German authorities reaffirm their commitment to the existing German mark/French franc parity. The Bundesbank reduces its repurchase rate by 15 basis points (to 8.60%) with corresponding reductions in Belgium and the Netherlands.

30 January 1993: The Irish punt is devalued by 10%.

In May 1993, with increasing speculation against the Iberian currencies, there was a further realignment: the Spanish peseta was devalued by 8 per cent and the Portuguese escudo by 6.5 per cent.

Then in July 1993, the speculators turned their attack on the French franc. There had been no realignment between the franc and the D-Mark since 1987. The French had been pursuing a policy of the *franc fort*, whereby maintaining the exchange rate was the dominant goal of monetary policy. But with the French economy sliding deeper into recession, and growing calls for cuts in interest rates, speculators believed that the exchange rate would have to fall.

The following is an extract from the *Guardian* of 3 August 1993:

> **Germany, July 29**
> Bundesbank decides not to change its key discount rate despite expectations of a reduction of at least 0.5%.
>
> **London, July 30**
> Shock waves from Bundesbank decision send foreign exchange markets into turmoil and push five ERM currencies to the bottom of their band.
>
> **Brussels, July 31 and August 1**
> Central bank governors and finance ministers meet over the weekend in an attempt to co-ordinate a response to the situation.
>
> **Tokyo, August 2**
> EC's failure to agree effectively leads to the collapse of the ERM sending the French franc plummeting.

The old ERM appeared to be at an end. The new ±15 per cent bands that were adopted that weekend hardly seemed like a 'pegged' system at all. However, the ERM did not die. Within months, the members were again managing to keep fluctuations within a very narrow range (for most of the time, within ±2¼ per cent!)

?? Go through each of the events and give a justification for any action taken by governments.

3. One means of achieving greater currency stability is for a group of countries to peg their exchange rates with each other and yet float jointly with the rest of the world.
4. The exchange rate mechanism of the European Monetary System is an example. Members' currencies have a central parity with the ECU and are allowed to fluctuate against it and each other within a band. The band was ±2¼ per cent for the majority of the ERM countries, but originally Italy (up to 1990) and then the new members, Spain, the UK and Portugal, adopted a wider ±6 per cent.
5. The need for realignments seemed to have diminished in the late 1980s as greater convergence was achieved between the members' economies. Growing strains in the system, however, in the early 1990s, led to a crisis in September 1992. The UK and Italy left the ERM and realignments of the peseta, escudo and punt followed. There was a further crisis in July 1993 and the bands were widened to ±15 per cent.
6. The ERM was seen as an important first stage on the road to complete European monetary union.

CASE STUDIES

THE MAASTRICHT TREATY
A timetable for EMU

In December 1991 the leaders of the twelve EC countries met at Maastricht in the Netherlands to negotiate a Treaty on European Union. The treaty was signed in February 1992 and was subsequently ratified by the individual member countries.

The Maastricht Treaty was a major move towards full economic, political and social union. It sought to develop a common European foreign policy and defence policy, and a common security policy (to encourage greater co-operation between the police), and in its social chapter (see Box 23.9) it set out a common social policy. It also made all EU nationals 'citizens of the Union', thereby granting them total freedom to live and work wherever they chose in the EU.

It also set out a detailed programme for economic and monetary union (EMU). The timetable for EMU was divided into three stages.

Stage 1

This was to be a preliminary stage, during which a Monetary Committee of the European Union would monitor monetary policy in the member states and provide advice to the Council of Ministers on monetary convergence. During this stage preparations would be made for the establishment of a European Monetary Institute (EMI), an institution which would be the forerunner of a European central bank.

It was hoped that stage 1 would start on 1 January 1993, but it could not begin until all twelve member states had ratified the treaty. As it turned out, it was not until the autumn of 1993 that the last country (Germany) completed the ratification process.

Stage 2

This would begin on 1 January 1994, at which point the EMI would be established. It would seek to co-ordinate monetary policy and encourage greater co-operation between EU central banks. It would monitor the operation of the ERM and take over the functions of the European Monetary Co-operation Fund (EMCF). Finally, it would prepare the ground for the establishment of a European central bank in stage 3.

During stage 2 the member states would seek to achieve convergence of their economies. In order to progress to full economic and monetary union in stage 3, a country would have to meet five convergence criteria:

- Inflation: should be no more than 1½ per cent above the average inflation rate of the three countries in the EU with the lowest inflation.
- Interest rates: the rate on long-term government bonds should be no more than 2 per cent above the average of the three countries with the lowest inflation rates.
- Budget deficit: should be no more than 3 per cent of GDP at market prices.
- National debt: should be no more than 60 per cent of GDP at market prices.
- Exchange rates: the currency should have been within the normal bands for at least two years with no realignments or excessive intervention.

By the end of 1996, the EMI would have to specify the details of the central banking system to be established in stage 3. Also by this date the Council of Ministers would have to decide whether the conditions had been met for the start of stage 3. The conditions specify that at least seven countries must have met the five convergence criteria. If they had, then the Council of Ministers would specify the date on which these countries would commence stage 3, the stage of full EMU.

Stage 3

It would commence at the earliest in 1997. If a date were not set by the end of 1997, a review would take place during 1998 and stage 3 would commence on 1 January 1999.

At the beginning of this stage, the countries which met the five criteria would fix their currencies permanently to the ECU, which would become a currency in its own right, and, it was later decided, would be renamed the 'Euro'. The national currencies would therefore effectively disappear.

At the same time a European System of Central Banks (ESCB) would be created, consisting of a European Central Bank (ECB) and the central banks of the member states. Like the Bundesbank (and since 1997 the Bank of England) the ECB would be independent: independent from governments and also from EU political institutions. Its board members would be appointed by the Council of Ministers for an eight-year term.

The ECB would operate the monetary policy on behalf of the countries which had adopted full EMU. It would be the sole issuer of banknotes (denominated in Euros) and would distribute them through the individual central banks. It would control the money supply and determine interest rate policy. It would take over the reserves of the member states and would use them to support the Euro on the foreign exchange markets.

Any member state not initially meeting the convergence criteria would proceed to full EMU when the criteria had subsequently been met.

The UK and Denmark negotiated an 'opt-out' from the Maastricht Treaty. They do not have to proceed to stage 3 if they so choose.

BOX 24.11

In March 1998, the European Commission ruled that 11 of the 15 member states were eligible to proceed to EMU in January 1999. The UK and Denmark were to exercise their opt out and Sweden and Greece failed to meet one or more of the convergence criteria.

All 11 countries unambiguously met the interest rate and inflation criteria, but doubts were expressed by many 'Eurosceptics' as to whether they all genuinely met the other three criteria.

- **Exchange rates.** Neither Finland nor Italy had been in the ERM for 2 years (Finland had joined the ERM in October 1996 and Italy had rejoined in November 1996), and the Irish punt was revalued by 3 per cent on 16/3/98. However, the Commission regarded these three countries as being sufficiently close to the reference value: both Finland and Italy had displayed sufficient stability during the two-year reference period, and the Irish punt had remained above its central rate in the ERM throughout the two-year period.
- **Government deficits.** Some countries only managed to achieve a deficit of 3 per cent or below by taking one-off measures, such as a special tax in Italy, and counting privatization receipts in Germany. Worries were expressed as to whether all countries could continue to keep their deficits below 3 per cent.
- **Government debt.** Only four countries had debts that did not exceed 60 per cent (France, Finland, Luxembourg and the UK). However, the Maastricht Treaty allowed countries to exceed this value as long as the debt was 'sufficiently diminishing and approaching the reference value at a satisfactory pace.' Only Germany had debts that were not diminishing, but since this was explained by the continuing high costs of German reunification and given that German government debt was predicted to fall in 1998, the Commission considered that even Germany met the debt criterion.

At a meeting of EU heads of state in May 1998, it was agreed that the 11 countries would join the single currency. By December 1998 the European Central Bank (ECB) would be formally established and the Euro would come into existence on 1 January 1999, but Euro banknotes and coins will not be introduced until 2002. In the meantime, national currencies will continue to exist alongside the Euro, but will be irrevocably fixed to it. Notes and coins of existing currencies will be in odd denominations of the euro.

On 1 January 2002 the ECB will introduce Euro banknotes and coins, and for 6 months these will circulate alongside the old currencies. On 1 July 2002 national banknotes and coins of the EMU countries will lose their legal tender status and will be withdrawn from circulation.

Performance of EU Member States in relation to Convergence Criteria for EMU (March 1998)

	Inflation (%)	Budget balance (% of GDP)		Debt (% of GDP)				Long-term interest rate	ERM band (± %)	Join euro in 1999?
					Change from previous year					EC Recommendations
	Jan 1998	1996	1997	1997	1997	1996	1995	Jan 1998	April 1998	25/3/98
Reference value	**2.7**		**−3.0**	**60.0**				**7.8**		
Germany	1.4	−3.8	−2.7	61.3	0.8	2.4	7.8	5.6	15	Yes
France	1.2	−4.2	−3.0	58.0	2.4	2.9	4.2	5.5	15	Yes
Italy	1.8	−6.8	−2.7	121.6	−2.4	−0.2	−0.7	6.7	15	Yes
UK	1.8	−4.1	−1.9	53.4	−1.3	0.8	3.5	7.0	free floating	No
Spain	1.8	−4.4	−2.6	68.8	−1.3	4.6	2.9	6.3	15	Yes
Netherlands	1.8	−2.3	−1.4	72.1	−5.0	−1.9	1.2	5.5	15	Yes
Belgium	1.4	−3.2	−2.1	122.2	−4.7	−4.3	−2.2	5.7	15	Yes
Sweden	1.9	−3.3	−0.8	76.6	−0.1	−0.9	−1.4	6.5	free floating	No
Austria	1.1	−3.8	−2.5	66.1	−3.4	0.3	3.8	5.6	15	Yes
Denmark	1.9	−1.6	0.7	65.1	−5.5	−2.7	−4.9	6.0	15	No
Finland	1.2	−2.6	−0.9	58.0	−1.8	−0.4	−1.5	5.9	15	Yes
Portugal	1.8	−3.2	−2.5	62.0	−3.0	−0.9	2.1	6.2	15	Yes
Greece	5.2	−7.4	−4.0	108.7	−2.9	1.5	0.7	9.8	15	No
Ireland	1.2	−1.1	0.9	66.3	−6.4	−9.6	−6.8	6.2	15	Yes
Luxembourg	1.4	1.8	1.7	6.7	0.1	0.7	0.2	5.6	15	Yes

ISSUES AND APPLICATIONS

ACHIEVING CURRENCY STABILITY

How to deal with speculation?

One important lesson of the expulsion of the UK and Italy from the ERM in 1992, the retreat from the narrow $\pm 2^1/_4$ per cent band for the remaining ERM countries in 1993, and the massive appreciation of the yen in 1995 is that concerted speculation has become virtually unstoppable. More than $1 trillion worth of currencies are traded daily in the foreign exchange markets. In comparison to this, the reserves of central banks seem trivial.

If there is a consensus in the markets that a currency will depreciate, there is little that central banks can do. For example, if there were a 50 per cent chance of a 10 per cent depreciation in the next week, then selling that currency now would yield an 'expected' return of just over 5 per cent for the week: equivalent to more than 1200 per cent at an annual rate!

So is there any way of 'beating the speculators' and pursuing a policy of greater exchange rate rigidity? Or must countries be forced to accept freely floating exchange rates, with all the uncertainty for traders that such a regime brings?

This box examines two possible solutions. The first is to reduce capital mobility, by putting various types of restriction on foreign exchange transactions. The second is to move to a new type of exchange rate regime which has the benefits of a degree of rigidity without being susceptible to massive speculative attacks.

Controlling exchange transactions

Until the early 1990s, many countries retained restrictions of various kinds on capital flows. Such restrictions made it more expensive for speculators to gamble on possible exchange rate movements. It is not the case, as some commentators argue, that it is impossible to reimpose controls. Some countries still retain controls, and the last ERM countries to give them up did so only in 1991. It is true that the complexity of modern financial markets provides the speculator with more opportunity to evade controls, but they will still have the effect of dampening speculation.

The following extract from *Euromoney* considers four types of control:[3]

1. *Capital controls* as provided for in the 1988 EC directive and in the Maastricht Treaty. According to Article 73c, the European Commission can consider 'special measures relating to capital transactions with non-EC countries'. Article 73f allows 'precautionary measures' if there is an extraordinary threat to the 'normal operation of economic and monetary union'. Article 73g allows members to take 'unilateral action to regulate the movement of capital and payments to and from non-EC countries'.
   Objection: This is anathema to the major EC members, although the Belgian finance minister briefly suggested use of such controls in August [1993].
2. *A transaction tax* on all foreign exchange deals in as many OECD countries as possible.
   Objection: Very complicated to apply. If too high ... it would hit trade and investment. It would also widen the bid/offer spread on all transactions. Richard Cooper, a Harvard economics professor, suggests ⅛% to ¼% ('to deter sloshing about'), but it is 'no panacea for governments stuck on particular exchange rates', and no solution to the problems of September 1992.
3. *A non-interest-bearing deposit* at the central bank equal to a bank's purchase of foreign exchange with domestic currency. Italy used a variation in the 1970s and Spain [in 1992].

24.8 European economic and monetary union (EMU)

Chapter 23 looked at the Single European Act and the removal of all trade barriers in the EU by 1993. But many of the advocates of a single market, including the President of the European Commission, Jacques Delors, argued for much more. The Delors report of 1989 advocated a complete European economic and monetary union (EMU). This would involve the complete economic and financial integration of the EU countries: not only a common market, but a market with a single currency, a single central bank and a single monetary policy. This European Monetary Union would be like the current 'British Monetary Union', the economic union of England, Scotland, Wales and Northern Ireland, or the Belgian–Luxembourg Economic Union.

The Delors plan paved the way for the Treaty on European Union hammered out at Maastricht in the Netherlands in December 1991. The treaty also covered moves towards political and social union, but it is its plans for monetary union that concern us here. This was to be achieved in three stages (see Box 24.11). During the first stage it was hoped that there would be growing convergence between the EU economies. At the beginning

BOX 24.12

Objection: There is a loophole, in the currency swap market. The measure also frightens foreign investors. In Spain it hit bond and equity markets.

4. *A capital charge* of 8% on the net open foreign exchange position of all institutions where prudential supervision is possible. This is one proposal, for banks, in a paper circulated by the Basle Committee on Bank Supervision.
Objection: Impossible to apply beyond the sphere of supervised banks and investment institutions. It is a prudential measure and should not be used for market volume control.

The main objection to all these measures is that they can only dampen speculation, not eliminate it. If speculators believe that currencies are badly out of equilibrium and will be forced to realign, then no taxes on capital movements or artificial controls will be sufficient to stem the flood.

Exchange rate target zones

One version of an adjustable peg system that has been much discussed in recent years is that proposed by John Williamson of Washington's Institute for International Economics.[4] Williamson's proposal has four major features:

- Wide bands. Currencies would be allowed to fluctuate by ±10 per cent of their central parity.
- Central parity set in *real* terms, at the 'fundamental equilibrium exchange rate' (FEER): i.e. a rate that is consistent with long-run balance of payments equilibrium.
- Frequent realignments. In order to stay at the FEER, the central parity would be adjusted frequently (say monthly) to take account of the country's rate of inflation. If its rate of inflation were 2 per cent per annum above the trade-weighted average of other countries, then the central parity would be devalued by 2 per cent per annum. Realignments would also reflect other changes in fundamentals, such as changes in the levels of protection, or major political events, such as German reunification.
- 'Soft buffers'. Governments would not be forced to intervene at the ±10 per cent mark or at some specified fraction of it. In fact, from time to time the rate might be allowed to move outside the bands. The point is that the closer the rate approached to the band limits, the greater would be the scale of intervention.

There are two main advantages of this system. First, the exchange rate would stay at roughly the equilibrium level, and therefore the likelihood of large-scale devaluations or revaluations, and with it the opportunities for large-scale speculative gains, would be small. Second, the wider bands would leave countries freer to follow an independent monetary policy: one that could therefore respond to domestic needs.

The main problem with the system is that it removes the pressure on high-inflation countries to bring their inflation under control.

?? Would the Williamson system allow countries to follow a totally independent monetary policy?

[3] D. Shirreff, 'Can anyone tame the currency market?', *Euromoney*, September 1993, p. 66.

[4] See, for example, J. Williamson and M. Miller, *Targets and Indicators: A blueprint for the co-ordination of economic policy*, Policy Analyses in International Economics No. 22, IIE, 1987.

of stage 2 (January 1994), a European Monetary Institute (EMI) would be set up. This is sited in Frankfurt and has taken over the role of the European Monetary Co-operation Fund. It has the role of paving the way for a complete monetary union (stage 3) by 1999 at the latest. This final stage would involve the creation of a single European currency – a European **currency union**.

How desirable is EMU?

EMU has the potential to bring several major advantages.

Elimination of the costs of converting currencies. With separate currencies in each of the EU countries, these transaction costs can be very large, especially when the various parts of a good are made in several different countries. By 1993 each of the twelve EU countries already did more trade with each other than with non-EU countries. With the further encouragement of trade and factor movements that the single market will continue to bring, these transaction costs are likely to rise as long as separate currencies remain.

DEFINITION

Currency union A group of countries (or regions) using a common currency.

Nevertheless, the elimination of these costs is probably the least important benefit from a single currency. The European Commission has estimated that the effect would be to increase the GDP of the countries concerned by an average of only 0.4 per cent. The gains to countries like the UK, which have well-developed financial markets, would be even smaller.

Increased competition and efficiency. Despite the advent of the single market, large price differences have remained between member states. Not only would a single currency eliminate the need to convert one currency into another (a barrier to competition), but it would bring more transparency in pricing, and put greater downward pressure on prices in high-cost firms and countries.

Elimination of exchange-rate uncertainty (between the members). Even with a narrow-banded ERM, realignments may still occur from time to time if separate currencies remain. As the events of 1992 and 1993 showed, this can cause massive speculation if it is believed that currencies are out of line. Removal of this uncertainty would help to encourage trade between member countries. Perhaps more importantly, it would encourage investment by firms that trade between these countries, given that exchange-rate uncertainty is a major deterrent to long-term investment by such firms.

Increased inward investment. Investment from the rest of the world would be likely to increase, attracted to a single market of up to 200 million customers, where there would be no fear of internal currency movements. EU countries, by contrast, which did not join, could find that inward investment was diverted away from them to the common-currency countries.

Lower inflation and interest rates. A single monetary policy would force convergence in inflation rates (just as inflation rates are very similar between the different regions *within* a country). Provided the European central bank is independent from short-term political manipulation, this is likely to result in a lower average inflation rate in the EU. This, in turn, would help to convince markets that the Euro would be strong relative to other currencies. The result would be less need to manipulate short-term interest rates to defend the currency and also a lower long-term rate of interest. This, in turn, would further encourage investment in the single-currency countries, both by member states and by the rest of the world.

Monetary union has been bitterly opposed, however, by certain groups. For example, the majority of the British Conservative Party (the 'Eurosceptics') see the adoption of the euro as a surrender of national political and economic sovereignty. The lack of an independent monetary and exchange rate policy is a serious problem, they argue, if an economy is at all out of harmony with the rest of the Union. For example, if countries like the UK, Italy and Spain have higher endemic rates of inflation (due, say, to greater cost-push pressures – perhaps caused by a lower growth in productivity than in other EU countries), then how are they to make their goods competitive with the rest of the Union? With separate currencies these countries could devalue or run a deflationary monetary policy. With a single currency, however, they could become depressed 'regions' of Europe, with rising unemployment and all the other regional problems of depressed regions *within* a country. This might then require significant regional policies – policies that might not be in place or, if they were, would be seen as too interventionist by the political right.

The answer given by proponents of EMU is that it is better to tackle the problem of high inflation in such countries by the disciplines of competition from other EU countries, than merely to feed that inflation by keeping separate currencies and allowing repeated devaluations, with all the uncertainty that they bring. If such countries become depressed, they argue, it is better to have a fully developed *fiscal* policy for the Union which will divert funds into investment in such regions. What is more, the high-inflation countries tend to be the poorer ones with lower wage levels (albeit faster wage *increases*). With the high mobility of labour and capital that will accompany the development of the single market, resources are likely to be attracted to such countries. This could help to narrow the gap between the richer and poorer member states.

Another problem for members of a single currency occurs in adjusting to a shock when that shock affects members to different degrees. For example, a sudden change in the price of oil would affect an oil-exporting country like the UK differently from oil importing countries. This problem is more serious, the less the factor mobility between member countries and the less the price flexibility within member countries.

This problem, however, should not be overstated. The divergences between economies are often the result of a lack of harmony between countries in their demand-management policies: something that would be impossible in the case of monetary policy, and more difficult in the case of fiscal policy, for countries with a single currency. Also, many of the shocks that face economies today are global and have similar (albeit not identical) effects on all countries. Adjustment to such shocks would often be better with a single co-ordinated policy, something that would be much easier with a single currency and a single central bank.

Even when shocks are uniformly felt in the member states, however, there is still the problem that policies adopted centrally will have different impacts on each country. For example, in the UK, a large proportion of borrowing is at variable interest rates. In Germany, by contrast, much is at fixed rates. Thus if the European central bank were to raise interest rates, the deflationary effects would be felt disproportionately in the UK. Of course, were this balance to change – and there is some evidence that types of borrowing are becoming more uniform across the EU – this problem would diminish.

The problem for economists is that the issue of monetary union is a very emotive one. 'Europhiles' often see monetary union as a vital element in their vision of a united Europe. Many Eurosceptics, however, see EMU as a surrender of sovereignty and a threat to nationhood. In such an environment, a calm assessment of the arguments and evidence is very difficult.

??

1. By what means would a depressed country in an Economic Union with a single currency be able to recover? Would the market provide a satisfactory solution to its problems or would (Union) government intervention be necessary, and if so, what form could that intervention take?
2. Is greater factor mobility likely to increase or decrease the problem of cumulative causation associated with regional multipliers? (See page 671.)

SECTION SUMMARY

1. The Maastricht Treaty set out a timetable for achieving EMU. This would culminate in stage 3 with the creation of a currency union: a single European currency with a common monetary policy operated by an independent European Central Bank.
2. The advantages claimed for EMU are that it will eliminate the costs of converting currencies and the uncertainties associated with possible changes in inter-EU exchange rates. What is more, a common central bank, independent from domestic governments, will provide the stable monetary environment necessary for a convergence of the EU economies and the encouragement of investment and inter-Union trade.
3. Critics claim, however, that it might make adjustment to domestic economic problems more difficult. The loss of independence in policy making is seen by such people to be a major issue, not only because of the loss of political sovereignty, but also because domestic economic concerns may be at variance with those of the Union as a whole. Countries and regions at the periphery of the Union may become depressed unless there is an effective regional policy.

??? END-OF-CHAPTER QUESTIONS ???

1. Assume a free floating exchange rate. Draw a diagram like Figure 24.6, only this time show an initial equilibrium national income with a balance of payments surplus.
   (a) Mark the size of the surplus.
   (b) Show the resulting shifts in the (*X–M*) and the *E* curves.
   (c) Mark the eventual equilibrium.
   (d) Show the size of the income and substitution effects (of the change in the exchange rate).
   (e) Under what circumstances will the income effect be (i) 'desirable'; (ii) 'undesirable'?
   (f) Could the income effect of the change in the exchange rate ever be larger than the substitution effect?
2. Compare the relative effectiveness of fiscal and monetary policy under (i) fixed; (ii) free-floating exchange rates.
3. What will be the effects on the domestic economy under free-floating exchange rates if there is a rapid expansion in world economic activity? What will determine the size of these effects?

*4. Using *ISLMBP* analysis, trace through the effect of (a) a deflationary fiscal policy and (b) a deflationary monetary policy under (i) a fixed exchange rate; (ii) a free-floating exchange rate.

5. Consider the argument that in the modern world of large-scale short-term international capital movements, the ability of individual countries to affect their exchange rate is very limited.
6. It is often argued that international convergence of economic indicators is a desirable objective. Does this mean that countries should all seek to achieve the same rate of economic growth, monetary growth, interest rates, budget deficits as a percentage of their GDP, etc.?
7. Do the exchange rate difficulties experienced by countries under the ERM strengthen or weaken the arguments for progressing to a single European currency?
8. Assume that just some of the members of a common market like the EU adopt full economic and monetary union, including a common currency. What are the advantages and disadvantages to those members joining the full EMU and to those not?

25 Economic problems of developing countries

25.1 The problem of underdevelopment

In this final chapter we turn to the economic problems of the poorer countries of the world. These include all the countries of Africa and Latin America and most of the countries of Asia. More than three-quarters of the world's population lives in these countries. As Theodore Schultz said when accepting the Nobel prize in economics in 1979:

> Most of the people of the world are poor, so if we knew the economics of being poor we would know much of the economics that really matters.

This first section looks at the nature and extent of their poverty and the means by which it can be measured. Section 25.2 examines the trade relations between the poorer countries and the advanced industrialised world. In section 25.3 the focus shifts to some of the internal problems faced by developing countries: problems such as the neglect of agriculture, the use of inappropriate technology and the rise in unemployment. The final section looks at one of the most serious problems facing poorer countries: the problem of huge international debts.

The gulf between rich and poor countries

The typical family in North America, Western Europe, Japan and Australasia has many material comforts: plentiful food to eat; a house or apartment with electricity and running hot and cold water; an inside toilet connected to an underground sewerage system; access to free or affordable health care and education; numerous consumer durables; holidays away from home; visits to the cinema, concerts, sports events, etc. These and many other features of life in the affluent countries are taken for granted by many of their citizens. There are some people, it is true, who are very poor. A minority cannot afford even the basics of life, such as adequate food, shelter and clothing. For most people, however, such poverty is something they never experience and perhaps only rarely witness.

In most of Africa, Asia and Latin America the picture is quite different. The majority of people live in poverty. For them life is a daily struggle for survival. Affluence does exist in these countries, but here it is the fortunate few who can afford good food, good housing and the various luxury items that typify life in the industrialised world.

A large proportion of the inhabitants live in the countryside. For many in Latin America and Asia, this means living in a family with many children and working on a small amount of land with too little income to buy adequate agricultural machinery, fertilisers or pesticides. With a rapid growth in population there is less and less land to go round. As land is passed on from generation to generation it is divided up between the offspring into smaller and smaller plots. Many who cannot make ends meet are forced to sell their land to the local landlords. Then as landless labourers they have to accept very low-paid jobs on the large farms or plantations. Others try to survive by borrowing, hoping to be able to pay off their debts with future crop sales. But often the only source of finance is again the local landlord who charges exorbitant rates of interest. As a result they end up in a state of 'debt bondage' where they can never pay off their debts, but year in year out have to give part of their crops to the landlord as interest.

Others come to the rapidly growing cities. In the cities at least there are some jobs. But far more people migrate to the cities than there are jobs available. Thus the number of unemployed in the cities grows inexorably. People are forced to do anything to earn a living: selling wares on street corners, or working as casual labourers, domestic servants or shoe shiners; some resort to prostitution and crime, others merely beg. All round the outskirts of cities throughout the developing world, shanty towns mushroom as the poor flock in from the countryside. Families crowd into one- or two-roomed shacks, often with no electricity, no water and no sanitation. There are schools in these towns, but often parents cannot afford to allow their children to attend. Instead they have to send them out to work to supplement the family's meagre income.

Statistics cannot give the complete picture, but they can give us some indication of the gulf between rich and poor countries. Here are some examples:

- 84 per cent of the world's population lives in developing countries but earns only 19 per cent of the world's income.
- The GNP per head of the 26 poorest countries of the world in 1995 averaged only $220. For the richest 26 it was $24 930.
- The average annual GNP-per-capita growth rate between 1985 and 1995 was 7.2 per cent in East Asia but was –1.1 per cent in Sub-Saharan Africa. It was 1.9 per cent in the advanced industrialised countries.
- The average life expectancy at birth in the 10 poorest countries of the world is 48 years. It is 77 years in the 10 richest countries.
- Developing countries suffer higher rates of inflation than advanced industrial economies. Upper-middle-income developing countries have higher rates than lower-middle-income countries, which in turn have higher rates than low-income countris. Between 1985 and 1995 the average annual rate of inflation was 256 per cent in Argentina, 400 per cent in Peru, 875 per cent in Brazil and 962 per cent in Nicaragua. In Latin America and the Caribbean as a whole it averaged 310 per cent. By contrast, it averaged 9.5 per cent in South Asia and 4.1 per cent in the advanced industrialised countries.

Table 25.1 gives more details.

The meaning of 'development'

Countries want to develop. But just what do we mean by 'development?' Clearly it is a normative concept. Its definition will depend on the goals that the economist assumes societies want to achieve. So how do economists define and measure development?

The basic needs approach

A starting point is to identify the basic needs that people have if they are to be able to realise their potential as

Table 25.1 Selected world statistics

	Low-income economies[1]	(Sub-Saharan Africa)	Lower-middle-income economies[2]	Upper-middle-income economies[3]	High-income economies[4]	All countries
Population (millions, 1995)	3180	583	1153	438	902	5673
GNP per capita ($ per annum, 1995)	430	490	1670	4260	24 930	4880
Population growth (average annual %, 1980–95)	1.9	2.9	1.6	1.9	0.7	1.6
Growth in GNP per capita (average annual %, 1985–95)	3.8	–1.1	–1.3	0.2	1.9	0.8
Inflation (average annual %, 1980–95)	31.6	29.7	118.5	206.3	3.9	30.6
Life expectancy at birth (years) (1995)	63	52	67	69	77	67
Number of people per doctor (1990)	6760	23 540	2850	640	420	3980
Infant mortality per 1000 live births (1995)	69	92	41	35	7	55
Adult illiteracy (% 1995)						
Female	45	54	26	14	<5	–
Male	24	35	15	12	<5	–
Urban population as a percentage of total population (1995)	29	31	56	73	75	45

[1] Those countries with a GNP per head in 1995 of below $750.
[2] Those countries with a GNP per head in 1995 of between $751 and $3100.
[3] Those countries with a GNP per head in 1995 of between $3101 and $9500.
[4] Those countries with a GNP per head in 1995 of over $9500.

Source: *World Development Report 1997* (World Bank).

human beings. Different economists have identified various lists of requirements, including the following items:

- Adequate food, shelter, warmth and clothing.
- Universal access to education.
- Availability of adequate health care.
- Availability of non-demeaning jobs.
- Sufficient free time to be able to enjoy social interaction.
- Freedom to make one's own economic decisions.
- Freedom for people to participate in the decisions of government and other bodies that affect their lives.

?? What other items might be included as basic needs?

There are four major problems with defining development in terms of a basic list of requirements.

The first is in deciding *what to include*. Any definition of *economic* development would clearly include people's *material* standard of living. But should development include social and political factors such as 'self-esteem', freedom from servitude and freedom of religion?

The second problem is in *measuring each of the items*. Some indicators, while providing only part of the picture of human welfare, are relatively easy to measure. It is possible to measure such things as income per head, literacy rates and mortality rates. The main measurement problem with these economic indicators is in acquiring the statistics. It is much more difficult, however, to measure the achievement of social and political objectives such as self-esteem.

The third problem is in arriving at a *single measure* of the level of development. You cannot add the average calorific intake to the number of doctors and nurses to the percentage of homes having various basic amenities such as running water. You can meaningfully add things up only if they are expressed in the same units, or if appropriate *weights* are attached to each of the items. Clearly the assigning of any such weights would be highly controversial.

The fourth problem is in deciding the importance of the *distribution* of the various items. If, say, the average calorific intake increases, but the poorest sections of the population have less to eat, has the country really experienced an increase in the level of development?

However, many economists argue that the basic needs approach does provide a useful 'checklist' to see whether a country's development is broadly based or confined to just one or two indicators.

?? Would it be possible with this basic needs approach to say (a) that one country was more developed than another; (b) that one country was developing faster than another?

Using GNP to measure development

The desire to have a single measure for development and thus to be able to make simple comparisons between countries has led to the universal use of real GNP per capita as the main indicator. It has some major advantages:

- It takes into account virtually all the goods and services produced in a country, and converts them into a single measure by the use of market prices.
- Although markets are by no means perfect, they do reflect the strength of demand and the opportunity costs of supply.
- The rules for the measurement of GNP are universally agreed.
- Virtually all countries compile GNP statistics.
- Although not every item that affects human welfare is included in GNP, a sustained rise in GNP is generally agreed to be a *necessary* condition for a sustained rise in welfare.
- There is a fairly close correlation between the level of per-capita GNP and other indicators such as mortality rates, literacy rates, and calorific and protein intake.

However, there are four fundamental criticisms of relying on simple GNP per capita as an indicator of development.

Many items are excluded. Much of production that does not get bought and sold will escape being recorded. This is a particular problem with rural societies which are largely subsistence based. People grow their own food, build their own houses, make their own clothes and provide their own entertainment. GNP statistics are therefore likely to *understate* the level of production in these societies.

On the other hand, as these societies 'develop', the size of the market sector is likely to grow. A larger proportion of people's consumption will be of items they have purchased and which therefore do enter into GNP statistics. Thus GNP figures will *overstate* the rate of growth of production and consumption.

As an economy becomes more urbanised, there is likely to be a growth in *external* costs of production and consumption, such as pollution and crime. Traditional ways of life will be destroyed; people may find themselves increasingly in a competitive, uncaring environment; aspirations will be raised by observing the lifestyles of the rich few, and yet the poor will not have the means of satisfying these aspirations. Again the growth in GNP is likely to *overstate* the growth in human welfare.

Market prices may be highly distorted. GNP is based on market prices, but these prices may be distorted. Markets

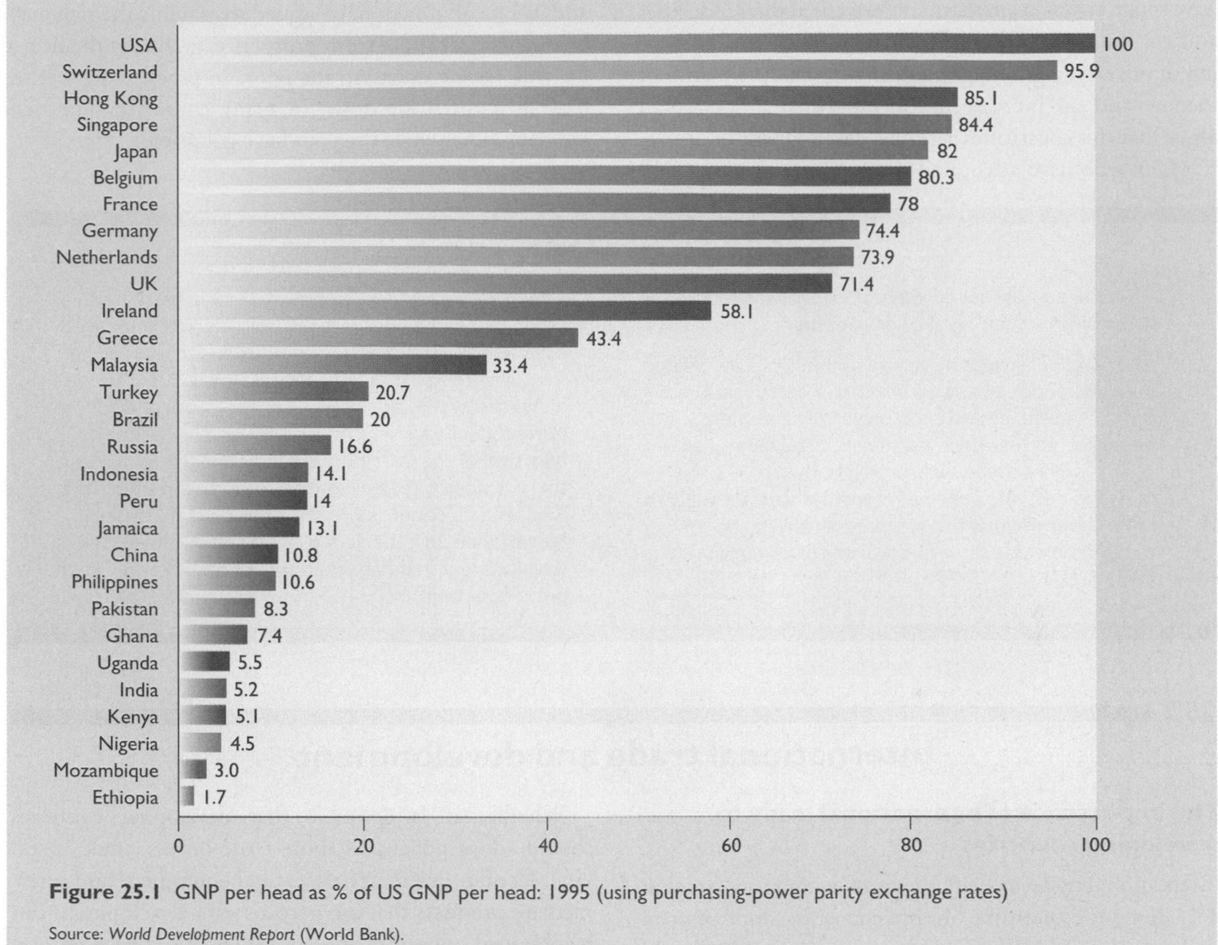

Figure 25.1 GNP per head as % of US GNP per head: 1995 (using purchasing-power parity exchange rates)

Source: *World Development Report* (World Bank).

are often highly fragmented, and there is little competition to ensure that prices reflect undistorted marginal costs. Companies often have considerable monopoly power to push up prices of manufactured goods; landlords often have power to push up rents; governments may impose price controls on food; employers with monopsony power may be able to pay very low wages.

?? How would a redistribution of income to the powerful be likely to affect GNP?

Exchange rates may not reflect local purchasing power. GNP statistics are initially compiled in terms of the domestic currency. For purposes of international comparison they then have to be converted into a common currency – usually the US dollar – at the current exchange rate. But exchange rates reflect demand and supply of *traded* goods; they do not reflect the prices of *non-traded* goods. Generally the price of non-traded goods and services in developing countries will be lower than the price of similar goods and services in advanced countries. The *level* of GNP is therefore likely to *understate* the level of production in poor countries. If, on the other hand, the proportion of traded goods increases over time, the *growth* of GNP will again *overstate* the growth in production. It is much better, therefore, to estimate GNP using purchasing-power parity exchange rates. Even if this is done, however, massive differences remain in GNP per head between rich and poor countries. This is illustrated in Figure 25.1, which shows GNP per head at PPP exchange rates as a percentage of US GNP per head.

The general conclusion from each of these three criticisms is that GNP figures for developing countries underestimate the true level of production and welfare, but overestimate their rate of growth.

Simple GNP per head ignores the distribution of income. Since the early 1980s, many developing countries have achieved relatively rapid growth in per-capita GNP as they have sought overseas investment, privatised their industries and cut the levels of public provision. But with a deepening of poverty, a growing inequality in the distribution of income and an increase in unemployment, few would argue that this constitutes genuine 'development'.

Many who have advocated the concentration on GNP and its rate of growth have argued that, while the rich may be the first to benefit from prosperity, gradually the benefits will 'trickle down' to the poor. In practice the wealth has failed to trickle down in many countries. The rich have got richer while the poor have got poorer.

SECTION SUMMARY

1. There are a number of ways of categorising countries according to their level of development.
2. The level of development of a country can be defined in terms of the extent to which it meets basic needs for human life. There is no universal agreement, however, about which items should be measured or about how to measure and weight them. Nevertheless the approach provides a useful indicator of whether development is broadly based and how rapidly the most serious problems of poverty are being tackled.
3. The most widely used measure of development is GNP. Nevertheless there are serious problems with using GNP: many items may be excluded, especially for a more subsistence-based society; prices may be highly distorted; exchange rates may not reflect local purchasing power; and the statistics ignore the question of the distribution of income. Nevertheless there is no other single measure of development that is used in all countries, and it does provide some guide, albeit an imperfect one, to relative levels of development in different countries and over different periods of time.

25.2 International trade and development

The importance of international trade to developing countries

International trade is one of the most contentious issues in development economics. Should countries adopt an open trading policy with few if any barriers to imports? Should governments actively promote trade by subsidising their export sector? Or should they restrict trade and pursue a policy of greater self-sufficiency? These are issues that we will be looking at in this section.

Table 25.2 The growth in the relative size of the export sector

Country[1] or group of countries	Exports as a % of GDP	
	1970	1995
Low-income economies (1–49)	7	19
India (27)	4	12
China (42)	3	21
Sub-Saharan Africa	21	28
Brazil (96)	7	7
South Korea (108)	14	33
Hong Kong (121)	92	147
Industrial market economies (108–33)	14	22

[1] Countries numbered in ascending order of GNP per capita.

Source: *World Development Report 1997* (World Bank).

Whether it is desirable that developing countries should adopt policies of more trade or less, trade is still vital. Certain raw materials, capital equipment and intermediate products that are necessary for development can be obtained only from abroad. Others *could* be produced domestically, but only at much higher cost.

As countries' economies grow, the proportion of trade to national income tends to rise. Table 25.2 shows exports for various countries as a proportion of GDP for the two years 1970 and 1995. Three general points emerge: smaller countries have a larger proportion of exports to GDP than large ones; exports form a smaller proportion of GDP in poorer countries than in richer countries; exports formed a higher proportion of GDP in 1995 than they did in 1970.

Trade strategies

As they develop, countries' policies towards trade typically go through various stages.

Primary outward-looking stage

Traditionally developing countries have exported primaries – minerals such as copper, cash crops such as coffee, and non-foodstuffs such as cotton – in exchange for manufactured consumer goods. Having little in the way of an industrial base, if they want to consume manufactured goods, they have to import them.

Secondary inward-looking stage

In seeking rapid economic development, most developing countries drew lessons from the experience of the advanced countries. The main conclusion was that industrialisation was the key to economic success.

But industrialisation required foreign exchange to purchase capital equipment. This led to a policy of **import-substituting industrialisation**, which involved cutting back on non-essential imports and thereby releasing foreign exchange. Tariffs and other restrictions were imposed on those imports for which a domestic substitute existed, or which were regarded as unimportant.

Secondary outward-looking stage

Once an industry had satisfied domestic demand, it had to seek markets abroad if expansion was to continue. What is more, as we shall see, import substitution brought a number of serious problems for developing countries. The answer seemed to be to look outward again, this time to the export of manufactured goods. Many of the most economically successful developing countries (especially Hong Kong, Singapore, South Korea and Taiwan) owe their high growth rates to a rapid expansion of manufactured exports.

We will now examine the three stages in more detail.

Approach 1: Exporting primaries – exploiting comparative advantage

The importance of primary exports

Despite moves towards import substitution and secondary export promotion, many developing countries still rely heavily on primary exports. These constituted 72 per cent of total developing country exports in 1970. Although this had fallen to 47 per cent by 1993, it was still much higher than the figure for advanced countries (18 per cent). For the low-income developing countries excluding China and India, both of which had had extensive programmes of industrialisation, primaries still constituted 61 per cent of exports in 1993. For many of the poorest African countries, the figure was over 90 per cent.

The justification for exporting primaries

Three major arguments have been traditionally used for pursuing a policy of exporting primaries. In each case the arguments have also been used to justify a policy of free or virtually free trade.

Exporting primaries exploits comparative advantage. Traditional trade theory implies that countries should specialise in producing those items in which they have a comparative advantage: i.e. those goods that can be produced at relatively low opportunity costs. For most developing countries, this means that a large proportion of their exports should be primaries.

The reasons for differences in comparative costs were examined by two Swedish economists, Eli Heckscher and Bertil Ohlin. They believed that comparative cost differences arise from differences in factor endowments. The **Heckscher–Ohlin theory** states that: *a country should specialise in those goods which are intensive in the country's abundant factor*. The more abundant a factor, the relatively cheaper it is likely to be, and thus the lower will be the opportunity cost of producing goods that are intensive in its use. Thus labour-abundant developing countries should specialise in labour-intensive products. By exporting these products, which will typically be primaries, they can earn the foreign exchange to import goods which use large amounts of capital and other resources that are in short supply.

According to this theory, international trade would lead not only to higher consumption, but also to **factor price equalisation**: i.e. the erosion of income inequalities between trading nations. For example, if wage rates are low in developing countries, trade will increase the demand for their labour-intensive products and thereby push up wage rates. International trade will also erode income differentials *within* countries. The demand for exports will increase the demand for the relatively cheap factors, and imports will reduce the demand for the

DEFINITIONS

Import-substituting industrialisation A strategy of restricting imports of manufactured goods and using the foreign exchange saved to build up domestic substitute industries.

Heckscher–Ohlin version of comparative advantage A country has a comparative advantage in those goods that are intensive in the country's relatively abundant factor.

Factor price equalisation The tendency for international trade to reduce factor price inequalities both between and within countries.

relatively expensive ones. Thus the cheap factors will go up in price and the expensive ones will come down.

??

1. What effect will trade have on the price of capital in developing and developed countries?
2. It is sometimes claimed that trade with developing countries is unjust because it leads to the importation of goods produced at pitifully low wages. How can the Heckscher–Ohlin theory be used to refute this claim? Is there any validity in the claim? (See Box 23.3.)

Exporting primaries provides a 'vent for surplus'. Trade offers a **vent for surplus**: i.e. a means of putting to use resources that would otherwise not be used. These surpluses will occur where the domestic market is simply not big enough to consume all the available output of a particular good. There is far too little demand within Zambia to consume its potential output of copper. The same applies to Namibian uranium or Peruvian tin. They can also occur where there is a lack of some complementary input, which can prevent the use of certain resources. For example, the opening of a mine or plantation can utilise surplus labour by producing for the export market.

Exporting primaries provides an 'engine for economic growth'. According to this argument, developing countries benefit from the growth of the economies of the developed world. As industrial expansion takes place in the rich North, this will create additional demand for primaries from the poor South.

Traditional trade theory in the context of development

There are a number of reasons for questioning whether the above arguments justify a policy of relying on primary exports as the means to development.

Comparative costs change over time. Over time, with the acquisition of new skills and an increase in the capital stock, a developing country which once had a comparative advantage in primaries may find that it now has a comparative advantage in certain *manufactured* products, especially those which are more labour intensive and use raw materials of which the country has a plentiful supply. The market, however, cannot necessarily be relied upon to bring about a smooth transition to producing such products.

Concentrating on primary production may hinder growth. The theory of comparative advantage shows how trade allows a country to consume beyond its production possibility curve (see pages 690–1). As its economy grows, however, this production possibility curve will *shift outwards*. By concentrating on primaries, the curve may shift outwards more slowly than if the country had pursued a policy of industrialisation. If this is true, in the long run the static benefits of free trade will be outweighed by the dynamic benefits of industrialisation.

The benefits from trade may not accrue to the nationals of the country. If a mine or plantation is owned by a foreign company, it will be the foreign shareholders who get the profits from the sale of exports. In addition these companies may bring in their own capital and skilled labour from abroad. The benefits gained by the local people will probably be confined to the additional wages they earn. With these companies being in a position of monopsony power, the wages are often very low.

??

Why does this argument make GNP a better indicator of development than GDP? (See section 14.5.)

Trade may lead to less equality. Trade shifts income distribution in favour of those factors of production employed intensively in the export sector. If exports are labour intensive, greater equality will tend to result. But if they are land or raw material intensive, trade will redistribute income in favour of large landowners or mine-owners.

Exporting primary exports may involve external costs. Mining can lead to huge external costs, such as the despoiling of the countryside and damage to the health of miners. Mines and plantations can lead to the destruction of traditional communities and their values.

Balance of payments problems may result. If a country pursues a free-trade policy, the production and sale of primary exports may not be able to keep pace with the increased demand for imports. The resulting balance of trade deficit will create various adjustment costs.

Trade may adversely influence tastes. The more freely a country trades, the more will people's aspirations for a 'better life' be fuelled. If people cannot afford to buy the goods imported from the affluent world, their frustrations are likely to increase.

DEFINITION

Vent for surplus Where international trade enables a country to exploit resources that would otherwise be unused.

CASE STUDIES BOX 25.1

WHO GETS FAT ON GATT?

If an OECD/World Bank study[1] is to be believed, the 1993 GATT agreement will bring a substantial increase in world income. The study estimated that, by the year 2002, this will be a staggering $213 billion per year (at 1992 prices). However, the developing world, despite containing some four-fifths of the world population, will gain only about one-third of the total benefit. In fact, some of the poorest regions of the world will end up actually losing. Sub-Saharan Africa, North Africa and the Mediterranean countries will between them lose an anticipated $7 billion a year.

The liberalisation of agriculture accounts for an estimated gain of $190 billion, with the main gainers being consumers in the rich countries. But, as the USA and EU remove export subsidies on agricultural products, and as surpluses fall, so agricultural export prices will rise. Food-*exporting* developing countries will benefit from higher agricultural commodity prices. However, after years of neglect of their agriculture and pressure from increased population, many developing countries are net importers of food. They will face declining terms of trade and a fall in their real incomes.

The ending of the old Multi-Fibre Arrangement, which restricted the access of developing countries' exports to the industrialised world, will help. But it will take until 2004 to be phased out. In the meantime restrictions on textiles, an area where the developing world has significant comparative advantage, will remain.

And what if further liberalisation is achieved? The OECD/World Bank study suggests that this will merely lead to further reductions in incomes for the poorest regions of the world (see the table).

Winners and losers from the Uruguay round

	Percentage change in real income by the year 2002	
	Effect of GATT round	Effect of full free trade
Indonesia	–0.7	–2.6
Mediterranean	–0.4	–2.4
Nigeria	–0.4	–1.8
Other Africa	–0.2	–0.9
Mexico	0.0	–0.4
USA	0.2	0.3
Brazil	0.3	0.4
India	0.5	1.8
Low-income Asia	0.6	1.3
Other Latin America	0.6	1.3
European Union	1.4	2.8
China	2.5	4.5

?? Could a rise in the world price of cereals and other foodstuffs benefit the poorest developing countries in the *long* run?

[1] I. Goldin, O. Knudsen and D. van der Mensbrugghe, *Trade Liberalization: Global economic implications* (OECD and World Bank, 1993).

These arguments cast doubt on whether a policy of relying on free trade in primary exports is the best way of achieving economic development. Various trends in the international economy have also worked against primary exporters.

Problems for primary exporters: long term

Long-term trends in international trade have caused problems for primary exporting countries in three ways: (a) exports have grown slowly; (b) imports have grown rapidly; (c) the terms of trade have moved against them.

Slow growth in exports

Low income elasticity of demand for primary products. As world incomes grow, so a smaller proportion of these incomes is spent on primaries. Since food is a necessity, consumers, especially in rich countries, already consume virtually all they require. A rise in incomes, therefore, tends to be spent more on luxury goods and services, and only slightly more on basic foodstuffs. The exceptions are certain 'luxury' imported foodstuffs such as exotic fruits. In the case of raw materials, as people's incomes grow they tend to buy more and more expensive products. The extra value of these products, however, arises not from the extra raw materials they might contain, but from their greater sophistication.

Agricultural protection in advanced countries. Faced with the problem of a slowly growing demand for food produced by their own farmers, advanced countries increasingly imposed restrictions on imported food. This was one of the major issues considered at the Uruguay round of GATT negotiations (see Boxes 23.7 and 25.1).

Technological developments. Synthetic substitutes have in many cases replaced primaries in the making of consumer durables, industrial equipment and clothing. Also, the process of miniaturisation, as microchips have replaced machines, has meant that less and less raw materials have been required to produce any given amount of output.

Rapid growth in imports

There tends to be a high income elasticity of demand for imported manufactures. The demand for imports of manufactured goods into the developing countries grows rapidly with the growth of their income. This is due partly to the process of the better off in these countries being able to afford luxury goods, and partly to the development of new tastes as people are exposed to the products of the developed world.

The terms of trade

Low price elasticity of demand for primaries. The overall demand for primaries tends to be relatively price inelastic. There is no substitute for food, and in the short run there is often no substitute for minerals. On the other hand, the demand for any *one* primary product, and especially the demand for any one *country's* primary exports, will be very price elastic: there are plenty of other countries producing substitutes. This will encourage countries to produce as much as possible (as long as price remains above marginal cost), but as all countries do the same, the low overall price elasticity will depress primary product prices.

Low price elasticity of demand for imported manufactures. Because of a lack of domestic substitutes, the price elasticity of demand for manufactured imports is low. This gives market power to the overseas suppliers of these imports, which tends to raise their price relative to exports.

The net effect of chronic current account balance of payments deficits and the low price elasticities of demand for primary exports and manufactured imports is a long-term decline in the terms of trade for primary exporters, where a country's terms of trade are defined as the average price of its exports divided by the average price of its imports (P_x/P_m). In Sub-Saharan Africa, the region whose exports contain the highest proportion of primaries, the terms of trade fell by nearly 23 per cent between 1980 and 1994.

Problems for primary exporters: short term

There are also problems for primary exporting countries in the *short term.*

The prices of primary products are subject to large fluctuations. This causes great uncertainty for primary exporters and makes it virtually impossible for the government to predict how many imports the country can afford. The current account of the balance of payments fluctuates wildly, which tends to cause large swings in exchange rates or requires massive government intervention to stabilise them.

Price fluctuations are caused partly by the low price elasticity of demand and supply of primaries, which we have just considered. They are also caused by substantial *shifts* in their demand and supply.

The demand for *food* is relatively stable, but that for minerals varies with the business cycle and tends to vary more than the demand for consumer goods. The reason is the *accelerator principle* (see section 16.4). Since the *level* of investment demand depends on the size of *changes* in consumer demand, investment will fluctuate much more than consumer demand. But since many minerals are inputs into *capital* equipment, their demand is also likely to fluctuate more than consumer demand.

The supply of minerals is relatively stable. The supply of cash crops, however, varies with the harvest. Many developing countries are subject to drought or flood, which can virtually wipe out their export earnings from the relevant crop.

?? If a disastrous harvest of rice were confined to a particular country, would (a) the world price and (b) its own domestic price of rice fluctuate significantly? What would happen to the country's export earnings and the earnings of individual farmers?

With a price-inelastic world demand and supply for primaries, shifts in either curve will lead to substantial fluctuations in world prices. The problem is most serious for countries that rely on just one or two primary products, such as Ghana on cocoa and Zaire on copper. Diversification into other primaries would help to reduce their exposure.

Approach 2: Import-substituting industrialisation (ISI)

Dissatisfaction with relying on primary exporting has led most countries to embark on a process of industrialisation. The newly industrialised countries (NICs), such as Malaysia and Brazil, are already well advanced along the industrialisation road. Other developing countries have not yet progressed very far, especially the poorest African countries.

CASE STUDIES BOX 25.2

WHEN DRIVING AND ALCOHOL DO MIX

A case of import substitution in Brazil

Two major changes in world trade hit Brazil in the 1970s. The first was the fourfold increase in world oil prices. Brazil has very little oil of its own. The second was the slump in the world sugar cane market as a result of northern countries' protection of their sugar beet industries. Brazil was a major cane sugar exporter.

Faced with a resulting large increase in its import bill and a slump in its sugar exports, the Brazilian government came up with an ingenious solution. It could use surplus sugar cane to make alcohol, which could then be used instead of petrol for cars. Large distilleries were set up to convert the sugar cane into alcohol. At the same time cars were produced (e.g. VW Beetles) that could run on alcohol rather than petrol. Thus by one measure two problems were alleviated.

Then with the decline in oil prices from the mid-1980s, the relative cost-efficiency of alcohol-powered cars declined: at times it was cheaper to import oil than to produce alcohol. This illustrates the danger of basing major schemes on terms of trade existing at a particular time. If these terms of trade subsequently change, the schemes could prove to be uneconomical.

?? Could a case be made out for taxing oil imports sufficiently to make it still profitable to produce alcohol?

The most obvious way for countries to industrialise was to cut back on the imports of manufactures and substitute them with home-produced manufactures. This could not be done overnight: it had to be done in stages, beginning with assembly, then making some of the components, and finally making all, or nearly all, of the inputs into production. Most developing countries have at least started on the first stage. Several of the more advanced developing countries have component-manufacturing industries. Only a few of the larger NICs, such as India, Brazil and South Korea, have built extensive capital goods industries.

The method most favoured by policy makers is **tariff escalation**. Here tariff rates (or other restrictions) increase as one moves from the raw materials to the intermediate product to the finished product stage. Thus finished goods have higher tariffs than intermediate products. This encourages assembly plants, which are protected by high tariffs from imported finished products, and are able to obtain components at a lower tariff rate.

One of the problems with ISI is that countries are desperately short of resources to invest in industry. As a result, a policy of ISI has usually involved encouraging investment by multinational companies. But even without specific 'perks' (e.g. tax concessions, cheap sites, the cutting of red tape), multinationals will still probably be attracted by the protection afforded by the tariffs or quotas.

Adverse effects of import substitution

Some countries, such as South Korea and Taiwan, pursued an inward-looking ISI policy for only a few years. For them it was merely a stage in development, rapidly to be followed by a secondary outward-looking policy. Infant industries were initially given protection, but when they had achieved sufficient economies of scale, the barriers to imports were gradually removed.

The countries that have continued to pursue protectionist ISI policies have generally had a poorer growth record. They have also tended to suffer from other problems, such as a deepening of inequality. The development of the modern industrial sector has often been to the detriment of the traditional sectors and also to the export sector.

The criticisms of ISI are numerous, and include the following:

It has run directly counter to the principle of comparative advantage. Rather than confining ISI to genuine infant industries and then gradually removing the protection, ISI has been applied indiscriminately to a whole range of industries. Countries are producing goods in which they have a comparative *disadvantage*.

?? If a country specialises in a good in which it has a comparative disadvantage, where will it be consuming with respect to its production possibility curve?

It has cushioned inefficient practices and encouraged the establishment of monopolies. Without competition from imports, many of the industries are highly inefficient and wasteful of resources. What is more, in all but the

DEFINITION

Tariff escalation The system whereby tariff rates increase the closer a product is to the finished stage of production.

largest or most developed of the developing countries the domestic market for manufactures is small. If a newly established industry is to be large enough to gain the full potential economies of scale, it must be large relative to the market. This means that it will have considerable monopoly power.

It has involved artificially low real interest rates. To encourage capital investment in the import-substituting industries, governments have often intervened to keep interest rates low. This has encouraged the use of capital-intensive technology with a consequent lack of jobs. It has also starved other sectors (such as agriculture) of much-needed finance, and it has discouraged savings.

It has led to urban wages above the market-clearing level. Wage rates in the industrial sector, although still low compared with advanced countries, are often considerably higher than in the traditional sectors.

- They are pushed up by firms seeking to retain labour in which they have invested training.
- Governments, seeking to appease the politically powerful urban industrial working class, have often passed minimum wage laws.
- Trade unions, although less widespread in developing than in advanced countries, are mainly confined to the new industries.

Higher industrial wages again encourage firms to use capital-intensive techniques.

It has involved overvalued exchange rates. By restricting imports, import substitution tends to move the current account of the balance of payments into surplus. This leads to an appreciation of the exchange rate. Governments often actively intervene to keep up the exchange rate as part of their fight against inflation.

But if, as a result, imported inputs are cheaper, this will discourage the establishment of *domestic* industries supplying those inputs. The spread effect of the industrialisation to supplying sectors will thus be reduced. Also a higher exchange rate discourages exports, since exporters will earn less domestic currency as the exchange rate appreciates.

With an overvalued exchange rate those goods with little or no protection will be cheaper. Due to pressures from the growing urban population for cheap food, governments are reluctant to impose tariffs on basic foodstuffs such as grains and meat. This then makes it difficult for local farmers to obtain a reasonable price for their crops, and thus discourages agricultural investment.

?? Why is an overvalued exchange rate likely to encourage the use of capital-intensive technology?

It does not remove the balance of payments constraint on development.

- Many of the new industries are highly dependent on the importation of raw materials, capital equipment and component parts.
- Foreign inputs, unlike foreign finished goods, are often supplied by a single firm which can thus charge monopoly prices.
- A large proportion of the extra incomes generated by these industries tends to be spent on imports by the new urban élites.

Protection has not been applied evenly. Many different tariff rates are often used in one country: in fact a policy of tariff escalation demands this. In addition, governments often use a whole range of other protectionist instruments, such as the licensing of importers, physical and value quotas, and foreign exchange rationing. The result is that protection is highly uneven.

Economists have developed the concept of **effective protection** to measure the true degree of protection an industry gets. Effective protection measures the extra domestic value added that protection gives an industry. By *domestic value added* we mean the difference between the world market price of the finished good and the cost of the imported inputs used to make the good.

The effective rate of protection is given by the formula:

$$\frac{V^* - V}{V} \times 100$$

where V is the free-trade domestic value added, and V^* is the value added after the imposition of tariffs. There are three variables that determine the rate of effective protection:

- The tariff rate on the finished good (the nominal rate of protection). The higher this is, the higher will be the value of V^* relative to V, and hence the higher will be the effective rate of protection.
- The tariff rate (or rates) on the inputs. The higher these are, the lower will be the value of V^* relative to V, and hence the lower will be the effective rate of protection.

DEFINITION

Effective rate of protection The percentage increase in an industry's domestic value added resulting from protection given to that industry.

Table 25.3 Growth rates and export performance of selected secondary outward-looking countries

	Average annual growth in real GDP (%)	Share of manufactures in merchandise exports (%)		Annual average growth rate of exports (%)	
	1970–95	1970	1993	1970–80	1980–95
Brazil	4.6	15	60	8.5	6.3
Malaysia	7.0	8	65	4.8	13.9
South Korea	9.2	76	93	23.5	11.3
Singapore	7.6	31	80	4.2	13.7
Hong Kong	7.5	96	95	9.7	15.4
All developing countries	4.1	27	53	3.9	4.6

Source: *World Development Report 1997* (World Bank).

- The level of value added as a proportion of the price of the finished good. The higher this is, the lower will be the effective rate of protection (assuming tariff escalation).

?? To demonstrate this last point, work out the effective rate of protection in the following three cases:
(a) Free-trade finished good price = £100; free-trade cost of imported inputs = £40.
(b) Free-trade finished good price = £100; free-trade cost of imported inputs = £80.
(c) Free-trade finished good price = £100; free-trade cost of imported inputs = £100.
In each case assume that a 50 per cent tariff is imposed on the finished good and a 10 per cent tariff on the imported inputs.

In many countries effective protective rates vary massively from one industry to another. For example, according to World Bank estimates, in 1980 effective rates of protection in manufacturing ranged from –85 per cent to 219 per cent in Brazil and from –62 per cent to 1119 per cent in Nigeria! Clearly such huge differences in effective protection impose massive distortions on the market.

?? Under what circumstances could the effective rate of protection be negative?

Income distribution is made less equal. Additional incomes generated by the modern sector tend to be spent on modern-sector goods and imported goods. Thus there is a multiplier effect *within* the modern sector, but virtually none between the sectors. Also, as we saw above, an overvalued exchange rate leads to a bias against agriculture, and thus further deepens the divide between rich and poor. Finally, the relatively high wages of the modern sector encourage workers to migrate to the towns, where many, failing to get a job, live in dire poverty.

Social, cultural and environmental costs. A policy of ISI often involves imposing an alien set of values. Urban life can be harsh, competitive and materialistic. Moreover, the drive for industrialisation may involve major costs to the environment, as a result of waste products from new industries.

Finally, import substitution is necessarily limited by the size of the domestic market. Once that is saturated, ISI can come to an abrupt halt. At that stage, further expansion can come only from exporting; but if these industries have been overprotected, they will be unable to compete in world markets.

This has been a long list of problems and different economists put different emphases on them. Neo-classical economists stress the problems of market distortions, arguing that ISI leads to great inefficiency. Neo-Marxist economists, on the other hand, stress the problems of **dependency**. Many of the new industries will be owned by multinational companies which import unsuitable technologies. The countries will then become dependent on imported inputs and foreign sources of capital.

Approach 3: Exporting manufactures – a possible way forward?

The countries with the highest rates of economic growth have been those that have successfully made the transition to being exporters of manufactures. Table 25.3 gives some examples.

DEFINITION

Dependency Where the development of a developing country is hampered by its relationships with the industrialised world.

The transition from inward-looking to outward-looking industrialisation

First we must be clear what is meant by 'outward-looking industrialisation'. It could simply mean an abandonment of biases in favour of import substitution. In other words, there would be a *neutral trade regime* where production for the home market and for export would get equal treatment by the government. A country could go further, however, and actively *promote* exports. It could, for example, subsidise exports, or give tax concessions to exporters. In most cases, however, when a country is referred to as 'outward looking', what is meant is simply that it is not biased *against* exports: that it is neutral.

But how is a country to move from import substituting to being outward looking? One approach is to take it industry by industry. When an industry has saturated the home market and there is no further scope for import substitution, it should then be encouraged to seek markets overseas. The trouble with this approach is that, if the country is still protecting other industries, there will probably still be an overvalued exchange rate. Thus specific subsidies, tax concessions or other 'perks' would have to be given to this industry to enable it to compete. The country would still be highly interventionist, with all the distortions and misallocation of resources this tends to bring.

The alternative is to wean the whole economy off protection. Three major things will need doing. There will need to be a devaluation of the currency in order to restore the potential profitability of the export sector. There will also need to be a dismantling of the various protective measures that had biased production towards the home market. Finally, there will probably need to be a removal or relaxing of price controls. But these are things that cannot be done 'at a stroke'. Firms may have to be introduced gradually to the greater forces of competition that an outward-looking trade policy brings. Otherwise there may be massive bankruptcies and a corresponding massive rise in unemployment.

The benefits from a secondary outward-looking policy

The advocates of outward-looking industrialisation make a number of points in its favour.

It conforms more closely to comparative advantage. Countries pursuing an open trade regime will be able to export only goods in which they have a comparative advantage. The resources used in earning a unit of foreign exchange from exports will be less than those used in saving a unit of foreign exchange by replacing imports with home-produced goods. In other words, resources will be used more efficiently.

It will lead to more employment. According to the Heckscher–Ohlin theory, the manufactured goods in which a country will have a comparative advantage are those produced by labour-intensive techniques. Export expansion will thus increase the demand for labour relative to capital, and create more employment.

It can lead to a more equal distribution of income. The increased demand for labour will tend to lead to a rise in wages relative to profits.

> ?? Will the adoption of labour-intensive techniques *necessarily* lead to a more equal distribution of income?

It removes many of the costs associated with ISI. Under a policy of ISI, managers may spend a lot of their time lobbying politicians and officials, seeking licences (and sometimes paying bribes to obtain them), adhering to norms and regulations or trying to find ways round them. If an outward-looking policy involves removing all this, managers can turn their attention to producing goods more efficiently.

Economies of scale. If the home market is too small to allow a firm to gain all the potential economies of scale, these can be gained by expanding into the export market.

Increased competition. By having to compete with foreign companies, exporters will be under a greater competitive pressure than industries shielded behind protective barriers. This will encourage (a) resource saving in the short run, both through their better *allocation* and through reductions in X inefficiency (see Box 6.4), and (b) innovation and investment, as firms attempt to adopt the latest technology, often obtained from developed countries. They cannot afford a 'quiet life'. They have to compete to survive.

Increased investment. To the extent that outward-looking policies lead to a greater potential for economic growth, they may attract more foreign capital. To the extent that they involve an increase in interest rates, they will tend to attract more savings. To the extent that they lead to increased incomes, additional savings will be generated, especially given that the *marginal* propensity to save may be quite high. The extra savings can be used to finance extra investment.

Drawbacks of an export-orientated industrialisation strategy

Many of the problems associated with a primary exporting strategy do not apply to a *secondary* exporting one. For example, the income and price elasticities of demand for manufactures are generally much higher than those for primaries. Nevertheless some of the problems of an outward strategy still remain.

The export of manufactures is seen by many developed countries as very threatening to their own industries. Their response is often to erect trade barriers. These barriers are often highest in the very industries (such as textiles, footwear and processed food) where developing countries have the greatest comparative advantage. Even if the barriers are *currently* low, developing countries may feel that it is too risky to expand their exports of these products for fear of a future rise in barriers.

?? Consider the arguments from the perspective of an *advanced country* for and against protecting its industries from imports of manufactures from developing countries.

The success of developing countries such as Malaysia and South Korea in exporting manufactures does not imply that other developing countries will have similar success. As additional developing countries attempt to export their manufactures, they will be facing more and more competition from each other.

Exporting manufactures may thus be a very risky strategy for developing countries. Perhaps the best hope for the future may be for a growth in manufacturing trade *between* developing countries. That way they can gain the benefits of specialisation and economies of scale that trade brings, while at the same time producing for a growing market. The feasibility of this approach depends on whether developing countries can agree to an open trade policy between themselves.

SECTION SUMMARY

1. Trade is of vital importance for the vast majority of developing countries, and yet most developing countries suffer from chronic balance of trade deficits.
2. Developing countries have traditionally been primary exporters. This has allowed them to exploit their comparative advantage in labour-intensive goods and has provided a market for certain goods which would otherwise have no market at home.
3. However, with a low world income elasticity of demand for primary products, with the development of synthetic substitutes and with the protection of agriculture in developed countries, the demand for primary exports has only grown slowly. At the same time, the demand for manufactured imports into developing countries has grown rapidly. The result has been a worsening balance of trade problem; and with a *price*-inelastic demand for both imports and exports, the terms of trade have worsened too. There is also the danger that comparative costs may change over time; that most of the benefits from primary exports may accrue to foreign owners of mines and plantations, or to wealthy élites in the domestic population; that mines and plantations can involve substantial environmental and other external costs; and that export earnings can fluctuate, given instabilities in supply and unstable world prices.
4. Import-substituting industrialisation was seen to be the answer to these problems. This was normally achieved in stages, beginning with the finished goods stage and then working back towards the capital goods stage. ISI, it was hoped, would allow countries to benefit from the various dynamic advantages associated with manufacturing.
5. For many countries, however, ISI brought as many, if not more, problems than it solved. It often led to the establishment of inefficient industries, protected from foreign competition and facing little or no competition at home either. It led to considerable market distortions, with tariffs and other forms of protection haphazardly applied and with resulting huge variations in effective rates of protection; to overvalued exchange rates with a resulting bias against exports and the agricultural sector generally; to a deepening of inequalities and to large-scale social and environmental problems as the cities expanded and as poverty and unemployment grew. Finally, the balance of payments was in many cases made worse as the new industries became increasingly dependent on imported inputs and as growing urbanisation caused a growing demand for imported consumer goods.
6. The most rapidly growing of the developing countries are those that have pursued a policy of export-orientated industrialisation. This has allowed them to achieve the benefits of economies of scale and foreign competition. It has allowed them to specialise in goods in which they have a comparative advantage (i.e. labour-intensive goods) and yet which have a relatively high income elasticity of demand. Whether countries which have pursued ISI can successfully turn to an open, export-orientated approach will depend to a large extent on the degree of protectionism they face from advanced countries and on the degree of competition they face from other developing countries.

25.3 Structural problems within developing countries

The neglect of agriculture

In their drive to industrialise, many developing countries have taken their agricultural sector for granted. The general view in the 1950s and 1960s was that agriculture was useful to the extent that it provided food for the expanding towns. But it was essentially seen as a resource to be tapped rather than developed. The key to growth and modernisation was industry, not farming.

The process of import-substituting industrialisation has been highly damaging to agriculture, especially in the poorest countries such as those of Sub-Saharan Africa. With a backward and run-down agricultural sector, with little or no rural infrastructure, many countries today face a food crisis of immense proportions. Harrowing scenes of famine and death from countries like Ethiopia and the Sudan have become all too familiar.

In the last twenty years, opinions have gradually changed. It is now realised that the relief of poverty, unemployment and the maldistribution of income can best be achieved by improving productivity and incomes in the rural sector. No longer is agriculture seen as a sector to be 'squeezed' like an orange. Rather it is seen as a sector that must be developed in harmony with the urban sector. Agricultural output must be increased for the benefit of rural and urban dwellers alike. At the same time industrial output can be given new markets in the rural sector if rural incomes expand. The following are some of the possible ways forward.

Price reform. The price of food needs to be raised relative to the price of industrial goods. This will increase the profitability of agricultural production and enable farmers to afford to invest in irrigation, agricultural implements, land improvement, etc.

Devaluation. If the currency is devalued, this will increase the price of food imports and thus make it easier for domestic food producers to compete. It will also increase the profitability of food exports.

Government support for rural infrastructure projects. If food is to be marketed, there must be adequate rural infrastructure. Government road-building schemes and the setting-up of marketing boards can make a dramatic difference to the viability of commercial food production.

The provision of finance. Farmers need access to cheap finance and not to be forced to borrow at sky-high interest rates from local moneylenders. This can be achieved by setting up rural banks specialising in the provision of finance to small farmers. These could be nationalised institutions, or the government could give incentives to private banks to expand into the rural sector.

The adoption of new technologies and practices. There have been rapid advances in agricultural technology in recent years. The development of new fertilisers, pesticides, simple but effective agricultural machinery, and most of all of new high-yielding strains of grain, especially wheat and rice, have helped to transform traditional agriculture in certain developing countries such as India. There has been a *Green Revolution*.

Other countries, however, and especially those of Sub-Saharan Africa, have made little progress in adopting these technologies. This is due partly to an inability to afford the new equipment, chemicals and seeds, partly to the lack of infrastructure to make them available, and partly to their unsuitability to the generally more arid African conditions.

Governments can help by funding research into the best farming methods and inputs for local conditions. They can also help by providing finance for the adoption of the new methods.

Education and advice. Many farmers are simply unaware of new more efficient farming methods. Training schemes or rural advisers can help here.

Land reform. As population grows, land holdings are divided and subdivided as they are passed from generation to generation. Thus many farmers operate on tiny plots of land that can never yield an adequate income. Increasingly, they get into debt and are forced to mortgage their land to large landowners at high interest rates, or to sell it to them at low prices. The number of landless labourers or farmers in 'debt bondage' therefore grows.

A solution to this problem is the redistribution of land. Clearly this cannot be done unless there is a government sympathetic to the rural poor and willing to take on the inevitable opposition from the large farmers. Often these large farmers are politically powerful and have the police on their side.

Two of the most successful developing countries, Taiwan and South Korea, despite having right-wing governments, underwent a radical redistribution of land from rich to poor in the late 1940s and early 1950s. In both countries the growth of the agricultural sector has been rapid and yet continues to be egalitarian, based as it is on small, but not tiny, peasant holdings. In both countries extreme rural poverty has been virtually eliminated.

The encouragement of rural co-operatives. If small farmers get together and form co-operatives, they may be able to afford to share agricultural equipment such as tractors and harvesters, and undertake irrigation schemes; they may be able to set up input-purchasing and crop-marketing and distribution organisations, and gain easier access to credit; they may be in a better position to negotiate with government agencies and be a channel through which the government can provide technological and financial assistance. In many countries, national or local governments have actively encouraged such co-operatives by providing subsidies, tax incentives and advice, and by passing favourable legislation.

Inappropriate technology

The technology employed in a country depends on the type of development strategy it is pursuing. Some strategies lead to the adoption of relatively labour-intensive technologies, others to relatively capital-intensive ones.

Neo-classical theory suggests that countries should use techniques that are intensive in their abundant factor. This is simply an extension of the Heckscher–Ohlin theory, only this time it is applied to the choice of techniques rather than to the choice of goods. The theory implies that (labour-abundant) developing countries should adopt labour-intensive techniques; techniques that use relatively more of the cheap factor (labour) and relatively less of the expensive factor (capital).

With the advent of policies of industrialisation, however, came strong arguments for adopting capital-intensive technology. Capital-intensive technologies were seen to be more advanced. These were the technologies that were developed in rich countries, countries with sophisticated research facilities. The argument here was that, despite having a higher capital/labour ratio, these techniques nevertheless had a low capital/output ratio. The equipment might be expensive, but it would yield a very high output and would thus cost less *per unit* of output.

> **??** If a modern capital-intensive technique has a higher capital/labour ratio *and* a lower capital/output ratio than a traditional labour-intensive one, what can we say about its labour/output ratio relative to the traditional technique?

A second argument was that, if multinationals were to be encouraged to invest in developing countries, they had to be allowed to bring with them their own technology – technology that was almost invariably capital intensive. In other words, the choice was not between more labour-intensive and more capital-intensive techniques, but rather between having *extra* capital (by allowing multinationals to invest) and not having it at all.

A final argument in favour of capital-intensive technology was that it provides a greater level of profit, and that this profit will then be reinvested, thereby causing a faster rate of economic growth.

Given these arguments, many governments of developing countries actively encouraged the use of capital-intensive techniques; some still do. But also there were other features of ISI that unintentionally led to biases in favour of capital-intensive technology. These included the following:

- Wage rates above the market-clearing level, driven up by minimum wage legislation, trade union activity, or firms trying to ensure that workers they had trained were not 'poached' by other firms.
- Low interest rates to encourage investment. The effect of this, plus relatively high wage rates, is to encourage the substitution of capital for labour.
- An overvalued exchange rate. This lowers the relative price of imported inputs, which under a policy of tariff escalation have low tariffs. This encourages the use of import-intensive technology, which also tends to be capital intensive.
- The ignorance of many multinational companies of alternative efficient labour-intensive technology.
- The bias of engineers. It is engineers rather than economists who are often instrumental in deciding which production techniques a firm will use. Engineers tend to be biased in favour of *mechanically* efficient techniques, which tend to be capital intensive, rather than *economically* efficient techniques, which may well be labour intensive.

> **??** What is the difference between mechanical efficiency and economic efficiency?

In recent years, with the criticism of ISI has come the criticism of capital-intensive technologies.

- Capital-intensive equipment may require more maintenance.
- It may have to be imported, and may use a high proportion of imported inputs. This will put a strain on the country's balance of trade. By using less domestic inputs there will be less spread effect to other sectors of the economy: there will be a smaller multiplier effect.
- There may be problems of hold-ups, breakdowns and incorrect usage due to problems in obtaining parts and an absence of properly trained maintenance staff.

CASE STUDIES BOX 25.3

INAPPROPRIATE TECHNOLOGIES
When 'modern' is not best

Marsden cites the following examples of the inappropriate use of capital-intensive technology in various developing countries:[2]

- The large public-sector shoe factory which operated at 20% of capacity because it had no means of reaching the small private shoe retailers who handled 90% of the shoe trade.
- The battery plant which could satisfy a month's demand in five days.
- The woollen-textile factory which had a 10 per cent material wastage figure (costing precious foreign exchange) because its management did not know how to set and control material usage standards.
- The $2 million date-processing plant which had been out of action for two years, ever since a blow-out in the cleaning and destoning unit, because there were no service engineers who knew how to repair it.
- The radio assembly factory whose production line broke down repeatedly because of the high rate of absenteeism among key workers . . .
- One country imported two plastic injection-moulding machines costing $100 000 with moulds. Working three shifts and with a total labour force of 50 workers, they produced 1.5 million pairs of plastic sandals and shoes a year. At $2 a pair these were better value (longer life) than cheap leather footwear at the same price. Thus 5000 artisan shoemakers lost their livelihood; this, in turn, reduced the markets for the suppliers and makers of leather, hand tools, cotton thread, tacks, glues, wax and polish, eyelets, fabric linings, laces, wooden lasts and carton boxes, none of which was required for plastic footwear. As all the machinery had to be imported, while the leather footwear was based largely on indigenous materials and industries, the net result was a decline in both employment and real income within the country.

[2] K. Marsden, 'Progressive technologies for developing countries', in R. Jolly *et al.* (eds.), *Third World Employment* (Penguin, 1973), pp. 320–2.

- Even if they do generate higher profits, there is no guarantee that these will be reinvested. They may simply flow abroad to foreign shareholders, or be spent largely on luxury consumption if the profits initially stay within the country (and a high proportion of luxury goods are imported anyway).
- Capital-intensive techniques often involve large-scale production. There have been many examples of countries opening up plants that are simply too large relative to the market. As a result they never operate at full capacity, and thus may operate inefficiently.

In addition, capital-intensive technologies have other detrimental effects. As we shall see shortly, they worsen the unemployment problem. Also, as these are large-scale technologies, the firms using them usually locate in the cities. This tends to worsen the problem of **dualism**. Inequality between urban and rural incomes tends to grow; and with relatively few workers being employed in these industries at relatively high wages, the gap between their wages and those of the urban poor tends to grow also.

The concentration of large-scale plants in cities can cause severe problems of pollution, especially if the government is not very strict in enforcing pollution control.

?? Why may governments of developing countries be less strict than developed countries in controlling pollution?

So what can be done to encourage a more appropriate technology? Part of the solution lies in correcting market distortions: there will probably need to be a devaluation of the currency and a rise in interest rates. This would remove two of the key factors favouring capital-intensive industry.

Then there will probably also need to be positive encouragement given to the invention or adoption of *efficient* labour-intensive technologies. This could involve government-sponsored research, information centres to provide details of the various techniques used around the world, education and training schemes for managers and workers, the provision of advice on production, marketing, distribution, etc., and incentives for inventions (such as subsidies or patent protection).

The government could help to encourage small businesses (which typically use more labour-intensive techniques) by, for example, setting up development banks which provide services specifically for small businesses and which grant loans at similar rates to those charged to large firms; encouraging the formation of co-operatives through tax concessions or subsidies, or by reducing the amount of

DEFINITION

Dualism The division of an economy into a modern (usually urban) sector and a poor traditional (usually rural) sector.

CASE STUDIES BOX 25.4

THE GROWTH OF URBAN SHANTYTOWNS

A consequence of rural–urban migration

Table (a) shows the extent of slums and squatter settlements in various cities in the developing world. In many large cities, more than half the population live in shantytowns. In Brazil they are called *favelas*, in India *bustees*, in Chile *cullampas* (mushrooms), and in Argentina *villas miserias*.

For many, life in the slums means living in makeshift dwellings made from scrap materials, with little or no work, no sanitation, no running water, no schools and no health care. In Bangladesh, infant mortality rates in the city slums are 50 times higher than in the impoverished countryside. Throughout the developing world, there are more than 100 million homeless children struggling to survive in the cities.

(a) Slum dwelling in developing countries

City	Population living in slums and squatter settlements (%)
Latin America	
Bogota, Colombia	60
Mexico City, Mexico	46
Caracas, Venezuela	42
Middle East and Africa	
Addis Ababa, Ethiopia	79
Casablanca, Morocco	70
Kinshasa, Zaire	60
Cairo, Egypt	60
Ankara, Turkey	60
Asia	
Calcutta, India	67
Manila, Philippines	35
Seoul, South Korea	29
Jakarta, Indonesia	26

Sources: *World Population Growth and Global Society*, report no. 13 (Population Crisis Committee, Washington), quoted in M. Todaro, *Economic Development in the Third World* (Longman, 1994).

The major factor contributing to the growth of these shantytowns has been the massive levels of rural–urban migration. Migration accounts for some 55 per cent of urban population growth in developing countries. But as table (b) shows, the percentage varies substantially from country to country.

(b) Rural–urban migration as a source of urban population growth: 1970–93

Country	Annual urban growth (%)	Share of growth due to migration (%)
Argentina	2.0	25
Brazil	3.2	31
India	3.3	36
Indonesia	4.8	60
Kenya	7.5	55
Nigeria	5.6	50
Philippines	4.4	45
Tanzania	8.5	62
Sub-Saharan Africa	4.8	42
All developing countries	3.3	40

Source: *World Development Report* (World Bank).

The combination of high total population growth plus rural–urban migration resulted in the urban population of developing countries rising from 809 million in 1975 to 1710 million in 1995 (an average annual increase of 3.7 per cent). Over 90 per cent of the worldwide growth in cities has been in developing countries.

Despite their dire poverty, some slum dwellers, by joint action and with security of tenure, have managed to bring dramatic improvements to their environment: installing running water and sewerage systems, helping each other build more substantial homes and providing simple health care.

red tape such organisations are likely to encounter; and providing small workshops at low or zero rent.

Finally, the government can actively encourage the economic development of the countryside and thus help to break down the dualism between the rural and urban sectors and stop the mass migration of people to the cities. Policies could include the building of roads, the provision of government rural advisory services on new techniques and business practices, the setting-up of rural banks, higher prices for food and the products of handicraft industries, and tax incentives for rural investment.

?? What difficulties is a government likely to encounter in encouraging the use of labour-intensive technology?

Unemployment

Imagine the choice of living in a large family in the countryside with too little land to be able to feed you and the other family members, or of seeking your fortune in the city where there are nowhere near enough jobs to go round. It is not much of a choice. But it is the sort of choice that millions of people are forced to make. Open

EXPLORING THE THEORY

UNEMPLOYMENT IN DEVELOPING COUNTRIES

Three simple models

In this box we will look at three models that have been developed to explain Third World unemployment.

Limited choice of techniques

The simplest version of this model assumes that there is only one technique available to firms and that just two factors of production are involved – labour and capital. Firms will thus face a right-angled isoquant. This is illustrated in diagram (a).

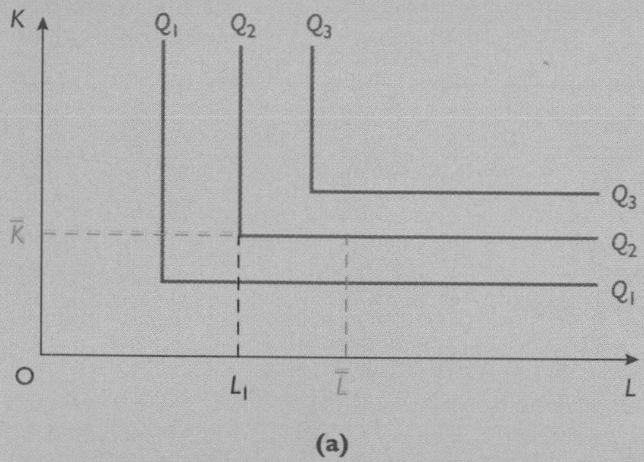

(a)

Each isoquant shows a particular level of output (Q). Given that there is only one choice of technique, involving a particular combination of labour and capital, then for each amount of capital used a *particular* amount of labour will be needed – no more and no less. Any extra labour will simply be idle.

For example, if each machine required one operative and if ten machines were available, then ten operatives would be required. An eleventh would add nothing to output. Similarly, if there were ten operatives available, an eleventh machine would be idle.

If, in diagram (a), the total supply of capital were $\bar{K}$, then firms would require L_1 of labour. But if the total labour force were $\bar{L}$, then $\bar{L} - L_1$ workers would be unemployed.

Thus the lack of availability of labour-intensive techniques means that there is not enough capital to employ everyone.

Capital-intensity bias

This model assumes that there *are* labour-intensive techniques available, but that firms choose not to use them. Assuming again that there are just the two factors, labour and capital, this time firms will face *curved* isoquants. In other words, the firm can choose to combine labour and capital in any proportions it chooses. This is illustrated in diagram (b).

Assume that the total supplies of capital and labour are $\bar{K}$ and $\bar{L}$ respectively. With a price ratio given by the slope of the isocost *AB*, the factor market will clear. All capital and all labour will be employed at point *d* on isoquant Q_1.

Managers, however, may have a bias in favour of capital-intensive techniques. Alternatively, the price of labour may be above the market-clearing level, or the price of capital may be below the market-clearing level, so that the isocost is steeper than *AB* (e.g. *CD*). In either case, if $\bar{K}$ capital is used, *less* than *L* labour will be employed. With an isocost of *CD*, only L_1 will be employed. $\bar{L} - L_1$ will be unemployed. There will also be a lower level of output, since production is now on the lower isoquant Q_2.

unemployment rates in developing countries are generally much higher than in developed countries: rates in excess of 20 per cent are not uncommon.

But even these high rates grossly understate the true extent of the problem. With the system of extended families, where the family farm or the family trade occupies all the family members, people may not be out looking for jobs and are thus not openly unemployed, but their output is nevertheless very low. There is simply not enough work to occupy them fully. This is the problem of **disguised unemployment**. Then there are those who manage to do a few hours' work each week as casual labourers or as petty traders. These people are **underemployed**. When you add the problem of disguised unemployment and underemployment to the problem of open unemployment, the problem becomes overwhelming.

The causes of the unemployment problem are deep seated and complex, but four stand out as being particularly important in most developing countries.

DEFINITIONS

Disguised unemployment Where the same work could be done by fewer people.

Underemployment Where people who want full-time work are only able to find part-time work.

*BOX 25.5

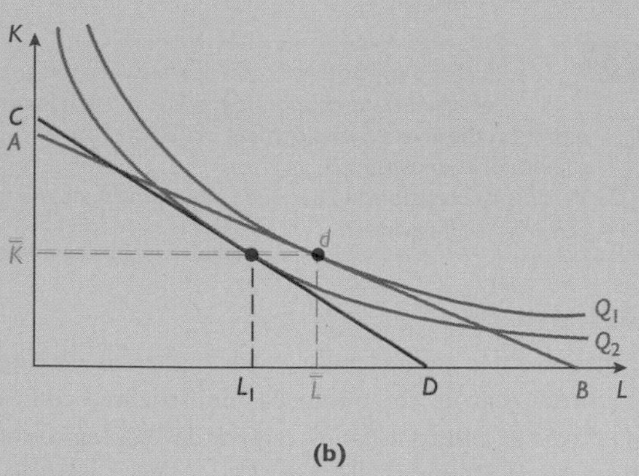

(b)

?? If there were three techniques available, what would the isoquant look like? Would it make any difference to the conclusions of this model?

Rural–urban migration

This model assumes that migration depends first on the difference between urban wages (W_u) and rural wages (W_r). The bigger the differential, the more will people wish to migrate. Second, it depends on the likelihood of getting a job. The more likely people are to find a job, the more likely they are to migrate.

These two can be combined in the concept of an *expected urban wage* (W_u^e). This is the *actual* average urban wage multiplied by the probability of getting a job. Thus if the average wage were £40 per week, and if there were a 50 per cent chance of getting a job, the expected urban wage would be £20. If the chance were only 25 per cent, the expected wage would be only £10, and so on. This can be expressed formally as:

$$W_u^e = W_u.L_m/L_u$$

where L_m is the total number of workers employed in the urban sector and L_u is the total labour supply (employed and unemployed). Thus L_m/L_u is the employment rate, which can be taken as an indication of the probability of getting a job.

So when will rural workers migrate to the towns? According to the model this will occur when:

$$W_u^e > (W_r + \alpha)$$

where α is a term representing the costs of migration. In other words, people will migrate when, after taking the cost of migrating into account, they can expect to earn more in the towns than in the countryside.

But as people migrate, W_r will tend to rise as the supply of rural labour falls, and W_u^e will tend to fall as the new arrivals in the towns increase L_u and thus reduce the likelihood of others getting a job. An equilibrium urban unemployment will be reached when:

$$W_u^e = W_r + \alpha$$

At that point migration will stop.

Thus in this model, urban unemployment will be greater (a) the higher is the level of the actual urban wage (W_u), (b) the lower is the level of the rural wage (W_r) and (c) the lower are the costs of migrating (α).

?? If more jobs were created in the towns, how, in the rural–urban migration model, would this affect (a) the level of urban unemployment; (b) the rate of urban unemployment?

Rapid population growth

With reductions in mortality rates (due to improved health care) which have not been matched by equivalent reductions in birth rates, populations in most developing countries have grown rapidly for many years now. The labour force has thus grown rapidly too. The growth in production has simply not been fast enough to create enough jobs for these extra workers.

Capital-intensity bias

As we have seen, import-substituting industrialisation has involved a bias in favour of capital-intensive technology. This has led to the production of goods and to the use of processes that provide only limited employment opportunities. As long as the relative price of capital to labour is kept low, or as long as there is a lack of modern efficient *labour-intensive* techniques available, or as long as multinational companies choose to bring in their own (capital-intensive) technology, so there will continue to be a lack of demand for labour.

Rural–urban migration

Throughout the developing world, people flock from the countryside to the towns and thereby swell the numbers of urban unemployed. But why do they do it? If life in the shantytowns is wretched, what is the point? The point is that for most of the migrants there was no chance at all of getting another job in the countryside, whereas in the towns there is at least some chance. If one in five migrants gets a job, then you might be the lucky one.

The decision to migrate thus depends on four main factors:

- The income differential between the countryside and the town. The more that jobs in the town pay relative to what the migrant could earn by staying behind, the more the person is likely to migrate. If their decision was to be totally rational, they would also take into account the differences in the cost of living between the two areas.
- The chance of getting a job. The higher the rate of urban unemployment, the less the chance of getting a job and thus the less likely the person is to migrate.
- The 'risk attitude' of the person: in other words, how willing potential migrants are to take the gamble of whether or not they will get a job.
- The degree of misinformation. People may migrate to the towns, attracted by the 'bright lights' of the city and the belief (albeit probably misplaced) that their prospects are much better there.

??

What would be the effect on the levels of migration and urban unemployment of the creation of jobs in the towns?

External influences

Most developing countries are highly dependent on international economic forces. If the world economy goes into recession, or world interest rates rise, or protectionist policies are pursued by developed countries, this will have a damaging effect on industry in developing countries. Their exports will fall and unemployment will rise.

There is no simple cure for unemployment in developing countries. Nevertheless there are certain measures that governments can take which will help to reverse its growth:

- The government can encourage the use of more labour-intensive techniques by adopting the sorts of policy outlined earlier.
- It can help to reverse rural-urban migration by reducing the rural 'push'. This will involve policies of encouraging rural development and thereby providing jobs away from the big towns.
- It can provide jobs directly by embarking on labour-intensive infrastructure construction projects. For example, it can employ gangs of workers to build roads or dig irrigation ditches.
- It can adopt policies that help to reduce the rate of population growth: policies such as educational and propaganda programmes to persuade people to have smaller families, measures to raise the economic and social status of women so that they have a freer choice over family size, and policies directed at tackling extreme poverty so that the very poor do not feel the need to have a large family as an insurance that they will be supported in their old age.

??

1. Is there any potential conflict between the goals of maximising economic growth and maximising either (a) the level of employment or (b) the rate of growth of employment?
2. What is the relationship between unemployment and (a) poverty; (b) inequality?

Inflation

Inflation rates are generally much higher in developing countries than in the advanced industrialised countries. The average annual inflation rate for developing countries between 1980 and 1993 was 73 per cent, whereas for developed countries it was 4.3 per cent (see Table 25.1 above for more details). They also vary enormously from one developing country to another, with rates of well over 100 per cent not uncommon, especially in certain Latin American countries.

Theories of inflation developed in the West (such as demand-pull and cost-push) have been inadequate to provide a full explanation of the problem. Whenever there is rapid inflation in developing countries there is also a rapid expansion of the money supply. But does this provide a *full* explanation? Is the expansion of the money supply the fundamental cause of the problem, or is the money supply merely growing in response to other deeper causes?

Structuralist economists have argued that the deeper causes of inflation are the structural rigidities inherent in developing economies, which frustrate attempts to expand the economy. The change from a traditional primary outward-looking economy to an inward-looking industrialised one demands fundamental changes in economic structures. There needs to be a supply of food to feed the cities, a supply of appropriately educated and trained labour (and not just a plentiful supply of unskilled labour), the provision of a transport and financial infrastructure, and so on. Inevitably, with all these extra demands for resources and facilities, bottlenecks will occur. There will be a shortage of tax revenues to finance all the desired government spending; there will be a shortage of foreign exchange; there will be a shortage of food;

DEFINITION

Structuralists Economists who focus on specific barriers to development and how to overcome them.

there will be a shortage of certain skills. In many parts of the economy there will simply be inadequate supplies to match the demand. The result is higher prices.

If supply bottlenecks are to explain *continuing* inflation, they must be validated by an increase in aggregate demand. Why will governments allow demand to expand? Structuralists explain this by arguing that very often governments simply cave in to price and wage demands arising from the bottlenecks. In addition, they may not have the political power to constrain the growth of credit or raise sufficient tax revenues to cover the growing levels of government expenditure. Alternatively, the government may choose to increase the size of the budget deficit quite deliberately in its desire to spend more on building the economy.

Monetarists challenge these arguments by claiming that there *has* to be an expansion of the money supply if there is to be sustained inflation, and that therefore the cure for inflation must be to slow down the rate of monetary growth. If bottlenecks *are* significant in developing countries, then it is the natural rate of unemployment they will affect, or the rate of growth of output potential. Monetarists therefore separate anti-inflationary policy (i.e. monetary policy) from supply-side policies to increase output and employment. As far as these supply-side policies are concerned, most monetarists argue that bottlenecks are best relieved not by 'throwing money' at them, but by freeing up the market and removing price distortions (such as artificially low interest rates, an overvalued exchange rate and controlled food prices).

For structuralists the cure for inflation lies ultimately in alleviating the bottlenecks. This will require more than simply freeing up the market (though for some this is an important ingredient). It will require measures such as a carefully designed system of education and training, the provision of transport infrastructure and schemes of rural development. Developing countries have too many problems of externalities and monopolistic vested interests to leave the relief of bottlenecks to the market. Nevertheless most structuralists do not dismiss monetary (and fiscal) policies as short-term devices for preventing structural rigidities causing inflation.

?? What common ground is there between structuralist and monetarist explanations of inflation and lack of growth in developing countries?

SECTION SUMMARY

1. The urban/industrial bias of many development programmes has led to the neglect of agriculture. The effect has been a deepening of rural poverty and a growing inability of the rural sector to feed the towns. Policies to reverse this trend include the raising of food prices, devaluation of the currency, government support for rural infrastructure projects, the provision of lower-interest finance to the rural sector, encouragement for the adoption of new labour-intensive techniques in farming and the use of new high-yielding seeds, land reform and the setting-up of rural co-operatives.

2. Development programmes have often encouraged the use of capital-intensive technology through policies of low interest rates, relatively high urban wages, an overvalued exchange rate or encouraging investment by multinational companies. These capital-intensive technologies were often seen as advantageous in that they yielded higher profits and thus more surplus for reinvestment. Often they were more sophisticated than labour-intensive techniques, and sometimes they had a lower capital–output ratio despite having a higher capital–labour ratio. Nevertheless, labour-intensive techniques may involve less maintenance and less reliance on imported inputs and foreign skilled personnel; the profits generated from them are more likely to be retained within the country; they are likely to create more employment and a more equal spread of the benefits of economic growth; and they may be less polluting.

3. Unemployment is a major problem for most developing countries, both in the countryside and in the ever growing shantytowns surrounding the cities. The causes are complex, but include rapid population growth, biases towards the use of capital-intensive technology, and a vulnerability to world economic changes. Urban unemployment has grown rapidly as people have migrated from the countryside, attracted by the relatively higher wages, the 'bright lights of the city' and at least the *possibility* (however remote) of getting a job.

4. Inflation too is a major problem for many developing countries. Again the causes are complex. At a superficial level, inflation is caused by excessive monetary growth. At a more fundamental level, the problem is one of structural rigidities, with supply being unable to expand sufficiently in response to demand stimuli, while the government, impatient for growth, runs large budget deficits and the people demand higher living standards.

25.4 The problem of debt

A serious consequence of the oil shocks of the 1970s and the reactions of the developed world to these shocks was a major debt crisis in developing countries. Attempts to service these debts – to pay interest and pay back capital (amortisation) – have caused severe strains on the economies of many developing countries. By the early 1980s the problem had become so severe that many developing countries found it virtually impossible to continue servicing their debt. There was a growing fear that countries would default on payment, thereby precipitating an international banking crisis.

Although today, from the perspective of the rich world, the debt problem is no longer seen as a 'crisis', this is largely because the world financial system has found ways of coping with the debt, and threats of default have subsided. From the perspective of the poor countries, however, the problems have generally not diminished. For many the debts are still mounting and the suffering of their people continues to grow. Table 25.4 shows the continuing (albeit slowing) growth of debt.

In this final section we look first at the origins of the debt crisis and then at schemes which have been adopted to cope with it. We then turn finally to look at ways in which developing countries themselves can attempt to tackle the problem.

The first oil shock and its aftermath: 1971–8

Between 1971 and 1973, developing countries' balance of payments had generally fared well, helped by a world commodity price boom. This position was then dramatically reversed after 1973 with the increase in oil prices and the resulting world recession. Oil imports cost much more and export demand was sluggish. The current account deficit of oil-importing developing countries rose from 1.1 per cent of GNP in 1973 to 4.3 per cent in 1975.

It was not difficult to finance these deficits, however. Flows of aid and loans from both governments and international agencies were increasing. The oil surpluses deposited in commercial banks in the industrialised world provided an important additional source of finance. The banks, flush with money and faced with slack demand in the industrialised world, were very willing to lend. As can be seen from Table 25.5, the biggest increase occurred in bank loans, which increased from $3 billion in 1970 to $12 billion in 1975. These flows enabled developing countries to continue with policies of growth.

After 1975, the balance of payments position of most developing countries improved. The reasons for this were as follows:

- The world recession of 1974–5 was short lived. Aggregate demand quickly recovered as mild expansionary policies were pursued. The rise in world demand helped developing countries to regain their growth in exports. Between 1973 and 1980 exports grew at an annual average of 4.6 per cent.
- Relaxed monetary policies in many industrialised economies, combined with the higher oil prices, led to rapid inflation. This helped to reduce the real value of developing countries' debt.
- The relaxed monetary policies also meant that interest rates rose less quickly than inflation. *Real* interest rates were thus low. This made the servicing of their debts relatively easy for developing countries.

The second oil shock and its aftermath: 1979–85

The second oil shock of 1979–80, like the first one, caused a large increase in the import bills of developing countries. But the full effects on their economies this time were very much worse, given the debts that had been

Table 25.4 Growth in debt of developing countries (average annual)

	1973–80	1980–5	1985–90	1990–5
All developing countries	22.6	14.6	7.2	7.4
Low-income countries	16.5	17.5	13.8	6.1
Middle-income countries	24.7	13.7	4.9	7.9
Sub-Saharan Africa	23.9	15.1	15.0	3.5
Severely indebted middle-income countries	25.2	14.1	12.9	4.8
Severely indebted low-income countries	–	18.1	8.5	2.5

Sources: *World Development Report 1991* (World Bank); *World Debt Tables 1995–96* (World Bank).

Table 25.5 Capital flows to developing countries: selected years ($bn)

	1970	1975	1980	1981	1983
Official aid	8.1	20.1	37.5	37.3	33.6
Official loans	3.9	10.5	24.5	22.2	19.6
Private investment	3.7	11.4	10.5	17.2	7.8
Bank loans	3.0	12.0	23.0	30.0	36.0

Source: *World Development Report 1985* (World Bank).

accumulated in the 1970s and given the policies adopted by the industrialised world after 1979.

Table 25.6 illustrates the worsening debt position after 1979, compared with that in 1974. These are averages for all developing countries. Some fared very much worse than this. For example, in 1984 the ratio of debt service (i.e. interest and capital repayments) to exports was 26.6 per cent for Brazil, 31.9 per cent for Egypt, 34.3 per cent for Mexico and 38.3 per cent for Bolivia.

But why were things so much worse this time?

- The world recession was deeper and lasted longer (1980–3), and when recovery came, it came very slowly. Developing countries' current account balance of payments deteriorated sharply. This was due both to a marked slowing down in the growth of their exports and to a fall in their export prices. Export prices of oil-importing developing countries fell by 2.1 per cent in 1981, 4.8 per cent in 1982, 1.0 per cent in 1983, 1.3 per cent in 1984 and 1.6 per cent in 1985.
- The tight monetary policies pursued by the industrialised countries led to a sharp increase in interest rates, and the resulting fall in inflation meant, therefore, that there was a very sharp increase in *real* interest rates. This greatly increased developing countries' costs of servicing their debts (see Table 25.6).
- The problem was made worse by the growing proportion of debt that was at variable interest rates. This was largely due to the increasing proportion of debt that was in the form of loans from commercial banks (see Table 25.5).

?? Referring to Table 25.5, how had the *proportions* of capital inflows into developing countries from different sources changed since 1970?

After 1979, many developing countries found it increasingly difficult to service their debts. Then in 1982 Mexico, followed by several other countries such as Brazil, Bolivia, Zaire and Sudan, declared that it would have to suspend payments. There was now a debt crisis, which threatened not only the debtor countries, but also the world banking system.

Coping with debt: rescheduling

There are two dimensions to dealing with debt problems of developing countries. The first is to cope with difficulties in servicing their debt. This usually involves some form of rescheduling of the repayments. The second dimension is to deal with the underlying causes of the problem. Here we will focus on rescheduling.

Rescheduling official loans

Official loans are renegotiated through the Paris Club. Industrialised countries are members of the club, which arranges terms for the rescheduling of their loans to developing countries. Agreements normally involve delaying the date for repayment of loans currently maturing, or spreading the repayments over a longer period of time. Paris Club agreements are often made in consultation with the IMF, so that a programme can be worked out with the debtor country for tackling its underlying economic problems.

The main recipients of official loans are low-income and lower-middle-income countries (the upper-middle-income countries relying largely on commercial bank loans). Between 1982 and 1987 demands by low-income countries for Paris Club renegotiations increased dramatically. By 1987 virtually all the Sub-Saharan African countries had sought repeated Paris Club assistance. By 1987 it was becoming clear that the existing arrangements were inadequate for many countries.

Table 25.6 The growth of debt: average of all developing countries: selected years

	1974	1980	1982	1984	1986	1990	1992	1994	1995
Ratio of debt to GNP (%)	15.4	21.0	30.6	33.6	37.6	33.2	35.7	37.6	39.6
Ratio of debt to exports (%)	80.0	86.5	131.3	143.4	201.7	161.6	166.7	150.0	151.4
Ratio of debt service to exports (%)	11.8	13.2	20.7	19.2	25.9	18.3	17.1	16.3	17.0

Sources: *World Debt Tables*: various years (World Bank).

ISSUES AND APPLICATIONS BOX 25.6

THE GREAT ESCAPE
The problem of capital flight

One of the more bizarre features of the Third World debt crisis has been the phenomenon of 'capital flight'. Countries deeply in debt have been forced to borrow more money to finance these debts. But much of this money, rather than being used to pay previous debts or to restructure the economy, has simply been put on deposit by private individuals and firms in foreign banks, or has been used to buy foreign property or stocks and shares.

Capital flight usually occurs when individuals or firms believe that they can obtain a better return for their money abroad (after taking risks into account). It can thus be caused by overvalued exchange rates (making foreign assets appear cheap), the fear of devaluation, high and fluctuating rates of inflation, political instability, poor domestic investment prospects, low real rates of interest or the corrupt obtaining of money and the wish to 'launder' it abroad.

Given the acute shortage of foreign exchange in highly indebted countries, capital flight is clearly a serious problem. Moreover, the volatility of such flows aggravates the problem of balance of payments instability. There is also the problem that it makes international agencies less well disposed to provide further financing to service debts.

So what can developing countries do to stop capital flight? One approach is to impose tough controls on capital movements. The problem here is that, with the ease of moving money around the world, such controls may be relatively easy to evade. The policy may also discourage inward investment if investors are worried about difficulties in withdrawing their money from the country should they so wish. The alternative approach, then, is to build up investors' confidence in the economy so that they will not wish to take their capital out. But this requires sound economic management by the government over a long period of time: something that may be both politically and economically very difficult to achieve.

?? Why may a considerable proportion of capital flight be included in the 'balancing item' of the balance of payments rather than in the capital account?

Then at the 1988 economic summit at Toronto, new improved Paris Club arrangements were agreed for *low-income* countries. The *Toronto terms* allowed for concessional (low-interest) debt to be repaid over 25 years, including 14 years' grace. In the case of non-concessional debt, three alternatives were open: (1) market interest rates, 25-year repayment, 14 years' grace; (2) concessional interest rates, 14-year repayment, 8 years' grace; (3) one-third of debt cancelled, market interest rates for remainder, 14-year repayment, 8 years' grace. By 1991, twenty countries had had their debt rescheduled on Toronto terms.

Then in 1991 *enhanced Toronto terms* were introduced for severely indebted low-income countries. Creditors were offered the alternative of writing off 50 per cent of a country's debt and rescheduling the remainder over 23 years, including 6 years' grace, or of charging a lower interest rate so as to make it equivalent to the first alternative.

In 1990 the Paris Club introduced new terms – the *Houston terms* – for severely indebted *lower-middle-income* countries. The terms allowed countries to repay their debt over 20 years with 10 years' grace.

In addition to the Paris Club terms, there have been increasing numbers of creditor countries cancelling debts.

Rescheduling commercial bank loans

After the declarations of Mexico and other countries of their inability to service their debts, there was fear of an imminent collapse of the world banking system. Banks realised that disaster could be averted only by collective action of the banks to reschedule debts. This has normally involved the creditor banks forming a Bank Advisory Committee (BAC) – a small committee that liaises with the country and the banks concerned. Such arrangements have sometimes been referred to as the 'London Club'. The BAC negotiates an agreement with the debtor country. The agreement can involve a simple delay in repaying loans for a number of months; or it can involve a more complex rescheduling of debt to cover a number of years, with the overall effect of lengthening the repayment period. When all creditor banks have approved the agreement, it is signed by each of them. As with Paris Club deals, rescheduling is conditional upon the debtor carrying out an adjustment programme supervised by the IMF.

The initial approach of banks after 1982 was to reschedule debt service for a short period (12–24 months). This was known as the 'short-leash' approach. The trouble with this approach was that debts needed repeated reschedulings. Thus in 1984 Multi-Year Restructuring Agreements

ISSUES AND APPLICATIONS — BOX 25.7

'ECOCIDE'
Debt and the environment

When faced with the pressure of mounting debts and the need to service them, most developing countries have sought to increase their export earnings. One way of achieving this is through the intensified extraction of minerals and ores or intensified farming. But a consequence of this may be massive environmental damage.

An example of a country forced into what has been called 'ecocide' in response to its huge debt burden is Brazil, with its Grande Carajas iron ore project. Proposed in 1980, the Carajas scheme has been estimated to cost some $62 billion and has involved massive deforestation of an area larger than France and Britain together. The Brazilians' willingness to incur such environmental damage was due to the fact that Carajas was seen as a 'national export project'.

Projects like Carajas and the cutting down of the rain forests to provide timber and to clear the land for farming have enormous long-term consequences. Unfortunately, most of the world's tropical rain forests are located in highly indebted countries (e.g. Brazil, Zaire, Indonesia, Peru and Colombia).

In recent years there has been growing international awareness of the scale of the environmental destruction that is taking place. In particular, the rich countries have begun to realise that they too might suffer from this destruction, with its consequences for global warming and the loss of many unique species of plants and animals. Increasingly, international agencies such as the IMF and the World Bank are taking ecological issues into account when considering appropriate development and adjustment programmes.

The Brundtland Commission's 1987 report, *Our Common Future*, stressed the need for 'sustainable development'. It is no good trying to secure 'development' for the current generation if, in the process, the environment is damaged and future generations suffer. This is a message that has been well understood by indigenous peoples for countless generations, especially those living on marginal lands: from the Aborigines of the Australian outback to the tribes of the African bush. It is seen as a moral imperative that the land bequeathed by one's ancestors should be passed on in just as good a state to one's descendants.

In 1992 in Rio de Janeiro, the United Nations Conference on Environment and Development (UNCED) put forward a programme for environmentally responsible development. In Agenda 21 it set out various policies that could be carried out by the international community. These included: targeting aid to projects which helped improve the environment (such as providing clean water); research into environmentally friendly farming methods; and programmes which help reduce population growth (such as family planning and education). The test of such sentiments, however, is action.

Nevertheless, there have been some examples of positive action by the international community. Returning to the case of Brazil: in 1991 an agreement was reached between the national government, local governments and various agencies in Brazil, along with various international bodies such as the European Commission and the World Bank, to launch a programme to protect the Amazon rain forest. For the initial phase of the project $250 million was provided, partly by Brazil itself, and partly by various industrial countries led by the Group of Seven. The project ranges from conserving certain areas to researching into environmentally friendly technologies.

One other development has been the advent of 'debt-for-nature' swaps. These are examined in Box 25.8.

??

1. If reductions in developing countries' debt are in the environmental interests of the whole world, then why have developed countries not gone much further in reducing or cancelling the debts owed to them?
2. Would it be possible to devise a scheme of debt repayments that would both be acceptable to debtor and creditor countries and not damage the environment?

(MYRAs) were introduced, which involved reschedulings of debt for longer periods (typically 9–14 years).

Then in 1985, with a slowdown in world trade and with an increased need for restructuring, US Treasury Secretary James Baker launched a new initiative. The *Baker Plan* called for banks to provide over $20 billion of new loans over three years to fifteen of the most highly indebted middle-income countries. In return these countries would have to agree to substantial market-orientated adjustment programmes, including trade liberalisation, reduction in public expenditure and an emphasis on growth through an enhanced role of the private sector. Additional loans, however, fell well short of the $20 billion. Banks were unwilling to supply extra money to deal with current debt-servicing problems when they saw the problem as a long-term one of countries' inability to pay. Nevertheless, banks were increasingly setting aside funds to cover bad debt, and thus the crisis for the banks began to recede.

ISSUES AND APPLICATIONS BOX 25.8

SWAPPING DEBT

A solution to developing countries' debt?

Faced with the inability of many developing countries to service, let alone repay, their debts, many banks have collaborated with debtor countries in ingenious schemes to convert debt into some other form. There are a number of types of these 'debt swaps', as they are called.

Debt-for-equity swaps

Banks sell a certain amount of a country's debt at a discount in the secondary market. The purchaser (a firm or a bank) then swaps the debt with the central bank of the developing country for local currency which is then used to buy shares in one or more of the country's companies. Sometimes debt–equity swaps are part of a privatisation programme, the debt being swapped for shares in a newly privatised company.

As far as the debtor country is concerned, this has the benefit of both reducing the debt and increasing the amount of investment in domestic companies. It has the drawback, however, of increasing foreign ownership and control in the country. Also, in the long term the increased outflow of funds in the form of profits and dividends may make the country's debt problem worse.

Debt-for-cash swaps

This is where the banks allow a debtor country to 'buy back' (i.e. repay) its debt at a discount. In order to do this the developing country will probably have to secure a loan from another source. The developing country gains from achieving a net reduction in its debt. The bank gains by achieving an instant repayment of a percentage of the original debt.

Debt-for-bonds swaps

Here debt is converted into low-interest-rate bonds. The developing country gains by having to pay a lower rate of interest. The bank gains by being exempted from any schemes that involve existing creditors jointly increasing their lending. Sometimes these bonds can then be swapped for equity.

Debt-for-nature swaps

This is where debts are cancelled in return for investment in environmental projects. Typically the scheme works as follows: the debt is sold to an international environmental agency at a substantial discount (or sometimes even given away); the agency then swaps this debt with the debtor country and receives an 'environmental bond' in exchange; this bond pays interest in the local currency which the environmental agency uses to finance conservation and other environmental projects. For example, in 1992 the Bank of America donated $2 million of Brazilian debt to the international agency Conservation International, which then used the bond interest to fund various Brazilian conservation projects.

The benefits to the developing country in terms of debt reduction and environmental improvement are obvious, provided that the agency uses the money wisely. The benefits to the bank are the immediate realisation of part of the money owed. And even when the debt is given away, the bank may still gain – from an improvement in its public image.

Debt-for-development swaps

Like debt-for-nature swaps, these involve the selling or donating of debt to an international development agency, which then exchanges it with the debtor country for bonds, the interest on which can be used for specific projects, in the fields of education, transport infrastructure, health, agriculture, etc.

Debt-for-export swaps

Under these schemes, banks arrange for developing countries to sell exports they would otherwise have difficulty in selling (perhaps because of industrial country protection), provided the revenues are used to pay off specific debt. Clearly the developing country can gain from the development of new export markets, but there is a danger that, by being a form of 'export protection', it could encourage the production of goods in which the country has a comparative disadvantage, and encourage inefficiency in production.

Debt-to-local-debt swaps

This is where external debt is converted into debt in the local currency (usually indexed to the US dollar). The original creditor sells the debt to a company which requires local currency to finance a subsidiary operating in the debtor country. The company benefits from a cheap source of local currency. The country benefits from a reduction in the need for scarce foreign currency.

Between 1985 and 1992 over $90 billion worth of debt conversion programmes were arranged. Of this the largest single category was debt–equity swaps, accounting for 38 per cent of the total. The amount of debt converted may seem substantial, but compared with the total level of debt, which stood at over $1500 billion in 1992, it remains small.

?? Would the objections of developing countries to debt–equity swaps be largely overcome if foreign ownership were restricted to less than 50 per cent in any company? If such restrictions were imposed, would this be likely to affect the 'price' at which debt were swapped for equity?

As banks felt less exposed to default, so they became less worried about it and less concerned to negotiate deals with debtor countries. Many of the more severely indebted countries, however, found their position still deteriorating rapidly. What is more, many of them were finding that the IMF adjustment programmes were too painful (often involving deep cuts in government expenditure) and were therefore abandoning them. Thus in 1989 US Treasury Secretary Nicholas Brady proposed measures to *reduce* debt.

The *Brady Plan* involved the IMF and the World Bank lending funds to debtor countries to enable them to repay debts to banks. In return for this instant source of liquidity, the banks would have to be prepared to accept repayment of less than the full sum (i.e. they would sell the debt back to the country at a discount). To benefit from such deals, the debtor countries would have to agree to growth-orientated adjustment programmes. Several such agreements have been negotiated, with countries buying back their debt at discount rates ranging between 44 and 84 per cent. Much of the debt reduction has involved debt swaps of one sort or another (see Box 25.8).

?? What are the relative advantages and disadvantages to a developing country of rescheduling its debts compared with simply defaulting on them (either temporarily or permanently)?

Dealing with debt: structural reform within the developing countries

Despite the fact that for many middle-income developing countries the debt problem is not as acute today as it was in the early 1980s, the problems still remain for most developing countries, and for many of the poorest countries the position is still deteriorating. What is more, most developing countries are under continued pressure to make painful policy adjustments.

Before it is prepared to sanction the rescheduling of debts, the IMF frequently demands that debtor countries undertake severe market-orientated adjustment programmes. These include the following:

- Tight fiscal and monetary policies to reduce government deficits, reduce interest rates and reduce inflation.
- Supply-side reforms to encourage greater use of the market mechanism and greater incentives for investment.
- A more open trade policy and devaluation of the currency in order to encourage more exports and more competition.

These policies, however, can bring extreme hardship as countries are forced to deflate. Unemployment and poverty increase and growth slows down or becomes negative. Even though in the long run developing countries may emerge as more efficient and better able to compete in international trade, in the short run the suffering may be too great to bear. Popular unrest and resentment against the IMF and the country's government may lead to riots and the breakdown of law and order, and even to the overthrow of the government.

An alternative, more interventionist approach to restructuring would include the following:

- Greater planning to encourage investment and infrastructure development.
- Reduction in imports if necessary by the use of tariffs, quotas and other forms of trade restriction.
- Policies to encourage greater self-sufficiency of the country.

The problem with this more interventionist approach is that, while avoiding excessive deflation, it may prevent countries becoming more efficient, and thus make it more difficult for them to reduce their debt burden in the *long* run.

But whether the approach is market orientated or planning orientated, there are substantial short-term costs for developing countries. Their balance of payments has to improve, and this means reducing the consumption of imports and diverting resources away from domestic consumption into exports. That means a reduction in their standard of living: a harsh penalty for some of the poorest countries in the world.

?? Imagine that you are an ambassador of a developing country at an international conference. What would you try to persuade the rich countries to do in order to help you and other poor countries overcome the debt problem? How would you set about persuading them that it was in their *own* interests to help you?

SECTION SUMMARY

1. After the 1973 oil crisis many developing countries borrowed heavily in order to finance their balance of trade deficits and to maintain a programme of investment. Despite this increase in debt, a combination of low real interest rates, a recovery in the world economy and high international rates of inflation allowed developing countries to sustain moderate rates of economic growth after 1975.
2. After the 1979 oil price rises, however, there was a much deeper world recession than in the mid-1970s, and real interest rates were much higher. Debt increased dramatically, and much of it at variable interest rates.
3. Although the problem for middle-income countries is now less serious, the situation is still deteriorating for many of the poorest countries.
4. Rescheduling can help developing countries to cope with increased debt in the short run. During the 1980s and early 1990s there were several initiatives to encourage rescheduling programmes. Official loans are renegotiated through the Paris Club. This will normally involve some combination of longer repayment periods, lower interest rates and grace periods in which payments may be delayed. Sometimes a portion of the debt will be cancelled. Commercial bank loans have also frequently been renegotiated through a Bank Advisory Committee of the banks concerned. This has normally involved delaying paying loans for a period of time and the extension of the repayment period. In addition, under the Brady Plan, countries have borrowed from the World Bank and other international institutions to buy back their debt from banks at a discount.
5. If the problem is to be tackled, however, then either debts have to be written off – something that banks have been increasingly forced to do – or the developing countries themselves must take harsh corrective measures. The IMF favours policies of deflation and market-orientated supply-side policies. An alternative is to pursue a more interventionist policy of restricting imports and encouraging investment in import-subsituting sectors of the economy.

??? END-OF-CHAPTER QUESTIONS ???

1. Compare the relative merits of using GNP statistics with those of various basic needs indicators when assessing both the level and the rate of a country's economic development.
2. If a developing country has a comparative advantage in primary products, should the government allow market forces to dictate the pattern of trade?
3. What are the advantages and disadvantages for a developing country of pursuing a policy of ISI?
4. Should all developing countries aim over the long term to become *exporters* of manufactured products?
5. How would you attempt to assess whether the technology used by an industry in a developing country was 'inappropriate'?
6. What policies could be adopted to reduce urban unemployment in developing countries?
7. To what extent was the debt crisis of the early 1980s caused by inappropriate policies that had been pursued by the debtor countries?
8. What are the advantages and disadvantages of debt swapping as a means of reducing the debts of developing countries?

Postscript: The Castaways or Vote for Caliban

The Pacific Ocean –
A blue demi-globe.
Islands like punctuation marks.

A cruising airliner,
Passengers unwrapping pats of butter.
A hurricane arises,
Tosses the plane into the sea.

Five of them flung onto an island beach,
Survived.

Tom the reporter.
Susan the botanist.
Jim the high-jump champion.
Bill the carpenter.
Mary the eccentric widow.

Tom the reporter sniffed out a stream of drinkable water.
Susan the botanist identified a banana tree.
Jim the high-jump champion jumped up and down and gave them each a bunch.
Bill the carpenter knocked up a table for their banana supper.
Mary the eccentric window buried the banana skins,
But only after they had asked her twice.

They all gathered sticks and lit a fire.
There was an incredible sunset.

Next morning they held a committee meeting.
Tom, Susan, Jim and Bill
Voted to make the best of things.
Mary, the eccentric widow, abstained.

Tom the reporter killed several dozen wild pigs.
He tanned their skins into parchment
And printed the Island News with the ink of squids.

Susan the botanist developed new strains of banana
Which tasted of chocolate, beefsteak, peanut butter,
Chicken and bootpolish.

Jim the high-jump champion organised games
Which he always won easily.

Bill the carpenter constructed a wooden water wheel
And converted the water's energy into electricity.
Using iron ore from the hills, he constructed lampposts.

They all worried about Mary, the eccentric widow,
Her lack of confidence and her –
But there wasn't time to coddle her.

The volcano erupted, but they dug a trench
And diverted the lava into the sea
Where it formed a spectacular pier.
They were attacked by pirates but defeated them
With bamboo bazookas firing
Sea-urchins packed with home-made nitro-glycerine.
They gave the cannibals a dose of their own medicine
And survived an earthquake thanks to their skill in jumping.

Tom had been a court reporter
So he became a magistrate and solved disputes.
Susan the botanist established
A university which also served as a museum.
Jim the high-jump champion
Was put in charge of law enforcement –
Jumped on them when they were bad.
Bill the carpenter built himself a church,
Preached there every Sunday.

But Mary the eccentric widow…
Each evening she wandered down the island's main street,
Past the Stock Exchange, the Houses of Parliament,
The prison and the arsenal.
Past the Prospero Souvenir Shop,
Past the Robert Louis Stevenson Movie Studios,
Past the Daniel Defoe Motel
She nervously wandered and sat on the end of the pier of lava.

Breathing heavily,
As if at a loss,
As if at a lover,
She opened her eyes wide
To the usual incredible sunset.

Adrian Mitchell[1]

??

1. Had the castaways reduced their problem of scarcity by the end of the poem?
2. Could the 'usual incredible sunset' be described as an economic good?

[1] In G. MacBeth (ed.), *Poetry 1900–1975* (Longman, 1979), p. 320.

Appendix: Sources of economic data

John Mark

This appendix gives details of the principal sources of UK data, but also draws attention to key European and international sources. Data are categorised according to the following headings with some rough correspondence to the order of the text:

1. General.
2. Consumer demand.
3. Production and sales.
4. Structure of industry, retailing and wholesaling.
5. Mergers and concentration.
6. Wages and salaries.
7. Income and wealth distribution.
8. Official reports on companies.
9. Agriculture.
10. Economic growth.
11. Employment and unemployment.
12. Prices and price indexes.
13. National income, expenditure and production.
14. Personal income, consumption and savings.
15. Investment, capital expenditure and capital formation.
16. Financial and monetary statistics.
17. Government expenditure and taxation.
18. Macroeconometric models.
19. Regional statistics.
20. Exports and imports and international trade and the balance of payments.
21. The European Union.
22. The economics of developing countries.
23. International sources.
24. Electronic media.
25. Guides to statistical sources.

1. General

Annual Abstract of Statistics, ONS. Furnishes a wide range of business, economic, financial and other data.

Digest of Environmental Statistics, annual, Department of the Environment.

Economic Trends, ONS, and *Economic Trends Annual Supplement*, ONS, monthly and annually respectively. They carry the principal macroeconomic series and the main economic indicators for the United Kingdom (output, employment, prices, earnings, monetary aggregates, government receipts and expenditures, etc.). The *Annual Supplement* presents long-run quarterly figures. *Economic Trends* (monthly) also includes cyclical indicators for the UK economy at the end of each volume.

Key Data, ONS, annually. Compact collection with over 130 tables.

Monthly Digest of Statistics, ONS. Collects together many series (national income, employment, agriculture, external trade, prices, etc.), mainly giving monthly data.

Pocket Britain in Figures, The Economist Newspaper, 1995.

Regional Trends, ONS, annually. Gathers the major statistical series (population, housing, transport, education, employment, income, etc.) on a regional basis.

Social Trends, ONS, annually. Features key social and demographic series (household data, income and wealth, the environment, leisure, transport, etc.).

UK Economic Accounts: A quarterly supplement to Economic Trends, ONS. Gives the latest national income and balance of payments figures.

United Kingdom Balance of Payments (*The Pink Book*), ONS, annually. The main source for the balance of payments.

United Kingdom in Figures, ONS, annually. A pocket-size leaflet with around 400 key statistical series.

United Kingdom National Accounts, ONS, annually. The 'Blue Book' gives detailed figures of national income, production and expenditures, etc.

2. Consumer demand

Business Monitor MQ24: Consumer expenditure, ONS, quarterly. Includes data of expenditure on durable goods and non-durable goods and services, etc.

Family Spending, HMSO, annually.

Household Food Consumption and Expenditure: Annual report of the National Food Survey Committee, HMSO.

National Food Survey: Compendium of results. Annual statistical supplement to the National Food Survey.

3. Production and sales

The pattern of the collection and publication of these data has been subject to many changes, the most recent of which was the merger on 1 April 1996 of the Central Statistical Office (CSO) with the Office of Population Censuses and Surveys (OPCS) to form the Office for National Statistics (ONS).

The Census of Production is conducted by the ONS and the industry reports carrying data on output, sales, value added, etc. will still appear in the *Business Monitor* series both as separate *Business Monitors* in the PA (Production Annual) series and in the *Annual census of production summary volume.*

The Census is part of a system of industrial statistics which includes inquiries concerning sales of manufactured goods by UK companies. Based on the new harmonised European-wide PRODCOM (PRODuction of the European COMmunity), the results are now published by Taylor Nelson AGB from the data supplied by the ONS (formerly CSO). These succeeded the PQ (Production Quarterly) and PAS (Production Annual Sales) series *Business Monitors*. The most recent list of what is now available is in the *ONS Catalogue 1996: The comprehensive source of national statistics*. See the following publications, among others, for some data:

Business Monitor PA1002: Annual census of production summary volume, annually. Collects together Census of Production data, although *Business Monitors* in the PA series are published when the industry data are available.

Business Monitor SDA25: Retailing, annually. Based on the annual services and distribution inquiries.

Business Monitor SDM28: Retail sales, monthly.

Input–Output Tables for the United Kingdom, ONS. Usually every five years with 1990 as the latest.

UK Markets, Taylor Nelson AGB. Quarterly and annual reports containing data on manufacturers' sales, imports and exports, net supply of the UK market, average price, trend data, graphics, etc. for the specific products covered by the PRODCOM system.

4. Structure of industry, retailing and wholesaling

Business Monitor PA1002: Annual census of production summary volume, annually.

Business Monitor PA1003: Size analysis of United Kingdom businesses, annually.

Business Monitor SDA25: Retailing, occasional.

Business Monitor SDA26: Wholesaling, occasional.

Companies, Department of Trade and Industry, annually.

Further details on markets are found by named company in many market research reports: Retail Business (Economist Publications), Mintel Market Intelligence, Market Research Great Britain, Euromonitor, ICC Information Group, Key Note Publications, Market Assessment Publications (MAPS), Marketing Strategies for Industry (MSI), etc.

Times 1000, Times Books Ltd, annually. This is a good example of the many business information sources.

5. Mergers and concentration

Acquisitions and Mergers Involving UK Companies, ONS, quarterly press release.

Acquisitions Monthly, Tudor House Publications.

Annual Report of the Director General of Fair Trading.

Business Monitor PA1002: Annual census of production summary volume, annually.

Financial Statistics, ONS, monthly, table 6.1c.

6. Wages and salaries (the labour market)

Census of Population, Office of Population Censuses and Surveys, various volumes.

Health and Safety Statistics, HMSO, annually.

IDS Management Pay Review, monthly, Incomes Data Services, on executive remuneration.

IDS Report, fortnightly, Incomes Data Services on agreements.

IRS Employment Review, twice monthly, Industrial Relations Services.

Labour Market Trends, ONS, monthly.

New Earnings Survey, HMSO, annually.

Social Security Statistics, HMSO, annually. Data on income support, housing benefit, pensions, etc.

Time Rates of Wages and Hours of Work, Department of Employment. Loose-leaf publication with monthly updates.

7. Income and wealth distribution

Economic Trends. Special section once per year (usually December or January) on the effects of taxes and benefits on the distribution of income.
Family Spending, HMSO, annually.
Inland Revenue Statistics, HMSO, annually.
Social Trends, annually.
Survey of Personal Incomes, HMSO, annually.

8. Official reports on companies

There are numerous reports of the Monopolies and Mergers Commission in particular and of other official bodies (both past and present). The libraries of the Office of Fair Trading and Monopolies and Mergers Commission have comprehensive lists.

OFTEL, OFGAS, etc. as regulators of the privatised natural monopolies provide data in their annual reports.

9. Agriculture

The Agricultural Situation in the European Union, Commission of the EC.
Agriculture in the United Kingdom, HMSO, annually.
The Digest of Agricultural Census Statistics, HMSO, annually.
Economic Report on Scottish Agriculture, HMSO, annually.
Statistical Review of Northern Ireland Agriculture, HMSO, annually.
Welsh Agricultural Statistics, HMSO, annually.

10. Economic growth

Economic Trends, monthly, appendix entitled *International Economic Indicators*.
International Financial Statistics, IMF, monthly.
Monthly Digest of Statistics.
UK Economic Accounts: A quarterly supplement to Economic Trends.
UK National Accounts.

11. Employment and unemployment

There used to be three official agencies. The Employment Department ran the Census of Employment and other inquiries. The Central Statistical Office collected employment data as part of the Census of Production. The Office of Population Censuses and Surveys is responsible for the decennial Census of Population, which also contains data on the labour force.

However, on 1 April 1996, the Statistics section of the former Employment Department and the Central Statistical Office and the Office of Population Censuses and Surveys merged to form the Office for National Statistics. Some major sources are now listed:

Annual Abstract of Statistics. Collects together data from the many labour market official sources.
Business Monitor PA1002: Annual census of production summary volume, and the many PA *Business Monitors* of the complete *Census of Production Report*.
Census 1991: Economic Activity: Great Britain and previous publications of the Census of Population.
Census of Employment Statistics 1993: Results for Great Britain, ONS. Comprehensive survey of employees in the UK, broken down by detailed industry groups, gender and full or part-time status.
Labour Force Survey Quarterly Bulletin, ONS.
Labour Force Survey Rapid Release, ONS.
Labour Market Quarterly Report: Great Britain, Department of Education and Employment.
Monthly Digest of Statistics. Collects together data from the specialised sources.

12. Prices and price indexes

Annual Abstract of Statistics.
Business Monitor MM17: Price index numbers for current cost accounting (monthly supplement).
Business Monitor MM22: Producer price indices, monthly.
Business Monitor MM23: Retail prices index, monthly.
The Grocer Price List, monthly, William Read Ltd, London.
Labour Market Trends.
The Monthly Digest of Statistics.
Shaws Retail Price Guide, monthly, EMAP Business Communications, Peterborough.

13. National income, expenditure and production

The primary source is *United Kingdom National Accounts*. The methodology is fully described in *United Kingdom National Accounts: Sources and methods, Studies in Official Statistics no. 37*, third edition, HMSO, London, 1985. Section 6 of the *United Kingdom National Accounts* contains updates of the methodology. Other data sources include:

Annual Abstract of Statistics, section 14.
Economic Trends, monthly.
Economic Trends Annual Supplement, annually.
Monthly Digest of Statistics, section 1.
UK Economic Accounts: A quarterly supplement to Economic Trends.

14. Personal income, consumption and savings

Economic Trends, monthly.
Economic Trends Annual Supplement.
Financial Statistics. See section 10.7.
Inland Revenue Statistics, HMSO, annually.
Monthly Digest of Statistics.
New Earnings Survey.
UK Economic Accounts: A quarterly supplement to Economic Trends.
United Kingdom National Accounts, chapters 3 and 4.

15. Investment, capital expenditure and capital formation

Economic Trends, monthly.
Economic Trends Annual Supplement.
Financial Statistics, sections 6, 10.4, 10.5 and 10.6.
Housing and Construction Statistics, Department of the Environment, quarterly and annually.
United Kingdom National Accounts, section 4.

16. Financial and monetary statistics

The following provide a range of monetary statistics:

Bank of England Quarterly Bulletin, Statistical Annexe. Some truncation since February 1992, but fuller details available usually on request.
Economic Trends, monthly.
Economic Trends Annual Supplement.
Financial Statistics, monthly.
UK Economic Accounts: A quarterly supplement to Economic Trends.

Many private sector organisations extract data from company reports, providing profiles on individual companies and defined business sectors. The various reports of *Business Ratio Plus*, published by the Inter-Company Comparisons (ICC) Information Group, are a good example. These typically give the profit and loss account and balance sheets and performance league tables of various components (size, profitability, liquidity, gearing, employee performance, etc.) by named company.

Many general sources, like *The International Stock Exchange Official Yearbook* and *Kompass: The authority on British industry*, exist. The market provides very well here, including a variety of stockbrokers' reports.

17. Government expenditure and taxation

Financial Statement and Budget Reports, annually, HM Treasury, HMSO. Gives the Budget measures, the finance of the public sector, summarises the medium-term financial strategy, etc.
The Government's Expenditure Plans. Now appears in many parts for the various government departments.
Inland Revenue Statistics, HMSO, annually. Compilation of wide range of data available from tax records.
Public Finance Trends, HMSO, annually. This new publication gives a full statistical background and commentary to public spending and revenues.
Summer Economic Forecast, annually, HM Treasury, HMSO.

Other sources include the following:

Annual Abstract of Statistics.
Economic Trends, monthly.
Economic Trends. Special section once per year (usually December or January) on the effects of taxes and benefits on the distribution of income.
Economic Trends Annual Supplement.
Financial Statistics, sections 1, 2 and 10.
HM Customs and Excise Report, annually.
UK Economic Accounts: A quarterly supplement to Economic Trends.
United Kingdom National Accounts, chapters 6, 7, 8 and 9.

18. Macroeconometric models

These make use of mainly national accounts data to estimate relationships combined in a set of equations which model the economy. Forecasts are made and simulation exercises performed. HM Treasury, the National Institute of Economic and Social Research, the London Business School and the Bank of England models are probably the best known, but many other organisations, both public and private, have a macro-modelling capacity.

Forecasts appear at regular intervals in the *National Institute Economic Review*, the *Economic Outlook* and the *Financial Statement and Budget Report.*

19. Regional statistics

Regional Trends is the main reference, but see also:

Northern Ireland Annual Abstract of Statistics.
Scottish Abstract of Statistics.
Scottish Economic Bulletin, biennially.
Welsh Economic Trends, biennially.

20. Exports and imports and international trade and the balance of payments

From 1993, following the completion of the single European market, the publications output is more complex than previously:

Business Monitor MA20: Overseas trade statistics of the United Kingdom with the world (including data for countries within the European Community: Intrastat). This is the annual volume bringing together intra-EC and extra-EC figures for the year.
Business Monitor MM20: Overseas trade statistics of the United Kingdom with countries outside the European Community (extra-EC trade), monthly.
Business Monitor MM20A: Overseas trade statistics of the United Kingdom with the world (including data for countries within the European Community: Intrastat), includes the monthly summary for intra-EC trade.
Business Monitor MQ20: Overseas trade statistics of the United Kingdom with countries within the European Community (intra-EC trade: Intrastat), gives more details of intra-EC trade, quarterly.

Other sources include the following:

Annual Abstract of Statistics, sections 12 and 13.
Bank of England Quarterly Bulletin, Statistical Annexe.
Business Monitor MQ10: Overseas trade analysed in terms of industries, quarterly.
Business Monitor MA4: Overseas transactions, annually. Has data on invisible earnings and payments.
Business Monitor MA6: Overseas travel and tourism, annually.
Economic Trends.
'External balance sheet of the UK', annual article, recently appearing in the November issue of the *Bank of England Quarterly Bulletin.*
Financial Statistics, section 10.8.
Monthly Digest of Statistics, sections 15 and 16.
UK Economic Accounts: A quarterly supplement to Economic Trends.
United Kingdom Balance of Payments (The Pink Book), annually. This is the basic reference here.

21. The European Union

The Statistical Office of the European Union (SOEU and Eurostat) co-ordinates the output of the various national statistical services. The many publications are placed within one of ten subject themes:

Theme 0. Miscellaneous (buff covers).
Theme 1. General statistics (midnight-blue covers).
Theme 2. Economy and finance (violet covers).
Theme 3. Population and social conditions (yellow covers).
Theme 4. Energy and industry (light-blue covers).
Theme 5. Agriculture, forestry and fisheries (green covers).
Theme 6. External trade (red covers).
Theme 7. Distributive trades, services and transport (orange covers).
Theme 8. Environment (turquoise covers).
Theme 9. Research and development (brown covers).

Each theme may then incorporate publications in the following series:

Series A. Yearbooks and yearly statistics.
Series B. Short-term statistics.
Series C. Accounts and surveys.
Series D. Studies and research.
Series E. Methods.
Series F. Statistics in focus.

A listing of EU statistical sources is available in *Eurostat Catalogue: Publications and electronic services*, which also details computer products.

Particularly useful publications are:

European Economy, annual report, statistical annexe. Incorporates many statistical time series for the EU countries, the USA and Japan for all years from 1960. Includes data on money, interest rates and exchange rates and the public sector as well as output, prices, wages, trade, etc.
European Economy Supplement A, monthly. Gives recent economic trends and economic forecasts for the EU economy as available.
European Economy Supplement B, monthly. Gives business and consumer survey results.
Eurostatistics: Data for short-term economic analysis. This gives statistics for the EU (12) countries plus some series for the EU (15) as well as the USA and Japan. A wide range of topics is presented, including the national accounts, employment and unemployment, production, energy, retail trends, agriculture, external trends, balance of payments, wages, prices and financial statistics.

22. The economics of developing countries

Commodity Trade Statistics, UN, annually.
Human Development Report, United Nations Development Programme, annually. Gives a wide range of social and economic data for virtually all countries of the world.
International Financial Statistics Yearbook, IMF, annually.
World Debt Tables, World Bank, annually.
World Development Report, World Bank, annually. Gives the world development indicators, etc. for more than 200 countries or territories.

World Economic Outlook, IMF, biannually.
World Economic and Social Survey, UN, annually.

23. International sources

Many international organisations put together available data. For instance, the OECD produces a range of monthly, quarterly and annual publications covering all the OECD countries. Notable are the biannual *OECD Economic Outlook* and the annual *OECD Economic Surveys*, which give an economic commentary, with statistical profiles of the member countries.. There are also *Main Economic Indicators*, monthly; *National Accounts*, quarterly and annually; *Quarterly Labour Force Statistics*; *Indicators of Industrial Activity*, quarterly; and *Monthly Statistics of Foreign Trade*.

See also *Government Finance Statistics Yearbook*, IMF, annually; *International Financial Statistics*, IMF, monthly; *Monthly Bulletin of Statistics*, UN; *Yearbook of Labour Statistics*, ILO; *World Tables*, World Bank, annually; plus references listed in section 22 above.

24. Electronic media

Information technology is continually changing the landscape of economic information. Many new series are available on-line to be accessed immediately on disk or tape. The Office for National Statistics, for example, has developed a World Wide Web (WWW) site on the *Internet*. Using a keyword index, users can interrogate both the catalogue and Databank listings and identify suitable publications and other data series.

With the continual addition of new series, for both official and commercial sources, the two volumes of the *Gale Directory of Databases*, Gale Research Inc., 1996, are full catalogues of what is available. The *On-line/CD-ROM Business Source Book 1995/96* (ed. P. Foster), Headland Press, is also useful.

Some good examples of the many series available are:

Databank, ONS. Has monthly, quarterly and annual series from data sets of Economic Trends, Financial Statistics, Price Indexes, Balance of Payments, etc.
Datastream. Provides data on economic series, company accounts, etc.
ESRC Data Archive. Contains raw data from many official inquiries.
New Cronos. This is Eurostat's reorganised database from 1995, including monthly, quarterly, half-yearly and yearly data, depending on the statistical fields covered. New Cronos is subdivided into further domains, each covering a specific sector of the economy. For further details consult *Eurostat Catalogue: Publications and electronic services*.

25. Guides to statistical sources

There are constant changes. For example, we are now operating SIC(92), the most recent Standard Industrial Classification, but many statistical series still reflect SIC(80). *Statistical News*, HMSO, quarterly, is the best early warning source. Periodically, supplements to *Statistical News* are published, detailing new surveys and departmental listings of publications.

Other guides provide information on recently published official and commercial statistical data:

Eurostat Catalogue: Publications and electronic services.
Government Statistics: A brief guide, ONS. Gives a synoptic review of leading official statistical sources.
Guide to Official Statistics, sixth revised edition, ONS, 1995, aims to be the most detailed guide to official statistics.
Macmillan Directory of UK Business Information Sources, third edition, by James Tudor, Macmillan, 1992.
ONS Catalogue 1996: The comprehensive source of national statistics, ONS. This is the most recent catalogue at the time of writing.
Review of UK Statistical Sources. A series of volumes written under the aegis of the Royal Statistical Society and the Economic and Social Research Council. They provide comprehensive guides and critical appraisals of the nature of the data available. Volumes 1–5 were published by Heinemann Educational Books, London; volumes 6–22 by Pergamon Press, Oxford; and volumes 23–9 by Chapman and Hall, London.
Sources of Unofficial UK Statistics, second edition, by D. Mort and L. Siddall, Gower, Aldershot, 1990.
UK Statistics: A guide for business users, by D. Mort, Ashgate, Aldershot, 1992.

Increasingly, guides to statistics which are more up to date are provided by the business sources listed under section 24 above.

It is worth pointing out that there are many books (as well as this one!) which continually draw upon statistical sources, giving the student a good feel for the subject. Some good examples are:

Buxton, T., Chapman, P. and Temple, P. (eds), *Britain's Economic Performance*, Routledge, 1994.
Johnson, C. and Briscoe, S., *Measuring the Economy*, Penguin, London, 1995.

Johnson, C., *The Economy under Mrs Thatcher 1979–1990*, Penguin, London, 1991.
Michie, J. (ed.), *The Economic Legacy 1979–1992*, Harcourt Brace Jovanovich, London, 1992.

Finally, *The Economic Review: Data Supplement*, Philip Allan, Oxford, is a useful annual adjunct to *The Economic Review*. It provides both data and some guidance to the interpretation and usage of economic statistics.

Index